Vitamin 3-D
New Perspectives in Sculpture and Installation

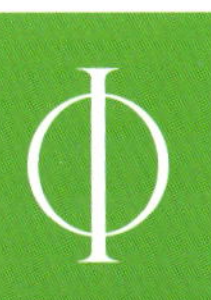

Nominators and Contributors

Nancy Adajania
Critic, cultural theorist and curator, Bombay
Negar Azimi
Senior Editor, *Bidoun*, New York
Sarina Basta
Curator, SculptureCenter, New York
Devrim Bayar
Curator and residency coordinator, Wiels Contemporary Art Centre; Editor in Chief, *Code* magazine, Brussels
Kirsty Bell
Writer, Berlin
Iwona Blazwick
Director, Whitechapel Art Gallery, London
Andrew Bonacina
Curator and writer, London
Thomas Boutoux
Curator and writer; founding member of castillo/corrales, Paris
Lindsay Brown
Writer, Vancouver
Adam Budak
Curator, Kunsthaus Graz
Jon Bywater
Writer; Programme Leader for Critical Studies at Elam School of Fine Arts, University of Auckland, Aotearoa, New Zealand
Giovanni Carmine
Director, Kunsthalle St Gallen
Luca Cerizza
Curator and writer, Berlin and Milan
Carolyn Christov-Bakargiev
Curator, Castello di Rivoli, Turin; Artistic Director, Biennale of Sydney 2008
Tyler Coburn
Artist and critic, New York
Suzanne Cotter
Director, Modern Art Oxford
Bice Curiger
Curator, Kunsthaus Zürich; Editor in Chief, *Parkett*
Penelope Curtis
Curator, Henry Moore Institute, Leeds
Trinie Dalton
Critic and writer, New York
Wouter Davidts
Writer, Antwerp
Lillian Davies
Curator, editor and writer, Paris
Diedrich Diederichsen
Curator and critic, Berlin
Florence Derieux
Curator, Paris
Dominic Eichler
Curator, musician and writer; Contributing Editor, *Frieze*, Berlin
Anne Ellegood
Curator, Hirshhorn Museum and Sculpture Garden, Washington, DC
Russell Ferguson
Curator and critic; Chair of the Department of Art, University of California, Los Angeles
Richard Flood
Chief Curator, New Museum, New York
Claire Gilman
Curator and writer, New York
Thelma Golden
Director and Chief Curator, Studio Museum in Harlem, New York
Ann Goldstein
Senior Curator, Museum of Contemporary Art, Los Angeles
Isabelle Graw
Publisher, *Texte zur Kunst*, Berlin; Professor of Art Theory, Kunsthochschule Städelschule, Frankfurt
Melissa Gronlund
Managing Editor, *Afterall* and *Afterall Online*, London
Bruce Hainley
Writer, Los Angeles
Kit Hammonds
Curator; tutor, Curating Contemporary Art MA, Royal College of Art, London
Glen Helfand
Curator; critic for *Artforum*; Associate Editor, *CMYK*; Adjunct Professor, Fine Arts, California College of the Arts, Oakland
Jens Hoffmann
Director, CCA Wattis Institute for Contemporary Art, San Francisco
Matthew Higgs
Director and Chief Curator, White Columns, New York
Laura Hoptman
Senior Curator, New Museum, New York
Anthony Huberman
Chief Curator, Contemporary Art Museum, Saint Louis, Missouri
Ronald Jones
Artist and writer, Stockholm
Geeta Kapur
Curator and critic, New Delhi
Céline Kopp
Curator and writer, Paris
Vasif Kortun
Director, Platform Garanti Contemporary Art Centre, Istanbul
Miwon Kwon
Associate Professor, Department of Art History, University of California, Los Angeles
Christy Lange
Assistant Editor, *Frieze*, Berlin
Sylvère Lotringer
Professor of French Literature and Philosophy at Columbia University, New York; General Editor, *Semiotext(e)*
Carol Yinghua Lu
Critic and curator, Beijing
Francesco Manacorda
Curator, Barbican Art Gallery, London
Chus Martinez
Chief Curator, Museu d'Art Contemporani de Barcelona
Rosa Martinez
Curator, Barcelona
Tom McDonough
Critic and Associate Professor of Art History at Binghamton University; Editor, *Grey Room*, New York
Charles Merewether
Art historian and curator, New Delhi, New York and Hong Kong
Dominic Molon
Associate Curator, Museum of Contemporary Art, Chicago
Shamim M. Momin
Associate Curator, Whitney Museum of American Art, New York; Branch Director and Curator of the Whitney Museum at Altria
Tom Morton
Curator, Hayward Gallery; contributing editor, *Frieze*, London
Gerardo Mosquera
Curator, critic and art historian, Havana; Adjunct Curator, New Museum, New York
Neil Mulholland
Writer; Director of the Centre for Visual and Cultural Studies and Reader in Contemporary Art Theory, Edinburgh College of Art
Julian Myers
Art historian, critic and professor, California College of the Arts, San Francisco
Bob Nickas
Curator and critic, New York
Hans Ulrich Obrist
Co-Director, Exhibitions and Programmes and Director of International Projects, Serpentine Gallery, London
Sally O'Reilly
Writer, London
Adriano Pedrosa
Critic and curator, São Paulo
Emily Pethick
Director, The Showroom, London
Jenelle Porter
Associate Curator, Institute of Contemporary Art, University of Pennsylvania, Philadelphia
Bert Rebhandl
Critic, Berlin
Beatrix Ruf
Director and Curator, Kunsthalle Zürich
Ralph Rugoff
Director, Hayward Gallery, London
Trevor Schoonmaker
Curator of Contemporary Art, Nasher Museum of Art at Duke University, Durham, NC, USA
Barry Schwabsky
Critic, London; Co-Editor of International Reviews for *Artforum*; critic, *The Nation*
Katy Siegal
Associate Professor of Art History and Criticism, Hunter College, City University of New York
Katie Sonnenborn
Writer; Director of External Affairs, Dia Art Foundation, New York
Beate Söntgen
Writer, Brussels
Rochelle Steiner
Director, Public Art Fund, New York
Francesco Stocchi
Curator and critic, Rome
Alina Tortosa
Critic, curator and writer, Buenos Aires
Lee Triming
Artist and writer, London
Marc-Olivier Wahler
Director, Palais de Tokyo, Paris
Gilda Williams
Critic, London
Rachel Withers
Writer, London

Phaidon Press Limited
Regent's Wharf
All Saints Street
London N1 9PA

Phaidon Press Inc.
65 Bleecker Street
New York, NY 10012

www.phaidon.com

First published 2009
Reprinted 2010
Reprinted in paperback 2014

ISBN 978-07148-6857-8

A CIP catalogue record of this book is available from the British Library

Design: Practise, London
James Goggin & Régis Tosetti
Printed in China

Translations
Texts by Giovanni Carmine and Luca Cerizza translated from Italian by Chris Gilmor. Texts by Florence Derieux and Marc Olivier-Wahler translated from French by Constance Gounod. Texts by Beatrix Ruf and Beate Söntgen translated from German by Michael Robinson.

Acknowledgements
The publishers would like to give special thanks to the artists, nominators and authors who contributed to *Vitamin 3-D*. We would like to thank the following galleries and institutions for their assistance:

Alison Jacques, London / Galerie Almine Reich, Paris / D'Amelio Terras, New York / Andersen-S Contemporary Art, Copenhagen & Berlin / Andrea Rosen Gallery, New York / Andrew Kreps Gallery, New York / Anna Helwig Gallery, Los Angeles / The Approach, London / Artangel, London / Arndt & Partner, Berlin / Artpace, San Antonio / Galerie Balice Hertling, Paris / Galerie Barbara Weiss, Berlin / Bellwether, New York / Blum & Poe, Los Angeles / Casey Kaplan Gallery, New York / Castello di Rivoli, Museo d'Arte Contemporanea, Turin / Catriona Jeffries Gallery, Vancouver / Cherry and Martin, Los Angeles / China Art Objects, Los Angeles / Galerie Chez Valentin, Paris / Galerie Christian Nagel, Berlin & Cologne / Contemporary Fine Arts, Berlin / Corvi-Mora, London / Daniel Reich Gallery, New York / Darren Knight Gallery, Sydney / David Kordansky Gallery, Los Angeles / DCA Dundee Contemporary Arts / Galerie Dennis Kimmerich, Dusseldorf / Doggerfisher, Edinburgh / Ellen de Bruijne Projects, Amsterdam / Elizabeth Dee, New York / Galerie Emmanuel Perrotin, Paris & Miami / Esther Schipper, Berlin / Galerie Eva Presenhuber, Zurich / Feinkost, Berlin / Fonds municipal d'art contemporain de la ville de Paris / Fonds régional d'art contemporain Champagne-Ardenne, Reims / Galeria Fortes Vilaça, São Paulo / Galerie Francesca Pia, Zurich / Galleria Franco Noero, Turin / Fred Mann, London / Galleria Civica del Comune di Modena / Galleria Galica, Milan / Gavin Brown's Enterprise, New York / Greene Naftali, New York / Galerie Guido W. Baudach, Berlin / Guild & Greyshkul, New York / Harris Lieberman Gallery, New York / Hauser & Wirth, Zurich, London / Herald St, London / Galería Heinrich Ehrhardt, Madrid / Hollybush Gardens, London / Hotel, London / Galerie Isabella Bortolozzi, Berlin / Johann König, Berlin / Johnen + Schöttle, Cologne & Berlin / Galerie Juliètte Jongma, Amsterdam / Karyn Lovegrove Gallery, Los Angeles / Kate MacGarry, London / Galerie Krinzinger, Vienna / Kurimanzutto, Mexico City / Level 2 Gallery supported by Catherine Petitgas, Tate Modern, London / LA><ART, Los Angeles / Lombard-Freid Projects, New York / Galeria Luisa Strina, São Paulo / Marc Foxx Gallery, Los Angeles / Mary Boone Gallery, New York / Mary Mary, Glasgow / Maureen Paley, London / Galerie Max Hetzler, Berlin / Max Protetch Gallery, New York / Galerie Meerrettich, Berlin / Galerie Meyer Kainer, Vienna / Michael Kohn Gallery, Los Angeles / MMK, Frankfurt / The Modern Institute, Glasgow / Galerie Neu, Berlin / Neugerriemschneider, Berlin / Galeria Nogueras Blanchard, Barcelona / PaceWildenstein, New York / Peter Blum Gallery, New York / Pinksummer Contemporary Art, Genoa / Raster Gallery, Warsaw / Ratio 3, San Francisco / Galerie Reinhard Hauff, Stuttgart / Richard Telles Fine Art, Los Angeles / Galerie Rüdiger Schöttle, Munich & Berlin / Sadie Coles HQ, London / Salon 94, New York / Sammlung Boros, Berlin / Secession, Vienna / Sies + Höke Galerie, Dusseldorf / Galleryske, Bangalore / Sprüth Magers, Berlin & London / Standard, Oslo / Stephen Friedman Gallery, London / Store Gallery, London / Stuart Shave Modern Art, London / VG Bild-Kunst, Bonn / Susanne Vielmetter Los Angeles Projects / Sutton Lane, London & Paris / Talwar Gallery, New York & New Delhi / Tanya Bonakdar Gallery, New York / Taxter & Spengemann, New York / Timothy Taylor Gallery, London / Galerie Thomas Flor, Dusseldorf / Vilma Gold, London / Galeria Vermelho, São Paulo / Walker Art Center, Minneapolis / Xavier Hufkens, Brussels / Yvon Lambert, Paris & New York / Zach Feuer Gallery, New York / Galleria Zero, Milan / David Zwirner, New York

Vitamin 3-D Photographer credits
Claudio Abate / Stefan Altenburger / Nick Ash / Giorgio Benni / A. Bessone / Giorgio Boata / Mary Boone Gallery / Mike Bruce / A. Burger / Dennis Cowley / Peter Cox / Marc Domage / Ivo Faber / Beto Felício / Brian Forrest / Jennifer French / Raphael Goldchain / Wolfgang Günzel / Marcus Haugg / Ilmari Kalkinnen / Andy Keate / Jan Kempenaers / Daenam Kim / Achim Kukulies / Edo Kuipers / Larry Lama / Guy L'Heureux / Ellen Labenski / Michele Lamanna / Kajsa Lindskog / Jochen Littkemann / Tom Little / Enrique Maciás / Jason Mandella / Roman März / Scott Massey / Isabella Matheus / Kerry Ryan McFate / Wit McKay / Wagner Morales / André Morin / Victor Muños / Ding Musa / Vincent Nevot / Holger Niehaus / Fredrik Nilsen / Al Nowak / Eduardo Ortega / Oliver Ottenschläger / Ludger Paffrath / Olivier Pasqual / Paolo Pellion / Mariano Peuser / Gene Pittman / Tom Powell / Adam Reich / Sabine Reitmaier / Daniele Resini / Charlie Samuels / Sebastian Schobbert / Matthew Septimus / Oren Slor / Andy Stagg / Daniel Steegmann / Tate Photography / Paolo Terzi / Tom Van Eynde / Simon Vogel / Jean Vong / Robert Wedemeyer / Joshua White / Stephen White / Walter Willems / Ellen Page Wilson / Jason Wyche / Michel Zabé / Jens Ziehe

Preface

Vitamin 3-D: New Perspectives in Sculpture and Installation is an up-to-the-minute survey of current global developments in contemporary sculpture and its close relative, installation. The vast medium of sculpture continues to be a central pillar of artistic practice, and *Vitamin 3-D* presents the outstanding artists who are engaging with and pushing the boundaries of the medium.

Vitamin 3-D follows the success of *Vitamin P: New Perspectives in Painting*, *Vitamin D: New Perspectives in Drawing* and *Vitamin Ph: New Perspectives in Photography*, presenting a cross-generational survey of contemporary artists from 27 countries. Chosen from more than 500 nominations by significant international critics, curators, art historians and creative writers, *Vitamin 3-D*'s 117 established and emerging artists were selected on the basis that they have made a significant contribution to sculpture and installation (in their broadest sense) during the last five years.

Vitamin 3-D allows the reader to look at the medium in detail, to study sculpture's unique properties in relation to itself, in relation to contemporary art and in relation to the world at large. An ongoing fascination with the key issues of modern sculpture, from the readymade to the specific object, today drives many artists to return to those issues again and again, with fresh and often surprising results.

In her evocative introductory essay for *Vitamin 3-D*, Anne Ellegood uses Rosalind Krauss's landmark 1978 essay 'Sculpture in the Expanded Field' as the basis to explore the wildly inclusive breadth and depth of work that the term 'sculpture' can now be applied to within contemporary practice — and the key historical moments that serve as the precedents for what we now understand as both sculpture and installation.

Sculpture continues to strike out into new territory, whether by harnessing the medium to confront today's commodity world in its own materials or conjuring visionary objects and environments never seen before. *Vitamin 3-D* contributes to these international debates on contemporary sculpture and installation while providing an accessible overview and a concise reference book.

Motley Efforts
Sculpture's Ever-Expanding Field

Anne Ellegood

· Sculptures

'Nothing, it would seem, could possibly give to such a motley of effort the right to lay claim to whatever one might mean by the category of sculpture. Unless, that is, the category can be made to become almost infinitely malleable.' [Rosalind Krauss]

A three-meter-high tall scrap of plain brown carpet upended and hanging on the wall, serving as the background for four short lines of white tape. Two very large mirrors joined at a right angle, mounted to the wall and rotating continuously. A boat built out of a disassembled shed and sent down river, where it is reconstructed into its original form and displayed in a gallery. Small sculptural forms made of paper, rocks, copper, plastic and tree branches, each acting as a character in a series of short films. Graphic silkscreen panels — their patterns inspired by mid-twentieth-century modernism and urban design — that can be moved around the room to serve as the stage for a series of performances. These are just a few descriptions of the innumerable works created during the past ten years that fall under the category of sculpture.

Thirty years ago, at the beginning of her 1978 essay 'Sculpture in the Expanded Field', Rosalind Krauss described a number of then-current types of artworks and actions that had come to be understood as operating under the umbrella of sculpture: an earthwork by Mary Miss, a Bruce Nauman corridor, Hamish Fulton's documented walks, Robert Smithson's mirror displacements and Michael Heizer's monumental cuts into the landscape.[1] Her concern that the 'rage to historicize', as she put it, ignored these works' important differences in favour of arguing for an evolution within the medium led her to speculate that the category of sculpture may, in fact, collapse under the weight of all that it was now expected to encompass.[2] Ultimately, however, Krauss argued that these wide-ranging practices were emblematic of a move away from modernism and into postmodernism. She understood that the enormous display of artistic cross-pollination and experimentation she was witnessing was something profoundly meaningful to the history of the medium and worthy of in-depth consideration. Recently, Johanna Burton has pointed out that this expanded, and nearly collapsed, category of sculpture, which in the intervening years since Krauss wrote her text has continued to absorb any number of different practices, may no longer suggest a crisis for the medium, but is simply its current 'state of being'.[3]

Today, the number of works to which we attribute the term 'sculpture' is almost breathtaking. While the types of large-scale interactive works and outdoor pieces far removed from urban centres that Krauss described emerged in the 1970s, room-size immersive 'installation', as it has been dubbed, has played a large part in sculptural practice during the last three decades. It is important to acknowledge that freestanding, autonomous sculpture and installation draw upon distinct historical legacies. Those who identify themselves as sculptors and those who make installations often look to divergent precursors and have distinct goals as to how viewers may experience their work. Nonetheless, the two categories may share more fundamentals than points of difference: both approaches embrace three-dimensionality as the physical manifestation of the work and both are acutely aware of the exhibition space or context as a site of presentation and display. In evaluating the most recent practices in sculpture, it seems that whether an artist creates singular objects meant to be observed in the round, or builds multi-faceted installations that inhabit the entire gallery and are intended to surround the viewer completely, these sculptural practices take on many of the same challenges and are preoccupied by similar questions and concerns. With such an incredible diversity of sculpture capturing our attention in contemporary art practice, how do we make sense of sculpture today? What are its unique challenges? And what are these questions and concerns, shared by its most striking and inventive practitioners?

We can likely agree that the field of sculpture continues to expand, and while it is tempting during these periods of rigorous activity and heterogeneity to search for some basic characteristics of the medium, to embark on an ontological investigation into sculpture seems to be heading in the wrong direction.[4] For it is not necessarily the 'nature of sculpture' that we are seeking to define here: we learned some time ago to be suspicious of efforts towards defining a medium solely through its physical attributes — in essence, to reduce or reify the medium to one dominant characteristic.[5] If postmodernism has a consistent argument, it may well be that medium-specificity, especially one inscribed within a hierarchy of media, often does not mesh with how contemporary artists are working.[6] Indeed, the most noteworthy sculptural production of recent decades has come out of artists feeling free enough to loosen themselves from the tethers of artistic tradition, to cross over and combine media, and to propose new possibilities for their chosen medium. These types of transgressions may have started with Marcel Duchamp and his readymades early in the twentieth century, but they began to gain real traction in the 1950s with Frank Stella's resistance to a predetermined picture plane for painting, Robert Rauschenberg's 'combines' of painting and sculpture, and the burst of happenings and performance onto the scene, which ignored traditional artistic mediums by way of a desire to combine art with life and embrace vernacular vocabularies of the everyday. The 1960s and early 1970s, of course, was a period of tremendous experimentation and inquiry into the question of just what constitutes a work of art. We witnessed the dematerialization of the object. Artists opened restaurants. Sculpture left the gallery and found itself in remote sites in the American West. Buildings earmarked for demolition became monolithic forms to be cut into, making us aware that absence can be every bit as physical as presence. Language, instructions and definitions — the very idea of art — were presented as the artworks themselves. This 'post-medium' condition, as it has been called, has engendered some of the most experimental and truly avant-garde practices of the twentieth century.[7] Artists often acknowledge what they understand to be the existing parameters of a medium, its history and its shifts over time, and then build upon and embellish, or try to tear down, what has become accepted practice. A desire to add to the category of sculpture things that had previously been denied its status — whether commodities purchased from a shop and displayed in the gallery largely unaltered, or a nearly invisible length of white rope nailed to the wall — has allowed artists to push against the methodologies of art history and to challenge that which we think we know.

There is no doubt that sculpture has proven itself to be an intensely malleable and generous medium. Of course, despite its heterogeneity, there is also no denying the unique physical, material and technical attributes that constitute the medium of sculpture and thus inform our analyses of any given artwork. While artists thrive on discursive space and a desire to offer something new (or at least something fresh and innovative), at a moment of arguably unprecedented activity within contemporary art worldwide, it certainly seems worthwhile to consider the ways in which they are approaching the medium of sculpture and to examine what continues to make this medium unique and distinct from others.[8] 'For', as Krauss so beautifully articulated, 'in order to sustain artistic practice, a medium must be a supportive structure, generative of a set of conventions, some of which, in assuming the medium itself as their subject, will be wholly "specific" to it, thus producing an experience of their own necessity'.[9]

What follows is a number of thematic sections aimed at beginning to articulate some of the myriad sculptural practices today. Specific artists discussed under any given category could easily be explored under another. Indeed, the headings themselves share characteristics and frequently overlap in meaningful ways. Of the number of artists addressed in these introductory remarks is necessarily limited, a mere teaser for the more in-depth descriptions to follow. If the 117 artists presented in *Vitamin 3-D* have anything in common, it may simply be the profusion of cultural and historical references, the range of materials and an eye towards experimentation. Each work can be appreciated for its sensitivity to form or its physical flair — these are, after all, objects in space that we encounter with our bodies — but the conceptual underpinnings are often as complex and layered as their forms and encourage a certain amount of unpacking. While many of the artists' preoccupations, inspirations and inquiries will be addressed, there are equally as many subjects and allusions that will remain unaccounted for in these pages. Each work acts as an orientation of sorts — a starting place from which to position oneself within a larger whole, and a fragment of a much longer conversation. The generosity of this work rests in its ability to keep giving. We will scratch the surface here, but if you keep digging, your archaeological investigation will reveal stratum upon stratum of historical precedent, critical inquiry and incisive material exploration in a field that continues to resist easy definition.

'Organized Chaos' [Mindy Shapero]

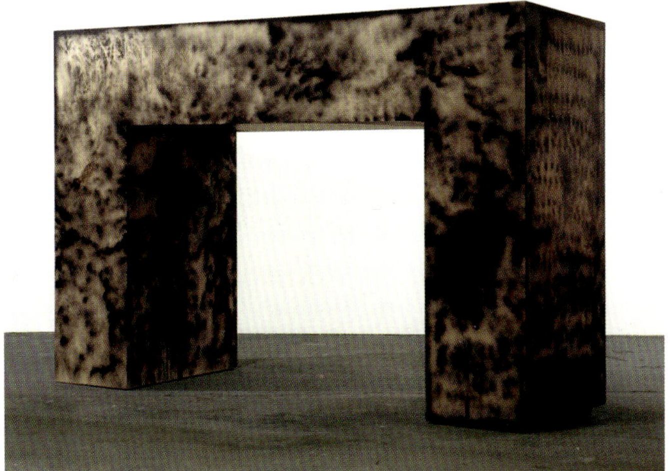

Sterling Ruby
Zen Ripper, 2008
Formica, wood
220 × 340 × 120 cm

Almost fifty years ago, Samuel Beckett said that it is the artist's task to find a form that accommodates the mess, and today his words continue to resonate with a fever pitch.[10] Contemporary sculptors try to make sense of the world around them by identifying paths to follow, or threads to pull, amid the glut of information, the profusion of visual images and the excess of physical objects. They recognize patterns in the chaos. They identify fragments as being part of a larger whole. They realize that entropy is an inevitable part of a natural cycle that indicates growth and life as much as it signals decay. In their negotiations with so much cultural, historical, and empirical information, the artist takes on such roles as archivist, historian, designer, engineer, scientist and translator, and while they find affinities, draw comparisons, point out differences and reconstruct events — in other words, distill the whirlwind into something to be contemplated — their works are also noteworthy for their sheer abundance. Sculptures by such artists as Rachel Harrison, Matthew Monahan, David Altmejd and Evan Holloway have been described as messy, decrepit, clumsy, precarious, expressive, flamboyant, corporeal, ambiguous and enigmatic (to use only a few of the colourful adjectives put into play). This embrace of disorder and precariousness would seem to indicate a deliberate move away from the relatively pristine surfaces and predetermined, sequentially ordered forms of Minimalists like Donald Judd, Carl Andre and Sol LeWitt, despite the influence of this movement on the history of the medium. Today's sculpture is not deconstructive. Its antecedents more typically reside in practices of construction and assemblage. Perhaps the text written across Sterling Ruby's large panel piece *Anti Print 3* (2005) sums up the sentiment best: 'Finish Architecture. Kill Minimalism. Long Live the Amorphous Law.'

Although artists like Tom Burr, Wilfredo Prieto, Eva Rothschild, Arcangelo Sassolino, Sterling Ruby and Jeppe Hein may be riffing on Minimalism, sculptors working today tend to eschew this type of 'simply order', as Donald Judd called it,[11] as well as the *a priori* formulas and systems of Conceptual art, in favour of practices that engage in improvisation and tap into the unconscious. Contemporary sculpture is remarkably expressive, more baroque than reductive. Repetition, composition and juxtaposition are integral to the artists' efforts to create a sense of order among the chaos, but there is also a consistent acknowledgement and mirroring of how the excesses of visual, physical and sensory input increasingly characterize contemporary life. Sculptors tend to articulate their relationships to *all this stuff* through strategies of assemblage and accumulation and by building installations that include an incredible range of objects.

One recurring approach to much contemporary sculpture is the use of everyday materials and found objects not historically associated with the medium. For some, these materials carry associations with their native homes — such as the nod to the reclamation and customization of objects common to Latin American cultures in Damian Ortega's explosion of a Volkswagen Beetle or Alexandre da Cunha's adoption of worn-out car tyres. For others, the perceived alchemical life of materials and a self-awareness and scepticism about bringing more objects into an already overloaded world leads to a disposition towards recycling, perhaps taking to heart Douglas Huebler's comment, 'The world is full of objects, more or less interesting. I do not wish to add anymore.' Hence Evan Holloway's incorporation of discarded batteries and Jedediah Caesar's encapsulation of his studio's detritus into blocks of resin. Simply put, these are the materials that make up our world and thus carry associations and allusions that the artists are intent to draw out.

'The "ghost haunting modernity": ornament and decoration.' [Jennifer Allen on Bojan Šarčević]

The baroque sensibility found in a number of current practices is not strictly a response to our high-speed information age or global economic systems of saturated commodification; it is also rooted in the natural world, architecture and design, which locate utility and aesthetics within pattern and decoration. In the past, patterns found in nature held the imaginations of artists, such as Robert Smithson and Eva Hesse. From Corinthian columns to mosaic tiling, architecture is a site of embellishment. Surface treatment has always been one of the concerns of sculpture; consider the patina on a bronze by Henry Moore or the industrially worked and scarred surfaces of the huge steel plates of a Richard Serra. Furthermore, artists have long looked for the eruptions, or the anomalies, within existing patterns.

Contemporary sculpture has not only grown to encompass numerous types of objects, materials and approaches to installation, but has also absorbed the surface itself. Decoration and patterning is as integral to the sculpture as its foundational support or interior structure. Ornamentation on the surface of art (and architecture), which Adolf Loos criticised for being 'degenerate' and a hinderance to culture's forward march in his influential 1909 text 'Ornament and Crime', is today hardly dismissed as redundant to the object; rather it is considered fundamental. Ornamentation, it seems, is no longer a crime, no longer synonymous with decadent culture. Instead, embellishment has been reclaimed by artists like Mitzi Pederson who has beautified the otherwise muted building materials of cinder blocks and planks of wood with black glitter and silver leaf. Revealing the level of ornamentation often found in modernism, despite its claim to simple clean lines and surfaces, Bojan Šarčević dispenses with the idea that decoration is superfluous to the integrity of the object. In *Keep Illusion for the End* (2005), the brass and copper adornment to the wood and poured concrete lines of the piece are fully integrated so that all its elements rely upon one another for the sculpture's sense of balance, scale and visual integrity. While these works are somewhat muted and understated, encouraging us to consider their surfaces through subtly reflective materials and modest visual allusions, Jim Drain's raucous psychedelia assaults the eye, its playful

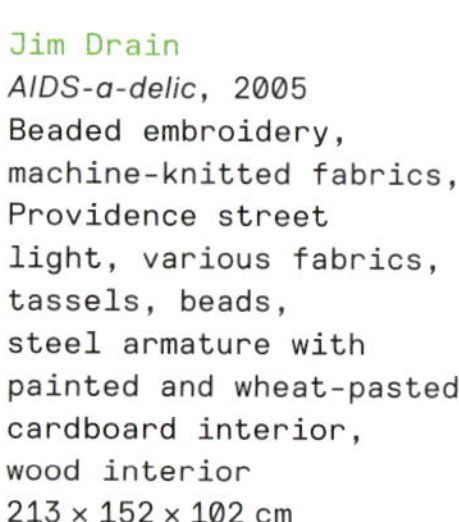
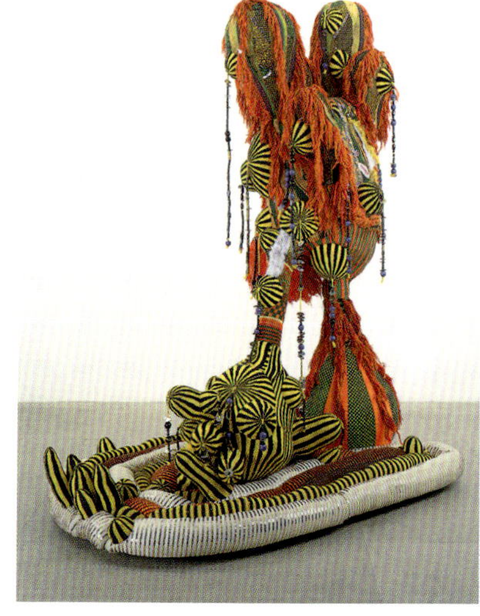

Jim Drain
AIDS-a-delic, 2005
Beaded embroidery, machine-knitted fabrics, Providence street light, various fabrics, tassels, beads, steel armature with painted and wheat-pasted cardboard interior, wood interior
213 × 152 × 102 cm

irreverence an irresistible riot. Creating sculpture and wall treatments in blindingly bold colour schemes, Drain voraciously adopts numerous familiar patterns — from tie-dye to camouflage to polka dots — and adorns his sculpture with all manner of textile-covered shapes and forms to create works with so much personality that they begin to take on anthropomorphic associations.

'I see public space as a place where you introduce a platform.' [Michael Rakowitz]

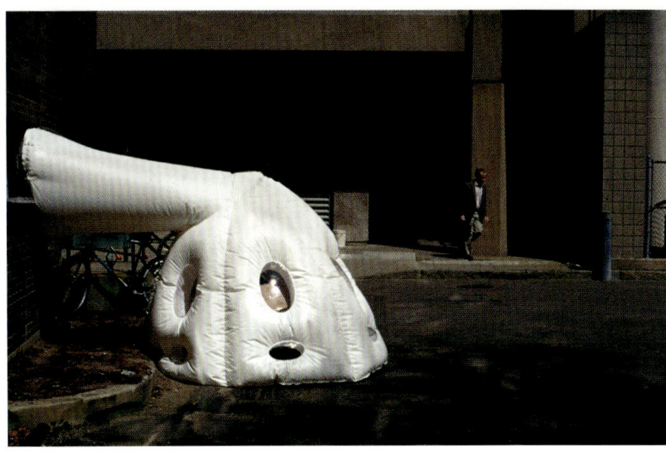

Michael Rakowitz
Bill Stone's paraSITE shelter, 1998
Plastic bags, polyethylene tubing, hooks, tape
Cambridge, Massachusetts

A sense of unconscious release, or primordial connection, in some contemporary sculpture has a direct relationship to a desire for action — for movement and gesture over stability or inertia. Sculpture often reveals the marks of its maker or embodies the physicality of its process of production: to roll, to crease, to fold, to twist, to crumple, to tear, to cut (to borrow some of Richard Serra's verb choices).[12] In some instances, this action extends past the activity of sculpting itself to create a performance space or a space of collective or public action. Mika Tajima's mobile panel dividers and Plexiglas boxes can be rearranged into a stage for performances with her band, New Humans (as well as for invited guests), the configurations shifting throughout the run of the exhibition. Action, accompanied by playfulness and absurdity, also characterizes the social activities of the artist-collective Gelitin, who in 2008 contributed an outdoor paddleboat lake, cantilevered from the side of the museum in the Hayward Gallery's 'Psycho Buildings: Artists Take on Architecture', and built a huge wooden arching playground for the group show 'The Hamsterwheel' during the 2007 Venice Biennale.

Some of these interactive environments bring to mind the work of artists associated in the 1990s with 'relational aesthetics', as dubbed by curator Nicolas Bourriaud. They aimed to enliven the exhibition space with collective activity by foregrounding the role of the audience, but also tended to work in highly aestheticized languages linked to the clean lines of twentieth-century modernist design or the projected illusion of cinema. Work by this more recent generation of artists tends to deflect this level of refinement, embracing lo-fi, makeshift processes of assemblage, often incorporating found materials and assuming a state of temporariness. While Gelitin's works can feel a bit like adolescent scatological pranks replete with shit and nudity, the artists are always at the centre of their rambunctious and energizing environments, participating in the scenarios they create and modelling an attitude of camaraderie that declares, 'everyone is welcome and anything goes'.

For some, there is a desire to create a site that can encourage social change. Michael Rakowitz's inflatable *paraSITE* sculptures function as temporary housing for the homeless by attaching to the heat-exhaust ducts of urban buildings. More recently, Rakowitz created a functional shop on Atlantic Street in Brooklyn for his project *Return* (2006), produced by Creative Time. Reconnecting to his Iraqi-Jewish ancestry, he resuscitated his grandfather's import-export business and began importing and selling dates from Iraq and shipping his customers' packages to Iraq free of charge. Rakowitz's social sculptures acknowledge the impact of nomadism, displacement and immigration on communities throughout the world and create safe havens or service-oriented sites that also function as spaces in which to gather and engage in dialogue. Tomas Saraceno's ongoing utopian endeavour *Air-Port-City* envisions a solution to the global population boom by creating connected floating structures hospitable to humans that would not only utilize the sky to decrease our impact on the earth but would offer an alternative lifestyle where new models for living and functioning as a community would be implemented. The sincerity and goal-oriented nature of these projects indicates that irony is largely dead. By contrast, these artists believe in art's capacity to implement change, or at least raise awareness, taking their works into the streets to reach those who are directly impacted by the troubling issues of our times.

'As if taking a page straight from Michael Fried's famous putdown of the movement's theatricality, his installation is a stage set for a scene taking place after an after-hours party.' [Holland Cotter on Tom Burr]

Theatricality has entered the realm of sculptural practice with tremendous vigour. While the majority of sculpture today does not function as a site for performance per se, many artists create complex, large-scale installations or objects consisting of distinct but connected parts that suggest the aftermath of an event or a moment within a trajectory of concurrent actions. These sites feel anticipatory, or like the calm after the storm. They function like an image captured within the relentlessness of time. The 'stage presence' that Michael Fried so maligned in his widely read and analyzed critique of Minimalism of 1967, 'Art and Objecthood',[13] is no longer necessarily a contemplative engagement with time and space but one that wears its flamboyant theatricality with aplomb. Sculpture-as-prop has a distinct and renowned historical relationship to performance and the theatre: we can recall such landmark collaborations as Isamu Noguchi's fabric-covered sculptures on the set of Martha Graham's *Judith* (1950); one of Robert Rauschenberg's early Combines *Minutiae*, originally created for Merce Cunningham's eponymous new dance in 1954; and Robert Morris's sculpture *Column*, used as a prop in a 1962 performance at La Monte Young's Living Theatre. Indeed, artists such as Rauschenberg, through his involvement with Black Mountain College, as well as Morris, performed with their sculptures on stage, choreographing movements in and around the works. While a specifically phenomenological engagement with the body, where

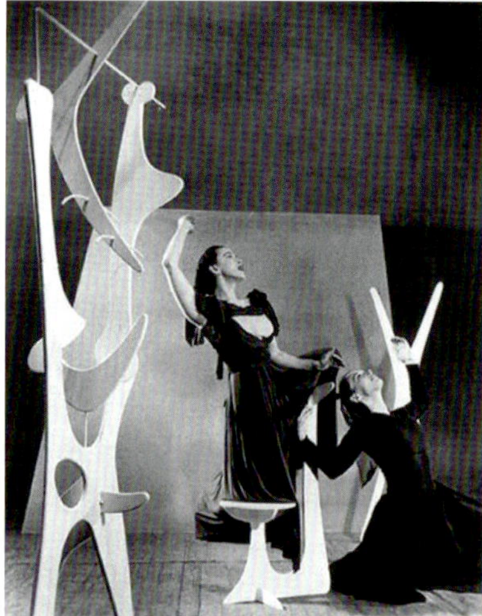

Isamu Noguchi
Stage set for *Hériodiade*, 1944–45, with Martha Graham and May O'Donnell

the viewer becomes more aware and attuned to the relationship of their body to its surrounding space, is undoubtedly one aspect of nearly all sculpture, the recent 'theatrical' work referred to here has a more visceral connection to the physical qualities of the body, taking up questions of sexuality, gender and identity, even when that body is absent from the actual sculptures and remains only as a trace. It seems abundantly clear that the generation following such protagonists in their own event-filled dramas as Paul McCarthy and Matthew Barney take no issue with overt theatricality.

Tom Burr's work is a case in point. His use of shiny black vinyl and the juxtaposition of flaccid forms with erect geometries have immediate connotations with the body and his incorporation of phrases like 'immediately after' into his titles underscores our reading of his sculptures as mise en scènes. For his 2006 project *Thirty Three Point Three Three Three* at the Museum of Contemporary Art, Los Angeles, Eric Wesley built a floor raised on stilts and used the existing walls of the museum to create a porous room, separate but integrated into the existing architecture. Well-lit and accentuated with a replica of a column and a framed window, the stark yet seductive space calls out for action, a stage awaiting its actors. Artists' renewed interest in the suggestion of action within sculpture might be the result of a number of impulses: a desire for their work to somehow *do* something, a general disdain for stasis in our high-speed society, or an affirmation and continuation of a postmodern intention to cross medium-specific boundaries and expand art's definitions.

'Most of my installations function similarly to architecture or design [...] One can enter them, touch them, but after the exhibition has ended most of them are destroyed.' [Monika Sosnowska]

Despite the many examples of non-traditional theatre taking place in car garages and on urban streets, theatricality often connotes the architectural structure of the stage. Architecture has long fascinated artists working in three dimensions, from Bruce Nauman's corridors to Dan Graham's pavilions, not only for the way in which it articulates space and references our lived environments, but also for its deeply psychological resonance. There are numerous associations with architecture in recent sculpture: spaces bursting with the abject detritus of neglected structures or the aftermath of a disaster; surreal spaces that play with scale to disorient the viewer; architectural frames embellished with materials, objects and images; and structures built out of such readily available commodities as stereo speakers and cardboard boxes. Mike Nelson's temporary sprawling installation *A Psychic Vacuum* (2007), a warren of rooms in the abandoned Essex Street Market in New York's Lower East Side, was a confusing funhouse experience, at once exhilarating and claustrophobic. Salvaging all his materials from the enormous waste of discarded debris in the city, Nelson studied the building's former life and its surrounding neighbourhood to reconstruct elements of the site while simultaneously creating an alternative universe. The sheer magnitude of effort and attention to detail allowed the work to vacillate between real and imagined space. This type of three-dimensional trompe l'oeil has gained currency of late and speaks to our society's need to consistently negotiate between actual experience and that which is mediated or simulated, as well as our increasing comfort with situations that straddle the two. While a project like Nelson's can feel monumental in scale, the experience of moving through his sites tempers one's awareness of all the activity outside and far surpasses the mere replication or mimesis of urban experience.

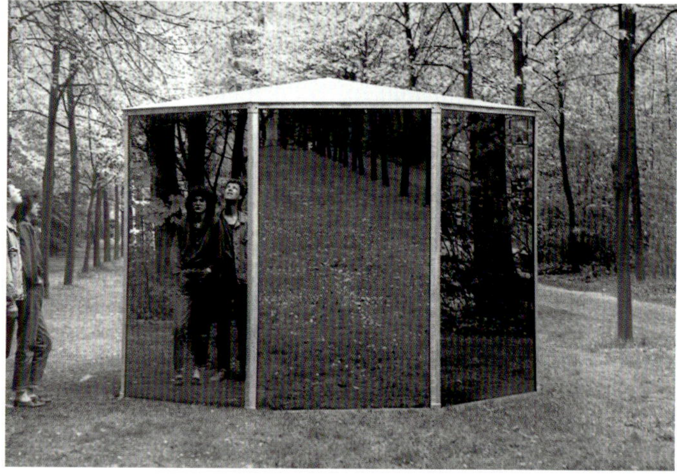

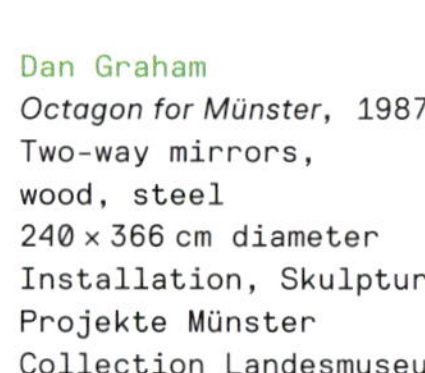

Dan Graham
Octagon for Münster, 1987
Two-way mirrors, wood, steel
240 × 366 cm diameter
Installation, Skulptur Projekte Münster
Collection Landesmuseum, Münster

These types of transformative experiences also take place within the gallery in works by artists such as Felix Schramm, who builds fragments of larger architectural structures that appear to be the remains of a natural disaster or violent upheaval. His piece *Misfit* at the San Francisco Museum of Modern Art in 2007 was wedged into the corner of the gallery — between floor and ceiling and columns — at a precarious angle, as if it had landed there after a hurricane, its sharp corners protruding outwards, calling to mind a site that has been abandoned by human inhabitants more than one of aesthetic contemplation. Monika Sosnowska is interested in the moments when architectural space takes on aspects of mental space. Her installations often play with scale so that rooms become increasingly smaller as one moves through the installation, or she forces viewers along a labyrinthine path, encouraging a sense of disorientation. While these sculptures borrow the visual languages of existing architecture — be it institutional, commercial or domestic — the spaces are resolutely psychological, able to transport us outside their specific references and into an awareness of our emotional responses to the sites in which we locate ourselves.

'The fundamental principle of my work is that it critiques capitalism in very specific ways [...] Leaf through a newspaper and you'll find horror stories from Iraq appearing side by side with underwear adverts. My work exaggerates this.' [Josephine Meckseper]

We have grown increasingly attuned to methods of presentation. The rigorous institutional critique initiated in the 1960s by such artists as Michael Asher and Hans Haacke and held aloft by later practices as divergent as Fred Wilson's reframing of cultural artefacts, Andrea Fraser's docent tours and David Wilson's Museum for Jurassic Technology set the stage for a proclivity towards evaluating not just art objects themselves but *how* they are displayed. Some sculptors who emerged in the late 1970s and early 1980s — Haim Steinbach, Jeff Koons and Allan McCollum — explicitly addressed the question of how objects are shown, both inside the museum and outside, in domestic and commercial spheres. Carol Bove and Josephine Meckseper form a bridge between realms of the personal/domestic and the public/commercial. Bove's selection of objects displayed on simple wooden shelves often carry associations with the politics and social changes of the 1960s and 1970s — one work includes a book by Aldous Huxley and the classic health manual that signified women taking control of their bodies, *Our Bodies Ourselves* — and yet they maintain a quality of personal idiosyncrasy, as if she were reinstalling found materials taken from a living room into the gallery. With strong feminist and anti-capitalist undertones, Meckseper transforms the gallery into a high-end boutique. Her pristine displays of such articles as women's underwear, plungers and stuffed animals encased in shiny glass and chrome cabinets are juxtaposed with imagery associated with ideological protest. Her highly charged combinations are unsettling for their powerful critique of our culture's propensity to fetishize revolutionary gestures and ultimately assuage them of their potential. Meckseper's displays make visible the prioritization of our consumerism and speak to our reliance on economic solutions to every problem that our society faces.

An interesting aspect of sculptors' recent interest in display is their integration of two-dimensional imagery into three-dimensional objects or within large-scale installations. Michaela Meise's *Hair* (2006) presents a celebratory scene from the film version of the musical as a sequence of images presented on top of an overlapping group of metal tables. Rachel Harrison's awkward architectural and columnar forms — which sometimes borrow the language of such display mechanisms as the shelf, the pedestal or the platform — serve as the surface upon which to present a range of photographic images, both from popular culture and captured by her own lens, or discarded amateur paintings which take up such subjects as food, celebrity and portraiture.

'At once insisting upon sensible, material fact and the ineffable meaning that exceeds it.' [Suzanne Hudson on Michael Queenland]

A desire to better understand the complexities of our social and political climate has led a great many contemporary sculptors to research and re-present the past. Their references range from the influential and infamous to the esoteric and largely unknown. The subjects that intrigue them may be political, literary, scientific, economic or artistic, triggered by personal experience or by the sense of curiosity typical of a historian or archivist. Michael Queenland has acknowledged that his childhood exposure to the Davidian church led to the creation of several works that examine those who opt to live outside the mainstream, whether because of pacifist or radical tendencies. Though some of his references may be unknown to viewers — Puritan theologian Jonathan Edwards, for example — his forms are abstractions of familiar objects that nonetheless remain recognizable. His show 'Bread & Balloons' featured several castings of these everyday objects, while his compositions make visual reference to Constantin Brancusi and the minimal forms of Shaker furniture. Similarly fascinated by some of the stranger moments in American history and larger-than-life historical figures' ties to ideological convictions and their ability to tap into huge reserves of ambition, Matthew Day Jackson has taken as his subject the mass suicide initiated by Jim Jones in 1978, the race to the moon, and Buckminster Fuller's utopian architecture. What, in part, is noteworthy in Jackson's work (as well as a number of artists, such as Matthew Monahan, Huma Bhabha and David Altmejd) is the unabashed return to a somewhat disfigured or truncated figure, often presenting parts of the body rather than the whole, and referencing ancient statuary, ritualistic totems and masks more than the history of the representation of the human figure in the arts during the past century. The figure was largely banned from the more commonly abstract avant-garde sculptural practices of the 1960s and 1970s, but it has remained largely whole, intact and, in fact, hyper-real in the sculptures produced since the 1990s by Charles Ray, Ron Mueck, and Paul McCarthy. However, it is not just the representation of the body, or the human image, that constitutes these more recent sculptures, but a notably corporeal and visceral display. These bodies are distinctly *material*, and the fact that we must share the gallery space in order to view or experience them can initiate a surprisingly emotional response that accompanies the intellectual discovery, which occurs as one roots around in the sculptures' many references.

The interconnected objects in Goshka Macuga's elaborate installations, including sculpture, drawings, textiles and prints, suggest an alternative history addressing

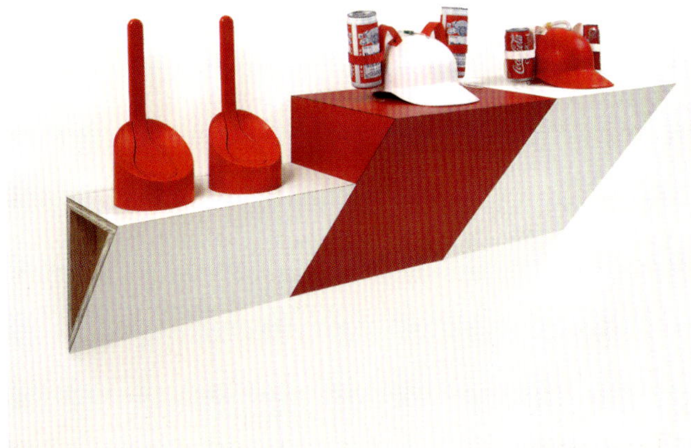

Haim Steinbach
Exuberant Relative #2, 1986
Plywood, plastic laminate, beer cans, plastic hats, scrub brushes
96 × 144 × 38 cm

provocative and speculative topics such as theology, spirituality and sleepwalking. While her practice is certainly research-based and draws upon the disciplines of history, archiving, cataloguing, collecting and curating, the resulting artworks are particularly compelling for their willingness to appropriate fragments and hearsay, and to demolish the hierarchies established between ways of gathering and disseminating information in order to present their own interpretations of these historical events or cultural phenomena, part uncovered fact and part embellished fantasy.

'His attraction to New Age beliefs and practices [...] is one born both of intense curiosity and scepticism [...]. Coffin favours the visual residue of do-it-yourself spirituality. He embraces complex ideas that lend themselves to clumsy visualizations, which humanize their coded beauty.' [Peter Eleey on Peter Coffin]

The representation and allusion that was so precisely excised from Minimalism and Conceptual art is back in full force. What may be surprising about this phenomenon is that in addition to the numerous social and cultural associations at play is a fascination with how sculpture may operate outside the hermeticism of the discipline of art history and in the realm of the sacred or the supernatural. Although artists remain sceptical of the notion of art as idolatry, or the supposition that individual works of art can carry an aura of subconscious universal appeal, it is not unusual today for artists to create sculptures that seek to have some relationship to veneration and ritual. This sacredness is not necessarily linked to specific ideologies, but rather to an exploration of the ways in which sculptural objects have functioned in earlier periods in relationship to activities that surpass the quotidian and extend into the extraordinary. These works tend to be open-ended so as to avoid advocating a particular position; rather, they encourage a level of receptiveness to things outside our daily experience that operate in territories of the unknown or the unexplained. Brian Jungen, for example, transforms vinyl golf bags into forms reminiscent of First Nation totem poles of the Pacific Northwest. Nathan Mabry utilizes the traditional sculptural materials of bronze and terracotta to create figurative and animistic forms and masks associated with ancient Mesoamerican statuary and spiritual objects.

Borrowing the display methodologies of the natural history museum and the accumulative gusto of the storage space, Francis Upritchard revels in the grotesque and the horrific as an expression of the unconscious. Abject and ritualistic, her objects are hybrid forms, and their sense of the uncanny is shared by a number of other contemporary sculptors who produce evocative forms that are deeply informed by things that elude physical description. Anna Sew Hoy locates power in menstrual blood and magical spells. Klaus Weber encourages altered states in his proposal for a public fountain laced with LSD. Peter Coffin explores the paranormal, belief in UFOs and the ability to communicate with plants. Some of these works may sound outlandish or absurd, yet it is clear that the artists' approach is not satirical, nor solely humorous in intention, however amusing the works may be. When considered thoughtfully, these works make apparent just

Nathan Mabry
A Touching Moment (?), 2006
Bronze
160 × 132 × 66 cm

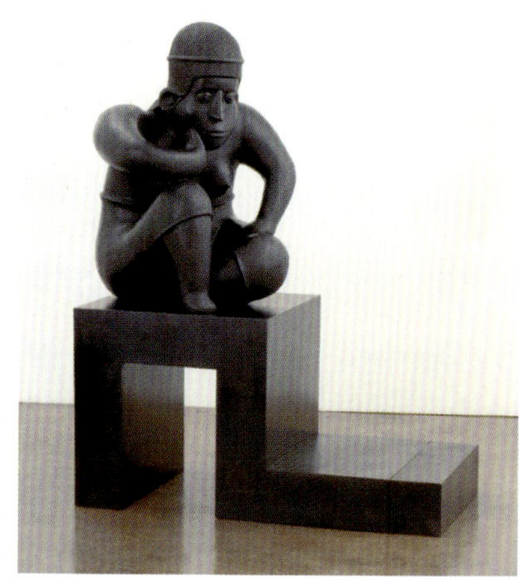

how instinctual and inevitable it is to search for meaning in our lives, and how ideas and beliefs can be translated into physical forms for our contemplation.

'Sculpture is something you bump into when you back up to look at a painting.' [Ad Reinhardt]

Contemporary art has witnessed a groundswell of activity in sculptural production in recent years. The reasons for this enormous interest in sculpture today are many, but the historical significance lies in the possibility that it indicates that the long-held hierarchy of mediums which holds painting to be superior to all others has finally been dispelled. While the diversity of sculptural practice is mind-numbing, making a survey such as this a somewhat daunting task, it is clear that many of the groundbreaking explorations and experimentations that occurred in the 1960s and 1970s to which Krauss was responding in her seminal essay cited at the beginning of this text have been widely absorbed and built upon by young artists now coming on to the scene. We no longer find a room full of dirt or a large hole in the ground to be a dubious sculptural gesture. We accept photographs taken to document a walk to be a valid material element of a larger sculptural project. We are far from the days when sculpture served the sole purpose of monument or memorial, when carving and casting were its primary techniques, or stone and metal its usual materials. Yet contemporary sculptors do not reject outright what by today's standards have become historical traditions of the medium. While the complete absence of the pedestal from the 1966 exhibition 'Primary Structures', organized by Kynaston McShine for the Jewish Museum, indicated a radical new direction for sculpture, taken up by a number of British and American artists — including Anthony Caro, Tony Smith, Robert Morris, Anne Truitt and Robert Grosvenor — and we have had very little use for the pedestal ever since, a number of artists working today have deliberately returned to it. The pedestal may act in its most conventional role as a nearly invisible display mechanism, but is more likely to be integrated into the work in a manner largely inherited from Brancusi. It is a pedestal, in other words, fully aware of its history.

This is just one example of how this generation of sculptors responds to the specific physical and technical challenges of the medium and the ideological debates that have played out within the genres or categories of the medium (as well as within individual practices). Today's practitioners know their history. Indeed, some have argued that artists have become too educated, relying on graduate degrees and the voracious consumption of theory to position their work. But, in fact, it is this level of engagement — a deep understanding of their medium — that serves as a continuous reminder of what is so compelling about sculpture and why these artists have taken it up as their primary medium. In a world fundamentally characterized by its physical nature, the materiality, tactility and spatiality of sculpture provides a direct line into our desire to examine and better understand our surroundings.

The field of sculpture has expanded so much that it has become harder and harder to define, yet these artists have managed to find a space for themselves among the crowds. Their works stand out for the same reasons that the best works of art in any medium draw our attention: their coupling of intellectual rigour and formal acuity, their relevance to the questions that preoccupy us in our daily lives, and their ability to capture our imaginations. However these works are also noteworthy for what they offer to our ongoing discussions and debates about the medium of sculpture. Sculpture's history is inscribed in these works' surfaces and embodied in their forms.

Sculpture is a stubborn medium. It inhabits space and demands our attention. It exposes itself, without illusion or sleight-of-hand, in all its materiality and stands bravely before us. It may be the scale of a city block or a piece of wood leaning against the wall like something belonging in the closet, but sculpture never fails to encourage us to look more closely at the world around us. As that world grows increasingly complex, ebbing and flowing between moments of profound connectivity and nearly insurmountable divides, sculpture offers us a space — an object or an installation — for interaction and contemplation. Among the chaos of our lives and even among the profusion of sculpture itself, the focus and sense of connection that sculpture provides — the way in which you can nearly touch the materials with your eyes or how its forms can trigger a memory — make it increasingly relevant. At this historical juncture, sculpture seems to fit our needs as a culture. Should this remain true, we can expect the field of sculpture to continue to expand. As it does, we can try to make some sense of it, while also relishing its unwieldy and generous nature.

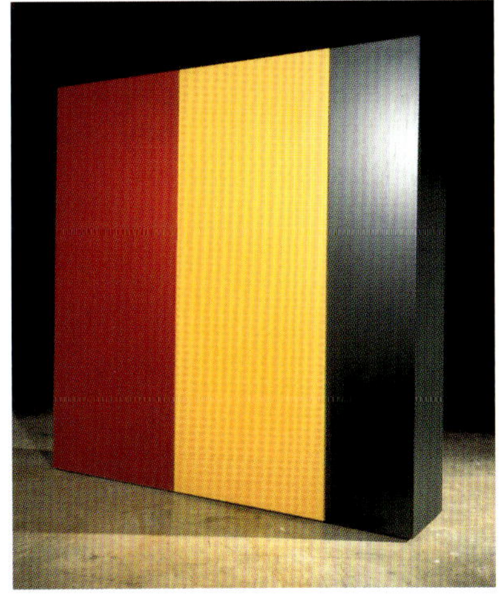

Anne Truitt
Knight's Heritage, 1963
Painted wood
152 × 152 × 31 cm

1 Rosalind Krauss, 'Sculpture in the Expanded Field,' in *The Originality of the Avant-Garde and Other Modernist Myths* (Cambridge: MIT Press, 1985): 276–290. Originally published in *October*, no. 8, 1979, 30–44

2 Johanna Burton acknowledges the relevance of Krauss's seminal essay to a discussion of sculpture today and works through her argument in 'Sculpture: Not-Not-Not (Or, Pretty Air),' in *The Uncertainty of Objects and Ideas: Recent Sculpture* (Hirshhorn Museum and Sculpture Garden, Washington, DC, 2006): 12–13.

3 Ibid, 13.

4 During moments of profusion, it can be a fruitful and meaningful exercise to examine the particulars of a medium, to return to specificity as definitions begin to blur, such as when Roland Barthes set out to uncover the essence of photography in *Camera Lucida: Reflections on Photography* (Hill and Wang, New York, 1981) and in Clement Greenberg's much analyzed considerations of painting and sculpture. However, these careful analyses can end up being too reductive, suggesting an end point in an evolution of a medium and thereby failing to acknowledge the capacity for mediums to continue to change over time. Moreover, these formalist approaches favour the notion of an 'objective truth' while often not adequately addressing the inevitable role of subjectivity in interpretation.

5 The best example of this is perhaps Clement Greenberg's claim that painting would find its essential meaning, its purest form, in flatness. He had a more difficult time, however, distilling sculpture to its essence. See Clement Greenberg, 'The New Sculpture,' in *Art and Culture: Critical Essays* (Beacon Press Boston, 1961) and, 'American-Type Painting' of 1955, Ibid, 208–229.

6 This hierarchy of medium is still alarmingly evident in many museum's structures and practices today.

7 While philosophers and theorists, including Jacques Derrida, Michel Foucault, Frederic Jameson, Walter Benjamin, Hal Foster, Rosalind Krauss and others, have examined the limitations of too predetermined and reductive a definition of artistic mediums and have acknowledged the layered and multifarious nature of artistic (and academic) practice, it is also the artists who, first and foremost, over the past few decades, have made this proposition, both within their works and in their writings and statements. They include Marcel Duchamp, Robert Rauschenberg, Donald Judd, Eva Hesse, Robert Morris, Robert Smithson, Joseph Kosuth, Marcel Broodthaers, Daniel Buren and, more recently, David Hammons and Michael Krebber, among others.

8 In recent years, several exhibitions have responded to the enormous flourish of sculptural practice within the contemporary art field by presenting heterogeneous surveys of the medium. While the curatorial approaches to the subject of sculpture naturally differed and the range of works varied from show to show, these exhibitions tended to present of a sundry assortment of relatively unstable, malleable, and found materials put together in a process that might best be described as aggregate assemblage. Although they emphasized the works' objecthood and materiality, the curators also consistently argued against the notion of sculpture as monumental, memorializing, or static. Relevant shows over the past four years (some of which have not focused on sculpture exclusively) include 'Formalismus: Modern Art Today' at the Kunstverein Hamburg (2004) curated by Yilmaz Dziewior; 'Make It Now: New Sculpture' at SculptureCenter, Long Island City (2005) curated by Anthony Huberman, Mary Ceruti, and Franklin Sirmans; 'Thing: New Sculpture from Los Angeles' at the Hammer Museum (2005) curated by James Elaine, Aimee Chaing, and Christopher Miles; 'Part Object Part Sculpture' at the Wexner Center for the Arts (2005) curated by Helen Molesworth; 'Gone Formalism' at the ICA, Philadelphia (2006) curated by Jenelle Porter; my show 'The Uncertainty of Objects and Ideas: Recent Sculpture' at the Hirshhorn Museum and Garden (2006); 'Unmonumental' at the New Museum (2007) curated by Richard Flood, Massimiliano Gioni and Laura Hoptman; 'Poor Thing' at Kunsthalle Basel, (2007) curated by Silke Baumann and Simone Neuenschwander; and the 2008 Whitney Biennial, curated by Henriette Huldisch and Shamim M. Momin.

9 Rosalind Krauss, *A Voyage on the North Sea: Art in the Age of the Post-Medium Condition* (Thames and Hudson, New York, 1999): 26.

10 In contrast, Theodor Adorno stated, 'The task of art today is to bring chaos into order,' in T.W. Adorno, *Minima Moralia*, translated by E.F.N. Jephcott (London, Verso, 1978).

11 Donald Judd, 'Specific Objects,' *Arts Yearbook*, 1965. Reprinted in *Donald Judd, Complete Writings 1959–1975* (The Press of the Nova Scotia College of Art and Design & New York University Press, Halifax & New York City, 1975): 181–189.

12 Richard Serra wrote this list in 1967–78 in order to remove metaphor from his sculpture and to root his practice in process, giving himself specific actions to enact upon his materials.

13 Michael Fried, 'Art and Objecthood,' in *Artforum* 5 (June 1967): 12–23.

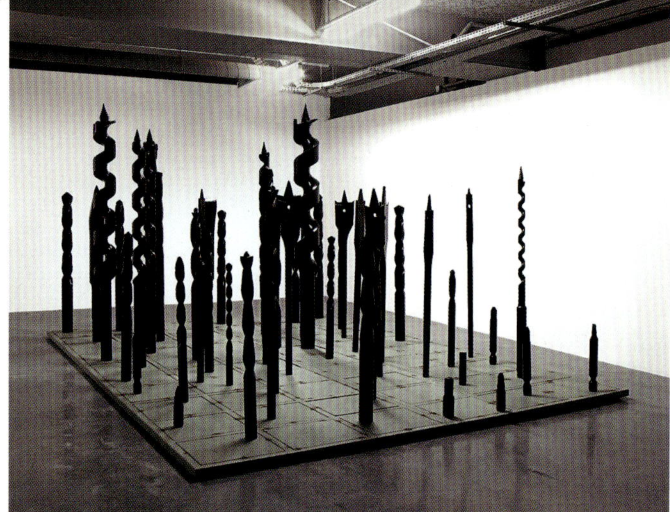

01

Since arriving in France from his native Algeria fifteen years ago, Adel Abdessemed has rapidly developed an expansive and diverse body of work addressing the complexities of selfhood in a globalizing world. Although he has strenuously disclaimed the rubric of the 'postcolonial' artist, he is unquestionably a postcolonial subject, caught between two cultures, between two identities, and his work exhibits the double consciousness that scholars of the cultural diaspora have signalled as characteristic of those who have been compelled to abandon stable ethnicities and nationalities. We might say that his art swings between the poles of an almost aggressively asserted personal autonomy and a lingering desire for an identity based within a hybrid sense of ethnic community.

This dynamic is particularly pronounced in his works that take up the theme of flight, itself an important trope of global population movements in the new century. *Habibi* (2004) is a large-scale sculptural installation (seventeen metres long), consisting of a resin and fibreglass human skeleton suspended from the ceiling in a posture of flight, accompanied by an aeroplane engine turbine that seems to be propelling the body through space. It is an image of migration as frictionless freedom, the human subject untethered to the earth and liberated from any constrictive bonds. The skeleton, which reappears in Abdessemed's work numerous times as a stand-in for the artist, is free from history, free from memory, a body stripped of all particularities and reduced to the bare signifiers of humanity: the bone structure and nothing more.

But this figure of a subject liberated from identity is countered by works such as *Bourek* (2005), the fuselage of a small private jet that has been twisted in upon itself to form a compact roll of metal. The title refers to the thin packets of pastry stuffed with ground meat popularly eaten as appetizers in Algeria and found throughout the Middle East and around the Mediterranean. *Bourek* expresses a longing for a lost home, through the bias of a food culture that the artist identifies with a maternal role. At the same time, however, this traditional signifier of the Algerian home is transformed, remade in a 'masculine' mode as a monumental (if still fragile) pile of twisted metal that resists nostalgic identification.

The collapsed body of *Bourek* also recalls another predominant element of Abdessemed's work: its frequent recourse to an implicit violence, whether in the form of sudden transformation (*Foot on*, 2005), implied threat (*Axe On*, 2007) or brute animal behavior (*Birth of Love*, 2006). But this violence, while unquestionably an element of Abdessemed's artistic persona, just manages to avoid the gratuitous by remaining tied to a larger social dynamic of North-South relations. *Salam Europe* (2006), sixteen kilometres of barbed wire wound neatly into a large circle, is a direct evocation of the violence attendant upon migration from North Africa to the European continent, and the brutality that frontiers still exercise in a supposedly global society. It is precisely this conflicted geography that subtends the conflicted subjectivity so eloquently explored in the artist's work.
[Tom McDonough]

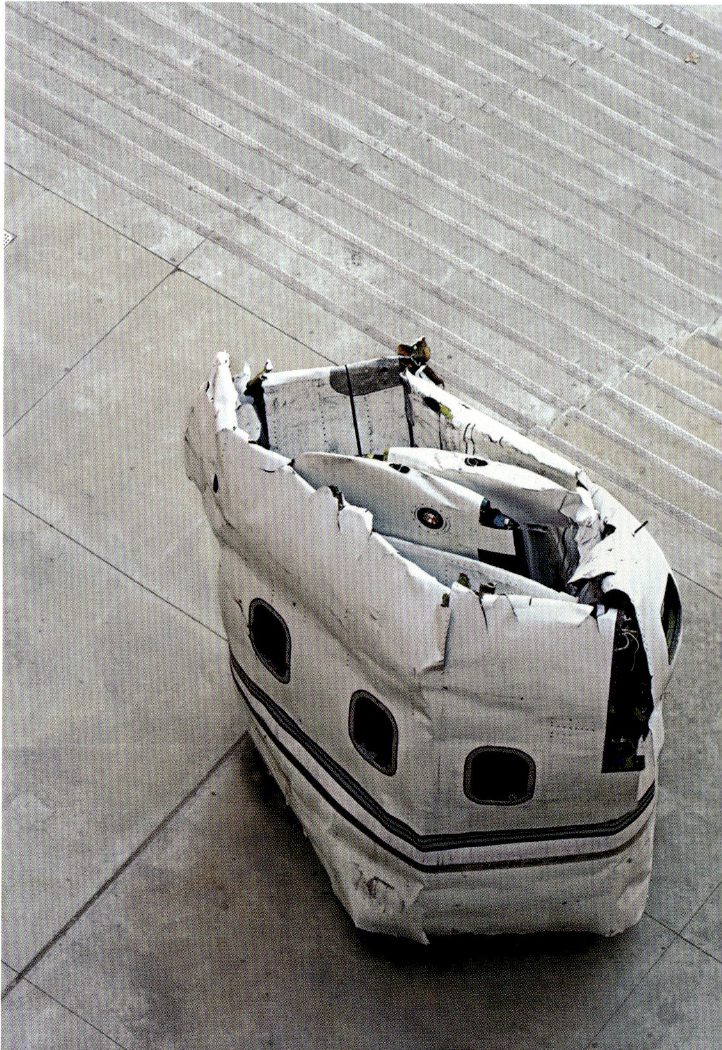

02

01 *Or noir*, 2007
23 drills, black marble
Heights vary from 127 cm to 255 cm

02 *Bourek*, 2005
Aerojet Commander plane
226 × 274 cm

03 *Axe On*, 2007
Knives
13 of 386 knives

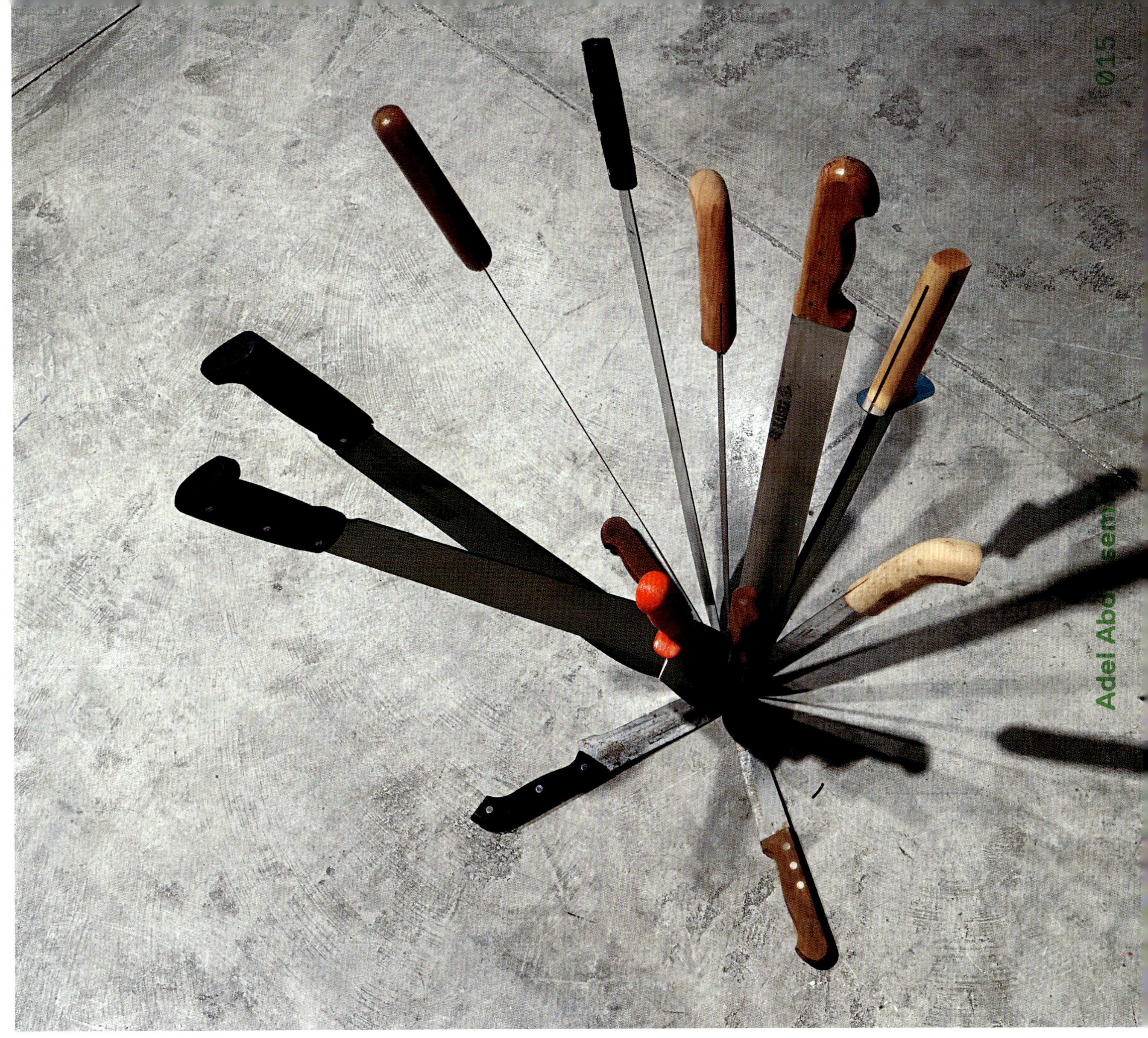

03

Overleaf:
04 *Habibi*, 2004
Resin, fibreglass, polystyrene,
airplane engine turbine
Length 17 m

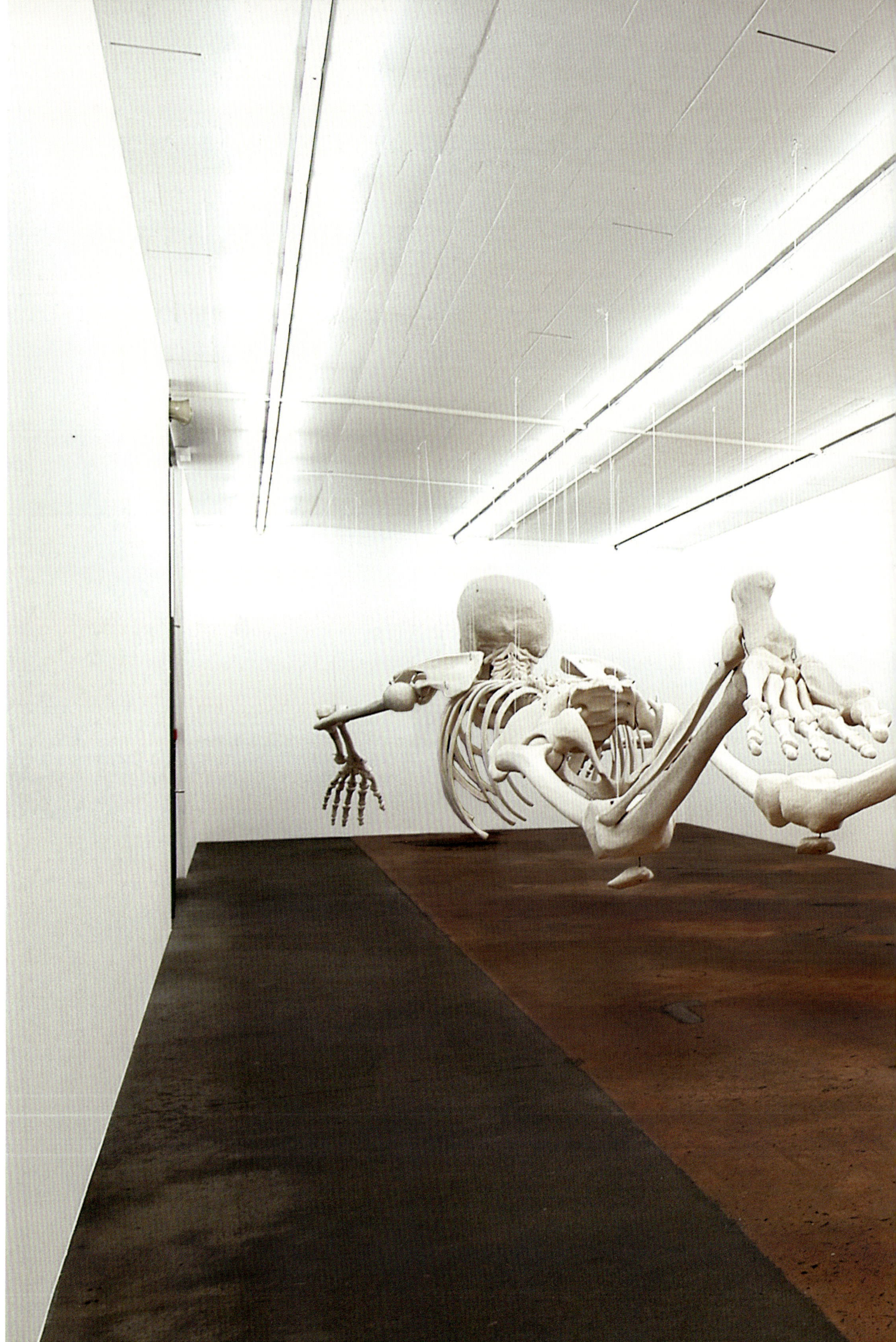

04

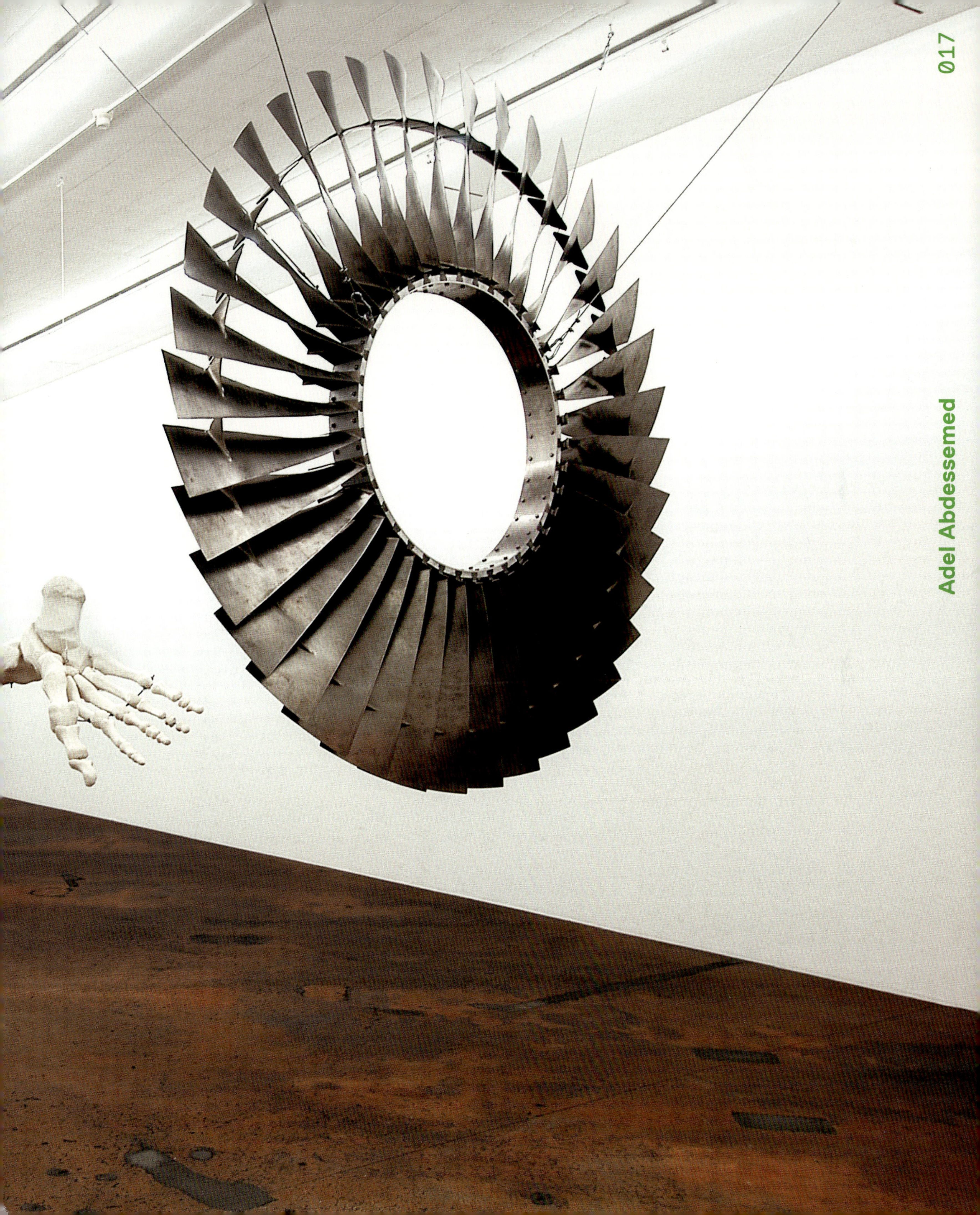

Adel Abdessemed

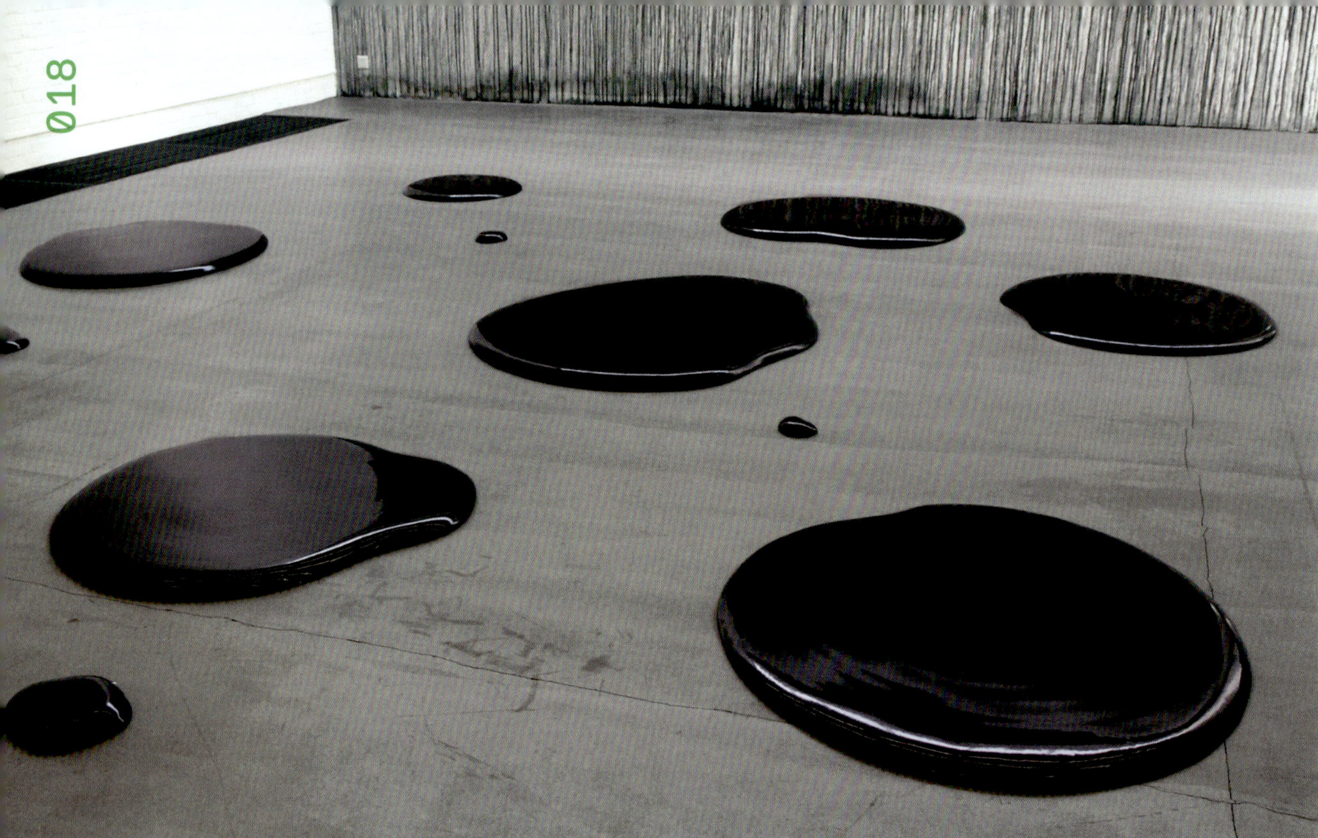

01

Ai Weiwei is an inexhaustible producer of opinions. People are as interested in what he says as they are in what he makes. His forceful blog writing and up front public speeches are as charismatic as his handsome and ambitious sculptures. Together with his extensive architectural projects, from the design of private homes to his involvement in the National Stadium in Beijing, the scope of his practice sees no bounds. His most sensational project to date was *Fairy Tale* (2007), a work he made for Documenta 12. The central idea of the project, to grant 1,001 Chinese people a visit to Kassel during the time of the exhibition, was so naïve and romantic that the complicated and prohibitive cost of its realization was almost dismissible and paradoxical. While *Fairy Tale* enabled Ai to carry out his own artistic ambition and social ideal uninhibitedly, the political undertone and humanistic concern of *Fairy Tale* was nothing personal or unreal. It was one of his persistent and daring crusades to question and challenge the concept of systems and the authority and elasticity of social structure.

Ai is also sincere in his belief in the transformative and transcendental potential of art. His determination and ability to revitalize and update traditional crafts and materials with contemporary concepts and aesthetics is exceptional and often generates extraordinary results. Wood and antique furniture-building techniques, porcelain and traditional firing methods have all found exciting new transformations in his practice, even when they were smashed or deconstructed. Their rebirth was always miraculous and revealing of his profound understanding of traditions, sophisticated stylistic choices and precise perception of scale.

While the usual attitude towards antiquity is one of absolute reverence and distance, Ai hasn't been able to suppress his impulse to constantly defy and redefine this relationship by interacting with ancient artefacts in many different ways. He has painted them in bright colours (*Painted Vases*, 2003), broken them into pieces (*Breaking Two Blue-and-White 'Dragon' Bowls*, 1996) and replicated them with great precision (*Blue-and-White Moonflask*, 1996). *Dropping a Han Dynasty Urn* (1995) is a series of three photographs that document the artist shattering a genuine 2,000-year-old Han artefact on the ground. The artist's matter-of-fact expression and deliberate performative gestures offset the provocative and subversive nature of his action. Adopting the same iconoclastic approach, Ai had a series of Ming and Qing Dynasty furniture pieces remade and altered using the same technical principle of constructing such classical furniture, yet they became purely formal objects stripped of their designated functions. He also took wooden beams from dismantled Qing Dynasty temples and had them carved into unusual, impractical shapes, including a bench in the shape of China (*Bench*, 2004). The same visionary nerve and visual sensitivity are also manifested in his inspirational makeovers of traditional artforms such as porcelain. He made large oil spills of irregular shapes (*Oil Spills*, 2006), a *ruyi* (a Chinese talismanic sceptre) made up of human organs (*Ruyi*, 2006), and dresses and plates of exquisite flowers. It is his deep-rooted distrust of tradition and establishment that motivates and marks his feverish and fruitful battle for creativity. [Carol Lu]

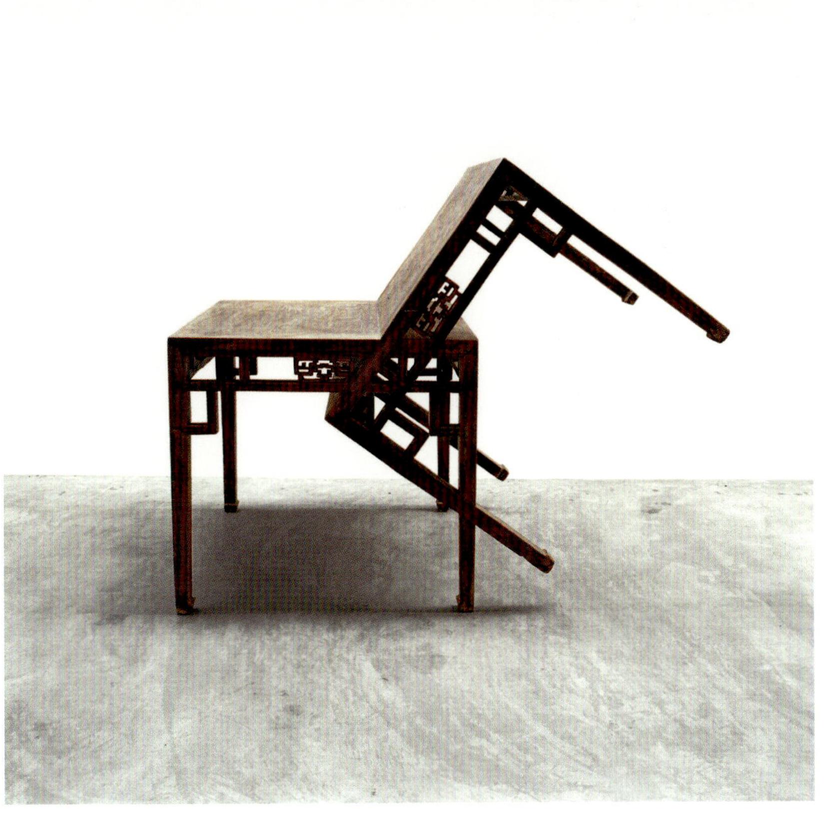

02

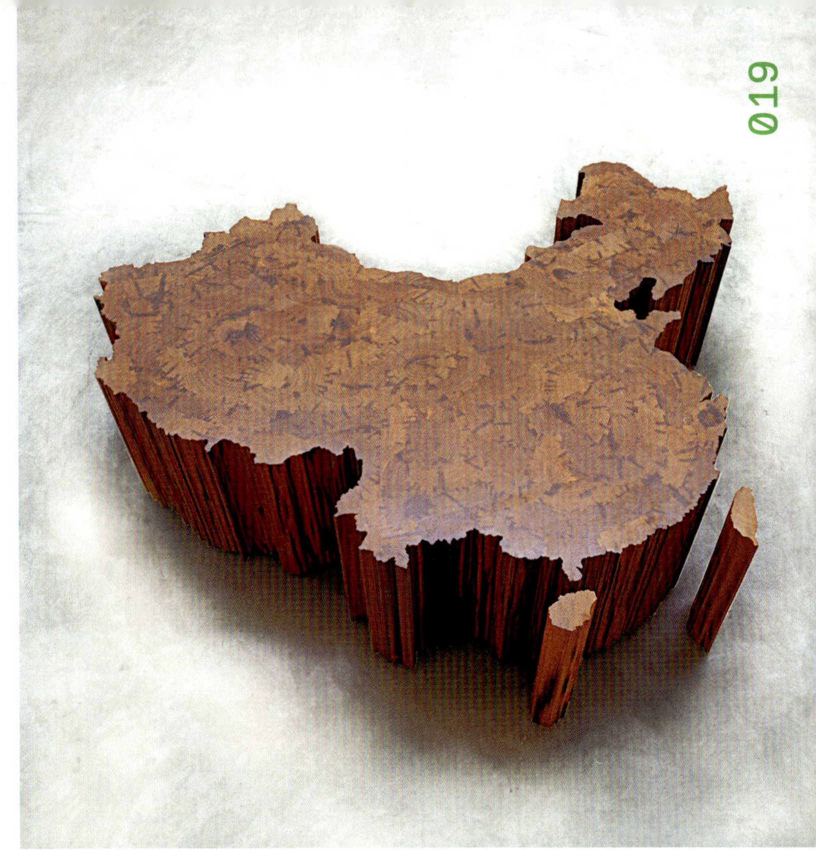

03

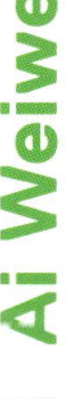

04

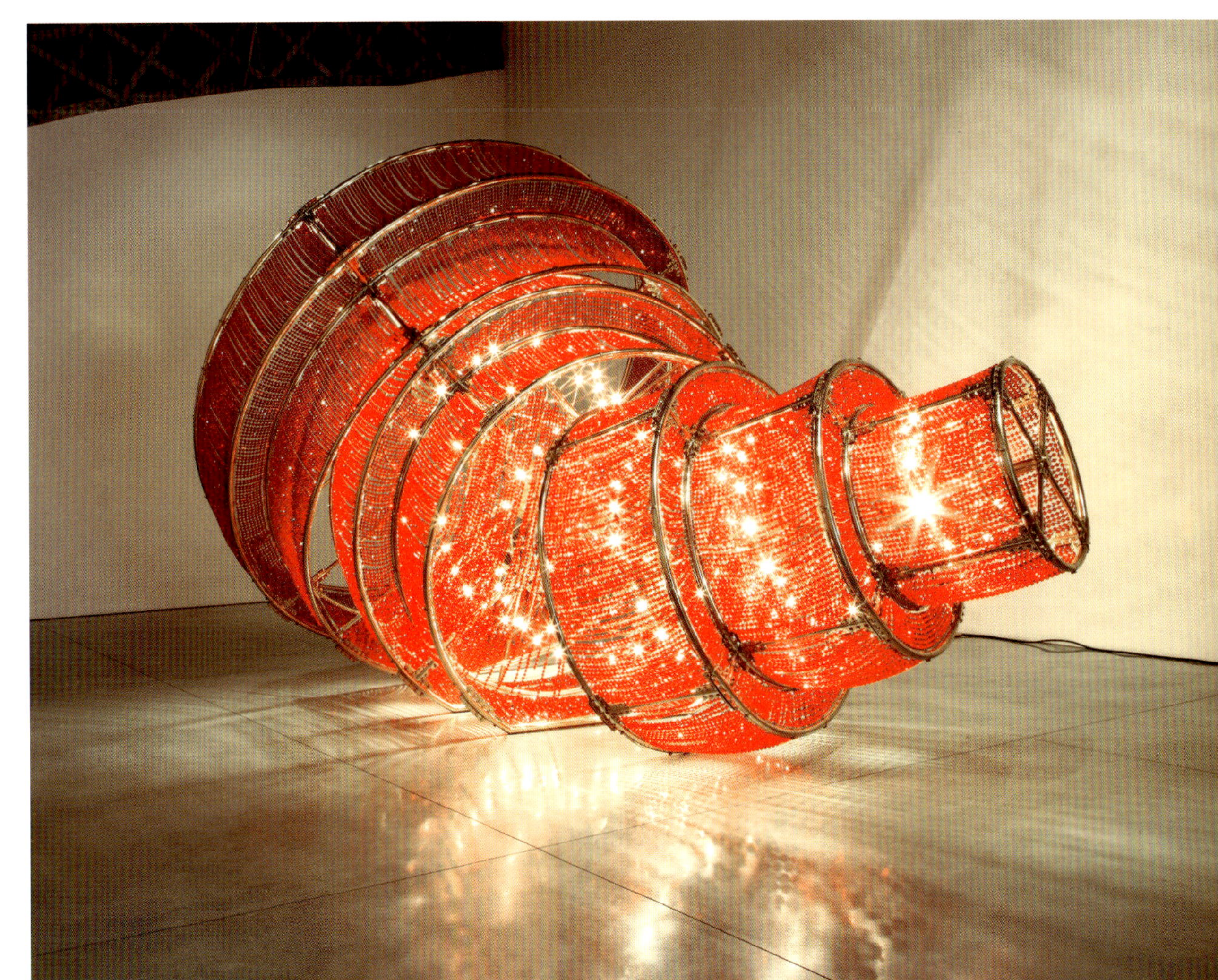

01 *Oil Spills*, 2006
Porcelain
12 parts
Diameters vary from 13 to 119 cm

02 *Two Joined Square Tables*, 2005
Tables from the Qing Dynasty (1644–1911)
136 × 168 × 92 cm

03 *Map of China*, 2004
Iron wood (Tieli wood)
from dismantled temples of the
Qing Dynasty (1644–1911)
51 × 200 cm

04 *Descending Light*, 2007
Glass crystal, lights, metal
400 × 663 × 461 cm

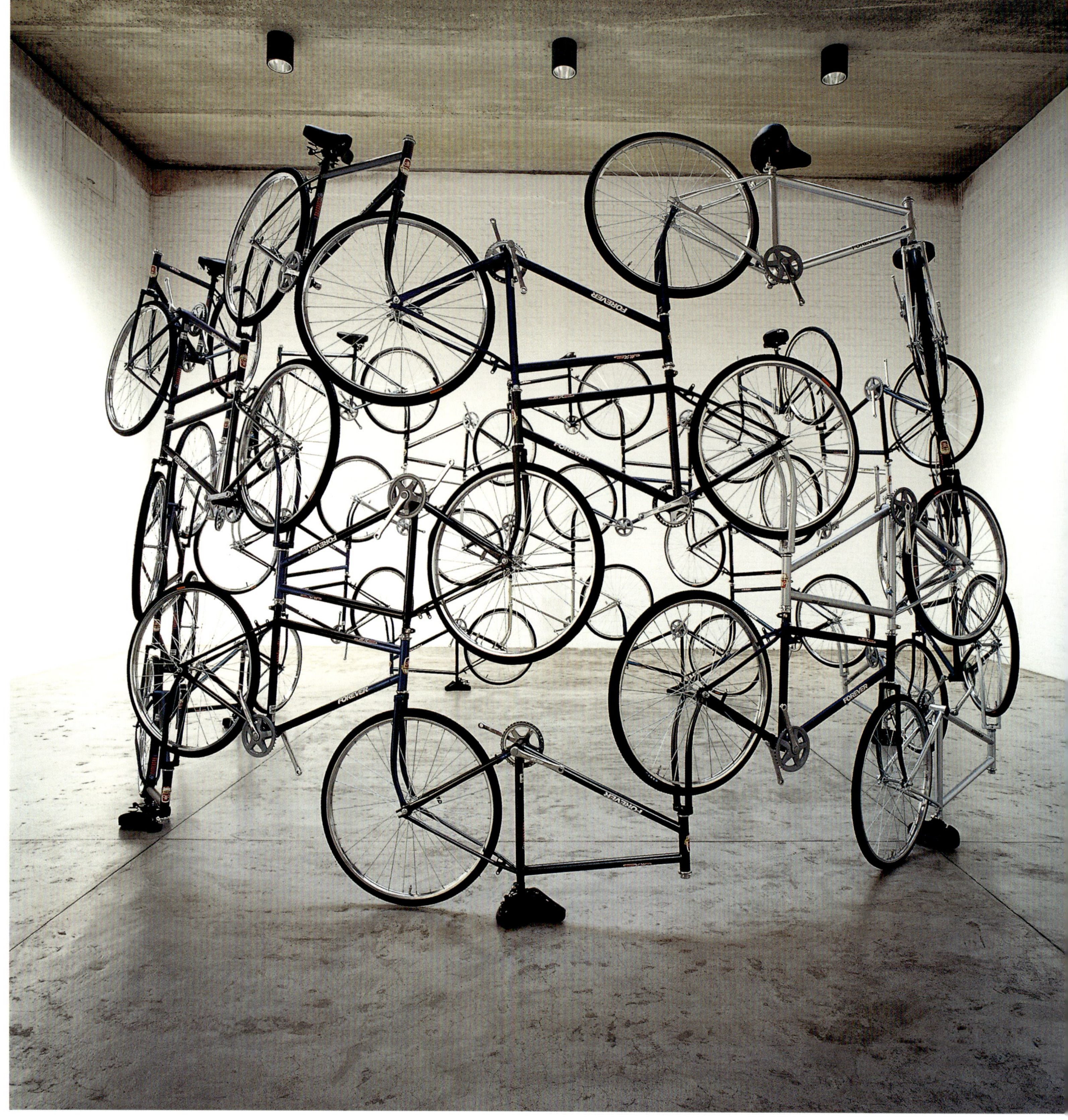

05

05 *'Forever' Bicycles*, 2003
Bicycles
275 × 450 × 450 cm

06 *Ton of Tea*, 2006
1 ton of compressed tea,
wooden base
100 × 100 × 100 cm

06

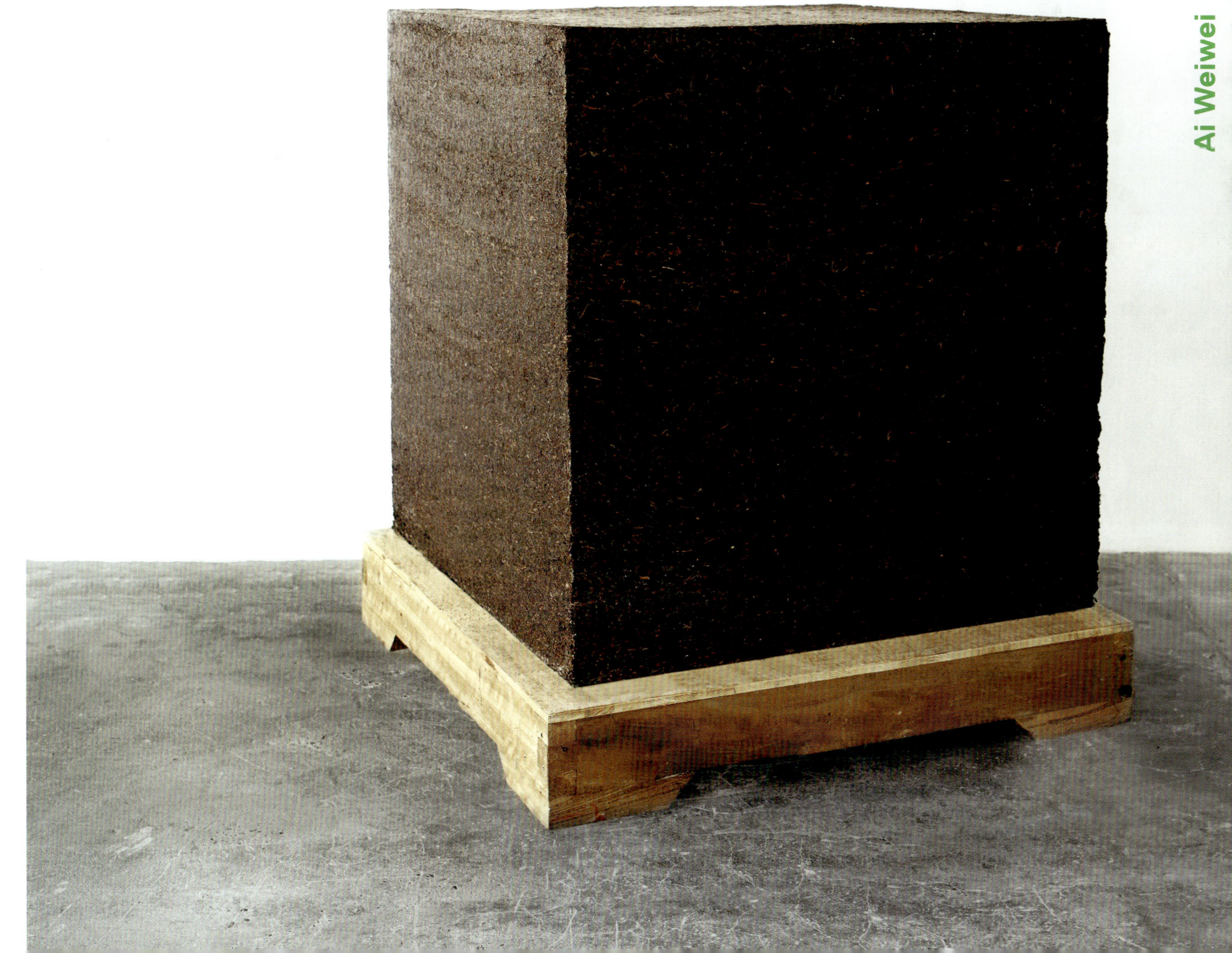

01

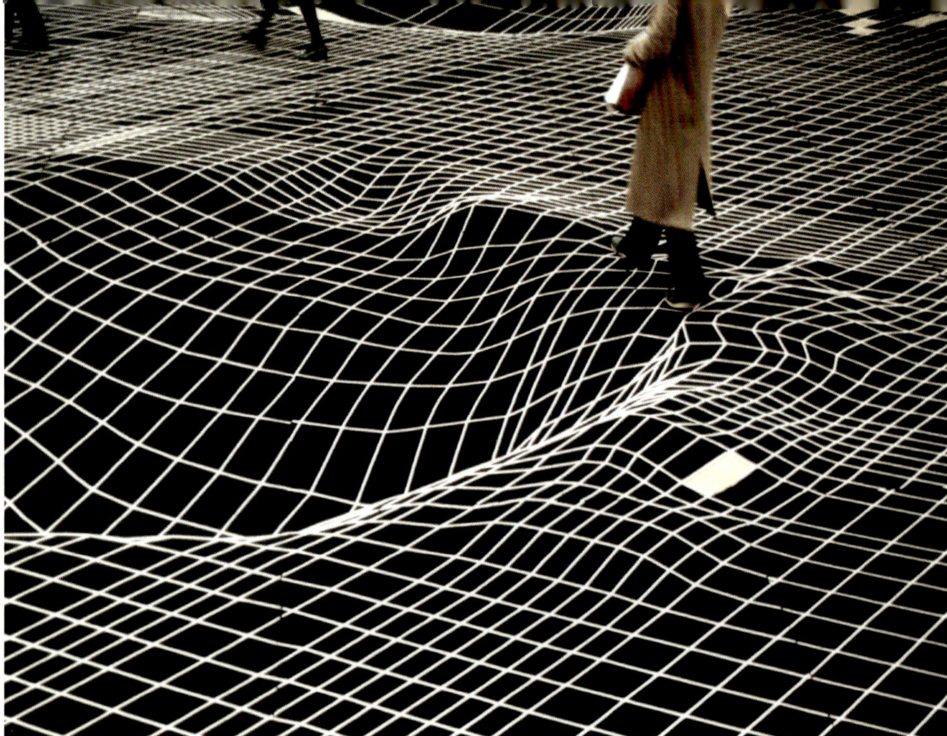

01 *Land Mark*, 1999/2003
Felt
5 × 29 m

02 *Returning a Sound*, 2004
Single channel video with sound
5 min. 42 sec.

03 *Clamor*, 2006
Plaster, foam, pigment, 1 tuba, 1 trumpet, 2 trombones, 1 flute, 1 drum kit, pre-recorded sound, live musicians
9.3 × 5.3 × 1.6 m

04 *Hope Hippo*, 2005
Mud, whistle, daily newspaper, person
Approx. 4.9 × 1.9 × 1.5 m

Despite their young age, the Puerto Rico-based artists Jennifer Allora and Guillermo Calzadilla are highly respected veterans of the international art world. Allora, who was born in the United States, and Calzadilla, born in Cuba, met for the first time in 1995 and have worked collaboratively ever since. Their work is best described as a post-Conceptual fusion of disciplines ranging from video, sculpture and performance to photography and sound. Their poetic and metaphorical pieces look at complex, highly topical issues such as war, migration, consumerism and national identity. Taking a critical and clearly political approach, often incorporating forms of protest, they simultaneously address politics, culture and history from multiple perspectives.

One of their best-known works, *Chalk*, underwent several incarnations between 1998 and 2002. It originally appeared in Peru's capital city of Lima during the 1998 Lima Biennial. The artists placed large chalk sticks all around the plaza housing the nation's government buildings. It is a local tradition for the public to circumnavigate the plaza every day at noon, protesting against government actions and policies. On seeing the chalk sticks, the protesters realized that they could voice their demands and criticism more permanently by writing on the pavement. Though it was site — and context — specific, *Chalk* also addressed broader issues related to the use of public space, democracy and possible modes of political action.

Another context-specific work, simple yet ingenious, is *Puerto Rican Light (to Dan Flavin)* (2003). At the Americas Society in New York, the artists took a 1965 fluorescent light sculpture by the American artist Dan Flavin, entitled *Puerto Rican Light (to Jeanie Blake)*, and powered it with electricity from car batteries charged with solar energy collected in Puerto Rico, thus creating and presenting 'real' light from Puerto Rico in a kind of representational implosion.

For a number of years, Allora and Calzadilla explored the history and contemporary realities of the small island of Vieques, off the coast of Puerto Rico, which until 2003 was a United States Navy bomb test site. In 2004, to commemorate the island's demilitarization, they created a film work there. Entitled *Returning a Sound*, it shows a young man on a motorcycle with a trumpet attached to the muffler. He tours through the lush, tropical landscape, creating various sounds on the trumpet by shifting gears in a sort of accidental anthem of triumphal reclamation.

Returning a Sound was the beginning of Allora and Calzadilla's interest in sound and its relationship to war and militarism. *Clamor* (2006) and *Wake Up* (2007) are two other pieces that combine sculpture, performance and sound. *Clamor* is a large-scale sculpture based on the architectural design of military bunkers from around the world in various historical eras. A live orchestra, hidden inside, plays a wide range of melodies related to war and militarism: songs that are used to get soldiers fired up, marching music and sounds that are used as weapons of torture. For *Wake Up* Allora and Calzadilla enlisted seven trumpet players to reinterpret 'Reveille', the well-known bugle wake-up call. The recording is played inside a large drywall sculpture through more than a dozen speakers. Several brilliant light bulbs are hidden inside the walls, their brightness synchronized to the volume of the bugles, creating an atmosphere reminiscent of an ongoing series of explosions. [Jens Hoffmann]

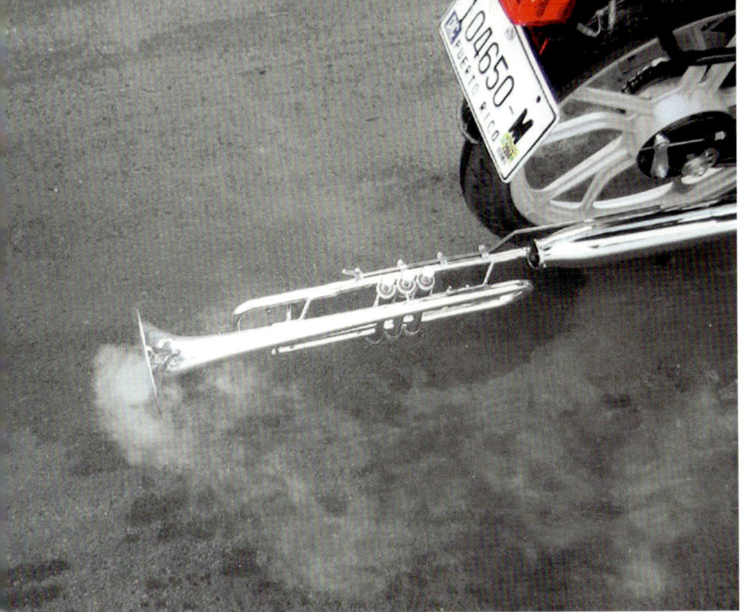

02

03

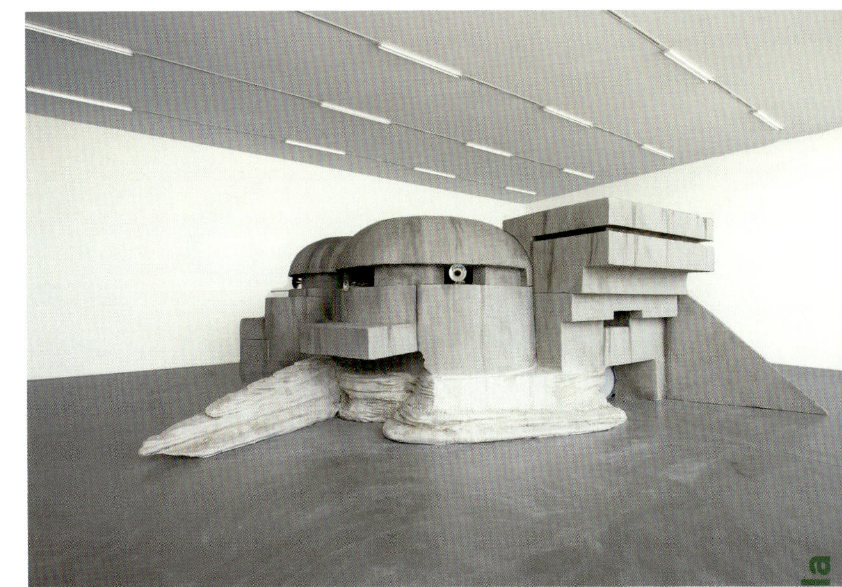

04

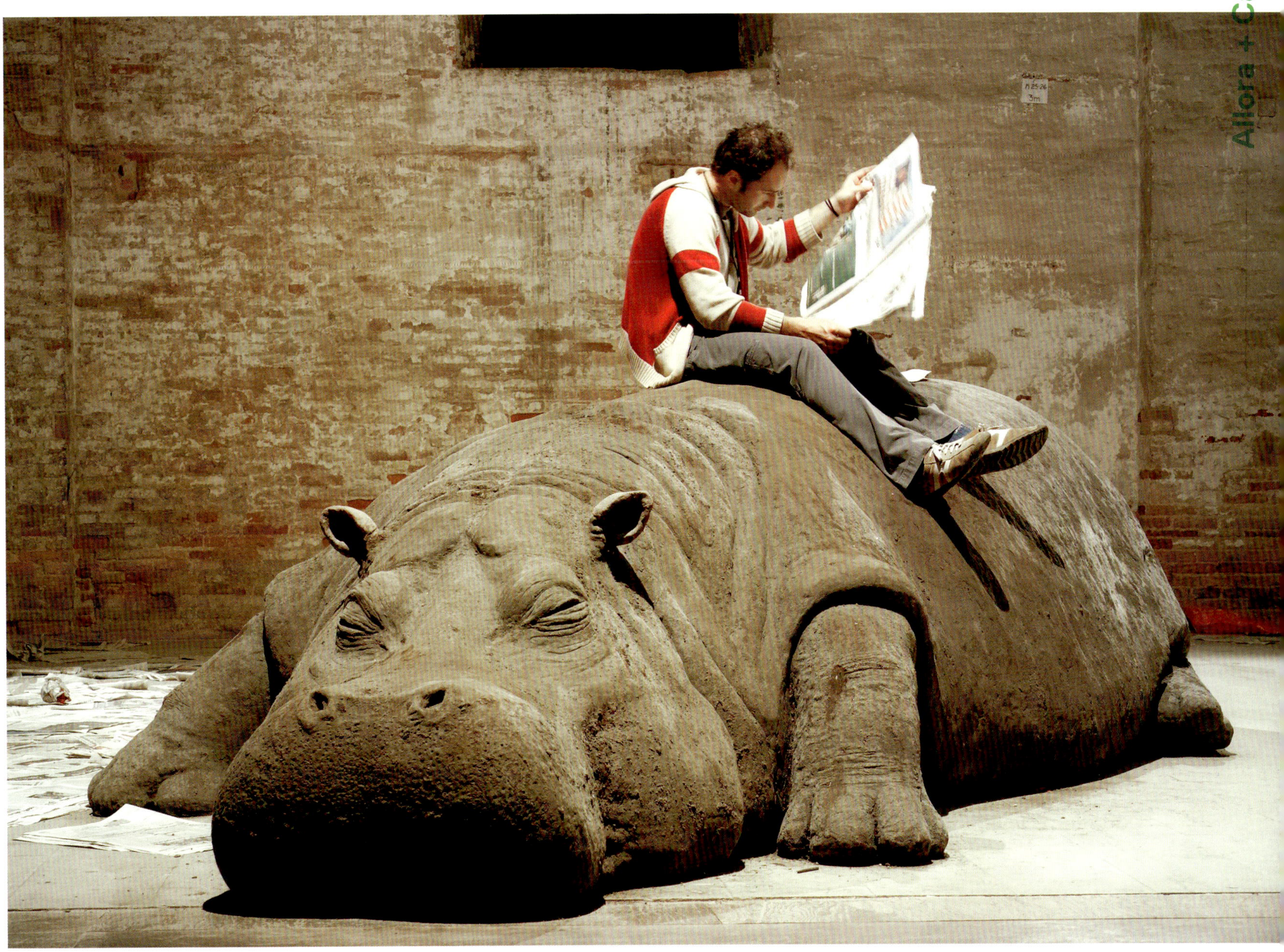

In ancient Greece, hybrid creatures — griffins, harpies, centaurs — embodied the spectacular and supernatural, simultaneously frightening and alluring in the impossibility of their dual physiognomy. Retaining a heraldic status up to the present day, these figures still lend significance to international currency, flags and emblems. Aware of the timeless power of the biologically unimaginable made flesh, Canadian artist David Altmejd has focused his endlessly inventive practice on the fantastical. He began his studies at the Université du Québec in biology, and since his turn to art he has continued his investigation of the natural and the artificial — and the overwhelming beauty
01 that arises from their collision.

Altmejd's sculptural beings and their distinctive habitats are born in his studio, and often continue to develop during their installation in galleries or museums, where he embellishes surfaces with glitter, glass beads or feathers. Emphasizing the handmade through his choice of media and finish, an infinite layering of details, Altmejd also makes a literal evocation of the hand in the form of life-size plaster casts, which regularly spring from a figure's back or a bird's wings or clutch at engorged sexual features.

In his works, Altmejd maintains the autonomy of individual elements, so that each one jars in contrast to its surrounding materials. There is a constant, almost violent, clash between media in works such as *Untitled* (2005), where a foam head, dressed in a synthetic blonde wig, is tangled with epoxy clay, paint, resin and amethyst quartz. His recent sculpture *The Center* (2008) combines diverse elements — wood, horse hair and glass eyes — in the fabrication of a colossal figure. Considering his productions as complex sculptural works, rather than installations, he also emphasizes traditional support structures — platforms, pedestals, vitrines and lighting. In *The University 2* (2004), he turns these framing devices into the very content of the work, further undermining the illusion of a cohesive whole.

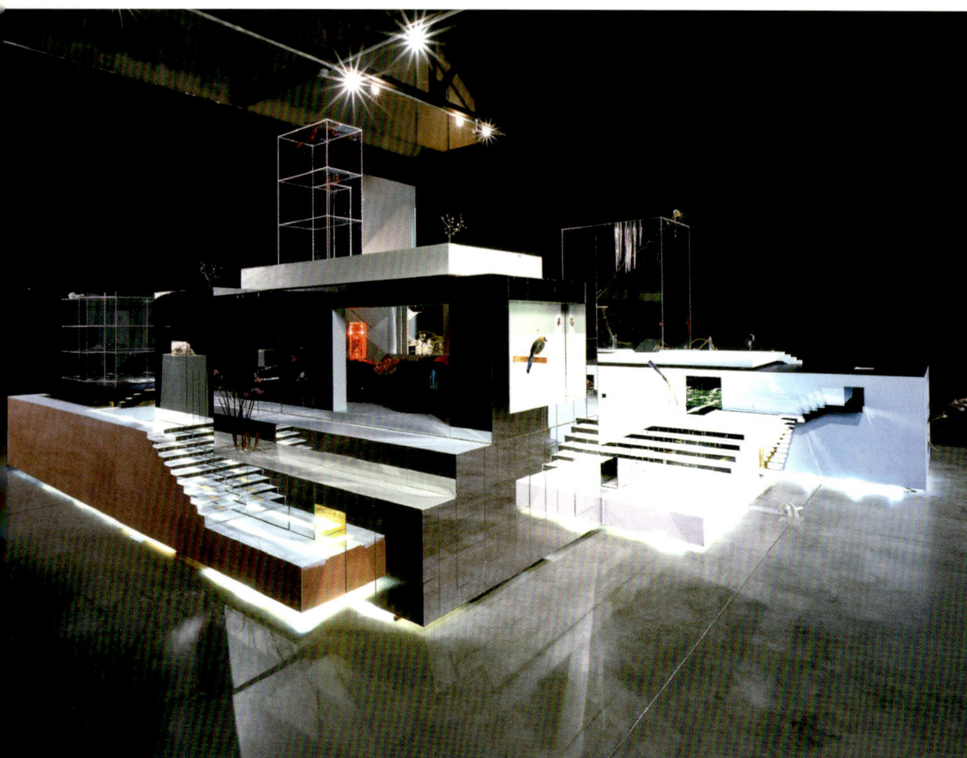

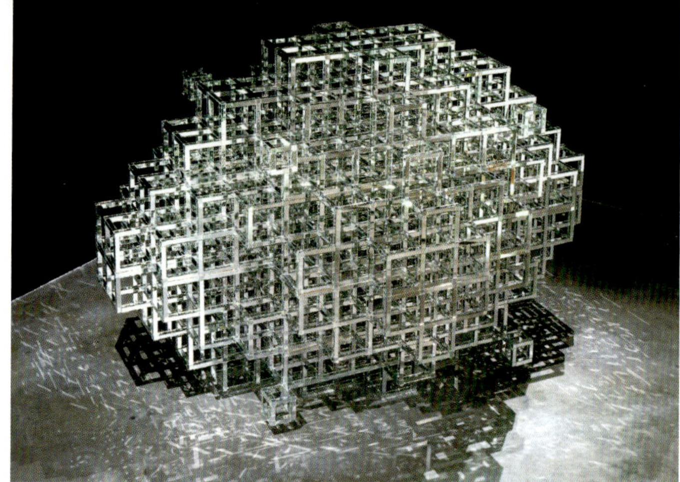

Applied to kaleidoscopic effect, Altmejd's consistent use of mirrors reveals his belief in the primacy of the act of looking. A streamlined example is found in *The University 1* (2004), an angular wooden matrix covered with mirrors to produce an amplification of form and space. Mirrors play a strong role in the fragmentation of *The Settlers* (2005), a furry creature adorned with reflective shards, white socks, black leather shoes and a digital Casio watch. Likewise, mirrored shrapnel dissects *The Glasswalker* (2006), another werewolf-like beast sporting laced-up leather shoes and white underpants. For his recent exhibition at the Museum of Contemporary Art, Denver, 'Star Power: Museum as Body Electric' (2007–08), Altmejd encased the galleries, as well as his sculptures, with mirrored panels, simultaneously fragmenting and magnifying the formal complexities of his work.

The seduction of Altmejd's work lies in his ability to place objects containing an uncanny degree of familiarity in intensely exotic situations. *The Index*, his project for the Canadian Pavilion in the 2007 Venice Biennale, created the atmosphere of an aviary — taxidermied birds and animals nestling among geological outcrops and tree branches bedecked with pine cones and glitter. In this magical environment Altmejd nevertheless kept at least one foot in the realm of the everyday. Although he cites Kiki Smith and Louise Bourgeois as references, curator Nancy Spector has compared his work to Matthew Barney's. This comparison, while not necessarily resonant on formal levels, acknowledges the artists' intensely visceral and conceptual narratives — and a shared sense of exuberant beauty on a par with the Baroque.
[Lillian Davies]

02

01 *The University 1*, 2004
Mirror, wood
168 × 180 × 269 cm

02 *The University 2*, 2004
Wood, paint, plaster, resin, mirror, Plexiglas, wire, glue, plastic, cloth, synthetic hair, jewellery, glitter, minerals, paper, beads, synthetic flowers, electricity, light bulbs
272 × 546 × 640 cm

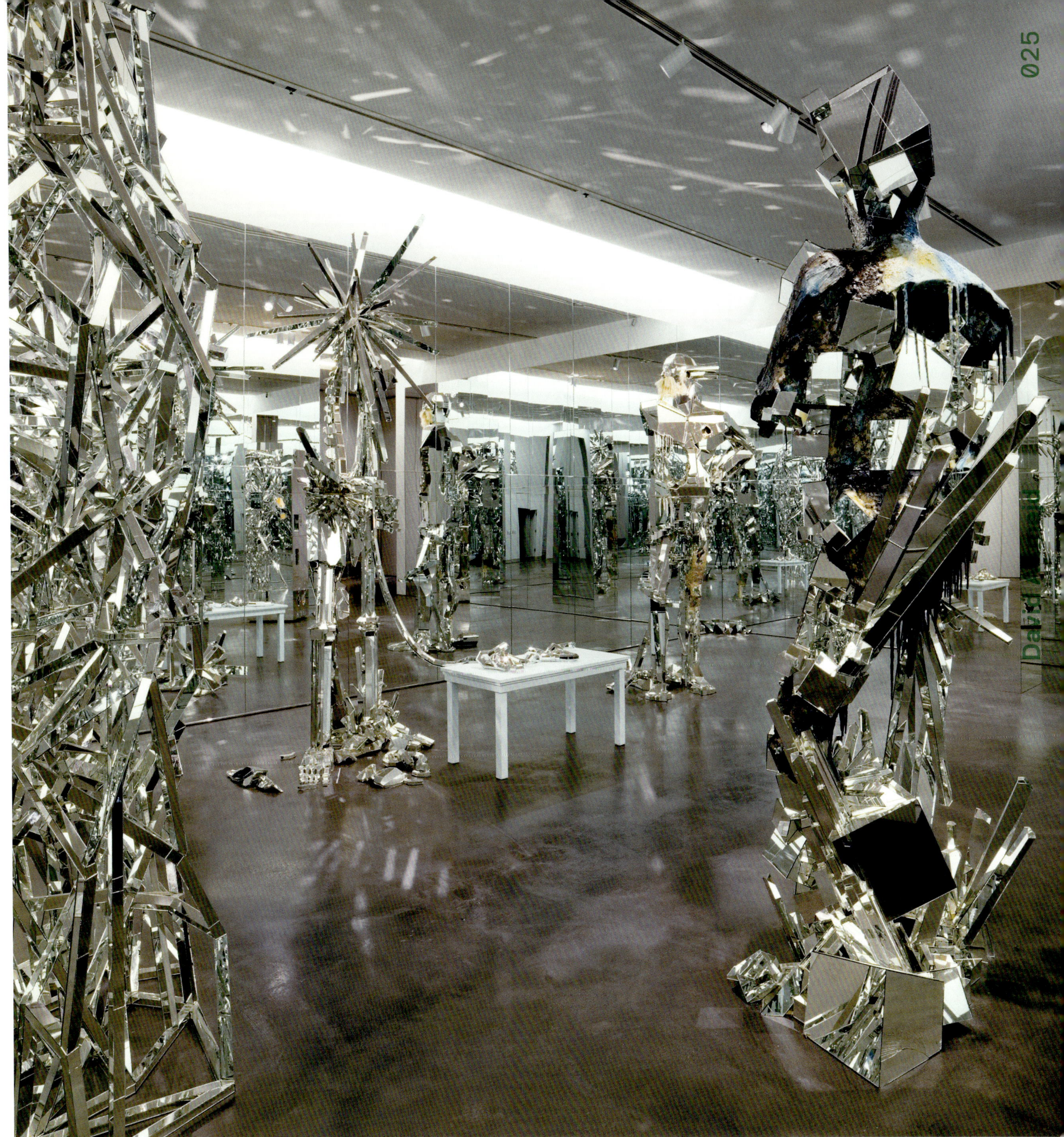

03

03 from left:
→ *Untitled*, 2007
Wood, mirror, glue
466 × 193 × 137 cm
→ *Untitled*, 2007
Wood, mirror,
paint, glue
452 × 416 × 340 cm
→ *Untitled*, 2007
Wood, mirror, epoxy clay,
paint, horse hair
383 × 125 × 104 cm
→ *Untitled*, 2007
Wood, mirror,
epoxy clay, paint
376 × 137 × 101 cm

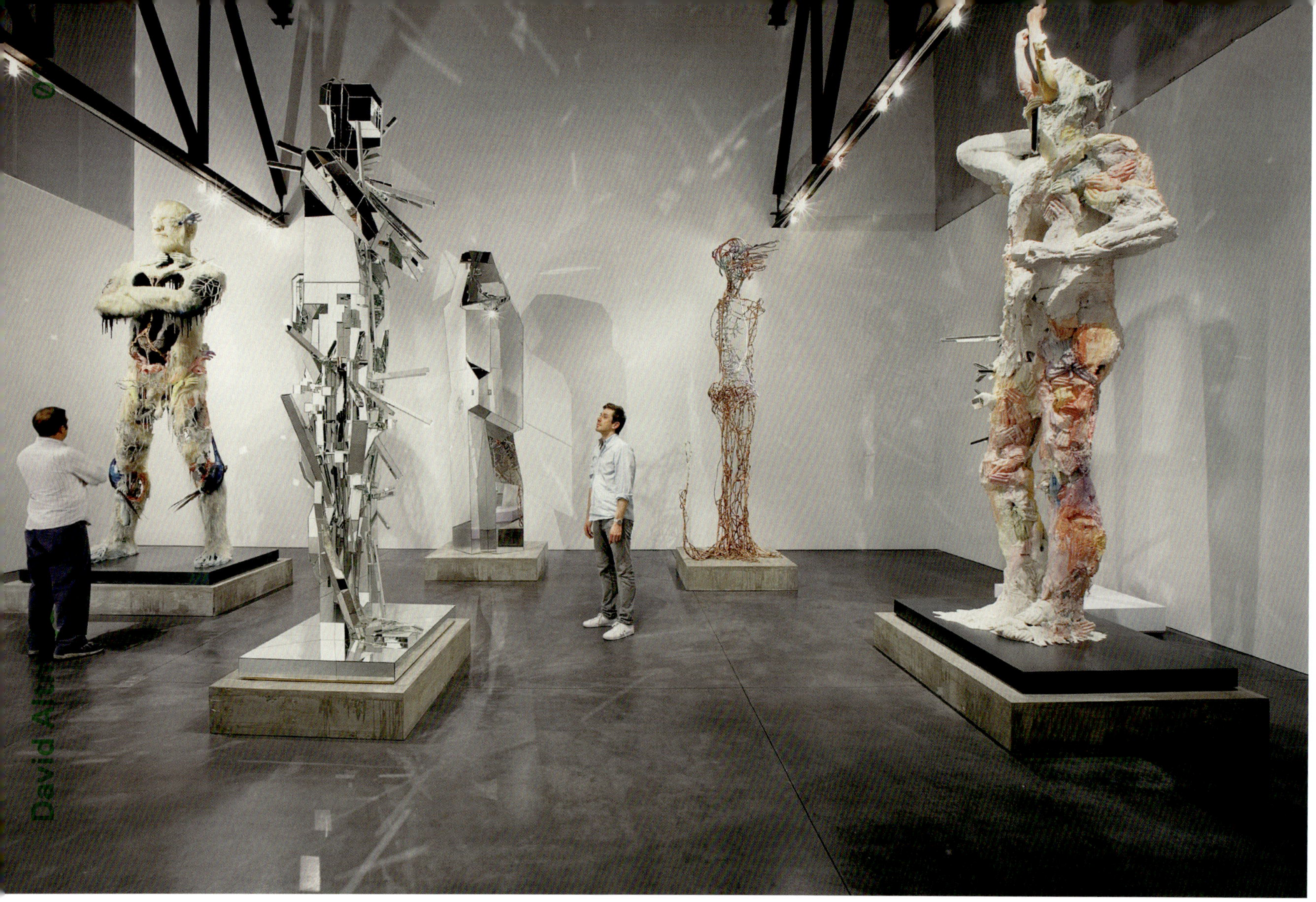

04

05

04 from left:
→ *The Center*, 2008
Wood, foam, epoxy clay, resin, horse hair, metal wire, paint, mirror, glass beads, plaster, glue, feathers, glass eyes
358 × 183 × 121 cm
→ *The Guide*, 2008
Wood, mirror, glue
367 × 123 × 91 cm
→ *The Quail*, 2008
Wood, mirror, glue, quail eggs
353 × 104 × 63 cm
→ *Figure*, 2008
Epoxy clay, wire, paint, glue, glass beads
363 × 114 × 102 cm
→ *YOU*, 2008
Plaster, wood, foam, paint, burlap, mirror, glue
414 × 155 × 122 cm

05 *Untitled*, 2006
Foam, synthetic hair, epoxy clay, paint, resin, amethyst quartz, glitter
28 × 25 × 24 cm

06 *The Center*, 2008
Wood, foam, epoxy clay, resin, horse hair, metal wire, paint, mirror, glass beads, plaster, glue, feathers, glass eyes
358 × 183 × 121 cm

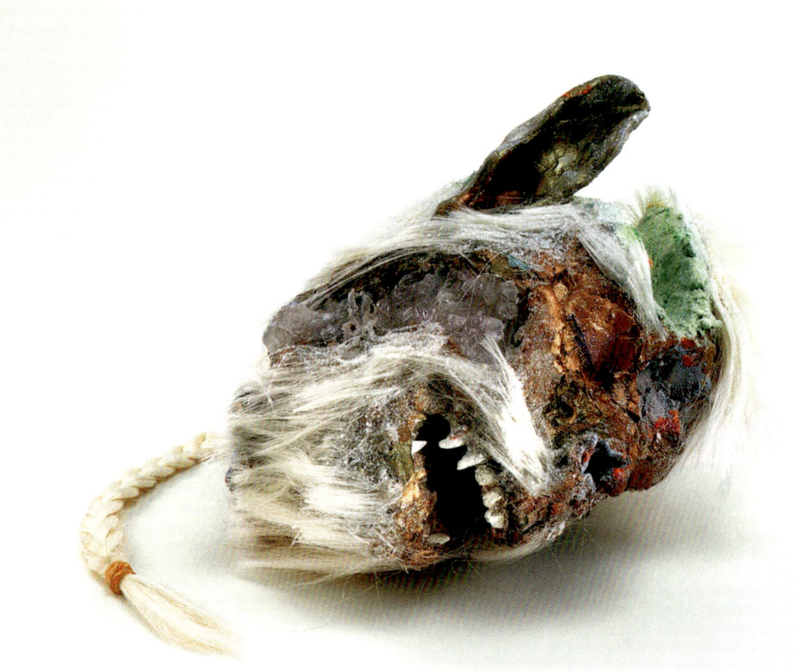

06

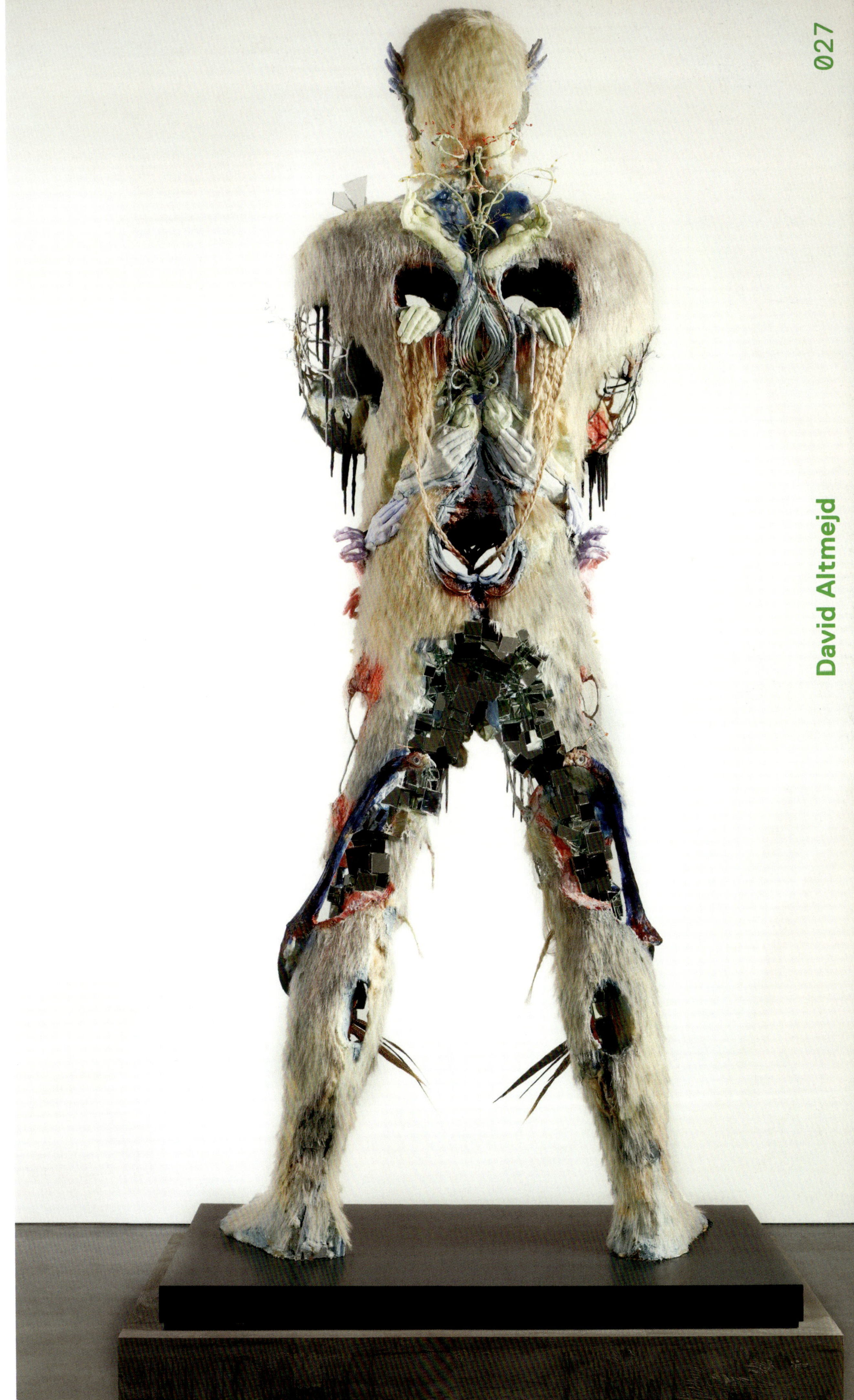

Micol Assaël's installations present an unrefined analogue world where the apparent menace of machines leads to introspection. Her works create wonder and disorientation in the visitor, who is not led to think analytically but rather to forget. It is difficult to remain inside such environments for an extended period of time, since they are situations in which human responses are stimulated to an unbearable degree. In *Mindfall* (2004 and 2007), for example, the artist placed twenty-one used motors on tables. A timer triggered them to twist rhythmically at maximum speed, creating a tense expectation of explosion. Analysis, interrogation and self-awareness of such works are only possible in retrospect, after the viewer has returned to familiar surroundings. Vibrant physical and psychological reactions, sparked by this return to consciousness, echo Kant's revolutionary theory of thinking based on the concepts of a priori and transcendental experience.

Assaël's study of philosophy and interest in physics and quantum mechanics are brought into an intimate realm where the spiritual and material are indistinguishable. Through her intuitive approach, atomic scale joins the theoretical, and, as the artist asserts, 'the human being is always a unit of measure'. Her attraction to isolated and gelid landscapes, such as Iceland and Siberia, is expressed in environments where familiar objects cohabitate with recreated natural elements or physical phenomena. If the former might embody a reassuring presence to hold on to, the latter expose the visitor to uncertainty and bewilderment, as in *Untitled* (2003), an iron room crossed by high voltage discharges and currents of strong wind generated by industrial fans. Recollection meets the unconscious, leading the visitor to play with hazard in an attempt to control it. Obsolete motors, electric fans, cold-storage rooms, lighthouses and electrical panels are all brought to a point of friction with the intention of reaching or crossing their limits. In *Altrove* (2008), for example, water and sparks cohabit menacingly, while in *Chizhevsky Lessons* (2007) electrostatic energy becomes visible through human contact. The drama involved when moving towards the unknown, failure and loss of control, bring to light obscure zones of inner consciousness. Assaël's attention is not on danger itself but rather on the insecurity that we face when taking risks. Her reiterated quest for new parameters seems to put her in a continuous state of emergency, in which new problems are created in an attempt to understand unexplained phenomena and the nature of things.

Although each work responds to its environmental surroundings, few of Assaël's installations should be considered site-specific. They are malleable and adaptable to new circumstances, and not wholly dependent on the milieux in which they are installed. These existential machines have brought about different collaborations with various professionals: physicians, engineers and musicians. However, the works always retain their equilibrium between the micro and infinity. As the conclusion of Kant's *Critique of Practical Reason* states, 'the starry heavens above me and the moral law within me'. [Francesco Stocchi]

01

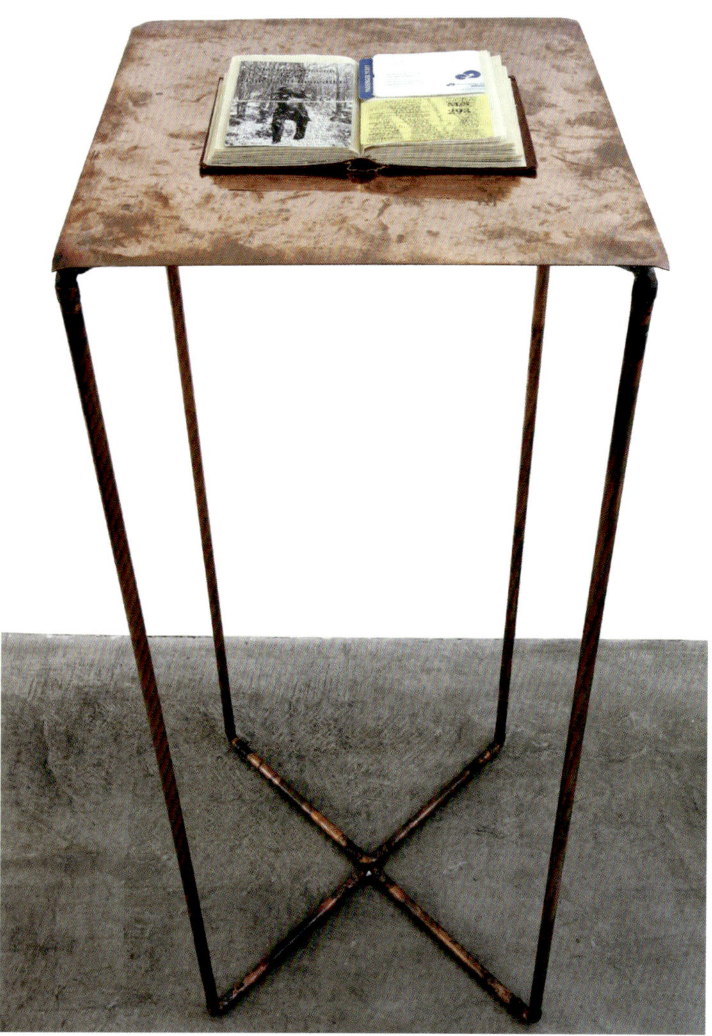

01 *Free Fall in the Vortex of Time*, 2006
Copper pedestal, book of drawings
120 × 40 × 40 cm

02 *Chizhevsky Lessons*, 2007
Copper plates, steel wires,
cascade generator, transformer
22.4 × 11.4 × 52 m

03 *Untitled*, 2001
Bed, glass, microspheres, iron,
sanitary ware, high-tension generator,
sparks, map of Iceland, glasses
18 × 8 × 3.5 m

04 *Mindfall*, 2007
Cabin with tarnished glasses,
electrical engines, electrical wires,
smoke, tables, chair
555 × 250 × 250 cm

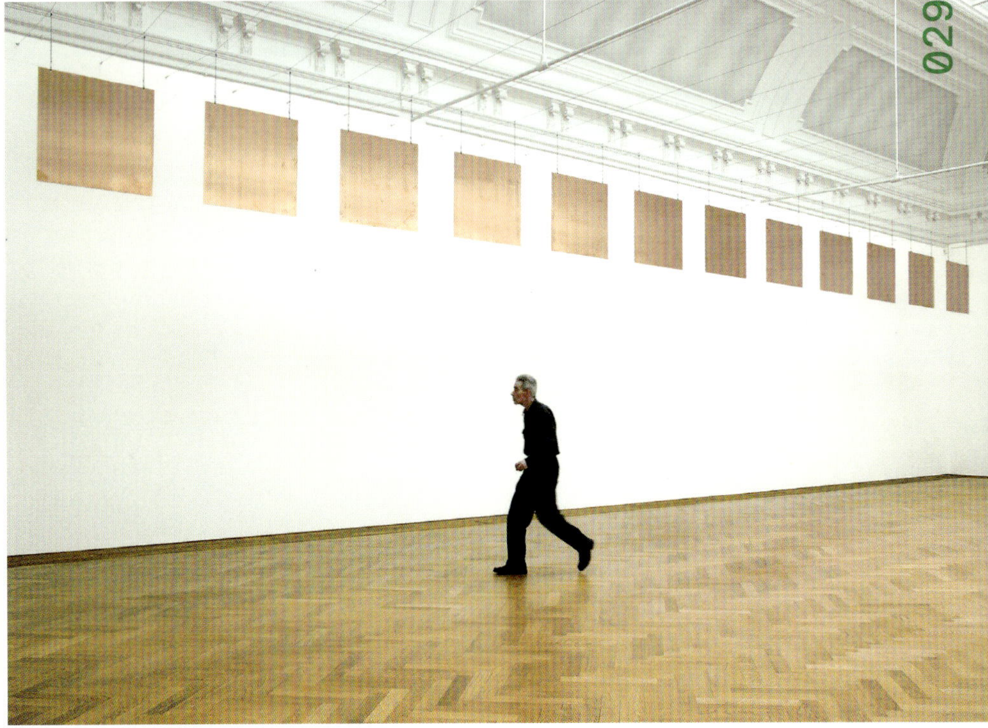
02

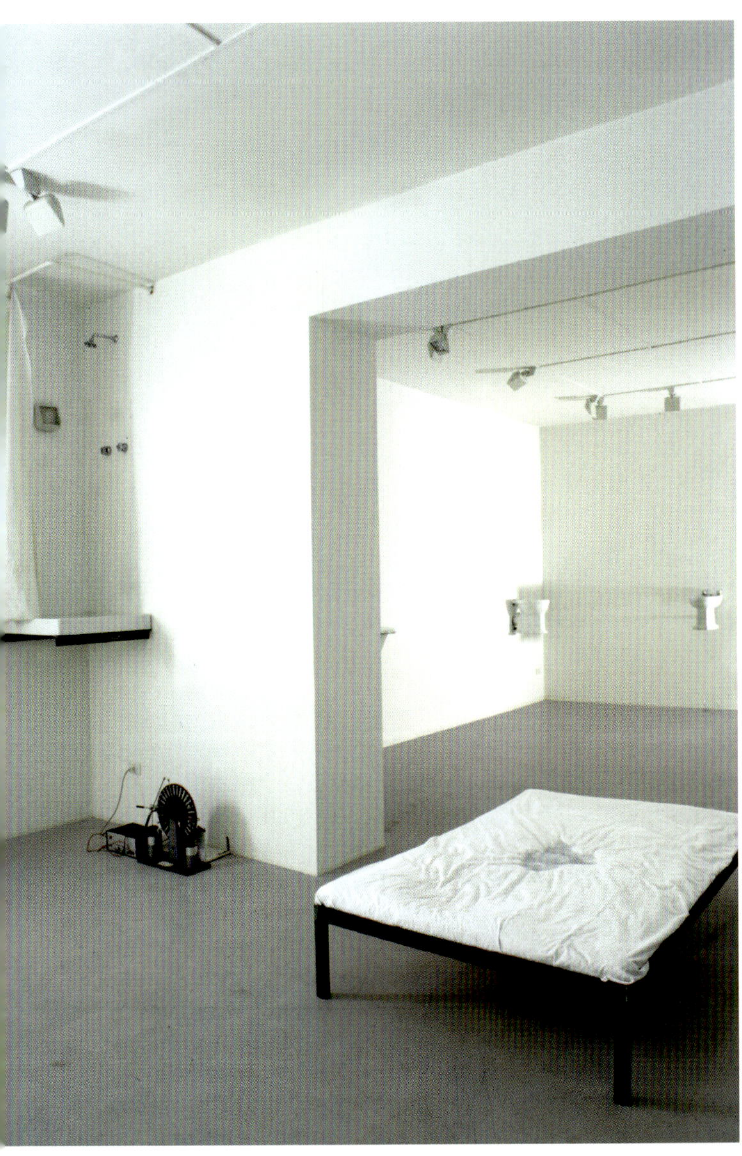
03

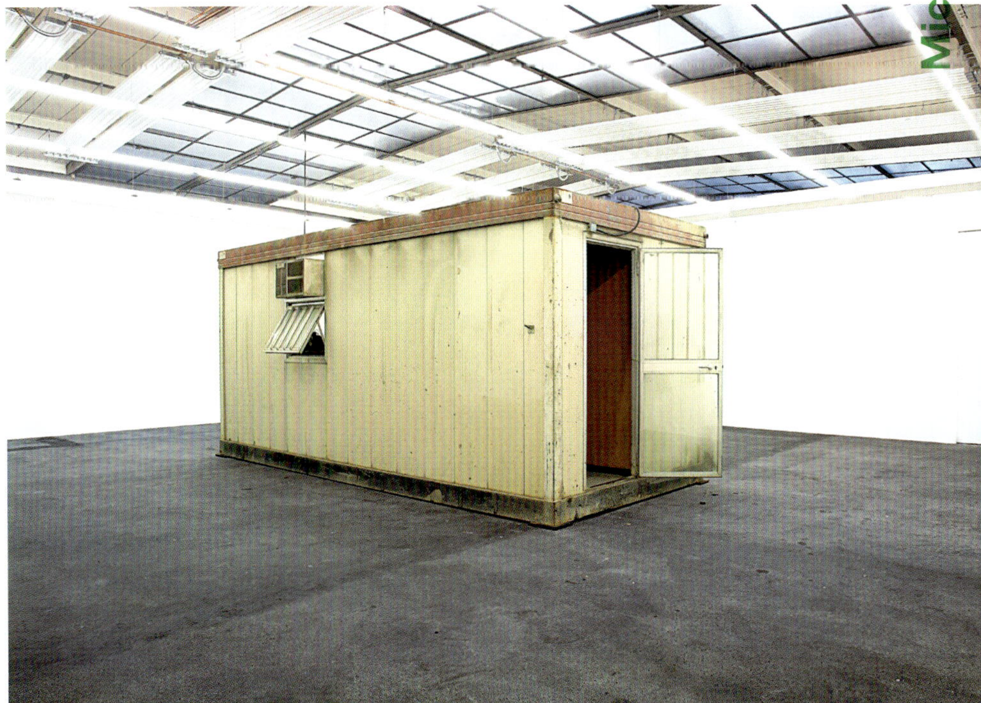
04

01 *Big Mouth 1, 2, 3*, 2008
Polished aluminium, coloured cast rubber
Approx. 260 × 170 × 65 cm

02 *Entr'acte*, 2007
Concrete, plastic awning, metal frames, mirror
Approx. 670 × 210 × 85 cm

03 *Spanner*, 2008
Chromed brass pipe, stretcher, rubber wire rope, painted metal rings
Length varies from 600 to 1200 cm

04 *Class reunion*, 2008
Coloured cast rubber, painted metal, coloured epoxy resin
Dimensions vary from 55 × 110 × 30 cm to 23 × 225 × 64 cm

01

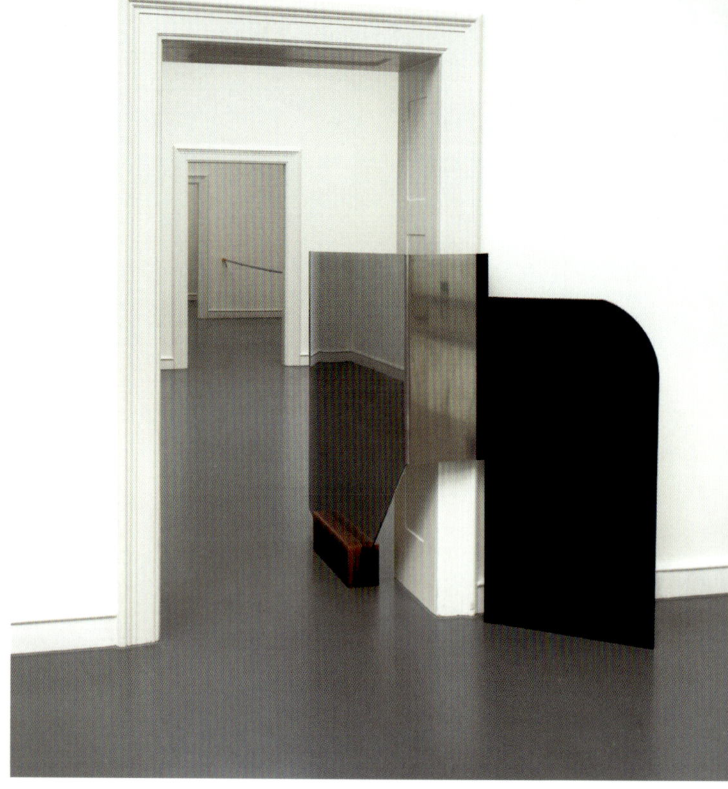

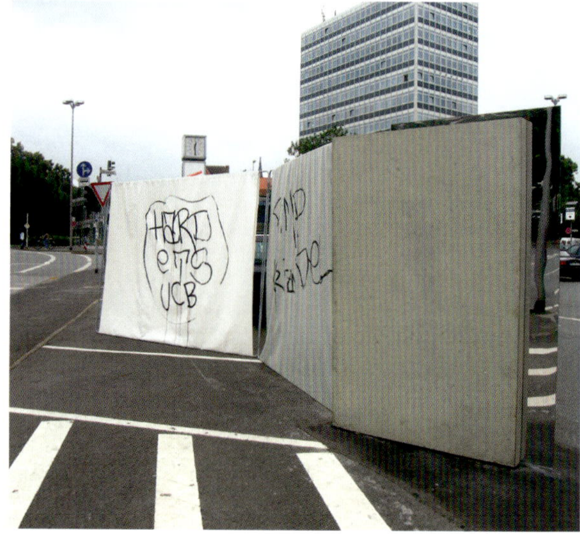

02

The aesthetic finesse of Nairy Baghramian's abstract and post-Minimalist sculptures and installations is immediately apparent whether one encounters a work like *Spanner* (Stretcher-Loiterer , 2008) — which consists of a filigree metal rod augmented like a bracelet with sections of chrome pipe and tensed between the walls of a given art space — or one of her recent multi-panelled metal sculptures wrapped around a threshold or delineating a fragment of a room within a room, such as *Entre Chambrage* (2008). But in order to fully appreciate the sophistication of her works beyond their formality, it's necessary to appreciate that they are all a matter of multi-faceted artistic negotiations. Typically, Baghramian's work sets up a constellation of thoughts, enquiries and responses that factor art historical precedents, questions of context and institutional framing, as well as the conditions of production and reception around contemporary art. Key to her work is how the theoretical concepts, drawn from art historical debates around Minimalism, literature and design history, are translated into specific materiality, manufacture and display decisions. Take, for instance, *Entr'acte* (Interlude, 2007), her anti-monument, anti-spectacle contribution to Skulptur Projekte Münster 07. This work consisted of a slightly forlorn-looking partition or paravent made from a sliver of Perspex mirror, cast concrete and a vinyl tarpaulin in a car park and intentionally abandoned to inevitable vandalism. Similarly ambivalent to the surrounding space was her first major exhibition at Kunsthalle Basel, 'Es ist ausser Haus' (It is outside the House, 2006). This presentation consisted of a series of works predicated on viewers imagining that one of the main load-bearing walls of the institution wasn't there. Only then could a relationship between the mirror panel on one side and the unmountable aluminium staircase on the other become clear. Her two-fold contribution to the 2008 Berlin Biennial involved a collaboration with, and homage to, Paris-based designer Janette Laverrière, whose career began in the 1930s.

Emerging after the identity-based political art of the 1990s, Iranian-born, Berlin-based Baghramian has intentionally confounded pre-existing models for an artistic position based explicitly on either her immigrant status, via post-colonialism, or her gender, via post-feminism. Yet the legacies of both also play their part in the coordinates of her work: *Empangszimmer* (Reception room, 2006), a concrete sculpture including a photograph taken in one of the former Shah's palaces, or her series of photographs taken in a Berlin women's refuge, *Halfway House* (1999), or more obtusely in her penchant for hot pink and inexpensive ornamental details. Accordingly, the reception of her work has involved a consideration of what properly constitutes 'the political' in contemporary art. It is in the uneasy relations and contradictions, which arise between materiality and conception, as well as the viewer's engagement and the artist's intention, that Baghramian's elegant works find their agency. [Dominic Eichler]

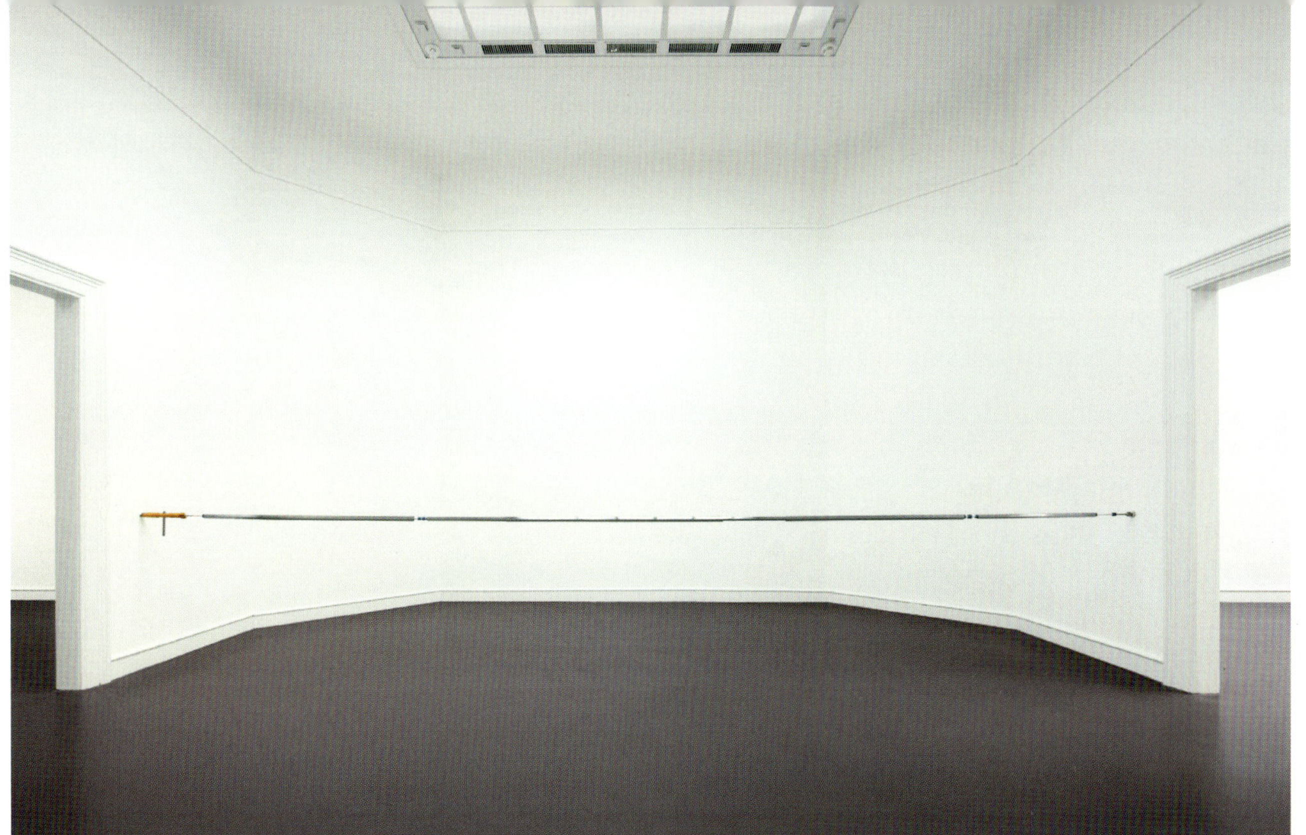

03

04

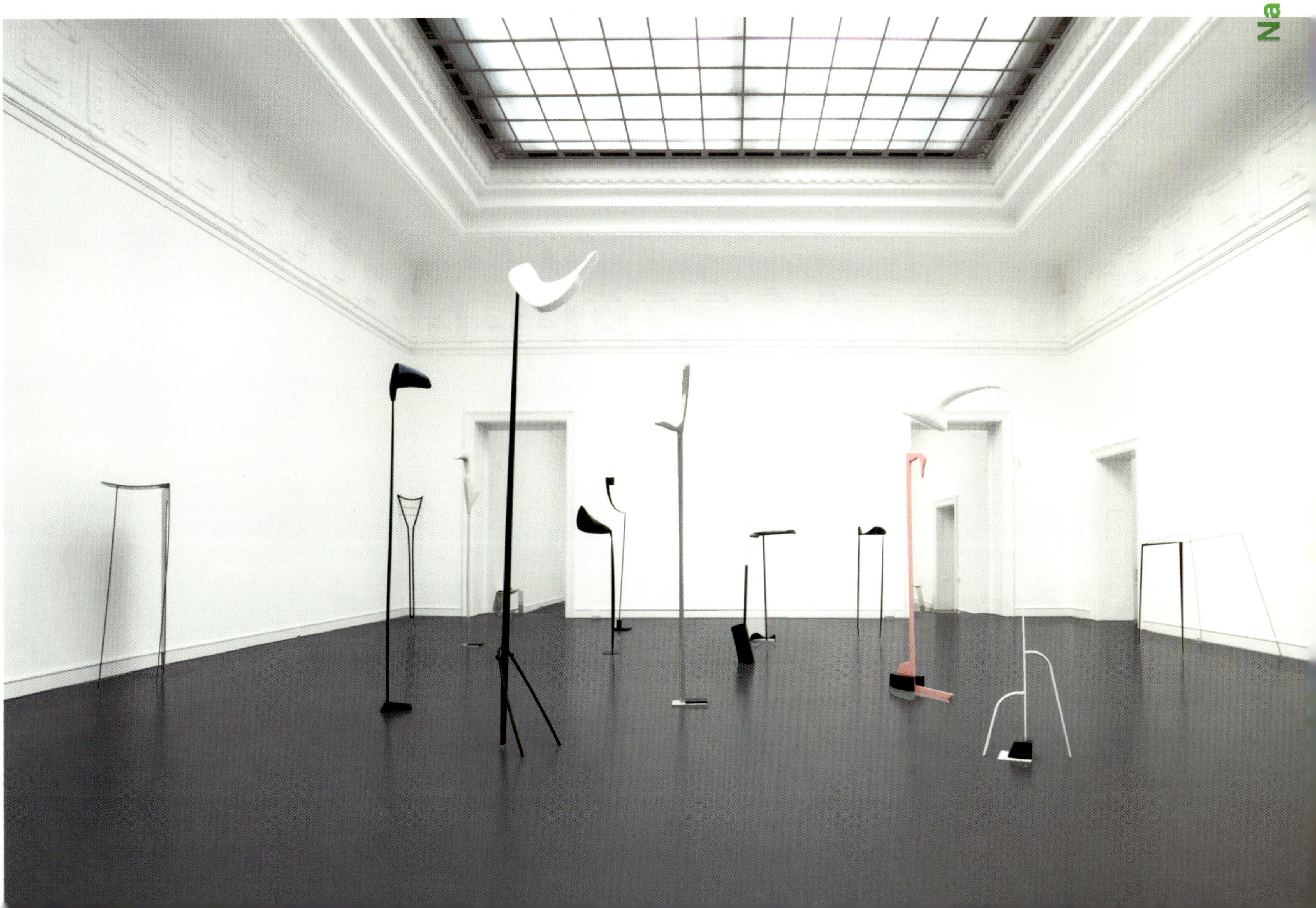

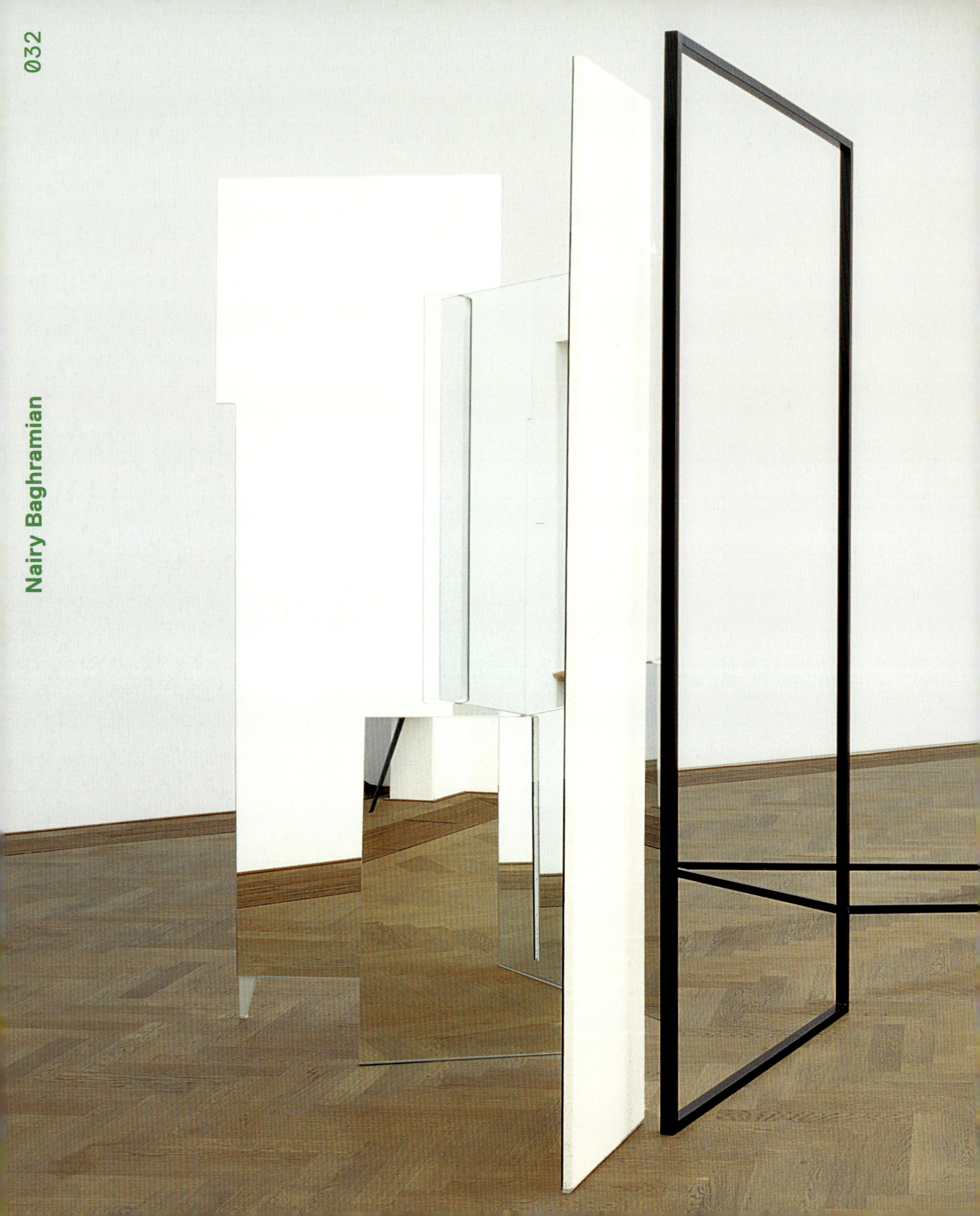

Nairy Baghramian

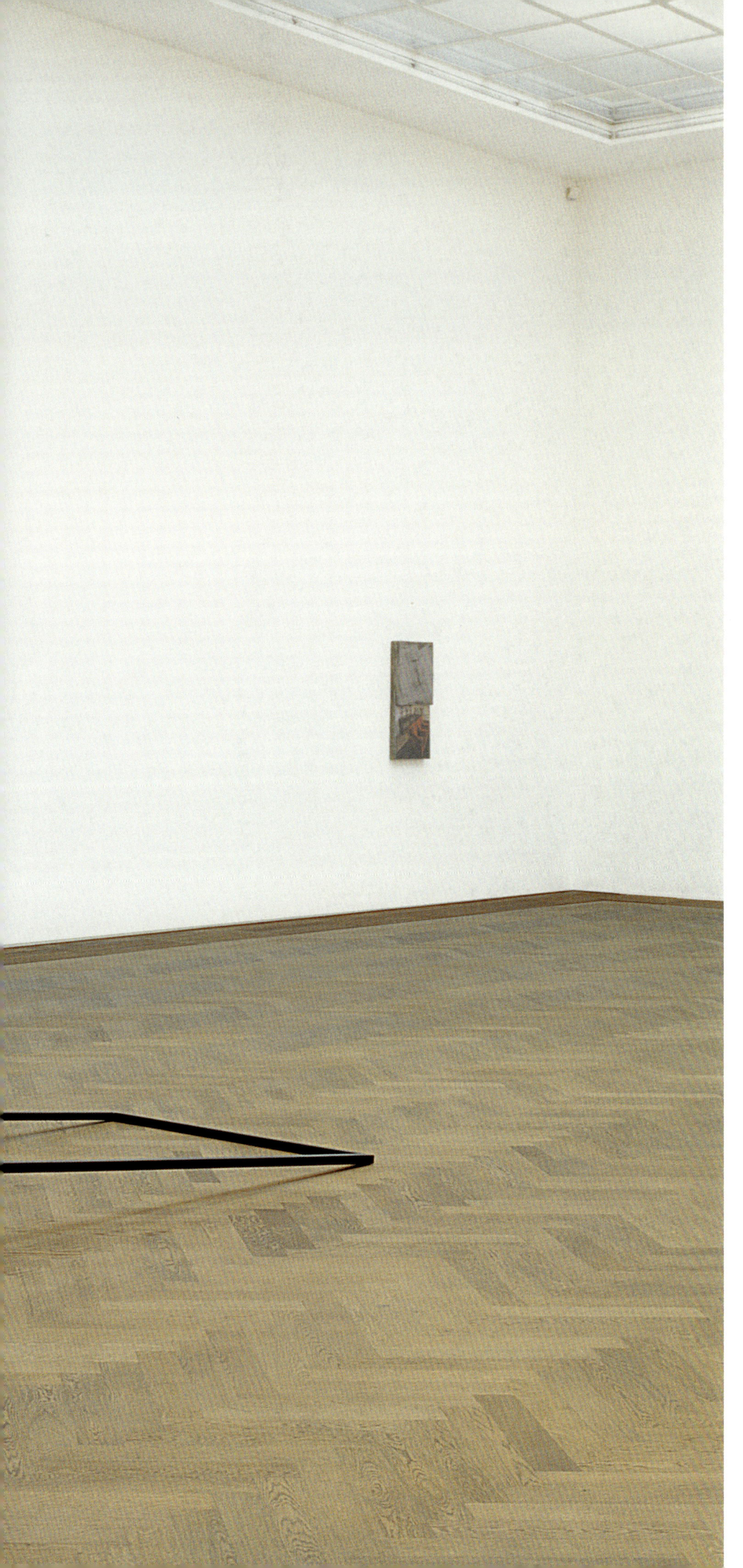

05 *The Pretty Corner*, 2006
Painted metal, mirror
Approx. 380 × 235 × 650 cm

Claire Barclay's exhibition at Camden Arts Centre in 2008, tellingly entitled 'Shifting Ground', revealed the way in which her work moves between sculpture, furniture and interior design. In this installation, Barclay combined rectilinear steel shelves with draped pieces of yellow and brown fabric — as if a modernist architect and an American Midwestern homemaker were meeting to converse in the living room. In an earlier work, *Hard Measure* (2006), a table, missing a leg and a top, is adorned with a swath of sagging brown suede and a slab of oak topped with several geometrically shaped brass weights. If ones sees these weights as Barclay's sculptures, then the remainder of the installation can be read as an elaborate base or a nearly complete domestic environment built especially for them.

In installations like these, organic forms frequently mingle with modernist ones, bringing traditional handicrafts together with the practical aesthetics of the Bauhaus or the luxurious modernism of Eileen Gray. Loose structures of steel and brass support fur and silk. Thin brass poles or wooden planks delineate vague furniture pieces, which Barclay adorns with painted mirrors or patterned cloth. A tension between objects seems to hold these compositions together like perspectival lines in a painting: diagonals prop up verticals, delicate objects dangle from sturdier frames. In *Silver Gilt* (2005), a comb and several shiny gold bowls hang from black leather strands. A circular metal disk in *After the Field* (2008) is wrapped with straw like a chic, updated dream-catcher. In *Venge* (2007), grease congeals in brass cups on the floor. There is an almost shamanistic quality to such installations, reminiscent of Joseph Beuys's collisions of materials such as fat, felt, iron and cement, but Barclay's works sidestep the materials' symbolic or political charge. Rather, her combinations of manufactured materials and site-specific forms suggest a looser, even decorative process, the way in which one might rearrange furniture and precious objects in one's living room.

It is as if Barclay is fashioning a new standard of style and interior design, a subject to which she alludes in an early piece from 2000, *Magazines*, which features hole-punched copies of *Wallpaper* magazine as decorative elements. Indeed, Barclay's installations look like domestic designs that are no longer in fashion but promise to return again in the future, like her furnishings for the interior of a geodesic dome in the desert of the American Southwest, fifty years from now. In Barclay's interiors, the basic structures of modernist design can mingle with New-Age paraphernalia, hunting tools and fetishized objects, and all these disparate functional objects, once stripped of their functions, can contribute to a singular design aesthetic. Barclay takes up handicraft and artisanal techniques like clay potting or weaving, even activities you might undertake as a child at summer camp, such as wrapping sticks in leather, but she does so not in an ironic way, to suggest a loss of authenticity. Rather, she fuses these traditional techniques and materials with the language of contemporary art to create a style that is at once antiquated and modern. [Christy Lange]

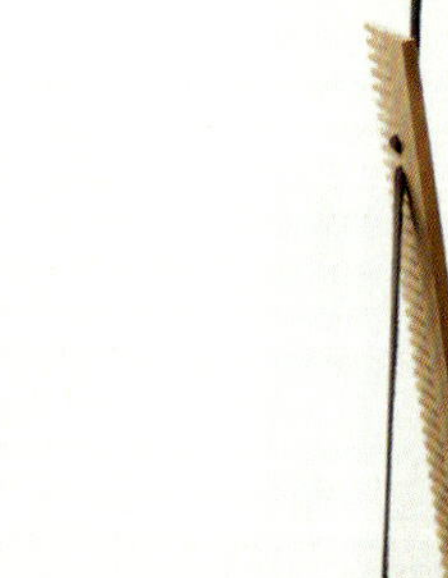

01

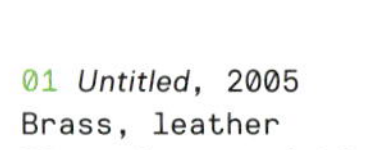

01 *Untitled*, 2005
Brass, leather
Dimensions variable

02 *Untitled*, 2005
Brass, printed fabric, leather
549 × 569 × 274 cm

03 *Shifting Ground*, 2008
Rendered straw bales, painted steel, woven straw, sewn fabric
100 × 150 × 100 cm

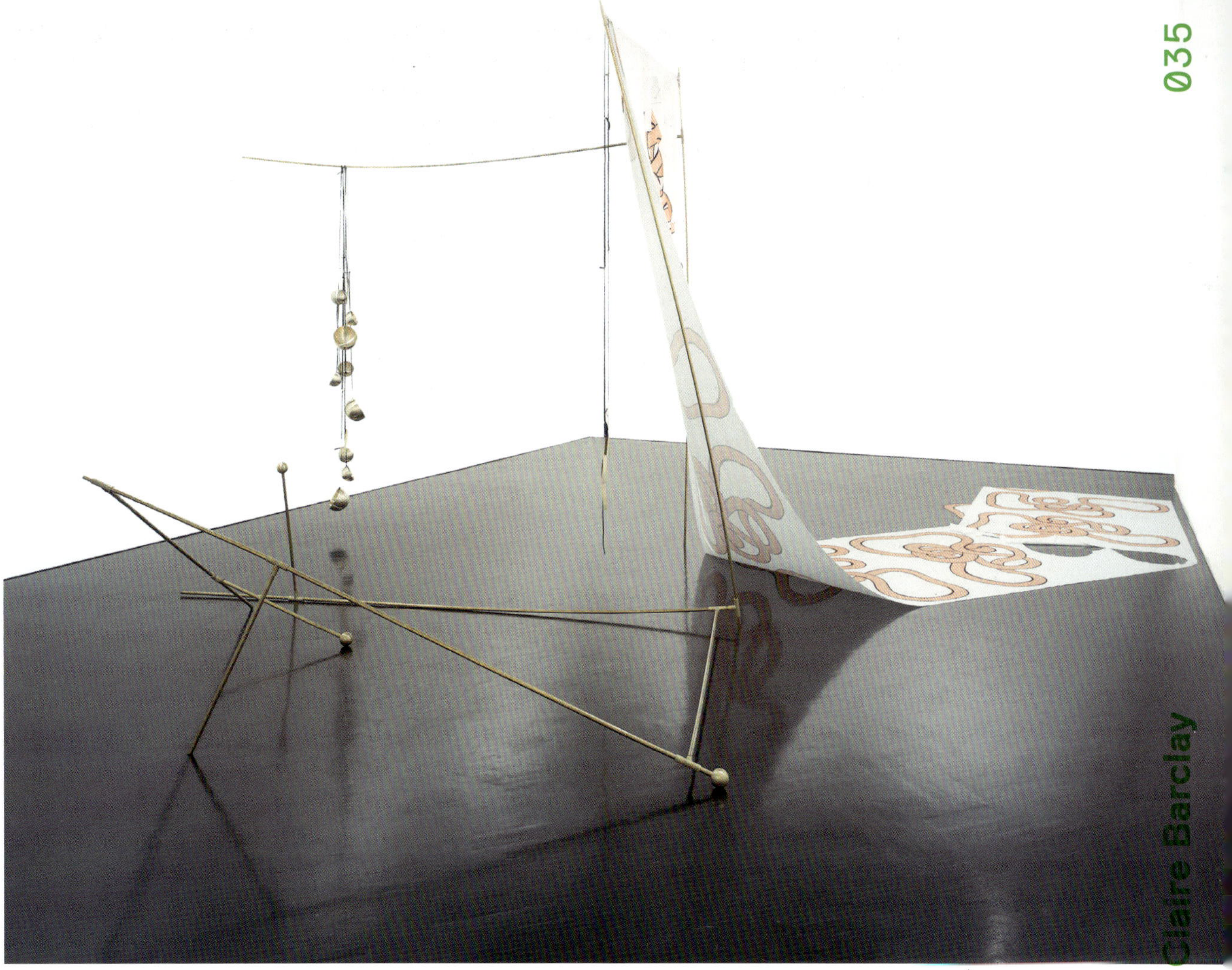

02

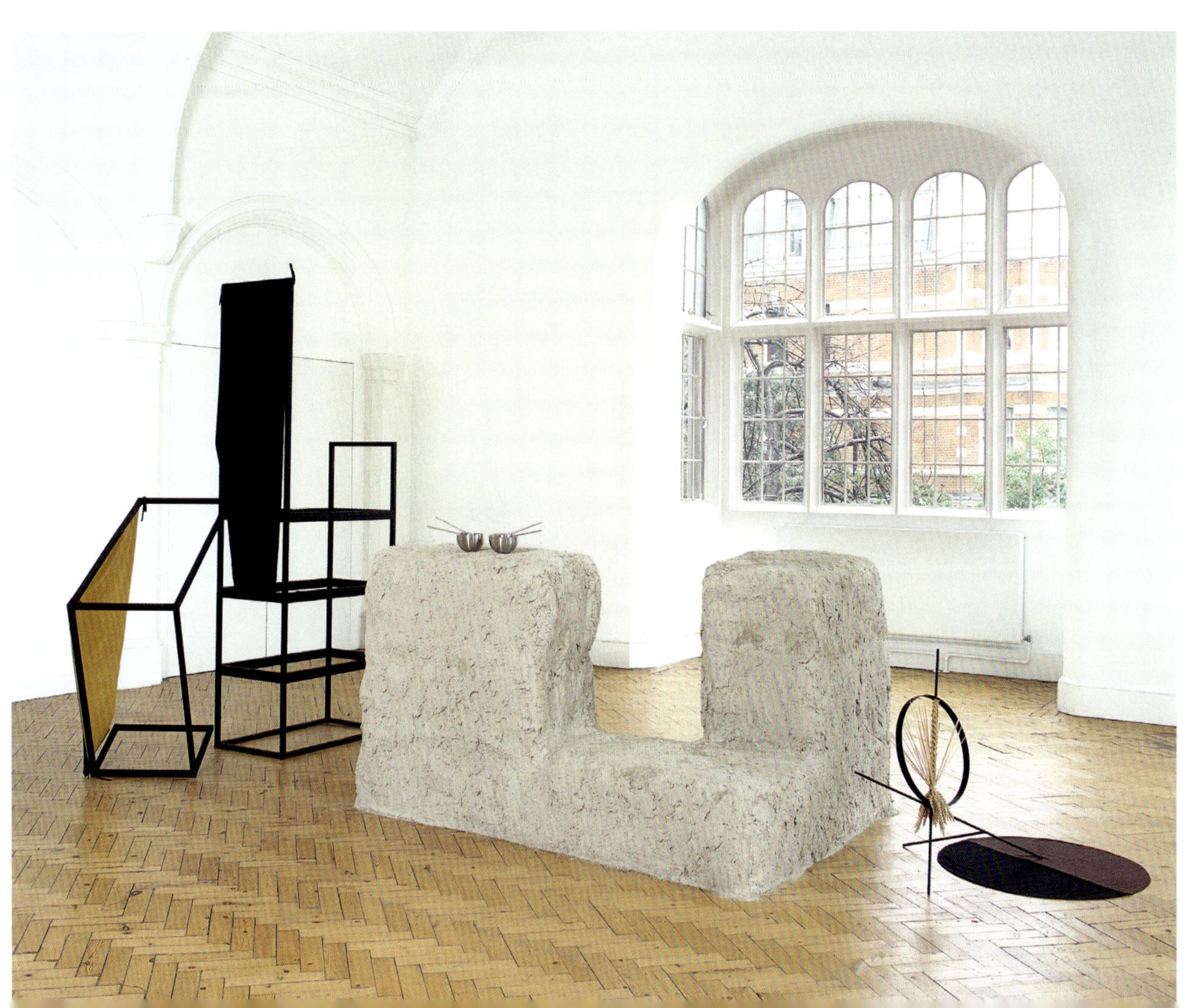

03

Frank Benson casts a potent spell on the items in his source pool. Banal, sometimes déclassé articles undergo acts of artful suspension: chocolate fountains halt mid-flow; bowling balls poise in columns; CD players, Styrofoam cups and plastic dishware melt, invert and contort into strange variations on standard-unit themes. The process by which these characteristically ephemeral commodities transform into art objects is precisely what engages their sculptural potential. Subtracted from consumer culture, they become the material remainders central to Benson's formal poetry.

Rather than work with readymades, Benson often fabricates his sculptures with the exact materials of the items that have inspired them. In *MDF (A)* and *MDF (B)* (both 2008), for example, two 2.5 centimetre thick pieces of Medium Density Fibreboard (MDF) seem to suffer from random warping but have been actually painstakingly assembled from 0.5 centimetre thick MDF sheets. Benson's professed interest 'in backtracking through the manufacturing and distribution process and intervening one or two steps before the object would become available to the public' here comes into play, as the commodified narrative halts and the residual objects accrue a minimalist air.

01

For *Chocolate Fountain #1* and *#2* (both 2008), Benson reconstructs a party staple in stainless steel (its original material), including the liquid chocolate, which covers the structure's tiers and basin with startling realism. Constantin Brancusi comes to mind, the fountains achieving a marriage of his *Endless Column* and steel pieces, and the heavy-lift table supports perpetuating their phallic sequencing. Rather than bringing the sculptures in line with his forebear's metaphysical formalism, however, Benson's allusion only draws the contemporary conditions of production into greater relief. His fountains' polished-steel facades lack none of Brancusi's material depth, but as re-enactments of present-day commodities, they incline towards the far side of the symbolic economy, where pure spectacle devolves into spectacular form.

By depriving his source objects of mobile positions in capitalistic flux, Benson also foregrounds the psychic charge subtending their market appeal. *Human Statue* (2005) dips deeper into the uncanny valley than anything concocted by the artist's former professor and employer, Charles Ray, its hyper-real manufacture and gauche referent coalescing to produce an alternatively disquieting and repulsing viewing experience. Smeared in silver paint and set atop a small pedestal, this life-size *David* poses a simple, material riddle, the solution to which does nothing to alleviate our suspicions about his verisimilitude. In fact, during the 2006–07 'Red Eye' exhibition of works from the Rubell Collection, certain visitors left money before the pedestal base, meeting *Human Statue*'s viewing contract with comparable ambiguity. As conventions of art spectatorship and consumer engagement double back upon each other, it becomes clear that the unstable status of this and other Benson works is no less than a mirror of our own. [Tyler Coburn]

02

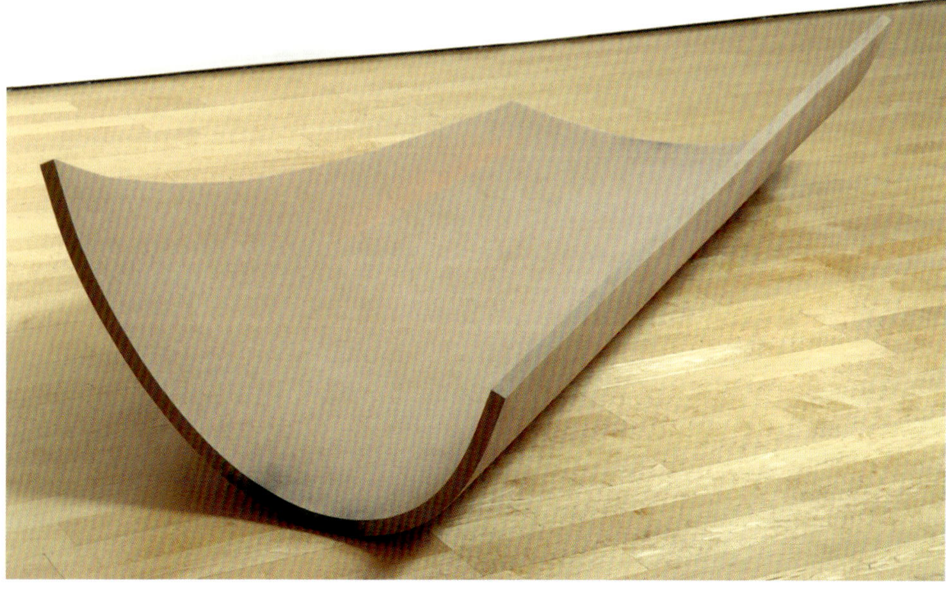

01 from left:
→ *Chocolate Fountain #1*, 2008
Polished stainless steel,
paint and powder-coated aluminium
Fountain 117 × 51 × 51 cm
Plinth 58 × 61 × 91 cm
→ *Chocolate Fountain #2*, 2008
Polished stainless steel,
paint and powder-coated aluminium
Fountain 117 × 51 × 51 cm
Plinth 58 × 61 × 91 cm

02 *MDF(A)*, 2008
MDF
50 × 104 × 244 cm

03 *Human Statue*, 2005
Forton MG, oil and
acrylic paint, wood
Figure 175 × 56 × 51 cm
Base 51 × 51 × 51 cm

03

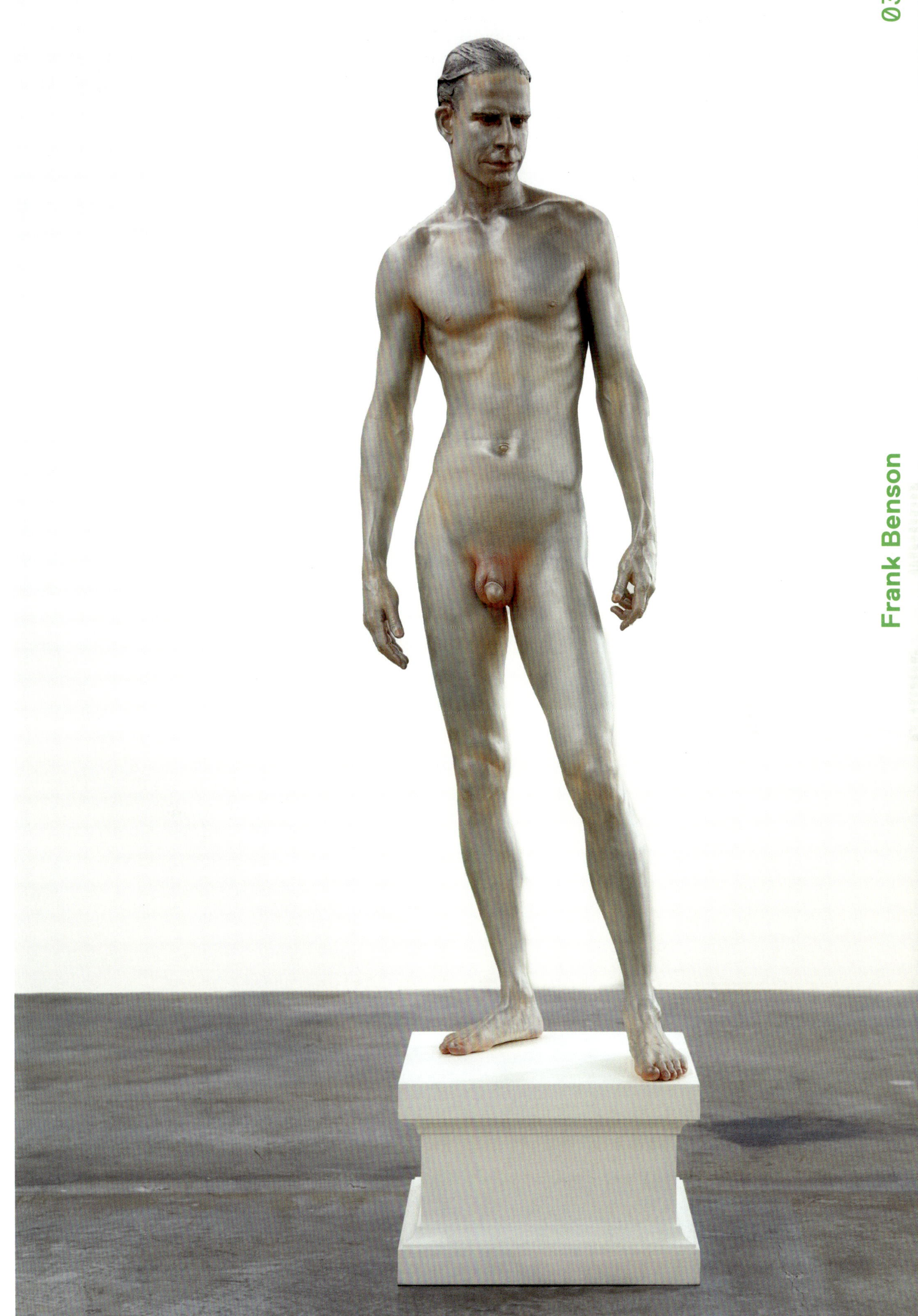

Michael Beutler's art is like a 'just-so story' but with reversed emphasis. 'Just-so stories' reliably provide logical explanations for which no tangible proof exists, whereas in Beutler's world, abundant with the physical proof of his art, plausible explanations are always in short supply. *Sputnik* (2005), an exceedingly convoluted claptrap contraption, slapped together from little more than plywood and packing tape, turns out long steel slats sheathed in wrappers of multi-coloured threads. The results look nice enough, but orphaned from any ideal of efficiency or apparent artistic (much less practical) efficacy, Beutler leaves you wondering, 'What gives?'

What gives, of course, is his see-sawing between ad hoc
01 nonsense and an ad hoc morality tale told through his idiosyncratic version of bricolage (a.k.a. DIY, a.k.a. creative resourcefulness whirling art out of whatever). Beutler, a twenty-first century bricoleur, creates something (kitschy coloured wood) out of nothing (ditched wood), turning *Sputnik* into a lo-fi moral compass about sustainability, a concept that our consumer culture will, in due course, consider indispensable. Offering ballast for this morality factor is his baloney factor — spinning a prettified object from trash in a kind of whistle-while-you-work approach — which any provocateur, including Rube Goldberg, would envy. Beutler doesn't make art so much as fiddle and tinker with it until it does something — usually something preposterously meaningful. In his art, the principled lay down with the bunkum.

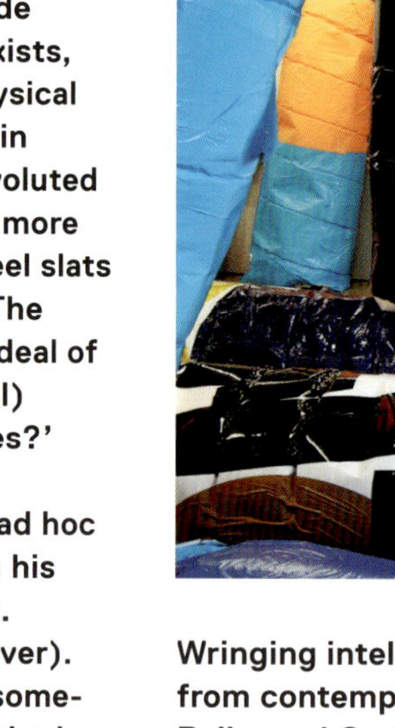

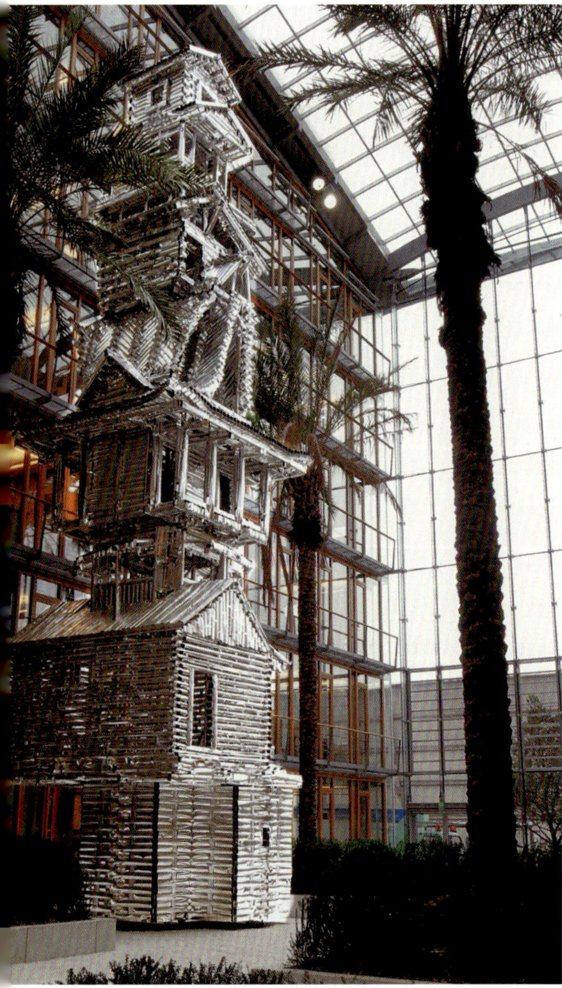

02

Wringing intelligence from impulse is his inheritance from contemporary German art: Joseph Beuys, Sigmar Polke and Gerhard Richter. The honorific shaman, the psychedelic mystic and the philosopher-artist oscillate between sarcasm and Romanticism in ways to which American art remains allergic but Beutler sensitive. Happy just tarting up wooden slats, what might such a pedigreed artist do, given the chance to build a monument? The *Aluminium Pagode* (2006) is a whimsical twenty-metre stack of improvised architecture that looks as if it has soft-landed amid Lufthansa's main administrative building in Frankfurt. The tower, the result of a Beutler makeover, converts the traditional pagoda tiers into eight garden sheds on a stick. True, each shed's style betrays a miscellany of cultural origins that ultimately stand in for wanderlust, Lufthansa's core business. But as another reversed 'just-so story,' set against the rational splendour of Lufthansa's glass and steel headquarters, this surrealistic apparition of humble materials (aluminium) and means (homemade) inexplicably takes over as the inner self of a multi-national corporation. 'Why?' Well, why not? With plenty of physical evidence but zero explanation, it appears from nowhere.

Beutler improvises talismanic experiences. Along the way he kicks open the door to a nonsensical world in an era defined by faith in the ascendancy of technical achievement — what Joseph Carroll has described as the eclipse of 'cultural capital' by 'scientific literacy'. We trail along Beutler's intuitive path, finding cast-offs magically converted into brassy art, and although we have no idea how we got here, we always arrive with pleasure.
[Ronald Jones]

01 *Kottgubbar*, 2008
Tetra Pak paper, fence wire, gift wrap, wallpaper paste, bamboo, cable ties, wood, rubber
4.5 × 2 × 3 m

02 *Aluminium Pagode*, 2006
Aluminium
17 × 5.5 × 5.5 cm
Permanent installation, Lufthansa Aviation Centre, Frankfurt Airport

03 *outdoor-yellow9*, 2004
Pecafil, cable ties
6 × 3 × 4 cm

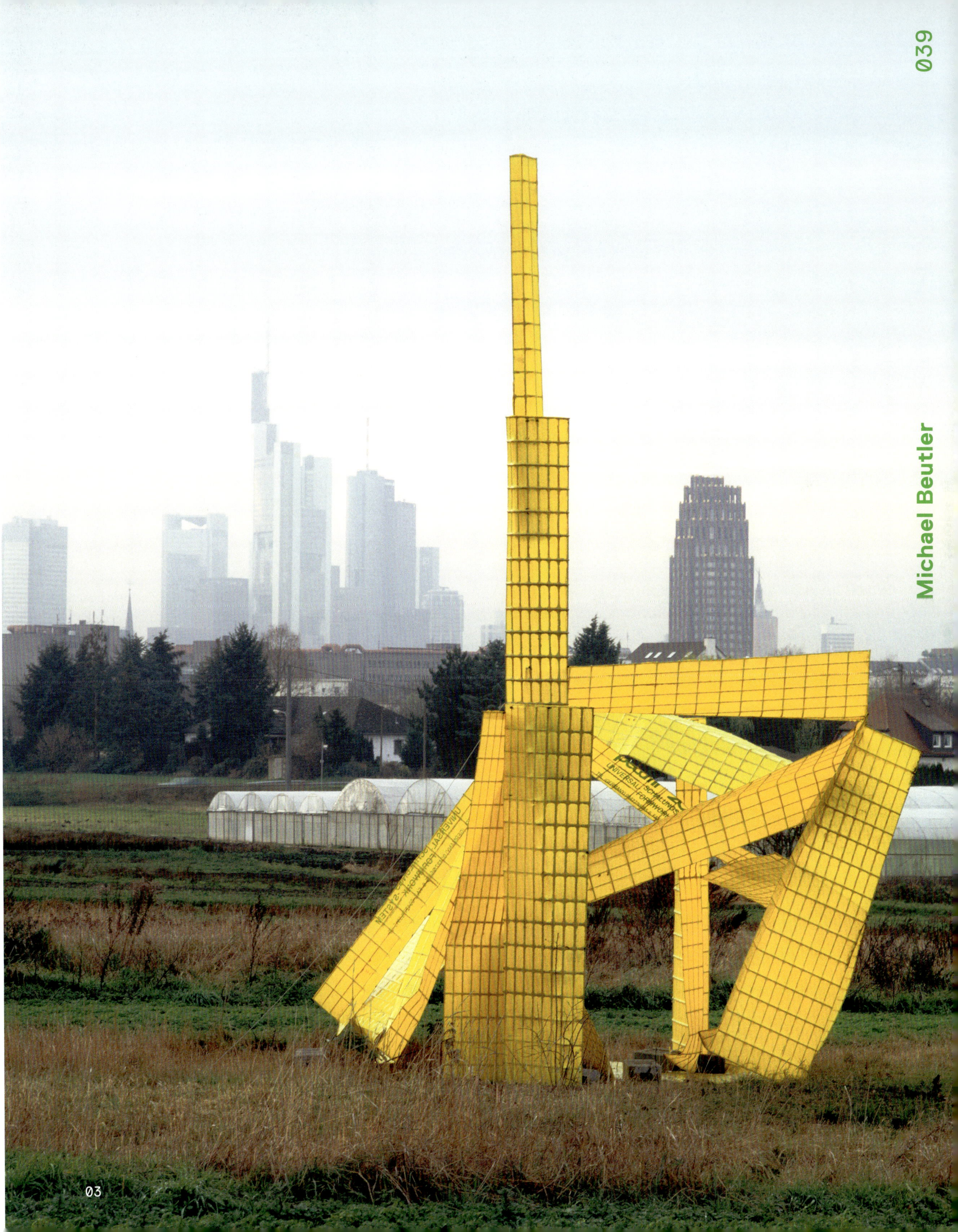

03

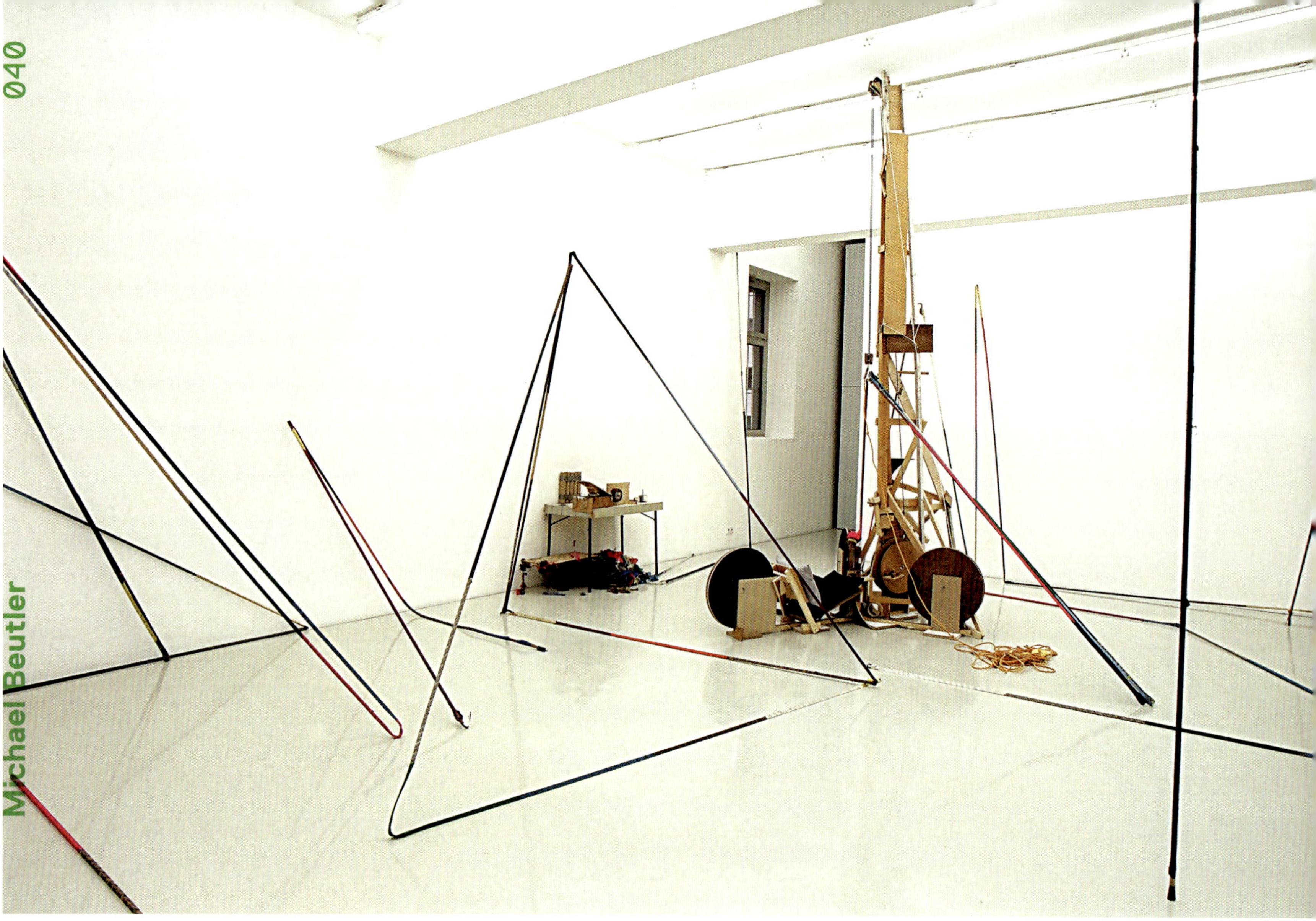

04

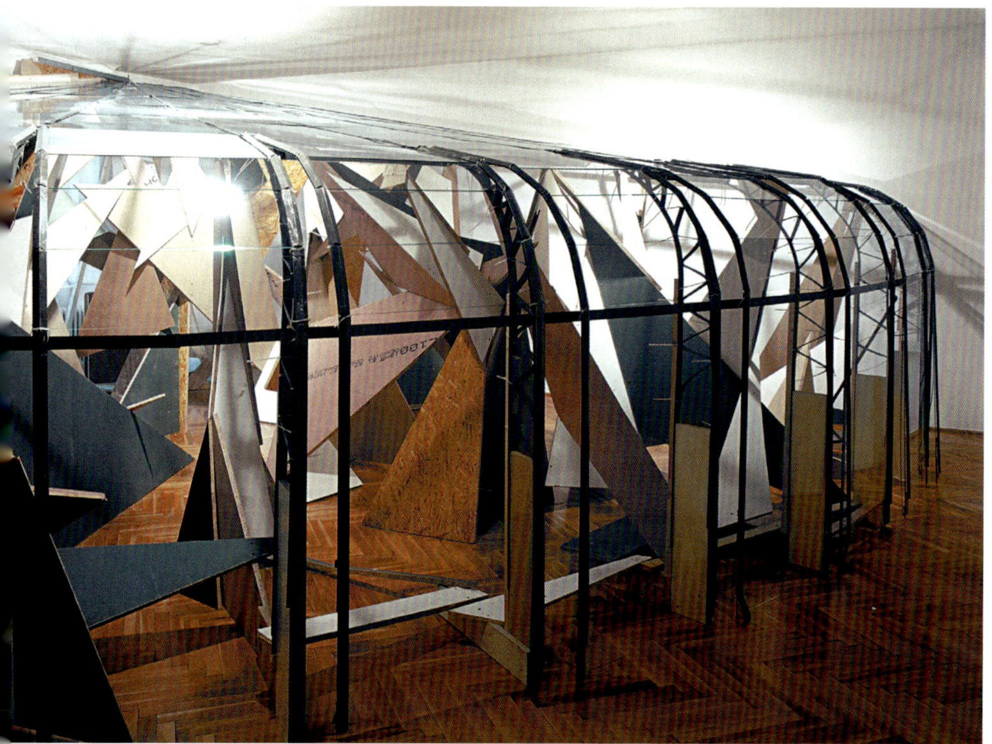

05

04 *Strandsegler 'Lolita'*, 2003
Band iron, lining,
wallpaper paste, wood
4.3 × 13 × 9 m

05 *Glashaus*, 2002
Glass, band iron, cable ties,
laths, chipboard, paper, wire
2.6 × 6.8 × 6.8 m

06 *Central Avenue*, 2005
Deer fence, paper
6 × 10 × 8 m

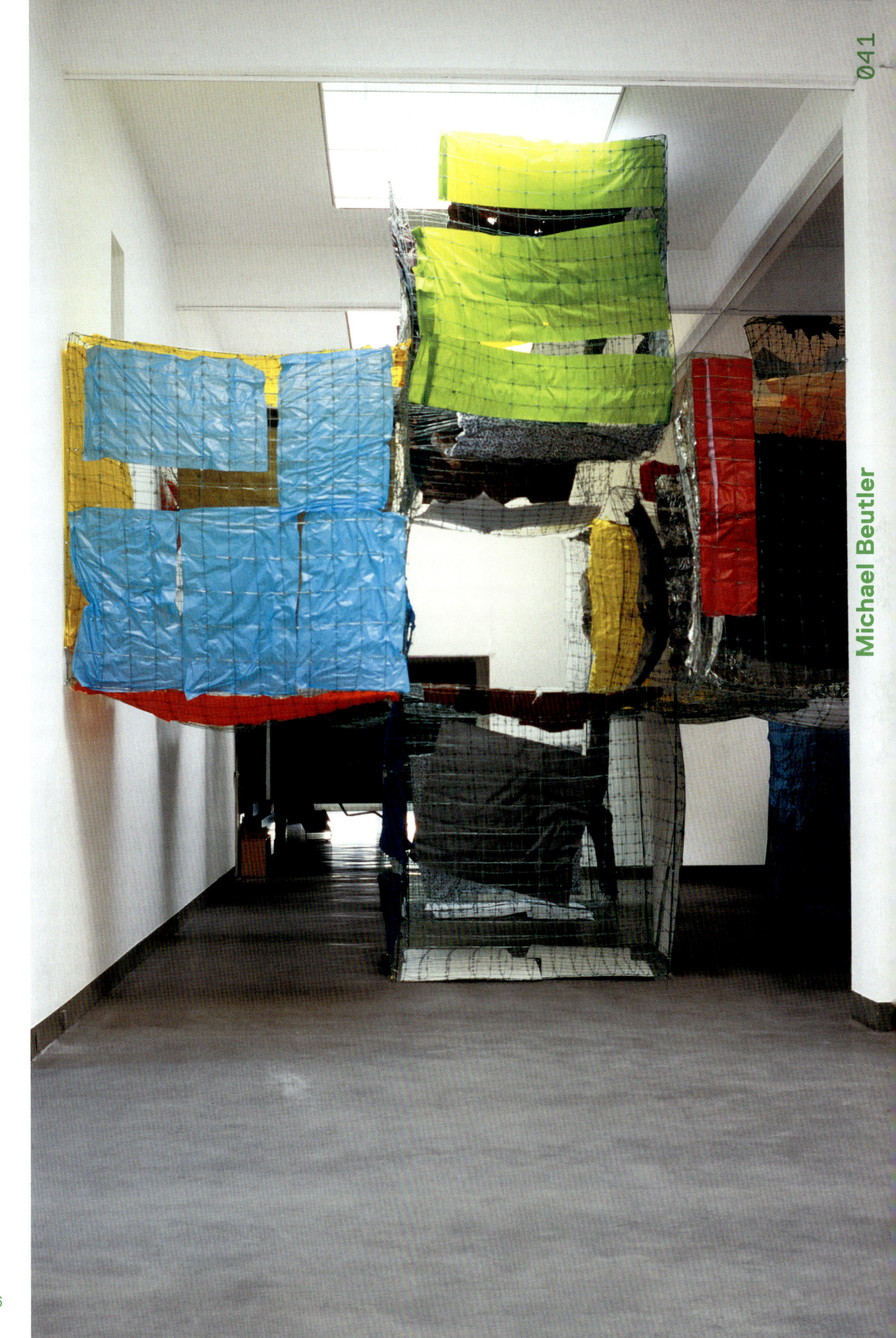

06

01 Huma Bhabha's Pakistani heritage informs her thematic fascination with ancient ruins and her formal interest in salvaging reusable materials, although she believes that her inadvertent expressions of concern with the after-effects of battle transcend nationality. Her monumental, figurative sculptures depict dismembered, burned-out figures that resemble archetypal rather than specific cultural remains.

To realize her 'characters', as she calls them, Bhabha incorporates architectural elements and utilizes industrial, construction-site materials to fuse her sense of extended history to her firm roots in the present. Like Robert Rauschenberg's assemblages, Bhabha's works are pieced together from detritus collected randomly — wood, Styrofoam, chicken-wire, rusted metal and plastic — into robotic, humanoid forms, twisted and destroyed by unspecified calamitous events that some viewers read as war. Her choice to give second life to throwaway materials comes, in part, from noting marked differences between what is considered trash by Americans and Pakistanis.

Though frequently described as post-apocalyptic, there is a romanticism inherent to Bhabha's monsters that distinguish them from sci-fi movie props. Applications of red or grey clay, carefully modelled around wire or metal armatures like skin, remind the viewer that these statuesque forms are embodiments of life. This is not to mythologize human suffering, but to encapsulate, through mass, colour, shape and texture, how memories survive the ages. In addition to the clay's enlivening effects, Bhabha's exposure of her figures' anatomies, consisting of foam blocks, cast-iron car parts, or broken furniture, introduces active relationships between the living and the dead, as did Egyptian tomb decor and other ritualistic arts dedicated to ancestral tribute. The desire she has to make her figures 'stand up' implies a hope for resurrection, and dictates her rigorous technical approach to ensuring that each character has a 'presence' that dwarves its life-sized scale.

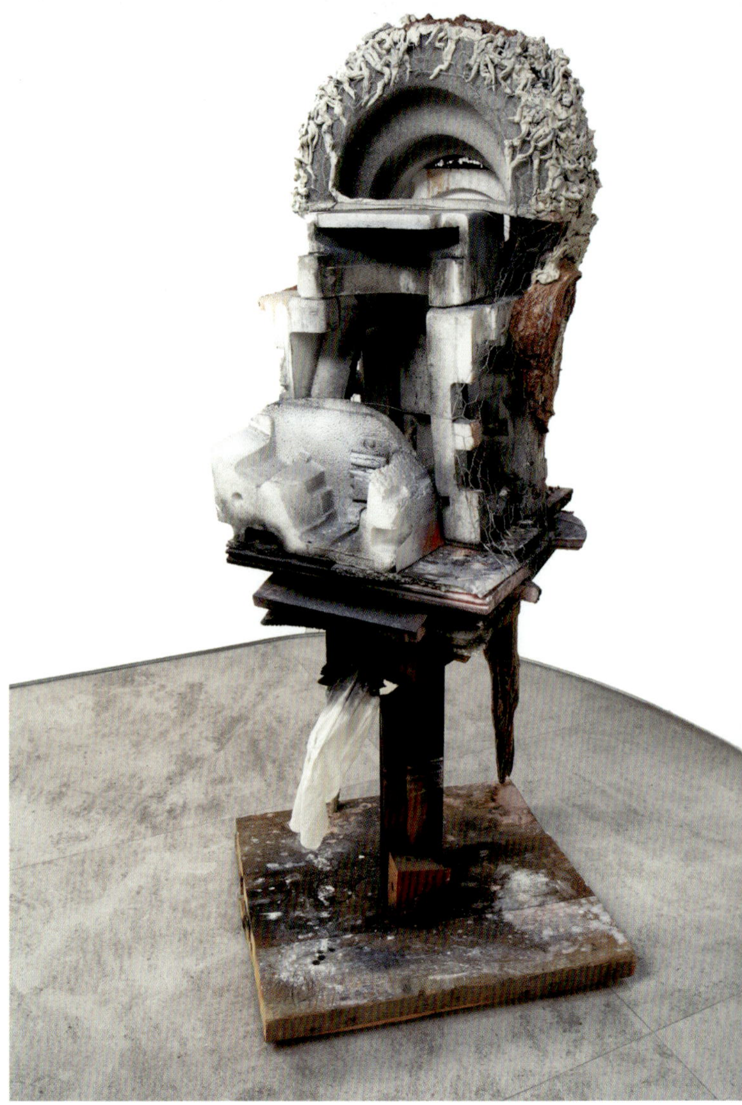

02

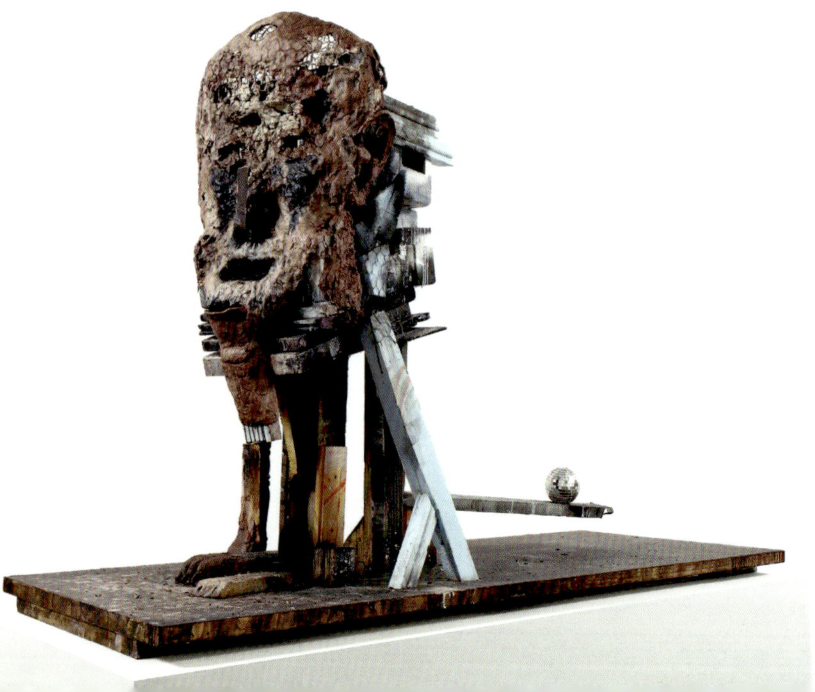

Bhabha exhibits photography, drawings and paintings alongside her sculptures to render more clearly the zones from which her beings have been rescued, although one can also glean narratives by studying their processes. Each figure begins as stacked Styrofoam, upon which materials are added and subtracted to create girth, connoting flesh. In a recent, untitled solo exhibition, Bhabha invited the viewer to travel, as she did, to generate the work. In one gallery, she exhibited photo-etchings of rubble piles and architectural ruins taken in her hometown, Karachi. The second gallery contained three small sculptures resembling a sarcophagus, a death mask and a pair of withered, amputated feet, likening the gallery to a tomb. The largest space housed a sculpture garden entitled *... and in the track of a hundred thousand years, out of the heart of dust hope sprang again, like greenness* (2007), after Omar Khayyam's twelfth-century book of verse *The Ruba'iyat*. A massive plinth built in four sections served as a landscape upon which two figures faced away from each other in the theatrical posturing of royal enemies. One, with an elephant's trunk connoting the Indian deity Ganesha, sat in a throne across from a standing, Styrofoam and wood cubist figure whose blank facial expression denoted physical and spiritual distance. In contrast, the sculptures that Bhabha has made since this exhibition, such as *Bumps in the Road* (2008), an homage to the image of Don Quixote and Sancho Pancha walking side by side, have pushed her characters into more abstract territory. [Trinie Dalton]

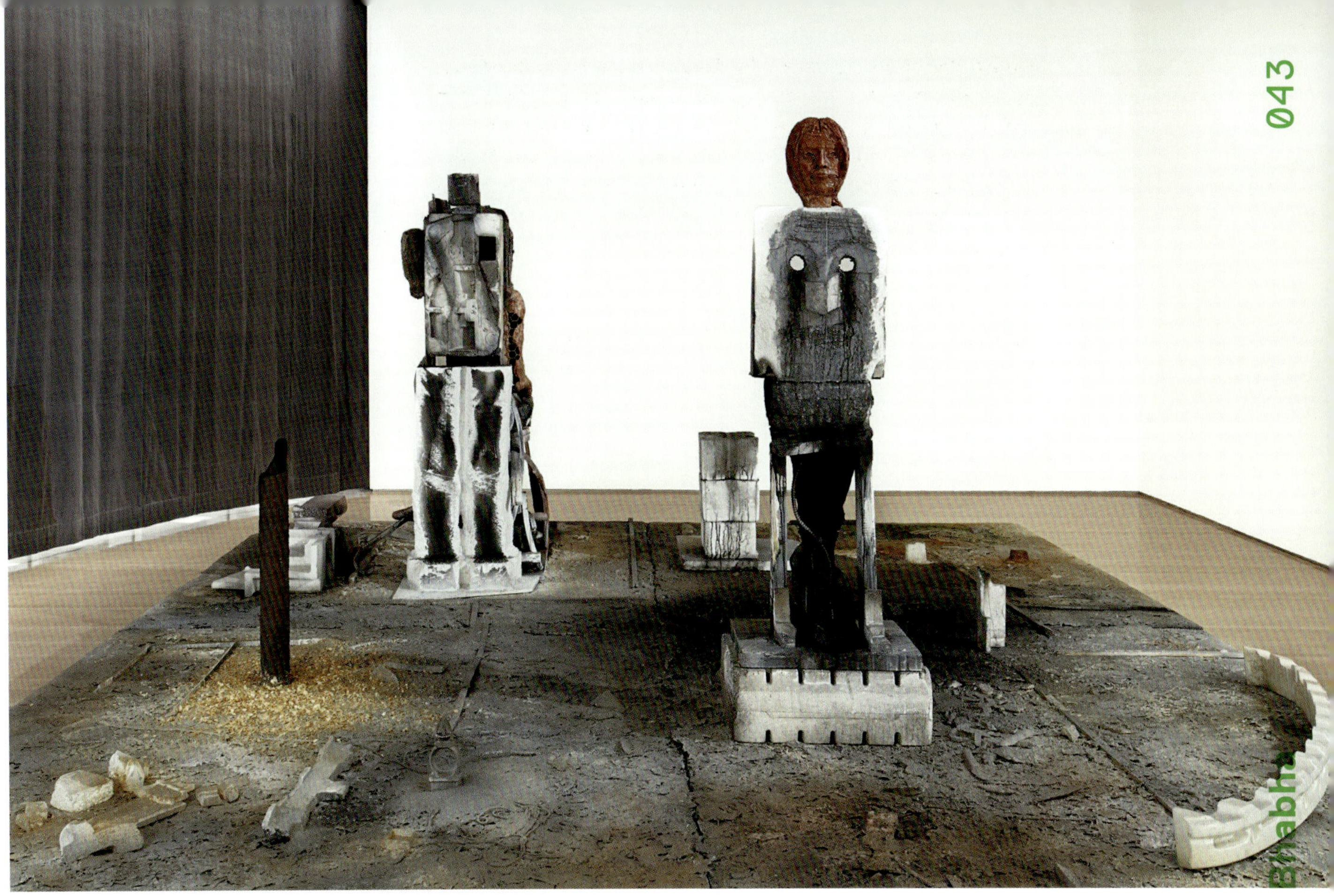

03

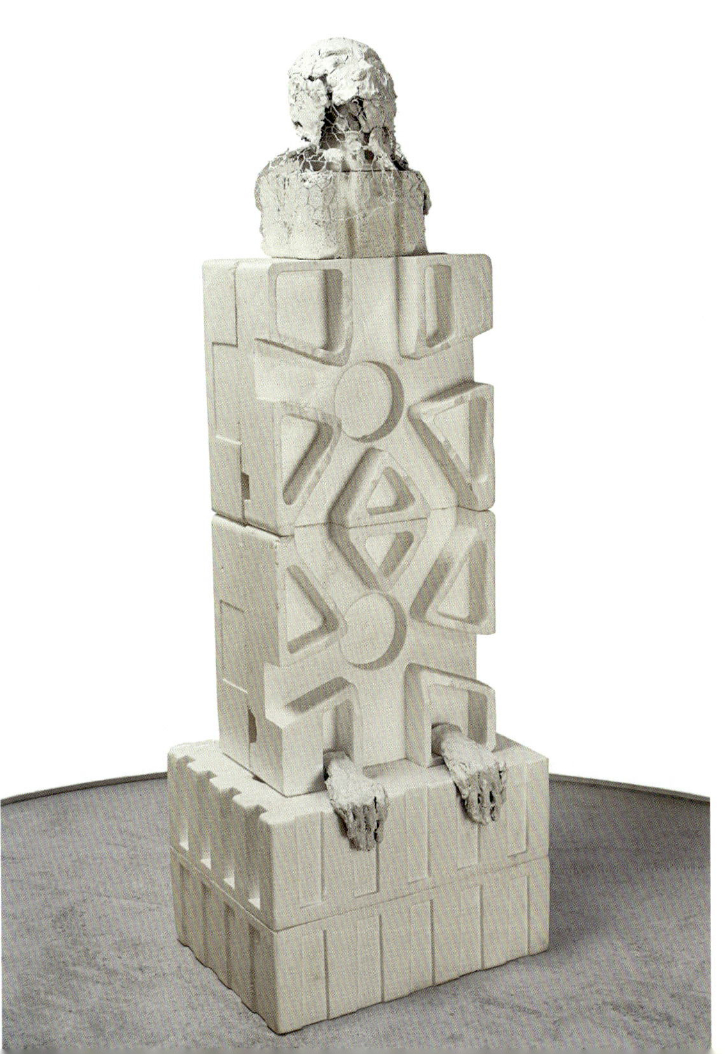

04

01 *Man of No Importance*, 2006
Clay, wire wood, bones, cotton fabric, iron, glass, acrylic paint, Styrofoam
104 × 76 × 165 cm

02 *The Main Player*, 2007
Clay, wire, wood, Styrofoam, metal stud, disco ball, iron, paper, acrylic paint
76 × 201 × 135 cm

03 *… and in the track of a hundred thousand years out of the heart of dust Hope sprang again like greenness*, 2007
Wood, acrylic paint, clay, Styrofoam, wire, leaves, ash, sand, iron, rust, plastic
427 × 366 × 185 cm

04 *Untitled*, 2006
Styrofoam, clay, wire, acrylic paint
59 × 51 × 165 cm

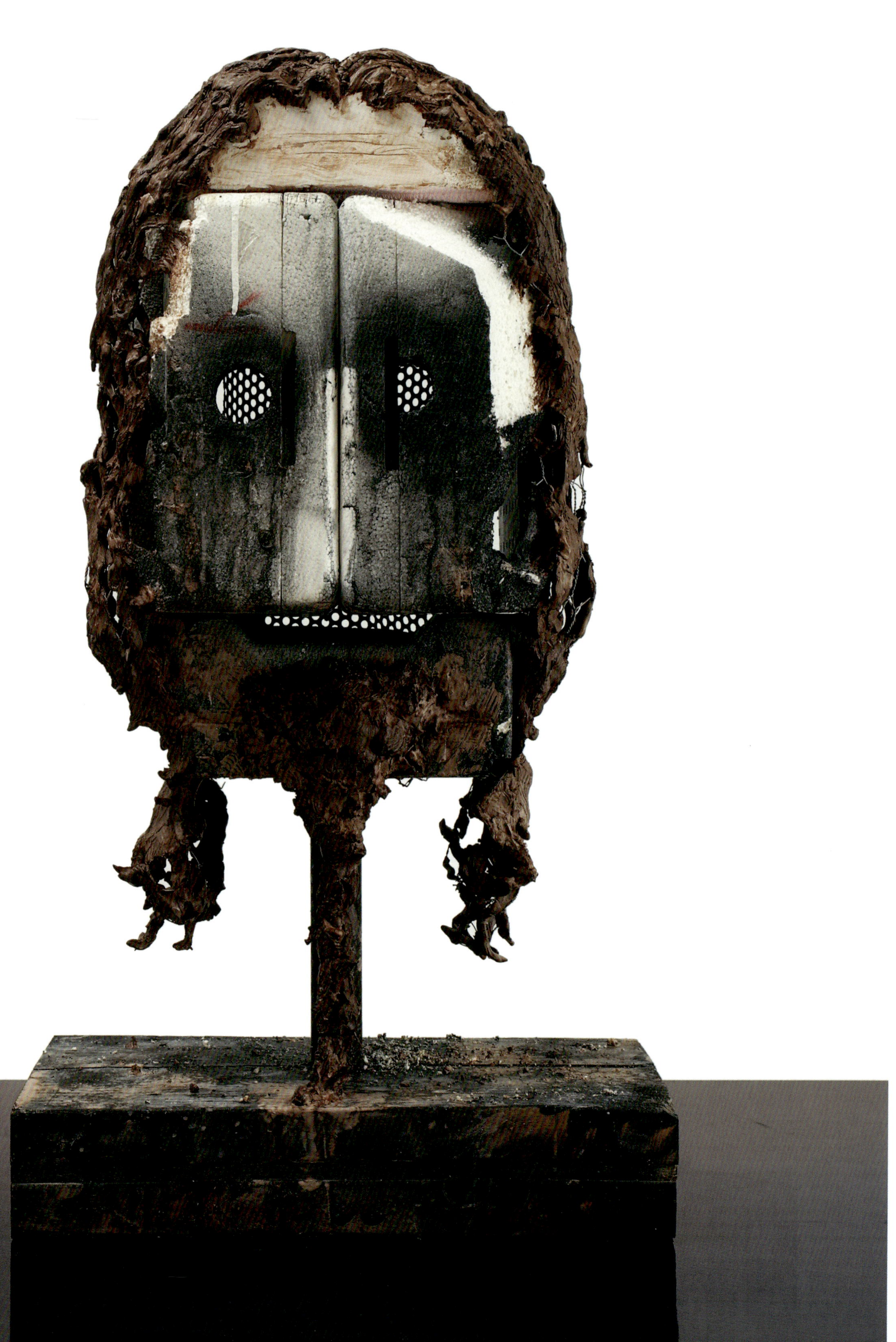

05

05 *J.C.*, 2006
Clay, wire, Styrofoam,
wood, iron, acrylic paint
47 × 31 × 83 cm

06 *Fear Eats the Soul*, 2007
Clay, wire, wood, Styrofoam,
acrylic paint, plastic
66 × 61 × 95 cm

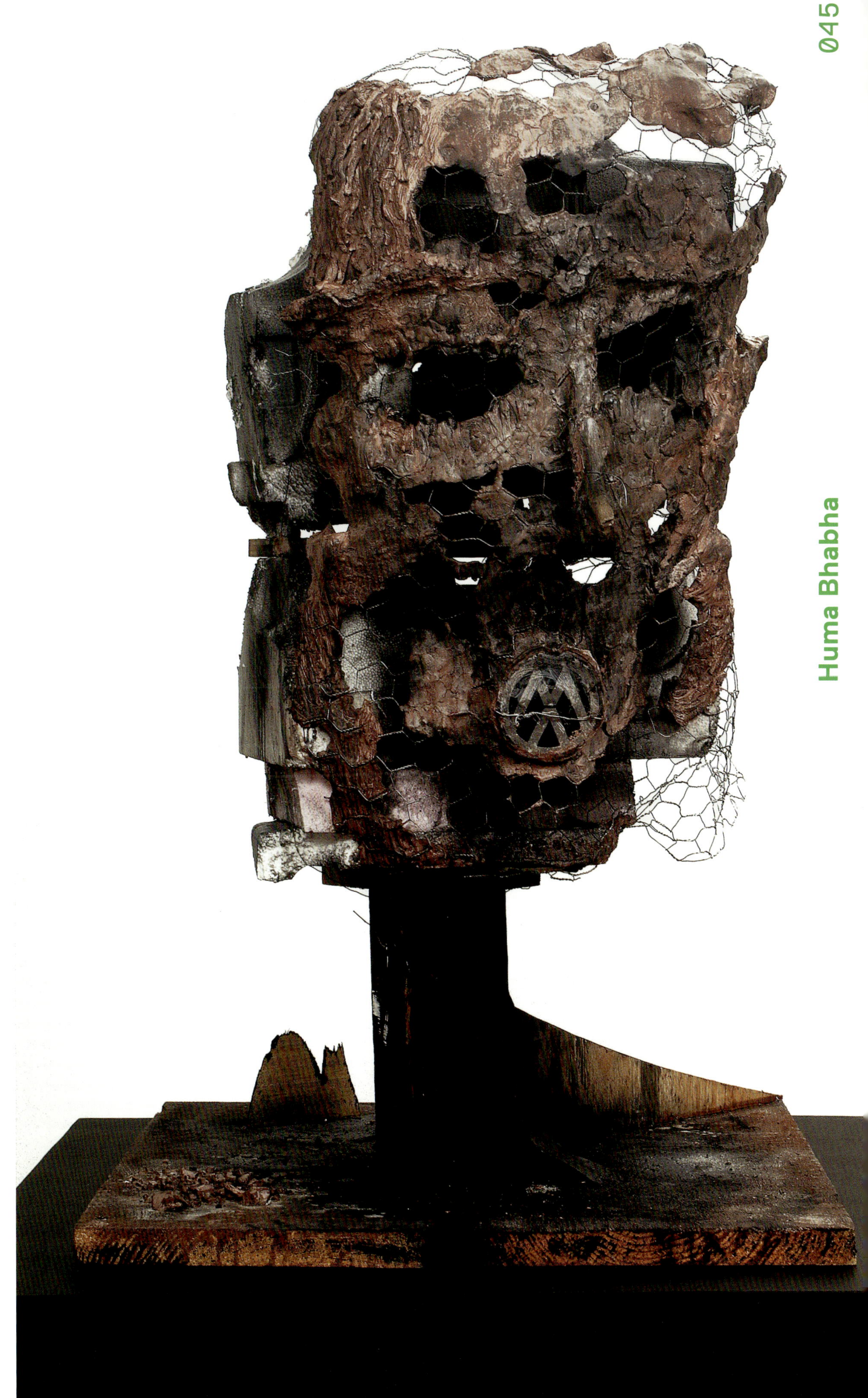

06

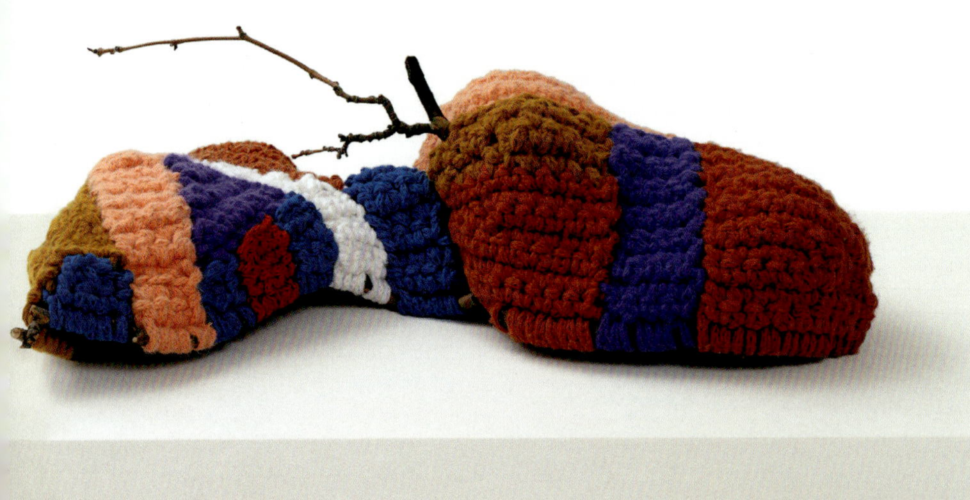

01 Alexandra Bircken may have originally studied fashion, but there is nevertheless something deeply unfashionable about her sculptures. The artist employs natural materials rarely used in contemporary sculpture, items that might be found in a wicker knitting basket or a woodsy backyard. Though she often works with the same materials used to make clothing, her sculptures don't always look comfortable in what they're wearing.

Bircken fashions her modest objects out of sticks, concrete, logs, tree branches, leaves, leather, wool yarn, plaster or fabric. Some of them rest on pedestals; others dangle from the ceiling. A few are big enough to function as improvised shelters, in particular the sculpture *Drape* (2007), which looks as if it could be a hobo's humble dwelling, cobbled together from broken tree branches and old garments. Others are so small that they resemble runts of the litter. *Wood* (2007), for instance, consists of a few upright branches huddled underneath a single swatch of fabric. As sculptures or home decorations, Bircken's works might be considered homely or ugly, even eyesores, but like shaggy mutts or ratty old blankets, they seem too loved or vulnerable to dismiss. Especially sympathetic are her rickety assemblages of spindly sticks snuggled into knitted patchwork sweaters. Some of these creations whimsically recall mushrooms, forest creatures or knobs on logs; others evoke comical scenarios, such as a 'spaceman' caught in a tree.

However Bircken's sculptures are not completely anachronistic to the language of contemporary art. Some of her compositions may look as accidental as a windblown plastic bag caught in a tree or as mismatched as a hand-me-down sweater, but each one manages to strike a balance between handmade, humble materials and a knowing nod to contemporary painting and sculpture. Her series of 'Units', for instance, are built within frames that look like empty blackboards. These rigid rectangular structures recall blank stretched canvases, while the geometric shapes suspended within them refer to abstract painting compositions, despite being made of soft or organic materials. Like oversized dream catchers, these webs of wires, fabric, wood and woollen forms create the impression of cracked glasses or decorated windows, but all within a uniformly sized frame. Some are composed like Peter Halley's fluorescent-coloured abstract paintings, translated into DIY materials. In *Unit 2* (2008), Bircken assembles fragments of wood leading to a central focus — a piece of stretched orange fabric decorated with thick grey wool and yellow paint. *Unit 5* (2008), meanwhile, displays red organza draped around a hooded vest.

While Bircken's methods and materials might playfully imitate failed rudimentary knitting projects like potholders or tea cosies, she displays them prominently, as a proud parent would tape a child's drawing to the refrigerator. Fragile as they are, they don't appear to be in danger of collapsing; rather, her sculptural components seem to be supporting each other. As Bircken puts it, 'Every single ingredient gives out some type of energy. I try to put them together as a whole, to give them a connection.' [Christy Lange]

01 *Gebilde*, 2005
Branches, wool
23 × 64 × 44 cm
Plinth
118 × 56 × 96 cm

02 *H*, 2007
Wood, branches, pigmented wax, screws
91 × 60 × 36 cm
Plinth
170 × 60 × 36 cm

02

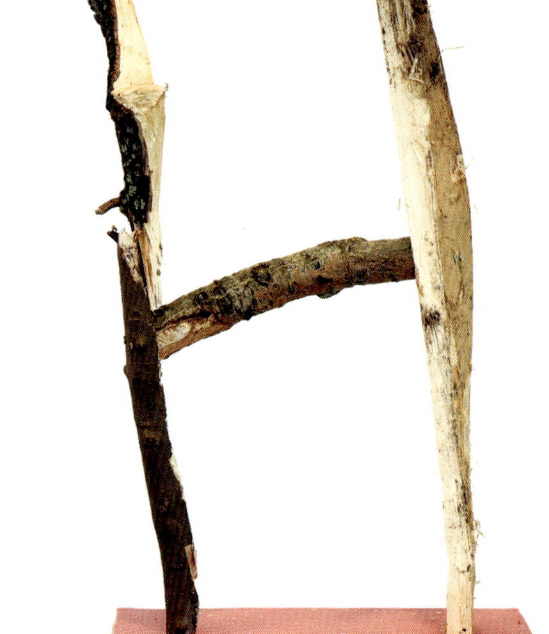

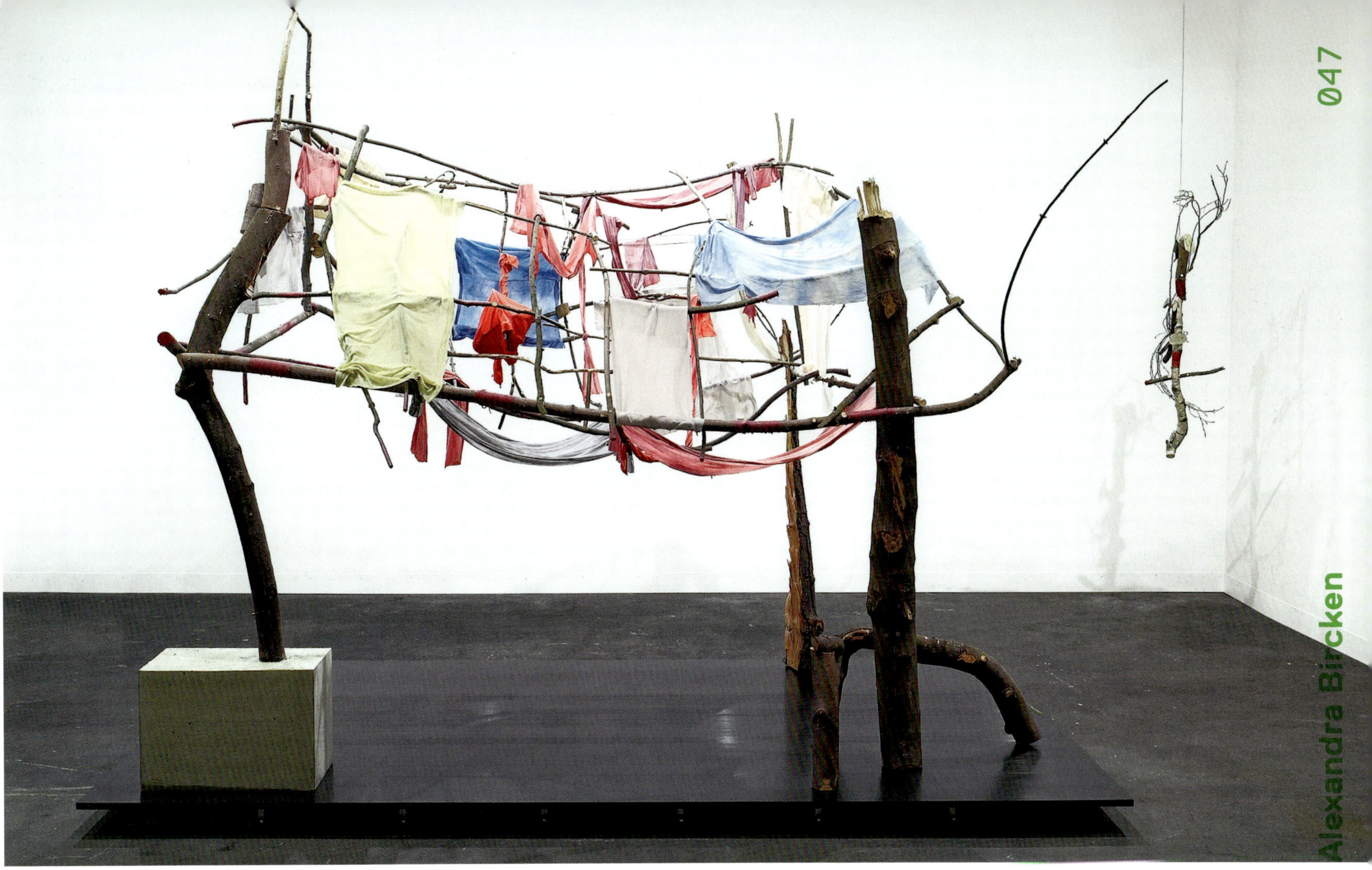

03

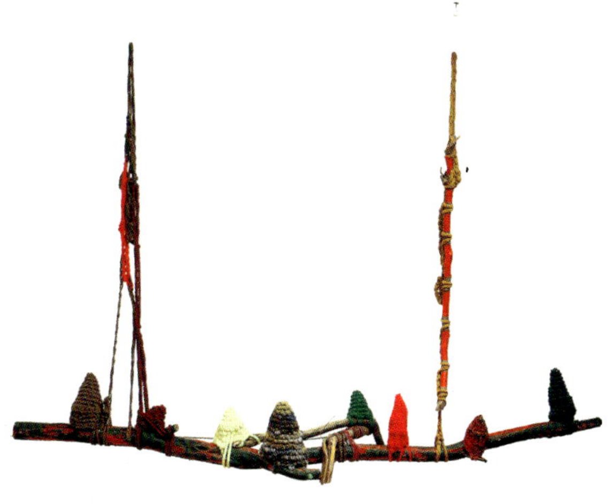

04

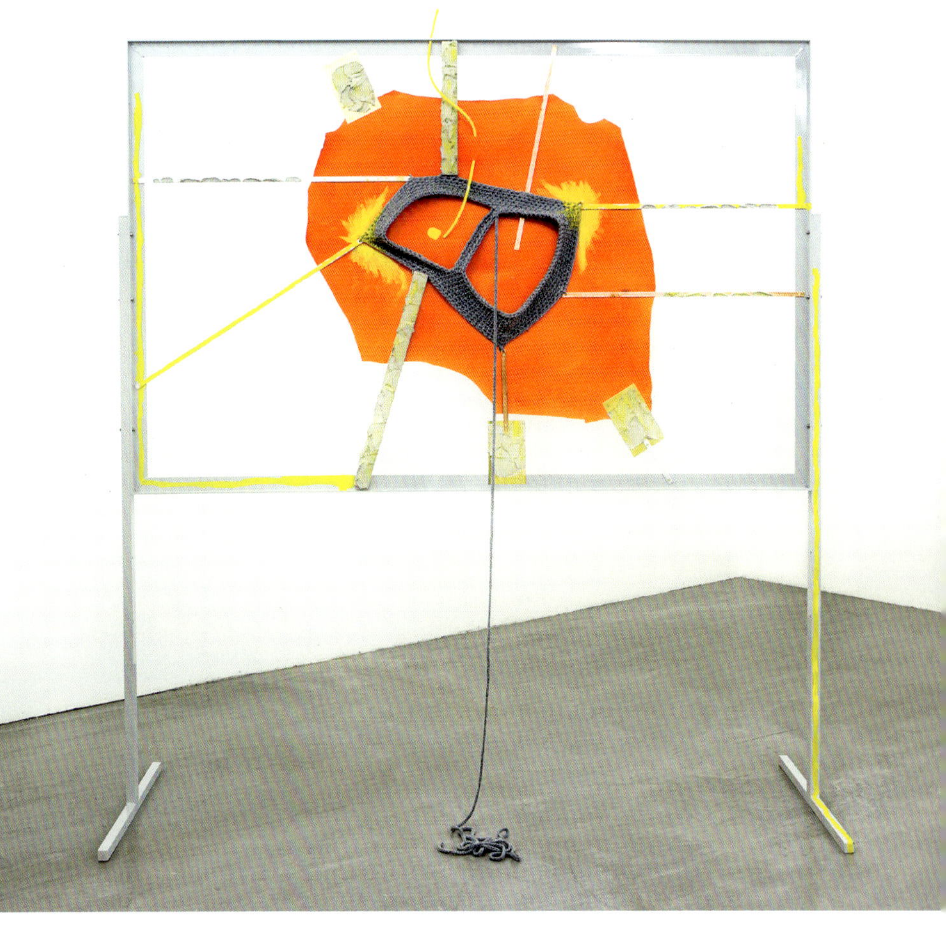

05

03 *Drape*, 2007
Branches, concrete, fabric,
wax, screws, wire, steel
240 × 300 × 236 cm

04 *Stammgäste*, 2006
Branches, wool, acrylic
145 × 59 × 220 cm

05 *Unit 2*, 2008
Painted aluminium, brass, copper,
acrylic paint, mortar,
leather, wool, plastic, pigment,
plastic tube, wood, screws
Height adjustable, frame 140 × 220 cm

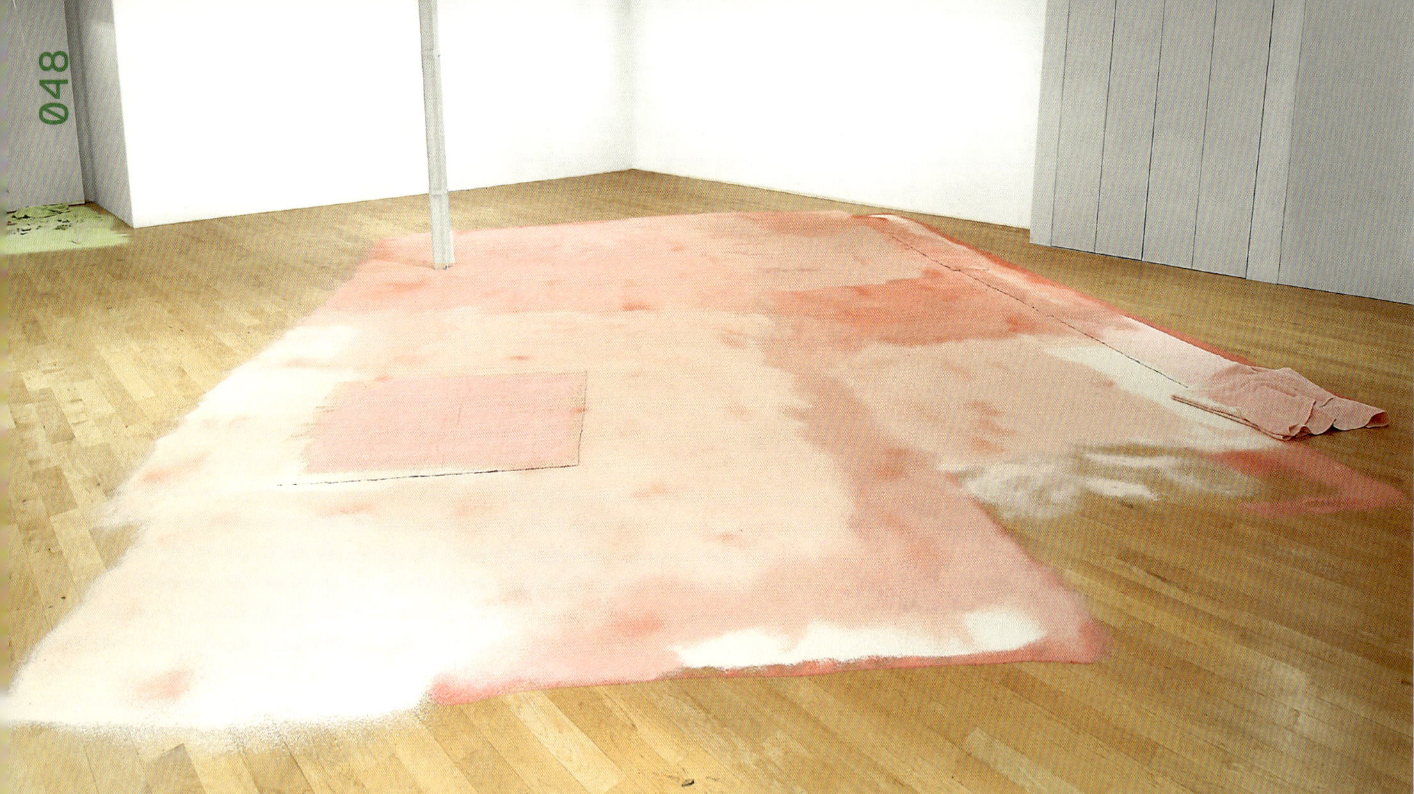
01

Karla Black

The first thing that typically strikes viewers about Karla Black's sculpture is what it is made of. On the one hand, she uses materials like paper, cardboard, plaster, fabric and polythene (the plastic used in shopping bags). Such things are hardly unprecedented in sculpture since the post-Minimalism of the 1960s (think of Eva Hesse), but they are striking here in their insistence on notions of impermanence, contingency and fragility, all of which are incompatible with the monumentality that for centuries was synonymous with sculpture. On the other hand, she also uses substances like toothpaste, shampoo, hand cream, petroleum jelly, nail polish and face powder which are 'end products' rather than working materials, rife with associations and certainly not easily associated with sculpture, even that of recent decades. Black often (but not always) uses materials of this second kind by piling, rubbing or smearing them on to the surfaces of the first sort — applying them, that is, as one might do to one's body, but also as paint is applied to a support.

Those materials convey a lot about what the work is. The fact that the materials are so mutable means that this is not the kind of sculpture that can be made at the studio or at a foundry and then transported to a gallery. The work is made on site; to move it could only mean to remake it. As a result, the sculpture is composed in relation to the space in which it exists; the architecture of the room is the work's support. However well planned it is, the work is also to some extent an improvisation, and this means that there is a performative aspect to it. But in tension with the work's relation to architecture and performance, and to the big abstractions of space and time, it also evokes intimacy, the private spaces and times in which one engages in self-care — an activity undertaken with a view to one's appearance in the eyes of others but at a temporary disengagement or detachment from those eyes.

So far, so good. But none of these considerations take into account the form of Black's sculpture, which is where it really comes into its own, although it is also the part least amenable to being put into words. For her materials and their implications are important above all for the complex and always-changing spatial and visual relationships that they make possible — relationships among each other, with floors and walls, and with the people who engage with them. What's so impressive is how these relationships always remain so unexpected. One feels that the decision-making that went into determining the relationship of part to part was always alert, nuanced and audacious. Other artists make you realize that anything can be sculpture. Black's makes you realize that sculpture can be anything. [Barry Schwabsky]

01, 03 *Punctuation is pretty popular: nobody wants to admit to much*, 2008
Chalk dust, towels, cellotape, cellophane, cling film, paint, washing-up liquid, anti-bacterial hand gel, body moisturizing creams, plaster powder
2 parts
700 × 600 cm

02 *There Can Be No Arguments*, 2008
Polythene, chalk dust, thread
230 × 570 × 475 cm

04 *Wish List*, 2008
Sugar paper, chalk, ribbon, hair gel, nail varnish, plaster powder, paint, petroleum jelly, polythene, rubber glove
600 × 400 × 300 cm

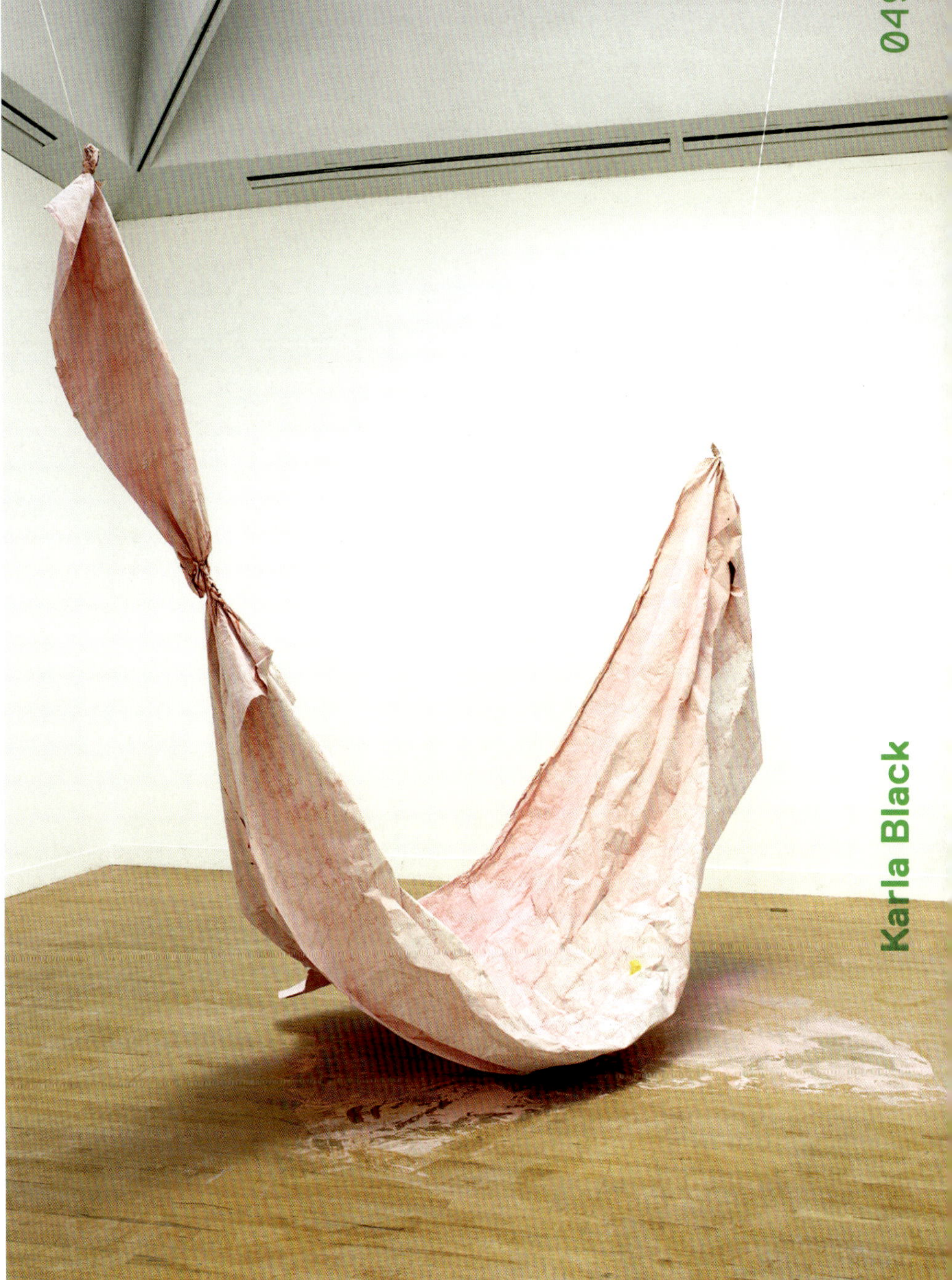

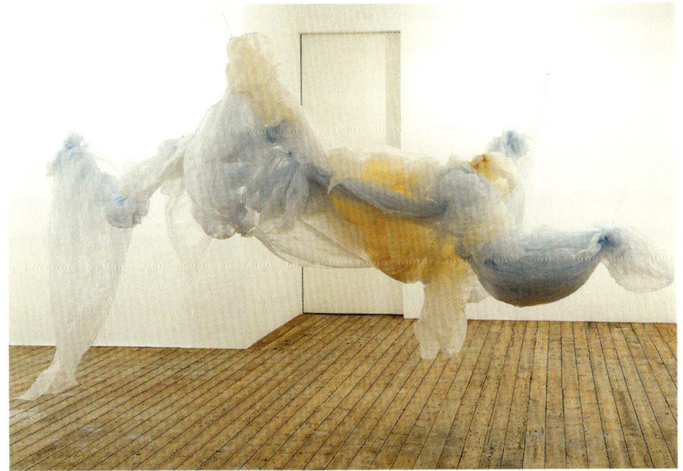

02

04

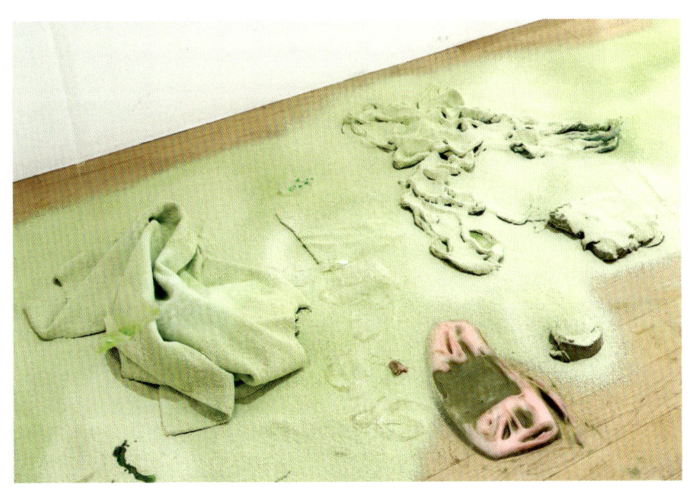

03

01

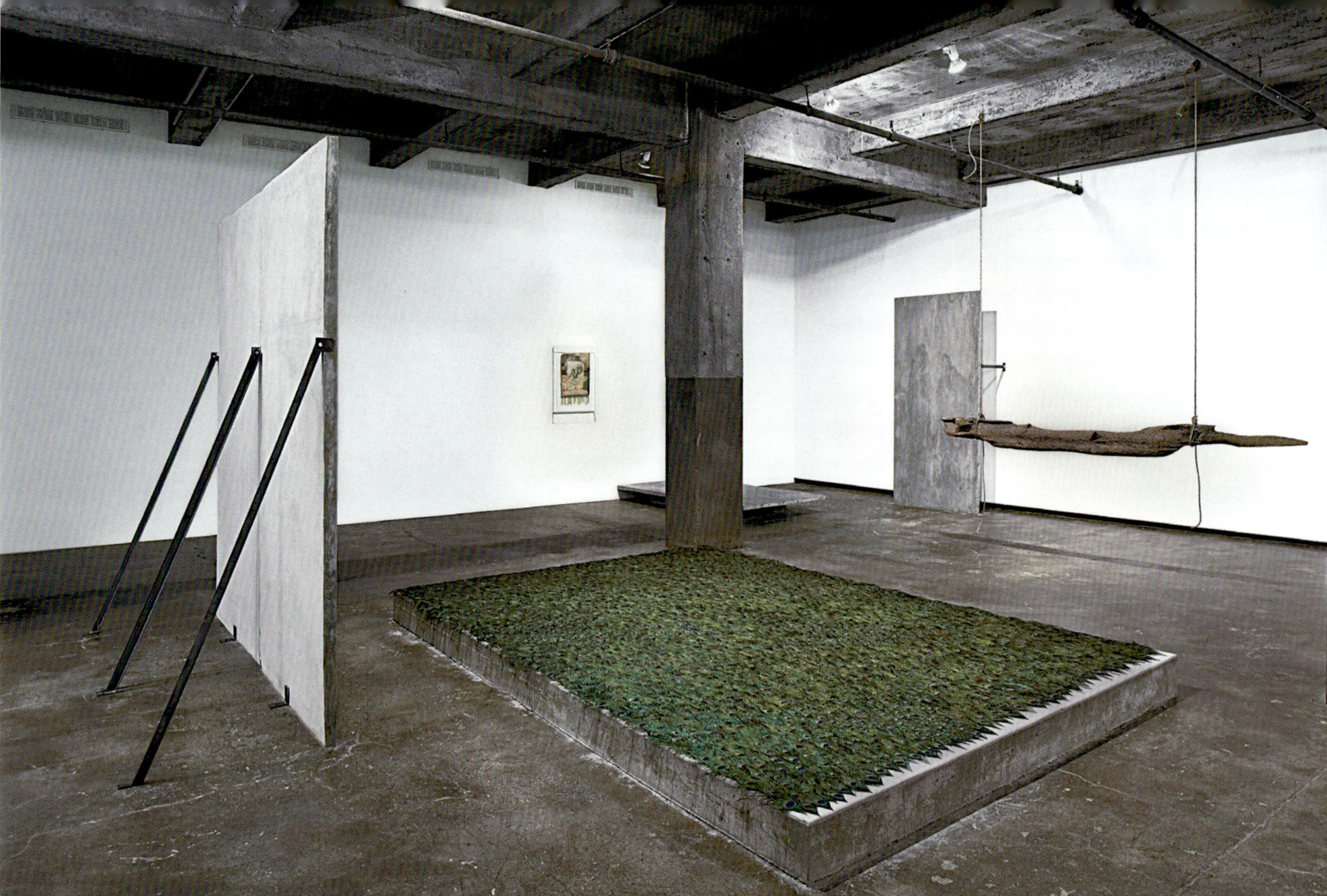

There is a theory that says in short that the progress of human intellectual evolution will eventually reach its apex in our return to our most primitive and perfect beginnings, without technology and at one with nature. This notion, that perfectibility could be reached all at once through an apocalyptic event (being bombed back into the Stone Age) or gradually, by stripping away the extraneous complexities of civilization — from monogamy to clothes — gained such currency in the late 1960s and early 1970s that it became an inspiration for a lifestyle. Utopian movements and the material culture that they spawn can date awfully fast, but the accoutrements of the Age of Aquarius are particularly fascinating and poignant for millennial adults because their wired lives are so opposite from what was dreamed of forty years ago.

Carol Bove's sculptures, wall drawings and arrangements of objects explore this gap between then and now, so small chronologically but in every other respect so enormous. Like an archaeologist, she carefully finds and examines key cultural artefacts from the period that roughly coincides with the year of her birth (1971), but then abandons dry science to connoisseurship. Displayed with an aesthetic appreciation and care appropriate to the most precious museum objects, elements as various as a table-top driftwood sculpture, a paperback copy of *Love's Body* and a peacock feather take on the significance of art historical objects.

Bove's best-known earlier works consisted of modernist steel and wood-shelving units that contained carefully selected groups of vintage books. 'Book families' or 'clusters' that might include titles by Lao Tzu, Marshall McLuhan, and Herbert Marcuse are arranged with an eye to thematic juxtapositions, but also to the compositional effect of stern geometries created by the combination of book stacks and minimalist design.

A consistent element in Bove's work has been its equal attention to elements of art and design. Later works have utilized classic wood and stainless steel Knoll side tables as supports for books and objects. Most recently, her installations have incorporated museum-like, minimalist bases of various materials, including cement, painted wood or Plexiglas. On these supports are various sculptural objects, such as pieces of driftwood, talismanic-looking stones, and notably, edition-sized sculptures that look all the world like Arnaldo Pomodoro's ubiquitous eroded bronze spheres or Richard Lippold's arrangements of slim brass rods. Clear products of the post-nuclear decades, artists like Pomodoro and Lippold strove to express through neo-primitivist forms the awesome horror of living in a world on the technological brink of annihilation, but succeeded in creating what most of us recognize as the quintessential corporate lobby sculpture.

Bove's assemblages expose the tragedy of objects and ideas that predicted a world in perpetual progress, a place where new would always mean better, and the garden, not the stars, was the destination. Failure, though, doesn't preclude beauty, and together Bove's objects create a particular aesthetic — call it the aesthetic of the lost cause — that doesn't make us nostalgic but, perversely, gives us hope. [Laura Hoptman]

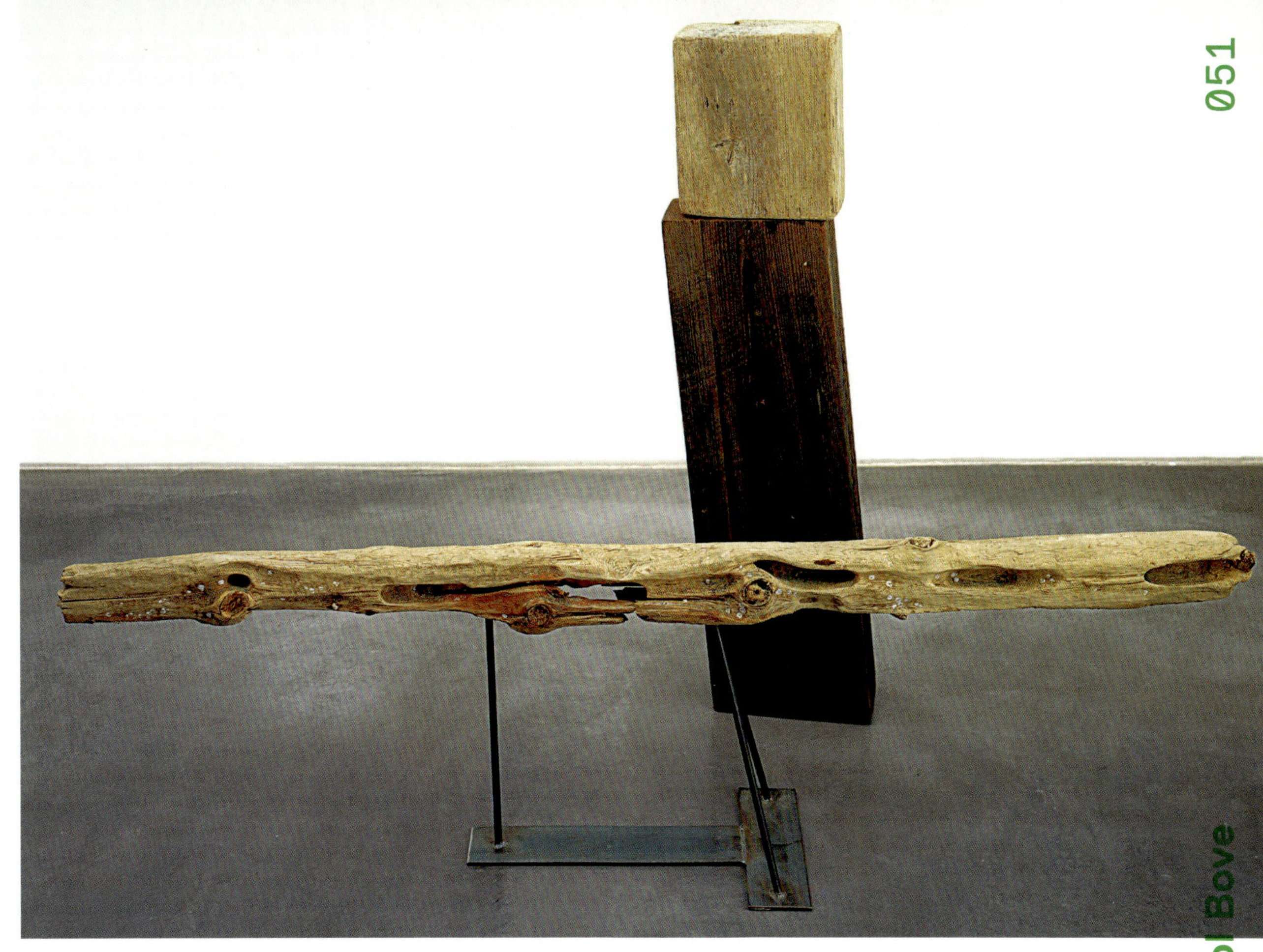

02

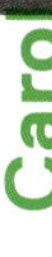

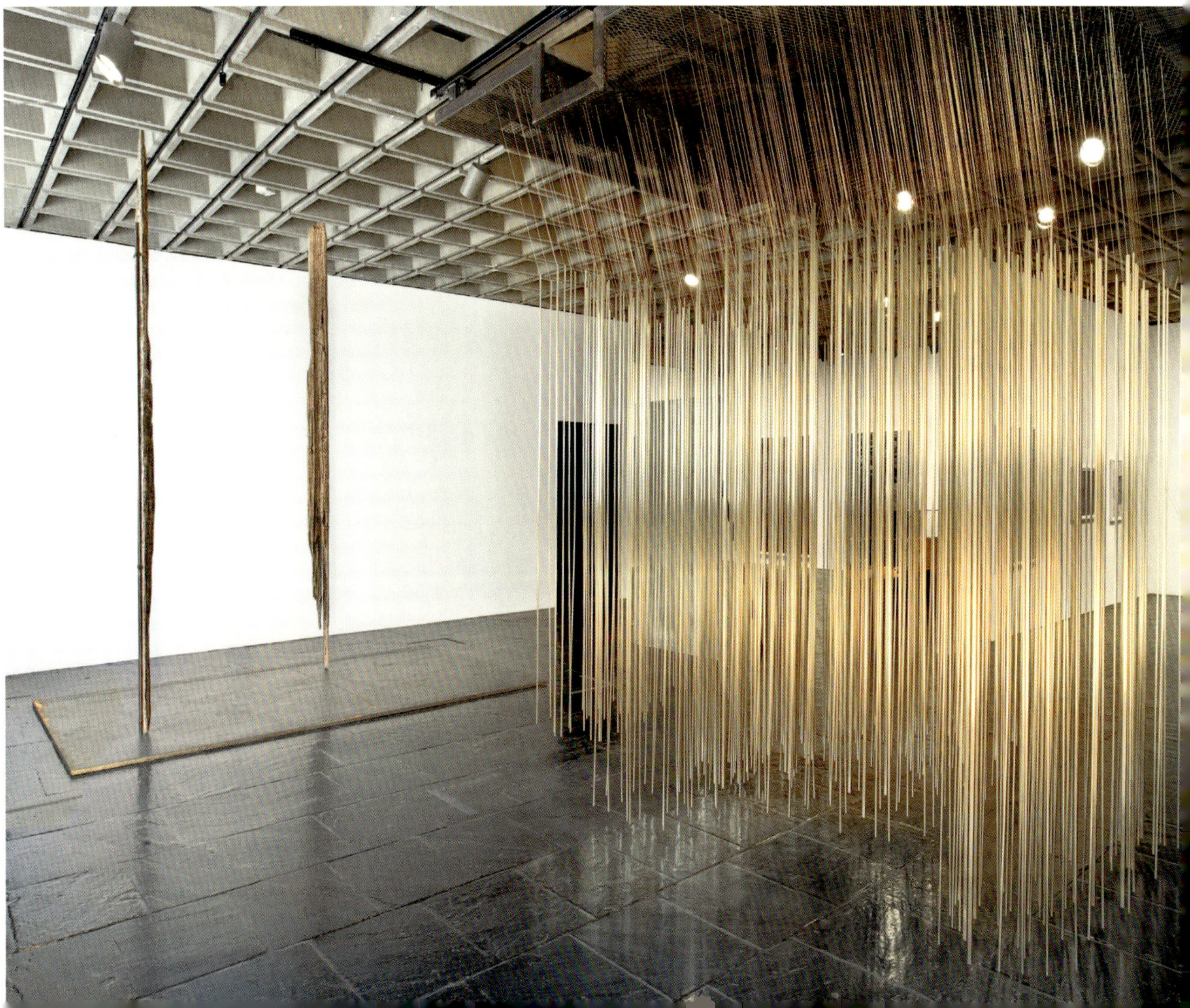

03

01 from left:
→ *Untitled*, 2007
Concrete
244 × 244 × 8 cm
→ *Untitled*, 2007
Peacock feathers, concrete
20 × 381 × 239 cm
→ Bruce Conner
September 13 1959, 1959
Mixed media assemblage with nylon stockings, black and white photograph, feather, plastic fringe, glass brooch, printed cotton fabric
56 × 38 × 2.5 cm
→ *Untitled*, 2007
Concrete
7.5 × 155 × 244 cm
→ *Untitled*, 2007
Concrete
244 × 122 × 7.5 cm
→ *Untitled*, 2007
Driftwood, rope
269 × 18 cm

02 *Machine Gun and Figure*, 2008
Driftwood and steel
Approx. 152× 122 × 122 cm

03 from left:
→ *Field Figures*, 2008
Driftwood, steel
397 × 351 × 213 cm
→ *The Night Sky Over New York, October 21, 2007, 9 p.m.*, 2007
Bronze, steel
371 × 488 × 244 cm

Martin Boyce's work is subliminal and visceral. It psychologically transforms common spaces into pleasure places: suburban swing parks (*Our Love is like the Flowers, the Rain, the Sea and the Hours*, 2002; *This is where we meet*, 2004), Riviera poolside playgrounds (*We are resistant, we dry out in the sun*, 2004) and abandoned outdoor ping pong tables (*We Pass Through Pools and Parkways. We Are Against Gravity*, 2007).

Boyce uses simple materials, the plain unencumbered surfaces of modern design. He remains ever true to Mies van der Rohe's 'less is more' credo, transforming his found materials as little as possible, narrating a scene through precise juxtapositions of readymades. In Boyce's minimalist world, Donald Judd's 'real materials in real space' transmogrify into real materials in surreal space.
01 He dreams of a murky modernism, sulkily conscious of its unfashionable machismo, guilty of its symbolic brutality, learning from Las Vegas, licking its Cold War wounds. In works of the 1990s, the design decade during which ornament was re-criminalized, broken ciphers of the Contemporary Style and Brutalist bric-a-brac were prevalent in Boyce's sculptural lexicon. The familial relations between Neo-Plasticism, Maison-Domino, Charles Eames' early military work (*Now I've Got Real Worry*, 1998), Arne Jacobsen's furniture and Miesian open-plan interiors play out conflicting gestures. Their seductive design qualities are overshadowed by their ritualistic and narrative values. A recurring leitmotif is the perspectival grid that features in Saul Bass' striking opening-title graphics for Alfred Hitchcock's *North by Northwest*. Boyce's omnipresent Bass grid functions spatially and metaphorically (*Ventilation Grills [your lost dreams live between the walls]* 2003). On the one hand it is a sculptural form, a prop for a regular modern curtain wall, an illusion of recessional space. On the other, it harbours all the hope of the gridiron-order that was once our modern vision. It acts as a lens, a way of re-imagining the future-perfect viewed through the alter-perspective of modernist memory.

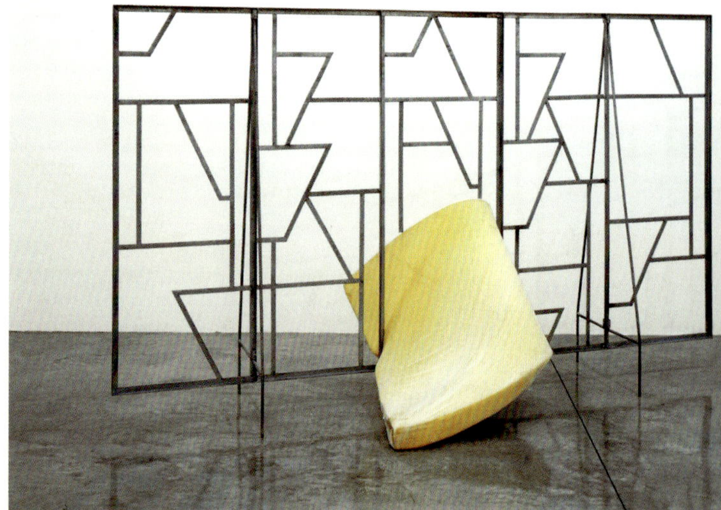

While the objects and materials exercised by Boyce in more recent installations tend not to have the same degree of readymade historical cachet, they show a greater confidence in his own practice and his considerable ability to produce designs on a par with those of his modernist mentors. His production of place is dramatically exuberant and all the more cinematic, enabling eccentric narratives to emerge from the cinders of modern nostalgia. His installations are oneiric, cities of dreams born in the dream factory. International Style skyscrapers, Tativille, Playboy pads, New Wave nightclubs are our utopic landfill; they give a new look to our new way of living.

Boyce has mastered the poetic use of carefully placed performing objects and illusionistic optical relationships. His unadorned configurations figure complex brooding landscapes. Chain-link fencing, modern steel benches, wire bins and steel gates limbo at acute angles, like short shadows cast by a high summer sun. Sculptures are bathed in the crepuscular light cast from fluorescent strips fashioned together to produce makeshift electric trees. Boyce practices a black art; his sculptural installations make the shadowy world of noir spring to life in solid silhouettes. [Neil Mulholland]

02

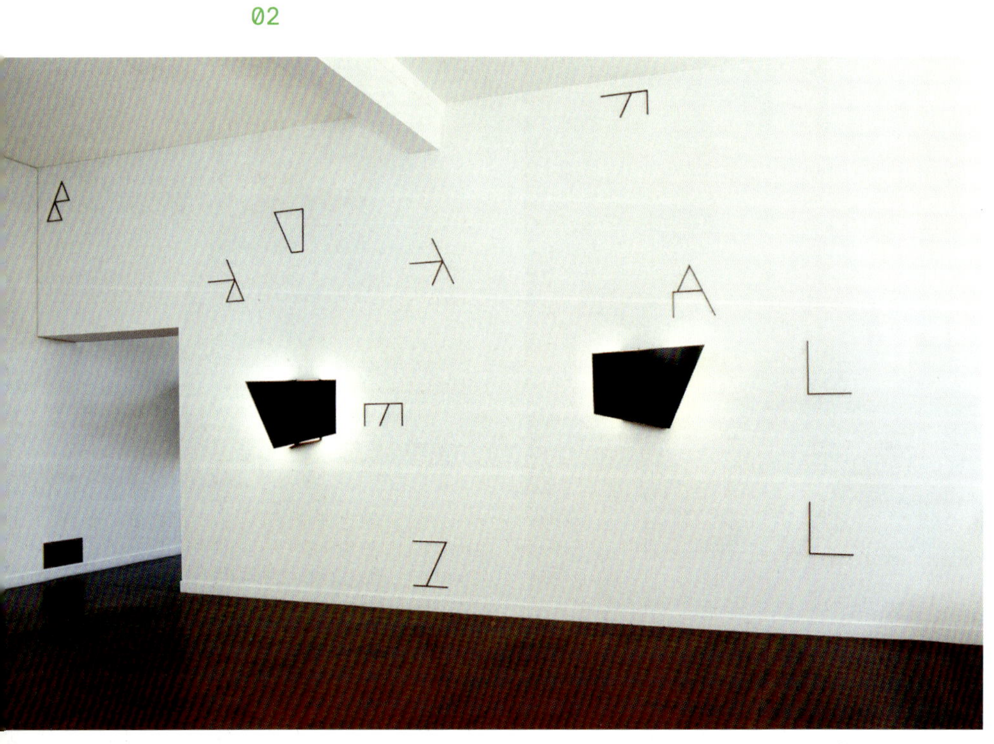

01 *Broken Branches and Flyovers*, 2007
Galvanized steel, foam
203 × 196 × 196 cm

02 *Broken Fall (That Blows Through Concrete Leaves)*, 2007
Burnished brass, lacquered steel, fluorescent light fittings
Dimensions variable

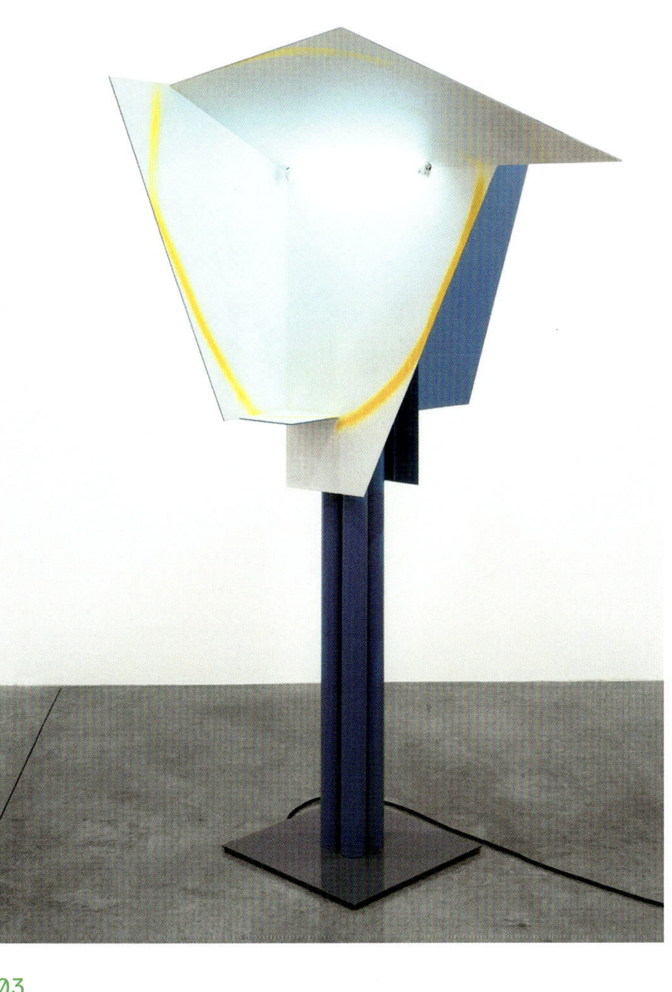

03

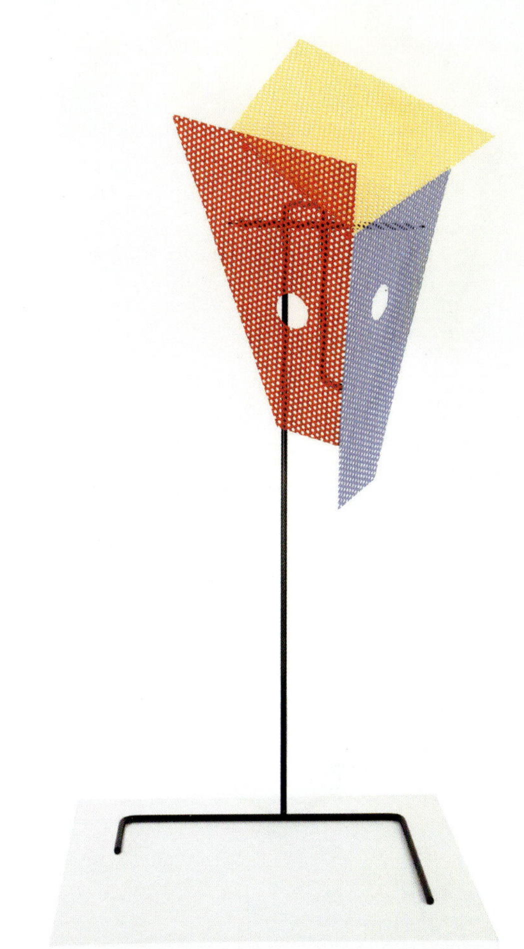

04

05

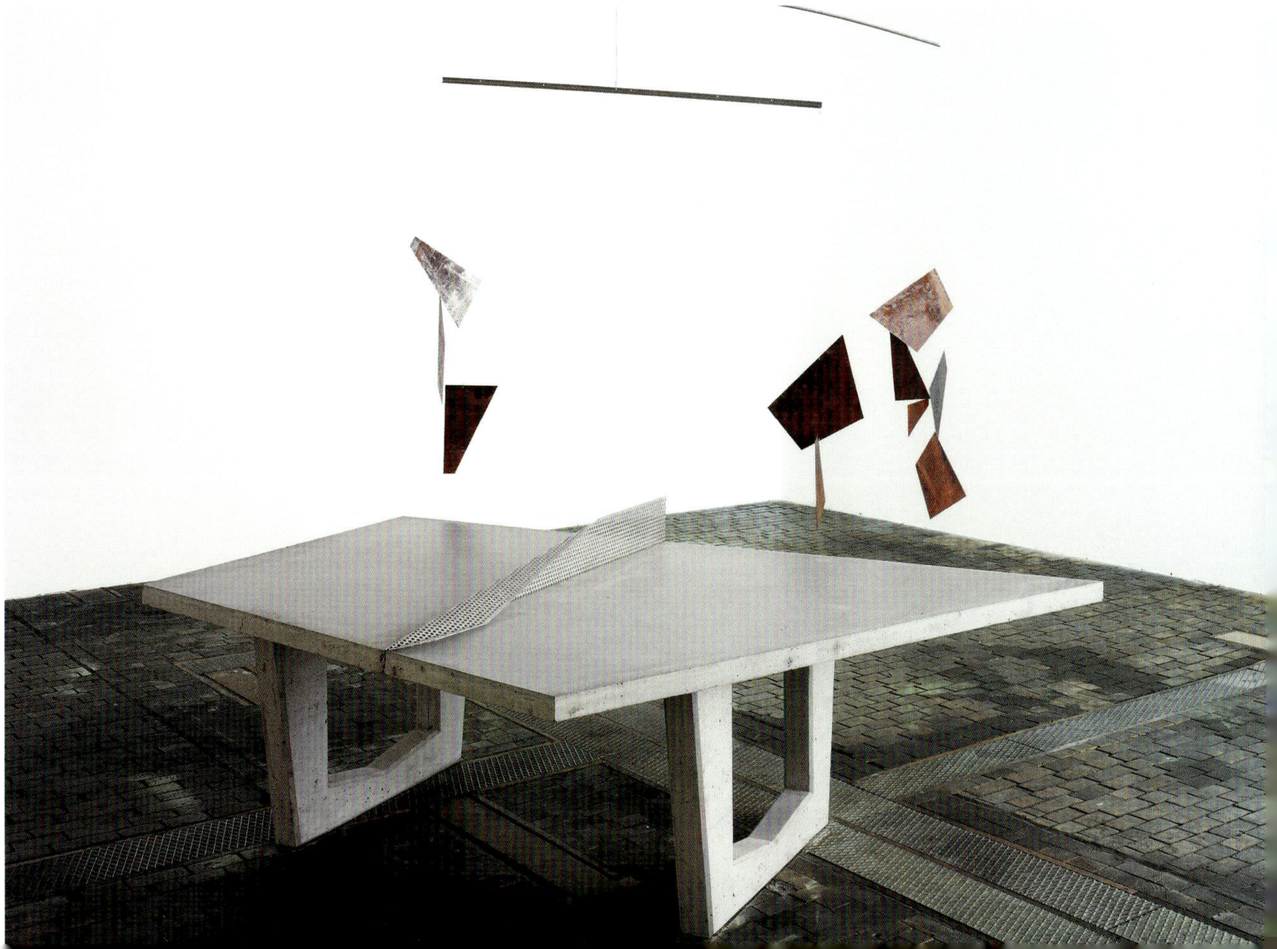

03 *Fluorescent Sunshine and Shivers*, 2007
Steel, powder-coated aluminium, light fixture and spray paint
215 × 176 × 150 cm

04 *Untitled*, 2007
Painted steel
71 × 37 × 23 cm

05 *We Pass Through Pools and Parkways. We Are Against Gravity*, 2007
Concrete, aluminium
Dimensions variable

Overleaf:

06 *Electric Trees and Telephone Booth Conversations*, 2006
3 painted plywood trees, 3 telephone booths (2 wall mounted, 1 free-standing), 3 lampshades suspended between trees, 1 climbing frame, 1 additional tree
Dimensions variable

054

Martin Boyce

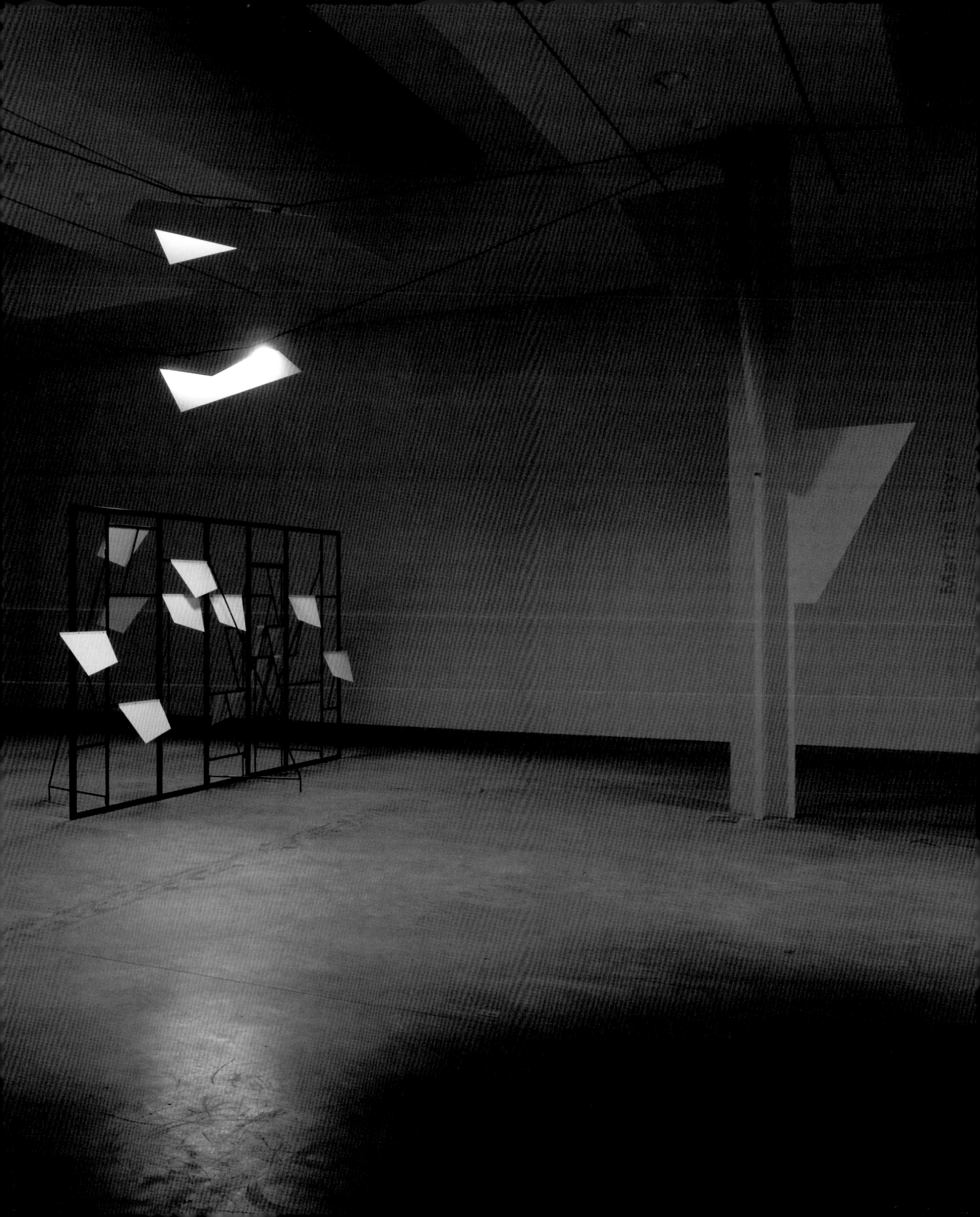

Few people know that Satyajit Ray, the most universally acclaimed director of Indian cinema, at one point wanted to make a science fiction film in Hollywood. Its working title was *Alien*, but its story was closer to what was to become Steven Spielberg's *E.T.* In fact, Ray claimed in an article written for a newspaper in Calcutta that his idea was instrumental in the latter's success. This would be just another apocryphal story from the mythology of global cinema had Matti Braun, the German-Finnish artist, not only thoroughly researched it, but eventually staged a production based on Ray's script. Braun's interest in the matter is not just a movie buff's fascination for the strange genealogies of films and films-never-to-have-been. His is an approach that deals with an archaeology of modernity. To him, the *Alien* project is situated at the crossroads of intercultural exchange and a history of progress that is not as linear as enthusiasts of the Western way of life would have us believe.

The way in which Braun revisits this topic is a telling example of his art in general. In 2003, for an exhibition in Freiburg, Germany, he created a lake within an entire gallery space, referring to the lake covered with lotus flowers in which the spaceship lands in *Alien*. He somehow 'realized' Ray's script, but not in its own medium, rather as a detour into more abstract territory and into the art system. In 2008, in his Berlin gallery show 'Lota', he came back to that scene by exhibiting photographs from his stagings of *Alien*, this time in combination with textile wall hangings, an abstract sculpture made of reinforced concrete and hand-blown glass objects.

Braun traces the trade routes of modernist and exoticist ideas around the globe. In *Özurfa* (2008), he created a dense web of references around the city of Urfa in Southeast Turkey. This richly historical site happens to be close to the birth place of Yilmaz Guney, who held a position within Turkish cinema similar to Ray's in India, a conscious reference on Braun's part that drew on the happenstance of that vicinity. One point that emerges in *Özurfa* (i.e. 'authentic' Urfa) is that authenticity is always a result of exchange and negotiation.

While cinema is his most frequent point of reference, Braun also takes a particular interest in design. In 2000 he was commissioned to create the interior design for the G7-summit. He made his contribution a homage to the design of Charles and Ray Eames, providing the functionality necessary for this meeting of top politicians, but at the same time creating an atmosphere like that of a science fiction film set. It was undecided as to whether the politicians were meant to be the aliens or those protecting mankind from alien experience. Braun certainly never shies away from exposing himself and the viewers of his work to spaces of uncertainty that are as challenging as any distant planet. [Bert Rebhandl]

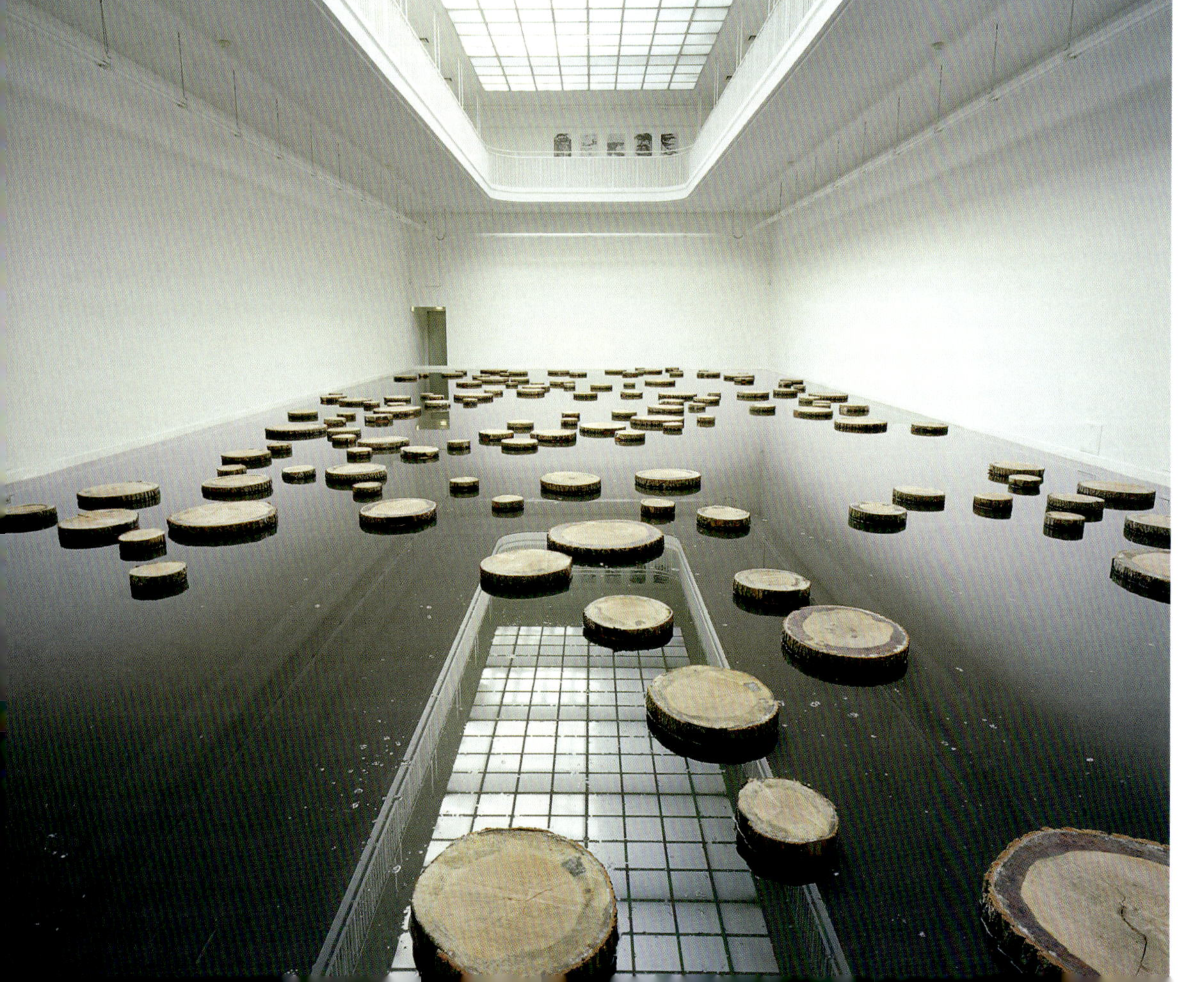

01

01 *S.R.*, 2003–05
Foil, water, wood
Dimensions variable

02 *The Alien (London)*, 2007
Set of 6 photographs
Each 27 × 30 cm

03 from left:
→ *Untitled*, 2008
25 flints, arrowheads, Faust wedges, scrapers, vitrine
90 × 116 × 76 cm
→ *Untitled*, 2008
4 pigeons, silver headdress, 3 silver anklets, vitrine
120 × 106 × 92 cm
→ *Untitled*, 2008
9 antique oil lamps, vitrine
96 × 84 × 88 cm
→ *Untitled*, 2008
11 antique Roman glass vases, vitrine
111 × 111 × 81 cm
→ *Untitled*, 2008
3 carp skeletons, vitrine
96 × 130 × 84 cm
→ *Yol*, 2008
7 film reels, vitrine
120 × 61 × 61 cm
→ *Özurfa*, 2008
Works on paper
13 parts
Sizes vary from 23 × 38 cm to 36 × 33 cm
→ *Untitled*, 2008
Wood, plaster, foam
328 × 333 × 14 cm

04 *Yol*, 2008
7 film reels, complete copy of 'Yol', vitrine
120 × 61 × 61 cm

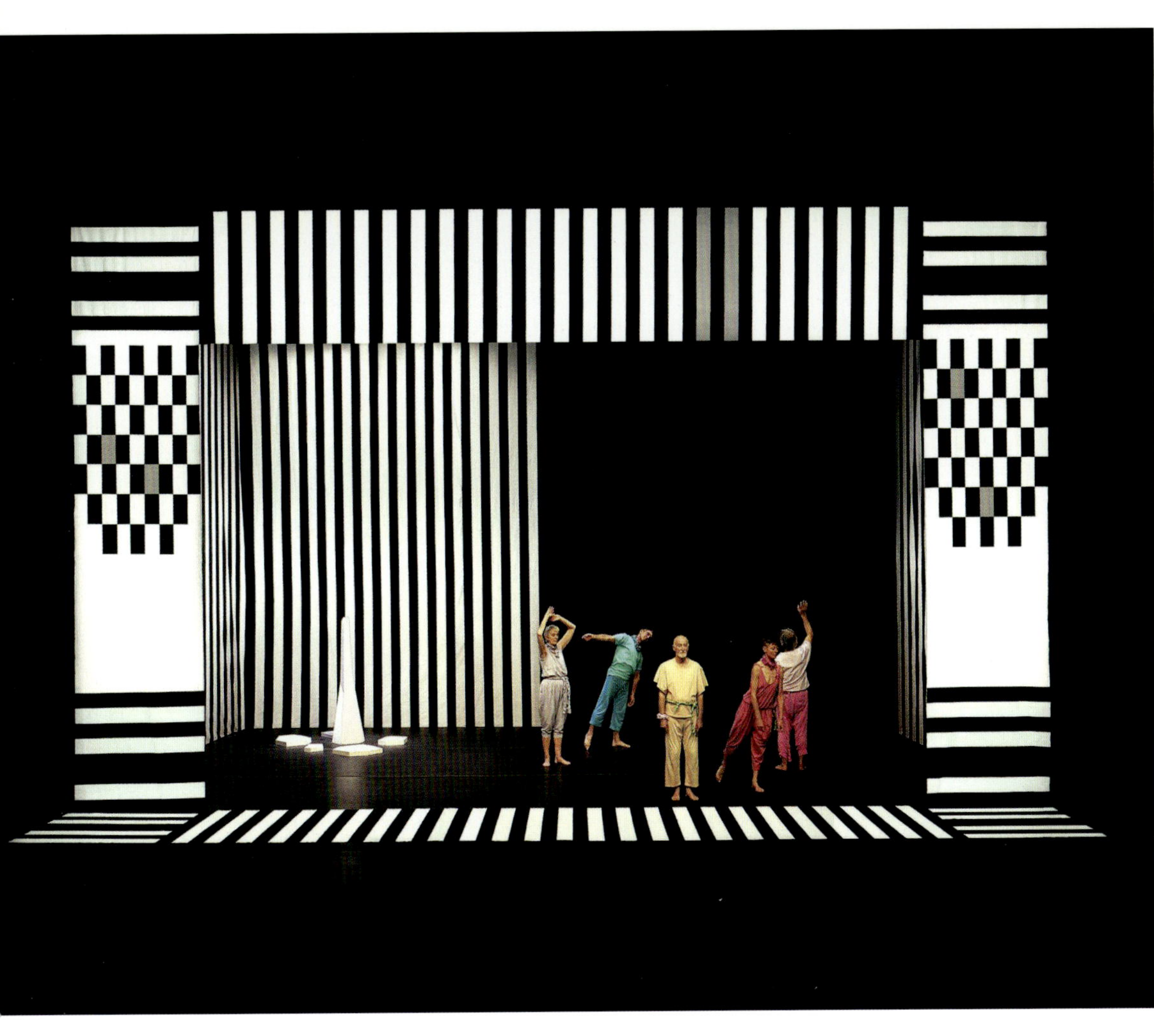

02

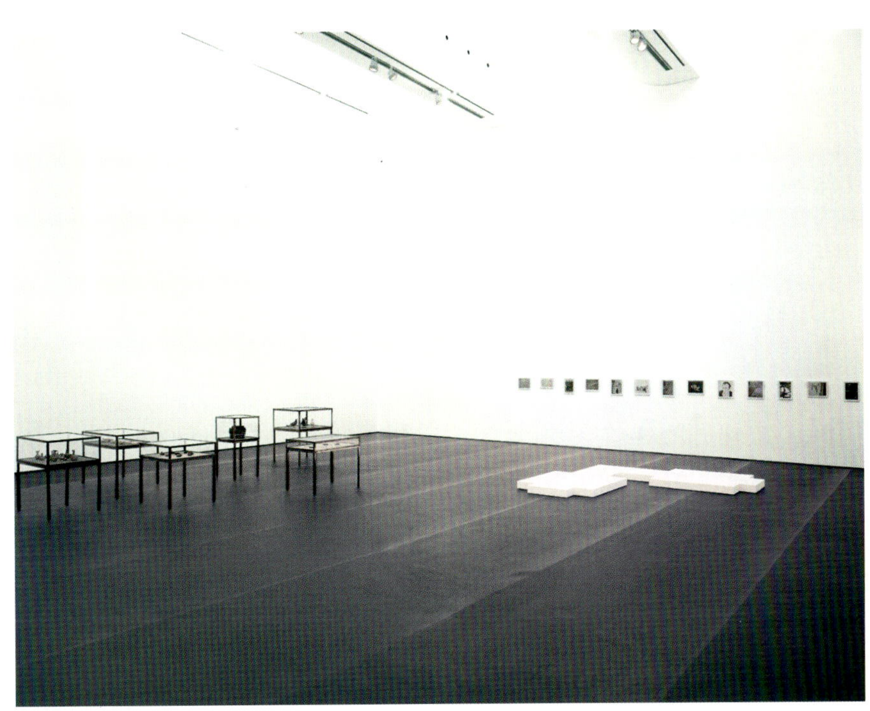

03

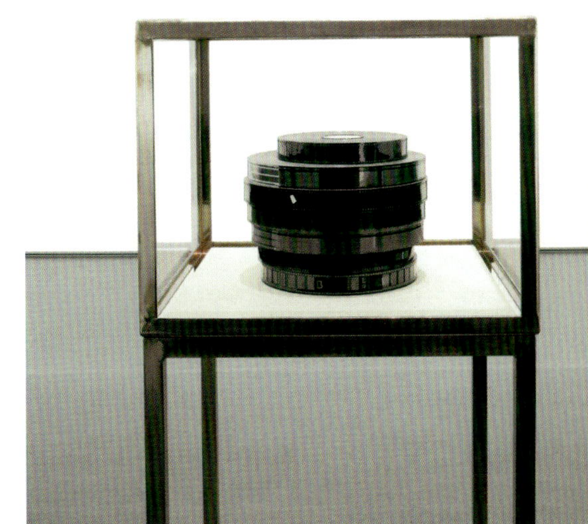

04

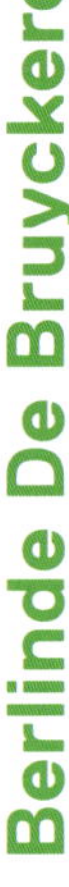

01

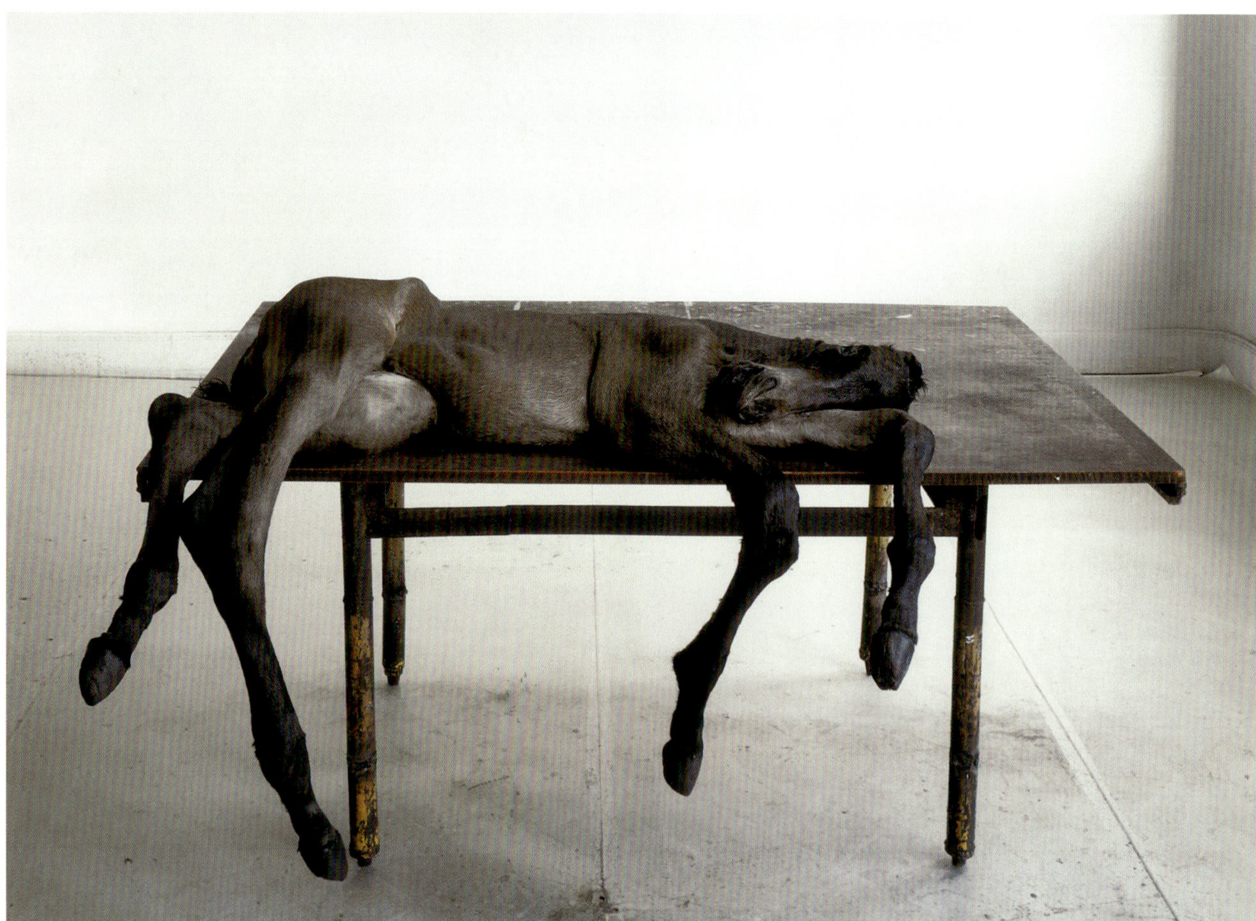

Berlinde De Bruyckere's is a baroque art, in the sense that it takes creature-suffering as its central theme, giving it a modern parallel in the work of Francis Bacon. She shows us figures that seem to be in pain, crouching or hugging themselves, seeking protection in the warmth of their own bodies. Some are firmly tucked up in blankets; the fabric hugs their bodies, is sewn to emphasize their curves, but also picks out points that reveal missing limbs. Many of the figures are fragmented or, conversely, expanded as a result of proliferations. Horses, sprained and mutilated, are shown directly on the ground or on table-like plinths and showcases. An accumulation of animal bodies presented like this resembles a battlefield, and yet the violent way in which the bodies are bent and fragmented is mitigated by the careful sewing of the hides. Such associations have become concrete references through the titles that the artist gives to her works — for example *In Flanders Field* (2000).

De Bruyckere also presents figures of almost Biblical stature, reminiscent of martyrs or the Crucifixion. Their wasted, twisted bodies evoke late medieval Flemish art, which is as important an influence on De Bruyckere (she was born in Ghent and still lives there) as the flesh prevalent in the work of an artist such as Rubens. To depict the human body De Bruyckere works with wax, which she pours into plaster casts made from living models. She captures the liveliness of the skin by mixing pale shades with strong colours that make the surface pulsate. The horse sculptures are also based on casts, in this case using silicone, of cadavers given to her by the Anatomy Department of the Faculty of Veterinary medicine at Ghent University. Using a block and tackle set up in her studio yard, she can position the animals' bodies as she wishes. Some of the horse sculptures hang from scaffolding, attached by one foot only, like slaughtered animals being bled, an image familiar from Rembrandt. But the bodies are shut off, covered with horse hide, a strange skin whose seams show that the hide has clearly been adapted to the mould, emphasizing the sense of protection. Like the fragmented human bodies, the mutilated horses also come together to form a new, complete whole. The visible seams are the characteristic scars of this ambivalent 're-membering', this way of closing a fragmented body to create an artistic whole.

De Bruyckere is a modern sculptor in the classic sense. According to one's viewpoint, the bodies seem almost abstract; figure and space are presented, as in a sculpture by Henry Moore, as a complex pattern of connections. As the drawings she uses to develop new ideas also show, De Bruyckere thinks in categories of volume, weight and tension. The effect made by the dismembered bodies develops only through the completeness of the sculptural form. [Beate Söntgen]

01, 02 *Lost II*, 2006–07
Horsehide, epoxy, metal, wood
152 × 164 × 98 cm

03 *In Doubt*, 2007–08
Wax, epoxy, glass, wood, iron
65 × 90 × 171 cm

04 *Pietà*, 2008
Wax, epoxy, metal, wood, glass, iron
59 × 85 × 242 cm

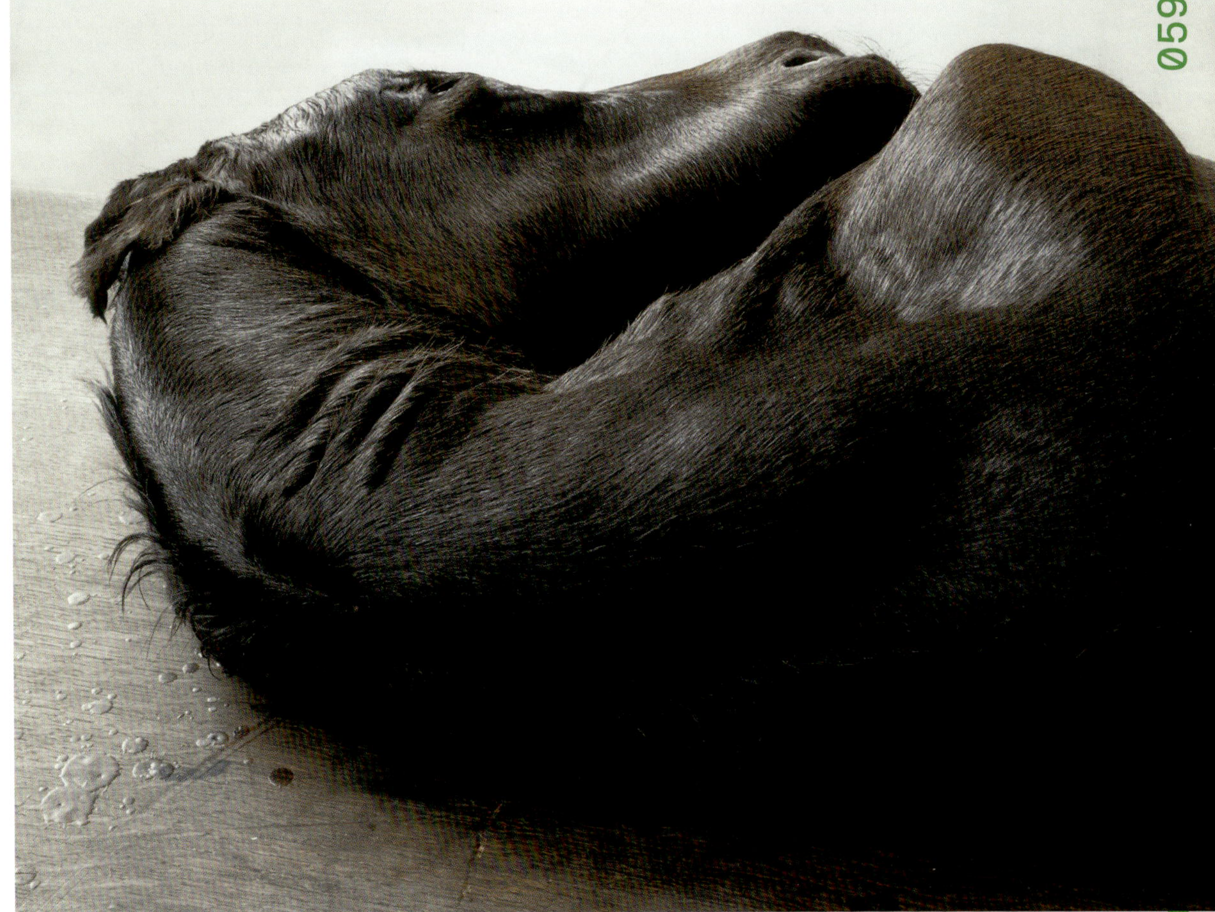

02

03

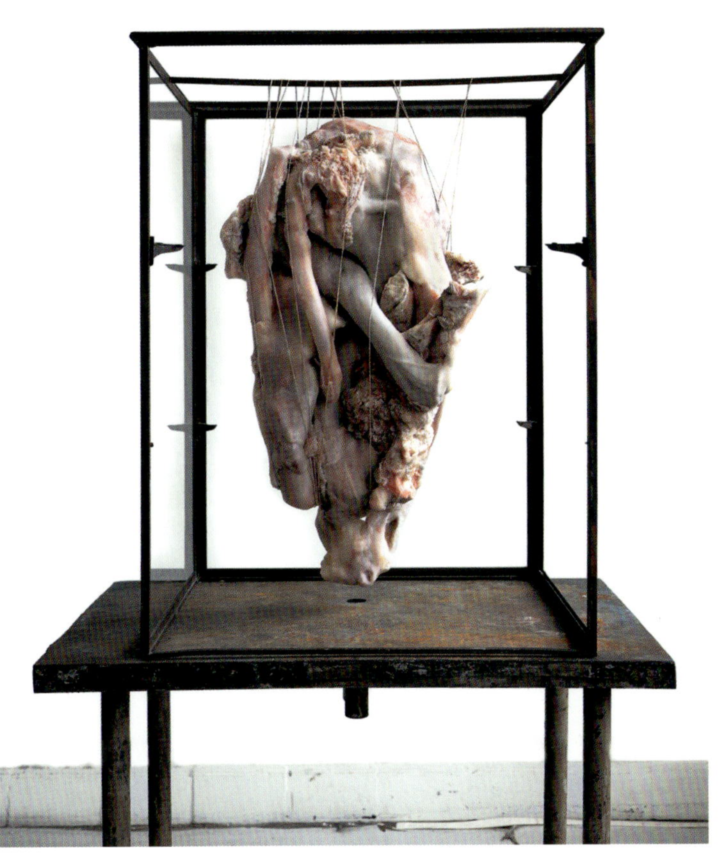

04

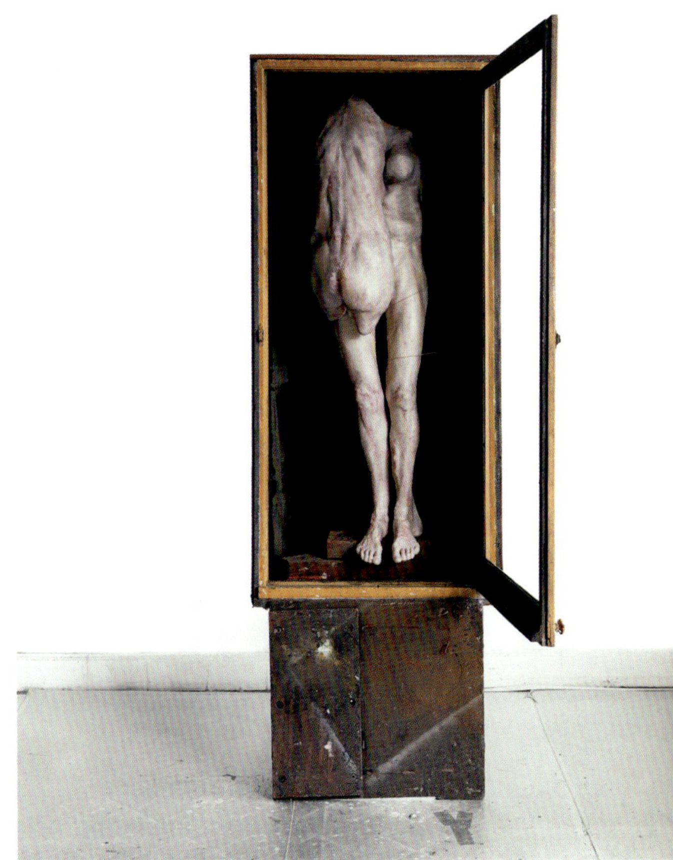

The Swiss artist Christoph Büchel is primarily known for his enormous installations — including *Simply Botiful* (at Hauser & Wirth Coppermill, London, 2006), *Dump* (at Palais de Tokyo, Paris, 2008) and *Deutsche Grammatik* (at Kunsthalle Fridericianum, Kassel, 2008) — which are hyper-realistic representations of specific situations. Viewers move through these inventions as if through a labyrinth, sometimes forced to navigate cramped spaces on their hands and knees and often losing all sense of direction.

Büchel's obsessively precise representations of reality seem to be more real than reality itself. Not only do viewers forget that they are in a museum, and thus inside a reassuring 'white cube', but they are physically
01 projected into other contexts that make up the contemporary world, familiar through mass media or personal experience. These are often contexts that we pretend not to see, or consciously choose to ignore. Büchel recreates these situations and spaces, dealing with current events and politics, and states his position on burning issues without moralizing. His work addresses a broad range of subjects: the Israeli-Palestinian conflict, the living conditions of refugees and illegal immigrants in the Southern Hemisphere, the military and imperialistic madness of the United States under George W. Bush, or the cultural prejudices that surround both faithful Muslims and musicians in a punk band.

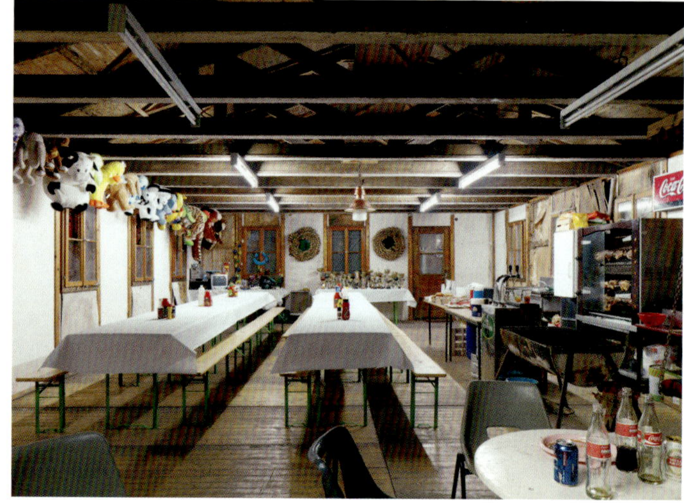

It is reductive to talk about Büchel's works as 'installations'. Rather, we should define them as real and genuine 'worlds'. This definition might sound overly poetic but, in fact, it is not so far from the truth: firstly because the artist controls, defines and sets in place every detail (both at a macroscopic and microscopic level, from the general architecture down to the smells drifting through the air), and secondly, and more importantly, because the work is precise, conceptual and dramaturgic, the result of a long process of research. Büchel creates true spatio-temporal miracles in which the line between artistic fiction and reality disappears. Moving through the various rooms or areas that make up the route through these worlds, viewers realize that they are in a truly organised system where nothing is left to chance. Every element has a precise role to play in the construction of a meaning, which goes well beyond that of simple hyper-realistic representation.

Büchel's artworks are allegorical representations in which the often tragic events of the modern society are re-elaborated, becoming grotesque representations or parodies of reality. However, what troubles us when visiting this realm is the fact that, despite a degree of irony, the parodies and grotesque aspects do not make us laugh. These installations serve to strip bare and expose the world we live in, which — as we all know — is no laughing matter. [Giovanni Carmine]

02

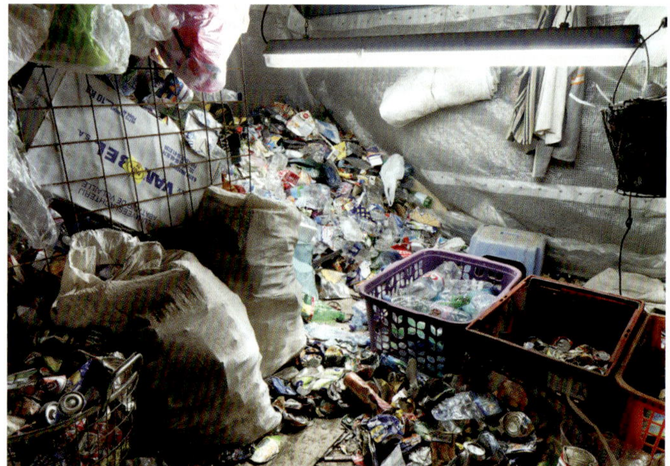

03

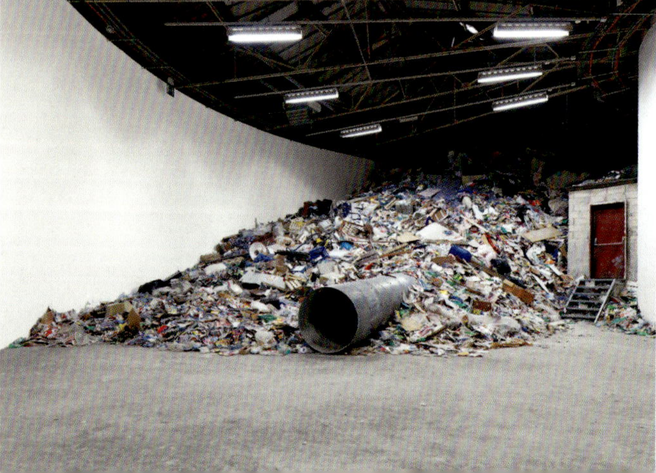

01, 02, 03 *Dump*, 2008
Mixed-media site-specific installation
Dimensions variable

04 *Simply Botiful*, 2006
Mixed-media site-specific installation
Dimensions variable

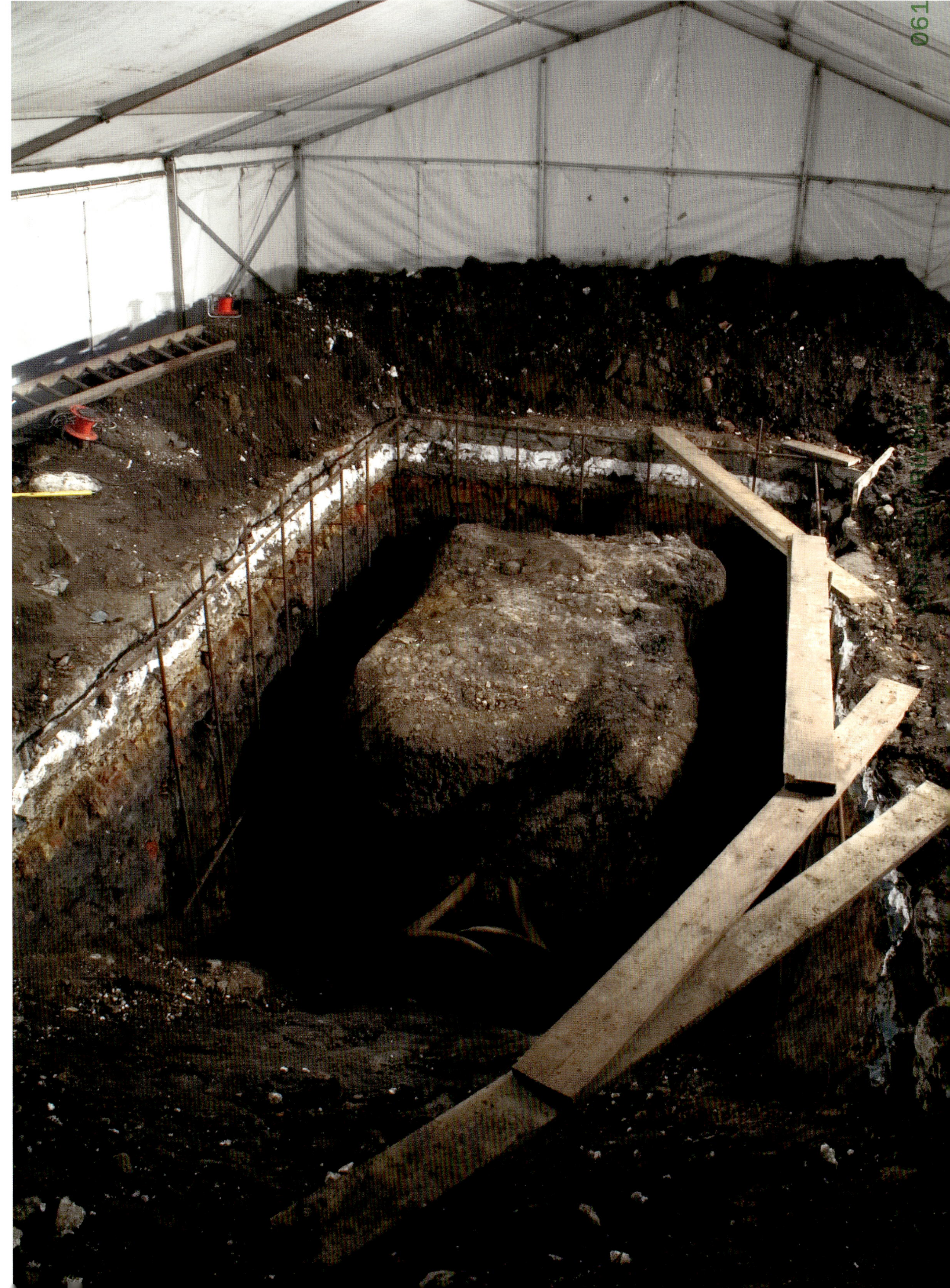

04

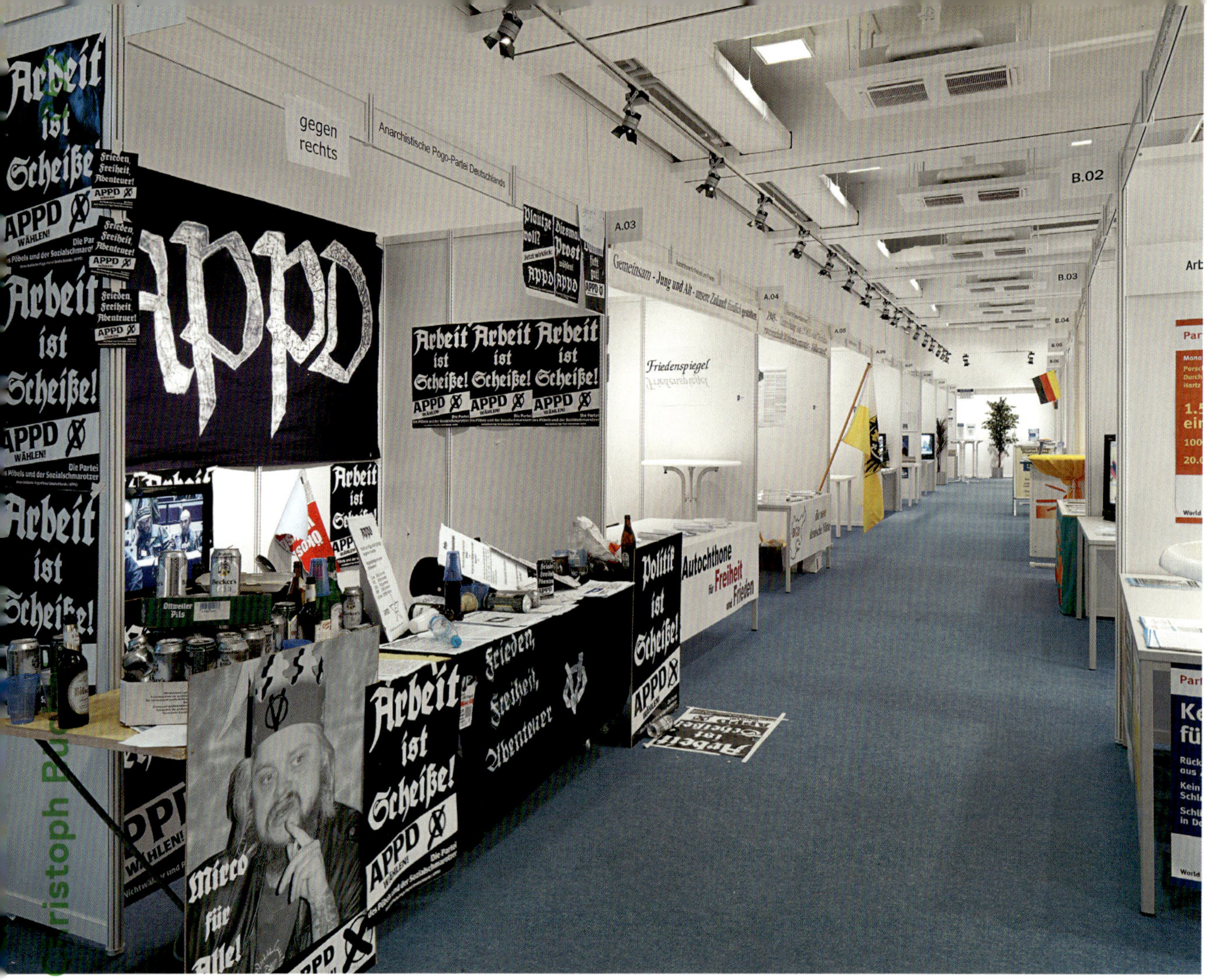

05

07

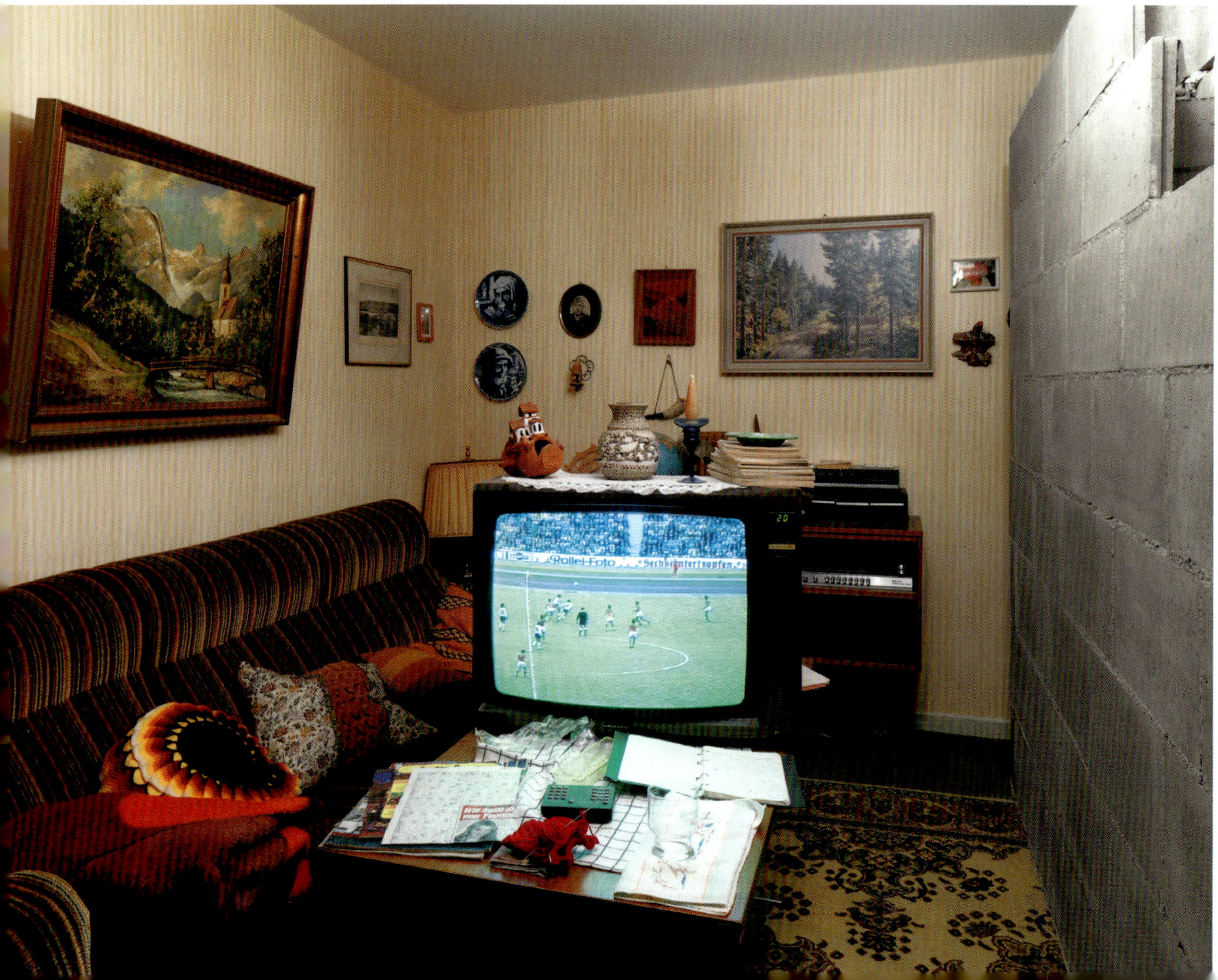

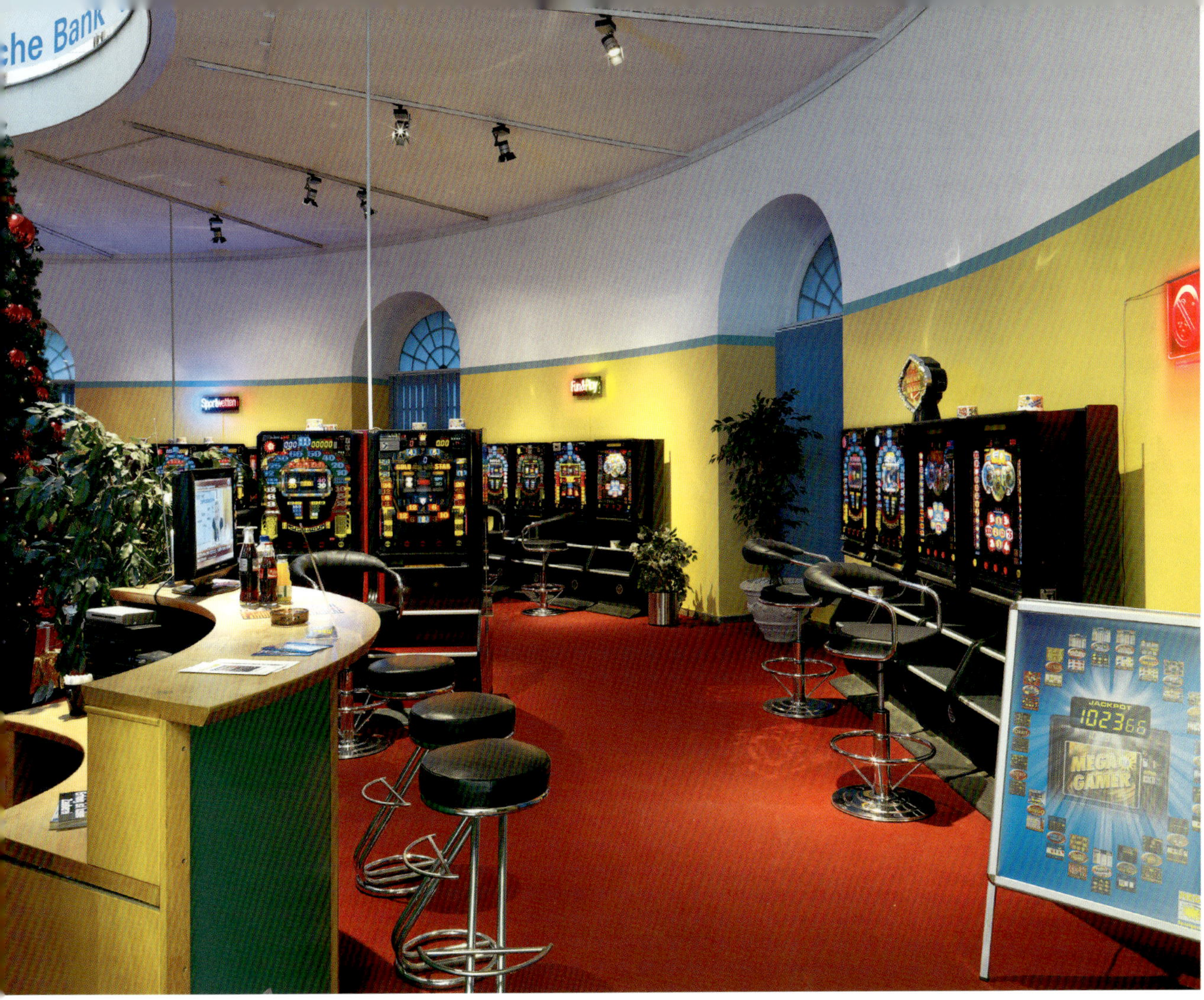

06

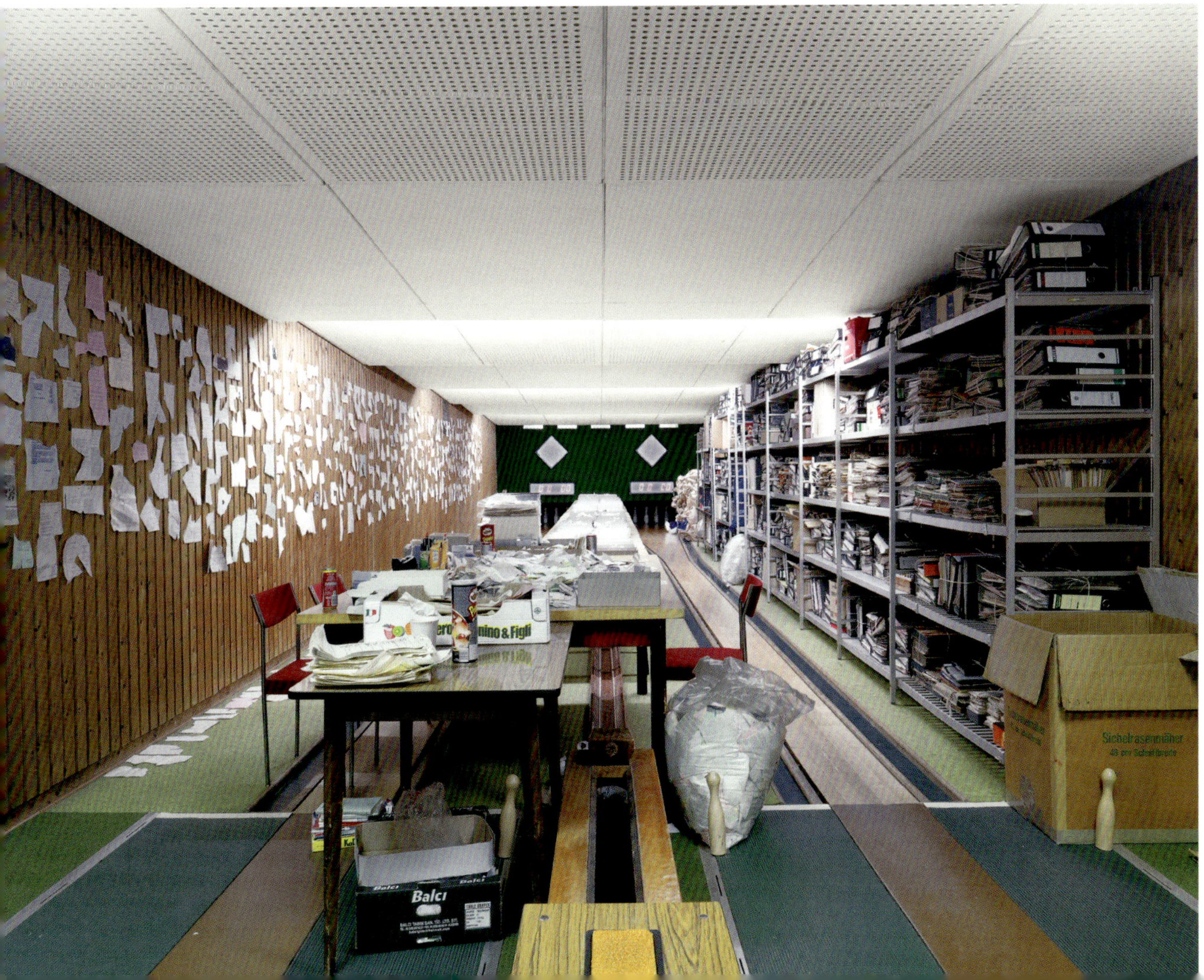

08

05, 06, 07, 08 *Deutsche Grammatik*, 2008
Mixed-media site-specific installation
Dimensions variable

In 2004, the Kulturbrauerei (a brewery turned cultural centre) in Berlin hosted an exhibition under the title 'Leichte Arbeit' (Light Work). The Polish artist Michał Budny was among the participants. He showed one of his 'impossible' sculptures, a ray of light made of paper. The intangibility of the natural phenomenon and the unimposing material that represented it form a relationship typical of Budny's sculptural work, in which he recreates everyday objects, usually from paper, cardboard and adhesive tape, with seeming ease. These might be useful things like cell-phones, but Budny also creates entire installations, such as *Projection* (2006) or *Slide Show* (2008), both of which were made in collaboration with Zbigniew Rogalski, and on one occasion even recreated the complete sleeping space of a homeless man. What he is up to, though, is by no means a minimalist form of realism, but rather a wry look at things seen from the perspective of an artist who works with perishable materials. The homeless man's shelter may be a makeshift solution, but in that sense it is closer to art than a comfortably furnished bedroom.

The still-life genre is a constant point of reference for Budny, who in his more recent work has increasingly incorporated spectatorship and the gaze into his objects. The exhibition 'Winter', held in Vienna in 2008, was conceived in two sections, one black and one white. The black section consisted of objects seen from the viewpoint of a drunk person at the moment of entrance into a dark room. The white section displayed of objects as they might look through a window in winter, when people retreat into homely spaces and the outside world becomes a kind of phenomenological theatre.

Budny speaks of 'models for mental use'. He creates a tangible world cut out of the mental space of perception. This world will always be fragmented, since totality is an illusion situated only in the brain. In the short video documentation of *Air* (2003), for example, he can be seen putting together geometric objects, eventually forming a kind of Rubik's Cube, a whole object out of pieces that originally seemed impossible to fit together. Budny likes to talk about 'errors' shaping a completely new kind of space. In this case, the wholeness would be the error, since reality never adds up to anything this complete. The cube is another 'impossible' sculpture, a makeshift thing-in-itself in a world still strongly determined by a Kantian view of perception. [Bert Rebhandl]

01

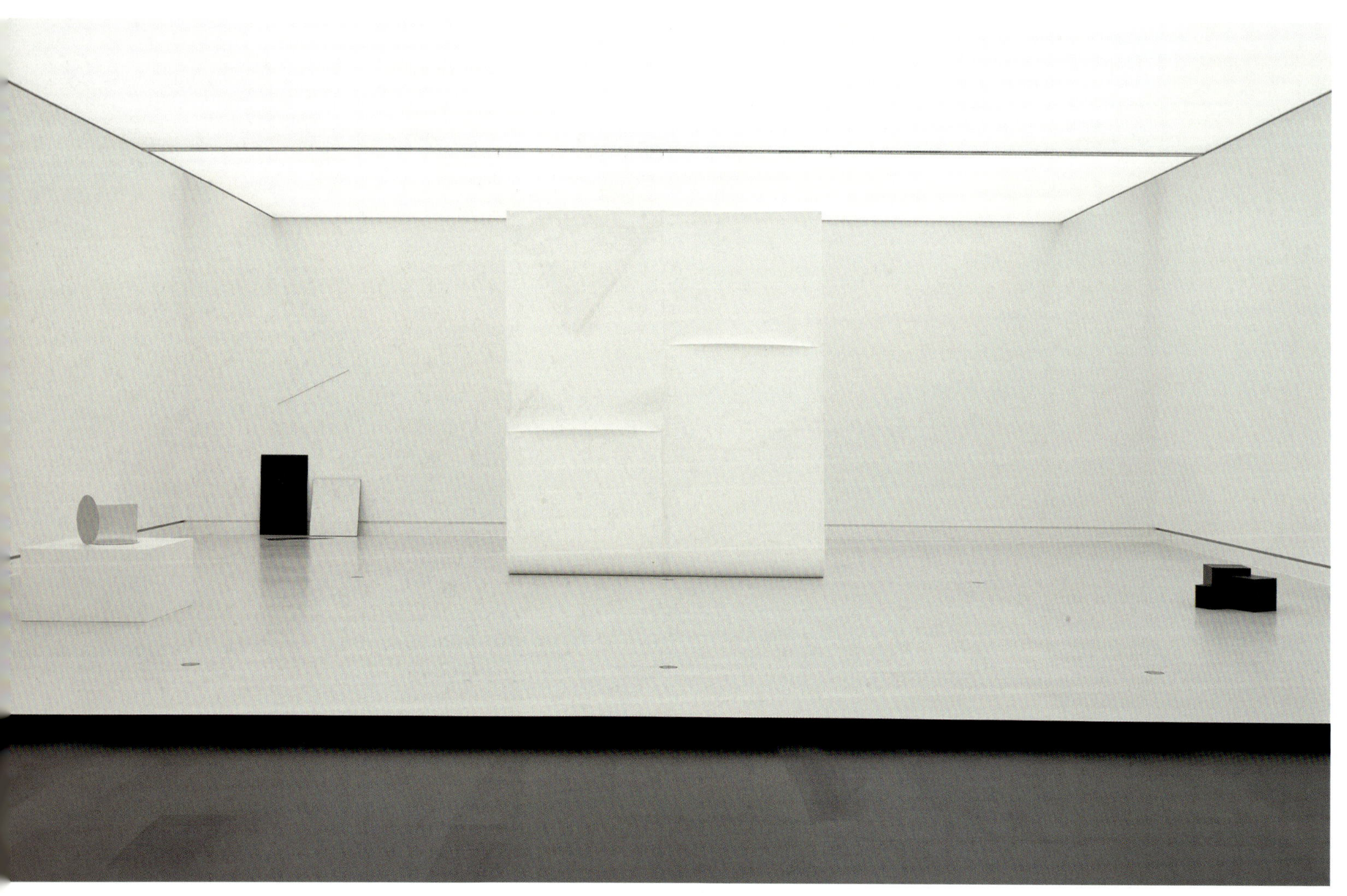

02

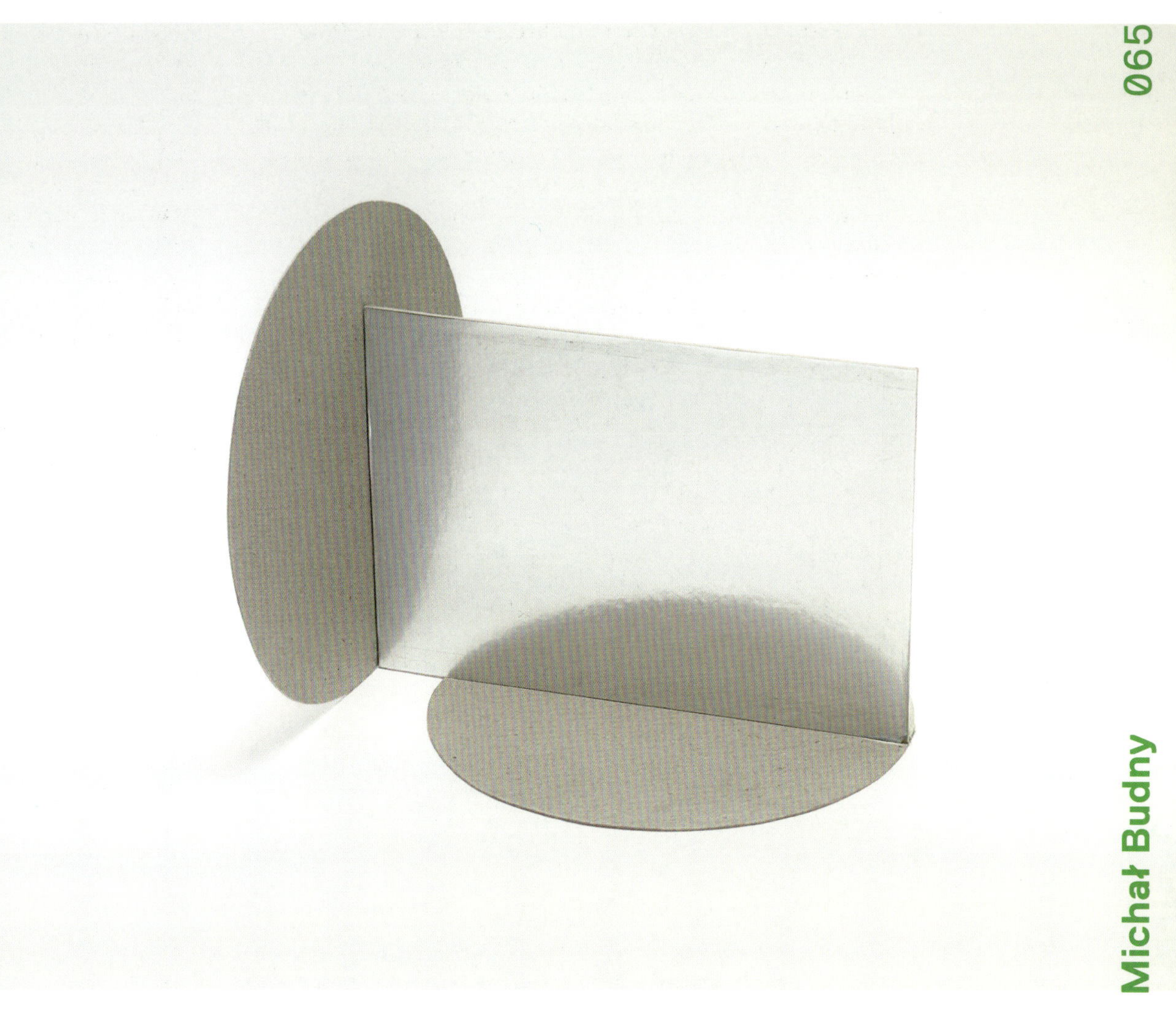

03

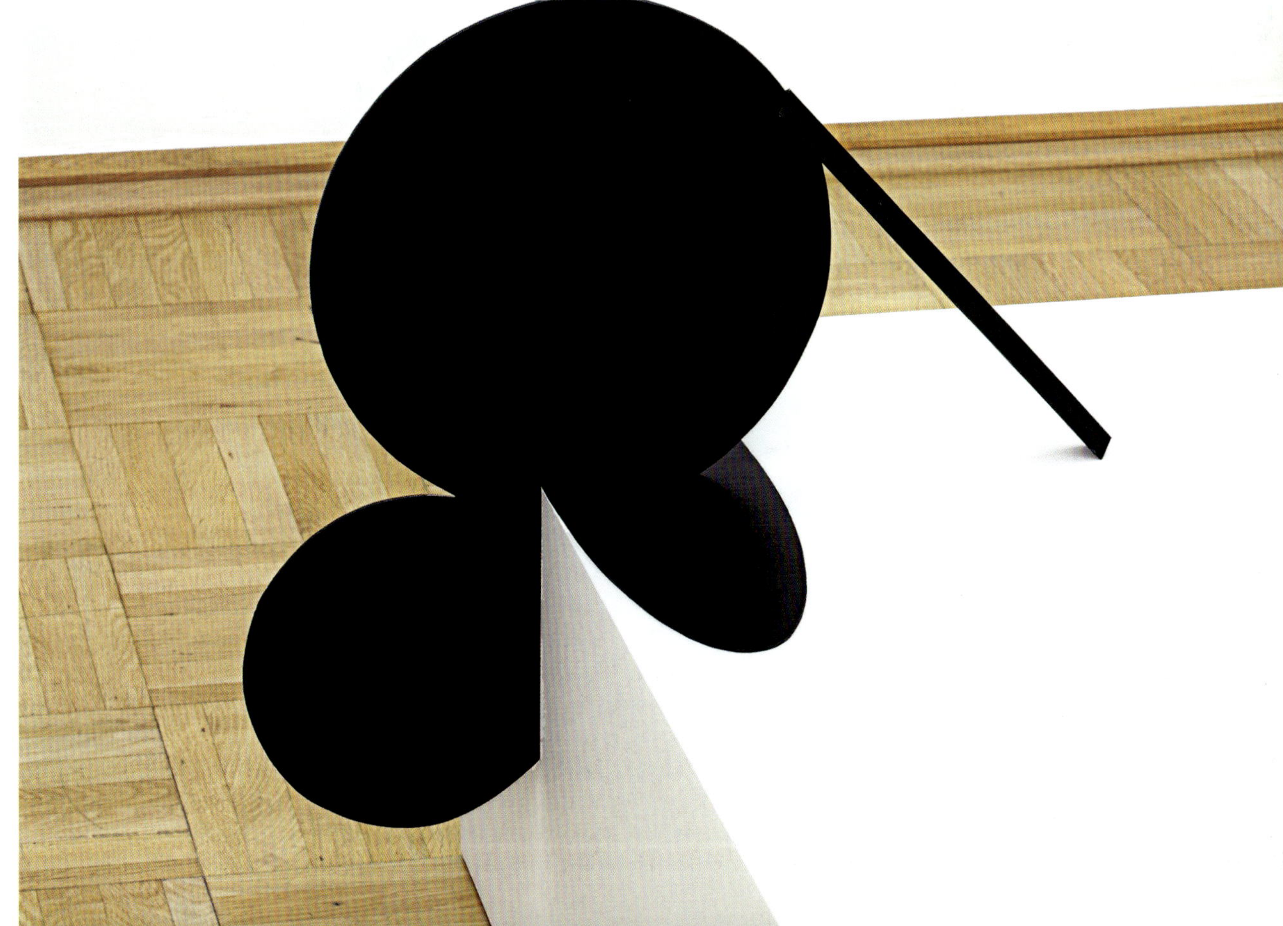

01 'Illusion and Consequence', exhibition view, Kunsthalle Mainz, 2008

02 *Transparency*, 2008
Cardboard, aluminium foil, tape
38 × 43 × 36 cm

03 *Untitled (Companion)*, 2008
Painted cardboard
3 parts
57 × 40 cm
57 × 17 cm
2 × 35 × 2 cm

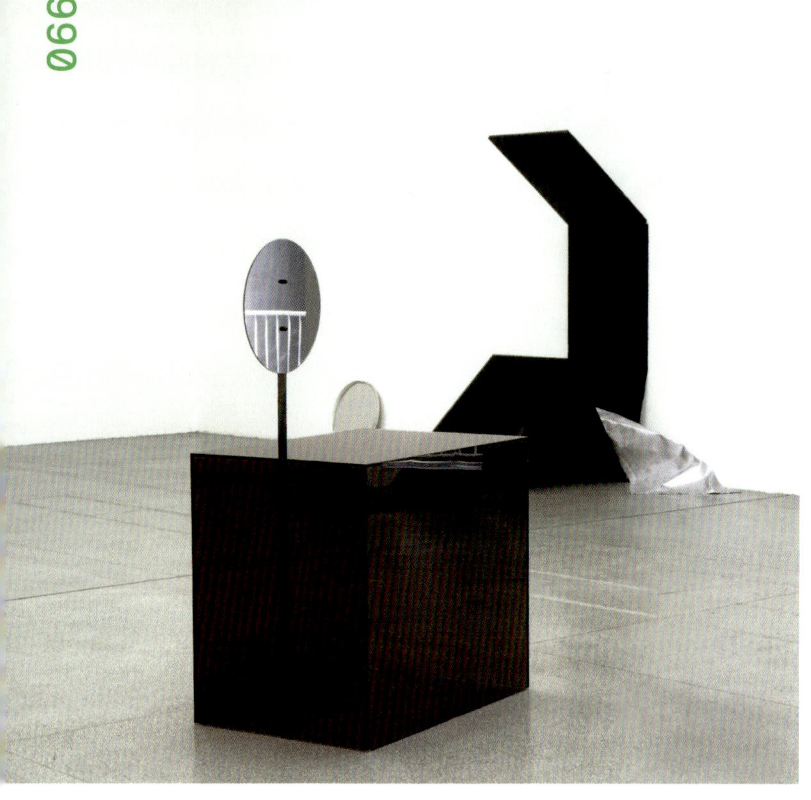

01

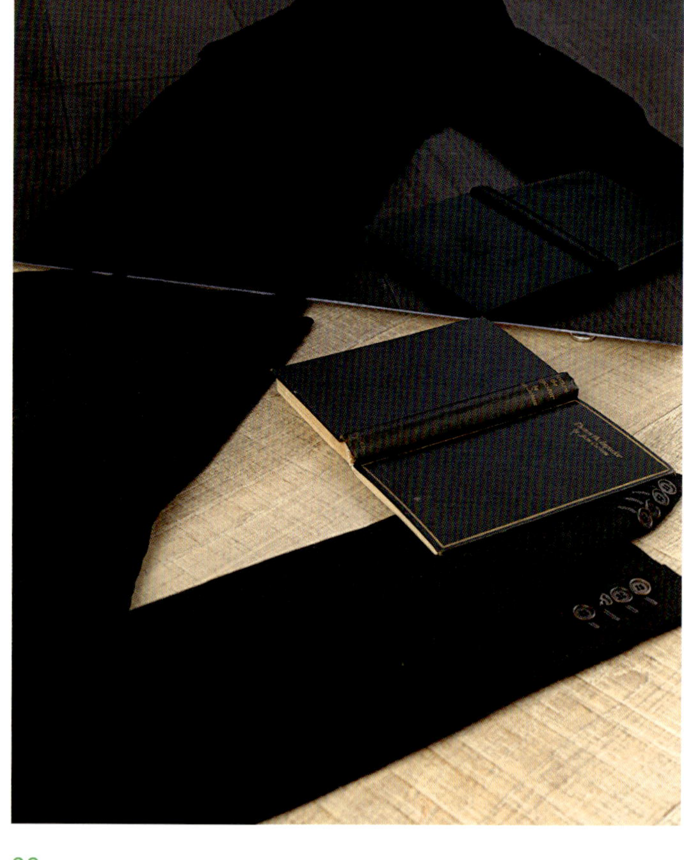

02

The phrase 'sexing up the dossier' applies nicely to Tom Burr's practice, which draws out the romantic desire and giddy anarchy hidden by works of art that strive for monumentality and autonomy. In Burr's hands, Richard Serra's Cor-Ten steel structures are coloured rich purple and downscaled in size, giving them the look of dividing screens in sitting rooms and boudoirs (*Deep Purple*, 2000). Minimalist objects are given use value and back-stage narratives — set against the floor like reclining lounges or suggestive of the body in repose. The sculpture *This Drinking Alone (The Deep Intoxication Series)* (2006) shows plaits of white-painted birchwood leaning against the wall, a long length of fabric draped across one of the folds, like a scarf across the neck of a poet in a bad B-movie.

Burr's works frame art as a drama to be enacted, and many of his pieces have the feeling of elements in a vast theatre set. An early series (*Unearthing the Public Restroom*, 1994) showed photographs of public toilets in New York City, popular cruising sites for gay men, that were then being closed down. His works make use of a specific form of metonymy in which the background site becomes a stand-in for the people who utilize them, conflating the architecture and the participants. In *Subterranean Park Rest Room Clip* (1997), two plush cinema seats sit on a raised platform like two old men — or new acquaintances — enjoying each other's company in isolation. The works evoke sadness as well as humour, sending up assumptions about the unity of the artwork by ratcheting up its theatricality and questioning the author's role as creator. Burr's more recent installations, in particular, suggest the multiple modes of authorship behind art production, as well as authorship destabilized by desire, or even by insecurity and mishap.

Collective participation and enjoyment is key, and the arrangement of his works suggests art-historical and literary references, as though presenting revellers at some re-enacted party. His show 'Moods' at Secession in Vienna (2007) invoked James Abbott McNeill Whistler, Jean Cocteau, Jack Kerouac and Jack Pierson through photographs and collages, while empty chairs were dotted about the room, some upright and others lying on their backs like upturned beetles. In contrast to this morning-after installation, the room was also filled with open metal structures in which works and chairs were set, almost like mini-studios, functioning as ciphers for the artist who works within them and suggesting pockets of productive solitude among the chaos of the space. The idea of a party was made more explicit in his 2008 show for the SculptureCenter in New York, in which his text *Ode to a Chair* (2006) was accompanied by jazz music, in a manner that explicitly recalled the environments of past poets and impresarios such as Frank O'Hara, Kurt Weill and Gertrude Stein. This idea of Minimalism as stage set implies an understanding of minimalist artworks not as autonomous or original items but rather as scripts or gestures that can be tried on and discarded — or given a second life, coded in opposite ways to their originals. [Melissa Gronlund]

01 *Dark Vanity*, 2007
Plexiglas, steel, mirrors, screws
157 × 91 × 91 cm

02 *Thomas the Impostor*, 2006
Plywood, perspex mirror, stainless steel hinges, book, suit trousers, suit jacket
152 × 81 × 84 cm

03 *This Drinking Alone (The Deep Intoxication Series)*, 2006
Painted birch plywood, satin, nickel gloss hinges
200 × 255 × 76 cm

04 *Deep Purple*, 2000
Wood, steel, paint
250 × 2500 × 44 cm

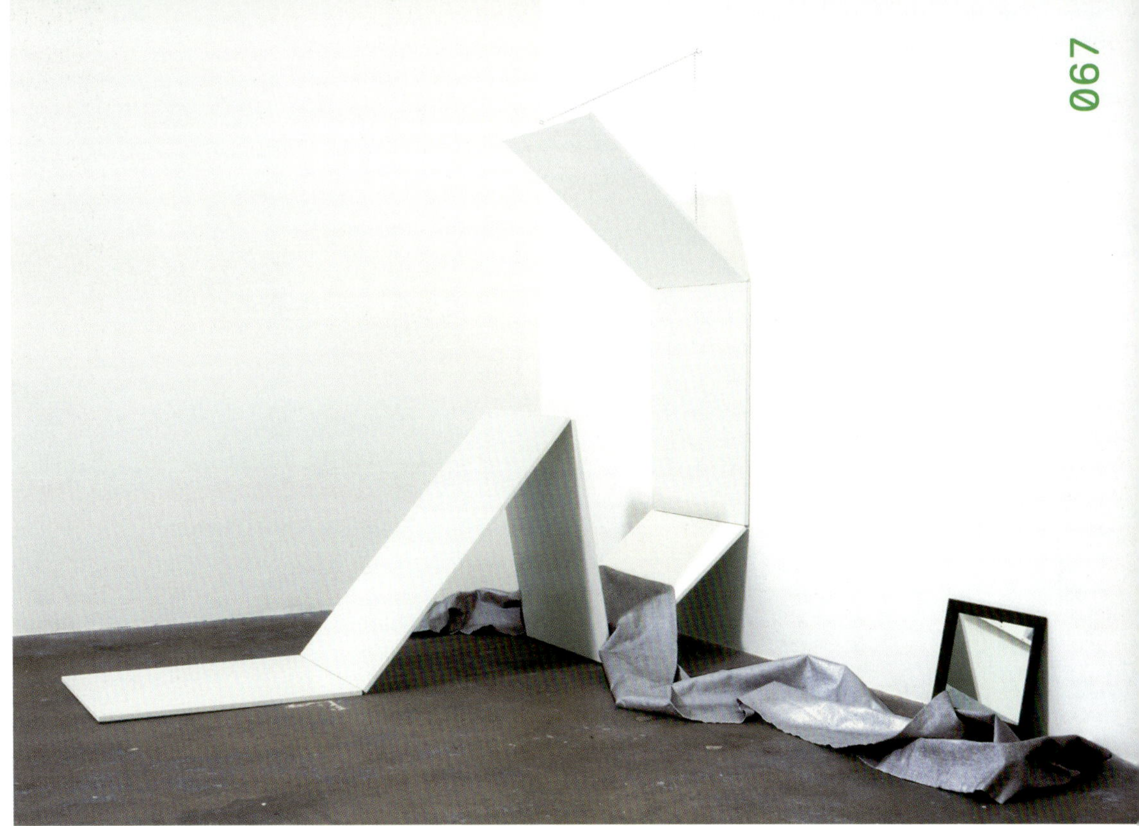

03

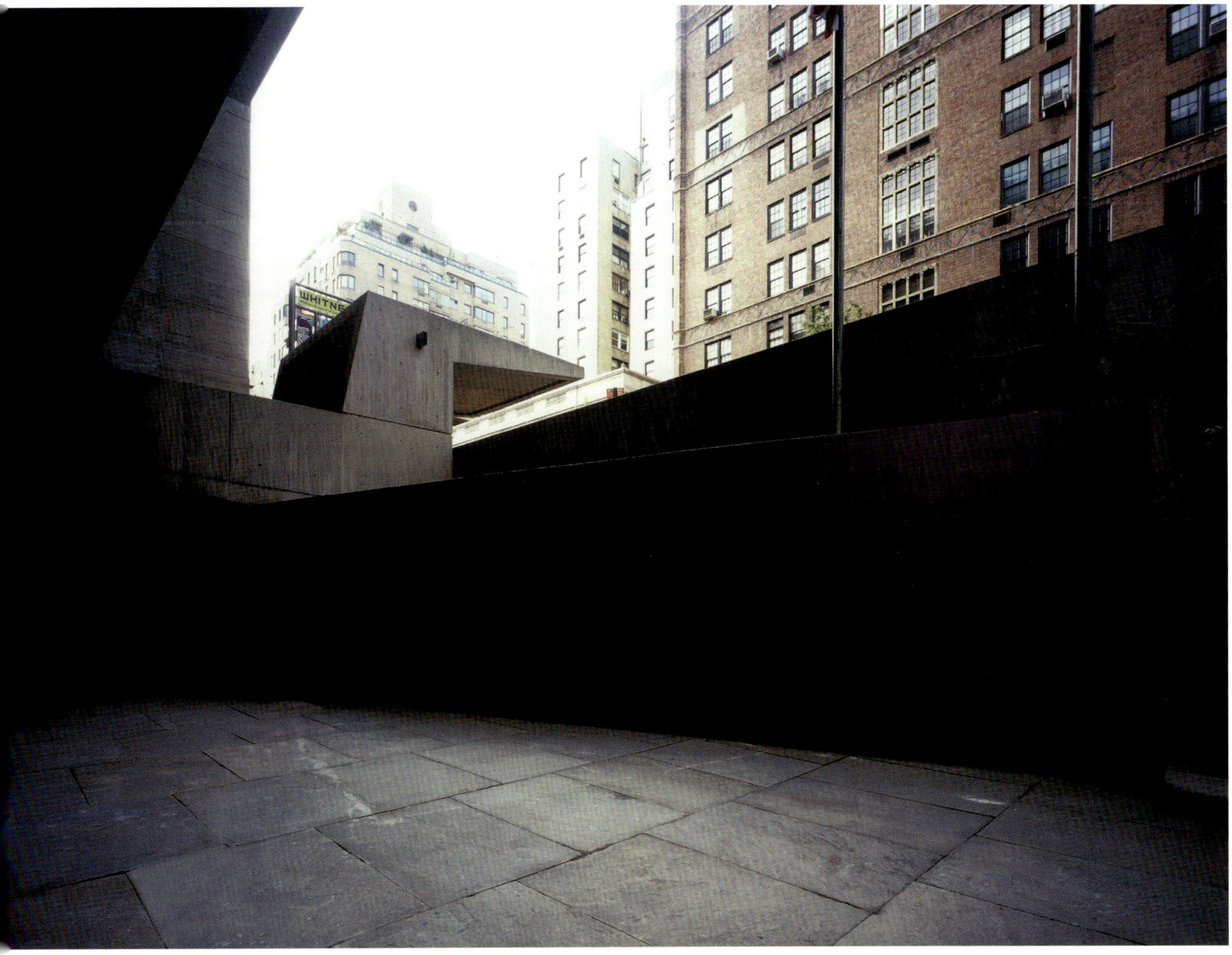

04

In 2008, Jedediah Caesar drove a large truck through the western United States, following a generally structured route but allowing for spontaneous shifts of location. This trajectory aptly describes an important aspect of his signature sculptural process, characterized by a tension between hard-won technical control and the vagaries of chance.

During his trip, Caesar collected masses of material, informed by the locale rather than predetermined. Each accumulated truckload was then sent ahead to the Orange County Museum of Art, where it was assembled and displayed on site upon his return. Constituting approximately ten truckloads of material, the piece became an extreme record of the trip, embodying place and time while also querying modernist monumentality: the fixed image/form belied by Caesar's notion of 'the object as an event'.

The project, *Californian* (2008), is a natural evolution of concerns that have occupied Caesar's sculptural investigations for many years. For nearly a decade he has created sculptures out of the collected detritus of his house and studio, which he preserves in blocks of coloured resin and industrially slices into units. The individual pieces, shown on the floor, leaning against walls or mounted as grids, constitute a material archive of time and space, simultaneously micro and macro, at one moment seeming to be physically organic, even cellular, images, at another suggesting a landscape or a lunar surface. In the 2007 installation, *City of Industry*, the constructions recalled schematic industrial landscapes or Minimalist forms, though impregnated with their own archaeology. A plywood floor acted as a stage for the sculptures and referenced the shipping pallets also incorporated into the work. The suggestion of transit and exchange is an important subtext in Caesar's recent work, part of an interest in the transitional spaces of production and dispersal.

The installation *Dry Stock* (2008) tracks what Caesar calls 'sculpture time', in which the information embedded in the sliced cross sections — mounted on the wall in a contiguous grid — serves as an extrapolated document of itself. While Caesar's interest in sequence and combination provides the guiding interest in each installation, the wall-mounted mural works engage directly with ideas of painting as a medium and process, the sculptural history of their making only adding to this conversation. Many tropes of modernist painting emerge in the accidental composition of each sliced 'painting' panel — a tiny pink 'Miró' repeats several times, while panels in a recent Paris installation (*The Ruinsed*, 2008) recall Lucio Fontana's 'cuts', Robert Rauschenberg's collages, and the target forms and mystical symbolic forms of Arthur Dove.

In a departure from his characteristic technique, Caesar created *Helium Brick (aka Summer Snow)* (2006) from a massive block of polystyrene, on to which he poured layers of jewel-coloured resins over the course of months. The toxic material ate away the support, excavating crevices that recall geological forms, which contrast with the sticky, unstable, artificiality of the resin. The corrosive process, much like in his previous resin sculptures, maintains a painterly tension between control and chance. Recently, Caesar remade this piece in black and white resin; this 'ghost' version, also entitled *Helium Brick*, follows a kind of reverse obsolescence, from colour to black and white. A self-aware gesture, the piece humorously riffs on seriality and repetition while continuing Caesar's sensual, intellectually rigorous investigations of material, image and space. [Shamim M. Momin]

01

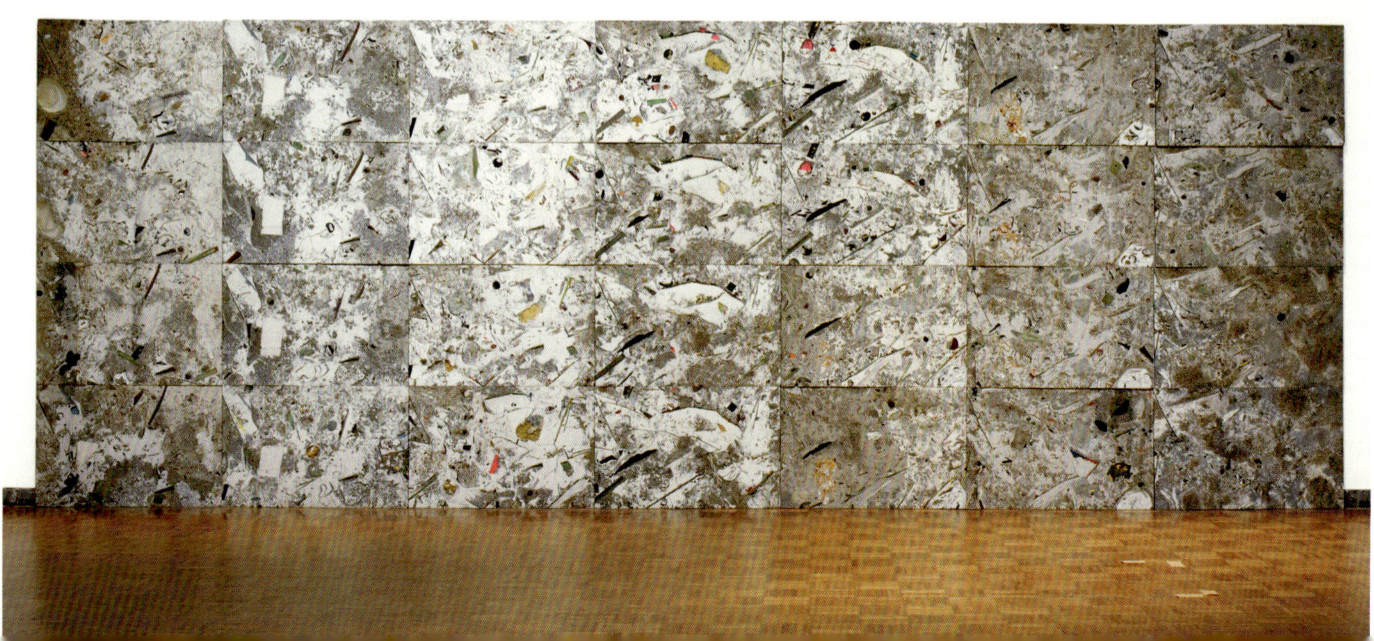

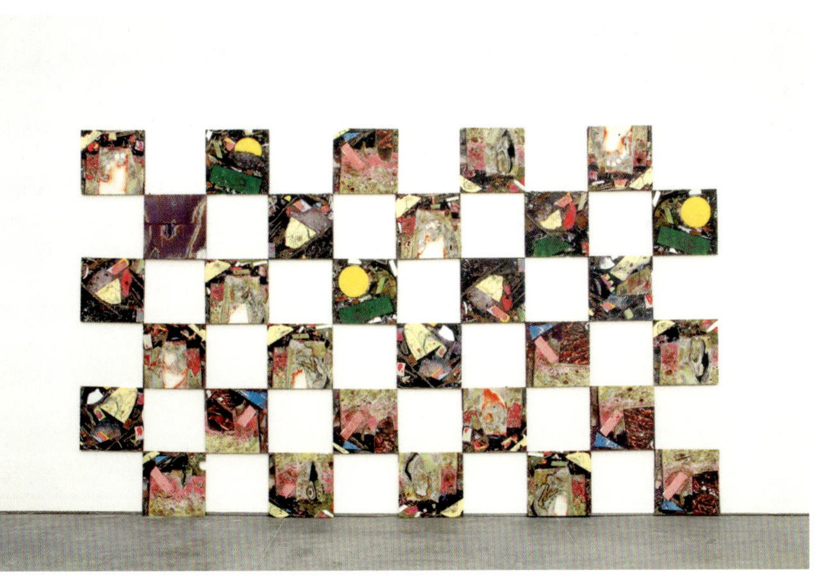

02

01 *Dry Stock*, 2007
Urethane resin, polyester resin, pigment, aluminium, titanium, wood, mixed media
29 panels (28 installed, 1 leaning)
Approx. 19 × 45 × 2 cm

02 *Check*, 2008
Urethane, pigment, mixed media
30 panels, each 28 × 29 × 1.3 cm
Overall 168 × 286 × 1.3 cm

03 *Helium Brick aka Summer Snow*, 2006
Resin, Styrofoam, wood, pigment
274 × 132 × 137 cm

04 *0,000,000*, 2007
Resin, plaster, dust, salt, dirt
18 parts
Diameters vary from 61 cm to 122 cm

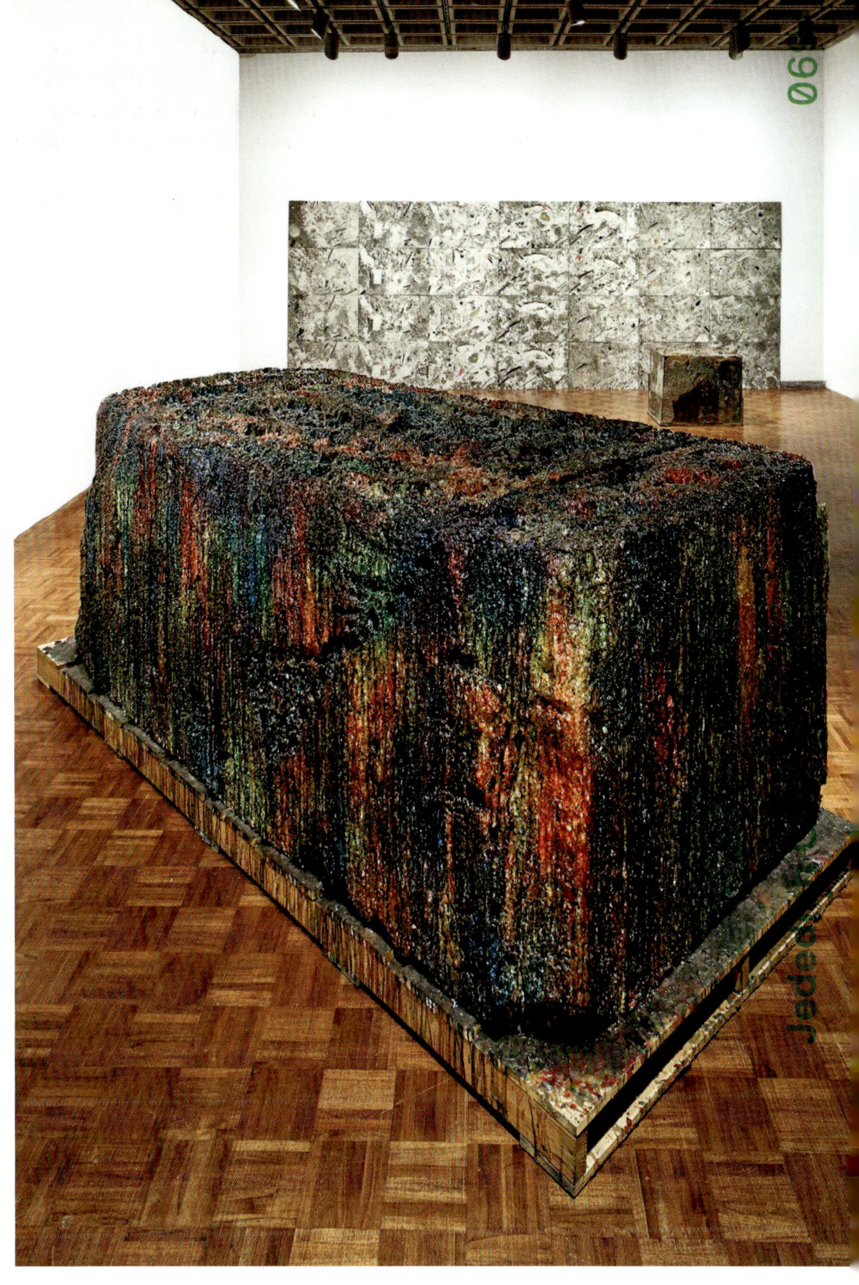

03

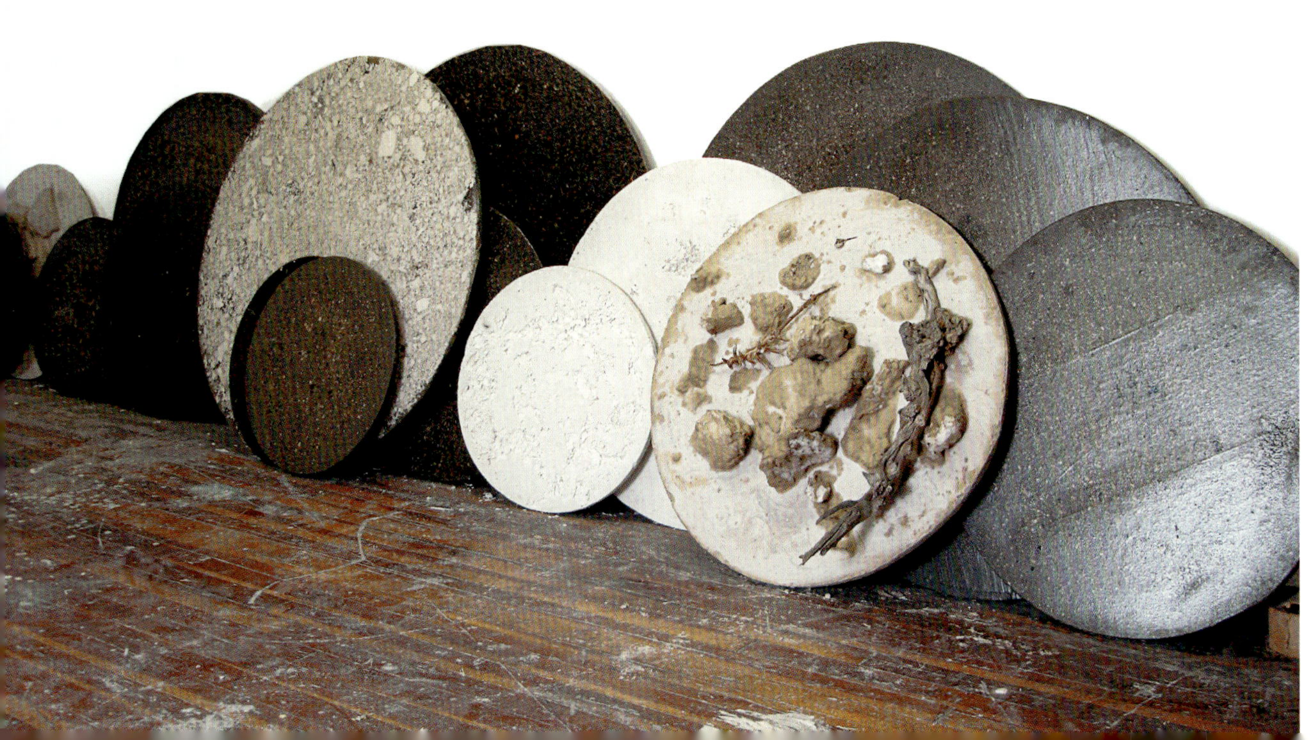

04

Valentin Carron's practice is an inquiry into the authenticity of the symbols and traditions that his home country of Switzerland holds dear. In his satirical sculptures, Carron questions whether such beloved nationalist symbols could be manufactured — or, more specifically, if he could manufacture them — and if there would be any difference between a local craftsman's version and his own. As he put it in a 2004 interview, 'I spend my entire days making life-size replicas of the objects I abhor.'

For Carron, the act of 'fabricating' these sculptures is both an act of artistic production and a kind of fakery. Synthetic materials are his favourites — Styrofoam, fibreglass, polystyrene and resin — especially when employed to recreate monumental sculptures, like *Untitled* (2004), a Styrofoam eagle perched on a pile of stones, light enough to topple over in a strong Alpine wind. In Carron's hands, local craftsmanship is recontextualized so that its provenance becomes questionable. He has inserted rustic wooden beams into the ceiling of a white cube to recreate the feeling of a mountain chalet, and has carved a life-size bear out of fake acrylic wood. In these iconoclastic versions of proud Swiss traditions, Carron replaces original materials with synthetic ones, exhausting them through both their literal and symbolic weight. In his series *Saison* (2008), Carron crafts impressive gem-like rocks out of Styrofoam — undoubtedly a reference to the polystyrene imitations of his fellow Swiss artists Peter Fischli and David Weiss — painting them to look like precious artefacts and thereby creating something between a relic and a readymade.

Carron also projects his sarcastic wit at other traditions that have been corrupted and misrepresented in the course of history. Obelisks, ancient crosses and military cannons are parodied with cheap, disposable materials. No artistic tradition is safe from his satirical grasp, not the sculptures of Alberto Giacometti, nor the artefacts of Native American cultures. In fact, Carron has created Native American dream-catchers — themselves already an interpretation created solely for tourists — stretched with paintings after Fernand Léger and adorned with fake plants. Carron has even turned to the heroes of modernist sculpture to strip them of their authentic origins, showing that a Constantin Brancusi or a Henry Moore can be convincingly replicated with industrial materials while remaining no less 'handmade' or 'original'.

Carron's replicas expose how desperate we are to preserve and display our national symbols, and how instrumental art can be in this process. Don't artworks, after all, become the same kind of precious historical proof of a culture's sophistication and uniqueness? Carron sardonically implies that a kitsch replicas are equivalent to authentic articles. At the point of origin of all the artistic traditions and icons we treasure, we might find something that looks synthetic or copied, or we might not find anything there at all. [Christy Lange]

01

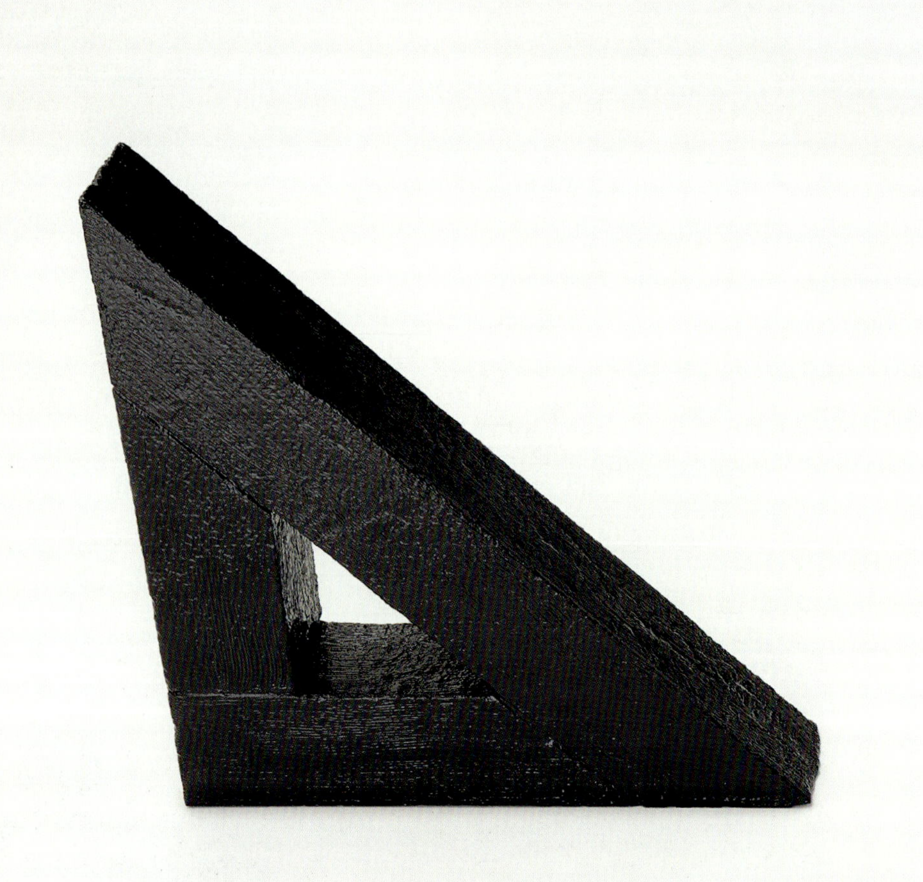

02

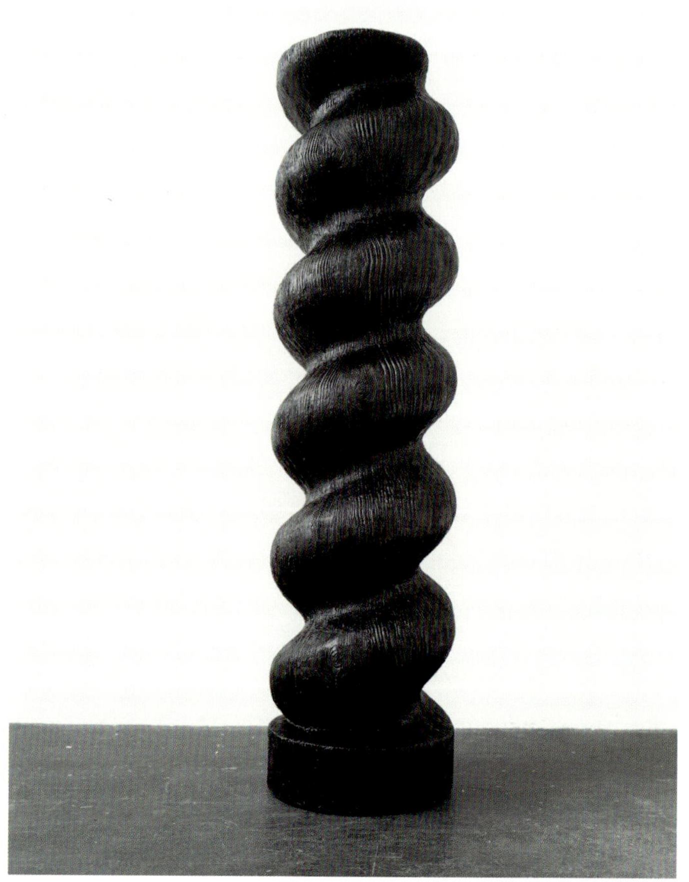

03

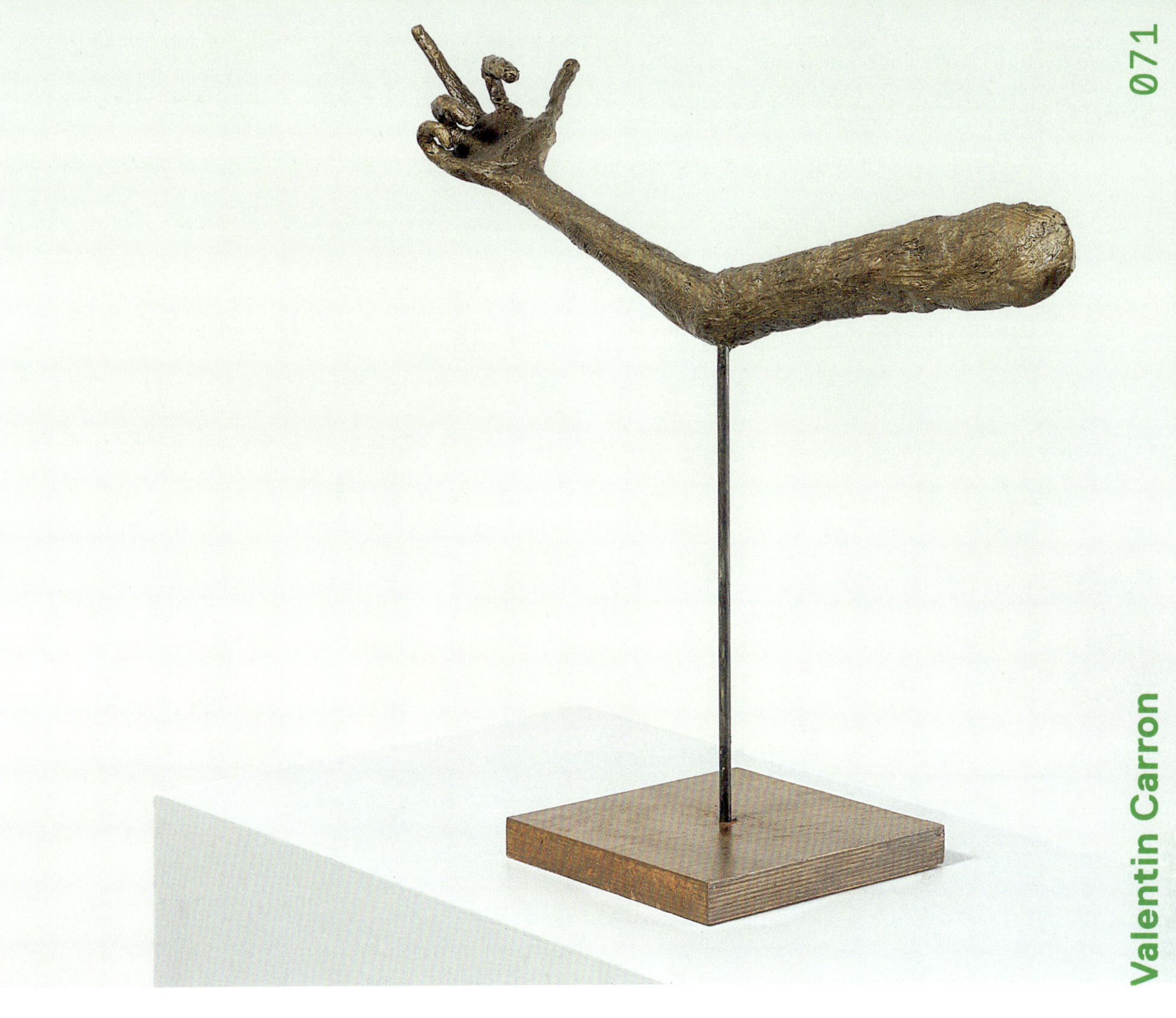

04

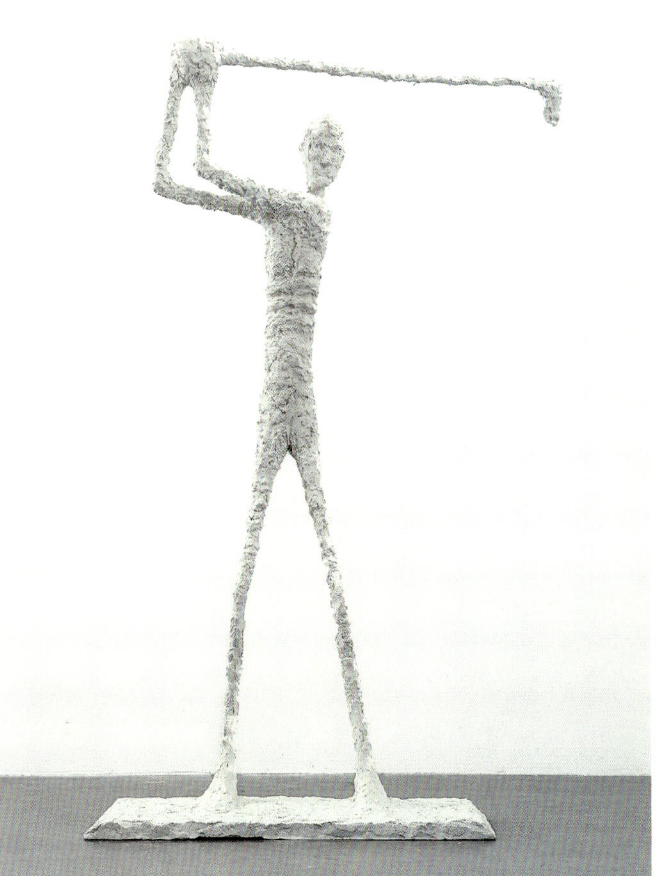

05

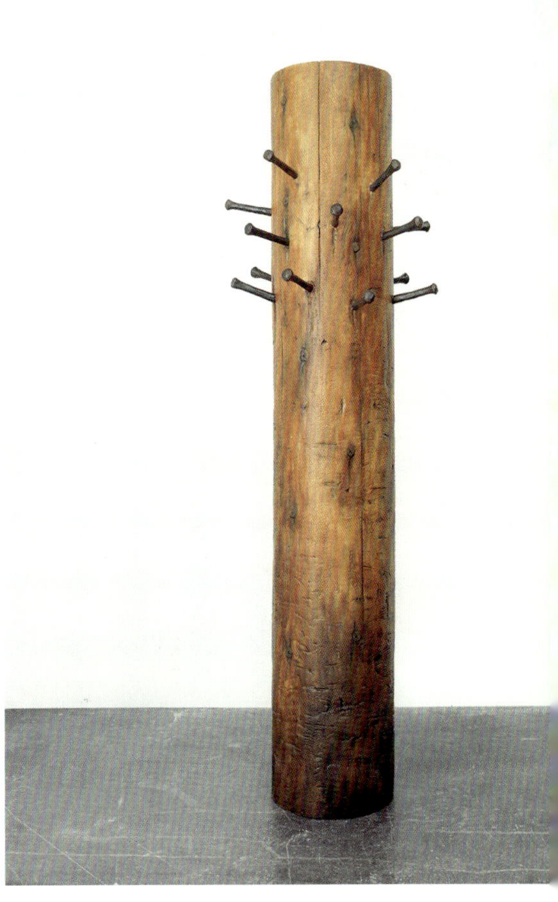

01 *Punish yourself (collection jaune souffre)*, 2007
Styrofoam, fibreglass, resin, acrylic paint
100 × 100 × 20 cm

02 *Deux jours pour convaincre*, 2007
Styrofoam, fibreglass, resin, acrylic paint
252 × 65 × 65 cm

03 *la main*, 2006
Wood, metallic structure, acrylic resin, paint
Sculpture 70 × 45 × 10 cm
Pedestal 75 × 25 × 25 cm

04 *L'homme qui swing (plâtre)*, 2007
Wood, metallic structure, acrylic resin, paint
220 × 114 × 52 cm

05 *Forza Ethiopia*, 2006
Carved polyurethane, epoxy, acrylic paint, metal
220 × 72 × 72 cm

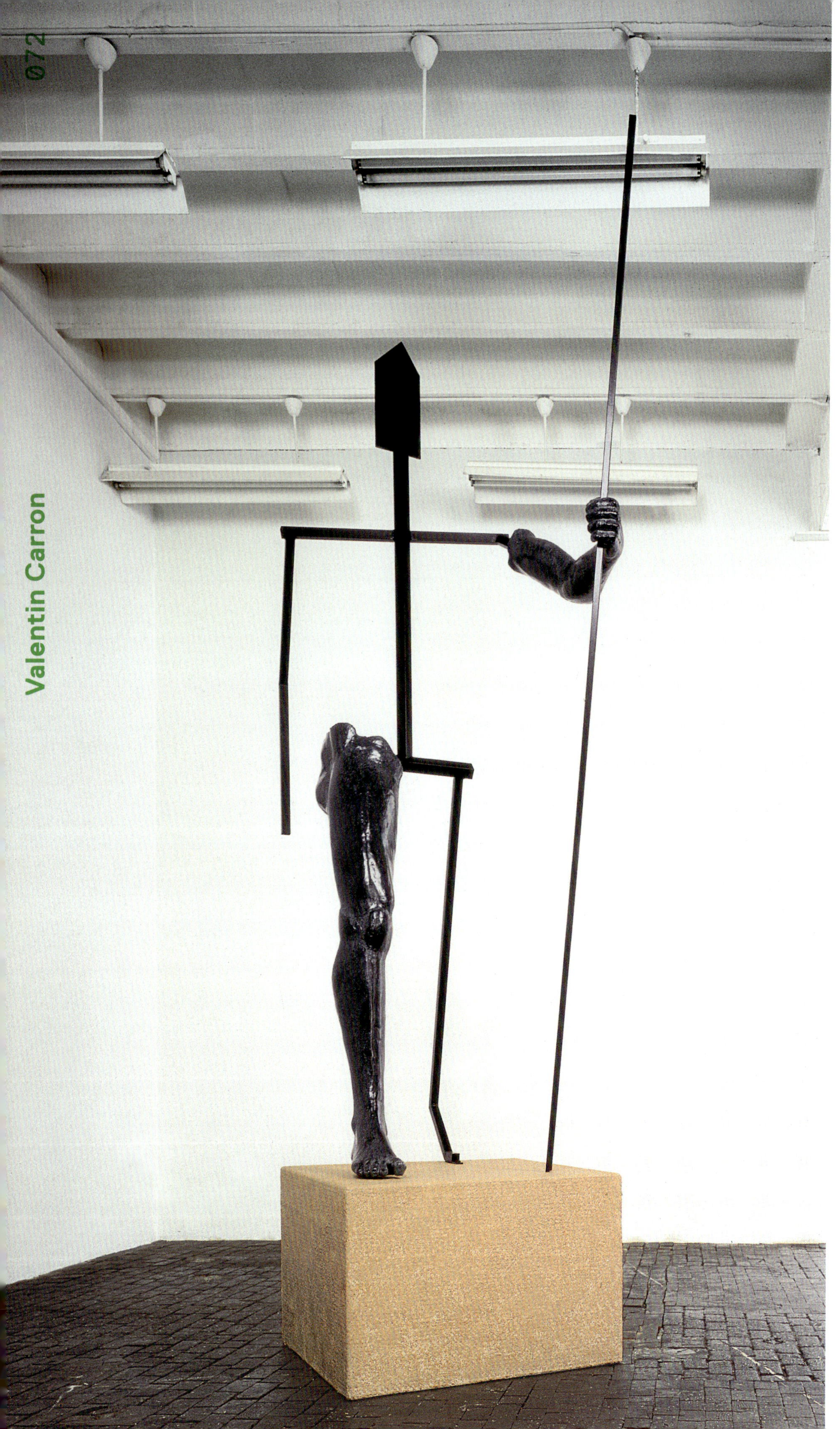

06

06 *Lasciatemi vivere la mia vita*, 2005
Metal, polystyrene,
fibreglass, acrylic resin, paint
370 × 160 × 90 cm

07 *Rance Club II*, 2006
Wood, plasterboard,
plaster, paint, sound
240 × 895 × 405 cm

07

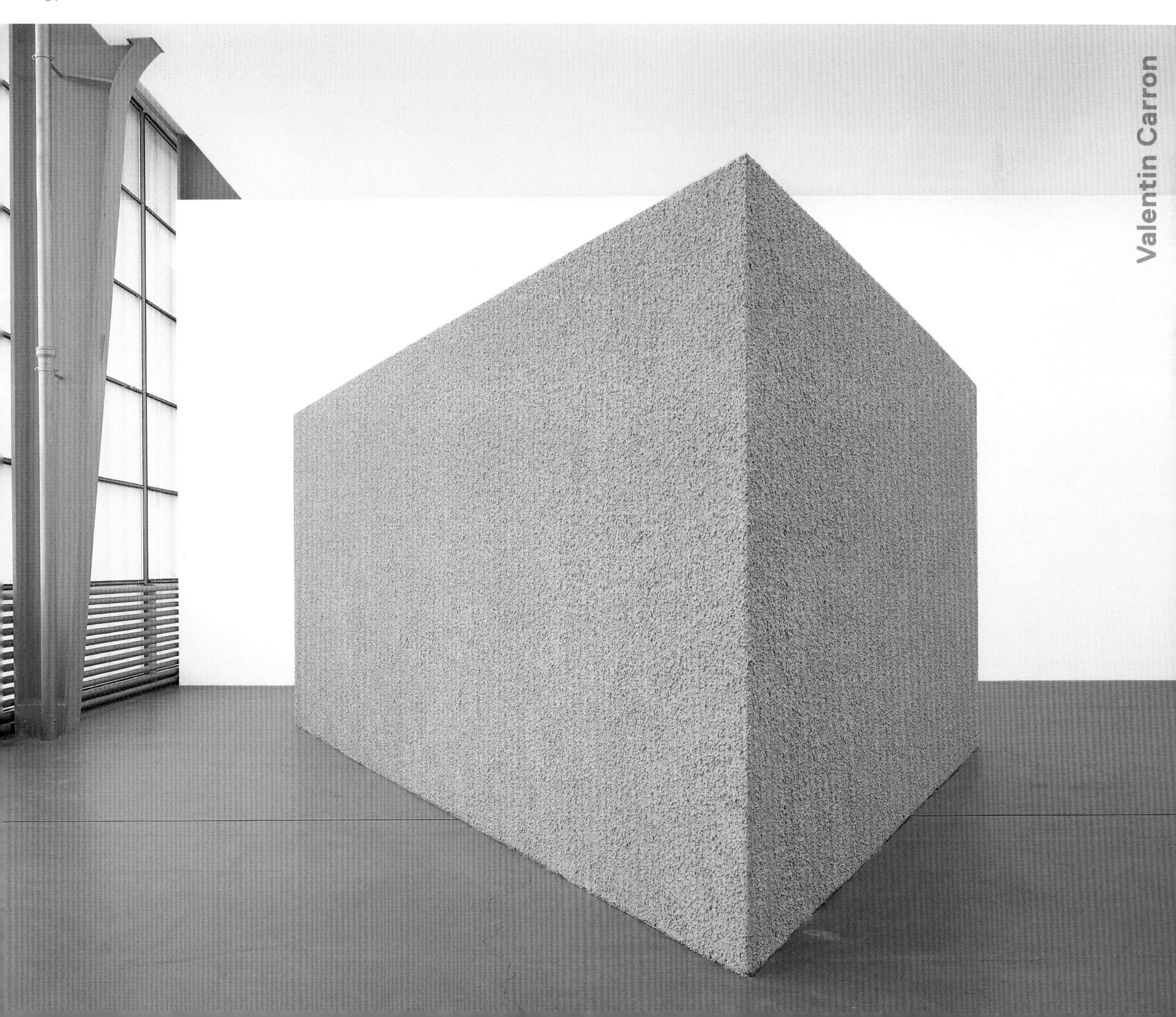

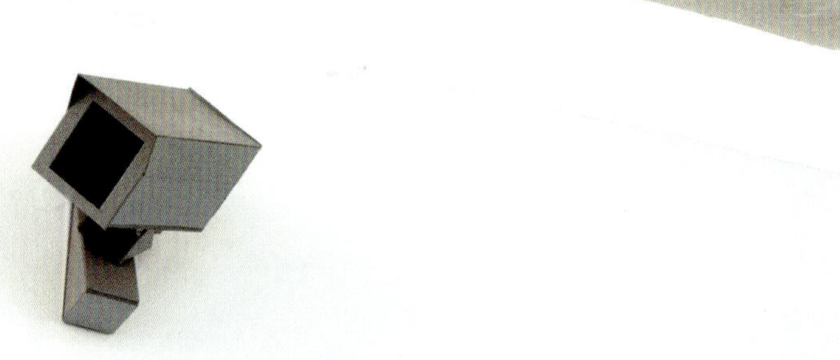

01 The work of Marcelo Cidade is deeply rooted in his experience of growing up in São Paulo. One of the largest urban conglomerations in the world, São Paulo is marked by its intense social contrasts and lack of urban planning as much as by its status as a major Latin American centre of commerce and the arts.

Cidade started out as an artist on the streets, doing mostly graffiti, or what Brazilians call *pichacao*, which, unlike graffiti in North America or Europe, does not originate in hip-hop culture but in a wide variety of sources that are more closely tied to the country's everyday realities. Since then, Cidade has expanded his focus to illegal activities in general, while also incorporating more critical contemporary art practices from Brazil, Europe and the United States.

His best-known work, *Direito de Imagem* (*Image Rights*, 2004), has appeared in a number of international exhibitions over the last few years. It is a group of strikingly authentic-looking cardboard copies of surveillance cameras that he places in strategic locations throughout museums and exhibitions alongside the real cameras. The work draws attention to the idea of 'Big Brother' and to his view of art-making as part of a larger practice of cultural resistance, which is closely monitored by the 'authorities' of both art and non-art institutions.

La Casa Encendida (2008) continues this investigation of art and its relationship to public space — specifically the limited space allowed for art in the public sphere. It is a small room of approximately four by four metres, closed off on all sides by metal shutters of the sort that are universally used to protect shops and windows. In a reversal of audience expectations, the graffiti is inside the space and can only be seen when the shutters are open.

Two other works with similar concerns are *Fogo-amigo* (2006) and *Intramuros* (2006), both exhibited at the 27th São Paulo Biennial. *Fogo-amigo* is a specially created device that blocks cell-phone signals throughout the exhibition space. It is not so much a comment on the excessive use of phones, nor a means of forcing audiences to pay attention to art, but rather the creation of a temporary autonomous zone where people cannot be traced via their mobile devices. *Intramuros* was placed on the walls of the exhibition space and consisted of improvised urban-defence devices — the bricks, cement and broken pieces of glass typically embedded in the tops of walls deter intruders.

Cidade has also been known to create pieces that are smaller, more poetic, and more formal in their concerns. One of these was an urban intervention entitled *In/Out* (2001), in which the artist (illegally) removed some of the famous paving tiles designed by Roberto Burle-Marx along Avenida Paulista, São Paulo's Fifth Avenue. He placed them in a gallery, making reference not only to Carl Andre's floor-based works, but also to the fact that pedestrians in São Paulo routinely walk over this iconic work of art without really noticing it. A more recent piece, *Amor e ódio a Lygia Clark* (2006), makes reference to the well-known Brazilian artist Lygia Clark and her 1968 piece *Hand Dialog*. It is made of two identical brass knuckles connected in the centre, rendering them useless for their original purpose and instead suggesting a gesture of reaching out or shaking hands. [Jens Hoffmann]

02

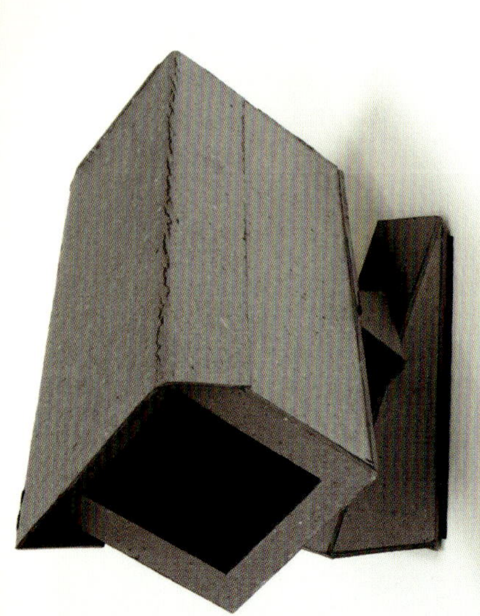

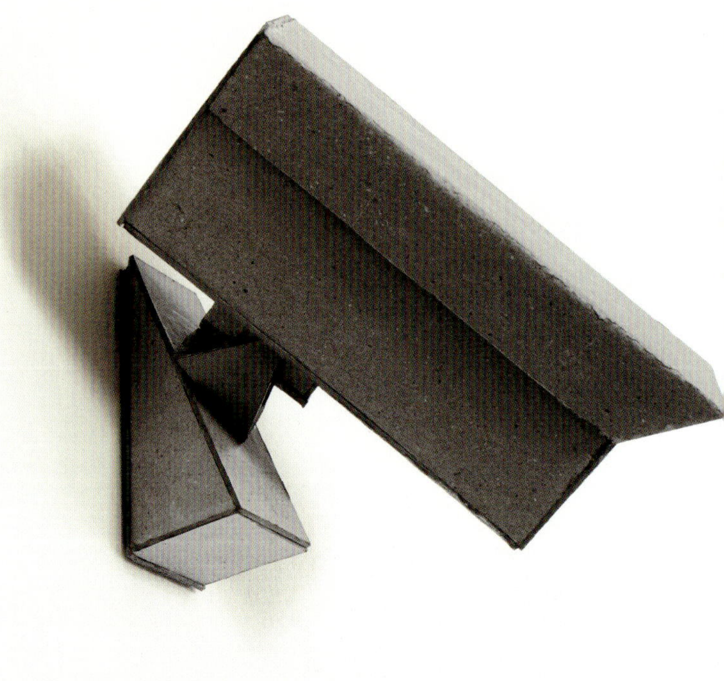

03

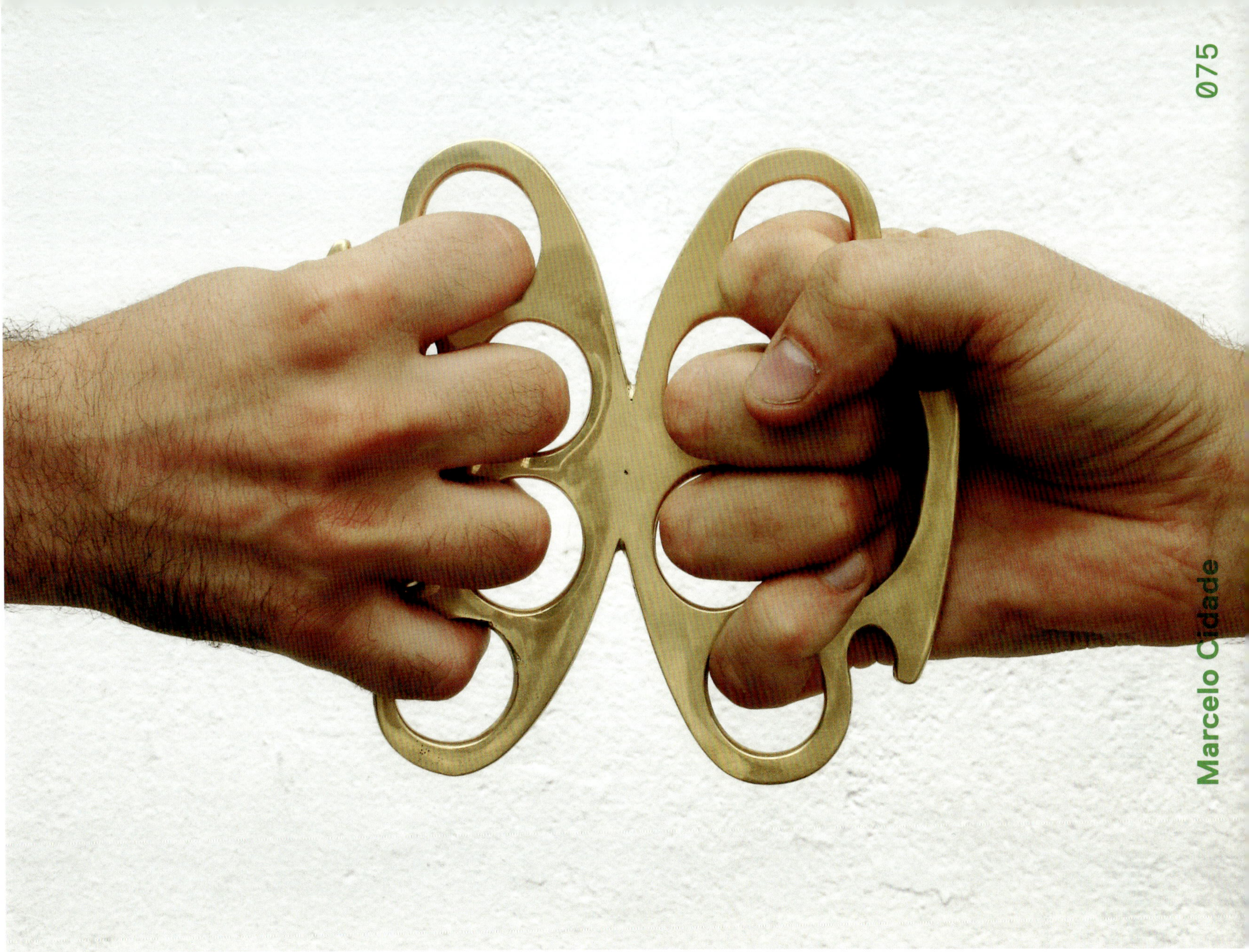

04

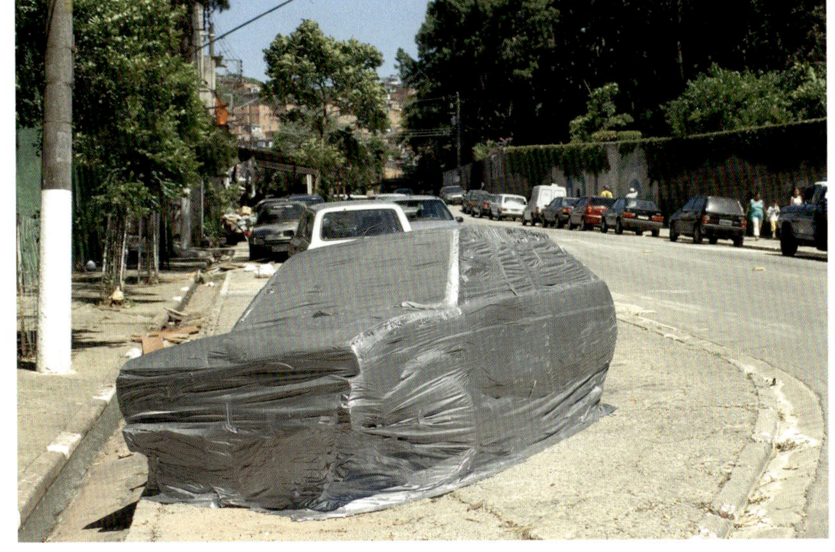

05

01, 02, 03 *Direito de Imagem*, 2004
Cardboard
Each 27 × 27 × 23 cm

04 *Amor e ódio à Lygia Clark*, 2006
Brass
14.5 × 13 × 0.5 cm

05 *Eu preciso estar seguro de você 2*, 2006
Photograph
40 × 60 cm

Overleaf:

06 *Imóvel*, 2004
Concrete bricks, trolley
190 × 55 × 100 cm

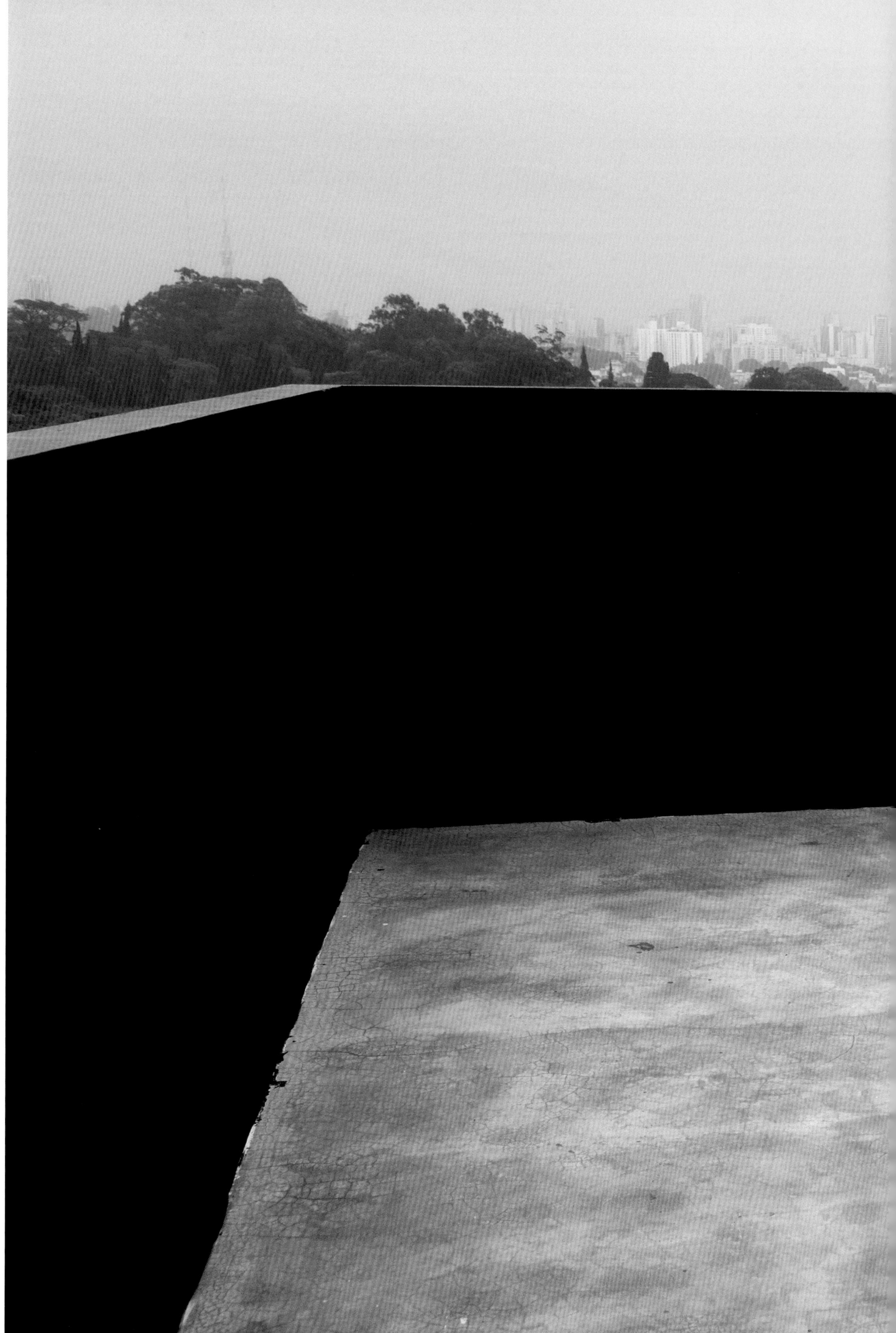

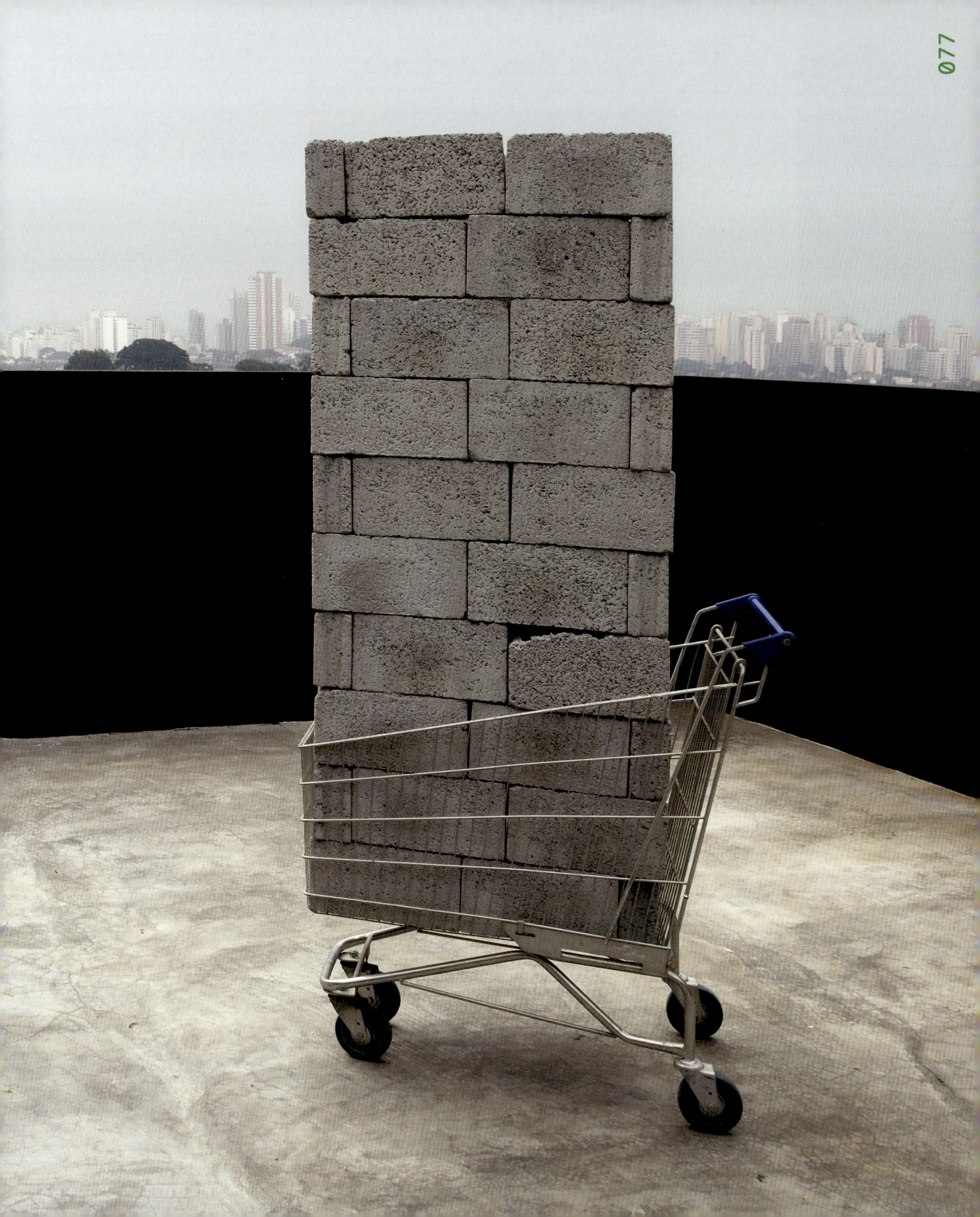

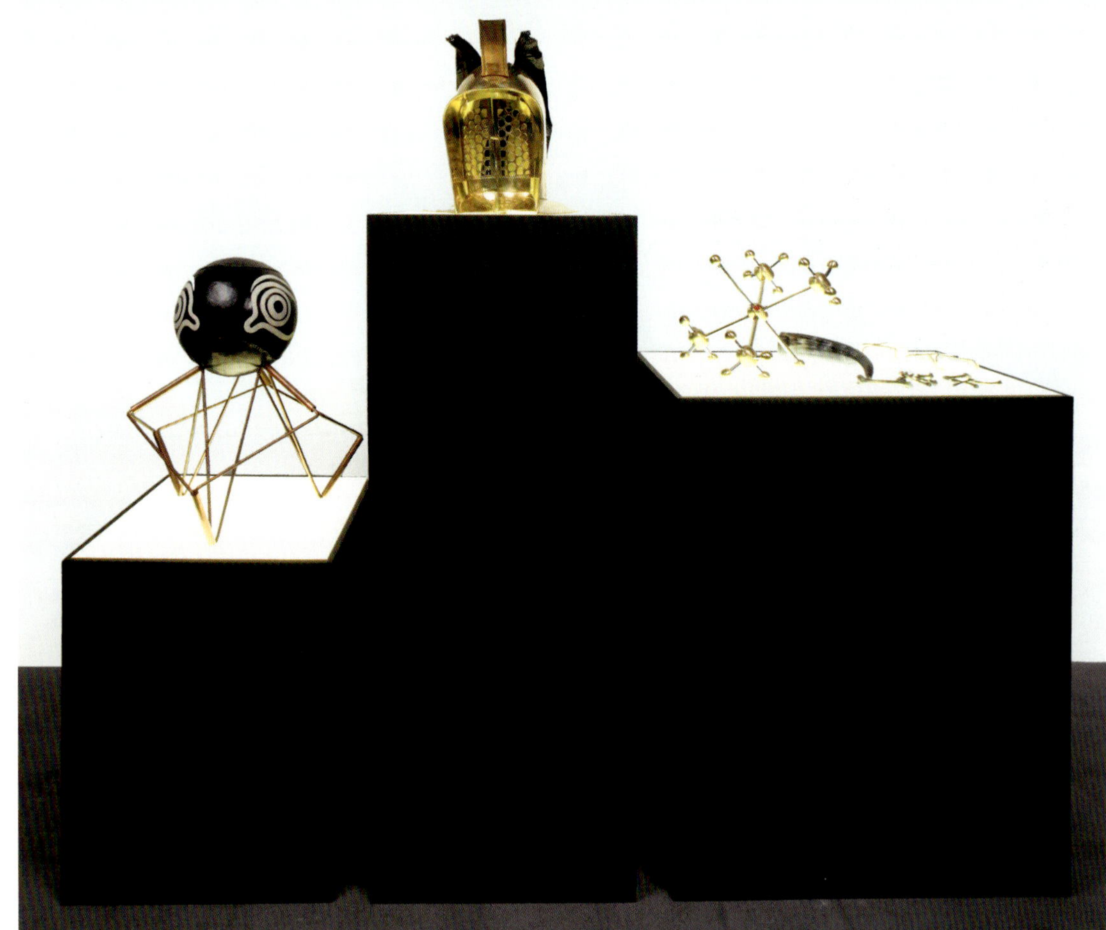

01

Science fiction's revision of the past to conjure the future is central to Steven Claydon's practice, yet his interest in the way in which objects and ideas are collected, categorized and displayed to build a historical narrative distinguishes his drawings, paintings and sculptures from sci-fi visions. His works often resemble artefacts from an ancient past through their use of materials like copper, marble or patinated bronze, and borrow from historical sources, whether text or image-based. But his juxtaposition of these old-fashioned references with new materials, such as mylar plastic sheeting and wigs, or with modern symbols, images and shapes, introduces an incongruity that emphasizes how artefacts and monuments can easily be fabricated to manipulate memory. This fictionalization of the past through false evidence dislocates reality, reconstituting history, which Claydon defines as a 'lateral mesh of causal events and absorbed protocol that informs our nature and forms our cultural conditioning'.

Although his works appear to be artefacts from an unknown universe, Claydon's arrangement of these objects points not towards archaeology but to a desire to examine what he calls the 'taxonomies of display': the ways in which 'institutions evolve modes of display to accommodate a lineal compartmentalization of events in order to rationalize them'. Aesthetically, his installations mimic this linearity through clean, geometric architecture, his discrete objects presented on black plinths, in light-boxes, or, if wall-mounted, on elaborate supports.

In his 2007 exhibition 'New Valkonia', a three-panelled folding frieze apparently depicting Greek gods running through outer space divided the gallery, presenting overlaps between past, present and future, and establishing a colour palette — black, orange and turquoise — for the entire show. In his display of objects from an invented European nation, Claydon exhibited three marble and copper busts: *Spaka Spou (Deposed Deity)*, *Patrician (Male) (Despotism and Tricks)* and *Patrician (Female) (Anthropods in Arcadia)* (all 2007). The female, sporting a bronze visor and a 1960s wig, seems infinitely cooler than the males, who resemble overwrought Greek philosophers, one with donkey ears. These busts point to a critique of sexism in Western history and underscore a need for citizens of any culture to reject imposed history in favour of judging events through multiple criteria. Pieces such as *Valkonian Objects* (2007) and *Chitin & A-Parallelism* (2007) display ritualistic items — bronzed bones, a large animal horn, crystals tied with twine, an intricately manufactured brass helmet — to remind us of how today's goods could become tomorrow's treasures. Images from current media, like a video-game monster hammered into the helmet and a frog patch sewn on to the folding screen, hint at a critique of consumerism. Wall-hung works, such the gold mylar silkscreened *Monopoly on Posterity (Battering Ram)* (2007), depicting an ape to connote evolution, and *Book Lungs* (2007), a Rorschach print with a hole punched through one side, read as sculpture due to their wrinkled three-dimensional properties and the hardware that suspends them away from the walls. Claydon's deeply imaginative presentation of these timeless relics urges viewers to interrogate the representation of history. [Trinie Dalton]

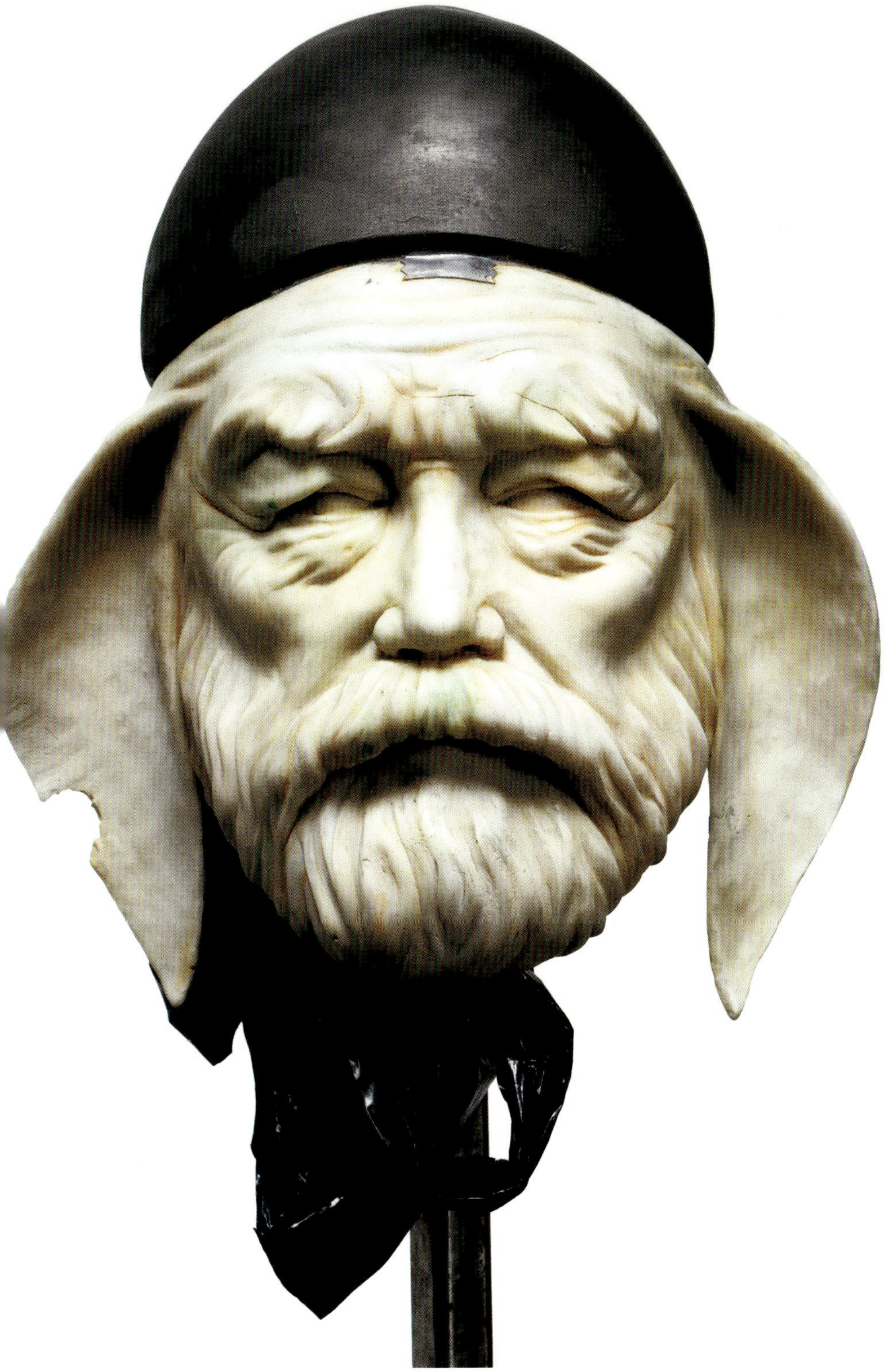

03

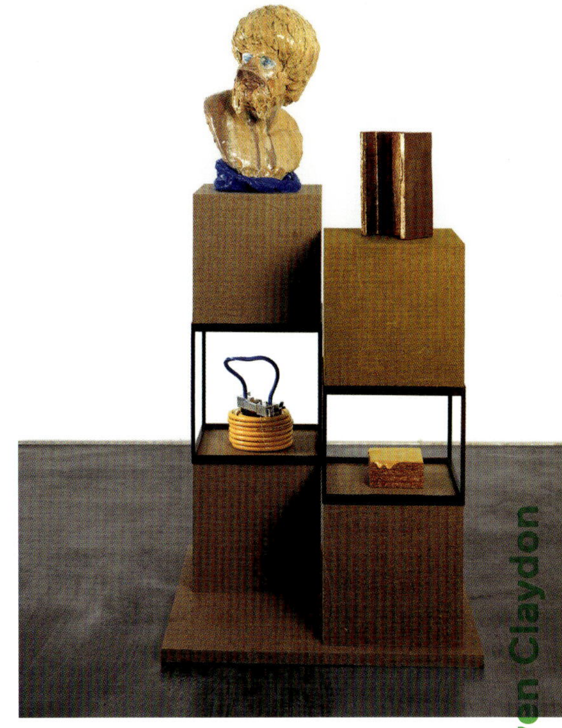

04

02

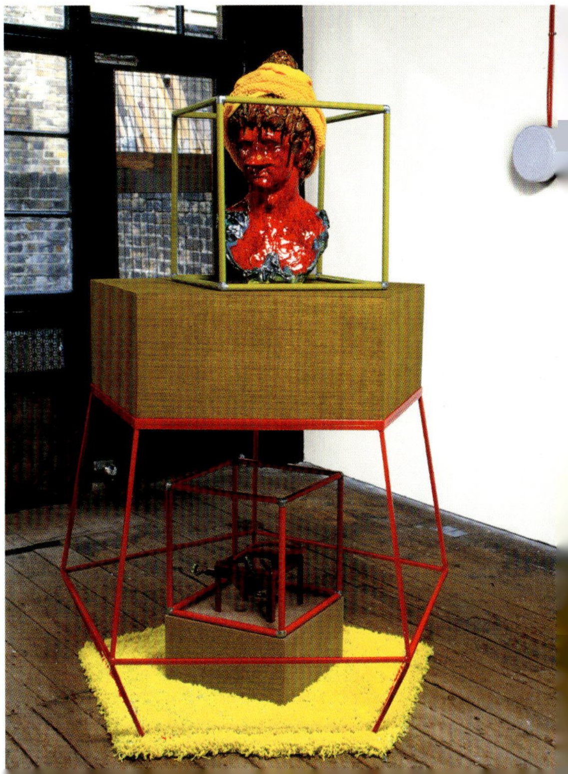

01 from left:
→ *The Ancients Set Great Store*, 2007
Copper, leather, paint
142 × 51 × 51 cm
→ *Chitin & A-Parallelism (New Valkonia)*, 2007
Brass, bull horn, plastic
196 × 51 × 51 cm
→ *Valkonian Objects*, 2007
Brass and steel, bull horn,
quartz crystals, bronze
128 × 76 × 51 cm

02 *Spaka Spou (Deposed Deity)*, 2007
Resin, graphite, marble,
steel, plastic, space blanket
180 × 38 × 38 cm

03 *A lark descending*
(Preparations for Leda), 2008
Ceramic, patinated steel, bukram-covered
plywood, air-hose, road-marking paint,
plastic bag
183 × 91 × 91 cm

04 *Omar (emergent)* 2008
Ceramic, powder-coated steel,
carpet, plywood, starched hessian,
found objects, aluminium

Recalling that there are two types of fools in literature might help to situate Peter Coffin's disparate and often deliberately contrarian practice. First there is the Shakespearean fool, whose nonsense expresses the real truth of a situation. Second, there's the fool who does away with the duality between ostensible and actual expression and delights in the shifting of appearances to prefigure unrevealed truths. Coffin is more likely the latter. His work carries a potentiality that is embodied in playful consideration and contemplation — evincible in titles such as *Music for Plants* (2002) and *Untitled (Log with Model of the Universe)* (2005). His loopy sculptures and conceptual acts are often performed deadpan — farce with no apology — giving few clues to their motivation. Rather, they engineer scenarios in which the impossibility of communication is a key subject and significance.

Music is a recurrent theme in Coffin's work, as are plants, fringe science, psychology and other subjects of curiosity. In *Music for Plants*, a CD compilation and live performance, Coffin invited musicians to perform for plants in a
01 greenhouse — a scenario that asks audiences to consider what connections might be possible between these members of different kingdoms. In *Untitled (Free Jazz Mobile)* (2007) musical instruments hang from a mobile, revolving freely and silently as viewers move between them, inviting a spatial parallel to the sonic experience of free jazz. *Untitled (Singing Tree)* (2006) uses scientific instruments to give a tree a singing voice, encouraging audiences to consider the tree's conscious potential and capacity to communicate — as well as its musical ability.

Coffin's matter-of-fact aesthetic suggests a commitment to interpretation, while his non-declarative approach has more to do with the drawing out of ideas. Artworks expose their own obviously constructed mechanisms, as in *Untitled* (2007), which features a meandering red balloon that traverses the gallery space on a carefully designed conveyor track. In an ongoing series, begun in 2001, he photographs 'auras' of friends and associates, asking the

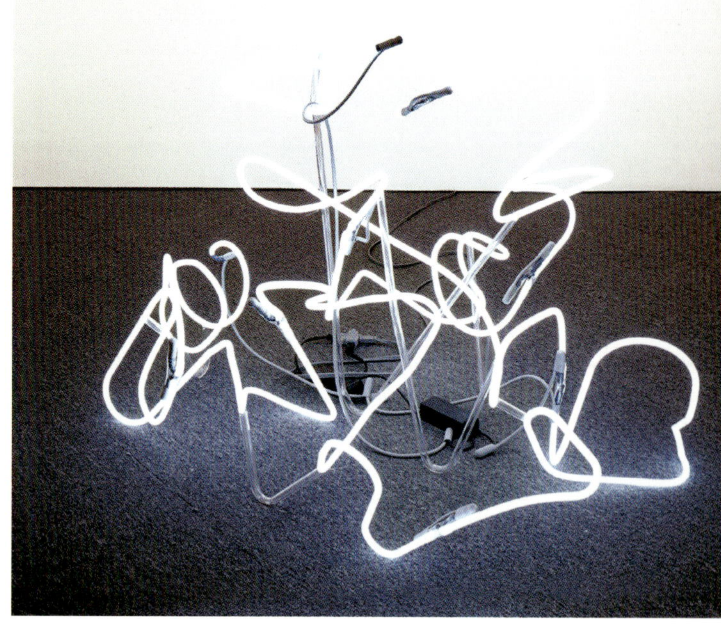

blurry colours surrounding his subjects' heads to testify to their true character and personality. Bruce Nauman's infamous credo becomes further abstracted and mysterious in *Untitled (Line After Bruce Nauman's 'The True Artist Helps the World by Revealing Mystic Truths')*, 2007. Nauman's sign is here just a tangle of neon tubing on the floor, its truism reduced to open-ended uncertainty.

Around, About Expanded Field (2007) renders several dozen classic sculptures from art history as free-standing silhouettes scattered about a dark space. These two-dimensional, matte black shapes, each functioning as a recollection of an image, are illuminated by stock aerial footage played on a video projector. While fields and streams roll by, the flattened sculptures cast their own shadows on nearby walls as if they were flying through the landscape. Like the full size UFO he set into orbit over the Baltic Sea in 2008 (*Untitled (UFO)*), these and other works provide a venue for viewers to project their own beliefs and imaginations without the hindrance of a fixed interpretation.

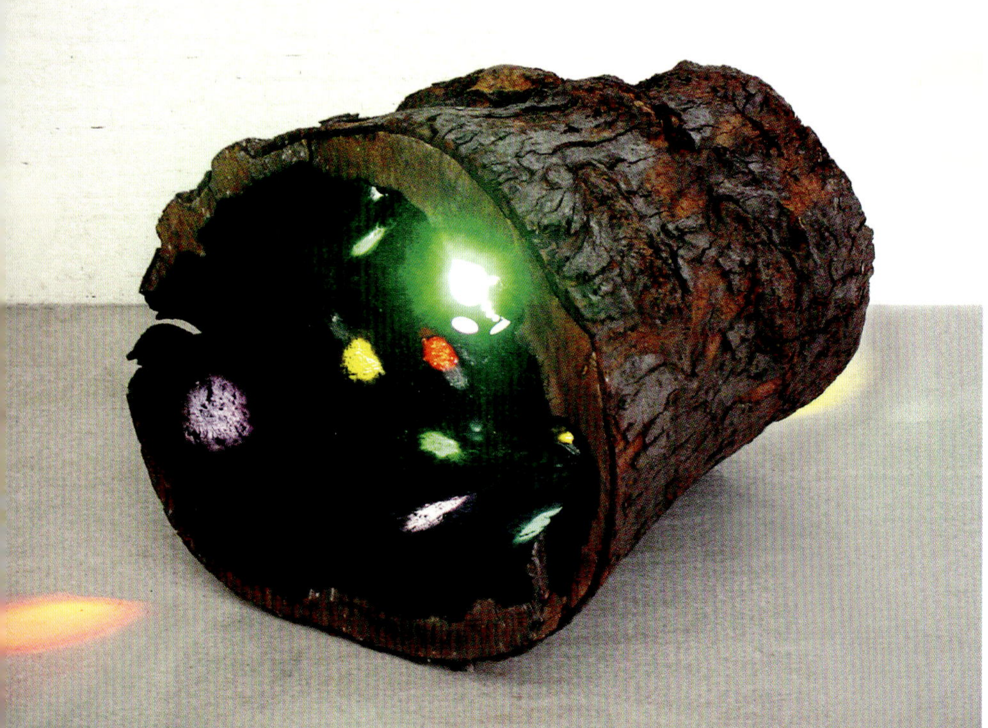

02

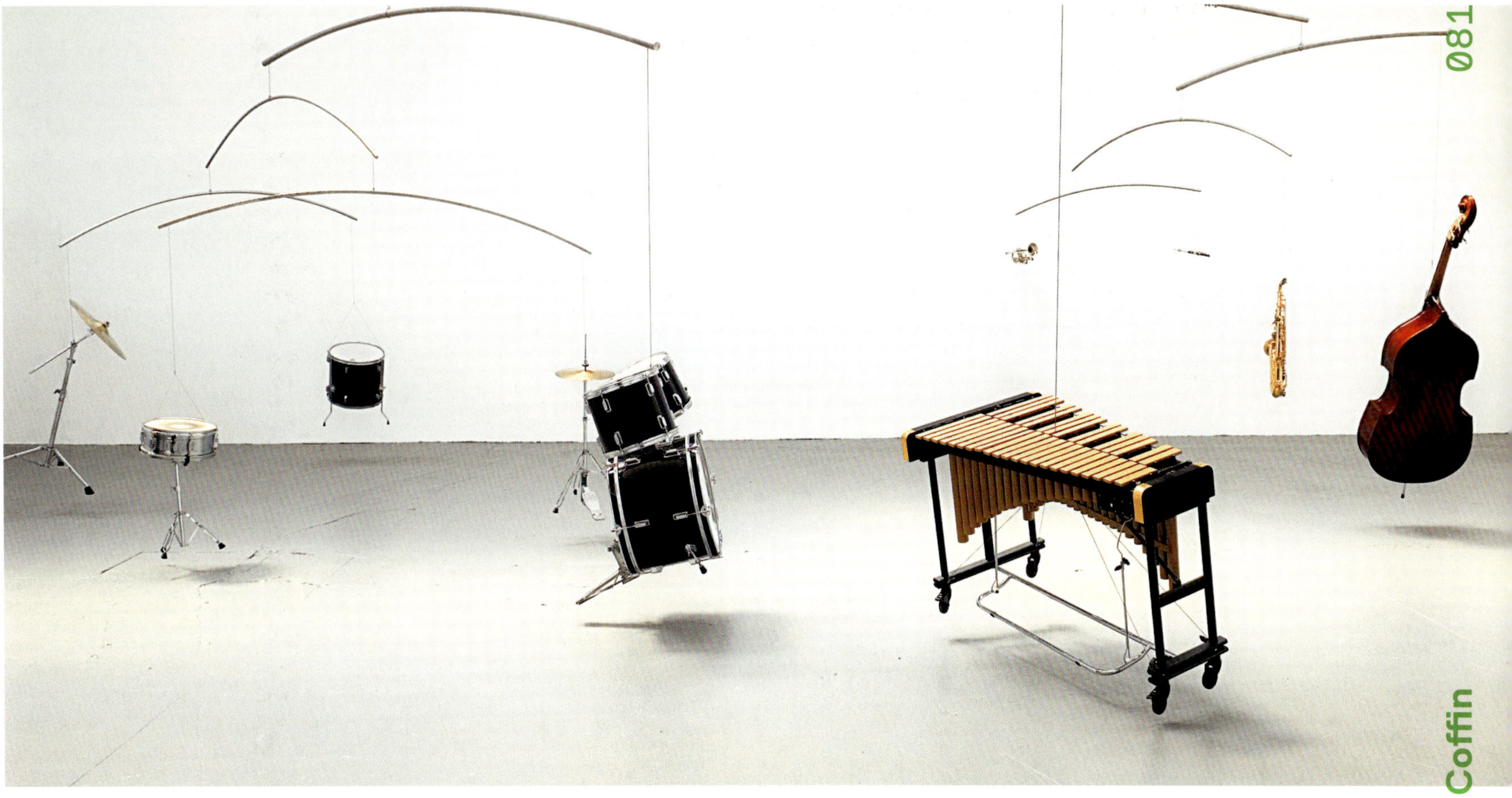

03

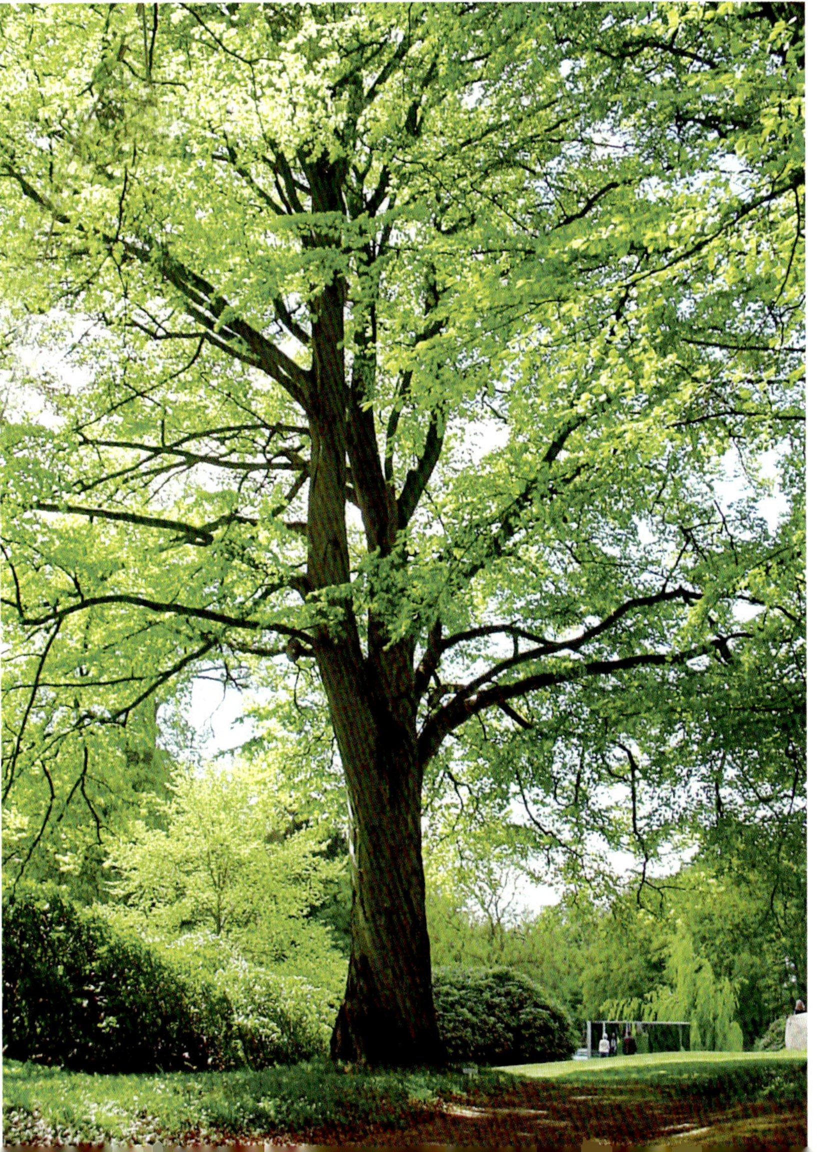

04

01 *Untitled (Line after Bruce Nauman's The True Artist Helps the World by Revealing Mystic Truths)*, 2004
Neon
122 × 122 × 122 cm

02 *Untitled (Hollow Log with Model of the Universe)*, 2005
Hollow log with moving light
76 × 76 × 152 cm

03 *Untitled (Free Jazz Mobile)*, 2007
Mobile structure, cables, musical instruments
Dimensions variable

04 *Untitled (Singing Tree)*, (with David Robert), 2006
Pin electrode sensors, signal amplifier, electronics, sound amplifier, horn speakers
Dimensions variable

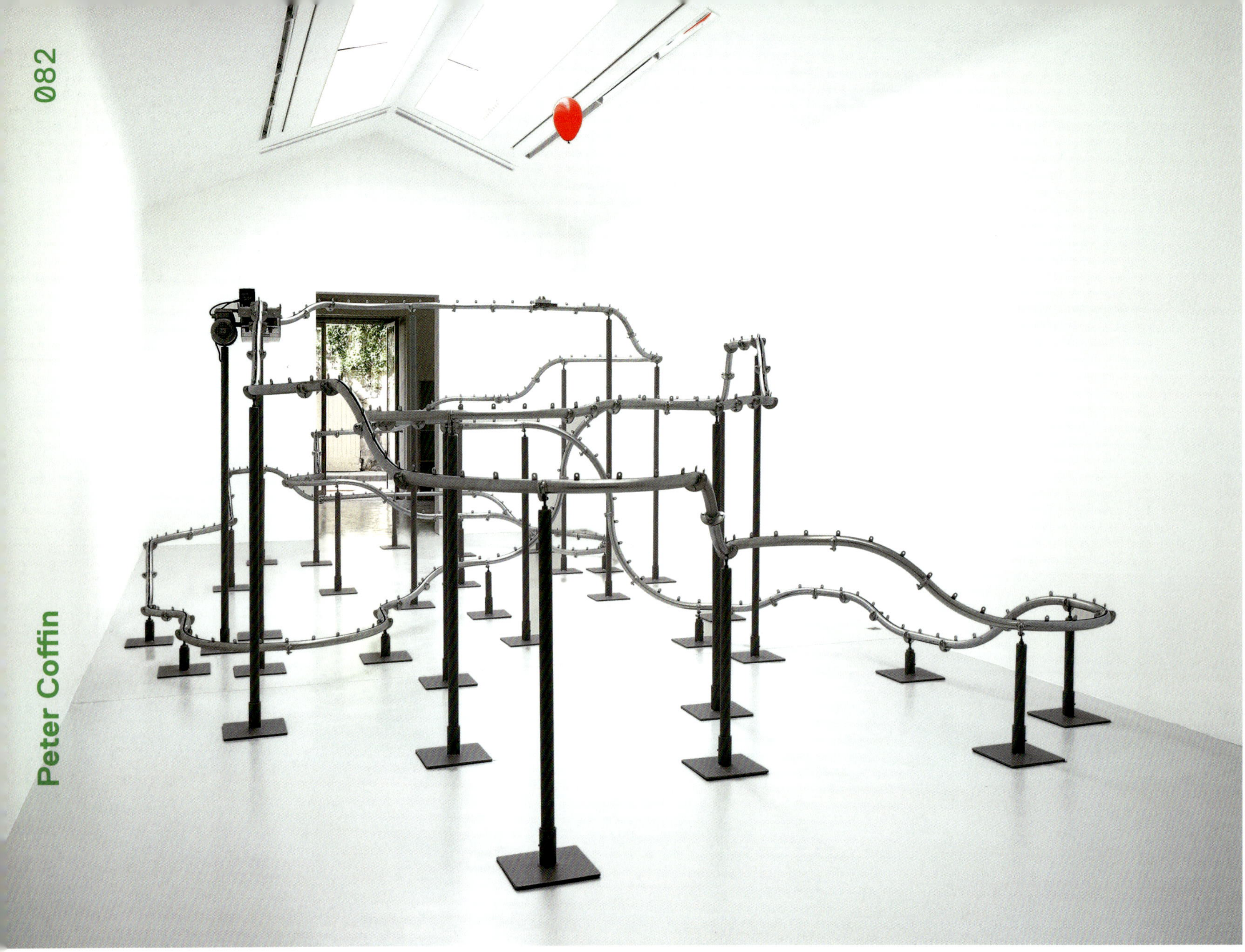

05

06

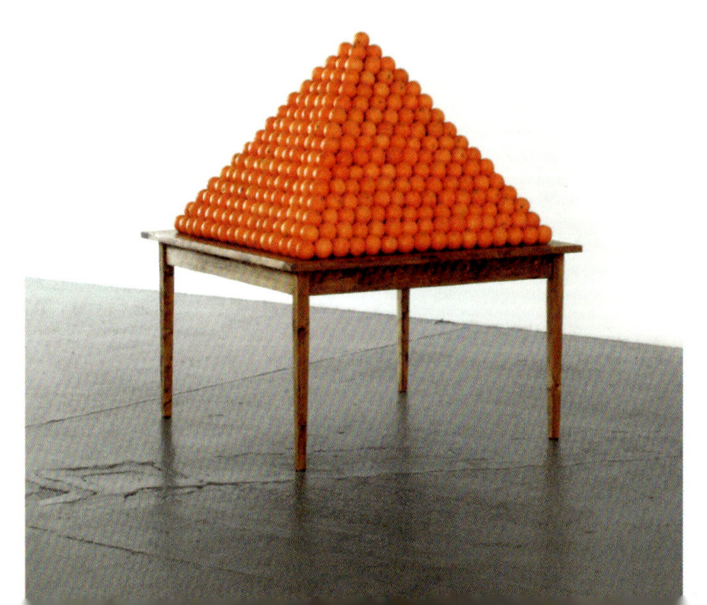

05 *Untitled*, 2007
Conveyor track, motor, release mechanism, balloon
243 × 548 × 1066 cm

06 *Untitled (Orange Pyramid)*, 2007
Table, oranges
137 × 109 × 109 cm

07 *Untitled (Spiral Staircase)*, 2007
Aluminium
670 × 670 × 213 cm

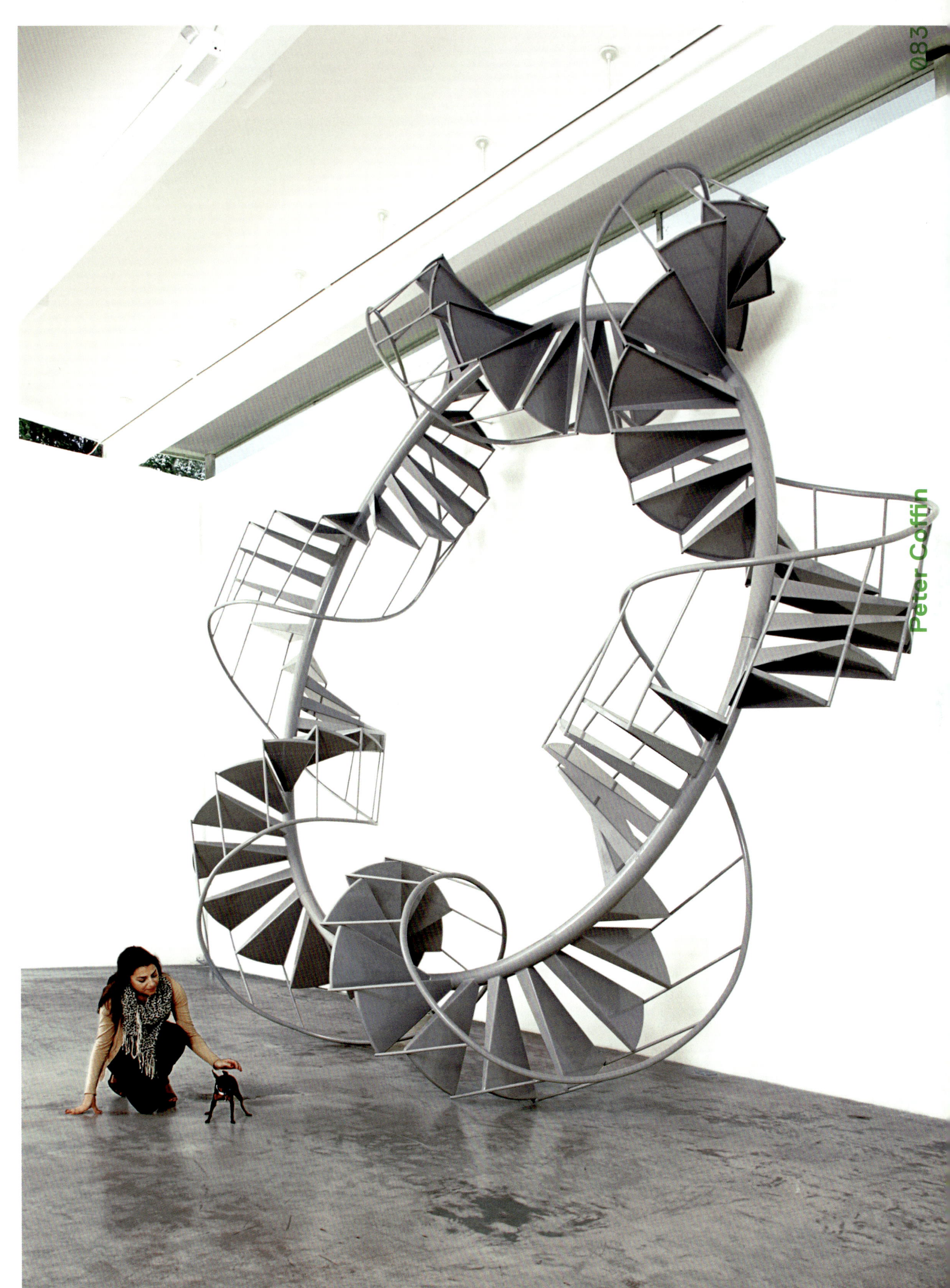

07

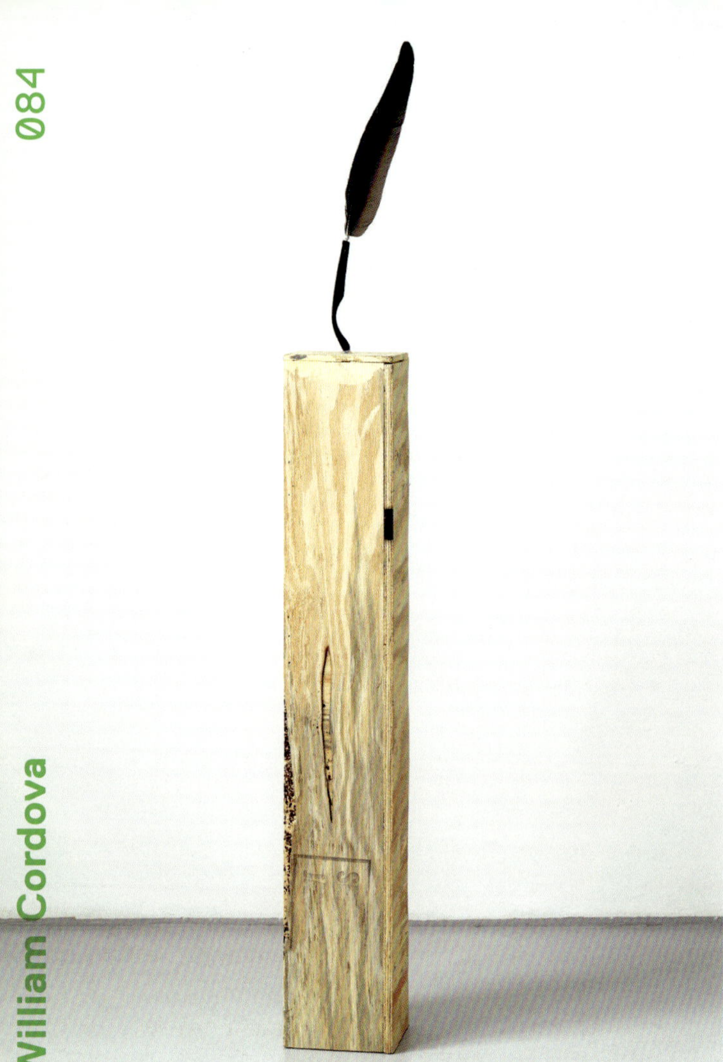

01

01 *Bird in Space (p'a Bobby Rush)*, 2007–08
Reclaimed wood from Chicago, found spectacles frame, Hyacinth bird feather
15 × 126 × 15 cm

02 from left:
→ *Badussy (or Machu Picchu after dark)*, 2004–07
200 reclaimed speakers, candy, currency, debris
244 × 518 × 244 cm
→ *World Famo Paintings*, 2004–05
100 individual framed drawings, ink, graphite, collage, wooden shelf, book cover
150 × 274 × 5 cm

03, 04 *San Antonio's greatest Hits (para Jose Angel Rodriguez, Rosie Castro y Mario Marcel Salas)*, 2008
4,000 vinyl records, Peruvian gourds, VHS tape, cigar, glass
427 × 31 × 31 cm

William Cordova reclaims and recontextualizes everyday objects to create mixed-media installations, using an assortment of unwanted or outdated materials such as old books, vinyl records, discarded speakers and bootlegged VHS tapes as the foundation of his work. His unassuming sculptures and installations function on multiple planes, employing a symbolic system of personal and cultural signifiers to impart historical significance to the work. Individually, the rough-around-the-edges objects may seem fragile and disjointed, like fragments from a conversation, but collectively they are coherent, street wise and enduring, locating beauty and meaning in the overlooked and underappreciated. Through them, Cordova reveals the histories of forgotten people and the memories of left-behind objects imbued with the reality of lived experience.

Cordova's work is in part a reflection of his transient lifestyle. Born in Lima, Peru, he relocated to Miami as a child and has been on the move ever since. For the past few years he has been moving from one artist-residency programme to another, with no permanent home. Thus while much of his work is very personal in nature, it is fundamentally more concerned with universal issues of communication, history and displacement. Consequently, a single motif or material may simultaneously allude to Cordova's nomadic lifestyle, his Afro-Peruvian heritage, a moment of historical significance and the various modern urban subcultures that interest him.

Large-scale works like *Badussy (or Machu Picchu after dark)* (2004–07) and *San Antonio's Greatest Hits (para Jose Angel Rodriguez, Rosie Castro y Mario Marcel Salas)* (2008), are built by stacking many elements on top of each other into a massive architectural monolith — in the first case, hundreds of second-hand stereo speakers, in the latter, thousands of vinyl records. These works possess fundamental characteristics common to many of Cordova's creations: an accumulation of found objects, a metaphorical use of materials, and a search for continuity through repetition. The gathering of carefully selected objects suggests makeshift shrines, perhaps as a way to mark territory and negotiate one's place within the ever-shifting landscape of today's world. Precise meaning is difficult to pin down, but Cordova offers us partially exposed clues from popular culture and social history as if dropping a trail of breadcrumbs to see if we can follow his lead.

As he moves fluidly between sculpture, installation, drawing and video, Cordova samples, loops and remixes his imagery, recreating ideas in different forms and contexts to produce original but interrelated works. Though his references may seem obscure, his work speaks of the complexity of the transmission of ideas and offers a multiplicity of interpretations. Odd juxtapositions of materials and motifs create new meaning as each viewer brings his or her experience to the work. Through such imagery he makes cultural and historical connections, but he leaves interpretation of meaning up to the viewer. With both veiled and direct references to underappreciated authors, artists and activists, Cordova's works function like murky history lessons, always tempting but never spoon-feeding his audience. The work is not meant to be deciphered, but rather explored. He is historian, trickster, philosopher and provocateur rolled into one, whose methods of obfuscation and misdirection pique our interest even as they keep us guessing. [Trevor Schoonmaker]

William Cordova

02

04

03

PROFESSIONAL
VIDEO CASSETTE
T-60PR
Shango

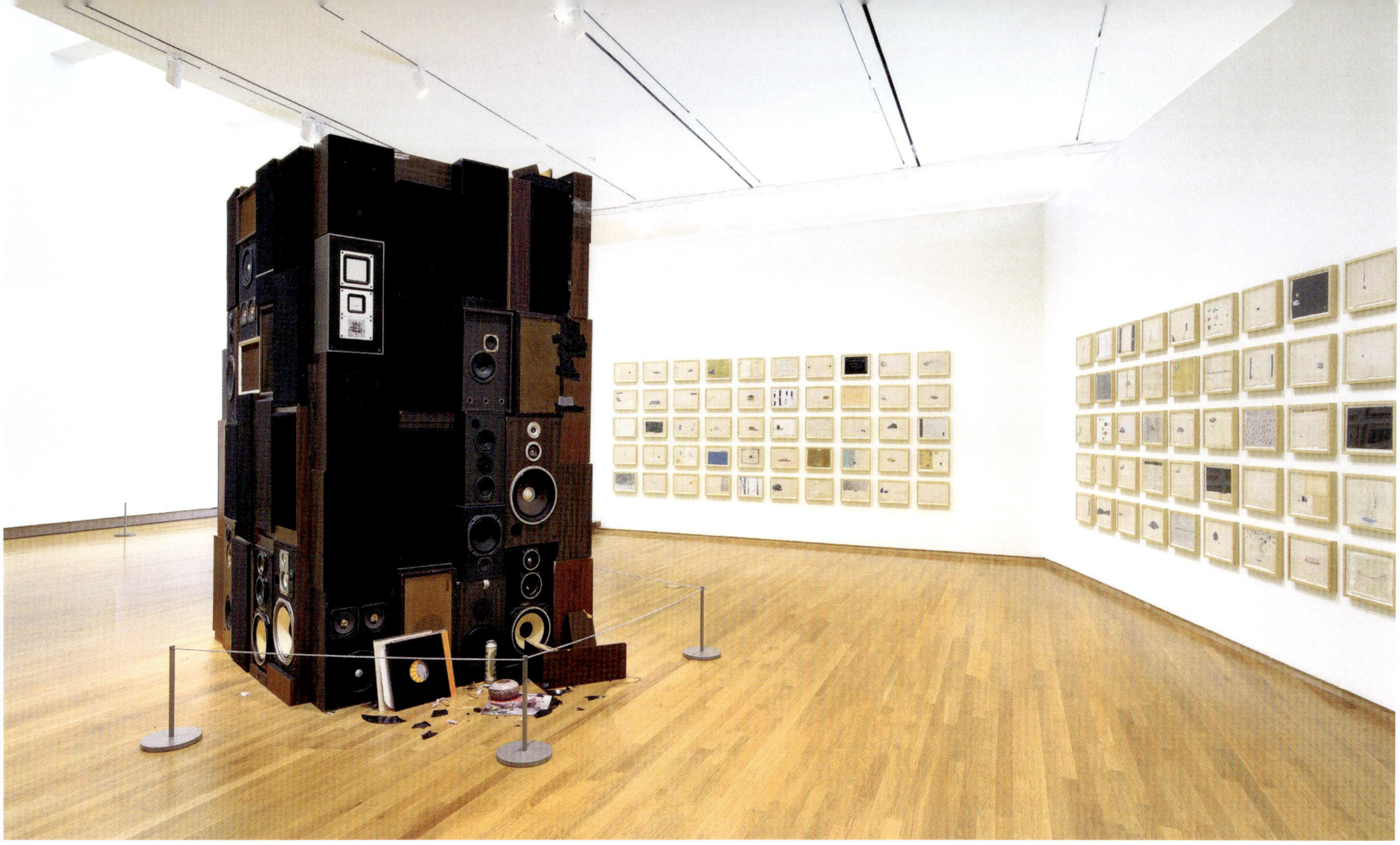

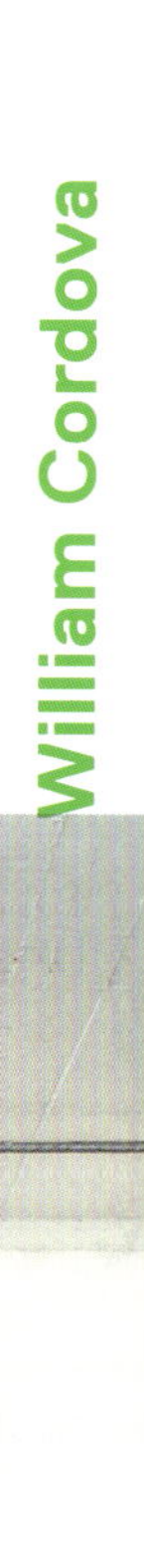

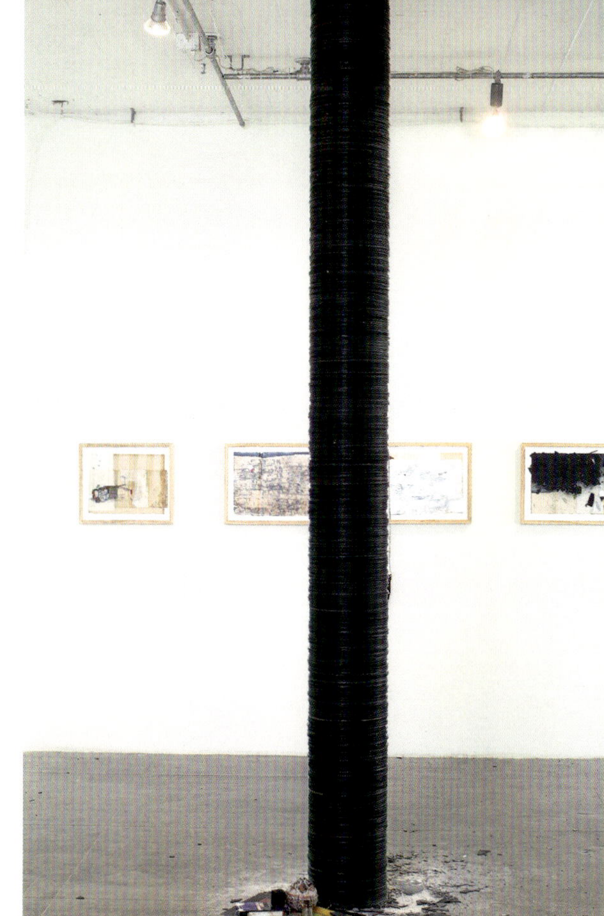

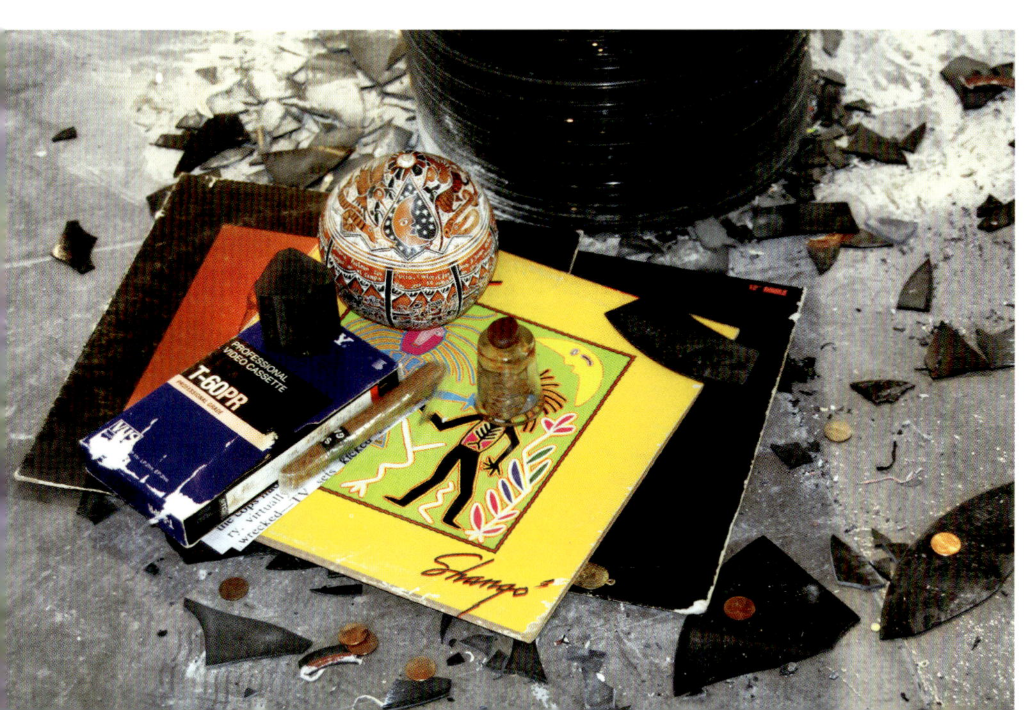

The Mexican-born artist Abraham Cruzvillegas follows a particular Latin American artistic trajectory in which a strong traditional craft sensibility and the tendency to reuse everyday objects is combined with the (Western) idea of the readymade. At first glance his works may recall pieces by his fellow Mexican artists Damián Ortega and Gabriel Kuri, but the severe play of forms, shapes and colours in his sculptures and installations, as well as their strong autobiographical and political references, distinguish them from those of his compatriots.

Cruzvillegas immersed himself in both fine arts and philosophy during his years at the University of Mexico (UNAM), and his dual interests are apparent in many of his pieces, which explore at their core the ideology of the object and the economic structure of Western society. Often stunningly handsome, they play with the idea of how we are seduced by beauty, only to break this fragile notion by juxtaposing it with something ugly and seemingly deformed. By appropriating everyday items and altering them, Cruzvillegas advocates a non-elitist approach to art-making and creates relationships between numerous — often seemingly contradictory — aspects of modern life. He frequently conserves the primary function of the objects he is using, relentlessly bringing them back to their cultural and utilitarian origins. A keen observer of the world around him, he uses everything from knives and plants to fish hooks, feathers, newspapers, candles, ropes and nails. He once even incorporated the jaw of a shark into an artwork.

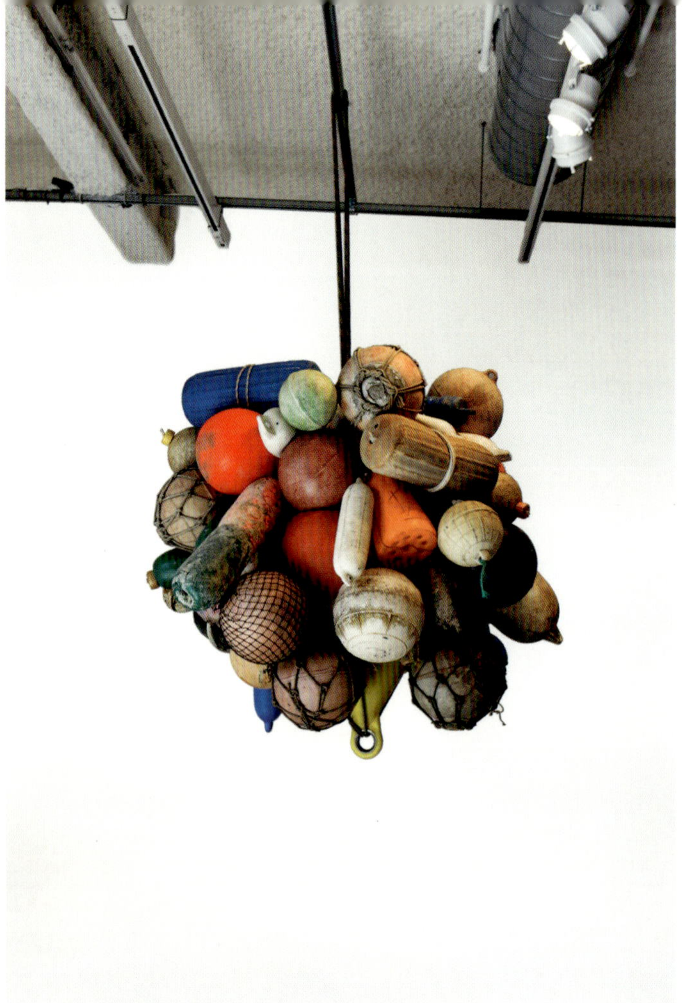

01

01 *Pending Sculpture*, 2008
Buoys, rope
270 × 170 × 170 cm

02 *El Nuevo Progreso*, 2003
Badminton shuttlecocks, steel wire
15 × 96 × 15 cm

03 *Bougie du Isthme*, 2005
Fishing poles, painted iron bottle rack, printed scarves, rubber
6 × 10 × 5 m

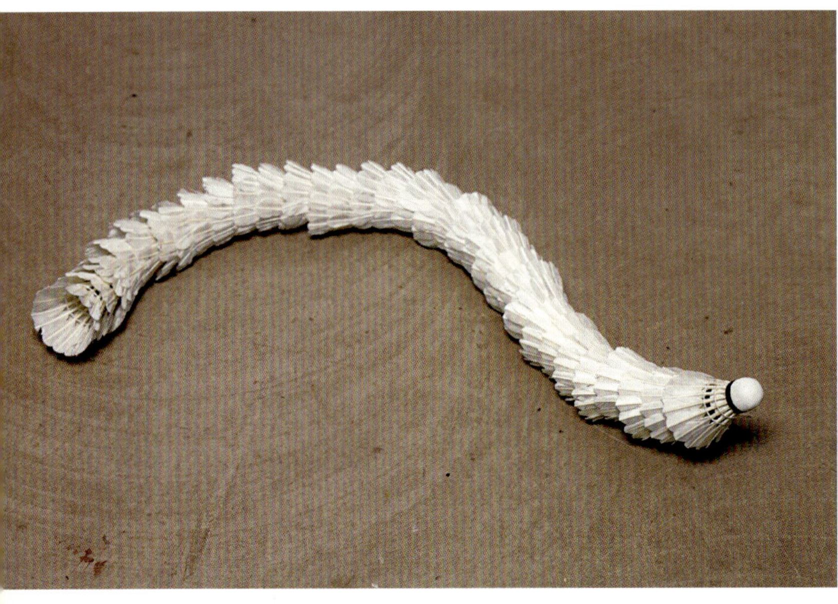

02

Though he is still an emerging artist, Cruzvillegas has been working in this field for more than a decade, beginning with appropriations of folk art made by his father. He gained a wider audience at the beginning of this decade during a boom of exhibitions focusing on the younger generation of Mexican artists. *Aeropuerto Alterno* (2002), shown at the 2003 Venice Biennale, became one of his trademark works. It consists of a handmade butcher's block into which the artist has stuck two dozen or so used knives of all sizes and shapes. The title suggests that the knives have flown in from different places to land in the wooden structure. Their arrangement also gives the impression of a floral bouquet.

A more recent work is *Canon enigmatico a 108 voces* (2005), in which the Spanish word *canon* takes on a dual meaning ('cannon' and 'canon'). It is comprised of 108 buoys found on the beach in Mexico, strung together and suspended from the ceiling like grapes on a vine. The play of shapes and colours inspires the viewer to contemplate faraway, exotic Mexican beaches. As in many of Cruzvillegas's works, the objects he uses are relentlessly utilitarian and mass-produced, yet somehow transformed so that they seem as if they were made exclusively for his works. [Jens Hoffmann]

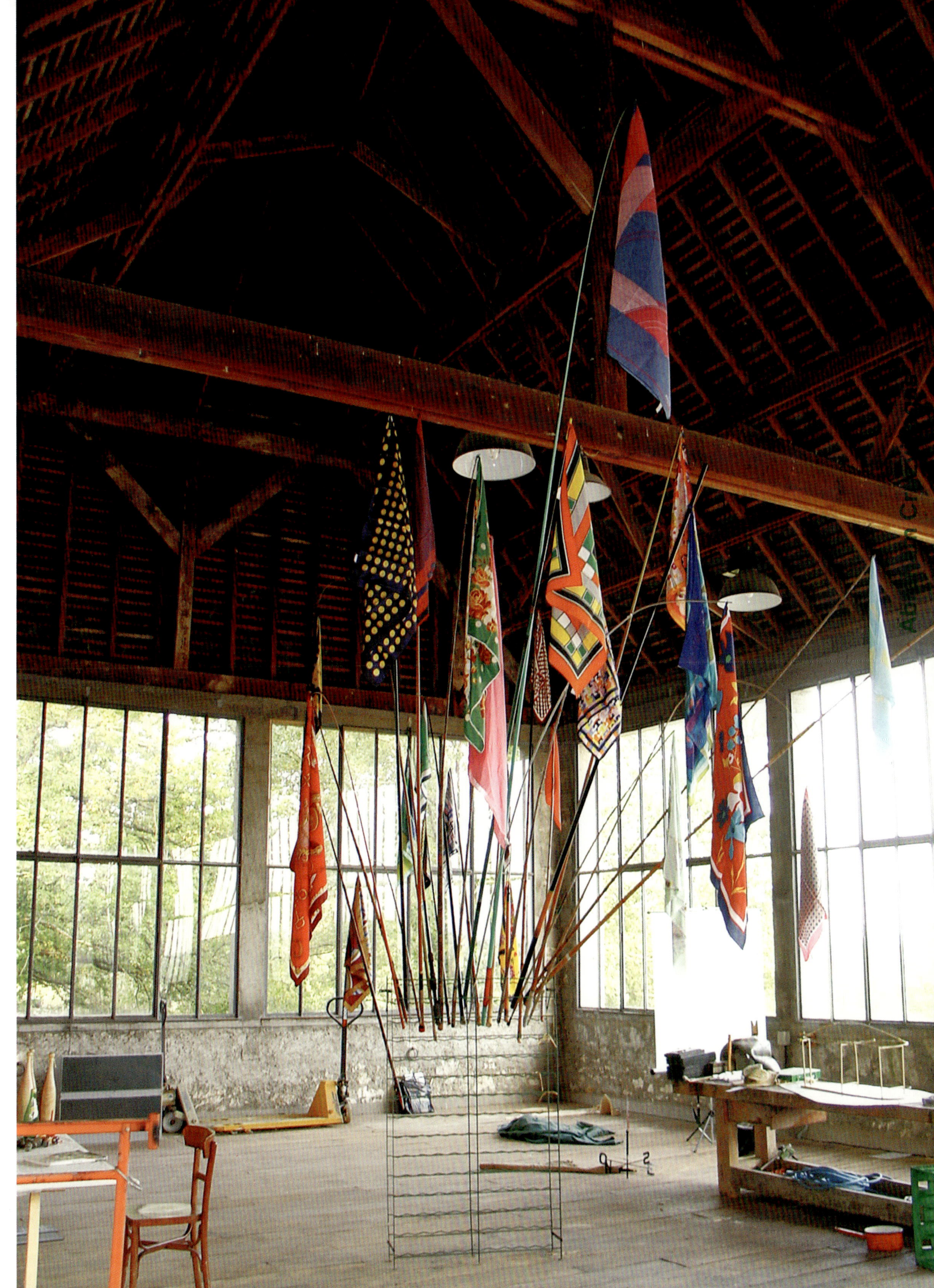

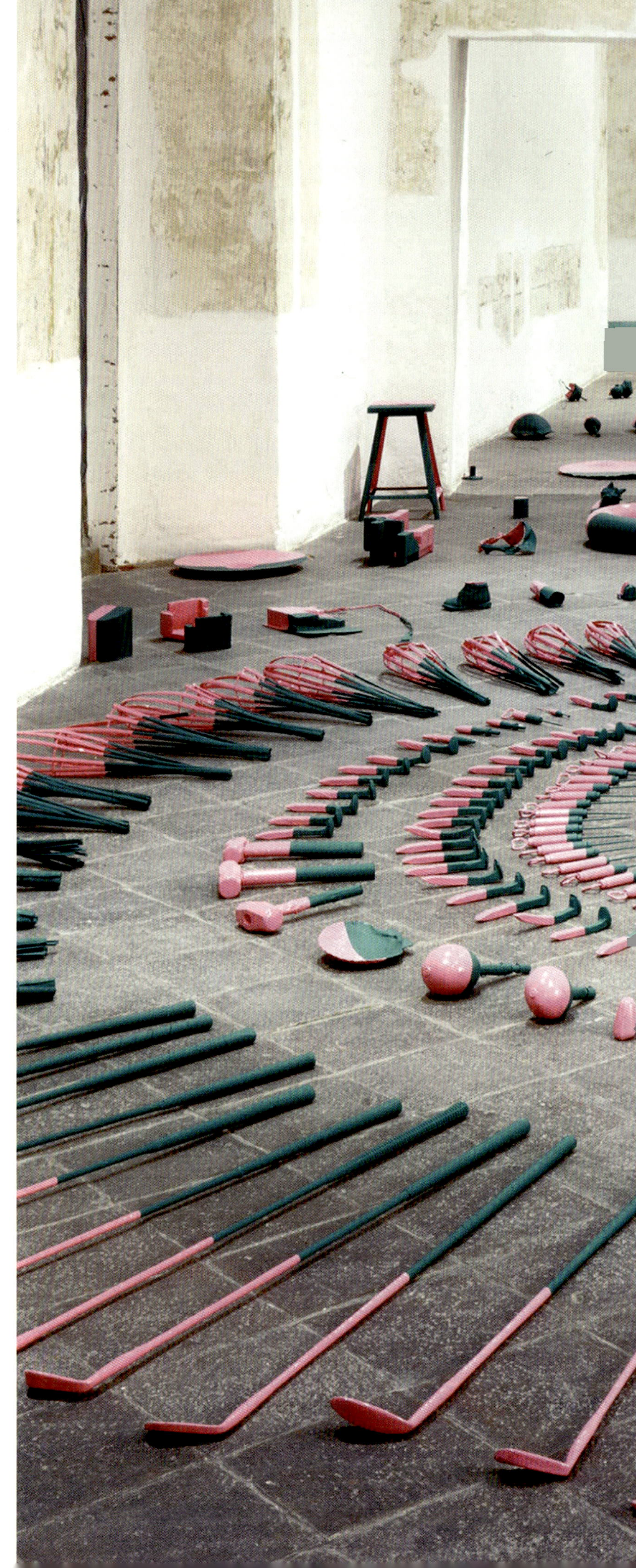

04 *Horizontes*, 2005
Acrylic enamel gloss pink paint and chalk-board green paint on approximately 400 found objects
Dimensions variable

04

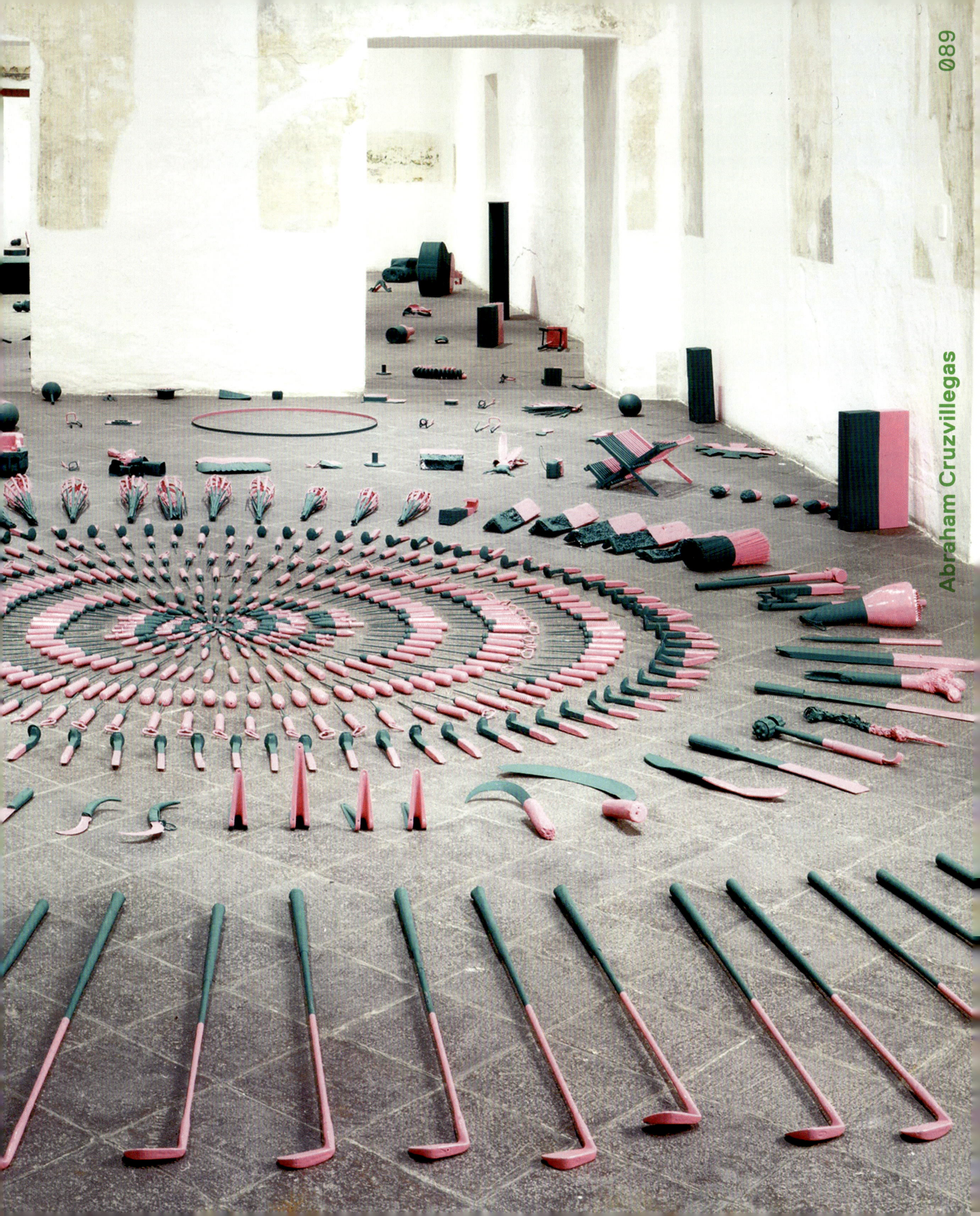

The London-based, Brazilian-born artist Alexandre da Cunha takes a transcontinental approach to art-making; he deploys a neo-formalist aesthetic that has emerged in Europe and North America over the last five years and fuses it with a specifically Latin American artistic sensibility that is based on a Post-Duchampian alteration of found objects. His work moves back and forth between the classic European legacy of modernism and a Brazilian incarnation of the same tradition. The latter has had a tremendous influence not only on Brazilian visual art but even more famously on the country's architecture; Brazil's Neoconcrete movement of the 1960s aimed to rejuvenate the individual's relationship to the surrounding world, and its legacy is still visible all over Brazil today.

But in contrast to those Brazilian forebears, for whom slogans and ideologies played an important role, da Cunha describes his practice as being more about techniques and materiality. Context is also crucial; he is deeply interested in the history and setting of modern and contemporary art in Brazil, particularly the fact that core aspects of Brazil's cultural identity are cannibalized from other cultures. He continues this tradition through the objects he chooses to appropriate — an act he describes as a 'tropicalization' of the readymade.

Most of da Cunha's works originate from intense observations of the everyday — specifically the ways in which people in Brazil improvise ordinary objects to create other useful items. He translates these improvisations into his own sculptural pieces through processes of decontextualization and modification. The resulting artworks, made out of inexpensive and sometimes defunct consumer items, often mimic modernist sculptures, yet their forms are rooted in everyday life. One of his best-known series, for instance, is a group of large ceiling-fan sculptures made from old skateboards and household utensils. Their titles are based on either the brand names of the skateboards or writings that their former owners scrawled onto them. The ceiling fan is obviously a reference to the climate and ordinary household decor of tropical countries such as Brazil. But da Cunha's method of appropriation goes beyond the straightforward reuse of the objects themselves. The found boards have scratches and stickers that tell stories — personal narratives of their former owners — and as cultural artefacts they refer to a particular lifestyle that is familiar to some and completely mysterious to others. We may see them as abandoned trophies, or fragments of secrets that da Cunha has found and exposed.

Recently, the artist's work has become more political and critical. For his 2006 *Velour Series* he used metal fittings and tape to cobble beach towels, curtain poles and ribbons into flaglike constructions. The towels' graphics are carefully selected; they show, for instance, tigers or girls in bikinis. Thus the flags are critical dissections of the idea of national identity, playing on the stereotypical iconography of tropical or 'exotic' countries by presenting lighthearted images associated with leisure culture as if they were official national symbols. [Jens Hoffmann]

01 *Ground*, 2008
Wooden handle, walking stick, cup, cork, bike bell, wood, rope, concrete
200 × 174 × 188 cm

02 *Bust I*, 2008
Mop, dyed wool, concrete
120 × 20 × 20 cm

03 *Velour Series*, 2006
Poles, broomsticks, curtain rails, tape, beach towels, fixings
260 × 40 × 40 cm

04 One Love, 2007
Printed fabric, copper piping, bolts
2 parts
190 × 160 × 215 cm
184 × 164 × 230 cm

01

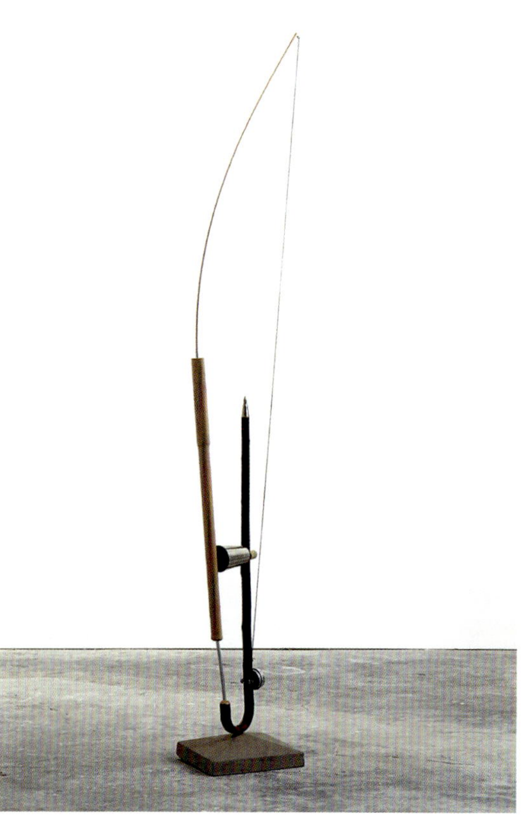

02

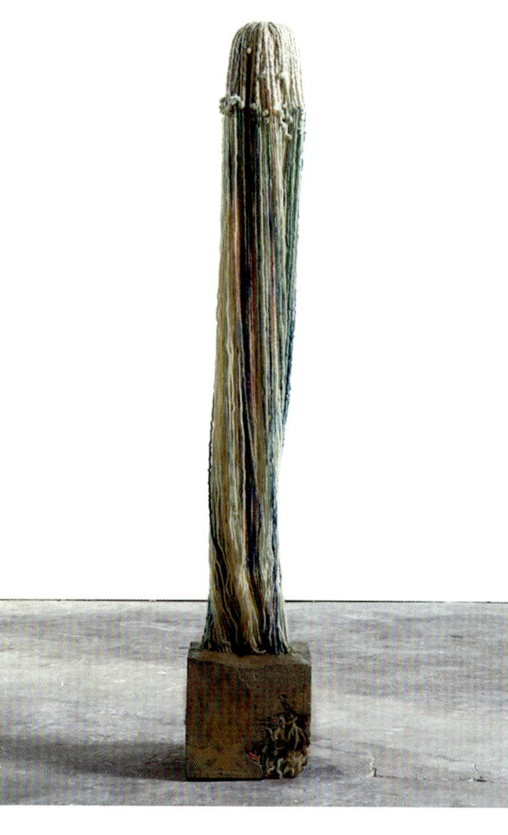

05 from left:
→ *Lavender*, 2006
Tapestry screen, bathroom mats, wool, stretcher
182 × 136 × 4cm
→ *Public Sculpture (Pouff 3)*, 2008
Concrete and foam
150 × 150 × 38cm
→ *Arcadia*, 2007
Tapestry screen, bathroom mats, yarn
182 × 136 × 4cm
→ *Noveau*, 2007
Tapestry screen, bathroom mats, yarn
182 × 136 × 4cm
→ *Chenille*, 2006
Tapestry screen, bathroom mats, yarn
182 × 136 × 4cm
→ *Jasmine*, 2007
Tapestry screen, bathroom mats, yarn
182 × 136 × 4cm
→ *Merino*, 2006
Tapestry screen, bathroom mats, yarn
182 × 136 × 4cm
→ *Public Sculpture (Pouff 2)*, 2008
Concrete and foam
150 × 150 × 38cm
→ *Public Sculpture (Pouff 1)*, 2008
Concrete and foam
150 × 150 × 38cm

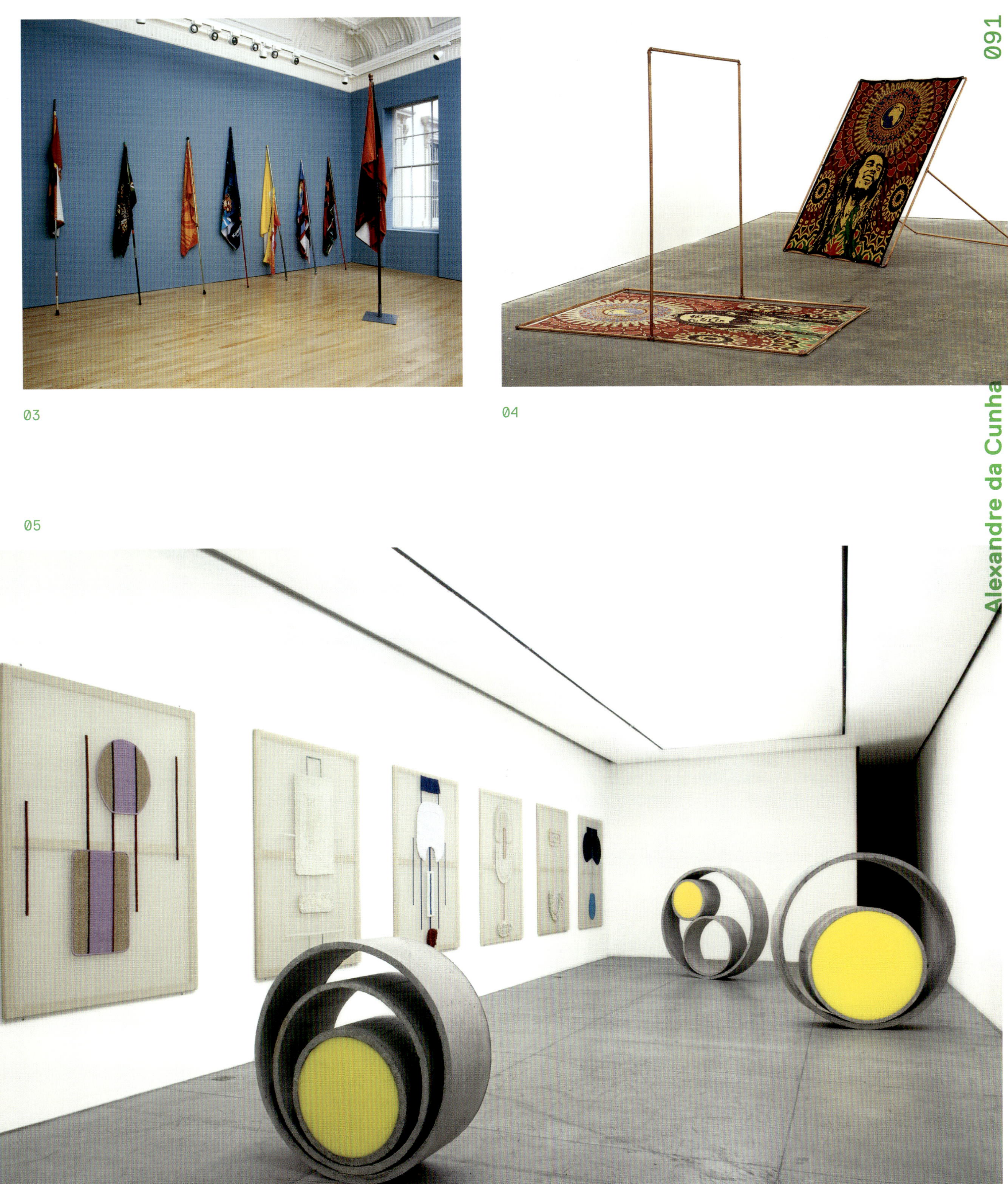

03

04

05

01

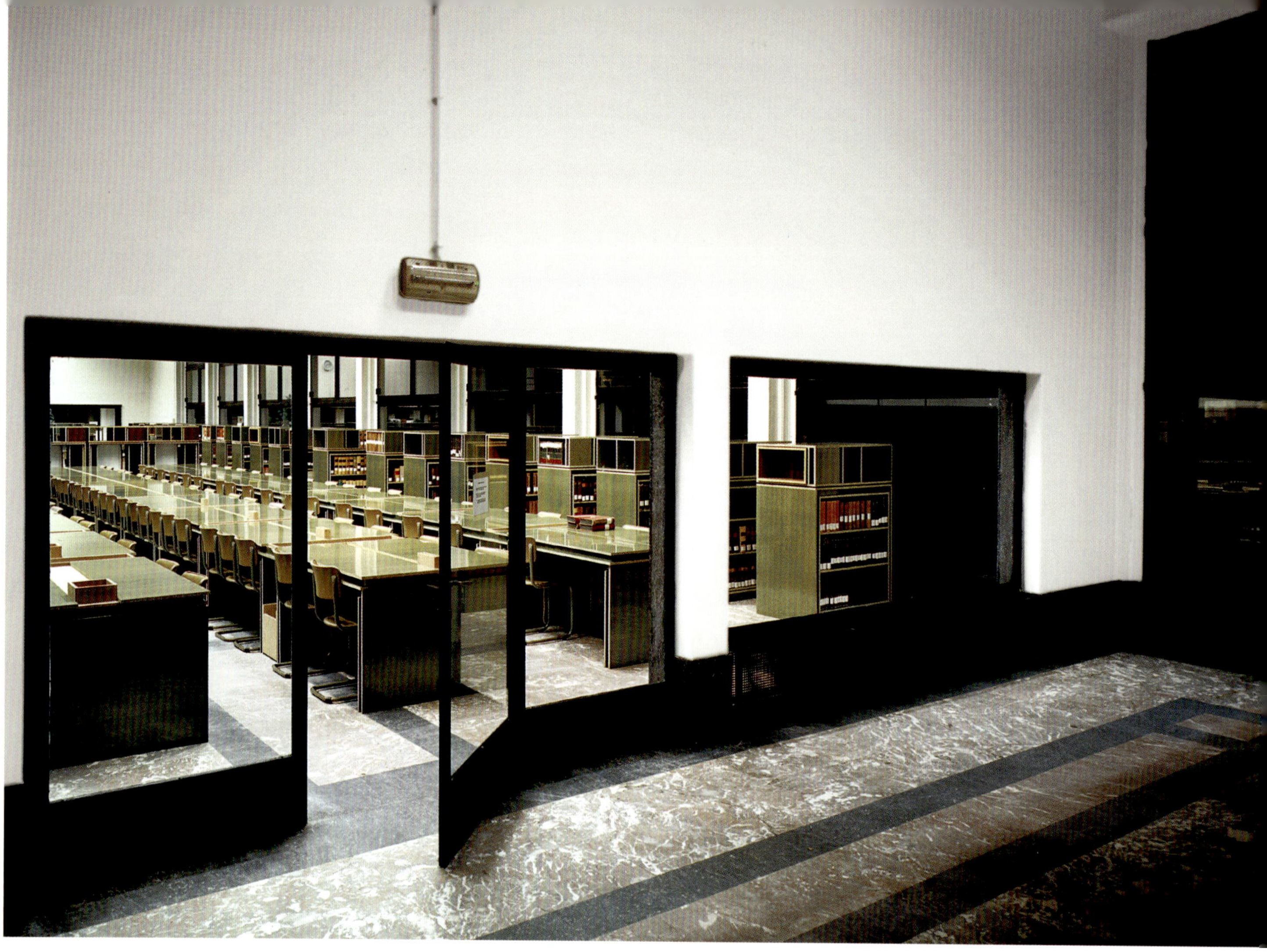

The work of Belgian artist Jan De Cock reads as a catalogue of sculptural encounters with sites and buildings of historical or institutional resonance — in some cases both — within the canon of modern art and architecture. In early 2004, he installed a bulky sculpture in the central reading room of Ghent University's main library building, designed by Henry van de Velde and better known as the 'Tower of Books'. He neatly wrapped every reading table and bookshelf with an elaborate sculptural skin of green fibreboard plates that delicately matched the modernist simplicity and classicist monumentality of van de Velde's design.

In recent years, De Cock has manoeuvred himself into such emblematic venues as the Palais des Beaux-Arts in Brussels, designed by Victor Horta (*Denkmal 23*, 2003); the Casa del Fascio in Como, designed by Giuseppi Terragni (*Denkmal 4*, 2006, in collaboration with Daniel Buren); Tate Modern in London (*Denkmal 53*, 2005) and the Museum of Modern Art in New York (*Denkmal 11*, 2008). The title of each resulting sculpture, *Denkmal* ('monument' in German), is followed by a number that correlates to the street address of its location. In Dutch, *Denk* means 'to think', while *mal* means 'mould'. Thus *Denkmal* does not merely convey a stately tribute to the site it occupies, but suggests that the work is a physical and mental container. De Cock's intricate constellations of frames, volumes and lattices insert a literal as well as metaphorical mould within and around the space, engendering a powerful material expression for the residual space of critical reflection and historical alertness.

Time and again, these labour-intensive and material-consuming wooden sculptures engage with both the distant and recent history of their respective locations, not by representing it, but by critically, and above all sculpturally, 'working it through'. De Cock's sculptural practice combines a radical commitment to places and spaces with a resolute investment in the making of material form. In doing so it subtly rearticulates the historical legacies of institutional critique and site-specific practice. Any dialogue between a *Denkmal* and the site it occupies is anticipated and 'framed' by the sculpture's obdurate material disposition.

De Cock's dialogue with history by means of sculptural form is further elaborated in his ambitious project for a twelve-part encyclopedia, of which he has published four volumes so far. The books are equally impressive, whether considered in material or conceptual terms, and to some extent act as sculptures in their own right. Here, De Cock lavishly documents his past projects through photographs, entwining them with myriad references to late nineteenth- and twentieth-century exponents of the modern avant-garde in such divergent domains as visual art, film, architecture and music. Figures ranging from Constantin Brancusi, Antoine Bourdelle and Jean-Luc Godard to Dan Graham, Miles Davis and Marcel Broodthaers reveal the rich artistic and intellectual tradition upon which De Cock fervently draws and aims to extend, and to which he ultimately aspires to belong.
[Wouter Davidts]

01 *Denkmal 9, Henry van de Velde University Library, Rozier 9, Ghent, 2004*
Chipboard
Approx. 48 × 15 × 7 m

02 *Modern is changing, fig. 3, 2008*
Chipboard, melamine paper, Kodak Yellow satin gloss enamel
Approx. 13.4 × 8.8 × 5.5 m

03 *Denkmal 9, Henry van de Velde University Library, Rozier 9, Ghent, 2004*
Chipboard
Approx. 48 × 15 × 7 m

04 *Denkmal 4, Casa del Fascio, Piazza del Popolo 4, Como*
(in collaboration with Daniel Buren), 2006
Chipboard, melamine paper, paint
14.6 × 4.6 × 4.1 m

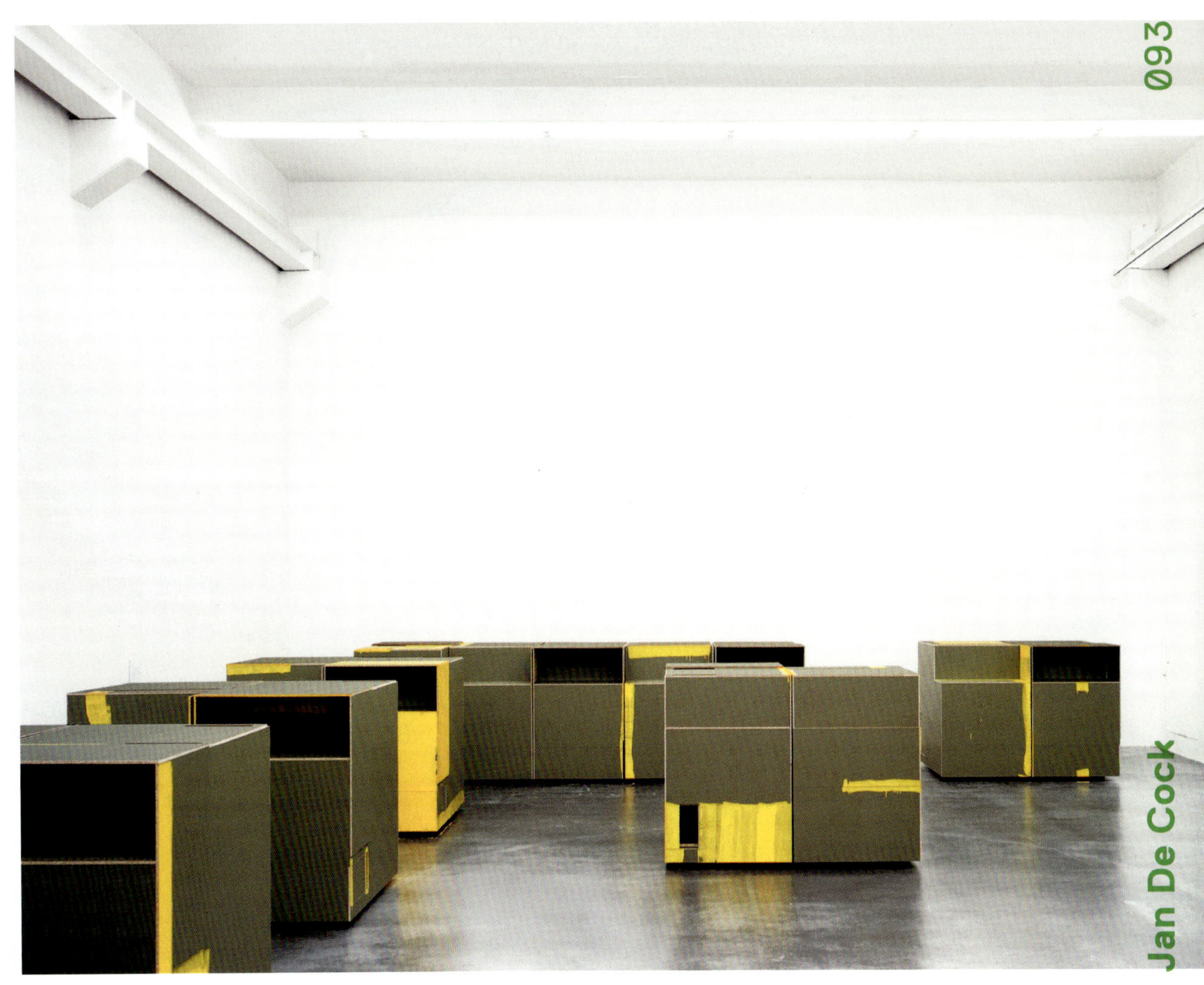

02

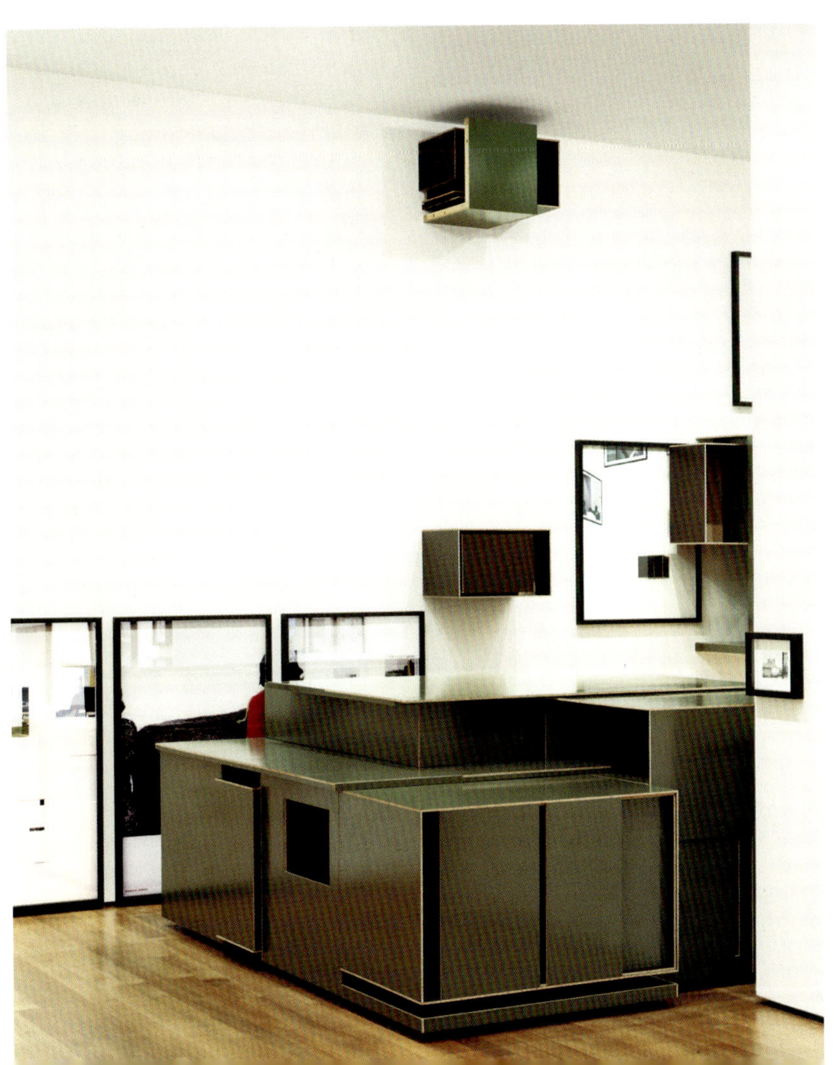

03

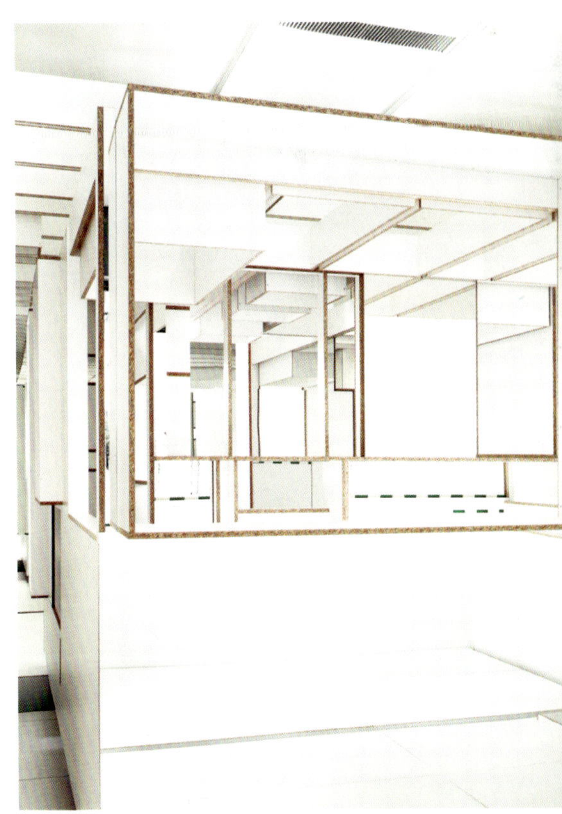

04

Thea Djordjadze

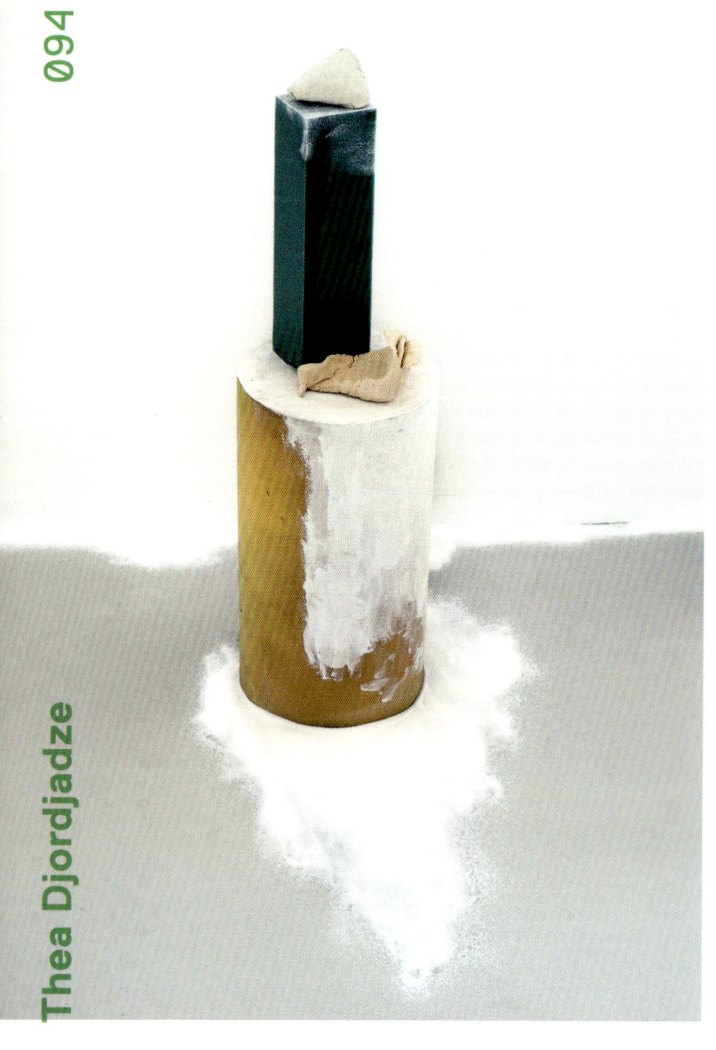

01

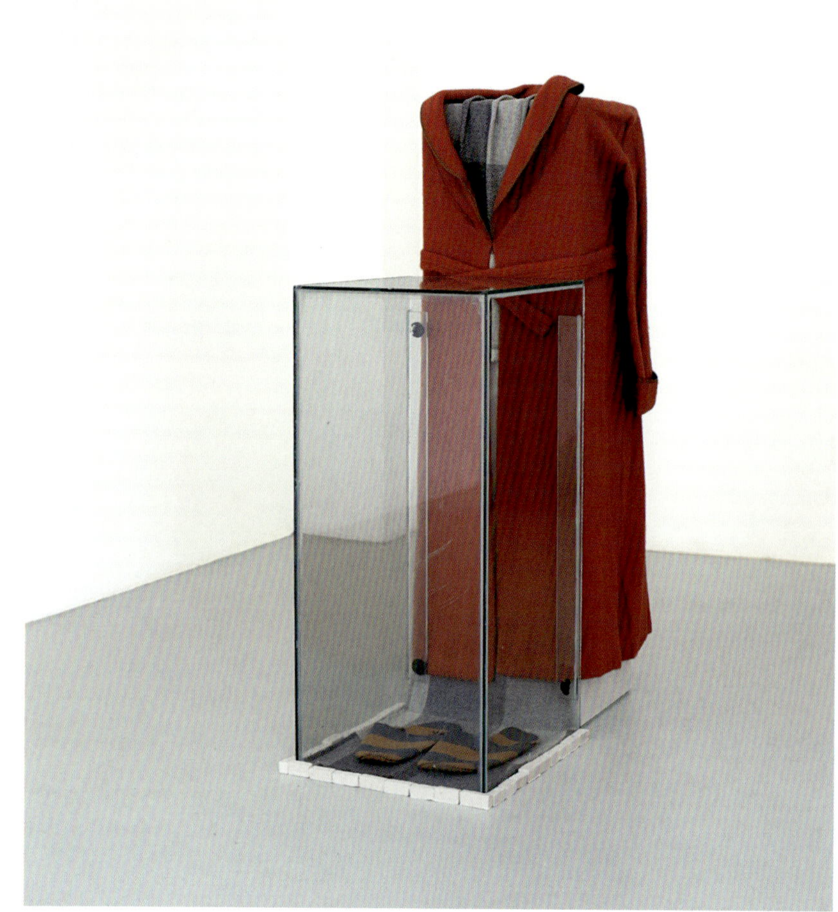

02

In her tactile sculptures Thea Djordjadze considers process as a perpetual conflict between form and material and between the work and the historical moment it relates to. She often renders her sculptures in found or everyday material, roughly moulding it into shapes reminiscent of formalism and, in particular, modernism. The result is an almost sullen or unwanted formal grace. The dialogue they initiate with history is similarly fraught. While Djordjadze often refers to a key moment in the past, her sculptures are more concerned with the operations of nostalgia and re-representation than they are with the moment itself. They seek, in Djordjadze's specific idiom, to represent the distance of the past as well as the past itself.

At the Berlin Biennial in 2008, she showed *Deaf and Dumb Universe*, an assembly of sculptures that took as their starting point the 'endless line' postulated by Austrian architect and designer Friedrich Kiesler, who created the exhibition architecture for Peggy Guggenheim's Art of This Century gallery. Presented as an array of spindly metal sculptures, uncomfortable wooden seats and bright white frames, Djordjadze's rendering of Kiesler's furniture appeared as if it had been found at the bottom of the ocean, its shine and sheen washed away and nothing left but its internal logic: the endless line running through the chairs and frames.

Her solo exhibition at the artist-run space Studio Voltaire in London in 2007, 'Possibility, Nansen', took as its starting point the Norwegian humanitarian and diplomat Fridtjof Nansen, the creator of the 'Nansen Passport', a type of passport given to Russian refugees escaping the civil war and famines of the early 1900s, their citizenship having been revoked. Djordjadze's show, made up of white plaster sculptures set on a floor strewn with coarse, crunchy salt, evoked the coldness and austerity of both Norway and Russia — a theatrical arrangement that flags up Djordjadze's interest in the phenomenology of the viewing experience. Two white plaster hoops set on a plinth that grew into and out of them, functioned both as armature in the psychological imagining of the state of 'Nansen' — evoking the clean abstractions of that modernist period encrusted with sea salt and brine — as well as Djordjadze's own style. Through this intermingling of the personal and the historic, Djordjadze stages the process of memory — a method of both reconstitution and, to an extent, destruction of the original.

These two facets involved in the process of recouping forms from the past were literally enacted in an exhibition staged at Sprüth Magers in Cologne with Rosemarie Trockel, her former tutor at the Cologne Art Academy. For the show Trockel and Djordjadze burned a series of sculptures and exhibited the ashes in the gallery space, illuminated by a series of cuts made into the black-painted walls. The 'show' was not only of artworks but also of the site — the site of production and destruction, and the site of the past's reconfiguration in the mind of the present. [Melissa Gronlund]

03

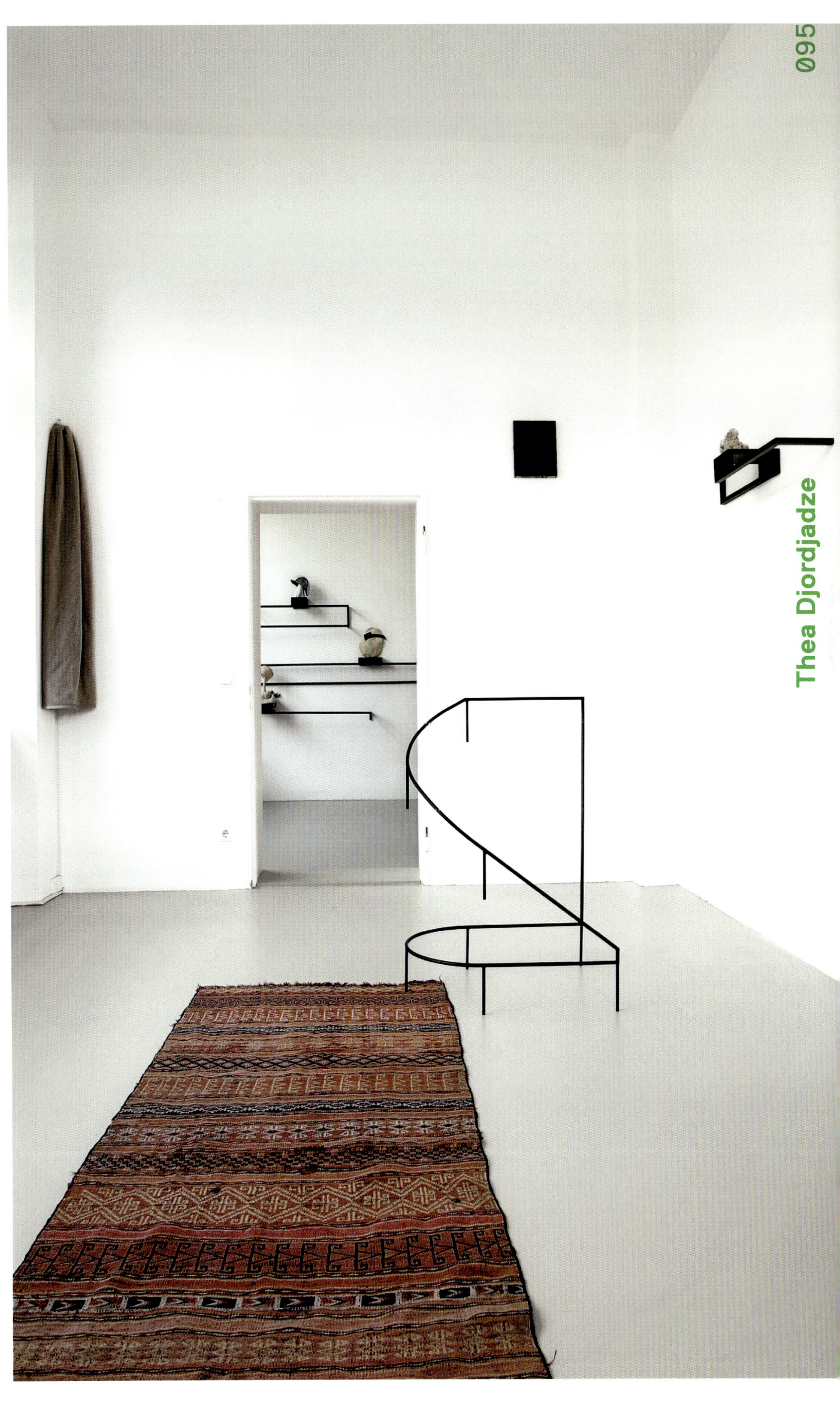

01 *Partly Departed*, 2007
Papier-mâché, foam rubber, paint, salt
105 × 31 × 32 cm

02 *Master Precision*, 2004
Fabric, clay, glass aquarium
80 × 35 × 40 cm
Plinth
112 × 37 × 37 cm

03 from left:
→ *Untitled*, 2008
Fabric
142 × 22 × 26 cm
→ *Untitled*, 2008
Wood, lacquer
119 × 248 × 30 cm
→ *The easy isn't done easy*, 2007
Steel, lacquer
100 × 70 × 50 cm
→ *Untitled*, 2008
Oil paint on canvas
30 × 25 cm
→ *Untitled*, 2008
Wood, paint, clay
22 × 100 × 22 cm

Trisha Donnelly is among the most elusive and indefinable artists working today. In the exhibition guide for the 2008 Yokohama Triennial, the location of her work was not specified on the floor plan but simply described as 'some other place'. This is typical of Donnelly's work, which is never obvious in any way and never suggests a simple interpretation. Resistance to a one-dimensional, 'fast' form of art consumption characterizes almost all of her work.

This inscrutability has not, however, prevented her from enjoying a successful career, or her work from being included in the collections of some of the world's most respected museums. In fact, her aversion to making things easy for art audiences — including critics, curators, collectors and the wider public — has actually aided her reputation in this era of the quick and uncritical ingestion of art. Donnelly grew up in San Francisco, a place that has throughout the last five decades consistently resisted art-world norms and doctrines. Like Wallace Berman, Jay DeFeo or Bruce Conner, Donnelly pursues artistic autonomy and independence.

There is, of course, more to her work than gestures of refusal to play by the usual rules of the game. Donnelly works in a wide range of media, including photography, film, video, audio, drawing, collage and sculpture. She once described her work as 'anti-materialist materialism', referring to the crystallization of a kind of non-object-based, even metaphysical, experience of the world into something material. But even this description does not fully explain the experience of seeing, hearing and feeling her pieces. Ultimately, she wants to create atmospheres of the non-existent.

In the beginning her pieces mainly took the form of highly subtle, almost ephemeral drawings and puzzling performances enacted in front of a live audience or a video camera. Since then, they have become increasingly cryptic and enigmatic.

Donnelly's sculptural work is as mysterious as most of her other pieces, yet, it feels almost inappropriate to talk about her art by focusing on specific media. In her spring 2008 exhibition at the Renaissance Society in Chicago, she again combined a wide variety of media to create a large installation consisting of a number of material and immaterial elements in which the gallery space turned into the work of art. This included the removal of all window frames in the exhibition space, the elimination of the freestanding walls, and the exclusion of the fluorescent tubes normally located on the gallery ceiling. In addition to these acts of subtraction, she included a sound piece in the space (a recording of church bells), a couple of benches that also functioned as the screen for the projection of one of the films depicting the movements of liquid, a few drawings, which were placed underneath the benches, as well as some photographs in a display case. Together, the installation clearly aimed at heightening the visitors' awareness of their own presence within the exhibition space, which, during the opening of the show, was activated through several events such as a dance party and a reading. [Jens Hoffmann]

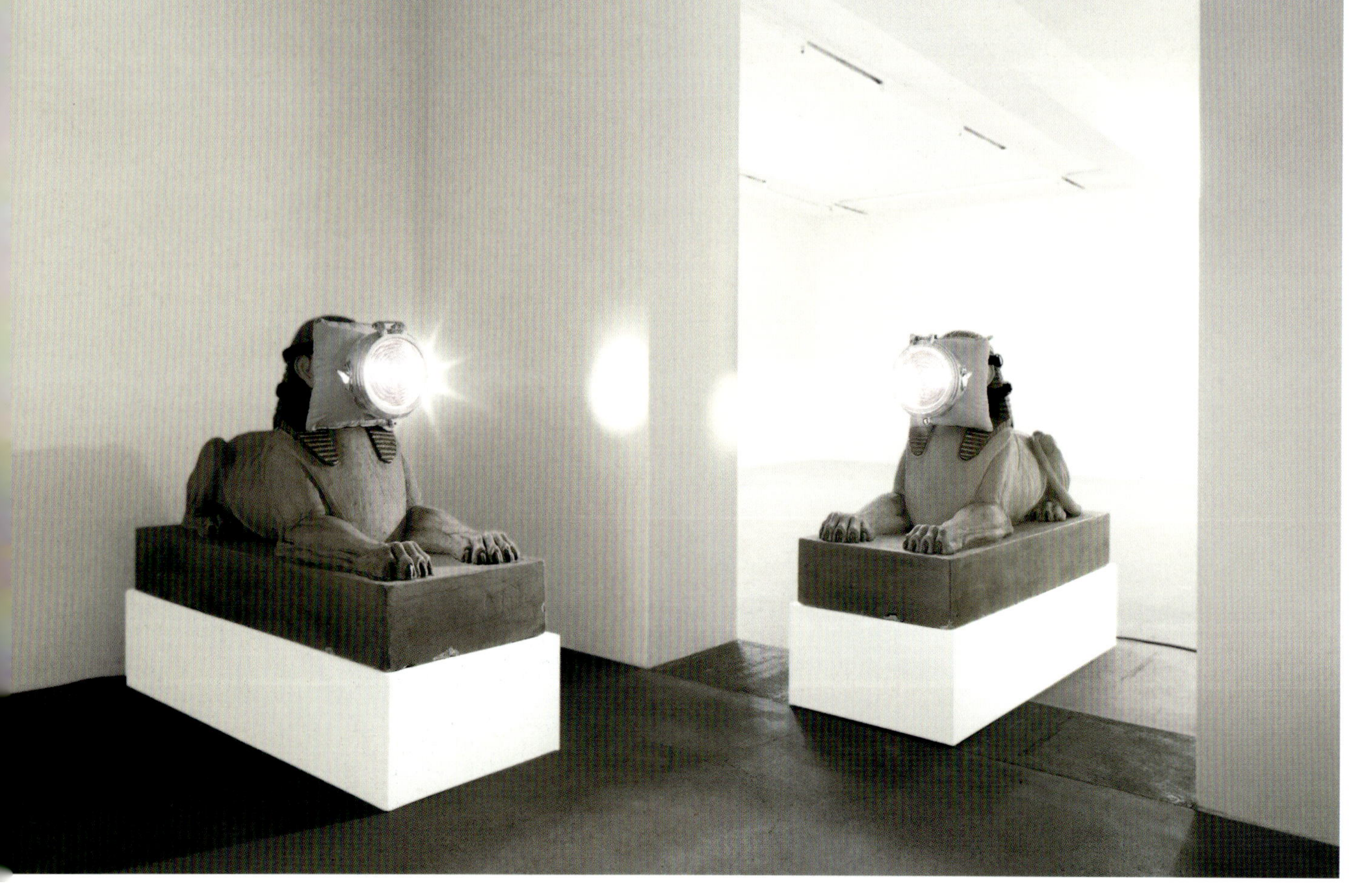

01

02

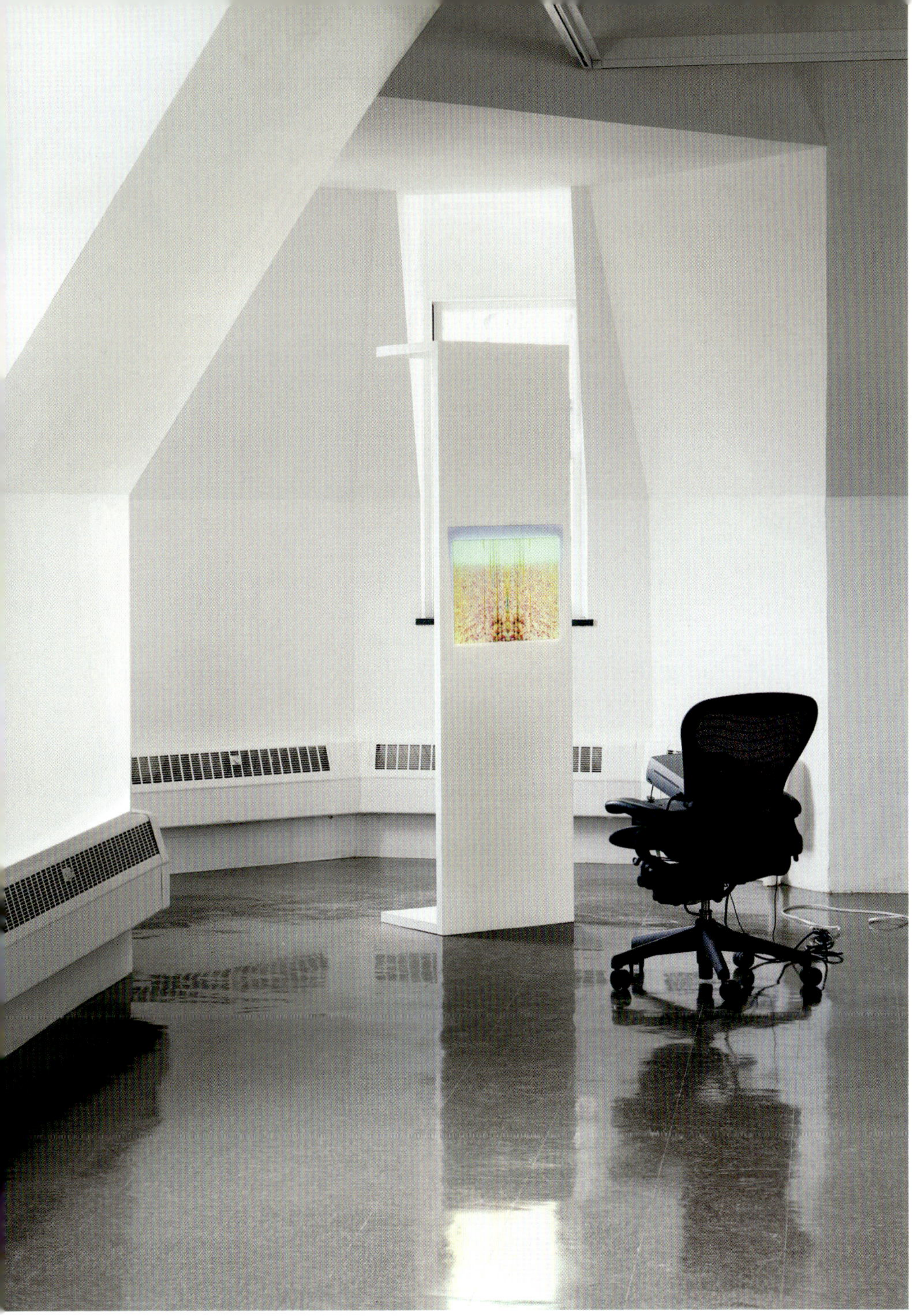

03

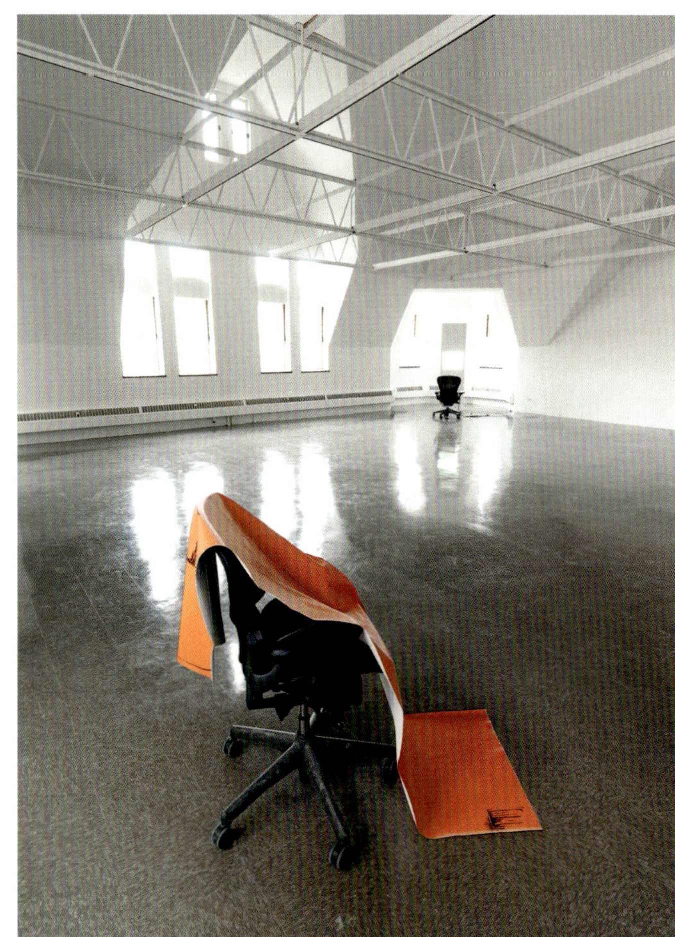

01 *Untitled*, 2008
Plaster, horse hair,
paint, pillows, belts, lamps
Each 91 × 152 × 58 cm

02, 03 'Roman', exhibition
view at Renaissance Society,
University of Chicago, 2008

Tara Donovan dignifies contemporary disposables, releasing these utilitarian objects from their quotidian tasks. Collecting common industrial products — pencils, paper plates, plastic wrap, sheets of glass — she launches them into a purely aesthetic realm. The sculptures and landscapes that she fashions from these goods deny their original function, further enabling the transcendence of matter. In a minimal yet commanding gesture, she shifts attention away from the cultural and environmental implications of consumer goods, and summons up the sublime.

Although the shape and finish of Donovan's sculptures alludes to the natural world — stalagmites, moss, coral reefs or cellulose — the majority of her original materials are the result of large-scale industrial production. This is a paradox that Donovan does not directly address but implies in her consistent choice of medium and through the scale of her works. In one of her early pieces, *Moiré* (2000), she creates soft and draping white coils with long reels of loosely spooled adding-machine tape. In *Haze* (2003), a vertical, wall-based work, Donovan mobilizes thousands of clear plastic drinking straws to evoke a wind blown snowdrift or pale honeycomb. Similarly, in *Untitled (Paper Plates)* (2005), she fashions a sprawling chain of irregular white spheres, recalling a coral reef or magnified leucocytes. *Colony* (2006) joins hundreds of yellow #2 pencils to construct a jagged landscape, while *Untitled (Plastic Cups)* (2006), a fifteen by eighteen metre expanse of disposable beverage containers, forms a gently rolling white terrain. Likewise, *Untitled (Mylar)* (2007) builds a cluster of reflective domes out of layers of polyester film. While these materials are a conservationist's nightmare, Donovan is not making a political statement or a critique of contemporary systems of production and consumption. Rather, she expresses an appreciation of the abundance of materials and the beauty that quantity and consistency can produce.

Donovan's subtle attention to the nature of form and material gives her gestures a strong visible presence. For example, *Untitled (Glass)* (2004) is a stack of rectangular panes of glass that she carefully cracks with a hammer each time the work is exhibited. The weight of the glass and the slow process of the tool's impact allow the transparent form to remain intact while revealing an infinite network of fissures and cracks — a record of the sculptor's encounter with her material. *Untitled (Toothpicks)* (2004) is also held together only by gravity and friction, while *Strata* (2003) is simply a coagulation of Elmer's paste, a glue for papier-mâché or collage. Donovan achieves density in these works by orchestrating clear or otherwise invisible everyday materials into a solid mass.

Like a magician, Donovan retains the mystery of her creations, but she never conceals the presence of her hand. Renewing familiar objects through their abundance, she elevates her chosen media beyond their everyday uses and environmental repercussions, evoking a blissful escape from reality. [Lillian Davies]

01 from left:
→ *Untitled (Pins)*, 2004
Straight pins
97 × 97 × 97 cm
→ *Untitled (Toothpicks)*, 2004
Wood toothpicks
97 × 97 × 97 cm
→ *Untitled (Glass)*, 2004
Tempered glass
97 × 97 × 97 cm

02 *Untitled (Toothpicks)*, 2004
Wood toothpicks
97 × 97 × 97 cm

03, 04 *Untitled (Paper Plates)*, 2005
Paper plates, hot glue
86 × 165 × 96 cm

05 *Untitled (Plastic Cups)*, 2006
Plastic cups
Dimensions variable

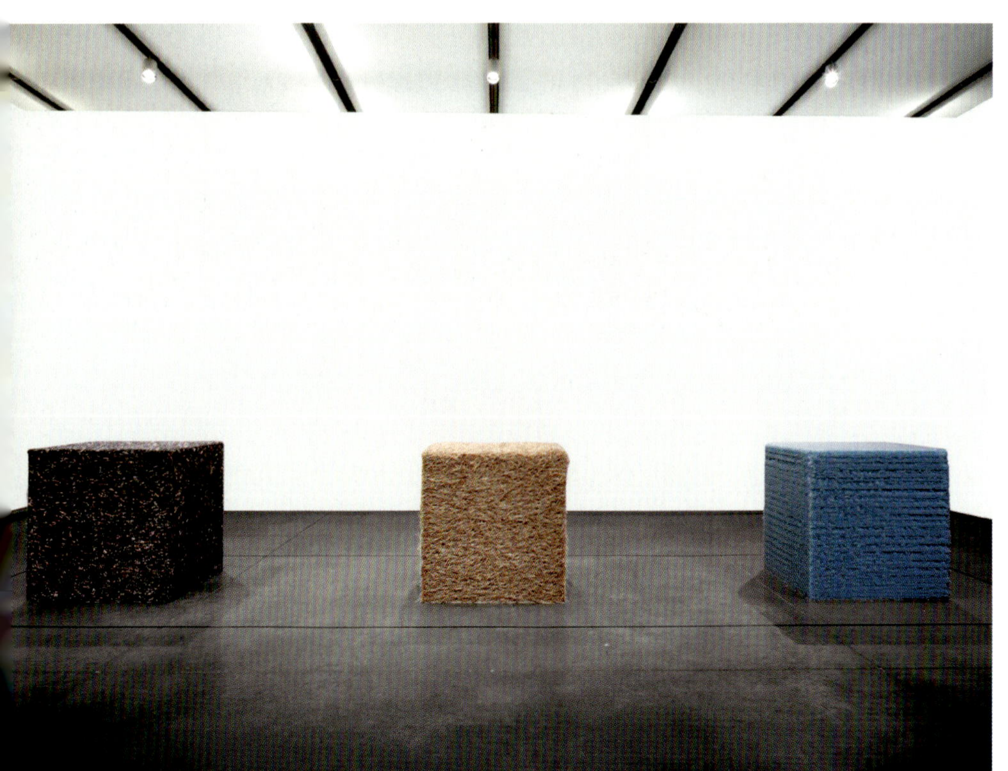

01

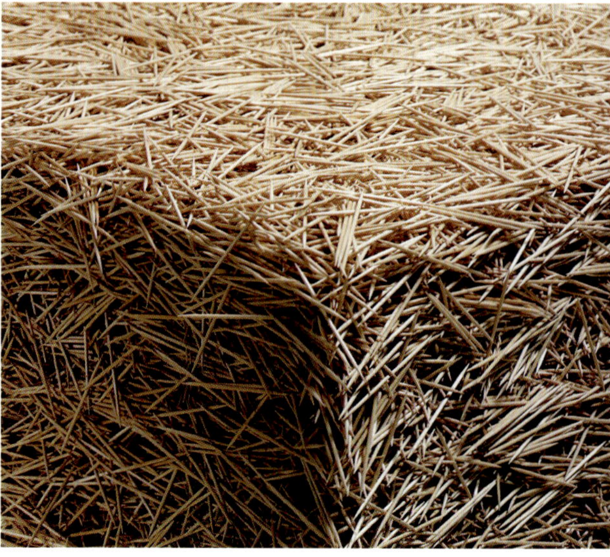

02

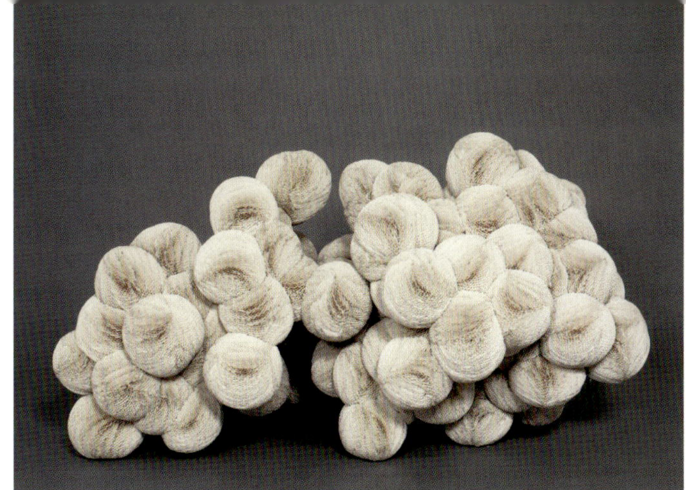

03

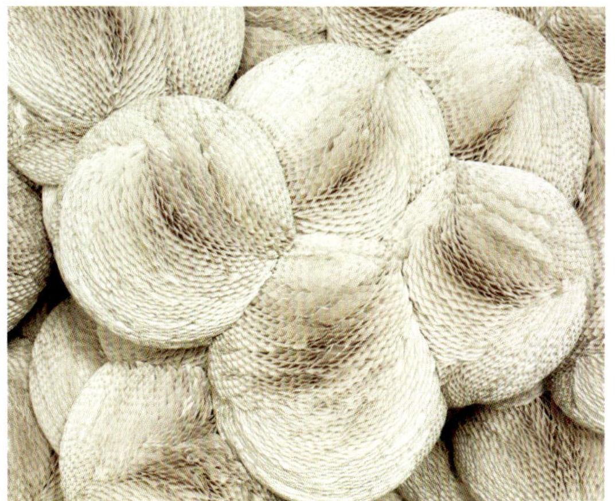

04

05

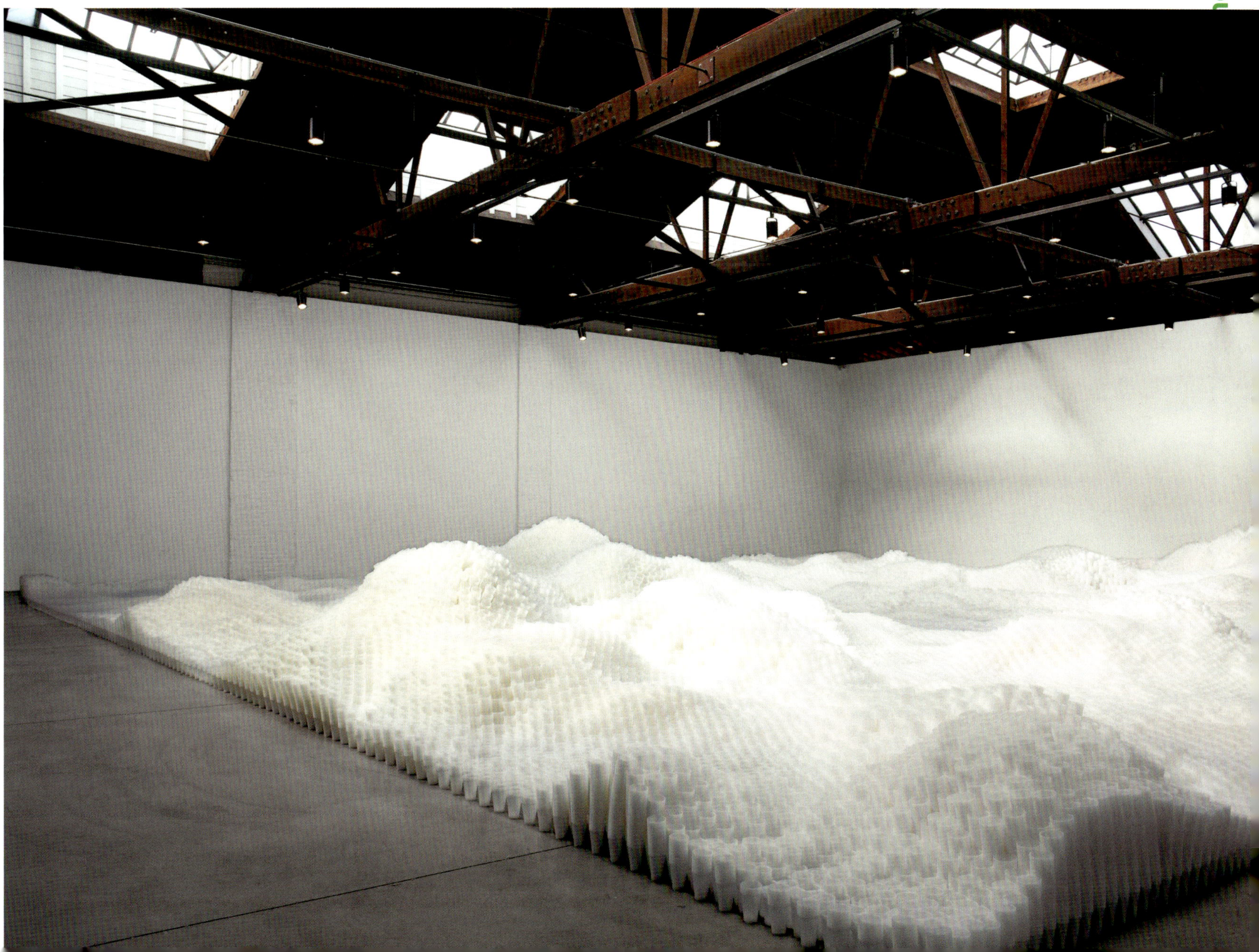

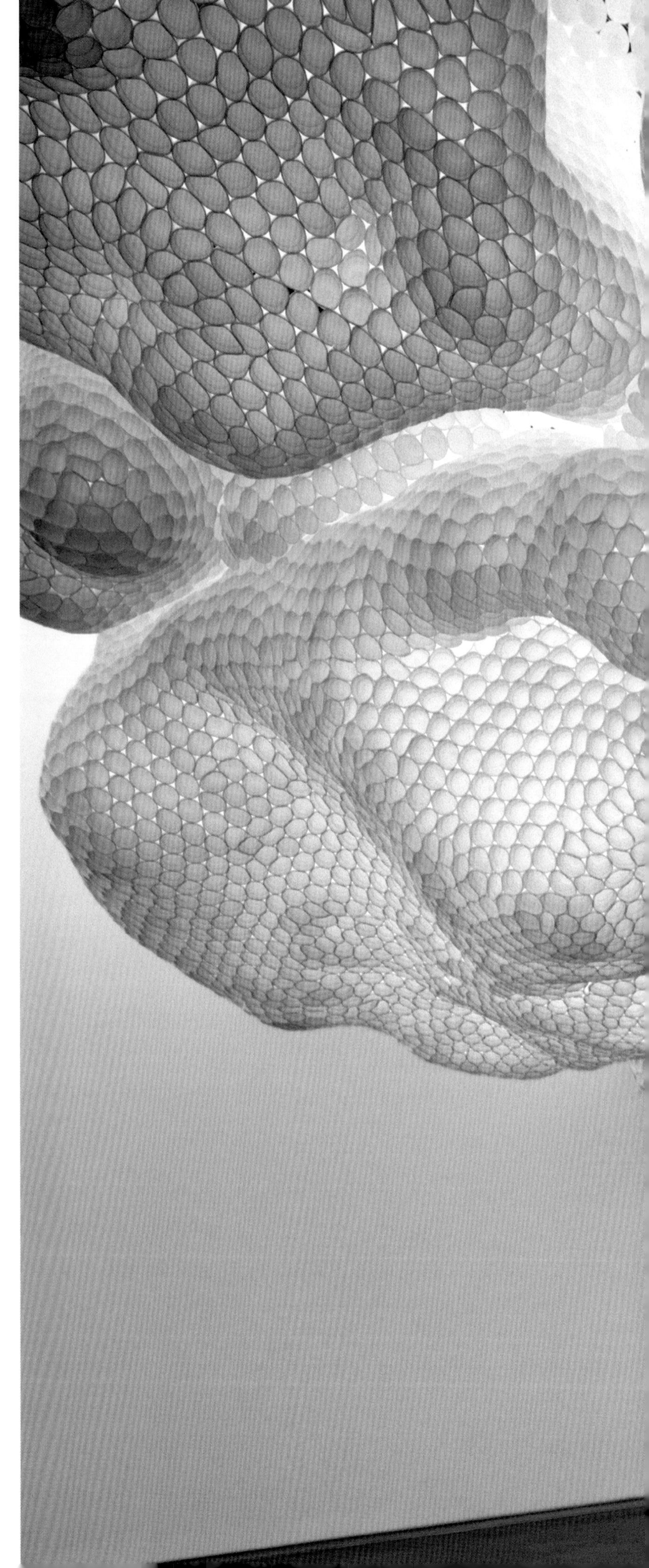

06 *Untitled (Styrofoam Cups)*, 2008
Styrofoam cups, hot glue
Dimensions variable

06

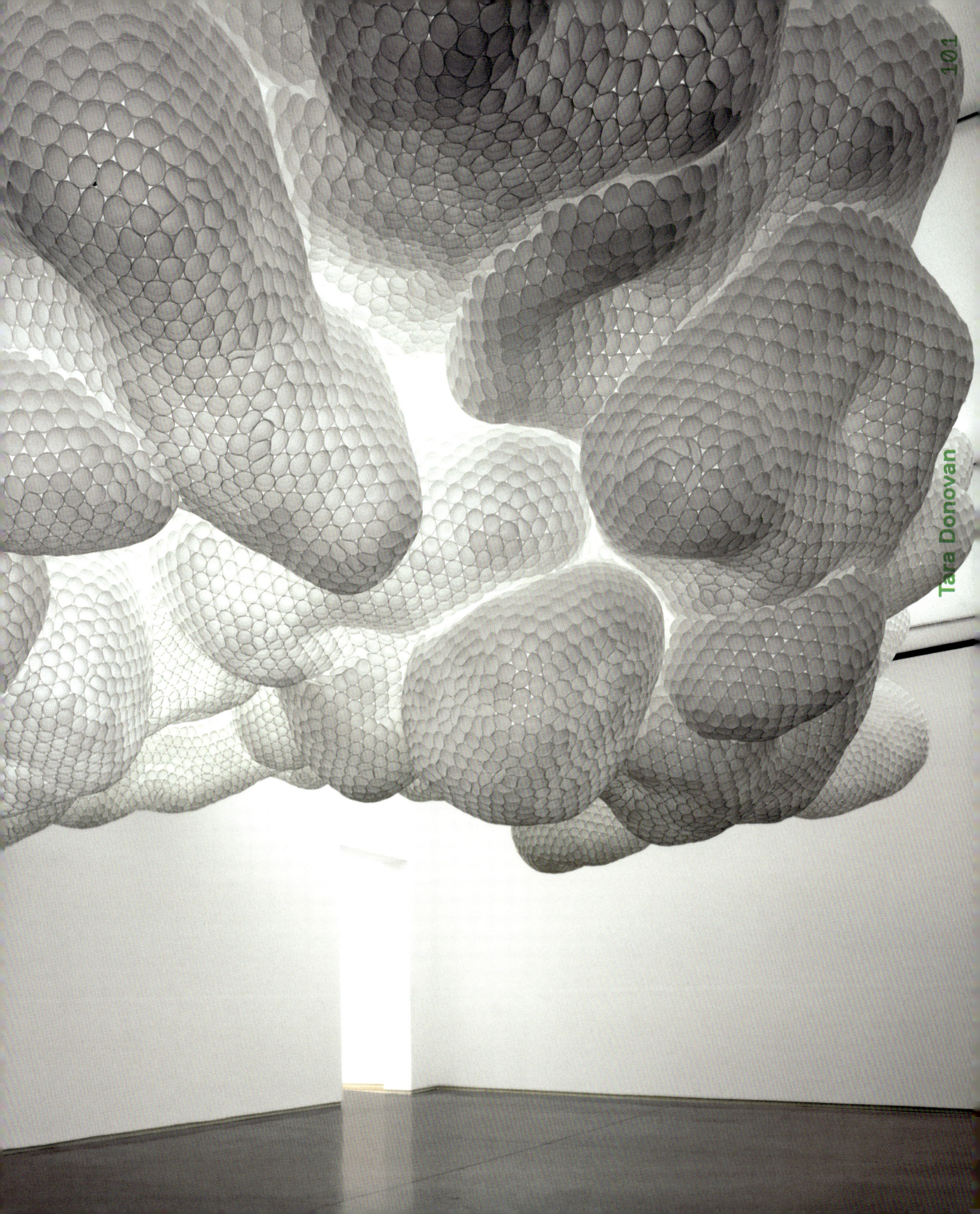

A free-spirited generosity and Jungian belief in collective creative consciousness informs Jim Drain's sculptural practice, whether he works solo or is immersed in collaborative endeavours. As Gorgon Radeo, his alter ego in the music and art collective Forcefield, Drain learned to knit, cladding himself and others in colourfully patterned, furred and fringed tribal knitwear that initiated his increasing interest in, as he says, 'the places where the body becomes obscured outwardly, through the display of deranged pattern and ornament'. After Forcefield dis-banded, Drain channelled his view that 'there is no making work alone' into formal gestures, sewing, gluing, dangling, braiding and mashing myriad pop cultural and craft items on to biomorphic forms that could arguably serve as stand-ins for the artists with whom he has collaborated. Certain bodies of work, such as his 2003–05 series of Yoruba-inspired hookahs and totem poles, exhibited with collages of wolves and children spiralling through concentric circles, Drain fondly calls 'ghost worship [...] a grieving [for the] wolf pack mind' — for the loss of group art-making. Now, however, while his use of decorative materials to express sensory overload still echoes his experiences of performing in a seminal noise band dressed as a living sculpture covered head to toe in weird sweaters, any historicism is funnelled into tactile, less humanoid shapes that offer equally synaesthetic viewing.

Jim Drain's shaggy, abstract sculptures have a shamanistic feel, as if drawn deep from his subconscious, conjuring open-ended symbols whose magic comes from their shocking juxtapositions of size, texture, materials and especially colour, as well as their brave use of neons, with which Drain strives for 'painful excitement'. Recent works trade knitted, kaleidoscopic, Op-art zigzags or stripes for bejewelled swaths of upholstery fabrics draped around wooden or metal structures, reiterating physical connections between solid, geometric forms and the human body. Some sculptures are comprised of actual furniture, including *Dress Up* (2007), in which a stack of coffee tables is transformed into an overgrown, pink, puppet-like mop dripping with white chains. Others employ puffy, sewn elements that either sag like Claes Oldenburg's soft sculptures or pop up erect, like sprouting plants. The stitched pillow form of *Orange Shadow* (2007), for example, resembles a helium-filled balloon or a tuba choked with orange fringe and serpentine coils of black and white chequered fabric. *Aids-A-Delic* (2005) is a topographic map of a giant's sandalled foot, whose pointy toenails recall a mountain range. The artist attributes his surrealistic style to 'not looking', and allowing the works to 'make themselves'.

Though Drain's work is psychedelic insofar as it mimics the colour collisions of art like that of the Mexican Huichols, it is not purely visionary. His work speaks to the history of modernism, directly borrowing from Cycladic, African or Middle Eastern art sources. The stuffed, intestinal coils that envelop nearly everything he makes recall soft toys, especially those used by Mike Kelley in the 1980s and 1990s. Drain's large-scale piece, *iii open iii closed* (2007), speaks to his split interests in ritualistic mysticism and academic art history. In it, doughnuts of fabric slung around poles make a raft to which a rag-rug sail is affixed, connoting an ocean of postmodern art supplies — and the ease with which the artist is capable of freeing them from previous associations. [Trinie Dalton]

01

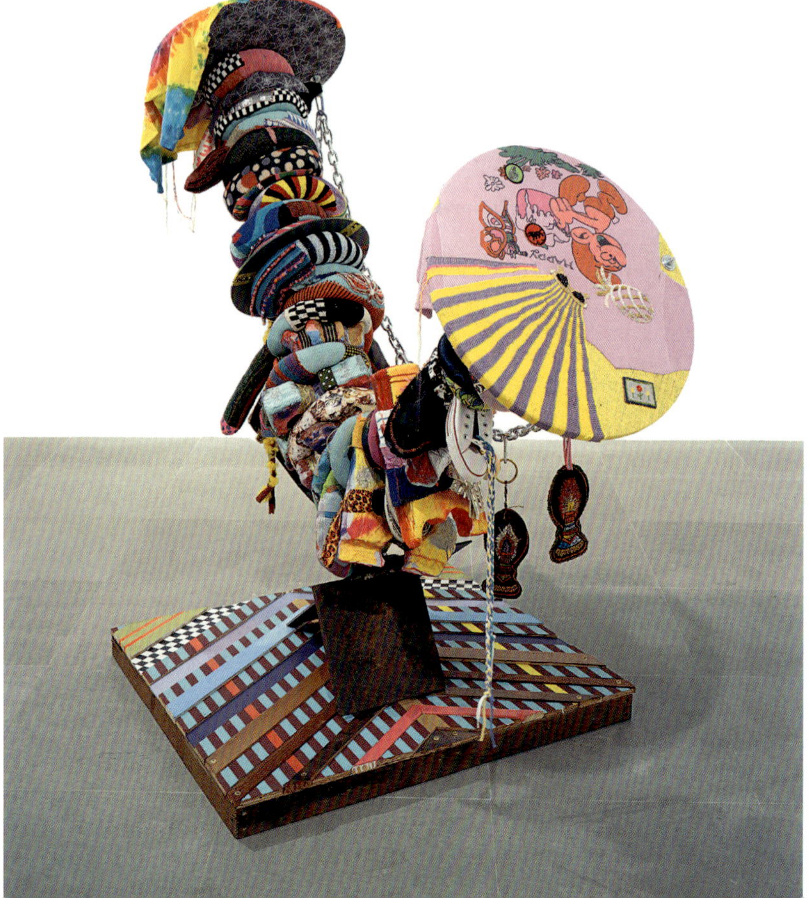

01 *Vagabond*, 2007
Galvanized steel pipe, steel plate, salvaged artwork base, hand-knitted doughnuts, plaster over cardboard giant beads, Olympic scarf, Happy Birthday Smurf T-shirt, machine-knitted and sewn embellishments, spray paint, chain, tie-dyed T-shirt, fashions, found crushed Arizona ice-tea can
178 × 109 × 203 cm

02 *Untitled*, 2006
RISD Museum of Art's totem pole, wood, Internet items, Marin County feathers, house paint, salvaged wood
427 × 427 × 122 cm

03 *Seahorse*, 2005
Machine-embroidered images, machine-knitted fabric, wheat-pasted and painted Styrofoam interior, threaded rod, wooden interior armature
170 × 119 × 48 cm

04 *Pinwheels* (with Ara Peterson), 2005
Foam core, glued coloured paper, fans, wood, cardboard, bearing hardware
Approx. 914 × 610 × 305 cm

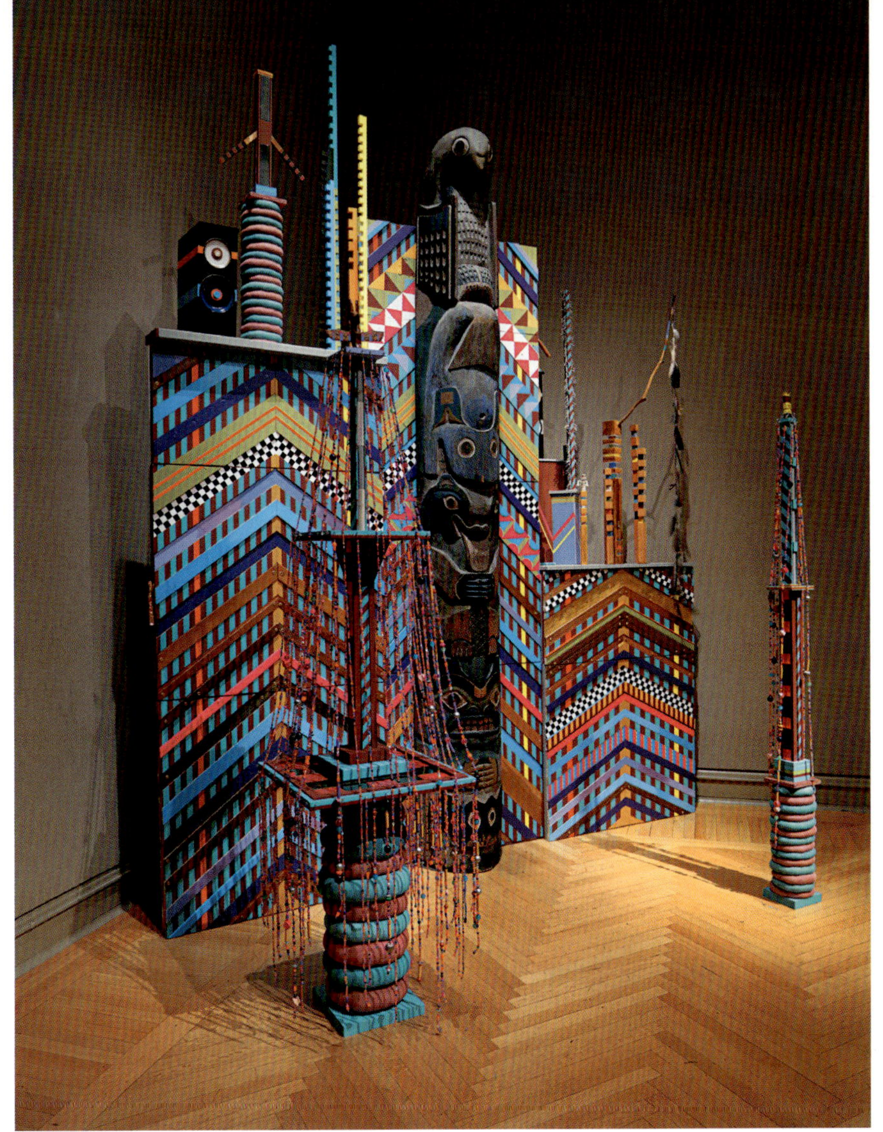

02

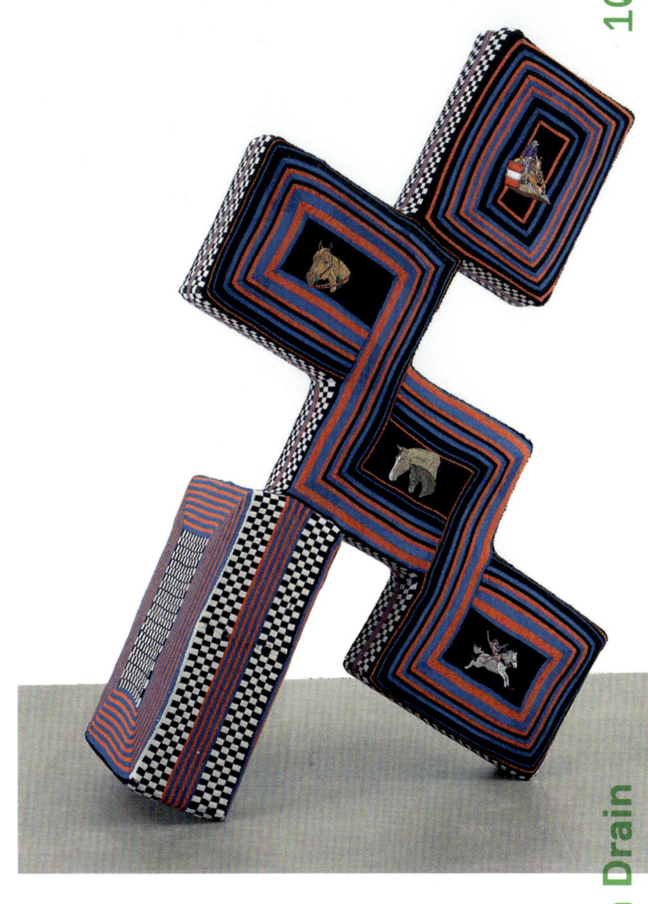

03

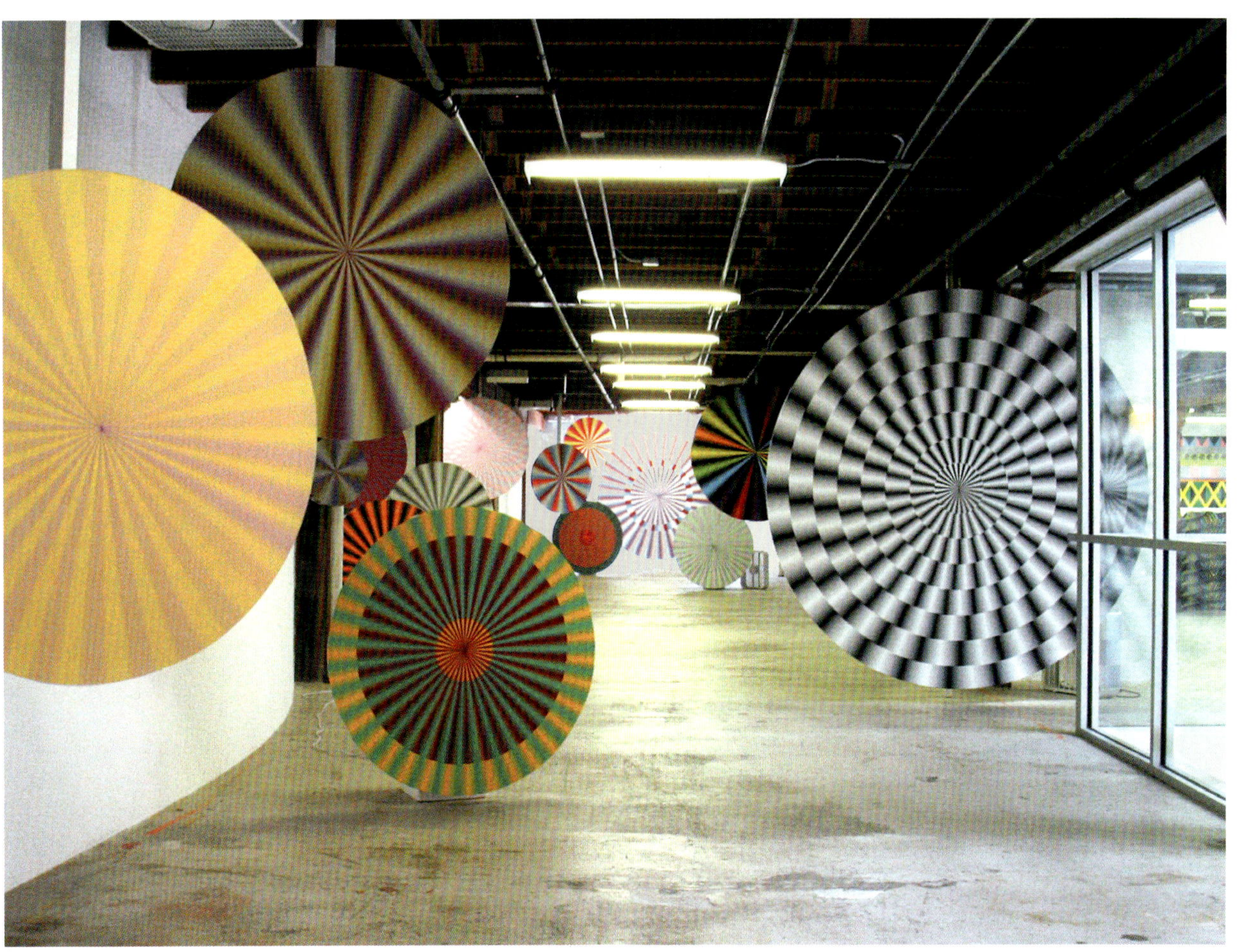

04

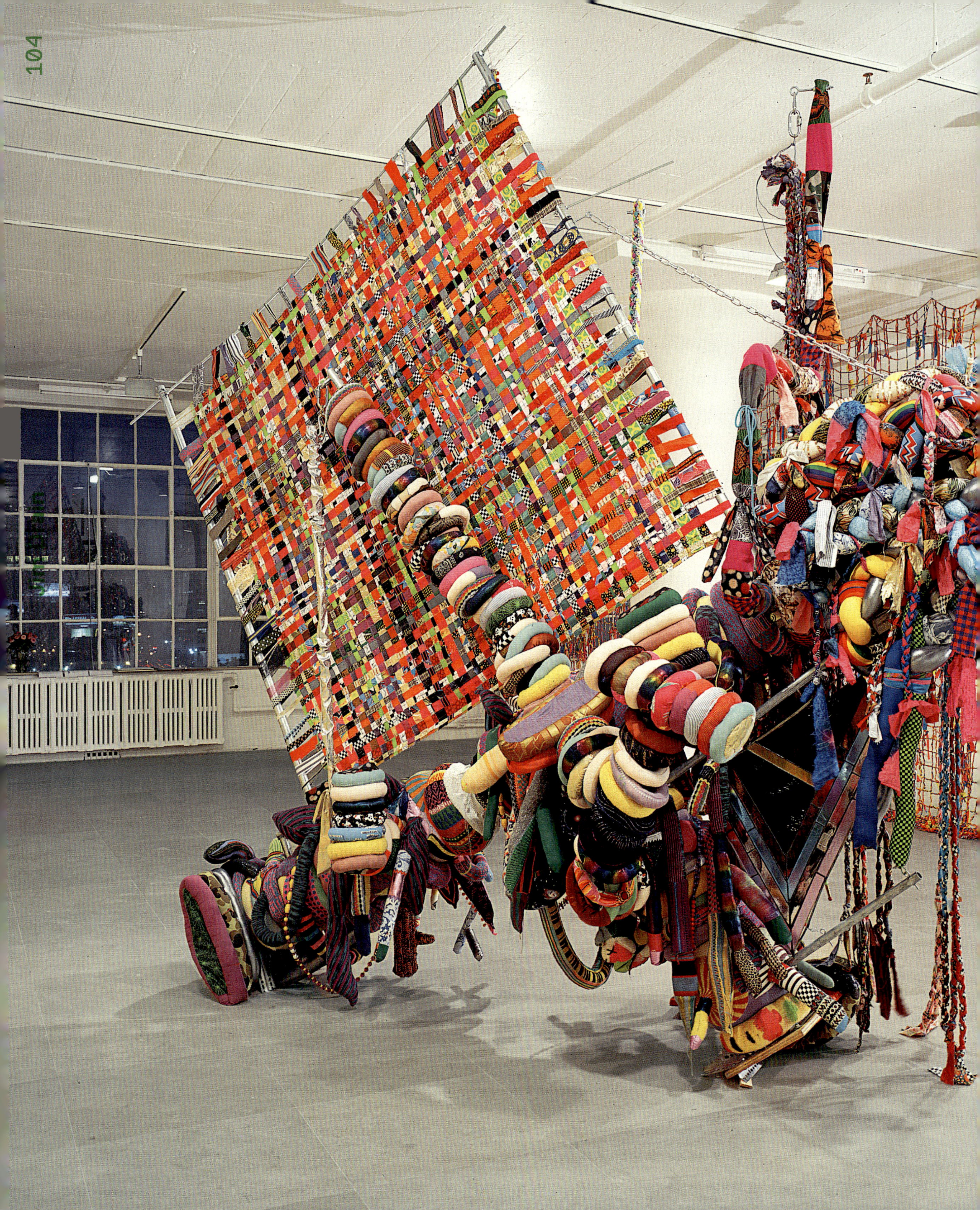

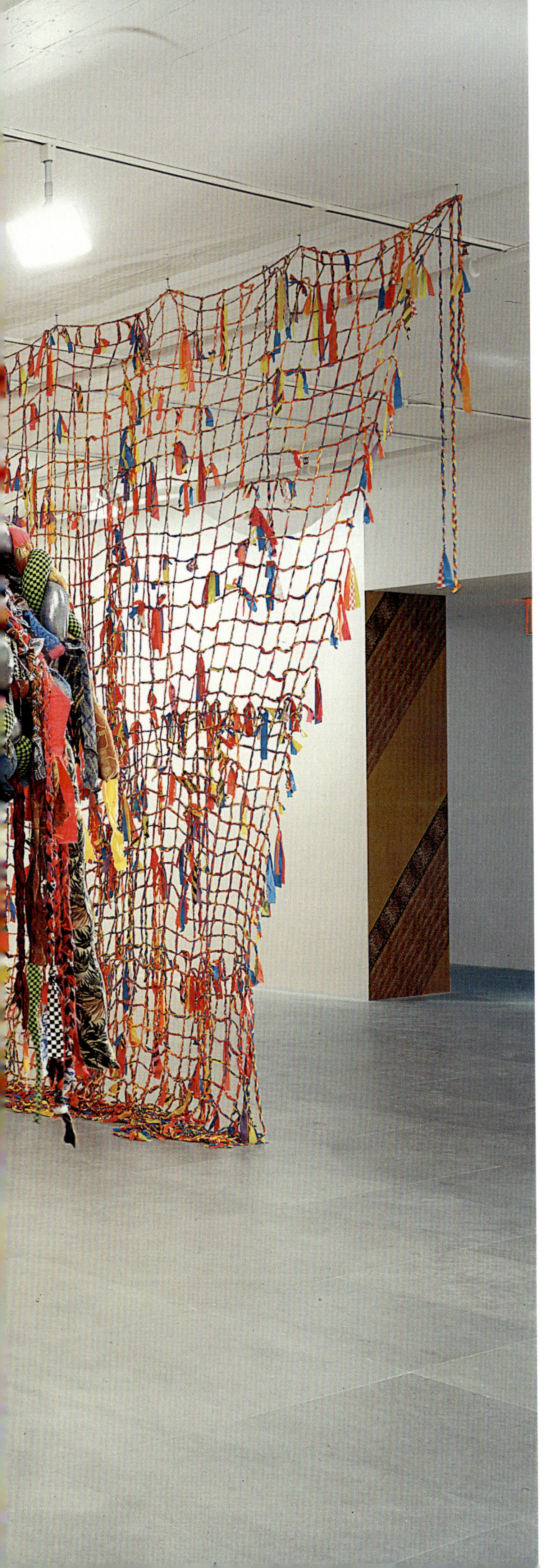

05 *iii open iii closed*, 2007
Scraps of knitted fabric, old textiles, ribbon, metal piping armature with a wooden frame, plywood, stained glass, aluminum head armature, paint, hand-sewn and beaded embellishments, galvanized chain, salvaged artwork scraps
347 × 140 × 401 cm

01

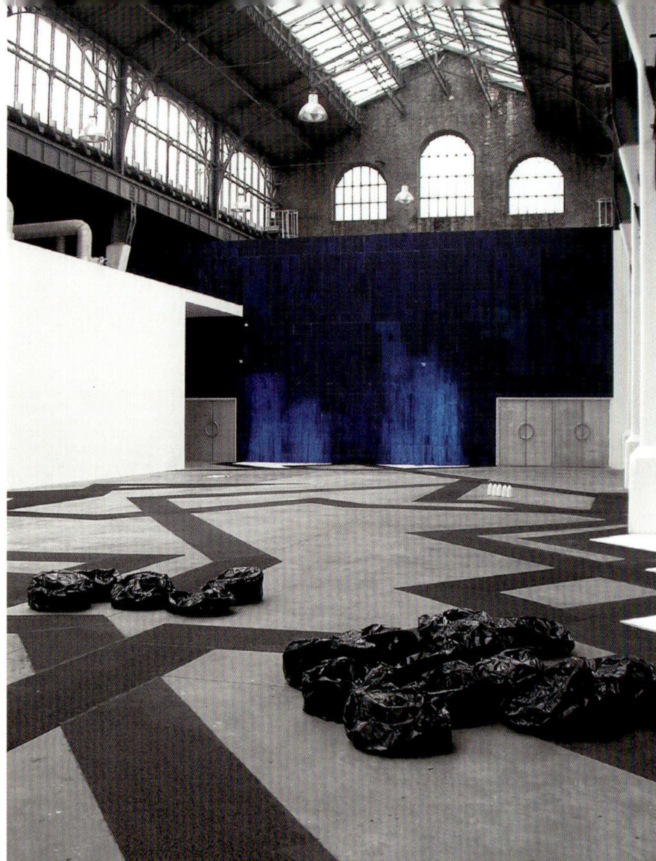

Latifa Echakhch's work is strongly influenced by her experiences as a Maghrebi immigrant living in France. She explores the codes and norms inherent to our societies while referring to a system of belonging and cultural attribution, within which she evolves as 'other' as well as woman. Echakhch is particularly interested in the concept of history and its processes of elaboration. Through her works, she underlines the recurring character of society's everyday practice of determination and constantly questions the clichés, generalizations and prejudices that ensue.

A piece of black tape is attached to a black and white television screen showing nothing but electronic 'snow'. The image evokes the millions of individuals pressing around the Kaaba at Mecca, a large black cube around which the international Islamic community gathers during the Hajj. Like much of Echakhch's work, *Snow in Arabia* (2003) is a simple and moving installation questioning how to define and identify a community in the age of mass media.

Echakhch takes images, objects and texts from given situations, which she then displaces and disrupts, to put into question their sense and appearance. She thus explores the links between a political and a socio-cultural reality. The mural painting *Resolution* (2003) takes up an expression that commonly appears in English as well as in French at the end of every UN security council resolution: 'Decides to remain seized of the matter/ Décide de demeurer saisi de la question'. The awkward phrase sounds like a poor translation in both languages, and this work challenges the role of an international committee that is authorized to make decisions during times of international crisis, while also questioning the role of the artist, suggesting her powerlessness to intervene.

The question of involvement is also addressed in the video *Untitled [11 March 2005]* (2005), which consists of a long-shot sequence of a street in Paris before, during and after a demonstration. The usual protagonists (stewards, politicians, demonstrators, police) appear on screen until the city cleaning services arrive, which methodically erase all traces of the event, until the demonstration begins again, in an endless loop. This cycle seemingly fails to fulfill the desire and expectation for change born in the last great collective contestation movement at the end of the 1960s. Yet at any point this vacated space could be appropriated and occupied by all.

By disrupting the relationship between the work and its exhibition space, through the modification or saturation of the latter, for instance, Echakhch resolutely appoints the spectator to the centre of her pieces' content. They form ensembles through which she expresses the complexity and contradictions of her research, and to an extent her own quest for identity. When, in 2006, she created the installation *Untitled (The Strangers)* for an exhibition in Romania, she demonstrated that her process did not limit itself to her own experience but tended towards the universal. By creating a large engraving of portraits, texts, as well as reproductions of artworks on a fifty square metre residential linoleum surface, she leaned into a section of that country's history, which she herself discovered. She began her research work on the avant-garde period in Romania, whose traces she could not find in museums, and as she became aware of the political reasons for this absence, she decided to rewrite history. Since the engraving on linoleum was the reproduction technique utilized to publish vanguardists' journals, which were then the principal vectors of modernity, she re-integrated an ancient means of communication within current social affairs. [Florence Derieux]

01 from front:
→ *Dérives*, 2007
Tar
Dimensions variable
→ *Vanités*, 2007
Black plastic
Dimensions variable
→ *Principe d'economie*, 2005
Bread made of sugar
Dimensions variable
→ *Principe d'economie II*, 2005
One kilo of sugar cubes
Dimensions variable
→ *A chaque stencil, une révolution*, 2005
A4 carbon paper, glue, alcohol
Dimension variable

02 from left:
→ *Fantasia*, 2008
Wooden flagpoles, metal wall brackets
Dimensions variable
→ *Speakers Corner*, 2008
Wood
40 × 60 × 40 cm
Tate Modern, London

03 *Erratum*, 2004
Broken tea glasses
Dimensions variable

04 *Principe d'economie II*, 2005
One kilo of sugar cubes
Dimensions variable

Overleaf:

05 *A chaque stencil, une révolution*, 2008
A4 carbon paper, glue, alcohol
Dimension variable
Tate Modern, London

02

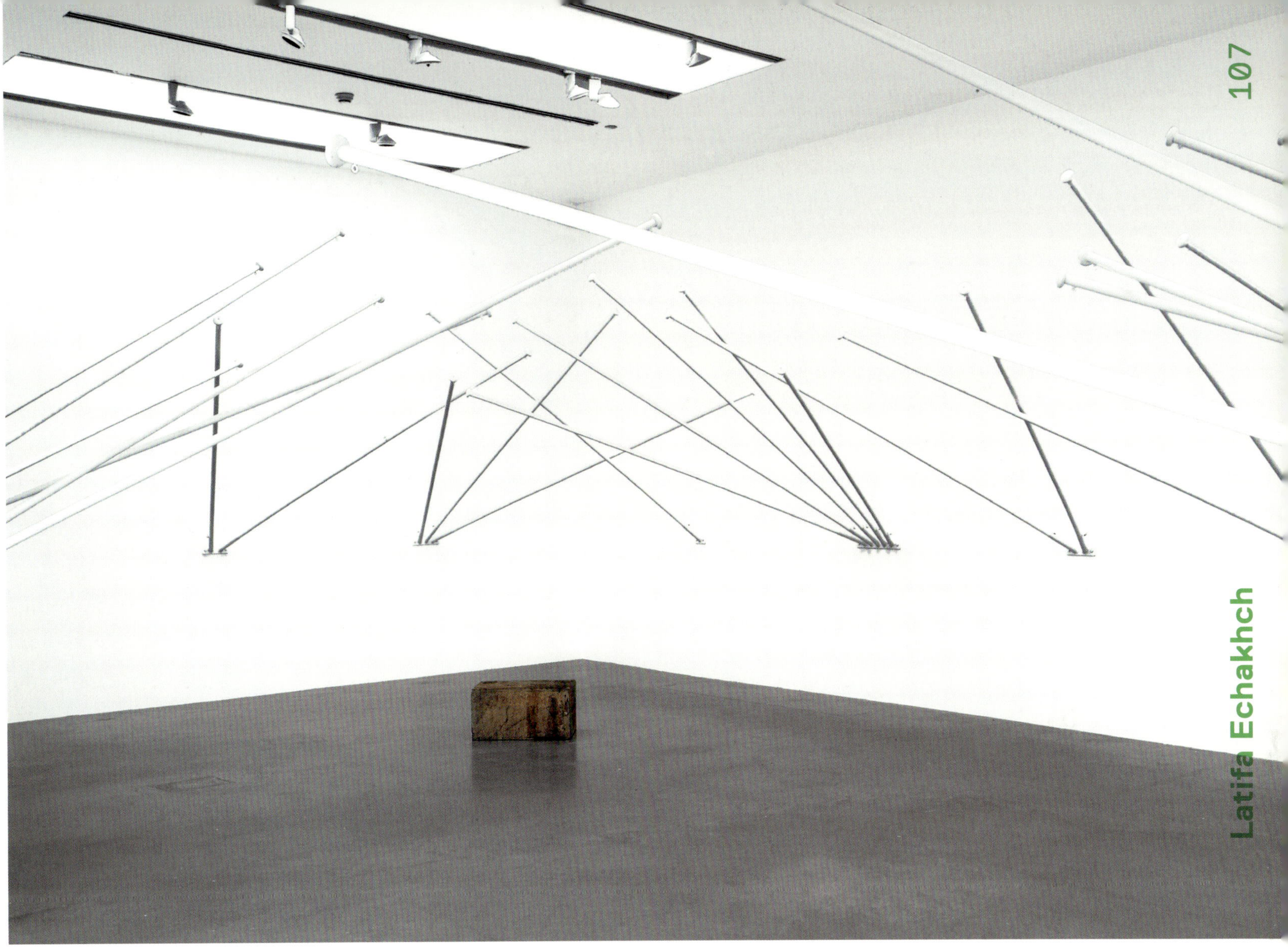

03

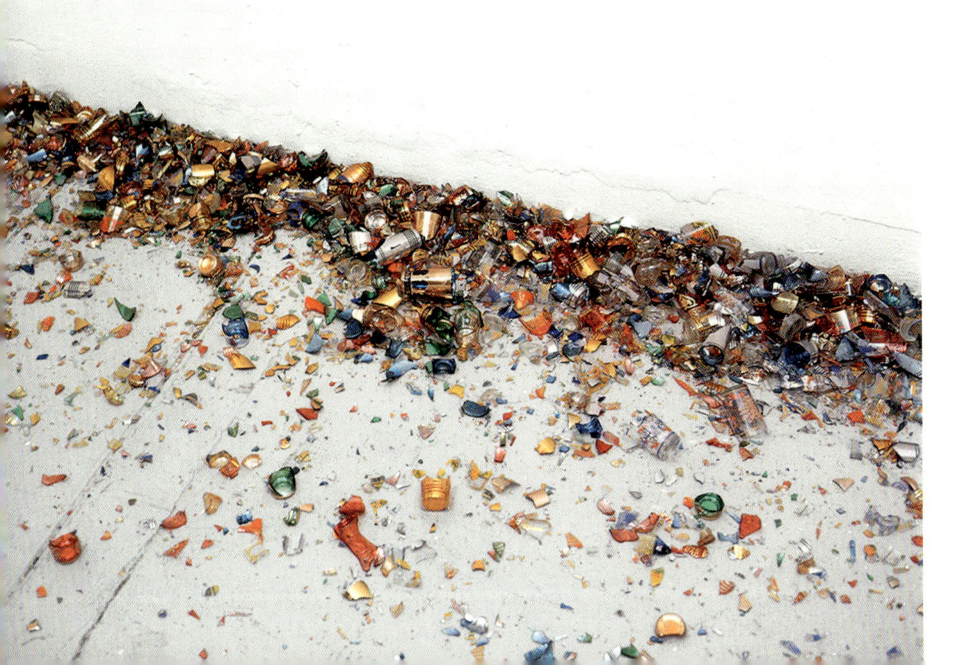

04

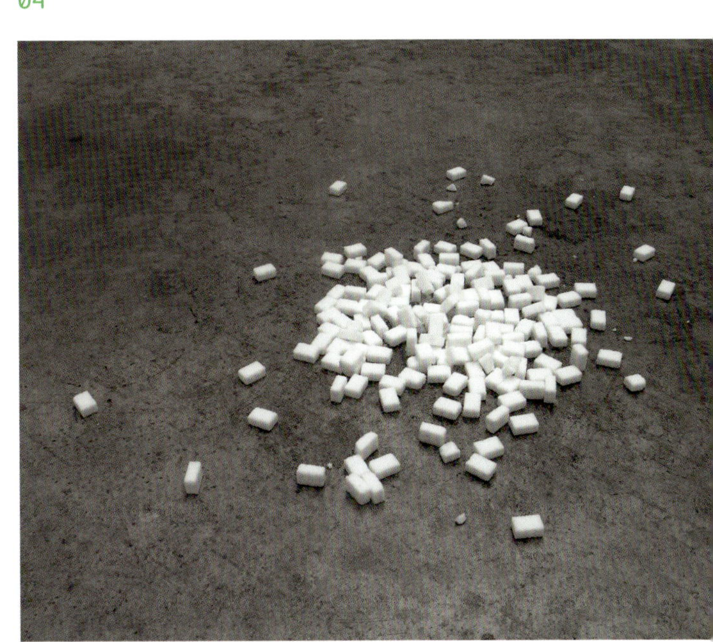

Latifa Echakhch

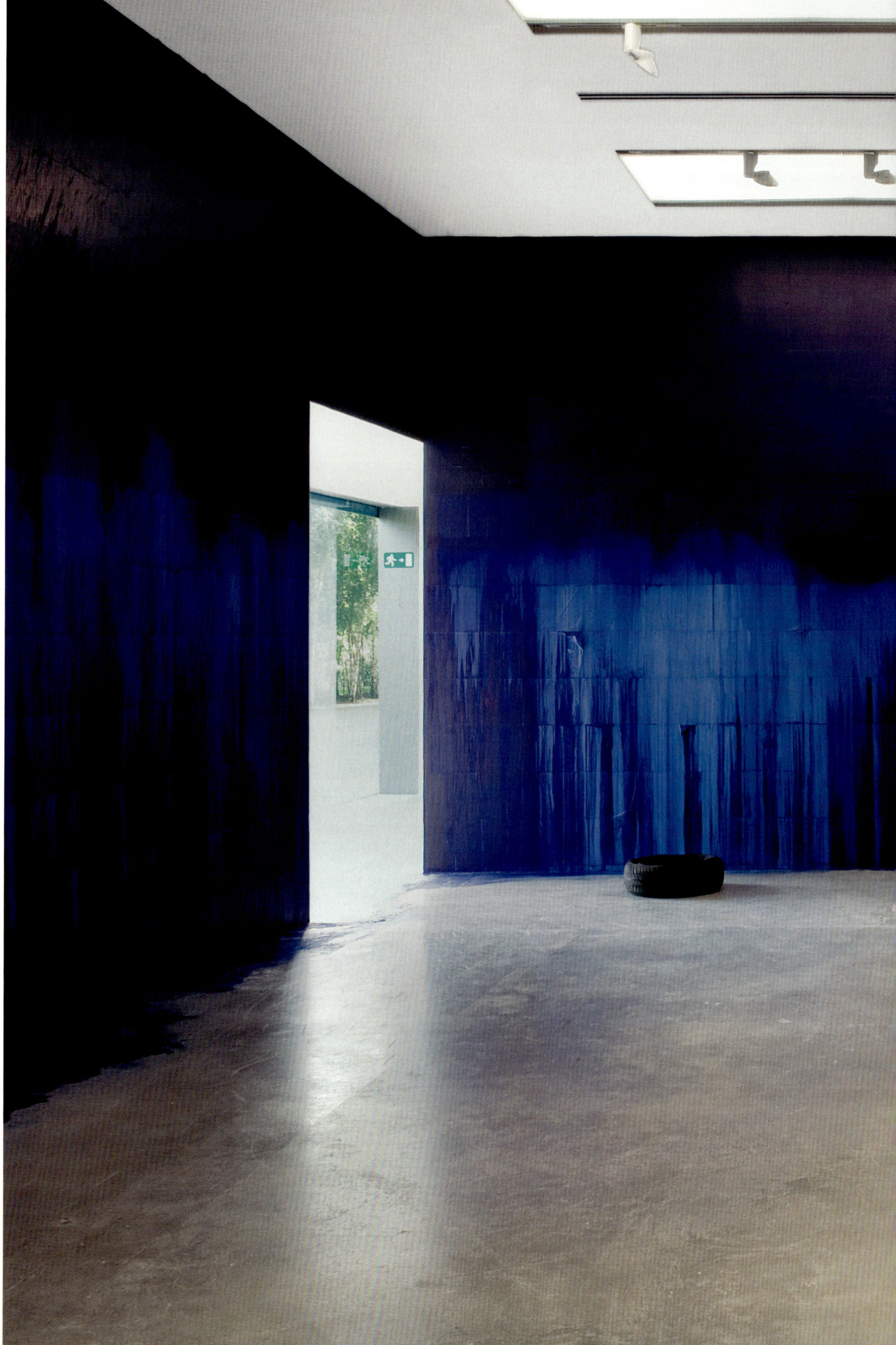

06

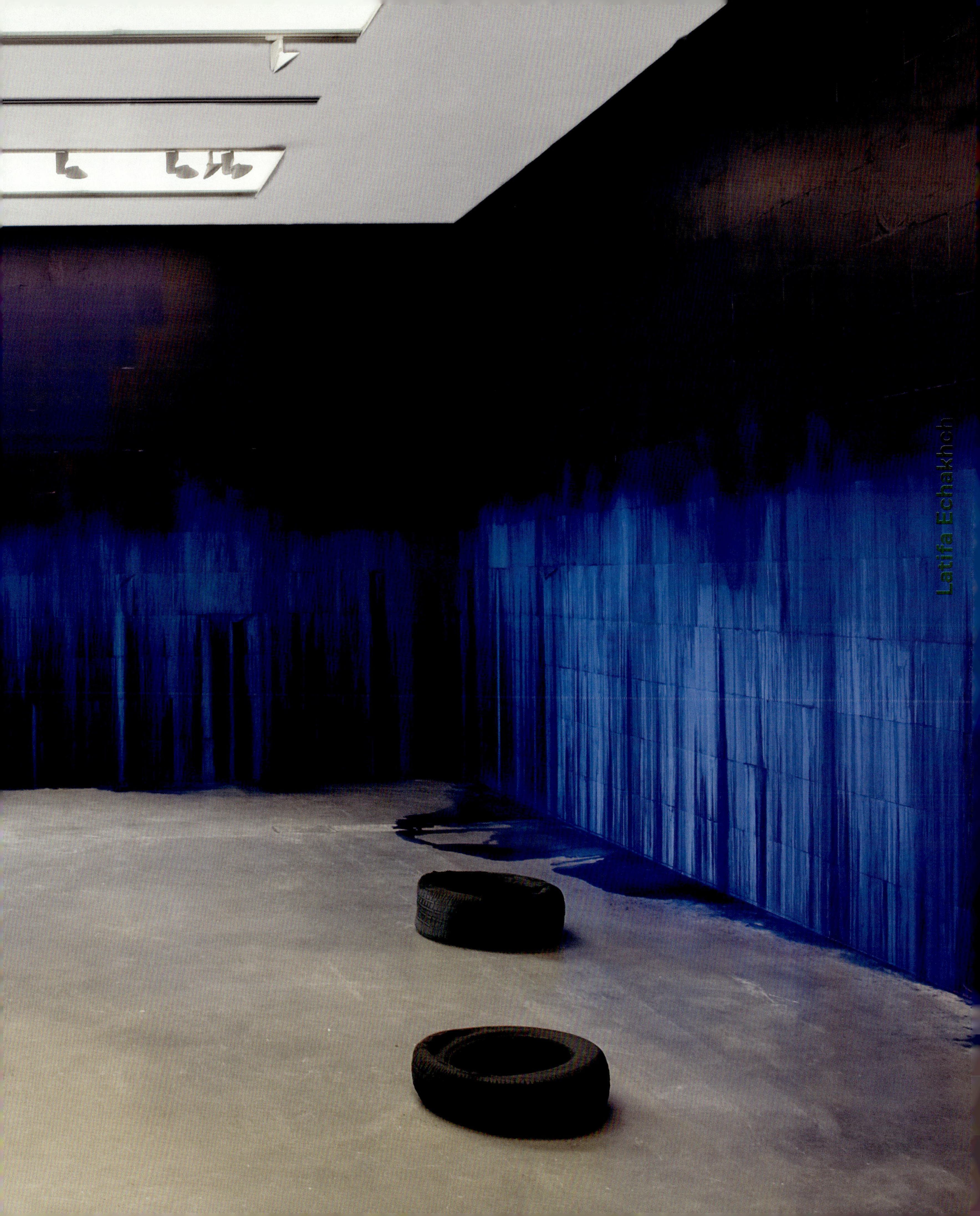

Iran do Espírito Santo's works trigger engaging plays in different fields and levels — between abstraction and figuration, geometry and nature, perception and representation, appearance and reality. Often fabricated by artisans and technicians, they have a highly slick and polished finish, and even if made with the artist's own hand (such as his laborious drawings or murals), no gestural traces are left behind. This distinguishes Espírito Santo from most of his compatriots, whose works often bear the traces of their fabrication, origin or history. In this sense, one could associate his work with the mid-century Concrete artists from São Paulo, with their passion for rigour, geometry and precision; nevertheless, Espírito Santo's works are both more ironic, humorous and duplicitous than those of his more severe and self-righteous predecessors.

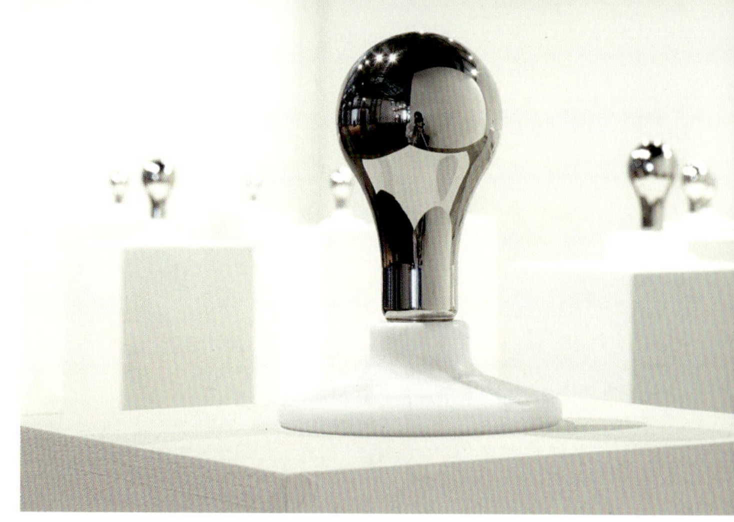

01

The series *Corrections*, which the artist began in 2001, is a good example. It consists of groups of six to eleven polyhedrons made of granite and arranged on the floor, apart from each other. The compositions resemble gardens of rocks that have been stylized and assume abstract geometric features, and the reference to the precursor of Minimalism, Tony Smith and his *Wandering rocks* (1967) is evident, yet here the sculptural pun is with representation, as the minimalist abstractions or reductions of rocks are indeed made of the real thing: granite, itself a traditional material of sculpture.

Restless, a series of that started in 1997, is another example. Each sculpture is a geometrically shaped piece of twelve millimetre thick glass cut at right angles resting against a wall. Although each object is made of a single piece of glass, its surface has been treated in up to three different ways — transparent glass, sandblasted glass and mirror. The effect is of several sheets of glass of different qualities propped against each other, one plane superimposed against the other one. The work is thus highly pictorial, and the reference to abstract geometry is both evident and playful (the Concretistas come to mind once again).

White box, Grey box and *Black box* (all 2003), made in white marble, sandstone and black marble respectively, establish further plays with geometric abstraction and the tradition of sculpture. Each one is a parallelepiped and is presented solemnly on a plinth, yet their small dimensions (12 × 33 × 23 cm) give away their quite ordinary model: a shoebox. In another play on form and material, the 2008 work *Deposition* consists of a large picture frame made of granite leaning against the wall. It is a clearly recognizable form, yet also obtuse as an object because it has the structure of conventional pictorial presentation but contains no image other than a black void of granite undifferentiated from the surrounding mat and picture frame. [Adriano Pedrosa]

02

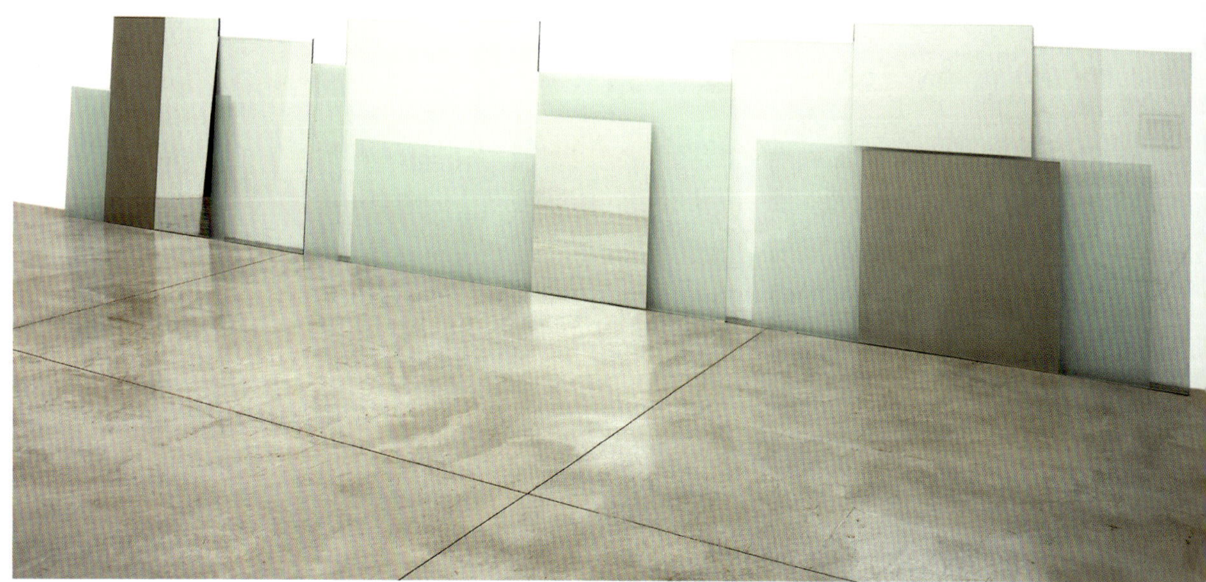

01 *Untitled*, 2005
Stainless steel, Teflon, wood
Approx. 17 × 6 × 4 m

02 *Restless 25*, 2005
Mirrored and sandblasted glass
142 × 733 × 1 cm

03 *Debris 17*, 2003–04
Sandstone
23 × 69 × 55 cm

04 *Water Glass 2*, 2008
Crystal
14 × 9 × 9 cm

05 *Can K*, 2008
Granite
42 × 31 × 31 cm

Overleaf:

06 *Corrections C*, 2007
Granite
Dimensions variable

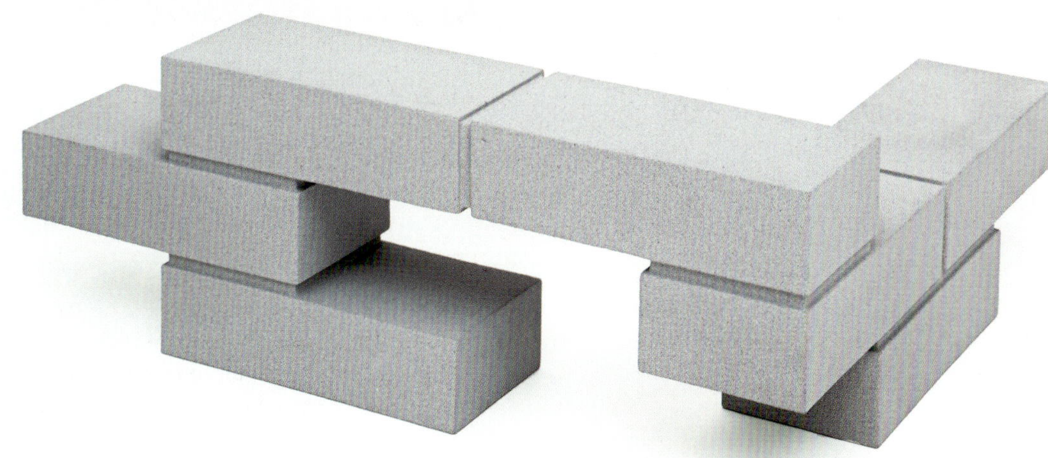

03

04

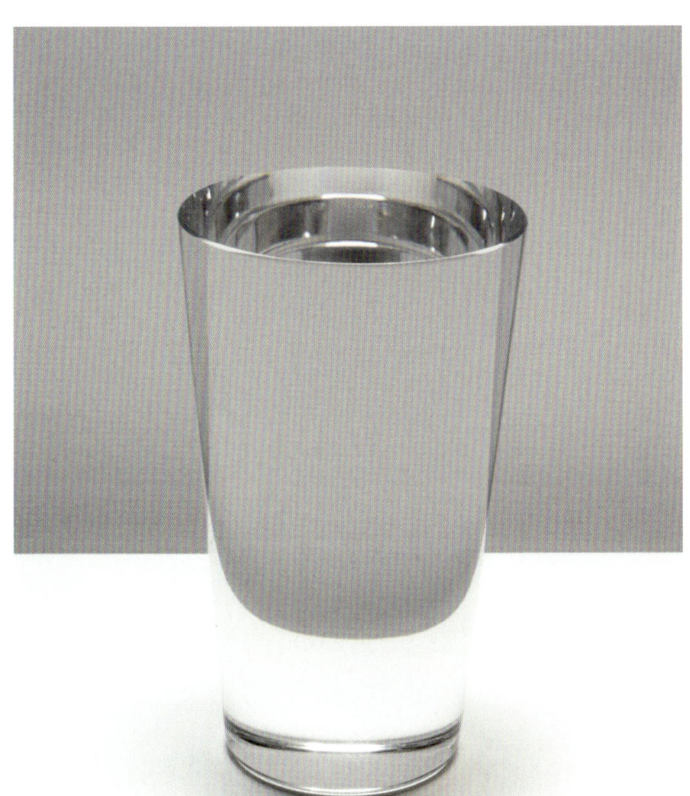

05

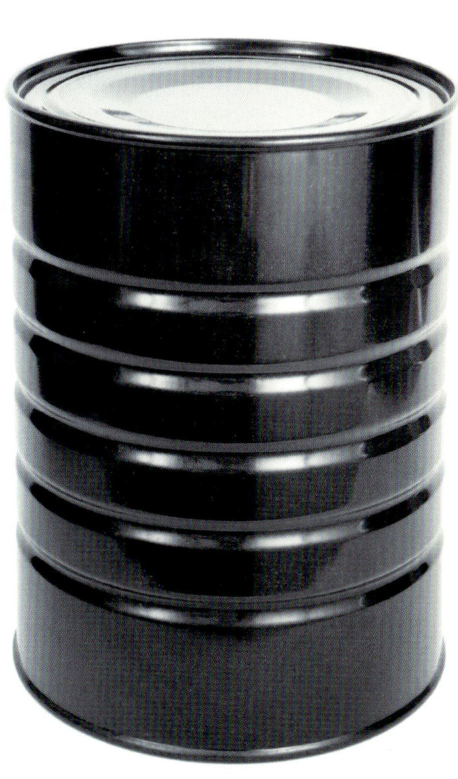

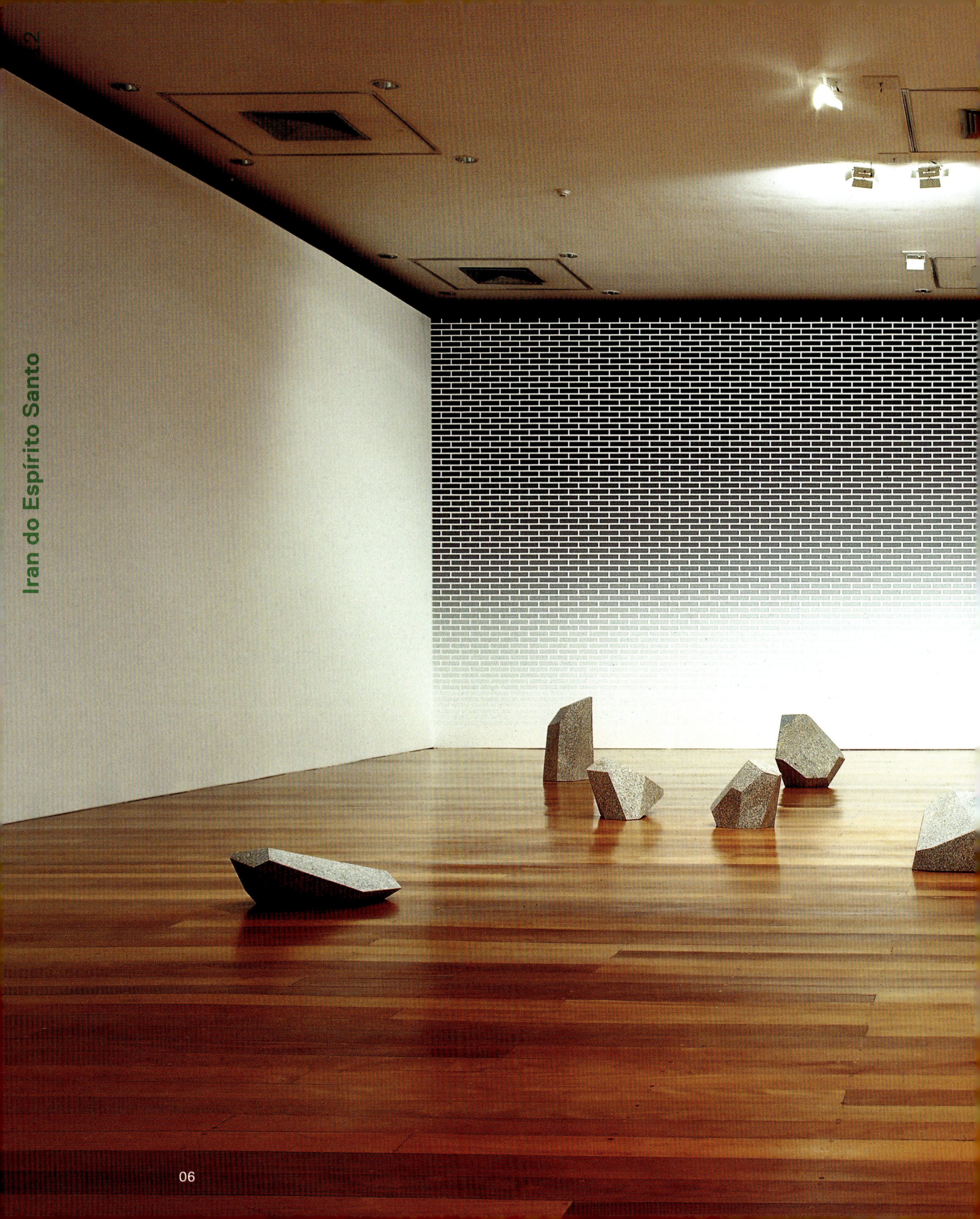

Iran do Espírito Santo

06

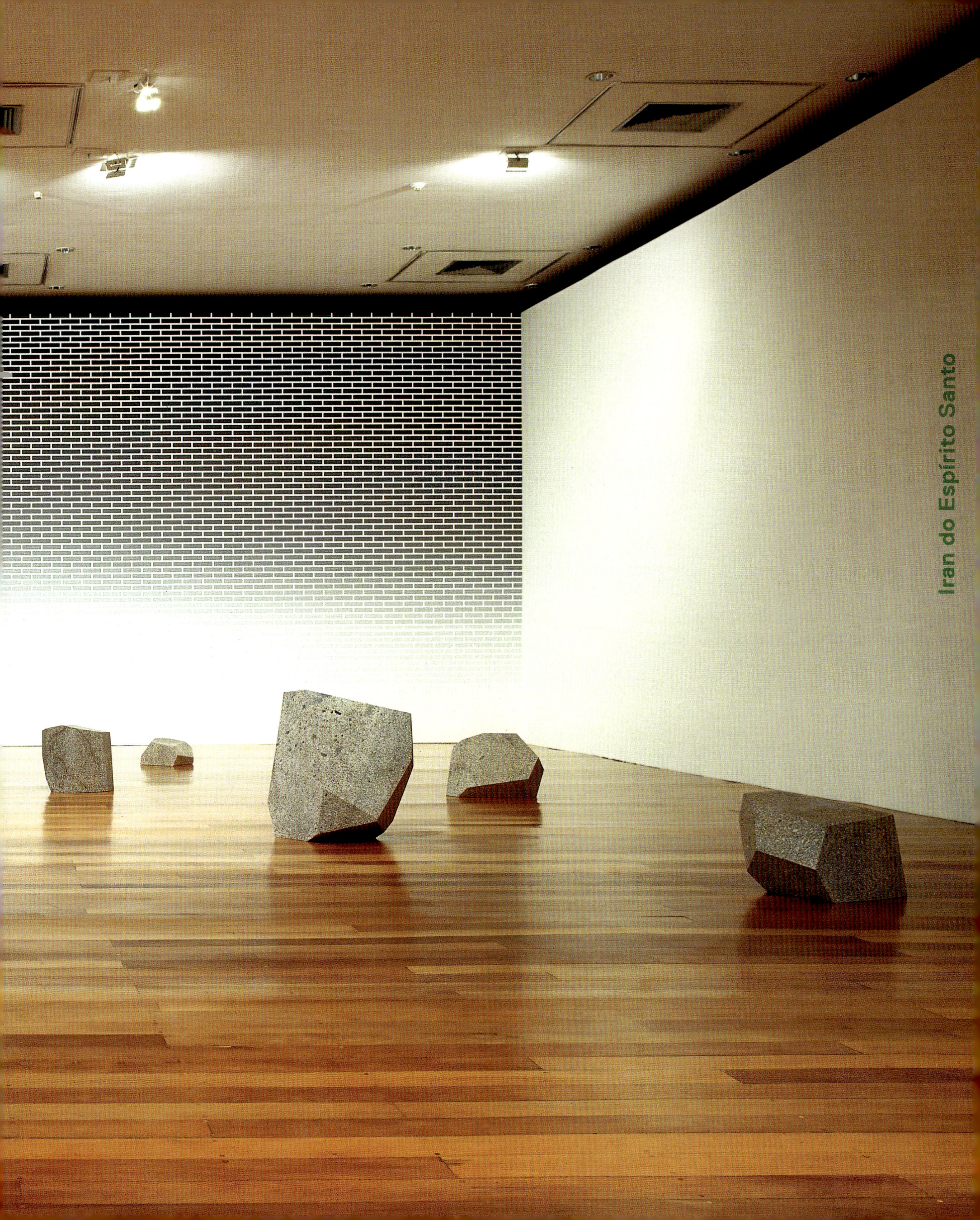

Iran do Espírito Santo

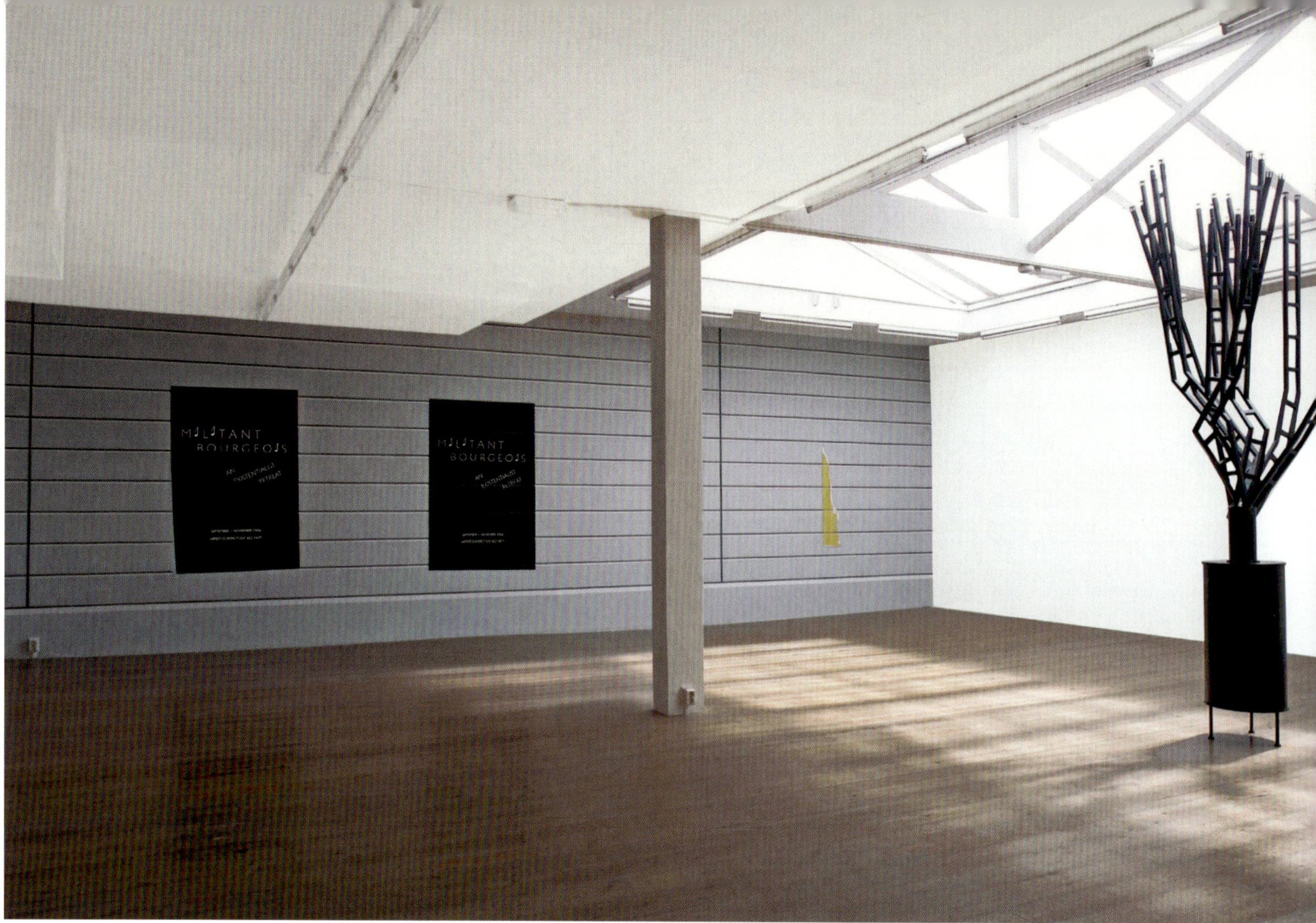

01

The work of art's autonomy, a belief asserting that the entirety of the artwork's meaning is located in the object itself, has been repeatedly challenged in the history of art. This tradition includes Duchamp's declaration about the viewer's contribution to the creative act, as well as Minimalism's theatrical emphasis on the viewer's experience. According to this approach, art objects are never isolated monads, but objects around which a web of negotiations is constantly at work. Chris Evans builds on this tradition by bringing to the surface the social, economic and cultural networks within which a work of art is produced, consumed and transformed.

Evans not only uncovers normally concealed parts of the art system but also actively intervenes in them. In the making of his work he typically involves actors from outside the cultural industry. For the project *Militant Bourgeois* (2006) he built an improbable retreat for artists, a residence placed under the orbital motorway in Amsterdam. Holland subsidizes its artists with a state patronage scheme offering stipends, residencies and grants. To refer to this tradition, Evans asked the living descendant of seventeenth-century art patron Baron Jan Six — famously immortalized an exquisite portrait by Rembrandt — to suggest the design of the chimney for the wood-burning stove to be placed in the retreat. This reversal of the commissioning process exemplifies Evans' mischievous act of collaboration. Scripting the process of artistic production, and giving the wrong roles to the actors in the play, makes apparent the theatrical situation that takes place between artist, producers, public, collectors and funding bodies.

Each of Evans' works takes part in a complex act of storytelling: sculptures, books, drawings and film scripts are indexes of a larger narrative, a web of fragments and processes from different worlds (economy, history, law, culture). Evans' works are like hints in a mystery novel in which the viewer has to play the role of an investigator to understand the whole scenario. The group of objects generated by a single project functions like images in a rebus: the viewer who engages with it will derive the pleasure of discovering a complex script hidden within.

In other works, actors are invited to perform a scripted role, local police officers are asked to make drawings of a judge that will preside over a rock representing the defendant (*The Rock and the Judge*, 2005–08); managing directors of global corporations are instructed to come up with ideas for a sculpture park in Estonia (*Radical Loyalty*, 2002–present); and four Italian politicians are briefed to suggest a sculpture symbolizing their notion of sacrifice (*As Simple as Your Life Used to Be*, 2007–08).

Evans' art seems to revolve around the notion of the monument and its discontents. The hidden relations behind the fruition of a cultural object for public use — for example, how beliefs, social status and ideological positions are negotiated in the work of art — are questioned through the invention of absurd alternative procedures to produce a sculpture. By orchestrating a series of relationships around the work, he aims to point out how meaning is only temporarily attributed to objects by a network of actors. Outside that, a sculpture might be viewed merely as an inert three-dimensional form. [Francesco Manacorda]

02

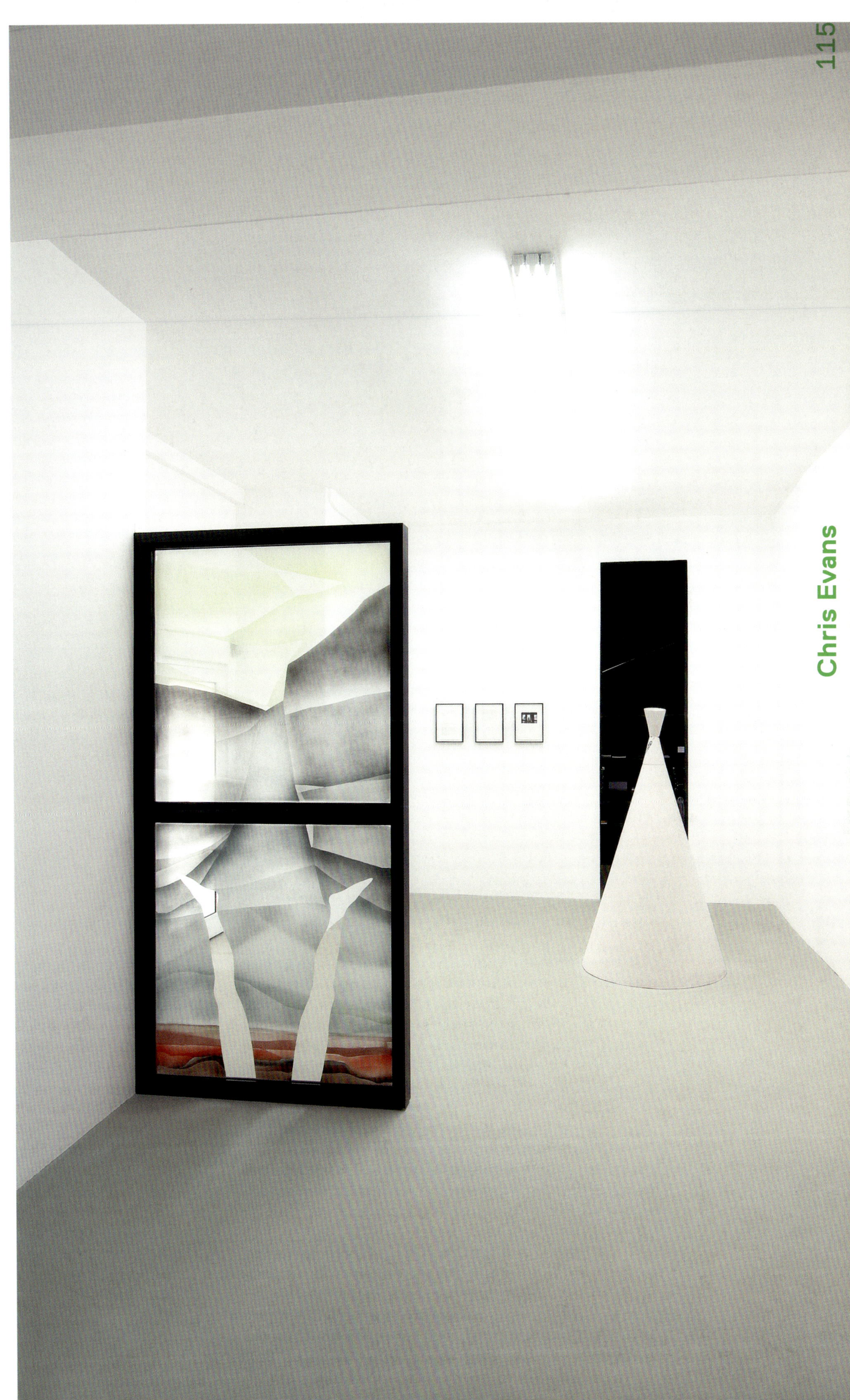

01 *Militant Bourgeois*, 2006
Iron and steel
woodburning stove
260 × 150 × 150 m
Wall painting
12 × 3 m
Video
14 min.

02 from left:
→ *I am in your foyer*, 2007
Airbrush on glass,
aluminium
260 × 100 × 10 cm
3 framed letters
32 × 23 cm
→ *Fantasist*, 2007
Video
4 min.
→ *You are the Sovereign*, 2007
Airbrush on
resin and ceramic
170 × 97 × 97 cm

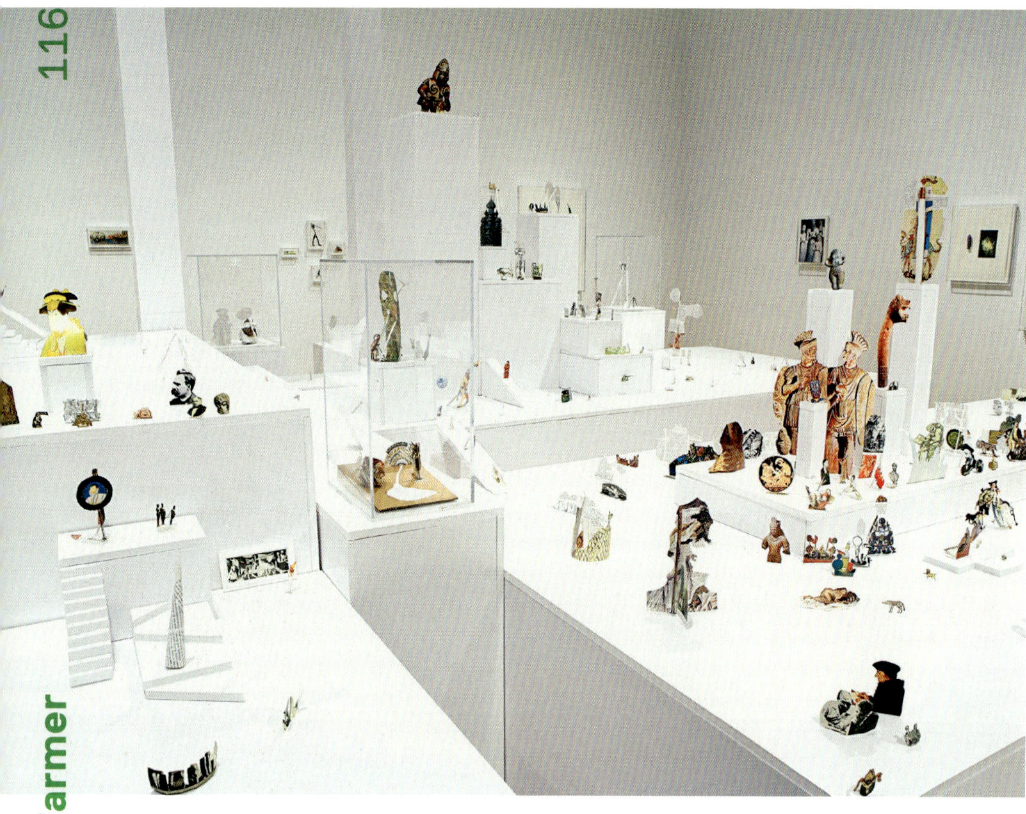

01

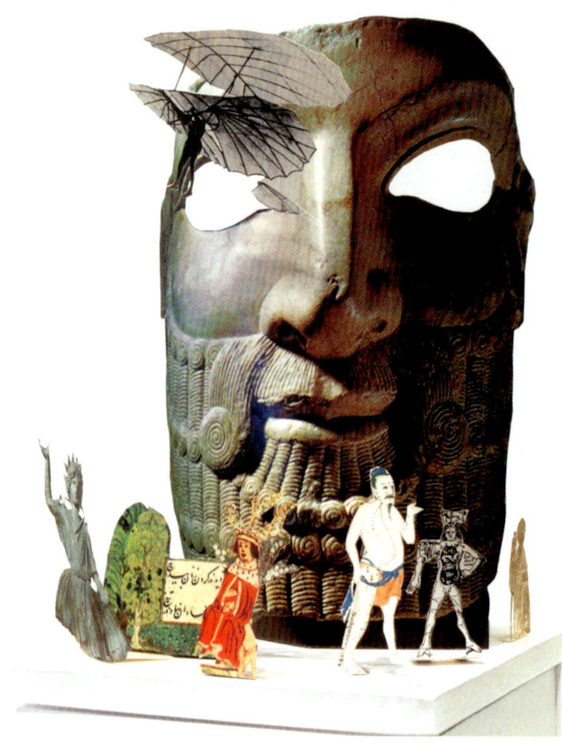

02

In its original form, Geoffrey Farmer's *Hunchback Kit* (2000) is a long, narrow transport case containing an eclectic miscellany of objects, from books and make-up to costumes and found objects, which can be used as props in 'conceptual adaptations' of Victor Hugo's *Notre-Dame de Paris*. Each unpacking of the kit sets the stage for new and unpredictable performances and configurations of its contents, dictated by specifics of site and the subjective interpretations of curators and public. *Hunchback Kit* exemplifies the formal, conceptual and textual unpacking that characterizes Farmer's practice, in which passages from art history, pop culture, film and literature are translated into intricately crafted and process-based installations that push literally and figuratively against the strictures of exhibiting, the making of art and its institutions.

Farmer's installations inscribe a literature of images and objects that remains porous to the slippages of meaning inherent in acts of adaptation and translation. *The Last Two Million Years* (2007) is an expansive (and ever-reconfigured) installation that emerged from Farmer's discovery of a 1970s *Reader's Digest* publication that somewhat audaciously attempts to present the entire history of humankind in a single illustrated volume. Freeing them from the pages of the book, Farmer arranged the cut-out illustrations across a series of platforms, replacing traditional categorizations with more intuitive combinations to create a wayward historical landscape that dismisses any singular account or point of view.

Projects such as *Airliner Open Studio* (2006) reveal the way in which Farmer employs the exhibition as a framework, and an inherently social space, within which any number of ideas are encouraged to take form. Constructed around a reclaimed 737 aircraft cabin, the work evolved as both a temporary stage set and rehearsal space. Built from real and fabricated parts — an ontological confusion with which Farmer recurrently plays — the set-up functioned in both filmic and theatrical terms; while some actions presented in real time exploited a direct relationship between viewer and performer, others, such as performative gestures recorded on video and displayed cumulatively in the space throughout the exhibition, created moments of greater intimacy that recalled the psychological explorations of 1970s video art. As in his earlier performative installations *Catriona Jeffries Catriona* (2001) and *Every Surface in Some Way Decorated, Altered, or Changed Forever [Except the Float]* (2004), *Airliner Open Studio* shifts the processes of production to centre stage and engages objects and individuals in an unstable choreography that flits between mutable form and uncertain signification.

If each of Farmer's installations in some way reflects on the act of making art itself, then his epic 2005 installation at The Power Plant in Toronto could be read as a full-blown manifesto for his creative methodology. *A Pale Fire Freedom Machine* was laid out like a vast processing plant in which hundreds of pieces of collected furniture were cleaned, sorted and incinerated in a fireplace originally designed by Dominique Imbert (later appropriated by French artist Xavier Veilhan for his 1996 installation *Le Feu*). Visitors were invited to print posters using ink made from the resulting soot. With its titular reference to Vladimir Nabokov's classic meta-fiction novel *Pale Fire* (1962), the work held up a mirror to its own construction, revelling in the creative process as a form of labour and the exhibition space as a workshop in which ideas are in a constant state of production and transformation.
[Andrew Bonacina]

01, 02 *The Last Two Million Years*, 2007
Images cut from found book,
foam core, tape, marble replica of book
Dimensions variable

03 *And Finally the Street Becomes the Main Character (clock)*, 2008
Wooden stage, computer-controlled soundscape, 8 speakers, styrene brick, glass shards, paint can, tree branch, paint tray, stool, artificial ivy, hand-carved wooden bowl, cardboard boxes, wooden mallet, protest sign, cardboard tubes, leather suitcase, folding chair, towel, sweater, desk lamp, string, blanket, light bulbs, tripod, sponge, lock box, tissue, paper bag, oil can, moth, thread, masking tape, felt books, rag, wooden figure, spoon, paint, styrene cup, chopstick, candleholder, ballet costume, brass sculpture, found wood, various framed works
490 × 600 × 180 cm

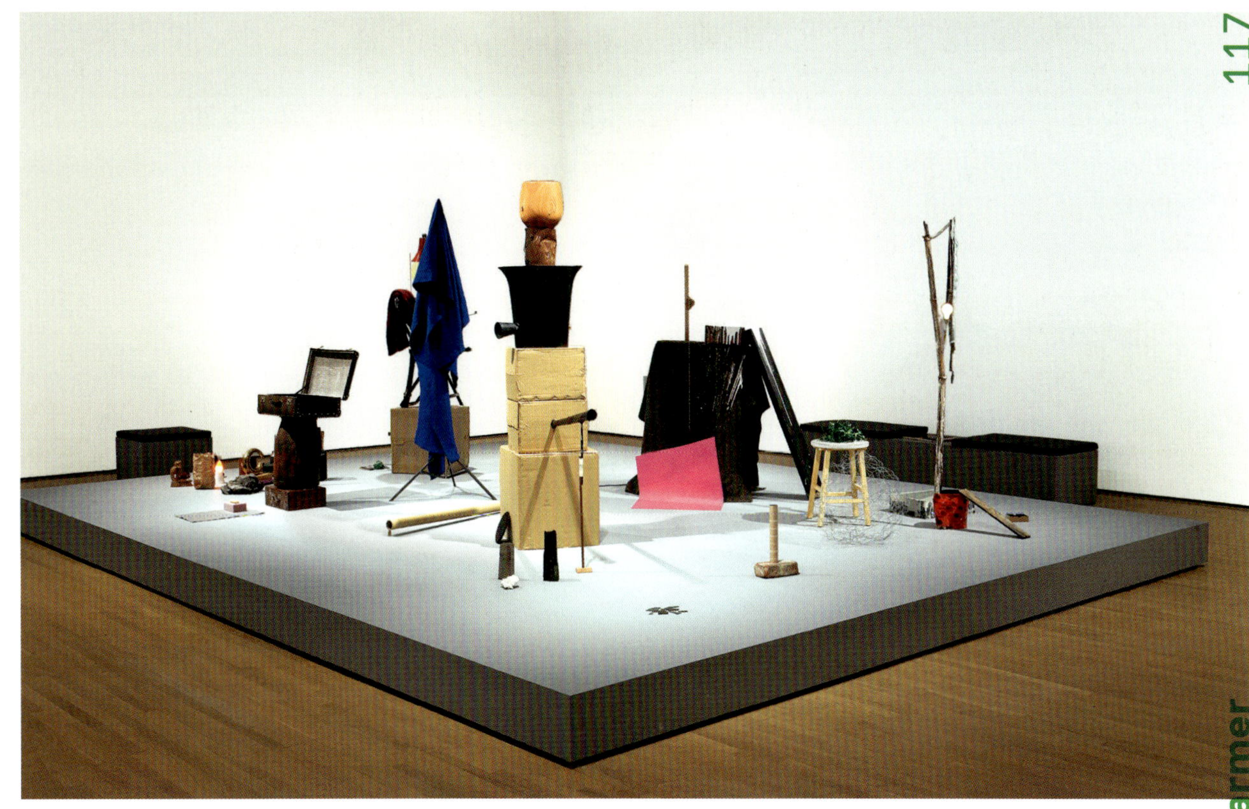

03

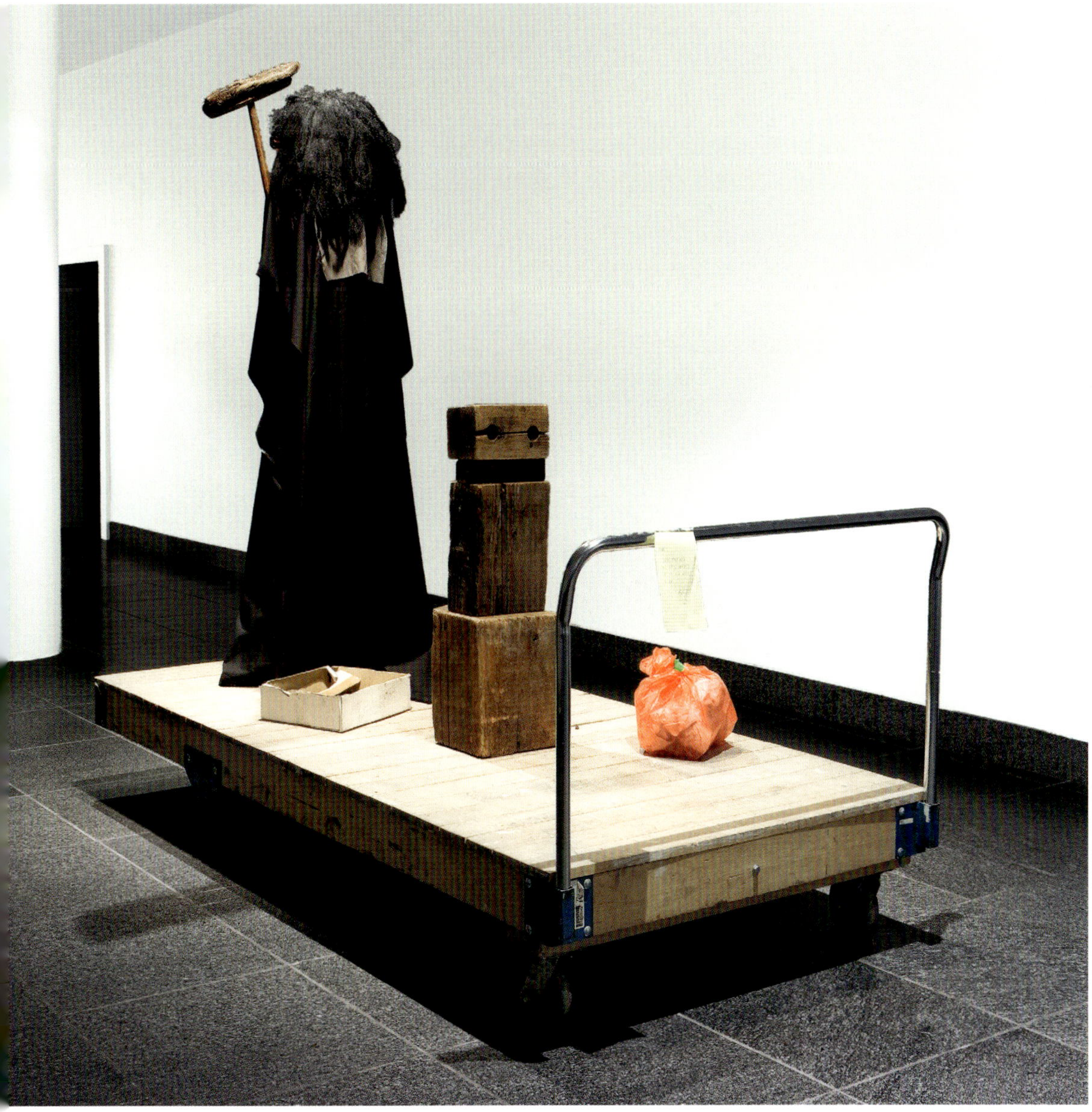

04

04 *I am by nature one and also many, dividing the single me into many, and even opposing them as great and small, light and dark, and in ten thousand other ways*, 2001
Various figures, wood, fabric, styrene, lights, brooms, chair, paper, wigs, shovels, costumes
Dimensions variable

Overleaf:

05 *Pale Fire Freedom Machine*, 2005
Found wooden furniture, fireplace, fire, fire extinguishers, sand blaster, axe, chopping block, paper, coveralls, tools, print shop, ink made from soot, found note paper
Dimensions variable

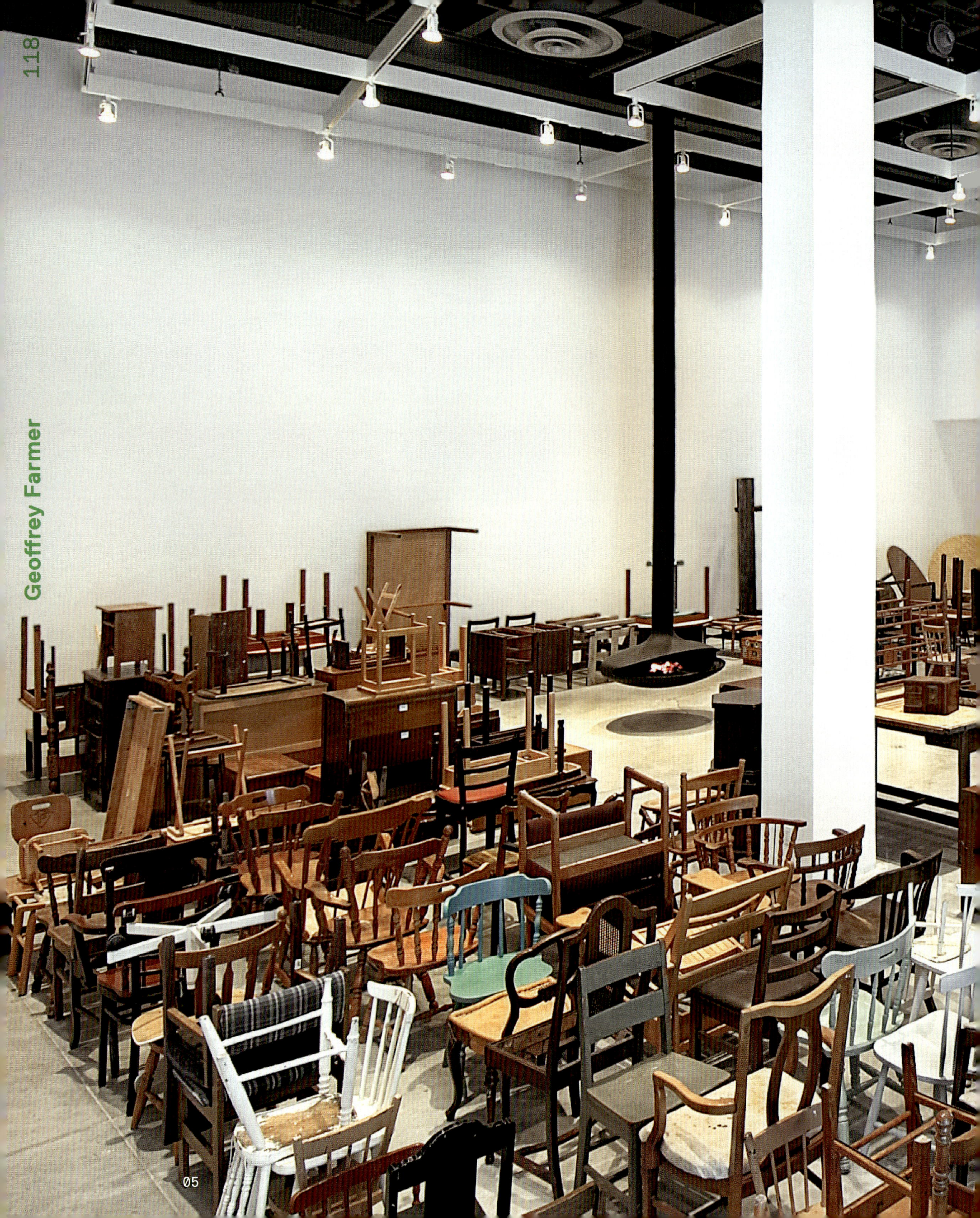

05

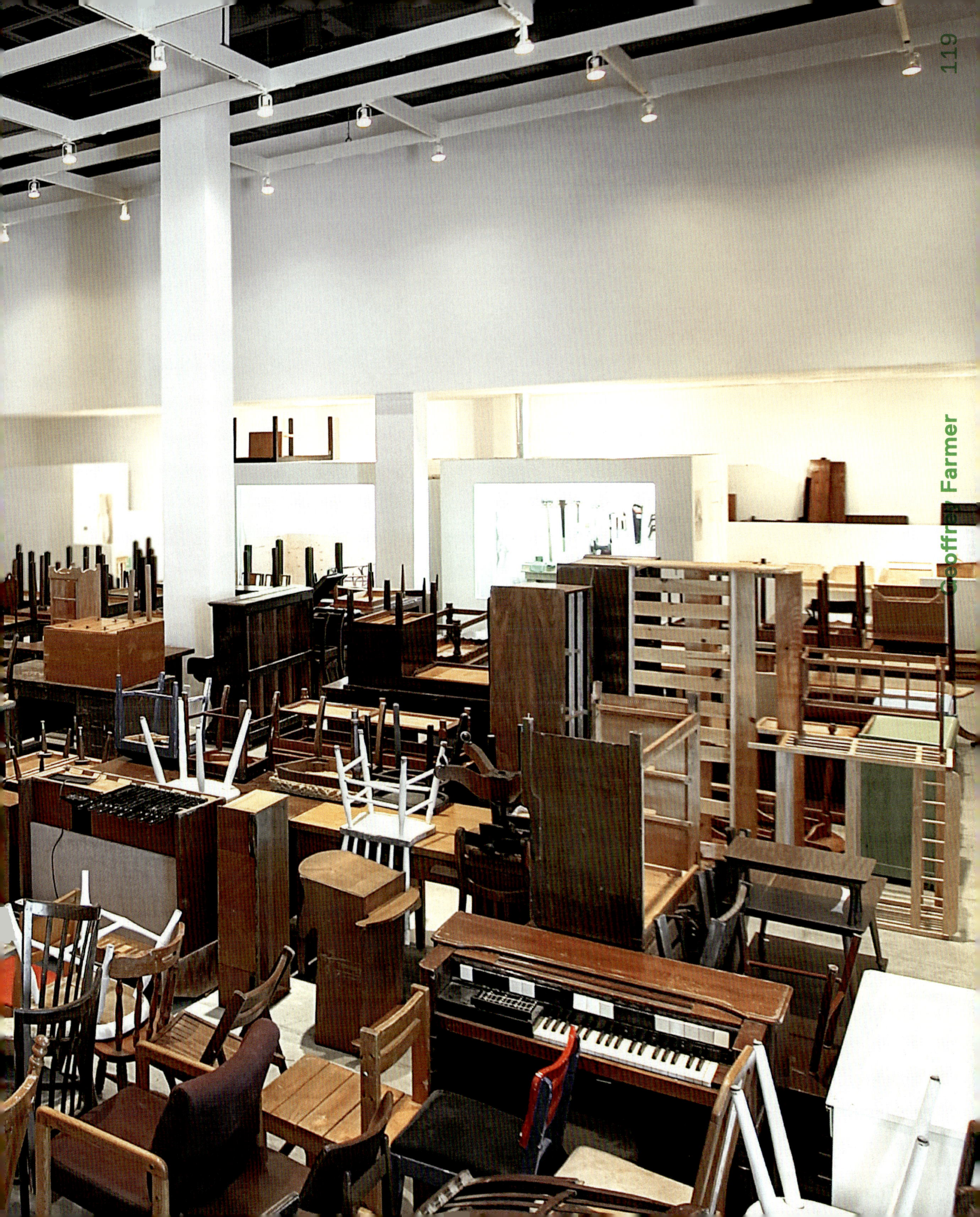

Born in Morocco, Mounir Fatmi currently works between Paris, Lille and Tangiers, straddling a geopolitical and socio-economic divide that has deepened following the events of 9/11. In his films, drawings, paintings, sculptures and installations, Fatmi investigates the complexities of tradition and contemporary politics on both sides of the Mediterranean and the Atlantic. Often incorporating found objects — VHS tapes and electrical cables, books and sounds — he uses a direct, at times ironic, visual language, subjecting social, religious and political belief systems to his own brand of dark humour. His work reveals the fragility of our present moment as well as the systems of communication that shape its interpretation.

In his sculptural installation *Obstacle/Mondrian Forest* (2007), Fatmi appropriates horse-jumping hurdles, elements that he commonly uses to suggest social and political barriers (while also alluding to the Arab equestrian tradition), and establishes a dichotomy between Piet Mondrian's hyper-modern concept of the 'New Plastic' and the natural world. Next to a banal photograph of a deciduous canopy, sixteen hurdle poles, one of them cracked and bent over a white bench, establish emblem and territory. The fifteen unbroken poles lean together against the wall, each half-painted after Mondrian and half with patterns of bold colours that are suggestive of national flags. In one breath, Fatmi indicts not only the tyranny of art history, lingering colonialism and modern
01 nationalism, but also the viewer's subservience.

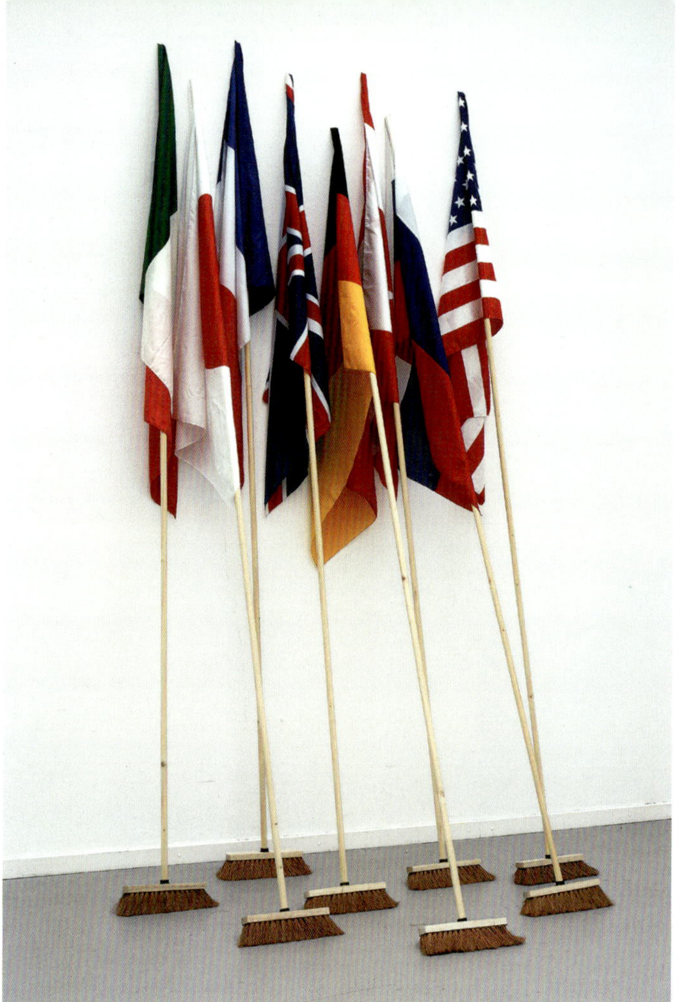

Through appropriation of the written word, which unites Judaism, Islam and Christianity as religions of the book, Fatmi implicates the increasingly strained dialogue between them. He uses popular and religious publications, wall texts and recorded sounds to cast language as both a constructive and destructive force. For example, *Save Manhattan 01* (2003–04) re-creates Manhattan's pre-9/11 skyline in the shadow thrown by a collection of texts. All published after 9/11 except for the two-volume Koran, which casts the silhouette of the Twin Towers, they propose literature as a regenerative, albeit divisive,
02 force. Formally similar, *Underneath* (2007), Fatmi's special project for the 8th Sharjah Biennial, mirrors the skyline of Dubai in white painted wood. The cityscape, projecting both above and below a table, is accompanied by a looming wall text: 'Guilty'. The word is spelled out not in French, not in Arabic, but in the international language of pre-emptive condemnation: English.

Adopting the strategy of comedy as a method of poignant commentary, Fatmi challenges both the East and West to an ideological battle. A potent interpretation of the tenets of Sharia law, his *Les Voleurs* (The Thieves, 2006) places a glistening sabre and five latex hands, their wrists slashed in bloody red, across the Saudi Arabian flag. He also turns his attention to Western propaganda in *G8 — The Brooms* (2004). A prescient work, foreshadowing French President Nicolas Sarkozy's wish following the riots of November 2005 to 'sweep up the scum' from the banlieues of Paris, the sculpture attaches the G8 nations' flags to heavy-duty brooms. In both works, Fatmi's joke is strongest in its allusion to a very serious reality.

Conjuring troubled cityscapes, political and ideological playing fields, spaces where abstract ideals are the foundations for architecture and action, Fatmi points to the philosophical, religious and political doctrines that shape the construction and legibility of these spaces. Equally, he reveals their very real potential for deconstruction. [Lillian Davies]

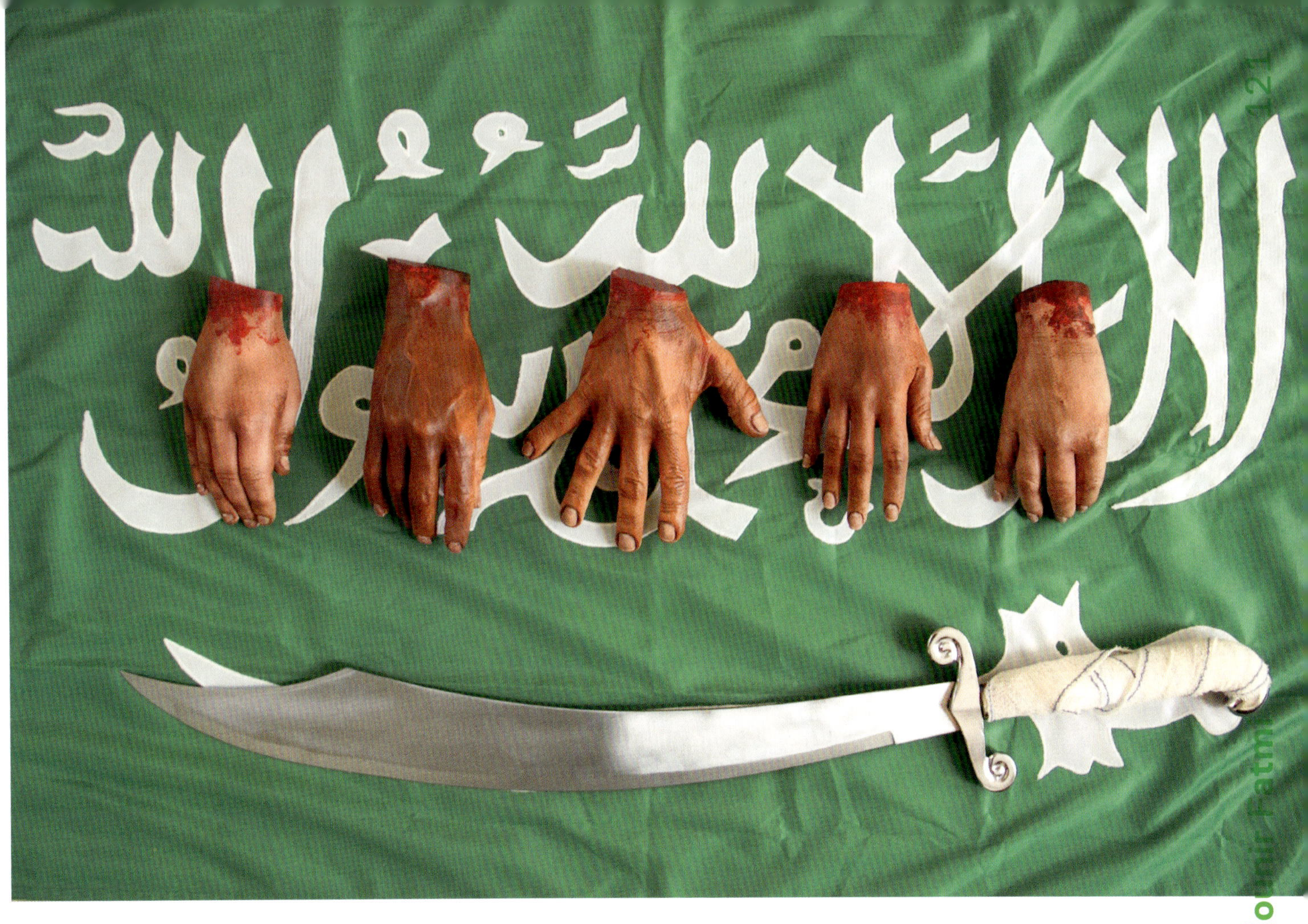

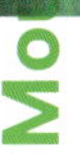

03

04

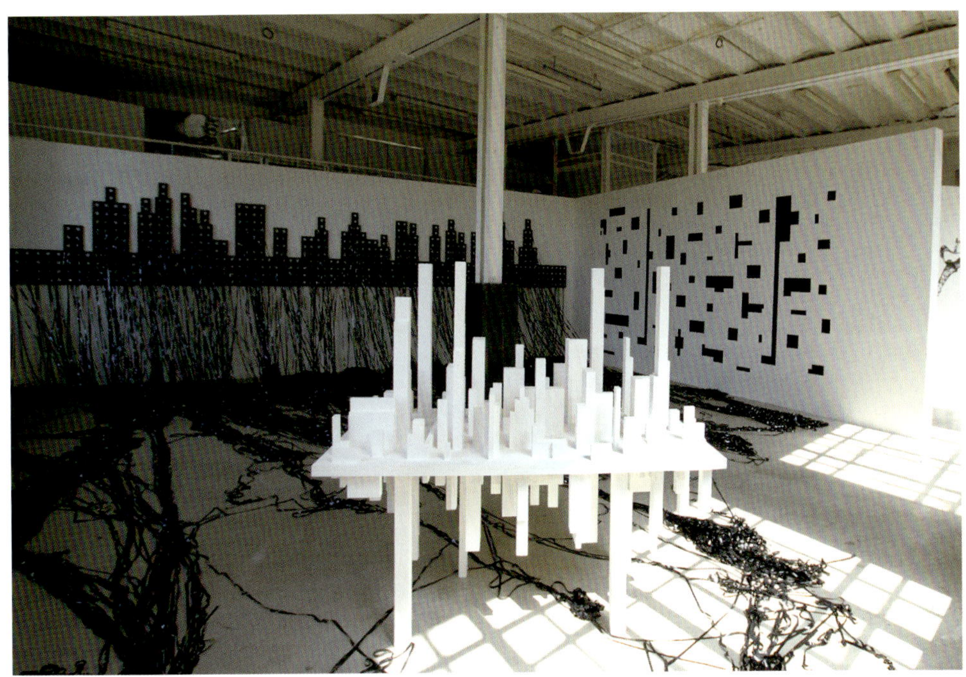

01 *G8 — The Brooms*, 2004
Brooms, flags
300 × 150 × 60 cm

02 *Save Manhattan 01*, 2003–04
Table, books published after 11 September 2001, light, shadow
120 × 90 × 140 cm

03 *The Thieves*, 2006
Latex, sword, flag
100 × 60 cm

04 *Underneath*, 2007
Wood, tables
2 parts
Each 160 × 90 × 75 cm

Imbued with a self-destructive impulse, Lara Favaretto's installations and performative interventions perpetually teeter on the brink of collapse. While objects remain central to her vocabulary, the temporal and social situations within which they are typically constructed form a reflexive space where they are called upon to unravel both physically and conceptually.

Her invitation to three masons to reduce three blocks of marble to dust in an early performance, *Doing* (1999), encapsulates many of the concerns that guide her work. Alongside frequent collaborations with so-called 'non-professionals' — an eclectic ensemble that boasts gypsies, farmers, royalty and choir singers among its number — as well as the use of the absurd and the surreal as tools of disruption, *Doing* represents a particular form of anti-economy in which non-productivity and obsolescence are used to question the roles and functions of art and artists in contemporary society.

01

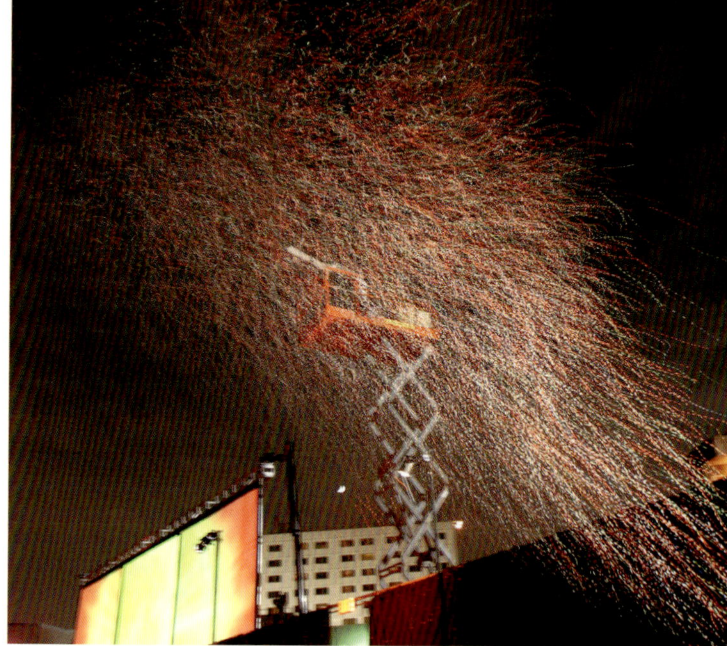

Displacement is a key strategy for Favaretto, subverting common objects and their traditional functions to create powerful but ephemeral images that insert a wedge into systems of logic. *I Poveri Sono Matti* (The Poor Are Mad, 2004) — a brightly coloured gypsy caravan suspended from a crane — has a back story that begins with a trip made by Favaretto to India to meet and travel with a group of gypsies. On her return to Europe she tracked down a dilapidated caravan, which she agreed with its owners to refurbish on the proviso that she would be able to borrow it for the duration of the work's installation at Turin's Castello di Rivoli museum. While the spectre of a caravan apparently floating in the sky creates a daydream moment — its romanticism heightened by the utopian image of social collaboration that brought it there — the equally powerful presence of the machinery holding it in place allows reality to intervene. As with *Doing*, which sublimated artisanal labour into an artistic act, this laying bare of the mechanism of the spectacle emphasizes the vacuity of the art object.

In *Cominciò ch'era Finita* (Begin as if it were finished, 2006) a salvaged and reconstructed army tent spins violently around a wooden platform, bearing a selection of enticing, gleaming objects that are glimpsed only momentarily during each rotation. As it spins, the canopy flaps scrape against the walls and columns of the exhibition space, eating away at both masonry and tent fabric. The promise of revelation — of sating the viewer's desire to 'reach' the contents of the work — is wilfully thwarted by the suggestion of the work's disintegration (and the possible collapse of the building itself), a refusal that challenges material and mercurial urges that assign value to object over concept.

Favaretto's objects and installations seem designed to frustrate, hovering disruptively between desire and satisfaction. Works such as *Confetti Canyon* (2001–05), a barrage of guns that scatters only colourful paper showers, or *Project For Some Hallucinations* (2007) — an invitation to the Queen of England to attend Frieze Art Fair, which was declined — draw on the language of spectacle and celebration while refusing access to the enjoyment of the spectacle itself. Her series of 'works' made for art-fair stands, consisting of scribbled questions — 'Why are you here?', 'Is it all true?', 'Is it all false?' — throw back at her audience the enquiries that she has dedicated her work to answering.
[Andrew Bonacina]

01 *Confetti Canyon*, 2001–05
Confetti, 3 fans,
hydraulic tubes, 3 tripods,
iron, polyurethane enamel
Dimensions variable

02 *I Poveri Sono Matti (The Poor Are Mad)*, 2005
Suspended caravan, 40 watt
electric light, 5 battery 160Ah,
CD player, remote control receiver,
2 60Ah batteries, Senhaifer
receiver, transmitter, dual tension
converter, remote control,
Relais-Interface, amplifier, speaker
250 × 700 × 350 cm

Overleaf:

03 from left:
Uomo Giallo (Fantaman), 2007
→ Iron slab, electrical box,
carwash brush, wires
204 × 146 × 83 cm
→ *Uomo Arancione (Thing)*, 2007
Iron slab, electrical box,
carwash brush, wires
205 × 146 × 183 cm
→ *Uomo Verde (Hulk)*, 2007
Iron slab, electrical box,
carwash brush, wires
200 × 68 × 60 cm
→ *Uomo Viola (Hawkeye)*, 2007
Iron slab, electrical box,
carwash brush, wires
150 × 300 × 100 cm
→ *Uomo Fucsia (Scarlet Witch)*, 2007
Iron slab, electrical box,
carwash brush, wires
205 × 198 × 85 cm

02

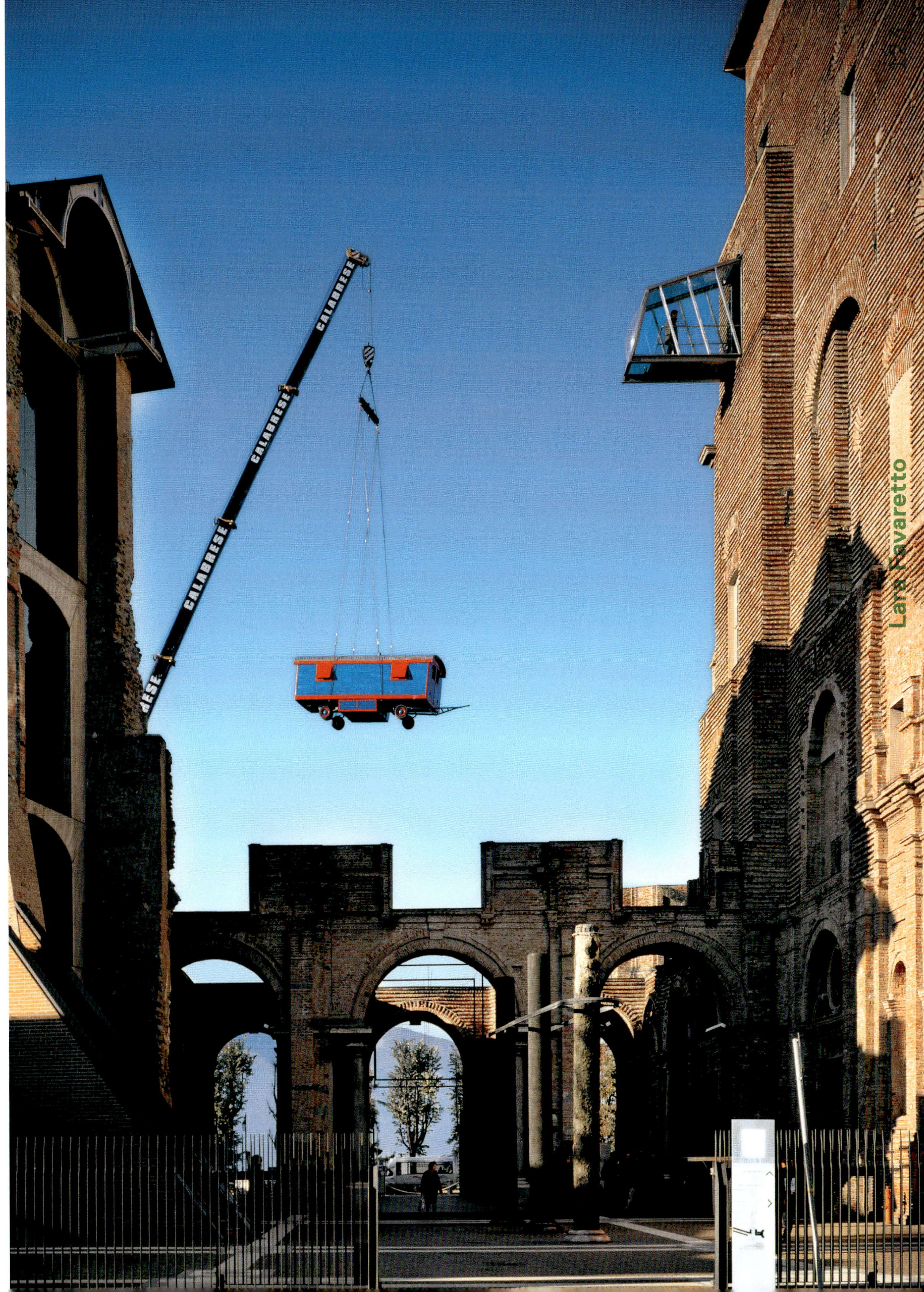

Lara Favaretto

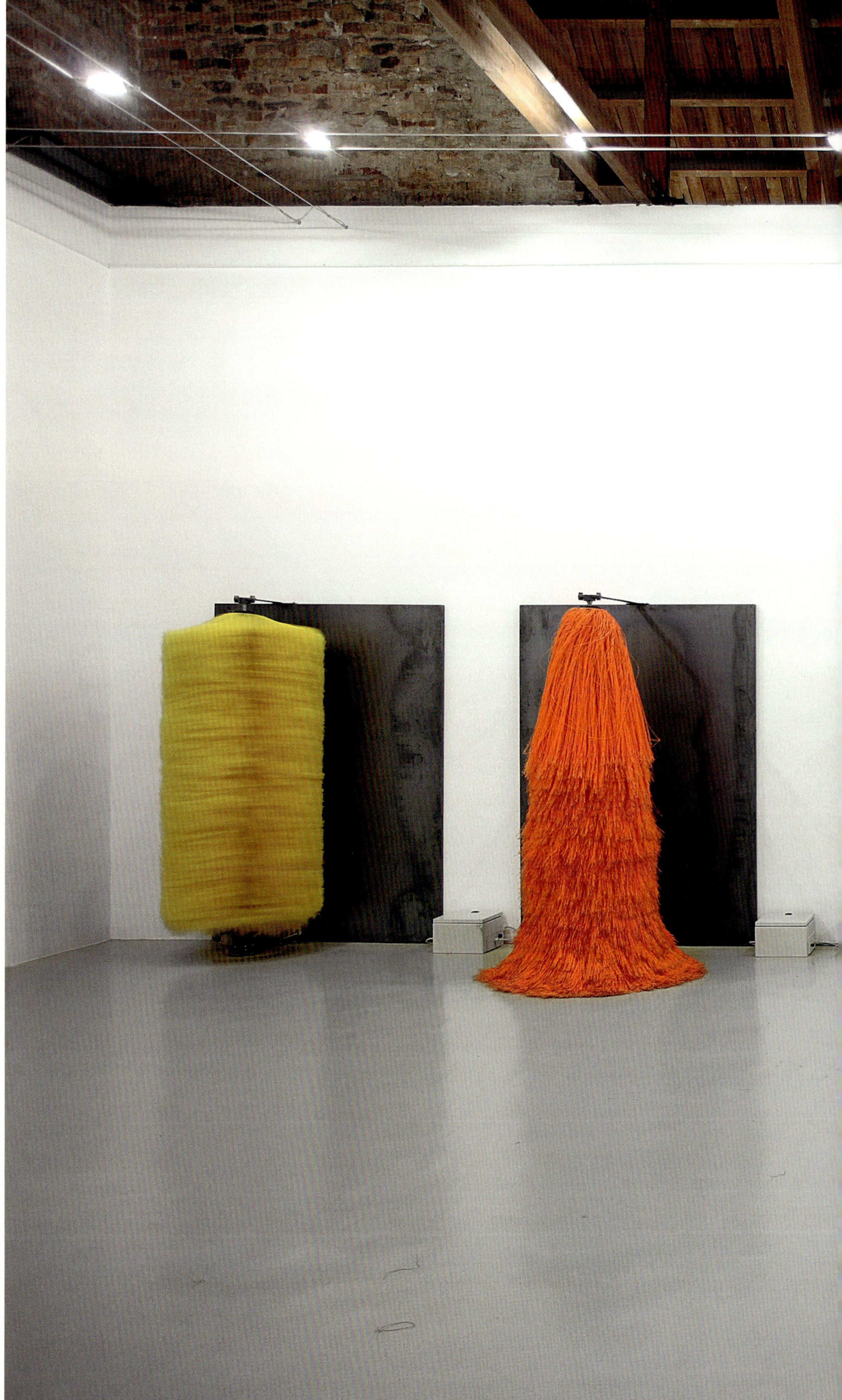

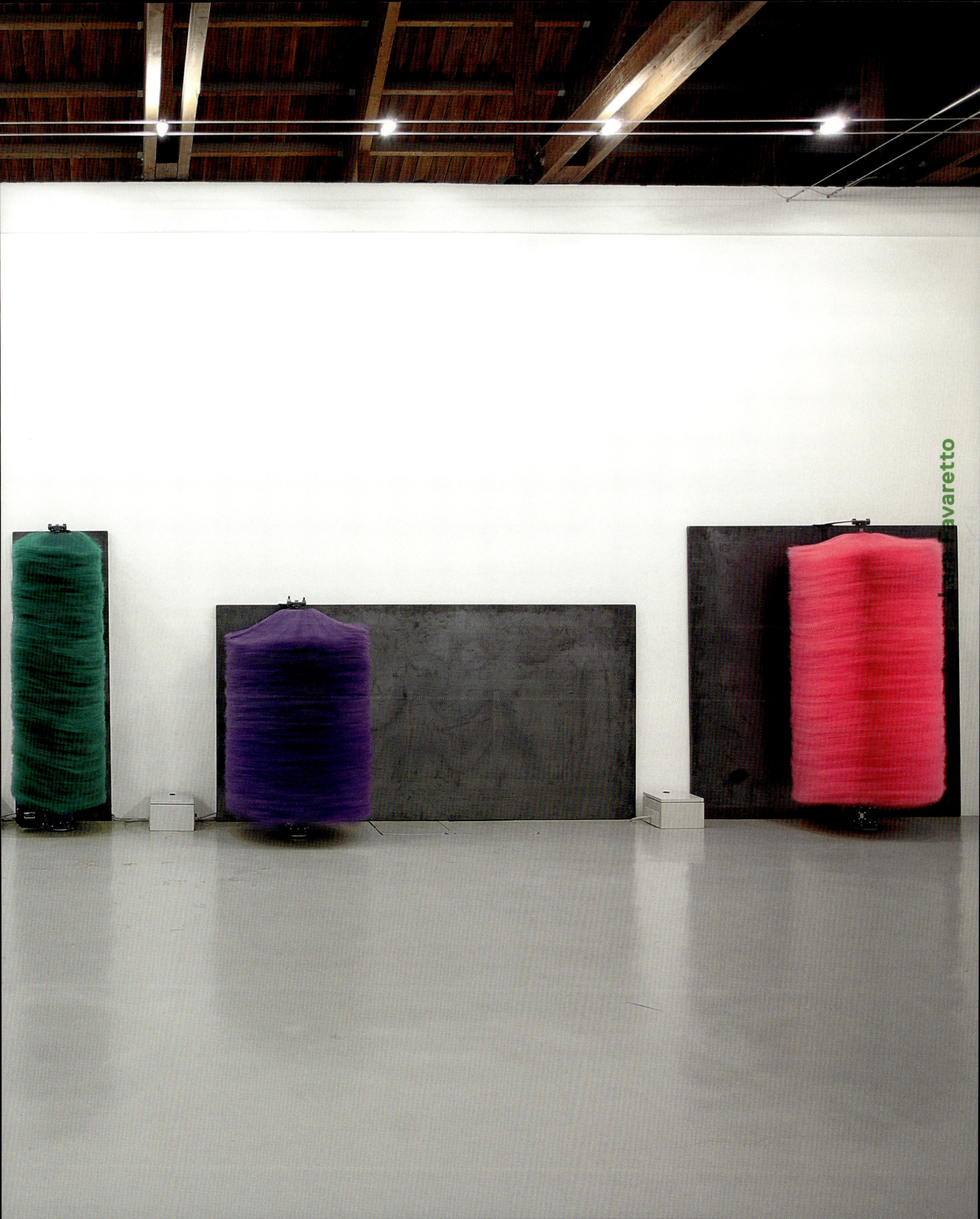

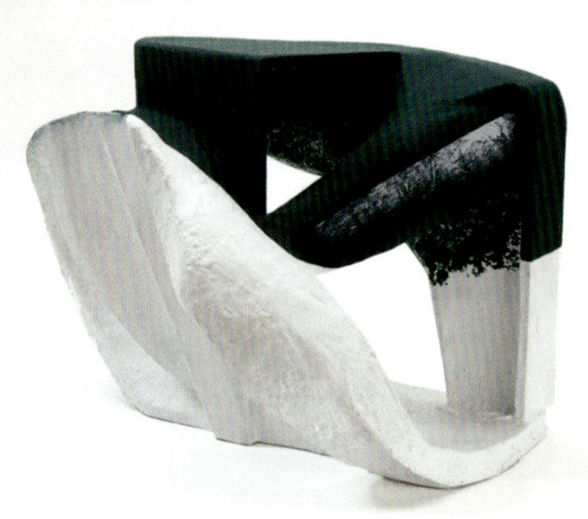

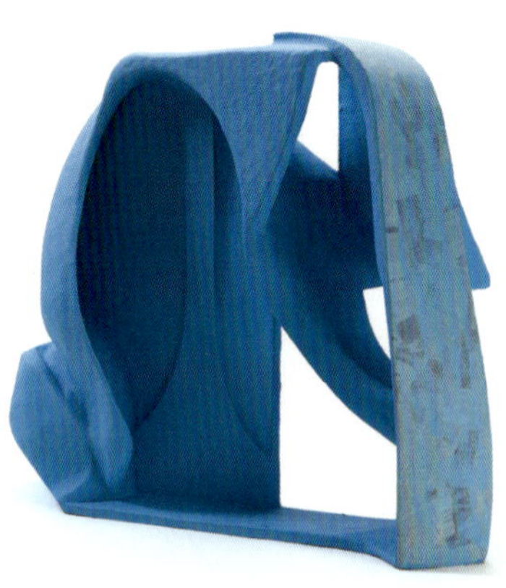

01

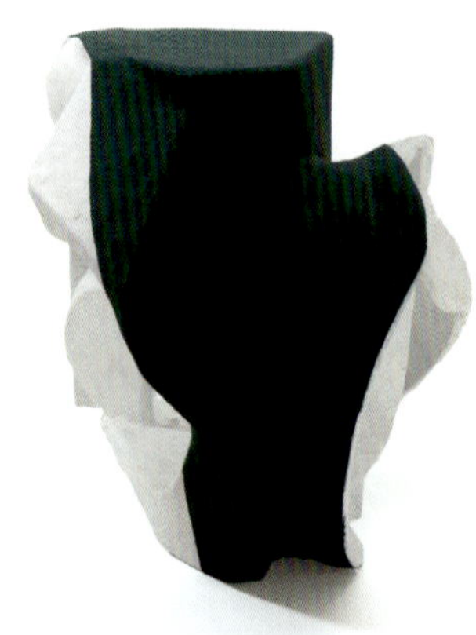

02

Awkward, eccentric forms and peculiar colour schemes are usually repellent artistic attributes. It's no small achievement, then, that Vincent Fecteau's modestly scaled freestanding forms, which are defiant in their ungainliness, simmer with a peculiar dignity and seductiveness. His objects, almost always made only of papier mâché and acrylic paint, are difficult to love but harder to forget. They're small enough to hold, but they're not exactly embraceable — it would be difficult to know where to find a comfortable spot. The twisting forms strike markedly different profiles as you circle them. Each oddly angled turn defies logic yet manages to be structurally sound. An ergonomically pleasing curve that curls to form an interior grotto — the semblance of a handle — invariably gives way to a thin, dangerously fragile-looking stretch.

These are works that exude complex personalities and deceptive demeanours. They are three-dimensional facades, carefully composed structures that look off-hand. The apparent errors in spatial judgement and colour choice are, in fact, the result of months of refining, tearing down, rebuilding, repainting and retooling. Fecteau's choices highlight his love of clumsiness and dramatic shift. The subtle gloss of an eggshell finish contrasts with a patch that has been painted another colour and coarsely sanded away. These abrupt juxtapositions are highly deliberate, in an intuitive way.

Fecteau has been making variations of these forms since the mid-1990s, but colour is a more recent addition, adding startling layers of formal evolution and character shading. Not every artist can handle tints that could have been hijacked from Julianne Moore's mad suburban house in Todd Haynes' *Safe* and maintain their subversive dignity.

Fecteau describes his practice as 'finding through making', and if this sounds like a road of indecision or uncertainty, it is only momentary. His sculpture gains potency and strength as layers of off-kilter choices accrue almost organically. All the strata of activity may not be visible, but they are perceivable. The materials are not weighty, but the tone of the works is extremely solid. The source of their gravity comes from the invisible hours of hermetic deliberation contained within their refined peculiarity.

There is a whiff of the architectural model to these works — Frank Gehry on a bender, Barbara Hepworth commissioned to design a residence — but pint-size potency is Fecteau's stock in trade. They are as perfectly comfortable in their dimensions as such awkward elements could be. Each of his sculptures could rest as comfortably on a dining-room table as on a museum pedestal. The choice of ordinary craft materials makes the works resemble amateur attempts at modernist form, a strategy that imbues them with a deceptively democratic flavour. It seems as if we could have made one at home, and yet their strangeness is so specific, their inscrutability so fascinating, that you can't help but acknowledge their singular source. [Glen Helfand]

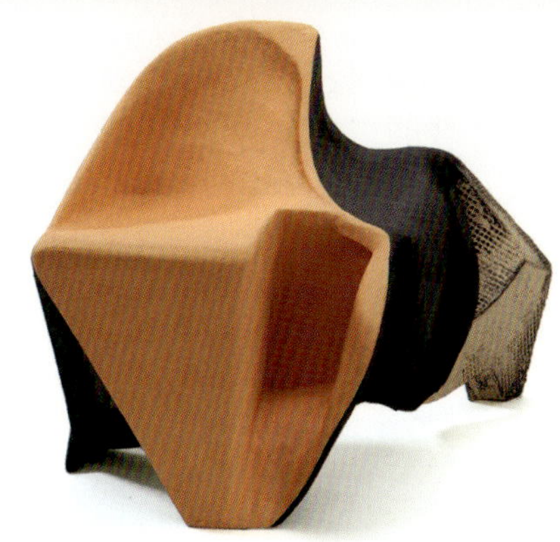

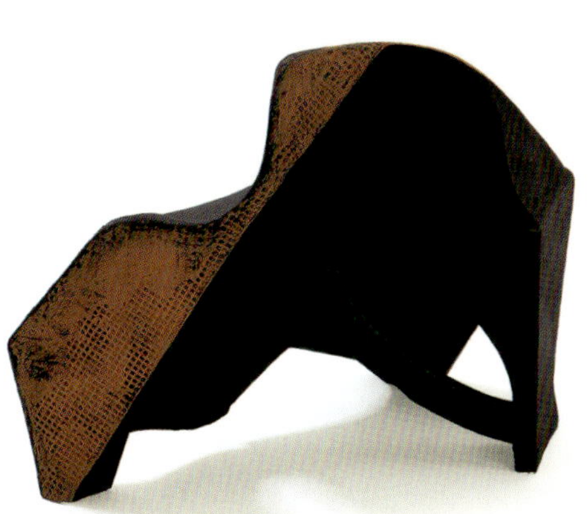

03

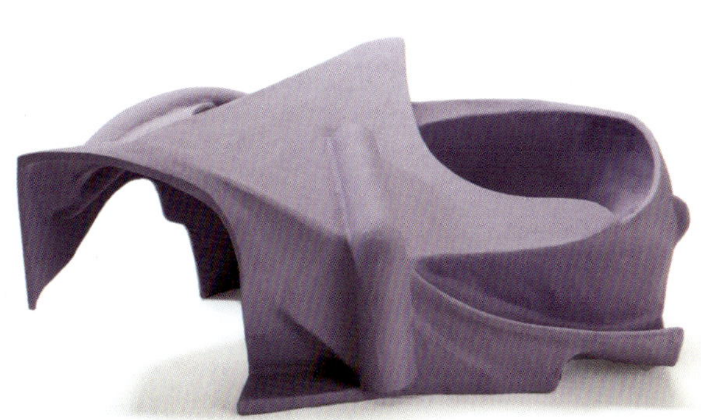

05

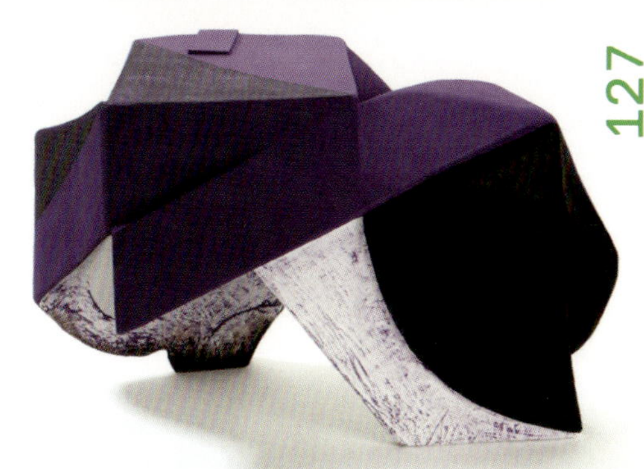

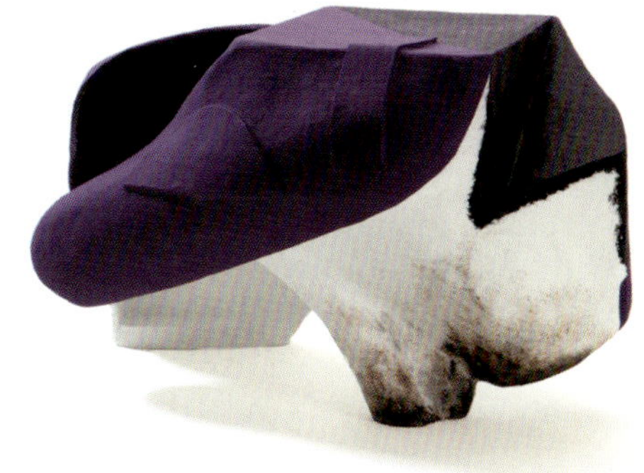

04

06

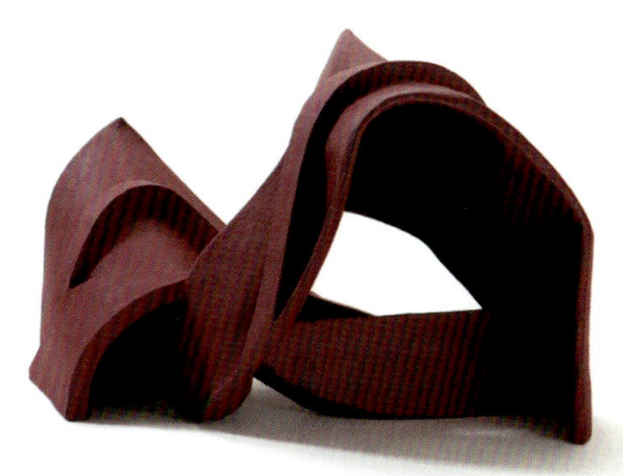

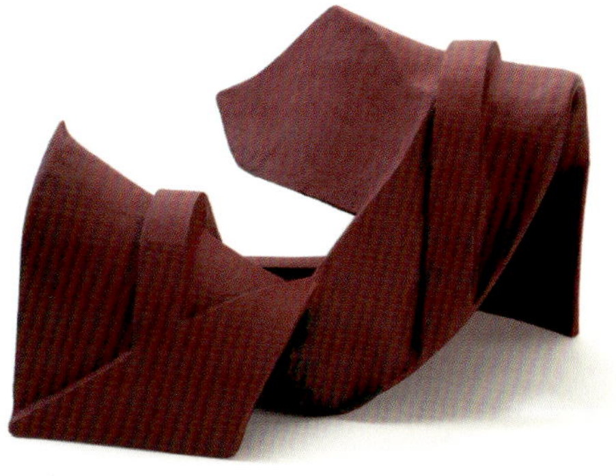

01 *Untitled*, 2008
Papier mâché, acrylic paint
65 × 83 × 32 cm

02 *Untitled*, 2008
Papier mâché, acrylic paint
51 × 72 × 48 cm

03 *Untitled*, 2008
Papier mâché, acrylic paint
51 × 56 × 56 cm

04 *Untitled*, 2008
Papier mâché, acrylic paint
40 × 72 × 48 cm

05 *Untitled*, 2008
Papier mâché, acrylic paint
38 × 83 × 62 cm

06 *Untitled*, 2008
Papier mâché, acrylic paint
45 × 61 × 59 cm

In 2004, Urs Fischer carved gigantic cloud-like holes in the walls of the Kunsthaus Zürich, creating panoramic views that gusted through his exhibition 'Kir Royal'. These abrupt changes in architectural scale perfectly suited the shifts in proportion that take place between his sculptures. Looking through one room into another, you could see a cartoony but human-sized skeleton prone on a bench, against a colossal captain's chair and an even larger packet of cigarettes. The effect was preposterousness on the scale of *Alice in Wonderland* or the disproportionate comb and soap in René Magritte's *Personal Values*. Like Magritte, Fischer stretches and shrivels commonplace objects to exaggerate the consequences once proportions of scale, as well as imagination, go crazy. He undercuts reality but without completely taking it away; when scale is this muddled up, the familiar regresses into an irresolvable dream.

01

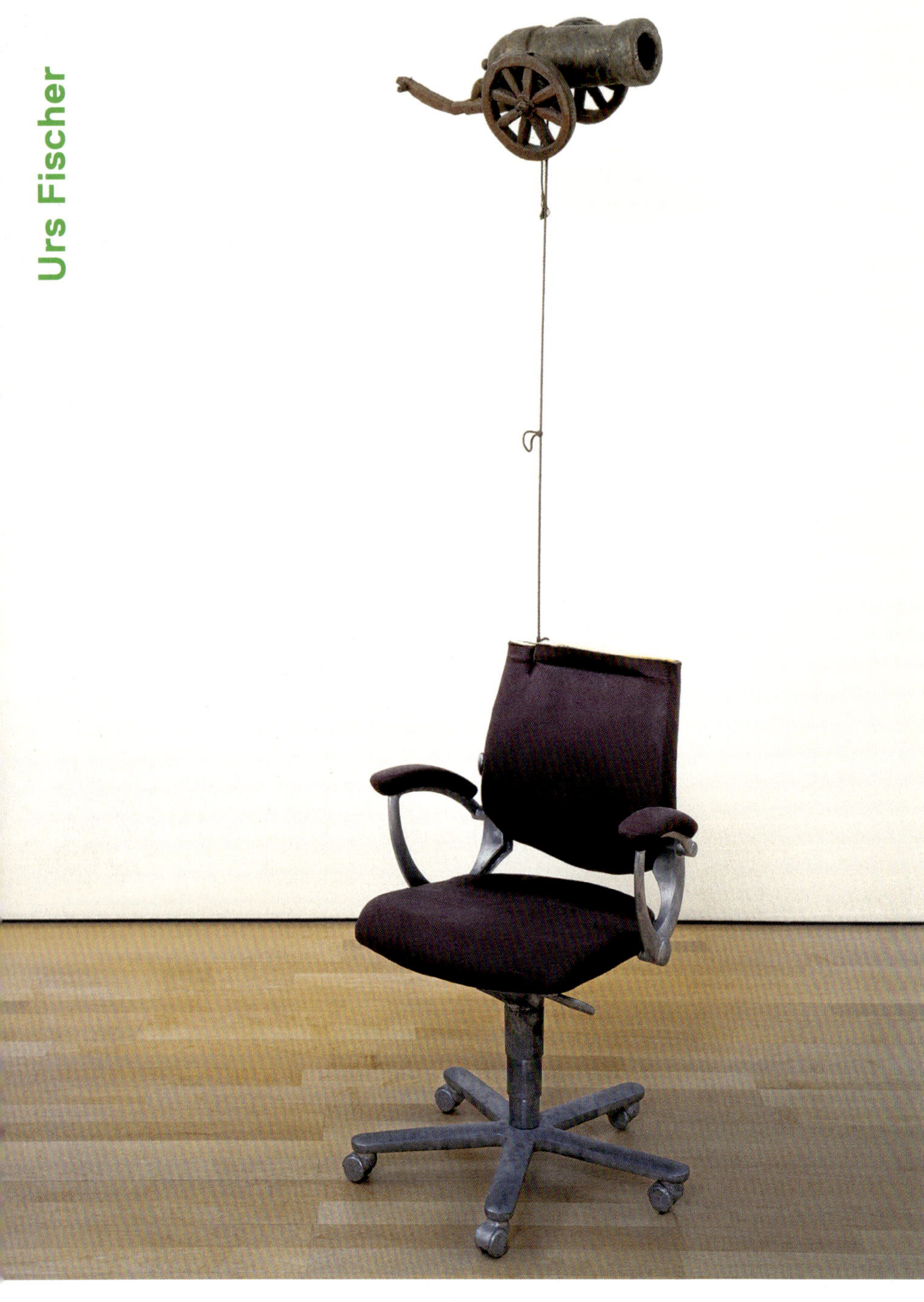

At face value, this slide between reality and fantasy, and the sharp changes in proportional ratios, make Fischer's work a Surrealist reverb. However, his vehicle for creating these follies is the still-life genre. In 1667, André Félibien, official court historian to Louis XIV of France, set down a hierarchy of genres, codifying art forms by calculating their capacity to interpret life through allegories of moral and intellectual consequence. He ranked *scènes de genre* — portraits, landscapes and finally still-lifes, understood as the inferior reportage of the everyday — beneath the *grande genre* of history painting. The hierarchy was his enduring legacy, and even today faint traces of his influence echo when pondering art's impact on an audience. Fischer traffics in the Vanitas still-life — meant to describe the transitory nature of existence. 'What I do in my studio — and actually we all do this,' he has said, 'is to plow through time [...] Every day. That applies to all forms of cultural activity, whether you're preparing a meal, taking a walk or making a work of art. We're creating nothing new; we're just developing what surrounds us.'

The everyday, transitory nature of time and the brevity of life recur as themes in Fischer's work through the symbols of the Vanitas: skulls (*Cockatoo Island Installation*, 2007), a candle (*Untitled Candle*, 2003), rotting fruit (*Untitled*, 2000). His *Chair for a Ghost: Thomas* (2003) can only invite to mind the ephemeral nature of life. Perhaps his most poignant Vanitas is *Bread House* (2004), a life-size Alpine cabin constructed of wood and loaves of bread, populated by four parakeets too young to fly. As time passes, and the house decays and crumbles, a tart stench rises, evoking death's closing stages, but all the while sustaining life amongst the birds. Allegories of moral and intellectual significance of such as *Bread House,* map time as a process of material transformation and decay while whispering a poetic *aide memoire* about our own mortality. [Ronald Jones]

01 *A thing called gearbox*, 2004
Cast aluminium, copper, iron rod, string, acrylic paint
231 × 68 × 68 cm

02 *Untitled (hole)*, 2007
Patinated cast aluminium
Approx. 540 × 340 × 270 cm

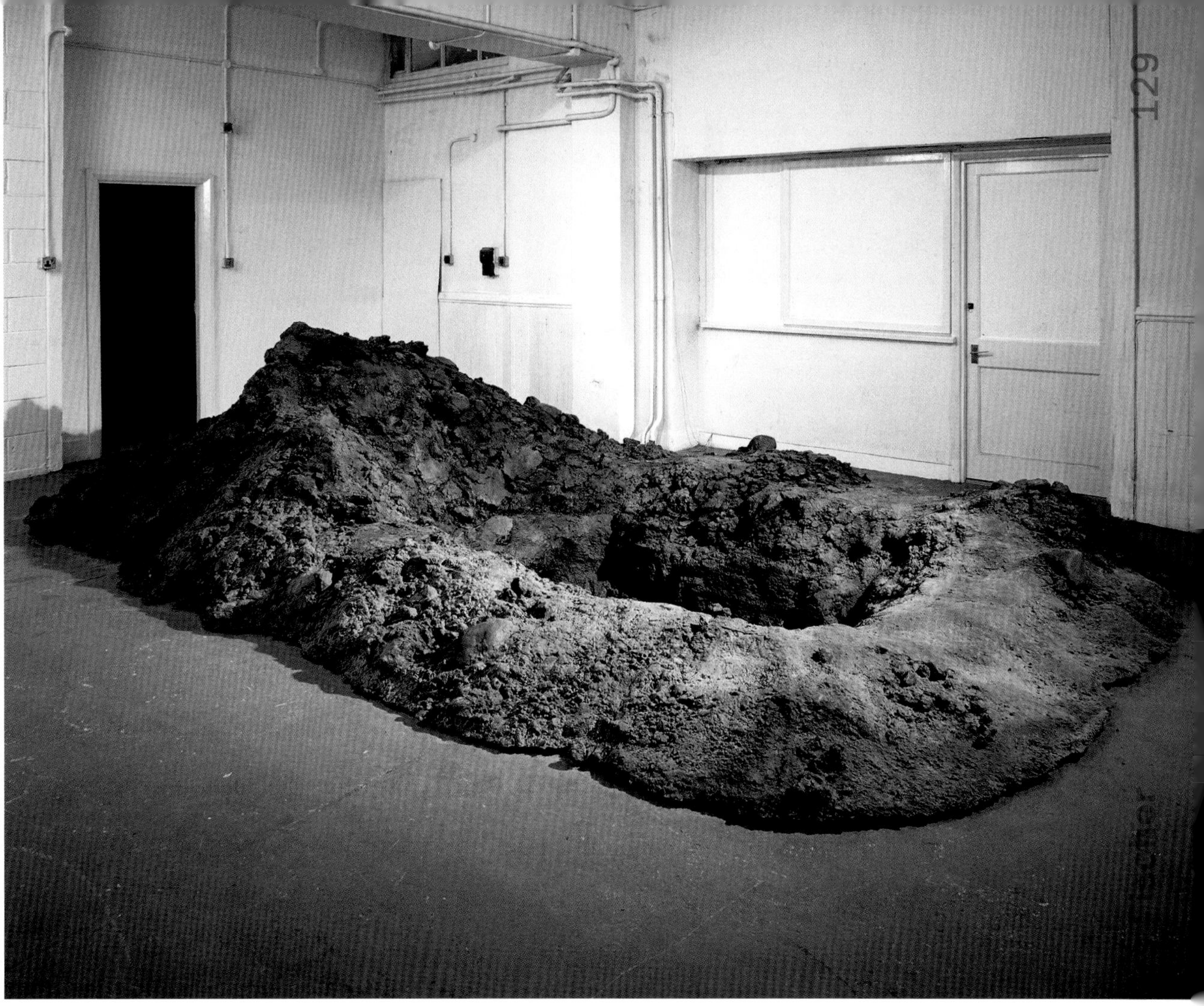

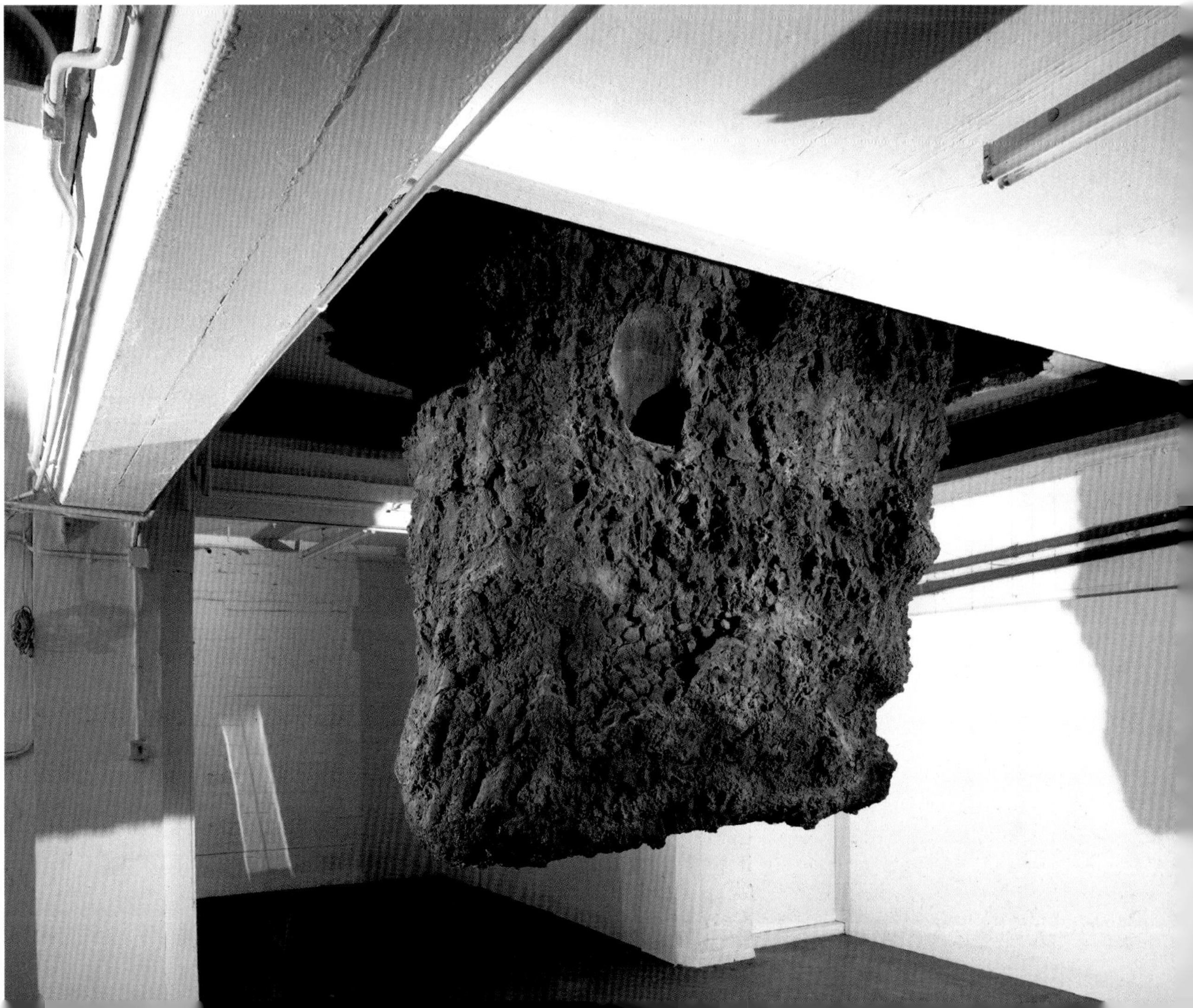

02

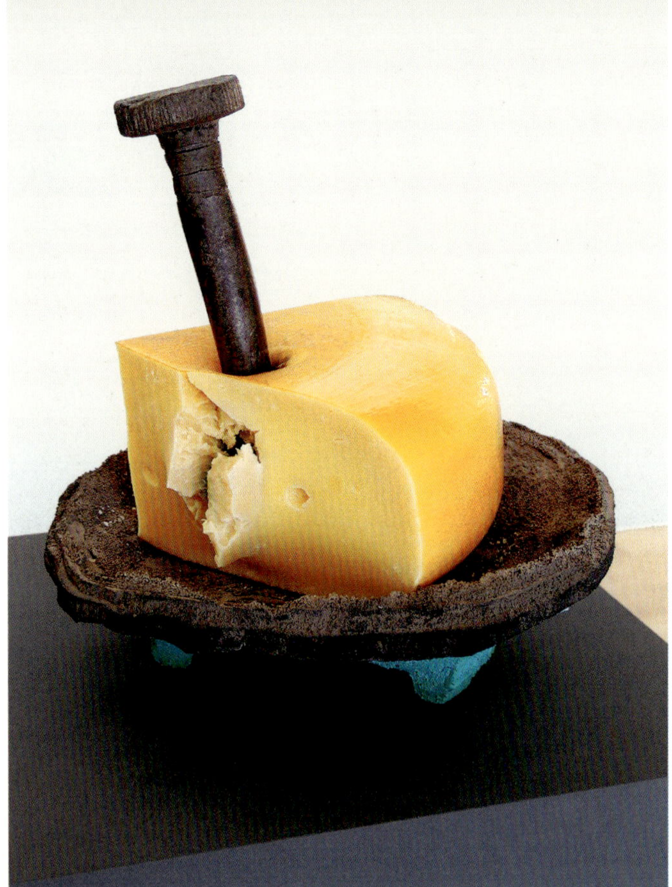

03

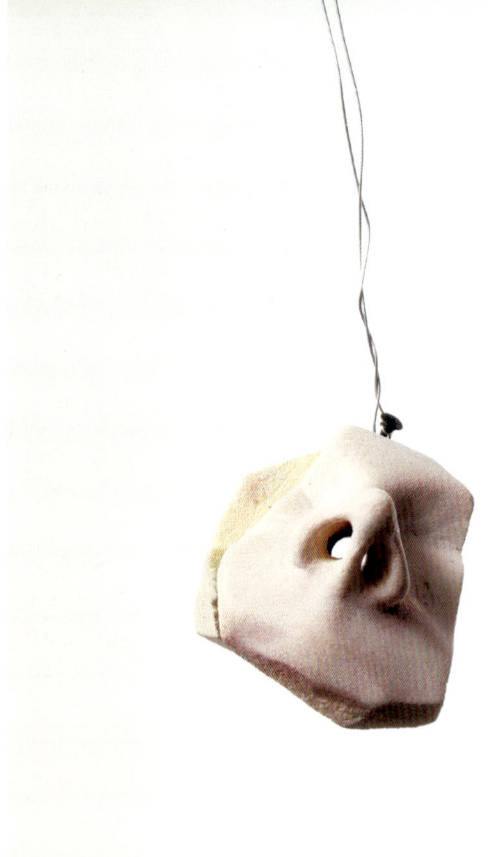

04

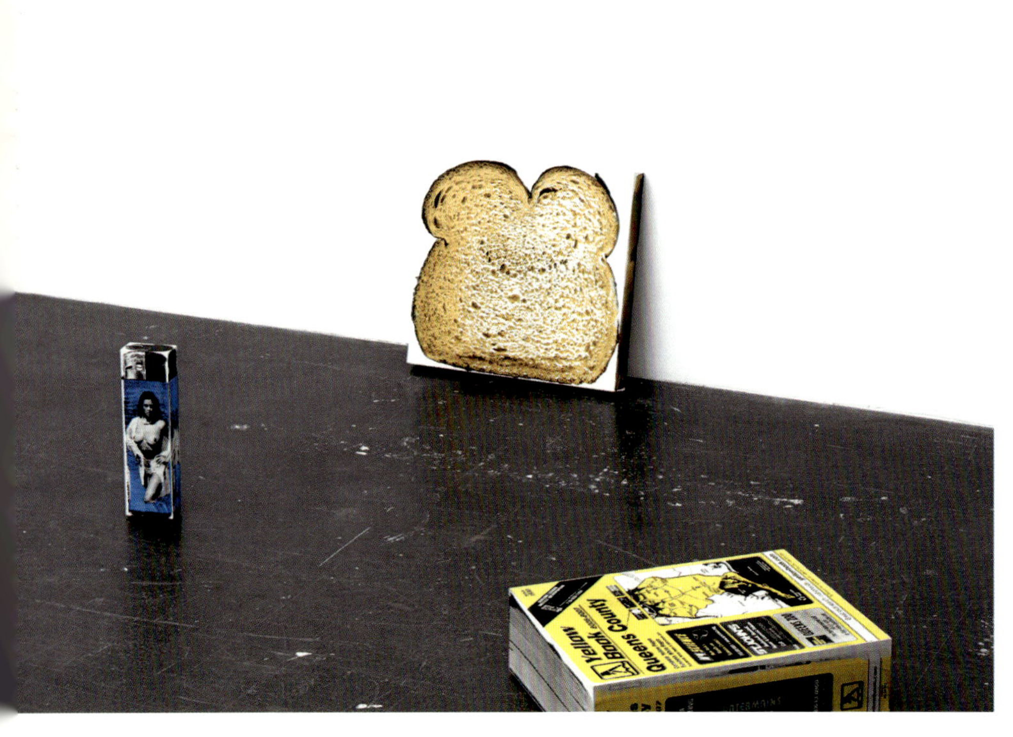

05

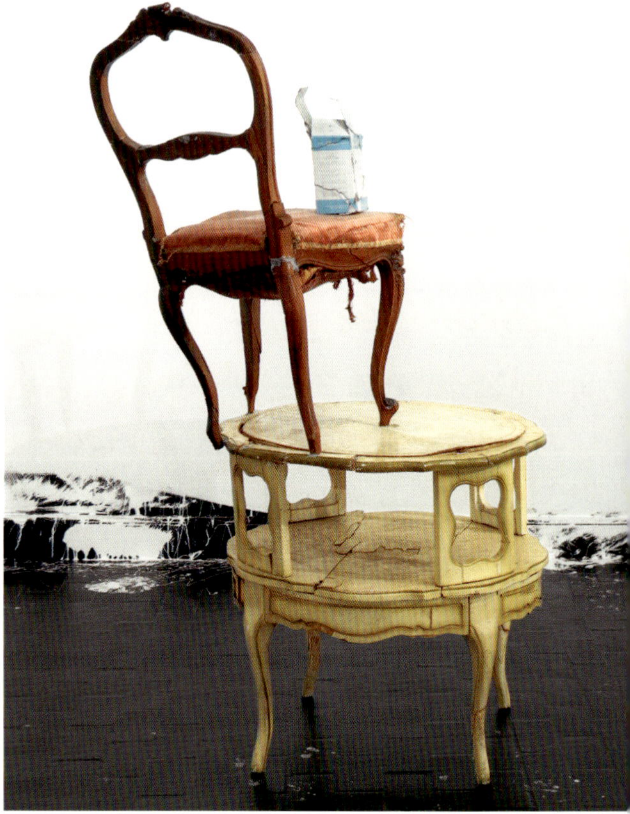

06

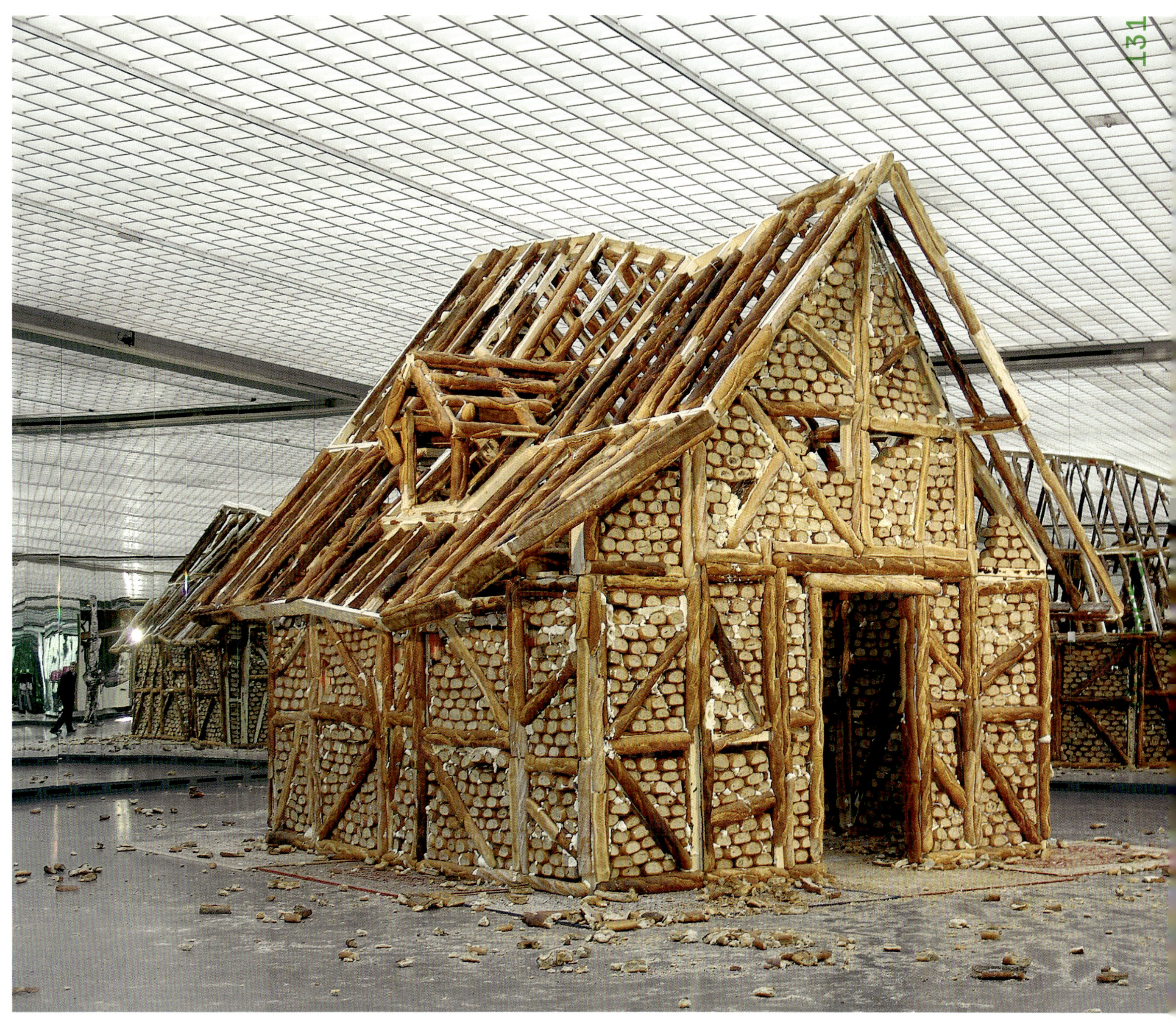

07

03 *Lie to a Dog*, 2005
Cast nickel silver, acrylic, metal pigments, Swiss cheese
24 × 28 × 25 cm

04 *Untitled (Holes)*, 2006
Carved polyurethane, plaster, acrylic paint, screws, wire
1 of 5 parts
Ear 13 × 34 × 9 cm
Nose 8 × 31 × 8 cm
Arse 15 × 19 × 13 cm
Willie 7 × 34 × 9 cm
Mouth 15 × 33 × 14 cm

05 *Untitled*, 2006
Screenprint on wood
3 parts
16 × 55 × 42 cm
37 × 11 × 5.2 cm
54 × 59 × 7.8 cm

06 *Addict*, 2006
Epoxy glue, found furniture, cardboard box
155 × 73 × 73 cm

07 *Untitled (Bread house)*, 2006
Bread, wood, silicon, screws, polyurethane foam, carpet
Approx. 500 × 600 × 500 cm

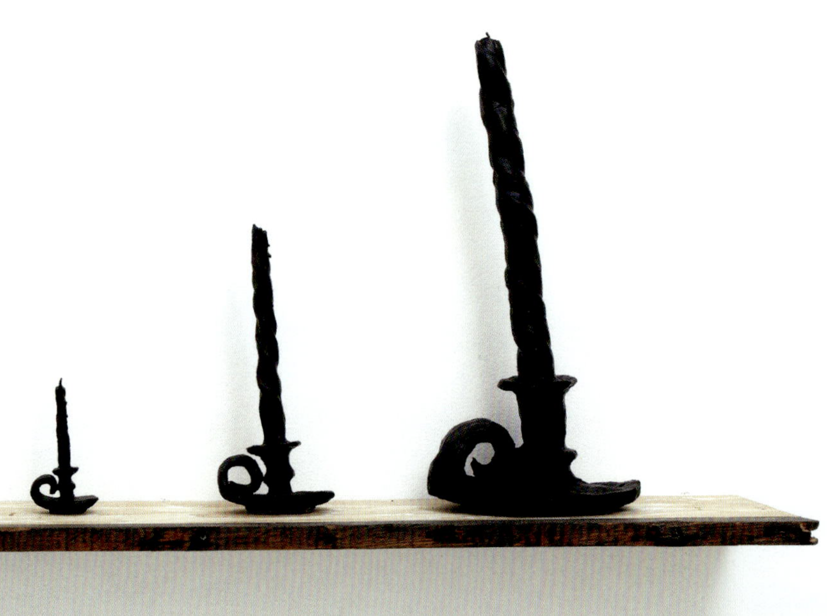

01

Daphne Fitzpatrick's sculptures do not directly resemble human forms, but their strong physical presences often encapsulate personas and emotions through her careful selection and organization of symbolic objects. Her installations, which have included photographs, drawings, found-object arrangements, videos and fabricated sculptures, express the paradoxes and ambiguities that riddle human existence, especially in regard to sexual desire and identity.

Fitzpatrick's approach to building her assemblages is intuitive, yet she consciously gravitates towards collecting objects and materials that have fetishistic associations, or widely recognized sentimental or commercial value, often pitting one against the other to humorous effect. Her works can be Chaplinesque, physically comedic visual puns that teeter, sag, dangle or balance erect. Many have phallic orifices, crevices, totems and poles to confuse and conflate sexual associations in an attempt to destroy gender stereotypes.

In *Split Rail/Pool Cues* (2007), two pool cues cut into a piece of found fencing; while they violently split the rail, their hand-carved crookedness and precarious balancing is peculiarly tender. In *Let Do It* (2007), a folded umbrella balances on its tip to support a beaver-fur top hat, upon which sits a slice of bread cast from plaster and painted in life-like replication. Like René Magritte's dream objects, these three items, juxtaposed in an intentionally ridiculous way, heighten the beaver-fur sexual pun and elevate the bread's value, as if the umbrella/hat combination is simply its pedestal.

Fitzpatrick's favoured materials — leather, rough-hewn wood, canvas, rubber, wax and gold — carry infinite associative weight. Combined into sculptures that are half found and half handmade, they act as catalysts to reveal the artist's nostalgic appreciation for child-like, tomboy-ish tinkering. Although her sculptures have a finished, formal aesthetic, their sense of craft as play combats the adult psychological complexities to which they allude, by reminding the viewer how identity is in part imagistically formed during early developmental stages. Fitzpatrick's use of belts, boots and Converse high-tops as motifs typify this child-like perspective on masculine fashion. She has built a giant leather belt (*Settling Knotty Points*, 2007) and oversized papier-mâché boots, and has hand-sewn life-sized sneakers out of canvas and rubber bath mats. She has also used actual leather straps and shoes in various sculptures, such as those crushed by a ship's mast in *King Neptune* (2007).

In her 2007 solo exhibition 'A Roll in the Hay', Fitzpatrick showed a video in which she took on the role of a nineteenth-century flâneur, dressed in hobo attire (including tattered boots) and strolling down Manhattan's Broadway. The video was part of the installation *Broadway*, a room lined with moving blankets. The video contextualized a suite of sculptures that combined old-fashioned and worn-out items with pristine and modern imagery to maximize sexual allusion and consumer critique. A homemade-looking can of beer hung from its plastic tab in *Tie a Pabst Blue Ribbon*, while *The sideways comfort business* consisted of a shelf supporting three phallic wax candles, each slightly bigger than the last. For *Delphinium Darling* and *Bottom Bottle*, she inserted cast sausages through small holes in glass jugs. Here, items with macho associations were admired, examined, restructured, remade and thus fetishized. To enter the gallery, one was required to walk up an antique fir ramp, *Ramp It Up*, another acute visual study of what objects and spaces represent in the human psyche. [Trinie Dalton]

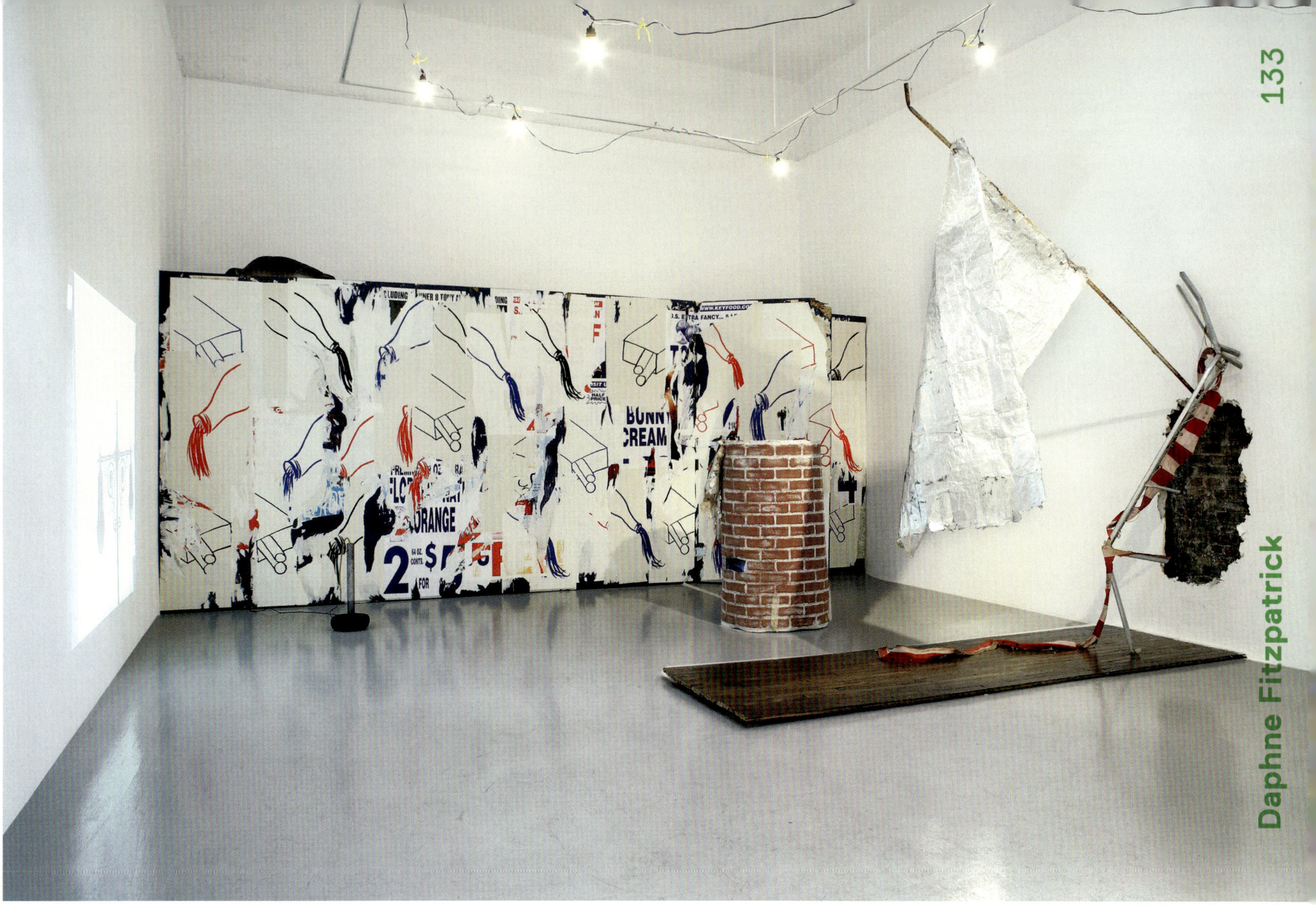

02

03

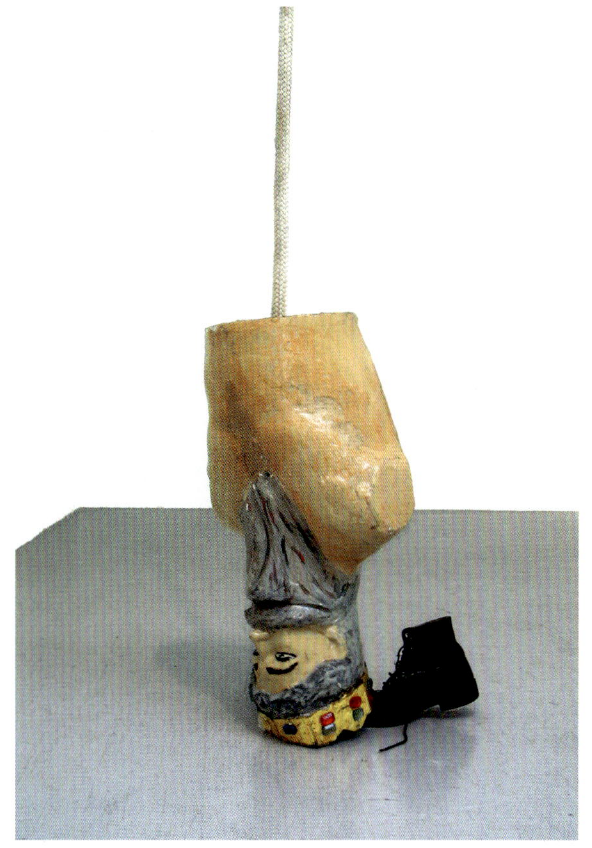

04

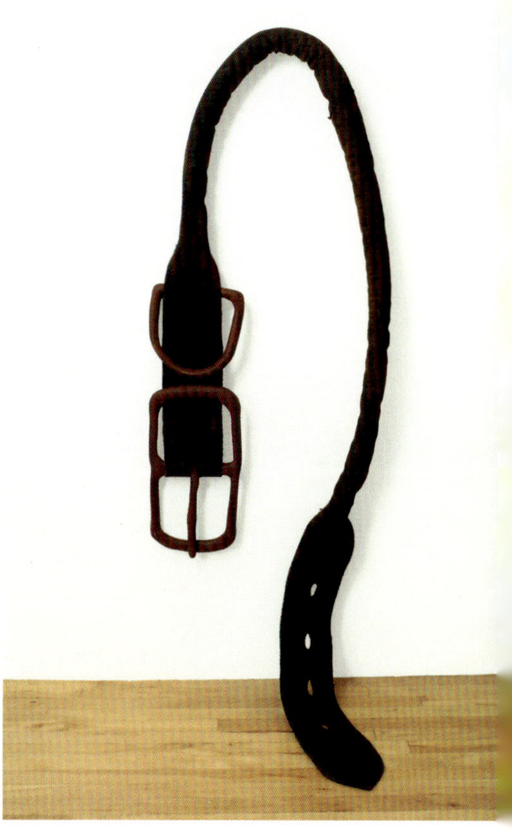

01 *The sideways comfort business*, 2007
Cast wax, plywood, oak
46 × 100 × 19 cm

02 from left:
→ *Broadway*, 2004–07
DVD
65 min.
→ *Sandmand*, 2007
Plywood, silk-screened drawings, packing blankets, 20 minute slideshow (images 2002–07), paint, sisal rope, fabric, lamp
610× 274 × 153 cm
→ *A roll of saran wrap and a bottle of beer*, 2007
Tire, pole, light bulb, plastic
61 × 33 × 26 cm
→ *Laughing in bed together*, 2007
Oak, steel, cotton, paper, silver leaf
335 × 102 × 29 cm

03 King Neptune, 2007
Plaster, fibreglass, concrete, plastic, nylon, leather, paint, cotton
510 × 46 × 31 cm

04 *Settling Knotty Points*, 2001–07
Leather, basswood, waxed thread
Approx. 310 × 26 × 2.5 cm

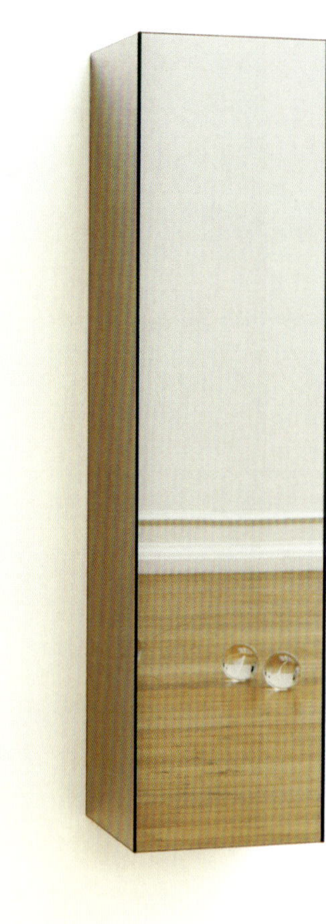

01

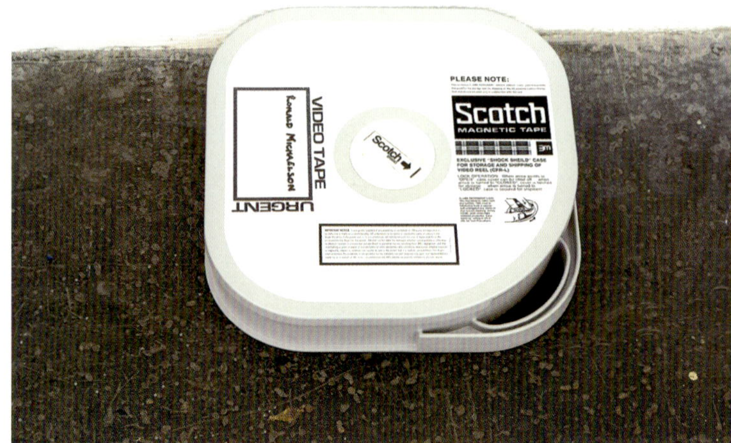

02

01 *She spoke in images like some new language — (Alchemy box #3)*, 2008
One-way glass mirrored box containing selected items, wall text
120 × 30 × 30 cm

02 *Captatio benevolentiae — (Alchemy box #14)*, 2008
Video canister
30 × 30 × 5 cm

The piece that perhaps epitomizes Ryan Gander's self-reflexive and polyvalent practice is *She spoke in images like some new language — (Alchemy box # 3)* (2008). A wall-mounted box made to the same proportions as Donald Judd's *Untitled: blue and yellow painted aluminium* contains, or so a wall text informs us, a book of matches from Hotel Galileo, Milan, with the penned inscription '1665 adore', varying lengths of wool, fax paper and self-adhesive magnetic strip, clothes dye, a holographic crystal and a page about lying torn from a book on body language, among other equally specific items. *Alchemy box* is typical of Gander's practice because it communicates an almost alarming self-assurance regarding its own interiority. The mute box is given a voice, of sorts, that imparts its contents matter-of-factly and invites us to conjure them through our mental efforts if we so wish. There is the sense, though, that their value as cultural signifiers is not dependant on their actuality. Rather than generating meaning for the benefit of comprehension, Gander is more intent on giving autonomy to significance, dissociating objects from systems of usage and placing emphasis on their back stories, whether discerned or imagined. In a related work, *Captatio benevolentiae — (Alchemy box # 14)* (2008), Gander claims that the sealed Kodak canister, which similarly may or may not contain the objects listed in the wall text, originally appeared in David Lamelas' *The Violent Tapes*. Gander corrals cultural history, alongside personal associations, into the forum of his own practice, not with glancing delicacy or eulogistic bombast, but with head-on opportunism.

At times Gander makes the title do the lion's share of the work in pinpointing meaning, as in *A sheet of paper on which I was about to draw, as it slipped from my table and fell to the floor* (2008). Without this explanation, one would not grasp the import of the etched image of a furling sheet of A4 at the heart of the hundred crystal balls strewn about the gallery floor. But then again, their physical presence does not necessarily substantiate the title's claim. Words, like objects, Gander suggests, are malleable and not necessarily coupled to truth.

The New New Alphabet (2008) translates the plasticity of words from conceptual to more tangible realms. Letter-forms produced as wooden printer's blocks were devised by Gander to print over Wim Crouwel's typeface, The New Alphabet, and make it more legible. Crouwel's typeface was designed in 1967 for display on early cathode ray tube screens, and Gander's overlay acknowledges the technological developments that have displaced the original to the realm of nostalgia. Presented unceremoniously on the floor, and cryptically divorced from the original typeface that they append, Gander's blocks require us to investigate his sources and, more importantly, to want to investigate them. Sculpture, for Gander, is a catalyst for curiosity and healthy scepticism. [Sally O'Reilly]

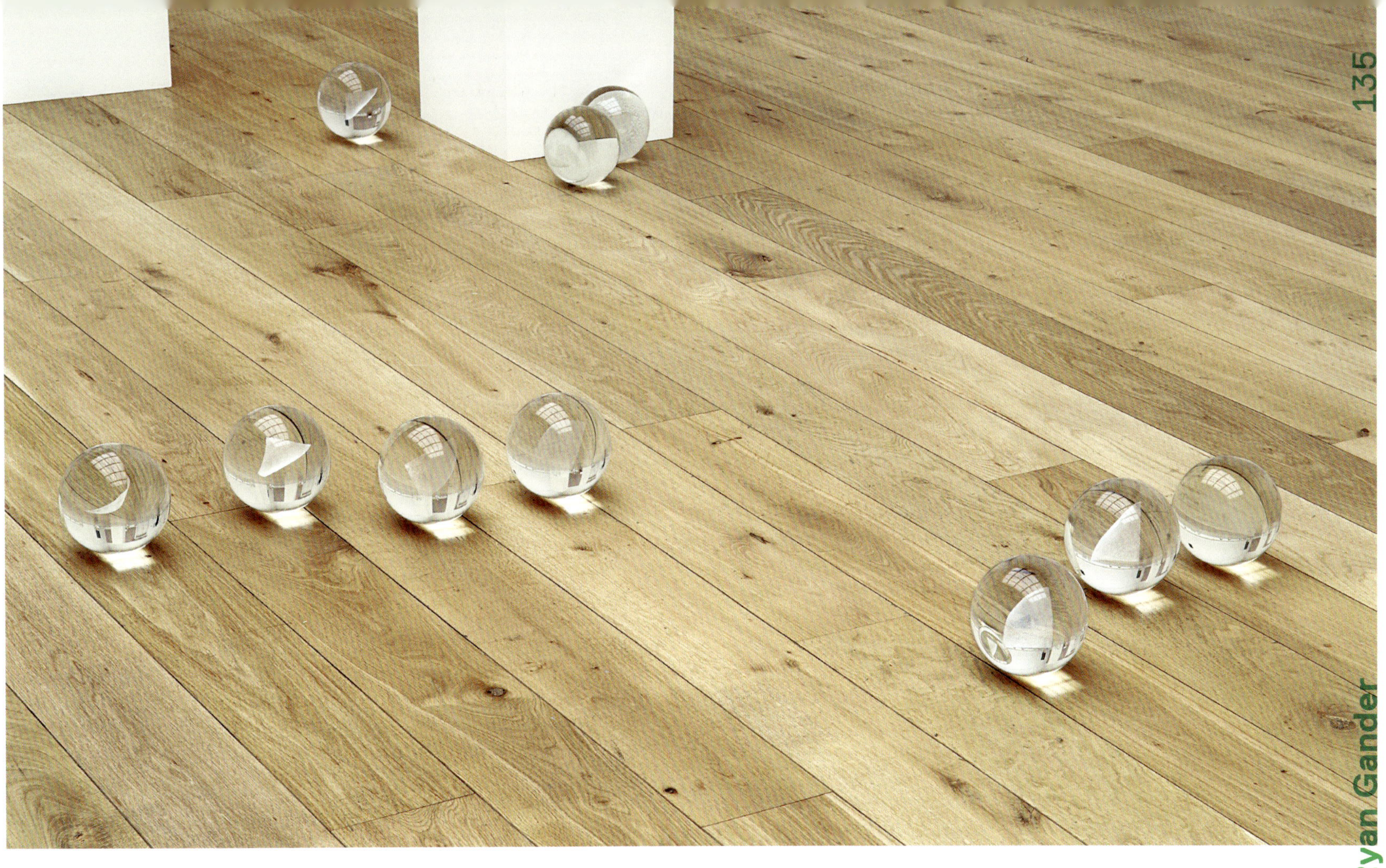

03

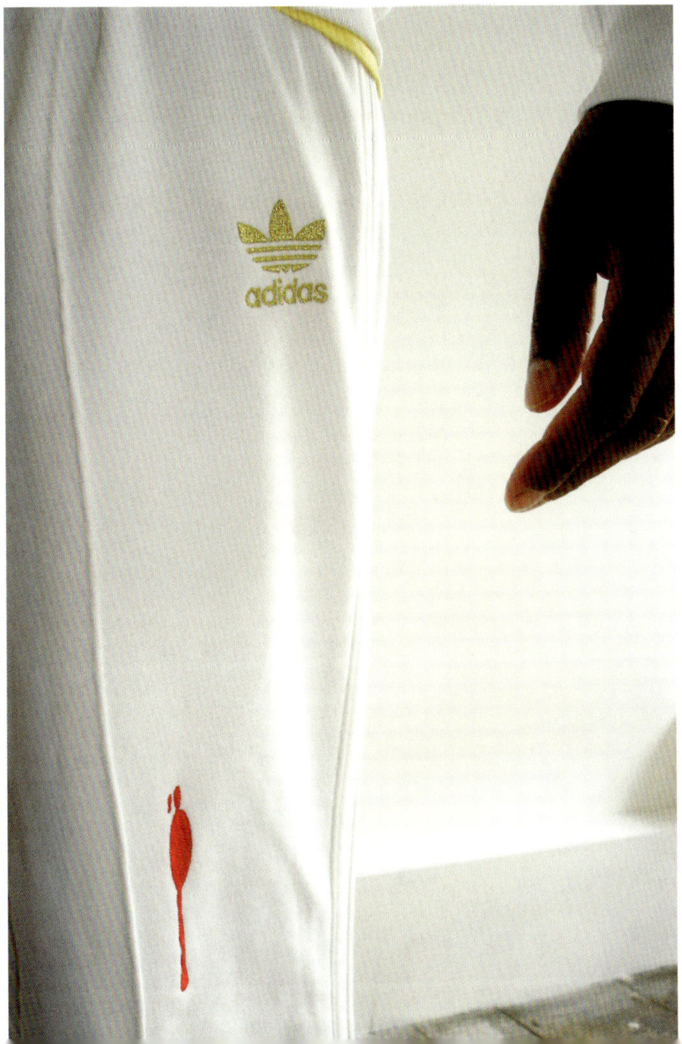

03 *A sheet of paper on which I was about to draw, as it slipped from my table and fell to the floor*, 2008
100 crystal balls
Each diameter 20 cm

04 *This Consequence*, 2008
Tracksuit with
embroidered blood stain
S, M, L, XL

05 *The New New Alphabet*, 2008
Printer's wooden blocks
42 × 33 × 18 cm

04

05

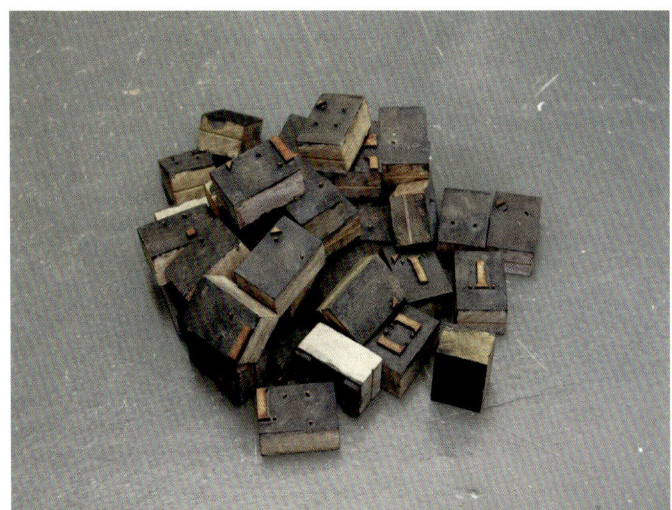

The collective Gelitin (Wolfgang Ganter, Ali Janka, Florian Reither and Tobias Urban) creates site-specific works that eschew the sculptural fetish in favour of interactive and malleable installations that invite a socially function. In *Otto Volante* (2004), for example, a fully functional roller coaster was available for use in the gallery space.

Inciting spontaneous situations that challenge conventions, Gelitin converts visitors into participants (or even into protagonists), encouraging self-reflection and a vivid biological perception of one's own body, used as an improvised sculptural material.

Simultaneously, the artists aim to redefine the public role of the artwork. Their sometimes extravagant social works construct situations around notions of encounter, congregation, obsession and play that occur in a framework between art and life. Adherence to normal social parameters is exchanged for a primal and childish, yet fearless, vision of our time. Their exhibition 'Chinese Synthese Leberkäse' (2006) at Kunsthaus Bregenz, for example, was introduced as follows: 'A monolithic exhibition by Gelitin. Welcome and drop your pants on the ground floor. A forest of poems surrounds the visitor, lures her into the elephant with its labyrinth of hand-knitted letters.' (The latter refers to *Das Kakabet*, a new font created and published in 2007.)

For *The Dig Cunt* (2007), a seven-day performance on Coney Island beach, the group would dig a hole in the sand each day and fill it in the evening. Friends and passers-by joined in with this exhausting, function-free labour, where collectivity became both the mode and the purpose of the work. The message is eloquent, real and direct. There are no special effects that might blur the relation between artistic production and public reception. Addressed to everybody and intelligible on multiple levels, Gelitin's works do not seek final solutions, definite explanations or appeal to historical references. The artists attempt to demystify art by reshaping popular icons. *Hase* (2005–25), for instance, is a sixty-metre pink woollen rabbit, sited in the mountains of northern Italy, where it will remain until it naturally degrades in approximately twenty years.

Gelitin is structured around an organized anarchy that transplants conventions through the use of universal body language and a disarming simplicity coloured by an improbably elegant kitsch. The quartet of artists, surrounded by a loose group of friends, highlights the difference between how to use something and the use of something within a context where the individual is protected by the collective. Since unconventional behaviour can easily be reduced to labelling, the quartet's name has already changed once and will probably change again, encouraging innovative external reinterpretations of its practice. Their work, defined by one of the members as 'very noticeable, but impossible to locate', yearns for continuous reshaping. [Francesco Stocchi]

01

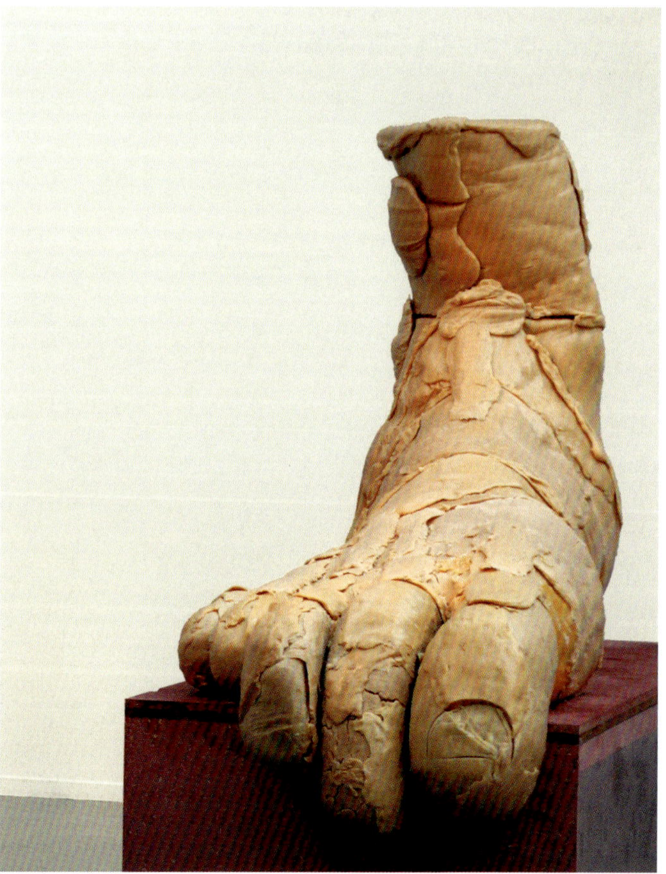

02

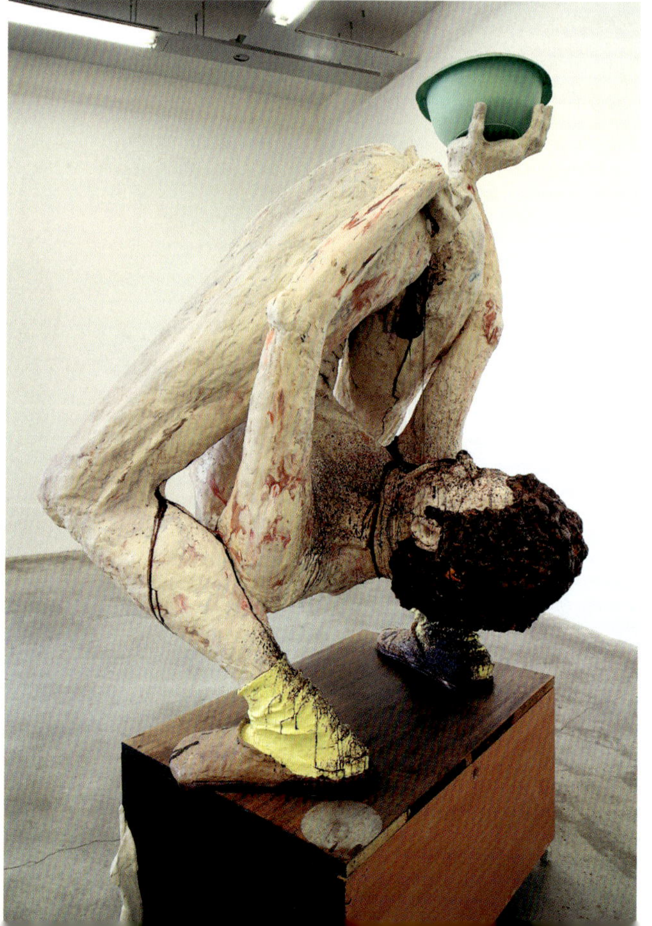

03

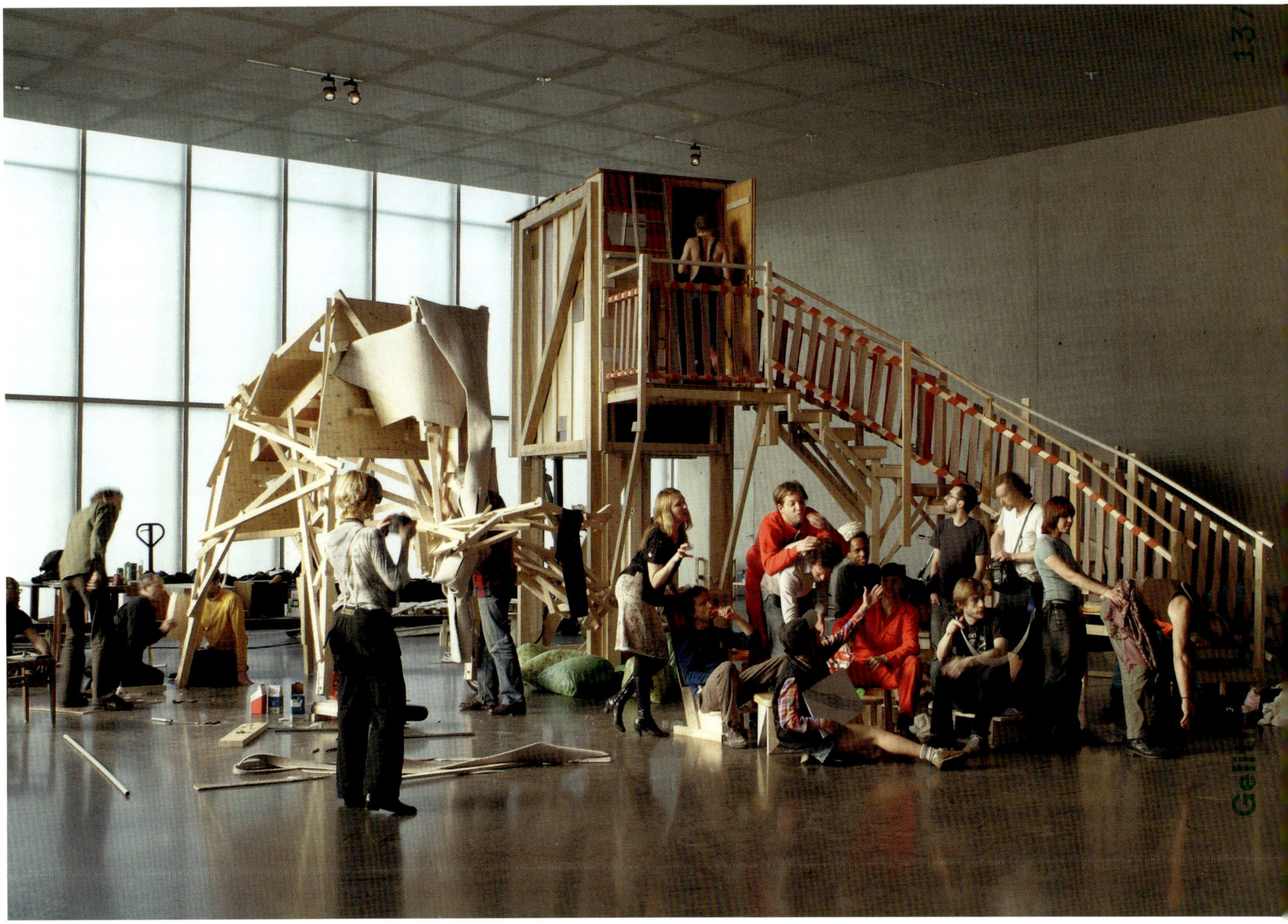

04

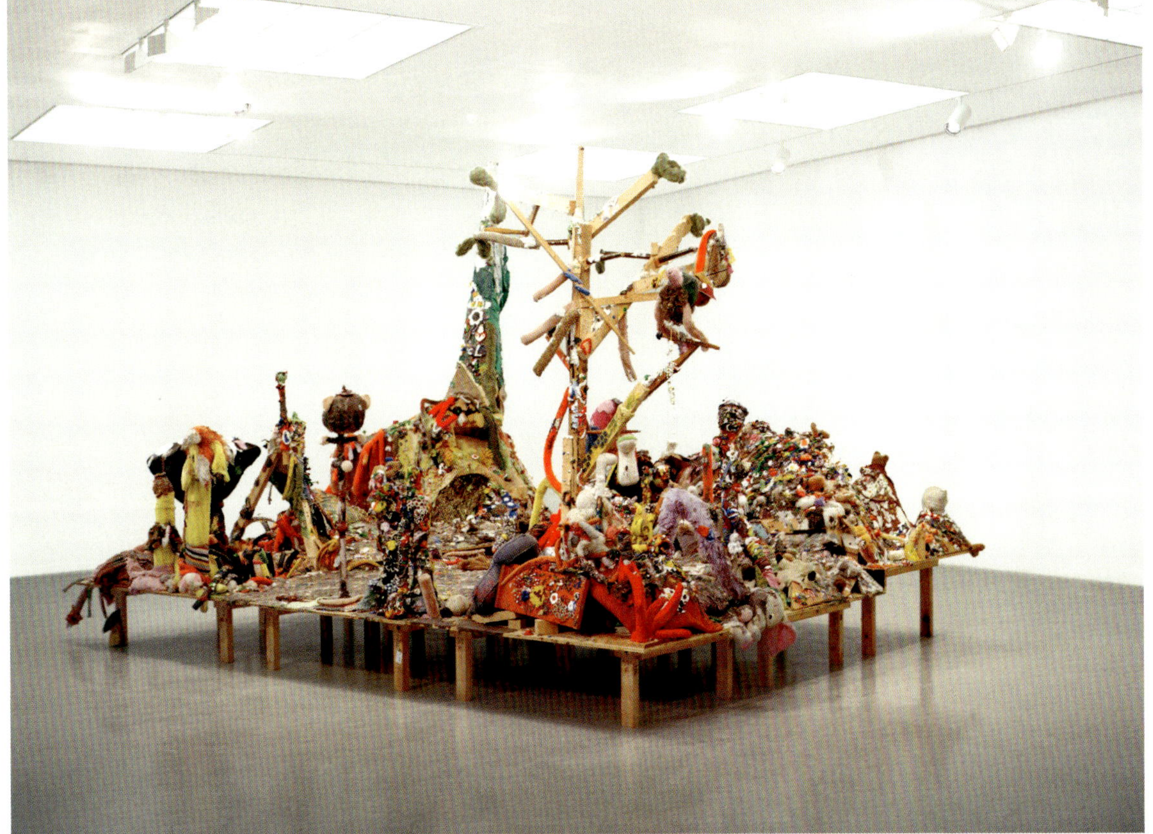

01 *Untitled*, 2008
Wood, cheese
Approx. 220 × 250 × 80 cm

02 *Schokolade Wasserfall*, 2006
Wood, plasticine, pump, heater, chocolate, strawberries
230 × 128 × 111 cm

03 *Chinese Synthese Leberkäse — Kacksaal*, 2006
Wood, toilet, mirrors
Approx. 5 × 2 × 7 m

04 *Skulptur für den flughafen*, 2005
Wood, stuffed animals, plasticine
495 × 375 × 300 cm

05

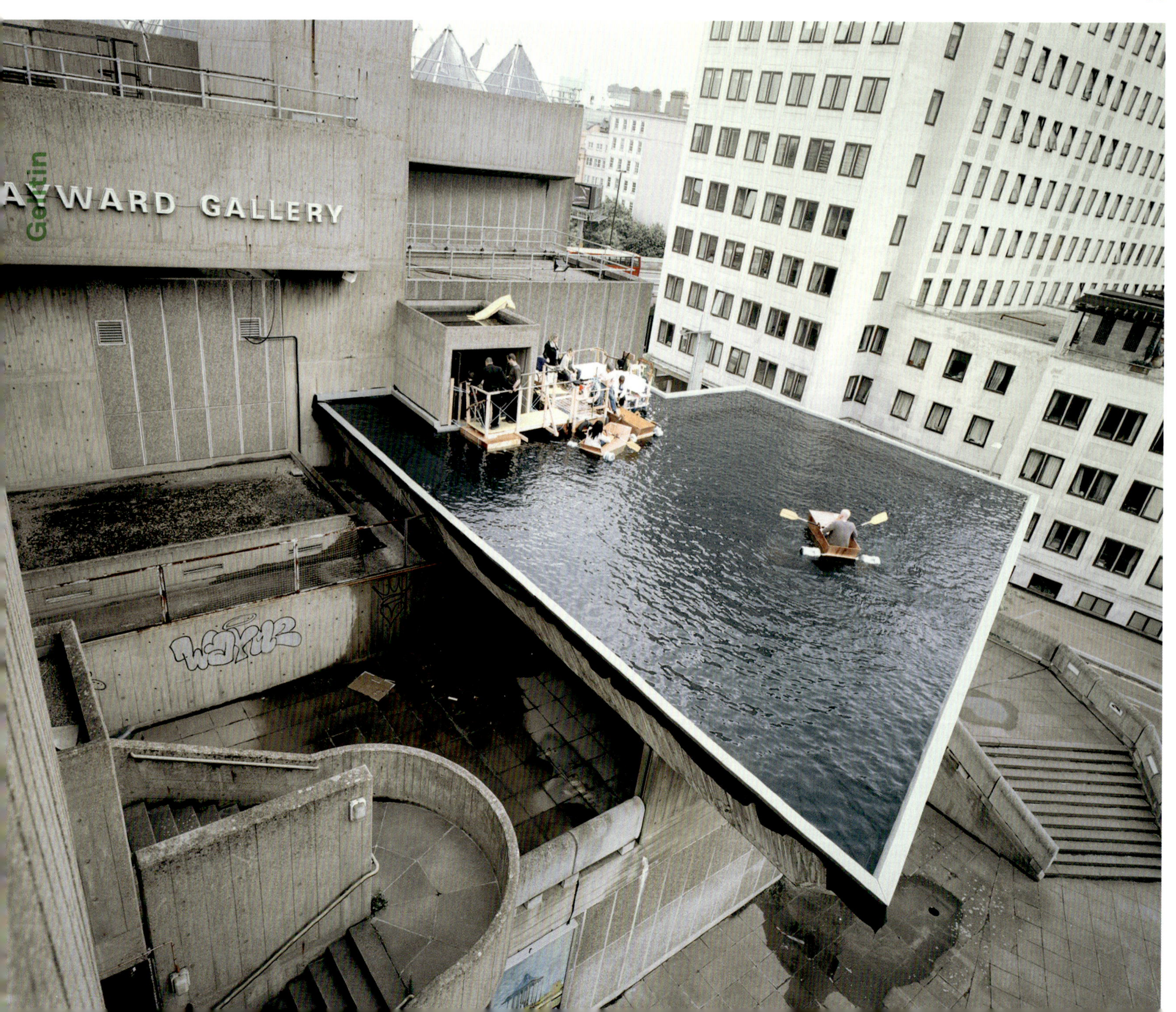

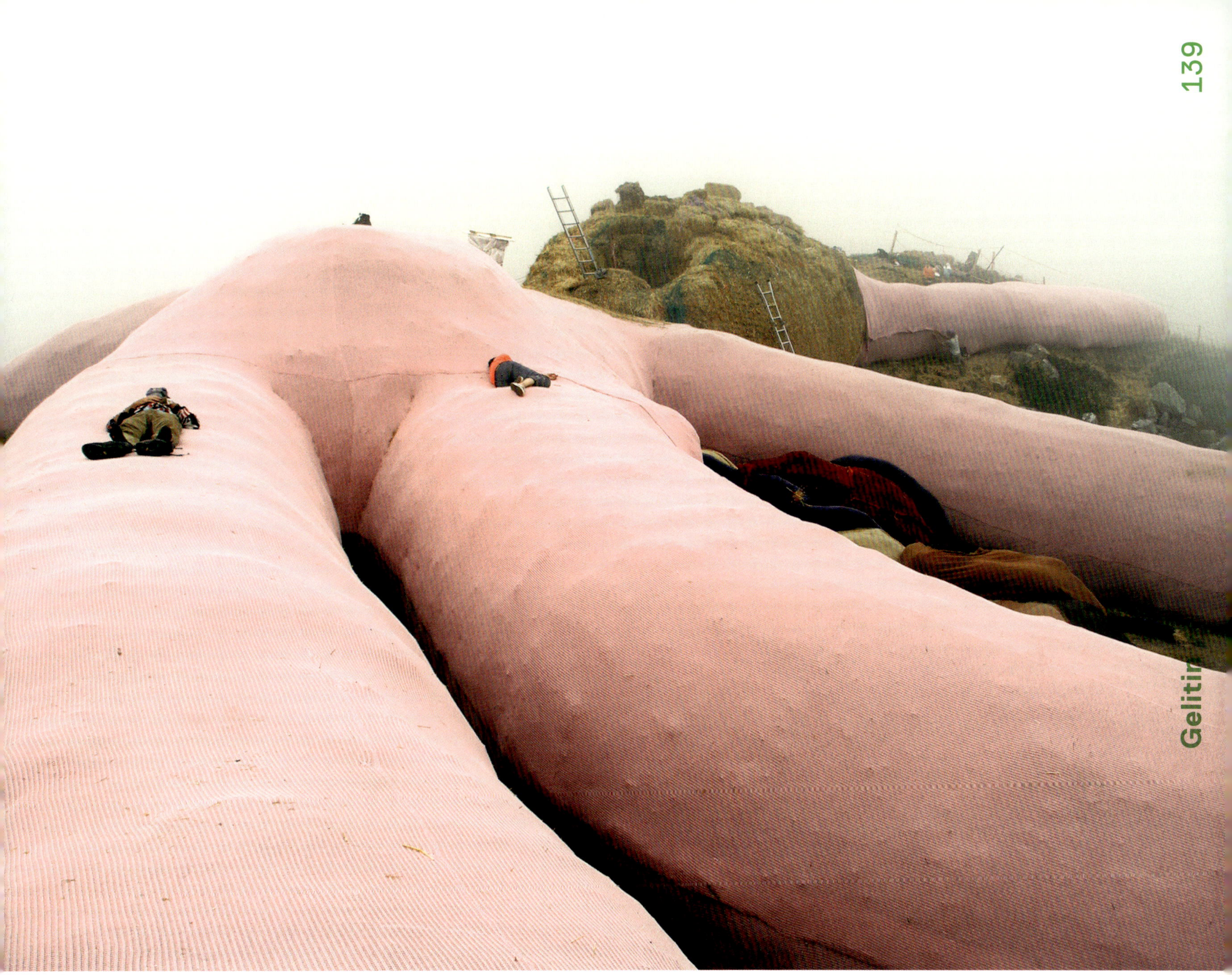

06

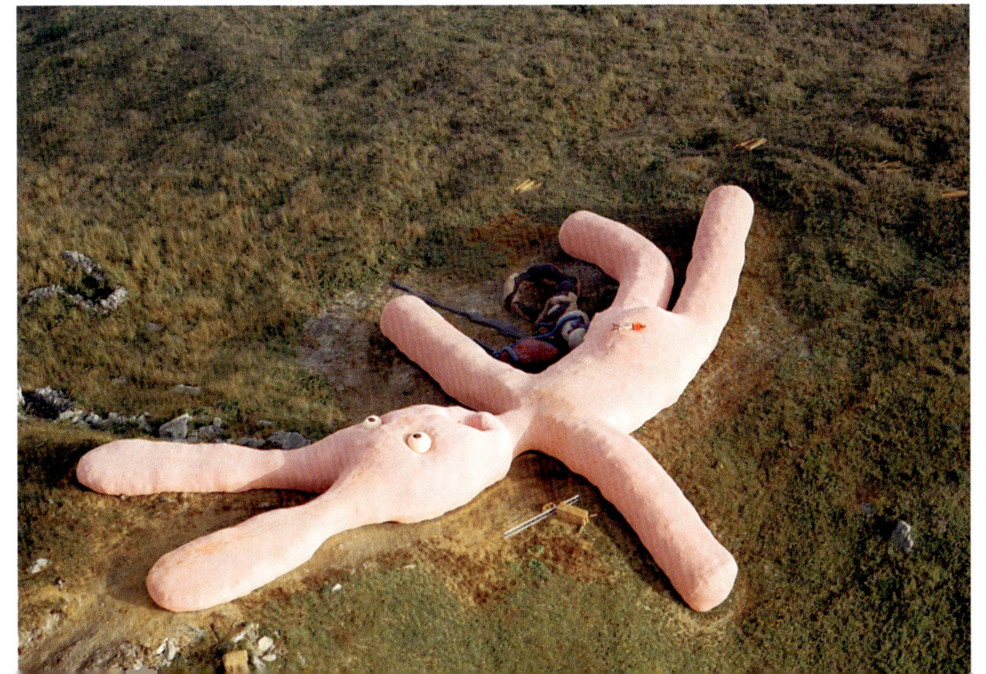

07

05 *Normally, Proceeding, and Unrestricted With Without Title*, 2008
Wood, paddles, water
Dimensions variable
Hayward Gallery, London

06, 07 *Hase*, 2005–25
Straw, wool
Approx. 3 × 60 × 40 m
Artesina, Italy

'Nothingness' has always fascinated scientists and artists, whether, for instance, in dissecting the vertiginous implications of a mathematical zero or exploring the impact of the void. Equally fascinated by this theme, Loris Gréaud rejects the notion that nothingness is invisible, working systematically with scientists, engineers, architects, writers and musicians to reveal otherwise. Nothingness and its corollaries (the void, silence, the invisible, the off-screen, immateriality and non-presence) are not conceived as the absence of something, but as an entity that the artist confronts in order to generate a paradoxical dynamic. Adjusting the scale of his works to the object of his exploration, he moves from a cosmic vision of the 'Great Void' (the seismic echoes of the Big Bang in *Tremors Were Forever*, 2005) to nano-sculptures invisible to the naked eye.

Since his first solo exhibition 'Silence Goes More Quickly When Played Backwards' (Le Plateau, Frac-Ile-de-France, Paris, 2005), works such as his flavourless sweets with the slogan 'A Taste of Illusion' (*Célador*, 2008), invisible architecture made of air currents (*Les Résidents 2*, 2005), his cinema for absentees (*Dark Side*, 2006), or his explorations of the utopian research of Buckminster Fuller's geodesic domes — founded on the principle of a perfect interpenetration between emptiness and fullness — have invited us to redefine our apprehension of the real within a broadened consciousness.

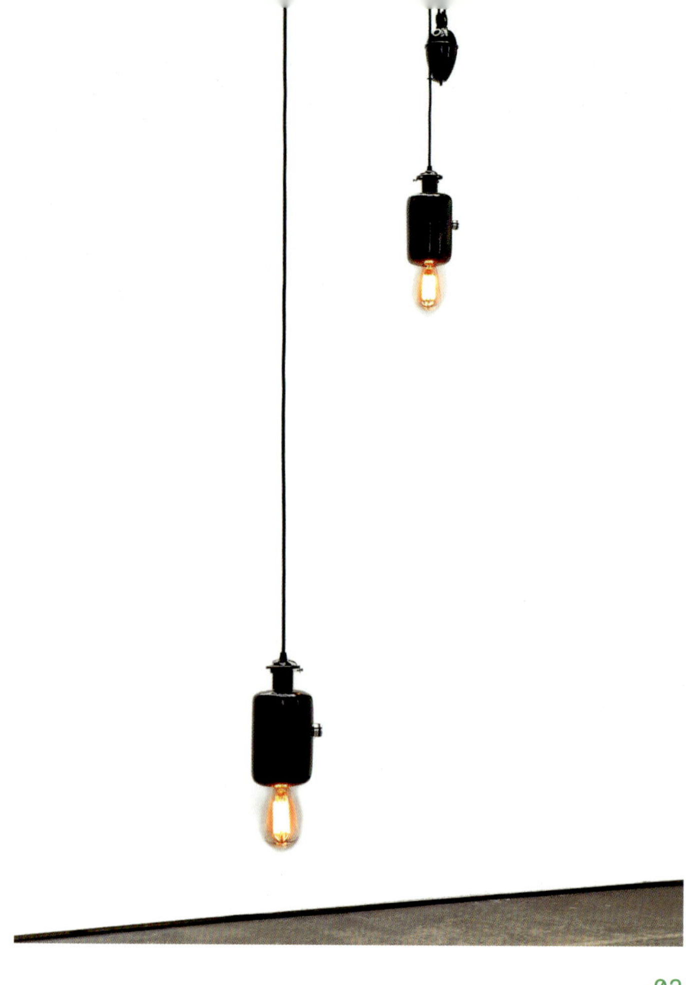

02

01

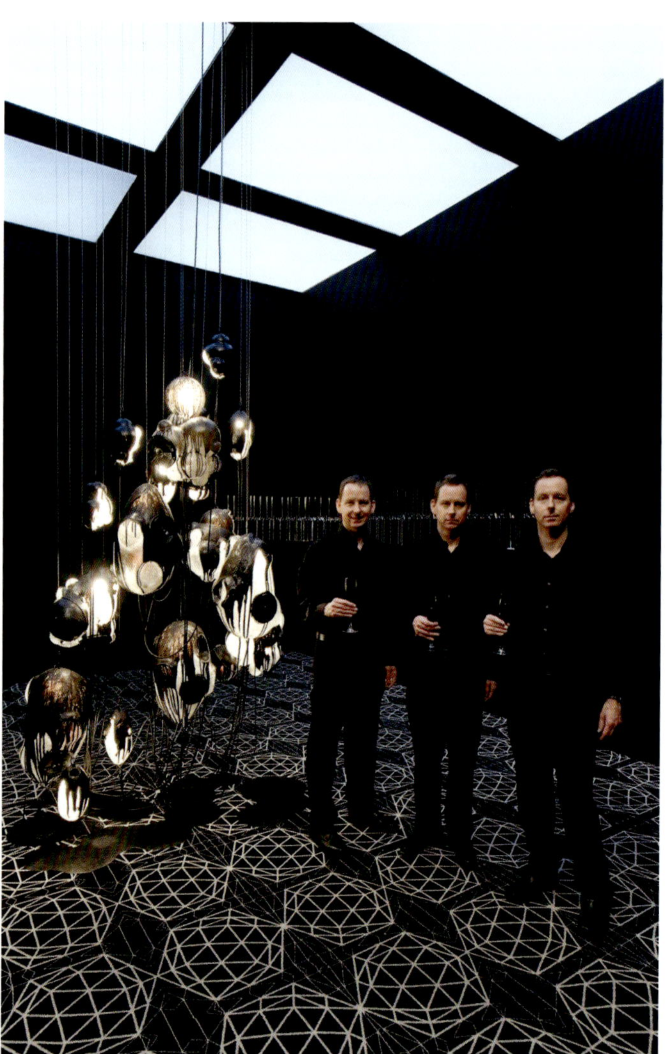

Gréaud's works cannot be considered as a simple sequence of isolated elements, but are part of a relentless attempt to create a true universe, where an exhibition escapes its own *exhibited* condition and instead takes the form of an opera, script, playground, museum, artist's studio or factory. A libretto can thus be at the root of both an opera and an exhibition ('Cellar Door', ICA, London, 2008). This model, based on the generation of repeated forms, defines his entire artistic path: his works are sampled and played out from one exhibition to the next, creating strange impressions of déjà vu (and, as with the black cat in the film *The Matrix*, every notion of déjà vu suggests a crack in the apprehension of reality).

Taking on board Arthur Danto's claims that there is no artwork without interpretation, Gréaud elaborates a formal grammar that translates theoretical or physiological codes into a visual language. In *Frequency of an Image* (2006), for example, the brainwaves of the artist can be translated into a code of pulsating lights. Skilfully mixing references and signs from different worlds, Gréaud launches incursions into the recent history of art and, in a quasi-pataphysical attempt, provokes interferences between Minimalist art and science fiction, paintball duels and Kurt Schwitters' *Merzbau*, chaos theory and a geometrically patterned carpet, the Milky Way and marketing techniques. To tackle such a project, one must abandon the reassuring comfort of a selective logic and venture into the meanders of Gréaud's vertiginous, schizophrenic mindset, embracing the 'obtuse meaning' of his work. [Marc-Olivier Wahler]

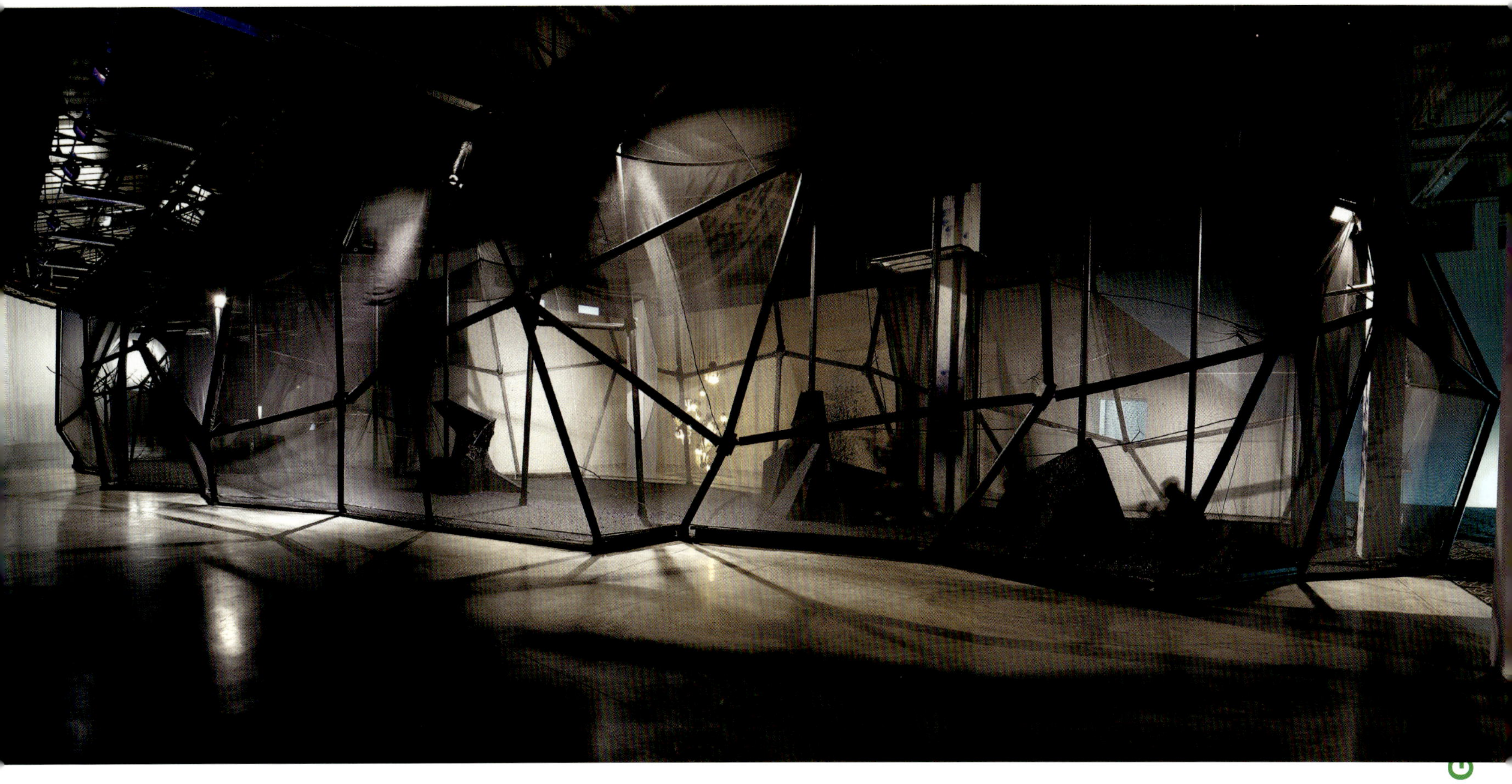

03

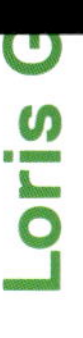

01 *Cellar Door (Once is Always Twice), Spore Speakers*, 2008
Resin, speakers, modified light bulbs
Dimensions variable
Developed by Vincent Nevot for Gréaudstudio

02 *Frequency of an Image (M46 Edit)*, 2007
Specific electronic device, resin, modified light bulb, M46 paint
29 × 15 cm

03 *The Merzball Pavilion* (with DGZ Research), 2007–08
Specially developed aluminium and epoxy painted canvas
9.2 × 5.8 × 26.5 m

04 *Neon Ball Bubble* (with DGZ Research), 2007–08
Neon, Inox steel structure, black Altuglass
4 × 4 × 4 m

04

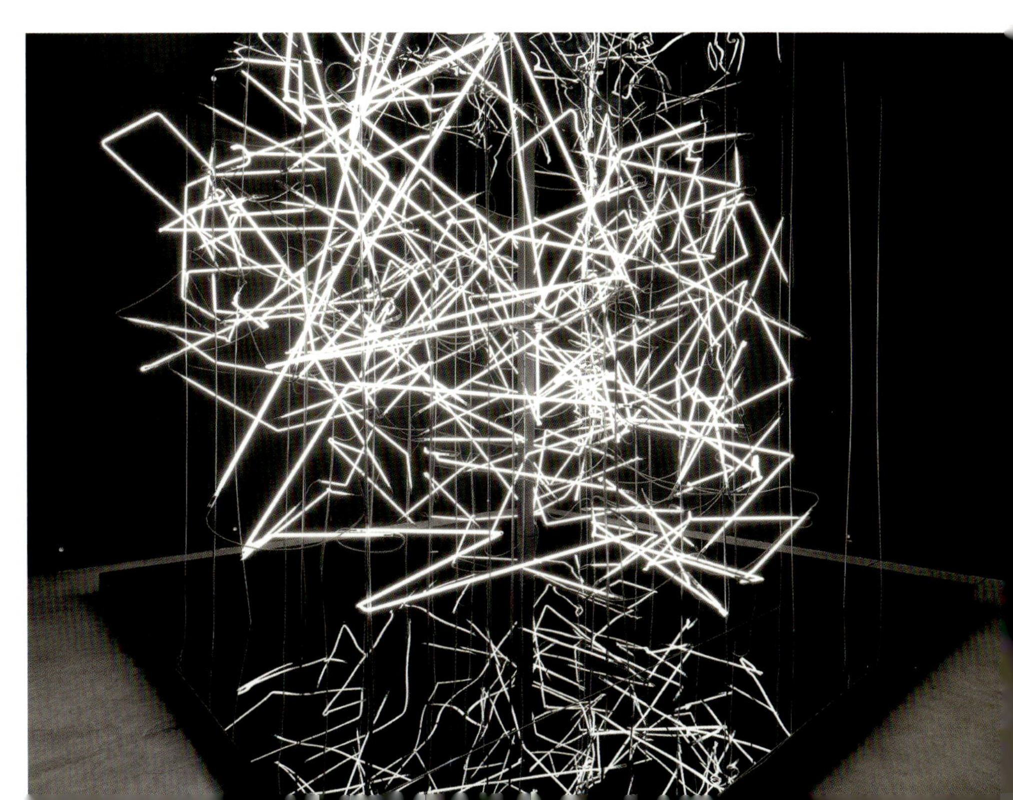

Rachel Harrison's work postures as sculpture, exists as sculpture and expands the vocabulary of sculpture while commenting on modes of representation. Often cumulative structures built from painted sculptural surfaces, inserted imagery and ready made goods, her works function as equations in which the whole informs every part and every part modifies the reading of the whole.

The array of works in her 2007 series *Trees for the Forest*, for instance, combines found flea-market portraits and stacked pedestal-like sculptures in ways that explore the interplay of forms, confusing distinctions between volume and surface. Subverting the expectations of high and low, found paintings float within the works, connoting a repertoire of art-historical references by virtue of their style and content. The portraits also act as decoys, initially luring the viewer's attention away from the abstract formal complexity of the pedestals, which upon inspection reveal themselves to be arenas for painterly and sculptural experimentation.

With her installations and freestanding sculptures, Harrison frequently plays sensual and perceptual games with the viewer. Instead of behaving as passive, static structures, the works' configurations serve as reminders that looking is a relational, time-based act that operates on a selection/exclusion basis. In *Amerigo Vespucci* (2007), for example, the viewer is confronted by a jagged, vividly painted sculptural pillar that has a bitten apple perched atop one side and, at the foot of the other, a propped photograph of actor Leonardo DiCaprio staring back. Impossible to see as a whole from any one angle, the work forces the viewer to make choices about how to approach it while its elements by turn enthrall or dodge the gaze; up close, the sculpture dissolves into a surface of elaborately applied paint.

While decoding and recoding the formal properties of sculpture, Harrison's work also plays off language structures and associations to sometimes create a humorous rebus-like effect. In 'If I Did It', the 2007 exhibition featuring *Amerigo Vespucci*, a group of totem-like sculptures dedicated to prominent male figures examined masculine personae and attributions of cultural and historical value as attached to such figures as Tiger Woods, Johnny Depp, Alexander the Great and Claude Lévi-Strauss. Generally constructed as erect sheaths, these complex abstracted forms function as allusive rather than descriptive portraits while referencing the conventions of twentieth-century sculpture.

In *Fats Domino*, for example, a Slim Fast can is placed on top of an abstract structure made of accumulated planes; a chunk has seemingly been removed from the structure's centre. Turning it alternately into a disproportionate column or a partial shelf, the Slim Fast can on display breaks with abstraction and reaffirms the existence of everyday human reality by inserting a reference to the body, canons of beauty and consumer culture. The celebrity images incorporated into the surfaces of many of these sculptures add to their anthropomorphic qualities.

Responding to some of the most important legacies of Modernism, Process art and Post-Minimalism while figuring references to totems, menhirs and other archetypal formations, Harrison's works detach themselves from the sacred realm of abstraction, grounding the viewer with elements from our everyday consumer reality. These works act like Andy Warhol's time capsules, congregating objects and references into cultural systems that could one day come to represent an era. [Sarina Basta]

01

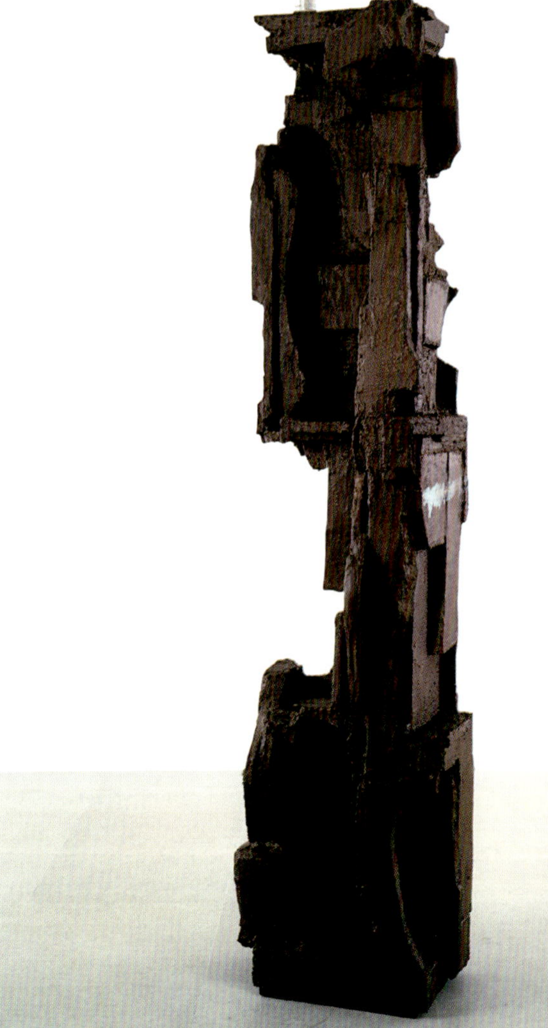

01 *Fats Domino*, 2006
Wood, polystyrene, cement, Parex, acrylic, Slim Fast Milk Chocolate meal option
267 × 64 × 56 cm

02 *Alexander the Great*, 2007
Wood, chicken wire, polystyrene, cement, Parex, acrylic, mannequin, Jeff Gordon waste basket, plastic Abraham Lincoln mask, sunglasses, fabric, necklace
221 × 231 × 101 cm

02

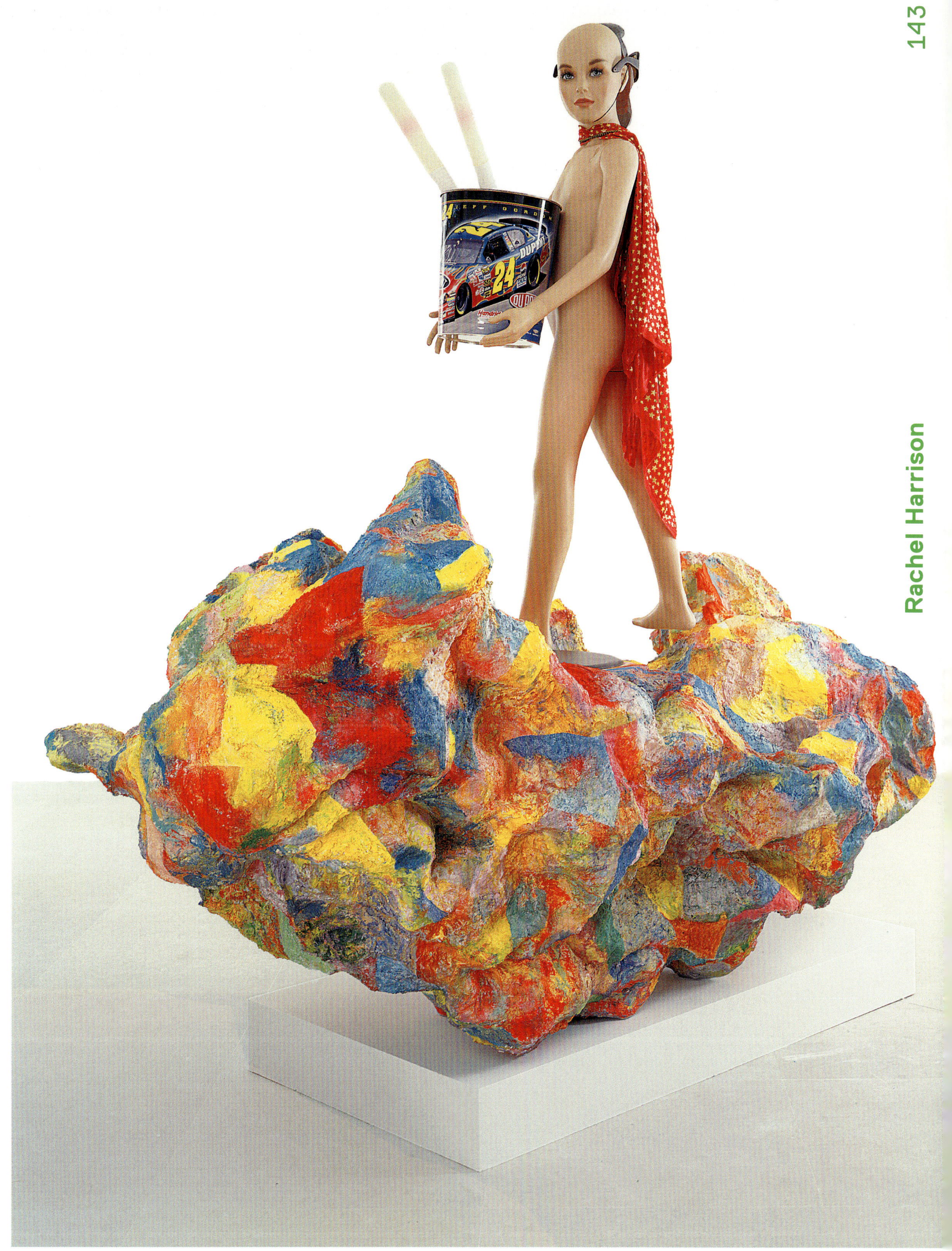

03 *I'm with Stupid*, 2007
Wood, polystyrene, cement, Parex, acrylic, child mannequin, papier-mâché skull, green wig, festive hat, SpongeBob SquarePants sneakers, Pokemon T-shirt, wheels, canned fruits and vegetables, artificial carrot, artificial feathers, artificial grass, Batman and Cat mask, necktie, scarf, plastic beads
165 × 79 × 61 cm

04 from left:
→ *Ma Bell*, 2008
Wood, polystyrene, cement, Parex, acrylic, telephone
37 × 61 × 226 cm
→ *Second Voyage of the Beagle*, 2008
58 digital inkjet prints
Each 41 × 29 cm
→ *One Ton Prop*, 2008
Wood, polystyrene, cement, Parex, acrylic, ski
84 × 48 × 201 cm
→ *Distinction*, 2008
Wood, polystyrene, cement, Parex, acrylic, framed mirror
38 × 40 × 178 cm
→ *Hammer and Lemon*, 2008
Wood, polystyrene, cement, Parex, acrylic, hammer, artificial lemon
41 × 38 × 148 cm
→ *Stump Speech*, 2008
Wood, polystyrene, cement, Parex, acrylic, toy gun
54 × 61 × 100 cm

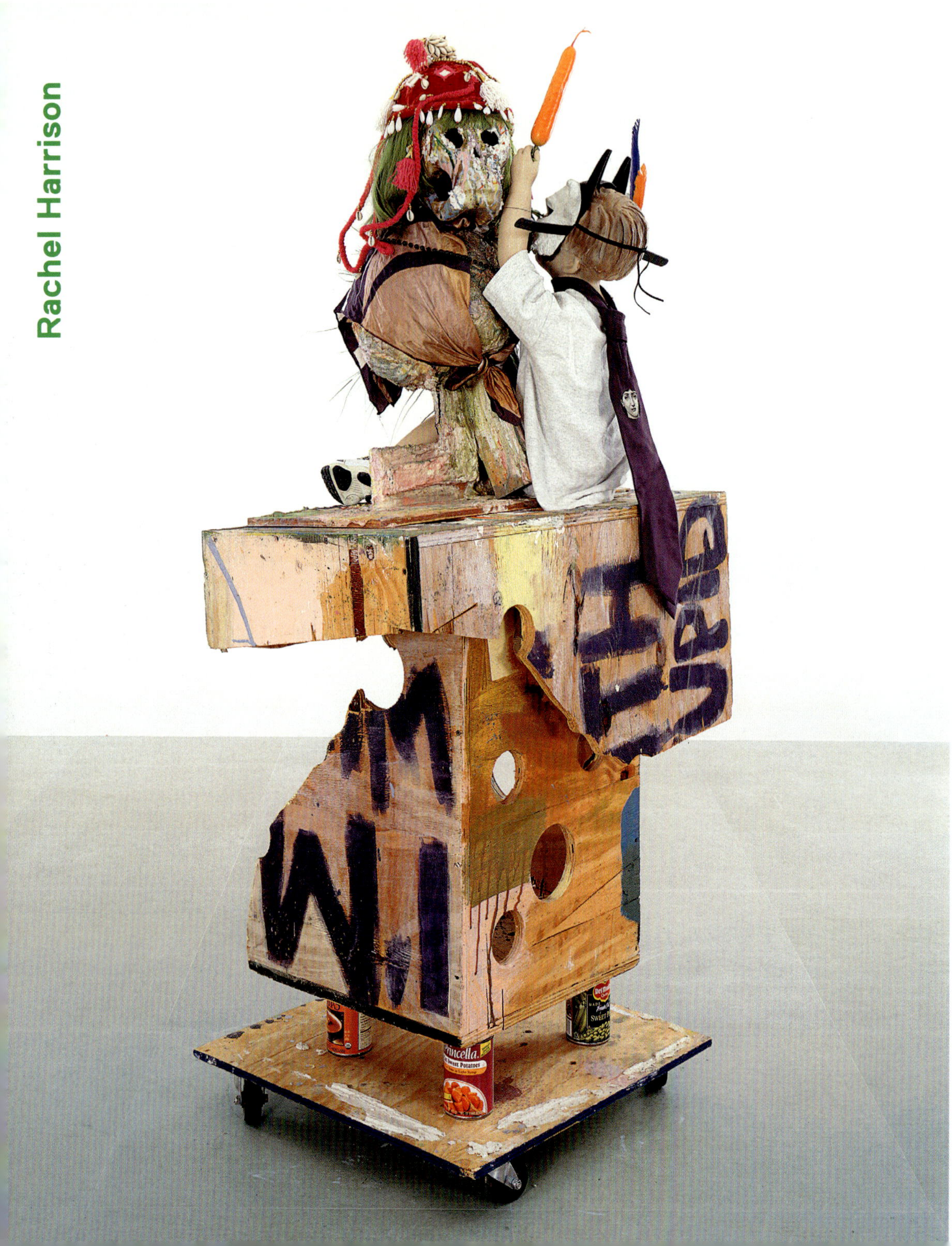

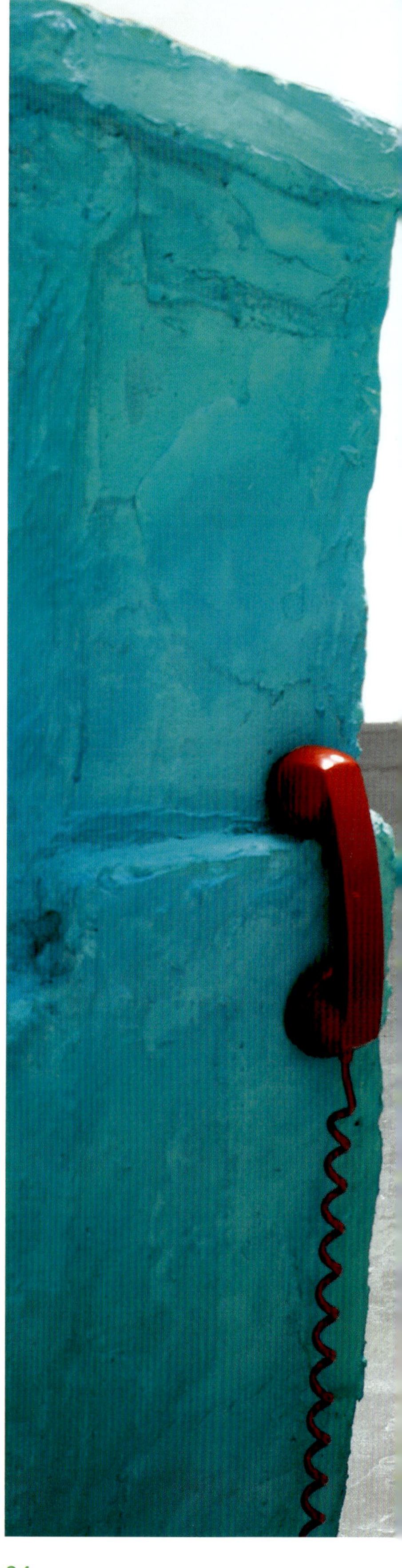

04

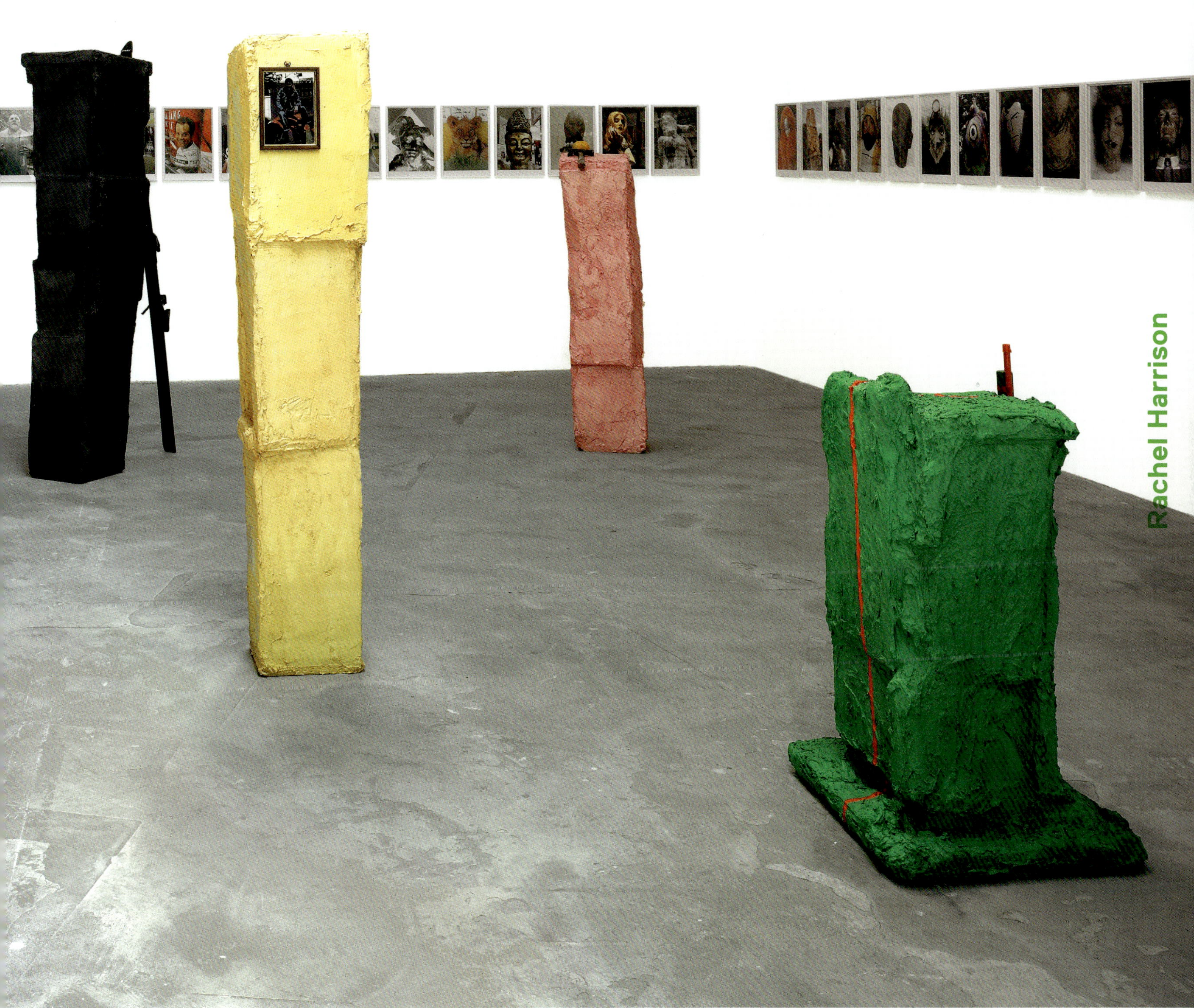

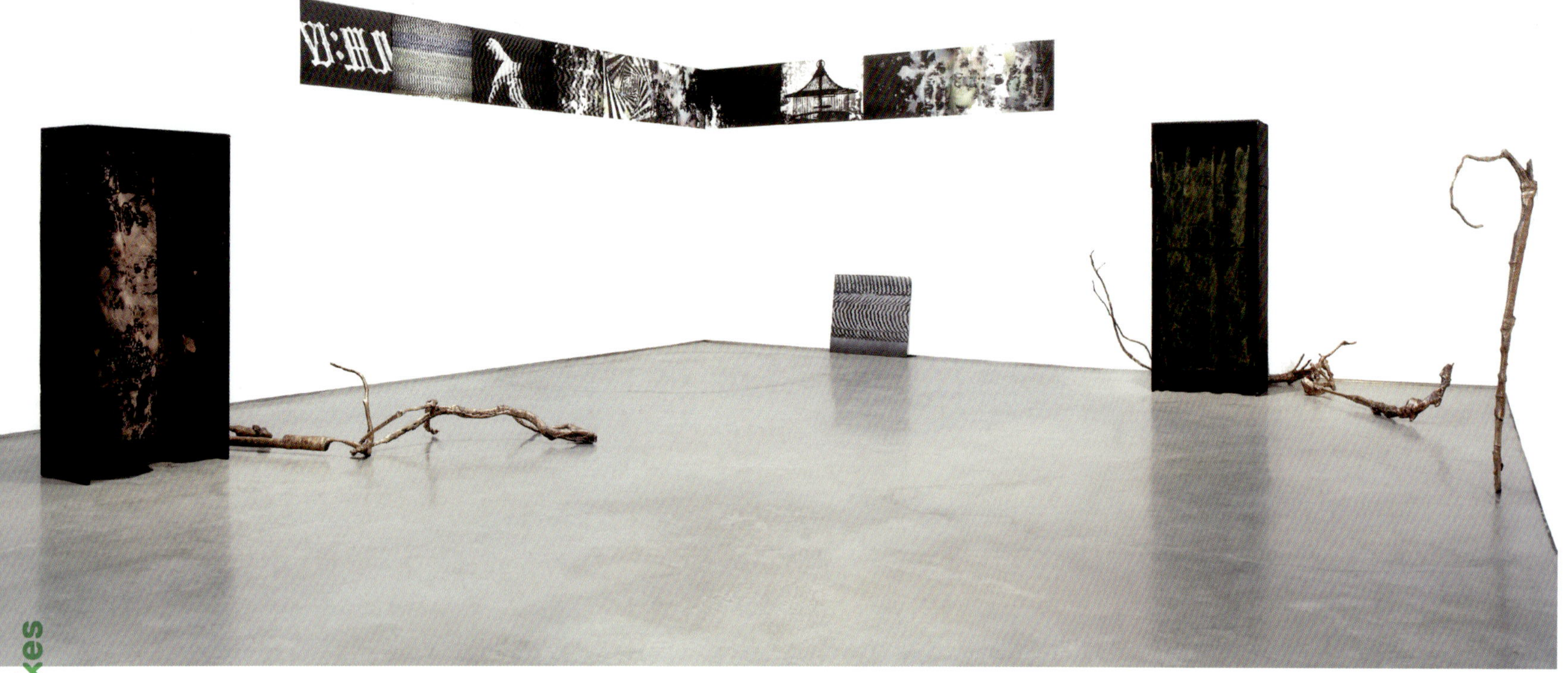

01

The unusual impetus for Jay Heikes' recent body of work was a joke — a rather generic, unfunny joke about a parrot's absurd stand-off with a one-eyed pirate. The joke was a generative element, its narrative and visual components tools in the artist's kit of parts. What began with Heikes 'performing' the joke on video segued into drawings made from the video stills, as well as painting, sculpture and installations, which he called 're-tellings' and with which he telegraphed the work deeper into the realms of metaphor. The joke figures in the work only obliquely, a frame of reference rather than a narrative illustrated. (In fact, it is only directly referenced in texts like this one).

This body of work seeks at once to interrogate and create language using codified motifs: clocks, beds, rooms, traps, hooks. For instance, the *Changing Room* sculptures are places where one could do just that — change. The roughly made boxes are variously sized: sometimes big enough for a human figure; sometimes a squat, horizontal box resembling a puppet theatre, replete with an awkwardly scaled and haphazardly constructed pair of laced-together jester's boots. The boxes' canvas curtains are painted with bleach that oozes like a primordial soup. All the works are parts of a narrative but are comprehended as abstract representations of broader ideas: limbo, stasis, repetition, voided histories and absurd gestures. It was Heikes' formal and conceptual explorations of topics from stage props to the existentialist playwrights Samuel Beckett and Jean-Paul Sartre that led to these particular works, which borrow the apparatus of theatre, performance and staging. Exhibitions are in themselves stages, after all.

Heikes employs a vast range of techniques, in part inspired by Arte Povera's tactic of using 'poor' (i.e., everyday) materials to great effect. His intensive material explorations took the joke through the paces of its inevitable degeneration and demise. The joke was a battery forced to corrode. This narrative mutation found its analogue in materials, in effect transferring concept to form. For example, a simple hooked cane morphed into an assemblage of wood and tape, cast in various metals. Some sculptures mix bronze and iron, a chemical composition akin to a battery, and like a battery they are decaying, changing — a relic produced by time.

Heikes' recent series of paintings on steel bring full-spectrum colour to his work. 'Fallen' pictures, they blur the line between painting and sculpture by resting heavily on the floor. They are pictures of static, an image borrowed from the television screen, or perhaps from the end of the video-recorded joke. Static is a condition of not moving, breakdown; it is leftover radiation from the Big Bang. Static is the end of the broadcast day and the painterly gestures bleached out of the changing-room curtain. Painting static freezes it just long enough for a new picture to emerge well the scrambled lines. The surface, marred by rust that slips out from under the applied colour, is entropic, constantly mutating by rusting away. For now, Heikes' work rests in the crux of a paradoxical condition of simultaneous stasis and entropy. [Jenelle Porter]

01 from left:
→ *A Broken Record Not a Broken Record*, 2007
Bronze, bleached cotton, wood, hardware, paper, latex
185 × 267 × 277 cm
→ *VI: III II*, 2007
Enamel, toner on paper
10 sheets
Each 81 × 102 cm
→ *Everything All at Once (Channel 4)*, 2007
Enamel on steel
83 × 89 cm
→ *A Broken Record Not a Broken Record Just a Sound*, 2007
Bronze, bleached cotton, wood, hardware, paper, latex
234 × 330 × 234 cm
→ *The Ninth Re-Telling*, 2007
Bronze
183 × 38 × 43 cm

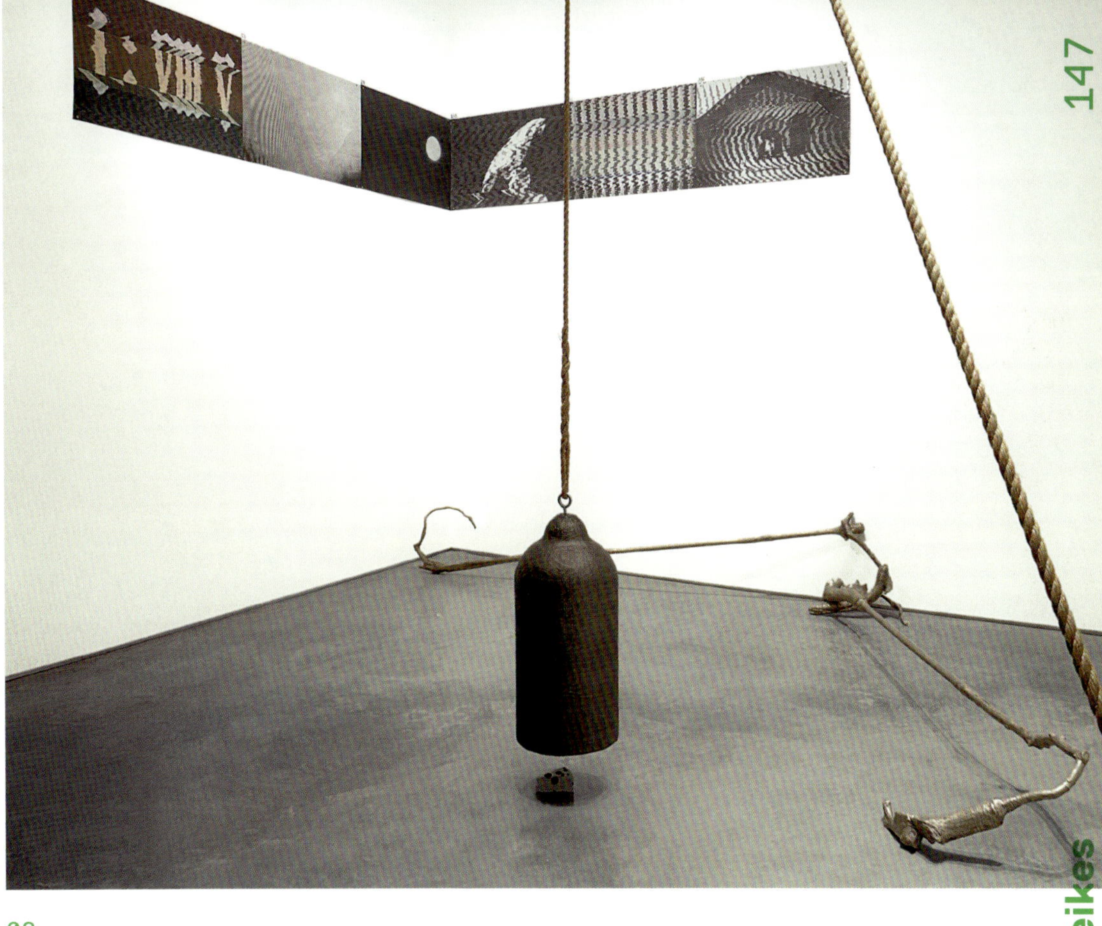

02

03

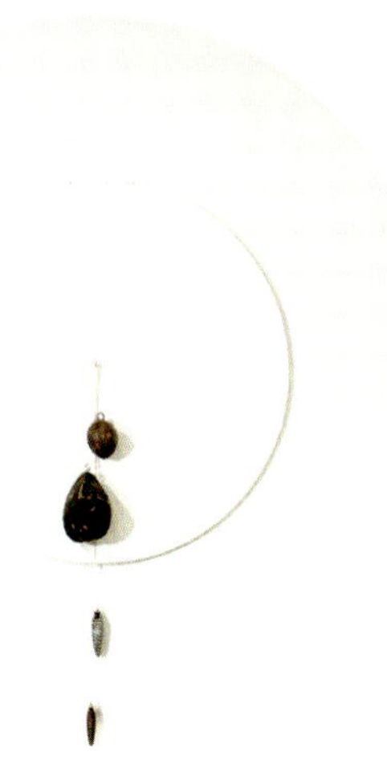

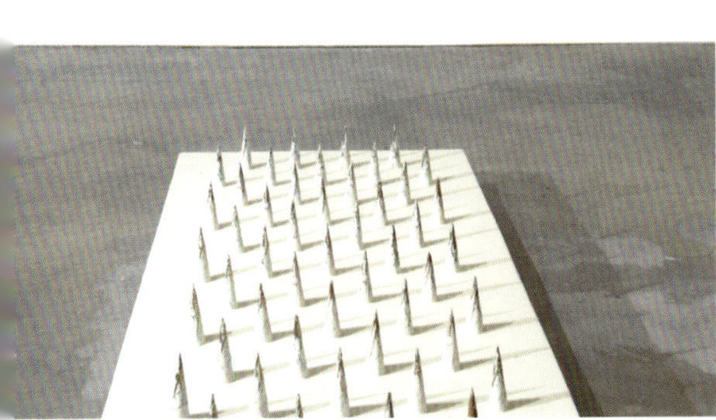

02 from left:
→ *I:VIII V*, 2007
Enamel, toner on paper
6 sheets
Each 81 × 102 cm
→ *Broken Record*, 2007
Bronze
2 parts
307 × 62 × 25 cm
340 × 62 × 25 cm
→ *Rules of Attraction*, 2007
Iron, bronze, hardware, rope, latex
Trap 83 × 36 × 36 cm
Cheese 5 × 9 × 12 cm
Rope dimensions variable

03 from front:
→ *The Soft Pillow*, 2007
Wood, string, latex, coconut, bronze, copper
25 × 213 × 81 cm
→ *6:30 Today, tomorrow and the day after that*, 2007
Bronze, wood, cement, plaster, enamel
244 × 244 × 15 cm

04 *Awkward Pause*, 2008
Bronze, iron, rust
13 × 119 × 76 cm

04

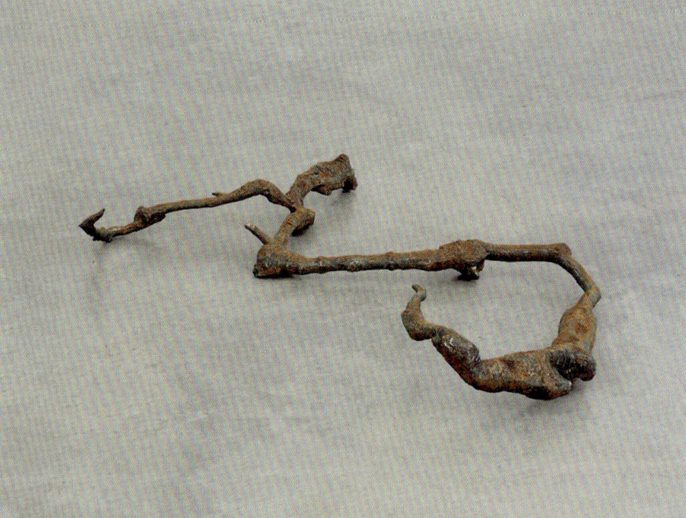

With a penchant for overstatement, reciprocity and enchantment, Danish artist Jeppe Hein examines the questions of perception and the artwork's relationship to the spectator. Accomplished in various modes of often 'interactive' sculpture, this critique often targets specific art movements. For example, while Minimalist objects have been said to be theatrical and reliant on some kind of phenomenological experience — requiring the viewer to realize their full potential — Hein lampoons this very observation by creating objects that literally are activated by the viewer: benches that jump when one sits down on them (*Moving Bench 2*, 2002), seats that spew water (*Private Rain*, 2005), sculptures that light up when no one is around (*No Presence [Yellow]*, 2006).

While Hein's work is clearly an art-historically literate critique, it also partakes of magic and wonderment. *No Presence [Yellow]*, which he showed at *Momentum*, the exhibition of Nordic art in Moss, Norway, utilizes the formal language of Minimalism, as well as mid-century Scandinavian design, while restoring a basic problem of perception — do things exist when we are not there to perceive them? — with a childhood sense of wonder.

In a suite of earlier pieces, Hein directs this brand of homage towards institutional critique, whose practical operations — a determination to use the physical infrastructure of the gallery as a metonymy for the institution itself — he subjects to literal battery. In *360° Presence* (2002) a large steel ball careers across the gallery, physically butting against the limits of the art space as, well as visitors and anything else in its path, while in *Moving Walls 180°* (2001) the walls of the gallery adjust slightly whenever a visitor is in the room.

Despite the almost comic scenarios effected by these sculptures, it is their relation to the viewer and his or her perception that forms the core of Hein's investigation. They are, in a way, humanist works that affirm the presence of the individual as primary, over that of the work itself. A suite of sculptures utilizing mirrors — with Dan Graham as a clear influence — multiply viewers' understanding of the space, the work itself and their perception of themselves. *Rotating Labyrinth* (2007) reconfigures the idea of theatricality as a mode of fracturing and partial invisibility, rather than one of amplified exhibition, by creating a rotating, round stage of mirrored columns. In a similar work, *Mirror Labyrinth Chiswick Park* (2007), a Stonehenge-like circle of mirrored columns reflects, literally, the site's shifts from natural to artificial environments. [Melissa Gronlund]

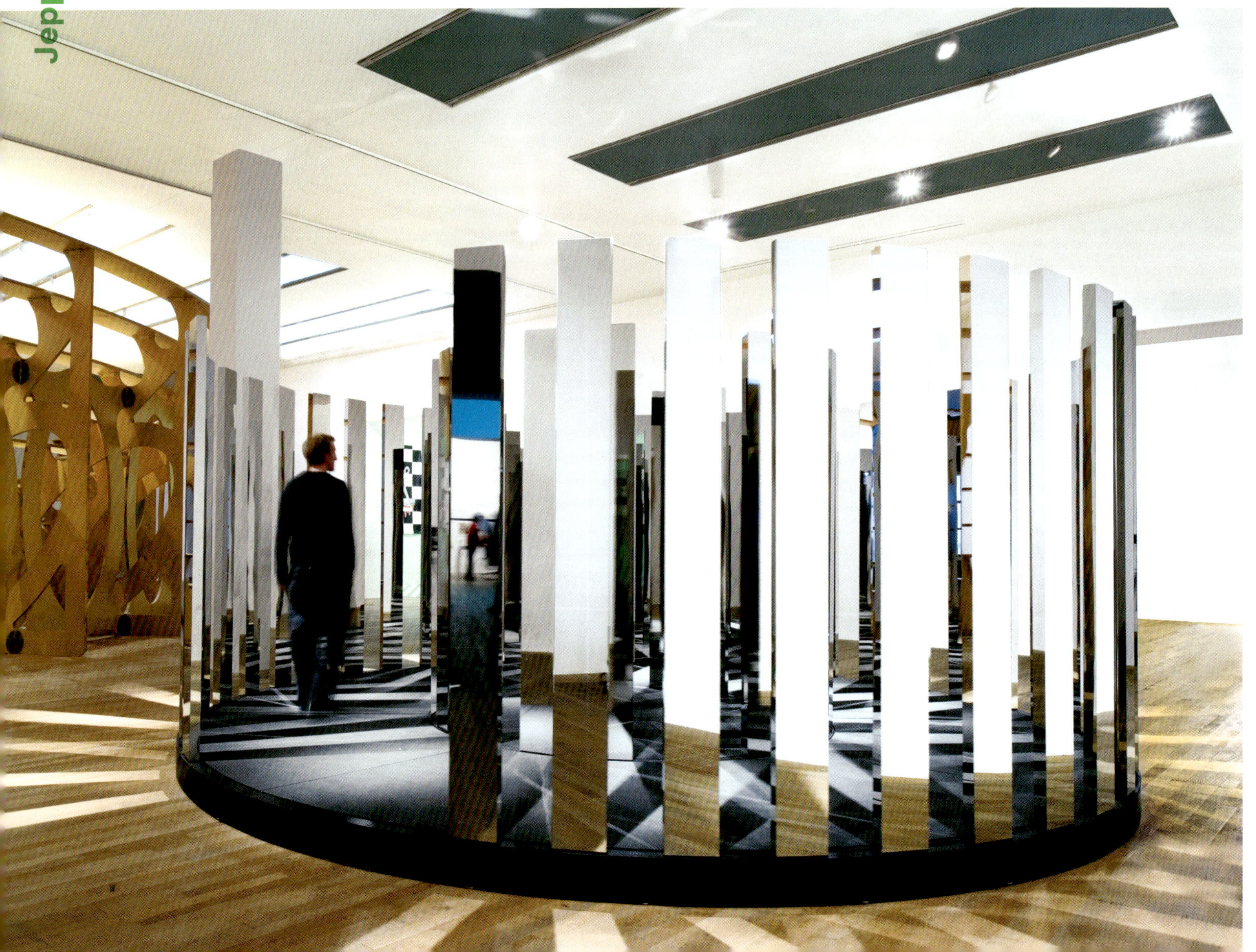

01

01 *Rotating Labyrinth*, 2007
Polished mirror, aluminium, electric motors, scroll, platform
550 × 550 × 220 cm

02 *Moving Bench 2*, 2000
Wood, electric motor, contact, wheels, pillow
70 × 200 × 40 cm

03, 04 *360° Presence*, 2002
Steel, electric motor, battery, sensor
Diameter 70 cm

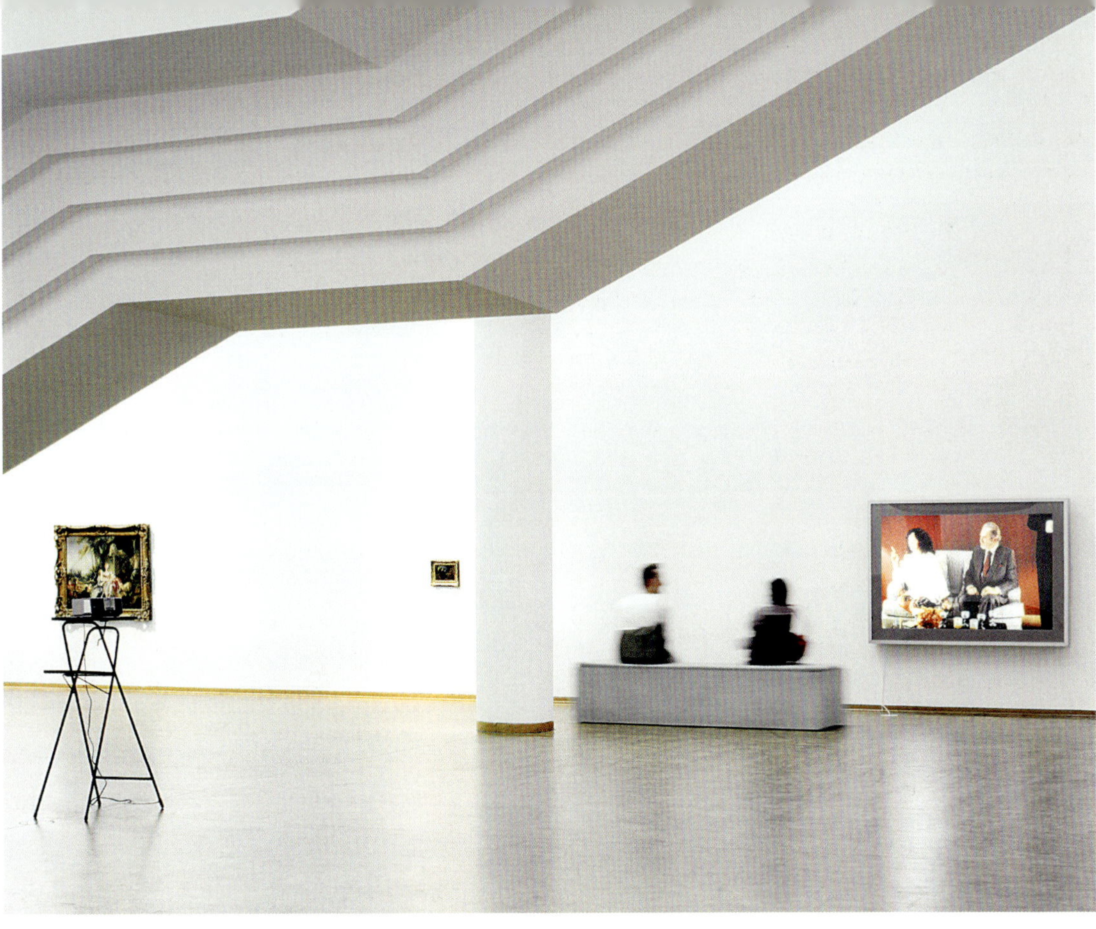

02

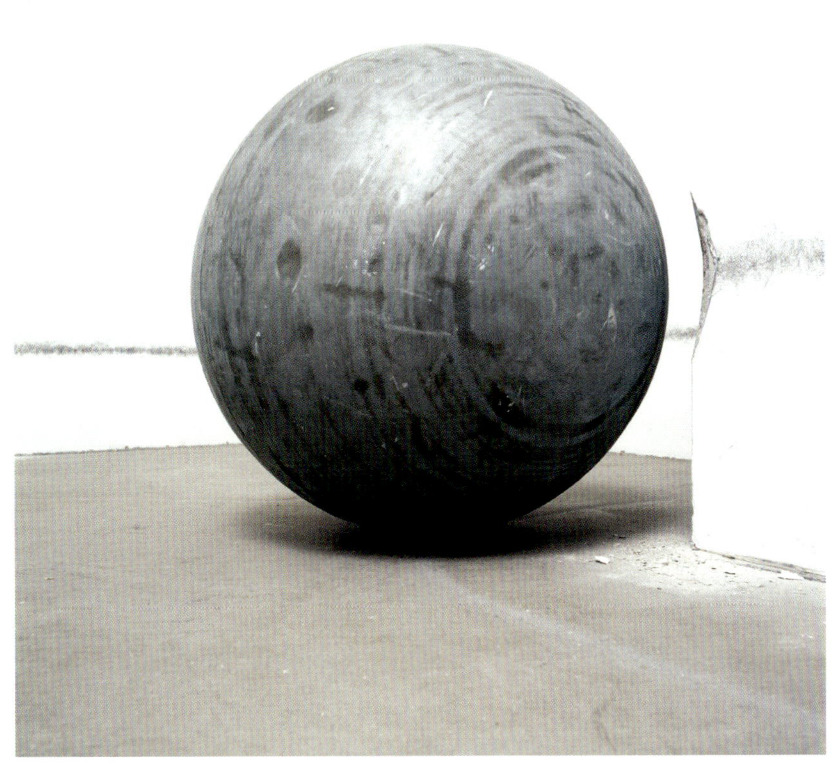

03

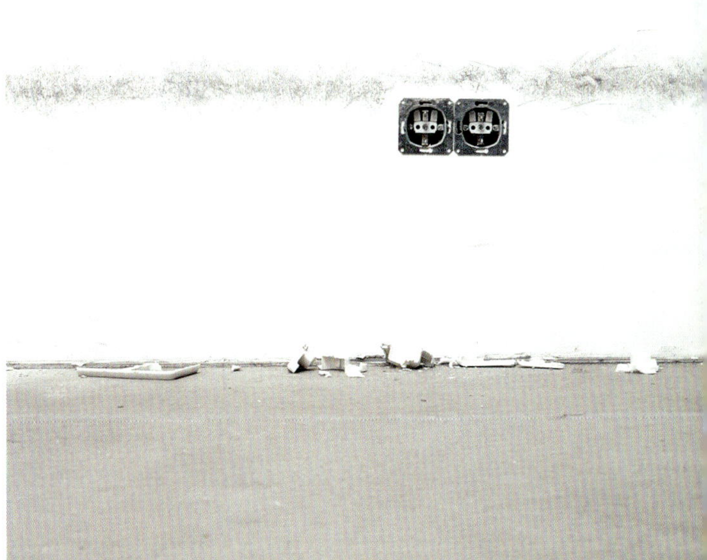

04

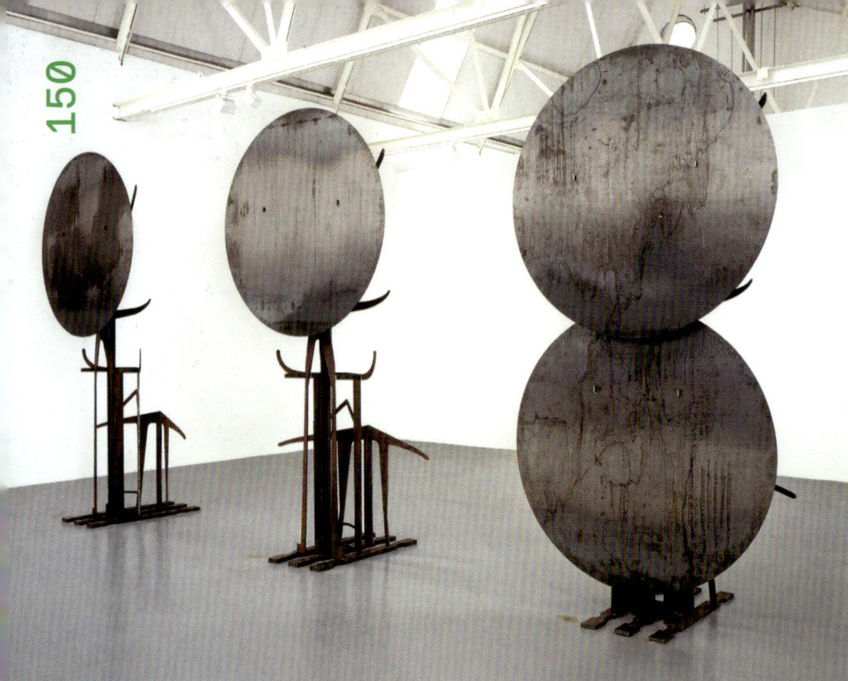

01

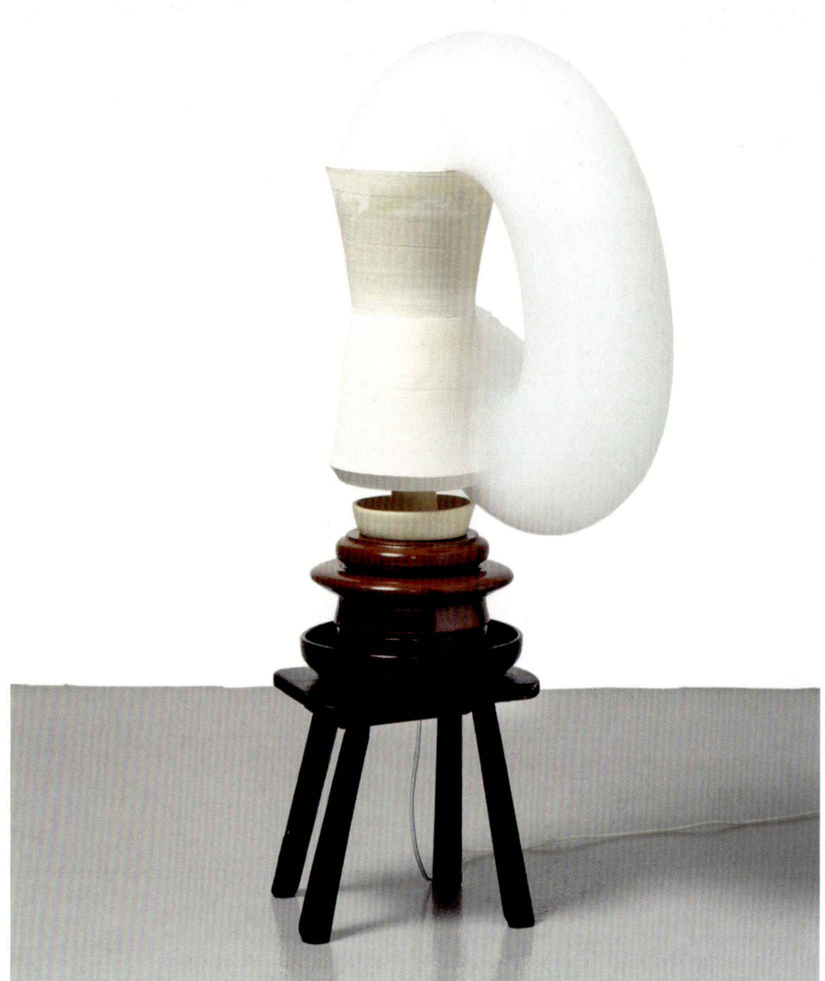

02

According to Aristotle's 'Politics', when the world's first sculptor, Daedalus, tired of the immobility of his marble carvings, he infused them with quicksilver, bringing them to life. Something similar might be said of the British artist Roger Hiorns, who vivifies his elegant yet brutal sculptures by introducing them to a variety of unexpected substances. In his work, silver panels are daubed with amyl nitrate, steel plates wear Guerlain's scent L'Heure Bleue, dangling ceramic urns foam with detergent bubbles, and engine filters are smeared with the brown, flaking remnants of a cow's brain. This is sculpture that struggles, if not for sentience, then for a kind of mournful, automaton existence. Caught between attraction and repulsion, greeting contemporary life with both hot blood and a numb heart, these works combine conceptual precision with a startling, visceral poetry.

Hiorns' practice suggests, at times, a religious observance or occult ritual. In two related, untitled works from 2006 and 2007, he applied a filter of his own semen to a single strip light in Cubitt Gallery, London, and another to one of the 2000-watt mercury lamps that illuminate the Parthenon at night. Through these anointments, he caused a fractional shift in the quality of light (imperceptible to the human eye) that fell on an exhibition space and an archaeological deposit, marking these two very different 'temples' as his own in a gesture that appears at once aggressive and impotent. Power, or rather its undoing, is a key theme in Hiorns' work. His *Untitled* (2008) consists of the powdery remains of a jet engine, ground into dust. Scattered on to the gallery floor, it suggests a lunar landscape — a destination that the engine, ground down into grey, elementary particles, could not hope to reach.

Hiorns is perhaps best known for *Seizure* (2008), a work achieved by introducing a large quantity of liquid copper sulphate solution into a condemned local authority bedsit, so that it formed sharp blue crystals on its every surface. If left to grow, they would have eventually destroyed the fabric of the building. The result was a glittering grotto, a fairy tale mixed with a sci-fi nightmare. *Seizure* embroiled its audience in a mutual toxicity and a mutual violence — flesh, here, was liable to be nicked, just as the crystalline shards were liable to be stolen as souvenirs. In this meeting of curves and edges, of subjects and objects, neither the work nor the viewer could survive each other for very long. We might imagine Hiorns' crystals as pathogens or malign tumours, but those are human categories, and human categories are unimportant in *Seizure*'s hermetic, mineral world. These blue growths did not — and could not — know what they had displaced or consumed. Their existence was one of perfect purposelessness, inexorably carried out. [Tom Morton]

01 *Untitled*, 2006
Steel, disinfectant
3 parts
Each 296 × 148 × 105 cm

02 *Untitled*, 2005
Ceramic, wood, compressor, foam
97 × 28 × 33 cm

03 *Seizure*, 2008
Copper sulphate
Dimensions variable

03

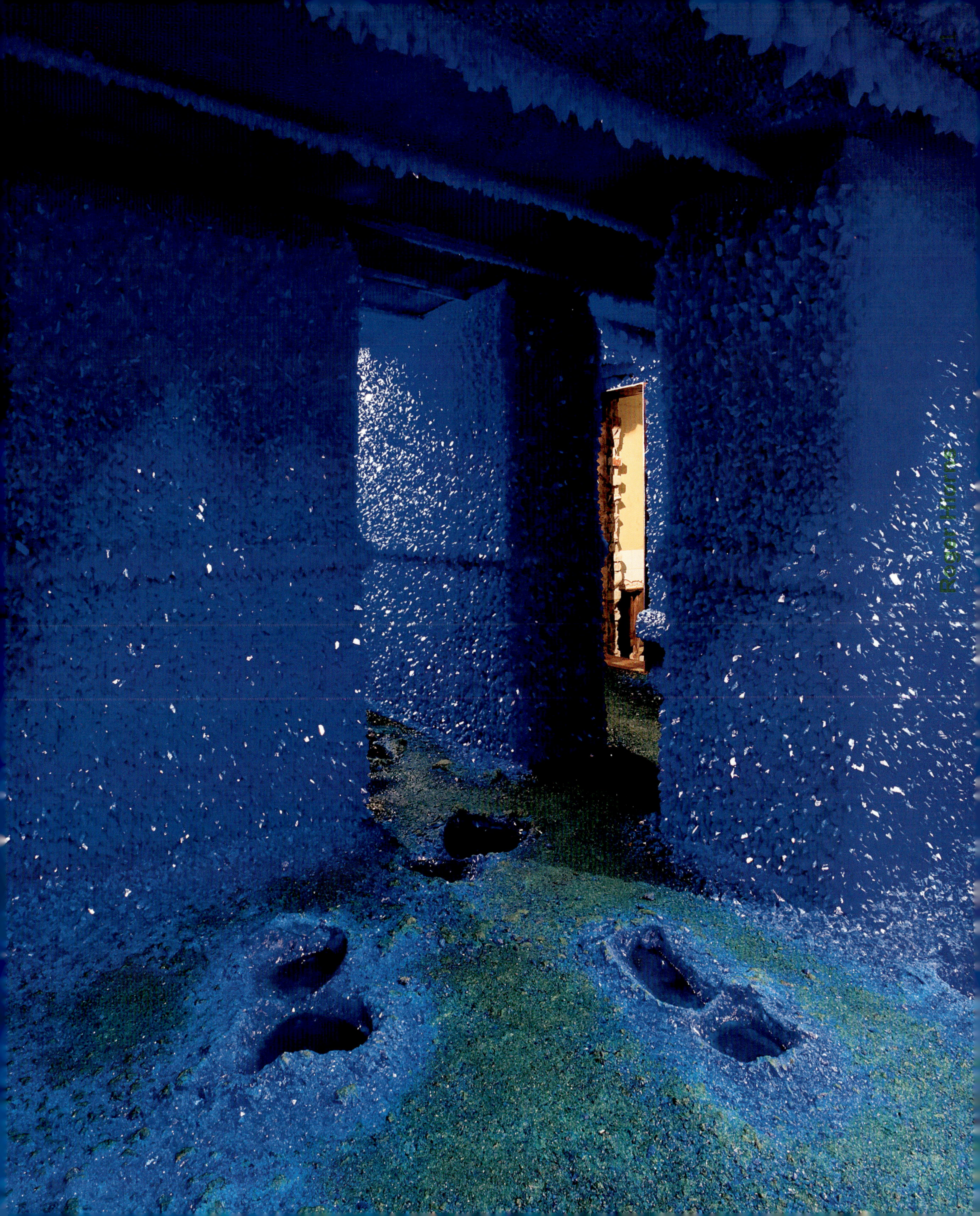

Imagine a big cube. There's an incredible racket issuing from inside it. The noise goes on and on. After a while, a man in a rumpled gold suit staggers out. His name is Evan Holloway, and he's been playing the drums.

Abstraction in Holloway's practice is never 'pure', no more isolated from discourse —political, historical, theological, philosophical — than is representation. (Which means, of course, that abstraction and representation aren't exactly separate categories here.) Accordingly, in his sculptures the formal always engages with a complex web of textuality. In *Drum Box* (1997, described above), what you see is, ostensibly, modernism; but what you hear coming from inside is something else entirely. In *Social Epistemology* (2006), Constantin Brancusi's *Endless Column* is conflated with the crass jocundity of a travelling fair, totem poles with the Hegelian dialectic, the groundbreaking 'Eureka!' moment with the bulbous, flashing noses of clowns and flying reindeer.

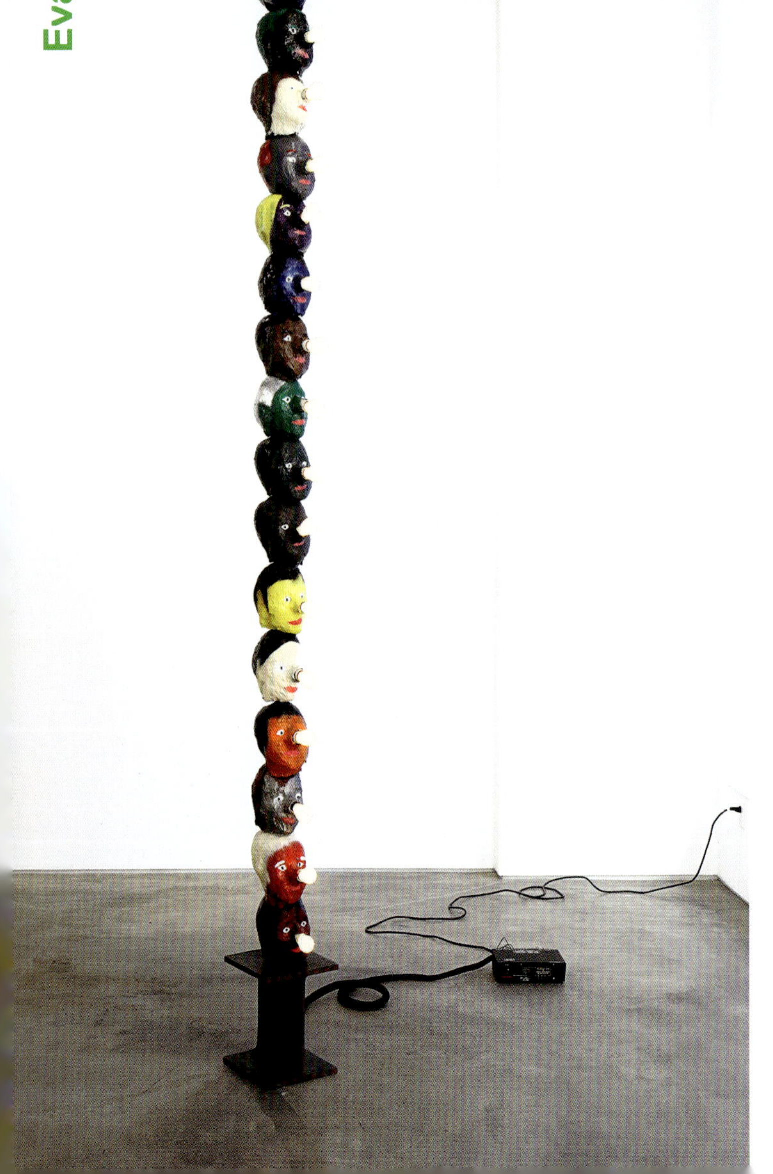

01

This coincidence of the formal with an invocation of the textual speaks as much about the human subject's relation to the larger world as the sculptural object's. In *Self-Portrait* (2005), a tangle of grey rods connects the letters of the artist's name to a crude, floating torus, like a follow-the-string maze in a kid's puzzle book. Naming and identity, game-playing, entropy and the formal language of high modernism become linked together in an uncertain relationship. The object resembles, among other things, a simple model of a set of physical forces — something to do with tornadoes or black holes. Within this model, the artist's name rests calmly, as if having coalesced from some abstruse vortex or, equally, as if about to be whirled into a mess of disjointed, meaningless letters.

Support structures, like the rods in *Self-Portrait*, often take on enhanced significance in Holloway's objects, becoming integral, sometimes predominant, sculptural elements. More than just a critique of the traditional object/base hierarchy, these structures come to evidence a common preoccupation in Holloway's work with the object/subject's relationship to formal systems, to transferences, migrations, collapses and transformations of energy and meaning. They can often seem to have a diagrammatic function, indicating, say, an entropic trajectory, a sequential progression, or a transition between states, systems and discourses. In much of the work, the artist comments, 'sequence determines form' (the letters in *Self Portrait* and *Carrion Flower ...* [2007], for example, or the numbers in *56–60* [2007]). 'These sequences are not "natural"; they are cultural data. The forms are therefore contingent upon familiar human stuff to give them meaning.'

The relationship of discrete objects to the larger world is, it could be argued, both the fundament of sculptural enquiry and a formal equivalent of the human condition. Holloway's sculptures each form a nexus where the complex traffic between 'object', 'subject' and 'world' can triangulate. In a neat looping motion, the investigation of basic sculptural problems (such as 'Where do the boundaries of the object lie?' or 'How can a formal system be represented in space?') generates sculpture that embodies these abstract relationships. [Lee Triming]

02

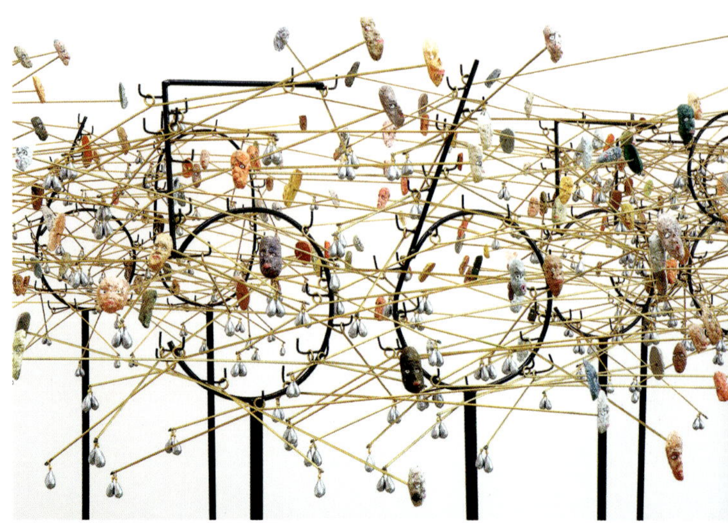

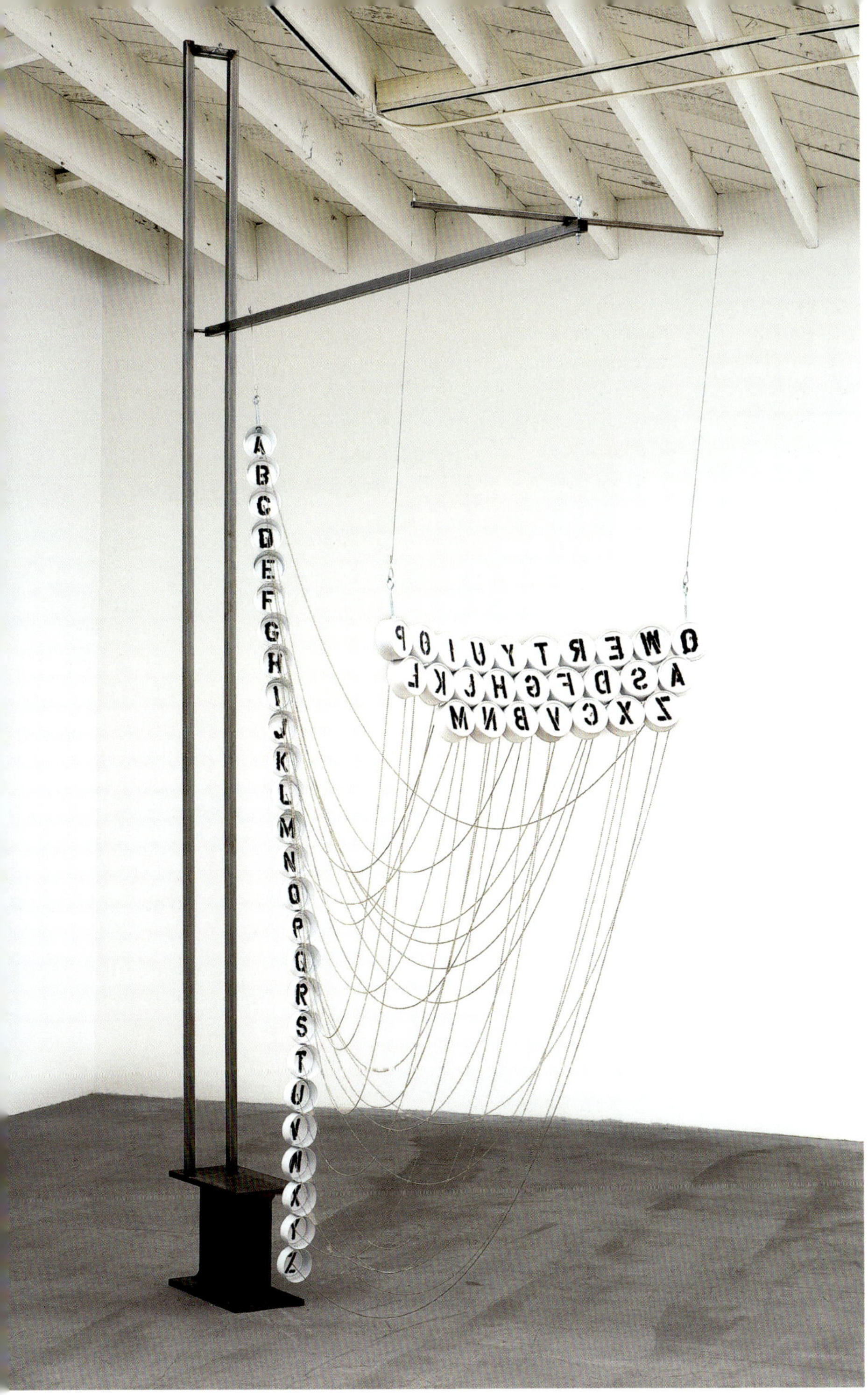

03

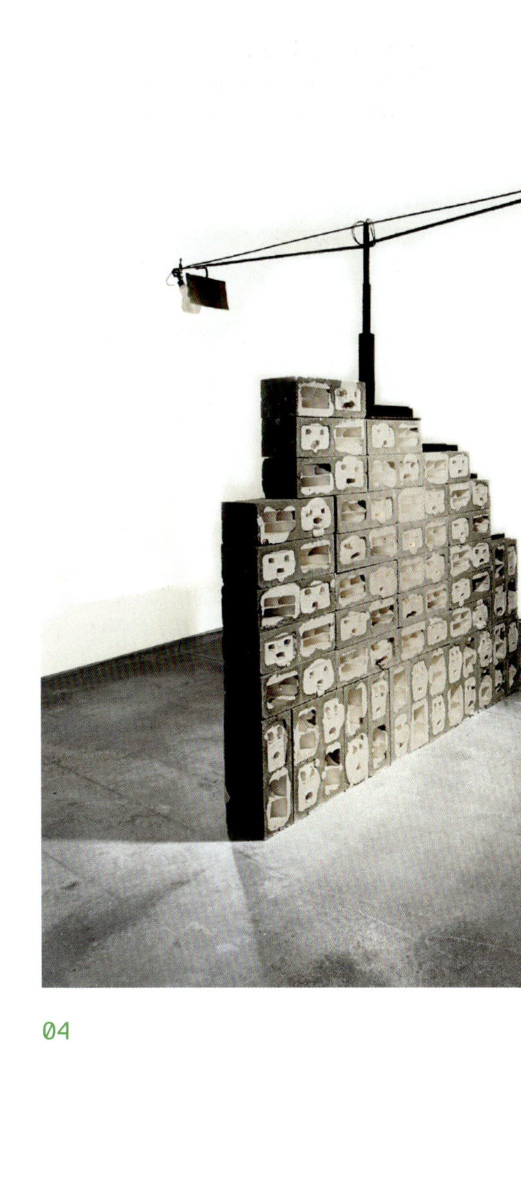

04

01 *Social Epistemology*, 2006
Steel, celluclay, acrylic medium, spray enamel, lighting, lighting controller
379 × 25 × 38 cm

02 *56–60*, 2007
Steel, brass sculptamold, lead, paint
Approx. 196 × 117 × 117 cm

03 *Carrion-flower*, 2006
'"It would be safe to say," says John Burroughs, "that there is a species of smilax with an unsavory name, that the bee does not visit, herbacea. The production of this plant is a curious freak of nature.... It would be a cruel joke to offer it to any person not acquainted with it, to smell. It is like the vent of a charnel-house." (Thoreau compared its odor to that of a dead rat in a wall!) "It is first cousin to the trilliums, among the prettiest of our native wild flowers," continues Burroughs, "and the same bad blood crops out in the Purple Trillium or Birthroot." Strange that so close an observer as Burroughs or Thoreau should not have credited the carrion-flower with being something more intelligent than a mere repellent freak! Like the Purple Trillium, it has deliberately adapted itself to please its benefactors, the little green flesh-flies so commonly seen about untidy butcher shops in the summer."'
Steel, aircraft cable, tuna cans, paint, rivets, hardware
320 × 203 × 81 cm

04 *Dialectic*, 2006
Cinder blocks, plaster, steel, brass, lighting, lighting controller
221 × 188 × 280 cm

05 *Closet*, 2005
Steel, plaster, vinyl, printed matter, copper, brass, printed T-shirt, velvet painting, wire hangers, paper
147 × 152 × 81 cm

05

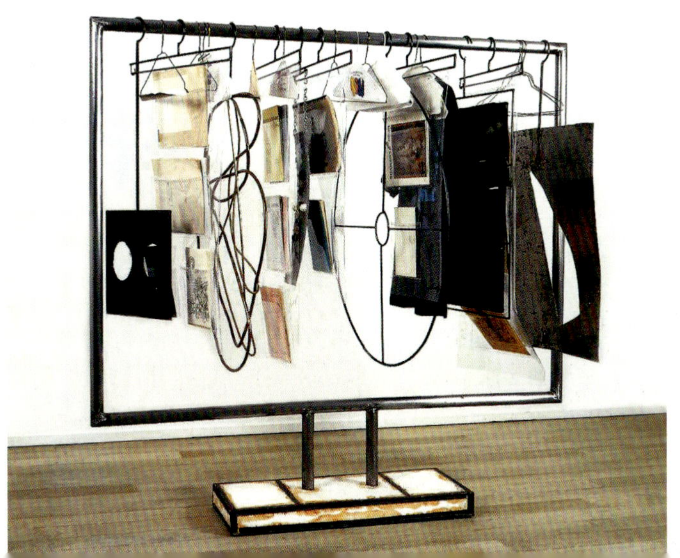

Christian Holstad's artistic output includes collages, drawings, room installations, sculptures — which are usually made by hand from textiles and everyday household objects — as well as music and performance (in particular with Delia Gonzales, Gavin Russom and Daniel Schmidt in the group Black Leotard Front). His is an ambitious project, examining elements of high culture and subculture in terms of their lost meanings and social criticality within the processes brought about by the commercialization of intellectual, spiritual and emotional values.

Holstad's hand-made aesthetic, a reversal of the commodified character of our various everyday cultural 'products', has as crucial a part to play in his art as the identification of homosexuality as his individual and cultural identity. He repeatedly contrasts, both ironically and in a utopian way, things that are supposedly 'natural' with socially and commercially contaminated individual emotions, longings and forms of expression. Consequently, he is an obsessive collector of images, objects and stories. He amalgamates these in his work, using an approach that goes beyond the traditional collage technique to create new surfaces intended to enable the de- and re-coding of what is shown, and at the same time to reactivate an individual emotional link to the things and subjects presented.

In his installation *Call of the Wild* (2004), for example, he brings together an embroidered, handcrafted, crocheted and sewn universe, consisting of a beached whale, a fireplace, a glitter curtain printed with a sunset and waves, a jumping tyre, murals and an indoor parabolic receiver. These elements create a charged, ambivalent atmosphere, something between romantic longing, campfire romanticism and intentionally kitschy irony. *Leather Beach* (2006) is his version of an S&M shop in midtown Manhattan, an area that in the 1970s was full of sex shops, gay bars, drag queens and the emancipatory atmosphere of free sexual choice until the AIDS crisis curtailed it. With this installation, Holstad created a cabinet of hand-sewn and hand crafted 'utensils' addressing the way in which society has thrust this sexual practice into the private sphere, while also exuding a dark atmosphere of wanting to join in.

It is perhaps most useful to see Holstad's work in the tradition of the filmmaker and performer Jack Smith, who was one of the influential figures in the camp, gay and underground aesthetic of the 1960s and 1970s. Holstad's work is shaped by the contents and forms of a reality that has made permeable the boundaries between 'high' and 'low', between mainstream and counterculture. He submits the essentials of the reality produced by the once effective phenomena of the counter culture to a revision process: gay culture, glamour, camp aesthetics and Goth culture are surfaces that he uses and examines for the possibility of re-contextualization and re-activation.

On the level of the picture, Holstad amalgamates ornaments with found photographs until everything is only pattern. He weaves them into a wildly proliferating collage, of which we ourselves become part. Image categories are permanently mixed up. Real objects and real people are transformed into reflections and oscillating formations that lead to other mental images: horror scenarios mutate into spirituality, pathos transforms itself into ornament — a theatrical scenario that permanently questions and redefines the meaning of images and reality. [Beatrix Ruf]

01

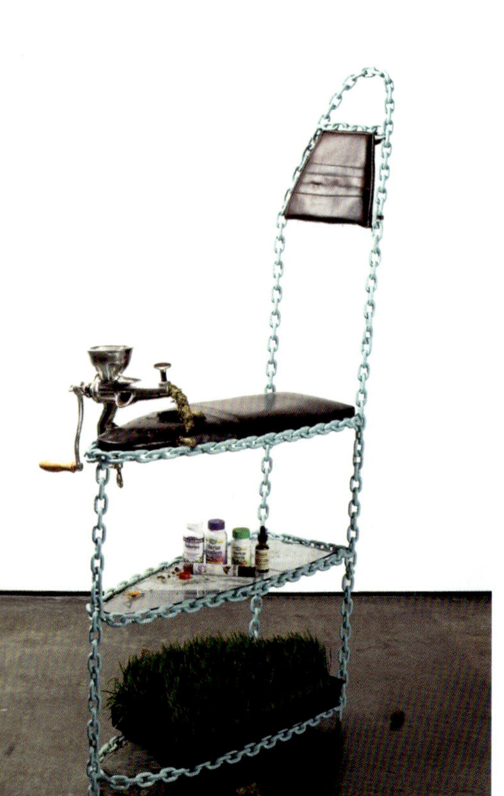

02

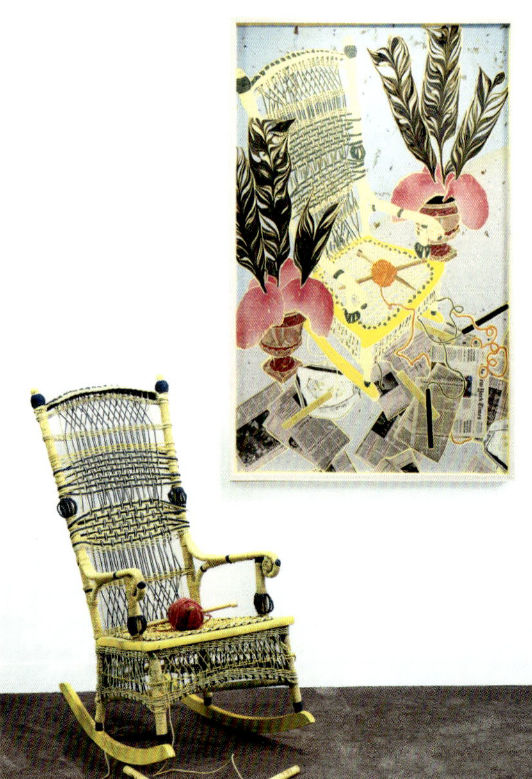

03

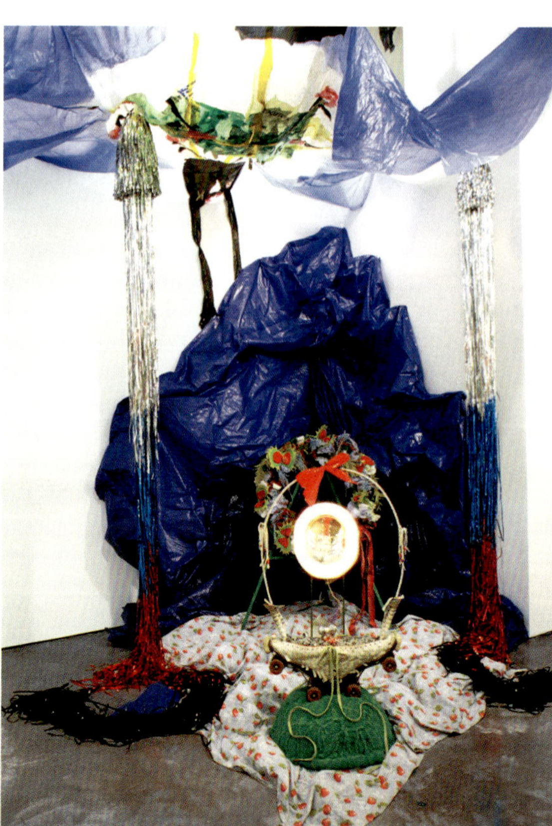

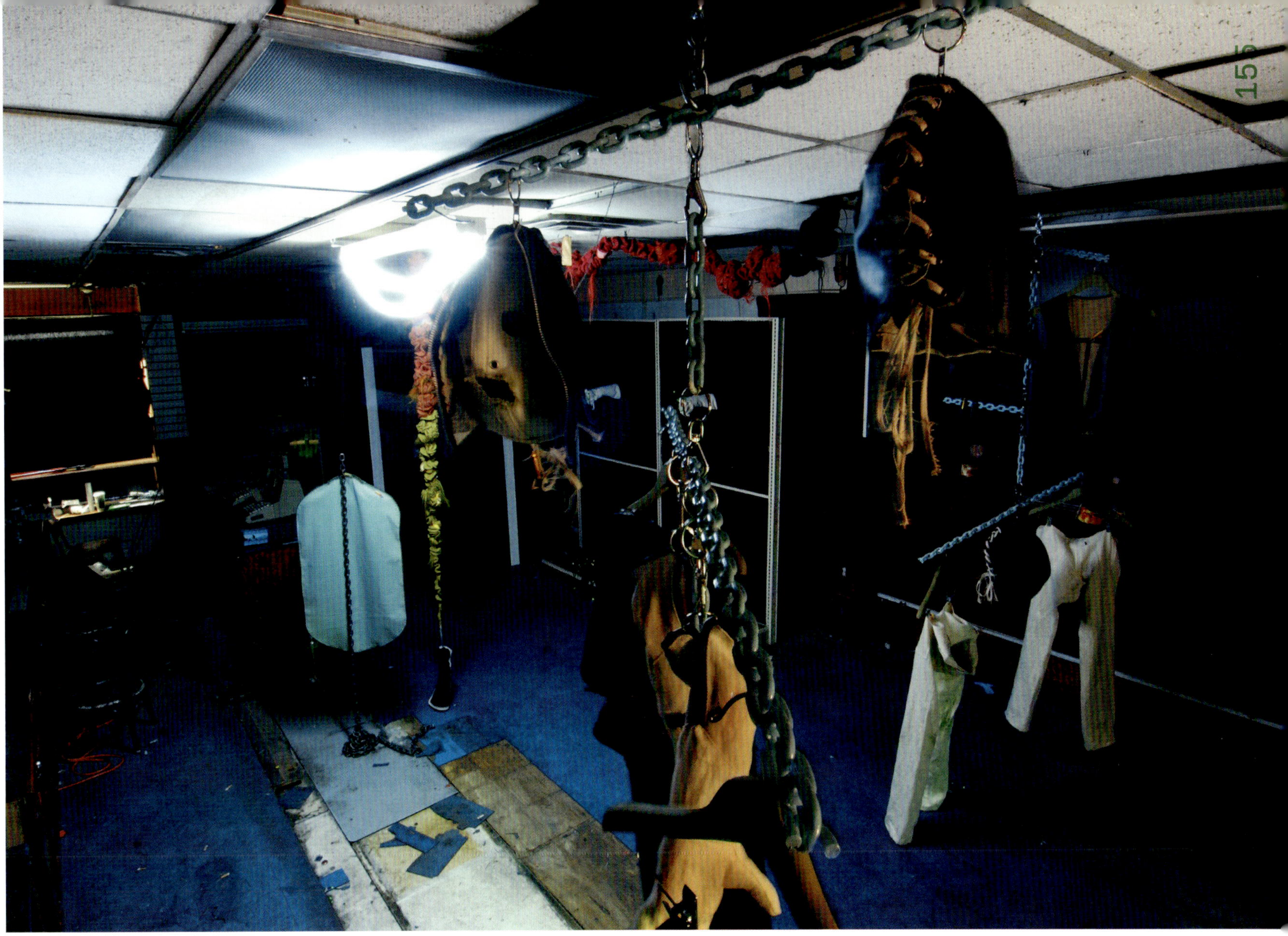

04

05

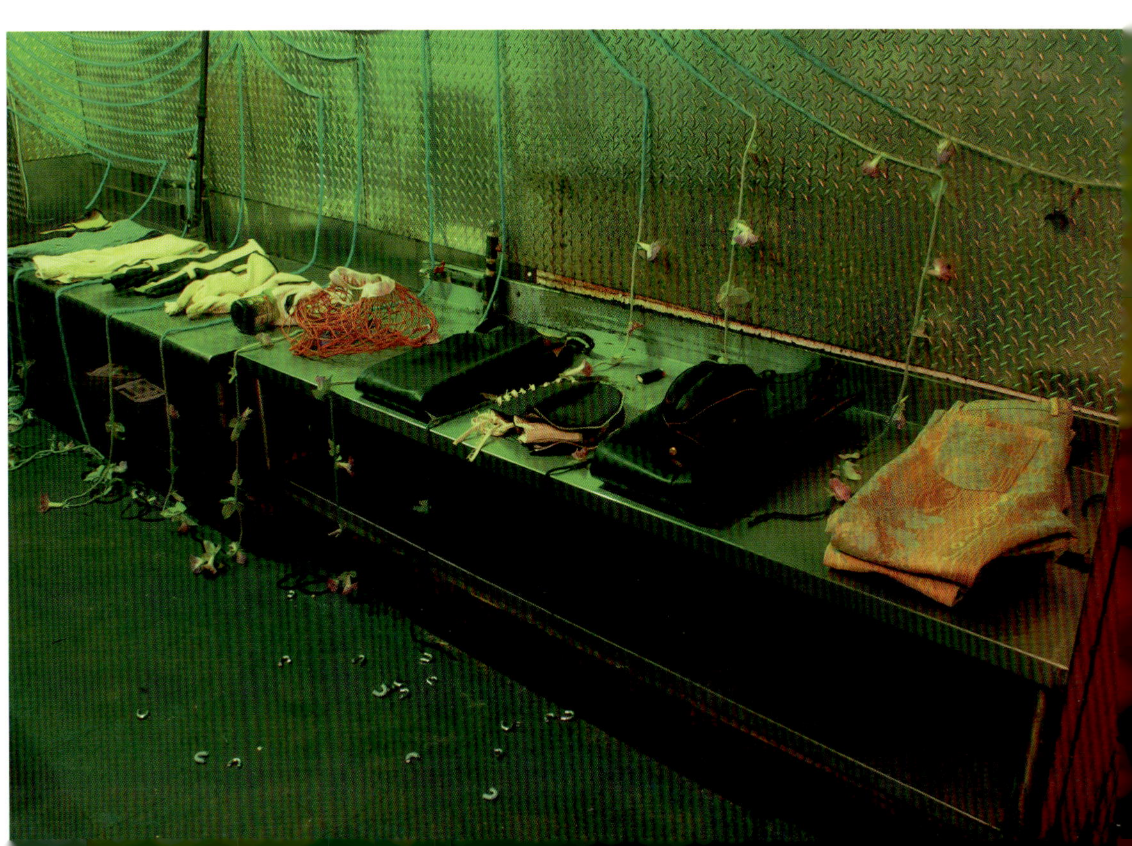

01 *Sissy Bar*, 2005–06
Vegetable, leather, chain, wheatgrass juicer, glass, wheatgrass, St John's Wort, American ginseng, Goji berries, Siberian eleuthero, valerian
137 × 76 × 32 cm

02 *Wickerwork Rocker (Sit Back and Try to Relax)*, 2008
Dynamite wicks, wood
102 × 152 cm
Collage on paper
105 × 92 × 61 cm

03 *Fear Gives Courage Wings*, 2003
Mixed media with lighted mirror, towel, iron rods, iron-on image, leather, plastic beads, sequins, roller skates, CD player, speakers, 'Guardian Angel' disco soundtrack
Approx. 137 × 107 × 107 cm

04, 05 *Leather Beach*, 2006
Mixed-media installation
Dimensions variable

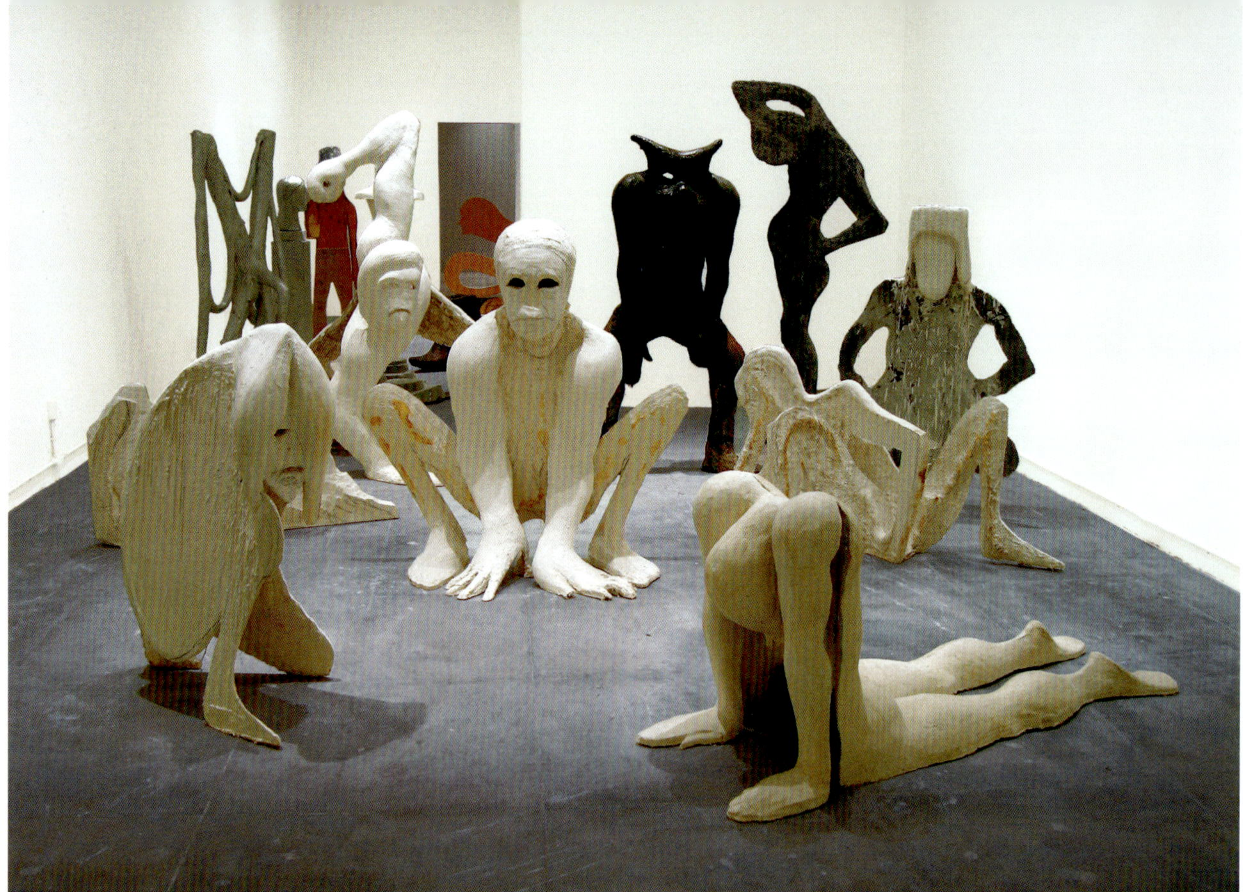

01

Plaster's alchemical properties and its malleable relationship to time — that is to say, its transformation from powder to liquid to solid, which begins slowly and speeds up as the plaster sets — attracts Thomas Houseago to the medium and serves as an apt metaphor for his interest in sculpture's timelessness. His monumental figurative works, drawn on boards that are laid flat to accept plaster pours before being assembled upright, show the wear and tear inherent to his process and recall, through his use of an 'old or tired medium', as he says, centuries of sculptures that use the human form as a blank canvas for artistic expression. Rather than viewing this notion of historical lineage as restrictive, Houseago finds freedom in linking art history to the contemporary. His plaster and wood sculptures, which depict aberrant, androgynous beings crouched, contorted, reclined or hunched over in awkward, uncomfortable poses, reference everything from the Golem to Michelangelo's marble statues, Goya's tortured monsters, Giacometti's wandering waifs, or Picasso's primitivist busts. Houseago's personal brand of primitivism, however, has nothing to do with robbing ancient cultures aesthetically, but rather with sculpting characters that strike archetypal poses to contain the 'weirdness of the third dimension' — a cosmos that is wild, unpredictable and fabulous. In this, his figures convey a theatrical surrealism and serve as architectural maps for his emotional landscape.

Houseago does not sculpt from live models. He originally aimed to dissect pop images of powerfully heroic men by riffing on recognizable, macho poses popularized by iconic celebrities like Marlon Brando or James Dean. He has an abiding interest in how postures communicate gender, and how gender is assigned to postures that read, for example, as aggressive or submissive, contemplative or active. His figures pit inside against outside, confuse back and front, and wear untranslatable facial expressions — hollowed-out eye sockets, pencil-drawn frowns that curl into smiles — to retain ambiguity. His European exhibitions from the 1990s featured suites of figures whose poses were only slightly exaggerated; it was their odd scale shifts, weight imbalances and colour variations that predicted Houseago's present focus on more haunted characters.

Having relocated to California from his native England, Houseago attributes this ghostly quality in some of his works to apprehensions and excitement about shedding cultural attachments. Works produced circa 2005 from his 'LA, first period', as he calls that time, are especially daunting. One figure, flattened onto the floor as if deflated, pushes himself up with his arms and hangs his head down in a gesture of failure. Another, squatting like a frog, wears a death mask. There are serpents climbing walls, headless torsos standing like zombies and black, horned demons ready to pounce.

Recently, Houseago has shifted emphasis away from the raw moods that his figures exude in favour of showing how their formal construction emulates natural shapes that he sees in the mountainous region where he lives. New figures have concentric circles rendered in graphite for eyes, recalling the owls' eyes he sees glowing at night from his porch. Tubes of hand-rolled plaster are pressed on to his figures to render muscles with fuller density, comparing human anatomy to the crepuscular folds found in eroding canyons. As the artist's observations of landscape have fostered an understanding of how geography emulates human form and vice versa, Houseago further deconstructs the figure, moving towards abstraction and the freedoms it implies. [Trinie Dalton]

01 The artist's studio, Los Angeles, August 2005

02 *Prop Mask*, 2008
Plaster, wood, hemp, graphite, oil bar
158 × 114 × 107 cm

03 *Quake Mask*, 2008
Bronze, redwood
254 × 81 × 140 cm

04 *Sitting Figure*, 2008
Plaster, hemp, iron rebar, graphite, oil bar, wood
234 × 168 × 117 cm

03

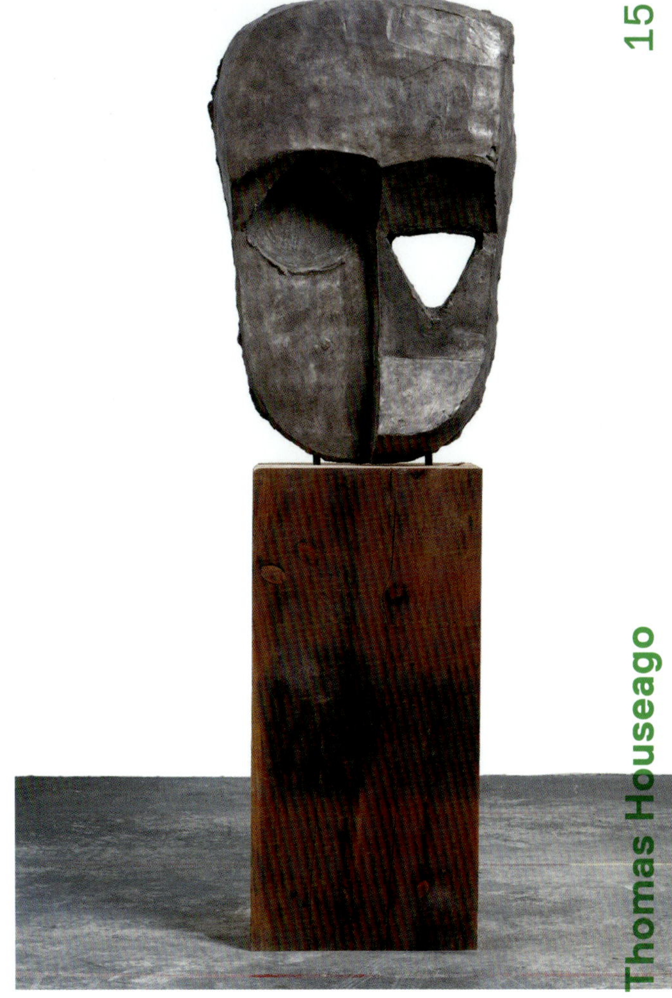

02

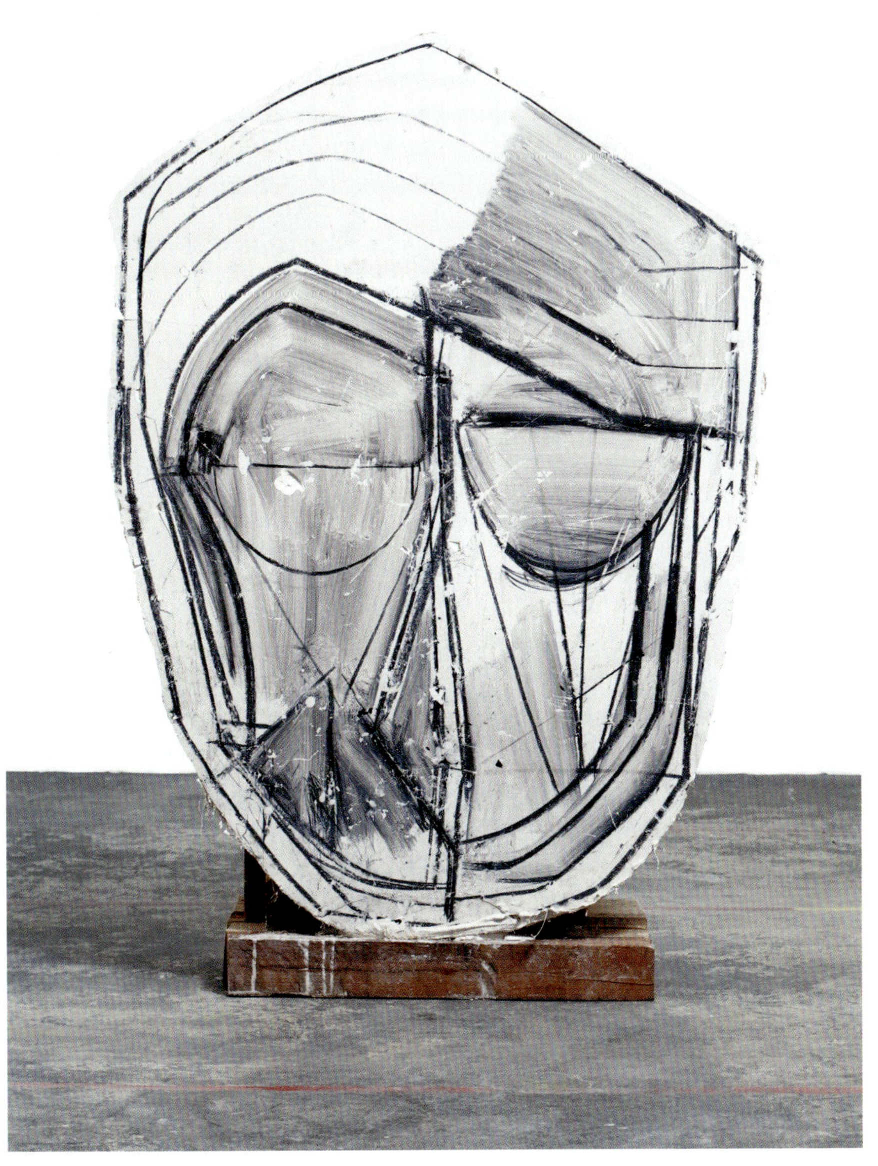

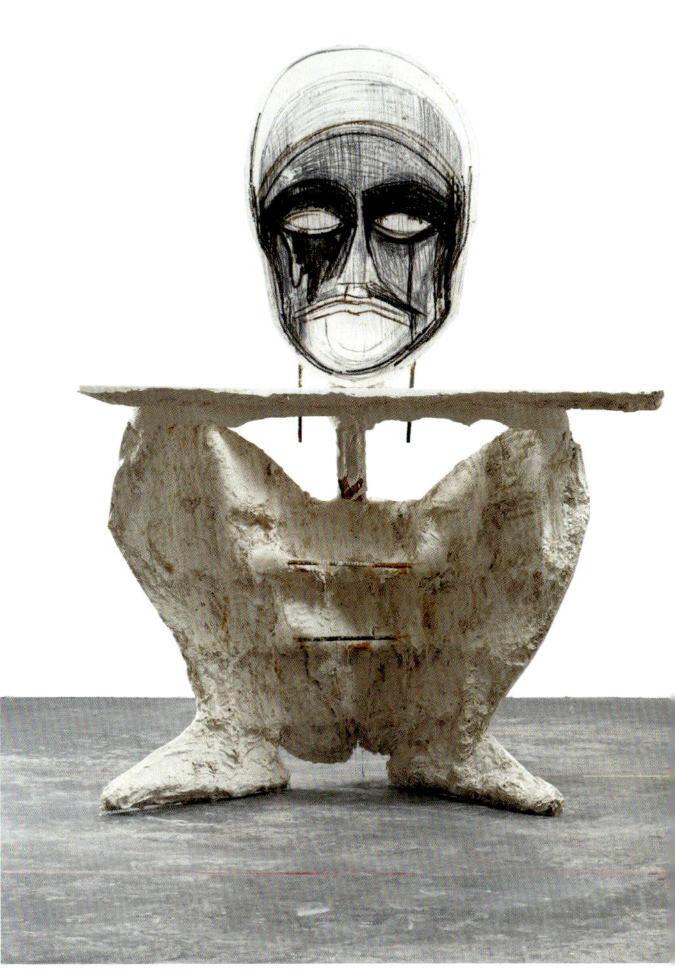

04

Through the use of elaborate crafts and the continuous reprocessing of available cultural material, Matthew Day Jackson's practice seems to aim at the creation of an alternative mythology. His work combines a variety of diverse elements, bringing together Native American traditions, modern art history, US politics, and psychedelic and popular culture, to name just a few. Like artefacts from a cult not yet fully understood, Day Jackson's sculptures, paintings, drawings and videos engage in the active rewriting of North American history in the form of a myth populated by heroes, demons, shamans and ritual objects.

His idiosyncratic pantheon is composed of a few recurrent 'idols' including Buckminster Fuller, Constantin Brancusi, the legendary Shoshone guide Sacagawea, Joseph Beuys, Eleanor Roosevelt, Piet Mondrian and the women's movement leader Elizabeth Cady Stanton. Some of them are depicted in the *Martyr Series,* a collection of portraits on dyed and burnt boards, encrusted with mother of pearl, abalone, colourful yarn and precious woods. The artist's use of folk craftsmanship lends his constellation of cultural icons an aura of spirituality that further interrogates the founding myth of the American dream.

In the celebrated book *The Savage Mind*, anthropologist Claude Lévi-Strauss likened mythical thought to bricolage, the particular kind of DIY practice in which fragments from objects that no longer function are used to create a useful item. In contemporary art, this practice, similar to what has been labelled as 'appropriation' or 'post-production', implies a digestion of received cultural elements that allows the construction of a new artwork with the leftovers from the past. Day Jackson's sculptures often take the shape of complex artefacts composed by way of cultural bricolage. *Sepulcher (Viking Burial Ship)* (2003–04), for example, is a life-size wooden ship built after the Nordic tradition of sea burial, but in which the sail is made of a patchwork of punk band T-shirts arranged within the compositional grid of a painting by Mondrian.

In a more recent work, *I Like America and America Likes Me* (2008), Day Jackson has built in felt the bodywork of a racing car suspended over human skulls. Inside the car a series of solar-powered fluorescent tubes reproduce the colour gradation of the rainbow. The driving seat of this spaceship is made from a cowboy saddle, while a felt space helmet rests on the navigator seat. The work clearly alludes to Joseph Beuys' famous plane crash and the title refers to the well-known performance in which Beuys, without touching American ground, tamed a coyote in a New York gallery. This science-fictional revision of Beuys' mythological founding narrative is combined with another of Day Jackson's heroes: Buckminster Fuller. The car's seemingly crashed windscreen is in fact a multi-coloured stained glass window, joined together in the same geometric structure as the famous architect's geodesic domes.

Through the mix of cultural and political elements and apocalyptic scenarios borrowed from science fiction, the artist attempts to write anew the history of ideas that forms our identity. Rather than proposing a unilateral version of our past, he provides us with a political cosmology that puts into question the way in which our secular or spiritual beliefs are organized. [Francesco Manacorda]

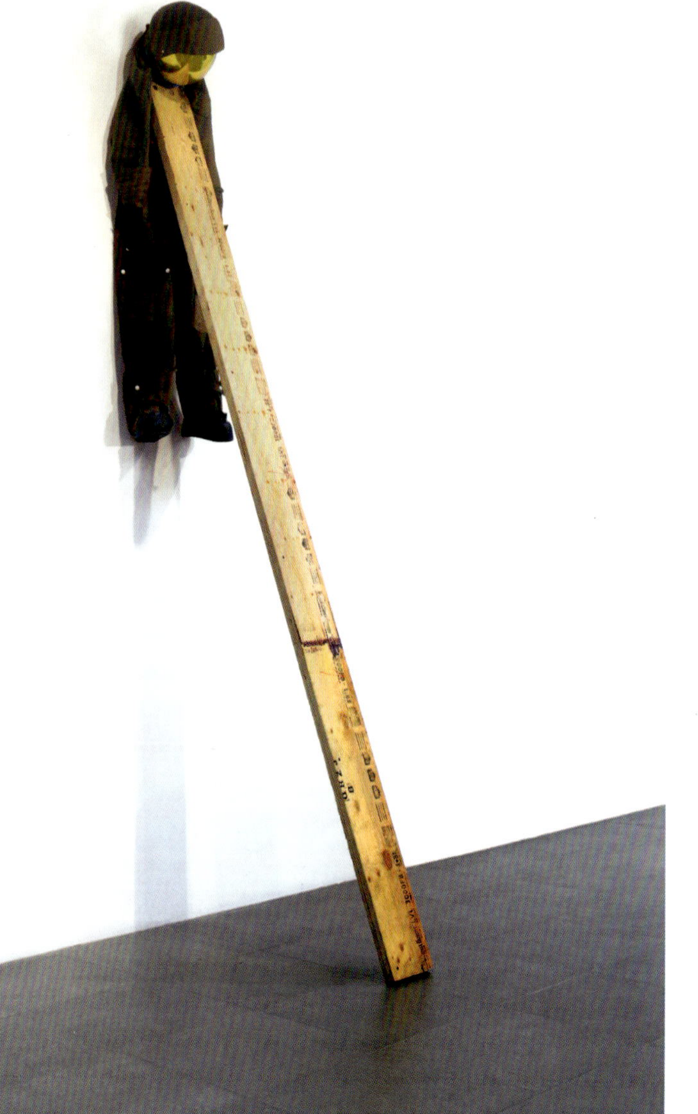

01

02

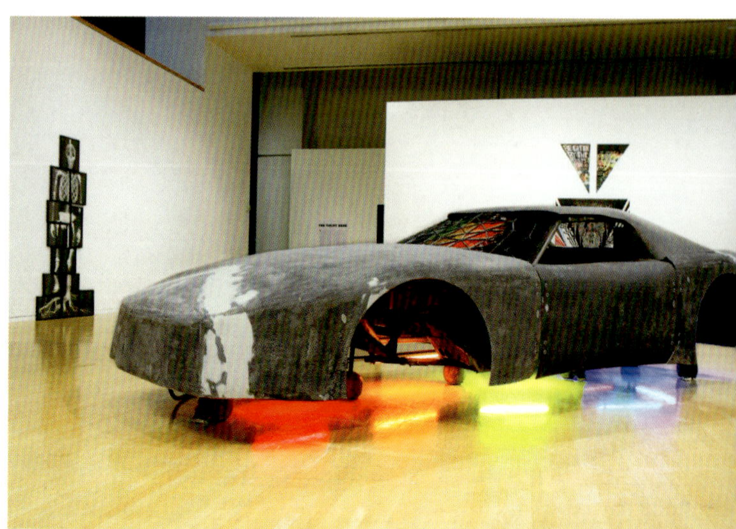

01 *Lonesome Soldier*, 2008
Vietnam-era military blankets, rubber, wood, aluminium, plastic
399 × 53 × 141 cm

02 *I Like America and America Likes Me*, 2008
Wool, felt, crashed race car frame (built by Skip Nichols), steel, fluorescent lights, epoxy, stained glass
117 × 233 × 458 cm

03 *Lean-to*, 2006
House wall from 2814 Glenview Rd, wood, column from Nebraska homestead
275 × 450 × 30 cm

04 *Against the Mythology of Linearity*, 2008
Acrylic, abalone, mother of pearl
17 × 200 × 500 cm

03

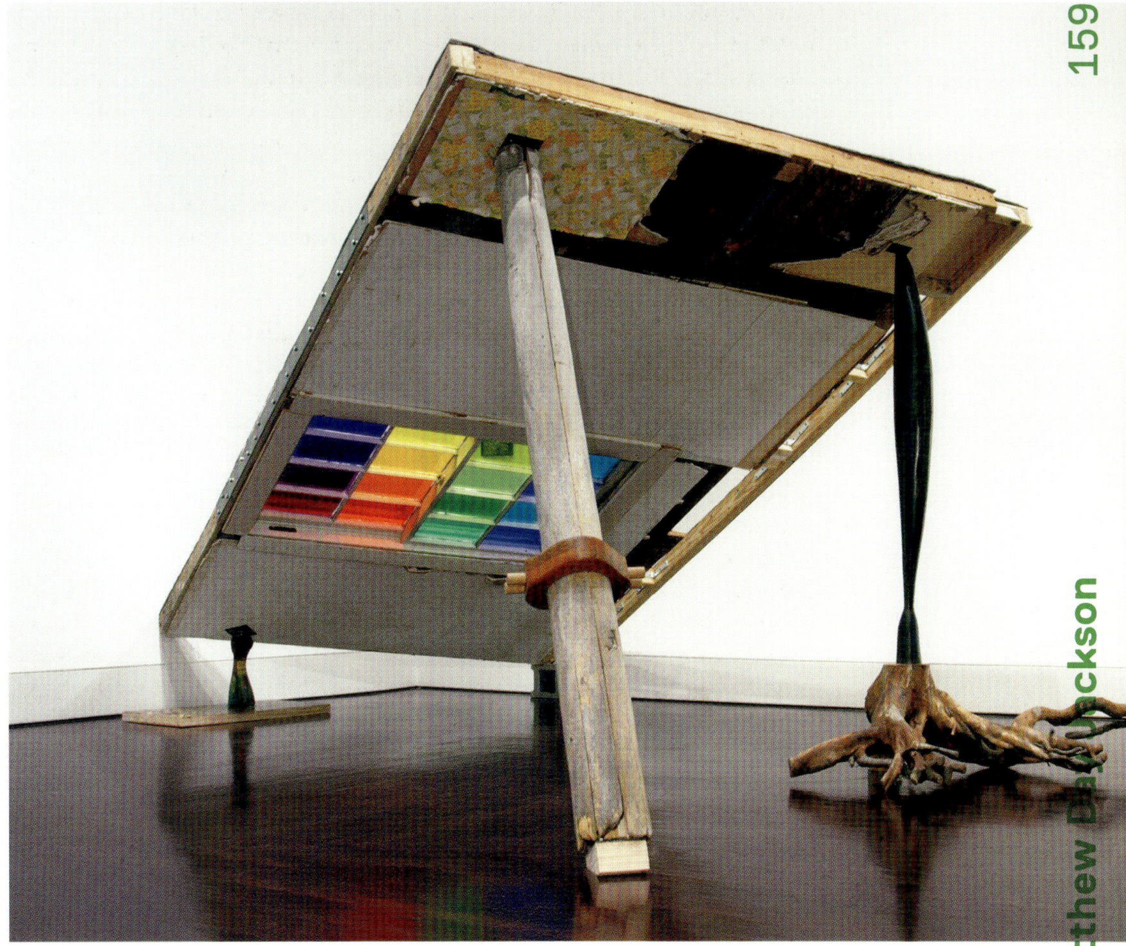

04

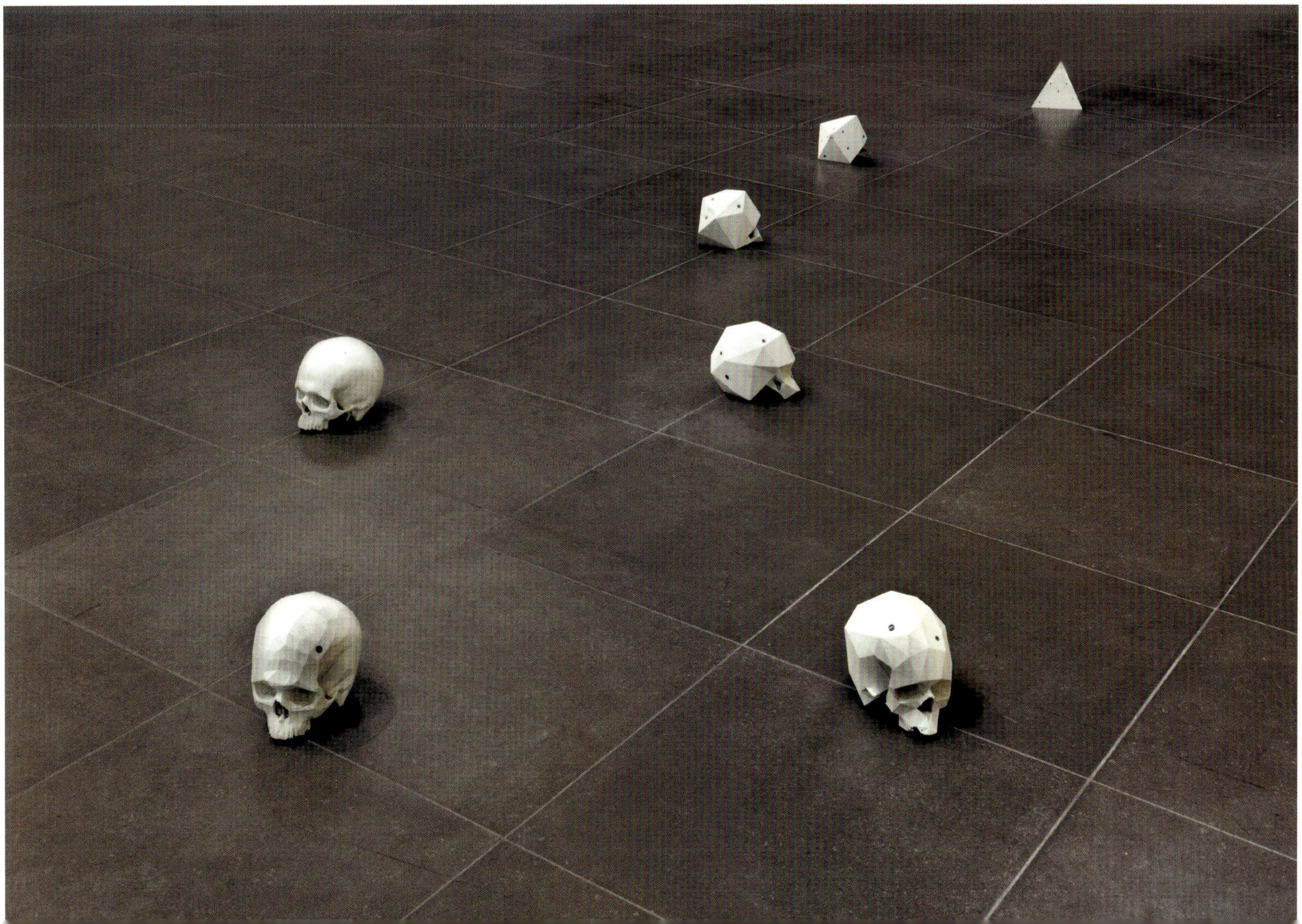

Koo Jeong-A was born in Seoul in 1967 and moved to Paris in 1991. After spending some time working in the studio of Christian Boltanski, she became known for her micro-interventions, consisting of collecting and placing poor and insignificant materials, including dust, boards and small objects. Ephemeral, fragile and furtive, her work is characterized by a response to place — our experience of our immediate surroundings. Her installations reveal a conception of place in which, contrary to appearances, nothing is left to chance. The almost-nothing is organized with an obsessive eye for detail and precision.

An interest in ephemeral architecture or modelling has consistently appeared in Jeong-A's work, whether in the form of houses made from sugar cubes or structures built from ground aspirin. *Cedric* (2003), an homage to the adaptable architecture of Cedric Price, is in keeping with this interest. Consisting of numerous small elements held in place by magnetic rods, the work changes as parts of the structure fall to the ground over time, creating a map or cloud formation on the floor adjacent to the structure (time-based, adaptable and relational, like Price's architecture).

Dreams and Thoughts (2003–08) extends Jeong-A's interest in architecture and its meeting with ephemerality and sensuality. The piece is made from 100 kilograms of chewing gum (a variety of flavours have been included over the years), the individual sticks, used like bricks to create a miniature cityscape, suggesting some kind of futuristic building complex. The visitor is first greeted with the olfactory presence of the work, for example the unmistakeable smell of Wrigley's Juicy Fruit, only later identifying the source and its physical conceit. The piece suggests both a temporary, edible structure and the notion that architecture, space or place could have a synaesthesiac effect. Our memory of place or our recollection of a building, for instance, is intimately tied to the accompanying sensory impression.

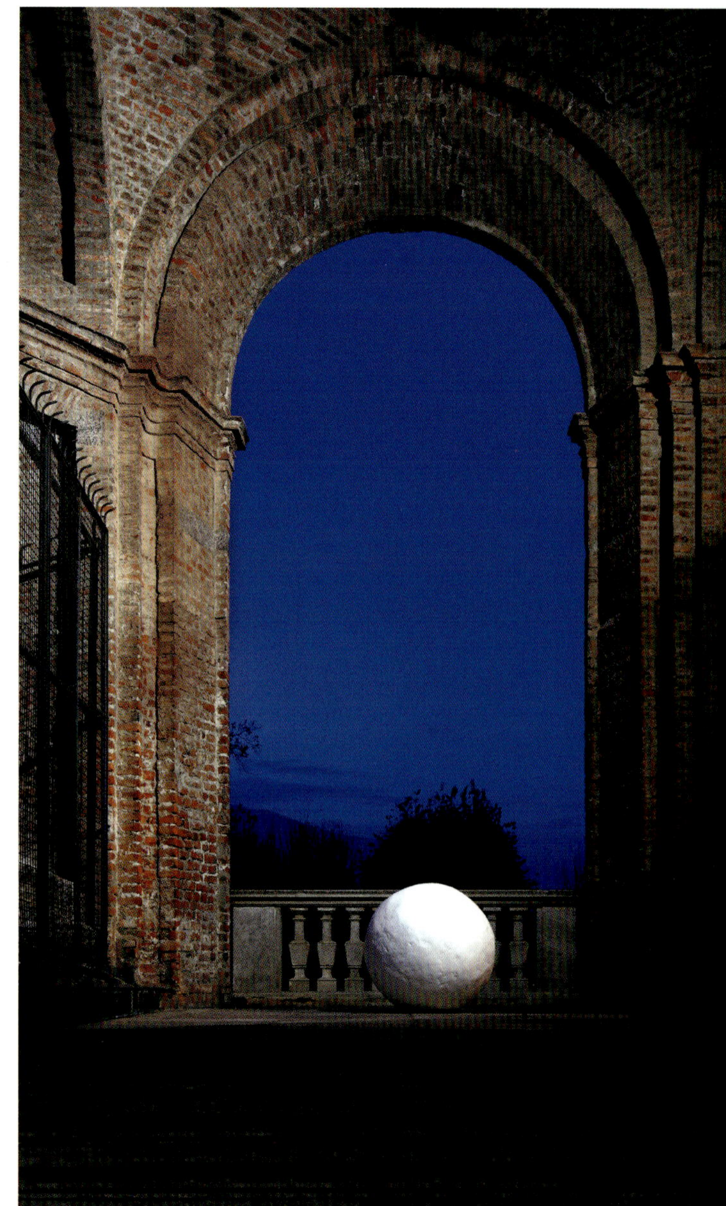

02

01

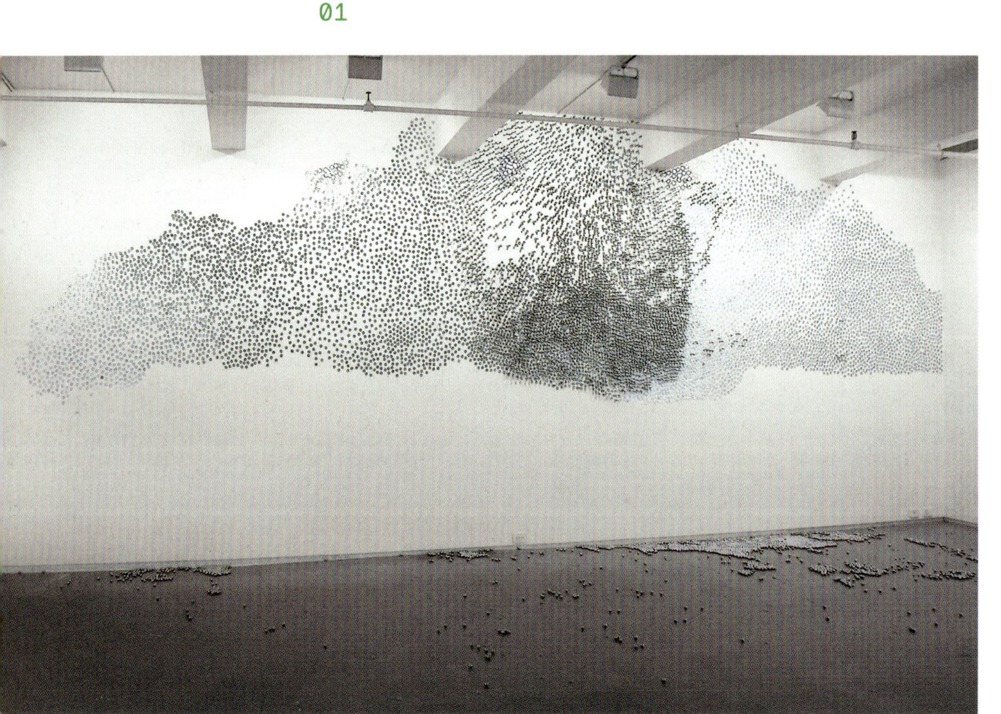

Most recently, Jeong-A has investigated this idea in a work that uses smell with quite different connotations. For the 2008 Turin Triennial she produced what appeared to be a giant snowball, or perhaps a fallen moon, illogically situated on the museum's steps in the sixteen degree warmth of a tepid Italian autumn. Closer inspection revealed, through smell again, that the work was something quite different. The unmistakeable smell of closets opened after a winter of hibernation demonstrated that this was, in fact, a giant ball of napthalene, the product used to repel moths during their summer egg-laying period. It was unclear if this was a comment on the more extreme fears of conservators in museums, who live in dread of moths, or if the work functioned as an interruption of our normal digestion of art, an olfactory blip in the otherwise visual overload of art. Jeong-A's work perhaps functions best as this kind of interruption or break in art viewing, encouraging the pause, often with an accompanying smile, that enables us to think differently as we continue on our visual journey. [Jens Hoffmann]

01 *Cedric*, 2003
Washers, magnetic rods, chrome steel balls
Dimensions variable

02 *Untitled*, 1998–2008
Naphthalene
Diameter 100 cm

03 *Dreams & Thoughts*, 2003
Chewing gum
Dimensions variable

04 *new song, o*, 2008
200 watercolours on paper
Dimensions variable

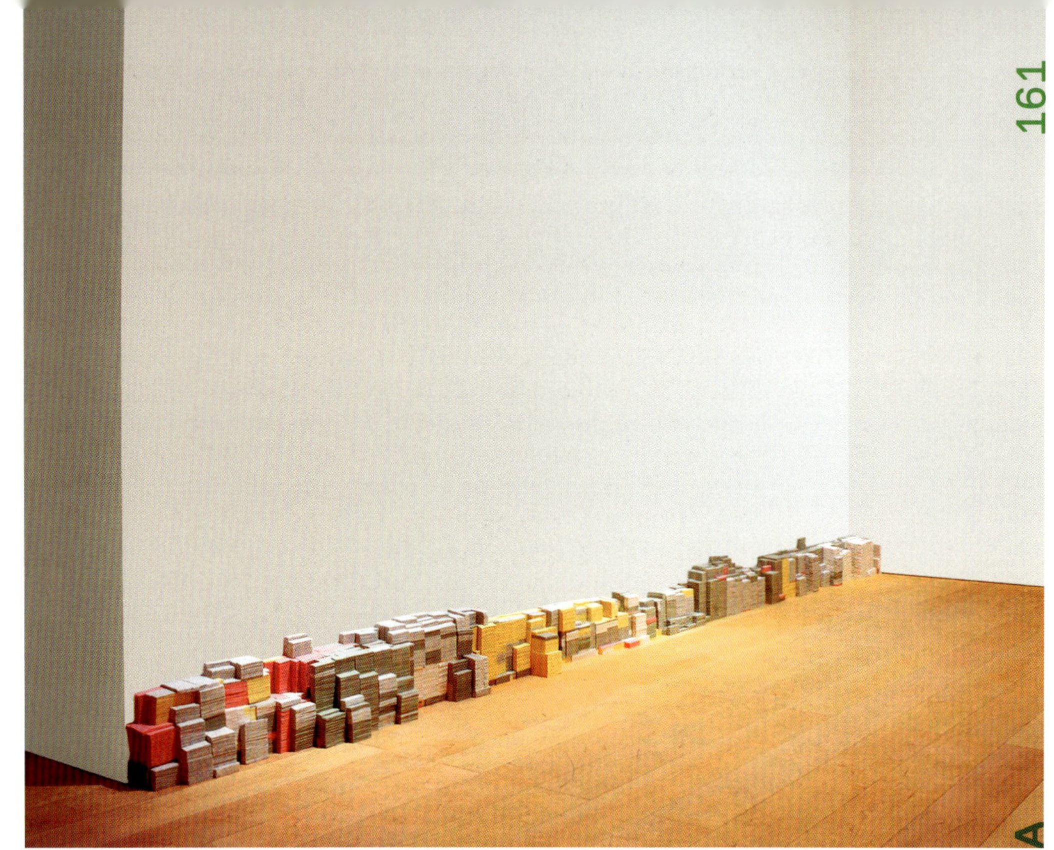

03

04

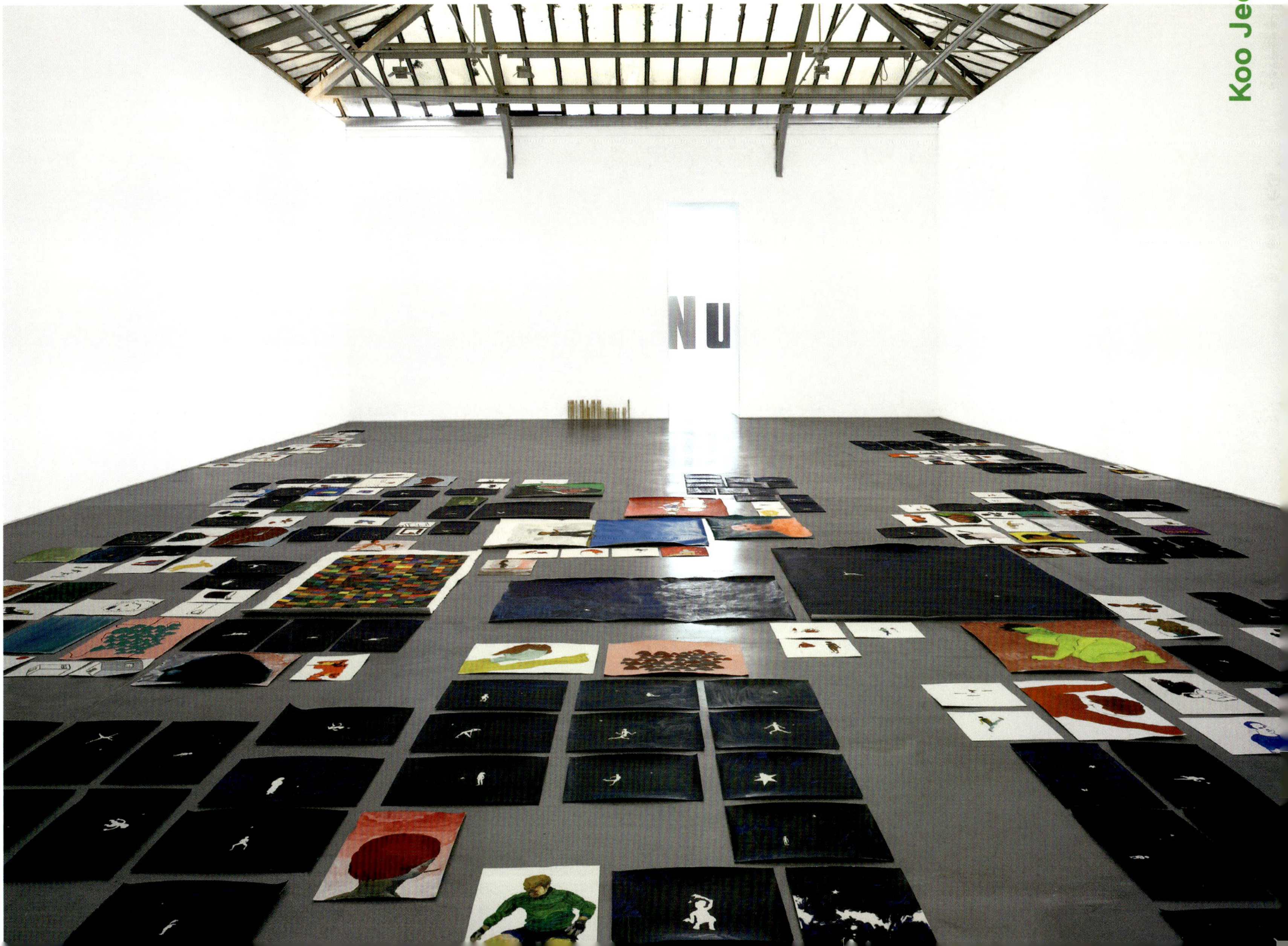

01 What comes across immediately in the work of Daniel Joglar is his sense of economy. His habit of using whatever materials are available, together with his deep and long-sustained impulse to hoard odd and disparate found objects without premeditated intention, could have led his installations to excess. But his inherent gift for poetic harmony guides his decisions judiciously throughout each work's development.

Joglar's regional culture and academic pursuits in chemistry, architecture, theology and philosophy are profoundly embedded in his work. His decision to become an artist, triggered by an ongoing search for meaning, earned him a place in the Studio Program for the Visual Arts in Buenos Aires, an artists' residency created by Guillermo Kuitca. The two years spent working in this context reinforced the penchant for experimentation he had acquired during his chemistry studies. While some of his colleagues lost themselves in this open-ended atmosphere, Joglar put to good use his chemistry experience, especially in the careful consideration of weight and measures.

His first table installations of simple stationary items were shown in a group exhibition at the Centro Cultural Borges in Buenos Aires. This event was followed by 'Geografía' in 2001, at the Dabbah Torrejón gallery, a show that held its own in terms of style and commitment, though unconsciously rooted in the River Plate constructive art tradition. Reams of pastel-coloured office paper in slightly undulating piles represented the different layers of land as it is conventionally drawn in geological diagrams. Pieces of tree trunk were sliced to show the age of the tree, while a wall installation of pick-up sticks closely followed the way in which they had fallen when dropped on the floor.

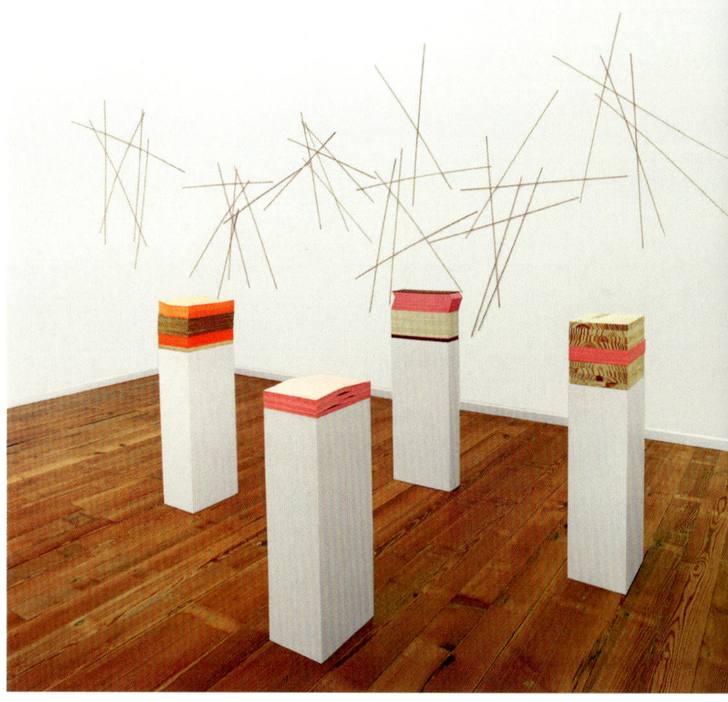

'Ants, spiders and bees', an exhibition of table installations at the Centro Cultural Borges in 2004, was inspired in Sir Francis Bacon's theories on how the different methods in which scientists work resemble that of ants, who collect, spiders, who knit their webs with their own substance, and bees who gather material and transform it. In 'Distant Sounds', Joglar's 2005 show at Dabbah Torrejón, he exhibited clean-cut, minimalist objects sparsely laid out on small classic French-style tables. Together, the cryptic arrangements evoked religious enigmas in the manner of cabbalistic riddles.

In 2006, Joglar liberated his work from a given surface by creating mobiles made up of light rods and circles, which swing in the air at the slightest breeze. In the same year, he mounted his first exhibitions abroad: at the Pontevedra Biennial in Spain and at the Blanton Museum of Art in Austin, Texas. For Pontevedra — a traditional Catholic fishing town — Joglar hung a large fishing net woven with green, luminescent rosaries, showing once more his grasp of the essential and the immediate.
His latest work includes periodic tables, an overt acknowledgement of his chemistry background and of his need to classify and systematize the objects that he so adroitly displays. [Alina Tortosa]

02

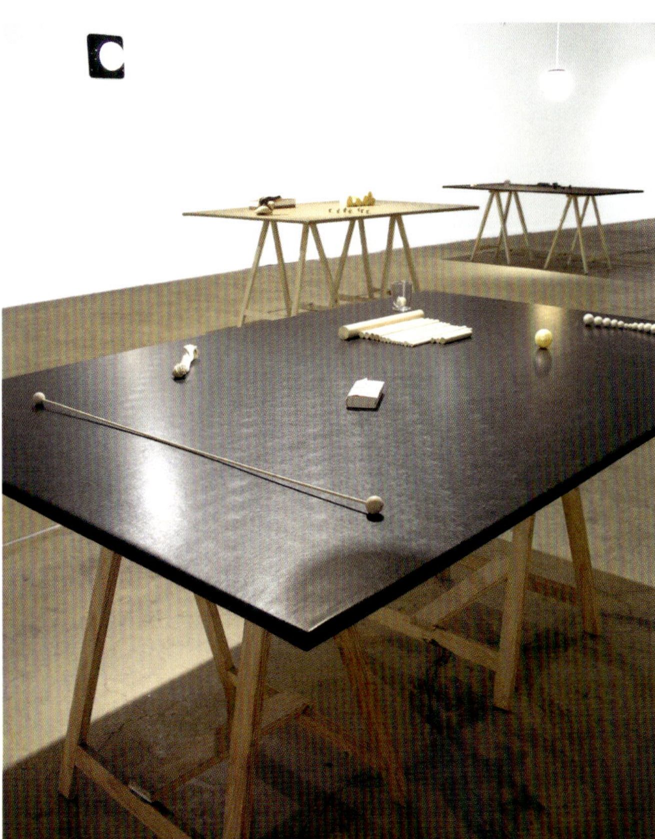

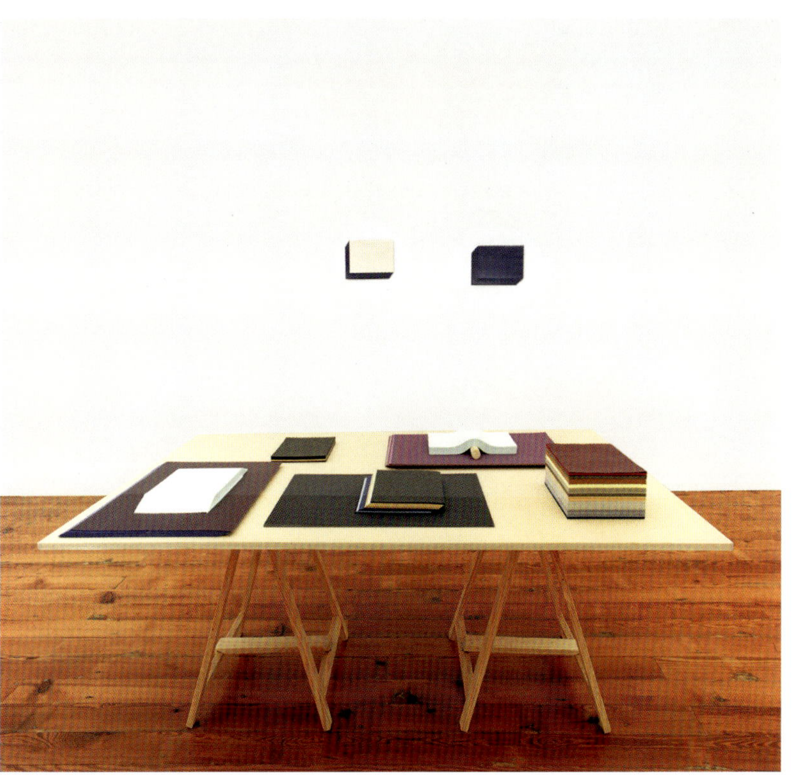

03

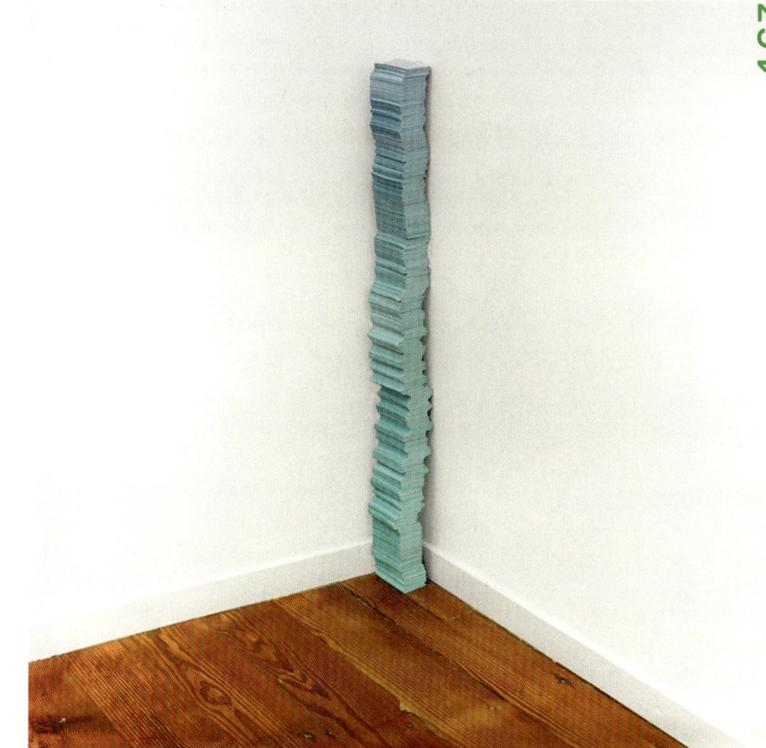

04

05

01 *Geography*, 2001
Paper, wood
4 parts
Each 22 × 28 × 80 cm

02 *Ants, spiders and bees*, 2004
Tables, leather, objects, lamps
Each table 180 × 120 × 80 cm

03 *El sial flota sobre el sima*, 2001
Paper, table
180 × 120 × 80 cm

04 *Relieve*, 2001
Cardboard
90 × 6 × 10 cm

05 *Distant Sounds*, 2005
Tables, objects and
musical instruments
Each table approx. 90 × 50 × 80 cm

Inspired by the intriguing forms of conceptual sculpture produced by recent graduates from art programmes in and around Los Angeles, in 2005 the Hammer Museum, with curators Christopher Miles, James Elaine and Aimee Chang, mounted the exhibition 'Thing: New Sculpture from Los Angeles'. Borne up by a flourishing object-based art market, the exhibition demonstrated, in Miles' words, 'a broadly shared drive toward specialization or focused investigation on the part of many emerging artists in Los Angeles: a reinvestment in objects.' 'Thing' used as its signature object a 2004 work by the artist Matt Johnson. Called *Bread Face*, it was a replica of a bread crust with two eyes and a mouth chomped from its square, made of cast plastic and oil paint applied with a trompe-l'oeil exactitude. Meticulously constructed, the object was both the incidental product of a child's primitive play and a weird artefact of a lost and tribal Americana.

Johnson's work invests singular objects with a dense play of meaning, often by consecrating impulsive or absurd gestures. Form emerges from the sorts of half-comedic feats of construction or defacement that one commits when drunk, distracted or bored. See, for example, *Matches* (2006) — miniature figures suspended in a moment of sexual congress, which seem to be constructed, on the fly, from paper matchbooks (actually cast in bronze) — or *Parlor Trick*, 2005, where two interlocked forks teeter atop a snapped toothpick (each made in bronze) stuck into the holes of a (found object) salt shaker. Exhausted or over-determined in the vicinity of art, sculptural impulses are discovered again in the offhand and everyday.

Several works riff on a history of art, which is both reified (as icons to quote) and clichéd (and ripe for parody). *Birth of Venus* (2007), *Tower of Babel* (2007), and *Pieta* (2006) each present irreverent and doodled approximations of old chestnuts of art history. *Reclining Nude* (2008) splices together styles and codes from different eras, forcing a rigid puritan chair to approximate the louche and half-pornographic pose of the painter's model. *The Pianist (after Robert J. Lang)* (2005), on the other hand, monumentalizes with a blue tarpaulin sheet a folded paper figure composed by the famous origami artist Robert Lang. At life size, the charming construction looks suddenly unhinged and hilariously Grand Guignol.

While those sculptural 'things' revive a familiar set of surrealistic manoeuvres — unlikely juxtapositions, everyday items in unfamiliar surroundings, shifts in scale — Johnson's best objects defy such categorization by constructing a deceptively artificial nature. In *Ventifact* (2006), for example, a sandstone rock is etched, as if by erosion, with the appearance of a human skull, putting forward the impression that death-rock romanticism extends deep into the natural order. *4Eva* (2006) similarly inscribes fleeting passions upon an apparently geological formation: a three-ton boulder of Pre-Cambrian granite imbued with quartz veins that brag, amusingly, about the rock's — and the artist's — persistence in time. [Julian Myers]

01

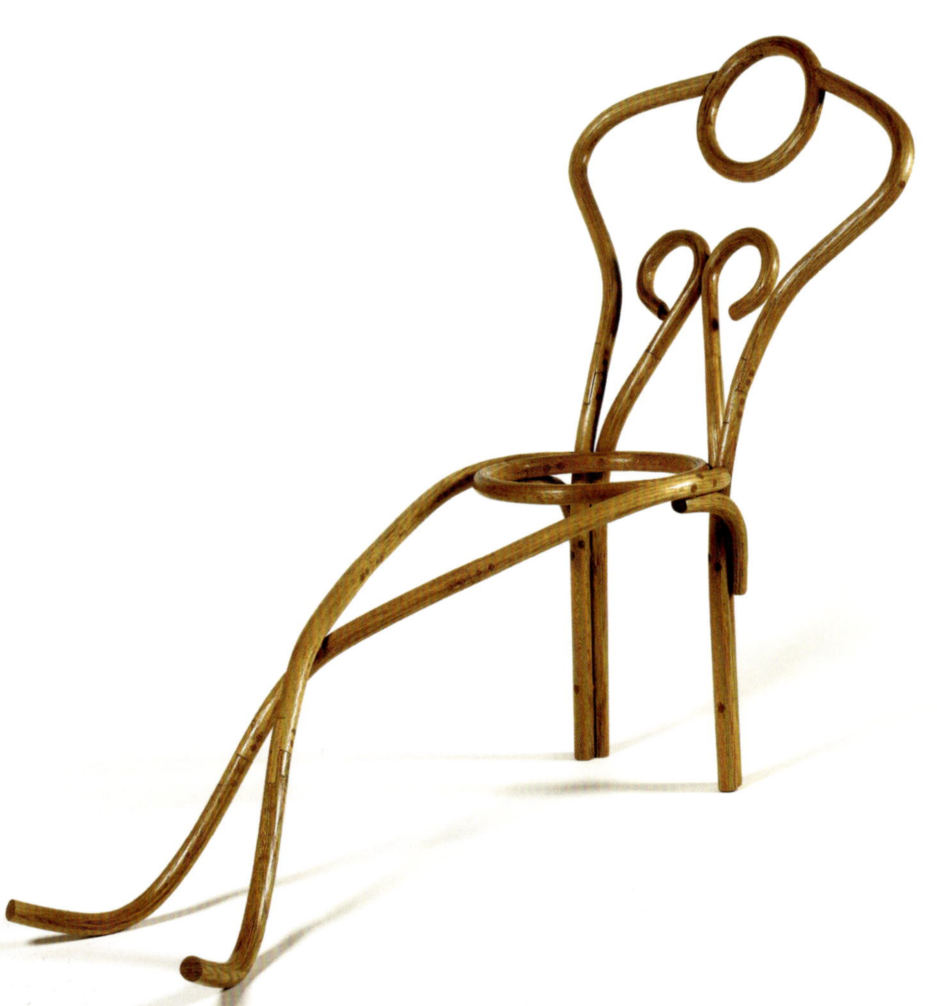

01 *Reclining Nude*, 2008
Steam bent and laminated red oak
165 × 119 × 71 cm

02 *4 Eva*, 2006
Granite with inlay
122 × 122 × 153 cm

03 *Ventifact*, 2006
Sandstone
41 × 38 × 48 cm

04 *Tower of Babel*, 2007
Stainless steel, paper
122 × 38 × 38 cm

02

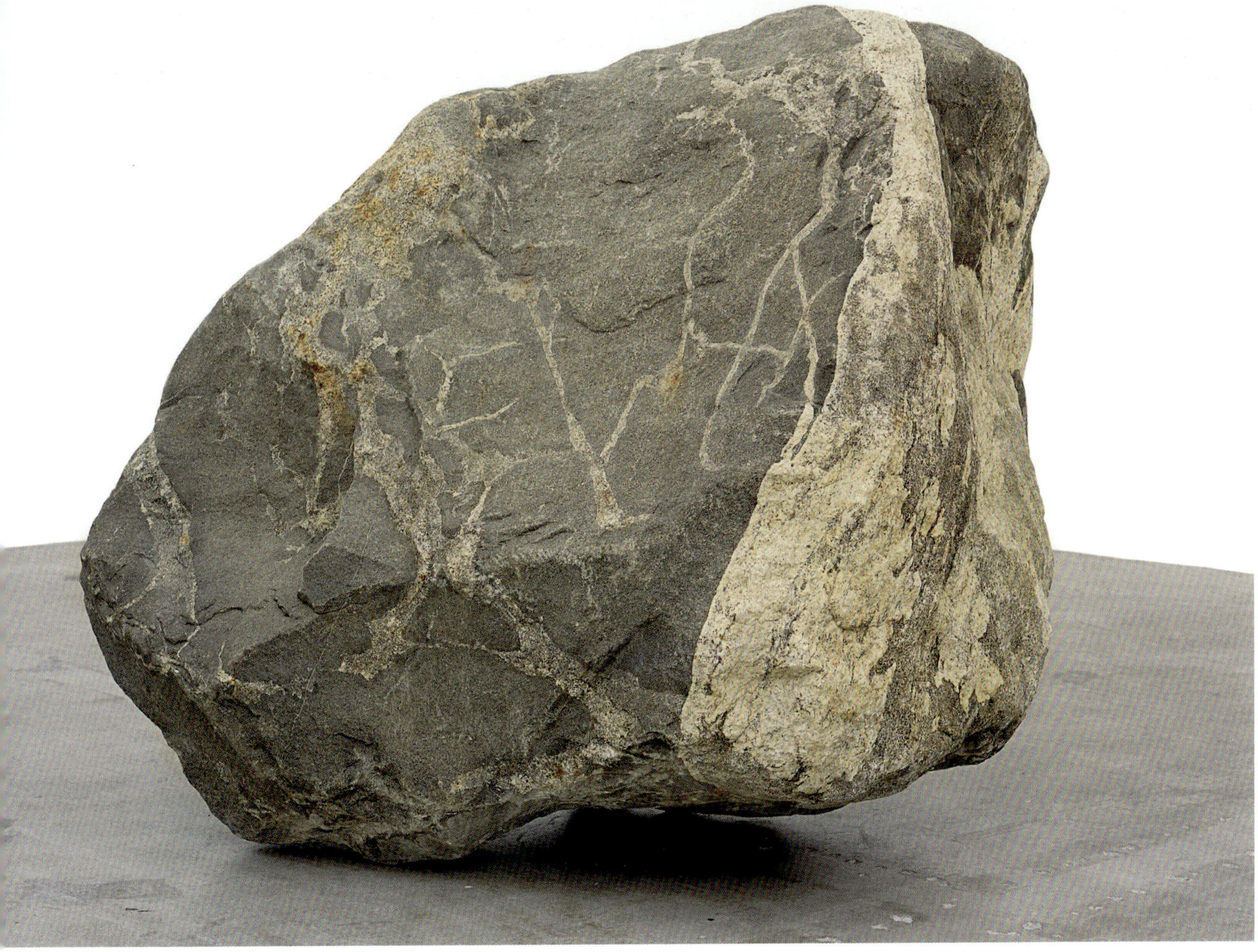

03

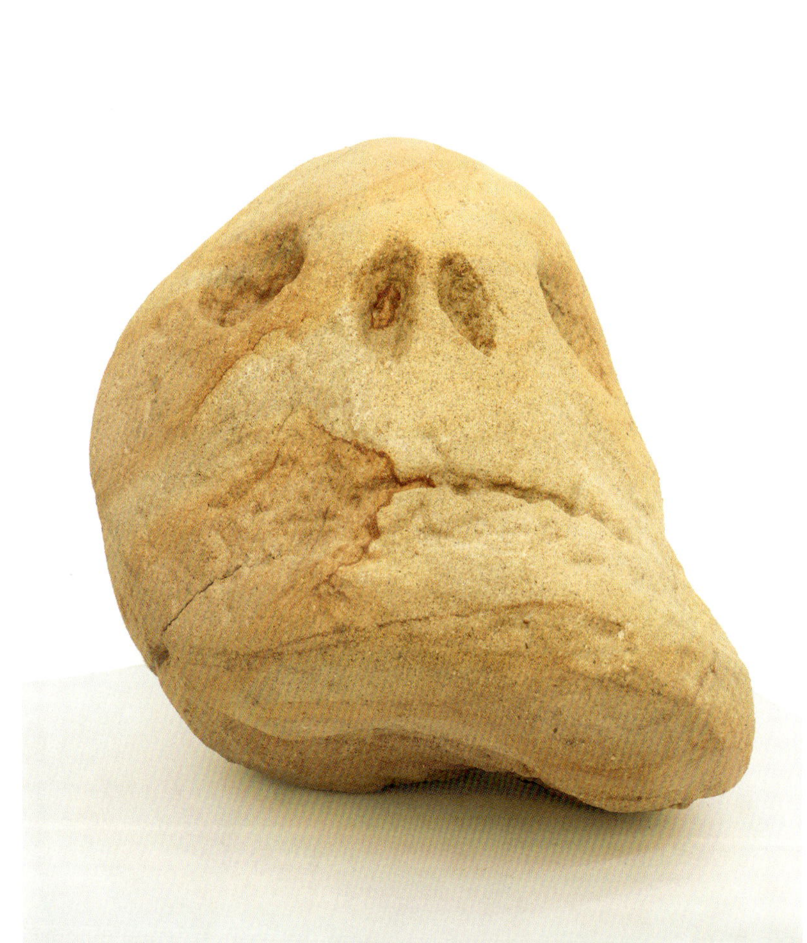

04

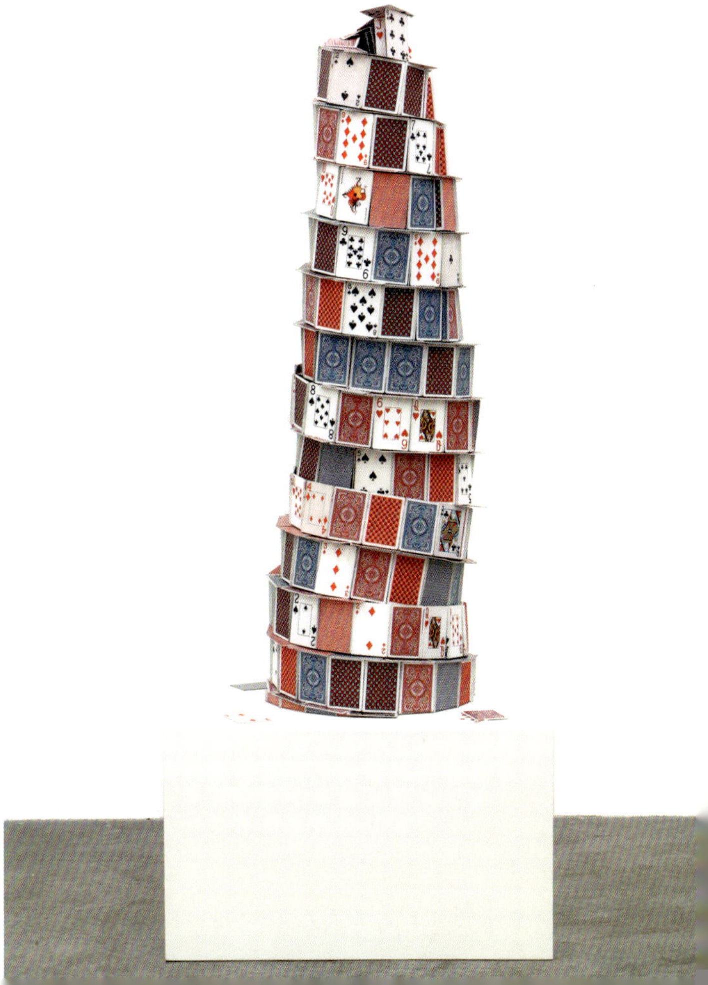

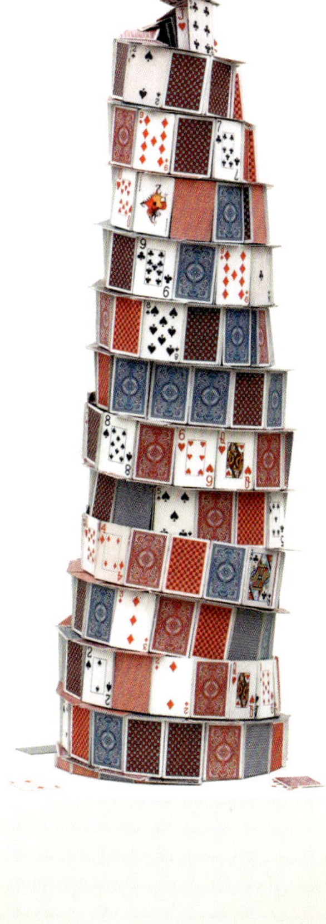

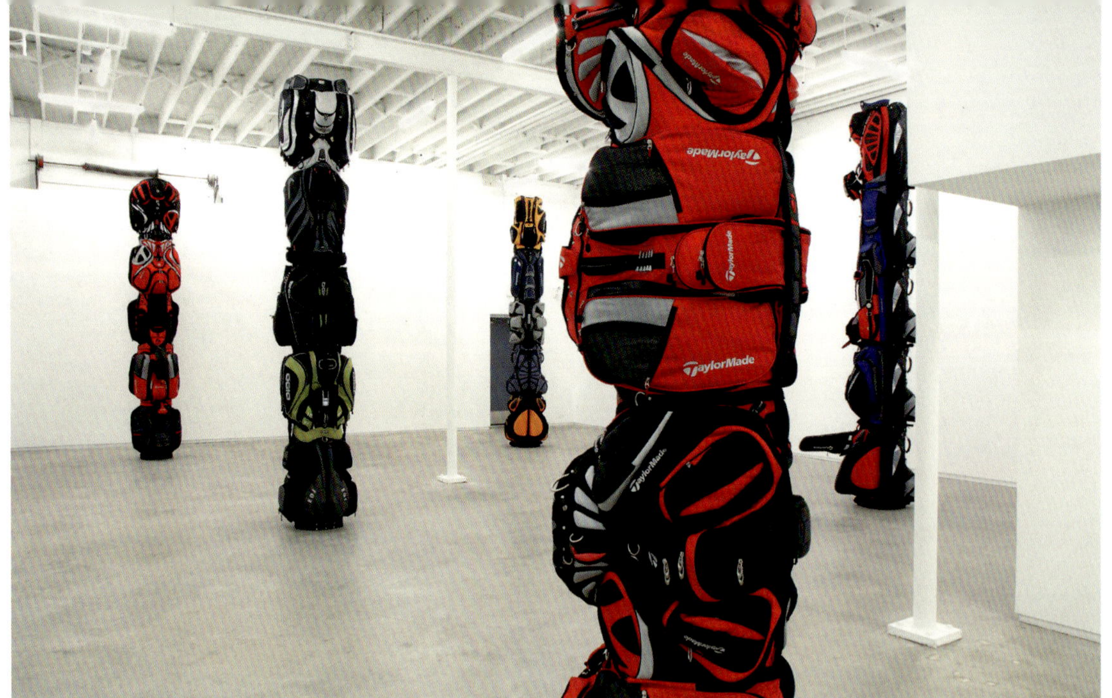

01

01 from left:
→ *2000*, 2007
→ *2010*, 2007
→ *1970*, 2007
→ *1980*, 2007
→ *1960*, 2007
Golf bags, cardboard tubes
Dimensions variable

Brian Jungen's *Prototypes For a New Understanding*, (1999–2005), his first widely known sculptural work, was a series of 23 handcrafted masks. Reminiscent of the masks of British Columbia's First Nations people, with their characteristic red, black and white ovoids, Jungen's masks carry the impression of cultural authenticity. On closer inspection, however, it becomes evident that they are only a freestyle, approximate rendition of traditional Northwest coastal craft, and that they have been fashioned from pieces of Nike Air Jordan basketball shoes. Like many of Jungen's later sculptural works, the masks propose a form of hybridity in which no element is ever fully assimilated within the other. More than simply addressing the commodification and fetishization of aboriginal culture, the masks propose a different understanding of cultural borrowing, hence their title.

Jungen, who was born to a Swiss father and a Dane-zaa First Nations mother in northern British Columbia, has said that his strategy of using hybrid materials derived in part from witnessing his family's practice of mending objects with whatever discarded materials happened to be at hand. He has turned this habit of bricolage towards a strategy for examining the intersections of the global economy, the discourses of art, aboriginal cultural stereotypes and his own mixed ancestry. Perhaps not surprisingly, he has pointed out that his own relationship to the masks, the shoes and his work's cultural borrowing is far from certain.

Jungen followed the masks with three immense whale skeletons assembled from white plastic garden chairs. Like the masks, the skeletons — *Shapeshifter* (2000), *Cetology* (2002) and *Vienna* (2003) — are hung as if in a museum of natural history, and in fact Jungen's works often project a sense of frozen, airless incarceration inside the gallery space. The title *Shapeshifter* simultaneously suggests his approach to sculpture in general, aboriginal myths involving human to animal transformation, science and fantasy fiction, the metamorphosis of past life into petroleum-based plastics, as well as the more mundane metamorphosis of one commodity into another.

In *Court* (2004), a basketball court is entirely constructed from the wooden surfaces of dozens of industrial sewing machine tables, the holes where the machines were once inserted making the court treacherous and suggesting the sweatshops where coveted basketball gear is produced. *Talking Sticks* (2005), wooden baseball bats laser-cut with phrases on the topic of labour, resemble native totem poles. Sport appears repeatedly as a concern in Jungen's work, perhaps because of its central role in the native communities of his background, but also because sports gear is as fetishized as native handicrafts and imagery, and because it can be made to stand in for commodities in general.

Jungen's work has increasingly engaged with architecture and its utopian social aspirations. His site-specific installation *Habitat 04 — Cité radieuse des chats/Cats Radiant City* (2004), was a rough model of Moshe Safdie's iconic Habitat '67, a social-housing complex built as part of Montreal's World Expo. The complex went drastically over budget, fell into disrepair and now exists as exorbitantly priced, privately owned condos. Jungen's replica, constructed from plywood clad in synthetic carpeting, functioned as an SPCA cat shelter and adoption centre. The structure was outfitted with video cameras, allowing viewers to monitor the cats. This amusing satire, in which the housing of abandoned animals is played off against the disturbing fact of their surveillance, suggests both the dreams and failures of the modernist social project. [Lindsay Brown]

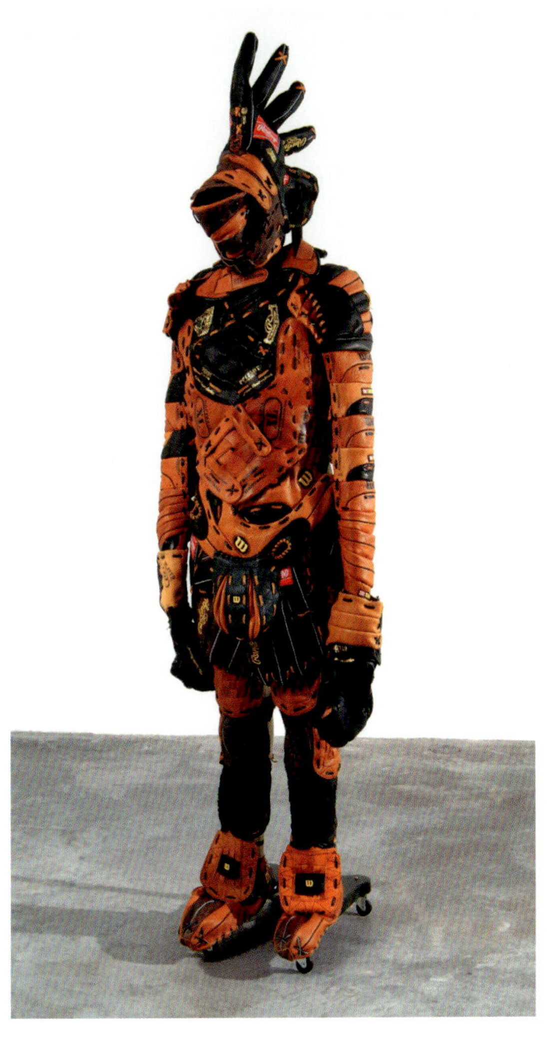

02

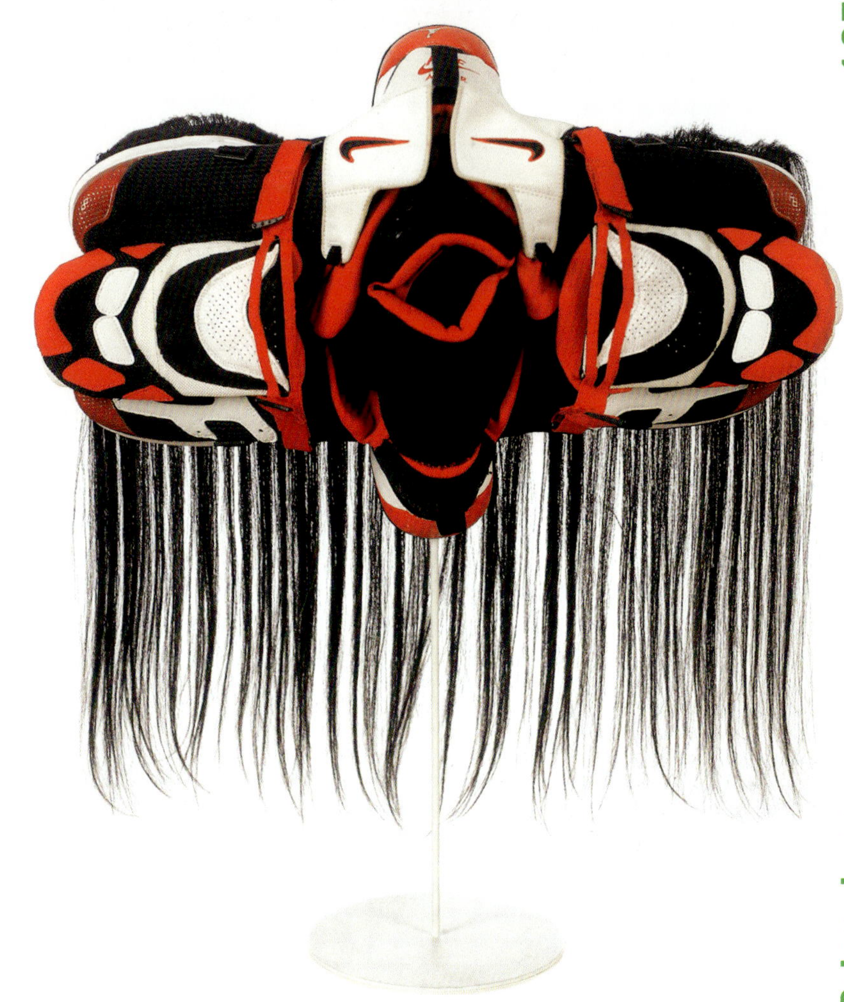

03

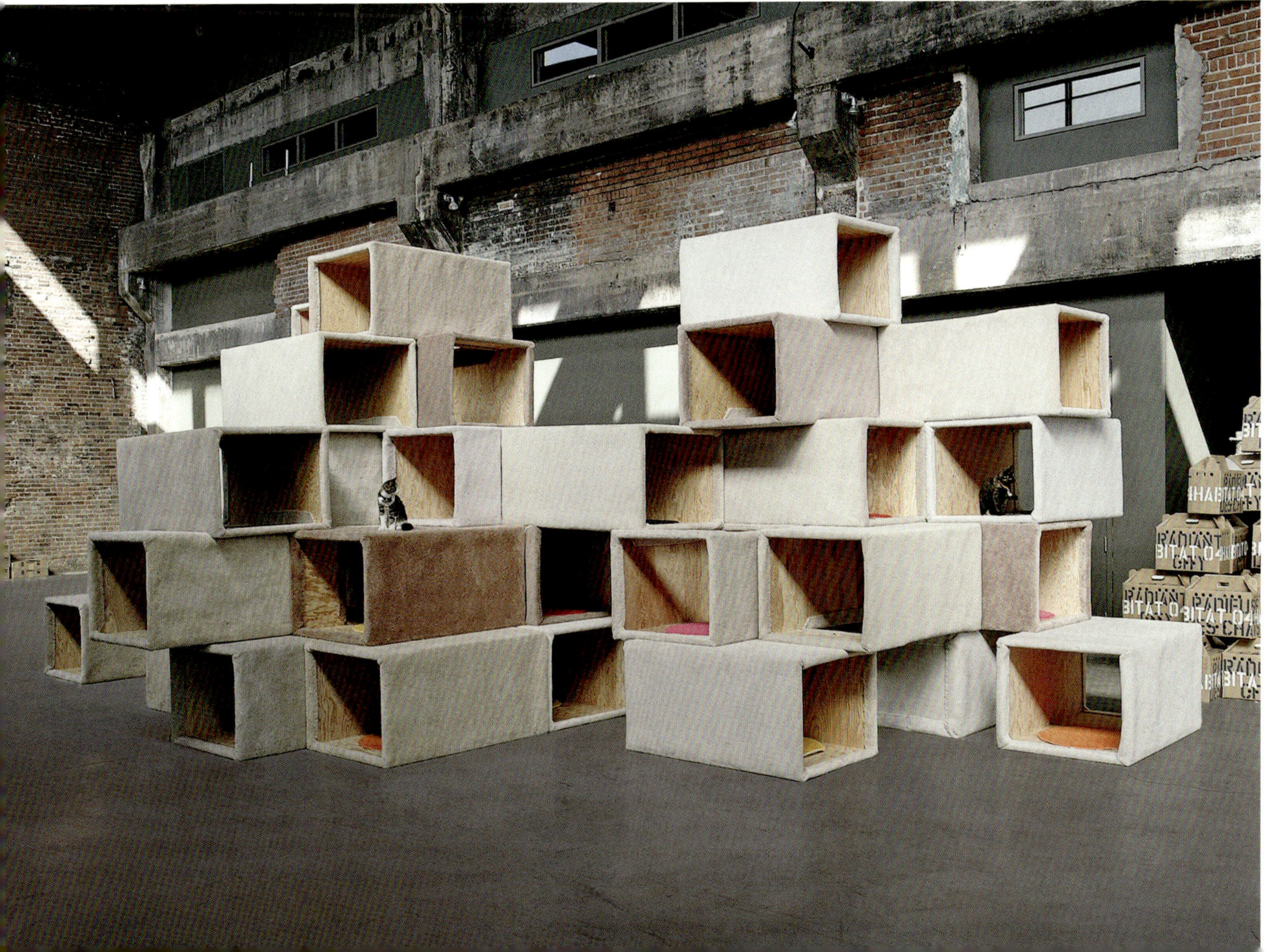

04

02 *The Prince*, 2006
Baseball mitts, dress form
208 × 61 × 232 cm

03 *Prototype for New Understanding #11*, 2002
Nike Air Jordan shoes, hair
67 × 59 × 25 cm

04 *Habitat 04 — Cité radieuse des chats/Cats Radiant City*, 2004
Plywood, carpet, cats
335 × 457 × 853 cm
Darling Foundry, Quartier Éphémère, Montréal, Quebec

Kitty Kraus's fascinating process of reduction in her work creates a sense of unease. At first glance her elemental formal vocabulary, her limited, almost achromatic colour range and her prefabricated everyday materials, such as glass, neon tubes, incandescent bulbs, adhesive tape, fabric, tar, ink and water, evoke the forms and propositions associated with Minimalism or the earlier Constructivist movement. But on closer inspection Kraus's seemingly orderly, geometrical world is characterized by fragmentation, dissolution, instability, destruction and loss of control.

Kraus cuts up suits and presents them as rectangles forming architectural islands in the space, as Minimalist floor works or as areas linking floor and wall. Panes of glass lean at strange angles to each other and to the gallery wall. These are disturbing definitions within the space, balancing at the limits of visibility, addressing viewers directly and disturbing their uninhibited movement around the gallery. They initiate an interplay between conscious visual perception and subconscious physical orientation.

But Kraus's objects also remind us of the human body, invoking the tripartite division of head, torso and legs through the use of geometrical forms. These non-figurative 'bodies' are trapped in a potentially threatened and constantly disturbing state of immobility. Evocations of the absence of the body, disembodiment through the imposition of geometrical form, the creation of boundaries and limits (through space, clothing, the physical nature of materials and the right angle), and the constructions created by this geometry are all central to her work.

In other pieces, Kraus captures the light from a lamp with six mirrors fastened loosely together to form a cube. Beams of light escape into the space through the imperfectly sealed edges — a spectacle that Kraus tries to reconstruct in countless drawings of reflection and deviations. But her attempts to perfect this process are what contradict the uncontrollable nature of handmade mirror cubes. At one performance, Kraus heated up a mirror lamp with an incandescent bulb to such an extent that the infinite reflection of nothing vapourized in the space in an uncontrolled explosion.

The relationship between geometrical and organic, controlled and spontaneous form is also addressed in Kraus's cubes of frozen water coloured with ink. These leave a random 'painting' on the floor as they melt in the heat of a light bulb frozen inside them. Sometimes Kraus transmits the sound made by the conflicting temperatures inside the ice via a microphone frozen within it.

Kraus's exhibitions are dramaturgically charged ensembles of encounters between the controlled and uncontrollable presence of bodies. But they are also dramaturgically charged links with the history of geometric art: Joseph Beuys' work on the physical state of materials, Richard Serra's 'splash' works, Blinky Palermo's use of fabrics and the seam, Bruce Nauman's work with solids and space and Isa Genzken's 1982 *Weltempfänger (World Receiver)*, with its radio aerial set in a concrete cube. The neon lamps and incandescent bulbs evoke works by Dan Flavin and Felix Gonzalez-Torres, who both use these materials to suggest death and decay. And the mirror cubes remind us of Michelangelo Pistoletto's *Metrocubo d'Infinito*, created in the 1960s. [Beatrix Ruf]

01

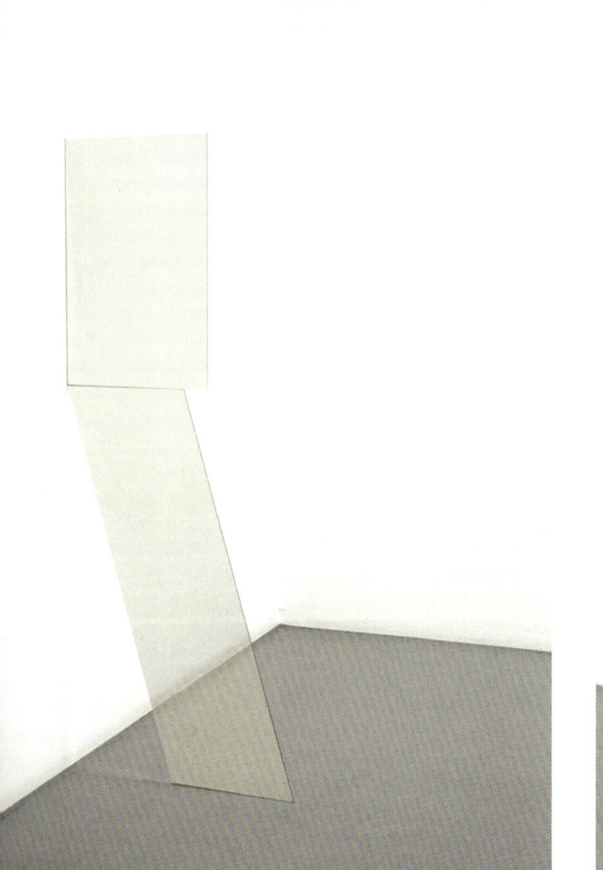

02

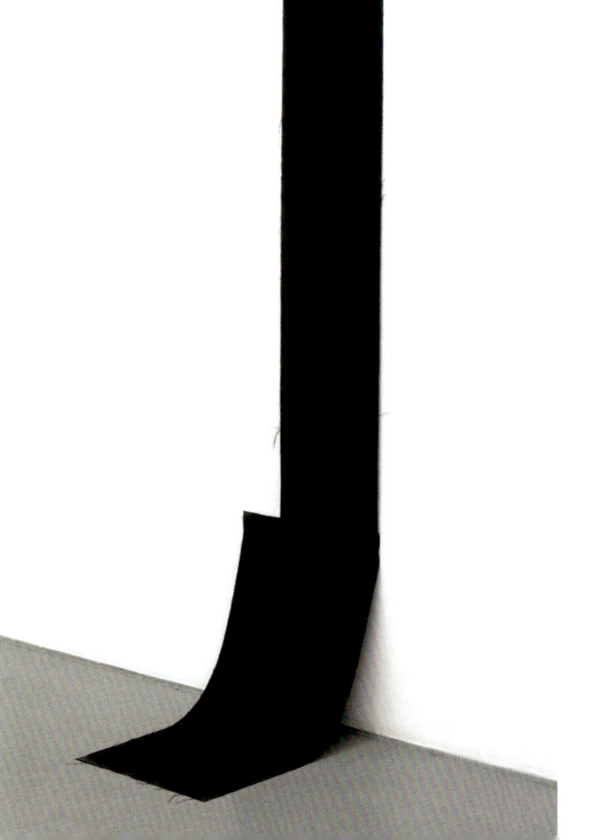

01 *Untitled*, 2006
Glass
171 × 68 × 0.5 cm

02 *Untitled*, 2008
Black suit cloth
146 × 46 × 45 cm

03 *Untitled (Mirror Lamp)*, 2006
Mirrors, light bulb
17 × 22 × 30 cm

04 *Untitled*, 2008
Ice, ink
Dimensions variable
Lamp
13 × 20 × 20 cm
Concrete plinth
20 × 20 × 25 cm

05 *Untitled*, 2006
Lamp, ice, ink
Dimensions variable

03

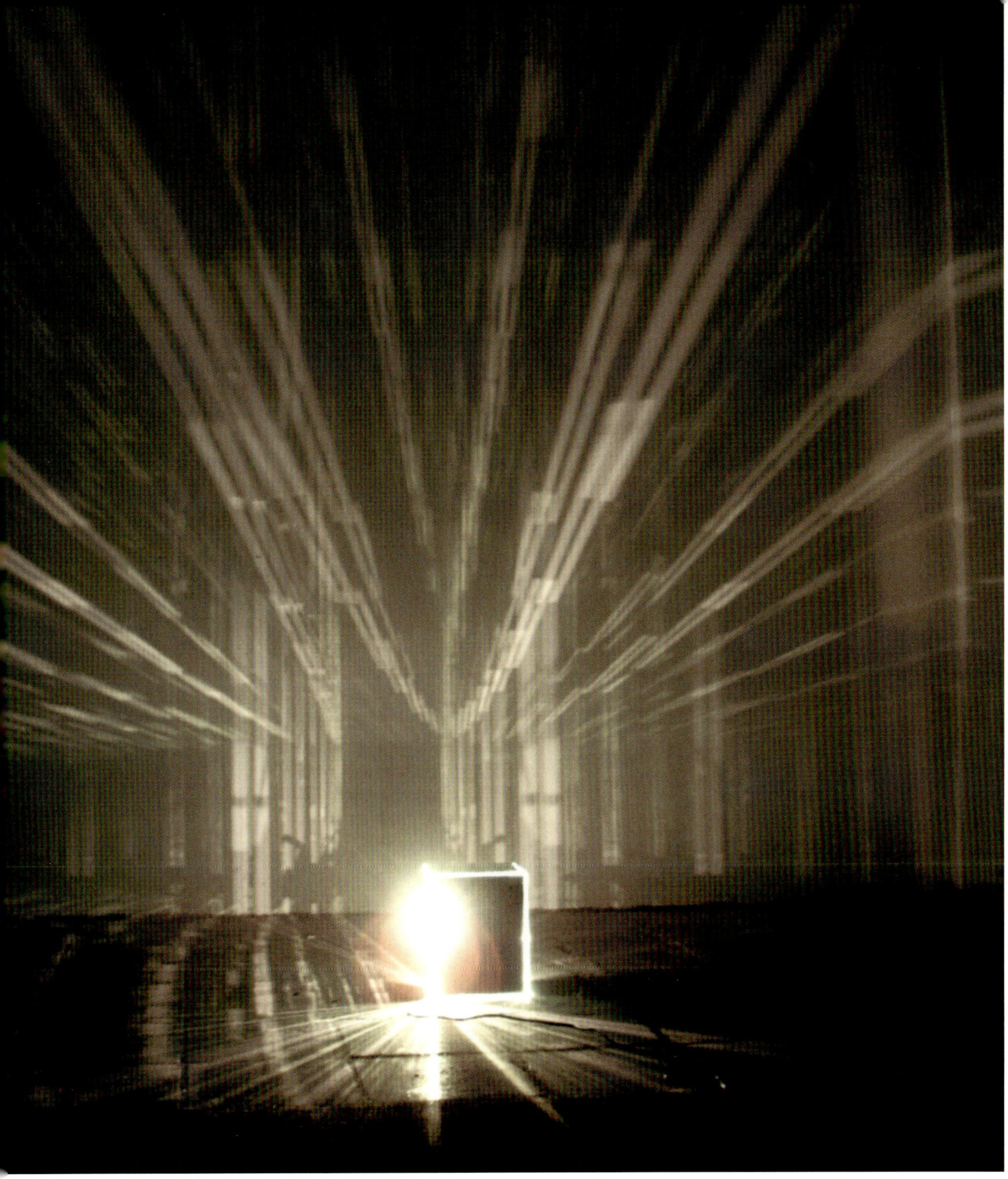

04

05

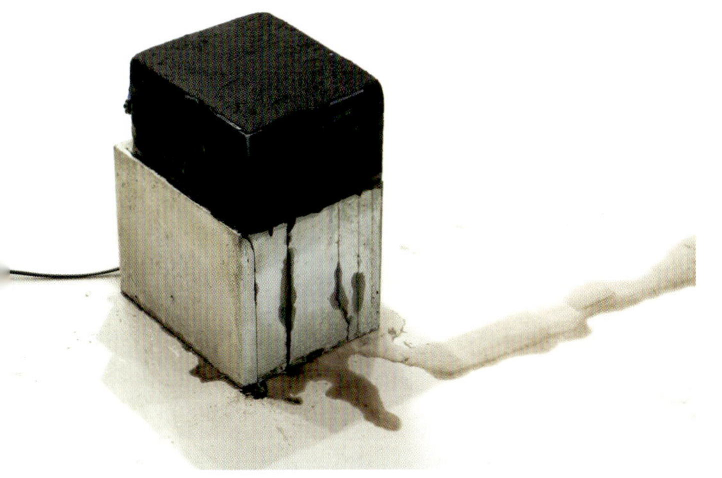

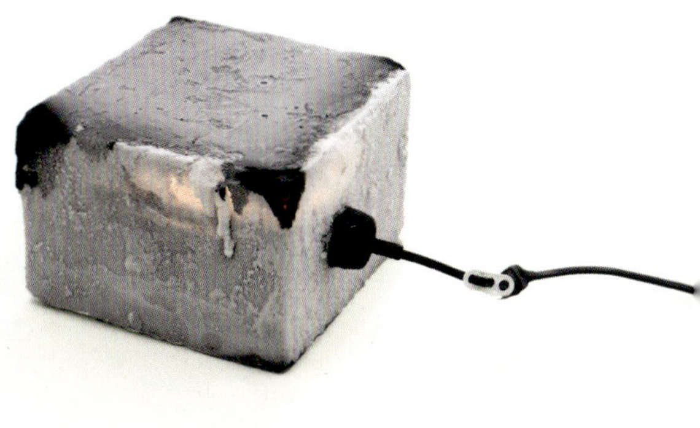

01 *A satisfied consumer*, 2008
Two tables, blue felt,
bits of washed-down soap
75 × 120 × 120 cm

02 *Model for a Victory Parade*, 2008
Conveyor belt,
aluminum can, perspex
51 × 223 × 71 cm

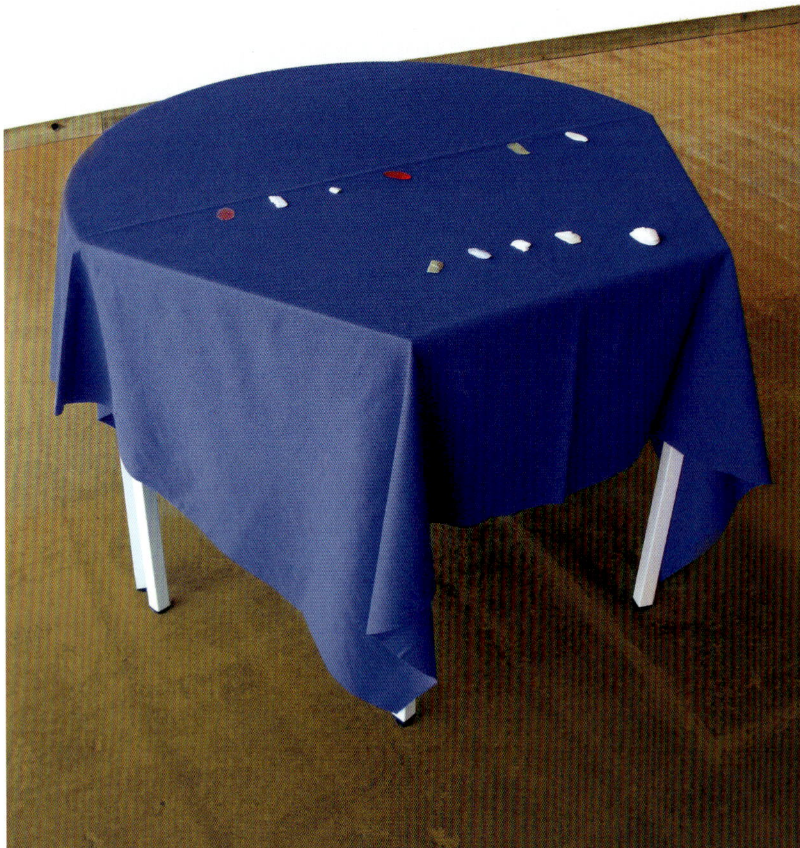

01

02

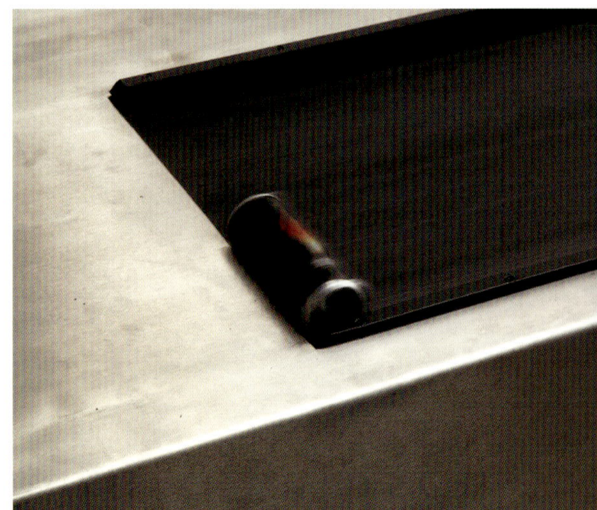

Gabriel Kuri studied in Mexico City and London but is now based in Brussels. From 1987 to 1991 he was active in an informal school run by the artist Gabriel Orozco that included Damián Ortega and Abraham Cruzvillegas. Known for his works made from altered commercial products, such as redesigned Kellogg's Corn Flakes containers, Kuri is also concerned with the import and export of culture, wealth and identity. He focuses frequently on the life of products that are manufactured in Mexico by US companies only to be re-imported as authentically 'American'. Orozco has used the term 'poetical activist' for Kuri's obliquely critical work.

His tapestry, *Untitled Leaflet Gobelin* (2002), mimics the process of production that characterizes contemporary economics but reinscribes a surprising value where normally we would expect to find none. Cheap advertising leaflets with a brief life were used as a cartoon to design the tapestry, ensuring a lasting life for the simple layout. Although no conscious reference is made, the labour in this work begs comparison with Alighieri e Boetti's Afghan-made wall hangings from the 1970s and a particular production of meaning through translation.

Untitled (2006) similarly involves a transformation of materials. Two cans poke out from the dismantled six sides of a cube, made of painted plywood and weatherproofed with roofing tar roll, calling to mind Arte Povera precedents. There is a Surrealist's affection for the unexpected encounter, the hybrid creation of montage and the transformation enabled by shifts in scale or focus in this work. There is even a palpable discomfort in examining some of Kuri's juxtapositions; things are out of place. Not all of his improbable combinations are constructed, however, and even those that are fabrications often suggest the kind of naturally occurring event or chance incident that we might stumble across in everyday life or create ourselves in the semi-conscious process of doodling. An apparently spotted tree trunk photographed by Kuri, for example, turns out to be a public dumping ground for chewing gum. Surprisingly, the random accumulation of gum has an unexpected beauty to it, as does the idea of the habitual behaviour that resulted in this sculptural form. What may have been one person's unthinking action has taken on a collective aspect, each individual adding independently to this collaborative effort.

Reflecting on the strategies of Arte Povera and Surrealism, Kuri's work is a fascinating example of the way in which contemporary artists continue to draw on art-historical models. Many of his works not only encompass such historic resonances but also express the artist's interest in the interplay between commerce and art. Similarly, a recent sculpture presented as part of the exhibition 'Model for a Victory Parade' (2008) comprises a simple conveyor belt with a squashed energy-drink can stuck at one end, perpetually tumbling in a frustrated attempt to 'check out'. This debris of an imagined ceremony, while holding multiple connotations, emphasizes the politics of energy consumption and, like much of Kuri's work, questions our own complicity in the production of events. [Jens Hoffmann]

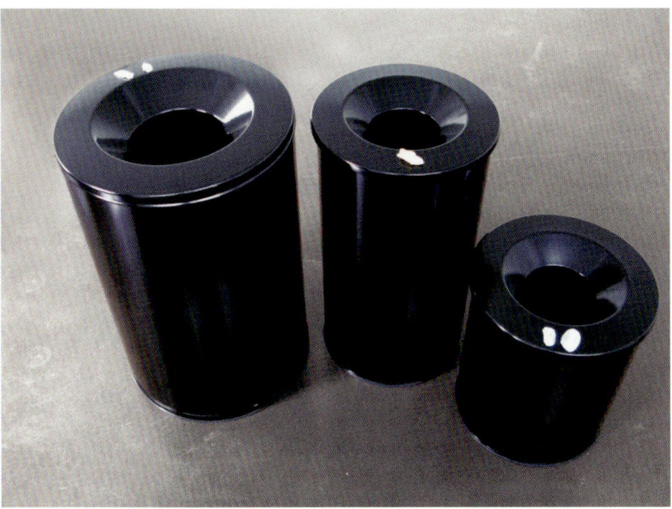

03

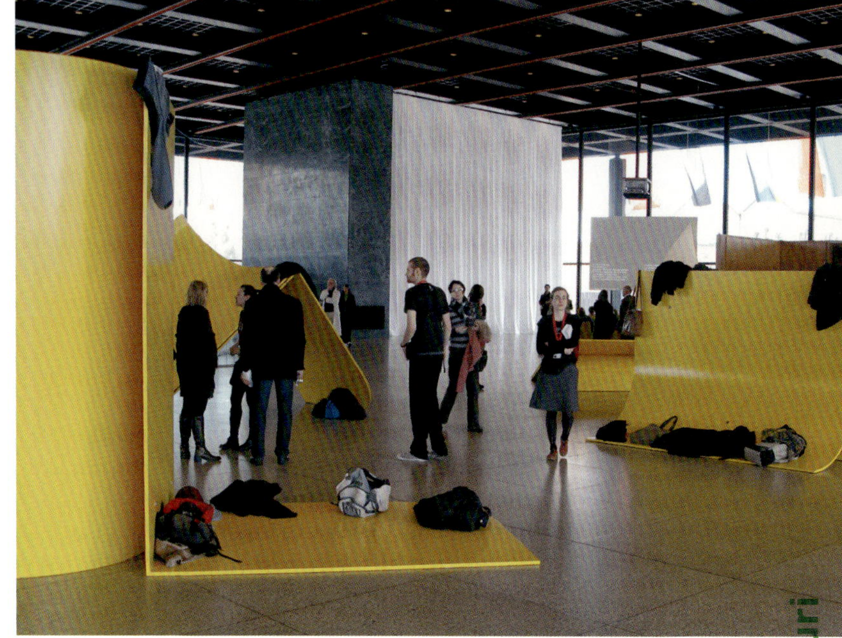

04

03 *The distance between producer and consumer (August 10)*, 2008
Metallic bins, washed-down bits of soap
3 parts
15 × 14 cm
60 × 37 cm
63 × 43 cm

04 *Items in Care of Items*, 2008
Painted steel, numbered magnetic discs, assorted items
Each 185 × 260 × 300 cm

05 *Complimentary Cornice*, 2008
Marble slabs, complimentary toiletries
132 × 191 × 3 cm

05

The most uncanny moment of the 2006 Berlin Biennial came for many visitors when they arrived at a room in the former Jewish elementary school for girls that displayed *Wagon* (2006), by Robert Kusmirowski. At first glance, this railway car looked deceptively like an authentic transportation device from the 1940s and therefore a possible instrument of the Holocaust. The site made the piece all the more resonant. However, on closer inspection it became clear that it was fake.

Kusmirowski, a Polish artist who grew up in the PRL (Polish People's Republic), elaborately replicates objects from a European past which is all the more elusive given that individual memory is always dependent on common narratives and tends to shape itself either in accordance with or through dissidence from official history. The PRL is now generally discredited for its oppressive politics and the poverty it brought upon its people, but for Kusmirowski it remains his Proustian point of origin, a paradise that depended on improvisation and the faking of items (the consumer goods of the capitalist world) that were out of reach. This notion of a parallel realm has become crucial to Kusmirowski's work, and he has turned his complicated nostalgia into a productive examination of collective memory.

Being a Polish artist after the fall of the Iron Curtain entails not only the liberty of access to the world art market, but also brings along historical connotations from which Kusmirowski has never shied away. *D.O.M.* (2004), his recreation of a multi-ethnic cemetery in Lublin speaks to a culture of loss and mourning that makes Poland a tourist destination, providing traces of an old Europe that was brutally destroyed in the twentieth century. Much of Kusmirowski's work plays with the concept of 'incontemporaneity' (*Ungleichzeitigkeit*), caused by the falling behind of the communist systems during the post-war period. In *DATAmatic 880* (2007) he reconstructed — as usual from cheap materials — a famous computer from the 1950s to set up a scene for himself as a time traveller. And a time traveller is truly what he is. He biked from Paris to Leipzig on a (fake) 1926 Wolberg bicycle and documented his trip with (fake vintage) photography. He then recreated an artist's studio from the times of the communist regime in Poland and duplicated it meticulously behind a mirror that didn't reflect.

In *Foreshore* (2008), a contribution to the Folkestone Triennial, Kusmirowski rebuilt three huts from a long-gone fisherman's quarter and set it up so that it would become accessible only during low tide, while at high tide it was under water. It was as if it had sunk under the surface of time in a loop that transformed progress — an obsession of the twentieth century shared by the communist and capitalist systems — into an eternal return of the same. Through his dubious remnants, Kusmirowski shows that the past can never to be a reliable point of origin, nor a site of belonging. [Bert Rebhandl]

01

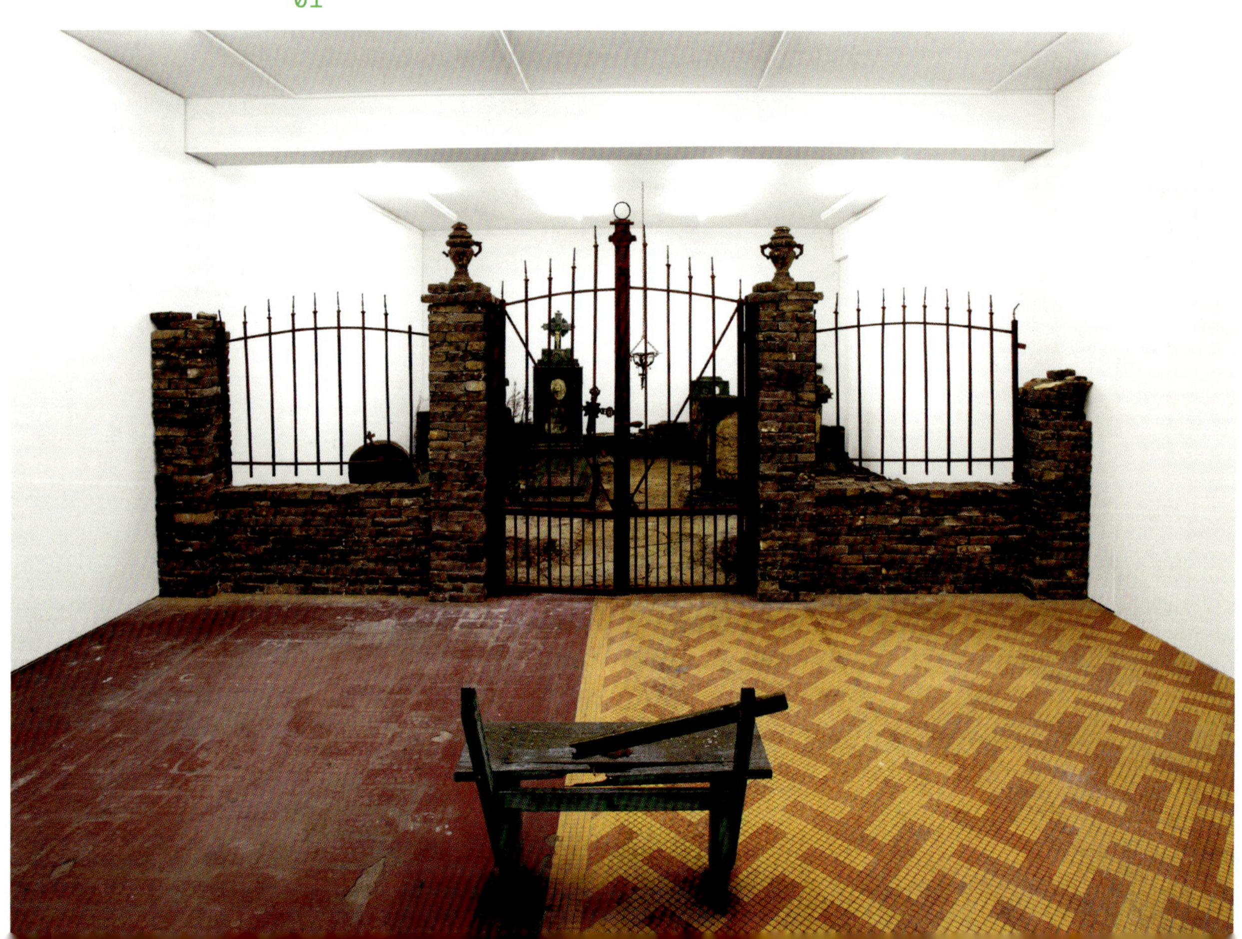

01 *D.O.M.*, 2004
Mixed media
Dimensions variable

02 *Double V*, 2005
Mixed media
Dimensions variable

03 *Die Ornamente der Anatomie / The Ornaments of Anatomy*, 2006
Mixed media
Dimensions variable

04 *Wagon*, 2006
Acrylic paint, paper, cardboard, wood
3 × 2.8 × 10 m

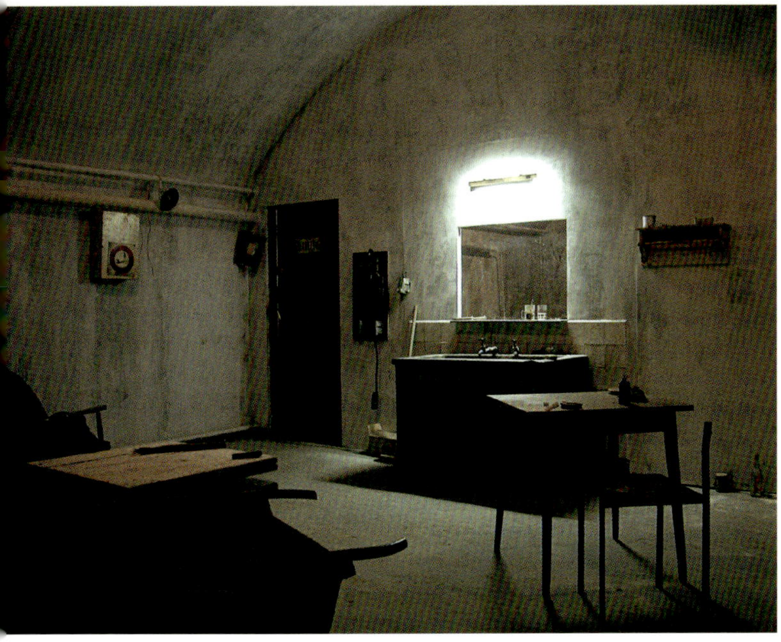

02

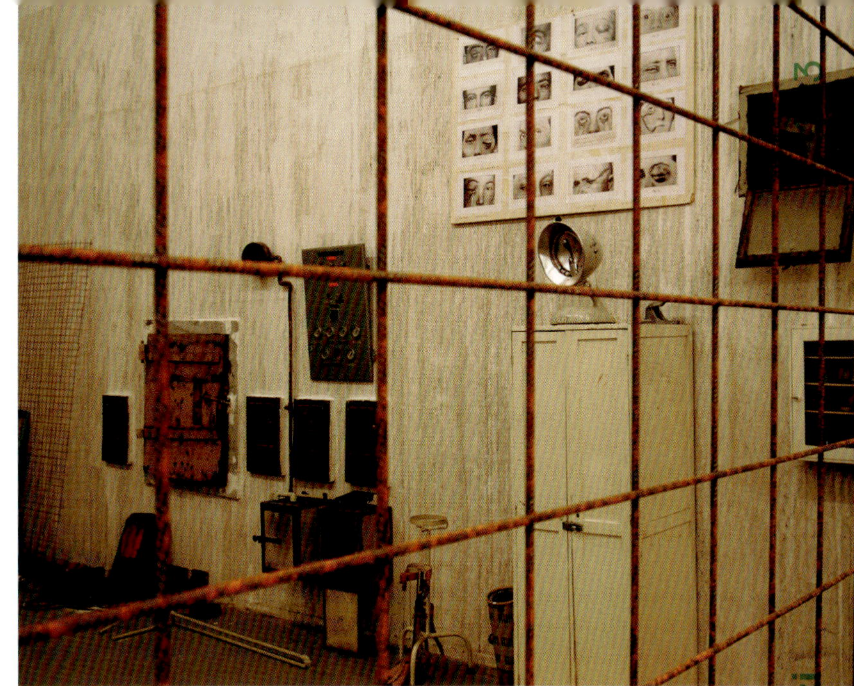

03

04

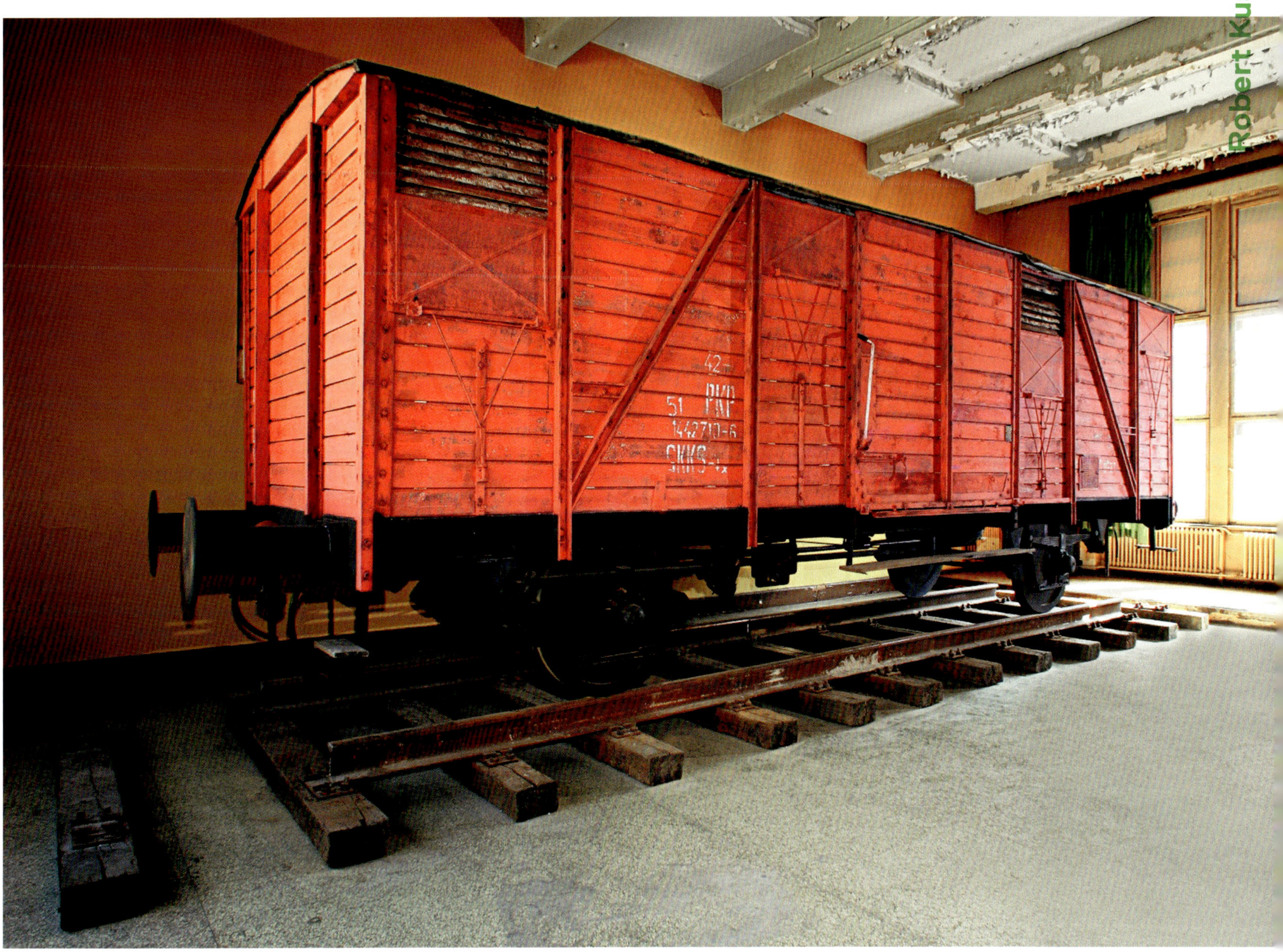

Whatever its bravura construction, consideration of the handmade and meditation on Shaker design, Lisa Lapinski's *Nightstand* (2005) monumentalizes, oneirically, the cluttered space between waking and sleeping (public life, privacy; consciousness, oblivion). Not a piece of furniture, but its opposite, expanding beyond all somnambulant recognition, it is usually displayed with its 'drawers' completely opened, a gesture not unlike a magician's, emptying his pockets and snapping his shirt cuffs for the 'nothing up my sleeves' bit. *Nightstand* posits craftsmanship as more than something not to be appropriated, questioning *techne* in the context of an art world that has almost forgotten it for 'design', with most cultural producers caring for little more than a product for production.

That Lapinski studied cabinet-making for two years at a local community college *after* receiving her MFA and putting together some of the most compelling shows anywhere surprises only if one ignores the forces accrued in her second solo outing, 'Untitled (Rimbaud Show)' (2001), inspired by Arthur Rimbaud. The hackneyed take on the rake Rimbaud leaving France and poetry for North Africa, and his plans to learn not just a trade but *all trades*, is abandonment. Actually, it was a move of transmutation and alchemy — words becoming things; thinking laboriously materialized — as well as a way for him to stop going mad in a withering absinthe atmosphere of expectation and 'promise' and a career in which he never had any interest in. Lapinski's 'Rimbaud' works on this theme (some of them mosques constructed of wallpaper and twigs), rather than being illustrative of the poet or his life, interrogated, in part, systems of belief — in what a career is, in what homage might be, in materiality and its relation to thinking, all the while literalizing *poesis*. Rimbaud had already deranged the senses; Africa allowed him to incarnate such effects and disappear into trade work. Lapinski took on his *techne* of autocivilization, learning glass-blowing, caning and cabinetry, among other skills. Yet it would be a mistake to think that this is what the work was 'about'; rather, it allowed the suture between *techne* and *poesis* to be examined.

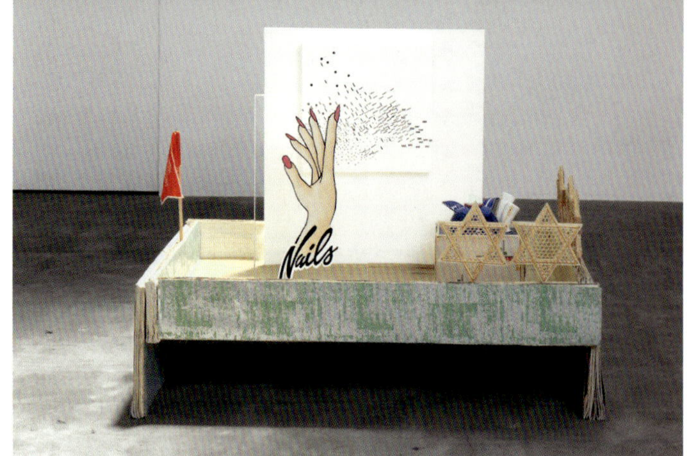

01

What makes Lapinski's project so compelling is that for all its references — whether to Ludwig Wittgenstein or to Los Angeles' own New Wave Utamaro, Patrick Nagel (and his beauty shop vixens), or to the 'faces' of Alexej von Jawlensky, or in the whimsy of restaging a photo of Frank Lloyd Wright's son, Lloyd, an ephebe seated upon the 'first' modernist chair, as a not so modernist drunk figure (*I Clown [Version A]*, (2008) — her steadfast pursuit of an irreducible quiddity remains, causing actuality to shimmer in its strangeness.

An ambassador from the community of the question, at a time when questions are out of fashion and expertise and knowledge are being reduced to forms of elitism, Lapinski discerns the available vernaculars and then overturns them: fences no longer fence; offices await their officials. Inspired by typical architectural 'makeover', in which display windows home to various Nagel-esque girls were 'hidden by' (or 'entombed in') Rudolf Steiner-ish abstractions when an actual LA building was repurposed from some adult usage to a kindergarten, Lapinski, for *Untitled* (2007), documented the abstractions *in situ* but also 'remade' the Nagels, placing them within cinderblock 'frames' in front of her home and photographing them — thereby revealing the figure of the body as originary non-representation. Lapinski draws attention to things made over, donning a different significance, but with her work she asks us to watch them until they change again into ____________ (fill in the blanks). [Bruce Hainley]

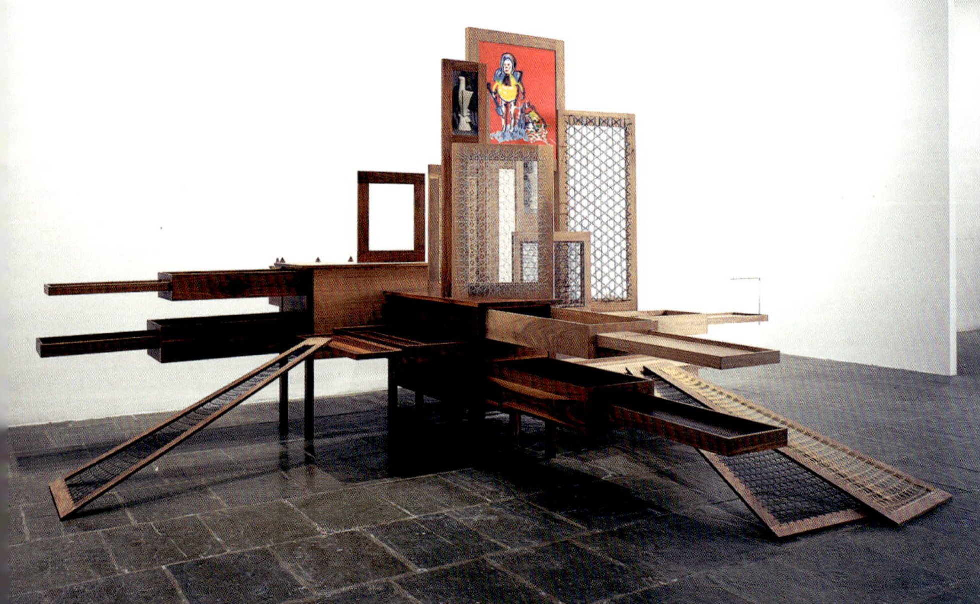

02

01 *Mimpy Mimp #2 (Aztec Register)*, 2004
Wallpaper, adhesive, paint, screen print, ceramics, fabric, wood
94 × 114 × 71 cm

02 *Nightstand*, 2005
Walnut, hardwood, polyurethane gel finish, paint, panel, canvas, photographs, cane, glass, feathers, hat form, screws and inserts, jewellery display hand, necklace
285 × 610 × 442 cm

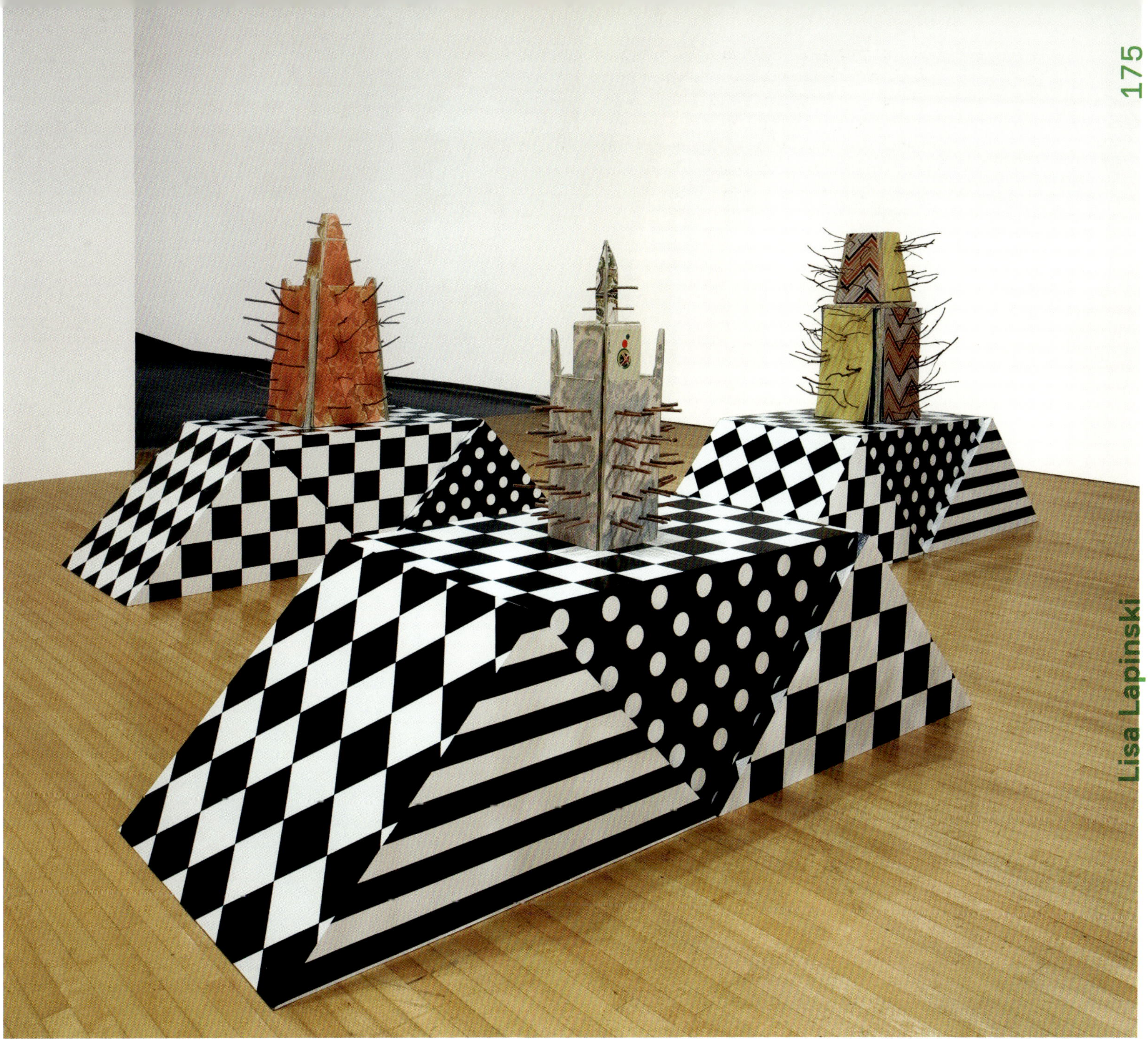

03

03 from left:
→ *Mosque of Mopti*, 2001
Wallpaper, adhesive and sticks
58 × 33 × 33 cm
→ *Mosque of Sankoré*, 2001
Wallpaper, adhesive and sticks
73 × 63 × 63 cm
→ *Mosque of Boré*, 2001
Wallpaper, adhesive and sticks
71 × 71 × 73 cm
→ *Three Stands for Mosques*, 2008
Plywood, Bondo and paint
3 stands
Each 45 × 90 × 65 cm

04 from left:
→ *Untitled*, 2007
Chromogenic print
127 × 102 cm
→ *Untitled*, 2007
3 chromogenic prints
Each 127 × 102 cm
→ *Christmas Tea = Meeting, Presented by Dialogue and Humanism, Formerly Dialectics and Humanism*, 2007
Wood, paint, paper, found Soviet ceramic vase circa 1980s, feathers, hat form
Dimensions variable

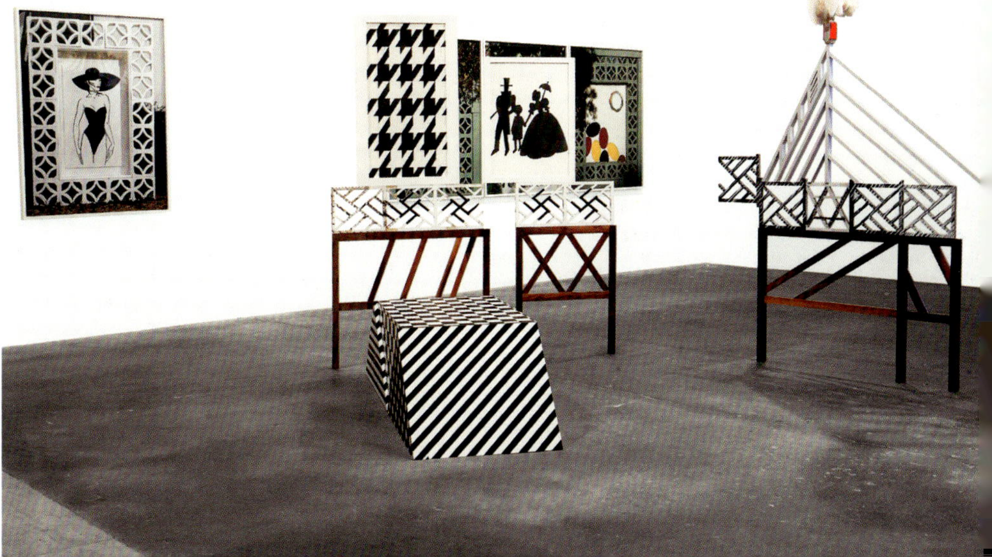

04

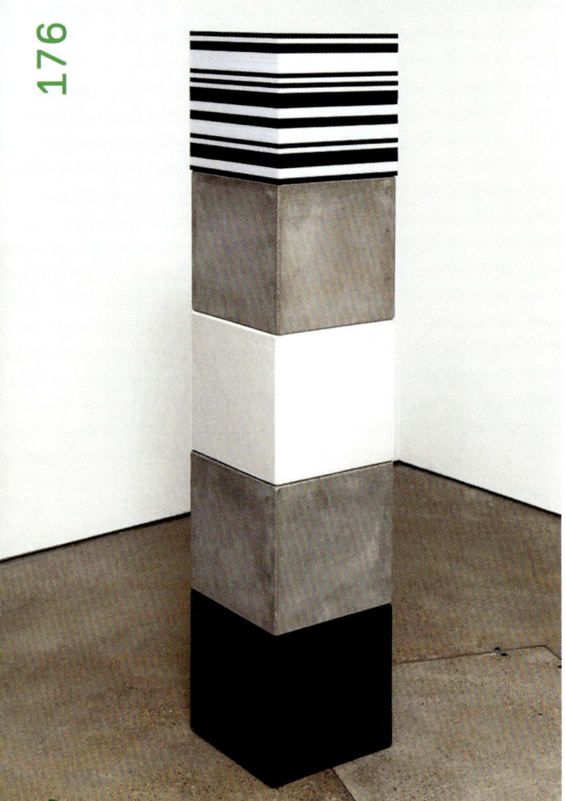

01

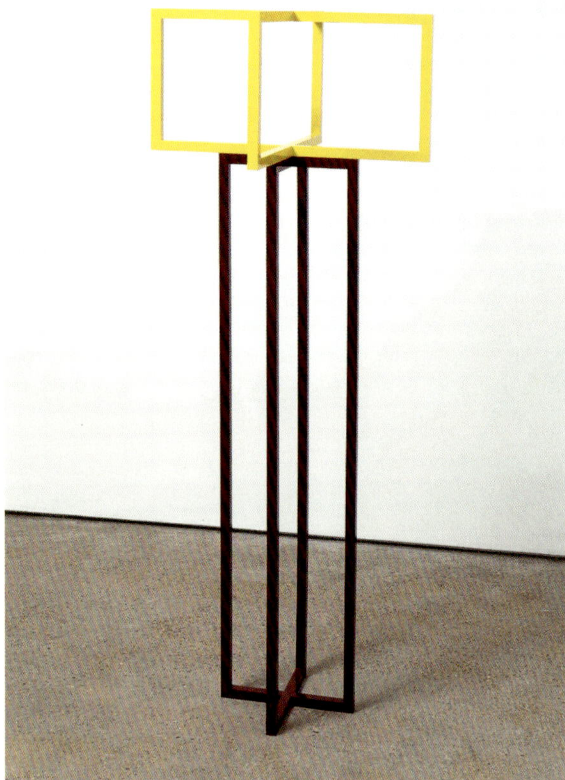

02

01 *III*, 2008
Concrete, Perspex
150 × 30 × 30 cm

02 *VIII*, 2008
Painted wood
150 × 60 × 60 cm

03 *VII*, 2008
Concrete, painted wood
151 × 30 × 57 cm

Through a distilled treatment of material, space and colour, Norwegian artist Camilla Løw activates the historical significance of sculpture, as well as its immediate spaces of encounter. Employing an elegantly direct aesthetic, distinct shapes and hues that she composes with a confident sense of beauty, Løw grants the viewer unmediated and intimate access to her work. Complimentary forms and spaces forgo illusion for transparency, with delicate and simple materials daintily balanced, stacked or hung. Despite her bold and precise forms, she creates a sense of the impermanence of their configuration — a subtle suggestion of the possibilities of movement and change.

Orchestrating visual harmony through a series of juxtapositions, Løw balances medium and shape, figuration and abstraction, as well as stereotypically masculine and feminine surfaces and colours. Modest media — painted wood, Plexiglas and poured concrete — are paired with a meticulous and polished method of construction. *VIII* (2008) poises delicate elements of brightly painted wood on top of solid concrete blocks which are left rough and unpainted. Embodying internal contradictions, this piece simultaneously contrasts with Løw's sturdier-looking monochrome or duotone constructions such as *III* (2008). She consistently renders pristine surfaces, although these are tempered with a visible craft-like method of composition. Instead of permanently fixing the elements of her sculptures together or to the wall, floor or plinth, she adopts a more casual manner, draping, suspending, stacking or leaning pieces — contrasting a moment of stillness with a kinetic potential.

The rich family of colours that Løw engages in her sculptures recalls Russian Constructivism, while the abstract forms allude to Minimalist sculpture by Donald Judd, Sol LeWitt or even Carl Andre. In addition, there are parallels with a certain contemporary pop aesthetic, such as that of Garry Webb or Jim Lambie. However, Løw seems more concerned about the resonance that this spectrum of references might have for each viewer than with explicit appropriation. Each allusion is gently filtered by her personal lexicon: Suprematist red becomes a little rosier, and Minimalist forms adopt the look of the handmade. Her latest series of works, *Straight Letters* (2008), references *pixação*, a form of sharply vertical graffiti found in São Paolo that is unique in its range of references to heavy-metal album covers and Celtic mythology. Løw does not seize on the specific political implications of her source material, only the variance of its formal aspects and the breadth of its stylistic associations.

Aware of the Greco-Roman lineage of Western sculpture and the medium's initial reflection on human form, Løw deliberately matches her sculptures to human scale. The construction of her sculptures is defined by her body, just as the experience of her work is defined by the viewer. The individual elements of each work are never too cumbersome or heavy to be carried, and are rarely fused together. Likewise, her sculptures are fully 'in the round', and respond to developing viewpoints. Stacked and often aligned within an exhibition, as in her recent shows 'Straight Letters' and 'Embraced Open Reassembled' (both 2008), Løw's incorporation of concrete blocks also implicates the position of the human form in urban space.

Through the presentation of her sharp and steady forms, Løw demands a physical engagement with her sculptures in space. This dynamic quality enables an instantly personal relationship with her work. [Lillian Davies]

03

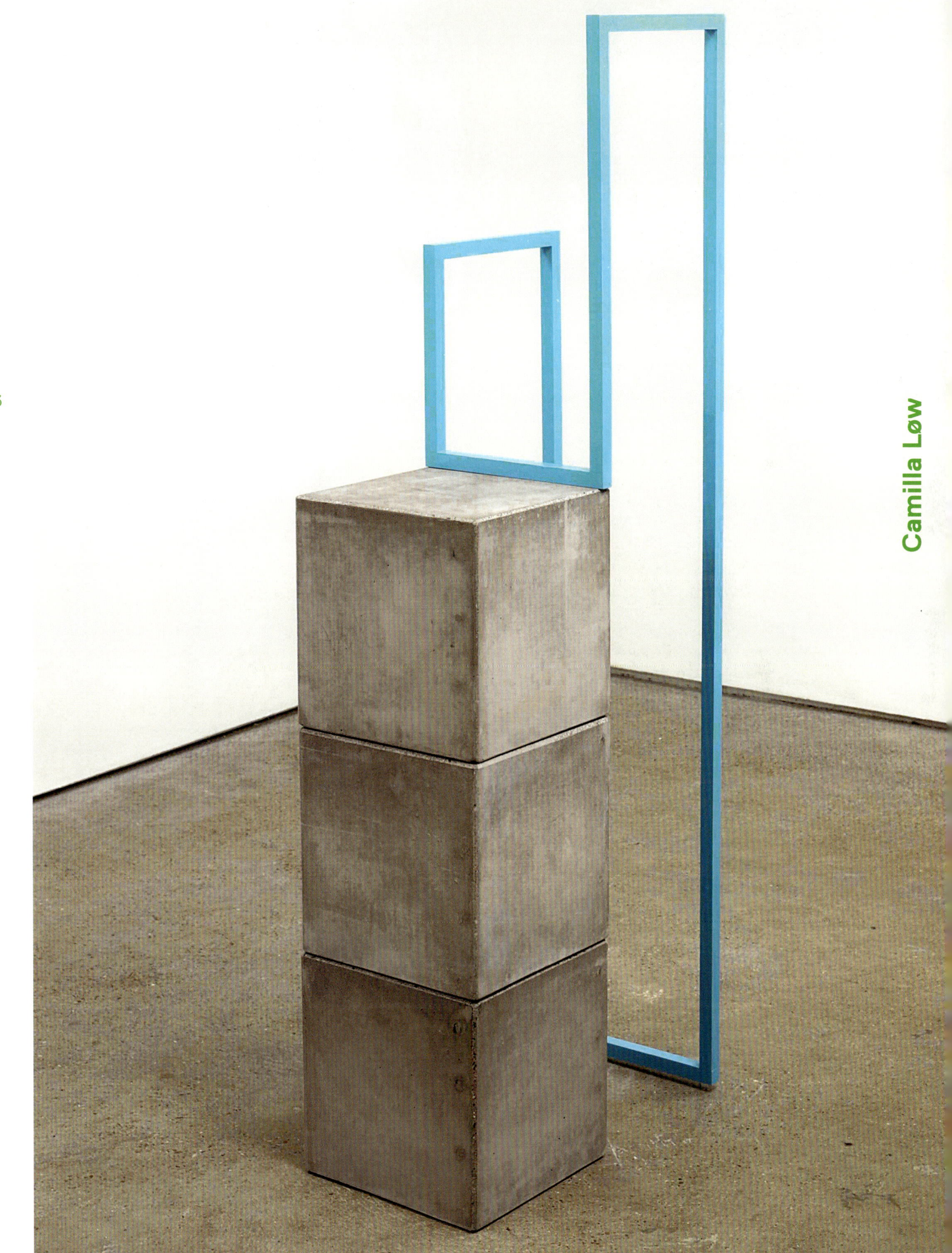

04 from left:
→ *VI*, 2008
Concrete, painted wood
151 × 30 × 30 cm
→ *IV*, 2008
Concrete, steel
150 × 30 × 30 cm
→ *III*, 2008
Concrete, Perspex
150 × 30 × 30 cm
→ *Numbers*, 2008
Perspex, string
60 × 60 × 2 cm
→ *VIII*, 2008
Painted wood
150 × 60 × 60 cm
→ *I*, 2008
Perspex
220 × 30 × 30 cm
→ *II*, 2008
Concrete, painted wood
150 × 30 × 30 cm
→ *V*, 2008
Concrete, painted wood
153 × 40 × 40 cm

05 from left:
→ *Ramona*, 2008
Perspex and metal
520 × 80 × 80 cm
→ *Arcade*, 2008
Wood, paint and concrete
150 × 53 × 46 cm
→ *High Rise*, 2008
Wood, paint and concrete
240 × 30 × 30 cm
→ *Digital*, 2008
Wood, paint and cord
270 × 90 × 90 cm
→ *4+4*, 2005
Wood and paint
139 × 9 × 9 cm
→ *Concrete*, 2008
Wood, paint and concrete
180 × 30 × 30 cm

04

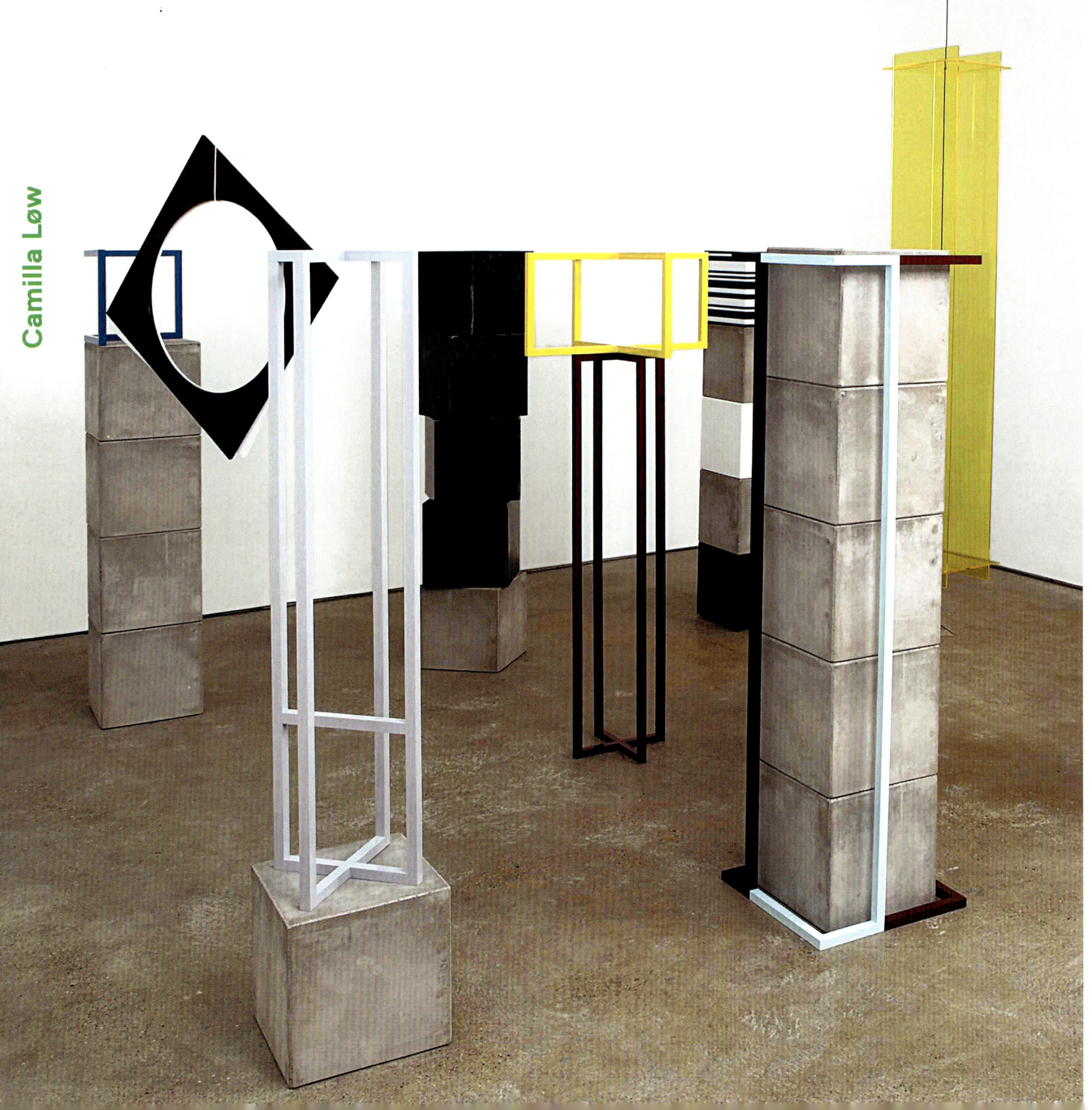

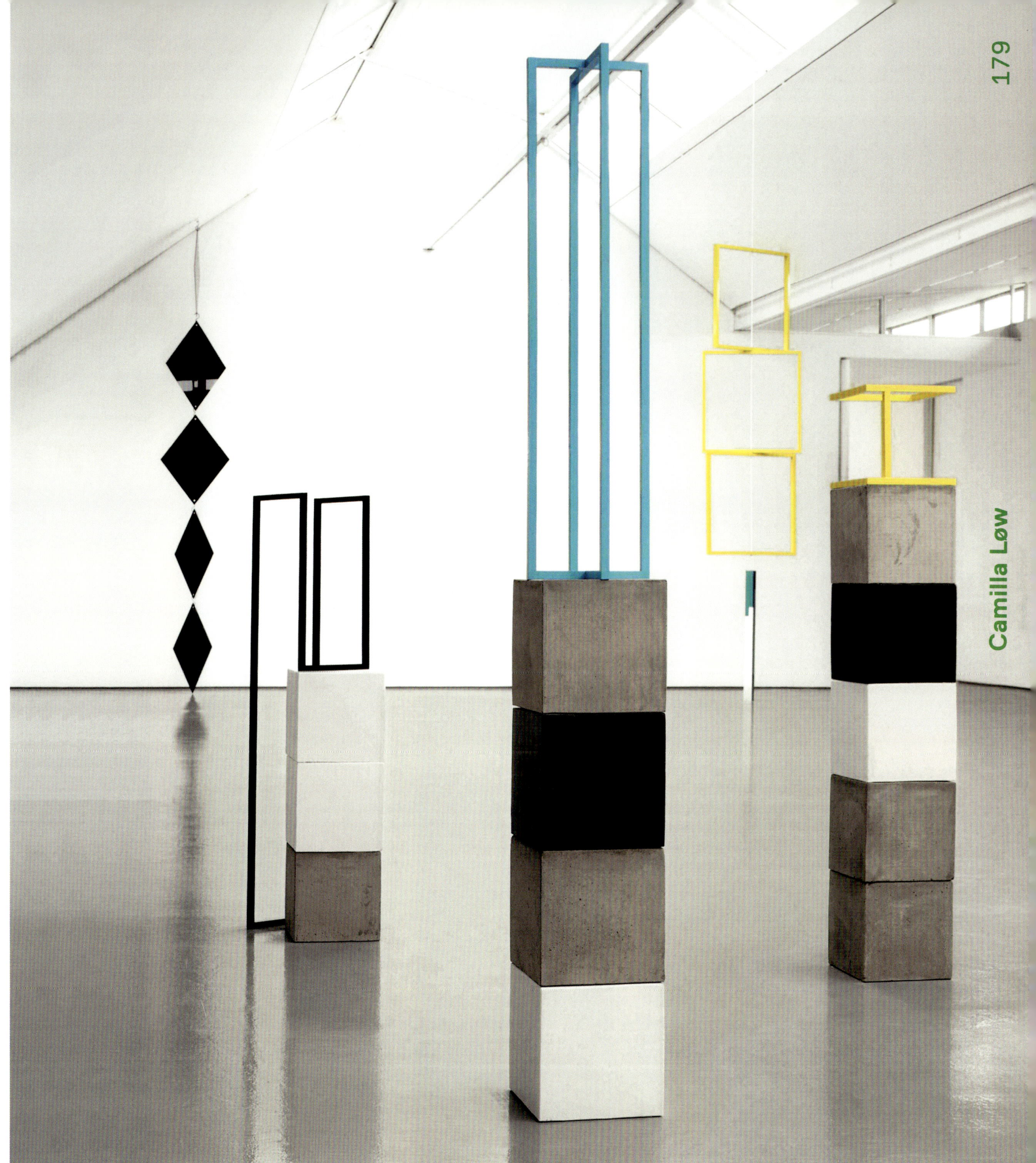

05

01 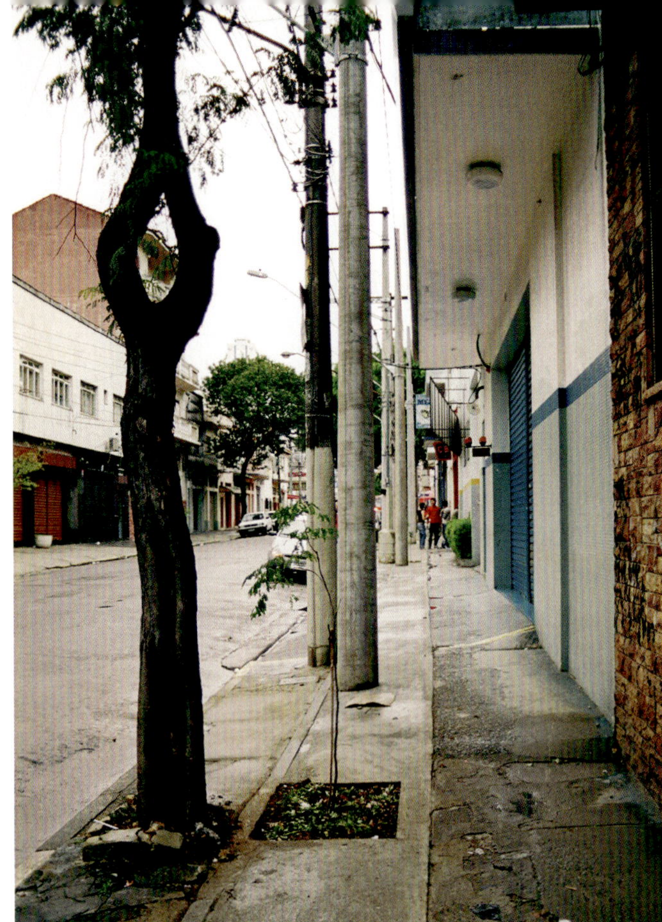

01 *Matemática Rápida (Quick Mathematics)*, 2006
Duplicated concrete sidewalk, including lamp-posts, tree planters, kerbstones
Length approx. 150 m
Brigadeiro Galvão Rua, Barra Funda, São Paulo

02 *Mau Gênio (Evil Genius)*, 2002
Scaffolding, plywood
Dimensions variable

03 *Cruzamento (Crossing)*, 2003
Plywood, 20 × 19 m
Intersection of Dois de Dezembro and Praia do Flamengo, Rio de Janeiro

One could contextualize the work of Renata Lucas in a São Paulo tradition of geometric abstraction and 1950s Concretism. Yet what gives her work distinction is the play she establishes between geometric abstraction on the one hand and architecture and urban planning on the other, through site-specific installations in galleries, institutions and the city streets.

Barravento (2001) consisted of a series of plywood panels, articulated by metal hinges, which covered up a small artist-run space in São Paulo. Architecture became interactive, and the reference to Lygia Clark's *Bichos*, a 1960 series of abstract geometric sculptures made with hinged aluminium sheets, was evident. The viewer's interaction through architecture reappears in Lucas's *Falha* (Failure, 2007), but this time the viewer is invited to play with plywood panels that cover the floor like a changing geometric game board.

Plywood panels also featured in *Cruzamento* (Crossing, 2003–04), a work that could never be conceived in countries with strict public safety regulations that hinder more experimental public interventions. Lucas used the panels to cover the intersection of two busy streets in Rio de Janeiro (2003) and São Paulo (2004). Here, abstract geometry can be seen in the clear reference to the element of the cross (in Rio) and of the square (in São Paulo), superimposed on to the dirty streets.

Mau Gênio (Evil Genius, 2002) was an installation at Museu de Arte da Pampulha, a former casino designed by Oscar Niemeyer in Belo Horizonte. Lucas filled the entire mezzanine level of the museum with scaffolding, bringing the raw element of building construction into the precious interiors. As one walked up the ramp leading to the mezzanine level, one could see the dizzying effect of the scaffolding's horizontal and vertical lines, drawn against those of the glazed windows behind them. One could climb up the scaffolding and from there discover new views of the museum's interior and exterior, including the Pampulha lake against which Niemeyer carefully set the building.

The artist's duplication and mirroring are strategies through which the geometric shows its mathematic features. In *Atlas* (2006) Lucas played with borders and territories, the public and the private, taking Galeria Millan Antonio in São Paulo as a central point of reference and dividing it into two parts. The section on the left was given to the next-door neighbour, a private resident who thus expanded her house temporarily to appropriate the gallery space, and whose fence was extended mimetically to include the new territory. The section on the right of the gallery was given to an auto-body shop located across from it, which then used the gallery space to park cars during the exhibition; again mimetically, Lucas appropriated the shop's facade colours to create a geometric composition. All that was left of the gallery was a narrow hallway separating the two sides.

In *Matemática rápida* (Quick Mathematics, 2006), made for the São Paulo Biennial in 2006, Lucas duplicated a series of elements found in a stretch of 150 metres of Rua Brigadeiro Galvão, where the artist lived at the time. A doubling of pavements, flower beds, trees and lampposts give the effect of 'one sidewalk walking over another', in the artist's words. The effect on the viewer is again one of dizziness, as if intoxicated by Lucas's poetic mathematics. [Adriano Pedrosa]

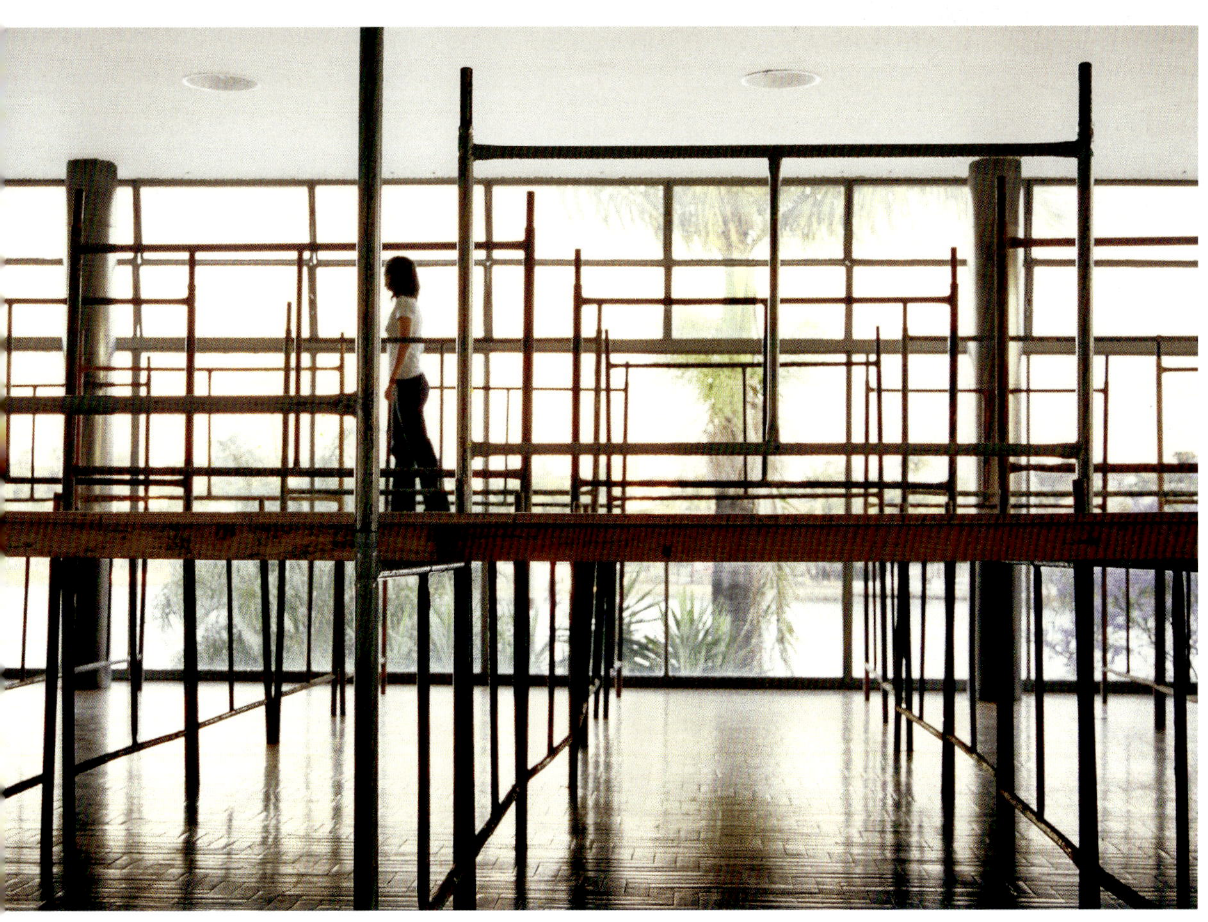

02

03

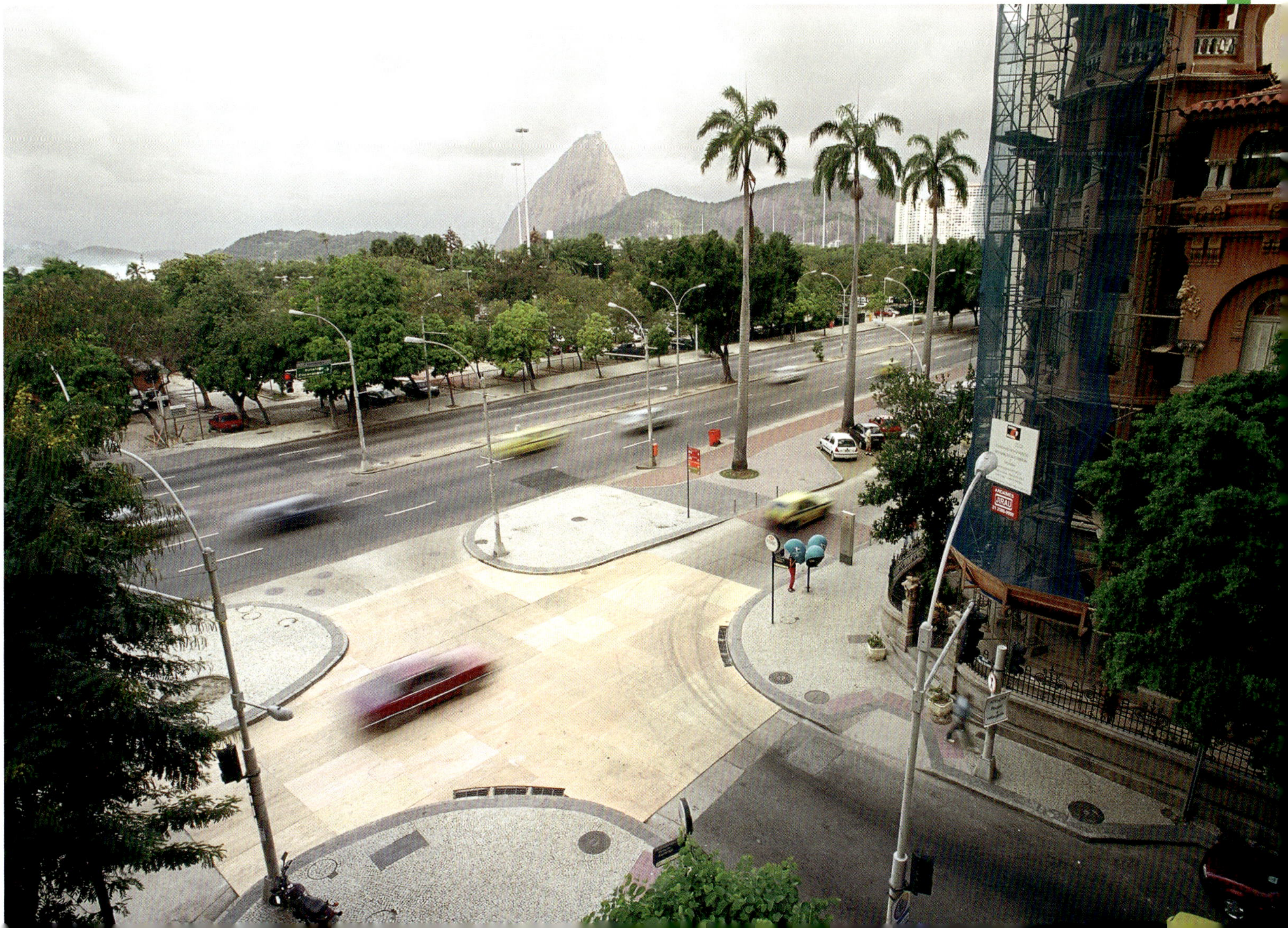

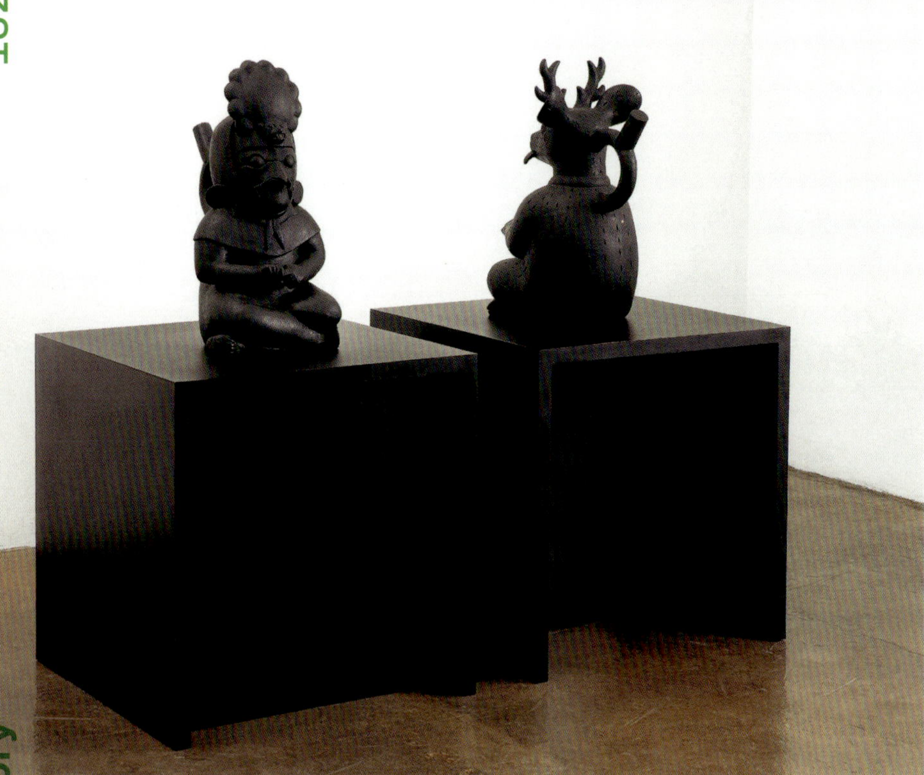

01

Although the targets of Nathan Mabry's iconoclasm may frequently change, his youthful irreverence towards sculpture, both past and present, has remained consistent since the relatively recent beginning of his artistic career. Mabry first garnered critical attention as one of the stand-out artists in the 2005 survey exhibition 'Thing: New Sculpture from Los Angeles' for his witty, bawdy sculptures, which freely turn totems, monuments and ritualistic objects into flagrant visual puns or unabashed mockeries.

Mabry comes from a lineage of LA-based artists who create satire on a monumental scale, such as Paul McCarthy (his professor at UCLA) and Jason Rhoades (whom he assisted). Taking his cue from their brand of unhindered postmodern sampling, Mabry quotes the spectrum of American sculpture in all its various incarnations, without preference or hierarchy, from ancient South American cultures to Native American objects to the now-canonized heroes of Minimalism.

Mabry's solo show in 2008 looked like something in a high-end gallery dealing in ethnographic antiques. Four classical graphite sketches of a standing nude woman hung on the wall, while the floor was occupied by bronze pedestals, which could have doubled as expensive coffee tables, adorned with vaguely 'antique'-looking figurines. The installation resembled a showcase at a Pottery Barn outlet until one noticed the grossly exaggerated breasts on the nude sketches and the raunchy gestures of Mabry's cross-legged figures.

The artist's previous series of sculptures in this vein, *A Very Touching Moment* (2004–07), also imitated small, squatting or sitting god-like pre-Columbian figures — imagery that Mabry borrowed from a book called *Sex and Sexual Magic in Ancient Peru* and updated for our times. He has placed his figures atop skilful bronze imitations of minimalist sculptures, thus downgrading them to mere pedestals. In doing so, he mocks several traditions at once: the sacred or ritualistic origins of the ancient artefacts, as well as the reverence with which we now look upon the tradition of Minimalism.

Mabry's works are not a lament about the commercial availability of objects and icons in today's marketplace. He is known for buying many of his materials on eBay, including a two metre tall replica of Rodin's *Thinker*, which he outfitted with a ghoulish mask that could be a sci-fi movie prop, titling it *Process Art (Dead Men Don't Make Sculpture)* (2008). By adding his own low-budget touch to an already fake cast of a neo-classical sculpture, Mabry gleefully contributes to the dilution of the idea of originality or 'inspiration'. By then casting it all in bronze, an artistic act symbolic of stasis and the memorialization of cultural symbols, he pinpoints the moment at which cultural objects lose their original meaning.

Mabry's series of ancient Aztec masks outfitted with 'grills' made of Swarovski crystals that spell out slang terms like 'O.M.F.G.' incorporate sources closer to home. Works such as *Mosaic Skull (OMFG)* (2008) quote Los Angeles hip-hop bling and teenage valley-girl slang — styles already known for their similarly sly and witty use of appropriation. He has also 'defaced' classical sculptures by fitting them with cheap, plastic Halloween animal masks. In his hands, the icons to which we turn for a dose of gravity or 'high art' become clowning faces and grinning gangsters laughing back at us. [Christy Lange]

02

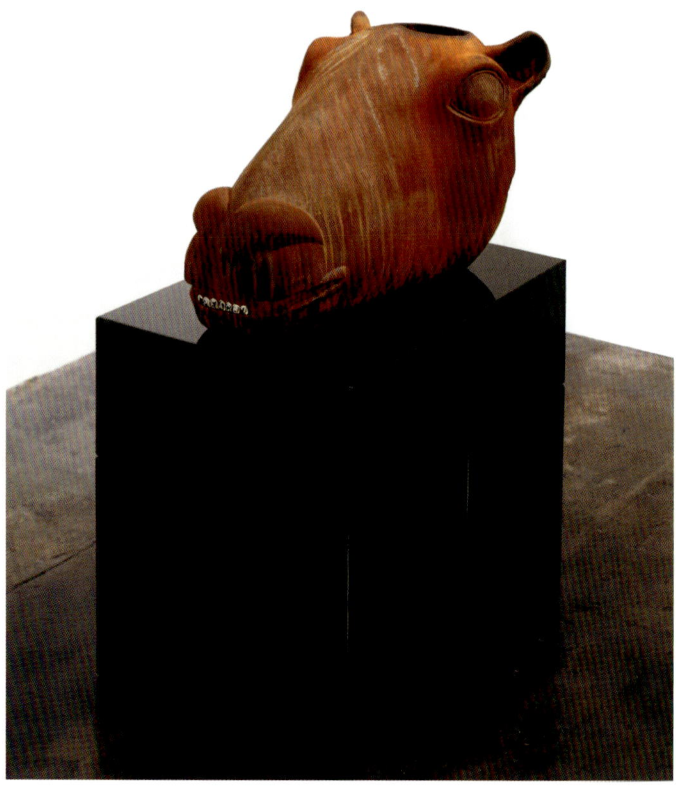

03

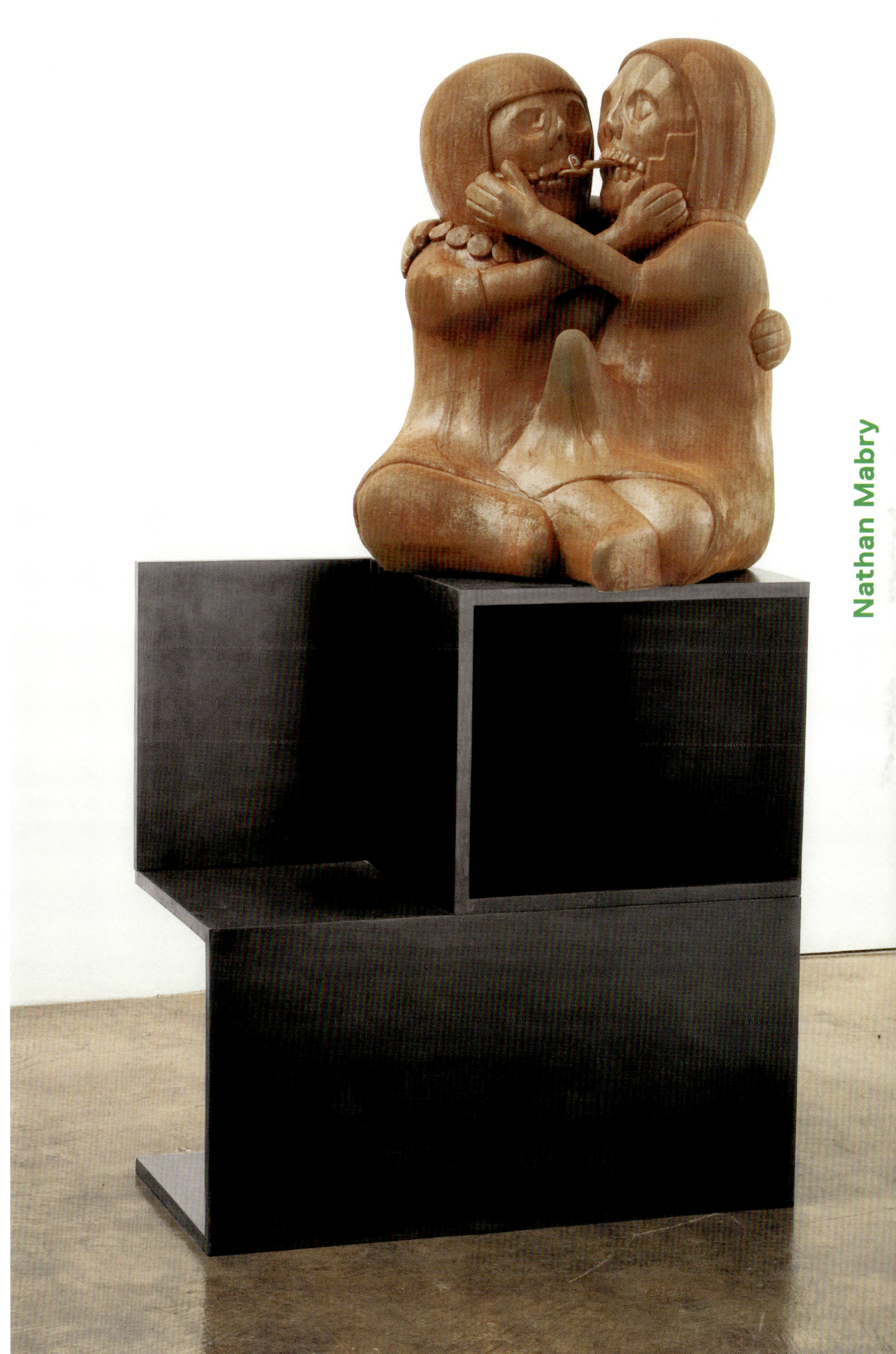

01 *It Is What It Is (The Old In and Out)*, 2008
Bronze
94 × 117 × 51 cm

02 *Conversation Piece (Jackin', Stackin' and Crackin')*, 2005
Terracotta, patina, wood, urethane enamel, white gold, synthetic diamonds
112 × 84 × 56 cm

03 *A Very Touching Moment (Pitching a Tent)*, 2006
Steel, silver, coral, turquoise
122 × 76 × 38 cm

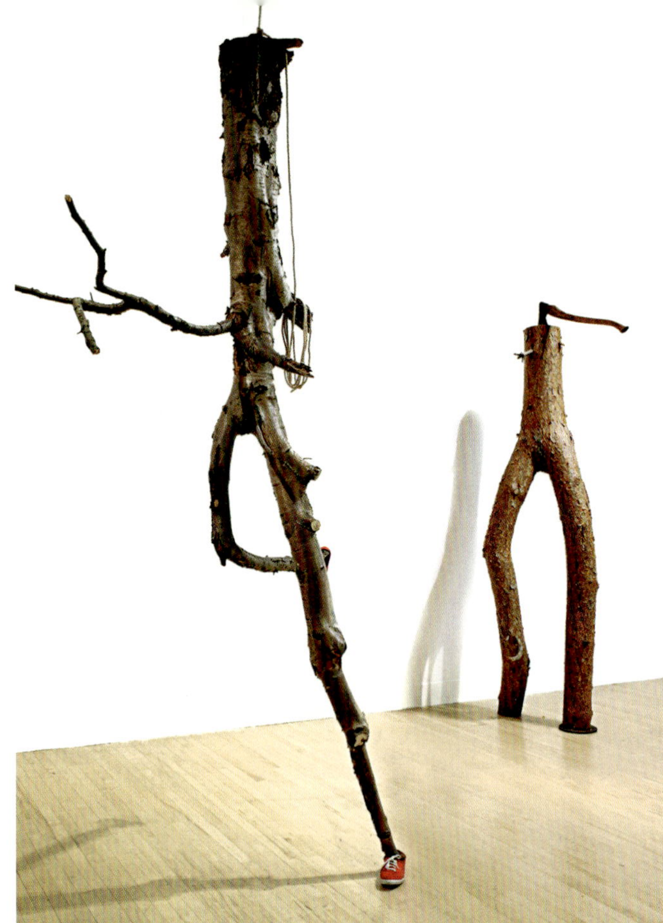

01

01 from left:
→ *Boy*, 2007
Wood, plimsolls
332 × 186 × 170 cm
→ *Girl*, 2007
Axe, facsimile of letter to Eileen Agar from Paul Nash
315 × 145 × 63 cm

02 *Sleep of Ulro*, 2006
Exterior view of *Element 4: Heaven*
Dimensions variable

03 *Sleep of Ulro*, 2006
Interior view of *Element 4: Heaven* (including David Thorpe, *The Kiff Plant*, 2005; Tony Matelli, *Weed*, 2006; botanical anatomical models by R. Brendel & Co. and various objects from the collection of The Manchester Museum, University of Manchester)
Dimensions variable

04 from left:
→ *Haus der Frau 1*, 2008
Glass, steel
340 × 480 × 100 cm
→ *Haus der Frau 2*, 2008
Glass, steel
120 × 700 × 100 cm
→ *Deutsches Volk — Deutsches Arbeit*, 2008
Glass, wood, steel
170 × 450 × 300 cm

Overleaf:

05 *Sleep of Ulro*, 2006
Mixed media
Dimensions variable

Alfred Barr's famous diagram used on the cover of his 1936 book *Cubism and Abstract Art* depicts the development of modernism and modern art in the form of a complex flowchart. Lines and curves trace connections and influences, and red text is used to introduce those external to the Western canon. A family tree of the historical references, artists, movements and methodologies that have featured in Goshka Macuga's wilfully promiscuous work would chart a similarly convoluted passage, though one guided by no rationale other than a personal logic and curiosity. Shifting between the roles of artist, collector, curator and archivist, Macuga uses art — her own and works by others — and artists' personal histories as material for the construction of an elaborate web of subjective re-readings and alternative historical narratives. These alternate histories are told through objects and intricately choreographed displays that resist traditional classifications and hierarchies of value.

The exhibition is a medium for Macuga, a mutable space in which stories are narrated and disparate histories can collide. Inherently site-specific, her displays typically begin with an elaborate research process that examines the fabric of the site itself — its physical confines and its archives, from which Macuga mines her subjects. In her 'Objects in Relation' exhibition at Tate Britain, her research in the Tate archives led her to the work of British landscape artist Paul Nash and the group, Unit One, which he founded in 1933. Selecting and displaying works by Nash, Henry Moore, Eileen Agar and Barbara Hepworth alongside natural elements such as rocks and tree branches, Macuga created a playful display in which historical fact mingled with personal anecdote and art with non-art objects that worked metaphorically to animate the lives of this group.

Her project in Mies van der Rohe's Neue Nationalgalerie for the 2008 Berlin Biennial centred around Lilly Reich, Mies' long-term partner and collaborator and a pioneer of exhibition design. *Deutsches Volk — Deutsches Arbeit*, *Haus der Frau I* and *Haus der Frau II* (all 2008) are replicas of Reich's design structures that support textiles commissioned from contemporary artists by Macuga. Like her *Picture Room* (2003), in which Macuga re-created Sir John Soane's ingenious folding display structure in order to show works borrowed from her contemporaries, Macuga's Reich project uses a historical framework within which to stage dialogue and to examine the dynamics at play in artistic collaboration.

Macuga's interests in the conventions of museological display often manifest themselves in large-scale architectural environments. For the 2006 São Paulo Biennial she created *Mula sem Cabeça* (Headless Mule, 2006), an elaborate construction formally inspired by the Oscar Niemeyer pavilion in which it was installed. It housed an array of items purchased in São Paulo that made reference to local folklore, art and design, religion and Brazil's colonial past. A museum in a museum, *Mula sem Cabeça* revelled in the unlikely marriage of Brazil's modernism with its spiritual values. *Sleep of Ulro* (2006) Macuga's most ambitious project to date, was an expansive *gesamtkunstwerk* in which works by artists such as Richard Hughes and Melvin Moti along with artefacts and scientific specimens borrowed from local museums were displayed in a vast architectural stage-set inspired by Robert Wiene's film *The Cabinet of Dr Caligari*.
A joyfully subjective cabinet of curiosities, *Sleep of Ulro* indexed Macuga's artistic processes and methodologies in a space in which historical narratives were rewritten at every turn. [Andrew Bonacina]

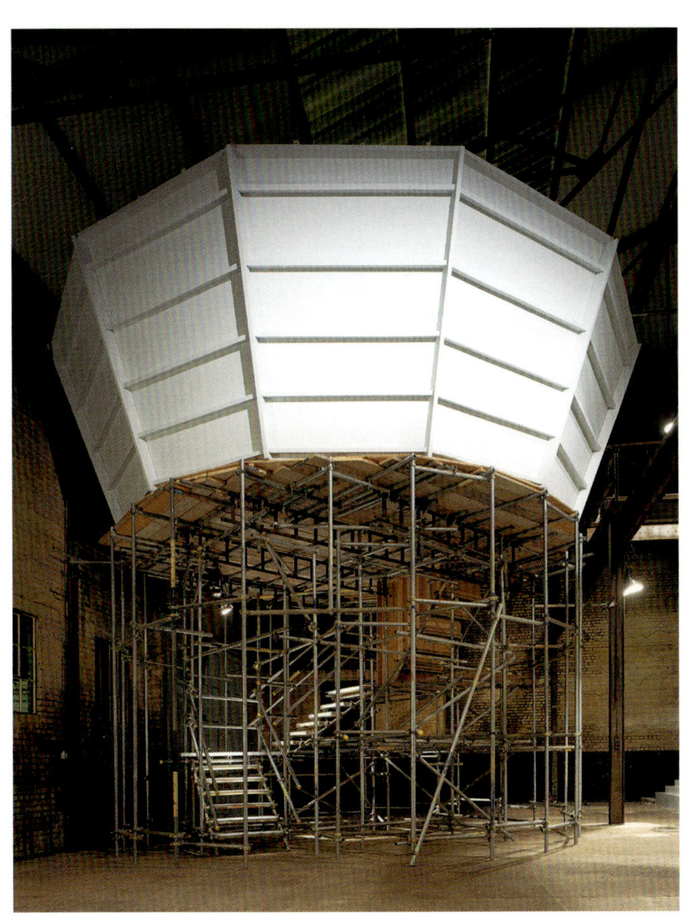
02

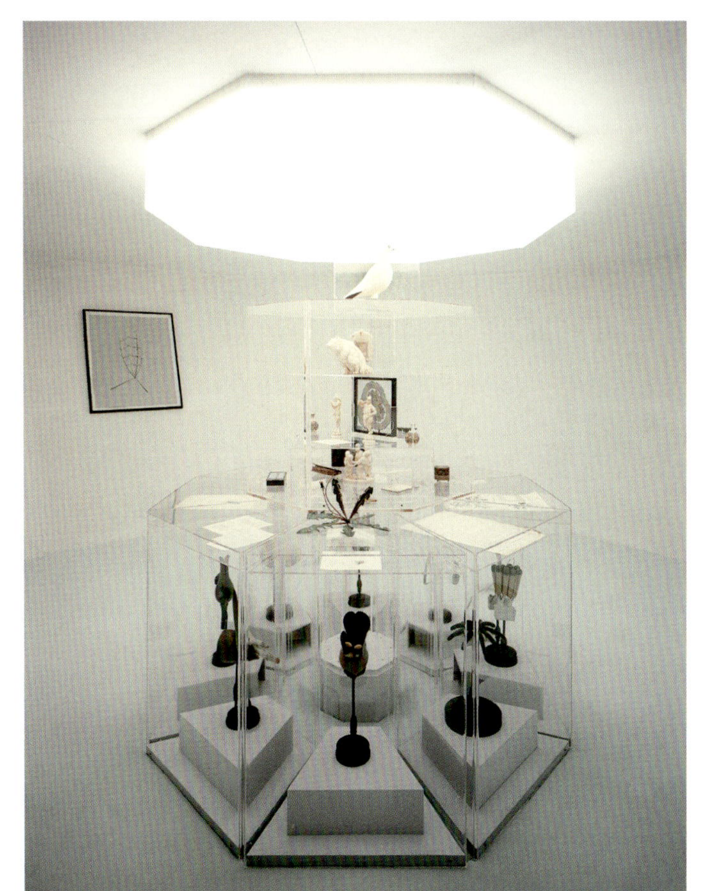
03

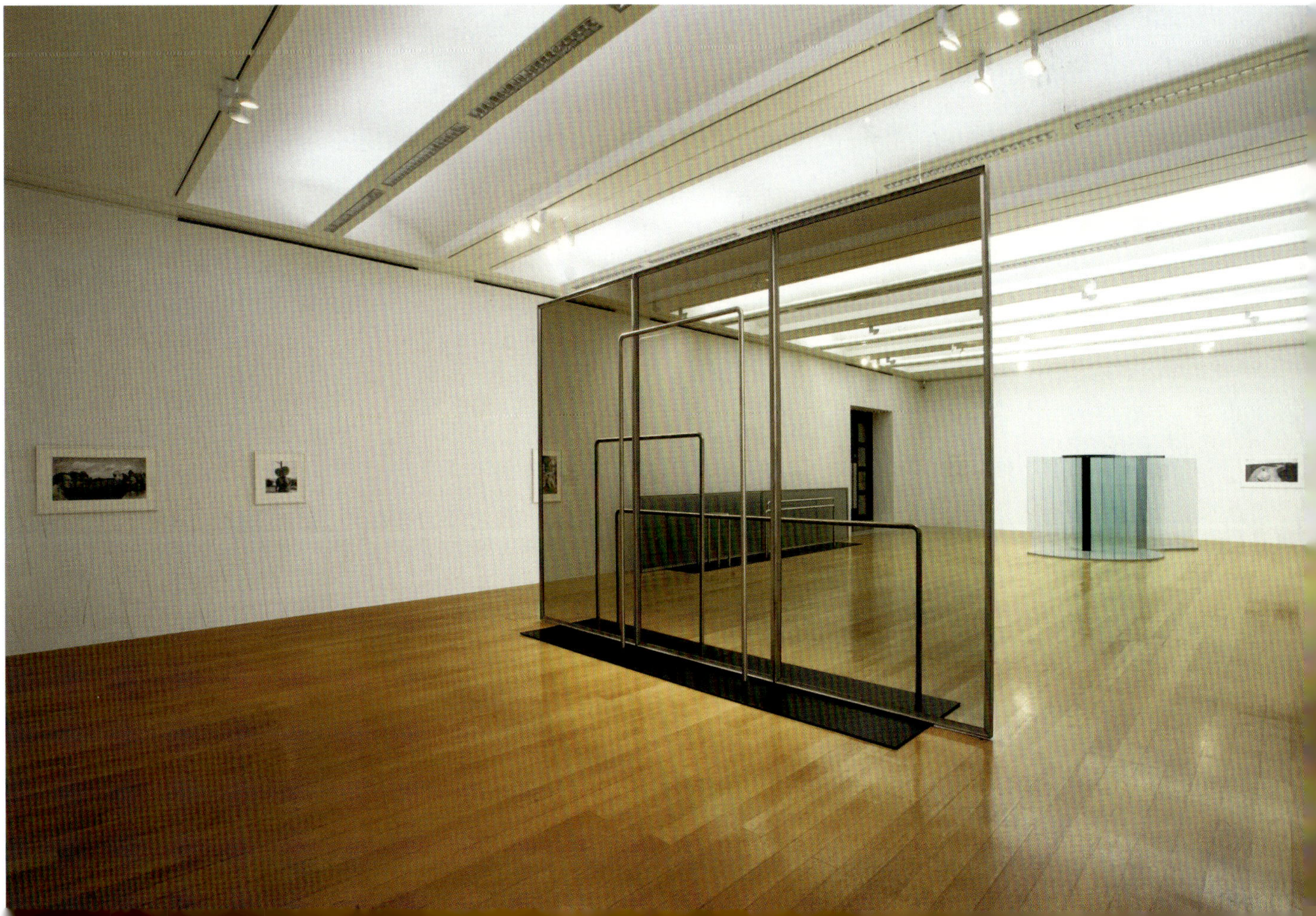

04

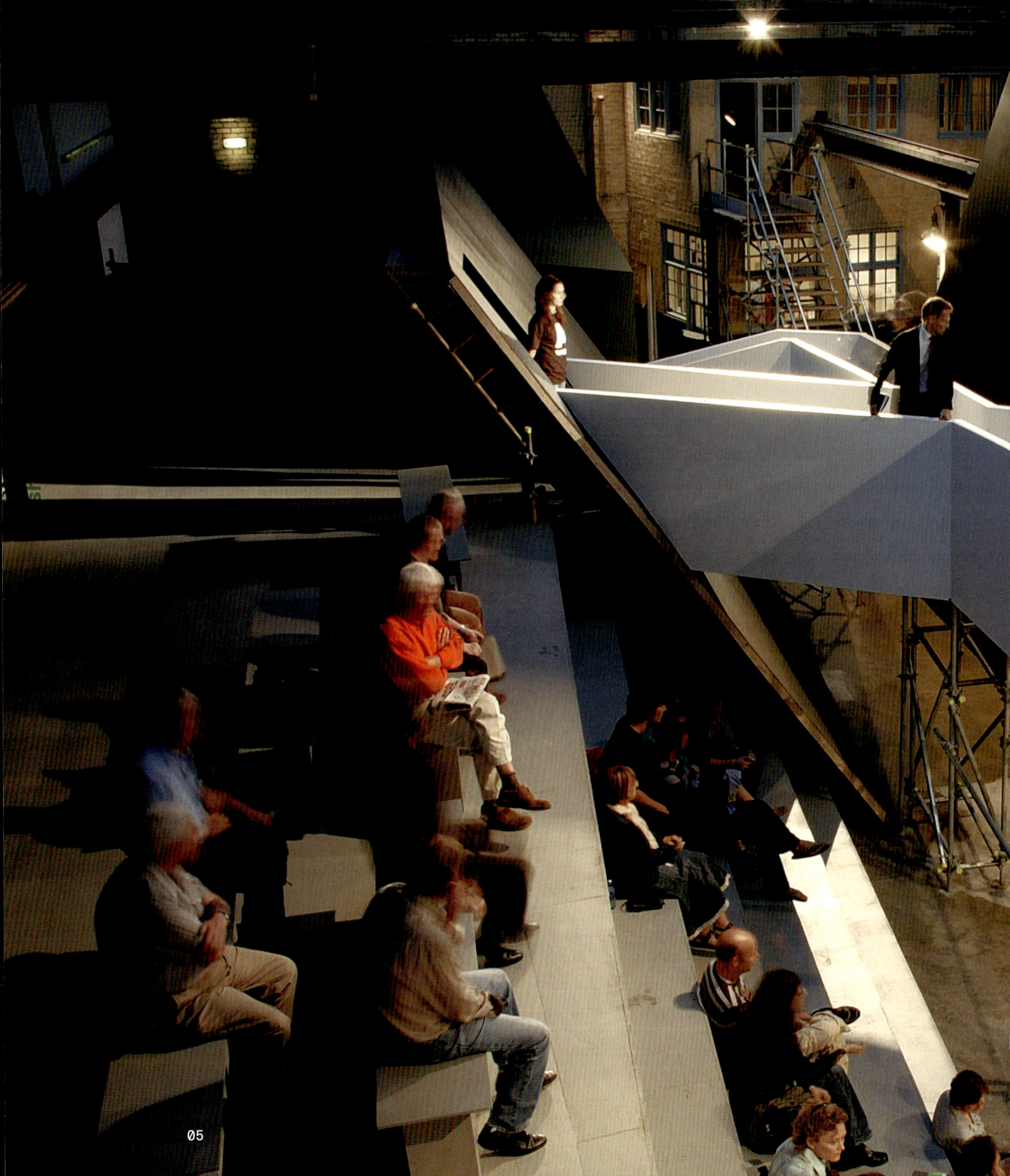
05

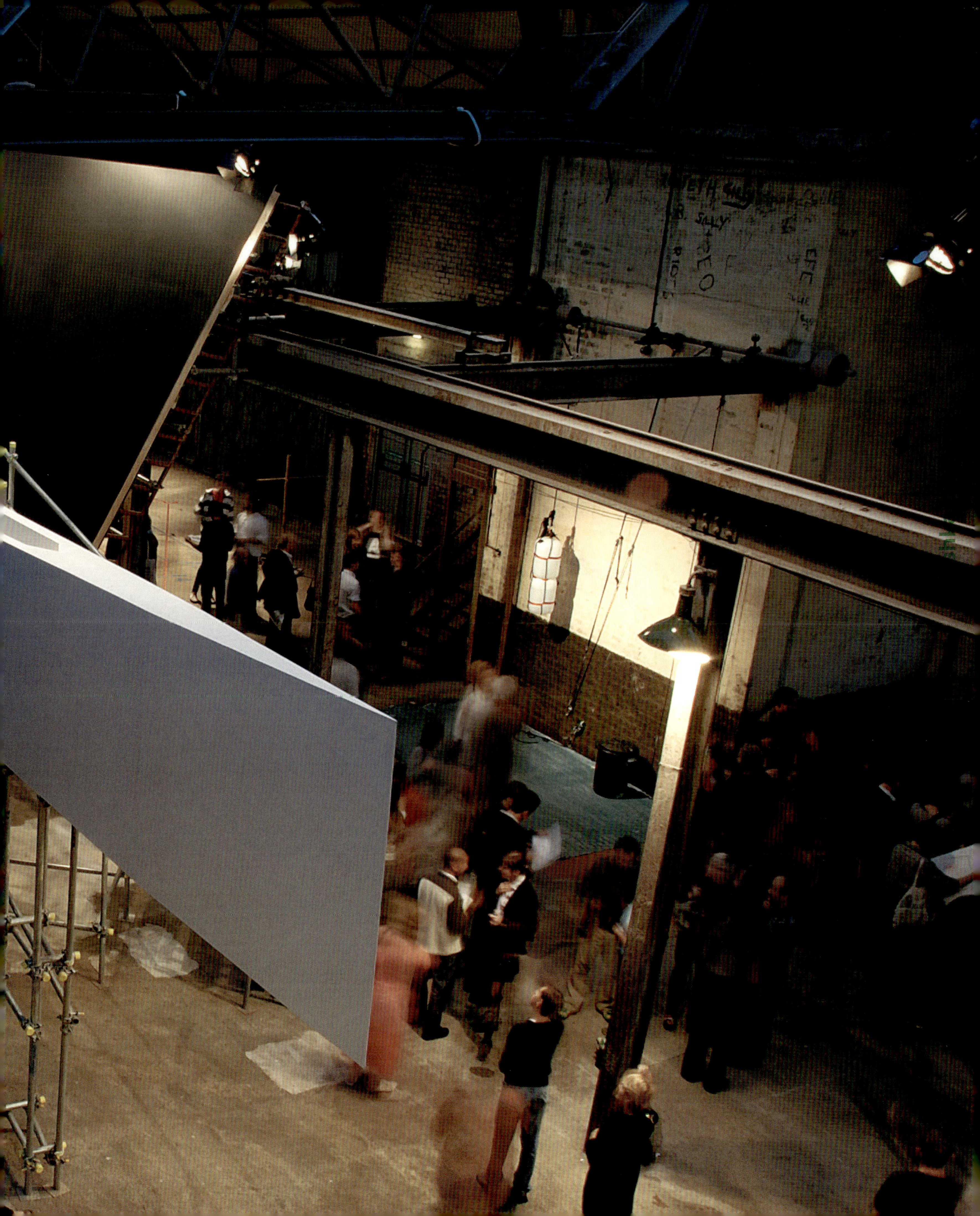

A sugar cube delicately balances between a cup and a human femur; the purpose of this feat is utterly unknowable, and yet the small knobble of bone that has apparently developed on the femur to achieve it evokes a grand narrative of purposeful biological and cultural evolution. This collaboration between the natural, hidden mechanics of our frame and one of our basic tools to perform a simple, pointless task has a formal clarity that verges on classicism and reads like a sentence written in a language just beyond our comprehension.

Mark Manders' *A Place Where My Thoughts Are Frozen Together* (2001) is symptomatic of his approach to associative thought processes and a genial co-authorship between artist and audience. He co-opts objects from the worlds of functionality and aestheticised design, combining them with votive imagery of his own concoction and laying them out in what he describes as a 'conjuring space'. Here, form and meaning coalesce and intermingle under his direction, to be expanded on and accessorised by the audience's impulse to create a narrative from fragmentary cues.

Throughout Manders' work the human figure, or a schematized version of it, recurs as a tool for generating empathy, hooking us into a nuanced psychological atmosphere where disruption and isolation are finely tuned with cadences of melancholy, vertigo or absurdist compulsion. The blank features of *Unfired Clay Figure* (2005–06), for instance, divert the interpretation from singular narratives of violence, instead suggesting classical metaphors of division, metamorphosis and self-replication. The objects schematically laid out on the floor relate back to what Manders considers his principle piece: *Inhabited for a Survey (First Floor Plan from Self-Portrait as a Building)* (1986), a drawing made up of writing and craft utensils arranged to describe the floor plan of a fictional building, which the artist refers to as a self-portrait. If we interrogate this shift of languages, from the tools of communication used in an unconventional way to empirically describe a non-existent space that is, in fact, an oblique metaphorical evocation, we can begin to grasp Manders' aspirations for his 'conjuring space'. His installations are an arena in which to summon significance through the interconnective languages of form, substance and personal and collective memory.

The discernible formal development between *Inhabited for a Survey ...* and *Finished Sentence* (1998–06) demonstrates how Manders reveals with one hand and obfuscates with the other. *Finished Sentence* is clearly an advanced version of the earlier piece, where the processes of embellishment, parody, specification and abstraction are laid bare. Yet the initial impulse behind these processes is never brought to light. Manders' language based on objects lacks the unifying specificity of one wrought from words, so that we can only evaluate how its semiotic values reaffirm, interrupt and obliterate our own. [Sally O'Reilly]

01

01 *A Place Where My Thoughts Are Frozen Together*, 2001
Painted porcelain, painted epoxy, sugar cube
Approx. 32 × 10 × 6 cm

02 *Inhabited for a Survey (First Floor Plan from Self-Portrait as a Building)*, 1986
Writing materials, erasers, painting tools, scissors
8 × 267 × 90 cm

03 *Unfired Clay Figure*, 2005–06
Iron chairs, painted epoxy, wood and various materials
225 × 150 × 300 cm

04 *Finished Sentence*, 1998–2006
Iron, ceramic, tea bags, offset print on paper
85 × 336 × 185 cm

05 *Fox/Mouse/Belt*, 1992
Painted bronze, belt
15 × 120 × 40 cm

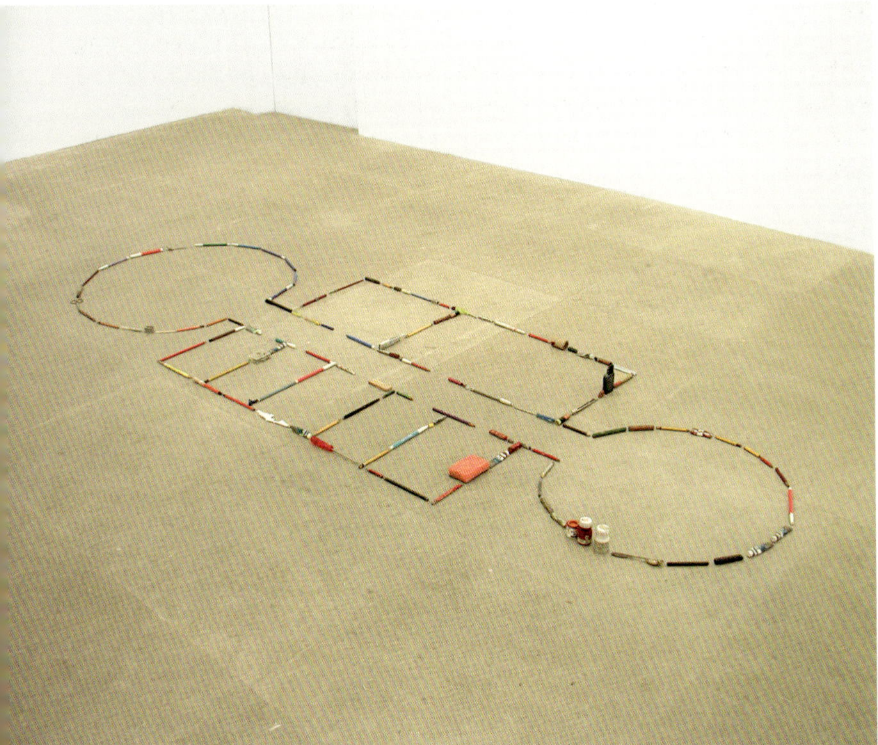

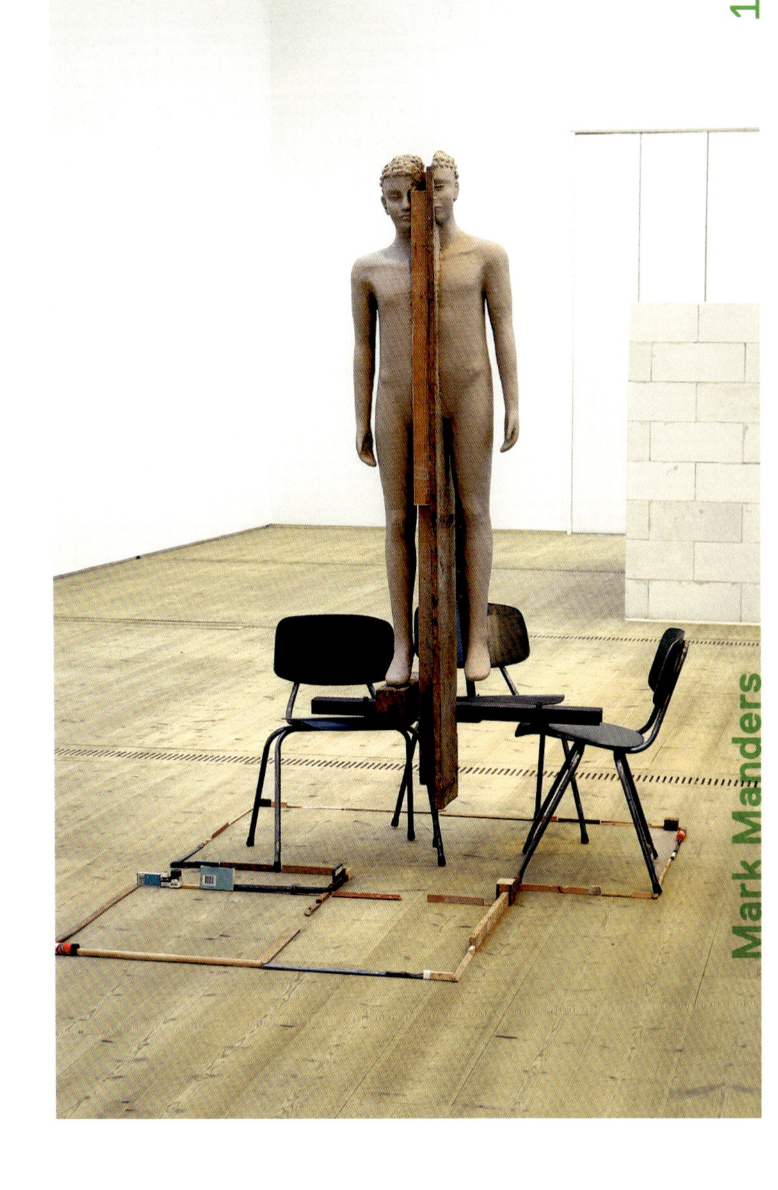

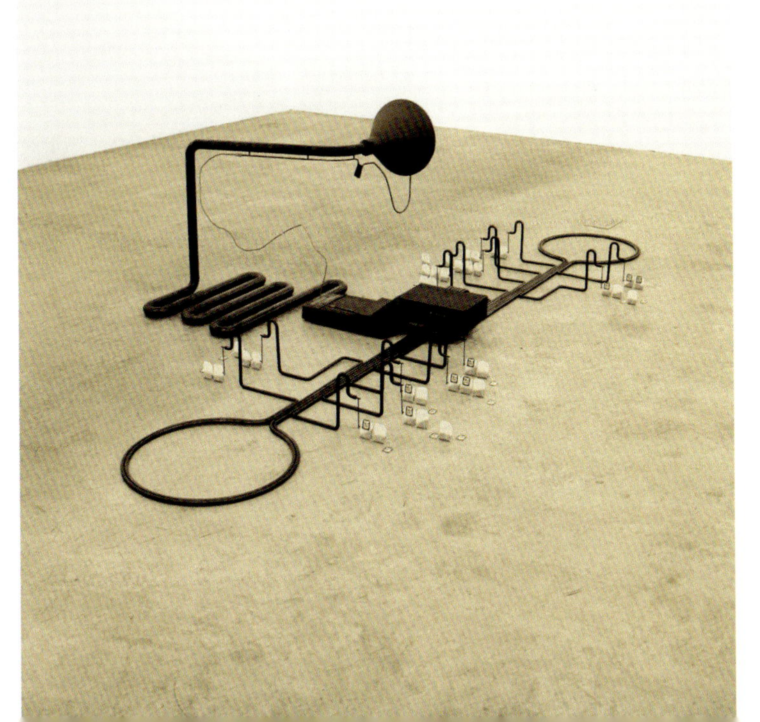

05

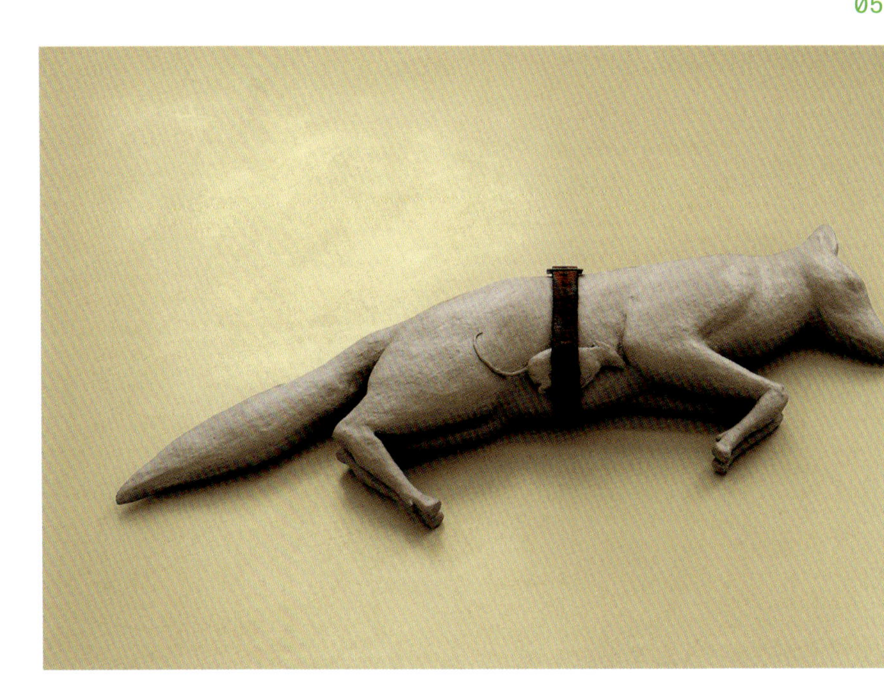

The work of Marepe (Marcos Reis Peixoto) is a fine example of how an artist can blend personal and regional references with the international language of contemporary art, making him at once local and global.

Presente dos Presentes (Presents for those Present, 2002) is an eloquent work that establishes dialogues between the local and the international, with poetic undertones. The work consists of a set of small sculptures of 'presents' made in clay in an irregular parallelepiped format, decorated with metallic paper of various colours, and wrapped in satin ribbons. The clay gifts can be seen, on the one hand, as a reflection of the lack of resources and as a signifier of a certain resistance to the capitalist and consumerist act of giving presents. On the other hand, they draw on a handmade traditional sculpture, if not with striking formalist features then with deep symbolic meaning and value — after all, there is nothing more valuable than our own soil.

In Marepe's series of *Embutidos* (Inbuilt, 2001–03) his interest lies in informal architecture. The sculptures (which exist both in full architectural scale and as scale models) use a multi-functional and flexible system of hinged wooden doors and boards through which a room may become a bedroom, a kitchen or a dining room by opening and closing tables, cabinets and ironing boards. *Embutido Recôncavo* (Inbuilt Recess, 2003), for example, is a wooden cube divided into four parts, articulated by hinges and elevated from the floor by wheels. Retractable furniture attached to the architecture allows the viewer to reconfigure it, proposing new architectures and mixing internal and external, public and private spaces. Here, there is a political and social connotation to the work; the precariousness of the construction recalls the informal architecture found in the poor areas of Brazil.

Pérola de água doce (Freshwater Pearl, 2007) was a work made on the occasion of the city of São Paulo's anniversary, on 25 January, at Bandeiras Bridge, which spans the polluted Tietê River. There, Marepe threw pearls into the river in a symbolic gesture that was both an homage to a lost beauty (in the past, pearls could be found in the Paulista rivers) and a call for protection from Oxum, who in the Afro-Brazilian religion of Candomblé is the deity of freshwater and symbol of pregnancy and fecundity.

Bringing together the traditional and the popular, the local and the foreign, the personal and the political, Marepe has been able to gather remarkable international recognition. In a context where all successful artists are from or move to Brazil's largest cities, Marepe has remained faithful to his roots and continues to live in his hometown of Santo Antônio de Jesus, a small settlement in the interior of Bahia, in the country's poor northeast region. [Adriano Pedrosa]

01

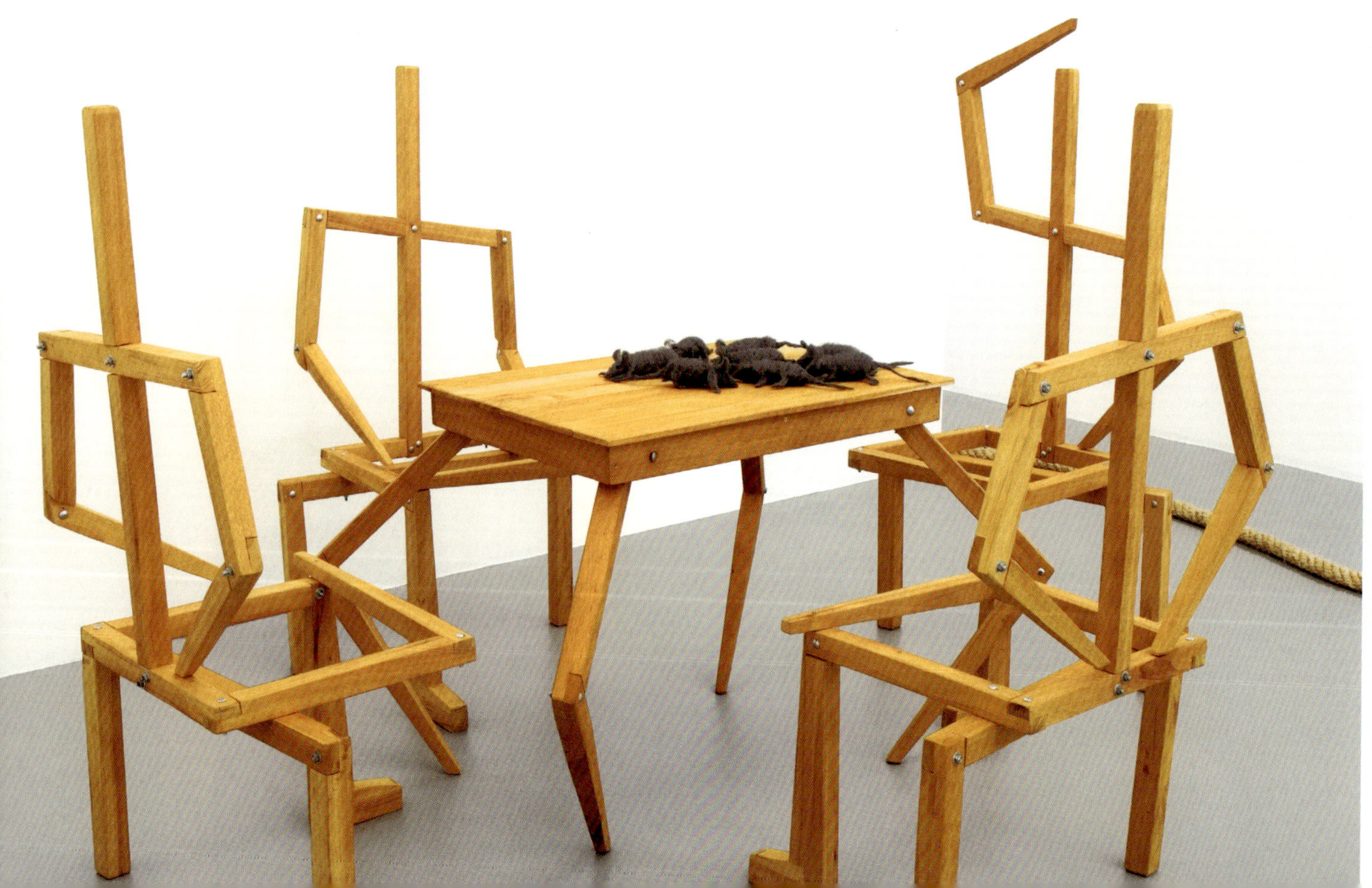

02

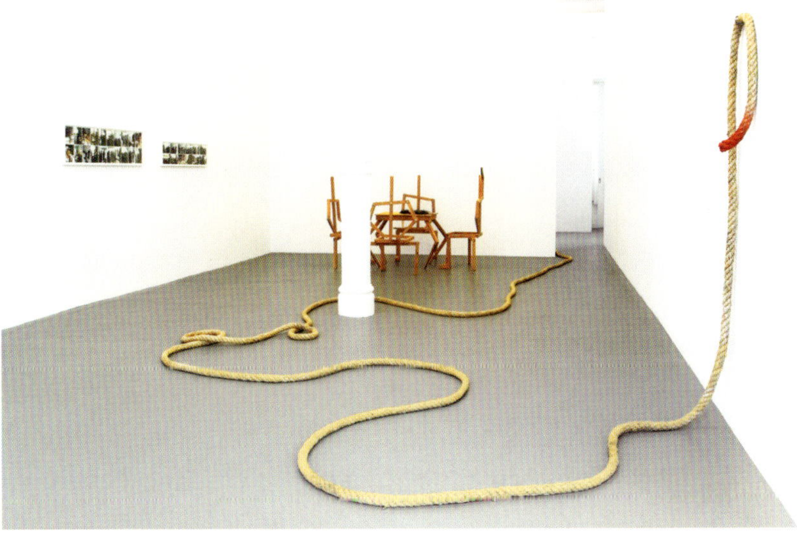

03

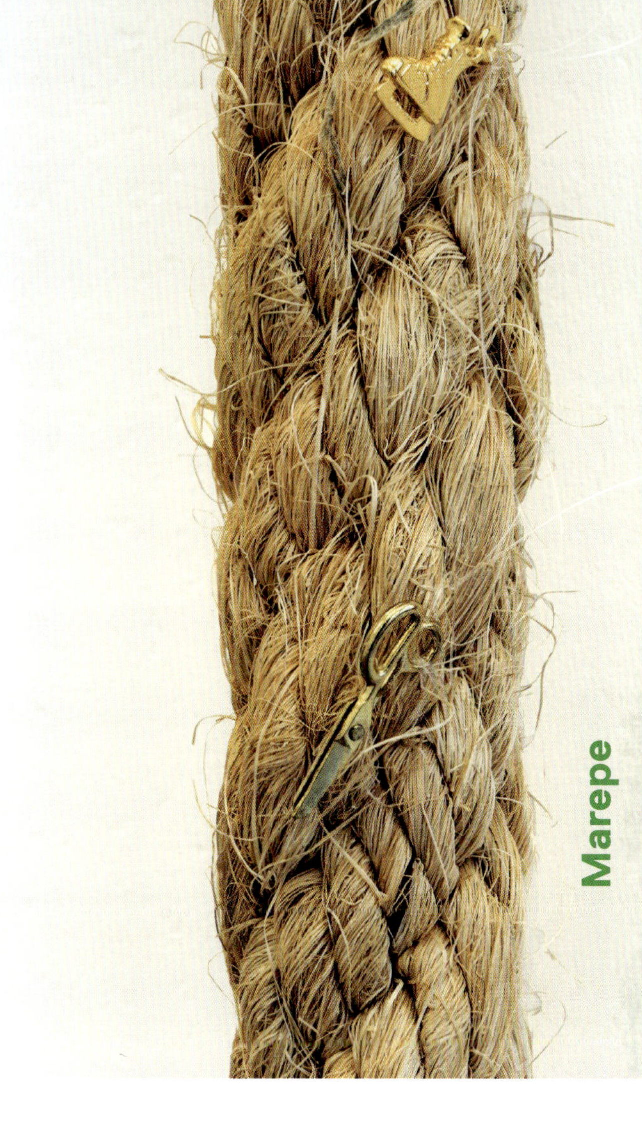

04

01 *Quatro cadeiras conversando*, 2007
Wood, steel, wool, metal
Dimensions variable

02 *Satélite Baldio*, 2005
Plastic, metal
Approx. 200 × 340 × 310 cm

03, 04 *Cordão umbilical*, 2007
Rope, acrylic, metal
Length 28 m

05 from left:
→ *Filtros*, 1999
Ceramic filter, wood benches, cups, water
12 parts
Sizes vary from 163 × 32 × 32 cm to 223 × 32 × 32 cm
→ *A Mudança*, 2005
Wood, metal, rubber, plastic, hinges
191 × 352 × 158 cm
→ *Andador*, 2005
Metal, fabric, rubber
322 × 259 × 288 cm

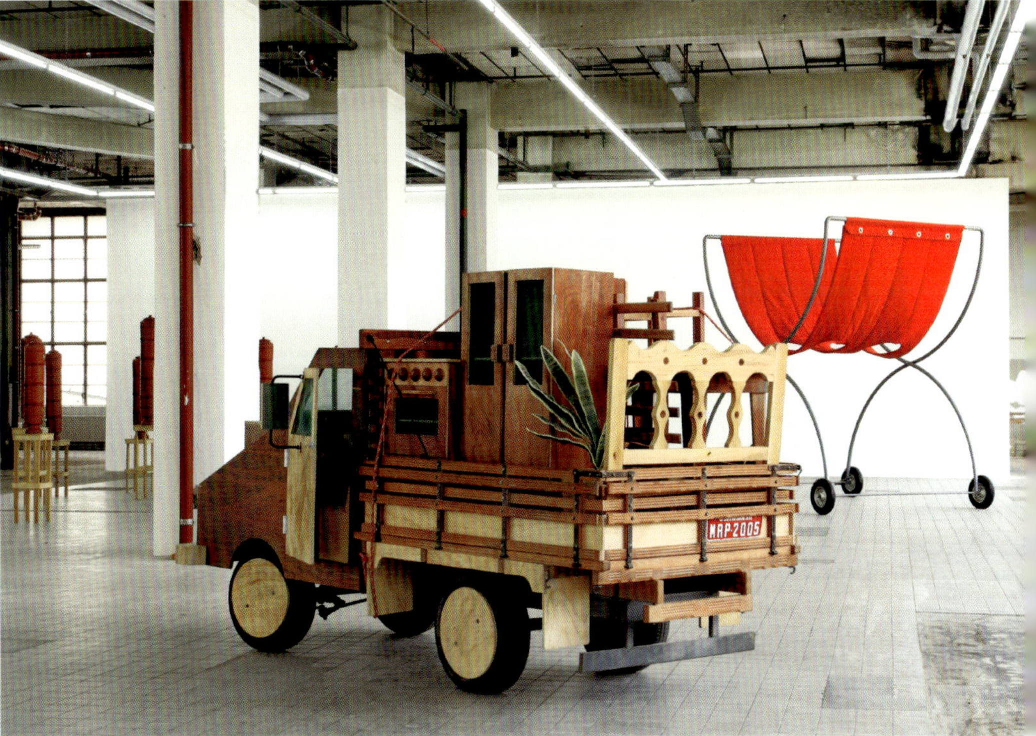

05

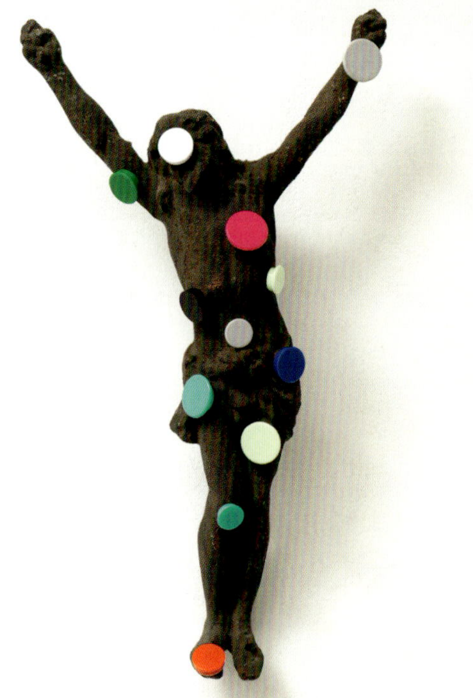

01

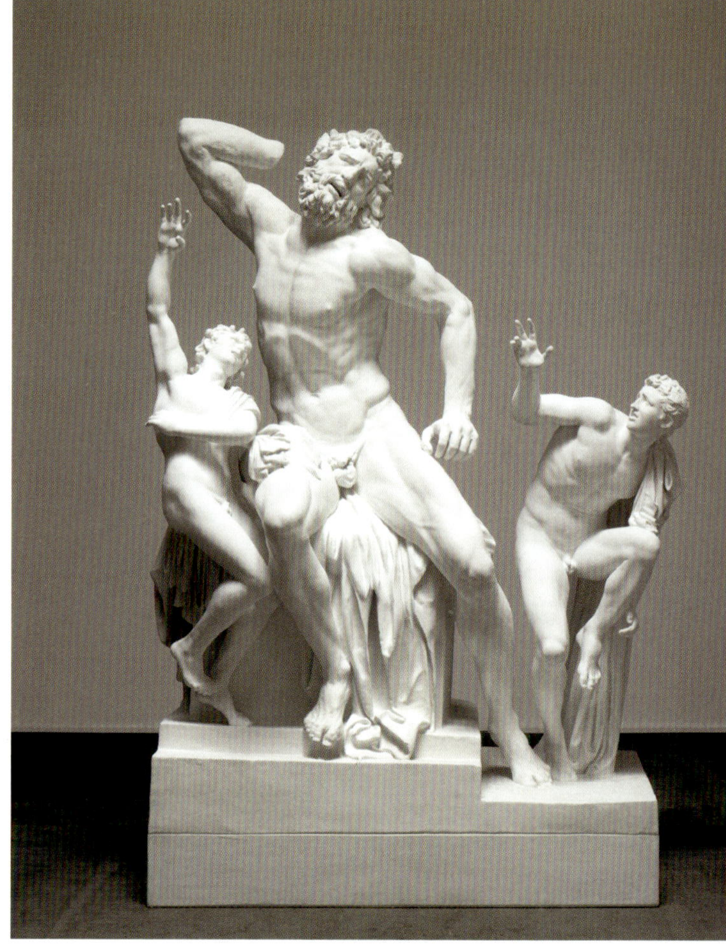

02

Many, if not all, of Kris Martin's works address time, whether it is the historical present of contemporary Europe, where he is based, or the immaterial time of the soul. Martin has stated that his interest in history and temporality is a natural result of his location: 'I enjoy the enormous advantage to live in the centre of Europe,' he says. 'When I look out of the window in my studio in Ghent, located on a little square, I see nothing but history [...] Jan van Eyck's studio is fifty metres from mine [...] I am a product of history.' Thus it is perhaps unsurprising that Martin's work is more likely to reference work from the Renaissance or Baroque than recent modern production.

One of his most ambitious works to date, *Mandi VIII* (2006), is a plaster cast of the famous Hellenistic sculpture of the struggle of Laocoön, although the baroque twisting forms of the serpents, whose attack the father and his two sons are desperately fighting off in the original sculpture, have been entirely removed. The alarmed expression and physical strain of the three figures suggest a fight to the death with an unknown and unseen tormentor — unnervingly apt for our current condition of alert.

Other works are no less dramatic in their merging of objects, philosophy and attitudes from vastly differing times. *Vase* (2005), appears, at least to the layperson's eye, to be a highly valuable Chinese vase. Standing taller than human height, it shows signs of repair following what seems to have been a tragic accident. In fact, Martin deliberately tipped over the vase and pieced together its fragments. The instructions accompanying the work, moreover, dictate that on every new showing (or at every change of hands) it must once again be broken and pieced together. As with the alteration of Laocoön, Martin deliberately plays with our desire for perfection, wholeness and a corresponding notion of beauty and value. His use of other people's artworks and artefacts within his own practice suggests at once a reverence for the culture that has preceded him and simultaneously a destructive, even patricidal stance.

This mixture of devotion and competition is apparent in a series of works based on texts, and in particular one relating to Martin's favourite book, Dostoyevsky's *The Idiot*. Martin went so far in his appreciation of this novel as to copy out the entire book (1,494 pages) in a beautifully hand-transcribed unbound edition entitled simply *Idiot* (2004–05).

Martin has also made works referencing Christianity, such as *Trinity* (2007), a triptych of watery ink drawings implying a mountainous support for the minute emblems of Father, Son and Holy Ghost, and *Pietà* (2006), a piece of found wood and crystal brought suggestively together to mimic the iconic pose. Asked about his relationship to Christianity, hardly a common topic in contemporary art, Martin says, 'I am a Christian because I am rooted in Christianity [...] It is hard for me to understand that people get sick and tired of their spiritual background. For me that is like a fish being sick and tired of water.' His security in his belief allows for his work to go beyond the confines of personal thought. It is, to put it another way, his firmly held faith that allows us to believe as well. [Jens Hoffmann]

03

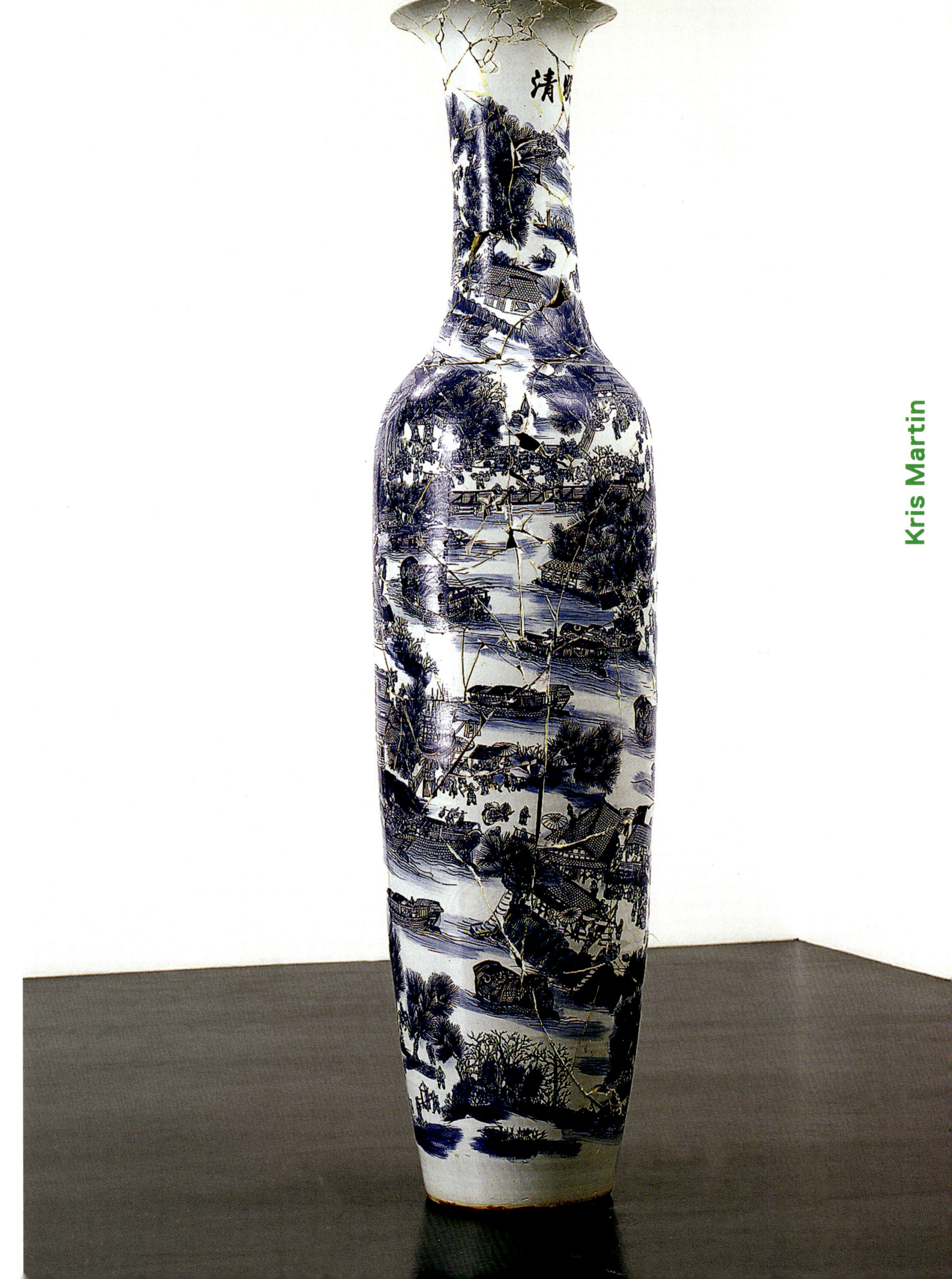

01 *Thirteen Idiots*, 2008
Iron, magnets
45 × 27 × 11 cm

02 *Mandi VIII*, 2007
Plaster
221 × 150 × 100 cm

03 *Vase*, 2005
Chinese porcelain, glue
Height 225 cm

Josephine Meckseper is known internationally for her sculptures and mixed-media installations, photographs and videos exploring the glamour of consumer fashion and advertising from a radical point of view located inside the world that she is displaying. Both art history and the very galleries in which she exhibits have been subjected to the same straight-faced treatment. In the ironically titled *The Complete History of Postcontemporary Art* (2005) objects displayed at incestuous proximity (toilet cleaners and perfume, fashion ads alongside a plunger) are reflected in Meckseper's signature mirrored showcases. At once standing to attention (like Jeff Koons' vacuum cleaners) and reversing themselves (reflected in the mirror the 'OUI' sign for the European referendum turns into a 'NON'), they keep alluding to the magic of the commodity brilliantly described in Karl Marx's *Das Capital*. In Meckseper's installations, objects stand for exchangeable human relations, but simultaneously they take on the attributes of fetishes (the furry rabbit and mannequin legs are classics). Similarly, conflicting ideologies and opposing political parties are reduced to empty tags and merely consumed as ideas.

01

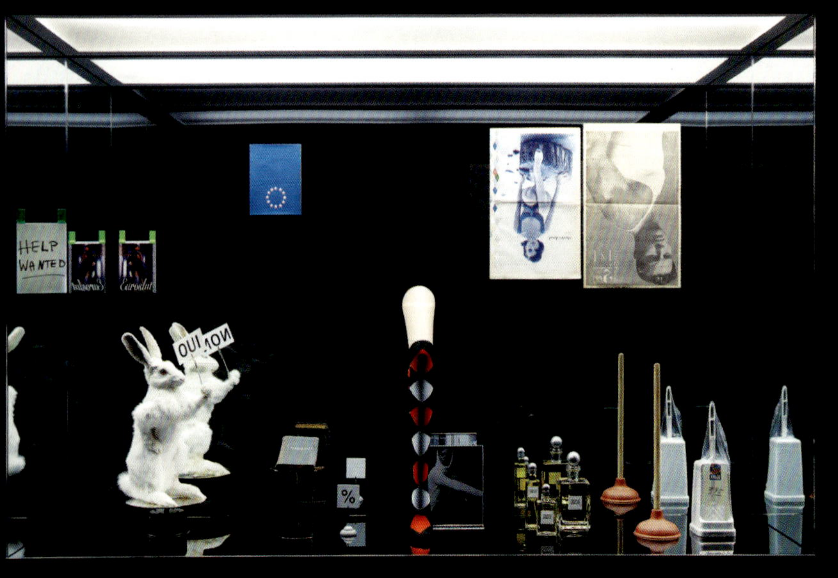

02

Occasionally the exhibition space itself is turned into a boutique in order to emphasize the continuum of art and commerce. In her mirrored shelves and chromed glass shop-windows, Meckseper subtly (or blatantly) introduces disruptive elements that upset the seductive display surfaces. Her *Talk to Cindy* (2005), for example, not only mirrors consumerist culture with a vengeance, but multiplies the same images ad infinitum. Instead of criticizing the consumer society, Meckseper keeps upping the ante on the principle of equivalence that regulates the capitalist system, sending it spinning into a kind of giddy delirium. In an art world which uses critique as some kind of disclaimer, Meckseper is the first contemporary artist to dare break what could be considered the ultimate taboo: not sex, but politics. Presenting imagery of protest culture and revolutionary myths side by side with art installations, she exposes consumerist and counter-cultural discourses as if they belonged together. In the process, she bewildered many well-meaning social critics, such as Okwui Enwezor and Christian Höller, who were otherwise ready to welcome her into the fold.

As early as 1968, in his *System of Objects*, Jean Baudrillard boldly anticipated that, in a consumer society, critique would become complementary and complicit to what it opposes: 'The revolutionary imperative is alive, but unable to realize itself in practice; it is consumed in the idea of Revolution. [...] All ideas, even the most contradictory, can coexist as signs within the idealist logic of consumption.' Like Emil Cioran or Jean Baudrillard, Meckseper doesn't project any ideological critique or advocate any cause but, taking its signs at face value, perversely allows the consumer system to hang itself.

Stylishly redolent of Constructivism and Minimalism, Meckseper's work sits uneasily between the cool irony of Andy Warhol and the interpolative slogans of Barbara Kruger. Her detachment may only be apparent, but what counts is the strategy she uses to register the ambivalent nature of contemporary reality. Instead of dismissing it, her strategy is to strip it bare in order to perform some kind of archaeology of the present. *Quelle International* (2008), a group of pictures reproduced on reflective Mylar culling fashion photographs from a mail-order catalogue popular in Germany in the 1970s, may go even further to suggest that showing contemporary reality for what it is would be enough. Time itself will eventually provide the necessary critical distance, turning her own work into an unsettling document.
[Sylvère Lotringer]

01, 02 *The Complete History of Postcontemporary Art*, 2005
Mixed media in display window
160 × 250 × 60 cm

03 *Shelf No. 31*, 2005
Shelf with mixed media
59 × 152 × 35 cm

04 *Untitled (End Democracy)*, 2005
Inkjet print, Plexiglas, plastic mannequin torso, metal stand, mirror on wood
144 × 121 × 121 cm

05 *USA*, 2007
Mixed-media sculpture on Plexiglas cube
74 × 21 × 21 cm

03

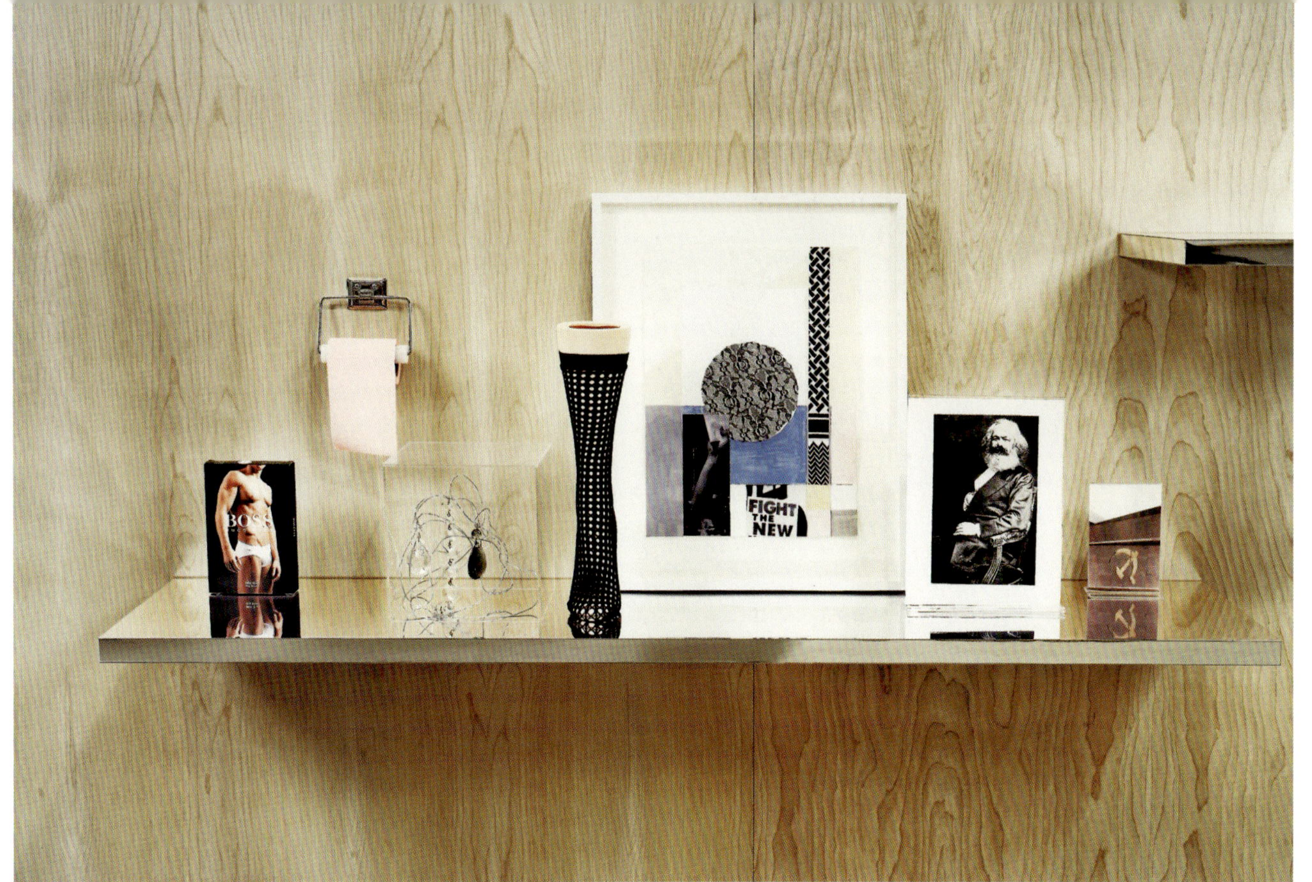

BOSS
FIGHT
THE
NEW

END
DEMO
CRACY
THAT FESTIVAL
OF MEDIOCRITY
VOTE
2008
COMMUNIST

U.S.A

04

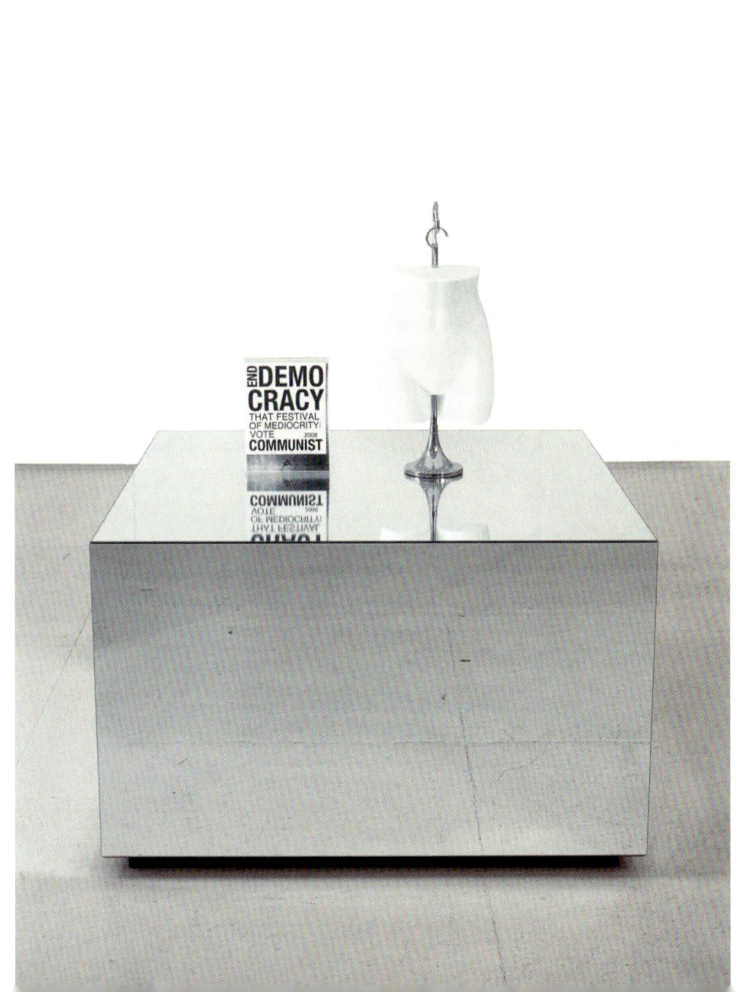

05

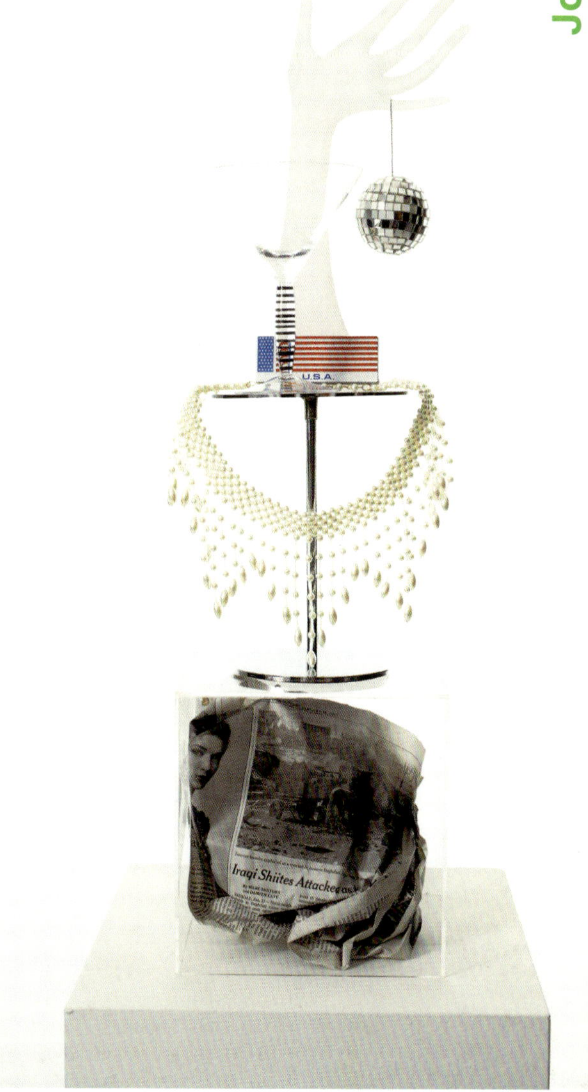

06

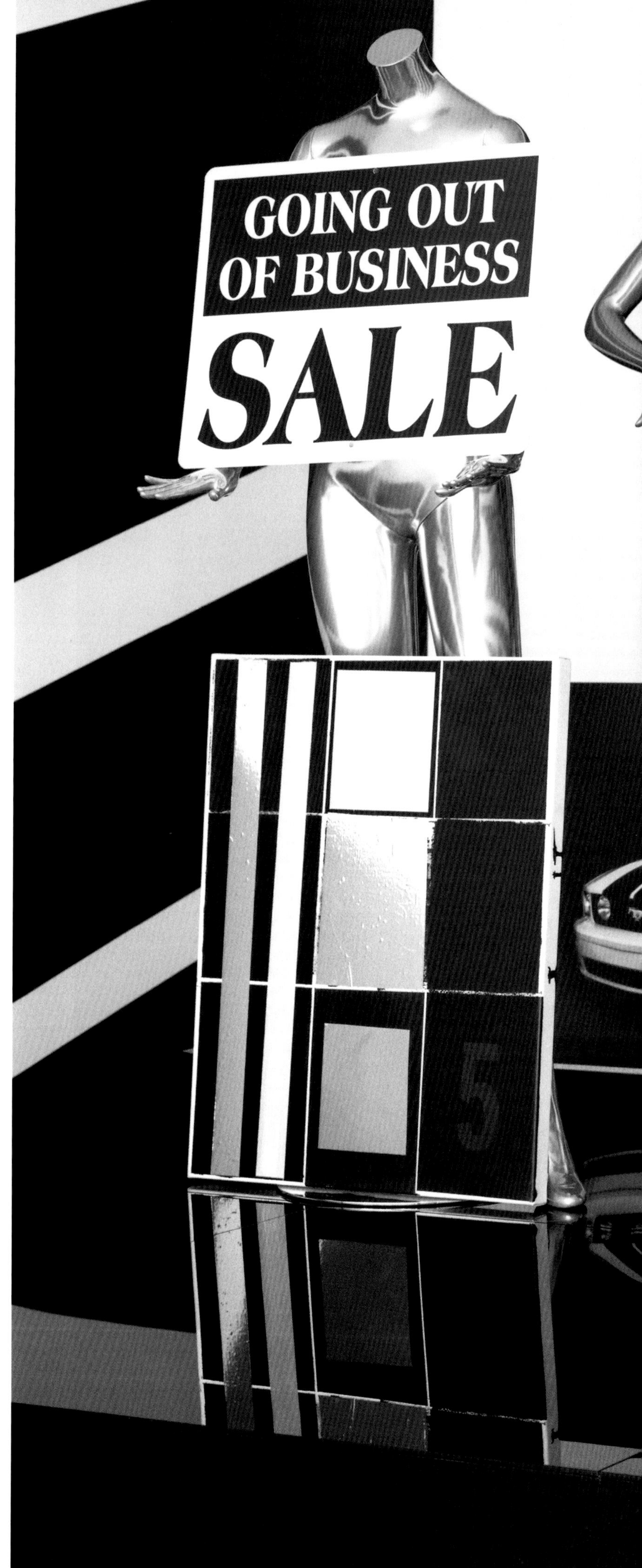

06 *Ten High*, 2008
Plexiglas platform, 3 mannequins, collapsible walker, cane, bottle of whiskey, Bible, ashtray with cigarettes, broken mirror on wooden panel, poster mounted to aluminium, mixed media on canvas, aluminium sign, T-Shirt, tie, fake vomit on Plexiglas
350 × 350 × 350 cm

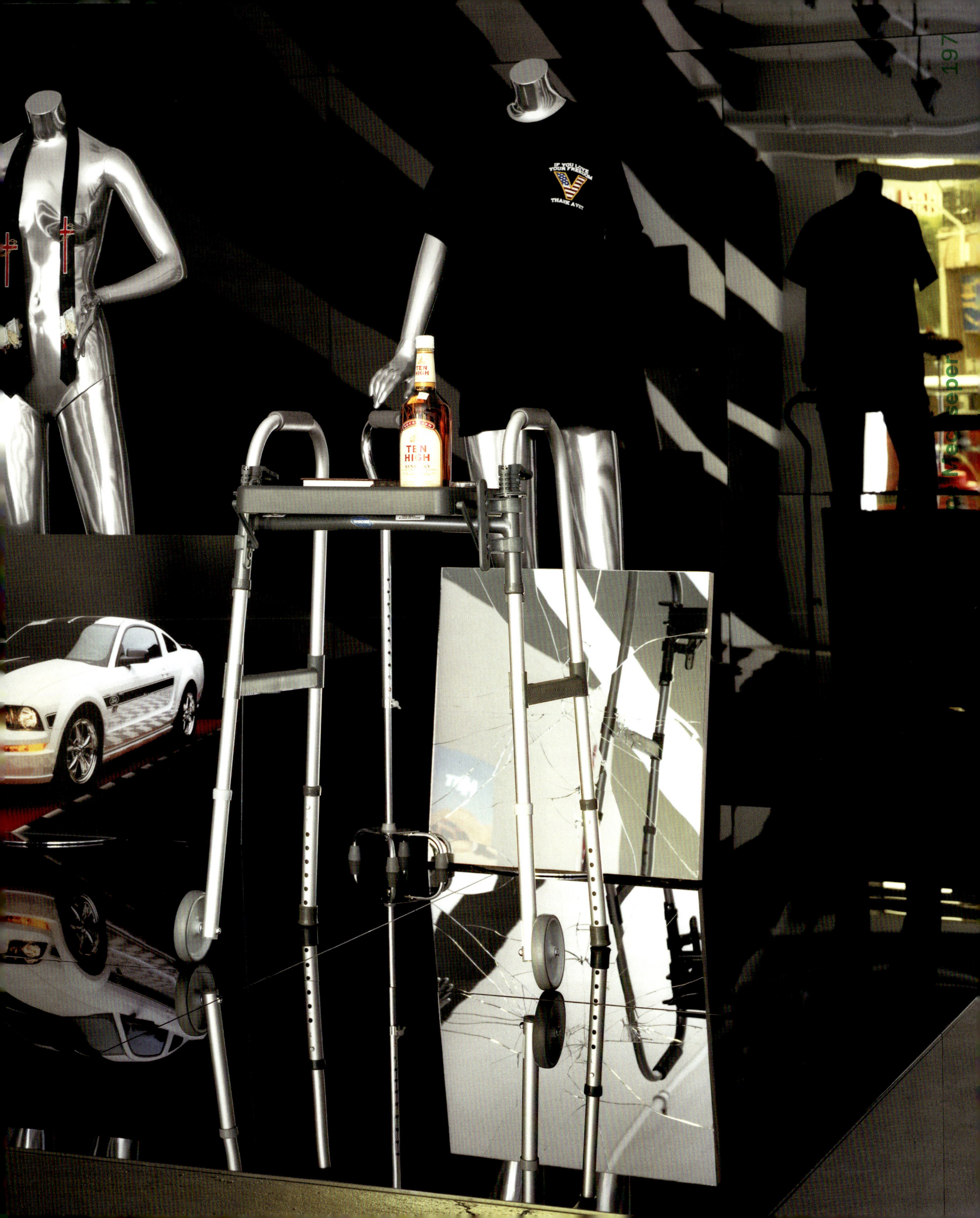
IF YOU LOVE YOUR FREEDOM
THANK A VET
TEN HIGH

Michaela Meise's *HaHaHa* (2005), six letters attached to each other to spell out the words of the title, gives no indication of what there is to laugh about. The way in which this work addresses its spectators is more like an instruction to laugh than a representation of infectious glee. But there is fun in Meise's piece, hidden within the contradictions of referentiality. After all, this is an artist who performed yoga-like movements in front of a wall displaying famous quotes out of Ludwig Wittgenstein (*Wittgenstein Exercise,* 2001), and *HaHaHa* can be viewed within this context. The Austrian philosopher gave a good deal of thought to *Sprachspiele* (language games), and *HaHaHa* is a piece at the margins of language, referring to movie theatre billboards as well as to abstraction, to nonsensical mumbling or to visceral utterance.

01

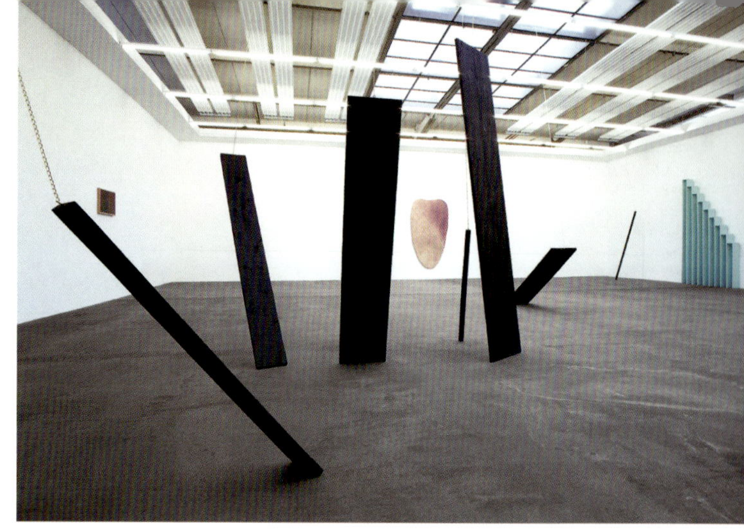

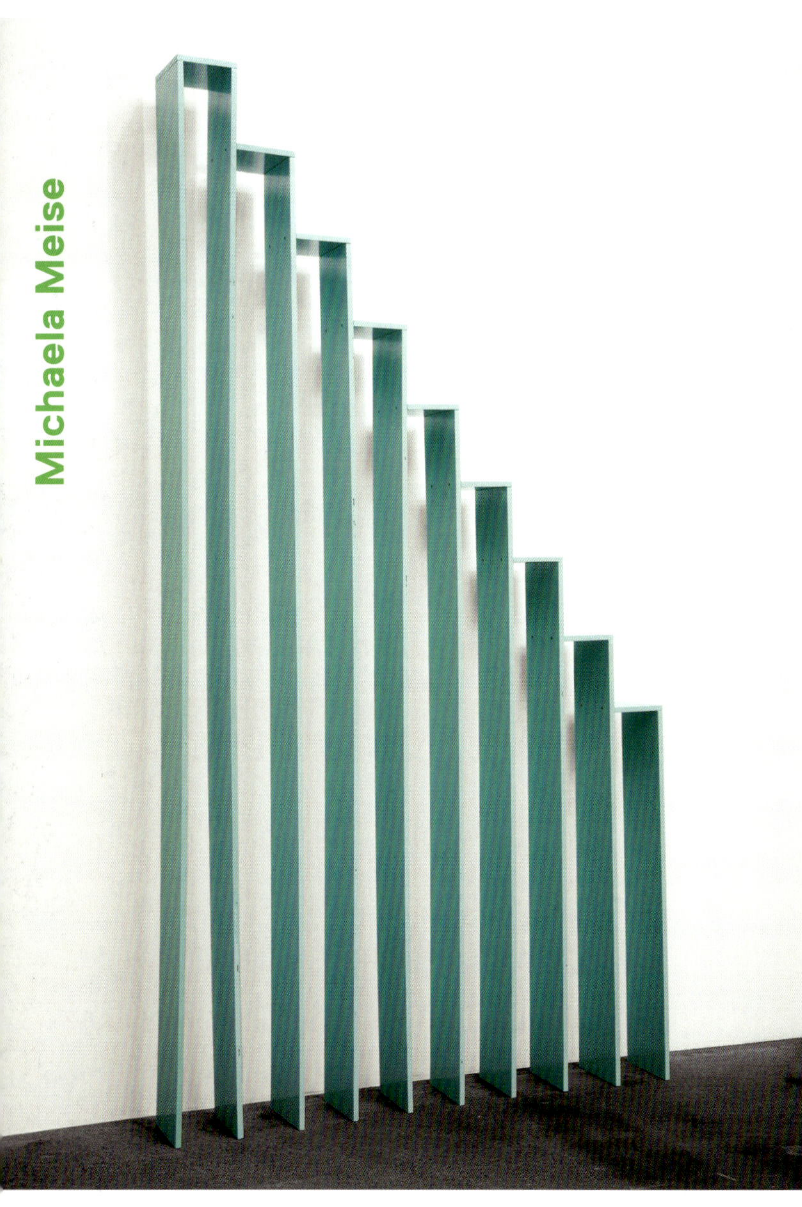

02

Tür auf, Tür zu (2007) presents objects that are essentially door handles mounted in a wooden structure but are no longer used to open anything: they are simply objects. Again, this is intended to be humorous, but it is not about to provoke a 'ha ha ha'. A chuckle, perhaps. Similarly ironic is *Treppe* (Stair, 2007), which doesn't lead anywhere but into the aporia of a wooden structure, gaining function only through its title.

There is no such thing as a signature piece by Meise; her strategies and approaches constantly shift. However, Minimalist and Post-Minimalist sculpture is a constant issue. She treats the sculptural elements in her work as being on the same level as any other medium or message that she employs, including books, watercolours, photography, quotes and icons. The simple cardboard structure *Nocturama* (2006), for example, acts as a lectern for an unexpected addition: W.G. Sebald's book *Austerlitz*. Sculpture may be about containment, but with Meise it is just as much about transparency. Or opacity: in *Großes Fenster* (Big Window, 2005) she erected a 'window' within a black frame on top of a base of Indiana limestone. The window is made of opaque straw-silk paper which means that one cannot see through it, plus the window is too high up.

Meise also mediates Minimalism with iconicity by implementing material from celebrity culture. In her *Missy Elliott cube* (2002) she displayed a logo consisting of the letters 'MSE', readable as an abbreviation of the pop star's name, but also of her own. She brings herself into the picture again in the photograph *Baby* (2007), which shows her with a baby and her name written on the wall behind her, albeit illegible, as it looks like a mix of hieroglyphic and Arabic lettering. These language games come very close to abstraction, but also to a preter-lingual realm of hieroglyphic communication. [Bert Rebhandl]

01 from left:
→ *Liegende*, 2007
Wood, stain, metal chains
Dimensions variable
→ *Colour*, 2006
Wood, arcrylic paint,
wax, resin lacquer
39 × 61 × 4 cm
→ *Zunge*, 2007
Wood, stain, wax
190 × 109 × 5 cm
→ *Treppe*, 2007
Wood, synthetic resin lacquer
250 × 136 × 19 cm

02 *Treppe*, 2007
Wood, synthetic
resin lacquer
250 × 136 × 19 cm

03 *Brain 1*, 2007
Wood, acrylic
100 × 128 × 84 cm

04 *Große Fenster*, 2005
Straw-silk paper, acrylic,
stain, block board, wax,
Indiana limestone
250 × 110 × 50 cm

03

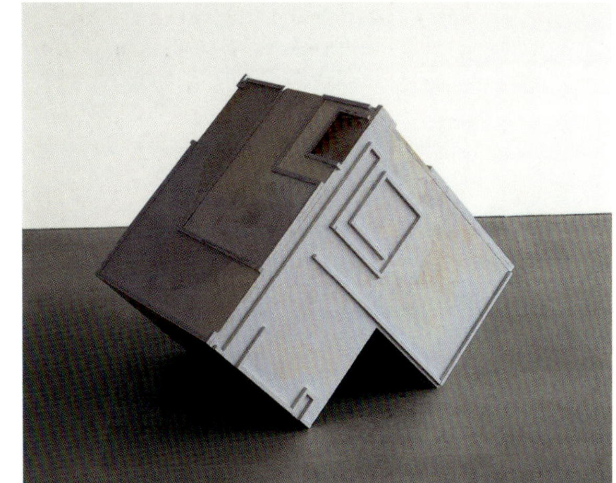

04

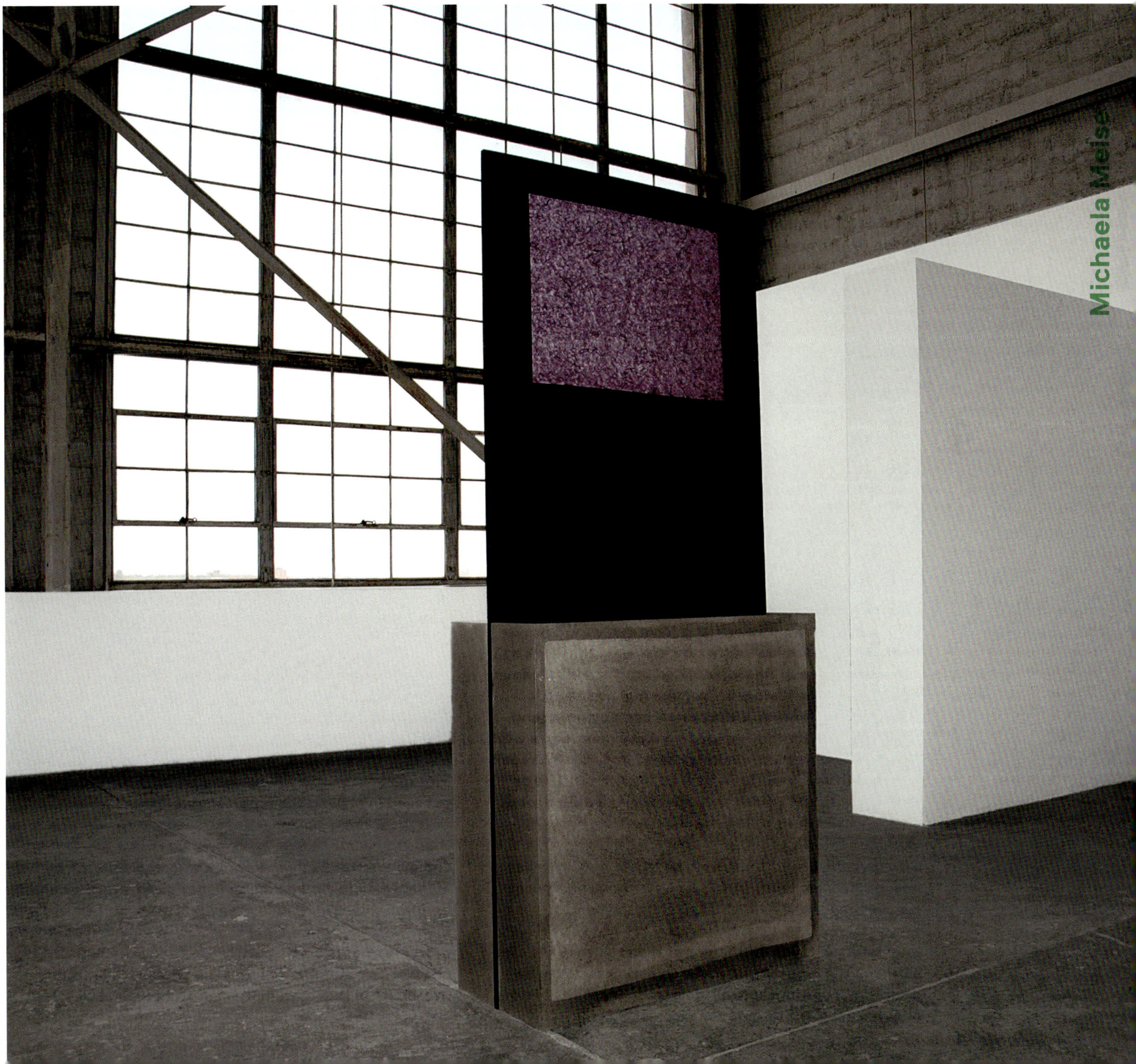

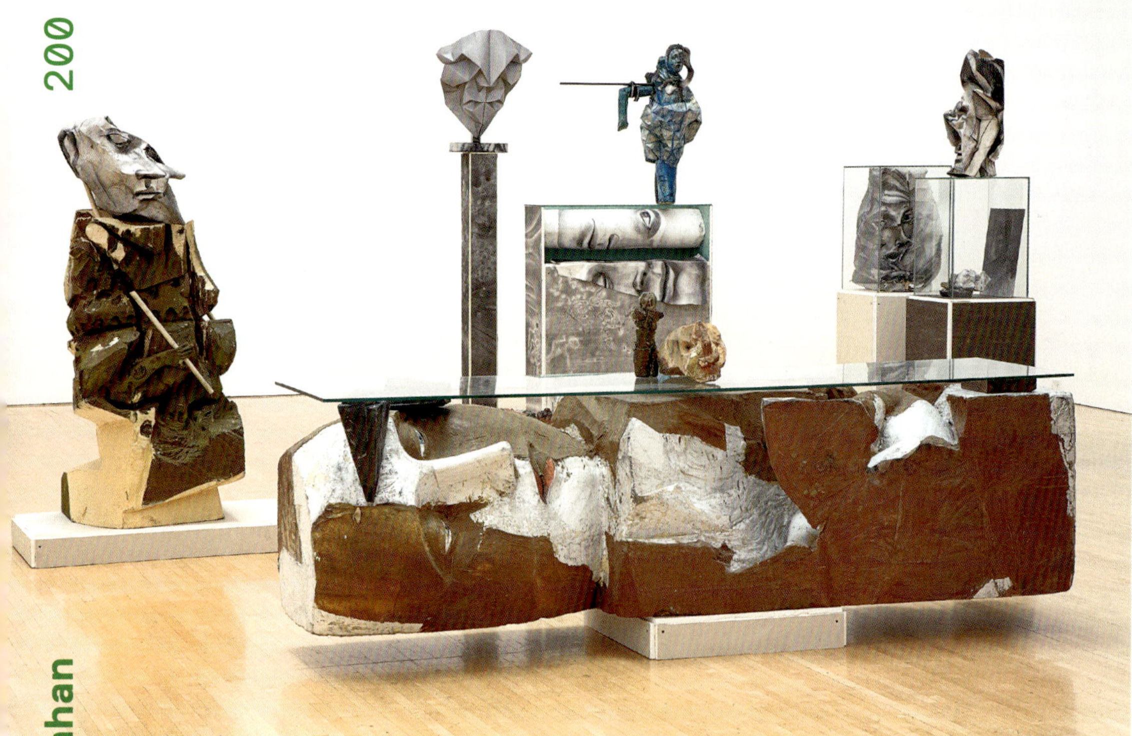

01

01 from left:
→ *Datong*, 2005–07
Foam, wax, silver leaf, glitter, cloth, string, glass, drywall
105 × 66 × 246 cm
→ *Mixed Messenger*, 2007
Foam, wax, pigment, wood, charcoal, paper, drywall
161 × 66 × 246 cm
→ *Rex*, 2006
Cloth and charcoal on paper, wood
216 × 30 × 16 cm
→ *Lover's Other*, 2002–05
Foam, wax, charcoal on paper, pigment, pins, wood, drywall
203 × 95 × 41 cm
→ *Knuf*, 1994–05
Charcoal on paper, wood, glass, dry wall
142 × 48 × 48 cm
→ *Sanitarium Artaud*, 1994–05
Drywall, glass, charcoal on paper on canvas, charcoal on muslin on panel, wax, floral-foam, pigment, matches
193 × 48 × 48 cm

02 *Untitled*, 2008
Glass, drywall, pigment, fabric strap, and wax
184 × 32 × 33 cm

03 *Untitled*, 2002
Folded plastic-coated fabric and paper
52 × 52 × 14 cm

In times when monuments to gods and men have been blown to smithereens or toppled from their pedestals, it only makes sense that a contemporary artist who sets out to make monumental figurative sculpture would make it as a readymade ruin. Los Angeles-based sculptor Matthew Monahan began his three-dimensional work by making masks, small enough to fit in one's hand, from folded paper that had been drawn on with charcoal. Vaguely cubist in their angularity (reinforced by the paper creases) and archaic in their glowering expressions, each of these works had a totemic weight that belied the lightness of its true materials.

These works are clear inspiration for the towering, full-figure sculptures that Monahan has produced over the past few years. Most of these objects are tall, imposing yet precarious towers of body parts: an armless torso, a head and two stolid, stump-like thighs that nevertheless read as complete, if monstrous, personages. Made from paper, dark green florist's foam and wax, however lightweight these sculptures are in reality, they look as if they were made of finely patinated bronze. This obvious reference to the history of monumental sculpture is reinforced by familiar art historical compositional and sculptural details that can be found in almost every work. Headless and limbless figures, angled in S-curves, recall classical Greek sculptures such as the Athena Nike or Rodin's be-robed Balzac. A head, balanced atop a torso on one ear, its face with half-moon eyes gazing towards the viewer, is a clear reference to Constantin Brancusi's *Sleeping Muse*, and a straining neck and torso recalls one of Michelangelo's slaves. The terrifying visages of the personages of Easter Island are also invoked, many faces have their 'o' shaped mouths and wide-open eyes. Interestingly, these evocations of the primitive, the classical and the modern can occur sometimes in a single sculpture. For Monahan, all idols throughout the history of culture are fair targets for excerption.

02

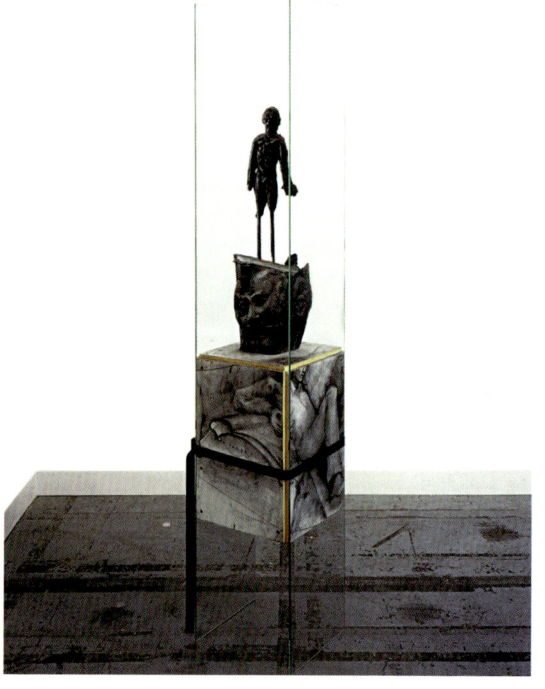

This historical gravitas, like the materials from which these sculptures are made, is trompe l'oeil; even the pedestals on which some of them are balanced or the Plexiglas vitrines in which some are encased do not succeed in making them portentous. Whatever civilization these relics have been rescued from, it was one that had no specific gods, nor particular heroes. By commemorating only the notion of commemoration, Monahan's pre-broken monuments give lie to the cult of hero worship altogether. They are the perfect embodiment of post-monumental times: huge but easily toppled, protected but not particularly precious (although one work memorably sports a headdress made from a five-dollar bill), frightening in an archetypical way, but also surprisingly, humorous. [Laura Hoptman]

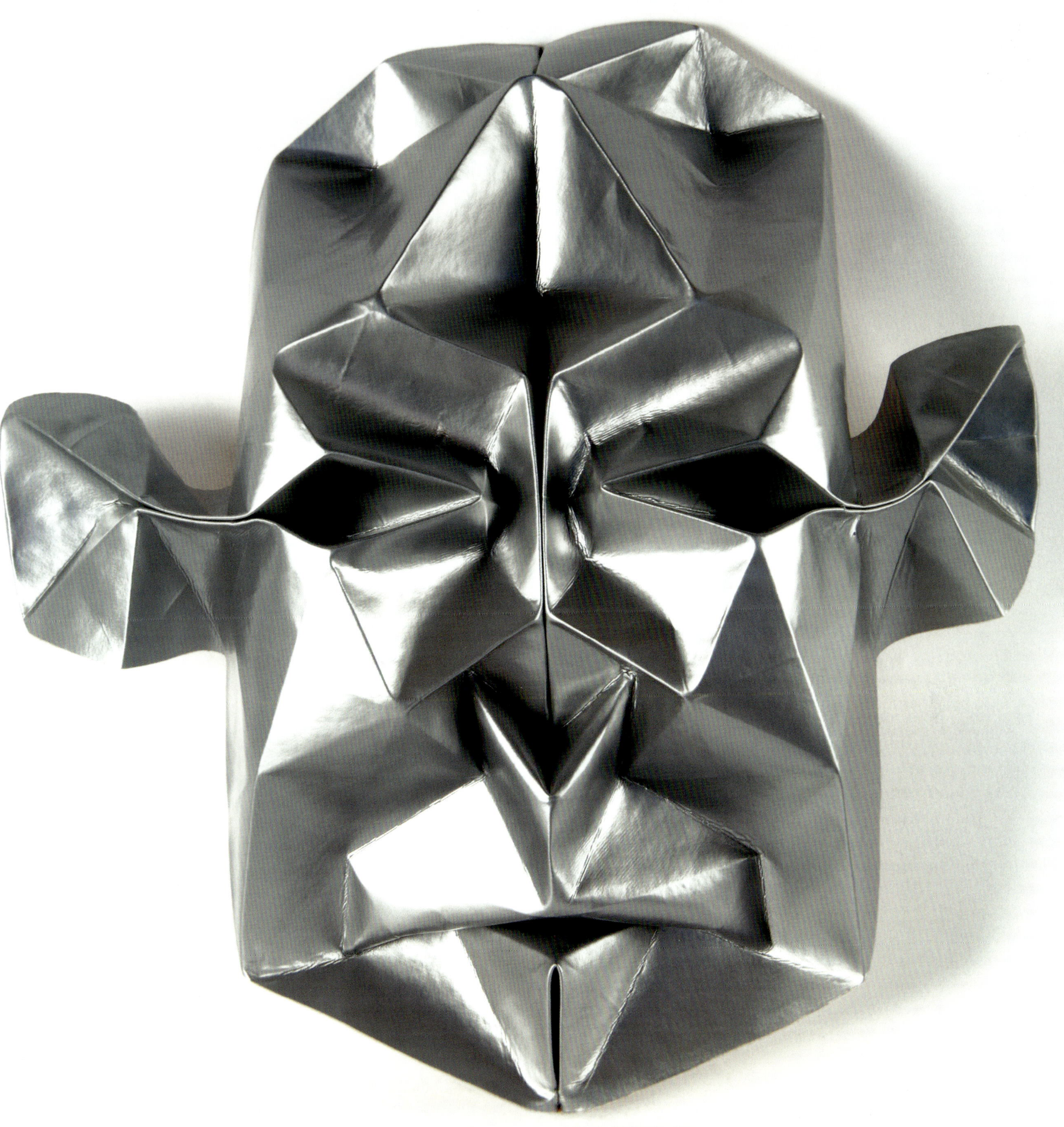

Matthew Monahan

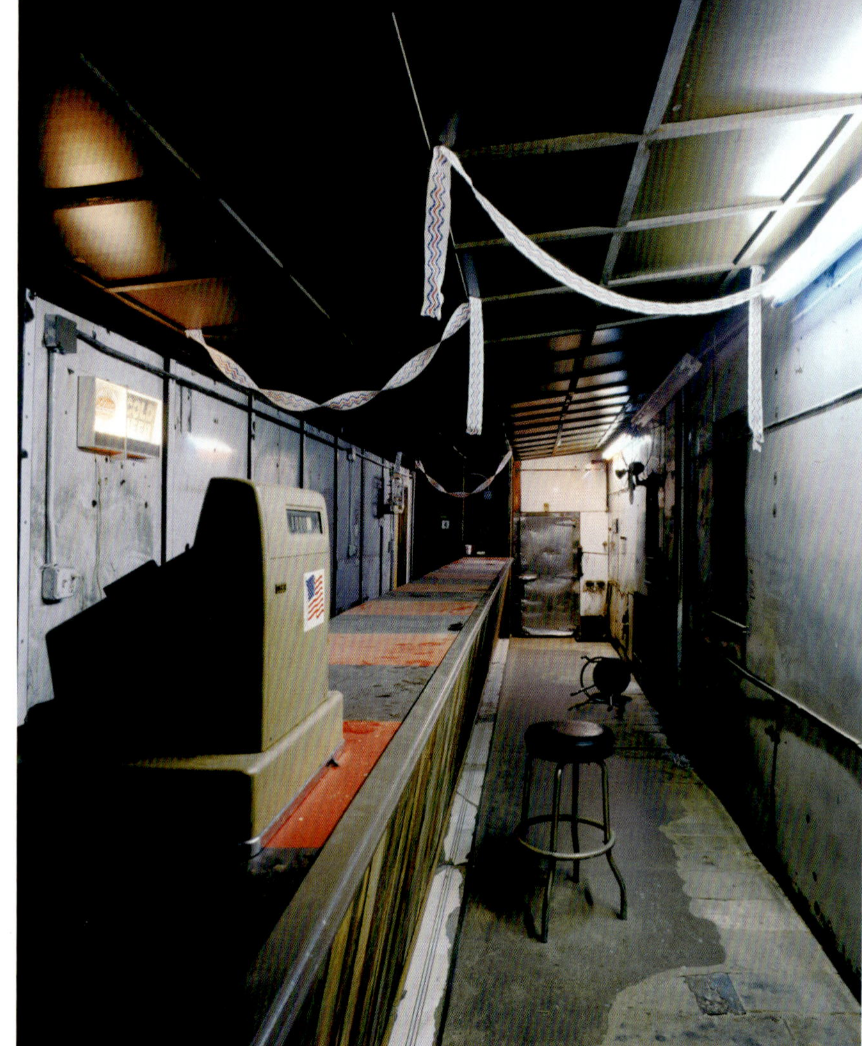

01

Initially, Mike Nelson's installations invite the adjective 'deceptive'. Pungently atmospheric and booby-trapped with clues to arcane narratives, they typically suggest theatrical sets or obsessively realized simulated worlds that have seeped from the pages of science fiction, the frames of film noir, or some other shadowy corner of twentieth and early twenty-first century subculture. 'Official' histories also appear, but only as they might trickle through to a twilight world of elusive, marginal characters, the absent inhabitants of Nelson's constructions: revolutionaries, drug dealers, gun runners, slaves, conspiracy theorists, religious radicals, vigilantes, backpackers, bikers or voodoo priests, to name just a few.

However, Nelson's deceptions are themselves a front; the underlying forms of his installations are just as significant, maybe more. Nelson's sketchbooks, a less celebrated but vital aspect of his practice, help develop the point. In them the artist calculates not only the physical nuts and bolts of each work (how battens will overlap, fixings attach, walls support ceilings and so on) but also its structural logic in relation to his oeuvre's themes. Certain formal devices recur, such as the labyrinth or the disjunction of interiors and exteriors. *Triple Bluff Canyon* (2004), for instance, reconstructs Robert Smithson's outdoor work, *Partially Buried Woodshed,* inside a gallery and invents the woodshed's interior elsewhere in the same gallery. Doubling and mirroring also fascinate Nelson. *The Coral Reef* (2000) and *A Psychic Vacuum* (2007) entice visitors into rabbit warrens of corridors and chambers and engender real panic by featuring, at different points in the maze, identical rooms. In other works, architectural structures exactly mirror one another. In *Amnesiac Shrine*, his 2007 Turner Prize installation, mirrored interiors filled with tiny sand dunes reflect miniature deserts into infinity. Here, Nelson 'mirrors' Robert Morris's canonical 1965 sculpture *Mirror Cubes*, but his version turns the earlier work inside out.

Indeed, recurrence itself recurs throughout the work. In the nineteenth century the labyrinth resurfaced from the distant past as a metaphor for the modern industrial city. In Nelson's work it morphs into a key for understanding the globalized world *in toto*. Global society is remade as an urban labyrinth, and its leaders (including John F. Kennedy, whose image Nelson uses more than once) are recast as the icons of dubious cults. Traces of the mythological Minotaur — disguised as an 'extremist' or 'gangster' — abound. Yet Nelson's reflexivity also determines our reception of this potent stew of references. Questers in the maze, we are asked to consider the monster as our own creation. By working out how Nelson's installations position us, their viewing subjects, in physical and historical space, we may learn about our own tactics for organizing time, memory and history. But ultimately Nelson is an artist, not a historiographer. There are no answers or explanations here, only patterns calculated to trouble, alert and, maybe, arm us in the real world. [Rachel Withers]

02

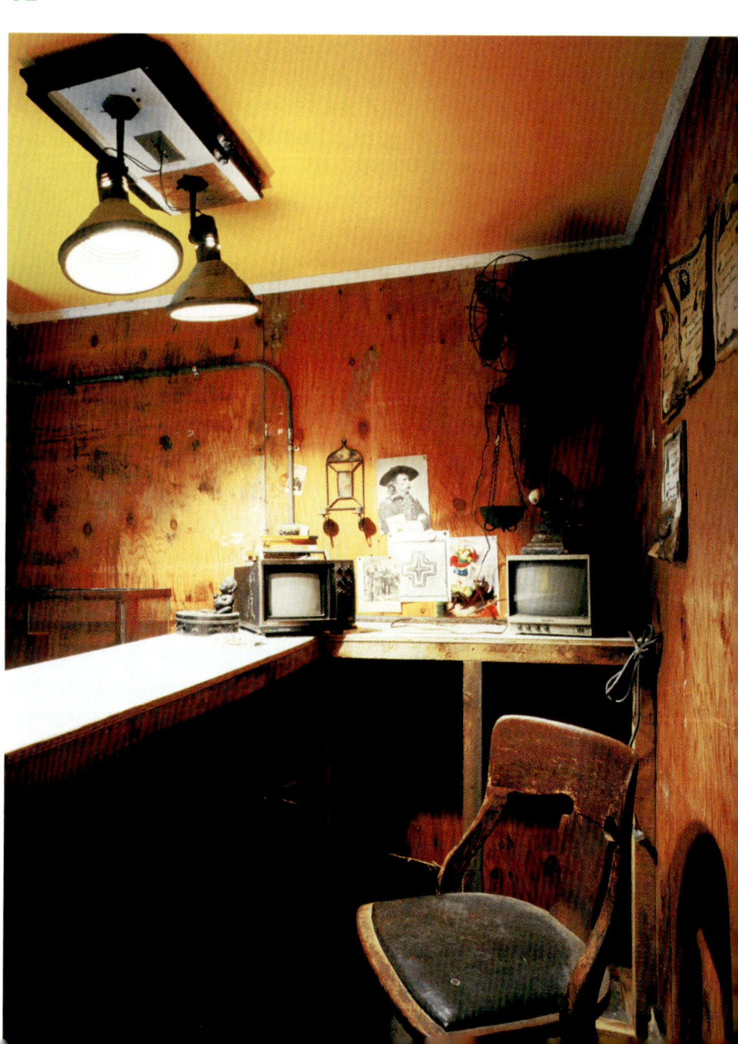

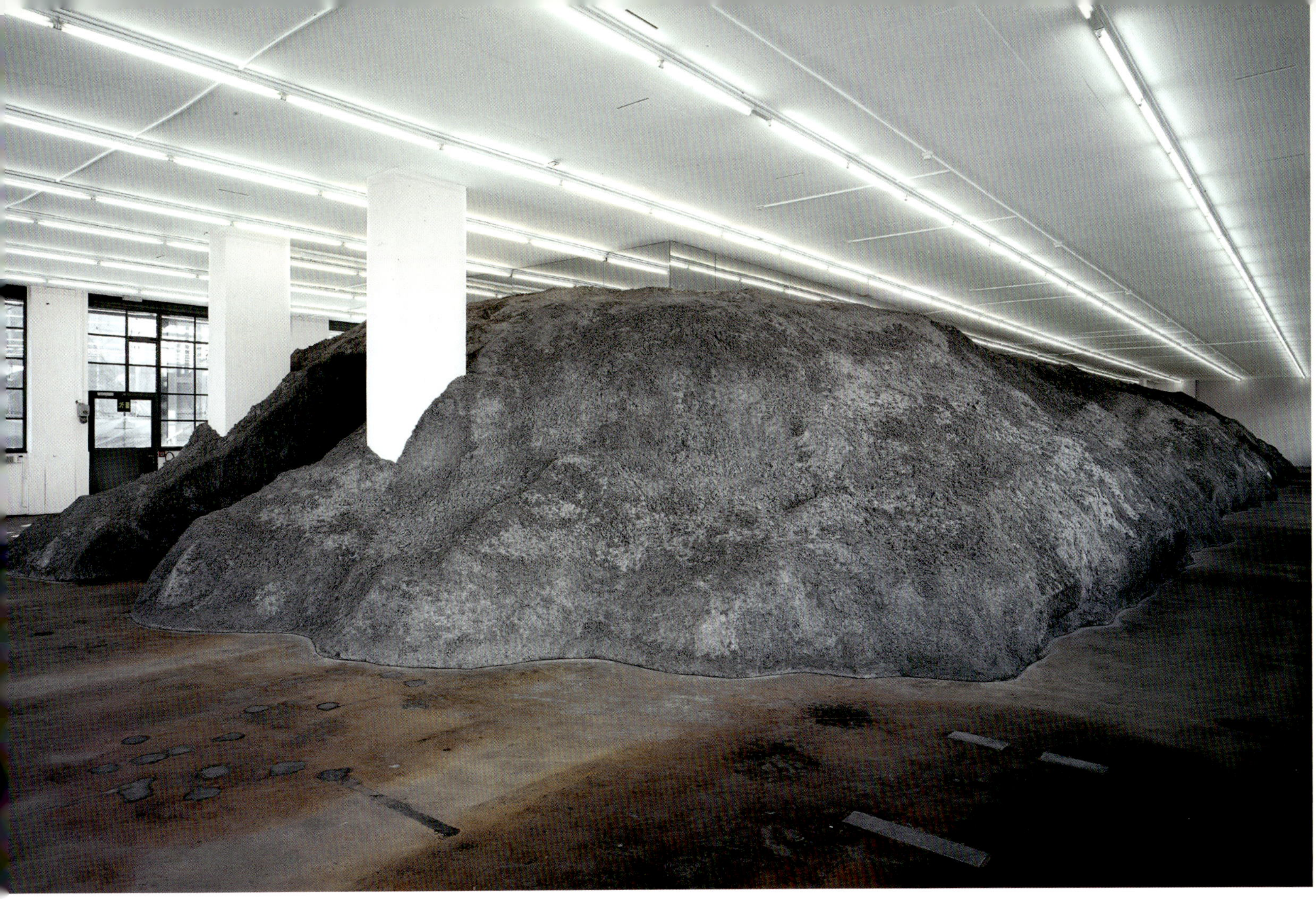

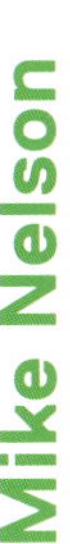

03

04

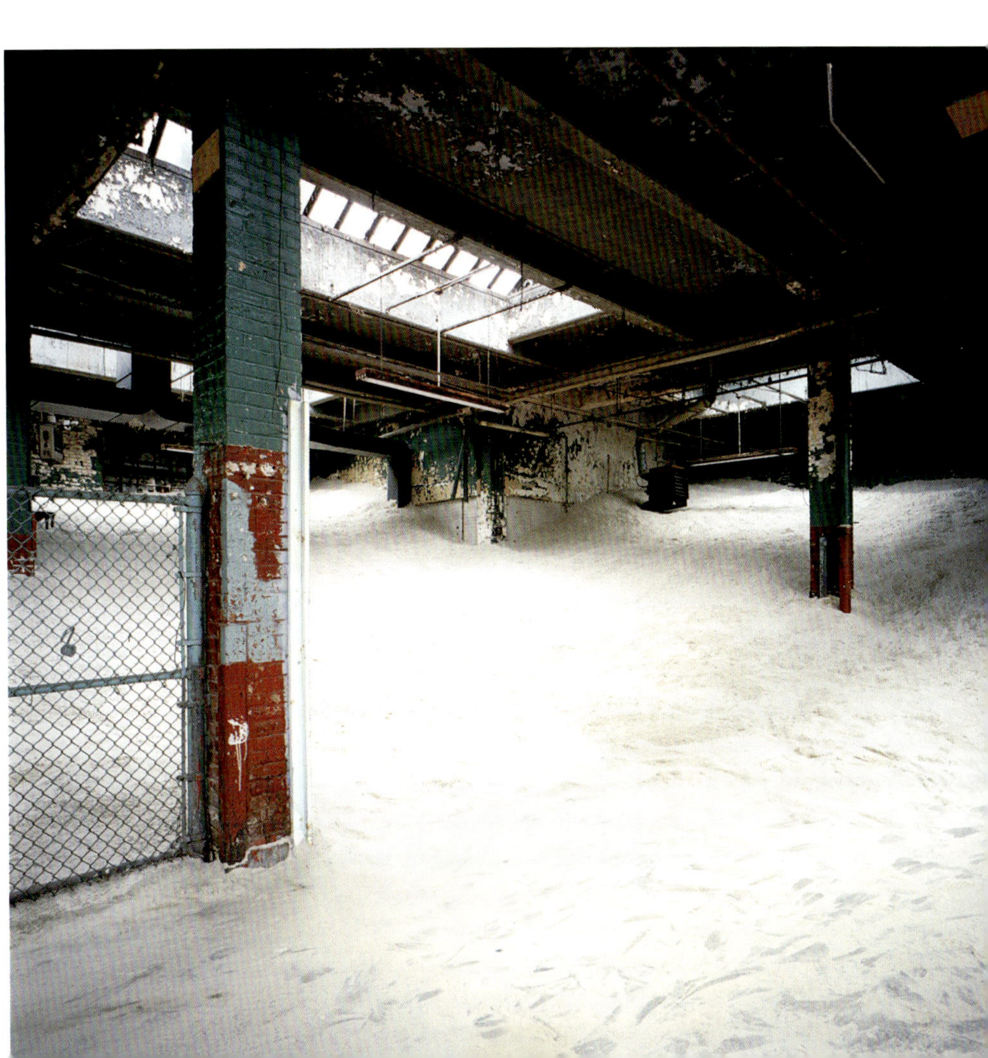

01, 02, 04 *A Psychic Vacuum*, 2007
Site-specific mixed-media installation
Dimensions variable
Old Essex Street Market, New York

03 *Studio Apparatus for MAMCO — An Intermediate Structure For A Museum: Introduction; Building Transplant In Three Sections; Towards A Revisiting Of Futurobjectics (As Voodoo Shrine); Mysterious Island* *
** see introduction*
Or
Humpty Dumpty, 2005
Site-specific mixed-media installation
Dimensions variable

Overleaf:

05 *Triple Bluff Canyon*, 2004
Site-specific mixed-media installation
Dimensions variable

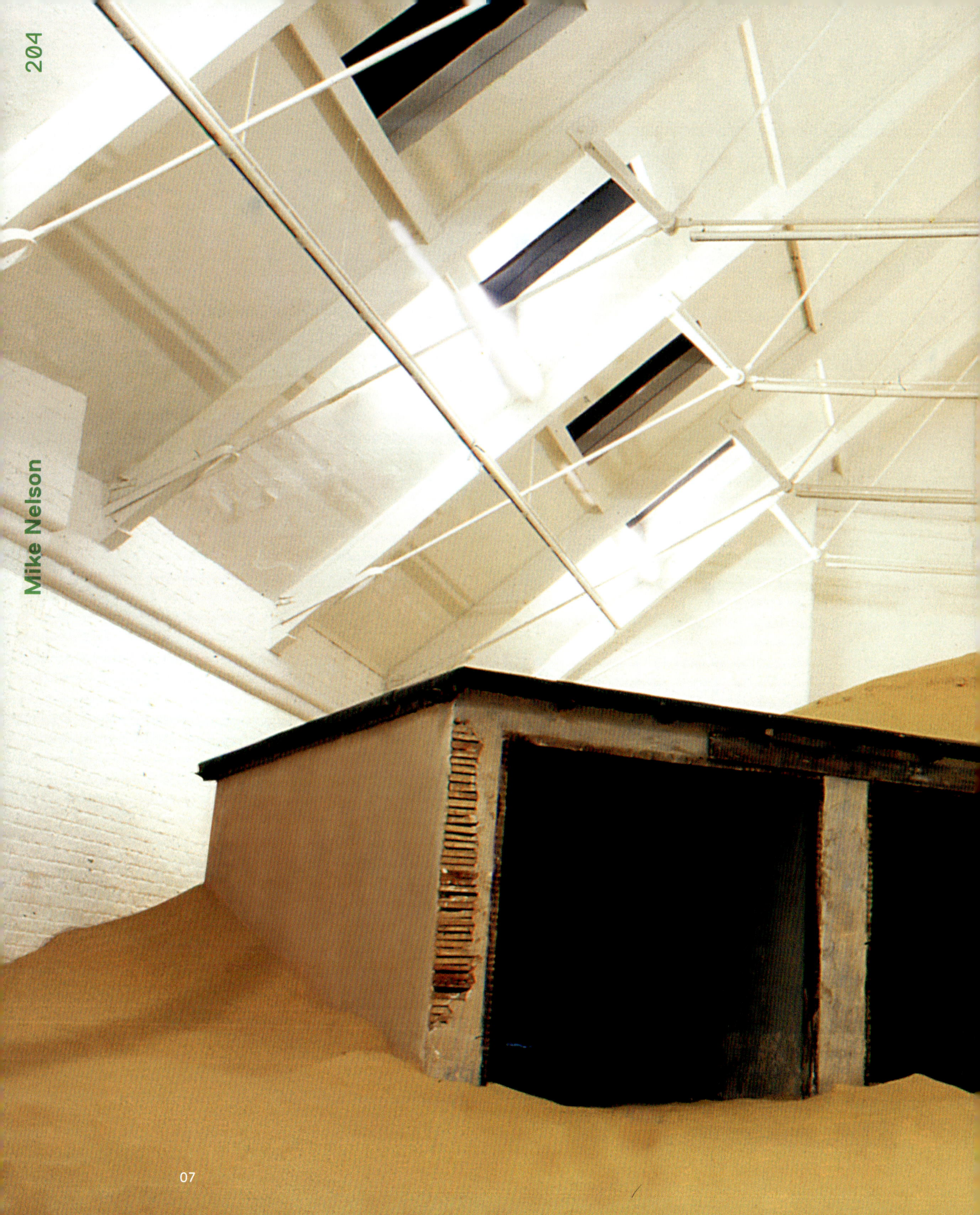

07

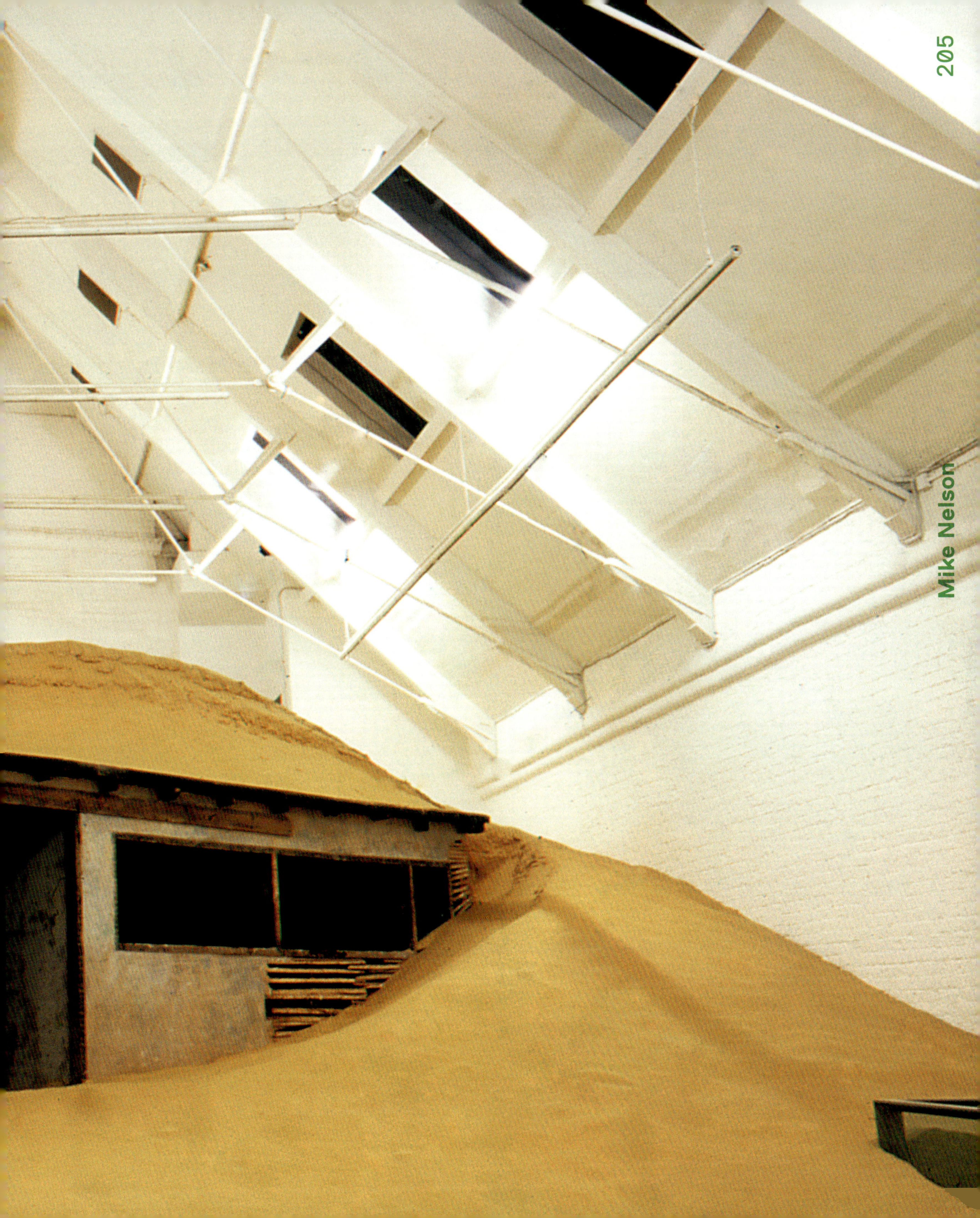

Ernesto Neto sculptures and installations are at once formal and interactive, abstract and figurative, full of bodily and geometric references, wishing to please and stimulate the mind and the senses. Neto started to work with what became his signature material in the late 1980s — women's stockings made of polyamide that were then filled with lead beads, an element that allowed the artist to experiment with an array of sculptural configurations. Through intelligent play with balance and weight, movement and rest, solidity and transparency, negative and positive space, these elements hung from the ceiling, crawled on the floor, rested on or penetrated one another, forming what the artist has called 'colonies' — in *Copulândia* (1989), for example.

Neto's sculpture developed in several ways, and in 1996, with the introduction of the sensual smells and earthy colours of different condiments and spices (such as annatto, cloves, curcuma and turmeric) into the now enlarged Polyamide containers, the work became multi-sensorial, gaining onomatopoeic titles such as *Piff, Paff, Puff* (1997). In the following year, the Polyamide material was further stretched and expanded to become room size, and the sculptural unfolded into the architectural. *Nave Deusa* (Goddess Ship), exhibited at the 1998 São Paulo Biennial, is one of the first examples of a series of *Naves* (Ships). Spectators could now enter the sculpture, touch its skin, poke their fingers through its orifices and smell the condiments that filled its uvulas.

The references go beyond the body, reaching out to physics, mathematics, geometry, biology and chemistry. Neto's use of the curve and the line, which appear in his sculptures and his drawings, depart from a very particular approach to geometry (one may think of Brazilian Oscar Niemeyer's curvaceous modernist architecture in a similar way). Fusion (of bodies, atoms, cells) is another distinct concept, and it becomes evident in one of Neto's most radical works, *O Casamento — Lili, Neto, Lito e os Loucos* (The Wedding — Lili, Neto, Lito and the mad ones, 2000). Neto's wedding with Lili, who was pregnant with their first son Lito (the name itself fuses those of the couple), was celebrated inside a giant Nave at the Museu de Arte Moderna in Rio de Janeiro, bringing together art and life — something that had been championed by mid-century Brazilian Neoconcrete artists Lygia Clark and Hélio Oiticica, to which Neto's work is deeply indebted.

Since then, Neto's Naves have hosted parties, have been taken to the desert, and have become increasingly complex environments, such as in *The Malmö Experience* (2006), some of them articulating labyrinthine sections, tunnels and rooms within which the spectator can walk, sit, lie or rest. On the other hand, the artist's installations can radically transform a pre-existing architecture while also incorporating it, as in the monumental *Léviathan Thot* (2006). One of Neto's most striking works, it was installed at the Panthéon in Paris, an eighteenth-century building originally constructed as a church. Referencing the biblical monster Leviathan, the work established a mesmerizing dialogue with neo-classical architecture, in which Neto's translucent materials hung and fell on many different levels as they bore the weight of white Styrofoam balls, delicately occupying the entire gargantuan space. Here, the colonies became a giant but gentle monster. [Adriano Pedrosa]

01

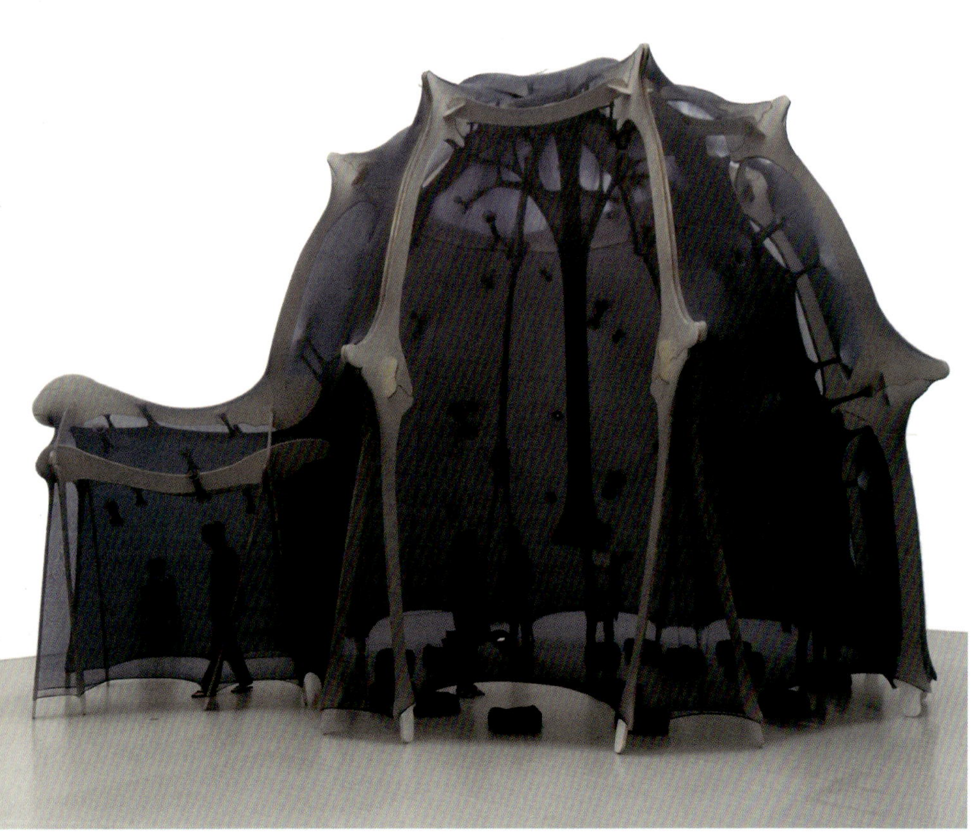

01 *Our mist into the myth*, 2008
Polyamide tulle, wood, turmeric and clove curry
6.5 × 7 × 9.3 m

02 *Leviathan Thot*, 2006
Elastane tulle, Styrofoam balls
Dimensions variable
Panthéon, Paris

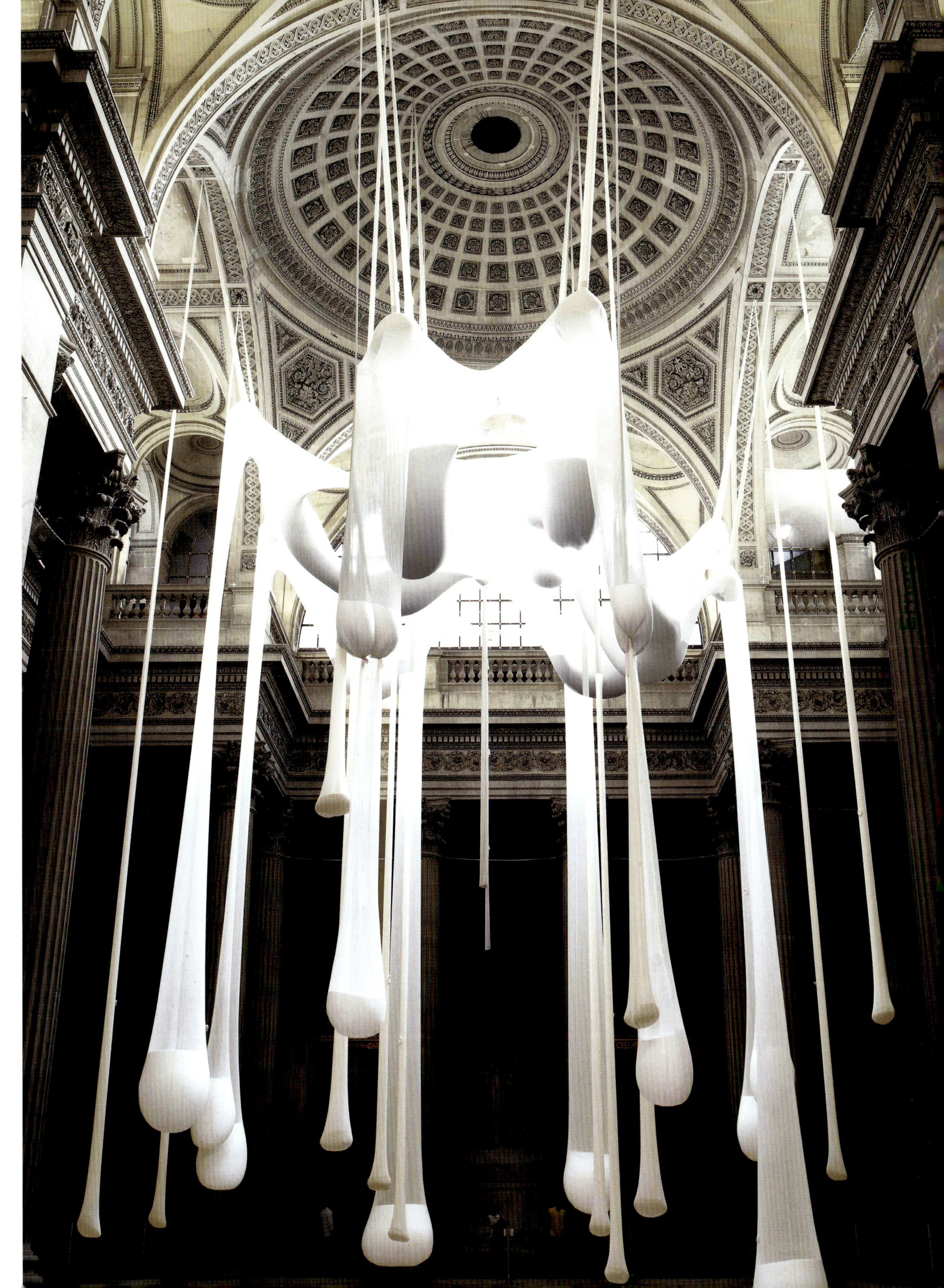

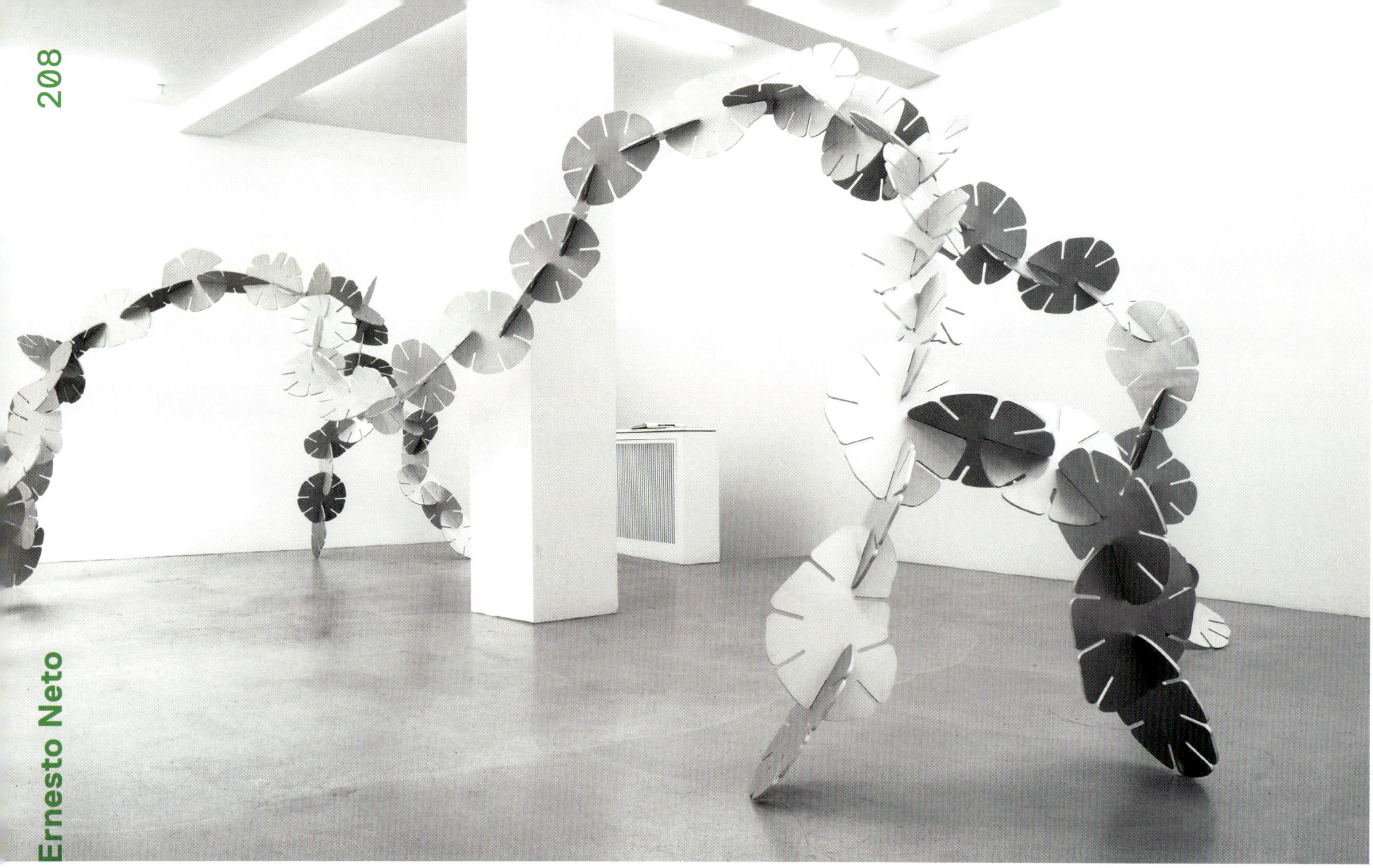

03

04

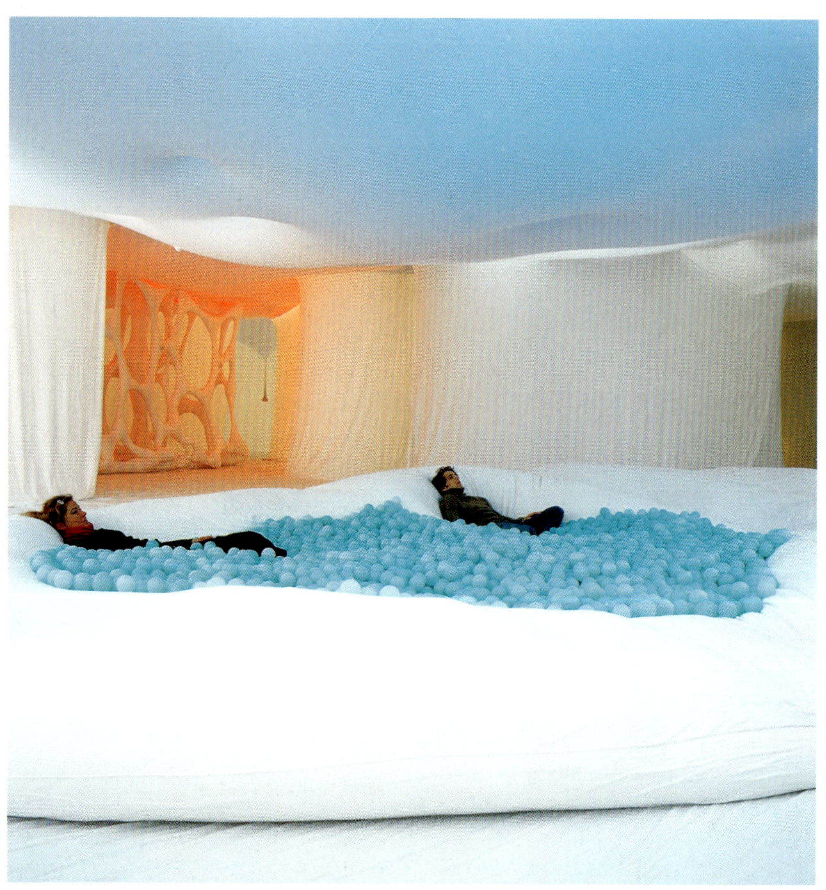

03 *Just... tick tack, bending the narrative*, 2008
88 interlocking aluminium panels
218 × 410 × 640 cm

04, 05 *The Creature, The Malmö Experience*, 2006
Cotton textile, polyamide tulle, polyamide stockings, cotton cloth, polyurethane foam, plastic pipes (bones), sand, polypropylene, glass beads, plastic spheres, polystyrene pellet, turmeric, clove, lavender, cumin, black pepper
3.5 × 65 × 23 m

05

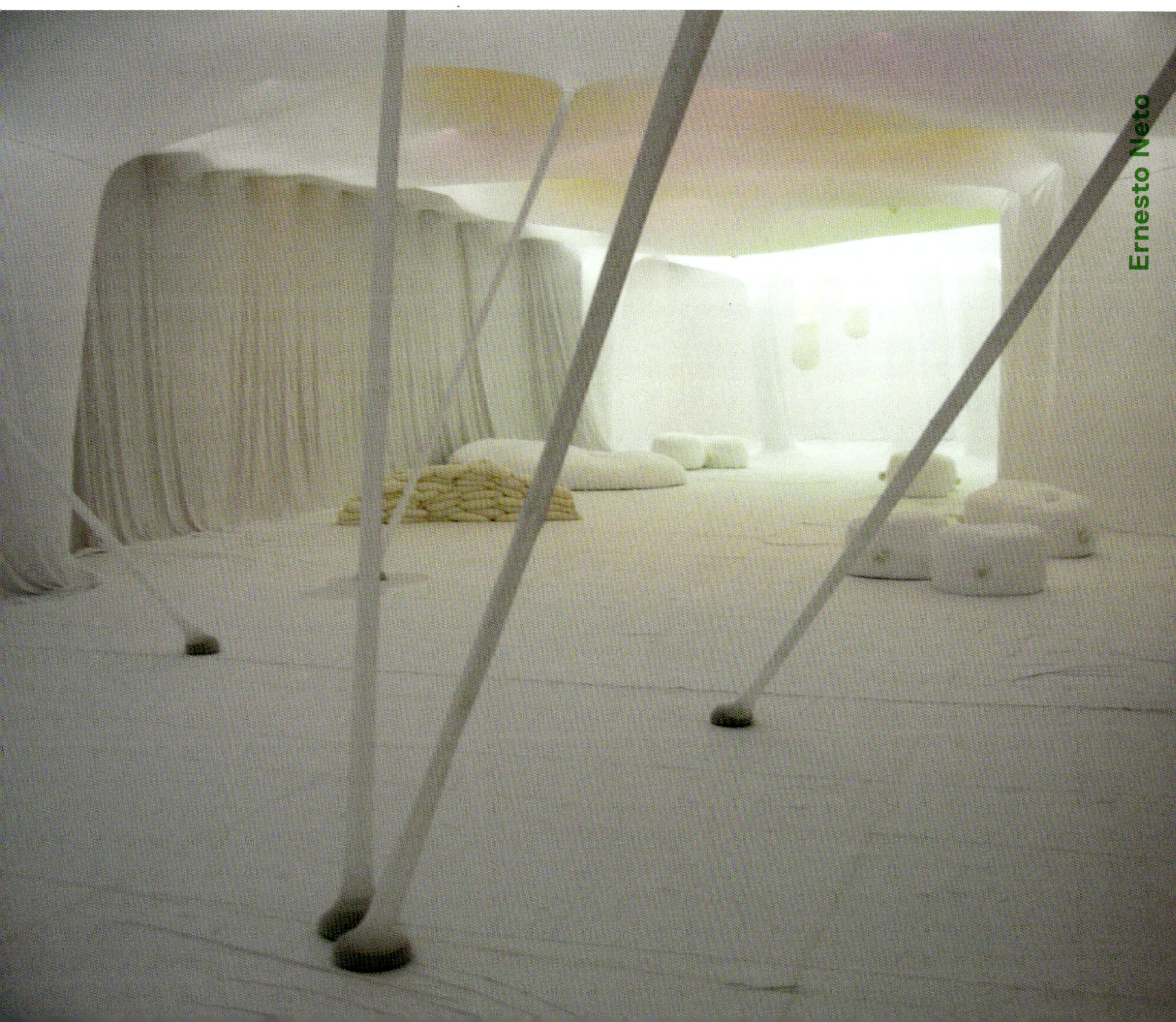

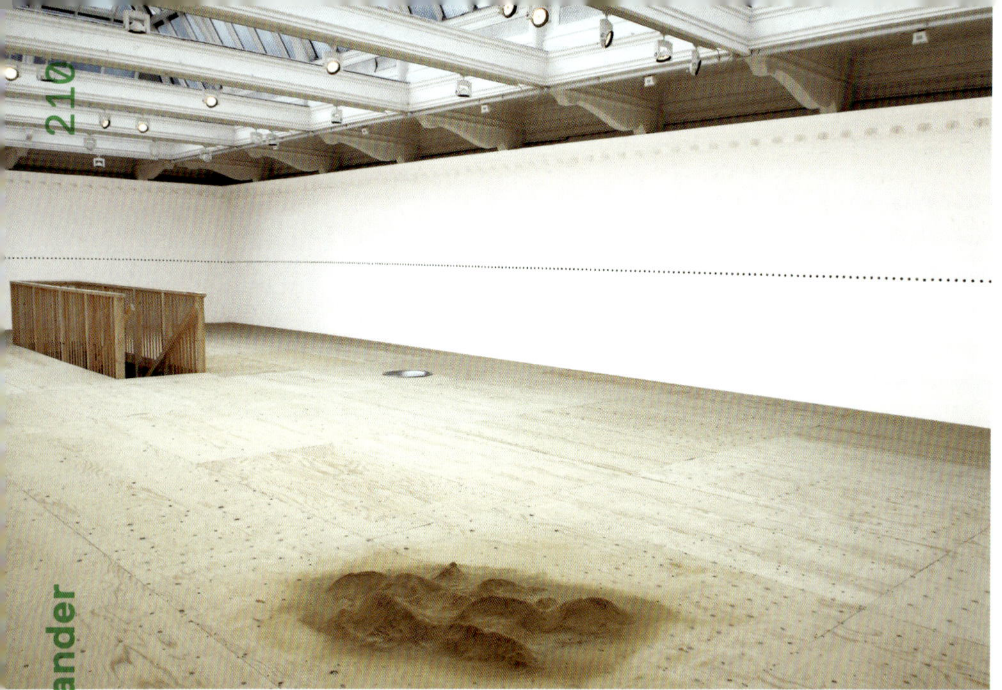

01 Rivane Neuenschwander's films, photographs, drawings, paintings and objects often attempt to discover poetic configurations of different systems, codes and orders. Thus her work is filled with calendars, maps, globes, numbers, alphabets, letters, recipes and measures that are interwoven with organic or bodily elements — peeled oranges, crawling ants, pouring rain — that seemingly contradict systemic codes.

Scrabble (2001), for example, is a room-size installation made up of cardboard boxes constructed to resemble architectural floor plans, filled with dehydrated oranges into whose skins letters were peeled. Exhibited at Portikus in Frankfurt, two sets of Scrabble in Portuguese (the artist's native language) and two in German were on display. A related installation, *Uma ou outra palavra cruzada* (One or Another Crossword Puzzle, 2007), takes the crossword puzzle (in the original Portuguese 'crossed words') quite literally: Portuguese sentences appropriated from street advertisements were suspended from the ceiling and crossed each other in mid-air.

Suspension is a recurring strategy. *Chove Chuva* (Rain Rains, 2002), exhibited at Museu de Arte da Pampulha in the artist's native Belo Horizonte, consists of a set of pierced aluminium buckets, hanging at different levels, through which drops of water 'rained' into other buckets positioned below. The work could represent the typical leaky roof of an under-funded museum, a situation not uncommon in Brazil. Its laborious maintenance throughout the exhibition, carried out by a member of the museum staff who from time to time would pour the contents of the floor buckets back into those hanging from the ceiling, gave the work a performative quality.

Esculturas Involuntárias (atos de fala) (Involuntary Sculptures [Speech Acts], 2001–03) represents a more focused investigation into sculpture. The work consists of a collection of small, handmade objects constructed by people during conversations in bars and restaurants. Here, the artist brings in her concern with language, as if these fragile and over-manipulated objets trouvés somehow represented the conversations (or 'speech acts') they witnessed. The work gives aesthetic significance to otherwise unassuming sculptural doodles and reveals Neuenschwander's interest in the output of non-artists, something that also comes up in *Ici là-bas aqui acolá* (an untranslatable and onomatopoeic conflation of French and Portuguese expressions for places, 2002).

'Suspension Point' (2008), Neuenschwander's exhibition at the South London Gallery, represents her tour de force. For this poetic, conceptual and formal articulation between sculpture, film, literature and narrative, the artist created another floor in the Victorian exhibition space, dividing the gallery's vast height into two. In this new architectural configuration, the viewer entered the gallery through a dark space in which, among other works, *Arabian Moons* was being projected. This sixteen millimetre film is made up of 1,001 frames that have been literally punched through the celluloid, thus projecting and magnifying uneven discs of light on to the wall, and calling attention to the material aspect of film. The title references the classic literary text *A Thousand and One Nights*, and its narrative unfolds as a palindrome — much like '1001' itself. On the upper, brightly lit floor, one encountered *Suspension Point*, in which the artist again divided the height horizontally through a series of holes drilled into the wall. Coming full circle, the dust produced by the drilling was used to create a delicate sculpture evoking mountains of sand — perhaps the background against which the narratives of 1,001 moonlit Arabian nights might have taken place. [Adriano Pedrosa]

02

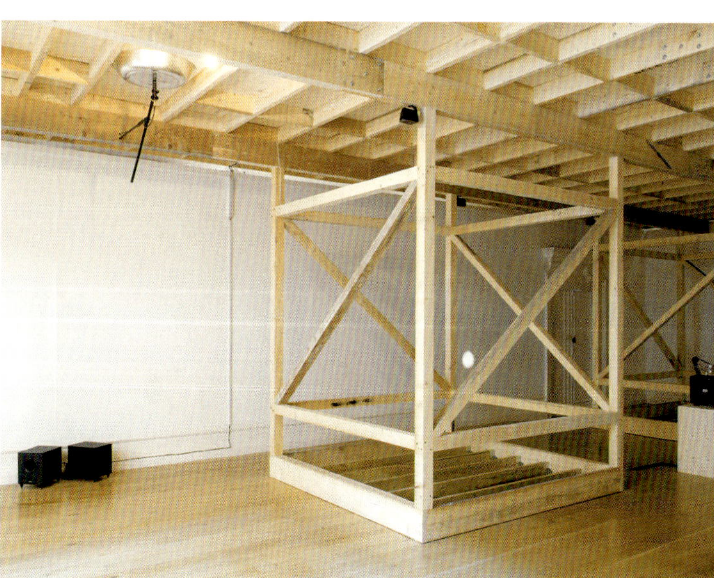

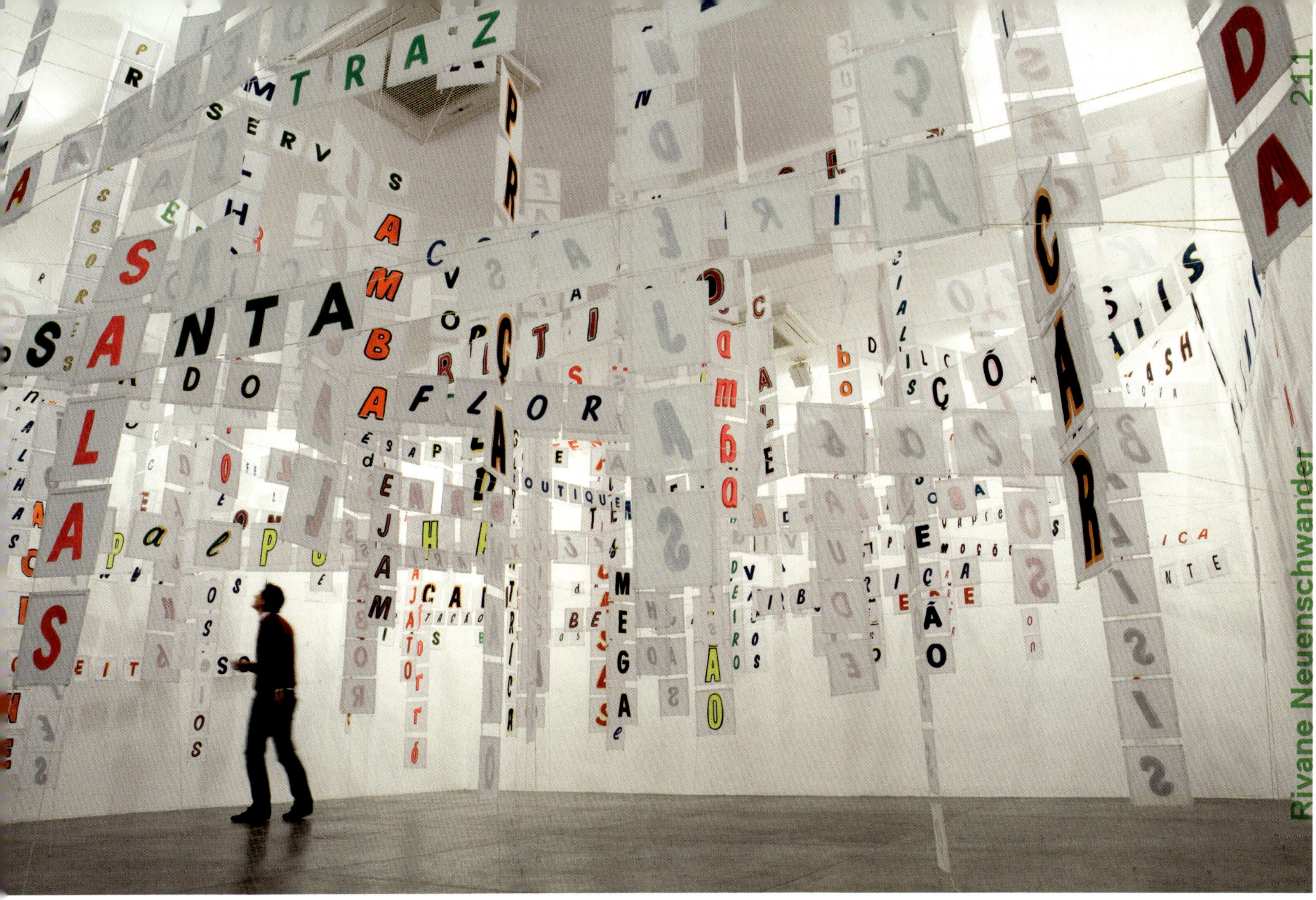

03

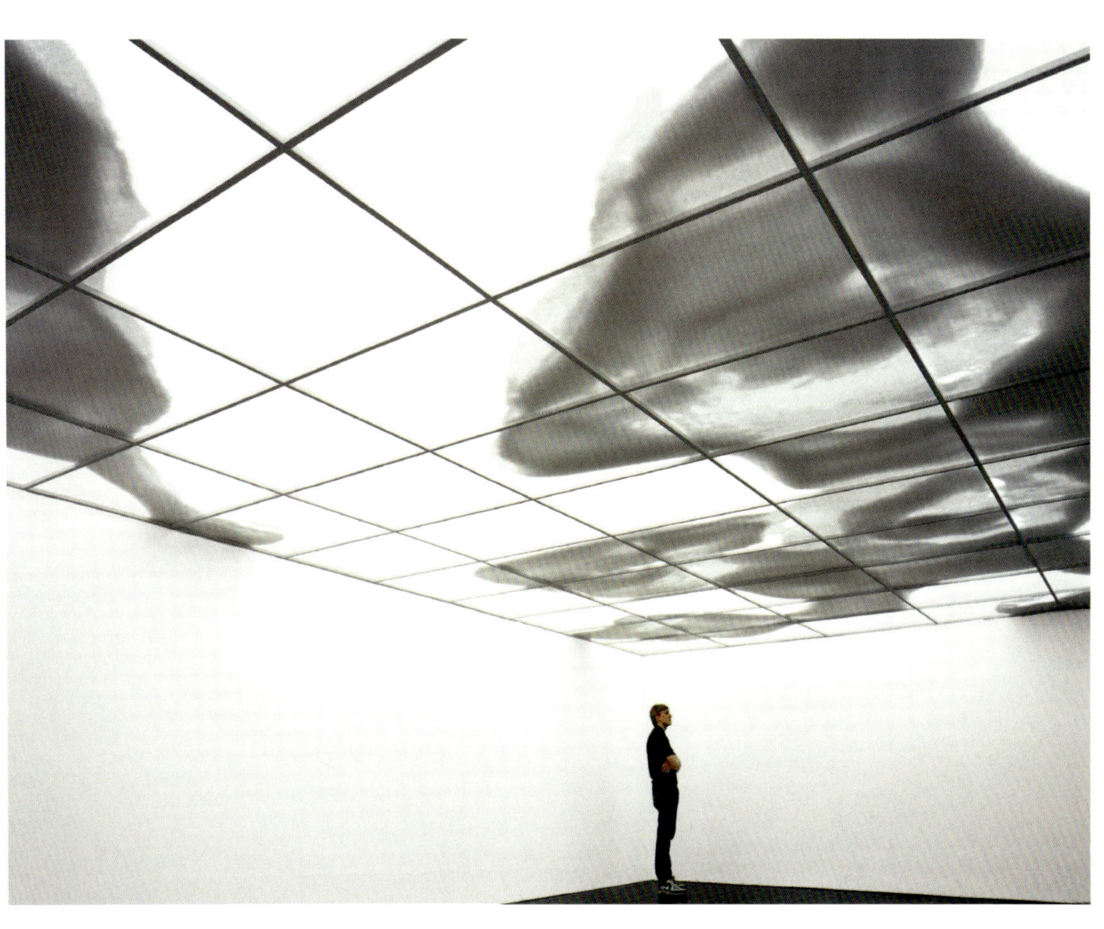

04

01 *Suspension Point*, 2008
Drilled holes, dust
Dimensions variable

02 from left:
→ *It's raining out there (Lá fora está chovendo)*
(with O Grivo), 2008
Aluminium basin, water
Dimensions variable
Audio loop, 18 min.
→ *Arabian moons*, 2008
Perforated 16mm film, projector
6 min. 20 sec. loop

03 *Uma ou outra palavra cruzada*
(One crossword or another), 2007
Reconfigured fabric street banners
Dimensions variable

04 *Continent-Cloud*, 2007
Correx, aluminium, Styrofoam
balls, fluorescent lighting,
electric fans, timers
Dimensions variable

In recent years, contemporary artists have exhibited a preoccupation with mobility by creating works that are meant to be experienced transitively, which are imbued with a sense of specific topology. This 'topographical impulse' refers less to an image of landscape than to the experience of its forms, such as moving through the spaces of an urban, post-industrial context. In Los Angeles-based Ruben Ochoa's particular brand of this mapping, the social dimensions of movement and boundary figure clearly: literally, as in *Class: C* (2001–02), for which he retrofitted his family's tortilla delivery van as a travelling art gallery, and more figuratively, as in his recent freeway project. In *Fwy Wall Extraction* (2006), Ochoa transferred what appeared to be a section of the freeway boundary wall to a gallery space and then seemingly replaced that same segment on the road with wallpaper simulations of the natural world obscured behind the concrete barrier. Visitors to the gallery soon discovered that the massive, Richard Serra-like form was an elaborate fake; as one moved 'backstage', it revealed its own construction, as did certain viewpoints of the wallpaper 'replacements' from passing cars. Ochoa's work, whether referencing the freeway boundary walls or the more conceptual barriers between neighbourhoods and communities, re-focuses attention on the socio-economic underpinnings of spatial flow and control.

Typically, Ochoa's projects have multiple, evolving incarnations: the extraction project gave rise to other recent works such as lenticular photographs (*What if walls created spaces*, 2007), depicting the freeway section that from one angle appears as a whole and banal view but from another dissolves into the same leafy flora as was pasted to the actual wall. In another piece that directly morphed from the project, *Remnants of a Fwy Wall Extracted / Wallpaper with the Sound of its Own Removal* (2006–08), Ochoa hangs the original vinyl paper that cloaked the concrete wall, accompanied by a recording of the sounds of its removal. Riffing on Robert Morris' 1961 work *Box with the Sound of its Own Making*, Ochoa again inserts a social / class dimension into the elite, hermetic project of art making by enfolding an idea of labour and industry within it. The images, scaled to the highway landscape, are monumental in the gallery space; however, their battered, curling surfaces mitigate against authoritarian objecthood. Hung close to but somewhat away from the wall, the scrolls of paper create a newly bounded space for the viewer to walk behind. The oppressive closeness of the corridor subtly evoked issues of power and control embedded in Ochoa's work.

Other recent works employ familiar urban materials to a similar end. Concrete and wooden pallets suggest stylized, broken sidewalks; chainlink fencing is employed for its references to protection / control, as well as for its stunning formal capacities; rebar — comprising the embedded structures that literally hold the city together — acts as a graceful minimalist gridwork of tree-like forms, melding nature and culture in a way both visually compelling and politically investigative.

The number of contemporary artists who, like Ochoa, mine American urban sprawl speaks to the metaphorical power of that subject, typically imbued with an insistence on finding interstitial spaces of transformation and resistance. In this way, the topographical impulse touches upon ongoing discussions of (and revisions to) the idea of site specificity, in which site has become a discursive space — the restive, in-between space of our contemporary moment. [Shamim M. Momin]

01

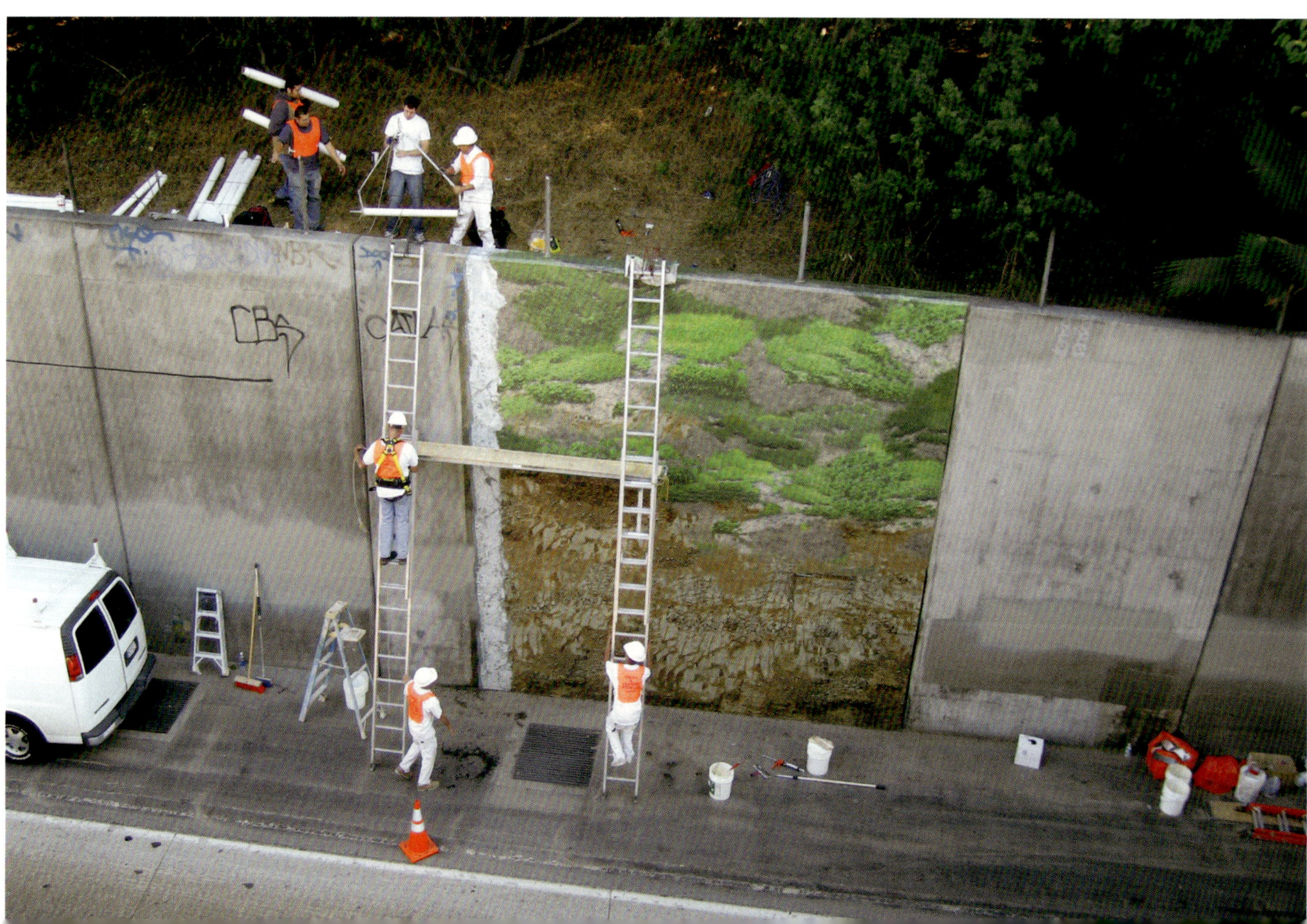

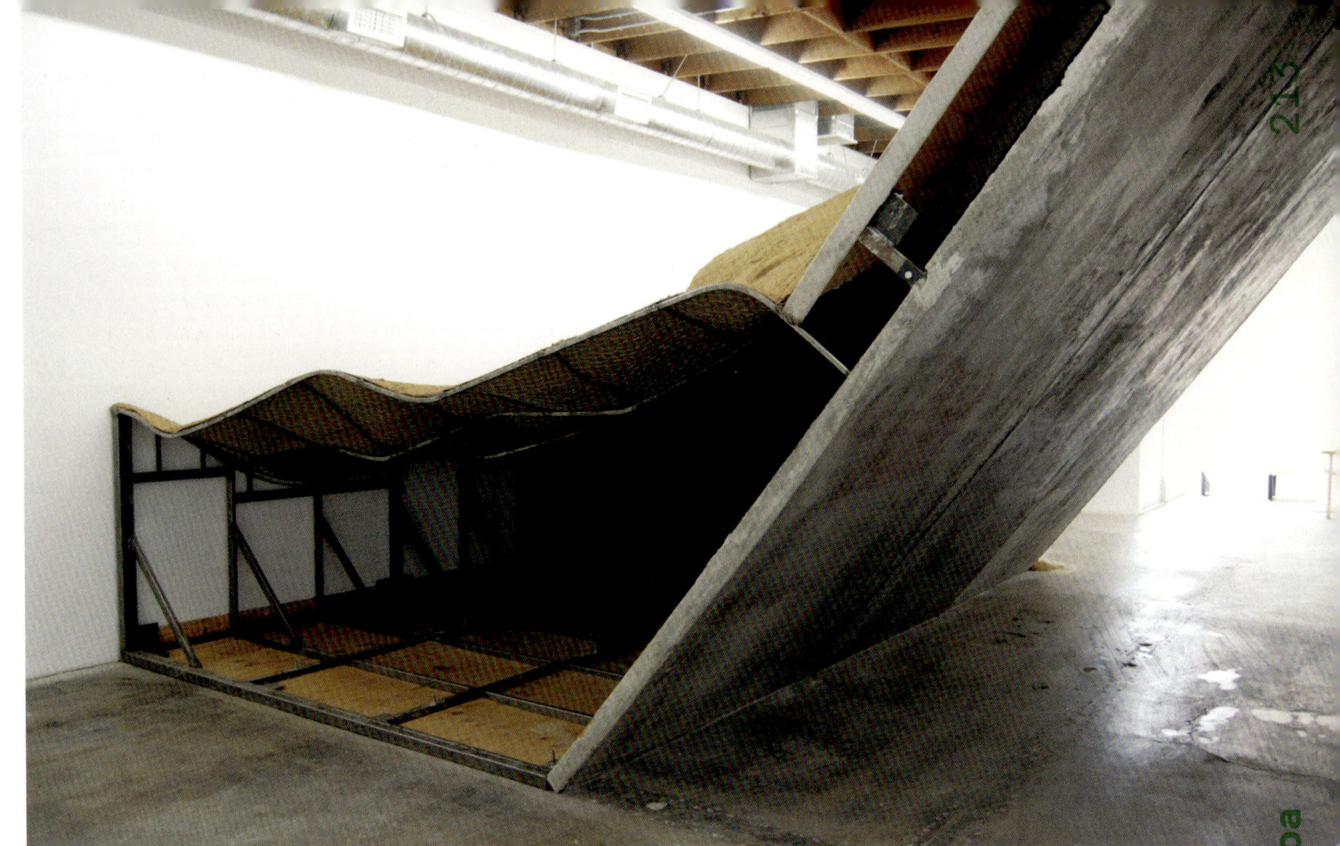

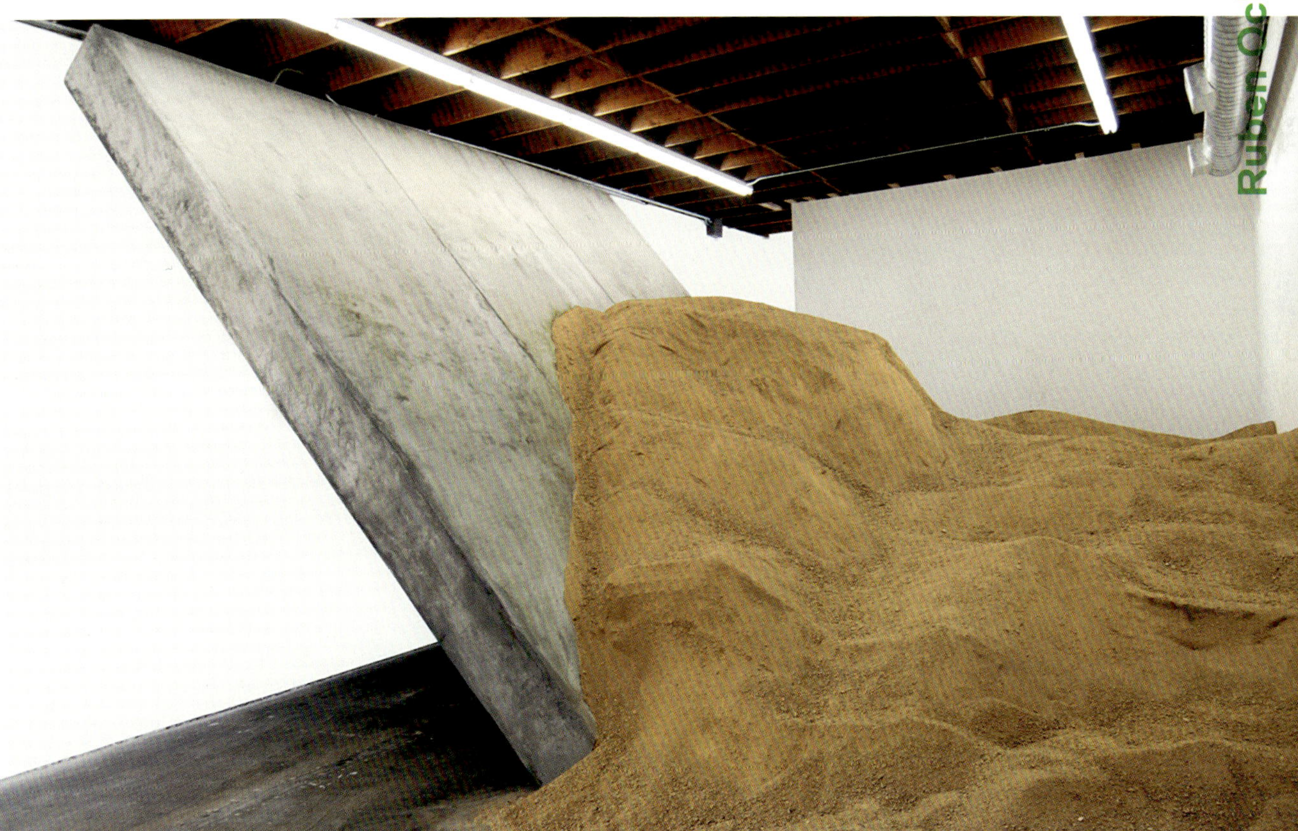

02

01 *Fwy Wall Extraction*, 2006
Site-specific installation
Interstate 10, Los Angeles
Dimensions variable

02 *Extracted*, 2006
Steel, wood, dirt, burlap,
wire mesh, EPS bonding cement
366 × 610 × 853 cm

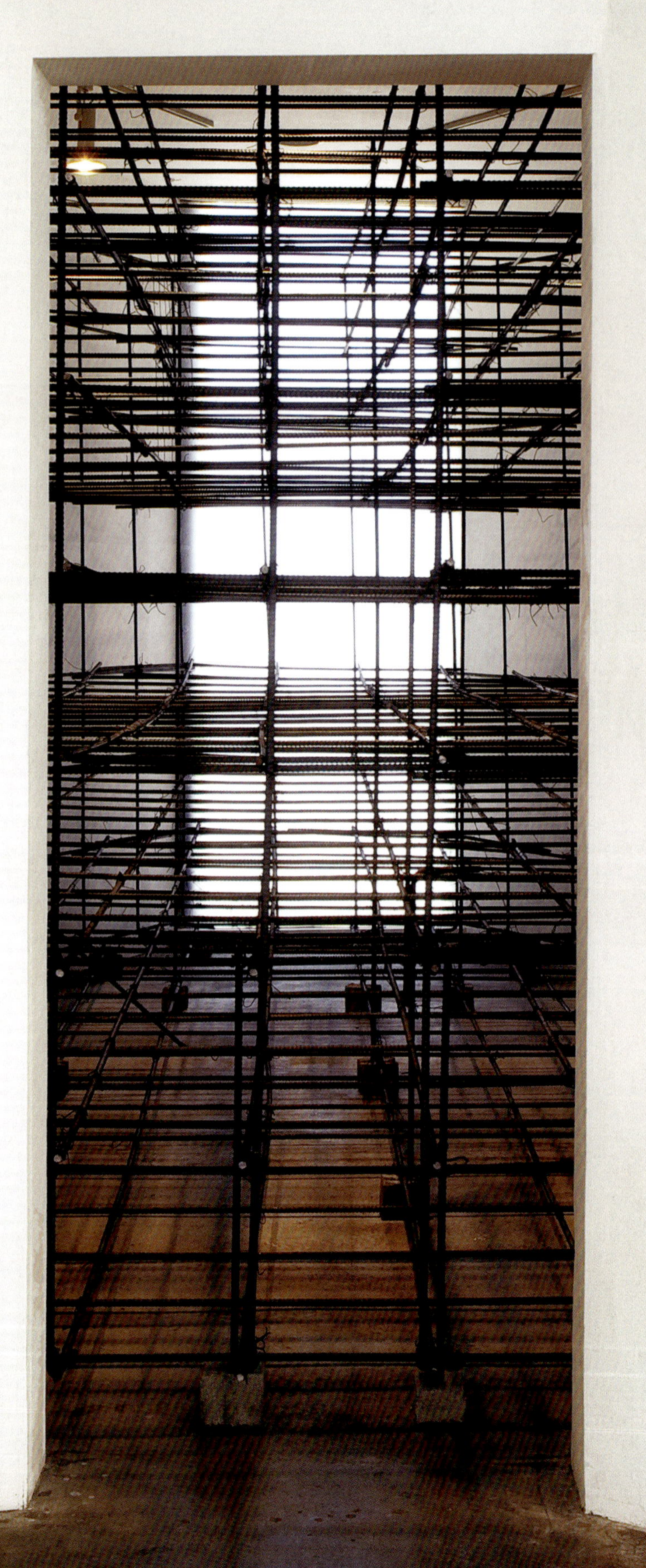

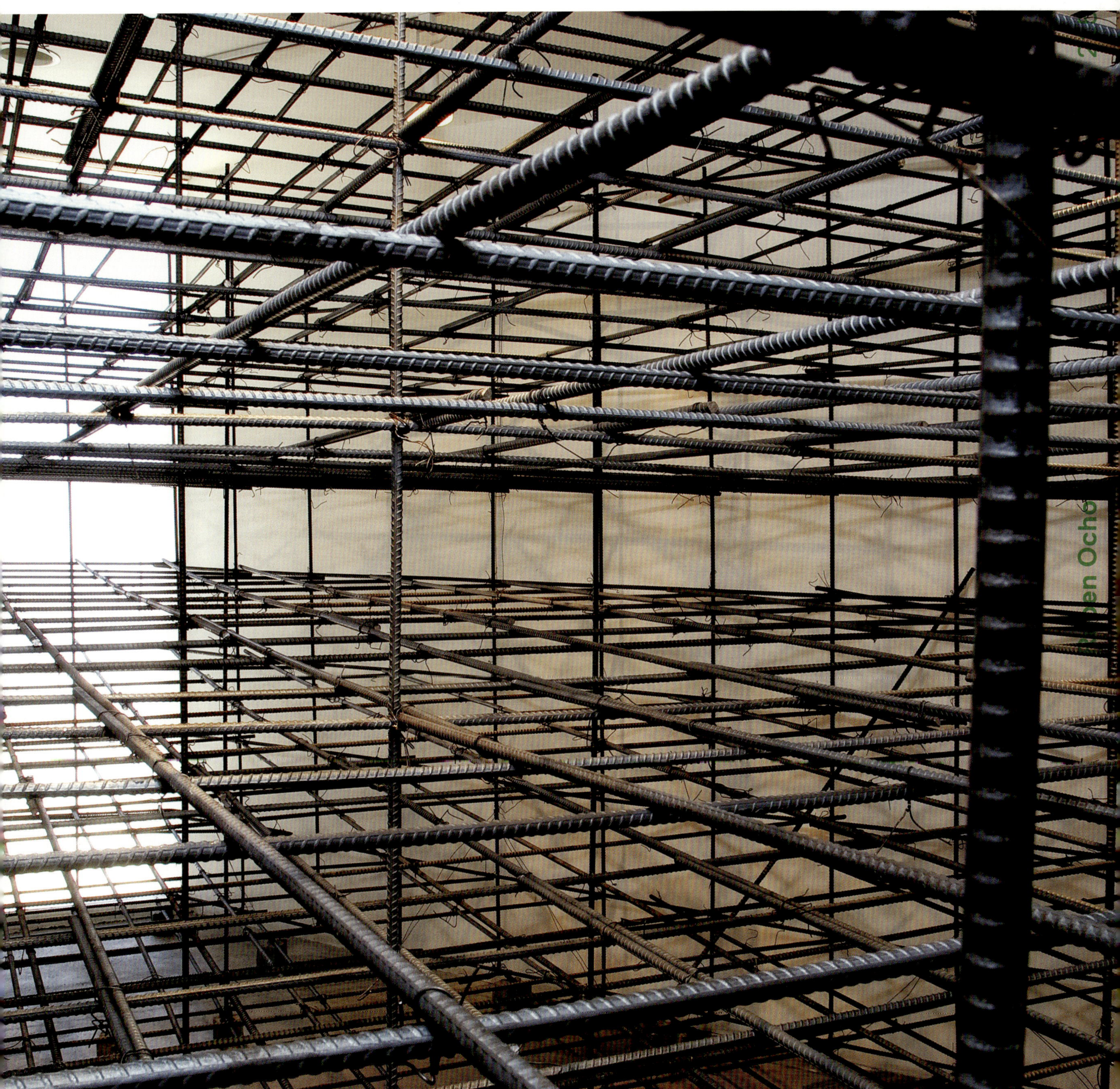

03

03 *If I had a rebar for every time someone tried to mould me*, 2007
Rebar, annealed wire ties, dobbie blocks
274 × 503 × 767 cm

The work of Damián Ortega is in many ways indebted to the Brazilian Neoconcrete movement, which in the late 1950s and early 1960s sought to infuse a free, experimental spirit into the rigid dogmas and abstract geometry of Concretism, reaching out to more subjective and expressive manifestations and, above all, life itself. Ortega's *Composición Concreta* (Concrete Composition, 2002) is a group of six photographs of different sections of concrete pavements that have been laid out and precariously patched up in geometric patterns of white, grey and brown. They contain very little of Concretism's rigidity and rigour in the geometry, and abstraction is an oblique reference — after all, there is nothing more figurative and impure than the dirty city streets portrayed here. In 2004–06, Ortega created a second group of works departing from these photographs; *Mampara — Composición concreta I–VI* (Screen — Concrete Composition I–VI), was made, not insignificantly, to be exhibited in São Paulo, the birth place of Brazilian Concretism. Each *Mampara* replicates the geometric design found in the pavement photographs, transforming them into folding concrete geometric screens that recall the sculpture of Neoconcrete artist Franz Weissmann.

Ordem Réplica e Acaso (Order, Replica and Chance, 2004) establishes similar plays between photography and sculpture, this time also connecting geometric abstraction with architecture. At the Museu de Arte da Pampulha, a former casino designed by Oscar Niemeyer in Belo Horizonte, Ortega created a series of twenty-four cubes, each made up of eight smaller articulated
01 cubes connected by metal hinges and together forming a 60 cm cube. The faces of the smaller cubes have the same bronze colour, reflective surface and dimensions as the mirrored tiles covering the museum's main wall. As in *Composición Concreta* and *Mampara*, Ortega submits a flat, real-life object to a process of abstraction in order to render it in three-dimensions. In appropriating Niemeyer, Ortega also references Lygia Clark, a Belo Horizonte native, and her famous series of *Bichos*, abstract geometric sculptures made up of articulated aluminium sheets joined by hinges. The photographic component of Ortegas work consists of a triptych (a module often used by Ortega) showing three possible configurations of all the twenty-four cubes in the space of the casino: a giant cube, a straight line duplicated in the mirrored wall and a sinuous Niemeyer-like line, respectively signifying order, replica and chance.

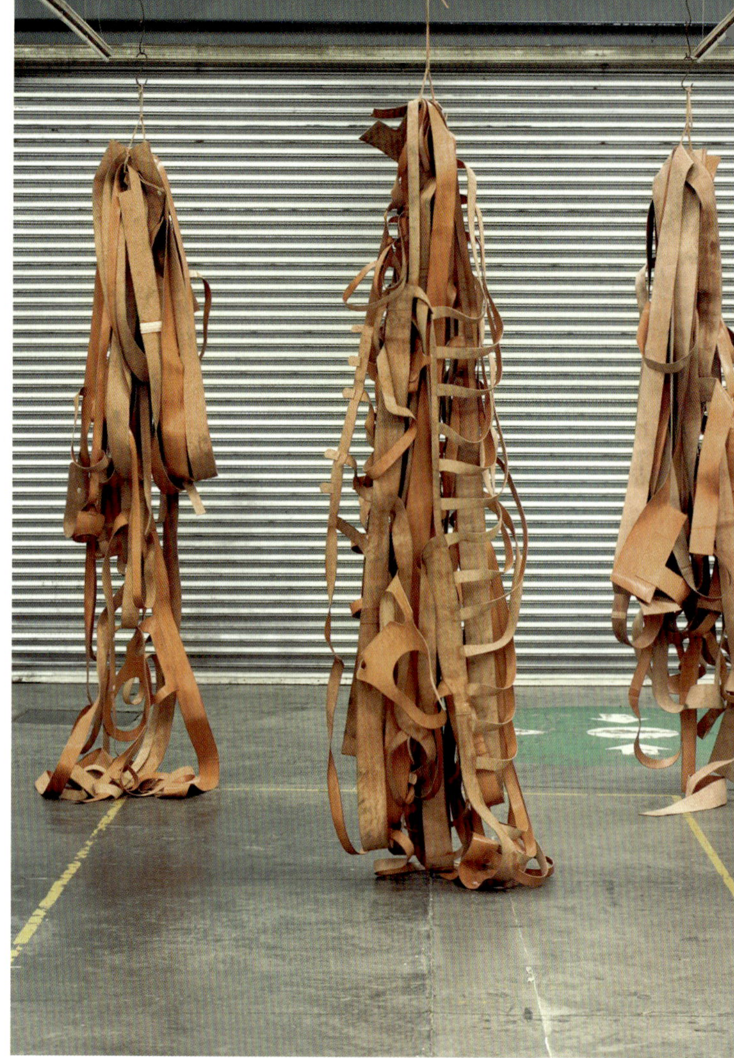

A similarly experimental approach to abstract geometry also informs Ortega's *Spiral of Violence* (2005). The work consists of a sixteen-panel window frame and its sixteen corresponding glass panels, all deconstructed and suspended in mid-air. Each glass panel has been marked by four intersecting horizontal, vertical and diagonal lines, the composition suggesting the British flag (a small sticker of the flag is found on one of the panels), which bear the traces of physical violence. One can consider this work an investigation into the possibilities of the smashed and transparent geometric plane, and in circling the suspended sculptural work one may be reminded of Hélio Oiticica's 1960 series *Relevos Espaciais* (Spatial Reliefs). The same sculptural suspension is found in other, more figurative works by Ortega, such as *Cosmic Thing* (2002) and *Miraculo Italiano* (2005). In *Spiral of Violence*, however, the geometric sculptural demonstration is imbued with violent, political tones, another lesson that Ortega may have learned from Oiticica. [Adriano Pedrosa]

01 *Piel-Skin, Centro Urbano Presidente Alemán C.U.P.A., 1950, Mario Pani, México D.F., L'Unité d'habitation à Berlin, 1956–58, Le Corbusier, Berlin, Germany, Przyczolek Grochowski Housing. L.C.S., 1963, Oskar Hansen, Warsaw, Poland*, 2007
Floor plan of three different apartments on natural cow leather strips, thread
Dimensions variable

02 *Ordem, Replica, Acaso (Order, Reply, Hazard)*, 2004
1 of 3 digital prints
Each 20 × 24 cm

03 *Spiral of Violence*, 2005
Glass, metallic window frame
Dimensions variable

04 *Cosmic thing*, 2002
Stainless steel, wire, 1983 Volkswagen Beetle, Plexiglas
Dimensions variable

Overleaf:

05 *Controller of the Universe*, 2007
Found tools, wire
285 × 405 × 455 cm

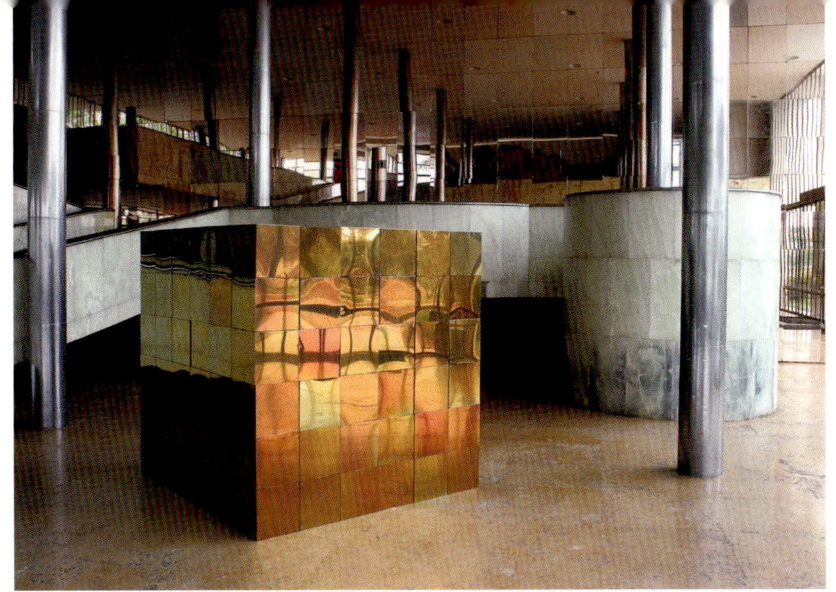

02

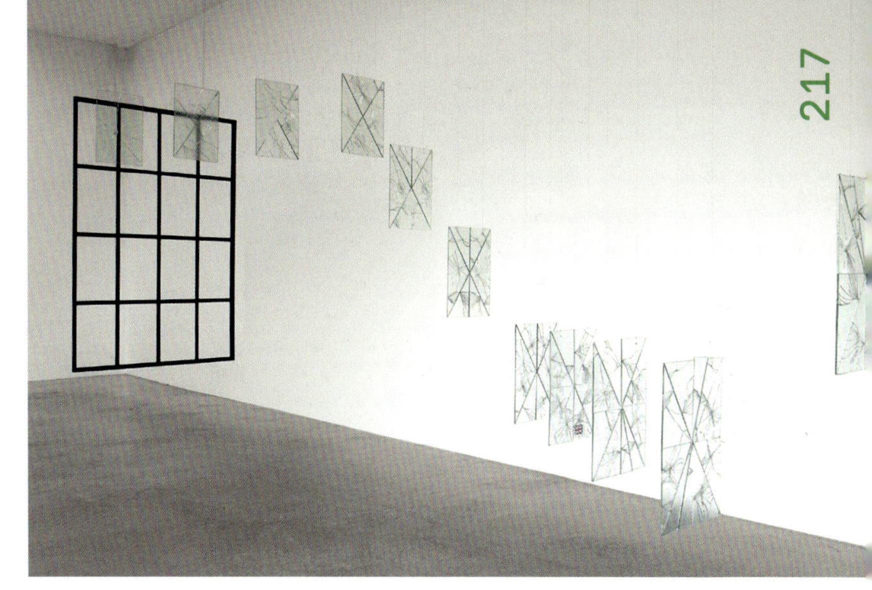

03

04

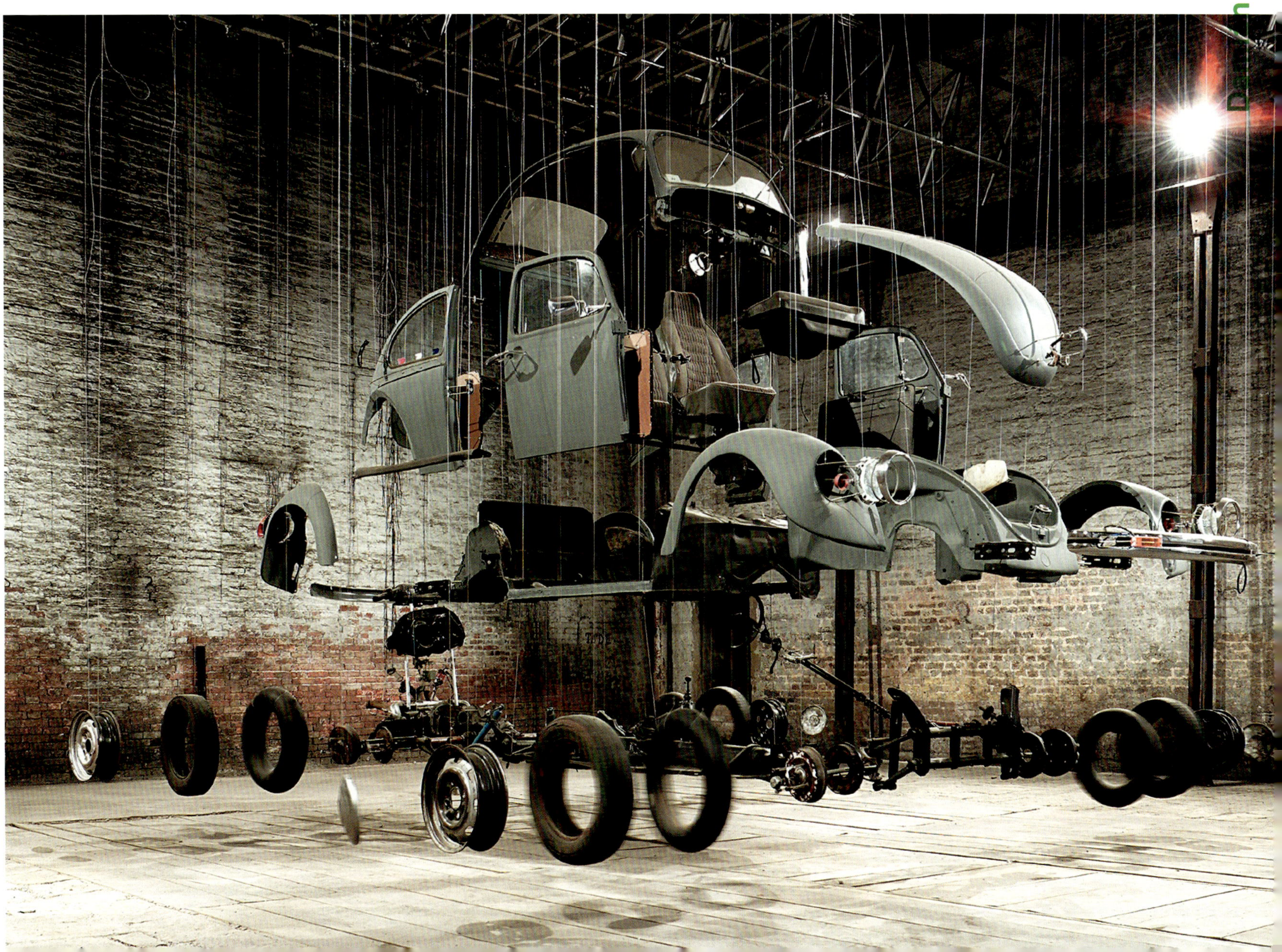

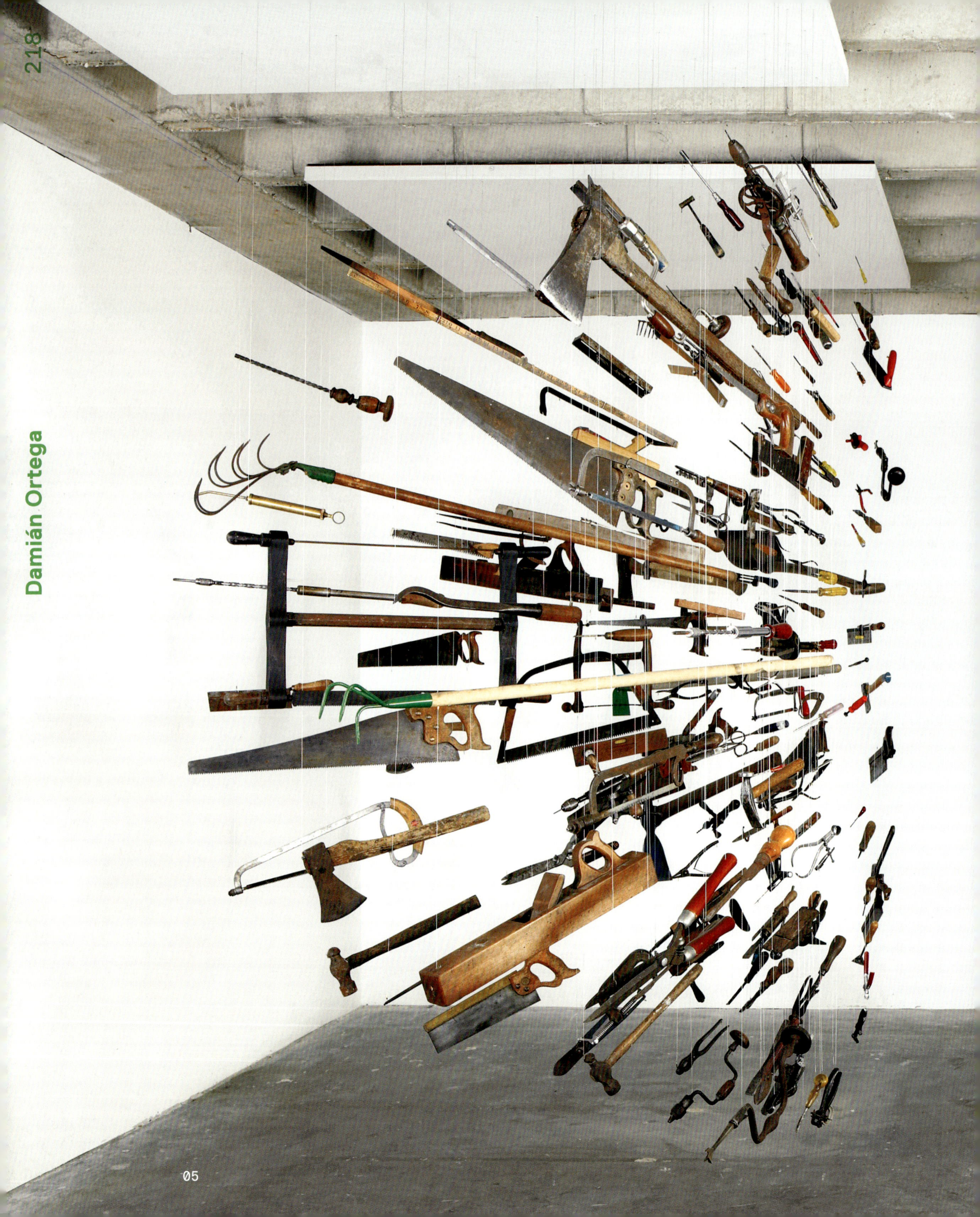

05

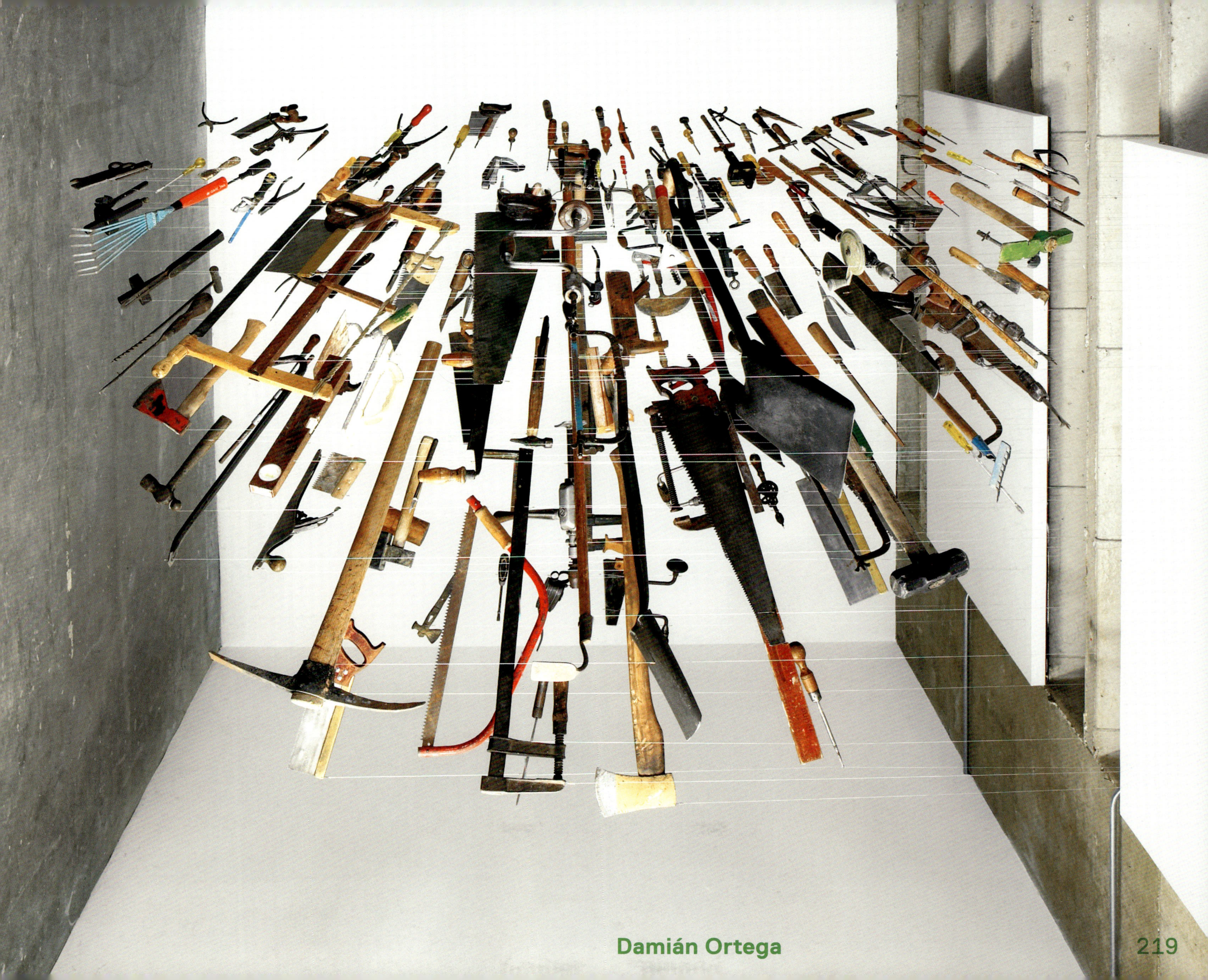

It is perhaps not surprising to discover that the West Coast sculptor Mitzi Pederson considers her works 'spatial drawings'; many of the finished three-dimensional works retain the lightness and ephemerality, the precarious 'barely-there' impression, of graphite on paper. Pederson's use of cellophane, plastic, sand and strips of wood reiterates in three dimensions the wash on paper, shading and linear mark-making that we tend to associate with drawing rather than sculpture. Although she is idiosyncratic in her language, one can identify the influence of an artist such as Richard Tuttle in her subtle combinations of carefully balanced forms; they have the same quality as his 'drawing in space'. *Sometimes when* (2007), for example, consists of two lines in space. The arched forms created out of wood mysteriously float, almost but not quite touching the ceiling and each other. Just as we follow the 'hand' when examining a drawing, when we look at Pederson's sculpture our eyes are drawn to track the arc of the two forms, tracing both the work and the dimensions of the space around it. *Sometimes when* is a typically minimal work with maximal effect.

The effect of light and shadow is no less important than the material aspect of Pederson's work. *Untitled (10 years later or maybe just one)* (2005) is one of a number of works that the artist has made from broken pieces of cinder block. Arranged in grid form, the pieces retain at least one right angle , which is such that once piled in the three-dimensional grid form they take on the attributes of architecture. Shadows pass through the gaps and spaces between the blocks like the play of light between buildings in a city: a New York skyline in semi-ruin. It is as if the cinder-block floor has risen up from the ground to form a new cityscape.

Untitled (ten years later or maybe just one) is perhaps less typical of Pederson's work in its fairly substantial materiality. In general her sculptures function through a process of subtly alerting the viewer to what might otherwise remain overlooked. The artist says, 'In my work I practice aspects of reconsideration. I'm interested in highlighting mistakes or changes and bringing attention to that which goes unnoticed.' Works such as *inflexicon* (2007) rely on viewers' movement around the work, their shadows and reflections incorporated as distorted forms into the sculpture. Similarly responding to the viewer's presence and enhancing the changeable, kinetic aspect of the work is the manner in which *sometimes when* floats and moves in the air as the spectator walks around it. During this process, light filters through, everyday materials are transformed into translucent beauty, and one begins to understand the 'reconsideration' of which the artist speaks.
[Jens Hoffmann]

01 *yellow and orange*, 2008
Cinder blocks, wood, glitter, glue, cellophane, aluminium tape
163 × 183 × 203 cm

02 *sometimes when*, 2007
Silver leaf, glitter, glue, wood
Dimensions variable

03 *Untitled*, 2008
Concrete, ribbon
101 × 500 × 91 cm

04 *Untitled*, 2006
Wood, acrylic, silver leaf, paint
Dimensions variable

05 *Untitled (ten years later or maybe just one)*, 2005
Cinder blocks, glitter, glue
Dimensions variable

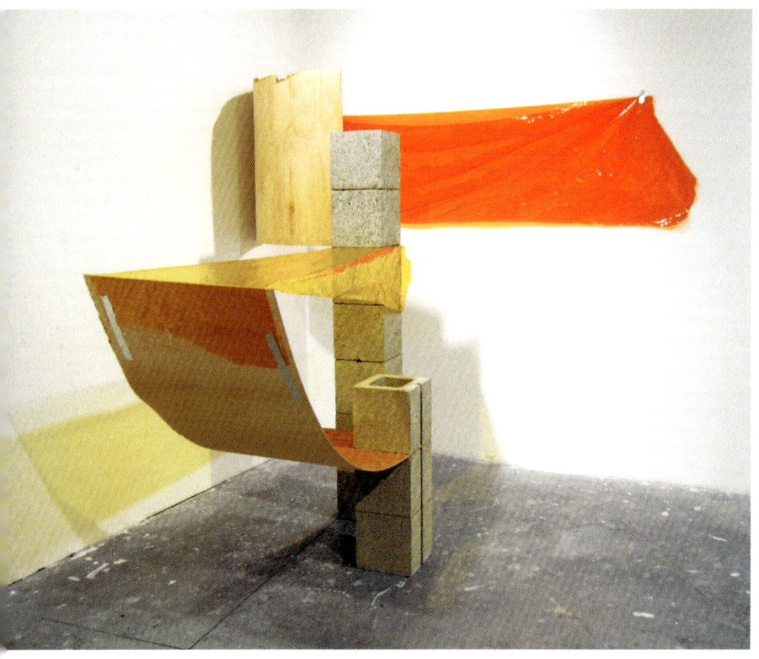

01

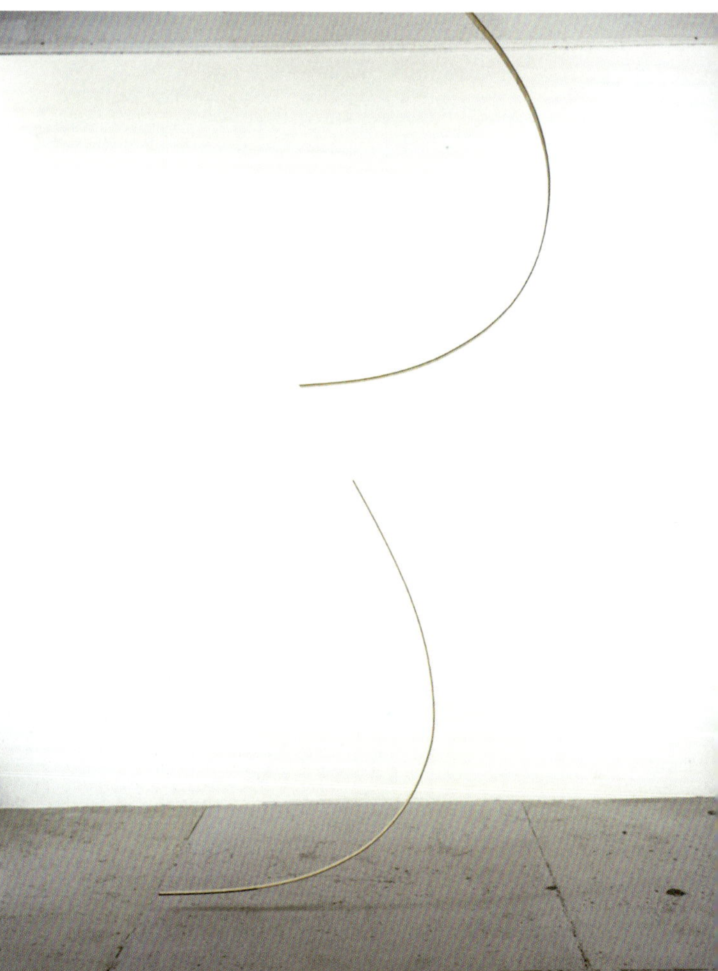

02

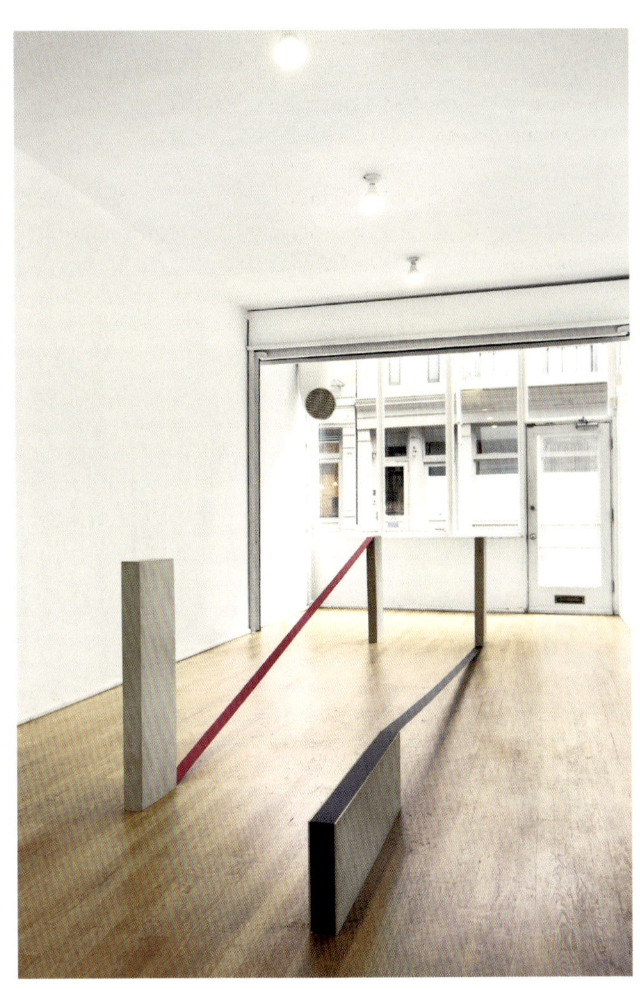

03

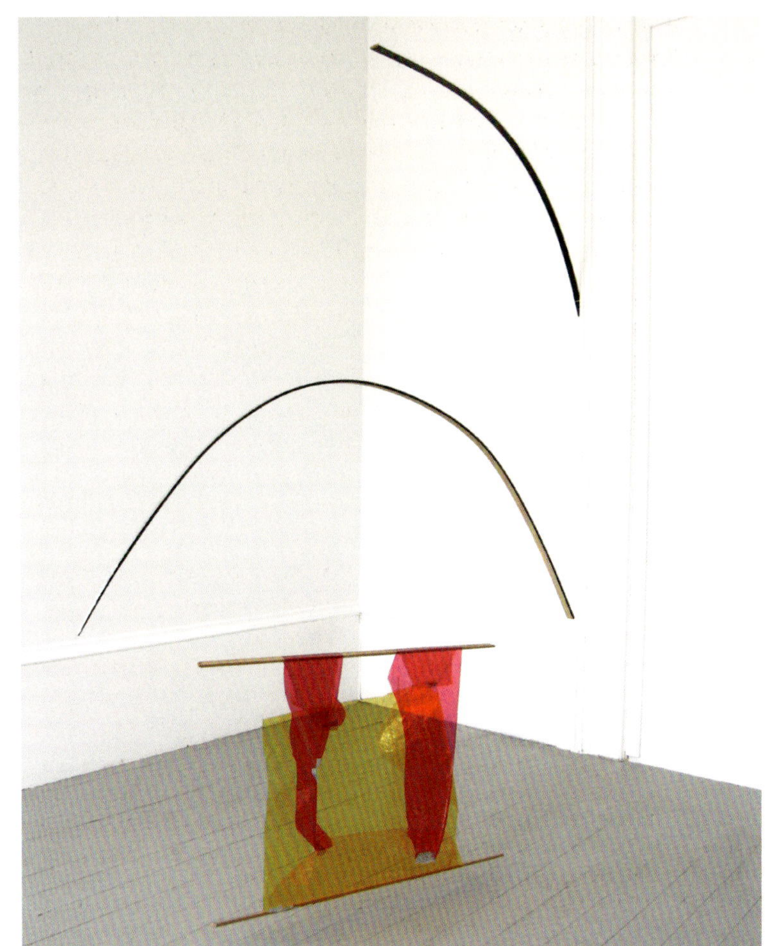

04

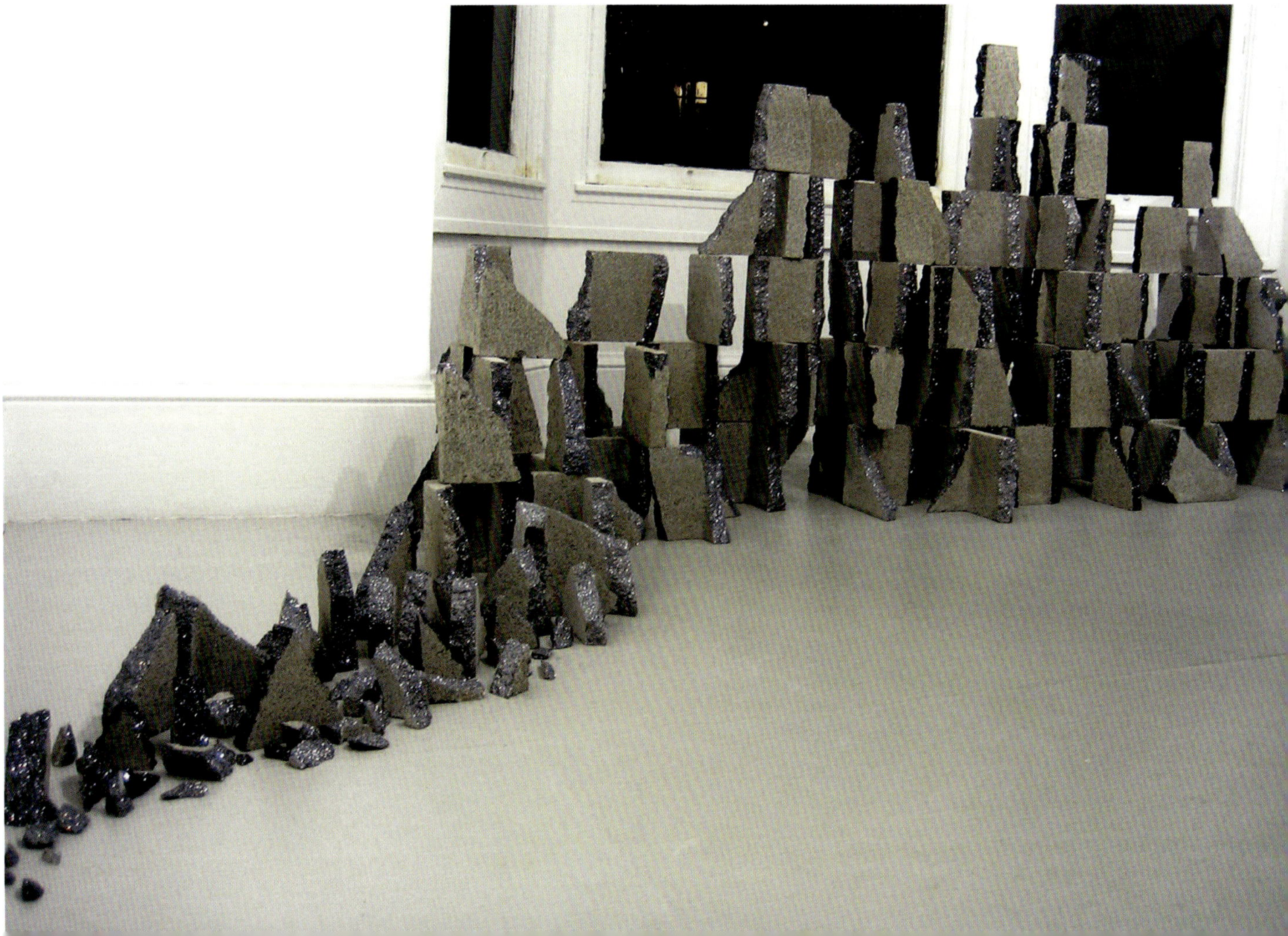

05

06 Front left:
→ *Untitled*, 2008
Wood, silver leaf,
sand, string, sequins
348 × 343 × 38 cm
→ *Untitled*, 2008
Wood, silver leaf,
sand, string
300 × 30 × 59 cm
→ *Untitled*, 2008
Wood, silver leaf,
sand, string
351 × 46 × 219 cm
→ *Untitled*, 2008
Wood, silver leaf,
sand, nails
0.3 × 53 × 191 cm
→ *Untitled*, 2008
Wood, silver leaf,
sand, string
201 × 227 × 9 cm

07 *Untitled*, 2008
Wood, paint
94 × 32 × 15 cm

06

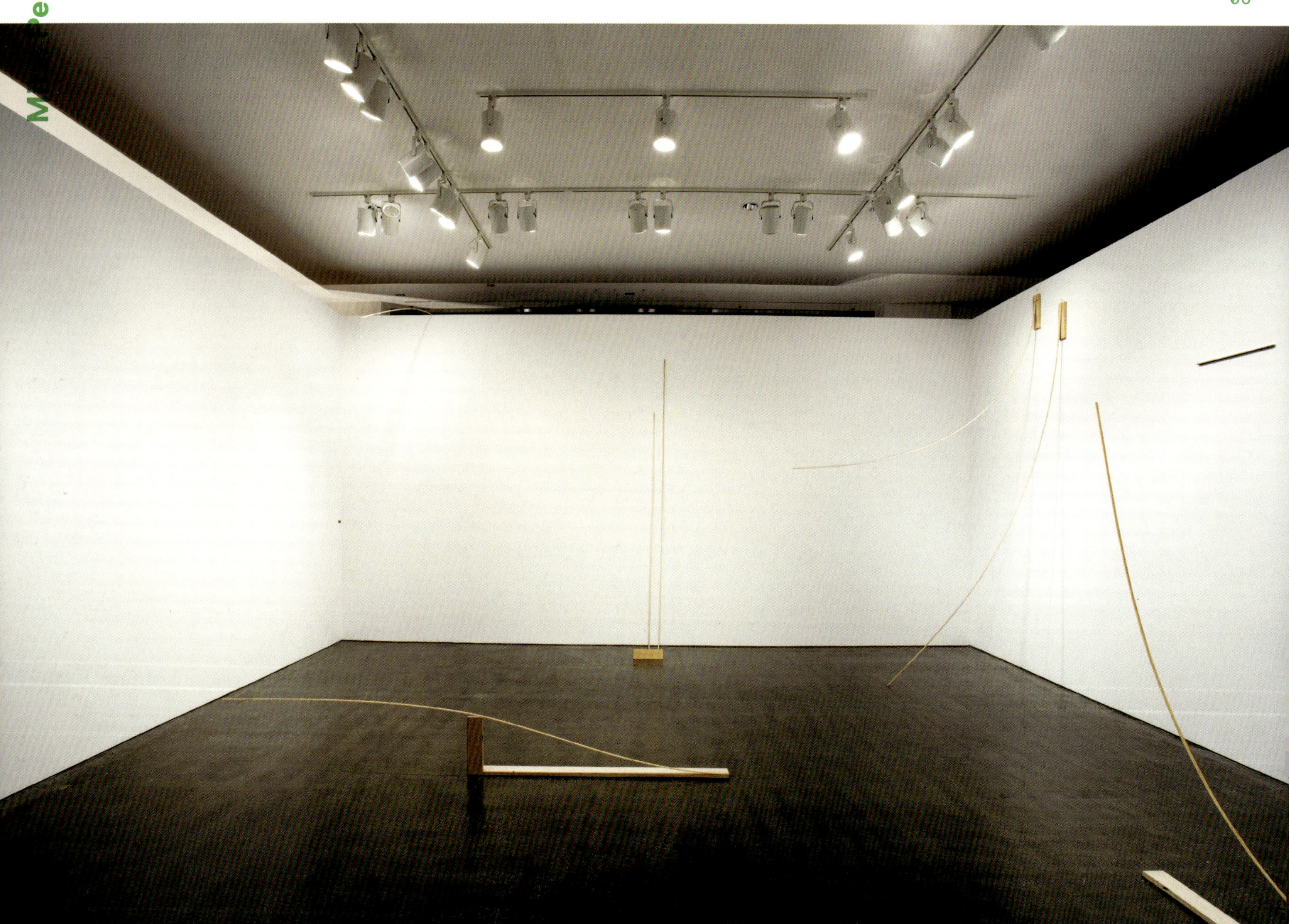

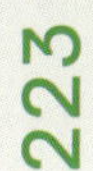

07

Mitzi Pederson

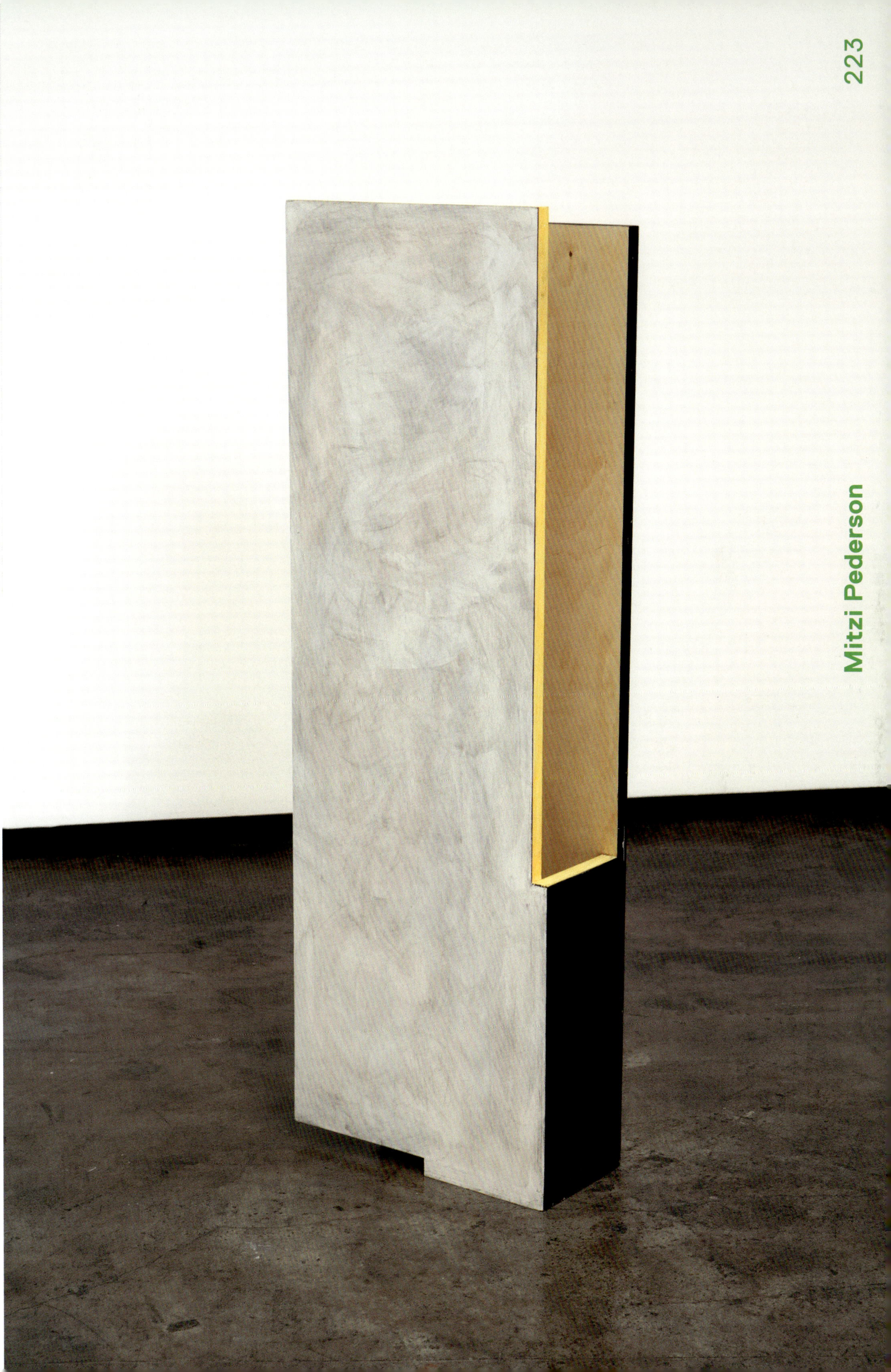

'Smash mechanical clocks, automated recordings, assembly lines, the object dejection of a grey morning in the city when you wake up depressed and pre-menstrual.' (Mai-Thu Perret, 'Some Notes on Time', in *The Crystal Frontier*, 1999–present)

Imagine dropping out, leaving the capitalist city in order to shape an autonomous community of women devoid of paternalist structure; a 'Year Zero' in the desert where psychedelic experiences let you start from the ground up; where the need for a sustainable architecture and a new Arts and Crafts movement is discussed experimentally, together with the necessity for geometry and the conception of clothes that will reflect the triumphant step of an emancipated new 'modern woman'.

Since 1999, Mai-Thu Perret has been writing fictional accounts of such experiences, building an archive of diary fragments, letters, schedules and song lyrics, supposedly emanating from members of 'New Ponderosa Year Zero', an imaginary female commune set in an indeterminate time somewhere in the desert of New Mexico. Entitled *The Crystal Frontier*, this unresolved script constitutes the underlying principle of Perret's production of hypothetical artefacts, either functional or reflecting the individuality of the members. The shift of authorship on to imaginary heroines allows Perret to produce a highly varied range of objects. In a hybrid mix of modernism, craft and esoteric aesthetics; housing for rabbits recalls 1950s modular architecture, furniture design resembles psychedelic devices, while ceramics, abstract banners and neon signs evoke Bauhaus or Constructivist models.

Through a multiplicity of potential 'authors', itself complicated by the use of appropriated texts, Perret's treatment of *The Crystal Frontier* is becoming increasingly flexible. Rather than serving as illustrations of the texts, her objects connect to a subtext filled with references that echo the wider signification of the fiction. In *Apocalypse Ballet* (2006), the five papier-mâché mannequins frozen in choreographic poses and holding neon hoops do not represent the women of the community. Neither functional objects nor monuments, the mannequins create a theatrical environment mixing references to modernist costume design, gymnastics and Busby Berkeley musicals. Perret decontextualizes these historical fragments to create a layered temporality, pulling the work towards a contemporary moment.

Perret's 2008 exhibition at the Kitchen in New York connected to *The Crystal Frontier* through themes of mysticism and revolutionary endeavour. Inhabited by a uniformed female mannequin sitting next to a Rorschach-patterned carpet, the exhibition's front room displayed wall diagrams of Korean shamanistic dance steps reduced to abstract symbols. Giant commas resembling quotation marks led the viewer towards another room to see *An Evening of the Book* (2007), in which three black and white silent films documenting the restaging of Vitali Zhemchuzhnyi's 1924 agitprop play were projected on wallpaper inspired by Varvara Stepanova. The films, pantomimes of the victory of revolutionary literature, show female dancers interacting with props including a giant book, hula hoops, a black banner and the over-sized commas. As the films ended, the lights came on, and the exhibition space was filled with the sound of Steven Parrino's 'Spider Song', which loosely conjured Marina, a member of 'Ponderosa', who faces her fear of spiders through creating rugs and decoration. [Céline Kopp]

01

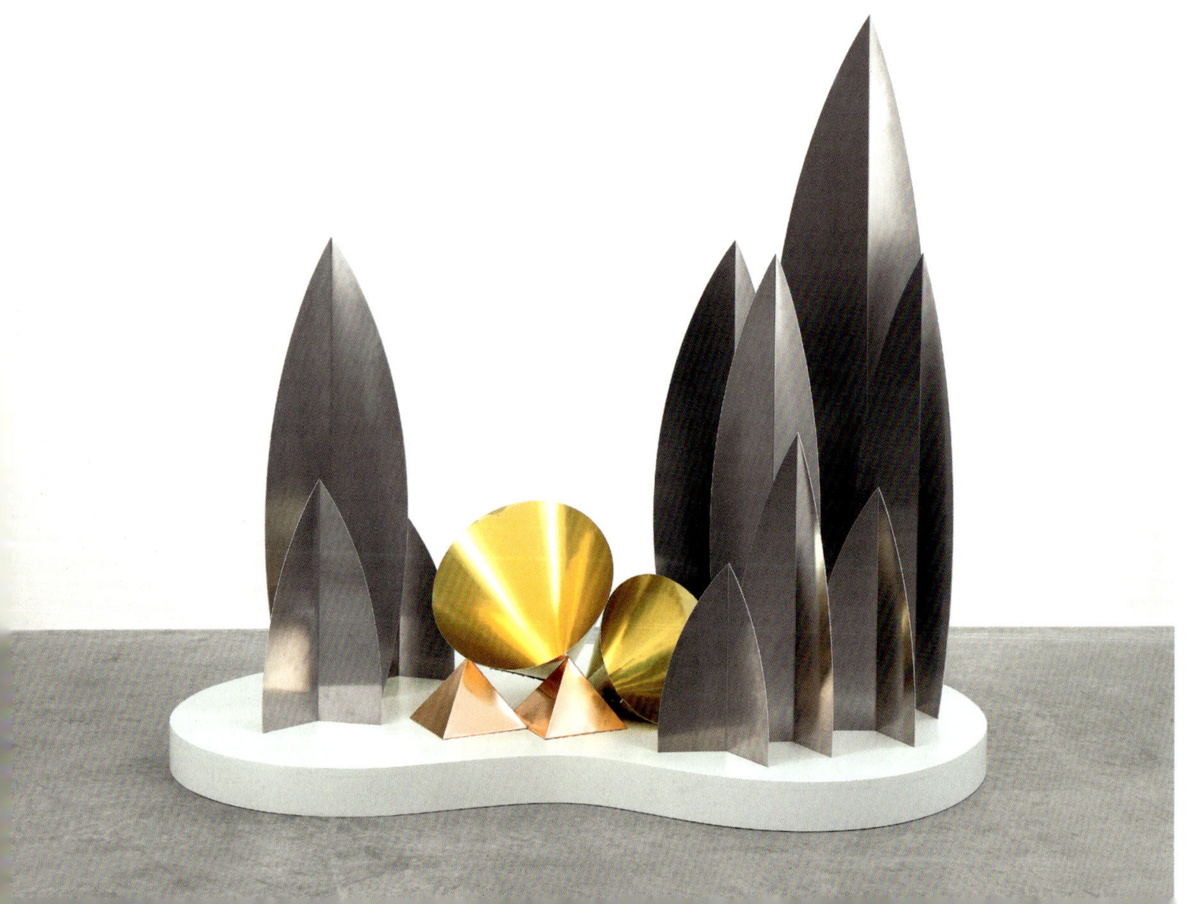

01 *White Sands*, 2008
Aluminium, brass, copper, lacquered wood
187 × 130 × 140 cm

02 *Apocalypse Ballet (neon dress)*, 2006
Figure in steel, wire, papier mâché, acrylic, gouache, wig, neon tubes, steel base
175 × 160 × 160 cm

03 *Heroine of the People (Golden Rock)*, 2005
Wire, papier mâché, acrylic paint, gold leaf
107 × 75 × 75 cm

04 *The Family*, 2007
Figures in wood, wire, papier mâché, acrylic, lacquer and gouache; wigs, clothes made by Susanne Zangerl and Catherine Zimmermann
170 × 192 cm
MDF base
12 × 250 × 160 cm

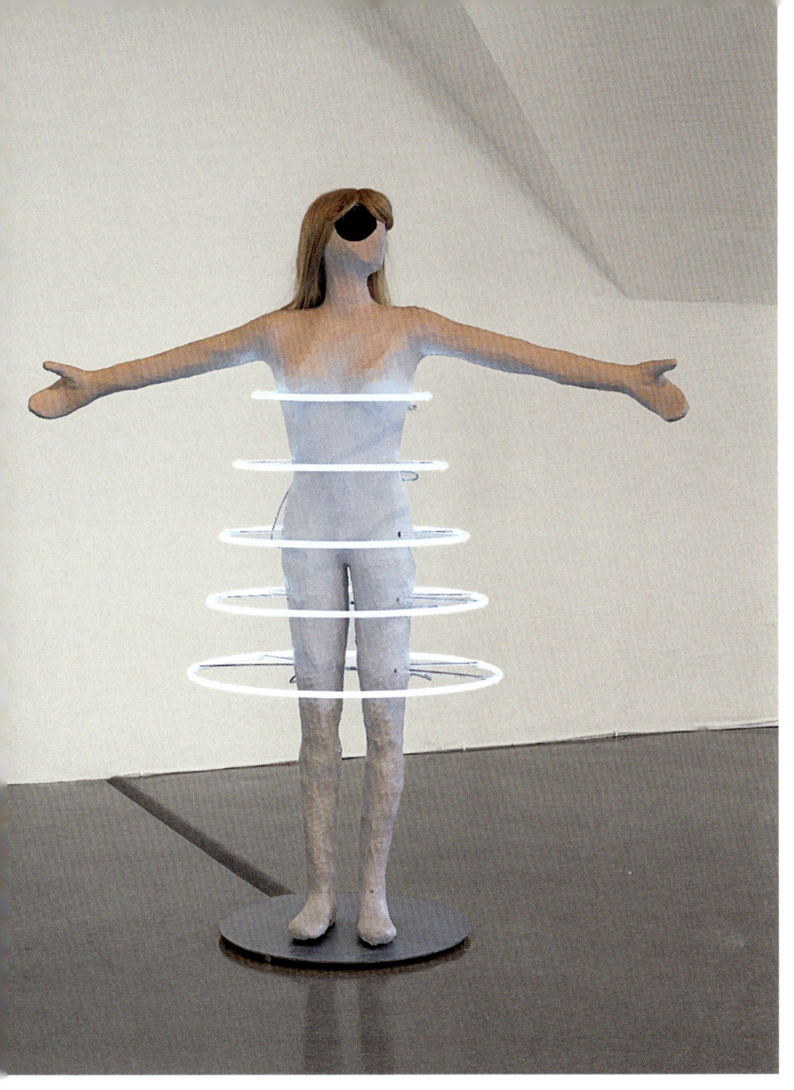

02

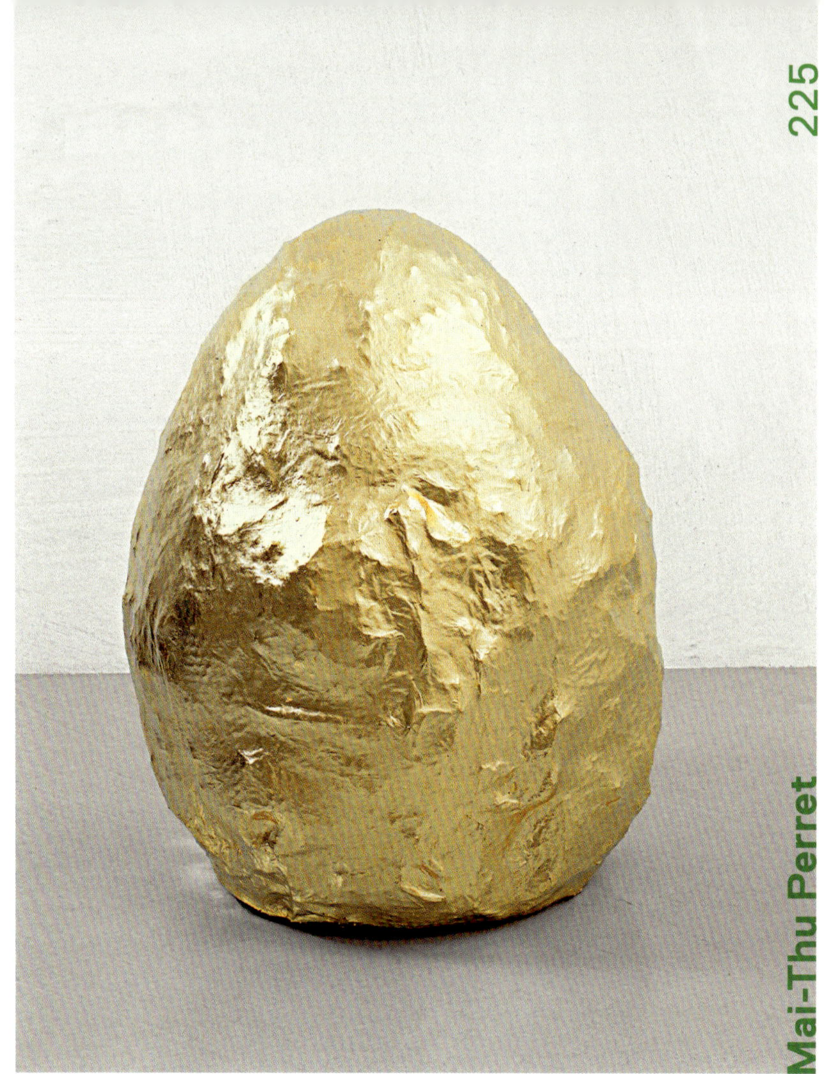

03

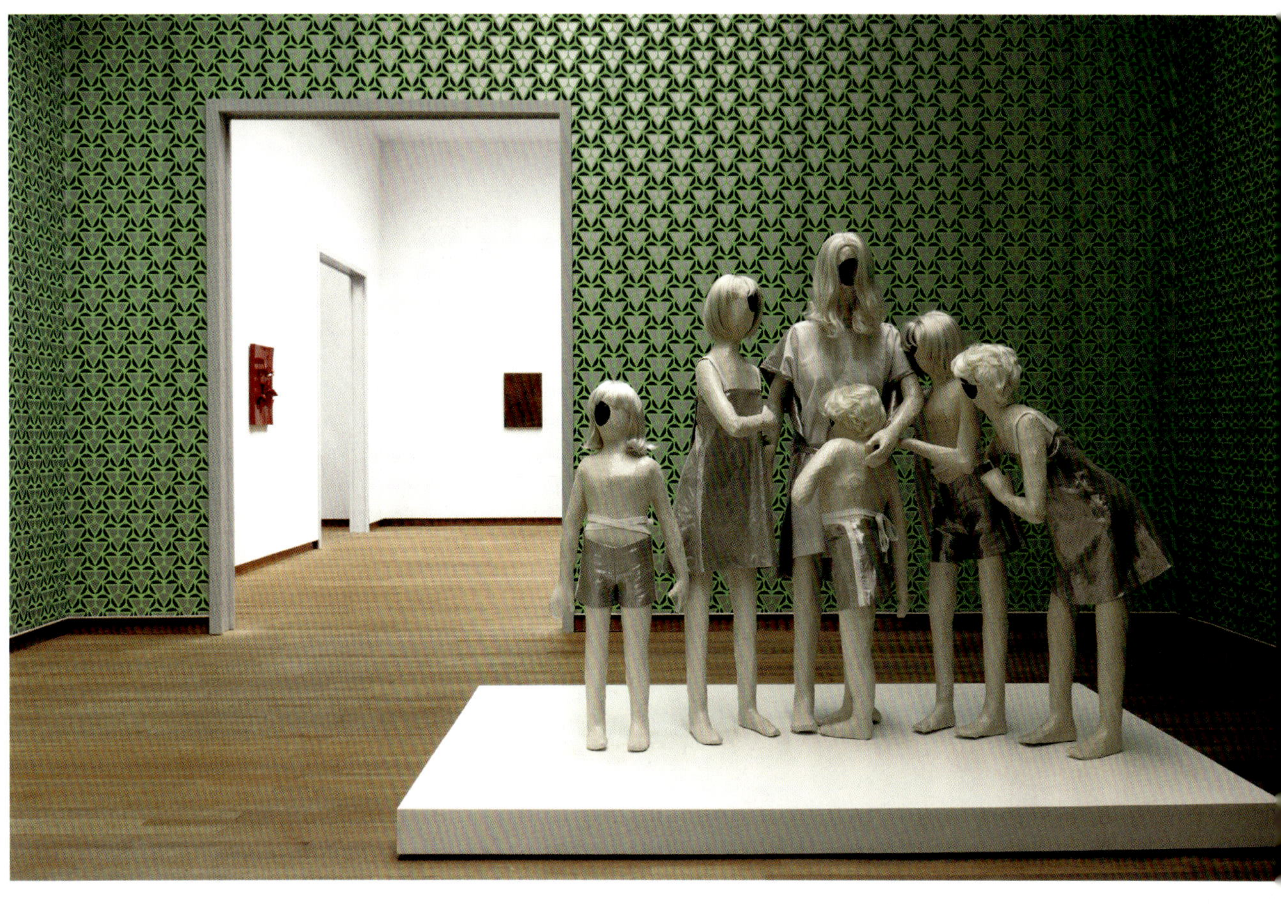

04

05

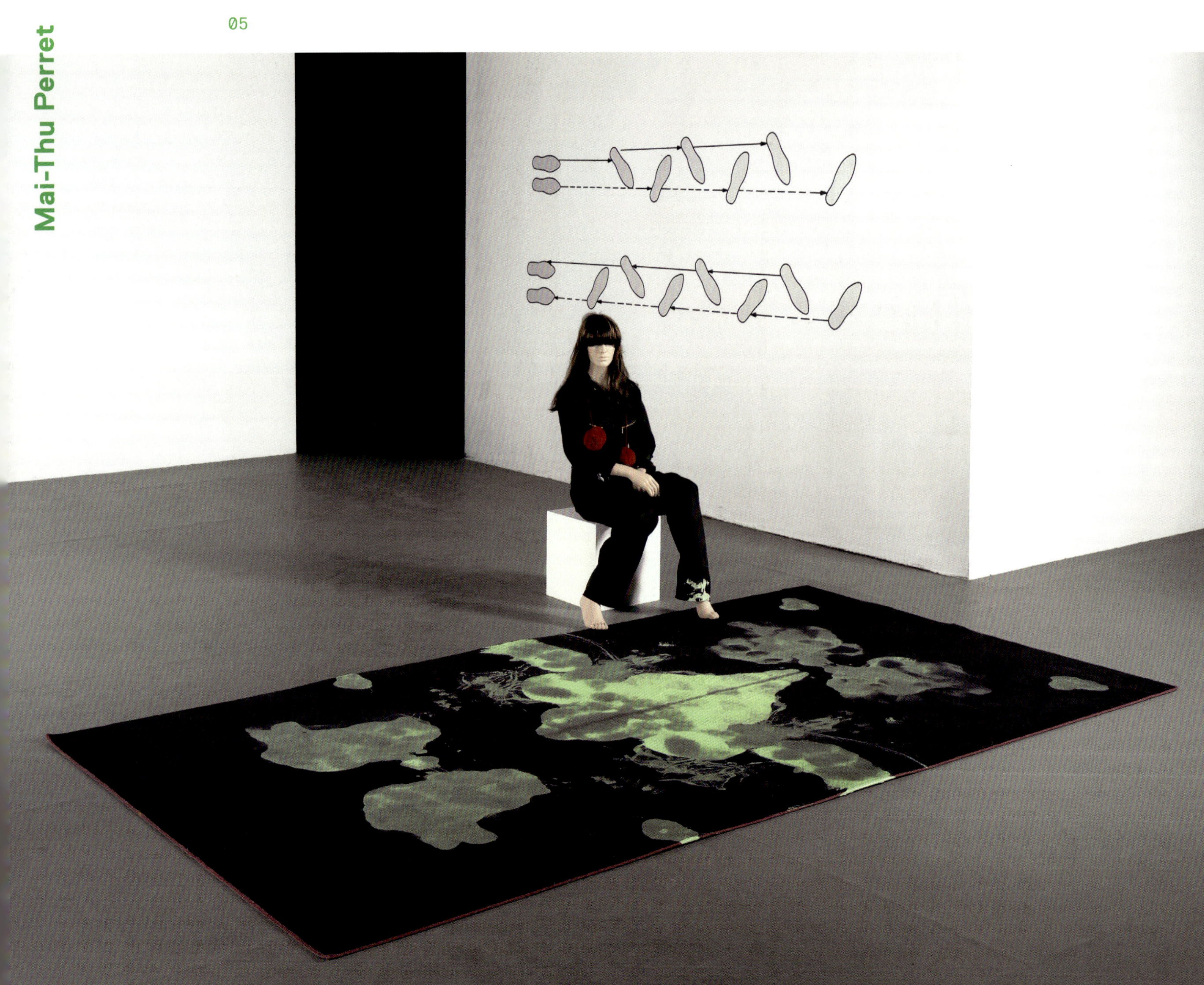

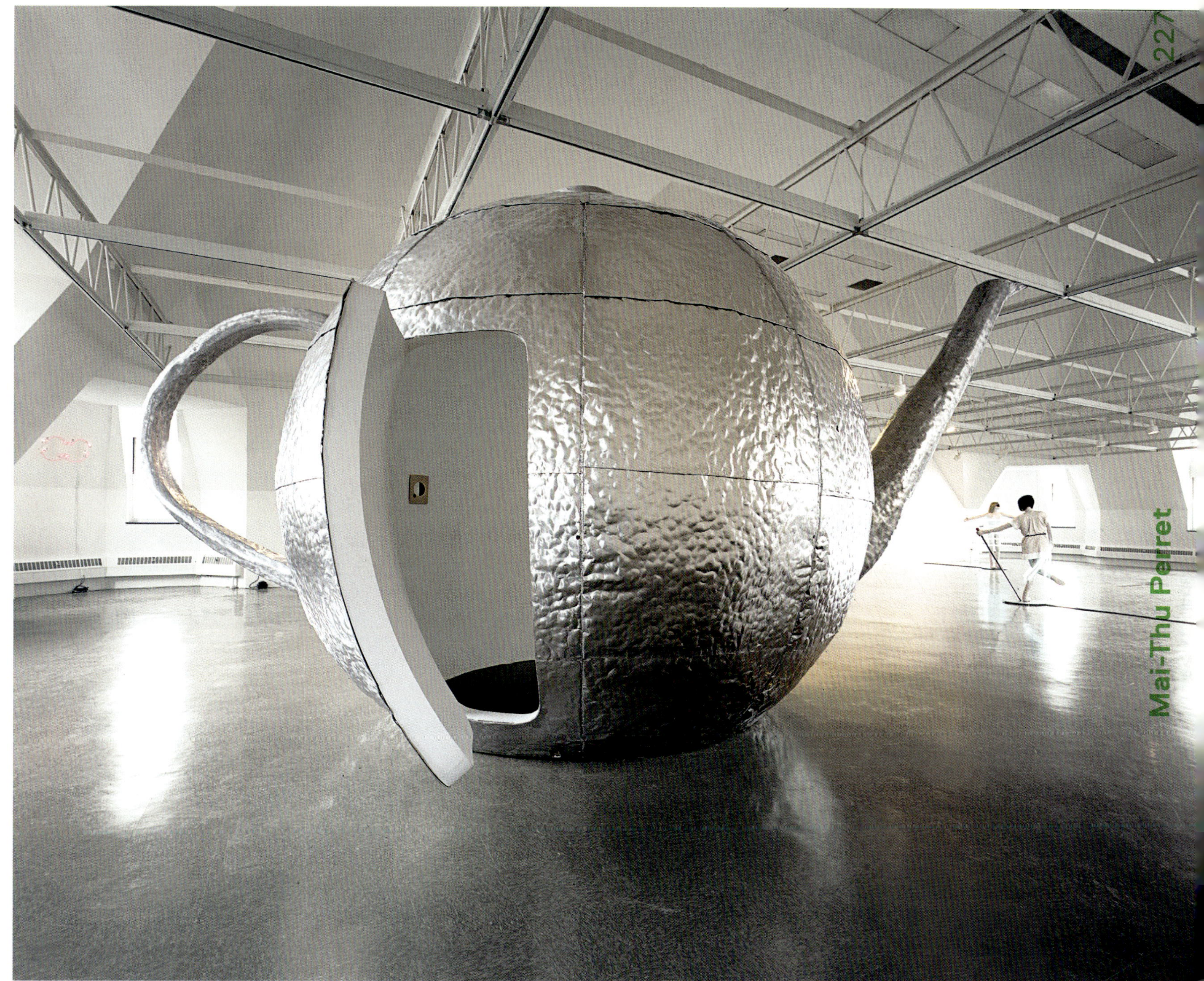

06

05 from front:
→ *Donna Come Me*, 2008
Mannequin, wig, uniform,
pom-poms, acrylic paint on carpet
Dimensions variable
Carpet
366 × 198 cm
→ *Taegamkori IV*, 2008
Acrylic paint on wall
Variable dimensions

06 *Little Planetary Harmony*, 2006
Aluminium, wood, drywall, latex wall
paint, fluorescent lighting fixture,
acrylic gouache on plywood paintings
356 × 643 × 365 cm

Sensitive to the multiplicity of perception, Dutch artist Falke Pisano investigates the possibilities of physical, conceptual and linguistic encounters with abstract sculpture. In addition to her photographs, diagrams and lectures charting an earnest grappling with the relationships between qualifying language and concrete object, she constructs elegant angular sculptures. Using the unadorned surfaces of some of her freestanding works as projection screens, as in *Object and Disintegration: The Object of Three* (2008), Pisano complicates the position of the art object in relation to artist and viewer. Her black and white video projections animate the sculpture's white painted surfaces with dynamic geometric shapes as well as texts that she has written concerning the developing associations between sculpture, creator and spectator.

Pisano also introduces her voice and image into some of these videos, channelling her performative practice. Reading her texts on the relationship of sculptor and sculpted, her voice holds a gentle, unassuming rhythm. She is questioning more than explaining, appropriating language not for its authoritative power but as a vehicle for research. Through writing, reading and voiceover, language also becomes a type of sculptural medium for Pisano — a means of eroding the edges of plastic form to forge a conceptual channel between object and language. Like her kinetic sculpture *l'Objet Complet [The undeniable success of operations]* (2008), her lectures, such as *A Sculpture Turning into a Conversation* (2006) and *Affecting Abstractions* (2007), emphasize time and establish sculpture's evolving context. Movement and narrative are necessary circumstances for her as she reveals the instability of form, as well as of vision and language.

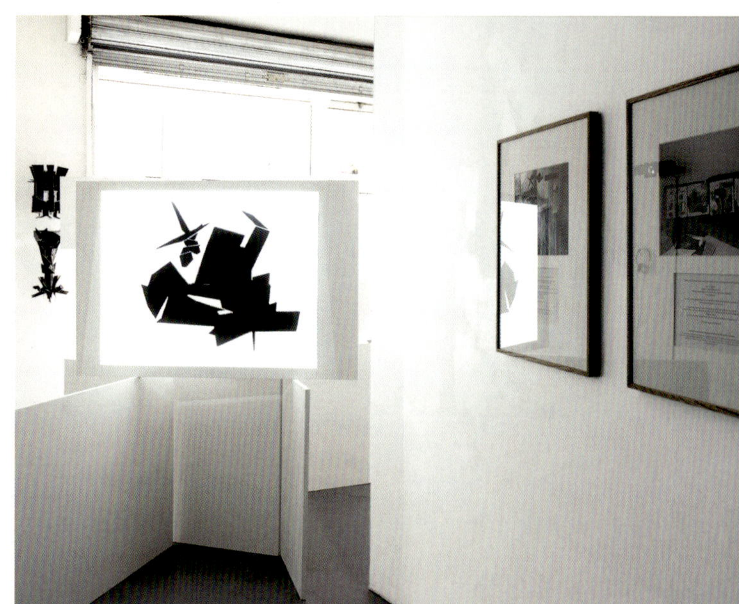

02

Pisano references modernism as a system of legibility that holds a series of forms together, as might a nail or glue. Works by Le Corbusier, Eileen Gray, Max Bill and Eduardo Chillida become more like found objects in her work as she modifies their structure and context to emphasize evolution. For *Rhythm in Space with Diamond* (2006) Pisano photographs black and white images of sculptures by Max Bill through the prism of a diamond, cropping and multiplying documents of the original forms. Similarly, for *Chillida (Forms and Feelings)* (2006) Pisano uses photographs of Chillida's sculptures in an art book as a starting point, and develops the images through collage. Expanding these appropriations into the sculptural realm, Pisano's black and white paper and foam-board models, *Object of Transformation* (2007) and *Conceptual Reconstruction* (2008), launch linear patterns into the third dimension. Again in *Module for 'Scenario for Form'* (2007) she reduces images of modernist sculptures, photocopied and pasted on foam-board, to a series of black and white shapes. Disconnected from a historical context, the forms become material for a new and temporary form.

Pisano's activation of a dynamic social sphere for sculpture recalls the work of Hélio Oiticica and his goal of exploding the static artwork and expanding its existence through the shared experience of movement and dance. Of course Robert Smithson's project of entropy also resonates in her recognition of the plurality of perception and the breakdown of the singular and permanent object. Ultimately what Pisano constructs is not only three-dimensional sculpture but also a dynamic system of vision and language in which production, subjectivity and perception are complicit in the ultimate dissolution of the object. [Lillian Davies]

01

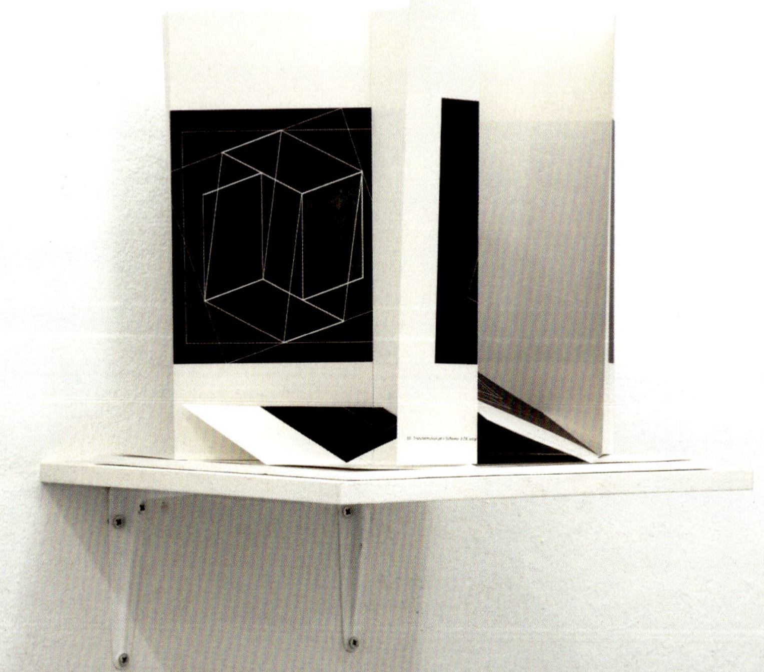

03

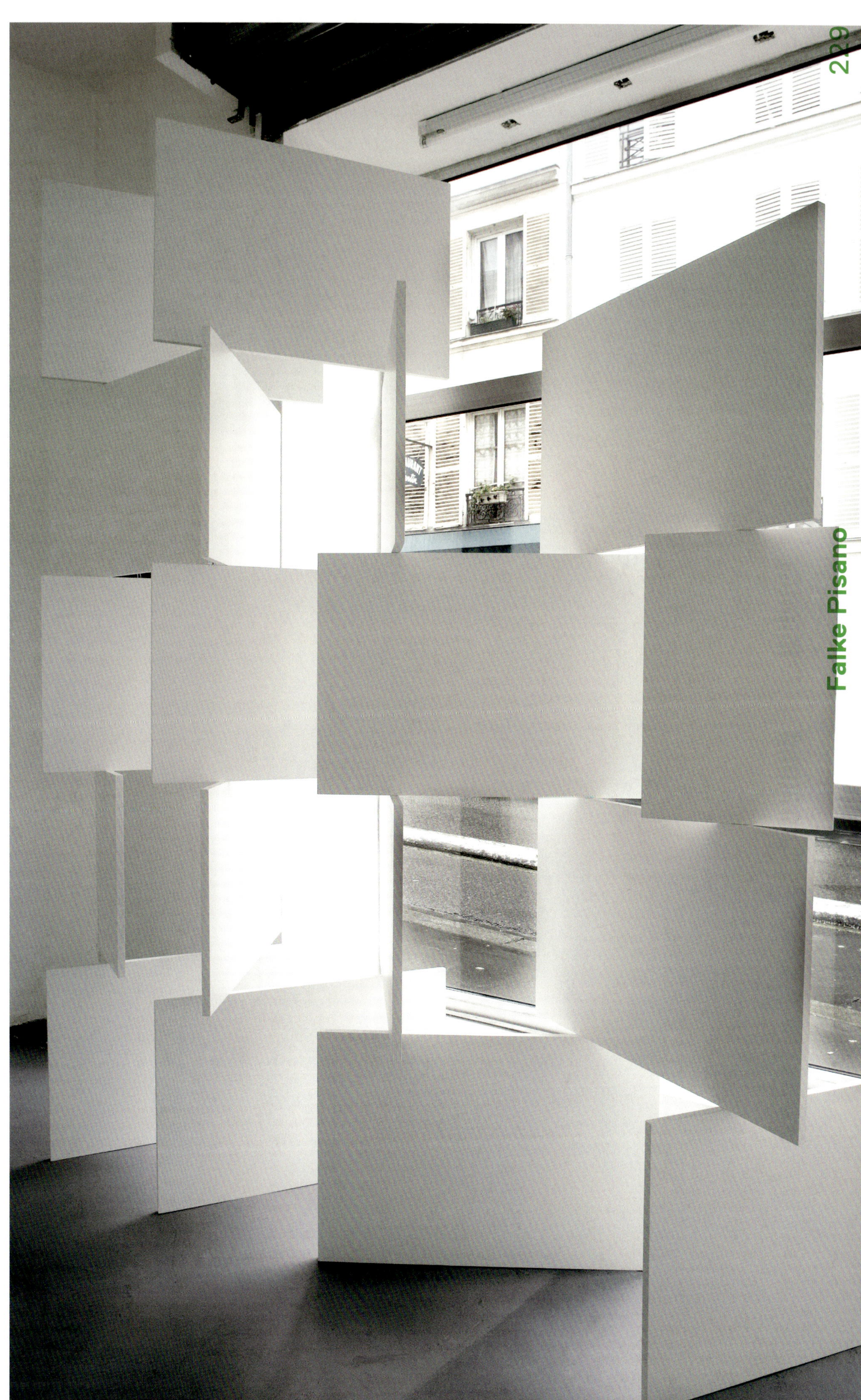

01 *Object of Transformation #1*, 2007
Paper, foamboard
30 × 30 × 30 cm

02 from left:
→ *Object and Disintegration: The Object of Three*, 2008
Wood, video projections with audio
180 × 200 × 200 cm
→ *Conceptual reconstruction concerning form: the object*, 2008
Black and white photographs, text
51 × 61 cm

03 *Screen (Parabolic Reflector*, 2008
Wood, mirror
220 × 250 × 75 cm

01

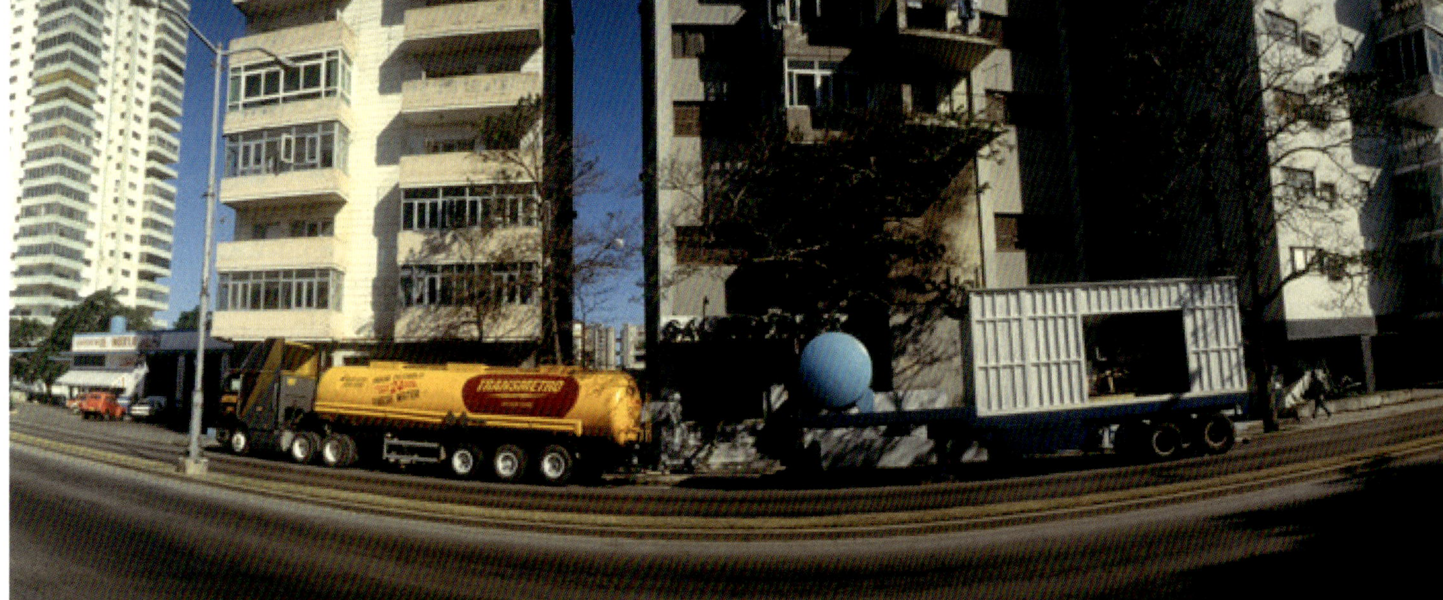

The young Cuban artist Wilfredo Prieto reflects the resurgence in Conceptual art currently taking place in Latin America. An inheritor of the political and sculptural practice of artists such as Cildo Meireles, Prieto presents a condensed and acute commentary on the current circumstances in which his work takes place. Much of his work has a purposeful dysfunctionality, and he seems to delight in absurdist humour. As we know from Freud, jokes work best by condensation: the neater the elision between things or the more unexpected the substitution of one for another, the more jarring the mental dislocation and the more psychologically penetrating the nervous laugh that ensues. One-liners by Prieto include the work *Mucho Ruido y Pocas Nueces* (2003), literally translated as 'A lot of noise and not many nuts' — or much ado about nothing — which took place at a Havana gallery. Arriving outside the space, one was led to believe that some kind of public work was taking place in front of the gallery, since a large water tanker and mobile generator were parked outside. When one followed the hoses and cables inside, it transpired that all of this paraphernalia in fact led to a measly potted plant that was being fed with a dribble of water and illuminated by a solitary bulb. Whether this was a commentary on bureaucratic excess or a piece of institutional critique about the state of the art world remained delightfully unclear. The work was ultimately a poignant commentary on any situation in which the means clearly overwhelm the ends.

Like most successful Conceptual art, Prieto's pieces alter their meaning according to context. *Apolitico* (2001) a work that has been realized in a number of different locations, is a case in point. Thirty national flags displayed on ceremonial flagpoles have been rendered in various shades of grey. Minus their identifiable colours, the flags become interchangeable, the nations and their pride reduced to a photocopied pallor. Interestingly, the identities of a few nations remain intact, however — among them Britain's Union Jack, the Swiss cross, the Japanese red sun and the American stars and stripes. Presented variously in Havana, Dublin, Paris, Siena and New York, the work calls into question the current circumstances of the country in which it is shown. The context in New York in 2008 called attention to the country's current foreign affairs, while the presentation in Havana suggested a polar position whereby the greying of the flags could be read as representing the detachment of the surrounding nations.

For the 2008 Frieze Art Fair in London, Prieto produced a work that again played on the ceremony of flags and nationhood while also commenting on the status symbols of the art fair itself. Running through the gallery space was an especially long red carpet (*Ascending Line*, 2008). Visiting dignitaries, or the curious, if driven to follow the course of this trail, would find that it led outside of the exhibition tent into the surrounding park. Its end was hoisted on to a flagpole where it dangled as a forlorn symbol of the fair's promises. [Jens Hoffmann]

02

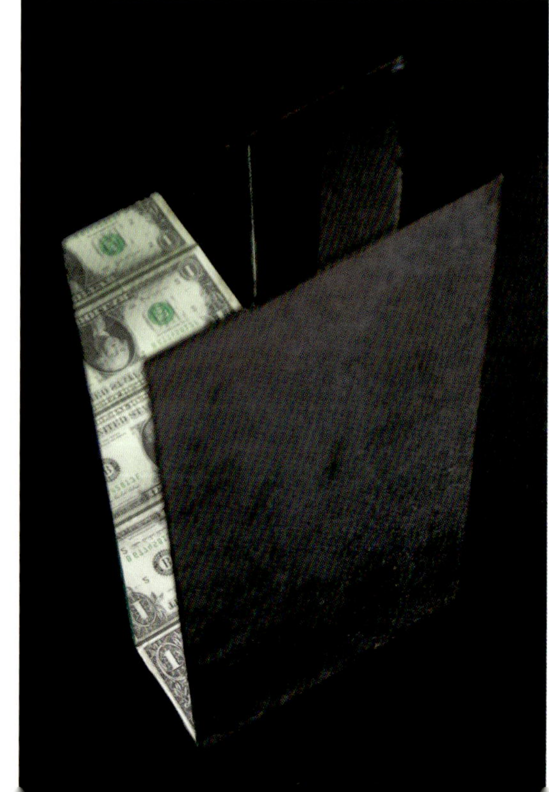

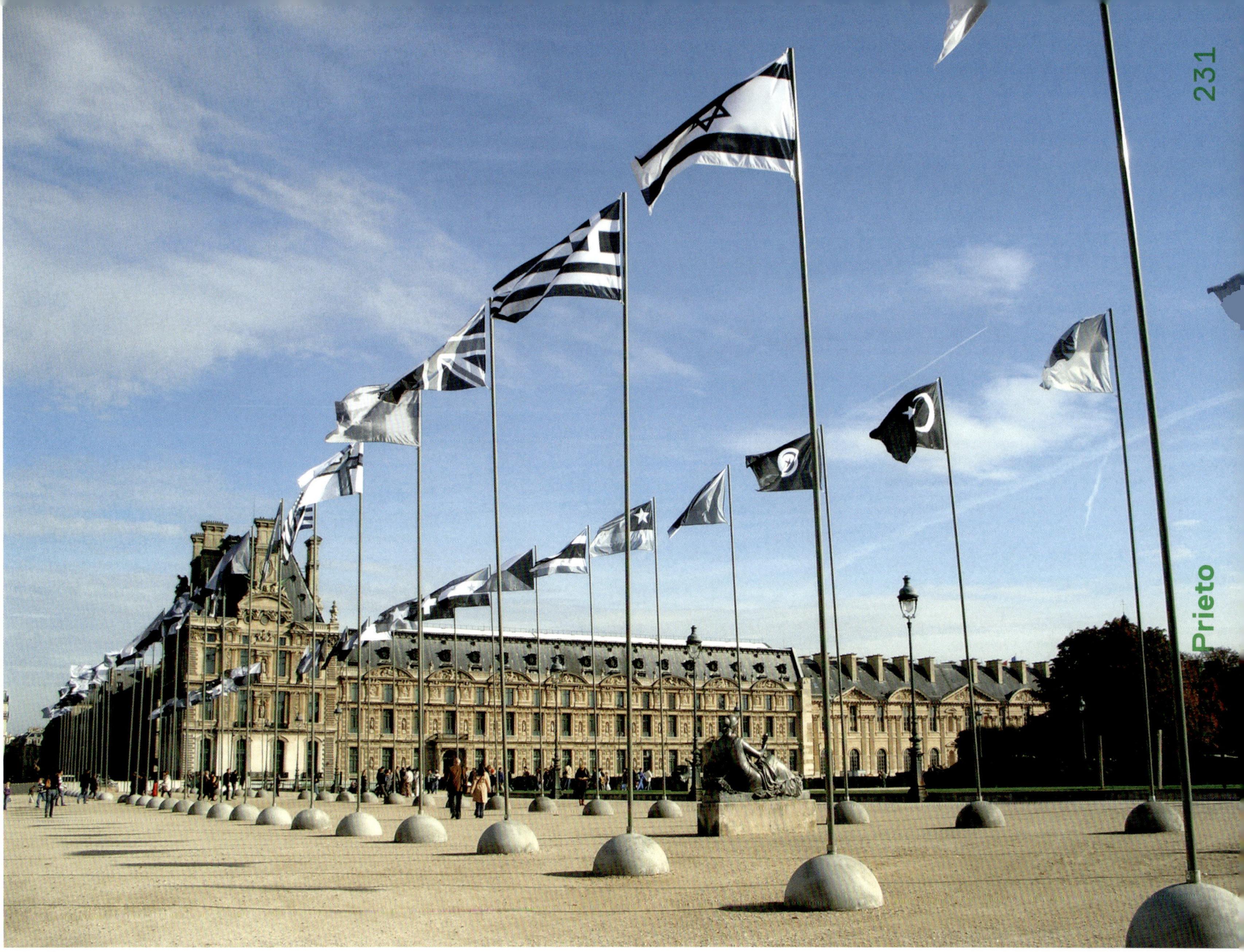

03

04

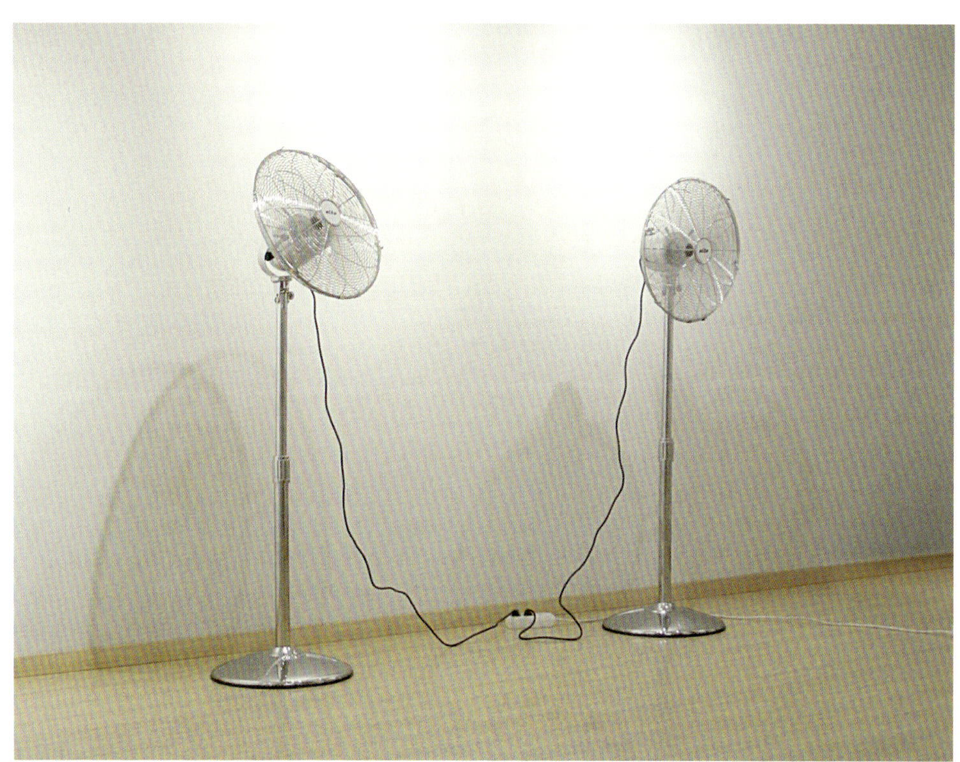

01 *Mucho Ruido y Pocas Nueces*, 2003
Power generator, water truck, water, hose, power cables, bulb, ornamental plant
Dimensions variable

02 *One Million Dollar*, 2002
One dollar between mirrors, security system
25 × 15.5 × 6.5 cm

03 *Apolitical*, 2001–06
Flags from every country designated by the UN in a scale of black, grey and white, with official design, dimensions and fabric

04 *Yes/No*, 2002
Two fans, one moving up and down (Yes) and one moving from side to side (No)
Approx. 170 cm high

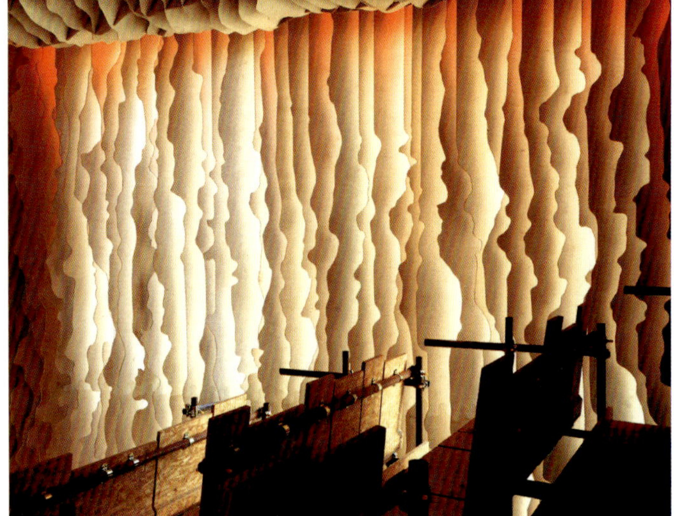

01

Tobias Putrih explores the way in which architecture participates in the creation of imaginary worlds. Within this premise, he has produced a variety of works including drawings, sculptures and mainly large-scale prototypes of cinemas, viewing machines similar to enlarged or modernized versions of the magic lantern. His architectural vocabulary is borrowed from the visionary structures and theories of Friedrich Kiesler, Charles and Ray Eames, Buckminster Fuller and Robert Smithson. Revolving around the Duchampian notion of the optical machine, Putrih's practice experiments with the three-dimensional mechanisms that allow the factory of dreams to sustain illusion.

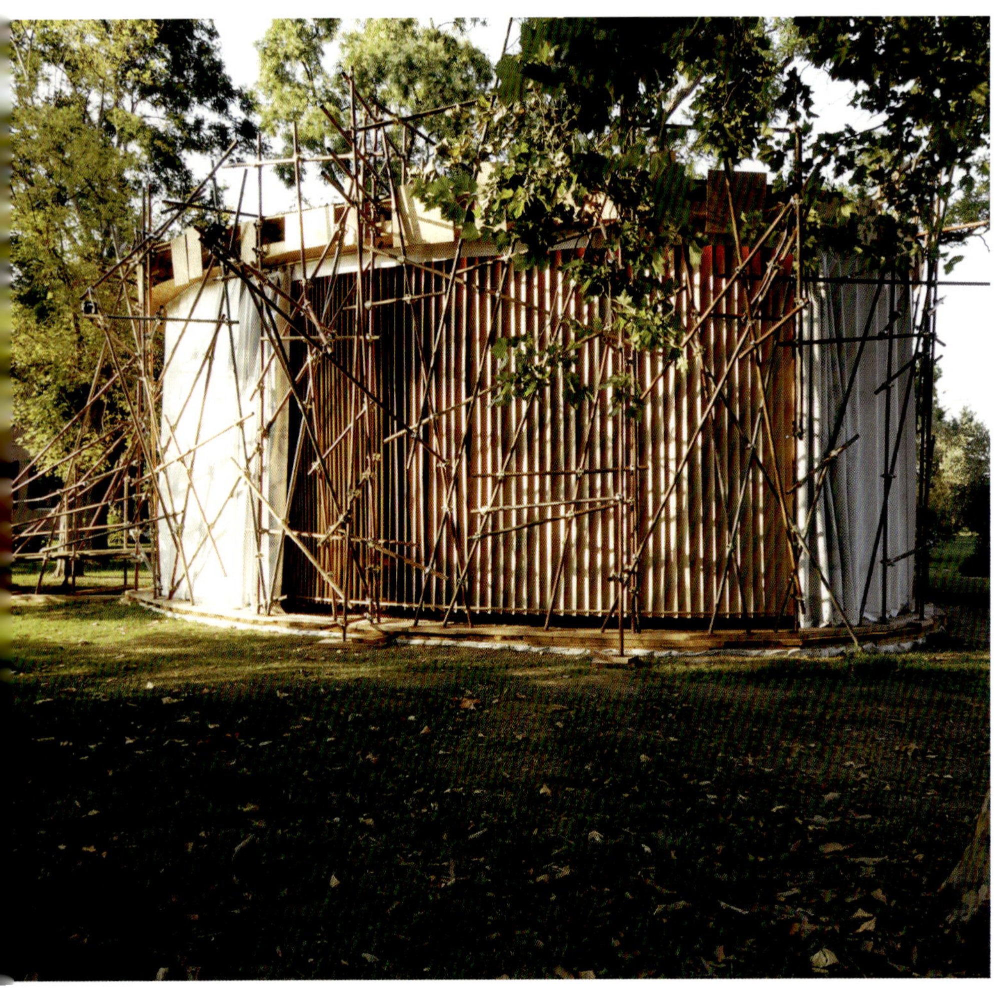

His smaller sculptural pieces often take the shape of models or studies not dissimilar to what could be found in an architectural studio as a means to visualize a future construction. However, the peculiarity of his works resides in its inefficient relationship to the function of the research. Rather than aiming at an innovative solution to the architectural brief, the artist strives to produce unresolved questions through his design and often points at the theatrical nature of cinema architecture. Movie theatres are typically designed as total stages set in which the spectator can make the transition into the imaginary realm of fiction. They facilitate the gradual shuttering of consciousness and allow viewers to liken film fruition to the experience of a dream. It is precisely this hypnotic function that Putrih wants to bring forwards with his work.

Lately, Putrih has built a series of pavilions as functioning cinemas, inside which he has projected selected films by other artists. For his Slovenian Pavilion at the 52nd Venice Biennale (2007), he built an outdoor auditorium that could host around thirty spectators. The sculpture directly referred to John Eberson, the inventor of the atmospheric cinema, a particular kind of movie theatre designed to simulate an outdoor setting, normally an exotic one such as the courtyard of a Moorish palace or a Venetian baroque square, in which the spectator would view the film. This double illusion fascinates Putrih because it makes of the architecture itself a film set in which visitors are both spectators and real-time actors among artificial scenery.

For his solo show at Attitudes in Geneva in 2008, Putrih built a cinema designed after Kiesler's Endless House model, inside which a programme of films relating to architecture was continuously screened. On two other occasions he has built environments in collaboration with artist-filmmaker Runa Islam, specially conceived for the projection of Islam's works. Putrih's work takes on the transitional nature of the subject that he investigates and becomes itself a portal to someone else's work. As in movie theatres, the container and its content feed each other in an osmotic relationship that allows one work to enrich the other.

Although his starting point is often linked to the formal and functional implications of architectural practice, Putrih is more like the figure of the Renaissance artist-scientist. Halfway between the inventor and the artist, he creates projects that can be seen as episodes of experimentation with machines to investigate the threshold between reality and fiction. Like a maverick designer, his prototypes always incorporate a future dimension that places them in the territory of utopian objects. [Francesco Manacorda]

02

03

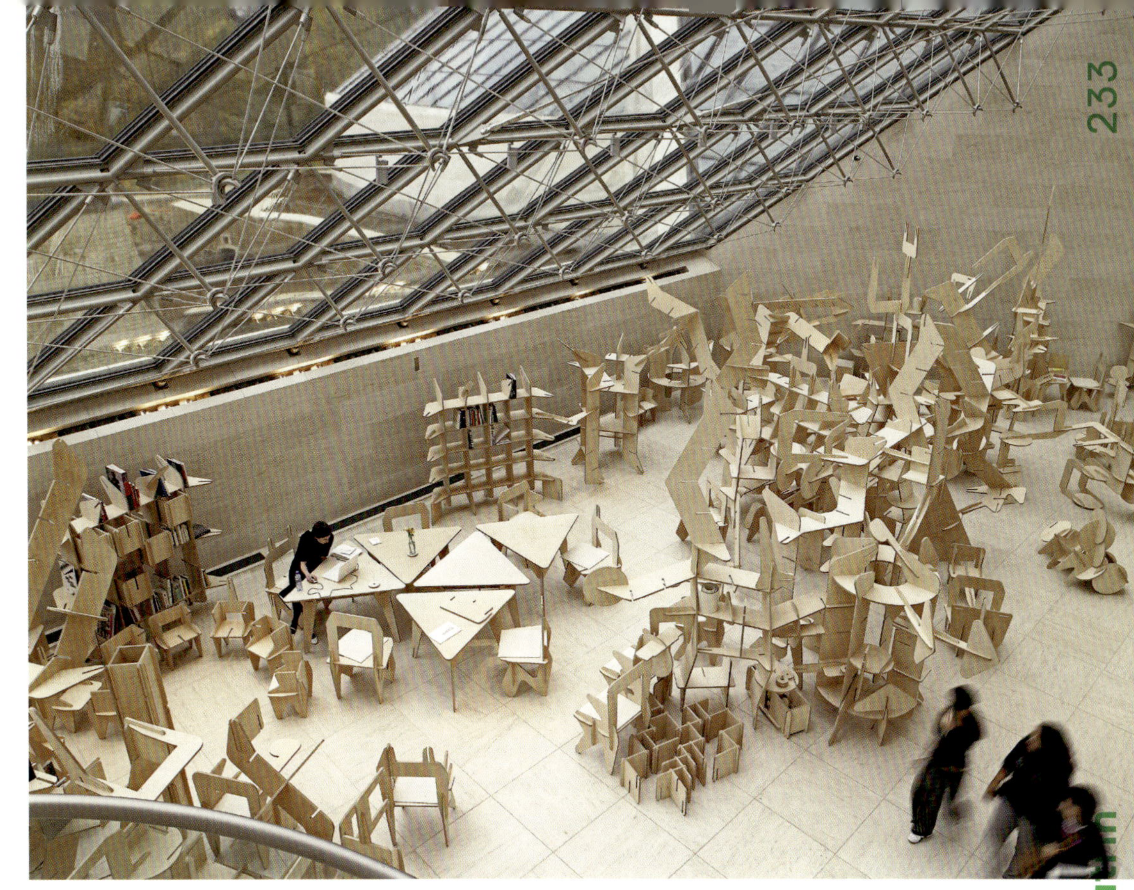

04

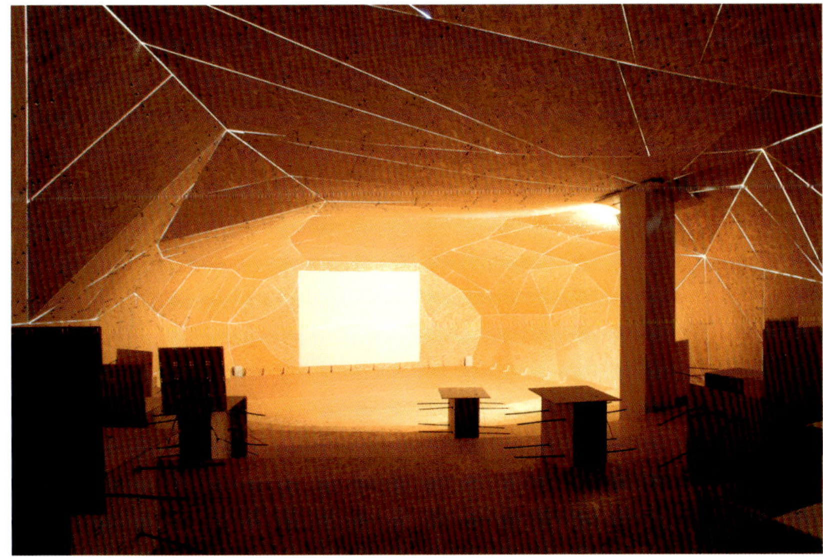

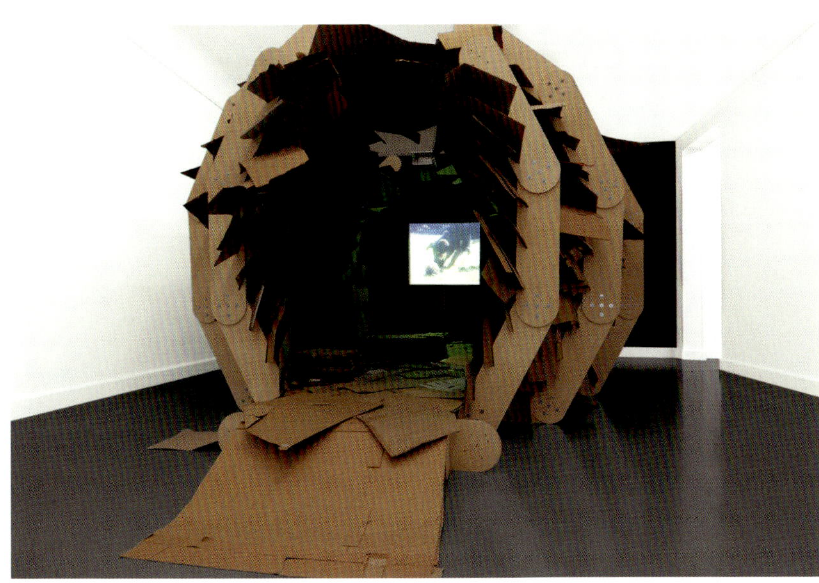

05

01, 02 *Venetian, Atmospheric*, 2007
Architecture by Tobias Putrih
and Luka Melon
Plywood, OSB plates, scaffolding,
PVC curtain, 16mm projectors,
digital projectors
Approx. 13 × 8 × 5.5 m
Island of San Servolo, Slovenian
Pavilion, Venice Biennale

03 *Mudam Studio*, 2006
In collaboration with Sancho Silva
Design by Tobias Putrih and Aleš Korpič
Plywood
Dimensions variable

04 *Cinema attitudes*, 2008
Plywood, OSB plates, steel scaffolding,
nylon ropes, screws, zip ties
13 × 6 × 3.5 m

05 *Argos Cinema*, 2008
Plywood, cardboard
Approx. 6 × 9 × 3.5 m

Overleaf:

06 *Re-projection (Modena)*, 2008
Steel hooks, monofilament, spotlight
Approx. 8 × 5 × 4 m

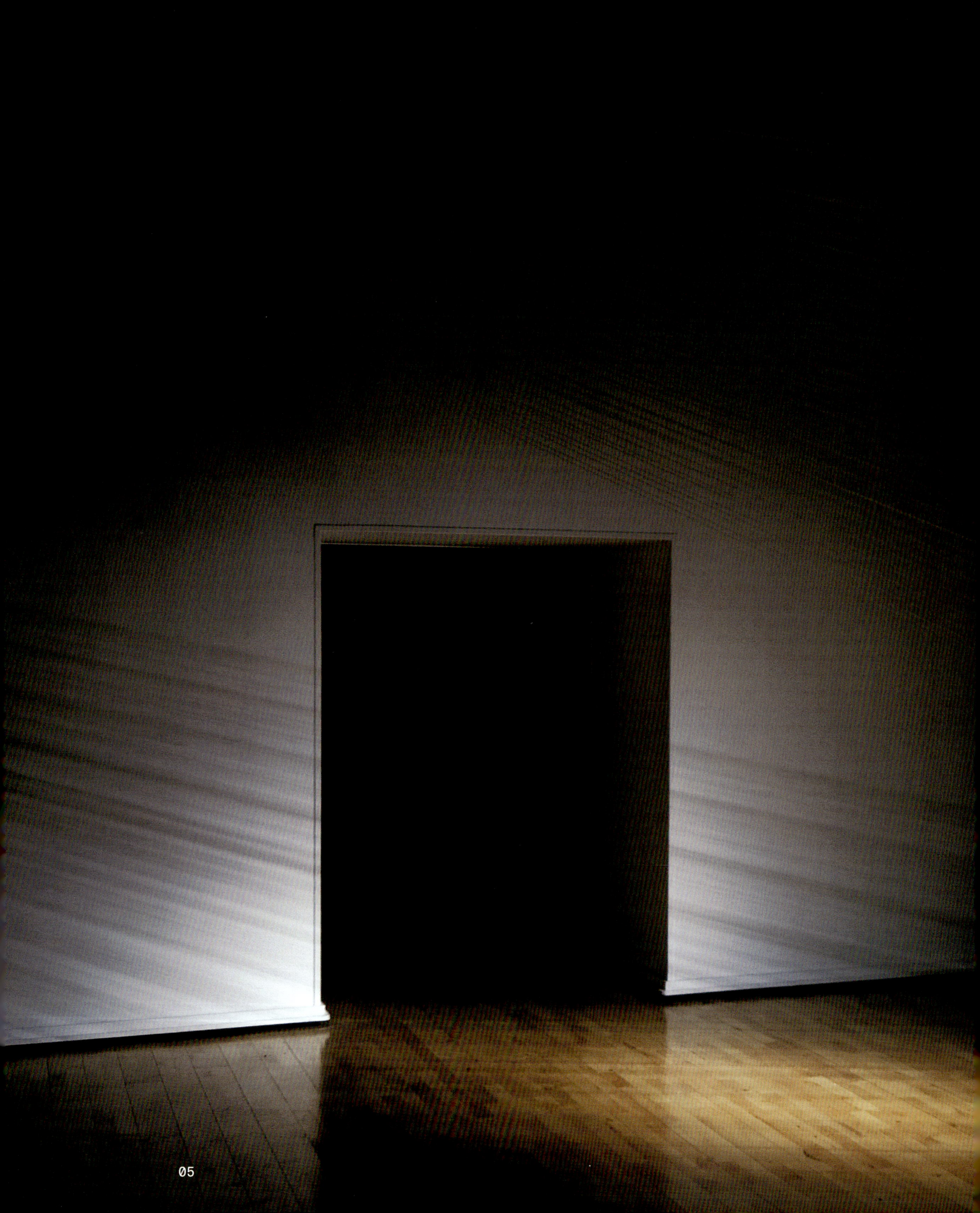

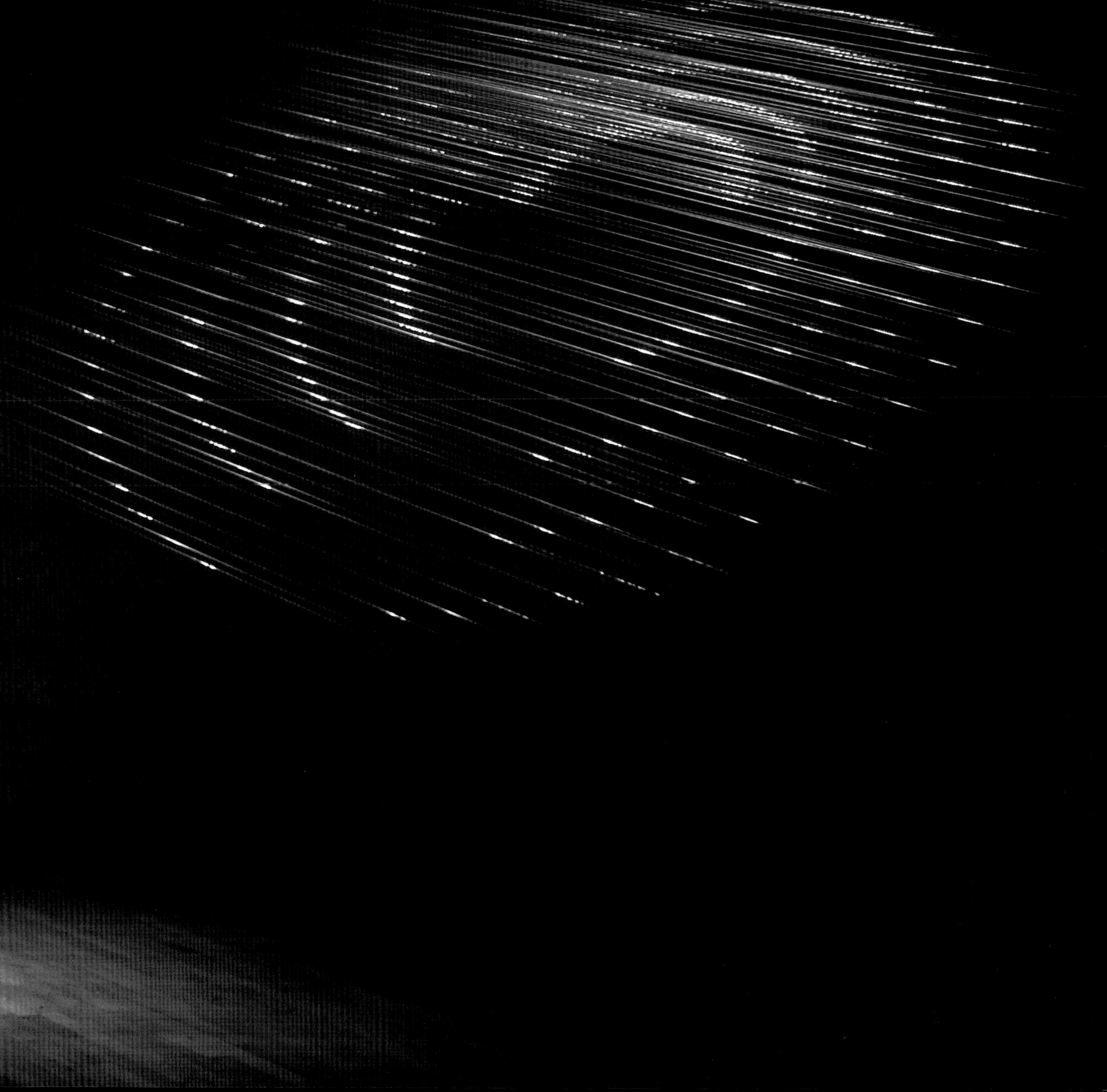

01

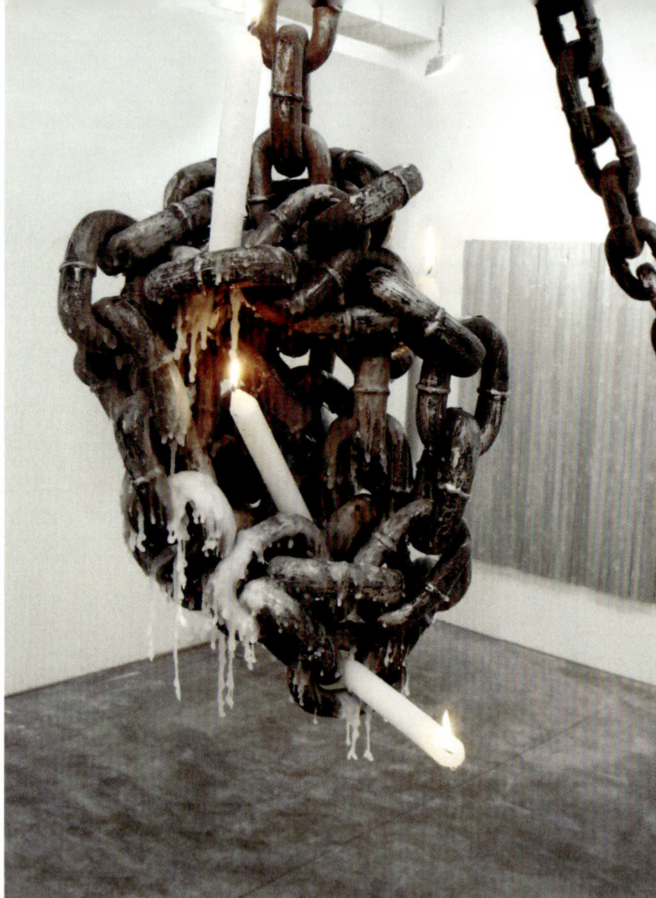

Michael Queenland excavates cultural and religious forms that have become detached from their original associations and functions. An early work, *Candle Piece* (2004), renders this interest with the most simple and elegant of gestures: a white niche in the gallery wall containing a single candle flickering with real flame. Yet upon closer inspection an electrical cord could be seen running from the candle base and into a socket in the wall.

Via subtle totemic sculptures of exquisitely cast and found materials, photography and reproportioned furniture installations — Michael Queenland's most recognizable forms — tangible objects explore a sense of symbolic organization and abstract liminality. Queenland operates within distinctly familiar forms yet subtly shifts their common context to evoke a sense of mystery and the sublime. His objects invite the viewer to witness private analyses and intellectual exercises, conflating the ideas of biography, the individual and personal exploration within a formal structure.

In one ongoing vein of Queenland's work, fanaticism — often religious — and the systems lifted from its communal applications in the splintered appendages of the American periphery are symbolized in near-fetishistic study. A wide range of isolationist movements and individuals show up in the works: Branch Davidians, Henry David Thoreau, Ted Kaczynski and the Seventh Day Adventists. *Shaker Unit* (2005), which refers to the latter group, offers striking evidence of Queenland's preoccupation with exercise and practice. The shelving unit, along with several other pieces of furniture, were built in collaboration with woodworking and furniture-design students during a residency in New Gloucester, Maine, and later shown in situ at the only currently active Shaker village, Sabbathday Lake, also in Maine. Yet, despite Queenland's insistence on following strict furniture building guidelines developed by the Shakers in the nineteenth century, he subverts the design and enlarges the shelves, benches and bedroom furniture, playing with the idea of disobeyed instruction, ideological translation and spatial transformation of the Shaker's simple yet strict design. Furthering the idea that each moment of translation shifts the objects into a space inhabited with a certain discomfort, the pieces were also chronicled as photographic evidence, assembled in a kind of Bernd and Hilla Becher typological format and shown alongside of their three-dimensional counterparts.

Queenland's 2007 solo show 'Bread & Balloons' similarly took on the gallery as a kind of theatre of presentation. The front gallery space, elegantly arranged and precisely perfect in its formal relationships, recalled an artist's studio (in this case Constantin Brancusi's), complicated by absurdist juxtapositions of forms — rustic breads rendered in black and white porcelain, balloons cast in plaster and presented on modernist pedestals or dangling from wax chains — raising questions of weight and gravity, and wryly subverting its modernist paradigms. Furthering his interest in the displacement and decontextualization, a narrow hallway created a transitional space — neither public nor private, but containing elements of both — between the presentational area of the gallery and the intimate back room, *Meant Every Other Way* (2007), in which live cats roamed freely.

Recent work such as *No Evil* (2008) or *Idle Youth* (2008), continue to explore Queenland's characteristic forms but introduce a quirky grotesquerie and anthropomorphic quality to his meticulous arrangements, furthering his ongoing investigation in to the possibilities of formal subversion and material meaning. [Shamim M. Momin]

01 *Midnight Curse*, 2007
Plastic chain, candles, wax, hardware, fire extinguisher dust
Length approx. 11 m

02 from left:
→ *Meant Every Other Way*, 2007
Two cats, constructed wood box and ledge, cotton lycra curtains, collected ephemera, cat food, kitty litter
Dimensions variable
→ *Untitled (HERSHEY)*, 2007
Collected ephemera
124 × 91 × 94 cm

03 *NO EVIL*, 2008
Cast aqua-resin, fibreglass, polyester filler, acrylic paint, balloon tie, string, paint bucket, metal, walnut wood base, rigid foam
38 × 38 × 211 cm

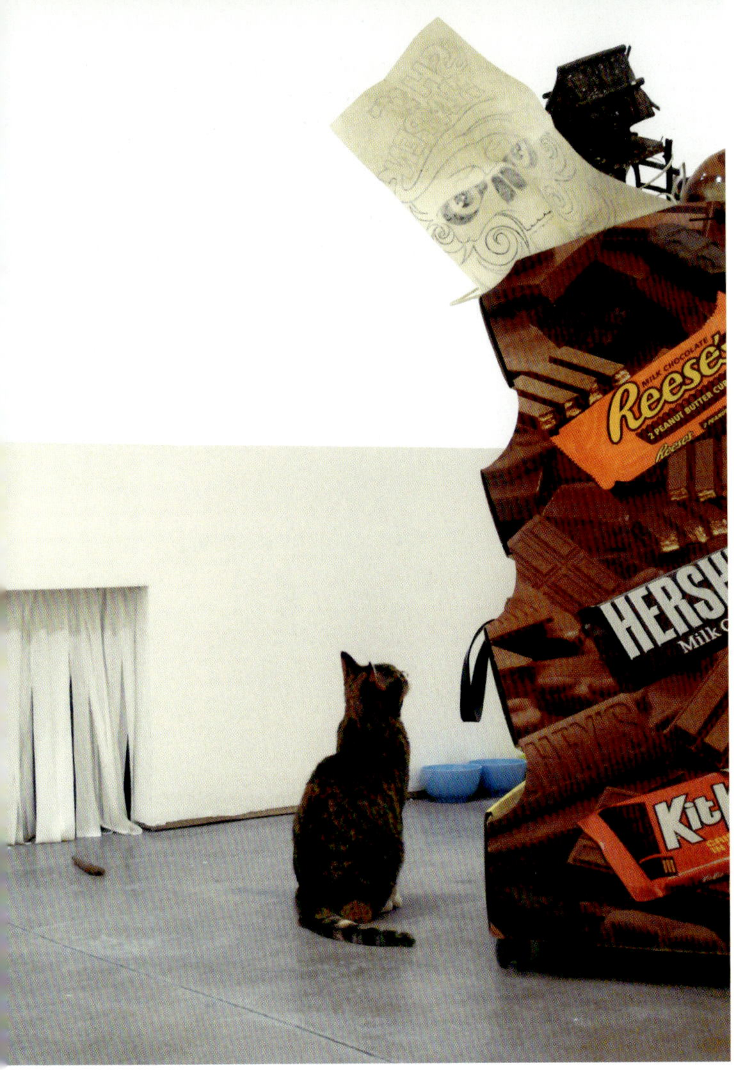

02

03

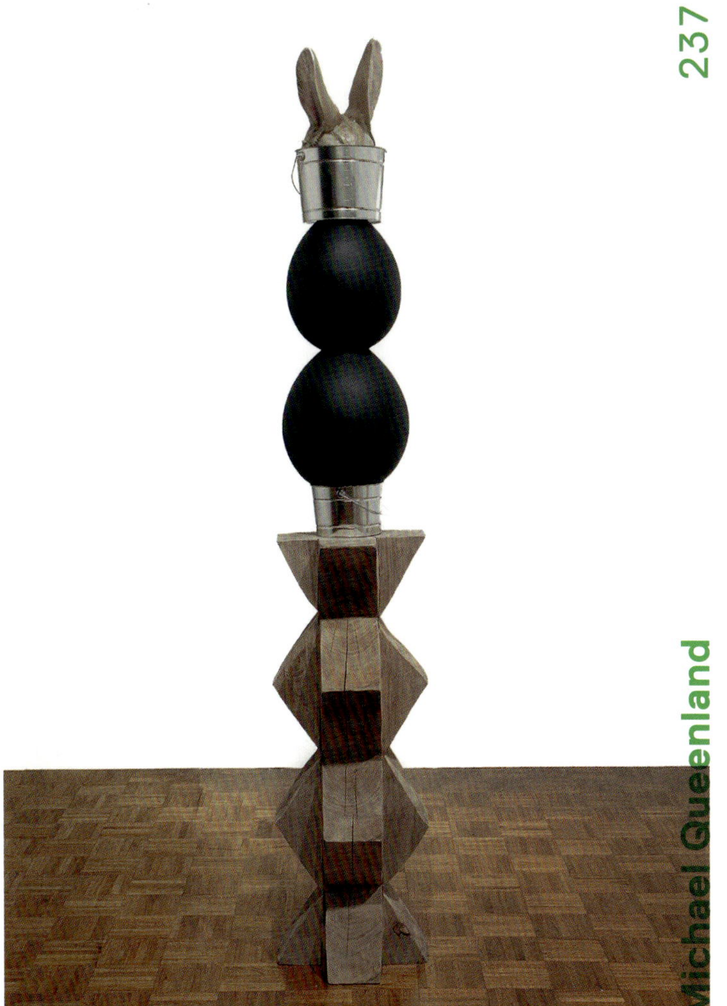

04

04 on platform from left:
→ *Untitled*, 2007
Plaster and fibreglass cast balloons
Dimensions variable
→ *Oh, Sister*, 2007
Wood, plaster
100 × 33 × 33 cm
→ *Untitled (Bread Basket)*, 2007
Wicker basket, porcelain
38 × 41 × 43 cm
→ *Balloon in Flight*, 2007
Wood, plaster
165 × 26 × 26 cm

background from left:
→ *Untitled (4)*, 2007
Digital c-print
152 × 127 cm
→ *Cheap Corridor*, 2007
Wood, sheet rock, glass doors
488 × 366 × 198 cm
→ *Abnormal Ladder*, 2007
Steel chain, plaster, wire, wax
427 × 31 × 31 cm
→ *Untitled (6 × 6)*, 2007
Wood, aluminium pigment
183 × 183 cm
→ *Midnight Curse*, 2007
Plastic chain, candles, wax, hardware, fire extinguisher dust
Length Approx. 11 m
→ *Untitled (7)*, 2007
Digital c-print
152 × 127 cm
→ *Untitled (4)*, 2007
Digital c-print
152 × 127 cm

01 Michael Rakowitz's mixed-media installations generate discursive narratives that emphasize how text influences visual art through the inclusion of sculptures, drawings and design elements in environments that encourage human discussion. Whether speaking with him as a participant in his own events, viewing his work or reading his written observations available as handwritten texts or on blogs, one is struck by how integral the history that informs each object is to the ongoing narratives that his objects inspire. Rakowitz's interactive work reinforces art history's overlap with commercial design and architecture, and his installations serve real purposes. He is best known for a series of inflatable homeless shelters called *paraSITE* (1997–present) which siphon heat from building vents to inflate nomadic homes, providing temporary solutions to homelessness while charitably highlighting socio-economic imbalance. Each white, billowy tent, loosely modelled after those used by Bedouins in Arabian deserts, is custom-tailored to its owner with pockets, windows and tunnels. The tents range visually from a Jabba the Hut lookalike to a two-domed bra-shaped inflatable made for a couple who demanded their own rooms. Since *paraSITE* began in 1997, his subsequent work has most often been exhibited in public to exemplify how, as the artist says, 'living, breathing projects are more exciting than having total control over an exhibition that begins and ends'. Rakowitz's work does function within a gallery setting, and as sculptures his discrete works innovatively employ such materials as air, memory and packaging from imported food that has weathered voyages across several borders. The artist considers his objects to be evidence of his endeavours to investigate political, economic and cultural belief systems through practical means of communication, regardless of medium. His impetus to capture 'moments of physical poetry', or chance occurrences in which humanity is revealed through the environment, is what methodologically distinguishes his practice from a designer's.

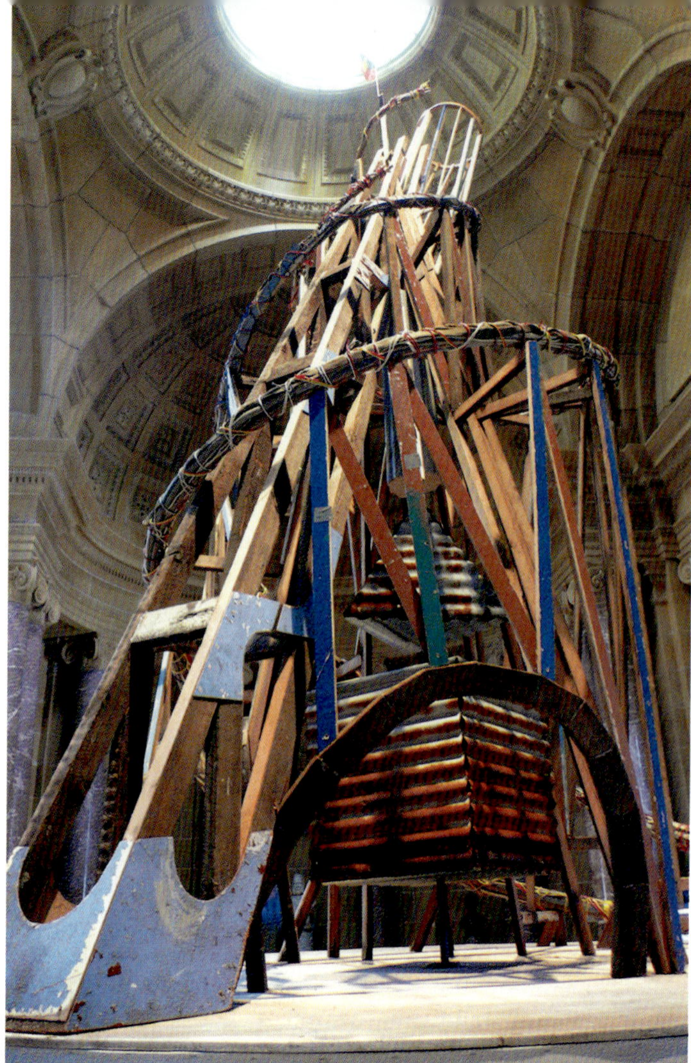

02

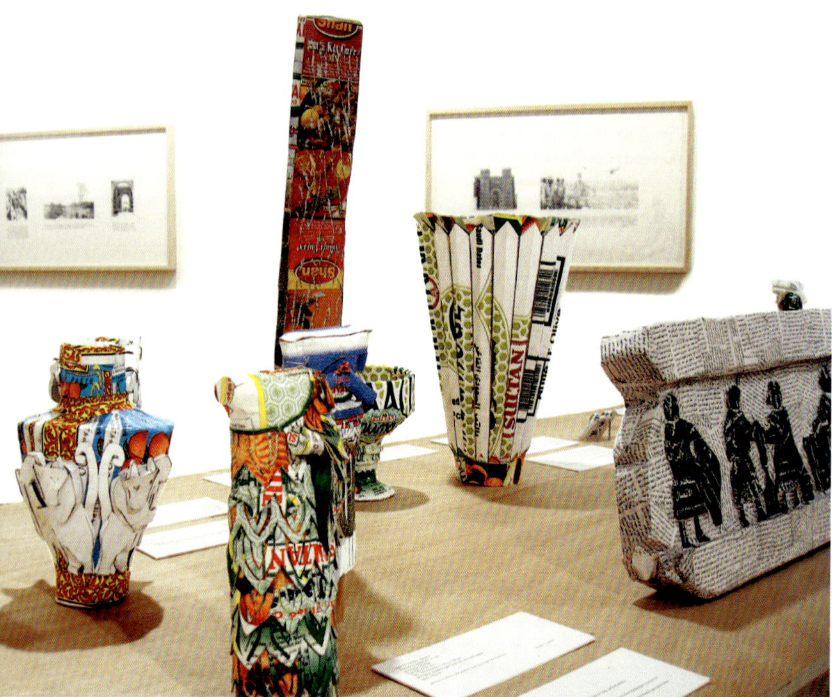

Each Rakowitz endeavour experientially contributes to and instigates the next, and his last two projects most specifically tie his Iraqi-Jewish heritage to a deep scepticism about the American war on Iraq. In 2006 Rakowitz's visit to a Middle-Eastern grocery store inspired *Return* (2006–present), for which he rented a Brooklyn shopfront to recreate his grandfather's shop with visual accuracy right down to every graphic design detail found on logos, window signage and stationery. Working as the sole shopkeeper, Rakowitz sold Iraqi imports and offered free shipping to Iraqi people wishing to mail items to their homeland. Using Iraqi-farmed dates as sculptural material, the artist shipped crates of the perishable fruits back and forth across Iraq, Syria and American borders traveling the same path as Iraqi refugees thus charting the customs holds and bureaucratic disturbances that Iraqi refugees try to avoid. Rakowitz's interest in foodstuffs as cultural signifiers also propelled *The invisible enemy should not exist* (2007), a project designed to interrogate the disappearance of artefacts stolen from the National Museum of Iraq, Baghdad, following the US invasion in April 2003. Reconstructing looted items out of food labels, cardboard and newspapers, he presented the intricately detailed sculptures on museum-like display tables alongside labels listing provenance details and quotes from people commenting on the looting and recovery of these objects, as well as graphite drawings that imagined the circumstances surrounding the plundered goods. All of these projects purposefully spark public conversation, enabling viewers to weigh levels of discomfort and feelings of foreignness against their own sense of belonging. [Trinie Dalton]

01 *White Man Got No Dreaming, Tower*, 2008
Demolished Aboriginal houses, wires, copper pipe, and wood
640 × 336 × 336 cm

02 *The Invisible Enemy Should Not Exist (Recovered, Missing, Stolen Series)*, 2007
Middle-Eastern packaging and newspapers, glue
Dimensions variable
Table
730 × 92 × 92 cm

03, 04 *Return*, 2006–present
Shopfront, shipping materials, Iraqi dates, date products
529 Atlantic Ave, Brooklyn

05 *Joe Heywood's paraSITE shelter*, 2000
Plastic bags, polyethylene tubing, hooks, tape
Dimensions variable
Battery Park City, New York

03

04

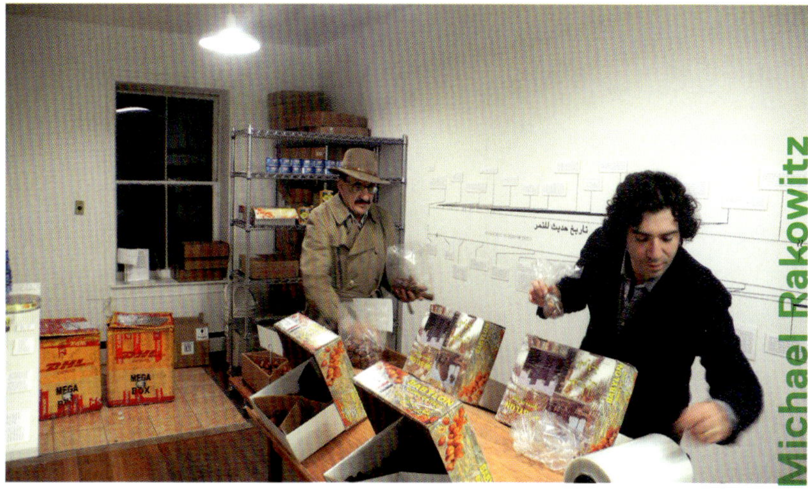

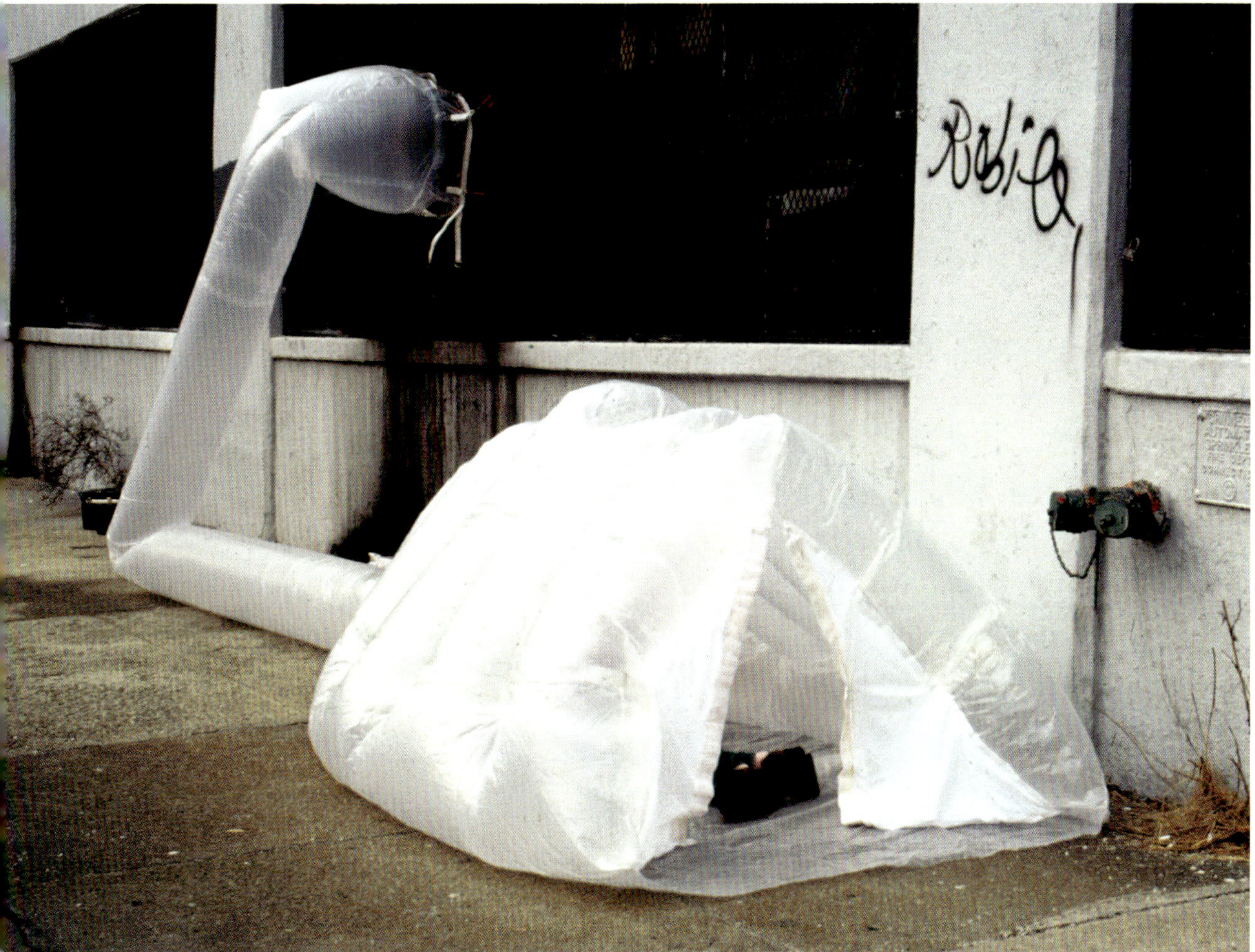

05

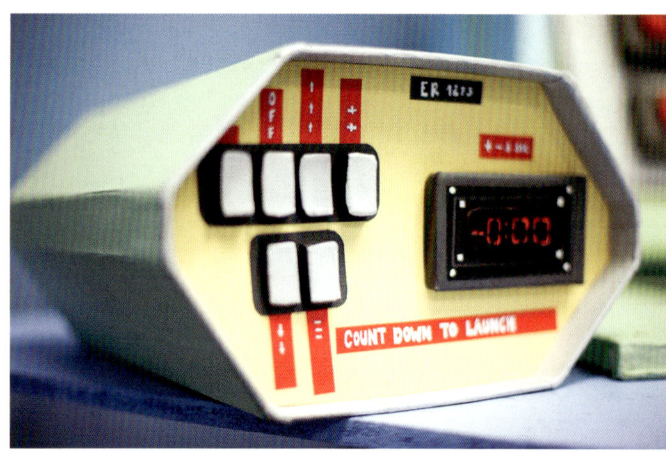

01

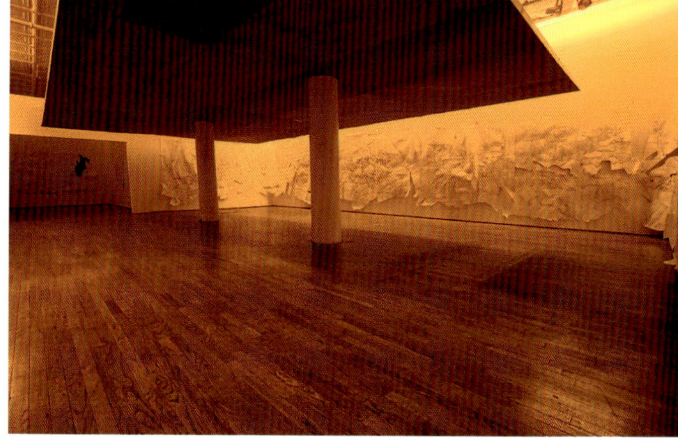

02

Lisi Raskin describes her multi-faceted installations recreating military architecture as 'experiential' sets that provide access into the real sites she visits in order to investigate her fear and fascination with possible apocalypse. Her stylized recreations of atomic shelters, bombing ranges and missile-launch test sites, and the objects found in those desolate places such as weaponry, high-tech equipment, security fencing and covert communication devices, conveys a sculptural aesthetic aiming to communicate three simultaneous narratives: the child's enjoyment of play-fantasy, the artist's study of memory's subjectivity relative to anxieties about impending disaster, and the tourist's documentation of industrial landscapes as a critique of technologies that endanger human lives.

In Raskin's environments, videos, photographs and drawings of the locales she visits adorn constrictive spaces filled with sculpted gear and furniture built of recycled wood and survivalist essentials like tarps and foil. What she calls the 'dorky' or 'wonky' accoutrements made from cardboard, coloured paper and elementary-school art supplies inject humour into her ruminations on who controls or provokes catastrophe. The handmade approach to creating sets in which war toys are 'krafty with a K', as she says, pits a craft-project aesthetic associated with motherhood and the classroom against a macho military realm that Raskin finds both terrifying and wondrous.

Raskin more directly challenges gender stereotypes by performing as a series of fictional, often male characters who populate her constructed worlds. While in residence in Berlin, she appeared in drag as Herr Doktor Hauptmann II, and she is currently writing a radio play for which she will play male and female characters reacting to the repression of gays in the military. The play is set in the Titan Missile Silo in Tucson, Arizona, which also inspired her 2007 installation *Topside*. While acting lends Raskin's sculptural practice an absurdist, perceptual dimension, the discrete objects she builds remind viewers how her subject matter is rooted in an absolute reality that induces panic and confusion. The artist reveals a soldier's dedication, 'If one can get scared enough, fear becomes a conduit,' she says.

This fear derives, in part, from Raskin's visit to see where missiles are launched and stored in the American Southwest. For *Topside*, Raskin built a Control Room, with curved walls mimicking the Titan silo, to house a scrupulously detailed control panel, monitors mapping out imaginary warpaths, and a hexagonal missile launch box. Tiny surveillance cameras lining the ceiling led further into Raskin's base, where a Missile Room displayed rockets in a bunker below a red-lit room lined with carved, chipboard netting that evoked camouflage.

For a previous exhibition, Raskin entitled a large-scale construction *Jack Shack*, implying from the outset the connection between sexual desire and male violence. Looking externally like a hobo's shelter, the inside revealed a bomb kit that appeared to be powered by beer, recalling Cady Noland's beer-can sculptures, which cover thematically similar territory. While *Jack Shack* presents a terrorist's botched science project, and *Topside*, with its geometric, 1950s modernist sheen, alludes to American defence stratagems, both projects invite the viewer to map out three territories: the gallery, the original site and the artist's imagination. Holistically, these installations simulate Raskin's apprehensions about forced geopolitical conflict and her sublimation of that apprehension through meditative aspects of artistic invention. [Trinie Dalton]

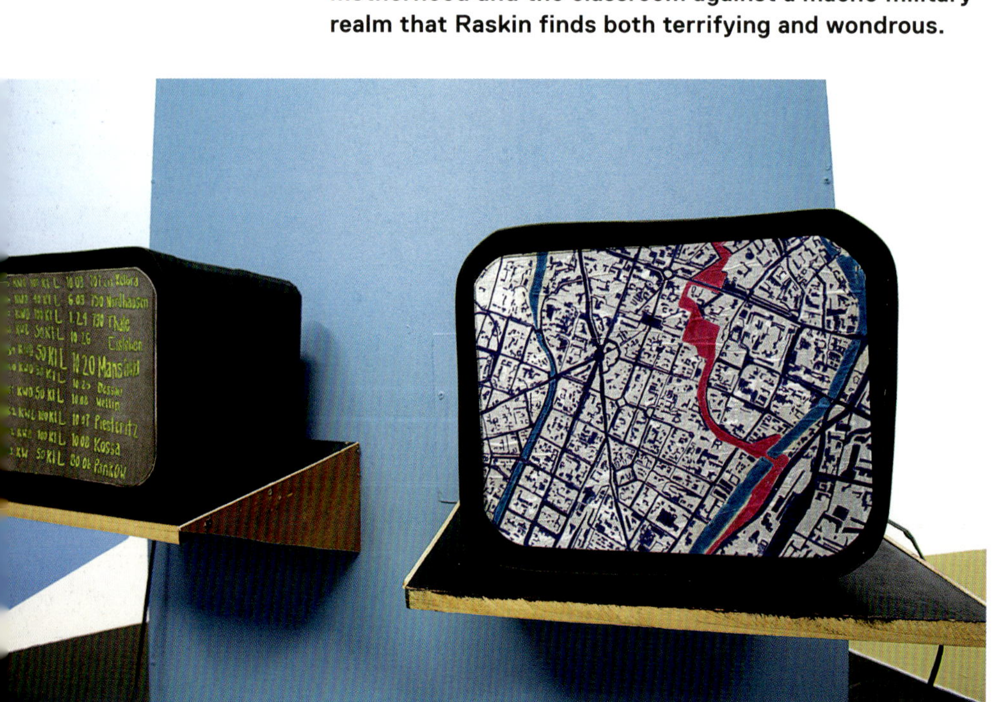

03

04

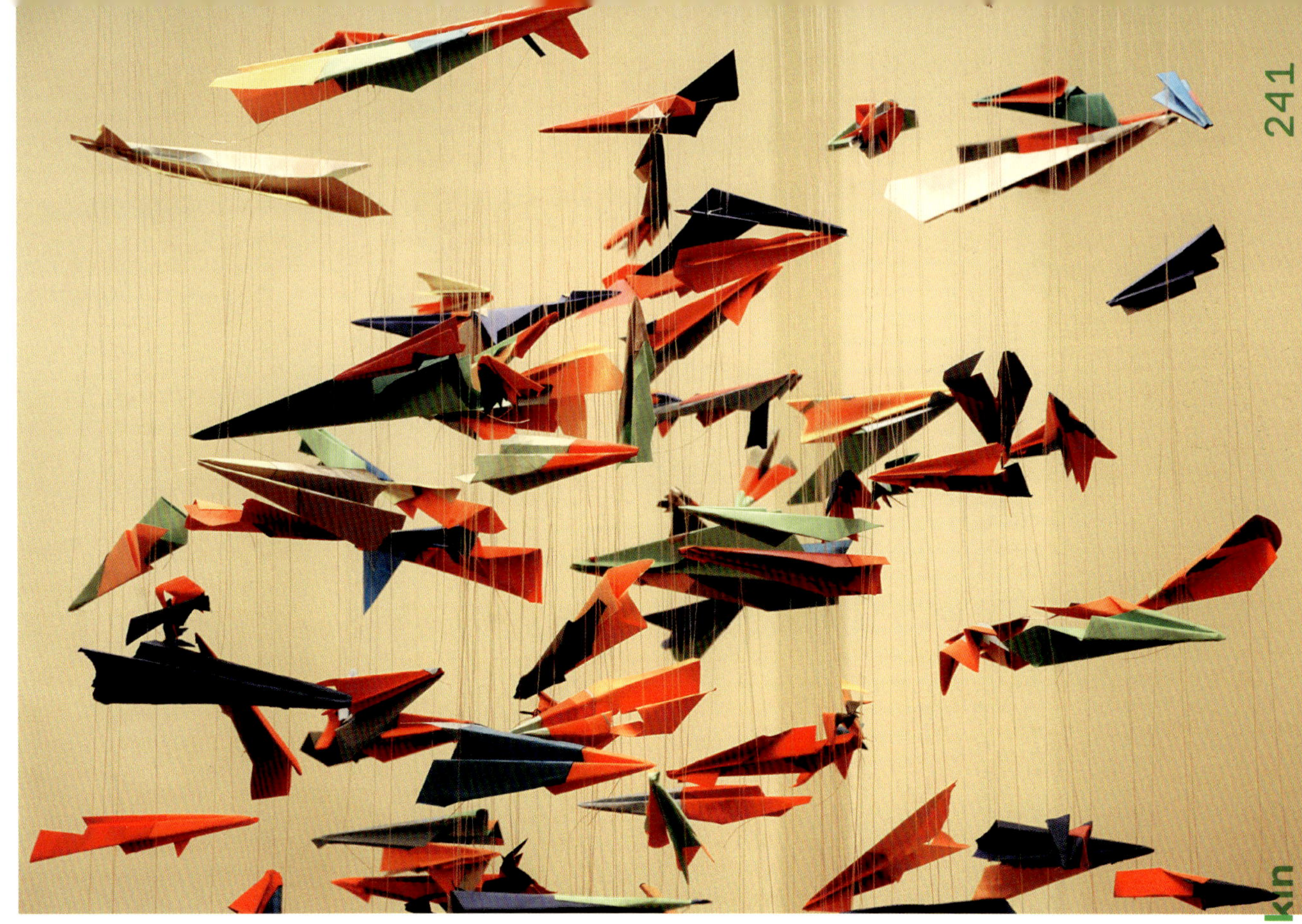

01 *Count-down to Launch*, 2008
Paper, chipboard, glue
18 × 20 × 46 cm

02 *Switchyard*, 2007
Collaged paper, luan, fluorescent lights, gels, graphite
366 × 671 × [illegible] cm

03 *Topside*, 2008
Surveillance monitors, paper, chipboard, wood, latex paint
2 parts
Each 142 × 140 × 140 cm

04 *Sunday Punch*, 2008
Paper, monofilament
61 × 51 × 46 cm

05, 06 *Jack Shack*, 2007
Paper, wood, tarpaulin, incandescent lights, fluorescent lights, gels, acrylic paint, latex paint, aluminium foil tape, Plasticine, glue, Styrofoam, rope, wire, pushpins, marker, blueprints, extension cords, beer cans and bottles, plastic bottles, bottle tops, cigarette butts, chair, typewriter, weathervane, analogue fixtures from nuclear power plants, dials, gauges, switches, heart-o-meter
250 × 430 × 310 cm

05

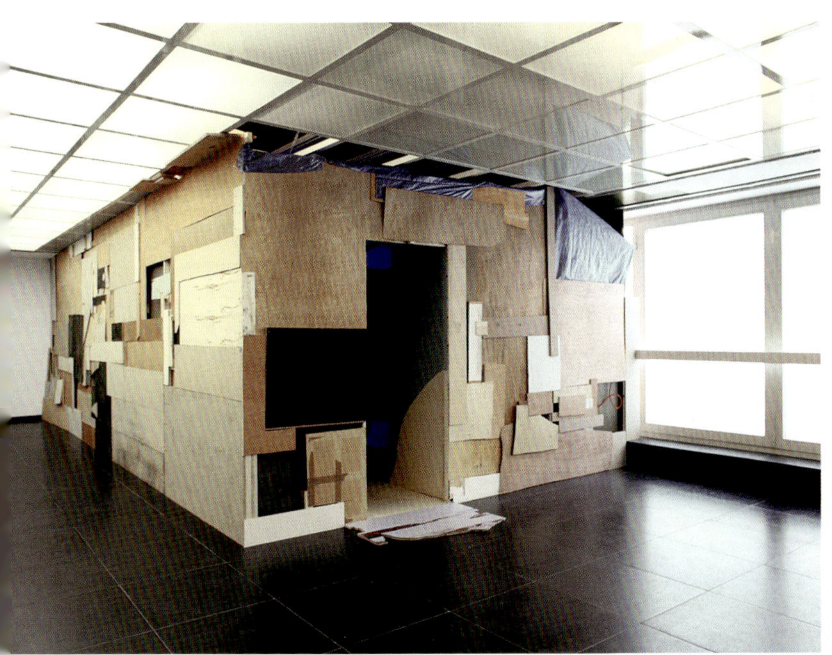

06

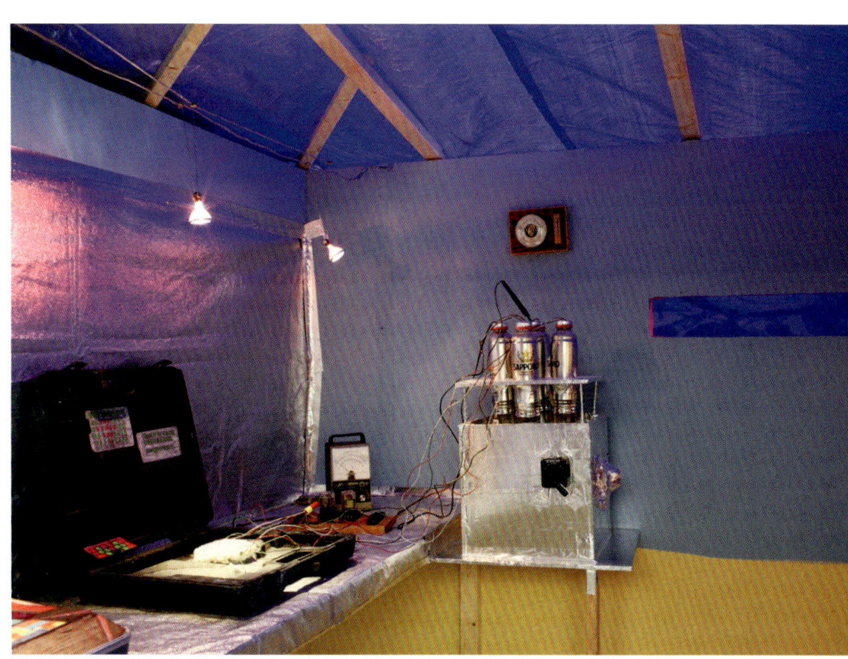

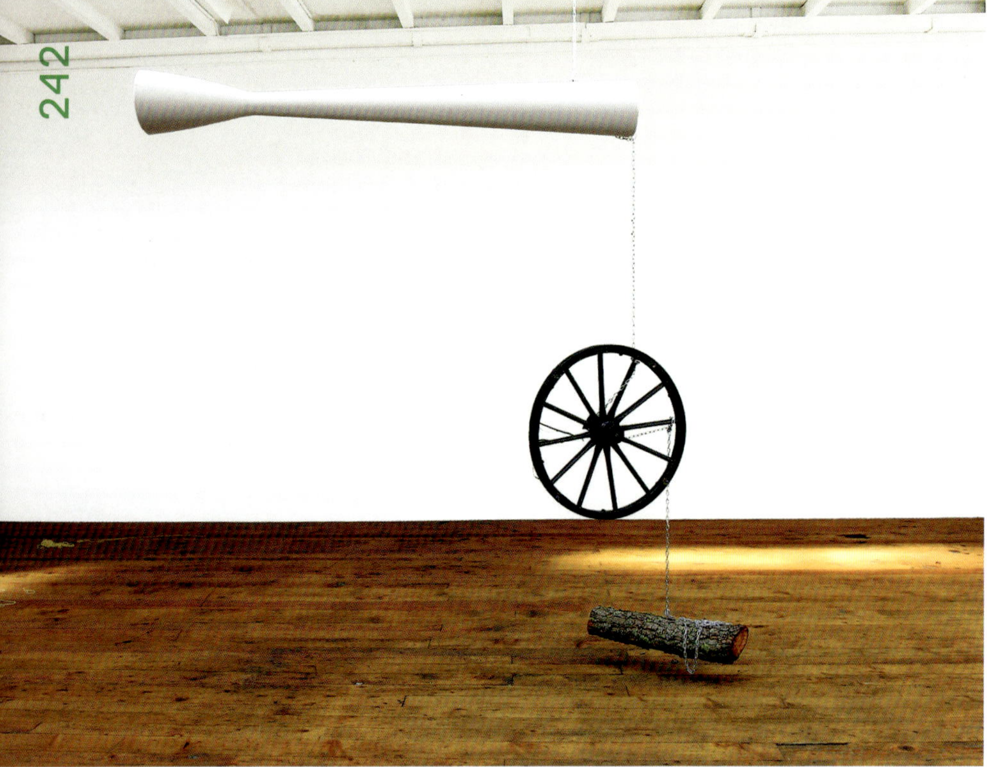

01

If one had to choose the single most important concept that recurs in David Renggli's work, it would be 'balance' — in both the literal and the figurative senses of the word. His art cannot be defined in terms of a particular medium or a specific subject. Instead, we should look to his artistic attitude, which is marked by continuous experimentation. Whether minimalist sculptures, photographic images or highly atmospheric installations, his works communicate a genuine desire to try new things and an enjoyment in ongoing research. However, this attitude of experimentation is not enough to explain the growing interest in Renggli's work. It is his skilful use of the idea of balance, giving his work a metaphorical underpinning, which ultimately grants it a universal validity.

In some of his works, the act of playing with balance becomes the dominant visual element and the principal formal component. For example, in *Flat Tire Make Higher* (2006) a log and a cartwheel are suspended from a tubular element that calls to mind a sculpture by Constantin Brancusi. The heterogeneous assemblage of objects becomes a 'surreal mobile', a kind of absurd spatial collage. Its title involves the viewer in philosophical and formal speculations. In this sense, Renggli's work is characterized by a powerful meta-artistic interest, due not only to its nods to art history but also to the direct thematic use of the classical elements that make up a work of art. The perspective, the way the light falls, the development of the space and the formal and tactile qualities of the materials play a central part in the work itself. We see this in the installation *The Night it Suddenly Became Bright Again* (2007); a theatrical beam of light sweeps across a darkened room, falling on the furniture, which, upon closer investigation, is made up of sawdust generated by the circular saw in the centre of the scene.

Everyday objects are the primary material for Renggli's compositions, in which — thanks to a strong shot of humour — the trivial lives effortlessly alongside the philosophical. His works can at times be read as still-lifes or picture-puzzles in which the viewer's visual intelligence is called upon and stimulated. However, Renggli does not seek to avoid abstraction, as we can see in the series of sculptures using chromed tubing (such as *Stripped Bike I,* 2007). Recalling the world of gyms and fitness, they create a filigree of delicate abstract lines that develop through the space. In moving between reality and fiction, perhaps in search of perfect balance, Renggli reminds us that art is still the perfect tool for sorting through and celebrating the complexity of the world. [Giovanni Carmine]

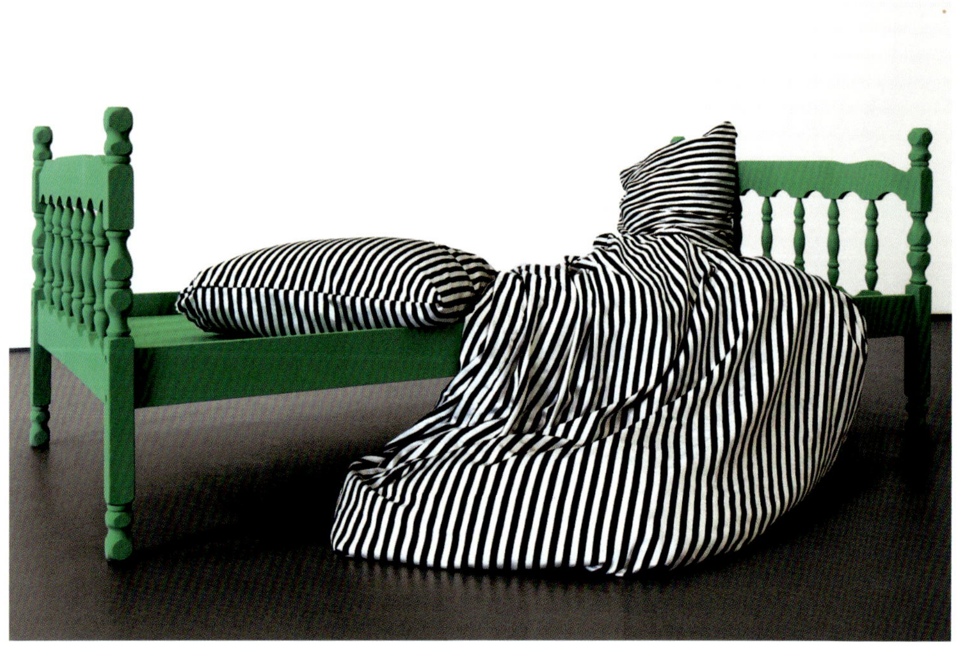

02

01 *Flat Tire Make Higher*, 2006
Wood, plastics, chain
380 × 260 × 110 cm

02 *While I Work my Bed Sleeps*, 2007
Wood, paint, pillow, duvet, fabric
75 × 200 × 90 cm

03

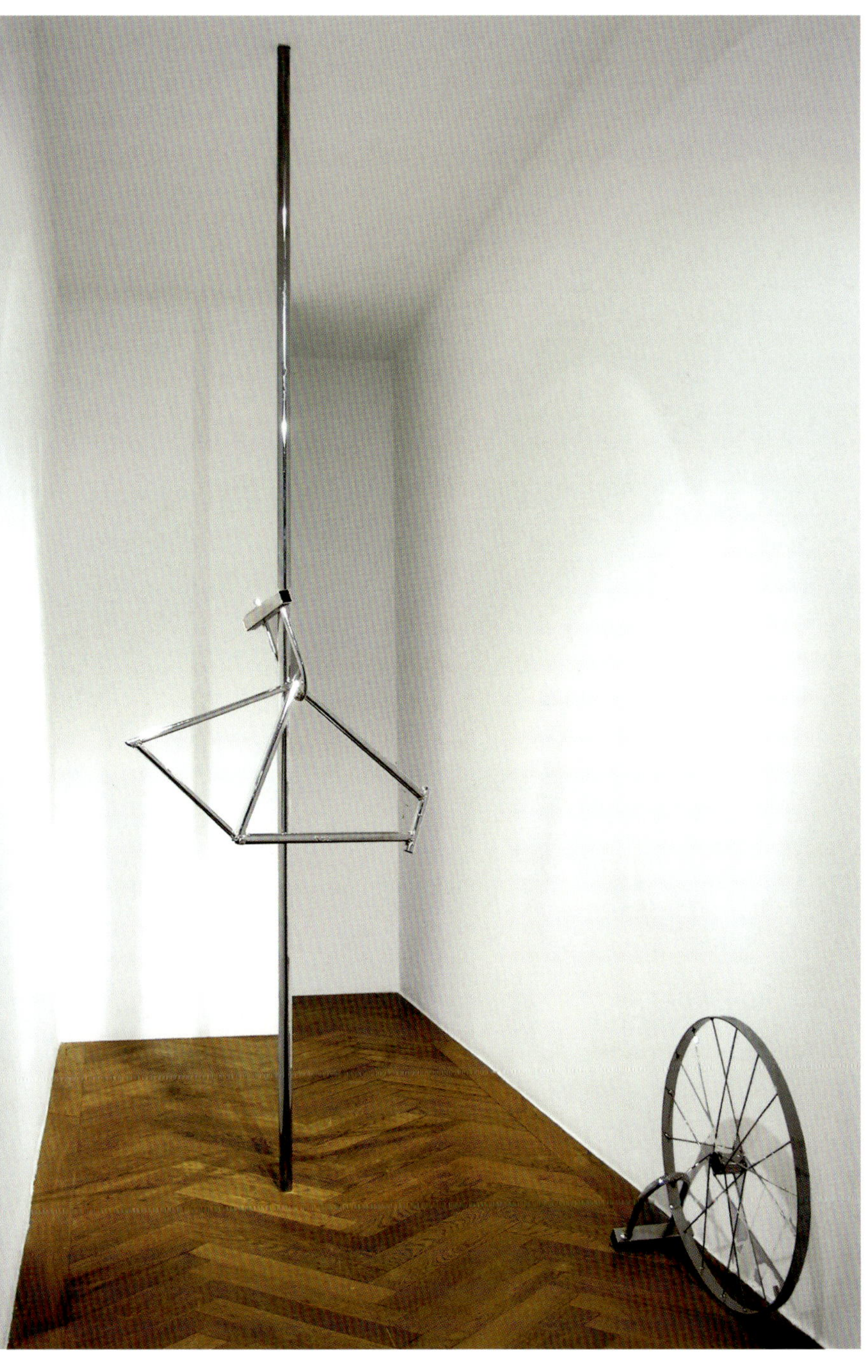

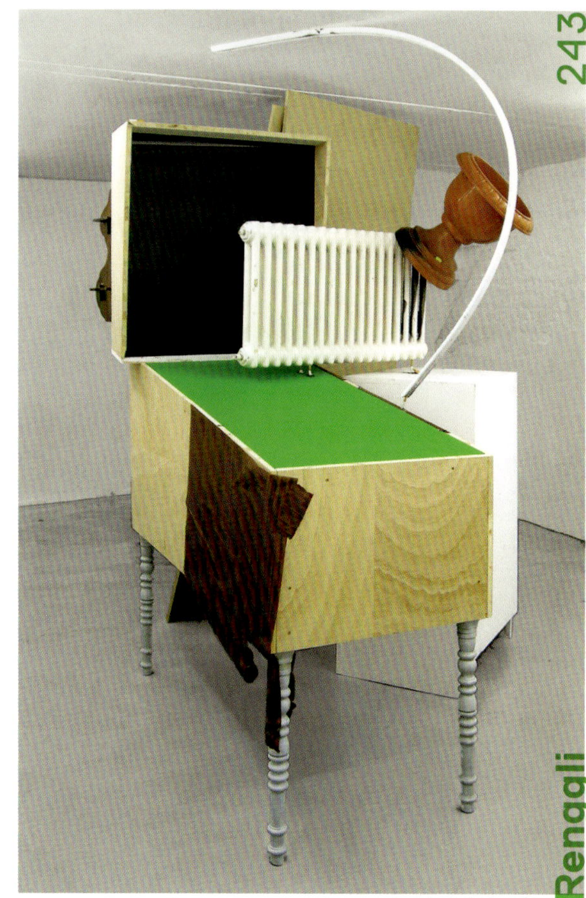

04

05

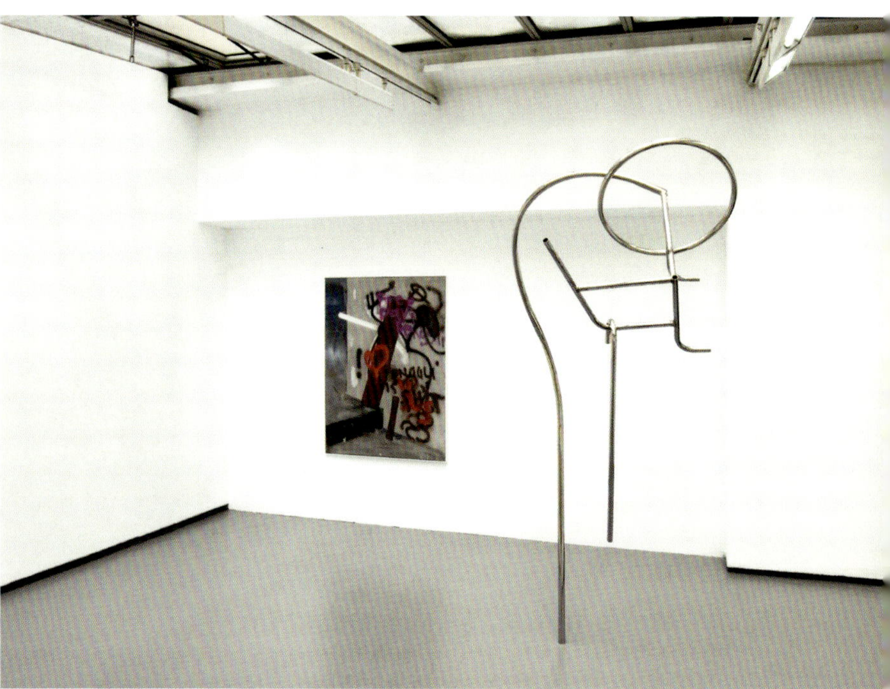

03 *Strippen für Piepen (Stripped Bike I)*, 2007
Metal, chrome finish
320 × 78 × 18 cm

04 *Compressed Pub*, 2006
Wood, felt, glass, radiator, adhesive foil, cigarettes, paint
200 × 180 × 200 cm

05 from left:
→ *Lass uns doch Kapitalistenschweine werden Nr. 7*, 2008
Paint, wallpaper, aluminium paper, spray paint, adhesive foil
144 × 100 cm
→ *Lieber ein Diplom als ein Titel*, 2008
Metal, chrome finish
250 × 145 × 90 cm

Overleaf:

06 *The Night it Suddenly Became Bright Again*, 2007
Wood, various objects, black paint, sawdust, mitre saw
250 × 850 × 450 cm

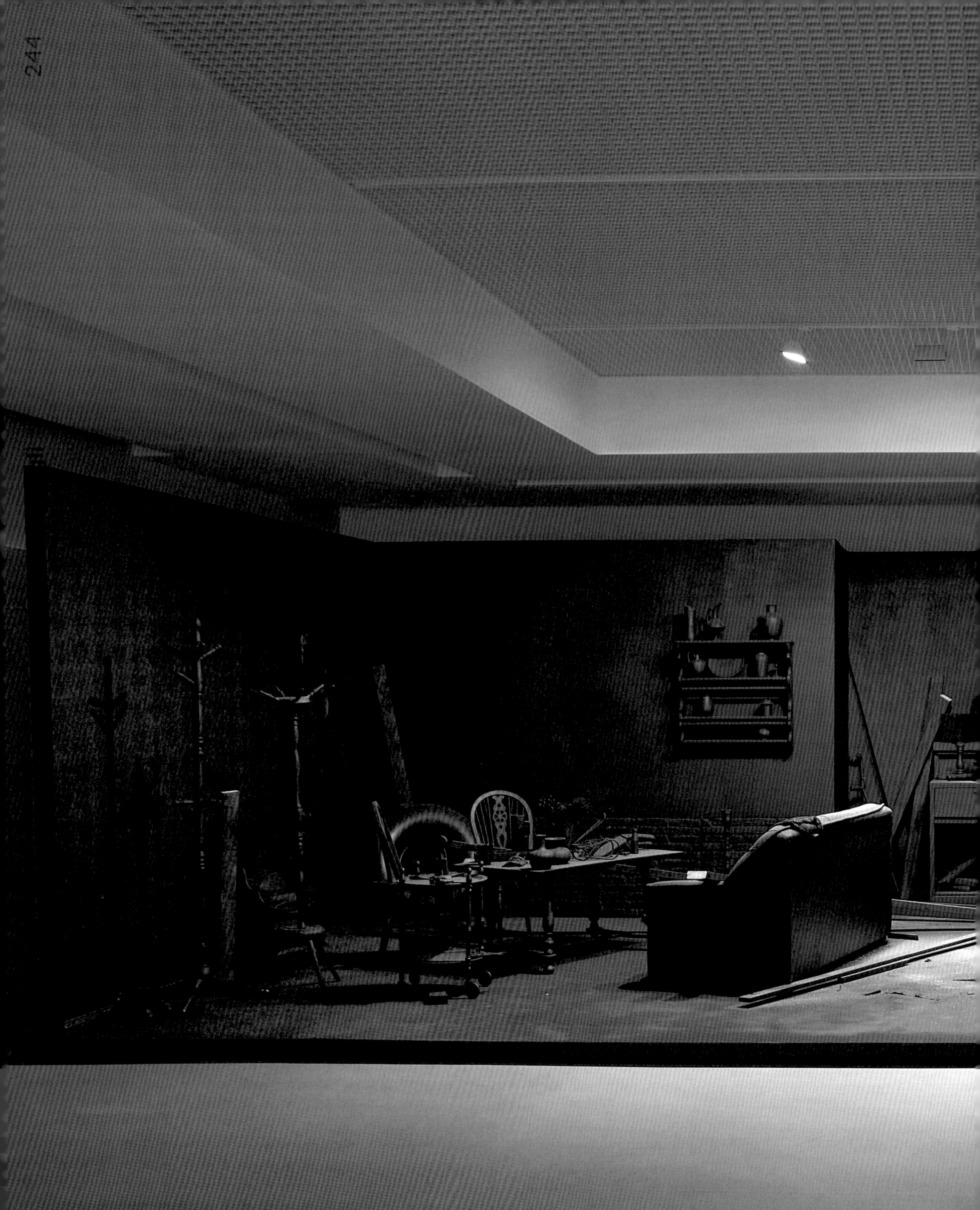

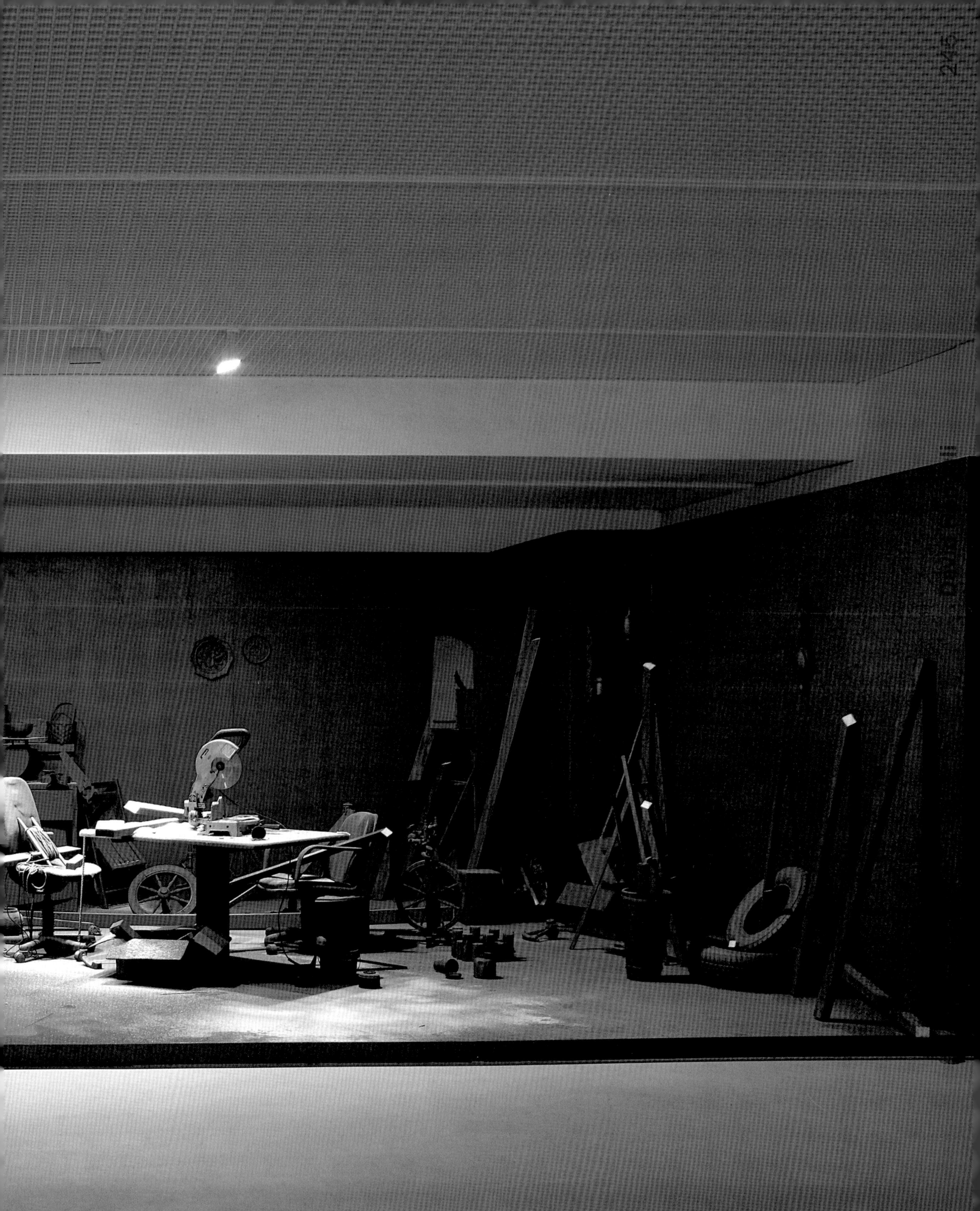

Mandla Reuter

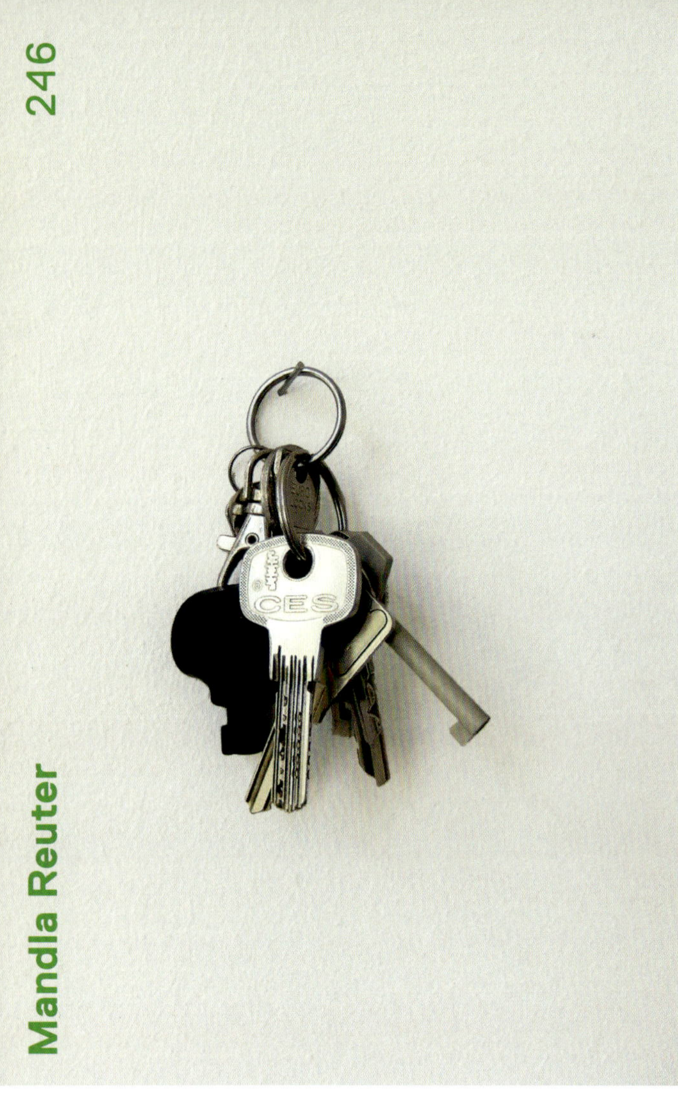

01

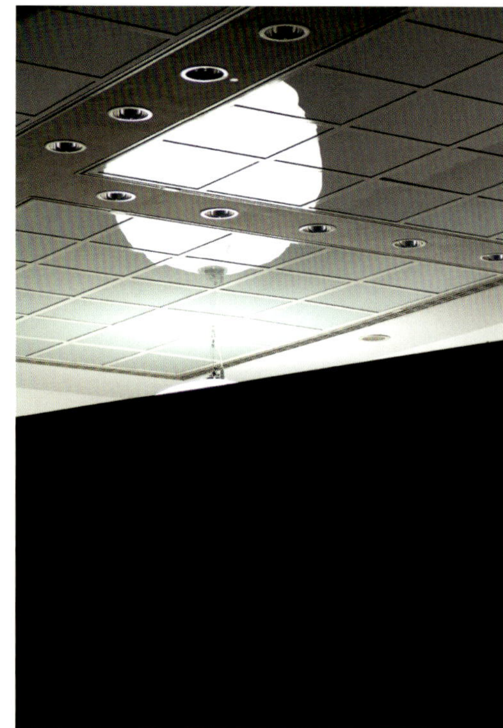

02

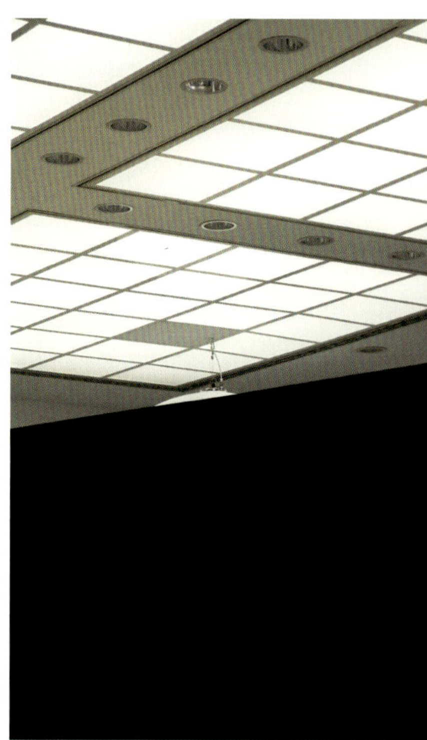

03

01 *BG*, 2007
Set of keys to every room in the building
9 × 5 × 5 cm

02, 03 *On and On*, 2007
Room lighting, balloon light, DMX controller
Dimensions variable

04, 05, 06 *Fourth Wall*, 2008
Electricity connection, cable, concrete, steel, connection box
Approx. 120 × 4 × 1 m

If one were to seek a key to the work of Mandla Reuter, the actual set of keys he displayed in his piece *BG* (2007) in the Berlinische Galerie would not be a bad starting point. Hanging on the wall of the gallery like a work of art, the keys were actually those to all the doors in the gallery building. A visitor could have used them to gain access to the 'backstage' of the institution, entering the director's office or the maintenance room, for instance. This visitor would have left with a different notion of the exhibition space, but just looking at the keys made a similar point.

The point of Reuter's works is not always execution: frequently they simply trigger thoughts, but they always somehow transform the spaces in which they are shown. Sometimes it only takes an electronically programmed light switch, as in *On and On* (2007), which interchanges a light source commonly used for theatrical and film productions with the normal gallery lighting. In this and several similar works with lighting, Reuter heightens our awareness of how spaces are framed according to certain situations and purposes. He also interacts with other aspects of the site. At Ursula Blickle Stiftung gallery he responded to the creek outside the space by playing a recording of the sound of Niagara Falls inside the space through speakers positioned in front of the window that gave a view of the creek.

In *Fourth Wall* for the 2008 SITE Santa Fe Biennial, Reuter installed a power supply that was strong enough to run a large-scale event or stage show. All that was on display in the white cube, however, was wiring that wound all the way through the building and a single electrical outlet. Potentiality is an important factor in Reuter's work. That his pieces consist of thoughts and ideas as well as objects places him within the tradition of Conceptual art. He does not consider it an orthodoxy to adhere to, but an open field of experimentation.

Pictures (2007) has so far been staged twice, once in Madrid and once in Hamburg. In both cases a small private space became a movie theatre — a thirty-five-millimetre projector was installed, a screen set up, and outside the venue was a huge billboard promoting the screening of *The Simpsons Movie*, which was out in theatres at the same time. This blending of realms that are commonly strictly separated is just another example of how Reuter examines spaces and sheds a different light on them. [Bert Rebhandl]

04

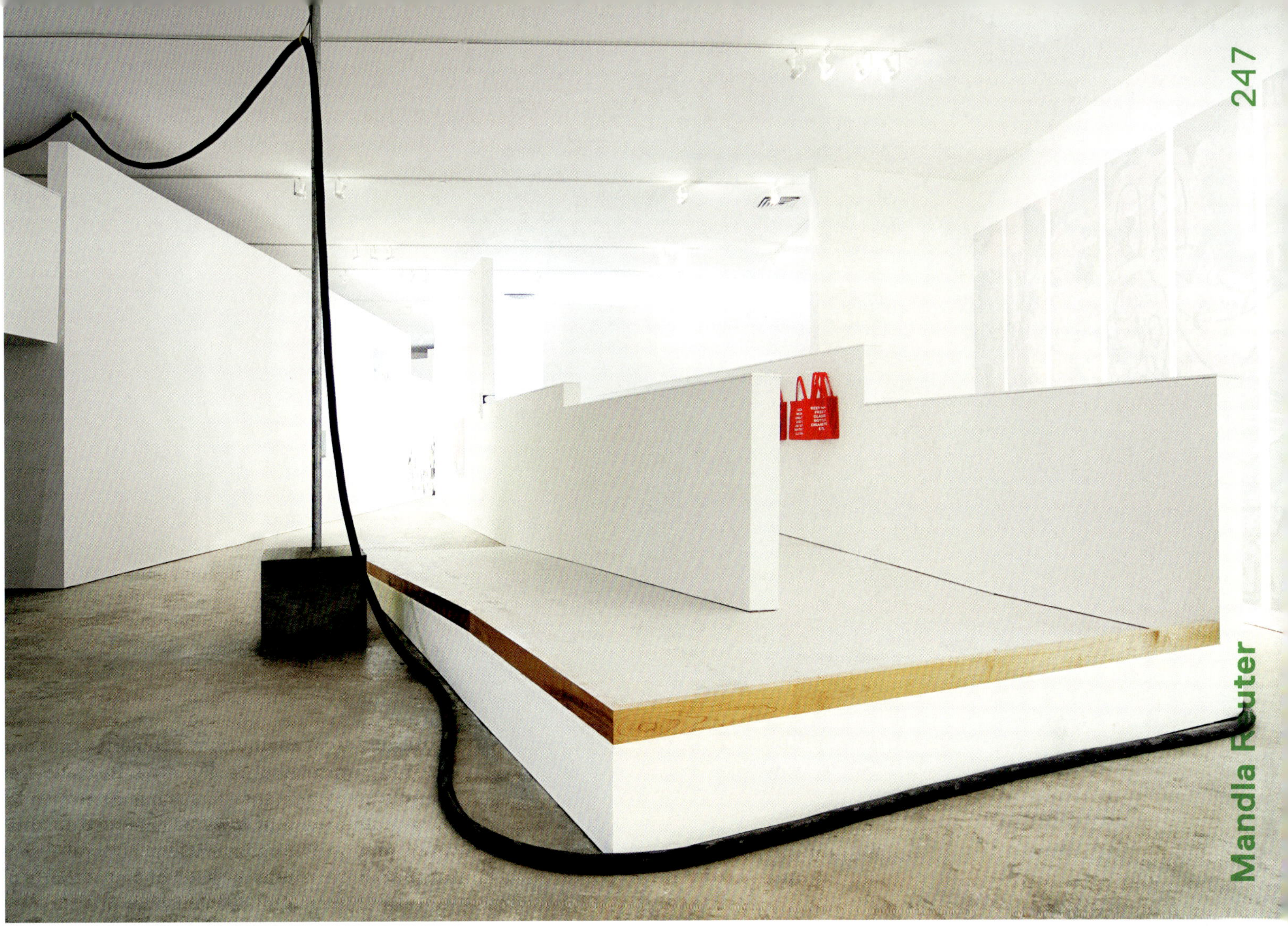

05

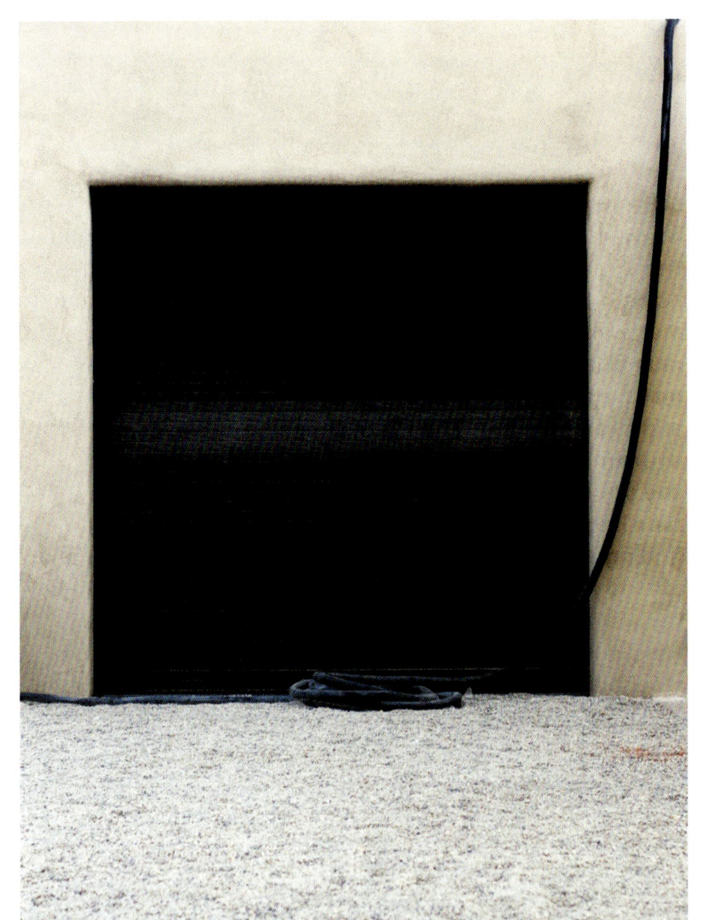

06

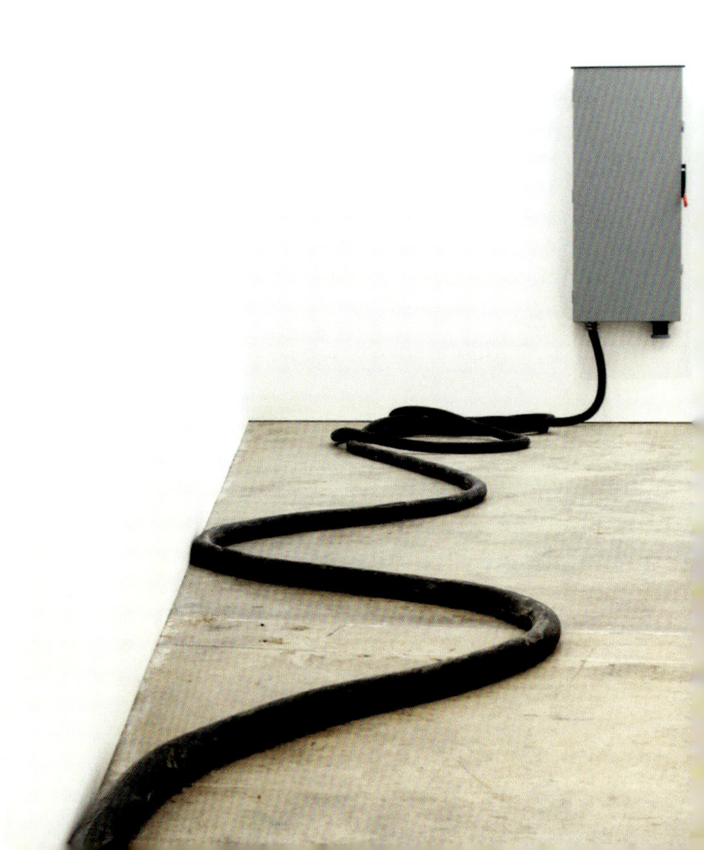

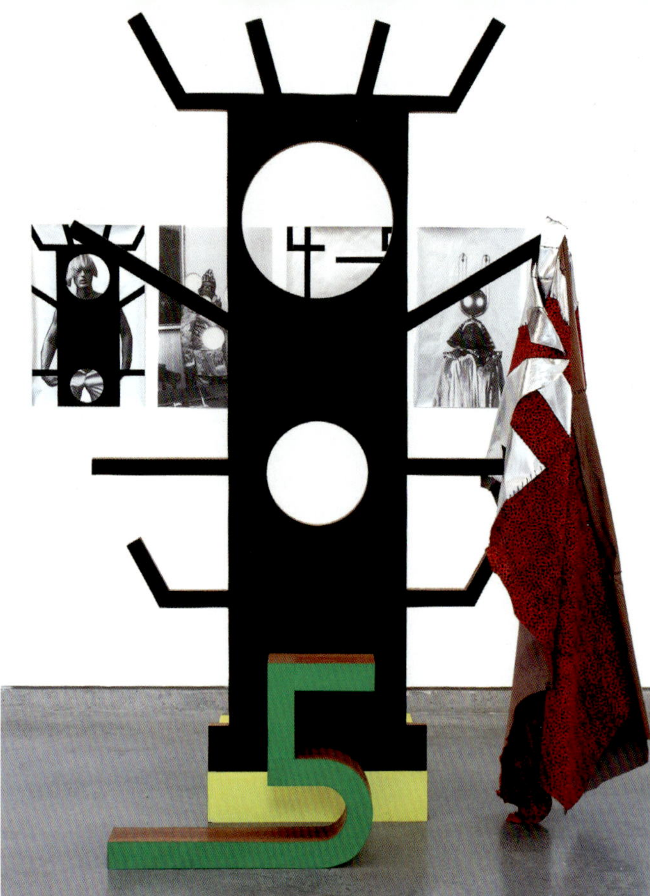

01

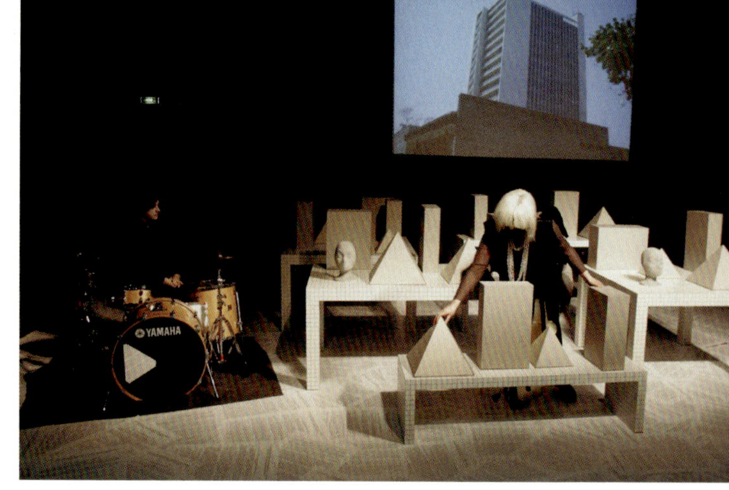

02

When trying to define any community or alternative culture, one first looks for its quintessential and 'pure' stage, the moment when the group could be identified by a common ideology, a posture, a sound or an aesthetic, before it was repackaged by the cultural industry. To Lili Reynaud-Dewar, such authentic and autonomous moments are nostalgic mythologies. In her work she appropriates elements from underground cultures and artificially reconstructs their roots to demonstrate eccentricity and opacity unprotected from outside interferences. Her allegorical sculptures and theatrical fables are devoid of transparent maxims, yet polarities collide in a burlesque mise en scène of cultural assimilations and resistance.

Allowing a range of vocabularies to co-exist in a mannered syncretism, Reynaud-Dewar reactivates forms from the historical avant-garde, merging them with elements from cultural movements that possess strong aesthetic and radical sensibilities (including post-punk, queer culture, voodoo and African-American culture). In her sculptures she plays with the proximity between generic abstract forms and culturally specific motifs. *Queen Mother Nanny of the Mountains* (2006), for example, is constructed with modernist geometrical forms and bold colours. Green, yellow and red, however, also represent the Rastafarian flag, and the overall shape of the sculpture, conceived from a frontal point of view with an axial symmetry, suggests possible uses as stage decor or a totem for initiation rituals. The black pyramidal hanging and burnt wood circle mimic ritual gates, underlining the creation of identity through staged artifices.

Drawing from aesthetic vocabularies that are unrelated to her own cultural background, Reynaud-Dewar assumes a fragmentation of her own voice to decentre the work's content towards foreign elements. This polyphony of voices questions cultural authenticity and the intrinsic representation of the author's own self in the creative process. Far from literal references, these appropriations function as allegorical characters, bringing contexts, motifs and myths together in a carnivalesque game in which aesthetic hierarchies, identities, radicalism and the mainstream are inverted by normally concealed energies.

Love=UFO (2008) is a complex example of this reversal mechanism. In this work, Reynaud-Dewar created an installation conceived as the decor for a performance featuring emblematic characters interacting with their self-images and opposites through multiple mise en abîmes. As in a narrative fable, each performer personifies a concept, from camp posture to Creole identity to noise music. These characters interrelate in an environment where each object brings new references to be multiplied in the never-ending effects of mirrors and make-up (with echoes of Robert Filliou, Bruce Nauman and Peter Saville). The Plaza Dressing Table, designed by Michael Graves for the Memphis Group, evokes the use of deviant taste as a critical tool, while a costume recalling Sun Ra's cosmogony suggests the possibility of finding a valid yet sardonic identity through humour, parade and mannerist celebrations. Although a fable typically leads towards a resolution, Reynaud-Dewar always keeps the audience at the core of the narrative mechanism by emphasizing the artificiality of the decor and showing the performers putting on make-up and arranging props. There is no narrative resolution, just a parade that surprisingly holds polarities together in an eccentric whole that seems to claim, 'We master rhetorical figures like magical formulas' (*The Center and the Eyes*, 2006). [Céline Kopp]

01 *Abacost!*, 2007
Wood, paper, leather, paint
Approx. 2.2 × 60 × 60 cm
4 collages
50 × 65 cm

02 *En réalité, le sphinx est il une annexe du monument, ou le monument une annexe du sphinx?*, 2008
Posters, mirror, drum kit, leather costume, chains, video, cardboard models, *Quasernea* tables from the *Misura M* series by Superstudio
Performance with Xavier Chabellard and Mary Knox
Dimensions variable

03 *Queen Mother Nanny of the Mountains*, 2006
Burnt plywood, fabric, photocopies, vinyl record and sleeve
Approx. 250 × 220 × 180 cm

04 *LOVE=UFO*, 2008
Wood, glass, leather, costume, screen-printed posters, video, performance
Dimensions variable

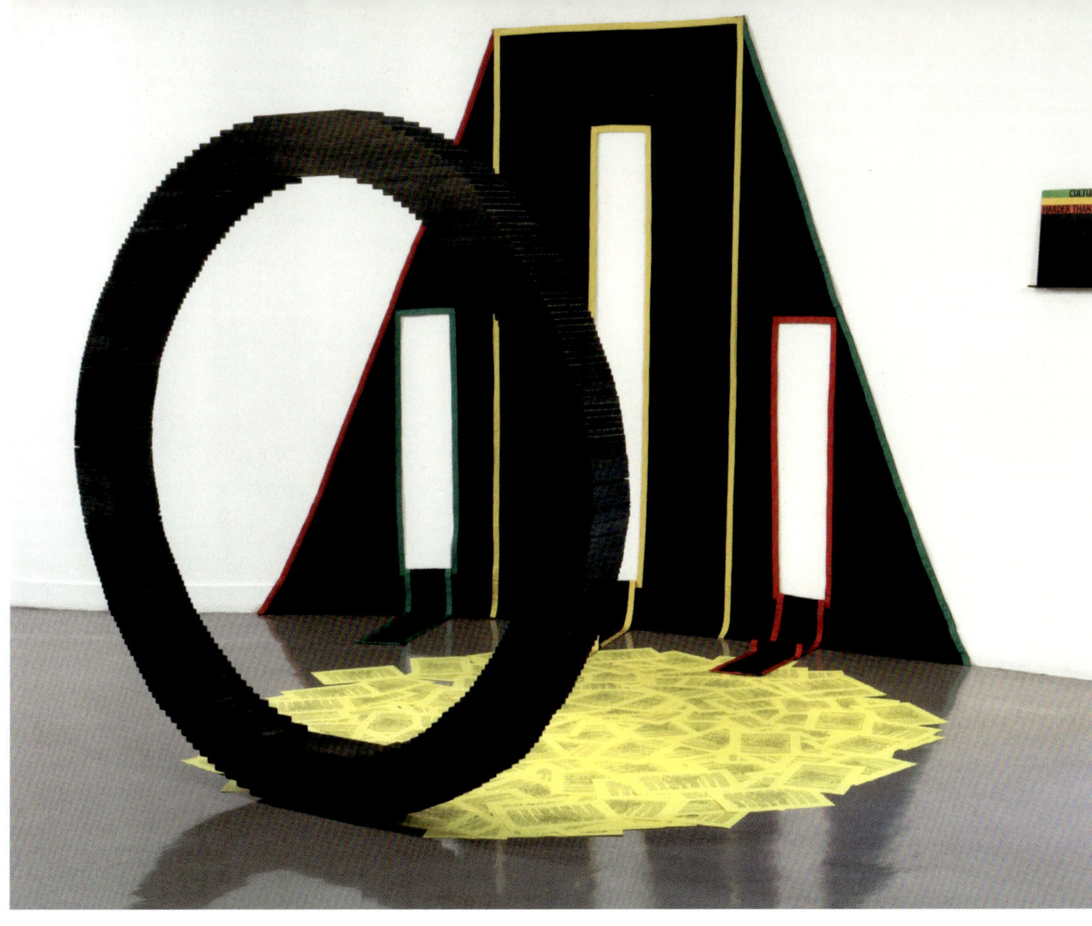

03

04

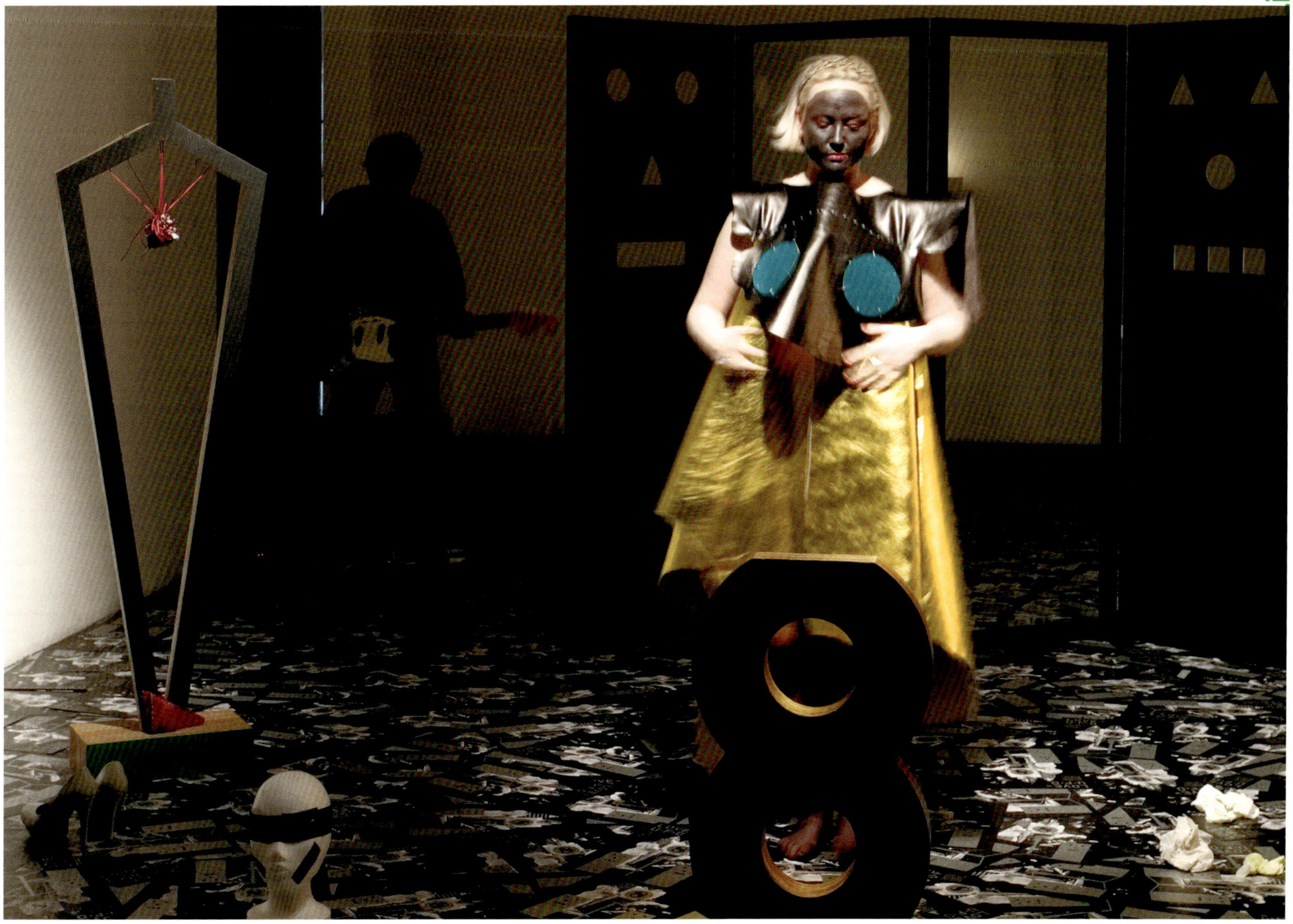

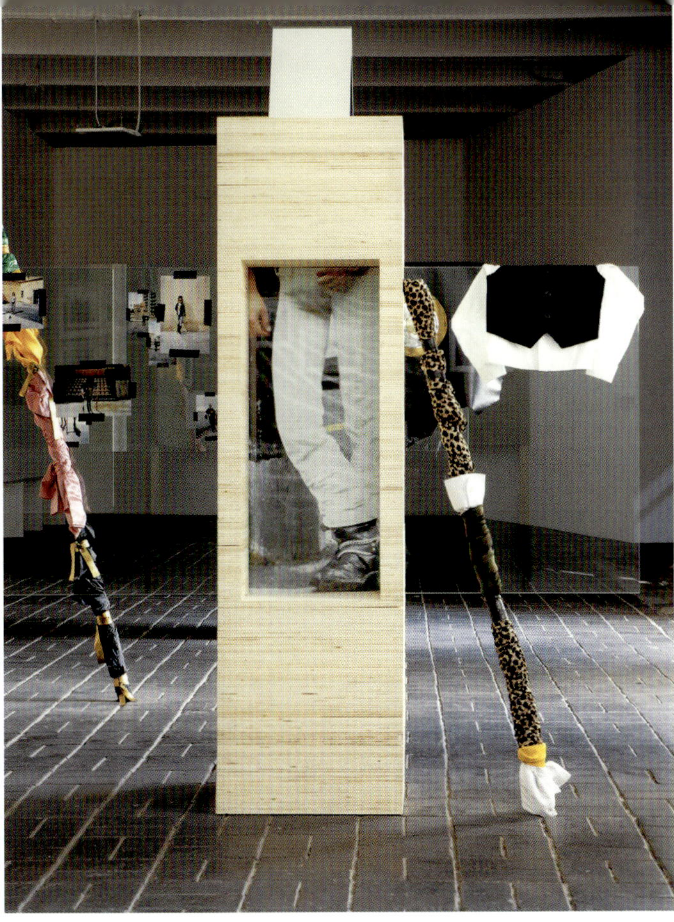

06

05 *Costume for performance (with child)*, 2007
Fabric, paper
90 × 100 × 5 cm

06 *Les Garçons Sauvages*, 2008
3 wooden columns, photographic prints, glass, prints, ceramic, fabric, mixed media
Approx. 170 × 40 × 180 cm

07 *In every room there is the ghost of sex*, 2008
12 screenprints, works by Ettore Sotsass, performance by Mary Knox and Lionel Fernandez
Dimensions variable

07

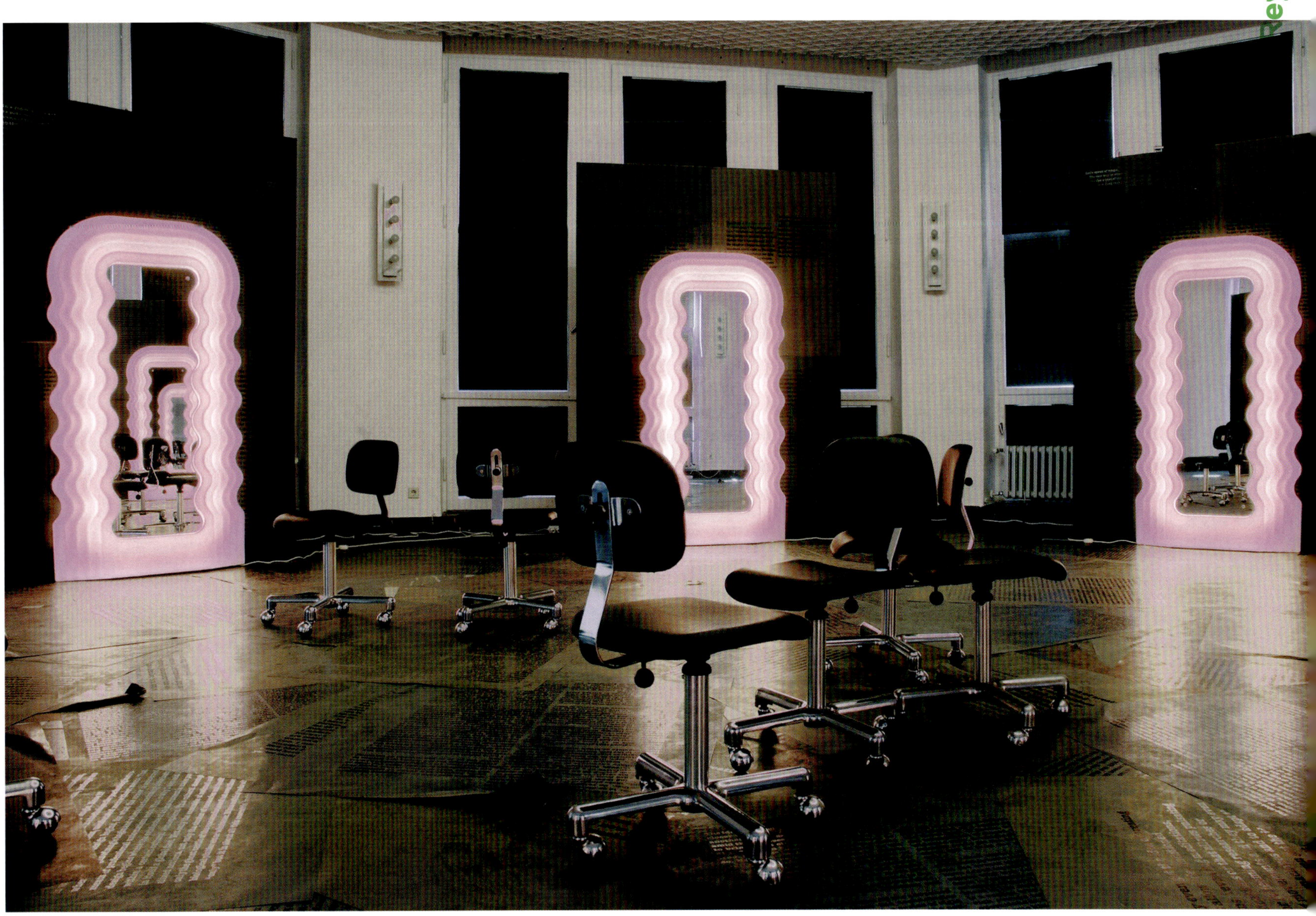

Eva Rothschild's sculptures evoke the tradition of Minimalism but are always reminiscent of something else: a traffic light woven from leather, curtains cut from strips of plastic and jewels, fetishes or objects borrowed from protest culture. The story of abstract art, through geometric forms such as the circle, sphere, square and triangle, is dispatched into a bazaar of meanings and projections. Current ideas of abstraction, representation and decoration are interwoven with models of longing that are projected on to these familiar forms.

Rothschild creates two and three-dimensional,obejcts, which make current again the formal vocabulary of 1960s art by charging it with contemporary content. They interrogate aesthetic models, faith models and social constructions of meaning. At the same time, the artist extends and tests her work by using unusual materials that are 'problematic' for art, mixing handicraft aesthetics with industrial processes, the former deriving from subcultures, the latter from Minimalism. Together they form a countercurrent to the commodified 'art object' that supplies a mass-cultural desire for content and meaning and at the same time resists it.

By using joss sticks in her work *Disappearer* (2002), Rothschild evokes a quasi-spiritual code familiar since the 1960s — incense, once an element of religious practice, stands in the Western world as a signifier of a vague form of Spirituality and an enlightened view of the world. *Burning Tyre* (2004), a used car tyre in which incense is burned, brings widely separate codes together: everyday object, minimalist circle sculpture, signifier of street counter culture and fragrant object of campfire romanticism. The 1960s subculture and the fetishization of the autonomous object are also to be found in Rothschild's frequent use of fringes, reminiscent of leather jackets and hippie carpet culture, as in her paper collages and her wall-mounted woven leather objects, such as *Good Relations*, 2007.

In Rothschild's work, the insignia of modernism are undermined by the irrationality, emotionality and disturbance of her subject matter. In works made of steel, Perspex or a combination of Perspex and high-gloss painted wood, as in *Pentagon* (2006), the artist encapsulates abstract signifiers to form a kind of handicraft Richard Serra sculpture that has the effect of both playing down and reactivating abstract forms. But the classic plinth/sculpture relationship also generates disturbing questions about the meaning and the status of objects in her work.

Rothschild is interested in the motives that make more of objects than their pure material quality suggests and in the spiritual longing that is directed at objects as projections. Her sculptures, 'decorated' with potential meaning, compel disturbances that unmask their potency to offer idealized, utopian affirmation steeped in mystification, triggering a longing for the autonomy of objects. [Beatrix Ruf]

01 *Disappearer*, 2002
Incense sticks
Dimensions variable

02 *Burning Tyre*, 2004
Tyre, incense
Diameter 58 cm

03 from left:
→ *Mr. Messy*, 2007
Armature, wire, plastic, painted steel
181 × 56 × 52 cm
→ *Jokes*, 2007
Painted oak, painted steel
258 × 68 × 74 cm
→ *Muscles* 2007
Armature, fabric, plaster, glass beads, paint, painted steel
220 × 85 × 77 cm
→ *Higher Love*, 2007
Leather, aluminium, steel armature
380 × 143 × 109 cm
→ *The Inside of Your Head*, 2007
Jesmonite, plaster, gesso, papier mâché, armature, painted steel
197 × 76 × 76 cm
→ Rising Sun, 2007
Woven paper
200 × 200 cm
→ *Cactus*, 2007
Steel armature, jesmonite, fabric, leather, paint
225 × 113 × 23 cm
→ *The Narrow Way*, 2007
Soft wood, leather, fabric, armature
304 × 370 × 62 cm
→ *The Rock and the Arch*, 2007
Polystyrene, jesmonite, ceramic tiles, grout, painted steel
311 × 447 × 144 cm

01

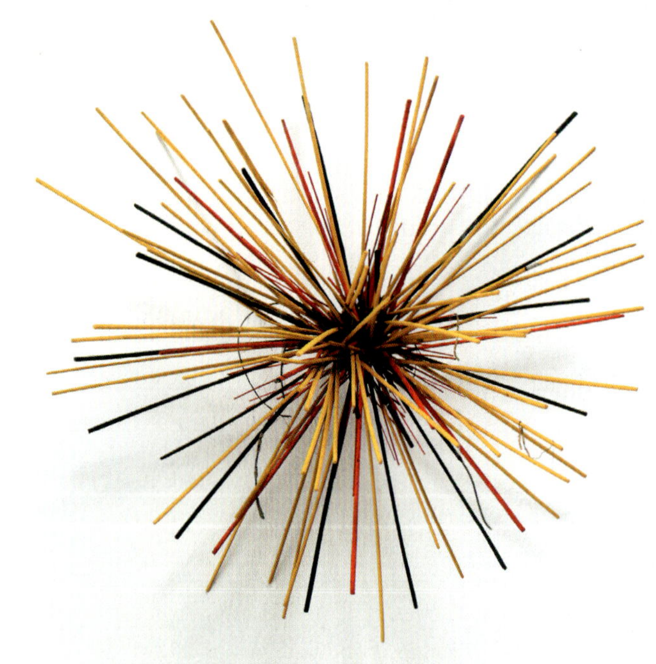

02

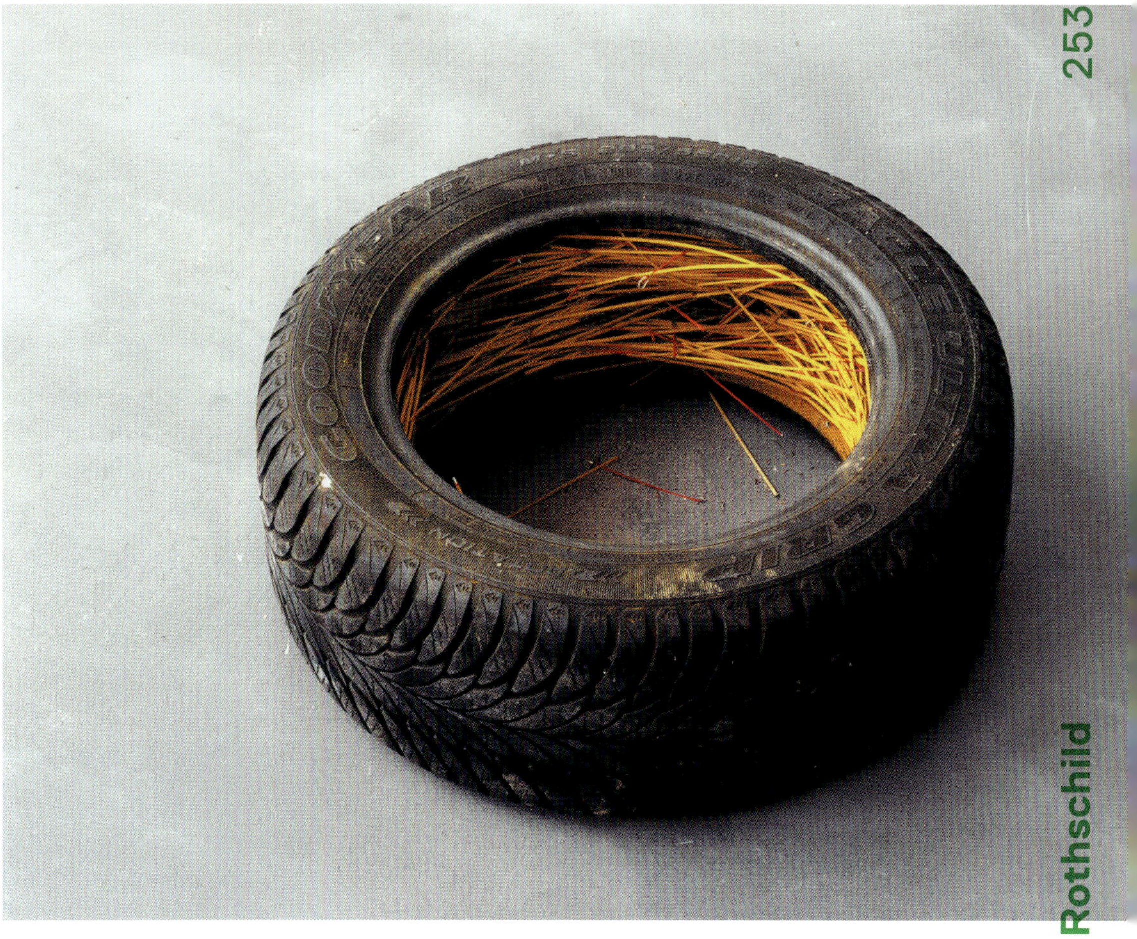

03

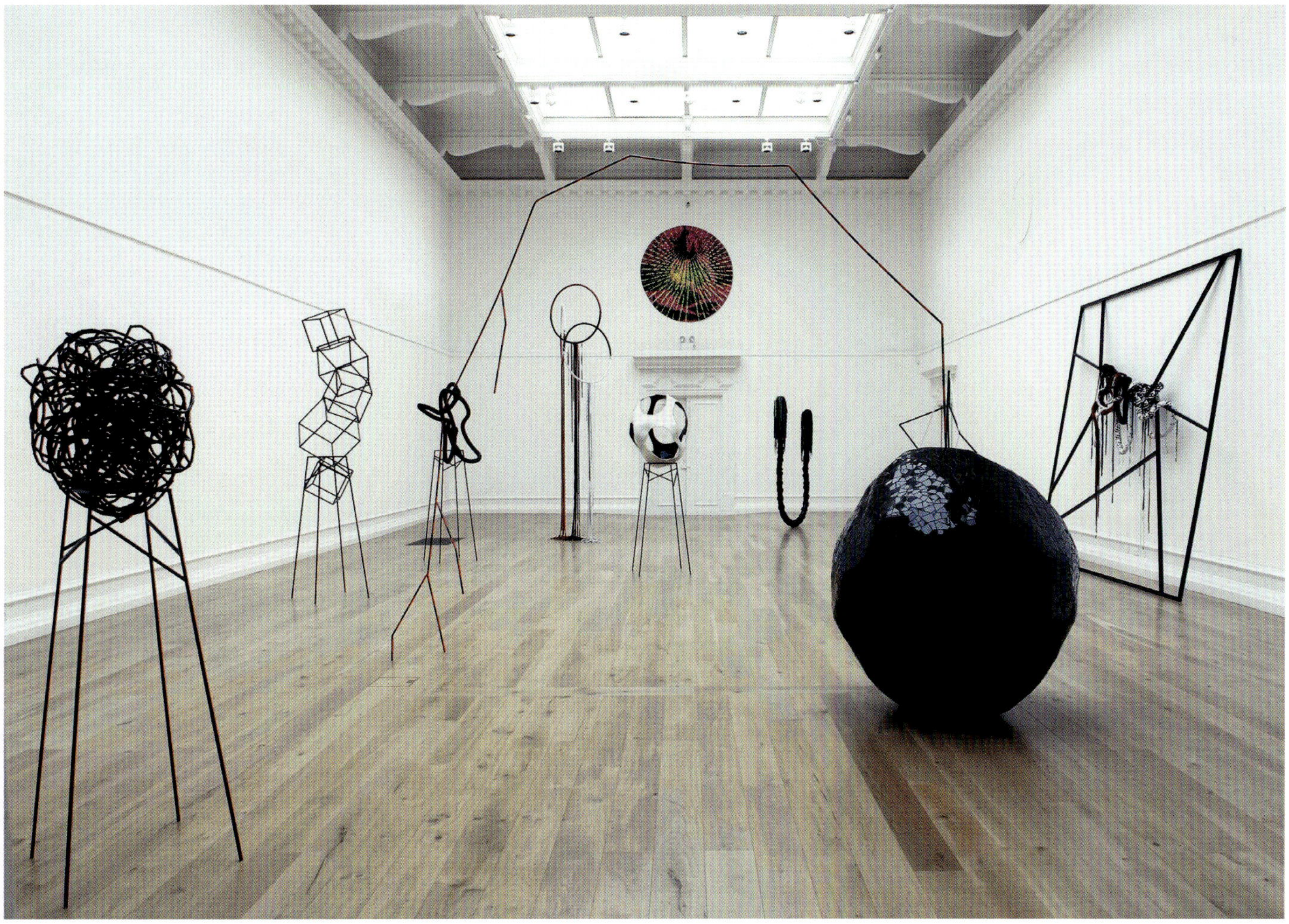

Heather Rowe's skeletal architectural compositions, typically referencing specific residential spaces, at first sight suggest a space either in a nascent stage of construction or one that is being dismantled. The ambiguity of this interpretation, an uncertainty about the 'time' during which the viewer is experiencing the work, is perhaps the crux of her investigation. While her practice is clearly linked to the architectural interventions of Gordon Matta-Clark, she synthesizes those elements with the destabilizing, fracturing tendencies of Bruce Nauman's installations, as well as the temporal and physical dislocation of Robert Smithson's oeuvre. Employing basic vernacular materials, Rowe creates something akin to a house turned inside out, revealing itself and its embedded personality to the viewer in uncanny, often physically disturbing ways.

In *Something Crossed the Mind (Embellished Three Times)*, her work for the 2008 Whitney Biennial, Rowe created an installation specifically designed for the space, a double corridor comprised primarily of two-by-four posts. While it is entirely permeable in all directions, it maps a kind of conduit slicing diagonally across the gallery space, thus in part steering the movement of the viewer towards the door of the next gallery, in part creating a barrier to the standard ambulation through the space. Closer inspection reveals incongruous details embedded within it: Rowe's characteristic insertion of shards of mirror, here dangerously wedged between the posts, fragments of found moulding and drywall painted in three shades of ochre. The familiar domesticity of certain elements combines with the opacity and often threatening character of others, highlighting the passage between spaces as well as challenging the viewer to engage with them. As one moves through the corridor, the mirrors refract both the space and one's own body in it, further undermining a sense of fixity and suggesting that all space is fundamentally in flux, interstitial, as variable as our experience of it and the world.

Similarly, in an installation entitled *On Returning* (2007), Rowe draws on the idea that one's memory of a space is a truer — albeit endlessly variable — record of architectural experience. A single large-scale sculpture positioned between the two main gallery columns, the work riffs on a late modernist house designed by Paul Rudolph in 1972, which had recently been demolished. Thus existing only as a record and memory, it becomes a perfect 'foundation' for the artist's exploration of architectural fragmentation and structural dysfunction/dispersal. Rowe inverts the plan of the house and reconnects the spaces at alternative angles. In her incarnation of the design, the facade of the house is mirrored and the two resulting structures are inverted and placed at an angle, essentially exposing the interior spaces as the exterior experience of the architecture. Again, she employs remnants of a fictional domestic space (a smashed window frame, tiled bathroom mirrors, a patterned curtain) within the structure, further enhancing the sense of vulnerability, a space stripped bare and revealed. At times, Rowe's constructions achieve a kind of psychological nakedness, nearly anthropomorphic in the emotions they seem to embody. [Shamim M. Momin]

01

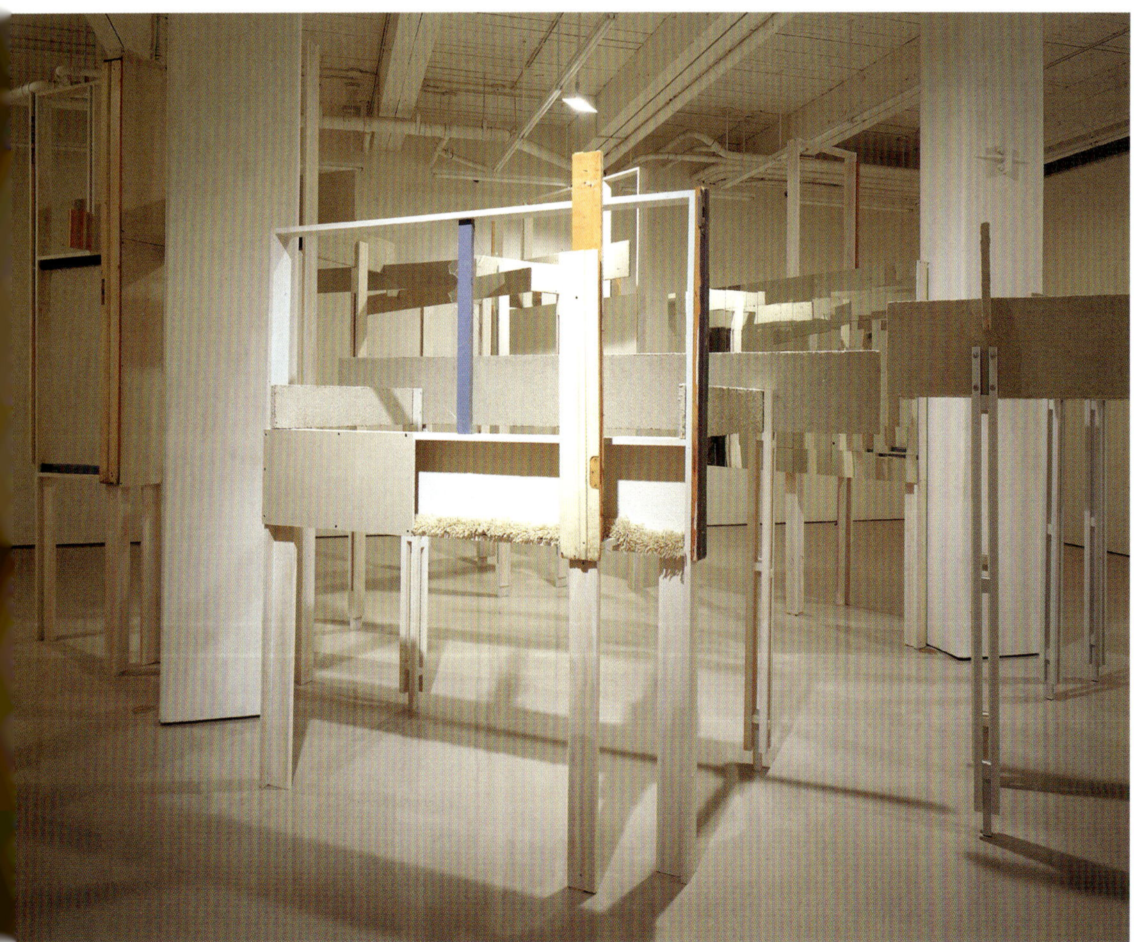

02

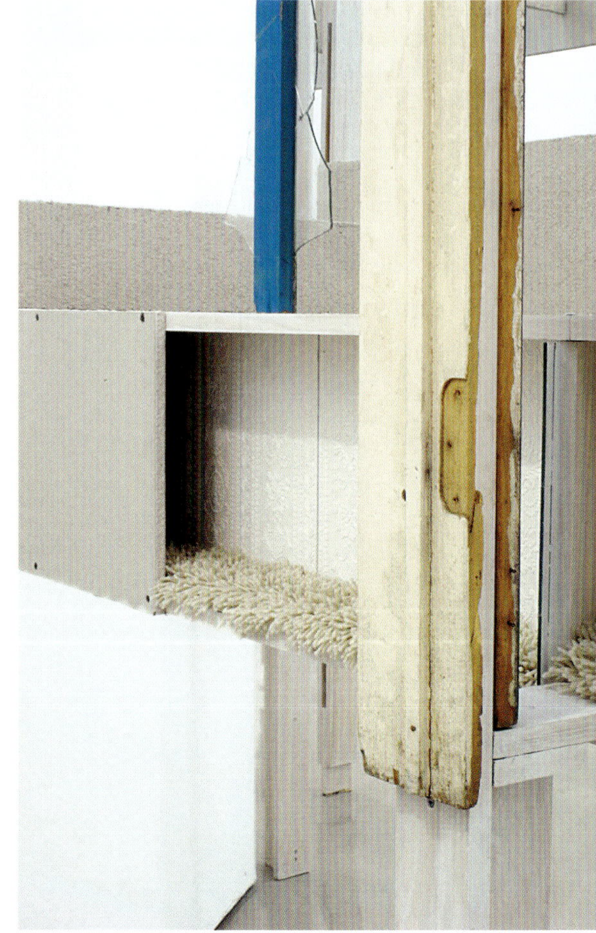

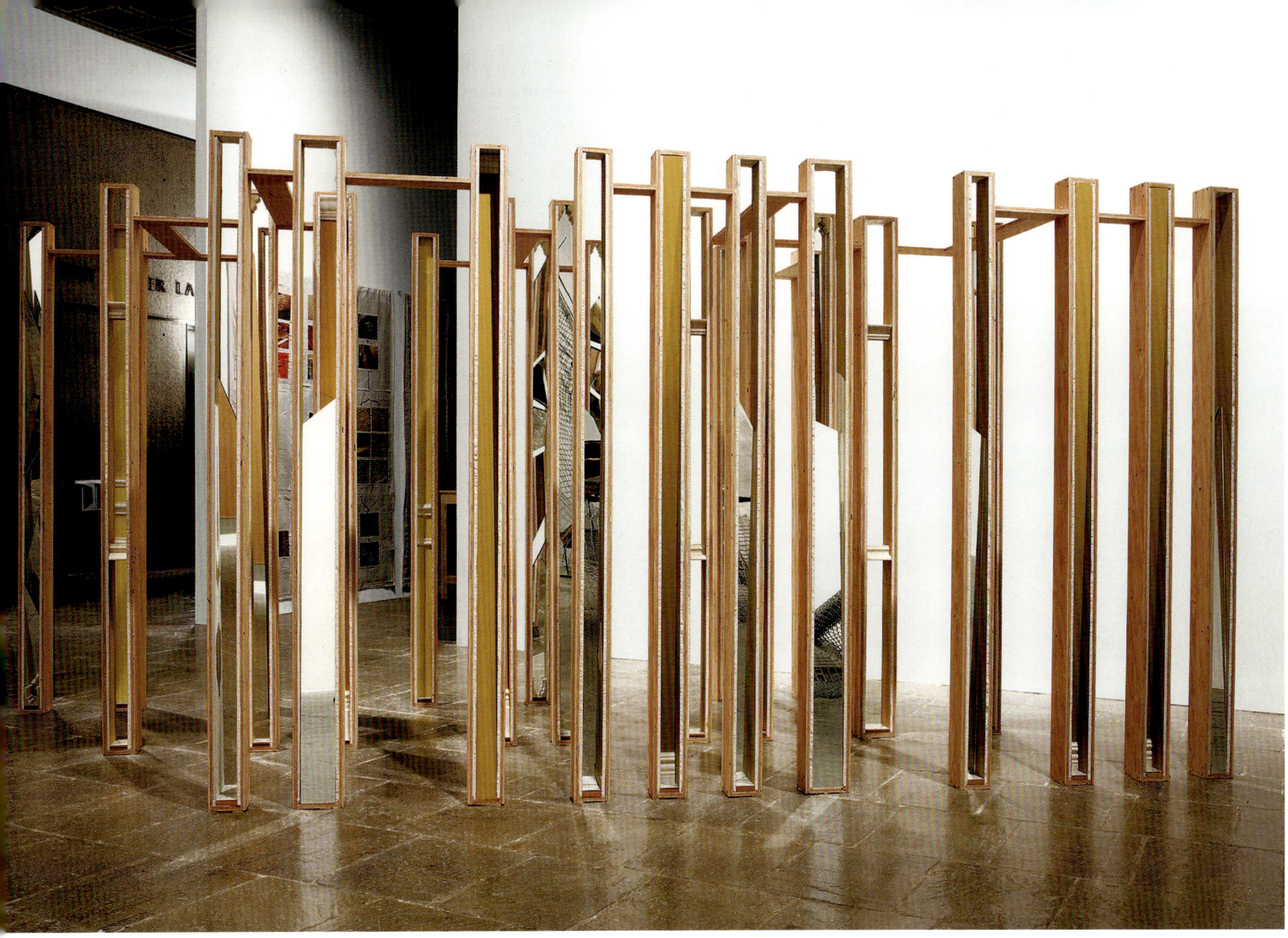

03

04

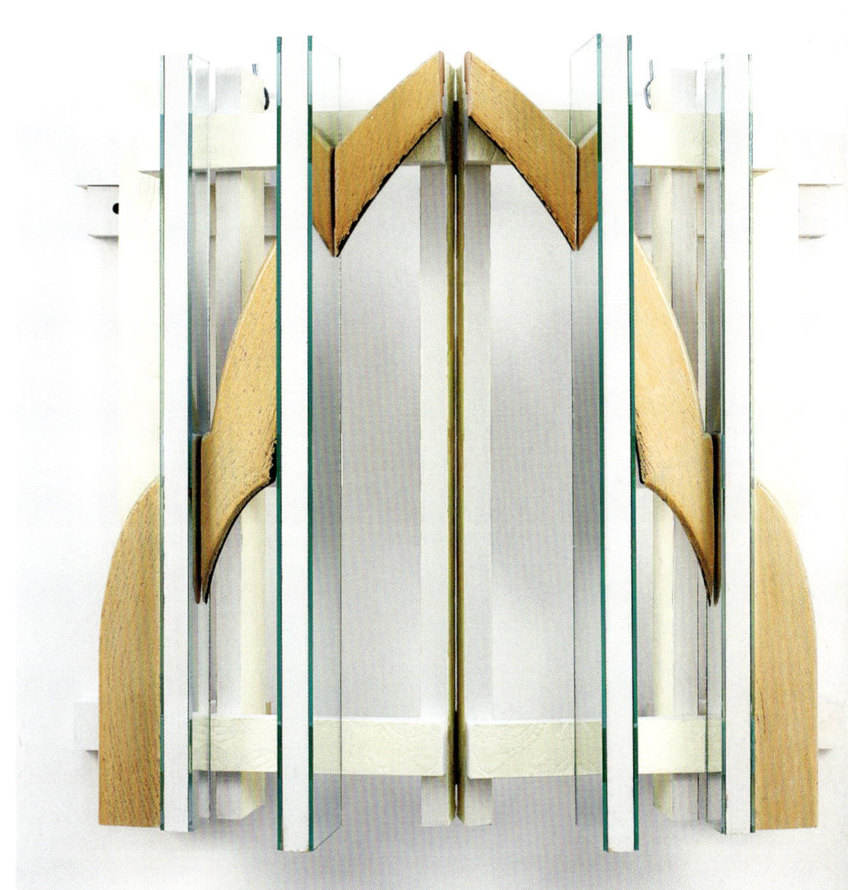

01, 02 *On Returning*, 2007
Steel, stucco, drywall, found window frames and door frames, shag carpet, wood, mirror, glass, hinge, curtain
Approx. 853 × 457 × 518 cm

03 *Something Crossed the Mind (Embellished Three Times)*, 2008
Plywood, drywall, wallpaper, mirror, moulding
549 × 221 × 244 cm

04 *Untitled 1*, 2008
Mirror, frame, wood, flocked wallpaper
64 × 55 cm

Sterling Ruby's *Kiss Trap Kismet* (2008) is a glistening red form, a totemic sculpture with threads of resin, characteristic of his webbed 'mandala' works, skeined over its surfaces and dripping on to its pedestal. The glistening red form resembles variously a wet tongue, a splayed vagina, a monumentalized candy-floss version of a spiritual talisman, or a ribcage/heart flayed to bone and sinew. Wrapping its low wooden base are the rhythmic words 'KISS TRAP KISMET GATE MOUTH AUTOASSASSINATOPHILIA IN TAKE' crudely lettered in red marker pen. The text was inspired by Ruby's interest in a 1970s social pathology study that aimed to systematize emotive types.

Ruby's practice engages an array of media: large-scale sculpture, painting, ceramics, photography and video. Enormous geometric sculptures tower, at times fully covered — 'tagged'— with graffiti, the lettering often minimally incised into the already grimy, debased Formica surfaces. (The artist draws his texts from various sources: art history/criticism, popular culture, graffiti and his own original writing.) The sculptural forms recall stepped juggernauts, historical monuments, iconic memorial arches, barriers and, on occasion, functional objects such as benches. The geometry, serialization and the modular, ordered forms of Minimalism frame a structure to his work overall but are corrupted by the intrusion of other materials and processes: the presence of the expressive hand, the incised text that breaks the objects' mute skin, or the Formica that he favours for its domestic evocation of efficiency and utility, in contrast to the 'macho' connotations of the monumental forms.

In 2008 Ruby completed 'The Supermax Trilogy' and in 2009 embarked on another triad of exhibitions, 'The Ripper Trilogy'. The former, a reference to maximum-security prisons, evoked issues of repression and control and culminated in a massive total environment, *SUPERMAX 2008*. Ceramic objects, slickly glazed, gnarled and organically shaped, suggest dismembered body parts. Huge, cantilevered, beam-like works lean somewhat impossibly across the room — 'physics sculptures' or 'headless dicks', as the artists calls them, referring alternately to the interest in weight and balance as well as more explicitly human concerns, including sexuality, gendering as a social construct, intimacy and expression. Similarly, the ceramics are both expressive body fragments, tropes of the feminine/feminism as well as material explorations of malleability made static, a meta-conscious evocation of process.

In 'The Ripper Trilogy' Ruby's set of thematics broadens from *SUPERMAX 2008* into an exploration of extremities of control and expression. Incorporating painting with sculpture, he uses a variety of non-traditional materials (nail polish) and techniques (spray painting) among more traditional ones. The atmospheric surfaces of the paintings include images that reflect the forms of his monumentalized geometric sculptures. It is clear that, for Ruby, expression and critical structure are not mutually exclusive. Rather, they now function as a set of tools, deliberately mobilized, in which meaning is part of that selection rather than purely in the process itself.
[Shamim M. Momin]

01

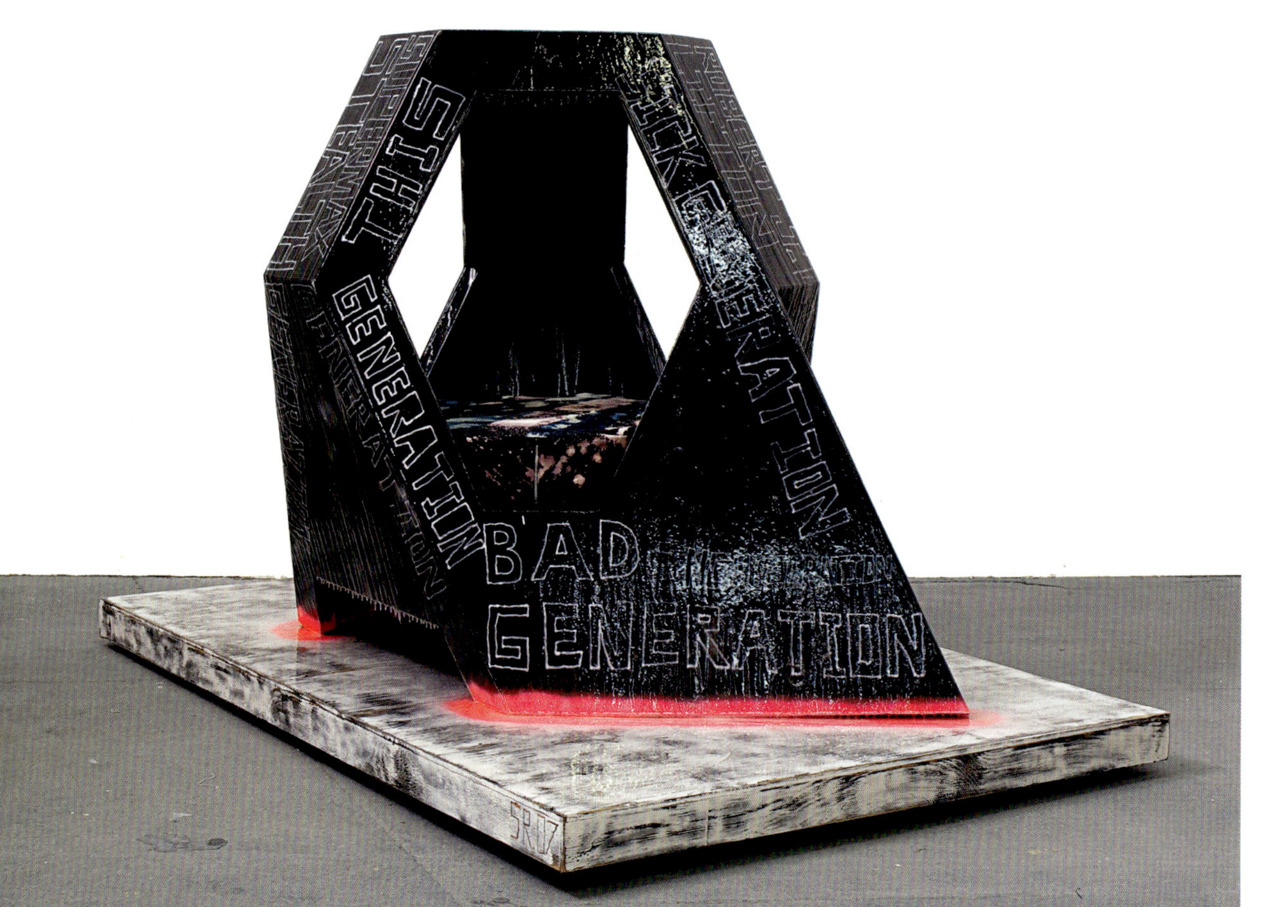

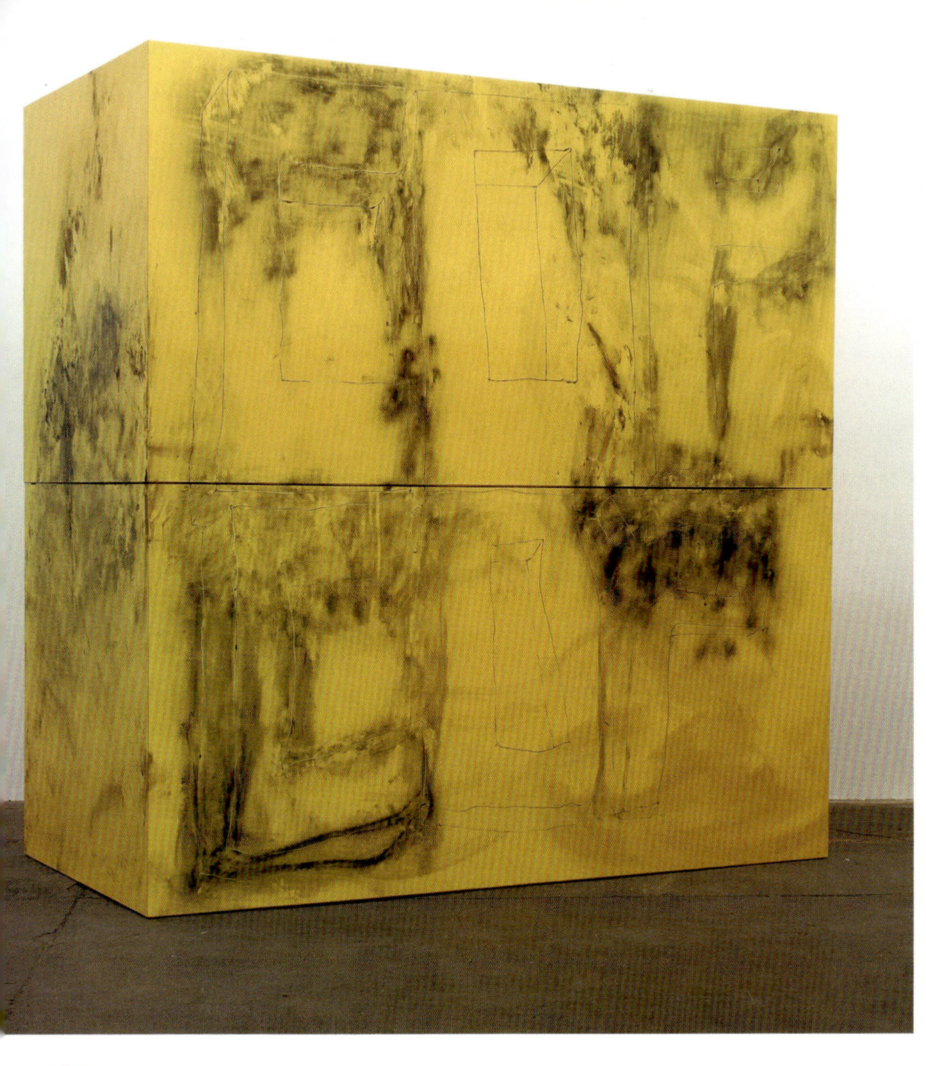

02

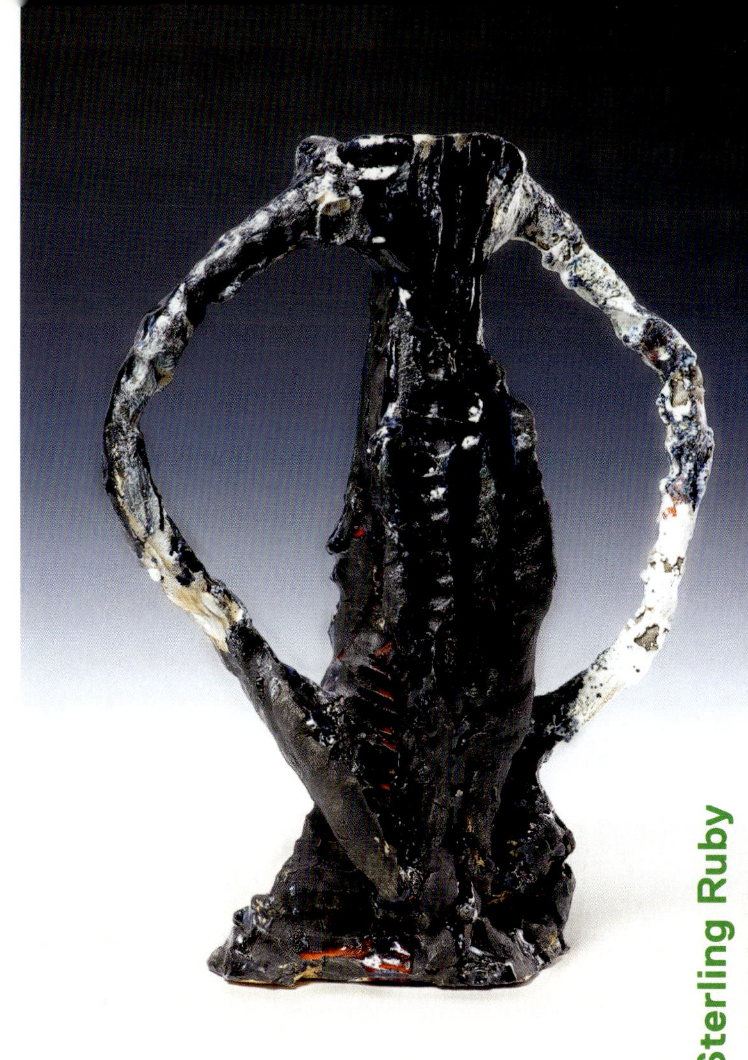

03

Sterling Ruby

04

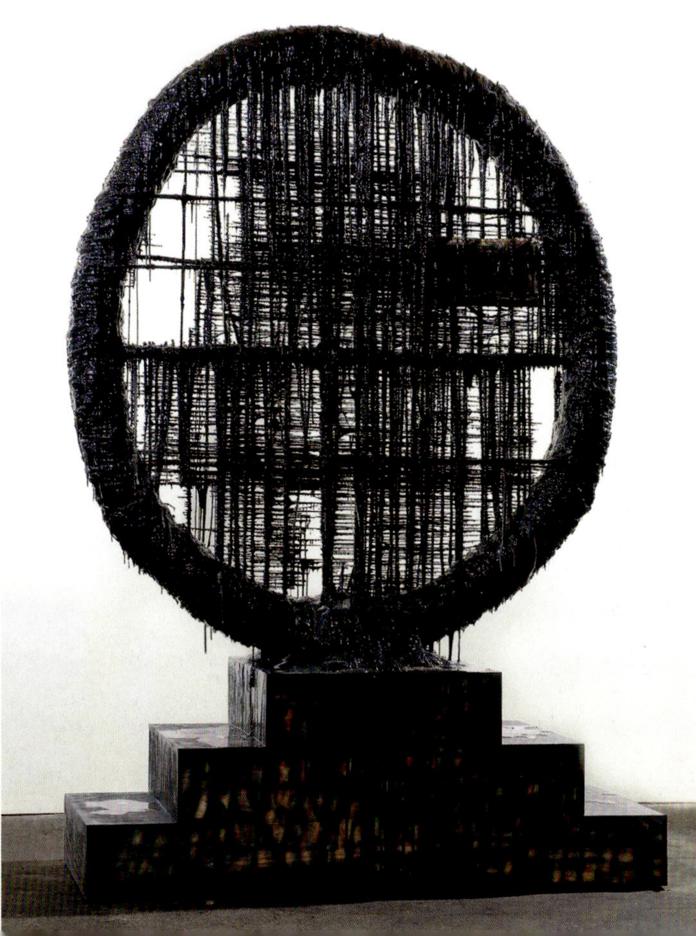

01 *This Generation,* 2007
Wood, clear urethane,
paint, denim, fibrefill
155 × 152 × 239 cm

02 *Cop, Cop, Cry, Cry,* 2008
Formica, wood
240 × 240 × 120 cm

03 *Blackout Romeo,* 2005
Ceramic, Formica, wood
48 × 41 × 14 cm
Plinth
101 × 51 × 51 cm

04 *Black Star / Prostitute's Bolster,* 2007
PVC pipe, urethane,
aluminium, spray paint, wood
350 × 230 × 80 cm

Overleaf:

05 'Supermax', exhibition view
at Musuem of Contemporary Art,
Los Angeles, 2008

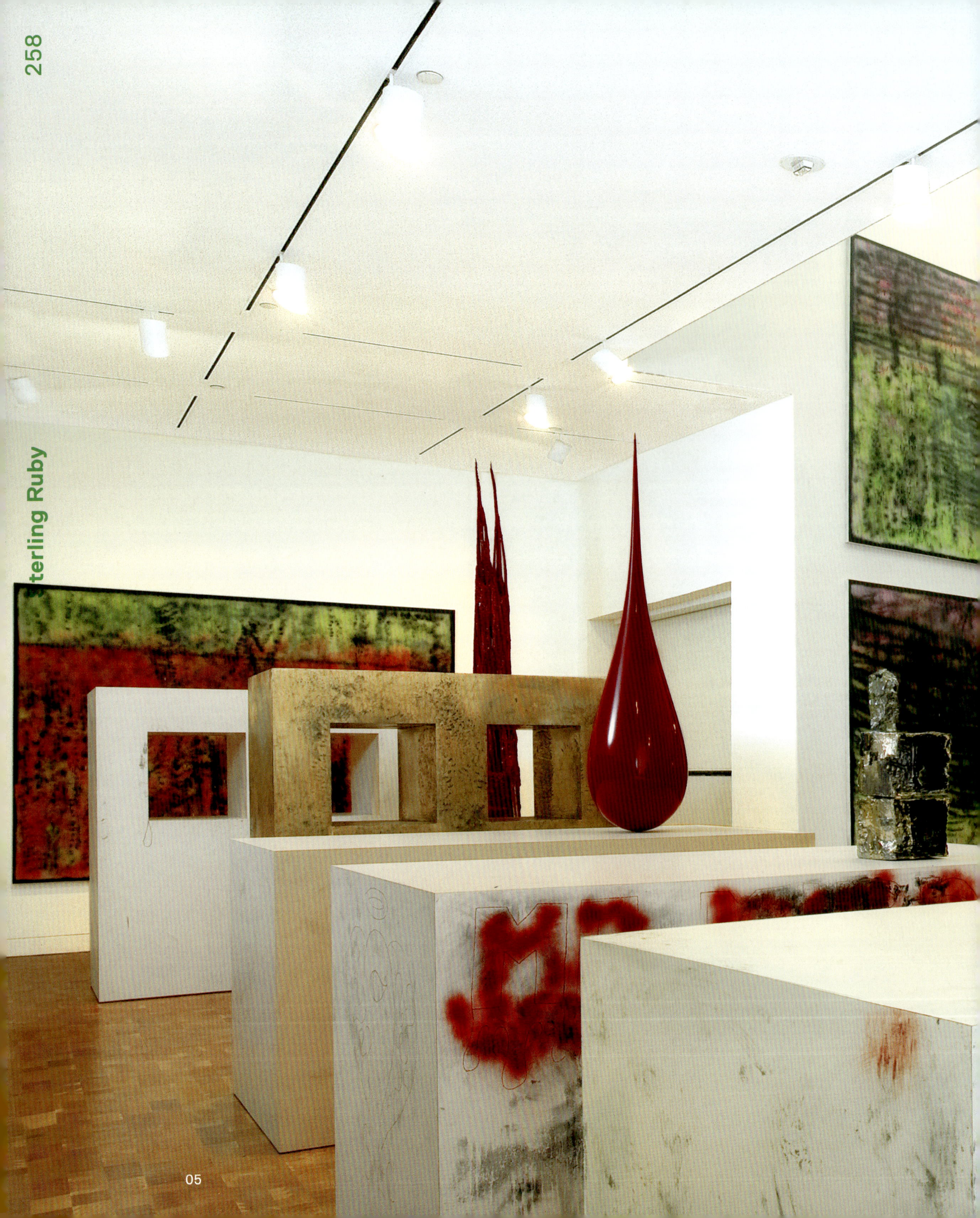

05

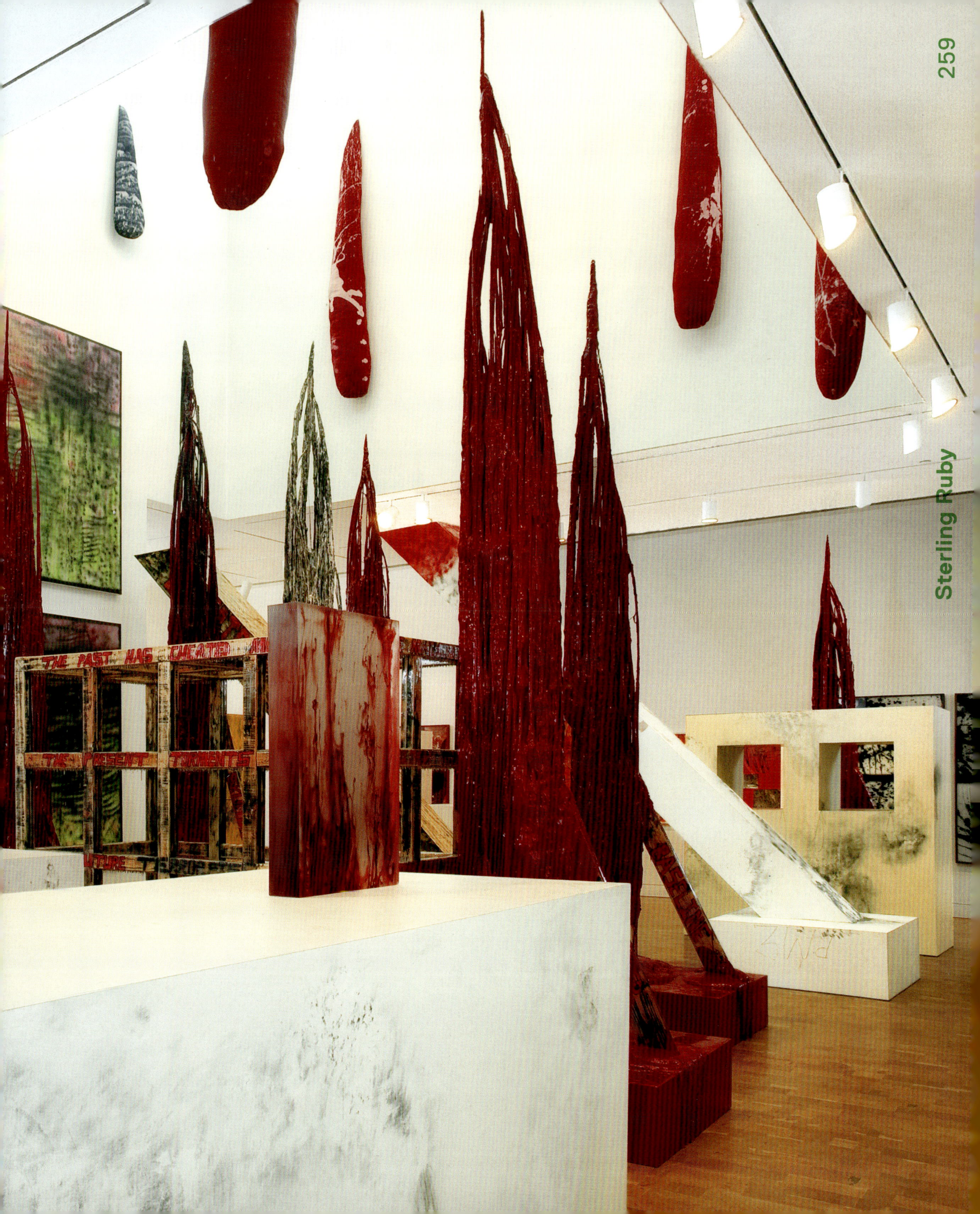
THE PAST HAS CHEATED
THE PRESENT TORMENTS

The sheer scale of many of Tomas Saraceno's sculptural installations relates to his involvement in and ambitions for architecture. In his gallery-based works the organic curves of his spaces within spaces abut the straight-edged gallery interiors, challenging authoritative rigidity and articulating the ideological potential and political implications of utopian architecture. His project *Air-Port-City* (2002–present) borrows from the legislative model of the airport, where international and local laws are invoked separately in different parts of the terminal. Saraceno's proposal is a city that is airborne and infinitely reconfigurable, with no fixed notion of place or nationhood. Each individual pod is free to relocate to wherever the inhabitant pleases, establishing concepts of synergy that are ultimately at odds with the restrictions of today's global situation, characterized by social insularity, impermeable borders and military invasion.

Contrasting the wildness of tree trunks in Arnhem's Sonsbeek Park with the manmade modular structures lodged between them (*Flying Green House*, 2008), Saraceno makes it clear that his proposed revival of nomadic culture adopts technological rather than bucolic intonations. His *Flying Garden* (2006) acknowledges how human intervention may be required to assist in the relocation of vegetation to new habitats as climate change continues to alter the terrain of the planet. Stocked with air plants, driving from the genus *Tillandsia*, which is native to Central and South America and Africa, these gardens provide an analogy for rootlessness and contingency as they ingeniously derive their nutrition from airborne sources.

In the tradition of past utopians, such as Buckminster Fuller, who grounded their visions in pragmatic technological enquiry, Saraceno employs up-to-date materials science. His current work with Aerogel, a super-lightweight insulating substance developed by NASA, explores the symbolic and practical potential of self-sufficient extra-planetary structures built from this potentially radicalizing invention. Rather than high-end application, Saraceno embraces the quotidian and socializing capacity of technology. His installation at the 2006 São Paolo Biennale, *How to live together* (2006) and *Observatory, Air-Port-City* (2008), which converted part of London's unforgiving concrete Hayward Gallery into a translucent clamber space, invited viewers into their supportive yet unsteady chambers. Here the ethics of leisure and collectivity were brought into focus as we took off our shoes, loosened our reserved and place our trust in an unorthodox construction.

If we think of architecture as any underlying structure, whether material or metaphorical, Saraceno's ambition to create a pliable, negotiable platform is profound. When applied to the knotty problem of extending productivity while conserving resources, his recurrent themes of gravity, mobility and visual motifs such as the unbroken horizon and geometric elegance signify a buoyant, forward-thinking attitude toward human intervention in nature's cycles and networks. If we acknowledge that we are an intrinsic part of these cycles, we may feel more invested, responsible and optimistic.
[Sally O'Reilly]

01

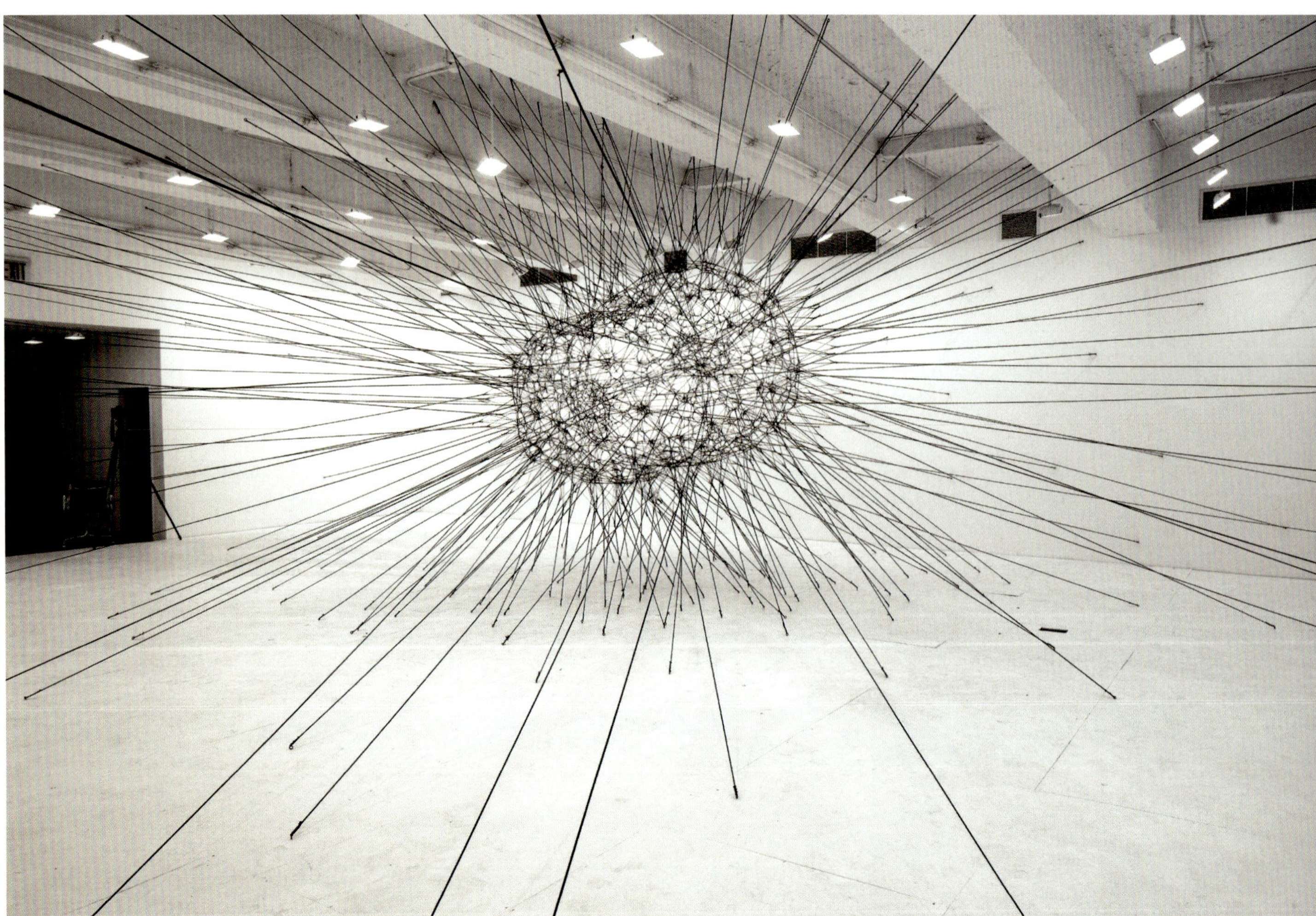

02

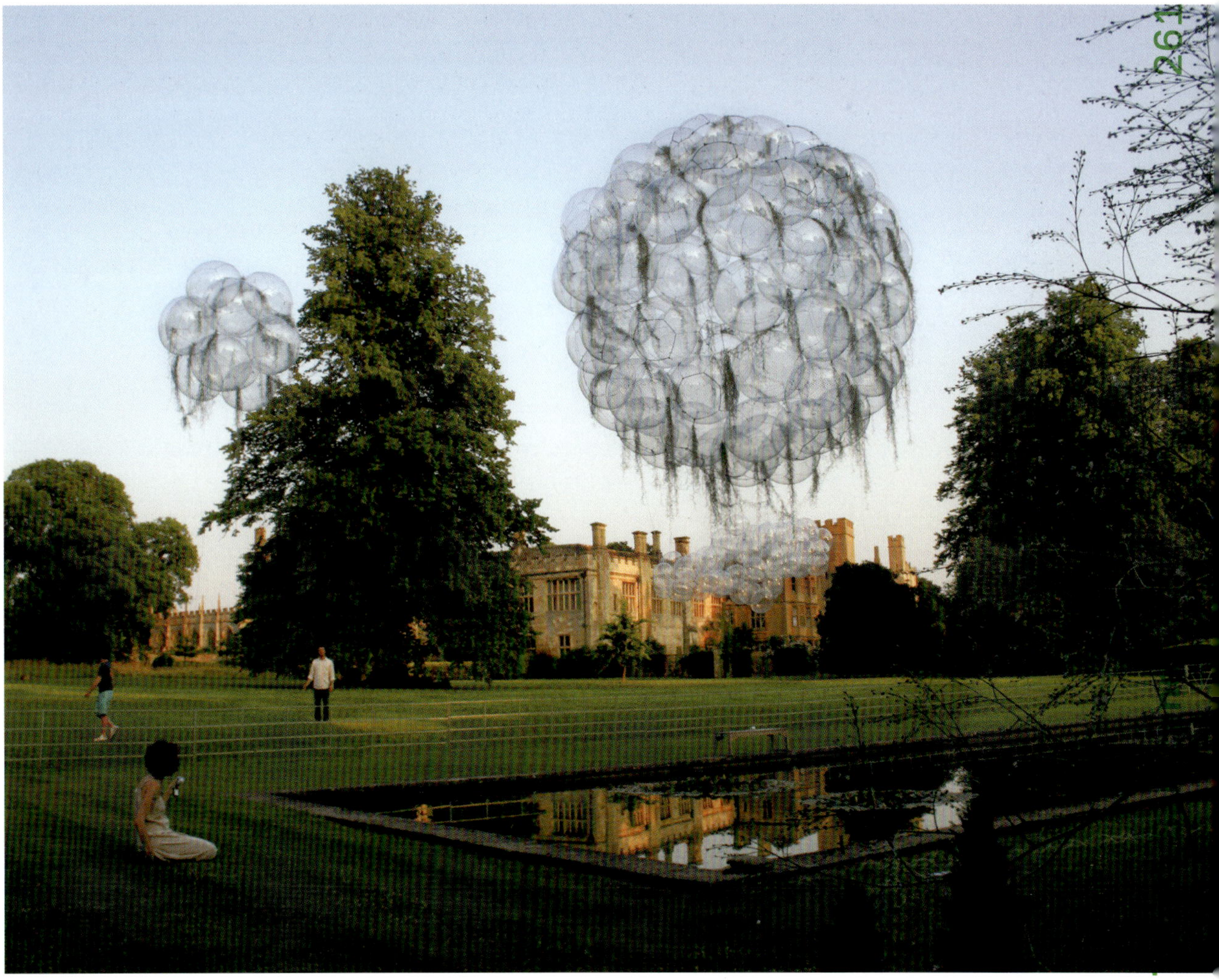

03

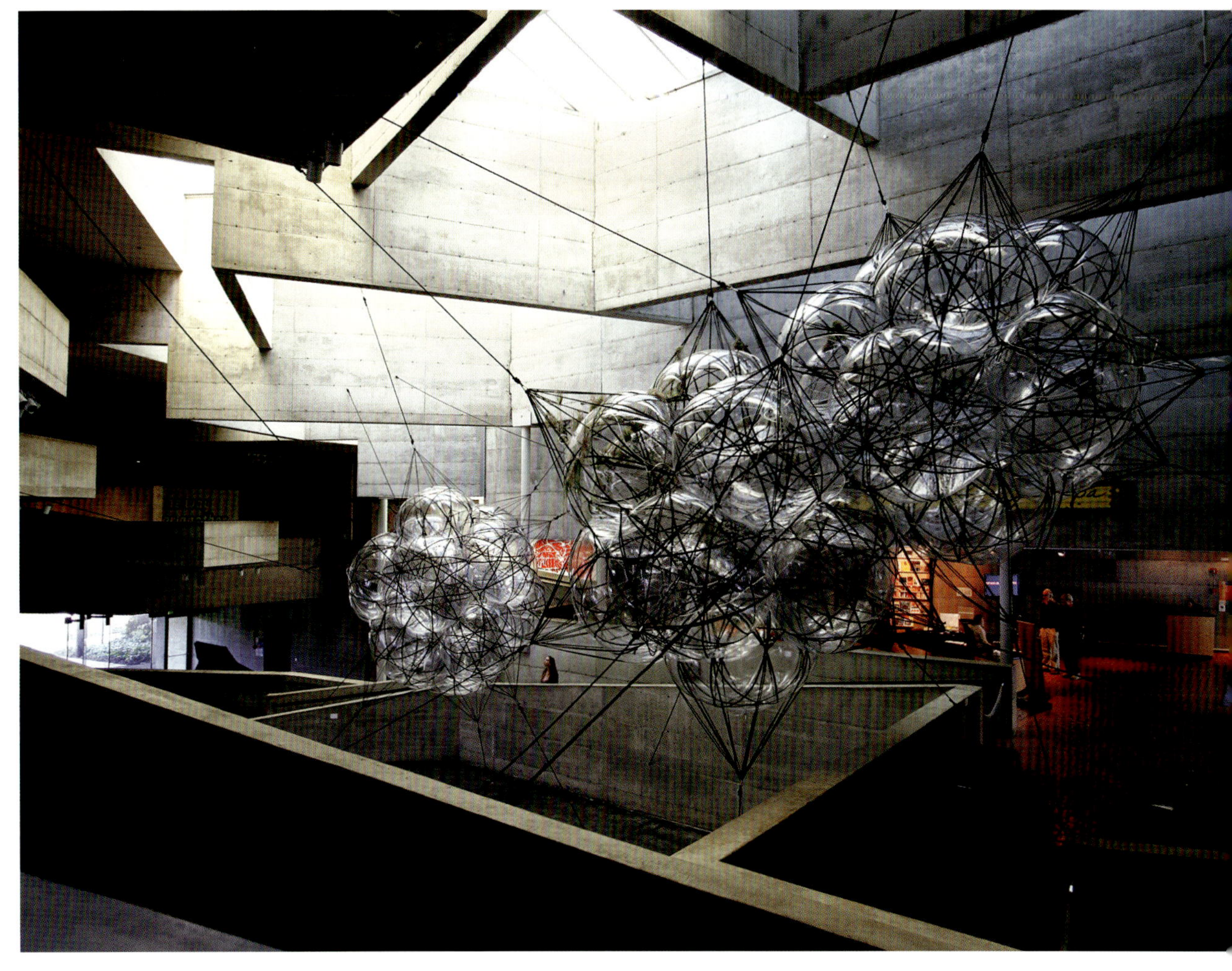

01 *Galaxy forming along filaments, like droplets along the strands of a spider's web*, 2008
Elastic rope
Dimensions variable

02 *Flying Garden*, 2006
Elliptical pillows filled with helium, elastic netting, Tillandsia plants
Variable dimensions

03 *Flying Garden, Air-Port-City*, 2007
Pillows filled with pressurized air, nylon, webbing, rope, Tillandsia plants
Each module 3.7 m

Overleaf:

04 *Observatory/Air-Port-City*, 2008
Pillows filled with pressurized air, metal dome, mirrored floor
Lower level approx. 50 × 50 m
Upper level approx. 22 × 22 × 22 m
Total height of metal dome 9.6 m

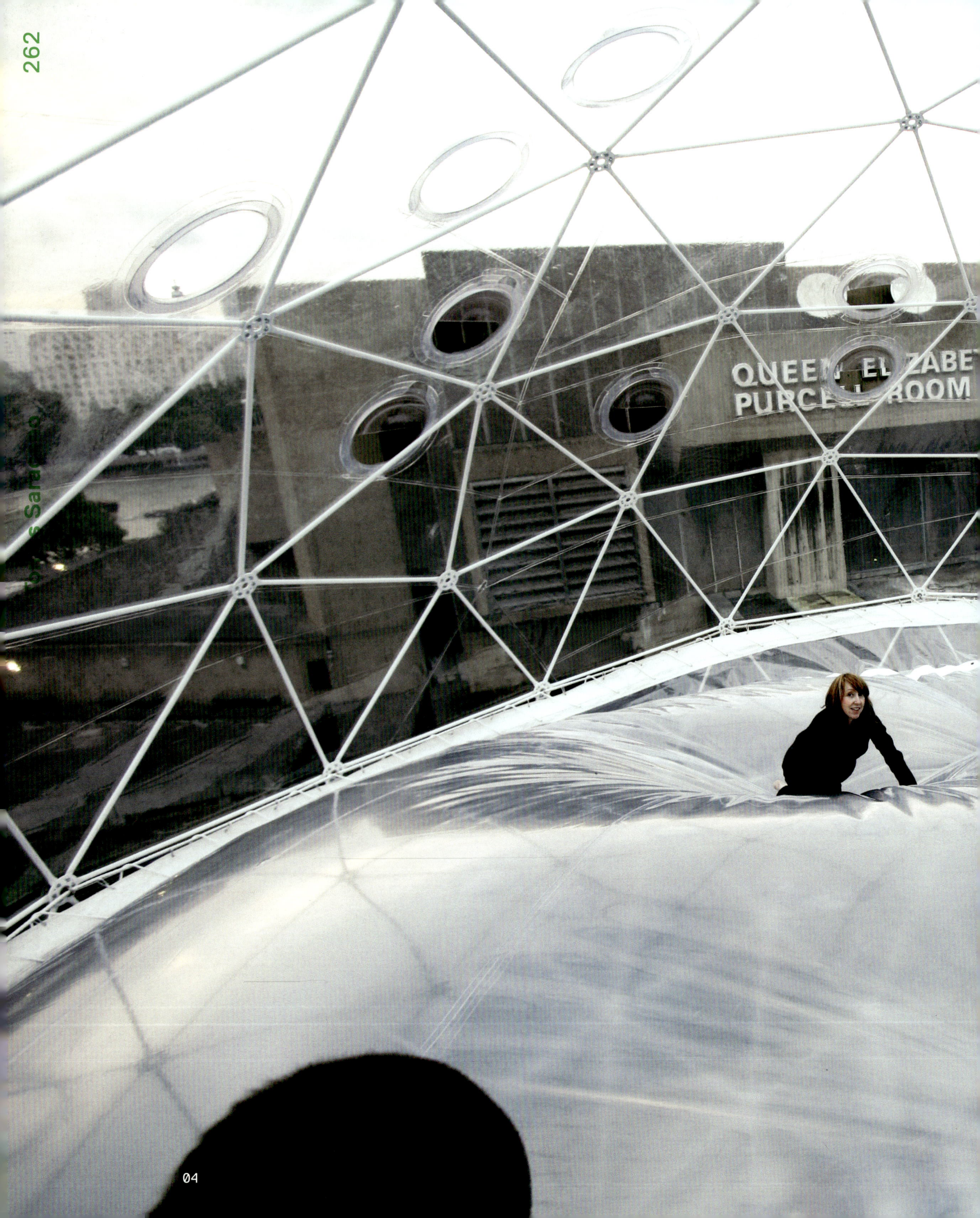

04

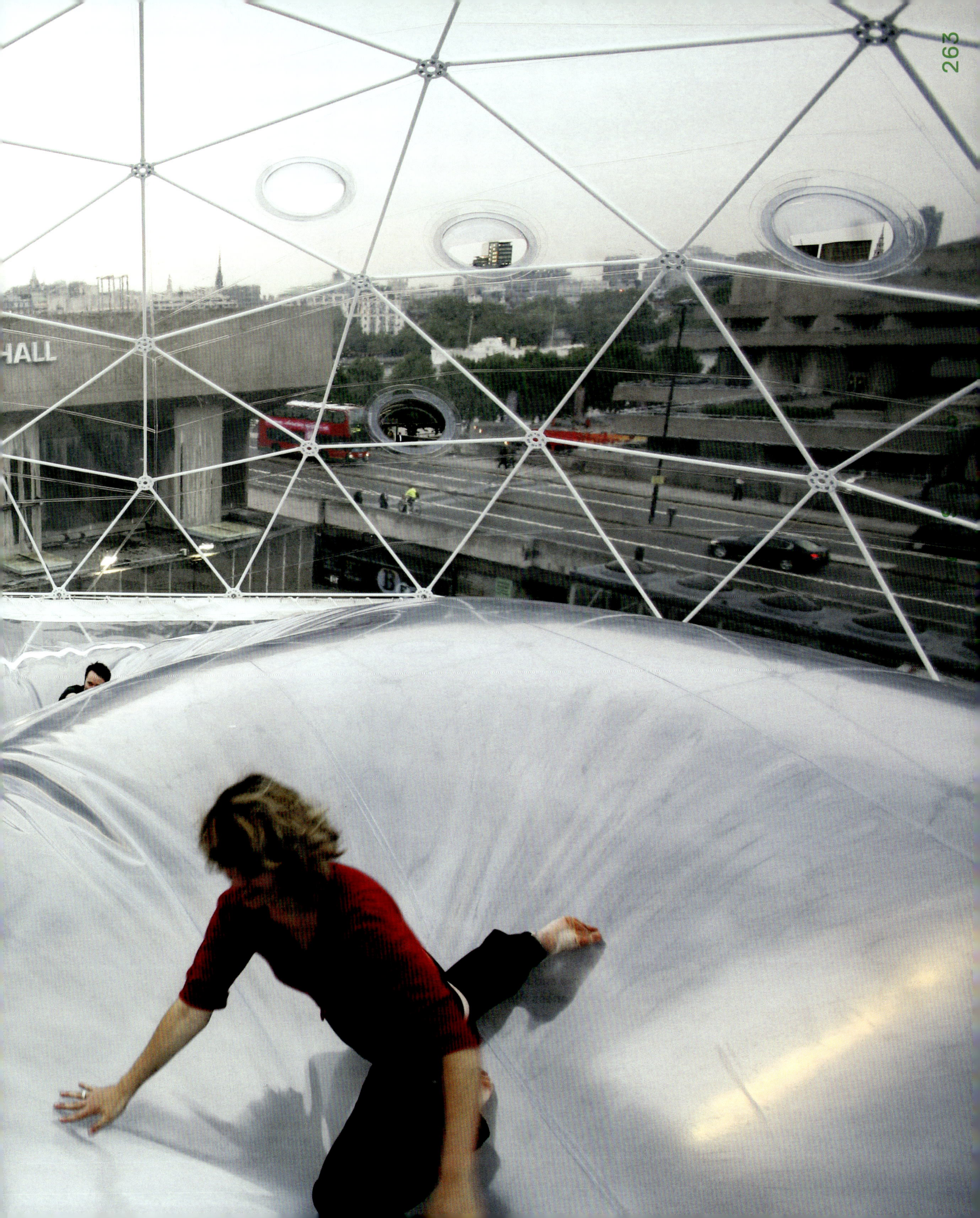
HALL

01

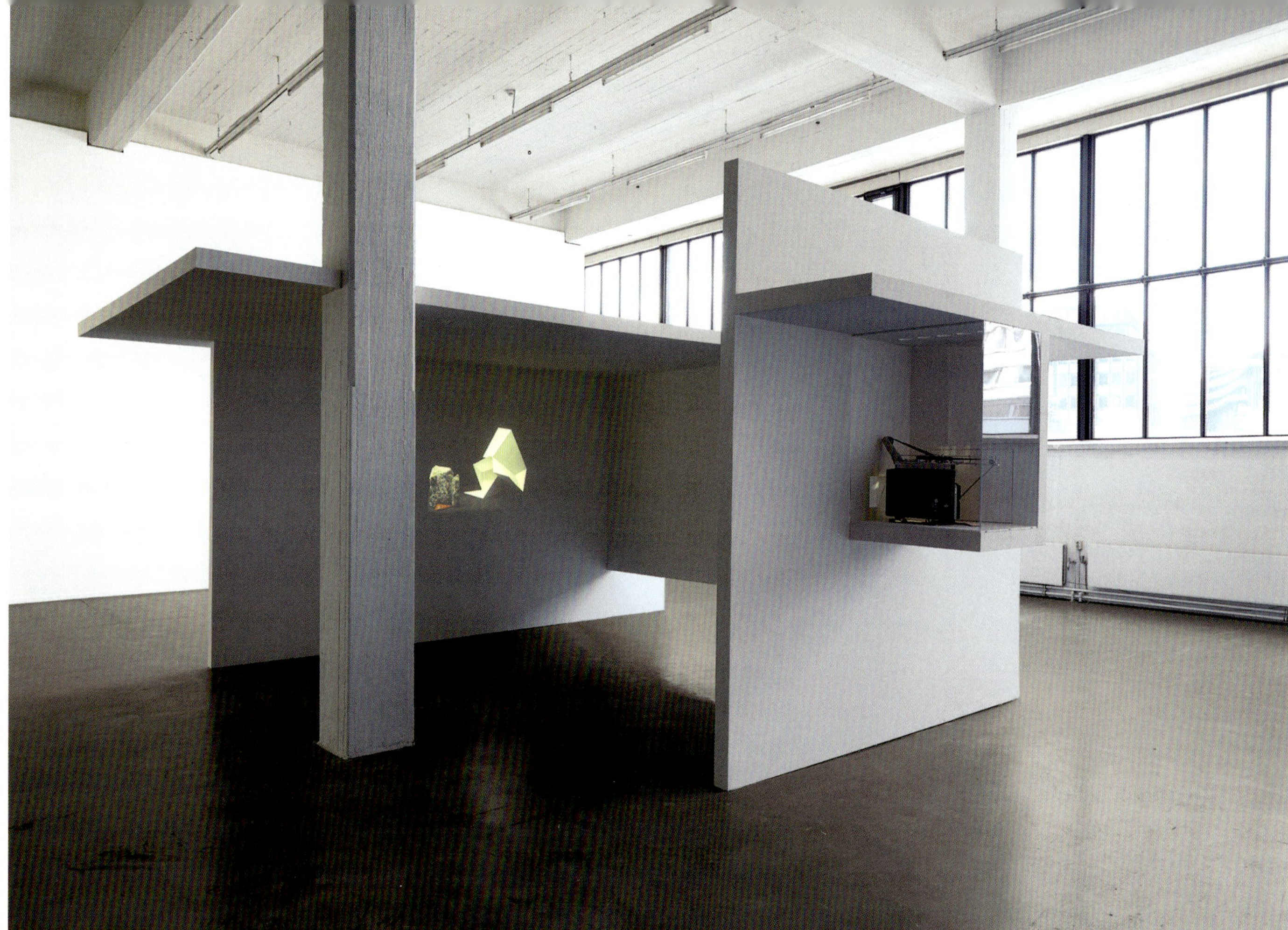

Bojan Šarčević's investigations into line and form address the patterns that remain when structures are removed or circumstances changed. Questions of the trace, ossification and adaptation run through his varied practice, which takes shape in sculpture, drawing, film and performance.

In a recent performance inspired by La Monte Young's instruction piece *Draw a straight line and follow it*, for example, Šarčević engineered an encounter in the Tate Modern cafeteria. In the piece, enacted by different performers, one collaborator would enter the room and gaze at another seated at a table. After a pause, the performer would walk up and draw a line through the other's hair with his or her fingers and walk away. (*A proposal conceived in my bed last night*, 2008). Such a performance, with a deadpan simplicity typical of Conceptualist instruction pieces, carried out Young's instruction so that the action became a light, almost intimately rendered trace of the earlier work. In a similar way, his films of triangular geometric shapes, his smooth wooden and metal sculptures and his architectural interventions create a seductiveness that allows for something latent — something sensed or remembered but not seen — to appear. In a 2002 interview he spoke of his work as if it were an infrastructure: 'I don't think existence is a structure; it rather needs an appropriate structure to appear and disclose its originality.'

In the wood and bronze sculpture *Replace the Irreplaceable* (2006), sinuous lines glide along the front of the architectonic sculpture, turning like a skater to swerve back around and skim the other side. A similar elegant swerve can be seen in the metal sculptures *Wanting Without Needing, Loving Without Leaning* (2005). In recent works, the curves that marked out blocks of space in earlier sculptures have grown thinner, into the spindly lines of wall-hung bronze sculptures such as *Untitled, Meanwhile* (2007), or into projected light in the suite of sixteen millimetre films titled *Only After Dark* (2007).

These various interventions into space have called to mind such masters of monumentality as Gordon Matta-Clark, as well as the more discreet interventions of Michael Asher — who, like Šarčević, grounds his formal explorations in wider social history. Šarčević specifically invokes the history of modernism and particularly its utopian desires and social aims, linking these to the question of the representation of the labourer. *Mies's Leftover* (2002) consisted of scraps of paper taken from an architect's office — paper that not only showed the literal models and drawings created in the office, but also presented the drawings as an index or a trace of a mental and professional process. The *Only After Dark* film suite was inspired by the time spent working in his studio, putting forward the artist as labourer, and suggesting that the work he or she exhibits is nothing more than the trace of his or her activity. By circling around history and its persistence as document, Šarčević re-imagines that history, sketched lightly in the present.
[Melissa Gronlund]

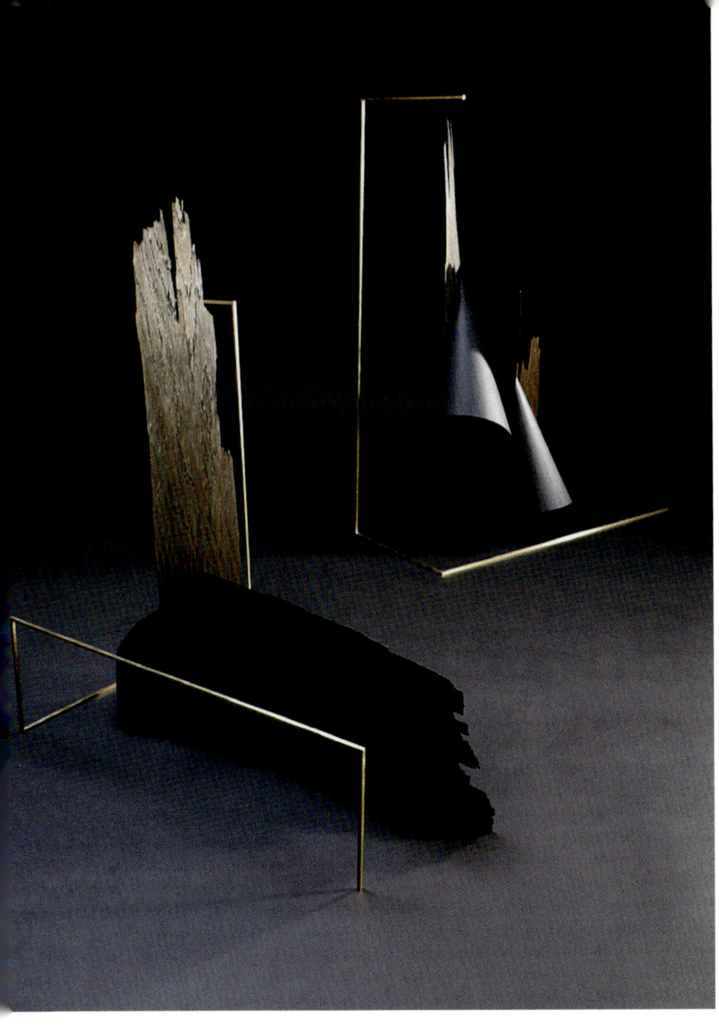

02

03

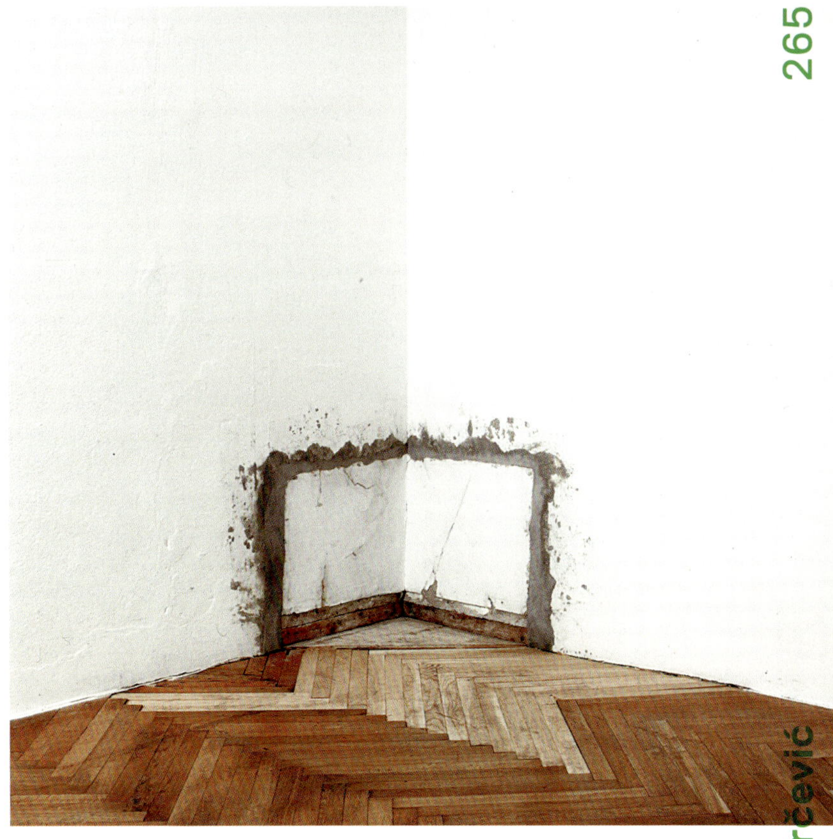

04

01 *Untitled (film 5)*, 2007
from the series *Only After Dark*
16mm film with colour and sound
2 min. 15 sec.
Plywood, Plexiglas
530 × 320 × 300 cm

02 *Untitled (film 4)*, 2007
from the series *Only After Dark*
16mm film with colour and sound
2 min. 29 sec.

03 *World Corner*, 1999
Bricks, plaster, wallpaper, wood
90 × 90 × 90 cm

04 *Replace the Irreplaceable*, 2006
Pear wood, brass
250 × 320 × 80 cm

'That which exists may be transformed. What is non-existent has boundless uses,' the Taoist philosopher Lao Tse famously asserted. Arcangelo Sassolino's practice, resulting from a compelling marriage between culture and industry, might well be built upon this statement. His intuitive approach brings about meaningful, unforeseen reactions within a determined aesthetic order. What absorbs Sassolino is not whether his sculptures look pleasing. Rather than an interest in the satisfying organization of planes, the Italian artist's obsession is rooted in the concept of a working mechanism: 'the form will then follow the function.' As a result, Sassolino's constructions are simple in appearance; organized within a symmetrical-order system, they produce an infinite number of asymmetrical arrangements that demand participation on the part of the viewer, as Victor
01 Papanek states in his studies on design.

A good example is *Untitled* (2008), a hydraulic piston lying on the floor, which is capable of exerting up to 60 tonnes of mechanical force on a metre-long rectangular block of wood held in place by steel cords. The instant a viewer walks into the space, this piston is activated by a small sensor pushing its arm at a barely visible speed of one millimetre per second. A cracking sound and strong smell of wood accompanies this action. When the visitor steps away, the piston stops. Breaking the entire block can take between fifteen minutes and several days, depending on the interaction of the viewer.

The purpose of Sassolino's sculpture is fulfilled through its function or method. His works make a truthful use of material; they never appear to be something they are not. There is no kind of illusion, just an expression of the tension between man and machine within a physical and psychological order.

02

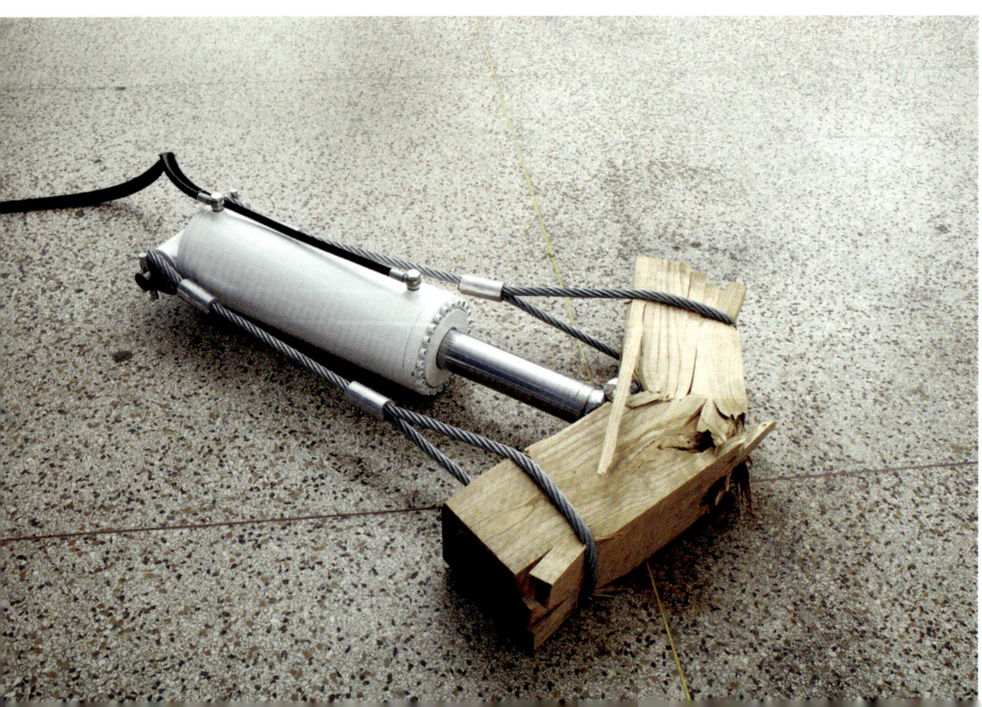

What happens when machines 'produce' art? Do artists then become engineers? What space is left for the artist's personality? To explore these questions, Sassolino constantly opens up his practice to collaborations with professionals, from physicians to architects and engineers. His constructions should be considered alternatively as sculptures and prototype machines, in some cases carrying a function, in some cases not. If function is absent, the aesthetic is then determined by the method, as in *Afasia II* (2008), the result of a long-term project developed with Italian engineering company Pietro Fiorentini. This work is a 600 kilogram container filled with thirty cubic metres of compressed nitrogen, creating a potentially explosive pressure of 250 bar (a fully inflated truck tyre is just seven bar). The form results from the differing approaches of engineers seeking to achieve the maximum possible compression without explosion.

A strong sensitivity to the interrelated perception of time defines Sassolino's sculptures, as in *Attrito Continuo* (2005–06). Here, a six tonne, two metre high rectangular solid block of concrete rotates on its axis. The sculpture is consumed by the slow friction of its own weight as its circulates around the floor, causing a monumental sonic wall of vibration. A complete rotation takes ninety minutes.

The aesthetic that defines Sassolino's work does not result from the pursuit of 'right' or 'wrong', as in an industrial process, but from the principle of cause and effect. Sassolino embraces concepts of failure, striving to control randomness without jeopardizing the drama of his works. [Francesco Stocchi]

01 *Untitled*, 2006
Steel, electromagnet, hydraulic system, PLC computer
420 × 365 × 180 cm

02 *Untitled*, 2008
Steel, wood, hydraulic system
120 × 100 × 25 cm

03

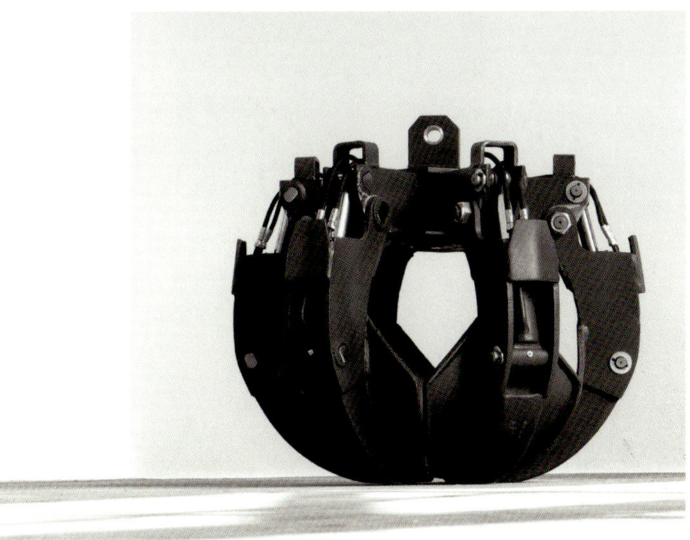

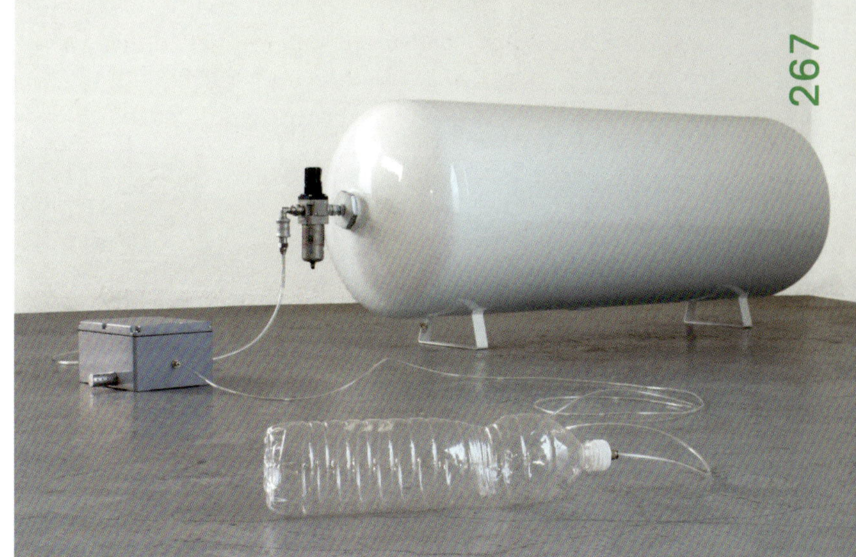

05

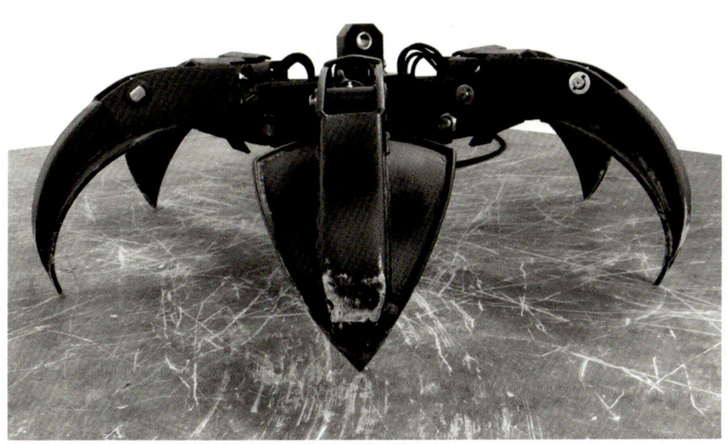

04

03, 04 *Untitled*, 2006–07
Steel, hydraulic pump
100 × 100 × 95 cm (closed)
195 × 195 × 60 cm (open)

05 *Untitled*, 2008
Tank 140 × 45 × 40 cm
Control box 20 × 18 × 10 cm
Bottle 36 × 9 × 9 cm
Plastic tubing 250 cm

06 *Afasia I*, 2008
Steel, compressed nitrogen,
glass bottles, PLC computer,
steel cage
300 × 500 × 2200 cm

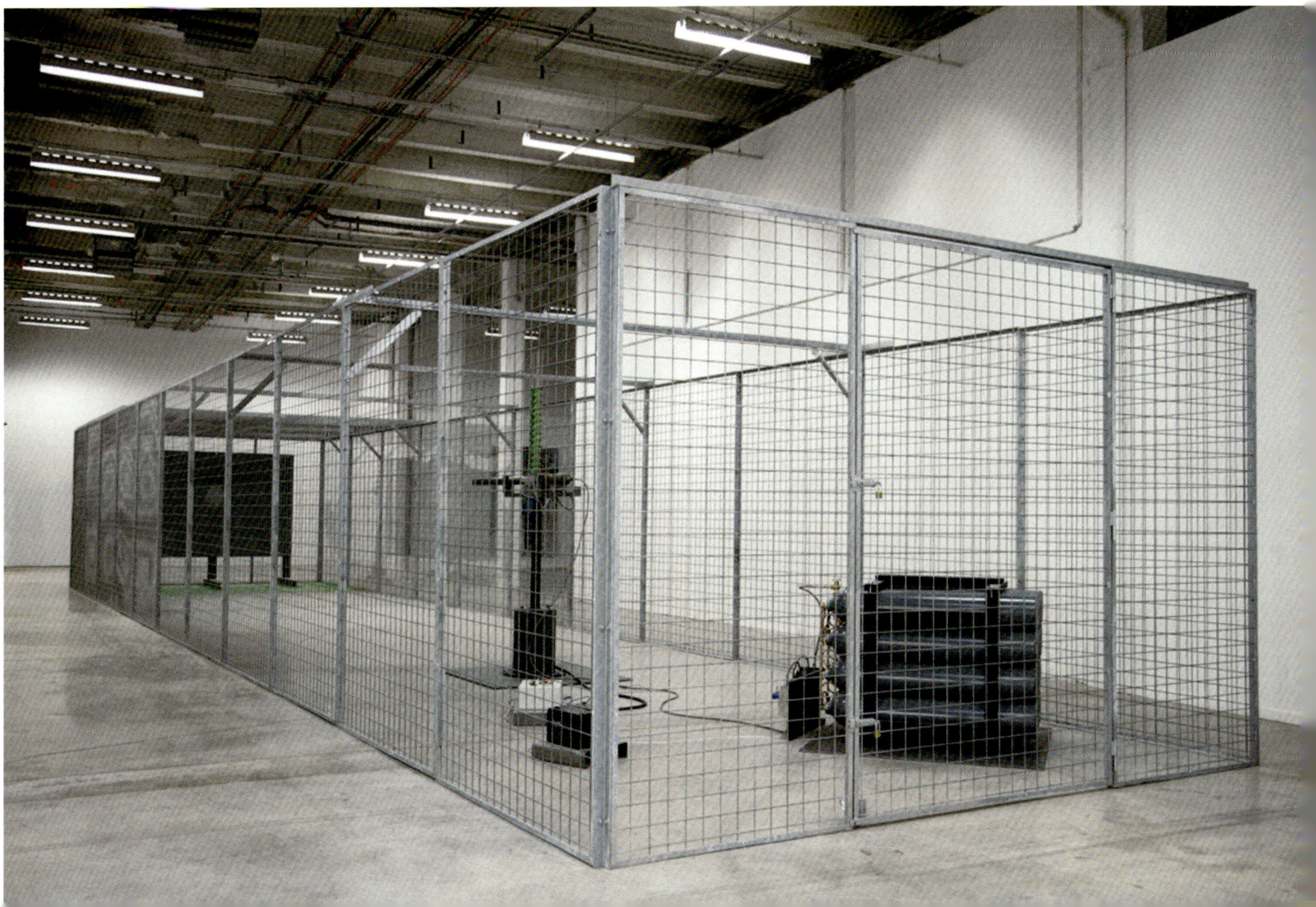

06

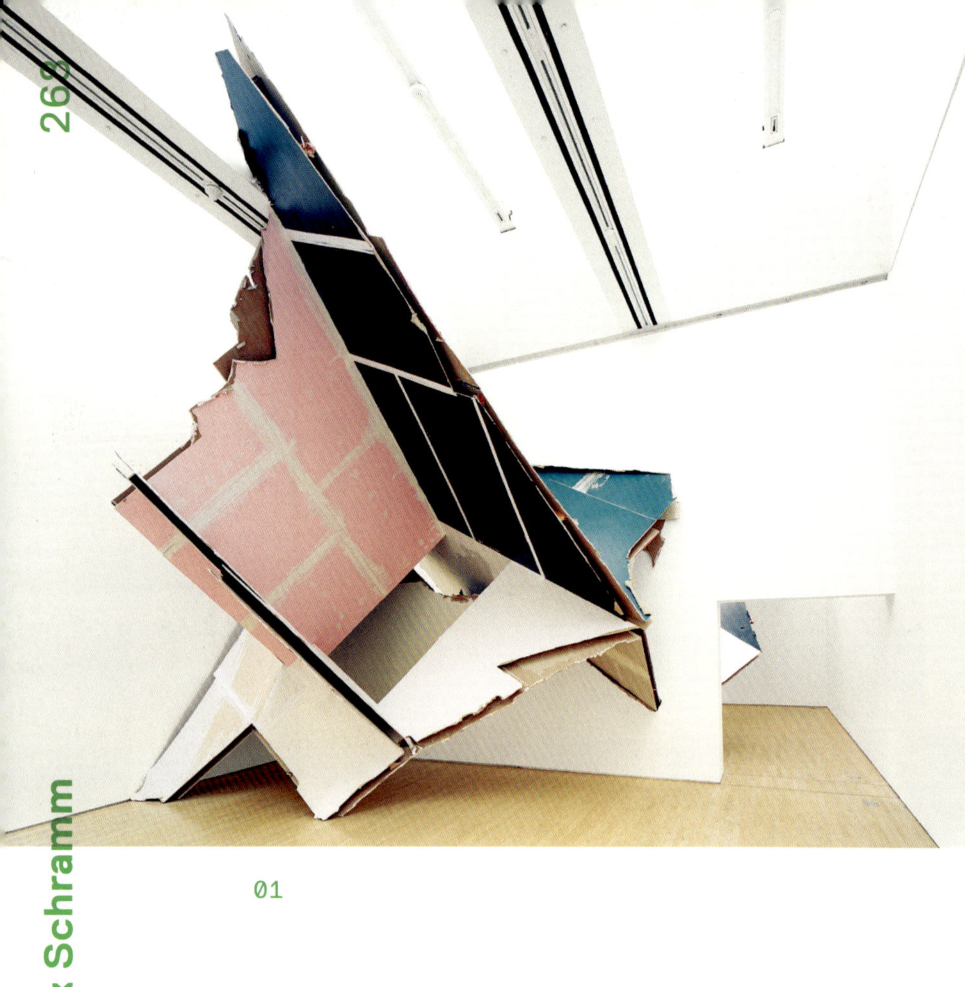

01

01 *Collider*, 2007
Plasterboard, metal, wood, paint, wallpaper
6.5 × 8 × 15 m

02 *Comber III*, 2006
Plasterboard, wood, paint
4.2 × 5 × 6 m

03, 04, 05
Savage Salvage, 2008
Plasterboard, metal, wood, clay, paint
7 × 9 × 35 m

We will never know what the inside of the World Trade Center looked like at the very moment when the first plane hit the towers on that day in 2001. The closest we may ever get is perhaps Felix Schramm's work *Collider*, which he built at the San Francisco Museum of Modern Art in 2007. As the title suggests, it was a collision of two things: the museum space and the artwork — drywall, paint, steel and wood, which were built into the galleries to give the illusion that disaster had just struck. Visitors could walk through the piece and experience spatial destruction converted into a temporal experience: the inside of the piece was also the inside of a moment, so to speak.

Critics and viewers tend to talk about Schramm mostly in terms of what he does to spaces — he simulates their detonation — but he does corresponding things to our experience of time. His work is about (paradoxical) stasis as much as it is about big bangs. Born in Hamburg in 1970, he studied in Düsseldorf under Jannis Kounellis, and within a few years he had made a trademark of what *Artforum* called 'intentional disarray'. His devastated fragments of walls and ceilings, built into the neat white cubes of gallery and museum spaces, create the impression that some super-monster or force of nature has thrown them into the site.

02

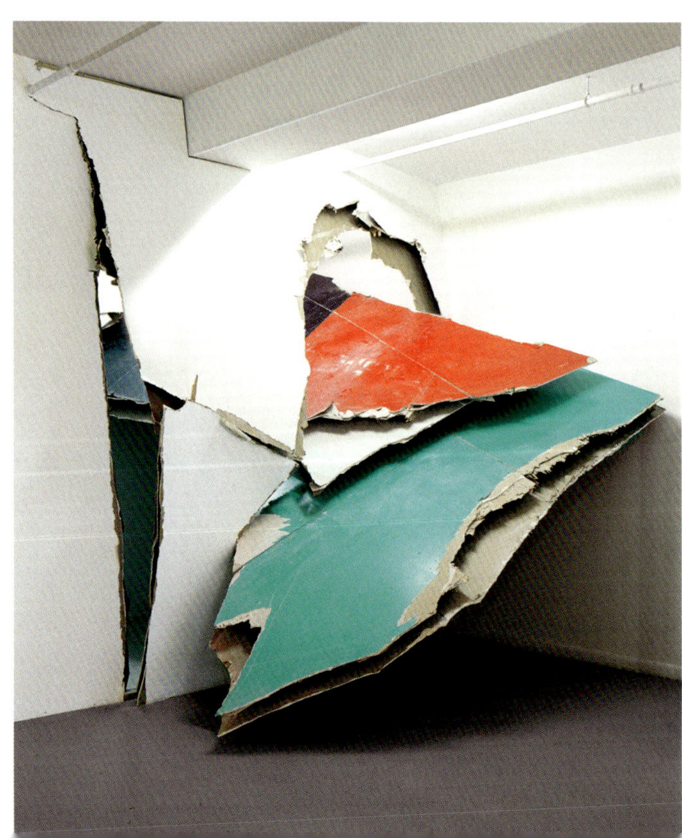

Occasionally Schramm's large structures, such as *Comber* (2005) or *Skaptor* (2004), are accompanied by smaller works like *Ringelringelreih* (2005) or *Soft Corrosion* (2007). In these he plays a record on a turntable, its balance and therefore sound distorted by a second hole drilled next to the central one. The turntable itself is connected to a unreliable and unstable electrical circuit. This double disruption of the wholeness of cultural production is another aspect of Schramm's post-catastrophe scenarios, the odd photo-wallpaper of an idyllic forest the only signifier of nature in works that are otherwise strictly edificial.

Schramm's art has frequently been discussed in relation to Gordon Matta-Clark's torn buildings, but it has been called 'depoliticized' in comparison to the socio-political and urbanist implications that were crucial to the American artist's approach. Perhaps Schramm is closer to another German artist, Gregor Schneider. While the latter builds intricate disruptions into private buildings, rendering them more or less inaccessible, the former throws gigantic pieces of wreckage into exhibition spaces that depend on accessibility. In doing so, he seems to disrupt any orderly consumption of art. But his unique feature is making the disaster area a walkable site, opening it up to monitoring in time and space. [Bert Rebhandl]

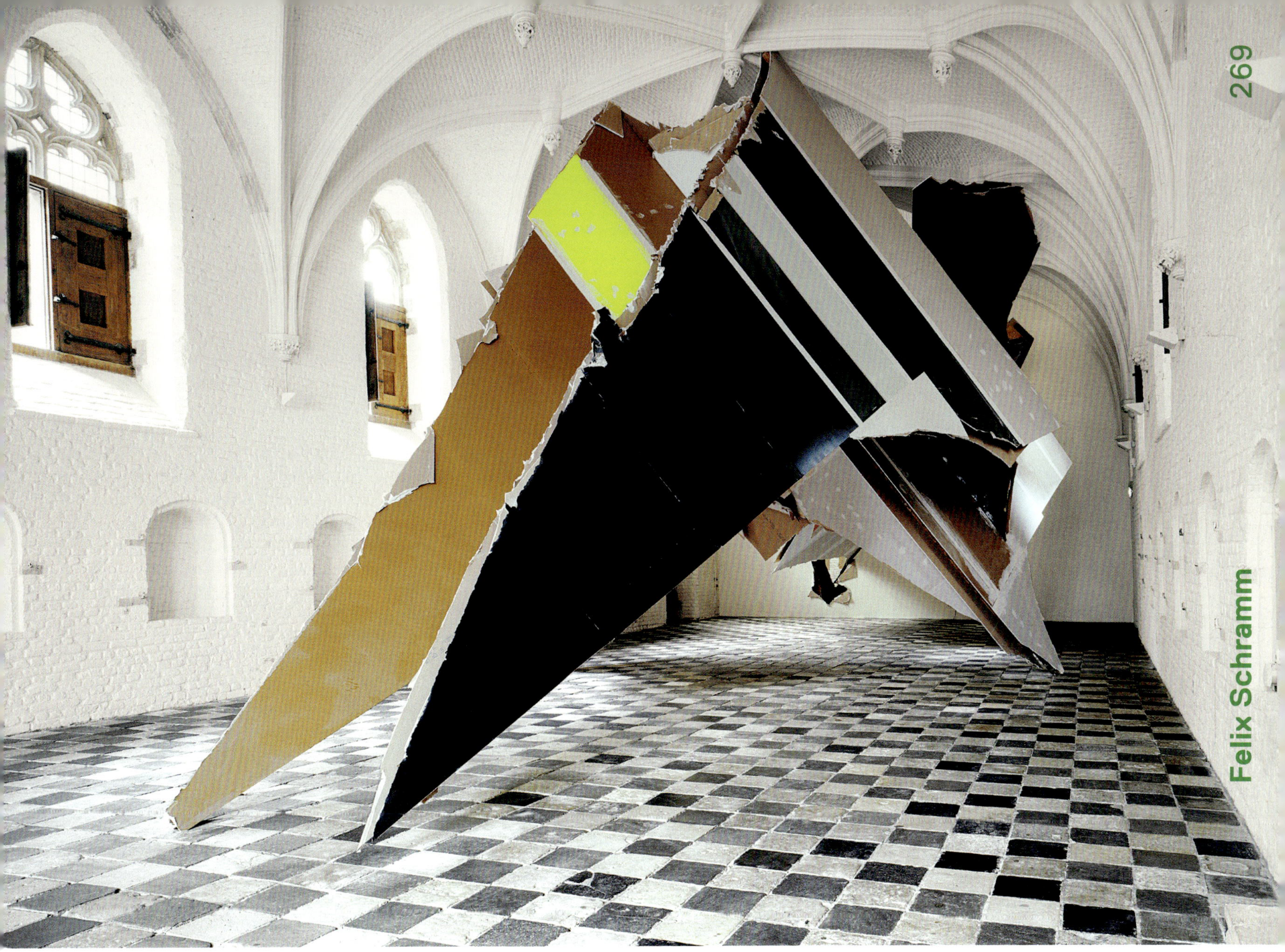

03

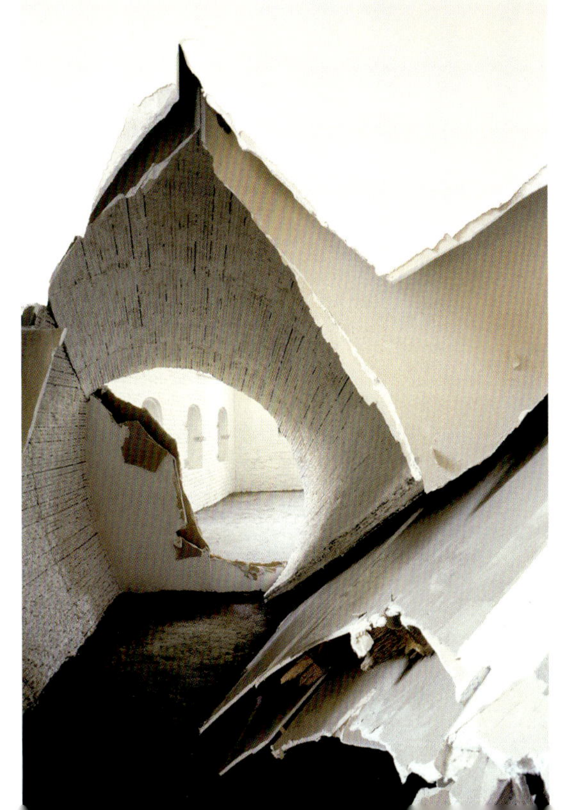

04

05

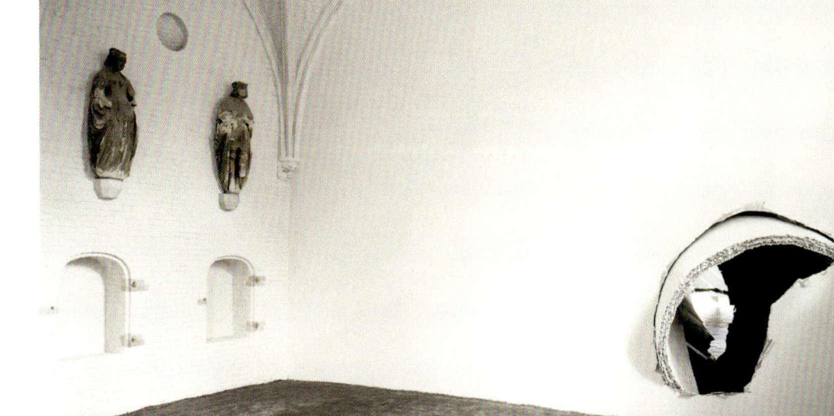

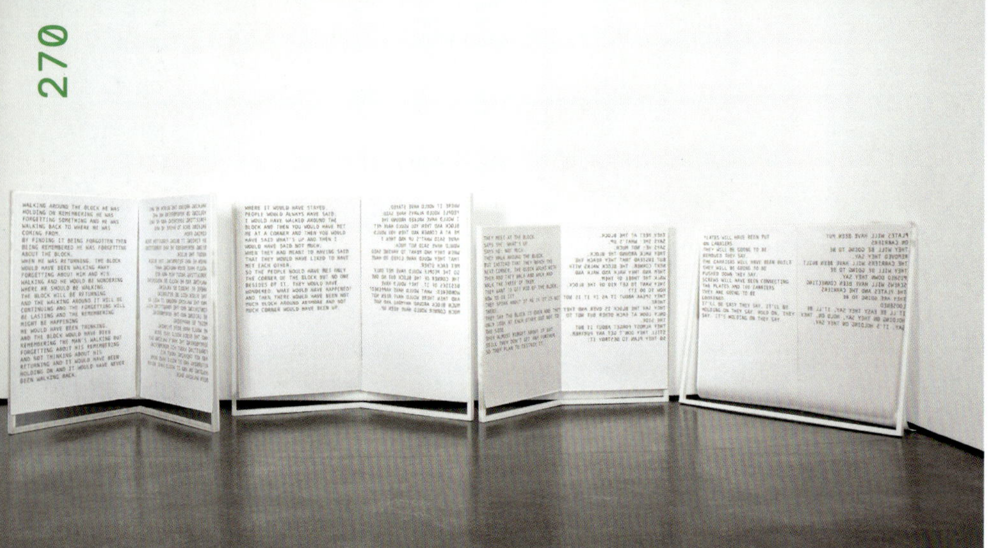

01 The accumulations of found materials in Nora Schultz's tentative assemblages seem intent on skirting any definitive form or meaning. Leaning, propped or carefully balanced, they remain contingent on each other, alternately supporting and being supported. Schultz's arrangement of objects and the intricate choreography of the relationships between them invites a 'reading' of their forms as if they were words or points of punctuation in a sentence, creating an opaque formal vernacular that teases with the possibility of decipherment.

Typically the result of an extended performative process, Schultz's exhibitions are layered like a palimpsest of gestures and formal manipulations that leave their traces on the surfaces of her assemblages. A series of photographs entitled *Countdown Performance* (2007) documents a piece of aluminium sheeting being formed and reformed into the numerals 0 to 10. Documentary in their appearance, the photographs literalize the sequential transformation to which Schultz submits her materials. Subjected to yet further adaptation, the piece of aluminium appears in another work entitled *Corner Panorama* (2007), which consists of a sheet of paper hung in the corner of a room and trailing on to the floor. The aluminium band, which was used as a drawing template for the delicate tracery of pencil lines that weave across the surface of the paper, assumes its final resting place on the floor at the base of the paper's folds, its zero configuration emphatically marking the end of its transformation.

Narrative becomes a slippery tool in Schultz's hands, stalled by repetition, doubling and an intermittent loss of sense. ***Block Letters*** (2007) is part sculpture, part text and encapsulates her interest in the materiality of language and the translation of formal configurations into textual exegesis. Around a delicate metal frame, which leans in the corner of a room for stability, are stretched panels of printed text repeated twice across four armatures. The text describes a couple who attempt to walk around an imposing building but find that the building 'walks with them'. Unable to ignore their uninvited companion, they agree to destroy the building. In its form, Block Letters is at once reminiscent of the open pages of a book and a paper architectural maquette, establishing a co-dependent relationship in which the structure and text rely on each other for support and meaning.

For the exhibition 'On Interchange' at the Museum Kurhaus Kleve, Schultz constructed an installation that charted a narrative through an elaborate sequence of interconnected references. *Dear Parrot* (2008) assembled disparate fragments — a multiple-exposure photograph of a pair of parrots, excerpts of a personal and unanswered letter from James Lee Byars to Joseph Beuys, an image of an installation by Lothar Baumgarten previously installed at the museum, a series of documents elucidating historical characters that she discovered in the museum's archives — into a precarious yet eloquent mise en scène. Woven around a central installation of plinths and reams of paper marked with coloured lines, created in a performance by the residual tangle of metal rods leaning against a nearby wall, the installation was not only an exploration of the gathered motifs and references but also a reflexive investigation into the act of art-making itself. [Andrew Bonacina]

01 *Block Letters*, 2007
Iron, lacquer, inkjet prints
Height 100 cm

02 *Untitled (foam mattress)*, 2007
Stainless steel, foam camping mat
71 × 110 × 90 cm

03 *Arrow Sculpture*, 2007
Stainless steel, sand, print, varnish
170 × 50 × 30 cm

04 *Countdown Krake*, 2007
Inkjet print on paper
60 × 140 × 140 cm

05 *Carriers in Search of the Time-Tilted Weight*, 2007
Metal, sandbags, found objects, frottage, photographs, foam mattress, cardboard, magazine
Dimensions variable

02

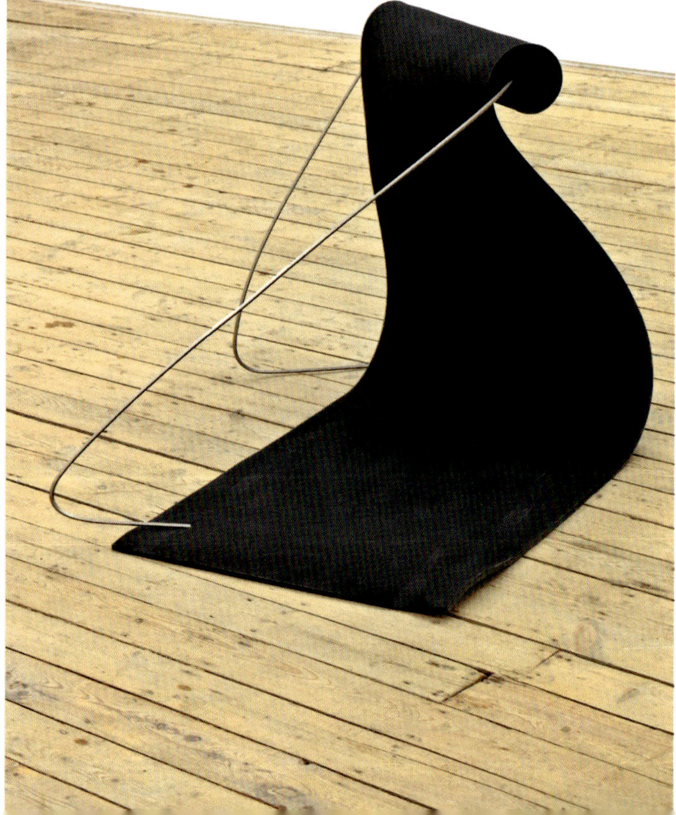

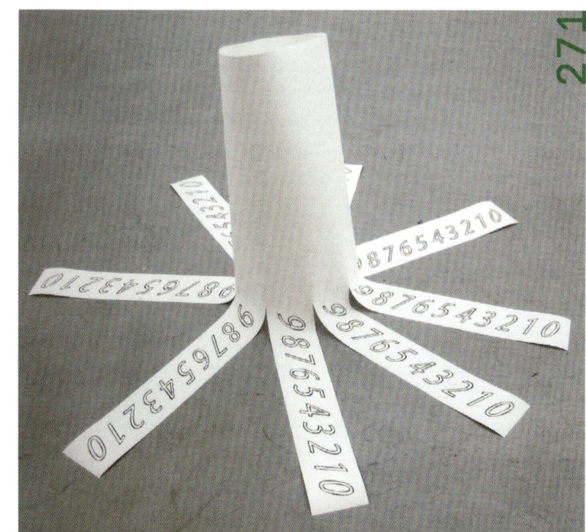

04

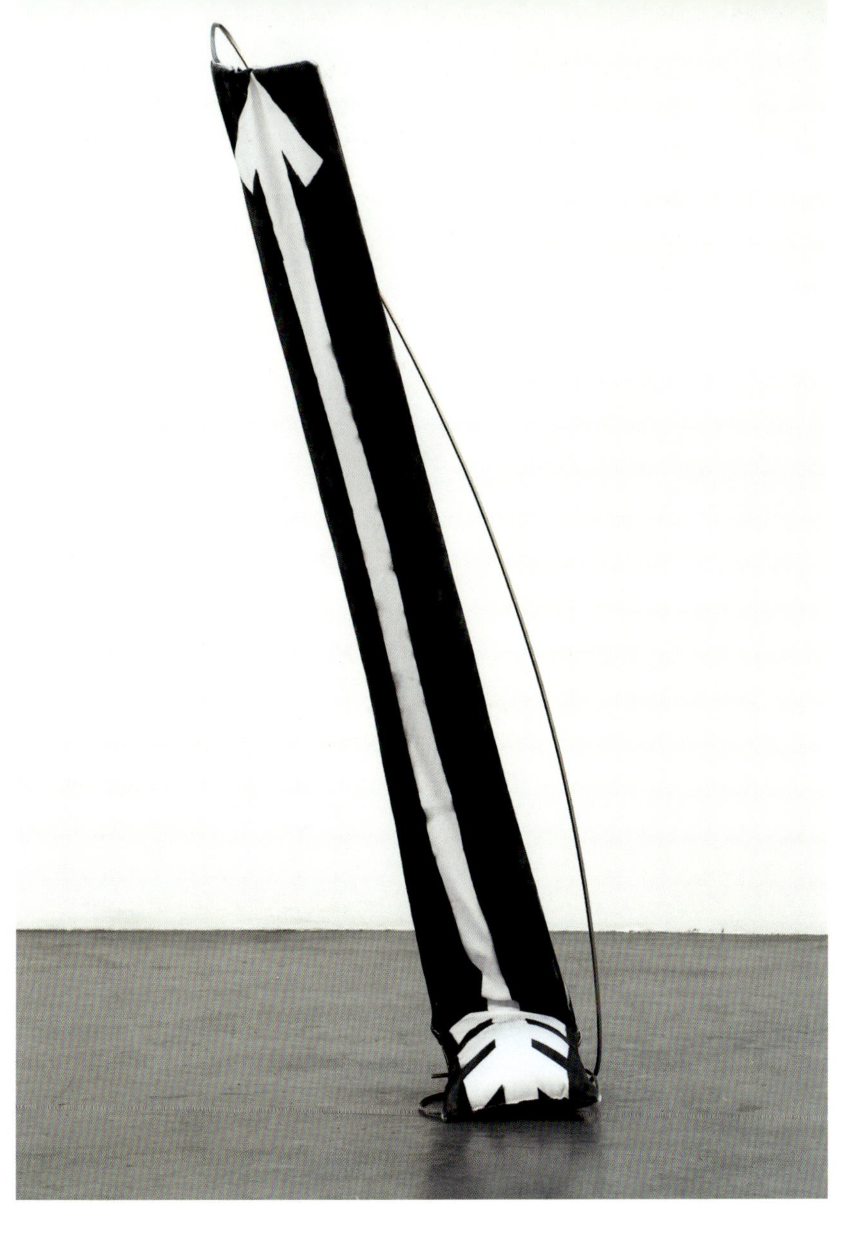

03

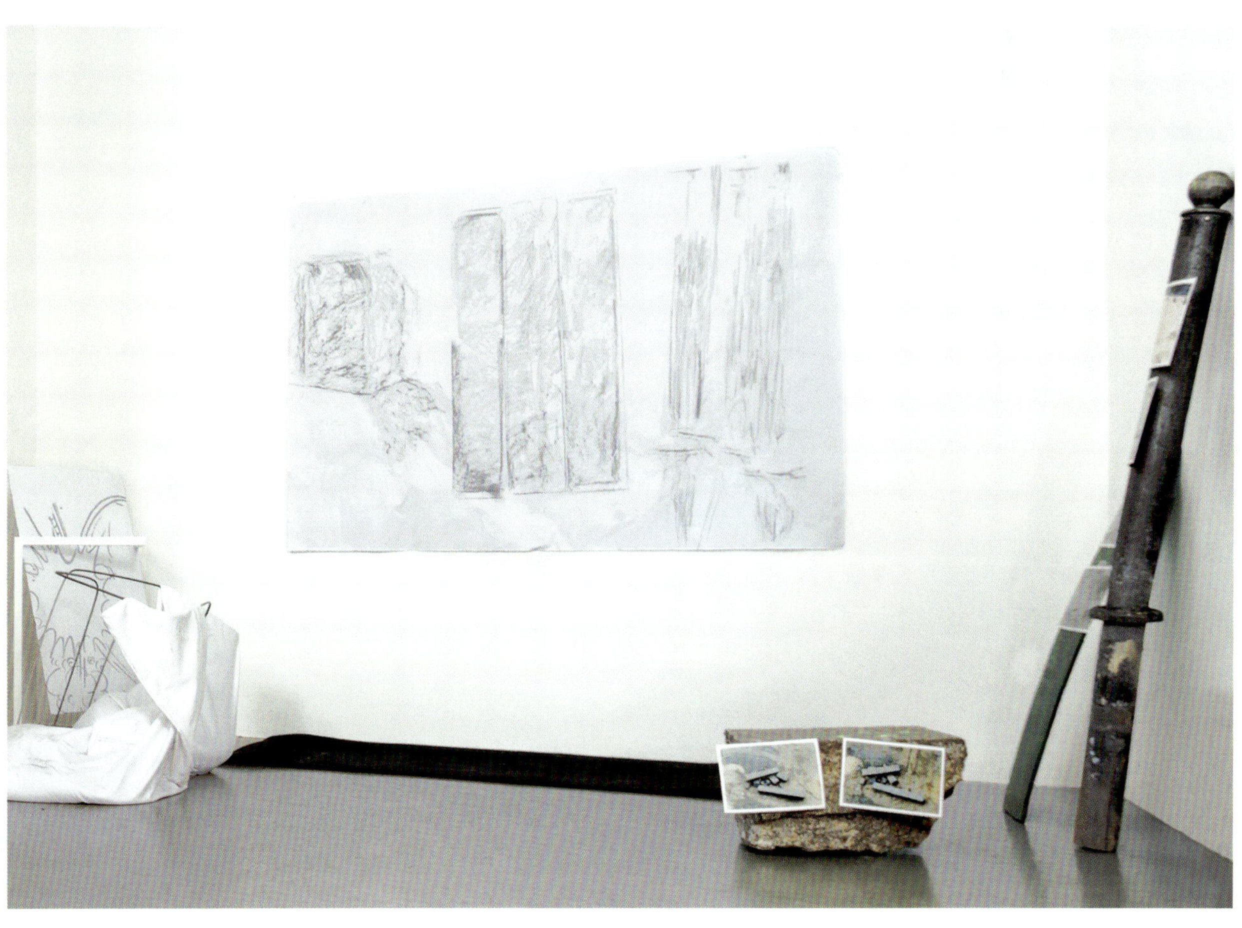

05

Can sculpture still be made today? On the evidence of Anna Sew Hoy's various productions, our answer might be 'not really' — at least not on the terms on which sculpture was once established. Not unless, as Rosalind Krauss suggested in her essay 'Sculpture in the Expanded Field', 'the category can be made to become almost infinitely malleable' — in which case, she claims, the term wouldn't be of much descriptive use. If sculpture in the 1960s had become 'a kind of ontological absence, the combination of exclusions, the sum of the neither/nor', today its sole condition is that it should preclude any condition whatsoever. Under this inverse injunction, anything goes and nothing goes; artworks in the vicinity of sculpture dramatize their perverse inclusivity even as they studiously avert the development of constructive order.

Sew Hoy's artworks navigate this weird situation with alacrity and wit, sewing together painted ceramic or plaster forms with found materials and consumer detritus. In her objects, wood, rocks, denim, beer cans, wire, power cables, beads, feathers, trashed cellphones and other 'objects and materials that people have a real connection to' find a place. We have a connection to these objects and materials because, through the mass production of consumer goods, we wear and own duplicates of these things, and because, through the turnover of styles or planned obsolescence, we have also disposed of them. In this way her work may invert the ambivalent strategies of Neo-Geo, replacing its fetishistic love of the brand new with an inventive and obsessive re-purposing of the hyper-disposable.

Unlike Kurt Schwitters, who imagined his found objects knitting together into a synthetic and abstract unity, Sew Hoy doesn't transform these materials into something else. The Sapporo beer cans knotted together in *Meteor* (2004) remain resolutely themselves, even if they find themselves in a new formal relationship (the artist has cited ikebana — Japanese flower arranging — as one model). Her title for the work is playfully descriptive: half ornamental, the work doubles as a representation, by way of spent aluminium, of the pocked surfaces of a rock hurtling from outer space. Indeed, asteroids, constellations, clusters, knots and lumps are her favourite shapes: they present an entropic world of possessions gone haywire, a loosely defined system of objects smelling faintly of Comme des Garçons #2.

Part of a thriving scene of artists, fashion designers and architects in Los Angeles — including the Sundown Salon and Assume Vivid Astro Focus, with whom Sew Hoy has collaborated — she incorporates their various tactics into artworks both posed and stylishly imperfect. When tossed onto a flat surface, altered shirts double as drawings; shredded stonewash denim is threaded through the holes of a coral-like ceramic tangle (*Arena*, 2006, part of her *Scholar Rocks* series). In a modernity that is increasingly planned and designed — and without a stable idea of 'nature' against which this abstract world might be judged or brought to view — neither the syntax proper to sculpture, nor the structural logic of the 'expanded' forms that Krauss puts forwards, seem to function as they once did. Sew Hoy's mirror blobs and bulging denim look to a distorted and awkward form of craft as a possible new nature for sculpture. [Julian Myers]

01

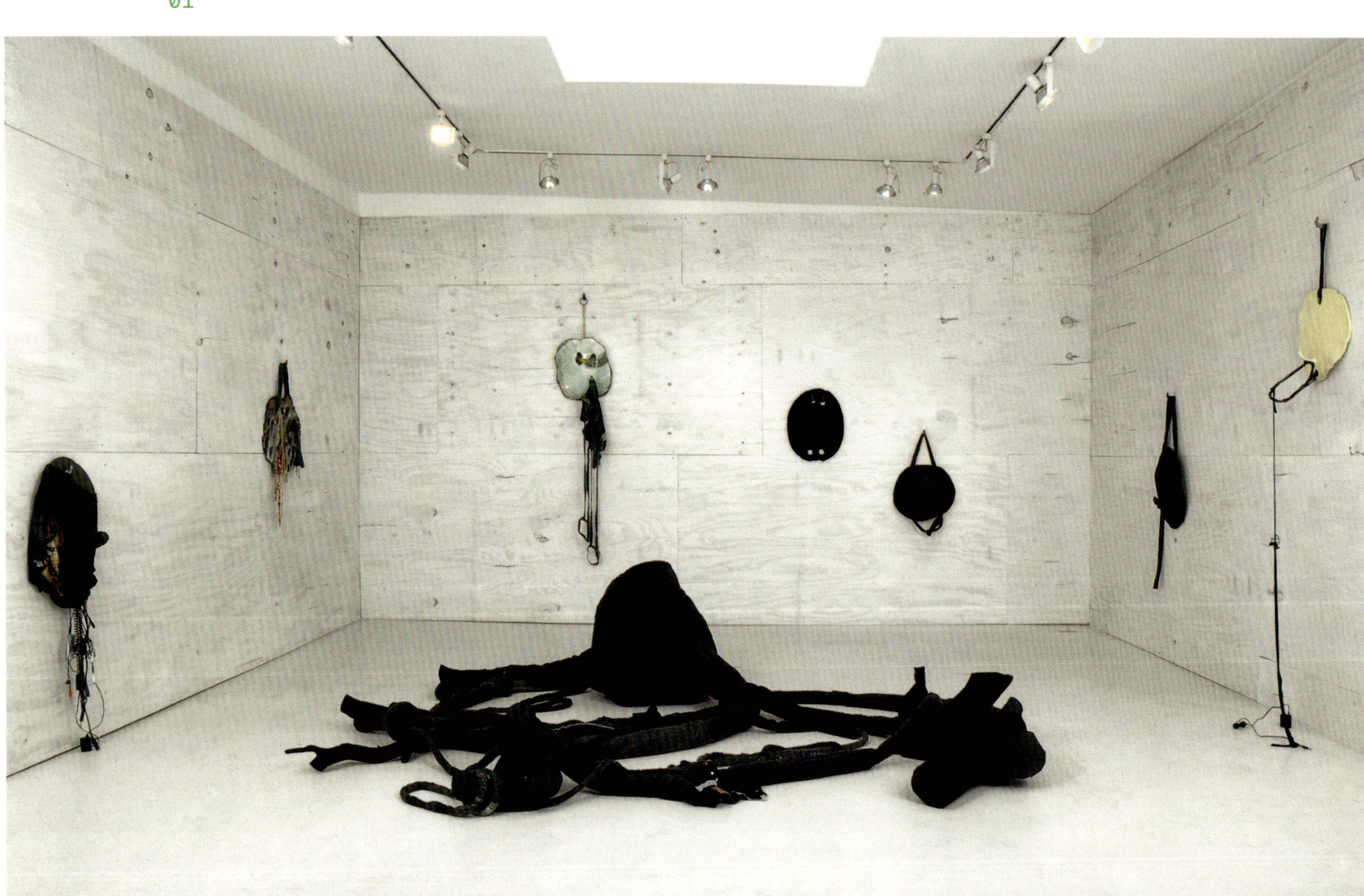

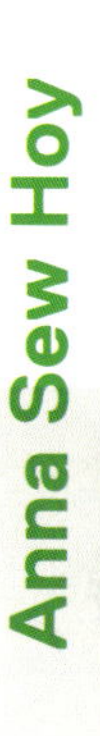

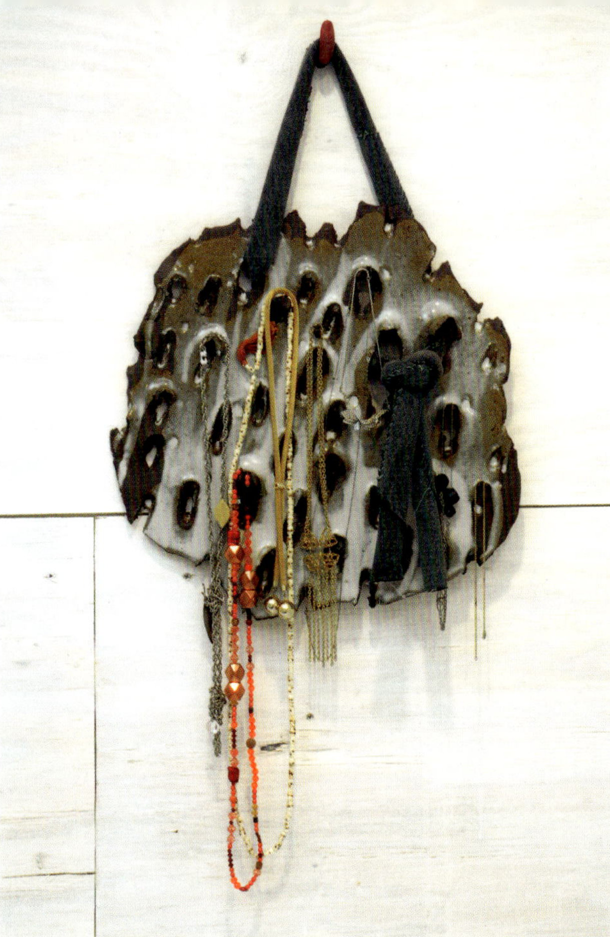

02

03

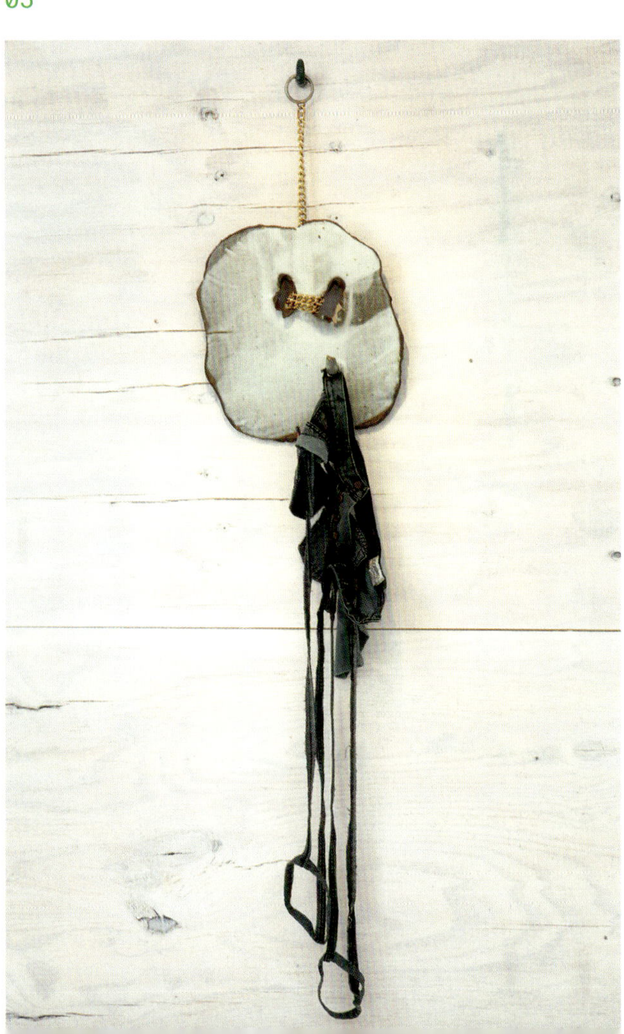

04

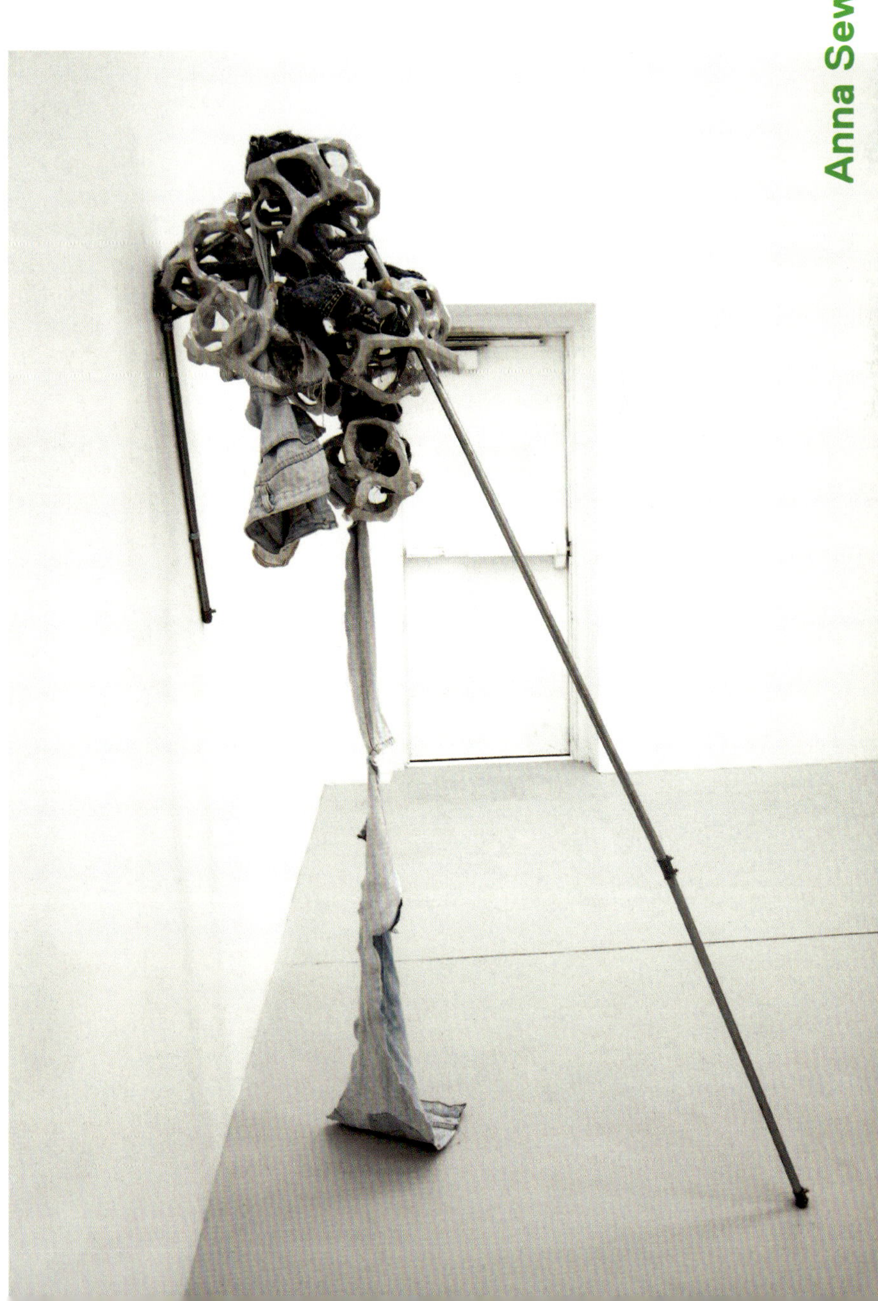

01 Centre:
→ *Circuit*, 2007
Wood, denim, flocking, polyurethane rigid expanding foam, paint
Dimensions variable

from left:
→ *Point*, 2007
Glazed ceramic, T-shirt, electrical cords, string, papier-mâché, paint, resin finger hook
122 × 45 × 19 cm
→ *Display*, 2007
Glazed ceramic, denim, necklaces from the artist's collection, resin finger hook
66 × 48 × 9 cm
→ *Two eyes*, 2007
Glazed ceramic, metal chain, denim, resin finger hook
190 × 44 × 13 cm
→ *Om*, 2007
Glazed ceramic, flocking, two resin finger hooks
53 × 41 × 13 cm
→ *Exploded*, 2007
Ceramic part, flocking, mud, papier-mâché, fabric and string, resin finger hook
76 × 48 × 13 cm
→ *Held*, 2007
Ceramic part, flocking mud, papier-mâché, fabric and string, resin finger hook
117 × 39 × 14 cm
→ *Speech*, 2007
Ceramic part, wire, acid wash cotton, resin finger hook, electrical cord
226 × 38 × 29 cm

02 *Display*, 2007
Glazed ceramic, denim, necklaces,resin finger hooks, screw
66 × 48 × 9 cm

03 *Two eyes*, 2007
Glazed ceramic, metal chain, denim, resin finger hook
190 × 45 × 13 cm

04 *Arena*, 2006
Iridescent glazed ceramic, electrical pipe, stone-wash denim
Height approx. 183 cm

Mindy Shapero's sculptures are suggestive of someone who spent many nights as a child reading fantasy novels by the dim light of a flashlight. Her works seem to spring from her own fertile imagination, while her delicate, humble materials oddly and obediently follow suit. But Shapero's works do not arrive fully formed — her sculptures bear the traces of an organic, time-consuming creative process. We can almost trace her floral blooms of eccentric thought through her compulsive layering of tiny confetti-like pieces of paper or her dizzying rainbow stripes.

Shapero's loopy, meandering titles introduce us to her quirky, ongoing fantasy narrative. These dictums and descriptions could be sentences stolen from the manuscript of an undiscovered mystic or a deranged street poet. (They have in fact blossomed into their own series of photocopied zines.) An exhibition entitled 'Inside the circle traps (in a zombie state walking around in tight circles from looking too deep into the blinded by the light; some get out and some don't)' (2005), for example, all at once suggests impending danger and infinite pitfalls. Yet the objects in the show look carefree and unbound, like little flying orbs that could serve as escape vehicles from any threat.

Shapero's eccentric and ecstatic sculptures, assembled from small pieces of paper, wood, metal leaf, mosaic and papier mâché, comprise her cosmos of 'monsterheads and circle traps'. Some lean towards the psychedelic, others towards folk art. Each is its own complex but nonsensical structure, bearing copious traces of its handmade origins. These fragile, precarious forms are constructed through a laborious process of layering, building and gluing — a method the artist may have tested at a young age by making things with Popsicle sticks and glue. It's clear that she derives a childlike pleasure from her painstaking process. The end results — kaleidoscopic circles or exploding rainbows, clouds and starbursts — become part of an accumulation of new-age talismanic objects. *The moment all the universes opened up to more, simultaneously right before they disappear into thin air* (2006) is a pyramid with strange mossy outgrowths made of multi-coloured confetti scraps. Another sculpture composed of painted discs precariously stacked on papier mâché rocks looks like a ritualistic object cobbled together by cave people — except that its fluorescent colours and its title, *The infinite truths of flatterland (hugging air till it hurts, and spinning out into other dimensions)*, (2006), suggest a leap into the future or onto another planet. An accompanying series of ominously hollow-eyed portraits, which she labels 'Ghosthead guides that will bring you to the ghosthead god', look like they could be members of a mysterious sect. Shapero's provocative, mystical titles might in fact be red herrings; her objects would have a cosmic, energetic charge even without them. These texts may not be clues to her work but rather a kind of eccentric poetry — a compulsive exercise of piling and layering words on top of each other that mirrors the way in which she handles her artistic materials. [Christy Lange]

01

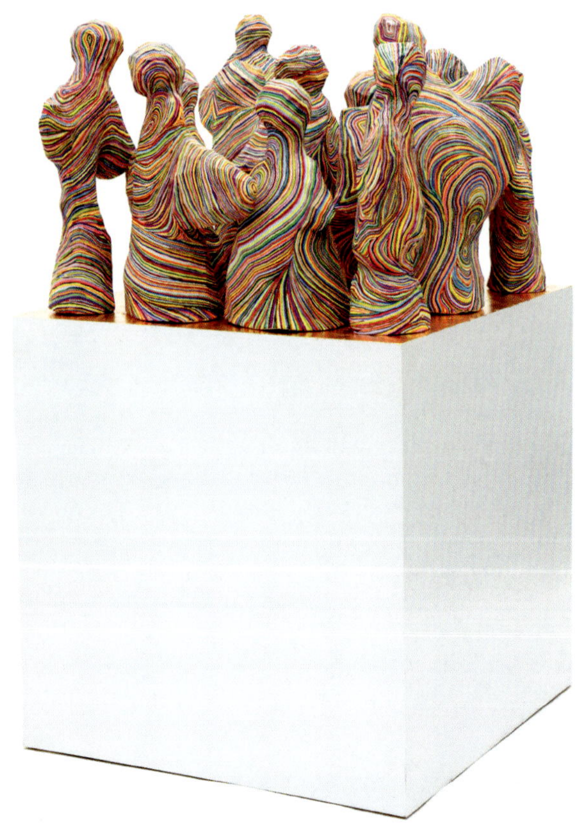

01 *Funerary Objects*, 2007
Papier mâché, acrylic
11 parts
Each 61 × 38 × 15 cm
Wood pedestal, latex, copper leaf
91 × 91 × 91 cm

02, 03 *Head*, 2007–08
Steel, acrylic covered paper, acrylic caulking
173 × 162 × 152 cm

04 *Inversion (seventh wonder)*, 2008
Wood, acrylic, gold leaf, Coloraid paper
Approx. 61 × 91 × 91 cm

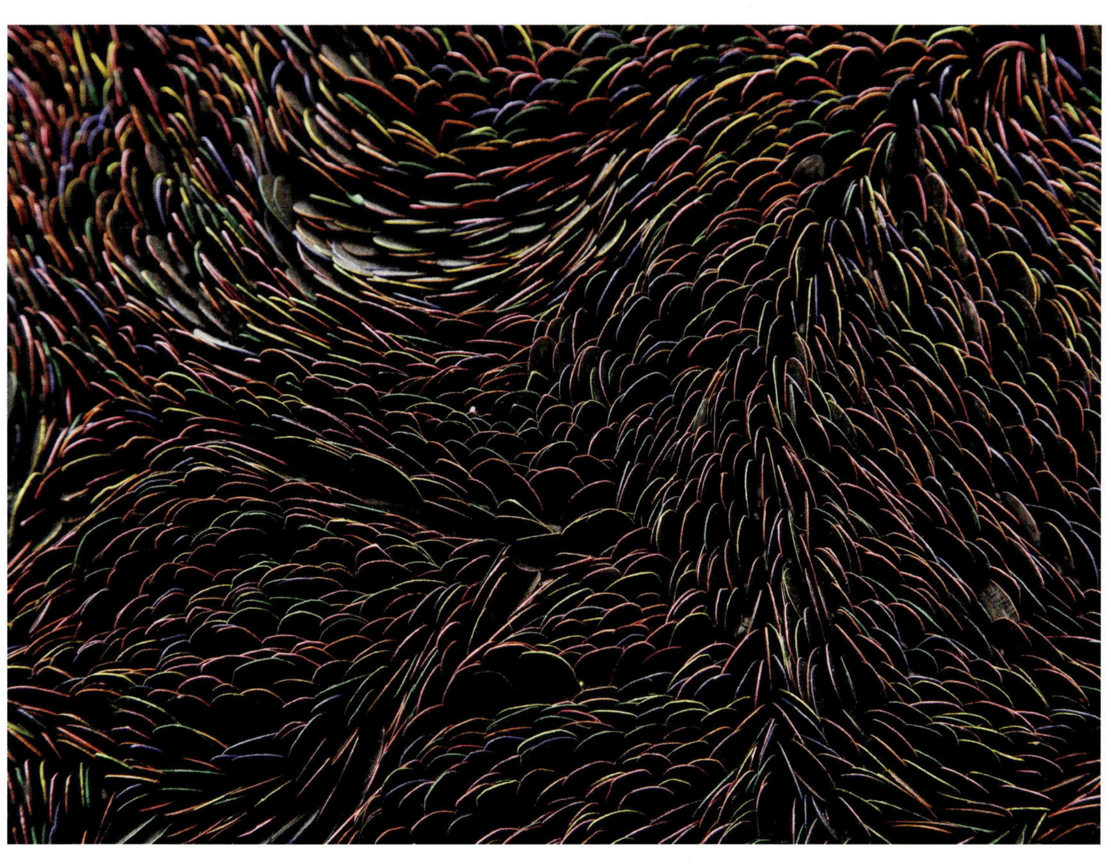

02

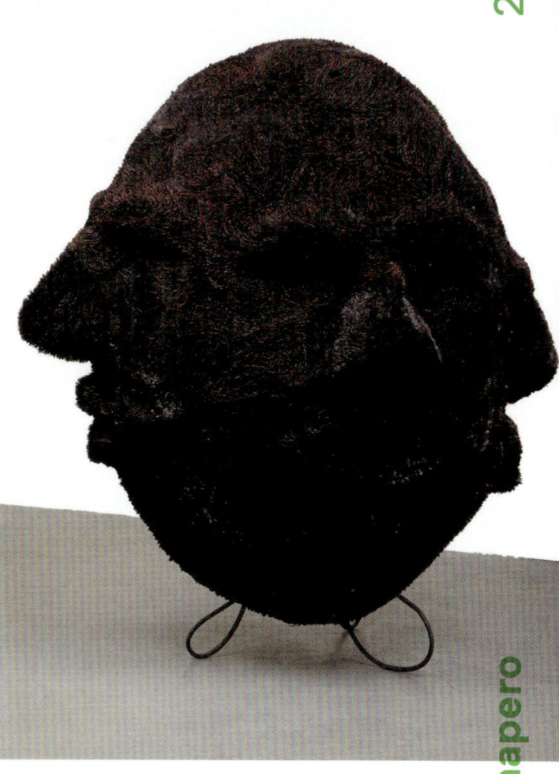

03

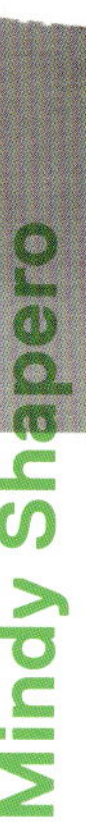

04

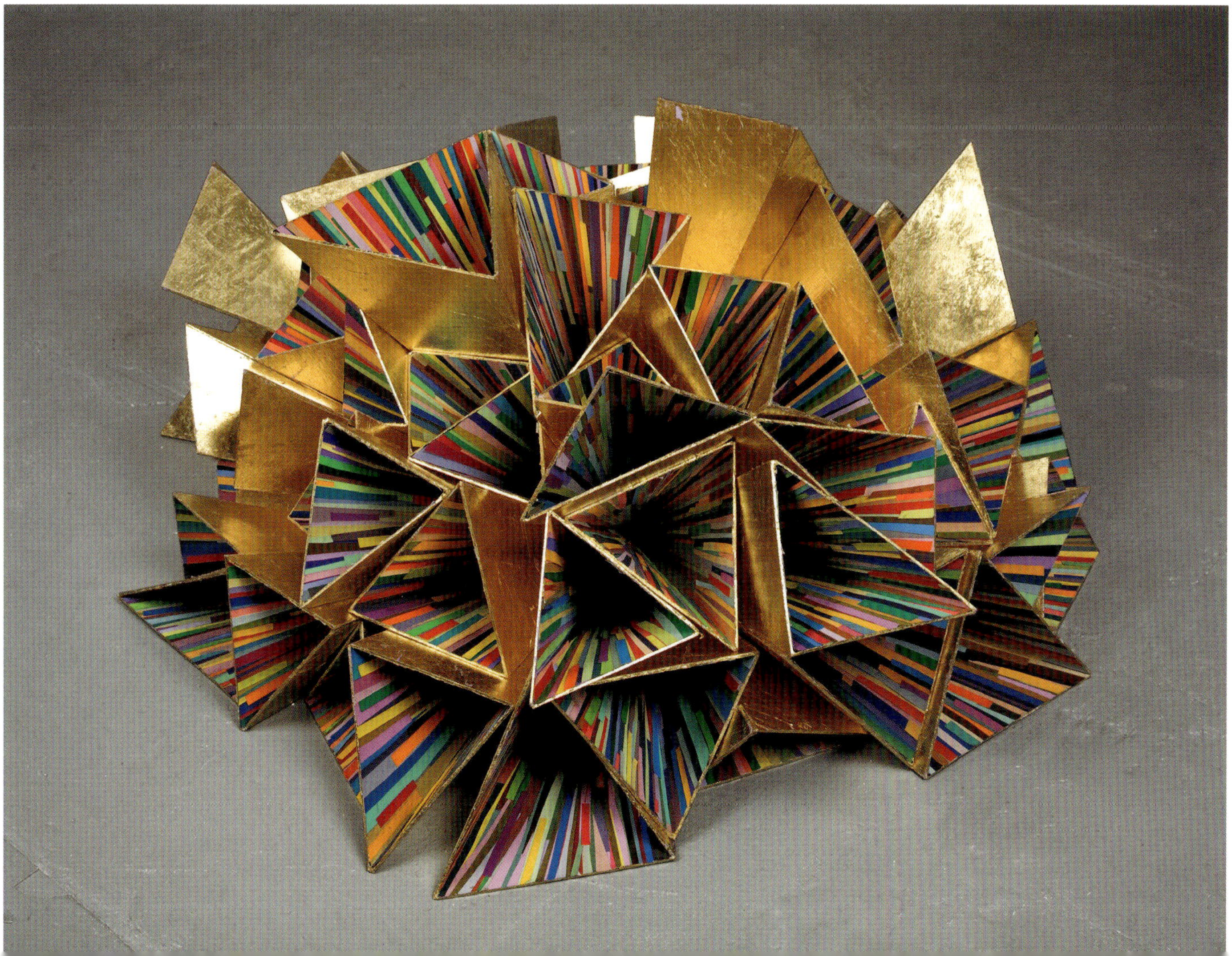

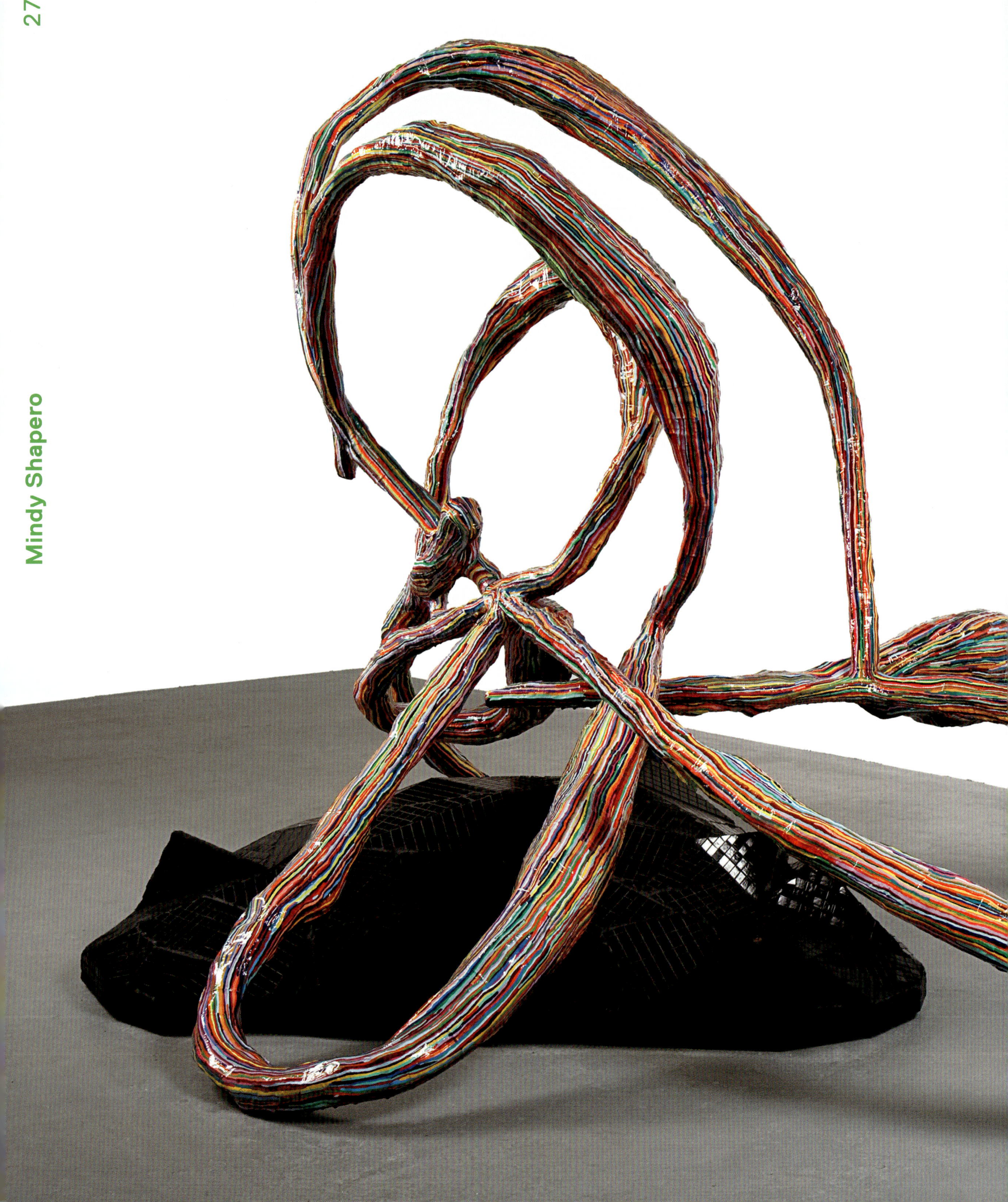

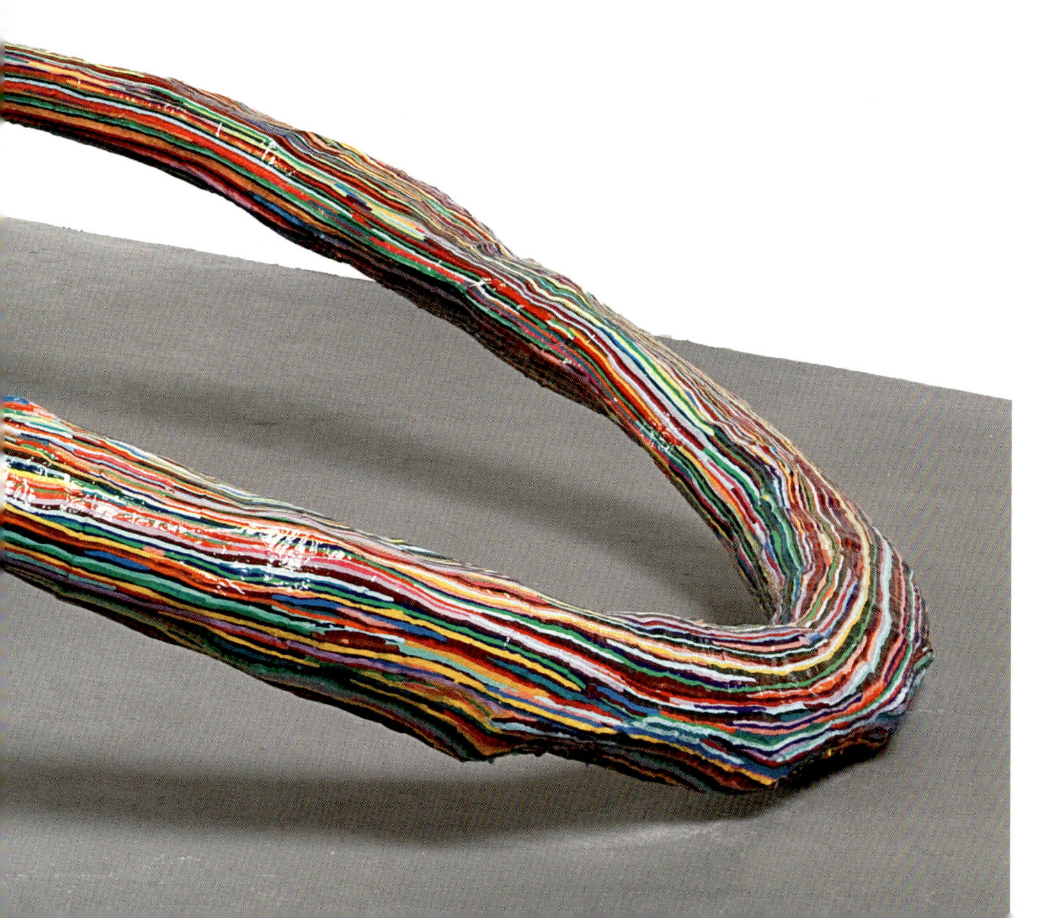

05 *Looping*, 2008
Steel, fibreglass,
epoxy resin, enamel paint
305 × 274 × 198 cm

In Ranjani Shettar's first solo exhibition 'Home' (2000), the ambition of the work was to capture the intrinsic beauty of the delicate fabrications made by birds, insects, bees or silkworms — cocoon-like forms, web-like constellations or clusters of berries. Yet made from plastic sheeting, rope and rivets, this work also showed the artist's commitment to exploring all manner of industrial materials in order to create a form of correspondence to the natural world that we inhabit and that surrounds us.

The early pieces were followed by such work as *Vasanta* (2004) in which thousands of hand-rolled beeswax nodes connect to a vast web of coloured strings. Reflected against the wall, they appear as a lustrous maze of cobwebs whose progressive changes of colour suggests that of the seasons. Soon afterwards, Shettar created *Heliotropes* (2005–06) out of thread and latex, which responded to the light in her studio, and *Just a bit more* (2005–06), a room filled with a delicate web of thread and hand-rolled beeswax. More recently, *Sun-sneezers blow light bubbles* (2008) was made with tamarind kernel powder paste and muslin used by local craft communities, as in the village of Kinnala, India, to make childrens' toys and religious idols. Shettar re-deploys these materials to create an immersive environment evoking the phenomenon whereby some people sneeze when exposed to the sun or bright light.

03

01, 02 *Vasanta*, 2004
Pigment, hand-rolled beeswax, strings dyed in tea
394 × 731 × 320 cm

03 *Sun-sneezers blow light bubbles*, 2008
Stainless steel, muslin cloth, tamarind kernel powder paste, lacquer
Dimensions variable

04 *Just a bit more*, 2005–06
Pigment, hand-rolled beeswax, strings dyed in tea
1100 × 730 × 370 cm

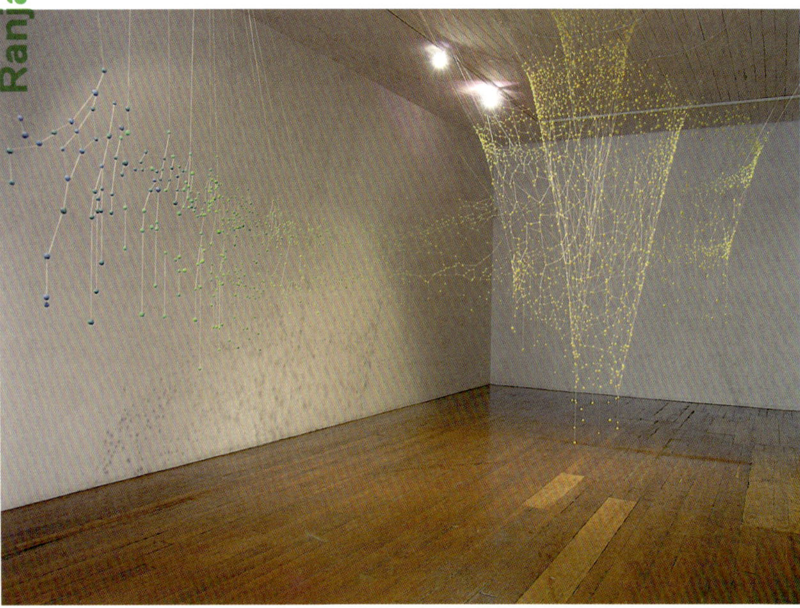

01

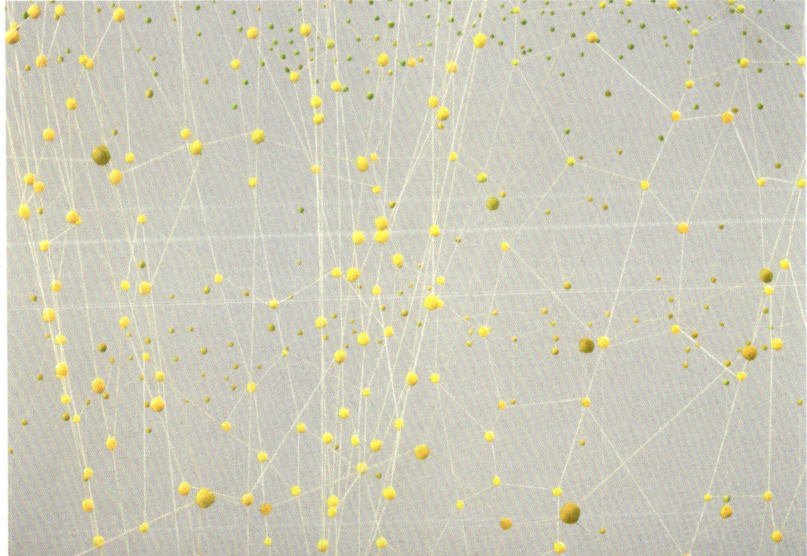

02

Through deploying this range of everyday industrial and natural materials, Shettar constructs environments that tacitly respond to the processes and forces shaping the growth and life of contemporary cities. This is nowhere found more clearly than in her own city of Bangalore, with its burgeoning Internet business and high-tech economic growth. Trained in sculpture at Chitrakala Institute of Advanced Studies, Shettar creates a world that does not simply respond to the effect that industrialization may have on the processes of urbanization, or on the local ways of life intimately connected to those of the countryside. Rather, she creates a delicate formal language, a tenuous network of creative exchange and correspondence between materials and environments through which to envisage other spaces, a setting that holds the promise of a transformative experience beyond the material everyday. 'Home is the body,' Shettar has remarked. 'The body is not the physical alone but the mental, emotional and the spiritual'.

Shettar's work belongs to a trajectory that is a counterpoint to modernist traditions, especially that of the Bauhaus. Significantly, this counterpoint has manifested itself most strongly and precisely in those countries where the influence of the Bauhaus has been more evident, such as in Venezuela, Brazil or Japan — in the art of Gego, Lygia Clark or Saito, respectively. Shettar's artistic project corresponds to these artists yet is distinctive in its form and trajectory. She proposes an extension into space that begins not by virtue of the laws of geometric abstraction, but of a tenuous relation to a world in which humans as sentient beings immerse themselves and belong. [Charles Merewether]

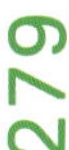

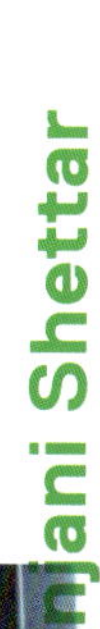

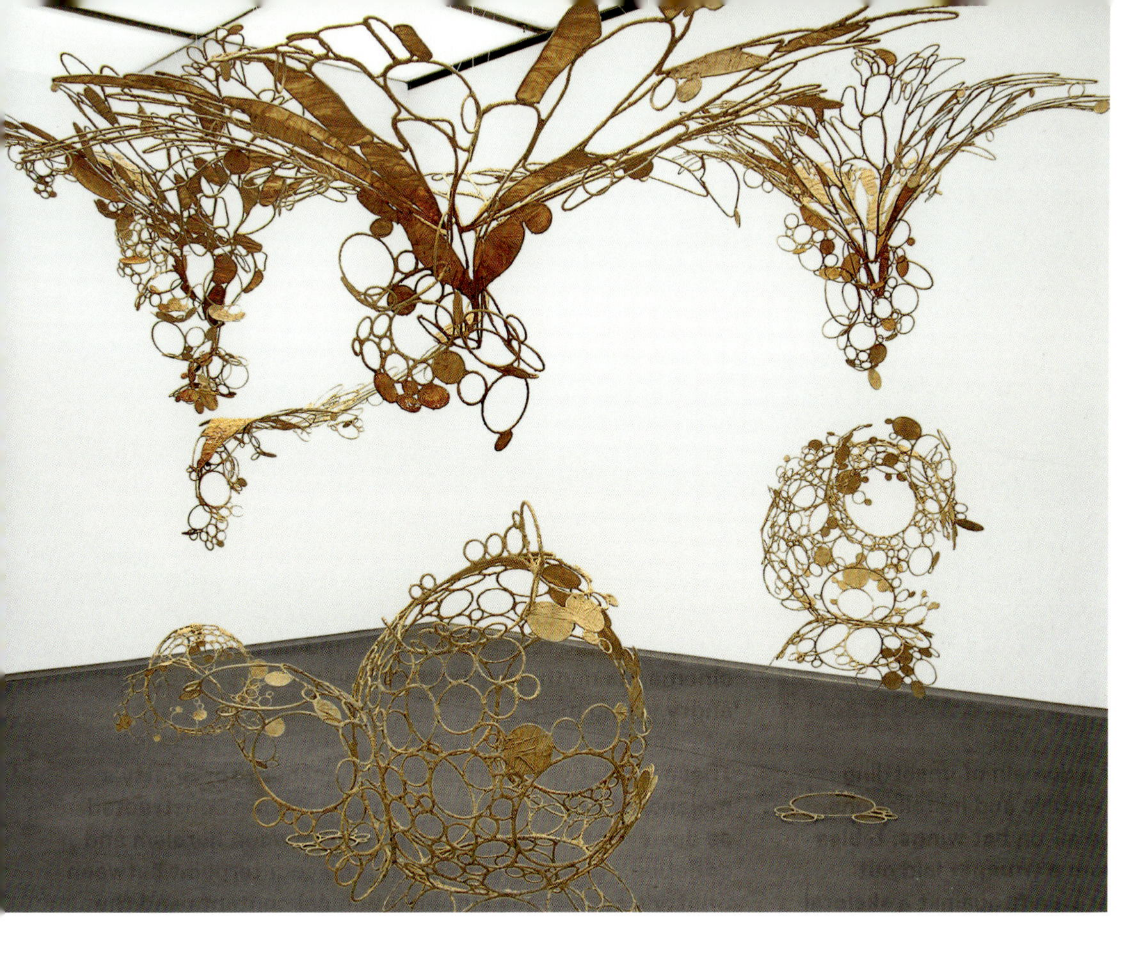

04

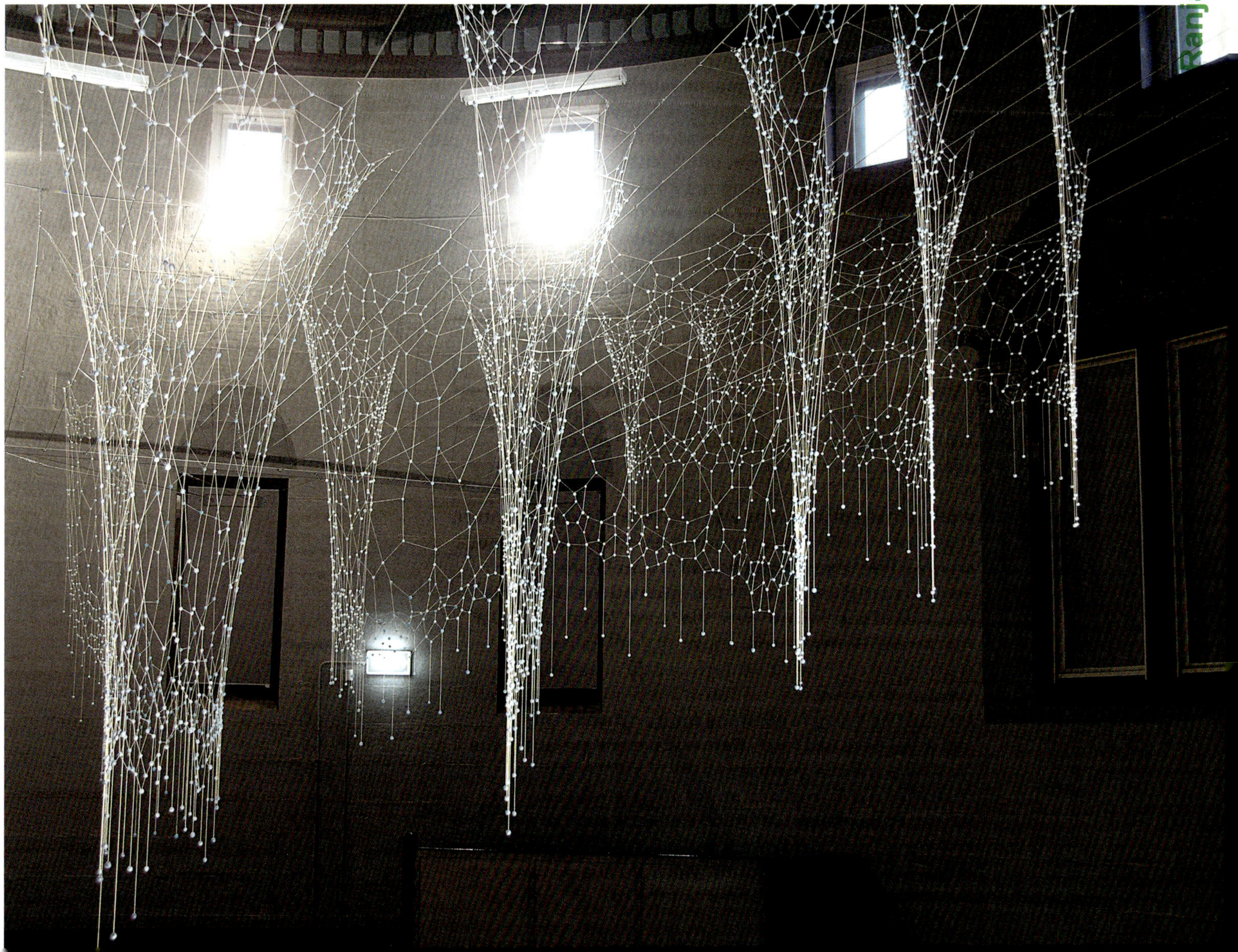

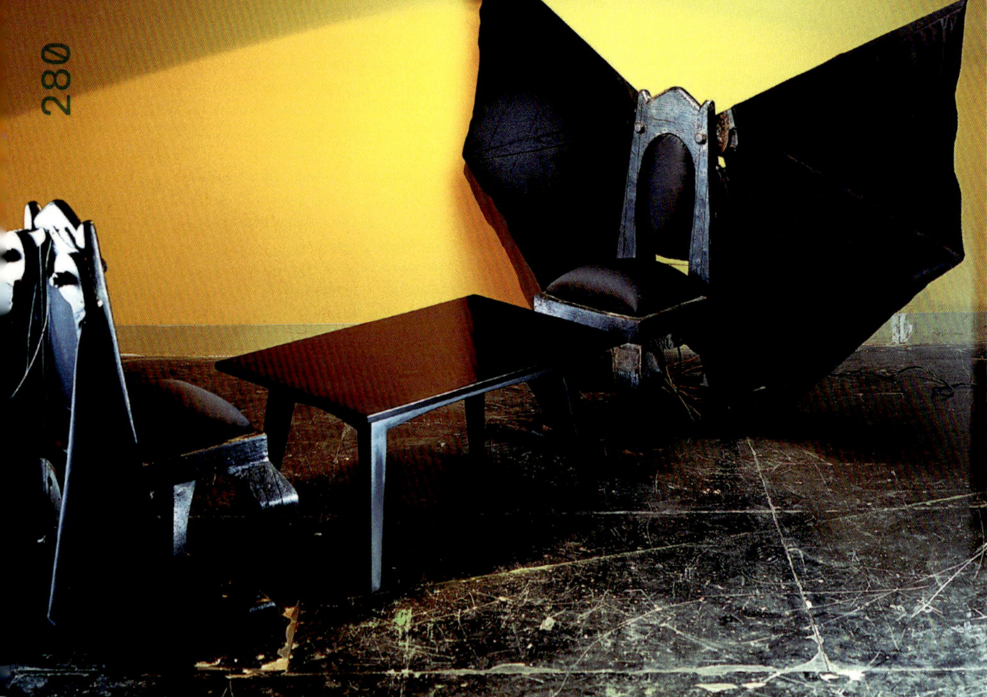

01

Sudarshan Shetty

Sudarshan Shetty reigns over a domain of unsettling paradox. In his sculptural ensembles and installations, chairs threaten to flap into the air on bat wings, tables shiver and tilt, blood pours from a trumpet laid out like an intestine and a hammer clangs against a skeletal buffalo's udders. A boat doubles as a cello, its oars scraping a sad music from its hollow thorax. His works are animated by DIY motors, black humour and quixotic wit.

Shetty was one of the pioneers of extended sculpture in Indian art. In the early 1990s, he rebelled against modernist sculpture in its fossilized, academic form, displacing its emphasis on monumentality, permanence and stasis with irreverence, provisionality and instability. His hybrid installations were not constrained by the canons of taste: they drew both on classical sources and the vibrant materiality of kitsch. Although he trained in painting at the Sir Jamsetjee Jejeebhoy School of Art in Bombay in the early 1980s, his art owes more to his term as a fellow at the Kanoria Centre of Arts, Ahmedabad, later in that decade. There, he interacted closely with colleagues at the National Institute of Design and the Centre for Environmental Planning and Technology. Through these conversations, Shetty honed his knowledge of the relationship between sculpture, design and architecture.

Vital to these discussions was the work of Robert Venturi, the theorist and reluctant guru of architectural postmodernism. Shetty's artistic choices are prefigured in Venturi's strictures against the International Style, his espousal of the 'hybrid' over the 'pure', 'distortion' over the 'straightforward' and, above all, 'ambiguity' over 'articulation'. Following Venturi, Shetty never deploys surface as a mere articulation of the work's inner structure, nor as a simple envelope for its dynamics of lift and drag, base and form. Rather, Shetty's surface is the face his sculpture presents to the world, switching from High Seriousness to street vulgate with polyglot facility as he integrates kitsch elements such as pink kite-paper, artificial flowers and plastic hearts into refined, retro-classical forms which are suggestive of the Pyramids, equestrian statues and the row of amphorae.

Another key to Shetty's art may lie in his quiet, largely unadvertised exploration of intimate realities associated with childhood, youth and family past. Born to a Bunt family from South Kanara with martial and mercantile traditions, Shetty grew up watching his father's long, leisurely-paced *Yakshagana* performances. These vivid encounters with a folk theatre form alternated with his exposure to 1980s Bombay, dominated by a dramatic and protracted textile-mill strike and by popular Hindi cinema, its mythology built around the persona of the 'angry young man'.

These formative experiences may account for Shetty's melancholic poetics. Many of his works are constructed as devices of imbalance, teetering between heroism and deflation, resilience and defeat. The counterpoint between Shetty's submerged autobiographical contents and the universalizing, almost mythic power of his devices allows him to negotiate productively between a voluble hybridity and a restrained classicism. [Nancy Adajania]

02

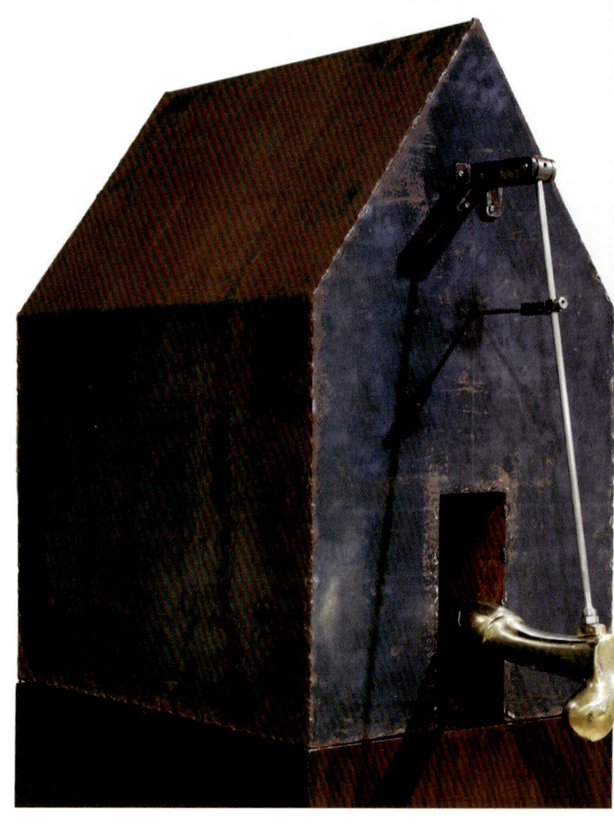

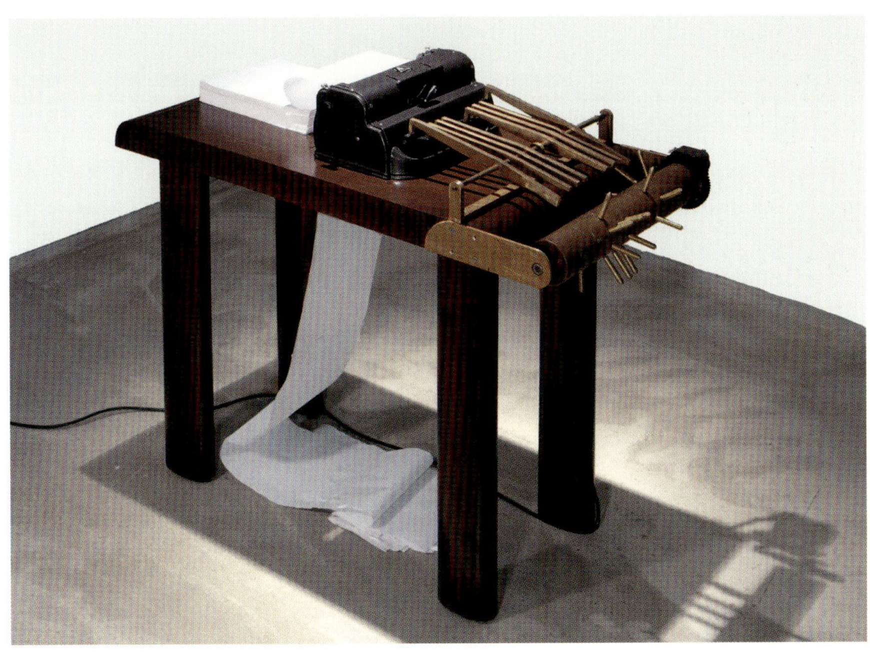

03

01 *Untitled*, 2001
Satin fabric, steel,
burnt wood, motor, mechanical device
Chairs 91 × 244 × 46 cm
Table 46 × 51 × 91 cm

02 *Untitled*, 2008
Cast brass, iron, motor mechanism
198 × 46 × 100 cm

03 *Untitled*, 2006
Modified brailer
Approx. 112 × 92 × 61 cm

04 *Untitled*, 2008
Wood, cast aluminium, motor mechanism
77 × 220 × 90 cm

04

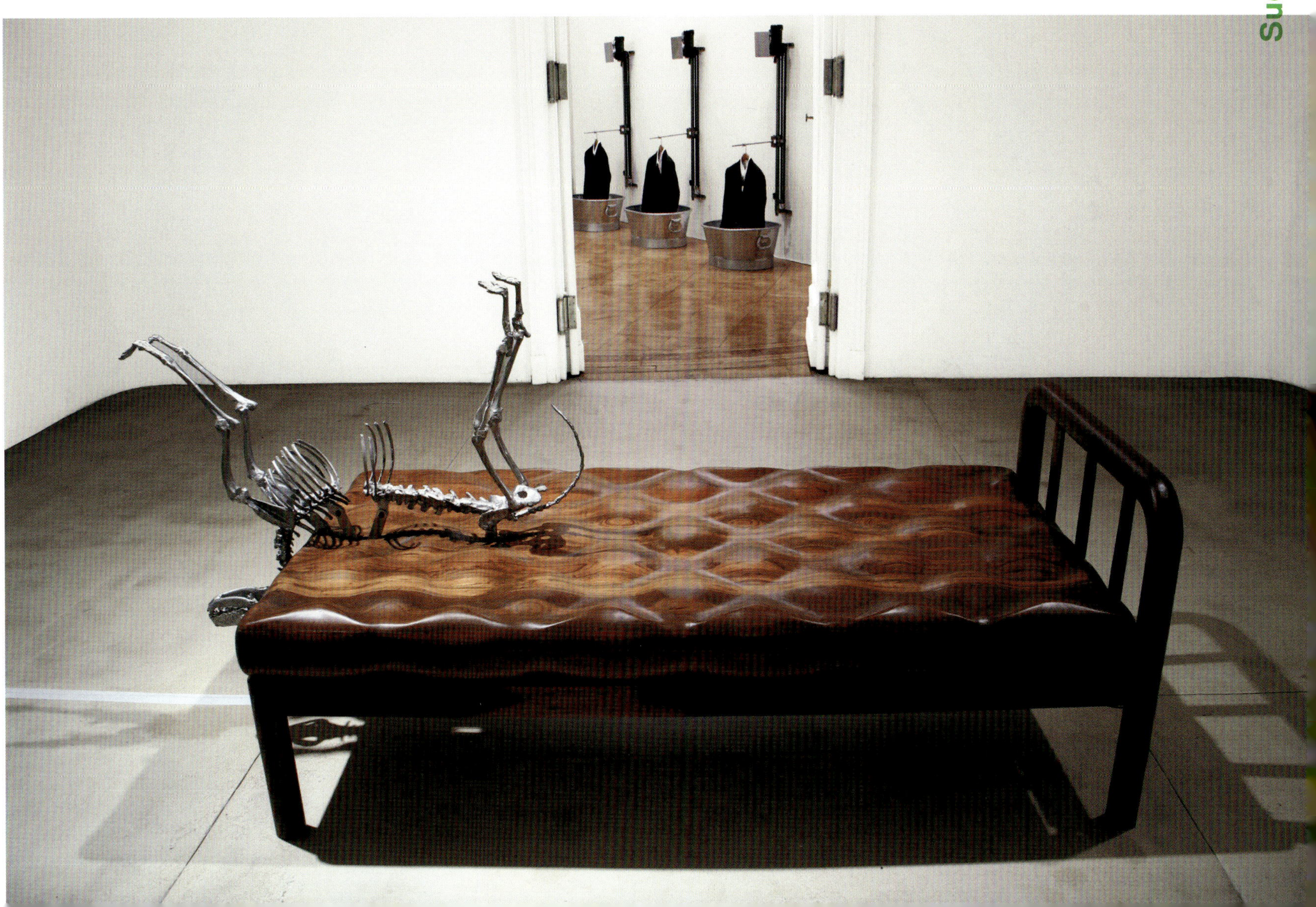

05

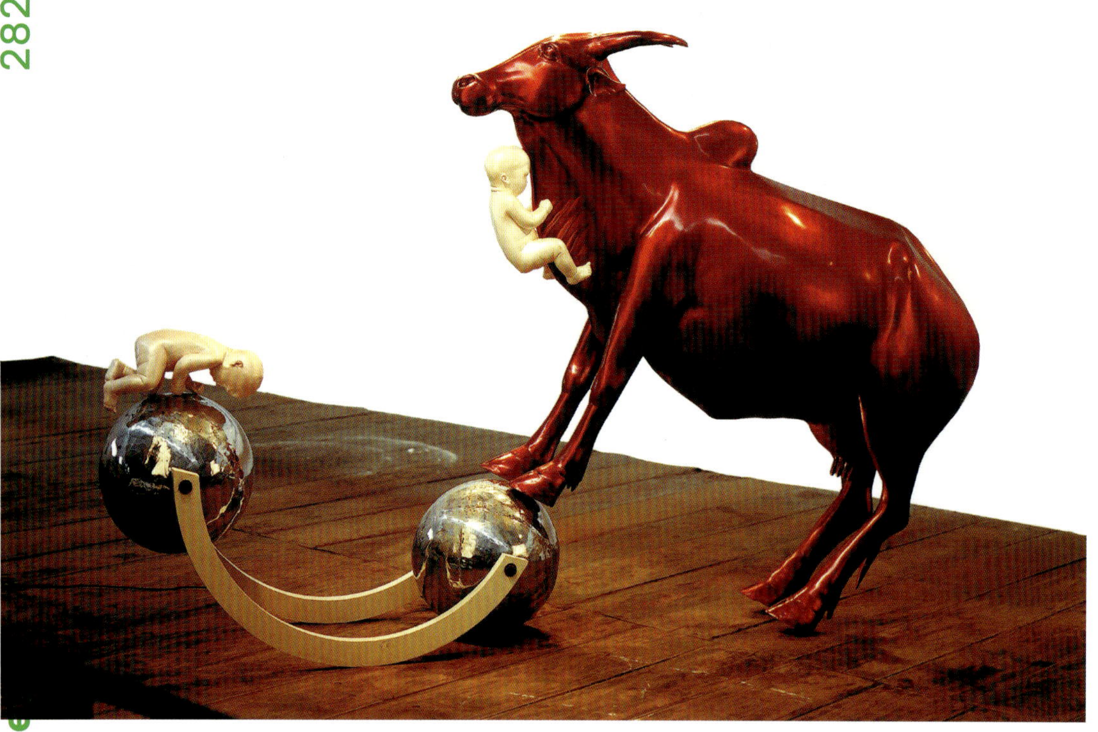

06

05 *Untitled*, 1998
Paint on fibreglass, wood, stainless steel
176 × 56 × 270 cm

06 *Untitled*, 2008
Life-size cast-aluminium dog skeletons, coloured acrylic casing, surveillance cameras, 9 flat-screen monitors connected to surveillance camera inside the dog skeletons
9 screens
Each 84 × 79 × 8 cm
9 dogs
Each 99 × 79 × 20 cm

07 *Pure*, 2007
PVC pipes, toilet bowl, steel stand, white powder-coated steel cabinet and glass shelving, glass containers, white-tinted water, plastic tubing, water pump, stack of white dinner plates
Tree approx. 290 × 213 × 122 cm
Cupboard approx. 213 × 178 × 61 cm
Dinner plate approx. 92 × 36 cm

08 *Untitled*, 2008
5 pairs of cast acrylic walking shoes, table, motorized mechanism
Approx. 185 × 77 × 52 cm

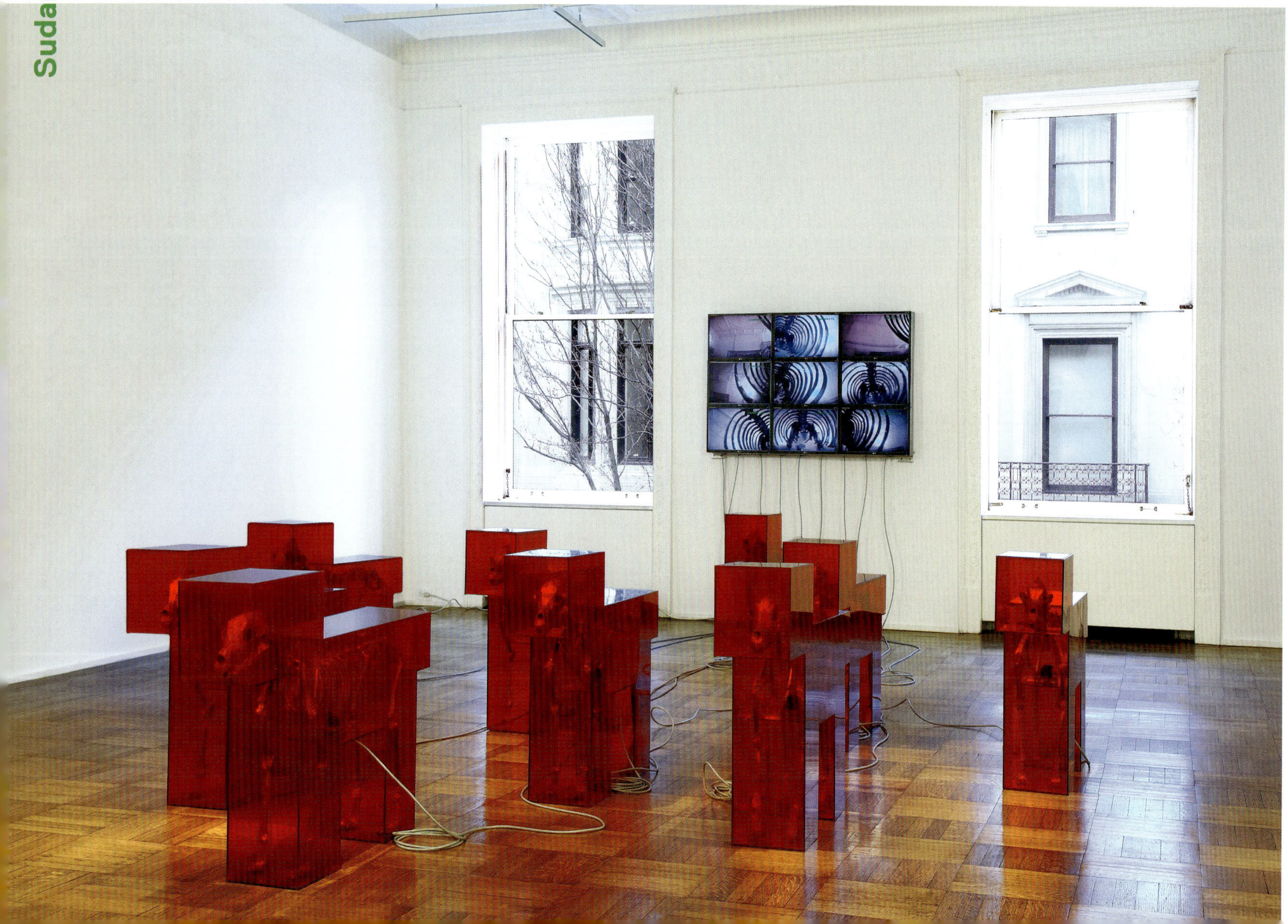

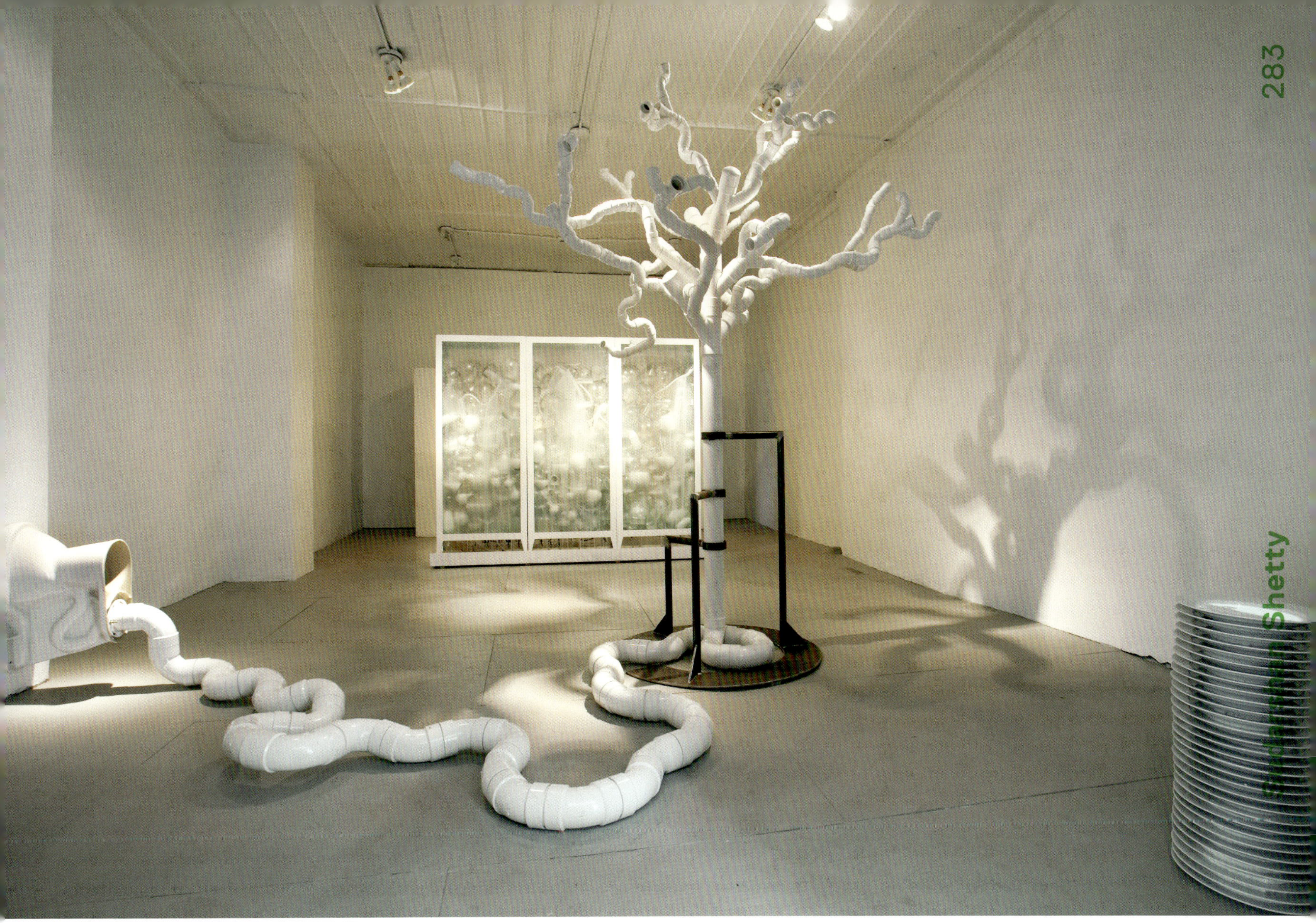

07

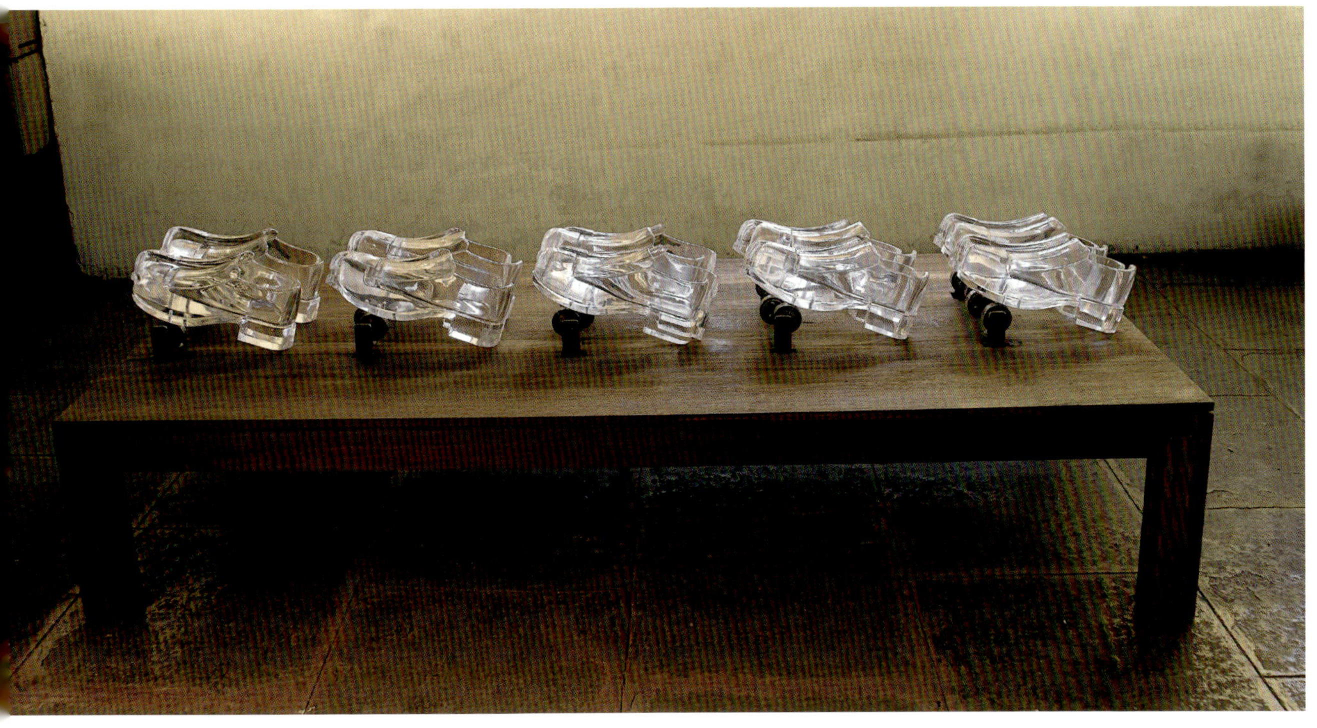

08

01

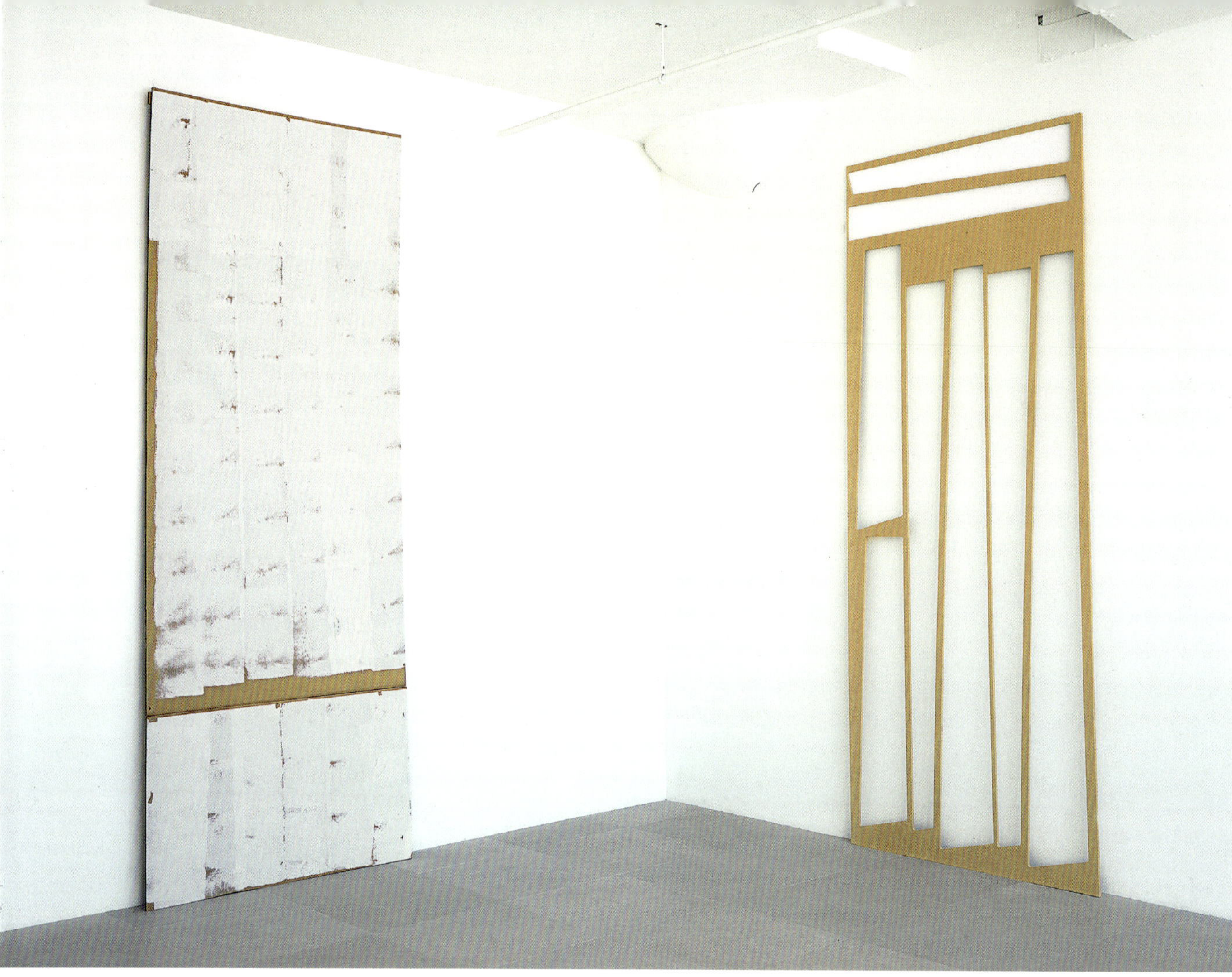

Gedi Sibony's makeshift sculptures, constructed from such crude materials as plywood, industrial carpeting, hollow-core doors and cardboard boxes, have drawn frequent comparisons to Arte Povera. This Italian 1960s movement also employed rough, unmanipulated elements and is typically understood to embrace a kind of anti-interventionist, return-to-nature agenda. The comparisons may seem accurate, but there is in fact nothing haphazard or essentialist about Sibony's work. By contrast, he carefully arranges his materials so that individual elements are challenged by their relationship with countering forms and gestures, including those posed by the architectural surroundings. For example, in a 2008 solo exhibition Sibony presented a large, sentinel-like rectangle of carpet extending all the way down the wall and neatly over the floor (*The Beginning is Near*, 2008). Beside it stood an open, rectangular floor sculpture (*Held Made the Road*, 2008) made of glued-together sticks and angled slightly towards the impassive wall piece. The sticks and carpet formed an unlikely but effective pair: open shape confronting closed shape, organic form facing geometric plane in an unsteady fellowship. Sibony achieved a similar effect at his 2007 solo exhibition at Kunsthalle St Gallen, Switzerland, in which he positioned a curving form made of sticks next to one of the gallery's rectangular support columns.

That meaning alters with context is even more pointedly revealed in the wood relief *Its Origins Justify its Oranges*, (2008), a simple, open frame crossed with wooden bars. In a 2008 gallery exhibition the relief sculpture was impossible to separate from its environment, a darkened gallery filled with the glow of yellow, pink and blue spotlights which both illuminated and dematerialized the work's surface and the space around it.

Theatrical motifs like spotlights and curtains are common in Sibony's work. *It Can Happen Because of Everything Else* (2007) consisted simply of a makeshift curtain pinned back to permit entrance to a group exhibition. A smaller untitled curtain occupied the same spot in his 2008 solo show at the same gallery. Such motifs make sense alongside Sibony's rough workshop materials, often likened to those used in set design. But beyond looking like stage props, Sibony's objects seem to inhabit the world of the theatre because, placed together and taken out of their everyday context, they exhibit a certain discomfort. They are, according to the title of Sibony's 2005 installation, merely *Disguised as their Material Properties*. Both cardboard and more than cardboard, sticks and more than sticks, they are activated by the artist and forced out of inertia, but like all actors they are ultimately unable to coincide with the roles they assume — which is to say that Sibony's sculptures are a lot like us: public and private, present and withdrawn, open to (and dependent on) the world around us, but ultimately inscrutable. [Claire Gilman]

02

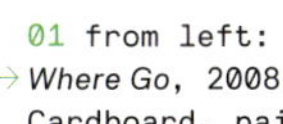

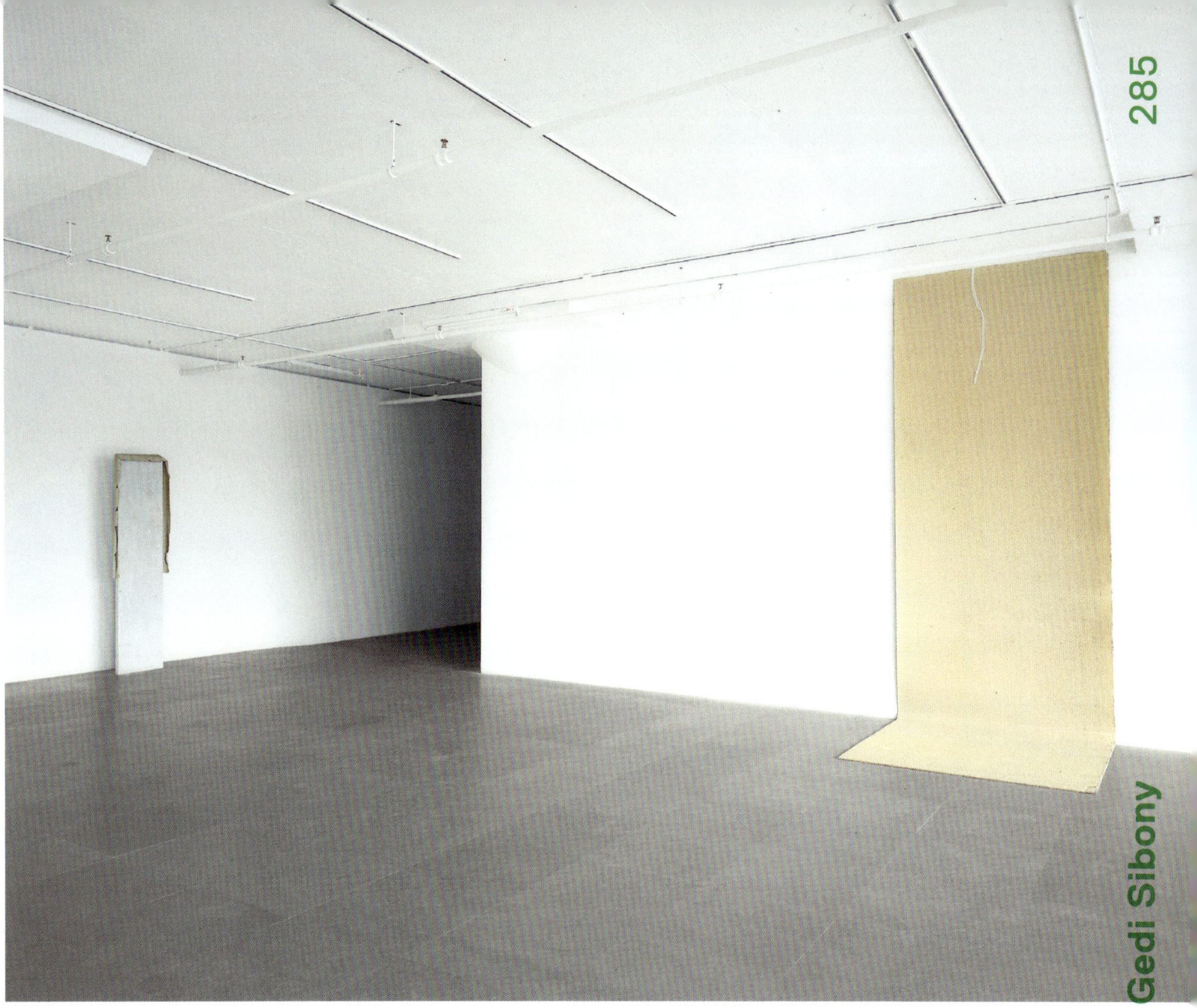

01 from left:
→ *Where Go*, 2008
Cardboard, paint
312 × 122 × 13 cm
→ *Where Now*, 2008
MDF
302 × 117 × 9 cm

02 from left:
→ *Partly Me Manners*, 2008
Door, paper
223 × 61 × 10 cm
→ *The Beginning Is Near*, 2008
Carpet, tape
345 × 152 × 152 cm

03 *The Middle of the World*, 2008
Vertical blinds
91 × 227 × 13 cm

04 from left:
→ *The Circumstance, the Illusion and Light Absorbed as Light*, 2007
Cardboard, vinyl window shades, plastic, plywood, hollow core door
Dimensions variable
→ *This One Too*, 2007
Plastic sheet,
Dimensions variable
→ *Revealing Itself With Suitable Attributes / With Nine Possible Classifications*, 2007
3 parts
Wood, framed paper, pedestals
Dimensions variable

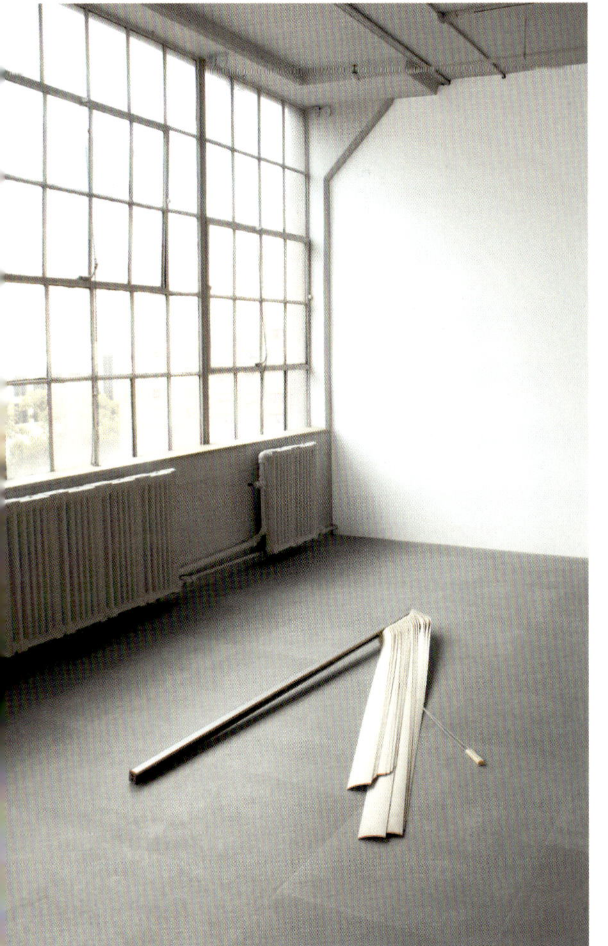

03

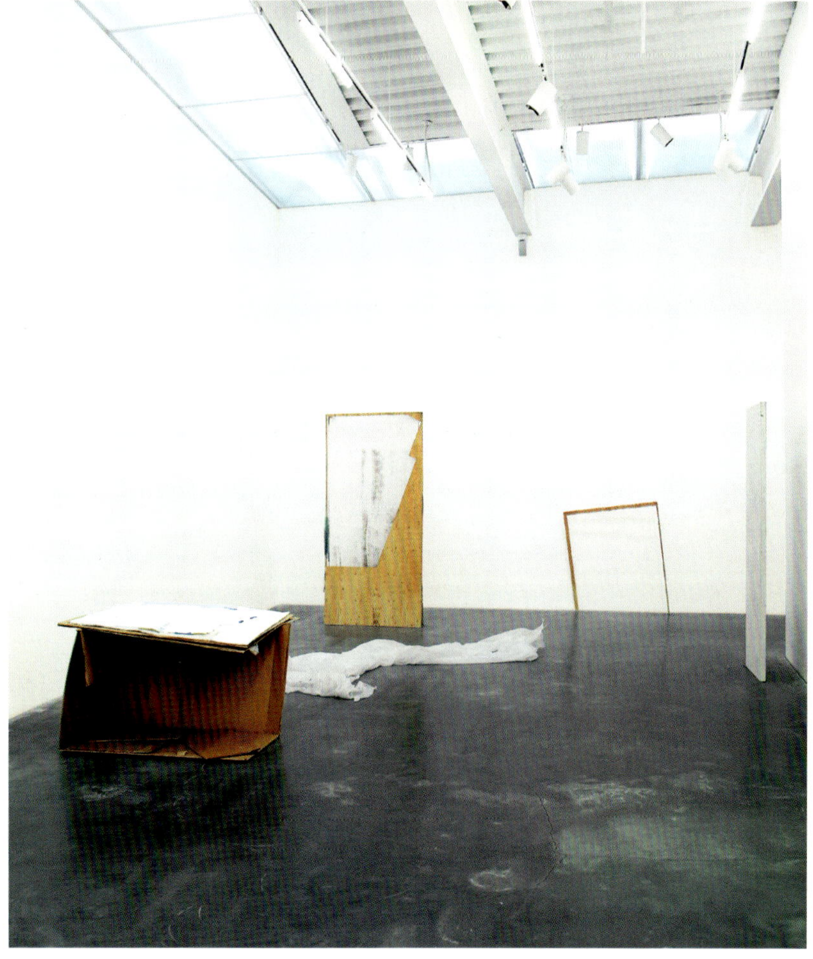

04

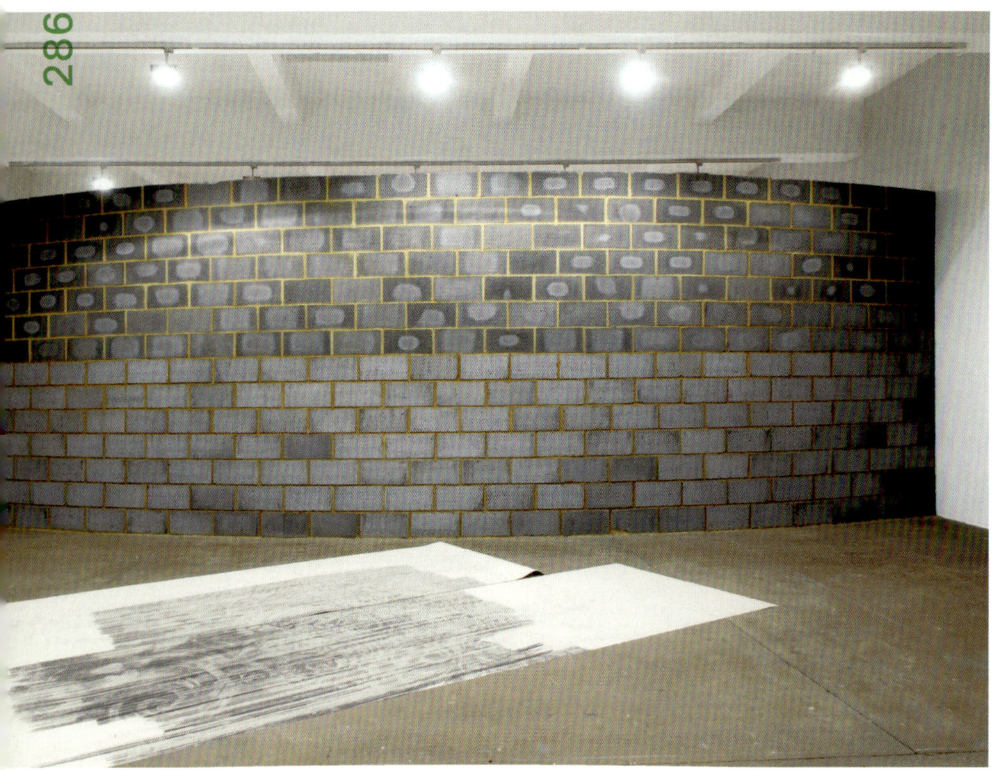

01

In her 2008 solo exhibition 'The Siege', Skaer used the same complex drawing process to reproduce Hokusai's famous woodcut *The Great Wave* and Leonardo Da Vinci's *The Deluge* — both images that depict nature in momentary flux. The show's title suggested opposing sides pitted against one another, as did the curving cinder-block wall that divided the exhibition space in two. While two drawings based on the source works were displayed on one side of the wall, on the other stood *Black Alphabet*, twenty-six reproductions of Constantin Brancusi's *Bird in Space* made of compressed coal dust and arranged like an infantry battalion. Among other objects were a set of rusted cast-iron teeth, tables used as printing plates and inky black prints lying as if discarded on the ground. Whichever side of the divide one stood on, a mirror on the ceiling provided glimpses of the other. These glancing views allowed visitors to draw their own connections between different artistic processes and materials. Skaer doesn't present any of these methods as stronger or more robust than another. For her, 'representation' is not a permanent condition, but a shifting power struggle — an ongoing battle between an object and its rendering in which no one comes out on top and no meaning or status is certain. Artworks, after all, are mortal too. [Christy Lange]

Lucy Skaer's works travel a long way, from objects to images of objects to the artist's reproductions of those images, until they no longer resemble each other and are related only in concept. Despite their abstraction, the subject matter of both Skaer's drawings and sculptural objects is rooted in the familiar. Images are selected because, in the artist's words, they 'typify an underlying social doctrine', where such doctrines might be systems of classification or simply a means of control. Although her works may make bounding leaps of logic and meaning from one to the next, they are united by her interest in diverse historical periods and the mortality of beings; she has made drawings of corpses and produced sculptures based on the skeletons of the Danse Macabre, leading the living to their graves.

Skaer is perhaps best known for her detailed drawings on a monumental scale, made with graphite, ink and paint and pinned to the wall, often unfurling all the way to the ground. Their subject matter, usually based on found photographs, veers from whales and horses to warships and prison cells. Many are intricately composed of small squares and spirals, executed with a laborious technique that the artist calls 'imprisoning'. As a result of this complex building process, each of her large-scale drawings has two lives: one on an abstract, micro scale and another on a more legible, macro level — similar to that of a digital image made up of individual pixels. Skaer's technique of moving from an articulate, hand-drawn technique to a larger, unrelated image illustrates the disjunction between an object and its representation. Her drawings are even further removed from their original sources in that they are virtually illegible when reproduced in photographs. In the process of rendering and re-rendering, their meanings have been dismantled.

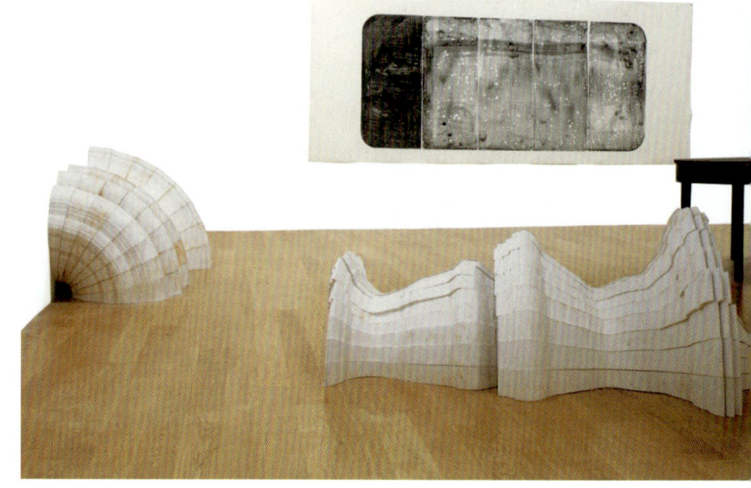

02

01 *The Siege (The Deluge [Expanded])*, 2008
Pencil on paper
300 × 450 cm

02 *Room of Lines*, 2008
Antique table, printing ink, paper
280 × 120 cm
Plaster
Approx. 150 × 120 cm

03 *The Siege (Black Alphabet)*, 2008
Coal
26 Parts
Each 125 × 17 × 17 cm

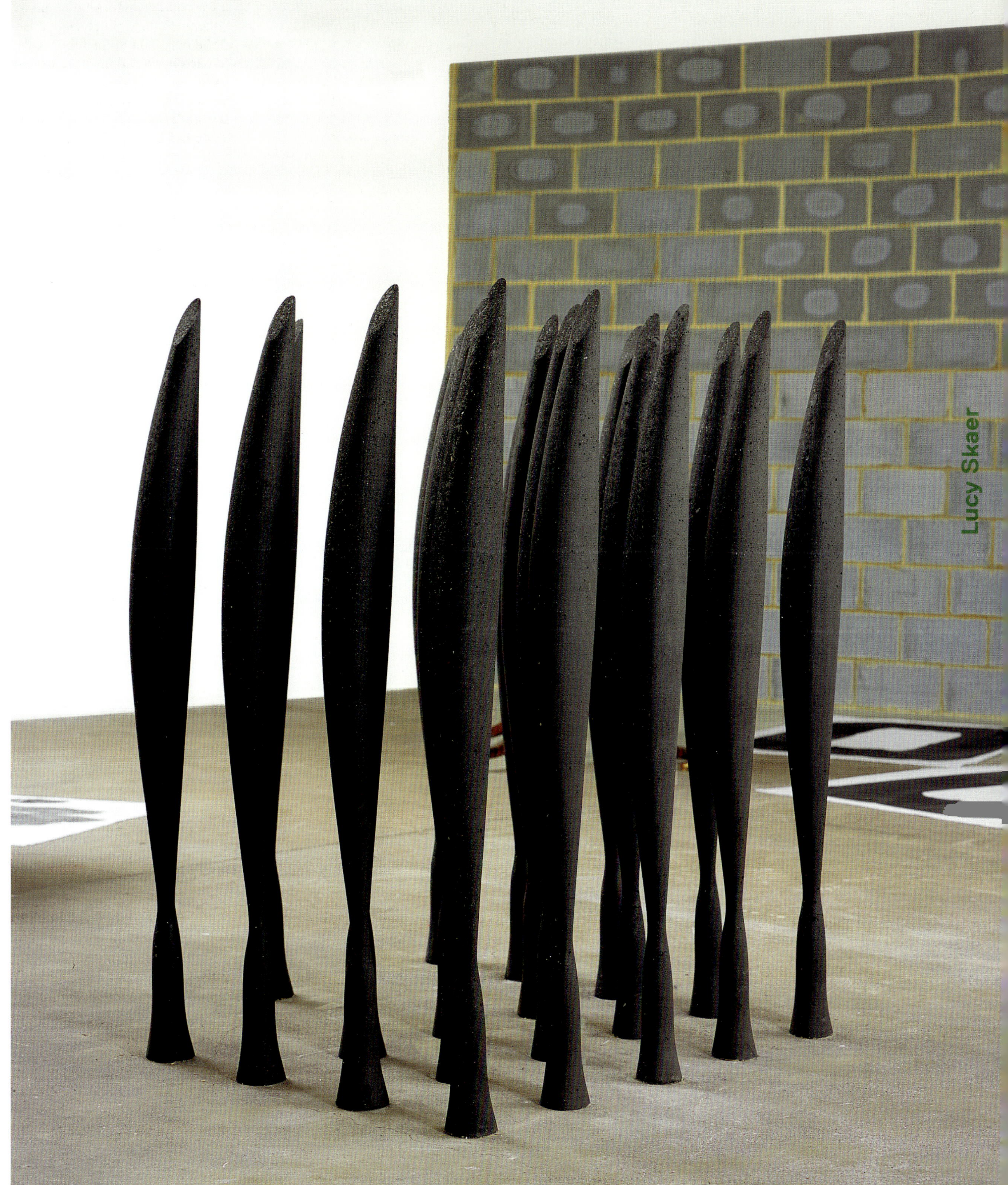

Growing up in Poland in the 1970s, Monika Sosnowska bore witness to the fading socialist architecture of the era. But she was also acutely aware that these structures had to be adapted and inhabited for future use. When looking at her site-specific architectural interventions, one can see a reflection of both a practical and exasperated attitude towards such conditions. Although there are many artists who explore the failures of modernist design and the follies of socialist architecture, Sosnowska's sculptural works are also experiential — we take part in them first hand, and in turn they have a psychological impact.

Sosnowska's improbable and impractical architectural installations aren't built with human comfort in mind. Instead they ask her viewers to adapt their bodies in uncomfortable ways, and are inflexible in their responses. *Corridor* (2003), for example, consists of a deceptively vast maze of dank, confining corridors painted in an institutional colour palette of eggshell and green. This seemingly endless series of doors lead to small claustrophobic rooms, or, more often, to locked doors and dead ends. Like the cramped 7 ½th floor in Spike Jonze's surrealistic film *Being John Malkovich*, they recall a bad dream or a clichéd movie nightmare of being trapped in an inhospitable or claustrophobic passageway that leads nowhere. *Untitled* (2004), likewise, is a plywood labyrinth that causes viewers to lose their orientation while exploring it, sometimes confronting others in the same situation. Created to occupy a position somewhere between a public and private space, *Untitled* has a way of making social encounters uneasy.

It's not just Sosnowska's viewers who are subjected to these awkward situations. Her sculptures themselves often seem to be uncomfortable in their surroundings. The artist commonly plays with their scale, fitting larger objects into smaller spaces, such as a painted steel cube that looks like a crumpled cardboard box crammed into a corner of a gallery (*Untitled*, 2006). These kinds of uneasy relationships between scale and surroundings draw attention to the institutional architecture in which they must be exhibited as much as to the sculptures themselves.

Sosnowska's works don't just highlight architectural obsolescence on a grand scale, they also expose its tiny faults and small failures. An installation such as *Fountain* (2006) shows that it doesn't take much to bring the surroundings of institutional architecture into focus. In this fairly seamless intervention into museum architecture, water drips slowly from the ceiling, forming a puddle on the grey carpet outside a bank of lifts. This negligible, unconcealed drip seems to symbolize the flaws in any building that would normally escape our attention.

In her best known installation to date, *1:1* (2007), created for the Polish Pavilion at the Venice Biennale, Sosnowska crammed a modernist steel architectural frame into the 1930s pavilion which is meant to showcase the country's most important artistic achievements. Normally a steel building of this scale would symbolize national pride, but here Sosnowska transforms it into a tilted, tottering steel carcass with bent legs and a crushed top, sitting awkwardly in its environment. The sculpture's crushed structure was not accidental or random — it was a feat of calculed engineering accomplished in the now disused Prefabricated House Factory in Poland. In this way, *1:1* becomes a symbol of a disillusioned past, but also a sign of an adaptable future. [Christy Lange]

01

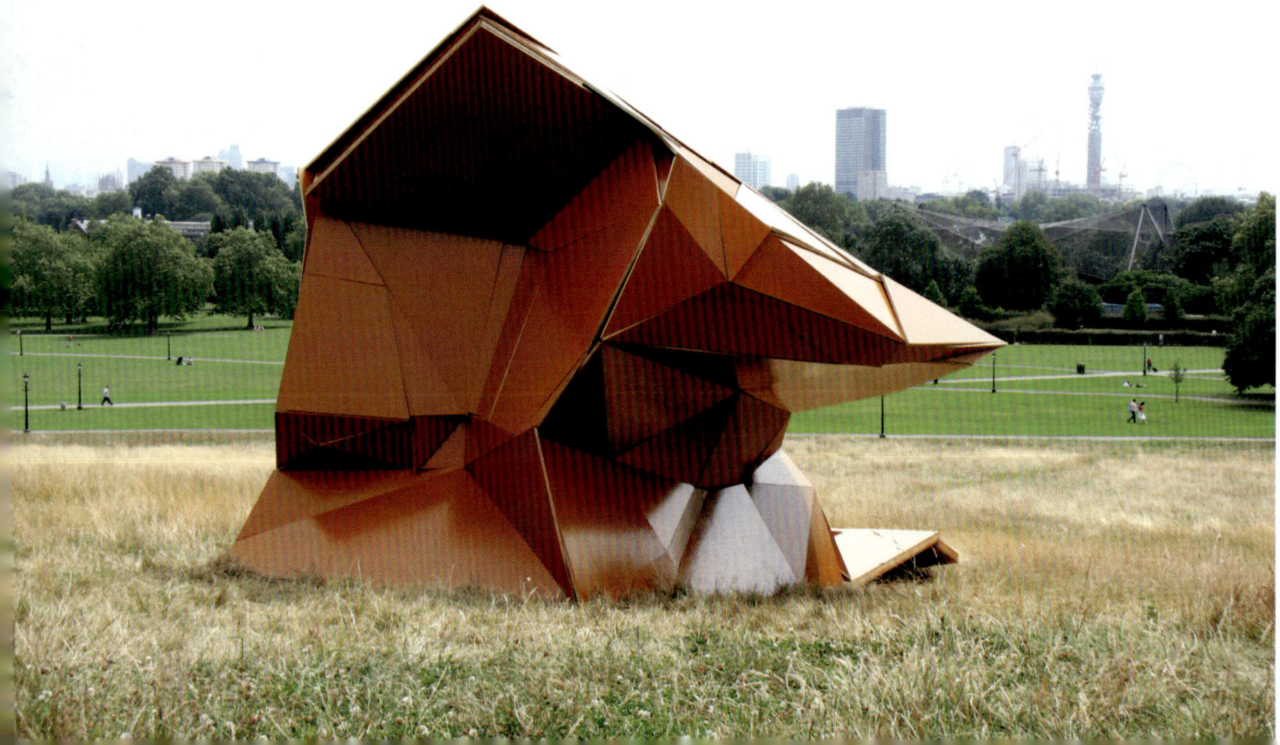

01 *The Wind House*, 2008
Steel, wood, paint
465 × 330 × 945 cm

02 *The Hole*, 2006
MDF, paint, fluorescent lights, halogen lamps, light fixtures
Approx. 7 × 9 × 6 m

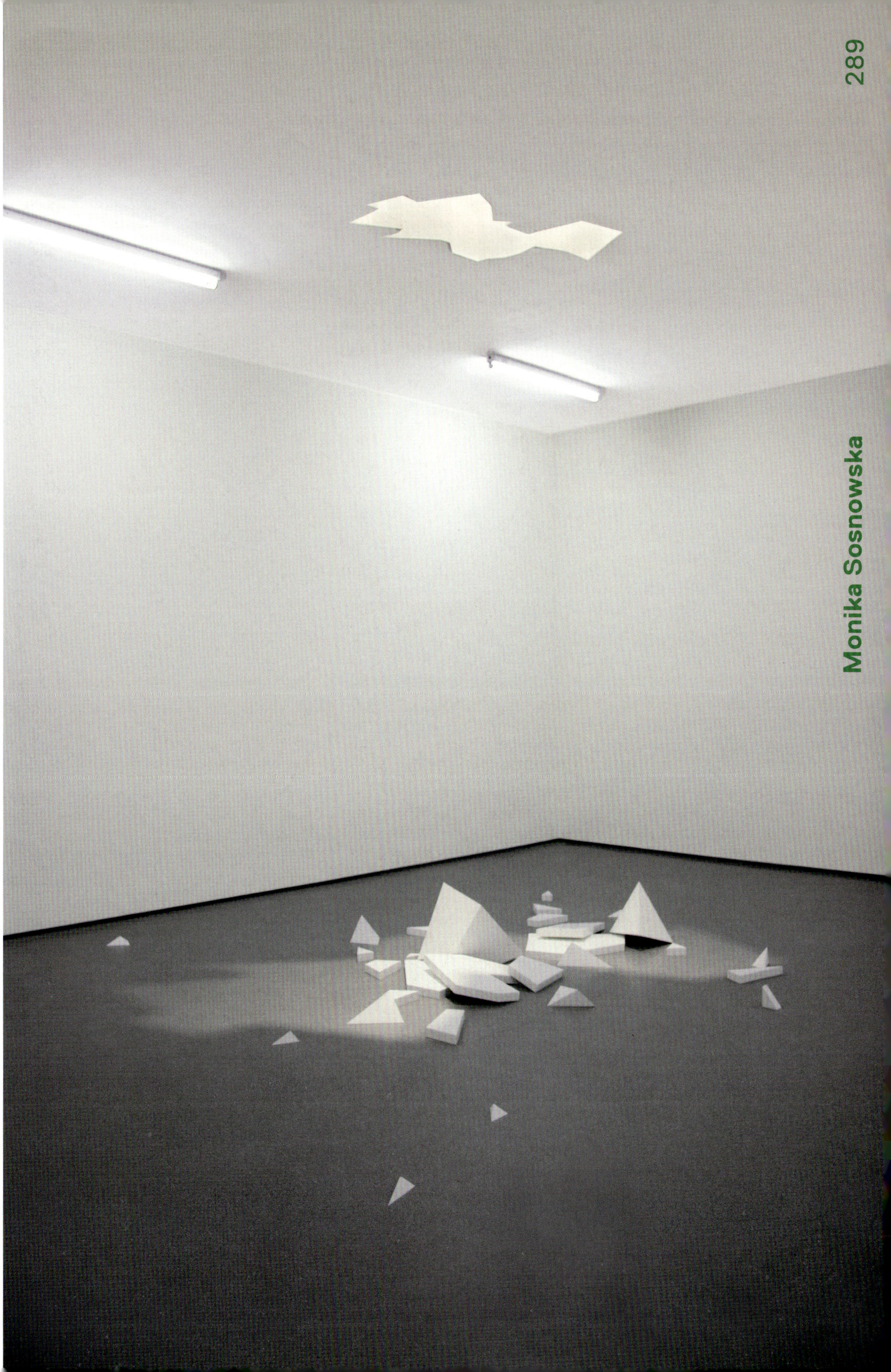

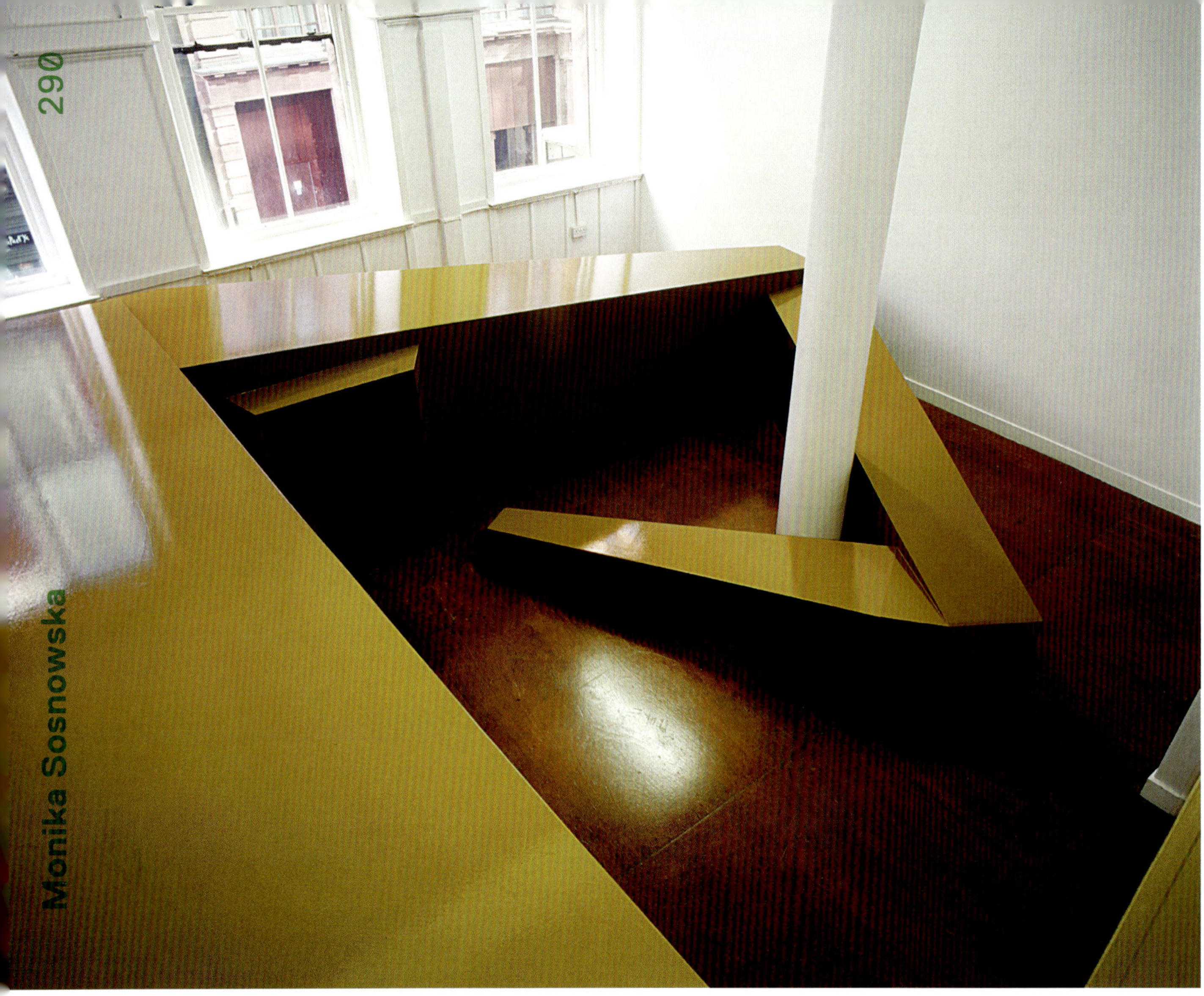

04

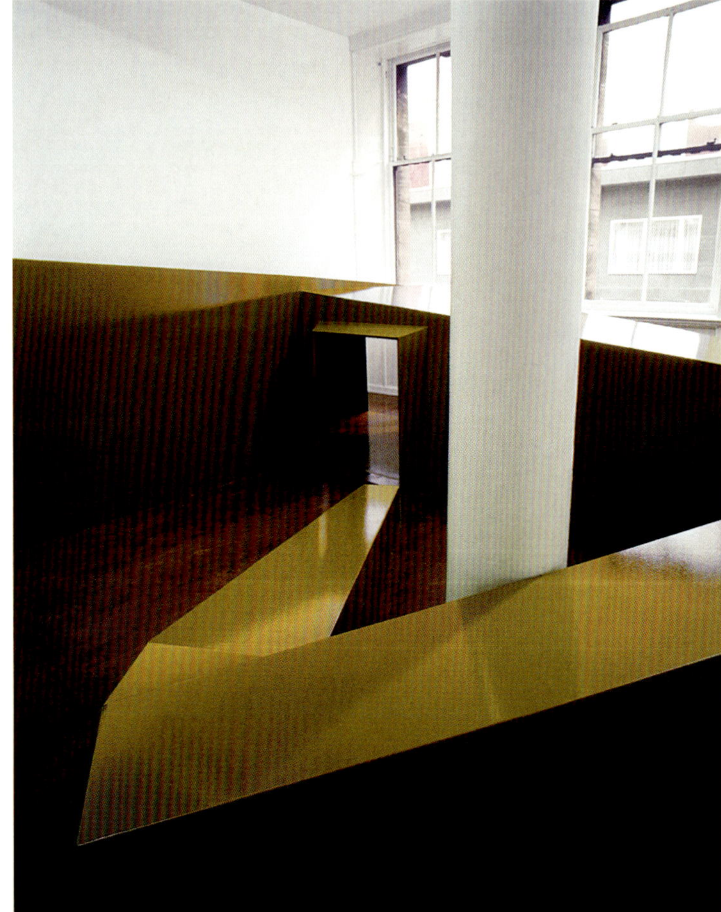

05

04, 05 *Untitled*, 2004
MDF, gloss paint
Dimensions variable

06 *1:1*, 2007
Steel
7 × 14 × 6 m

06

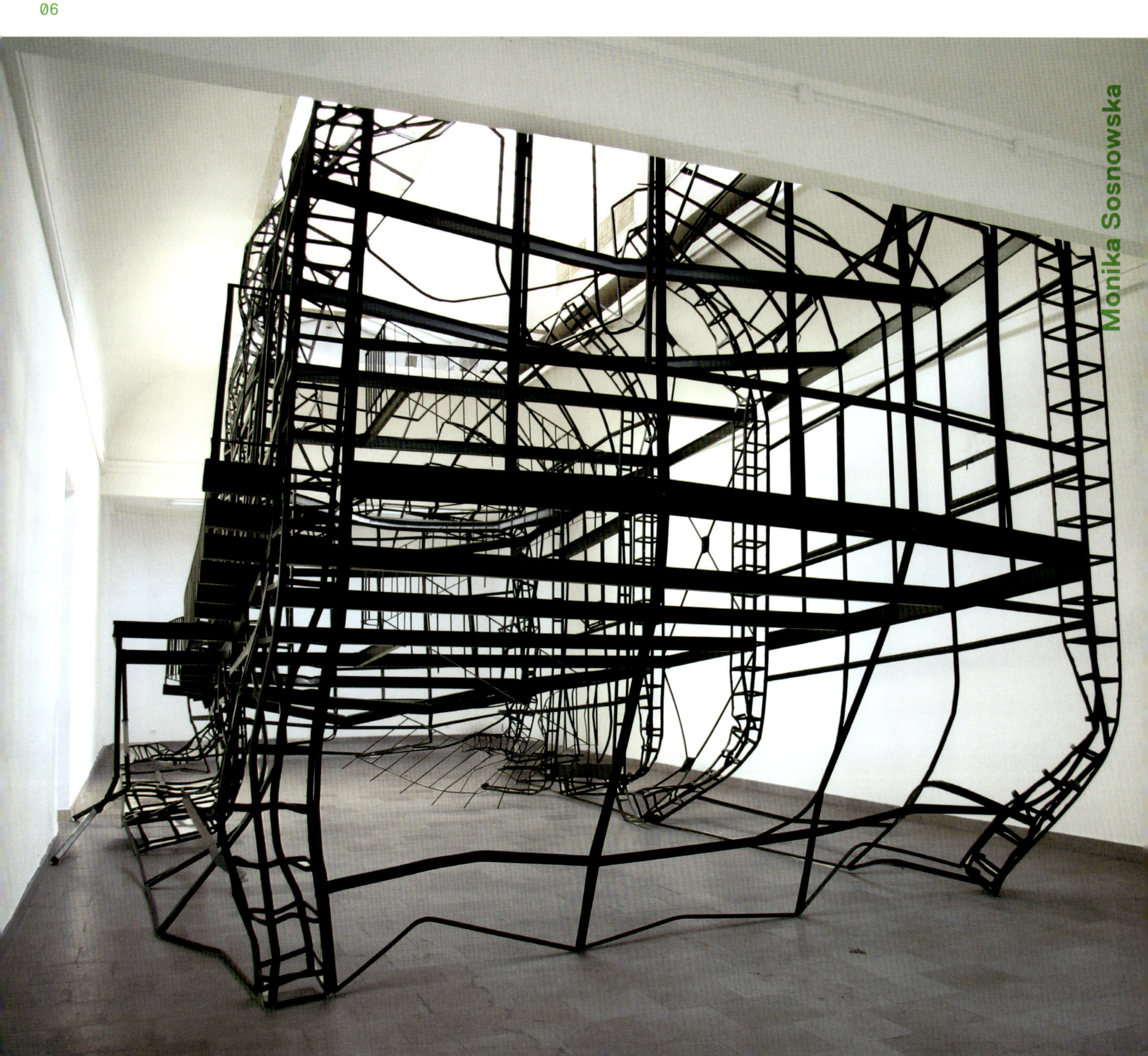

Simon Starling

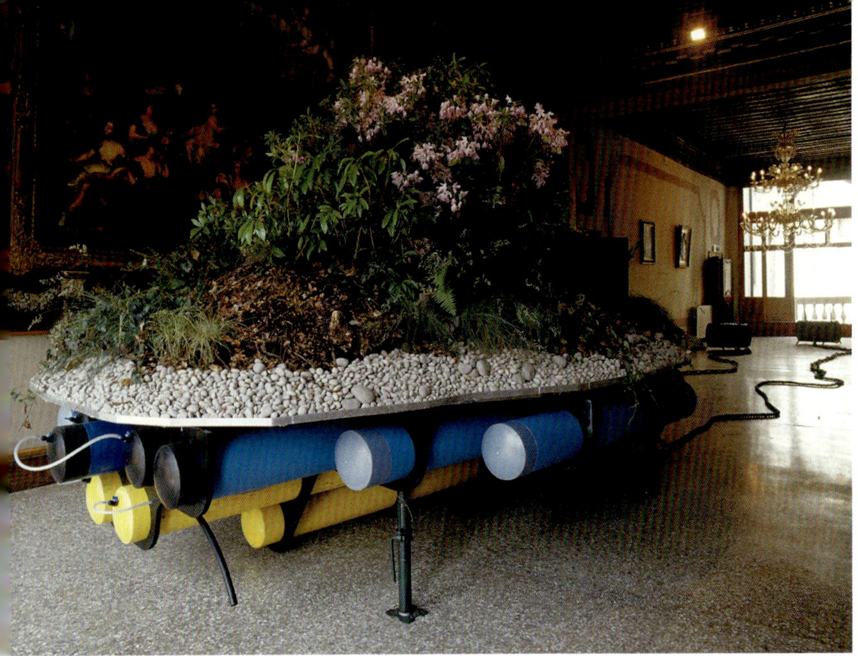

01

Simon Starling makes constructed scenarios that, far from suggesting a linear, controllable model of historical causality, emphasize the unpredictable, convoluted consequences of human actions. He often draws connections between allegorically and literally transformative energy sources to critique a pressing ecological situation brought to the precipice by Western consumerism. *Infestation Piece (Musselled Moore)* (2006–08), for instance, conflates art-historical and ecological incidents in a single, apparently autonomous figurative sculpture. The figure is a steel replica of Henry Moore's *Warrior with Shield*, which Starling submerged in Lake Ontario for a year and a half, where it provided anchorage for a colony of zebra mussels. These molluscs were introduced to the lake in the mid-1980s via the bilge water of trading ships, irreparably upsetting the ecosystem. Moore, too, has been described as an interloper of sorts, his work often embodying the notorious 'plop factor' of public sculpture that makes no effort to relate to its surroundings. *Infestation Piece*, then, draws a parallel between ecological accident and cultural colonialism.

Starling's work is diametrically opposed to Moore's formalism and 'truth to materials'; the story behind his work's manifestation is as important, or perhaps even eclipses, its physical fact. His processes of construction are eclectic and often protracted: while *Infestation Piece* harnesses the habits of living creatures, *Island for Weeds (Prototype)* (2003) references technology as an interruptive and controlling force. A series of pipes provide and self-regulate the island's buoyancy, keeping its cargo of rhododendron ponticum plants afloat. Now a familiar and tenacious irritation in the Scottish landscape, this non-indigenous plant again raises issues about the impact of human action on natural systems, posing such questions as whether a line can be drawn at all between nature and technology. In contrast to Moore's public sculpture, however, the issues that the island raises were considered too contentious for a piece of public art, and the piece was rerouted from its intended site in Loch Lomond to the more liberal environment of the art gallery.

Starling's transformations are often brought about by an epic and symbolic journey. In *Kakteenhaus* (2002), a cactus is housed in the red estate car that transported it from the Tabernas Desert in Spain to the gallery in Frankfurt. The cactus had been planted as a prop in a spaghetti western by Sergio Leone, while the reconfigured car engine provided the conditions for its survival in the gallery, making it a thoroughly unnaturally occurring specimen. Starling's position on the place of technology in environmentalism is not didactically posited, though, and while the poetics of his alchemical renovations are not without critical pronouncement, their ambivalence mirrors an attitude in the West to technology that is at once celebratory and suspicious. [Sally O'Reilly]

02

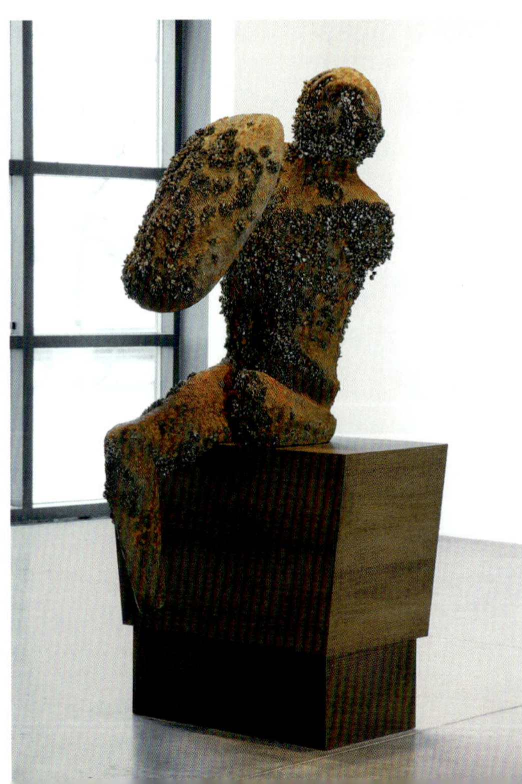

03

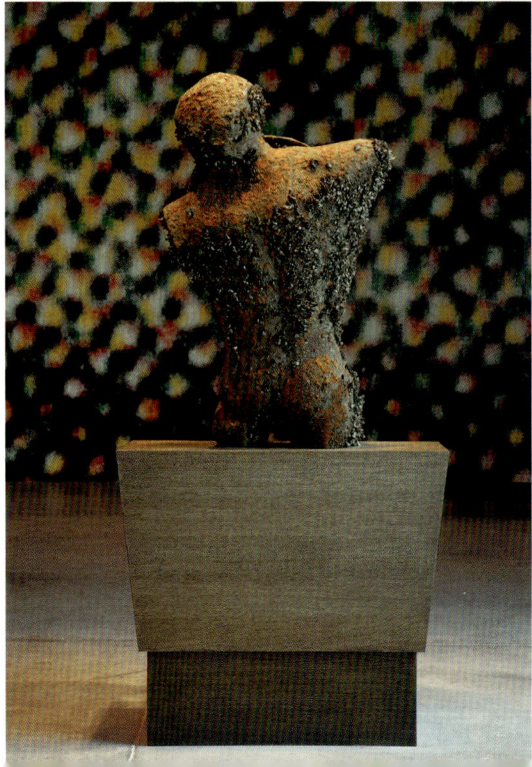

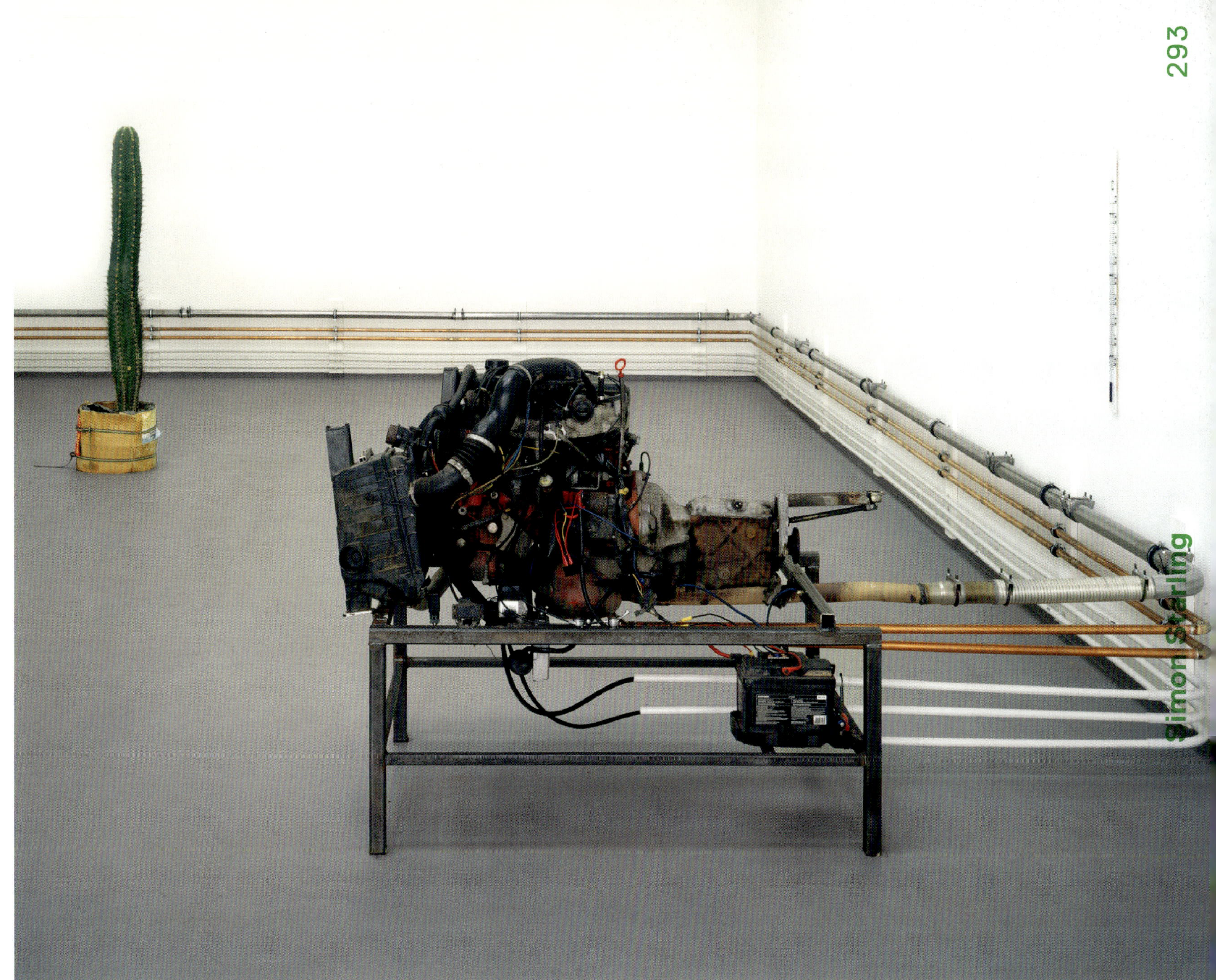

04

01 *Island for Weeds (Prototype)*, 2003
Steel frame, sealed plastic pipes, plastic tubing and fittings, pebbles, soil, plants, anchors, rope, chain, stands
Approx. 450 × 350 × 300 cm

02, 03 *Infestation Piece (Musselled Moore)*, 2006–08
Steel, mussels, wood
162 × 76 × 76 cm

04 *Kakteenhaus*, 2002
Volvo 240 estate, cereus cactus, piping, cables, text
Dimensions variable

05

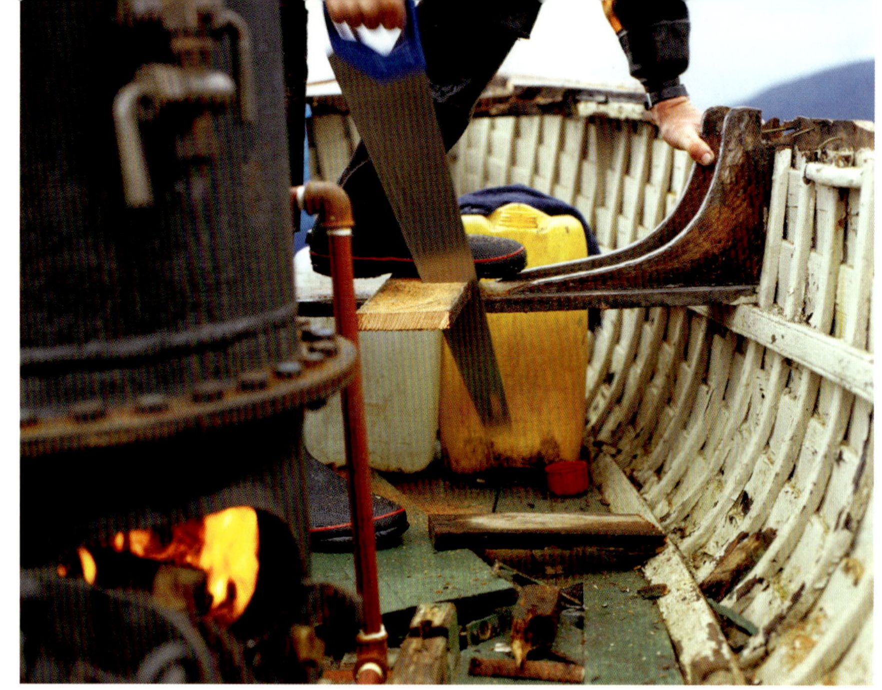

06

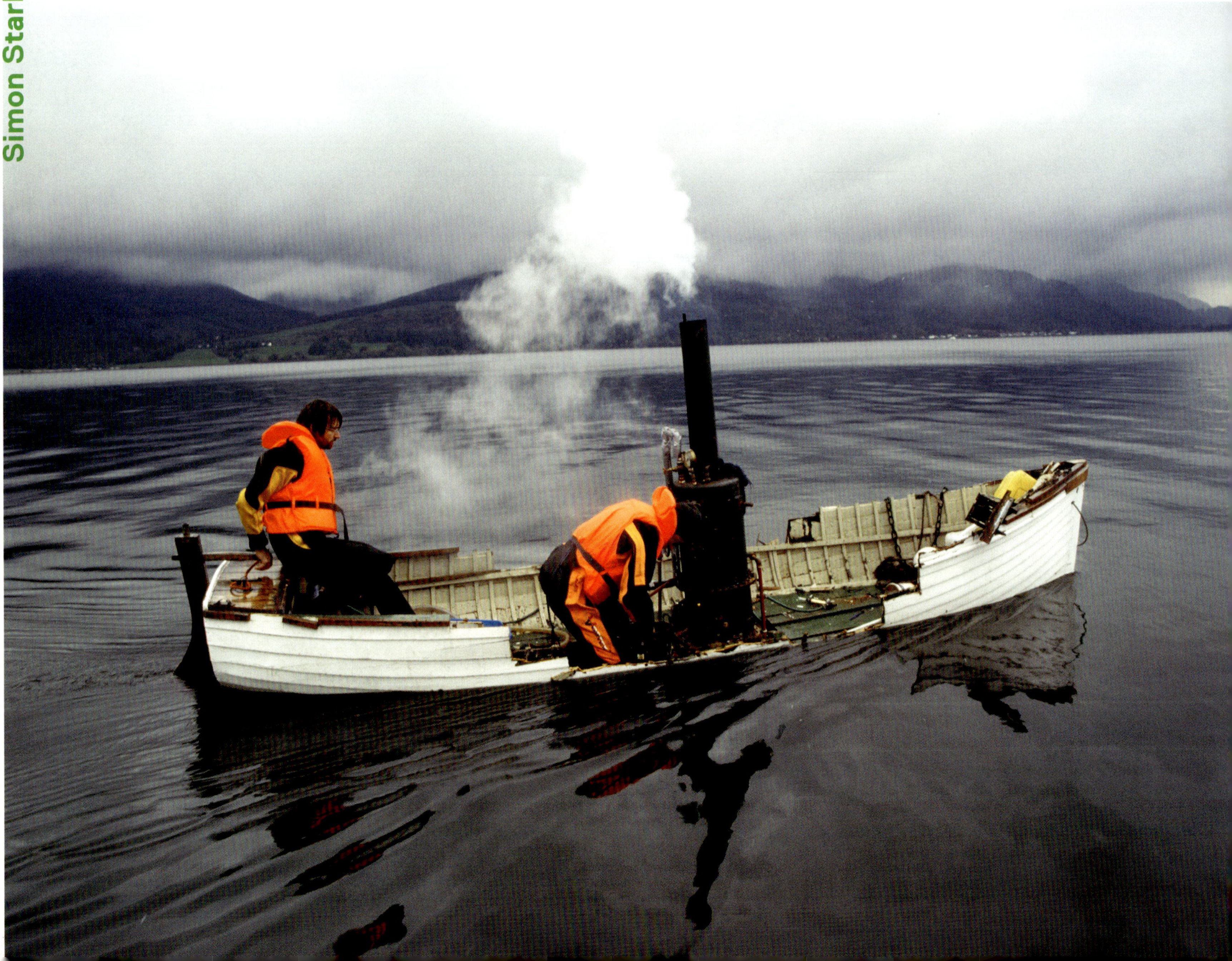

05, 06, 07, *Autoxylopyrocycloboros*, 2006
38.6 × 7 cm colour transparencies,
Götschmann medium format
slide projector, flight case

07

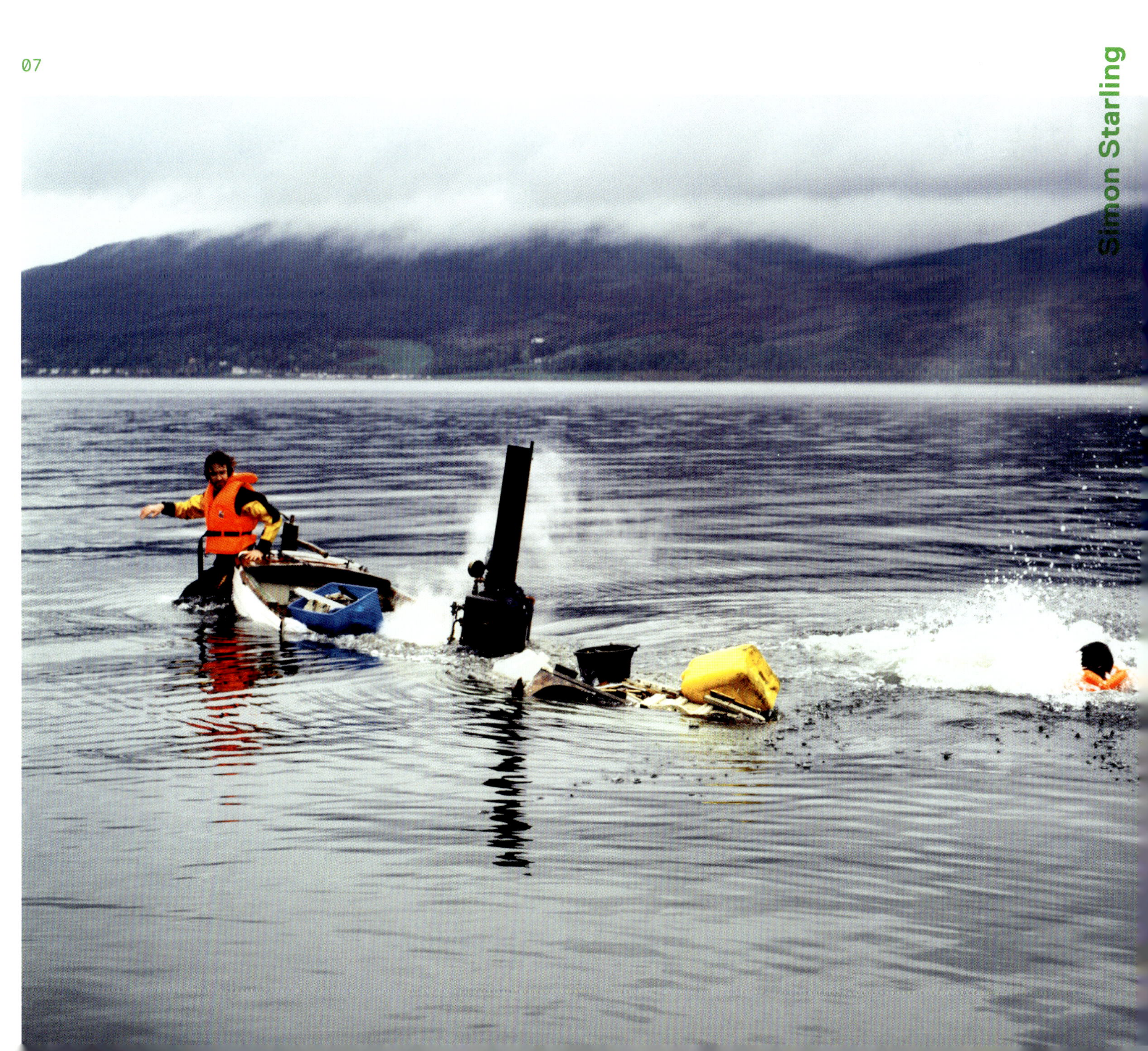

Katja Strunz's work has always played with modernist forms, but her statements over the years have gradually expanded and become more substantial. Many of her early works are fragile, whimsical, even nostalgic, incorporating delicate, found or recycled materials such as yellowed pages torn from old books or discarded metal pieces. In *Visionary Fragment (für Antoine Augustin Cournot)* (2005), she cast slices of honeycomb in bronze, while her installation *Yesterday's Echoes* (2005) consisted of found copper and other bits of antique metal instruments arranged in little mushroom and umbrella shapes that sprouted from the floor. Such works were often directly connected to specific eras or places: titles like *Whose Garden Was This?* (2005) suggest the passing of time or obsolescence — subjects of particular interest to Strunz, whose studio is located in the former East Berlin. In *Brunnen* (Fountain, 2000) she introduced into the gallery a set of old copper stairs that she had found in a defunct Berlin swimming pool.

The work in Strunz's solo show 'Einbruchstellen' (Points of Rupture, 2008) represents an even bolder entry into space. The forms seem to have expanded from her previous work, taking on the characteristics of the definitive, even muscular gestures associated with Minimalism. The exhibition was populated with large-scale sculptures of white, black and pink lacquered wood and steel, which protrude from the wall or rest on the floor. The majority of these are composed of Strunz's signature forms: triangular shapes of folds or pleats, which create dynamic angles, shadows and negative spaces. Strunz transforms creased or crinkled metal into what look like collapsible fans or Japanese screens.

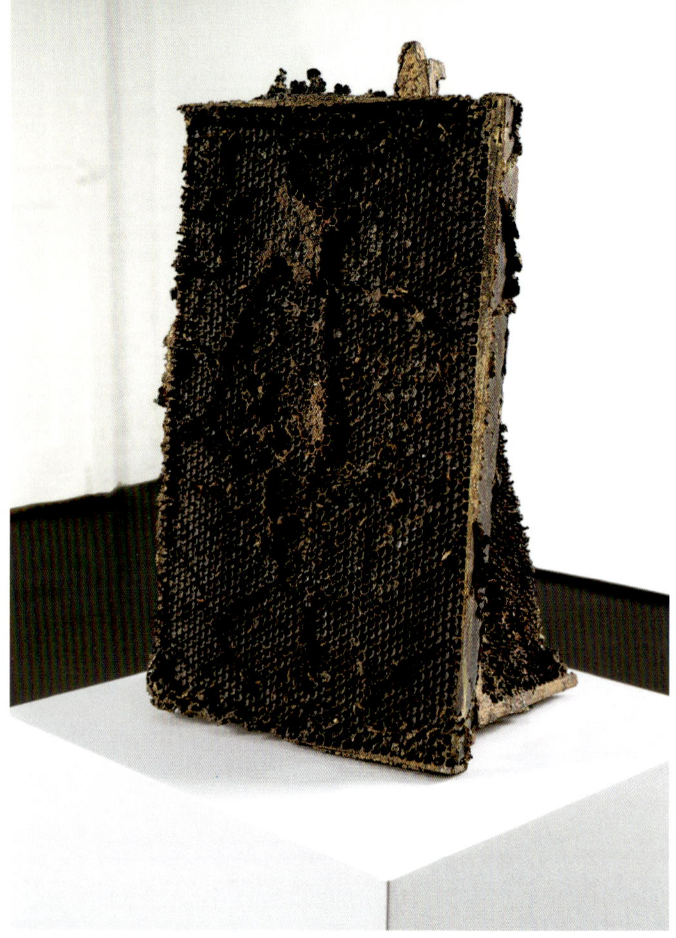

01

These sculptures have a solid, furniture-like presence, though they aren't rigidly geometric; they also incorporate a sense of unfolding or disassembly. *Einbruchstelle* (2008), a floor-based steel and wood sculpture, looks like a giant paper plane that has crash-landed into its black podium. *Memory Wall* (2008), a series of cubes mounted on the wall, resembles an upturned Carl Andre floor piece, one whose squares have been damaged, oxidized, burned or are slowly drifting away from each other. Standing in front of the sculpture creates a momentary sense of vertigo, as if one is looking down on the tops of skyscrapers.

But Strunz also manages to make her heavy, solid materials defy their weight and take on the grace and lightness of origami figures or ornamental napkins. Her smaller-scale wall sculptures incorporate the same dynamic angles and sharp incisions as her collages, and refer to Russian Constructivist and Suprematist sculptures. They also continue her investigation into the idea of time, though more literally — many of them resemble kinetic sculptures or clocks whose hands nonsensically point to folded planes of metal. Some have two mirrored and folded sides, as if imitating a butterfly's wings. Although Strunz's newest works may be edging towards the monumental, they nevertheless retain a patina of the past, suggesting that the promises of modernism haven't held up as well as we might have hoped. [Christy Lange]

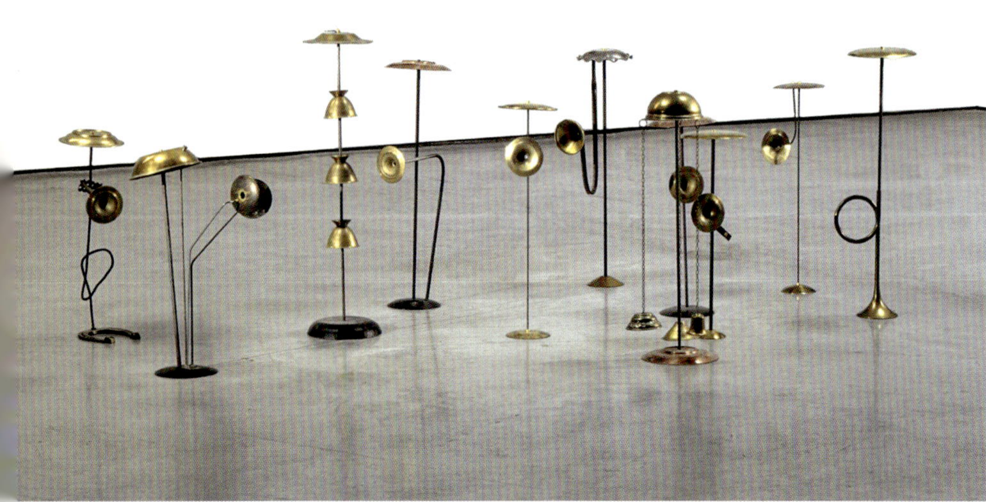

02

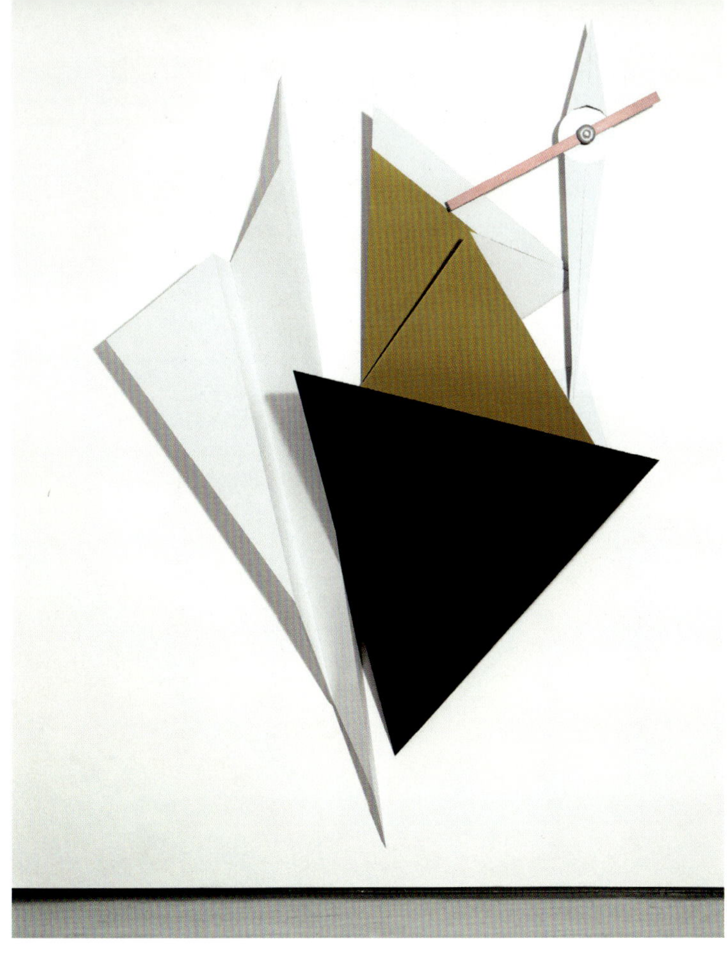

03

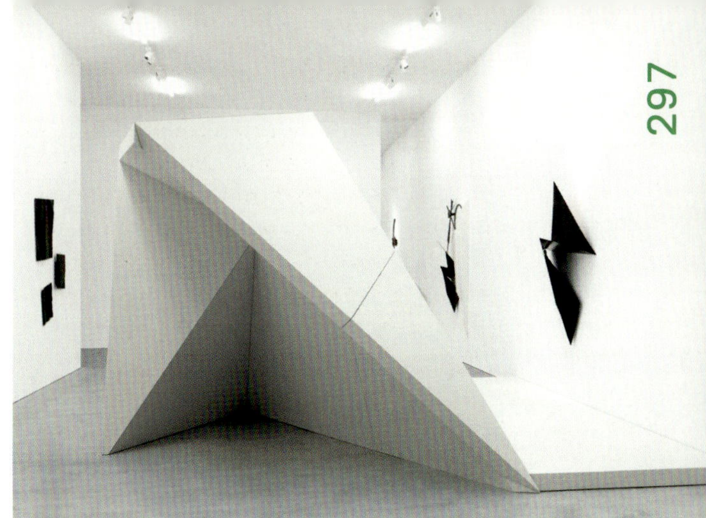

04

01 *Visionary Fragment (für Antoine Augustin Cournot)*, 2003
Bronze-cast honeycombs
39 × 22 × 24 cm

02 *Yesterday's echoes*, 2005
Various metals
Approx. 45 × 120 × 120 cm

03 *A drop in time*, 2008
Wood, steel, paint
285 × 205 × 37 cm

04 *Der müde Traum*, 2008
Wood, paint
330 × 550 × 550 cm

05 *Einbruchstelle*, 2008
Wood, powder-coated steel, paint
175 × 348 × 260 cm

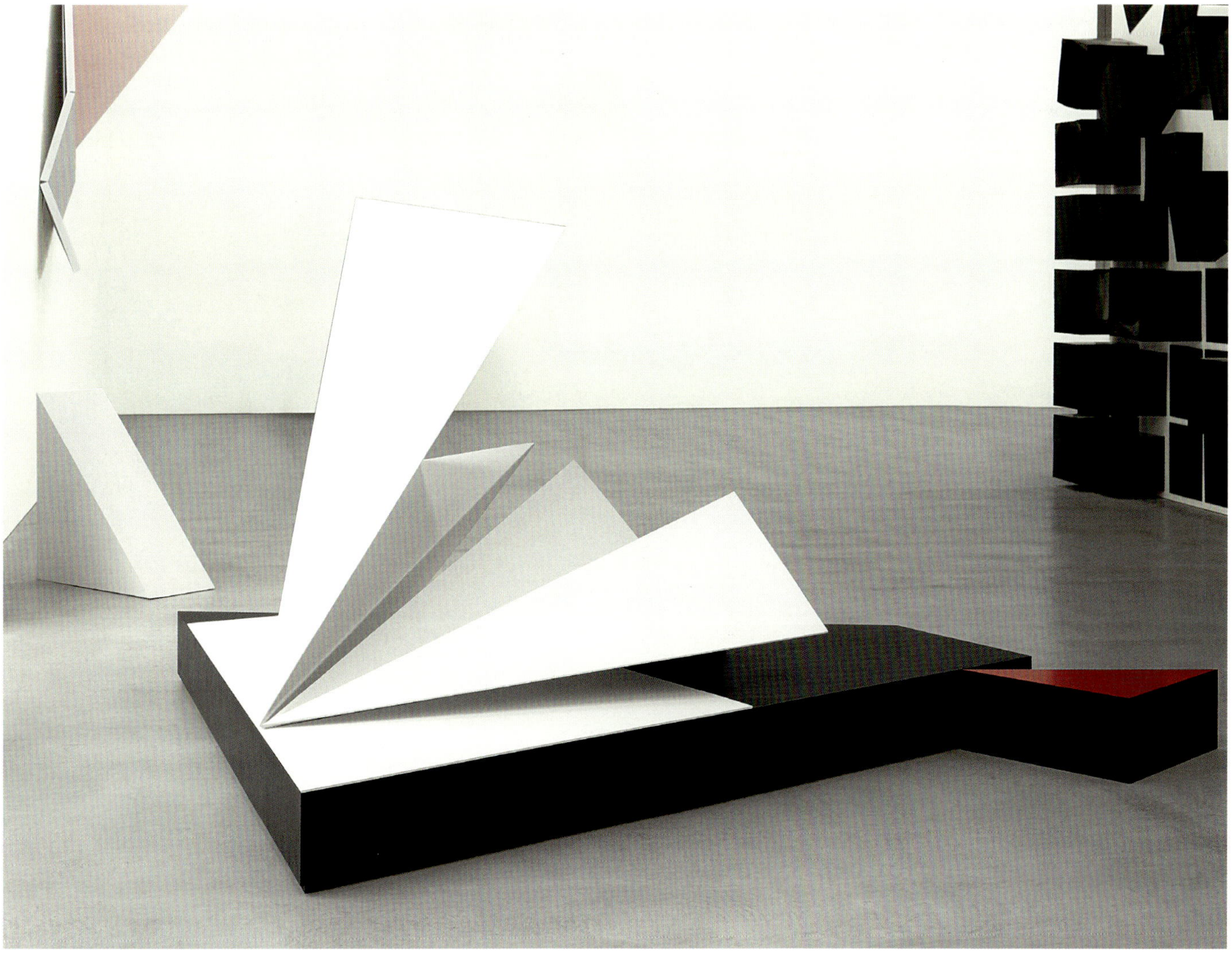

05

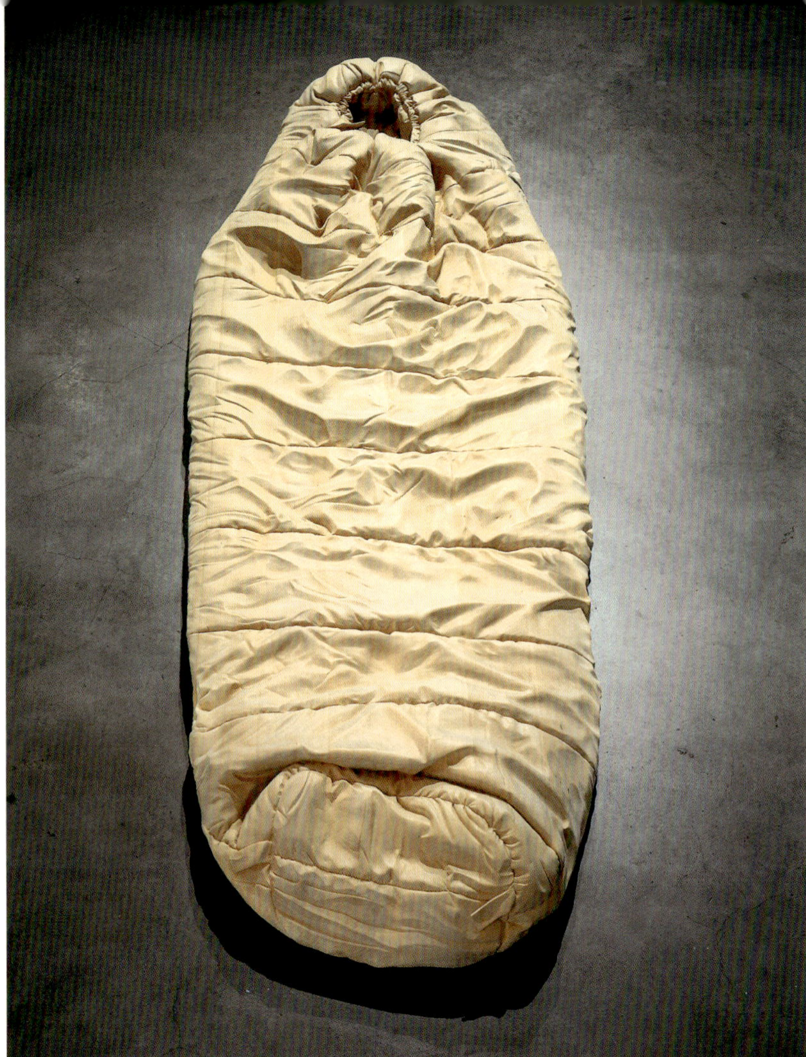

01

Ricky Swallow's meticulously crafted carved-wood and cast sculptures critically refresh one of art's most historically familiar seductions. The many hours expended on making these fragments, objects and tableaux charge them with a corresponding power — through a level of detail, a surprising likeness — to slow down and take up time. They may appear obvious in this respect, yet their interest lies in the complex way in which they refract time and our sense of it. As objects of durable contemplation, they project futures as they simultaneously recall multiple pasts.

Come Together (2002), a bean bag with a skull nestling in its folds, and the similarly full-scale sleeping bag *Sleeping Range* (2002) replay a Baroque sculptural trick, freezing the nuances of cloth into a rigid medium. The crumpled paper rendered in hardwood in *Fig. 1* (2008) likewise makes the heavy appear light and thus allows the effortful to feel effortless.

This hard-won ability to catch and absorb attention might at first seem to contravene what Jacques Rancière has called the postmodern 'formal imperative of non-resemblance', but these works do relate to photography and the readymade. Swallow's dry naturalism and everyday subjects — like a graffiti-scarred succulent from a Los Angeles garden (*Field Recording / Highland Park Hydra*, 2003), or a lost high-top sneaker stuck in branches (*The Bricoleur*, 2006) — are markers of his works' relationship to the present.

Come Together (2002) recalls Bernini's *Death* flying up through diaphanous marble in his monument to Pope Alexander VII in St Peter's Basilica in Rome. Looking from Swallow's skull to the winged skeleton, the seventeenth century work anachronistically evokes heavy metal album art. Correspondingly, we might wonder what a bean bag — already a symbol of a certain moment at the end of the Western twentieth century — will mean in four hundred years time.

More bones, *The Exact Dimensions of Staying Behind* (2005), a seated skeleton in wood, leaning on her staff, or *Tusk* (2007), a sculptural X-ray of a handshake with medical white finish, echo in a different way a well-worn theme: the reminder that time will indeed pass, and that the surest consequence of this passing is death. Content like, form and technique, though, is clearly up for scrutiny as part of the works' subject.

In *Last of the Unnatural Acts* (2007), a portrait of musician John Phillips — the photograph from the cover of his 1970 solo LP, *John the Wolf King of L.A.* — is cast in bronze and paired with a matching miniature of Donatello's *Saint Mary Magdalen* on a separate plinth. In his post-Woodstock moment, as ex-leader of The Mamas & the Papas, Phillips seems as bedraggled by success as he is by the weather. Here and elsewhere, Swallow dwells on the end of the 1960s and the dawn of the 1970s, a time that entangles crises in the promise of the popular, of genre, and — perhaps most poignantly — of virtuosity. [Jon Bywater]

01 *Sleeping Range*, 2002
Laminated jelutong
503 × 180 × 51 cm

02 *Fig. 1*, 2008
English limewood
17 × 24 × 20 cm

03 *Younger Than Yesterday*, 2006
English limewood
20 × 20 × 20 cm

04 *Private Dancer*, 2002
Laminated jelutong
58 × 58 × 20 cm

05 *The Bricoleur*, 2006
Jelutong
122 × 25 × 25 cm

06 *Tusk*, 2007
Bronze with white patina, aluminium rod
50 × 105 × 6 cm

02

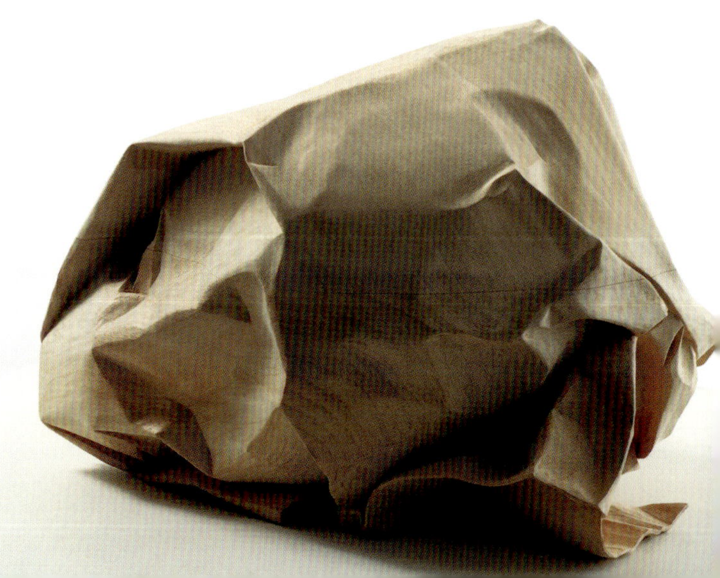

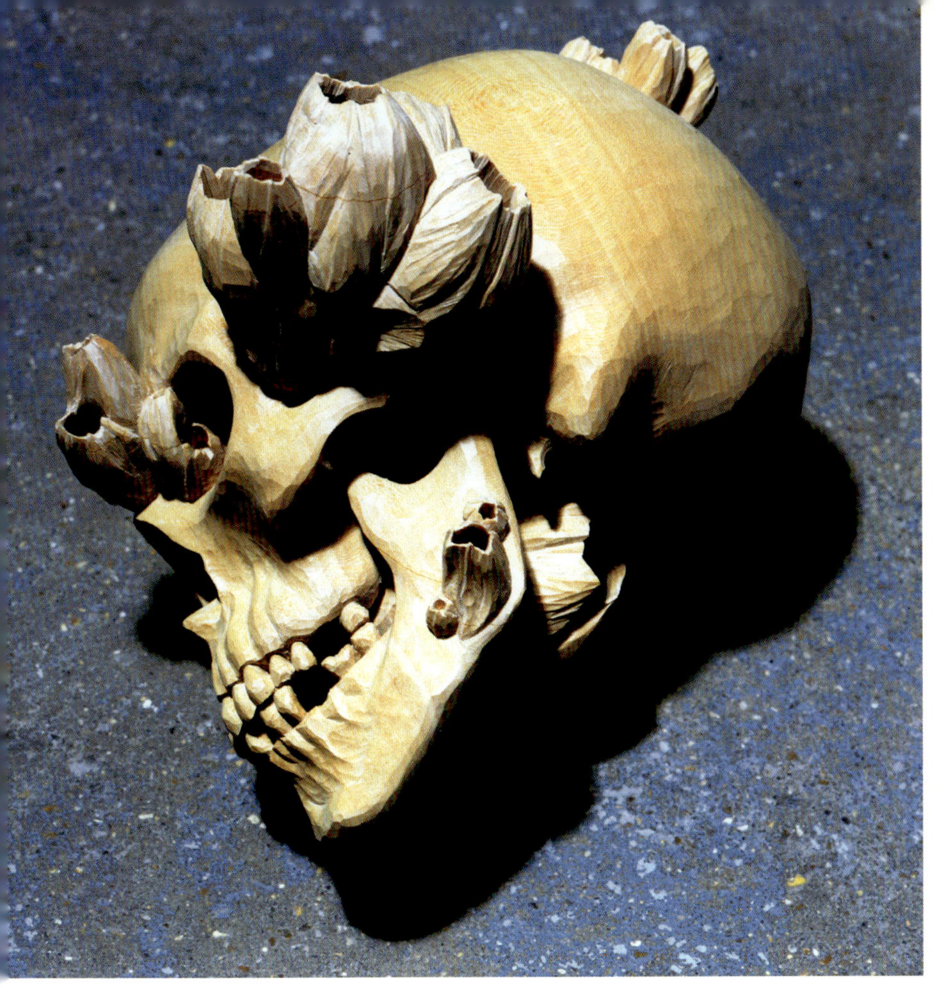

03

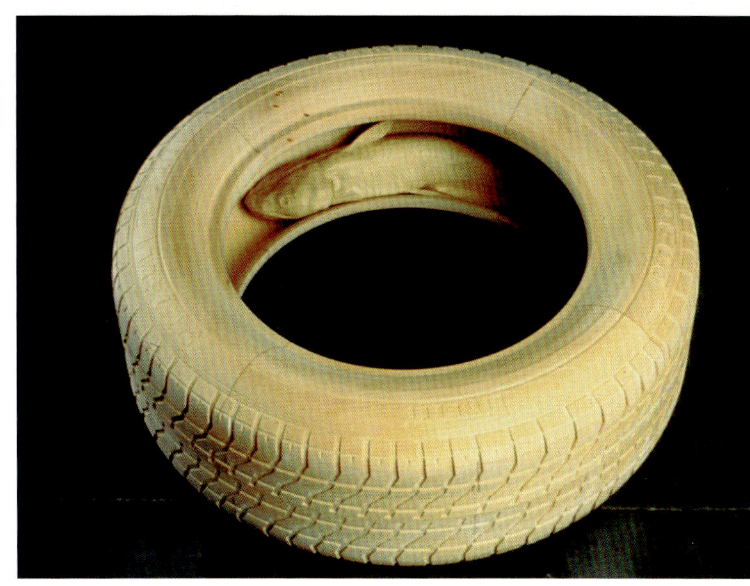

04

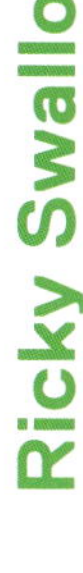

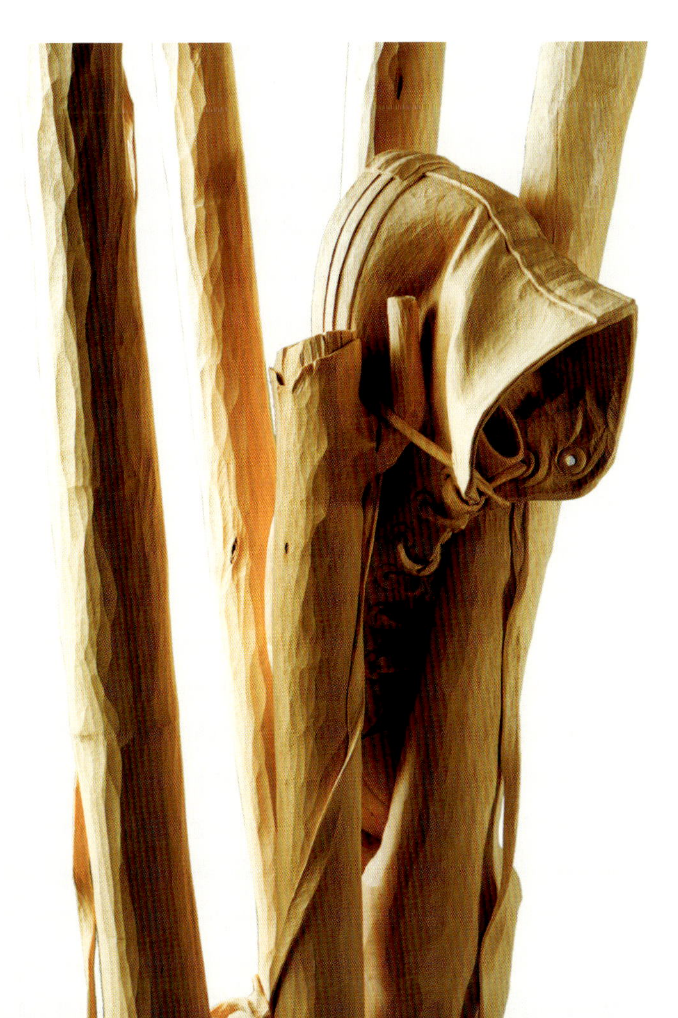

05

06

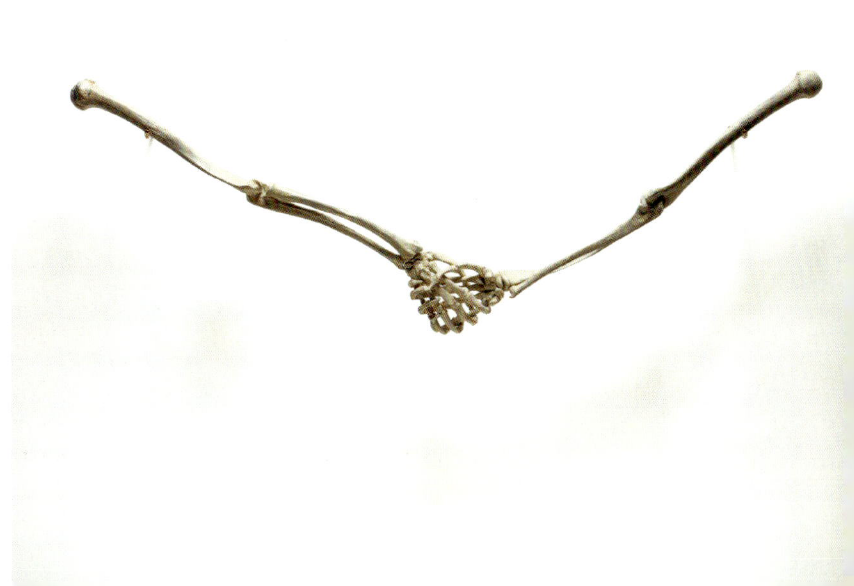

Mika Tajima makes hybrid artworks that blur traditional definitions and elude straightforward characterization. A single object — for example a double-sided, free-standing, silkscreened panel — is simultaneously aligned with the fields of painting, sculpture and architecture. Individual artworks are frequently repositioned for use in multiple projects, reflecting an inherently unfinished character and her preference for exploring the 'means' rather than the 'ends'. Such was the case in the 2007 exhibition 'Disassociate' in which elements figured first as objects in the gallery, then as the backdrop for a performance and ultimately as visual components of a video. Other works are designed to be modular, allowing time, circumstance and personal preference to factor in their ultimate shape and design.

When working in two dimensions, Tajima builds out surfaces in an additive fashion that moves towards a third plane. Starting with a solid-coloured foundation, she superimposes elegant graphic tessellations composed of texts or patterns appropriated from myriad sources including Bauhaus design, modernist furniture and scientific diagrams. Some are covered with opaque Plexiglass and others with mirror, a material Tajima uses regularly as a means of extending into the physical space beyond the work itself. Others might host individual silkscreen prints pinned directly on top of the picture plane, or support small props scattered on the floor. As a result, Tajima nearly always denies her viewer full access to the visual information she has assembled, preferring to offer clues that hint at the complexity underlying each work. Such obstruction creates a tension between the visible and the hidden that is a hallmark of Tajima's practice.

Like the architecturally scaled panels she conceived for *The Double* (an installation inspired in part by Mick Jagger's 1970 cult film *Performance*), Tajima's artworks often toe the line between functional objects (recalling studio, workshop or stage equipment) and sculpture, and in many, implied action lies latent. Louvered barriers, such as *Appearance (Against Type)* (2008), evoke theatrical sets, and a series of text 'ladders' (*Thin Line*, 2007) made from vertically oriented letters that serve as both rungs and rails, suggest physical engagement.

01

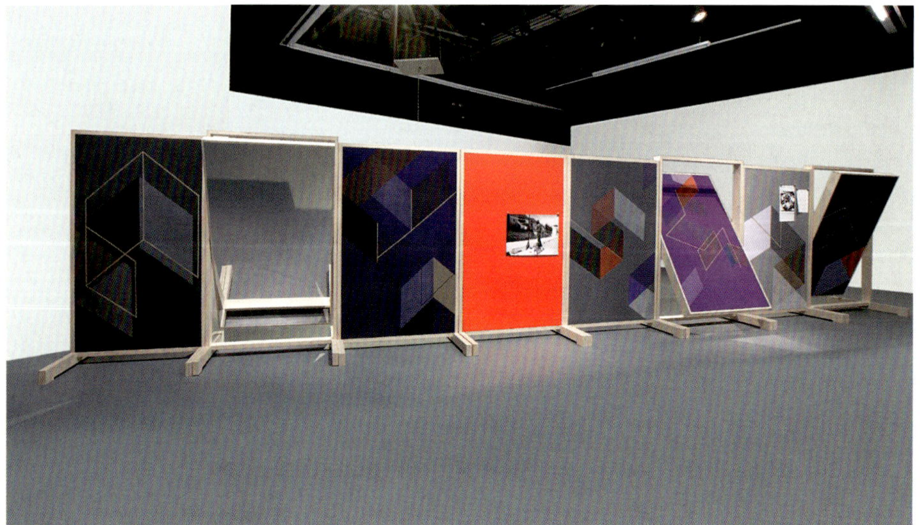

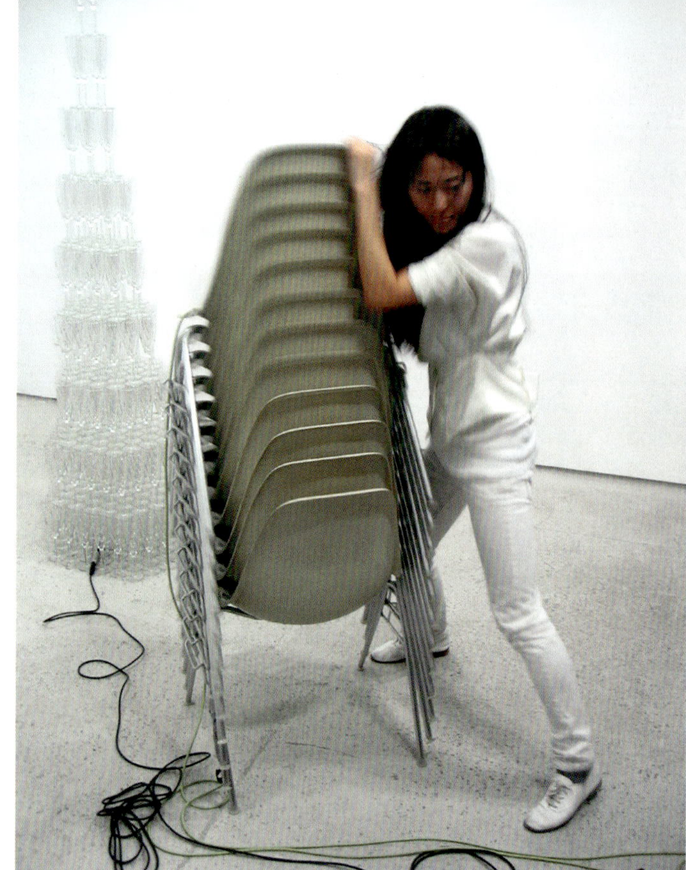

02

Some installations even assume the literal appearance of performance sites, inviting slippage between traditional categories of the visual arts (employed) and the performance arts (implied), as well as Tajima's position as artist and the viewer's place as performer.

Such designations are reversed, however, when Tajima uses her installations as sites for, and tools of, performance by New Humans, the collaboration she co-founded in 2003 with Howie Chen as a branch of her artistic practice. New Humans invite an ever-changing group of artists and musicians to participate in discrete projects and noise events that Tajima initiates, designs and often directs. For her, the unpredictable frictions of group endeavours become one more tool for leveraging modes of production and typologies of display. Like Tajima's discrete artworks, New Humans' initiatives comprise a series of interlocking elements that are firmly disassociated from any finite interpretations. The structure allows Tajima to infiltrate her own installations and challenge the hegemony of both the artworks themselves and her own role as an artist. [Katie Stone Sonnenborn]

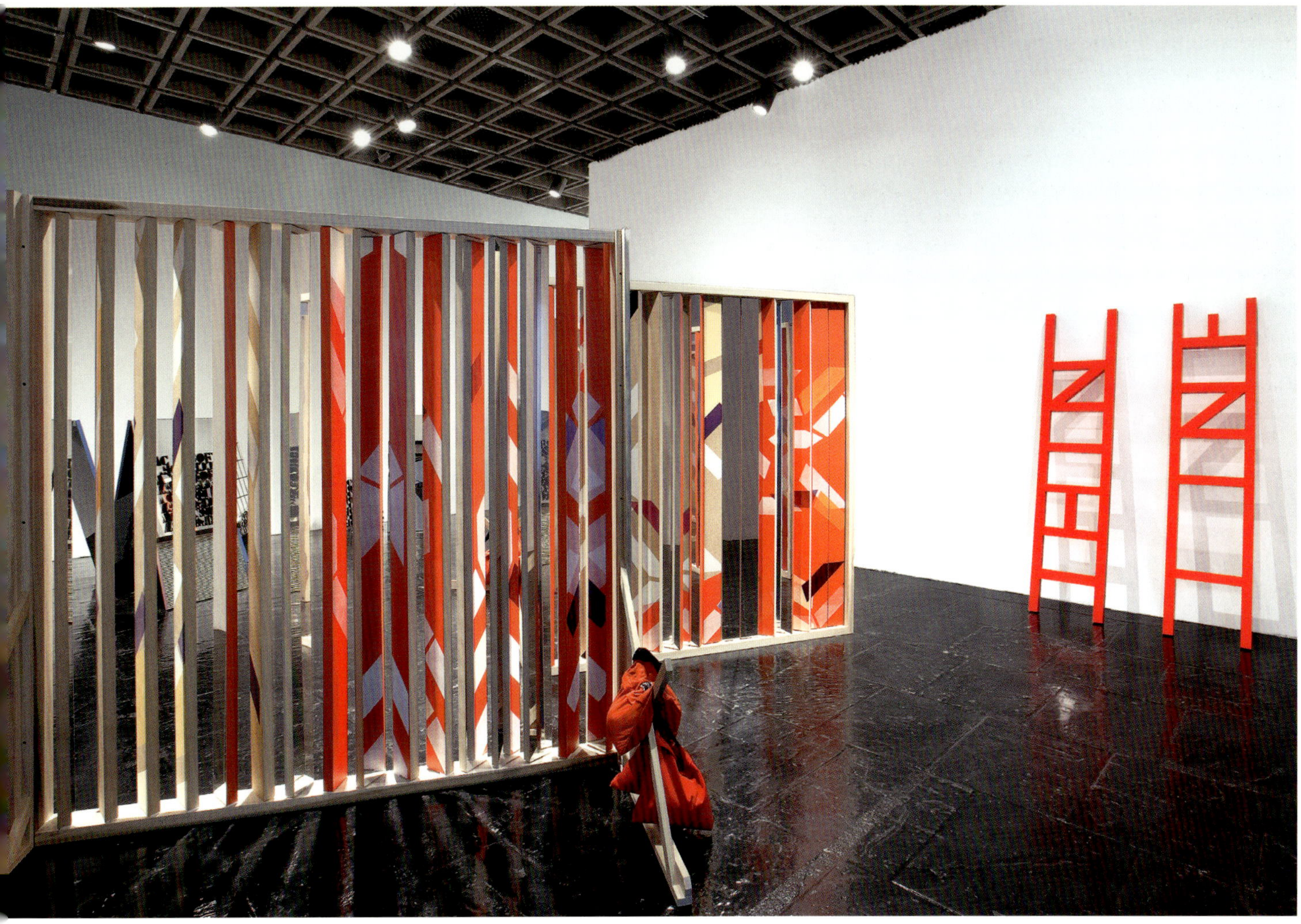

03

04

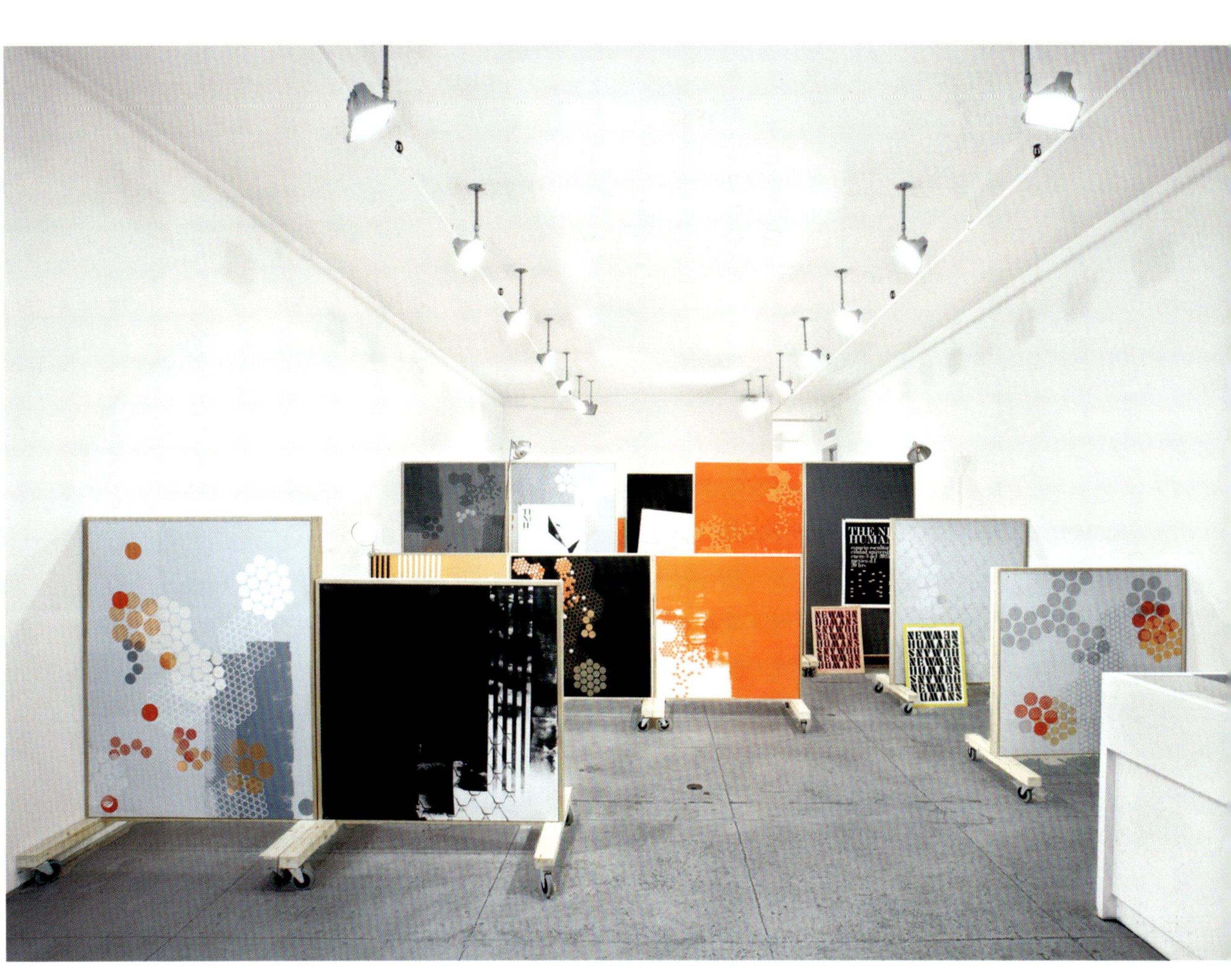

01 *The Double*, 2008
Silkscreen, canvas, acrylic paint, gold leaf, wood, mirrored aluminium, paper, pins
8 parts
Each 168 × 122 × 10 cm

02 from left:
→ *Avoidance of Something*, 2007
Eames stacking shell chairs, champagne glasses
152 × 46 × 46 cm
→ *Disassociate*, 2007
Performance

03
→ *Appearance (Against Type) 1, 2*, 2008
Silkscreen, MDF, wood, mirrored aluminium, Formica, acrylic paint, sandbags
2 panels
Each 183 × 183 × 76 cm
→ *Thin Line*, 2008
MDF, lacquer
41 × 183 × 5 cm

04 *Disassociate*, 2007
Silkscreen, canvas, acrylic paint, gold/silver leaf, wood, mirror, paper, pins, lights
Sizes vary from 122 × 122 × 10 cm to 244 × 122 × 10 cm

Drawing on a vast array of languages that range from sculpture to installation, from drawing to collage and from video to sound, Luca Trevisani's works are like documentations of the metamorphic possibilities of many kinds of materials. By turn they recall the phases of a chemical reaction, a physics test, an experiment in equilibrium, geometrical measurements or botanical studies. Trevisani is at the centre of a laboratory where many scientific processes are continually played out and questioned.

He is not seeking to reconstruct an 'authentic', pre-modern, natural condition. Rather, his work speaks of a modern-day reality, or even more so of a future reality. It has overtaken the 'solid' modernity of rational planning, the production line, serial manufacture and Euclidian geometry and has entered into a second modernity — one described by the sociologist Zygmunt Bauman as 'liquid'. In the same way that liquids and fluids do not define space or fix time, 'liquid modernity' is made up of elements of lightness, transferability, speed and reduction. Just like Trevisani's work, this new condition contains multiple levels of hybridization, preferring movement to stasis, multiplicity to uniqueness and difference to singularity. Trevisani's works have a traversal nature in relation to their references and sources: from martial arts to Arte Povera, from Epicurus to computer technology and from traditional Japanese art to modernist architecture. A huge range of materials are brought into dialogue with each other as part of the same sphere of meaning and modified into new and precarious structures. Trevisani moves laterally, as if through a system with multiple entry points. His work is part of a constant flow — of data, materials and transforming images — that does not permit either hierarchies or a solid state, a defined form. In the words of Gilles Deleuze and Felix Guattari in Anti-*Oedipus*, his works are 'partial objects that are by nature fragmentary and fragmented'.

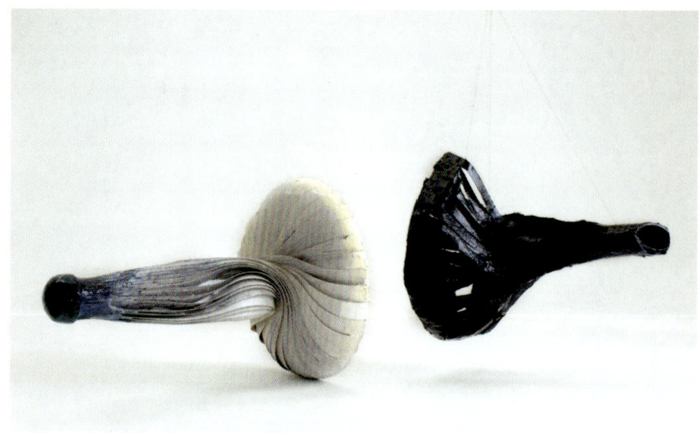

01

Ultimately, this is a continuous interrogation of the process that lies behind the birth and the identity of a form, the playing out of its own creation. In his bulimic but coherent effort to embrace the possible idea of 'totality', Trevisani creates a universe of signs that are engaged in continuous interaction. He shows us this condition of impurity in which, as Primo Levi said, 'matter is matter, neither noble nor vile, infinitely transformable, and its proximate origin is of no importance whatsoever.' As a consequence, the authority of form and image, and of the artwork itself, its possibility of being a definitive and meaningful entity is weakened and called into question. For Levi, talking about chemistry was the same as talking about society and politics. Similarly, Trevisani's formalism and his attention to organic and changeable materials speak of a modern-day condition and, metaphorically, of the possible social and political consequences. [Luca Cerizza]

02

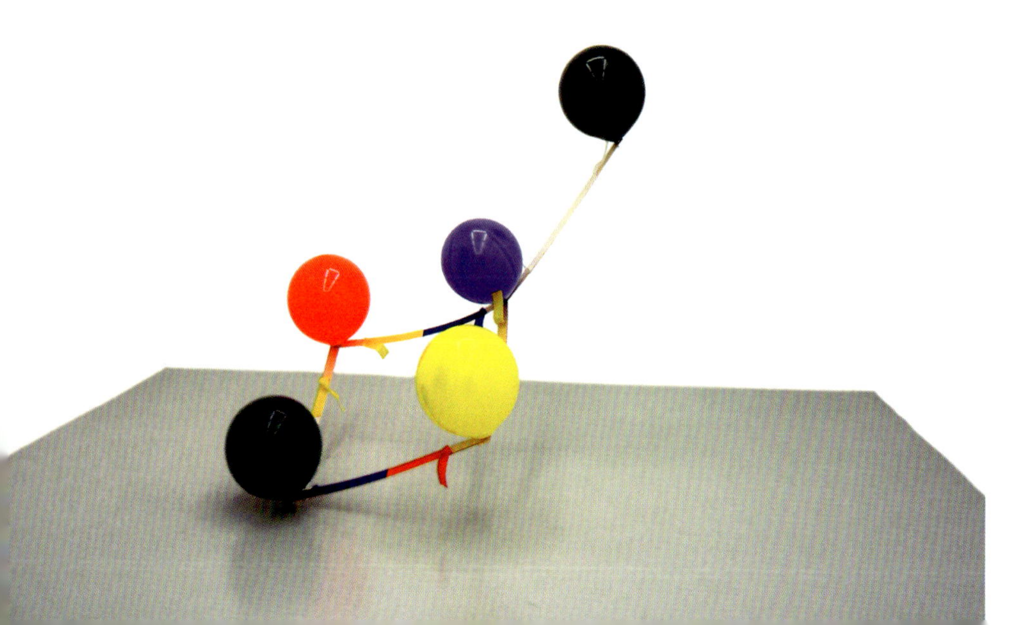

01 *White as the milk, black as the ink, please concoct*, 2008
PVC, wood, milk, ink, glue
2 parts
100 × 100 × 130 cm
70 × 80 × 100 cm

02 *The weaving constellation*, 2005
Wood, balloons, helium
50 × 120 × 240 cm

03 *Every basin is a mixing bowl*, 2008
Fishing rod, recorded audio tape, objects
250 × 30 × 150 cm

04 *Seven boards of skill*, 2008
Copper, cork, aluminium, cinefoil, tape, clam
60 × 45 × 30 cm

05 *Gibbosa e sfuggente*, 2006
Rapid prototyper nylon
Each 12 × 12 × 12 cm

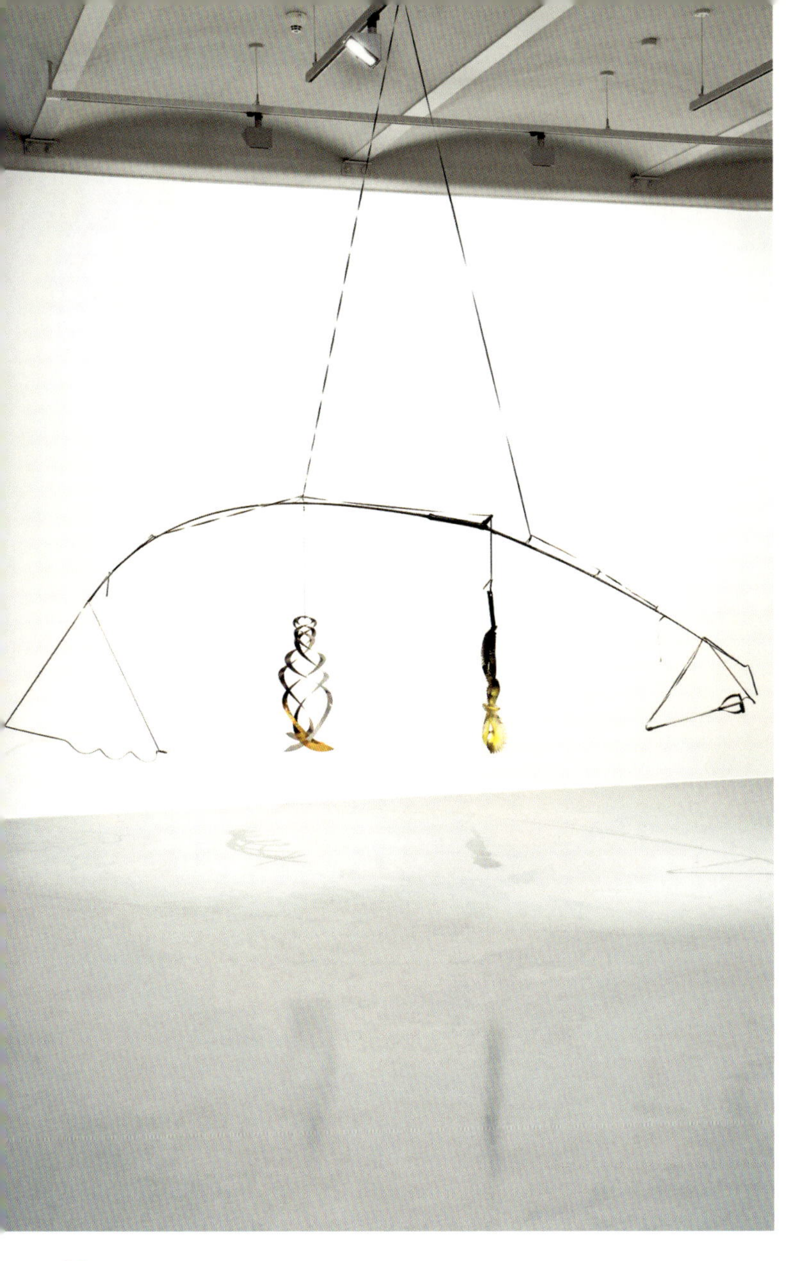

03

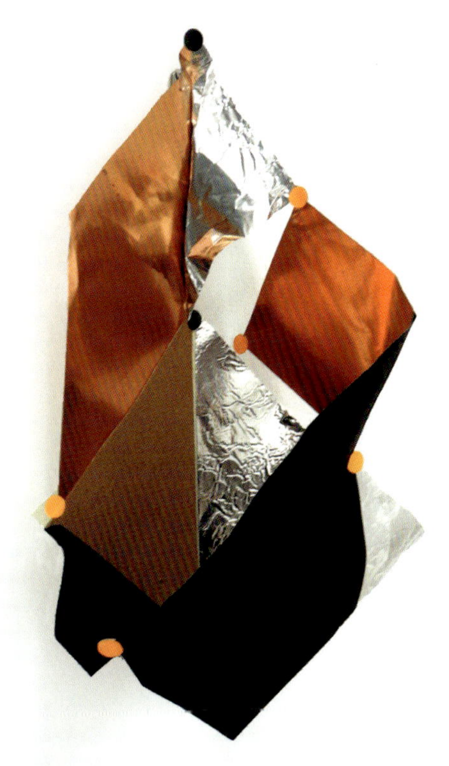

04

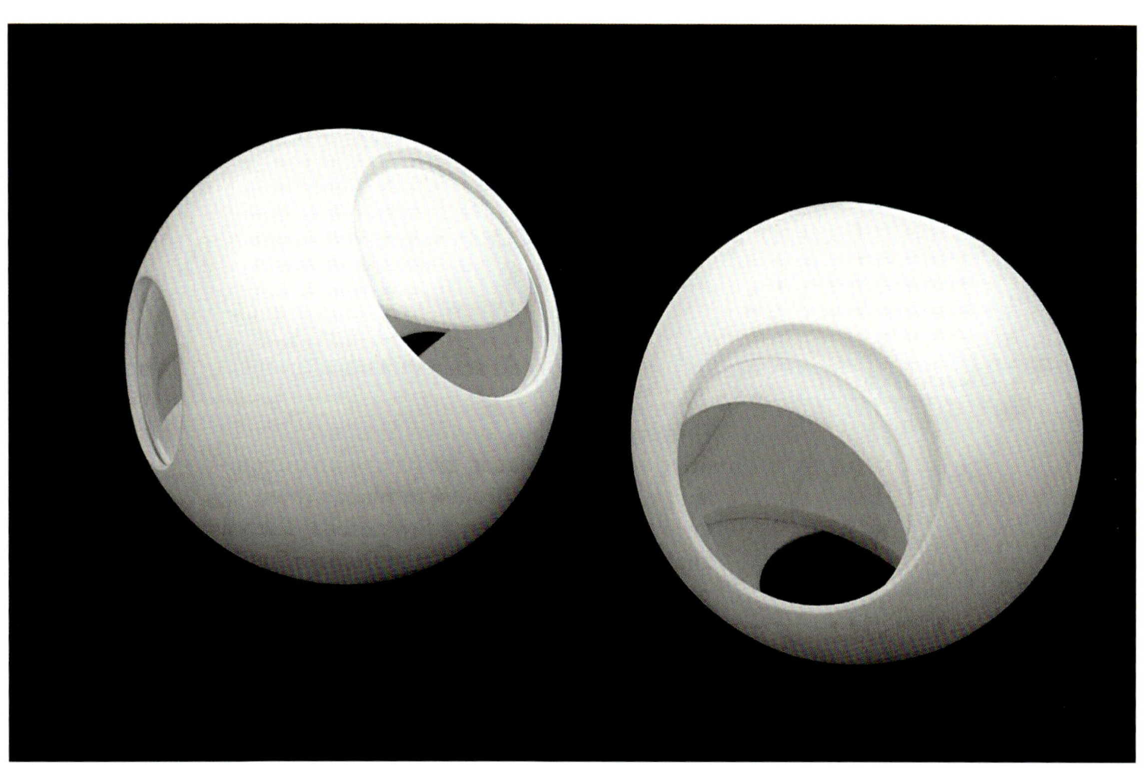

05

01

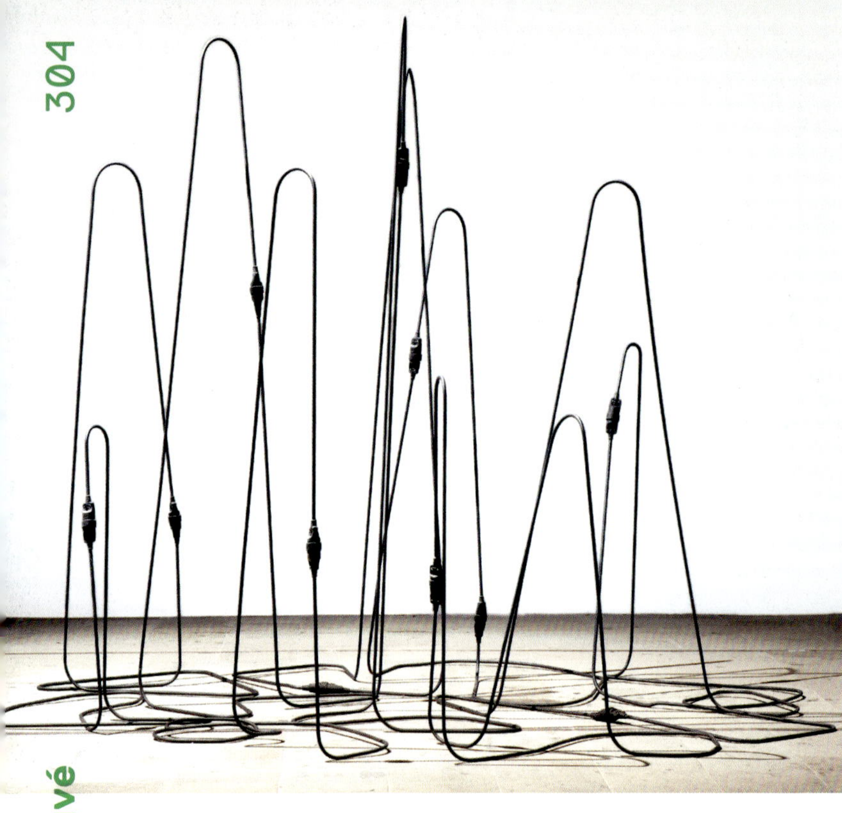

02

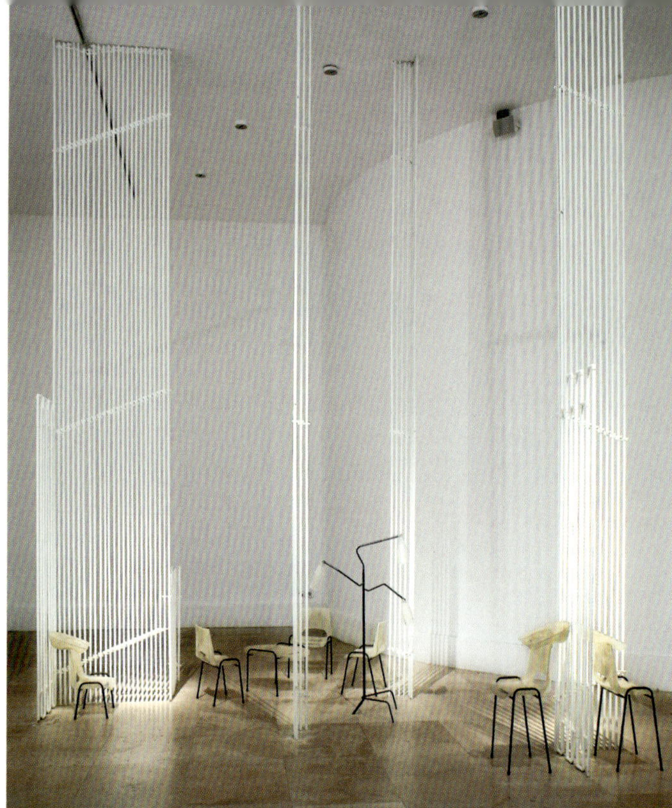

Tatiana Trouvé's sculptural installations vaguely indicate or delineate rooms, but not ones you'd want to inhabit for any length of time. What look like pieces of furniture seem to be arranged in practical constellations, but it's nearly impossible to determine their exact function — one can only imagine what that vinyl-covered table or that heavy metal ball connected to a rope might be used for, but they're probably best left undisturbed.

Many of these installations are in fact models of modules from a fictional office called the Bureau d'Activités Implicites (*Bureau of Implicit Activities*, or BAI), which Trouvé began formulating in 1997. Originally built to accommodate the bureaucratic paperwork involved with her job applications, rejection letters and grant applications, the BAI began as an architectural manifestation of Trouvé's artistic frustrations and failures. This fictional matrix consists of various fantasy modules that correspond to her own conceptual categories, including spaces designed to make 'waiting' more productive, a 'reminiscences module' which can't be entered, and modules with filing cabinets full of records of unrealized projects. Although Trouvé built the BAI according to functional architectural rules and guidelines, these are rules oriented more towards a corporate office than an artist's studio.

Trouvé now only makes reduced scale models of the BAI, while the project itself remains dormant and perpetually incomplete. These installations look like provisional spaces — waiting rooms or places for having an uncomfortable procedure performed. Trouvé furnishes them with cold, sterile materials, adding a few details, such as draped animal skins, which make them more hospitable but also define them as useless. Trouvé's designs borrow heavily from hospital furniture, gym equipment or bureaucratic instruments; they look almost functional but cruelly instrumentalized, like a dentist's office from a nightmare, furnished with plastic chairs with transparent attachments at head height.

Trouvé has dedicated her recent exhibitions to her series of 'Polders' — site-specific installations that originated from the recyclable materials from the modules of the BAI. Polders incorporate industrial materials like iron, copper pipes, resin, Formica and Plexiglas. The artist refers to these works as 'prisoners of a dimension that is not their own' and in fact their dimensions do look warped or compromised. Furniture is made at half its normal scale and often looks skewed and perverted, as if designed for an incredibly specific torture. Pipes resembling expanded heating units stretch from floor to ceiling, suggesting the bars of a cell. One Polder is a series of steel garment racks and metal bars with black leather-covered apparatuses that look like narrow punching bags hanging from hooks or chains. The overall effect is like being inside a slaughterhouse without any meat.

'I wanted my Polders to work like outgrowths, to serve as the beginnings of a mental space,' Trouvé said in a 2005 interview. 'I've created spaces that are x-rays of architecture, which materialize what the eye cannot delimit or define.' Although they may not look like it, Trouvé's sculptural installations are time-based conceptual projects — some only exist in her mind or would not be temporally possible to realize, like elevator doors designed to close over a span of ten years. In fact, the sculptures she exhibits are models for possibilities that only she envisions: 'I think they have within themselves the thrust of a design, that idea of the project, that formulation of something that is coming into being.' [Christy Lange]

01 *Untitled*, 2007
Metal, rubber
218 × 268 × 240 cm

02 *Polder*, 2005
Metal, cement, imitation leather, wood, rope, plastic
210 × 350 × 500 cm

03 *Untitled*, 2007
Metal, epoxy paint, Formica, wood, leather, resin
190 × 800 × 500 cm

04 *Untitled*, 2007
Cement, Plexiglas, Formica, metal, leather, marble, bronze, wood
300 × 610 × 421 cm

03

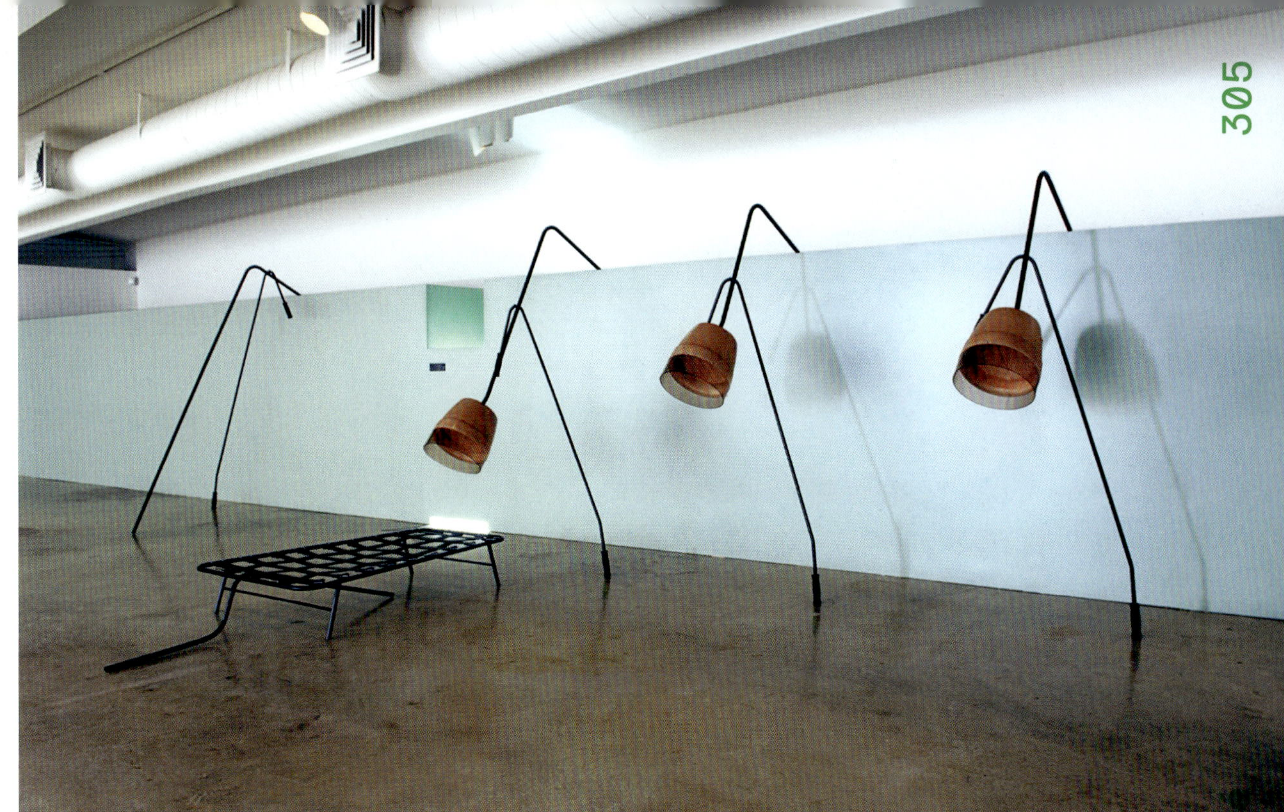

04

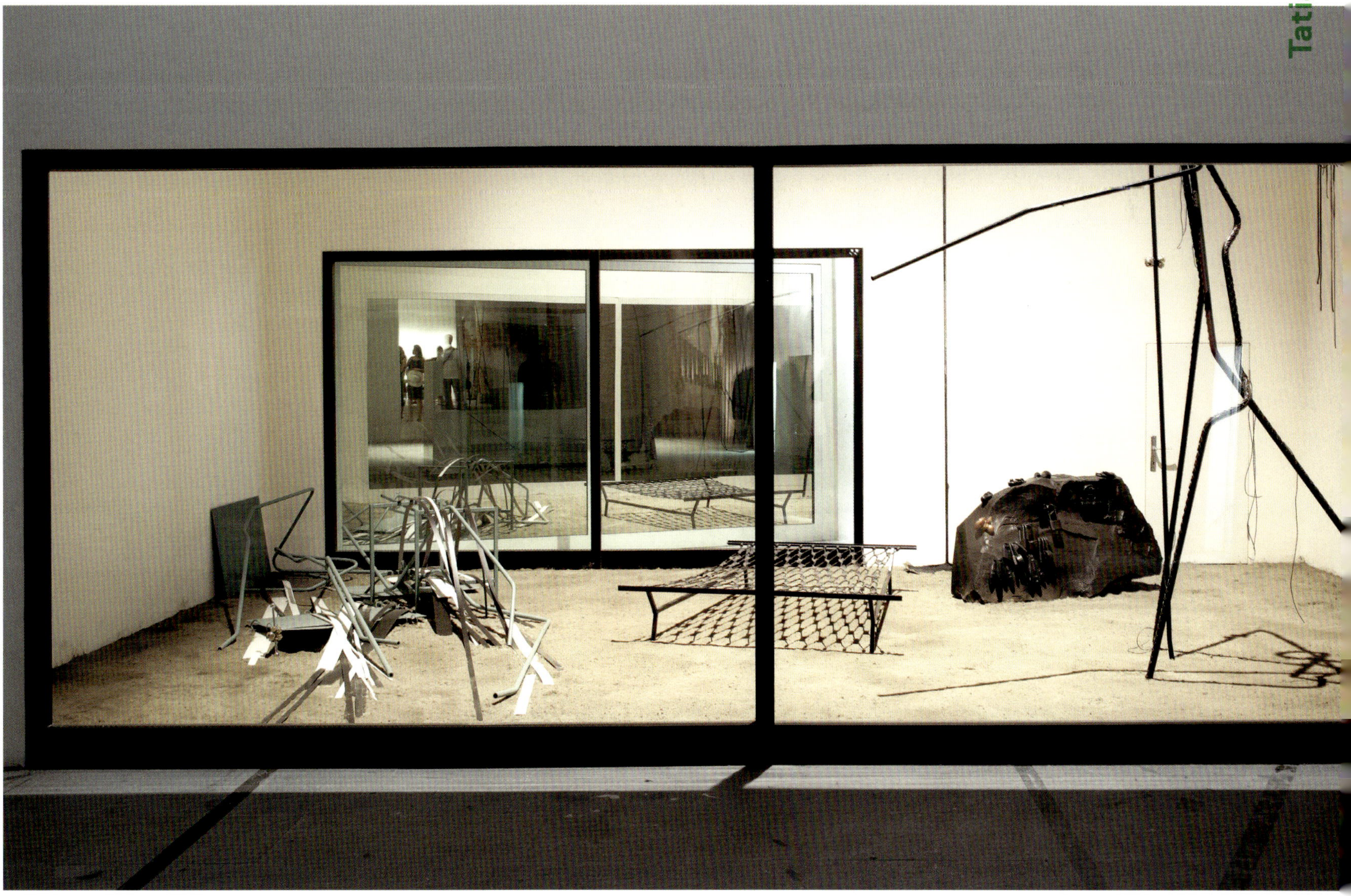

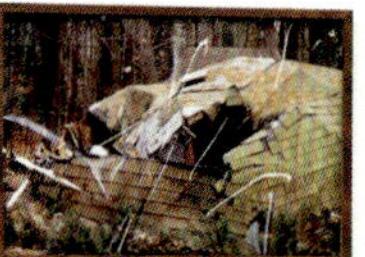

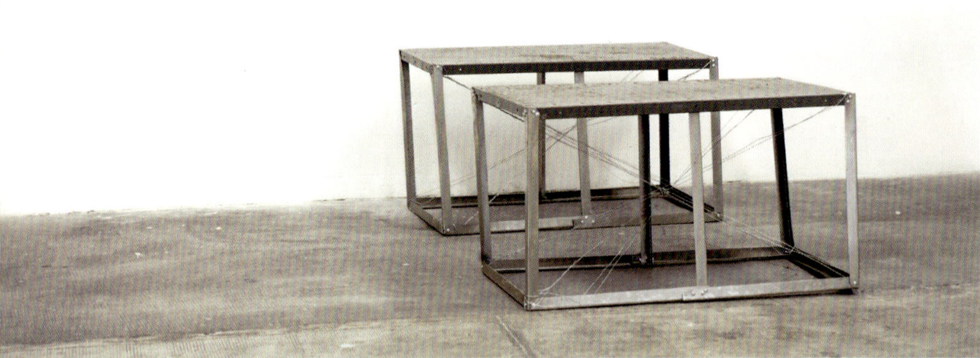

01 ‘Two years ago, taking a rifle, a handful of beaver traps, and about $200 in bulk food, I headed into the woods. Except for brief intervals, I’ve been in the woods ever since. For the most part, I’ve gotten my living from the woods: cutting cedar shake bolts, thinning trees and running a small winter trap-line for winter meat and needed cash.’ For two years these words served as the opening lines for speeches that Oscar Tuazon gave at art institutions, schools, galleries or symposia. Every aspect of his appearance — a cross between a hippie and a lumberjack, with long hair, bushy beard and thick plaid shirt — matched the story. Except that there he was behind a microphone, reading from notes and presenting slides of the wood-and-concrete sculptures he had been exhibiting in typically white-walled art spaces over the course of those same two years.

Tuazon is an American architect, artist and fiction writer. Since graduating, he has collapsed the three disciplines and aspirations in a series of shows — including ‘I’d rather be gone’, ‘Where I lived, and what I lived for’, ‘Kodiak’, ‘A vow of Poverty’ and ‘I was a stranger’ — in which he consistently investigated how theories of personal freedom and autonomy can be embodied in architecture, and how to build and live with minimal resources and minimal needs, in remote locations.

Tuazon’s early projects made direct reference to historical or current practices of architecture without buildings, as well as the subcultures of DIY and self-sufficiency. These include Steve Baer’s design processes for Drop City, which from 1965 to 1971 was home to the first hippie commune in America; VONU, a libertarian, off-the-grid living practice centred in the American West in the 1970s and 1980s that intended to allow its practitioners to become invisible to governmental and commercial surveillance and documentation; and *Dwelling Portably* a thirty-year-old zine written by and for a close community of hardcore hippie survivalists dispersed throughout the woods of the American Northwest. Tuazon uses elements of their low-tech designs, as well as techniques taken from their how-to manuals for building temporary, mobile and invisible shelters, to conceive his architecture-cum-sculpture, which often emerges raw and sharp-edged, combining concrete and urban debris, wooden pallets, melamine boards, steel scraps or glass fragments — materials usually gathered from the areas surrounding the exhibition site, where he always works firsthand.

Tuazon has also embarked on a long-term project of designing a full-scale house, which he builds in fragments: a corner here, a stairway, heating system or elements of a kitchen there. This project allows him to develop his own approach to secondary-use design and to edit his knowledge as he builds and experiments with materials, structures and ideas, playing with the limits at which constructions can physically fail or collapse. The project *Kodiak*, carried out in 2008 with his brother Elie Hansen, consisted of building a cabin in the wilderness on remote Kodiak Island, Alaska, and then constructing an architectural fragment at the Seattle Art Museum, more than 1,400 miles away, which mirrors and completes the original shelter. Tuazon uses the exhibition site as a fictional apparatus, giving the viewer the fragmentary sensation of being, or wishing to be, somewhere else, living a different kind of life. [Thomas Boutoux]

02

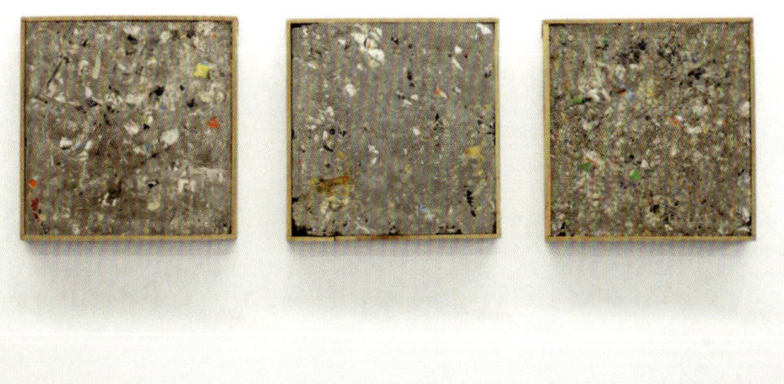

01 *Two possible benches*, 2008
Steel sheets, steel brackets, wire
2 parts
Each 120 × 60 × 40 cm

02 *Papercrete prototypes*, 2008
Mixed concrete and newspaper, wooden frame
3 parts
Each 42 × 42 × 6 cm

03, 04 *A Vow of Poverty*, 2008
Concrete, steel, plywood boards, wooden beams
Dimensions variable

04

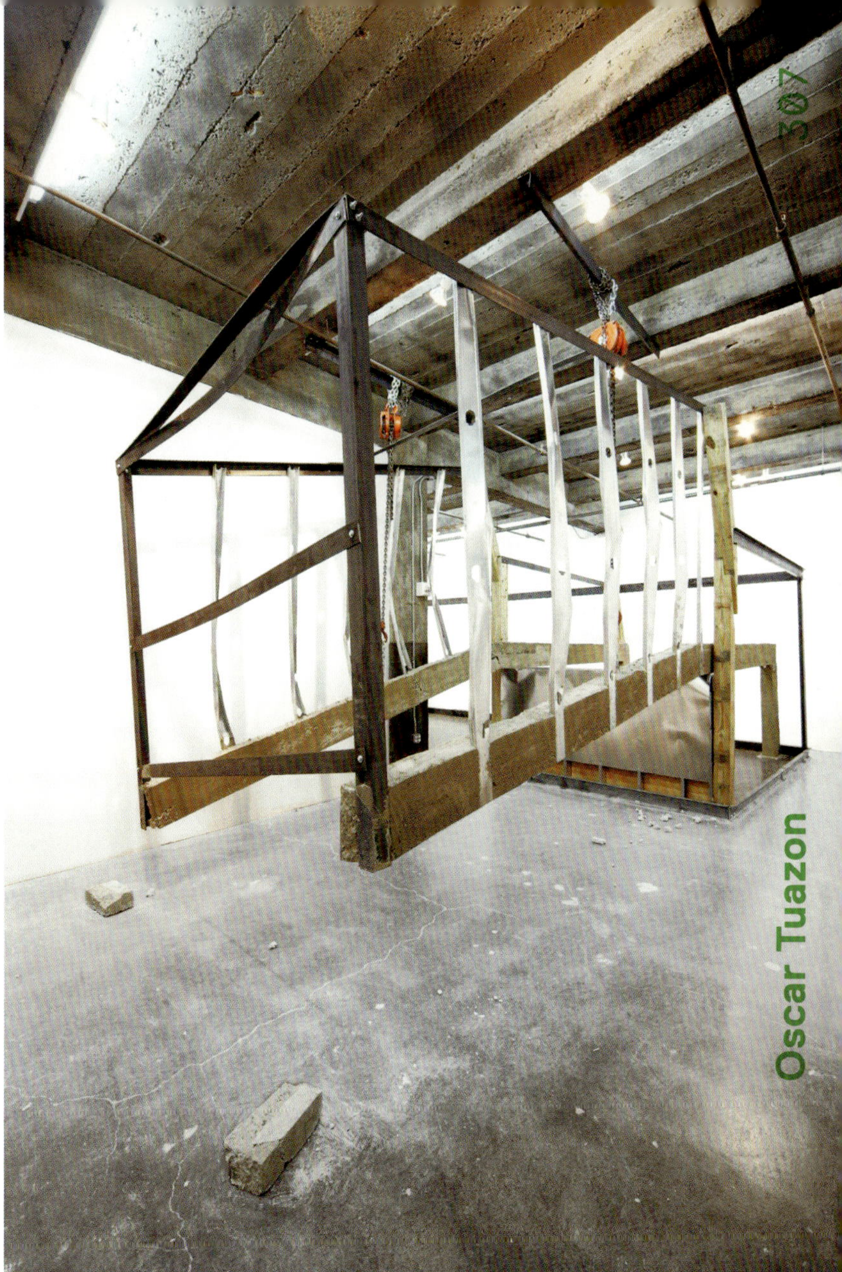

03

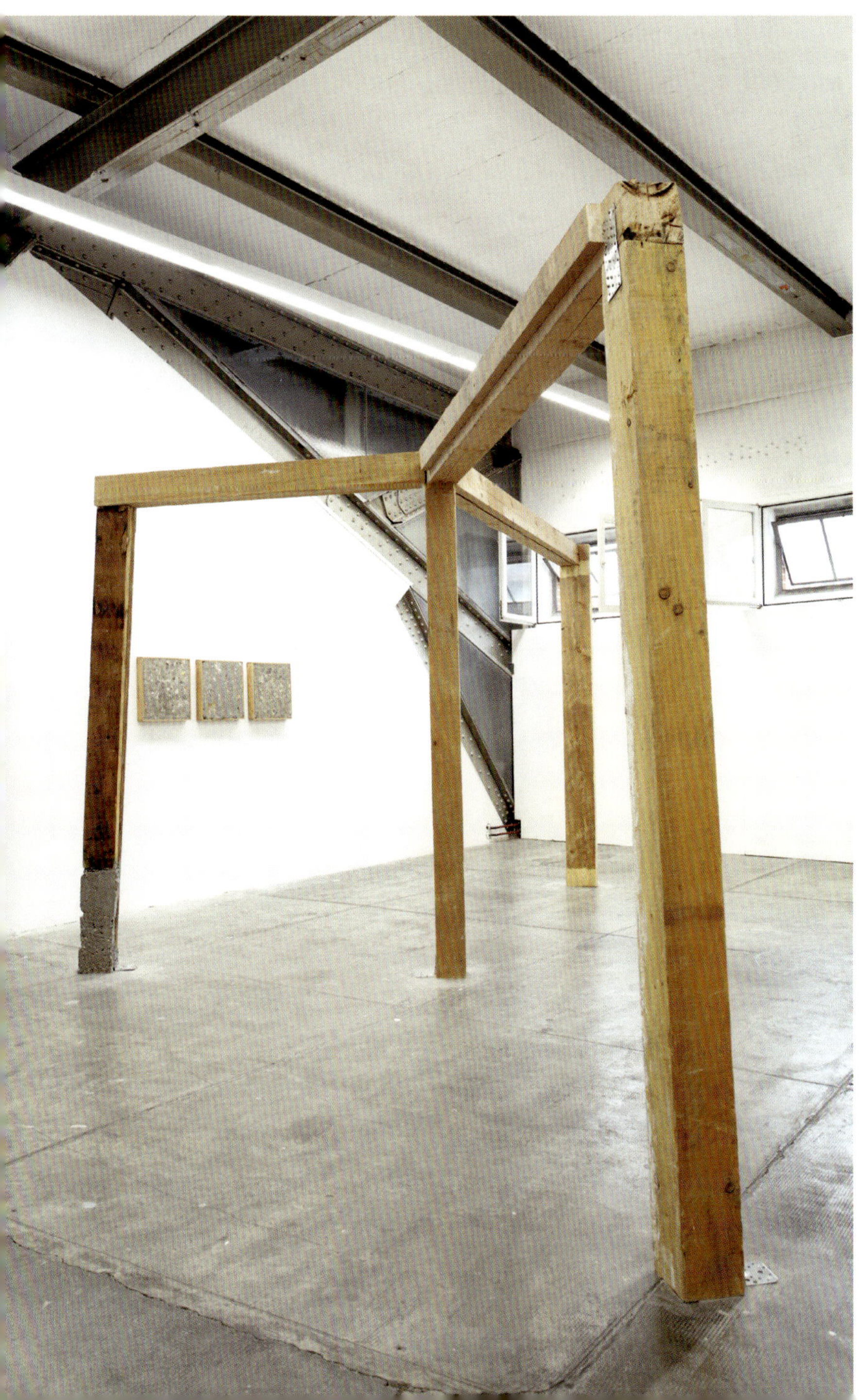

Mistakes are central to Francis Upritchard's practice. Her misremembering of human and animal form creates botched anatomies that verge on the comically grotesque, while the wider consequences of cultural appropriation and misrepresentation provide a solemn political undertone to her displays of reconstructed cultural and ethnographic artefacts.

The not-quite-right flattened groin of *Yellow Figure* (2007), the ludicrously simplified body of *Sloth Creature* (2004) stretched out like a parody of a sloth, and *Jealous Saboteurs* (2005), an unruly family of hockey-stick alligators, swing between tragic and comic. This sort of slippage becomes more sombre, though, at the level of colonial and historical distortion, as Upritchard hints at the dangers of displacement and misunderstanding between cultures. Converting jars and vases found in junk shops into the canopic urns used by ancient Egyptians to preserve the body's vital organs to be buried alongside mummified remains, Upritchard stoppers them with the heads of ambiguous dog- or horse-like creatures instead of the baboon, jackal or falcon of the funerary tradition. While this makes for beguiling curios, her strategies of display — the sobering cabinets, plinths and bell jars — remind us that in the museum the ethnographic consequences of misrepresentation are more serious. *Head II* (2004), for instance, represents a fantastical 'what if' scenario in which a Maori shrunken head, usually taken from a tattooed and revered member of a tribe, has been culled from a rotten-toothed colonialist only to be sold back to Western bounty hunters looking for authentic Maori keepsakes. The implied back story to *Head II* is as grim as its suppurating, ratty-haired appearance.

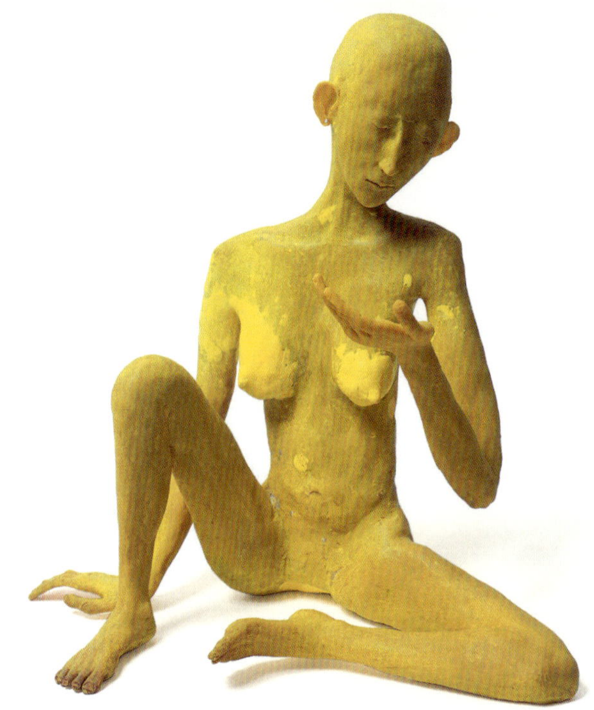

02

01

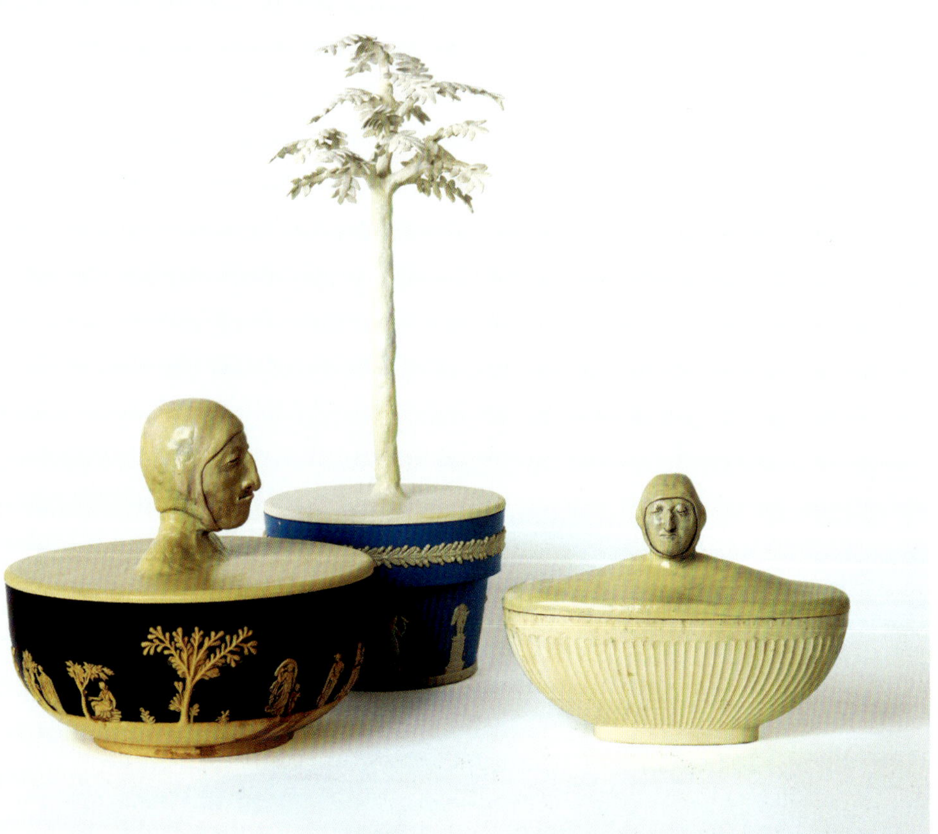

Upritchard considers all of her works to be portraits, even the mummy in *Save Yourself* (2003) and the lamps whose shades become masks that stare rather grumpily back at us. Such objects are, after all, expressions of ideologies, beliefs, daily habits and aspirations. The odd conjunction of contemporary kitsch and ancient forms makes explicit the composite nature of Western society, where travel, an impulse to collect and a compunction to re-educate have combined to infect, cross-pollinate and export wholesale from other cultures. Indeed, ritualistic and spiritual phenomena from ancient civilizations, primitive tribes and indigenous peoples have entered popular culture, oral history and the arts to an almost intractable extent.

Issues of global politics and the failings of Western historiography aside, Upritchard's practice is ultimately a tactile one. Her manner of making is rooted in bricolage and craft, with the serendipity of her found pots providing a manufactured surface against which her hand-hewn interventions play. The series of figures *Balata Men* (2004) is made with a malleable natural latex that must be worked with underwater, where it cools and sets within one hour, intensifying the hands-on aspect of production. Upritchard cuts through the aura of history and otherness ascribed to ancient museum artefacts to rediscover a surface fashioned by a single pair of hands. [Sally O'Reilly]

01 from left:
→ *Before*, 2008
from the series *Roman Plastics*
Found plastic vase,
modelling material, paint
21 × 23 × 23 cm
→ *Strong Tree*, 2008
from the series *Roman Plastics*
Found plastic vase,
modelling material, paint
33 × 18 × 18 cm
→ *Pre-Roman*, 2008
from the series *Roman Plastics*
Found plastic vase,
modelling material, paint
17 × 22 × 10 cm

02 *Yellow Figure*, 2007
Modelling material,
foil, wire, yellow paint
32 × 33 × 17 cm

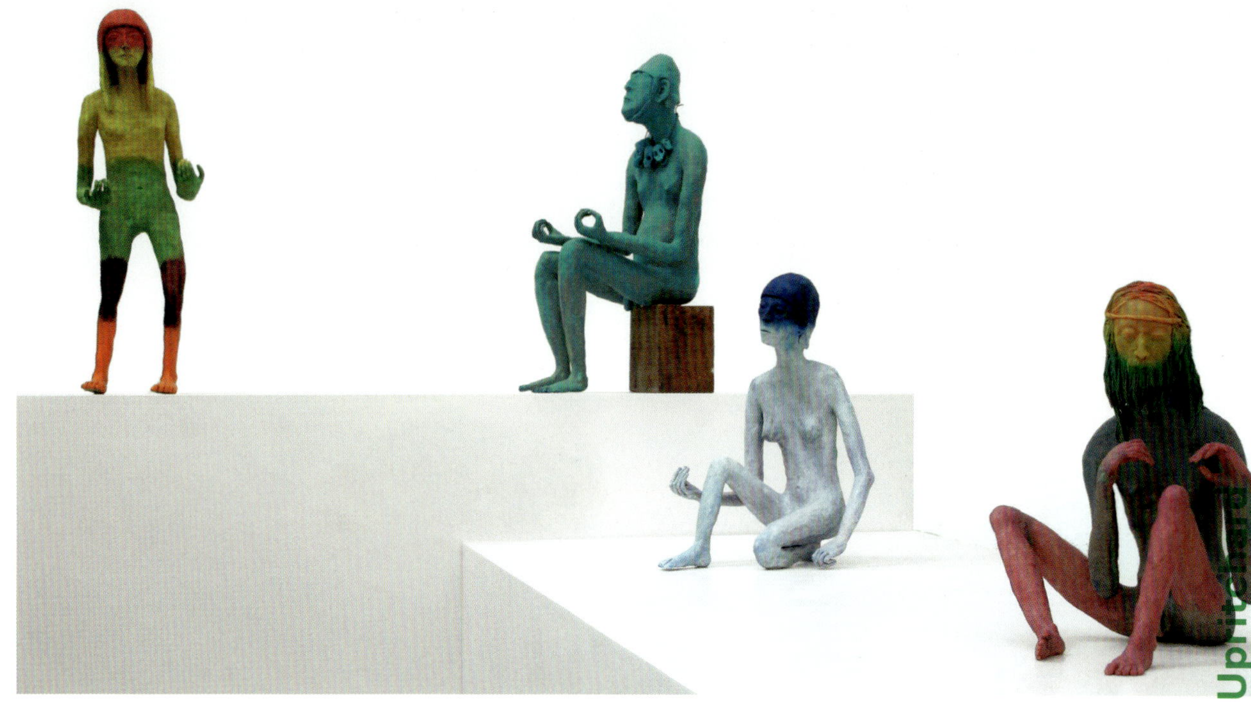

03

03 from left:
→ *Amelia*, 2007
from the series *Plastic People*
Modelling material,
foil, wire, paint
64 × 17 × 20 cm
→ *Prugal*, 2007
from the series *Plastic People*
Modelling material,
foil, wire, paint
65 × 25 × 27 cm
→ *Softly*, 2007
from the series *Plastic People*
Modeling material,
foil, wire, paint
41 × 23 × 29 cm
→ *Clan of Rob*, 2007
from the series *Plastic People*
Modelling material,
foil, wire, paint
35 × 28 × 27 cm

04 *Lamps*, 2005
Ceramic
2 parts
Each 61 × 18 cm

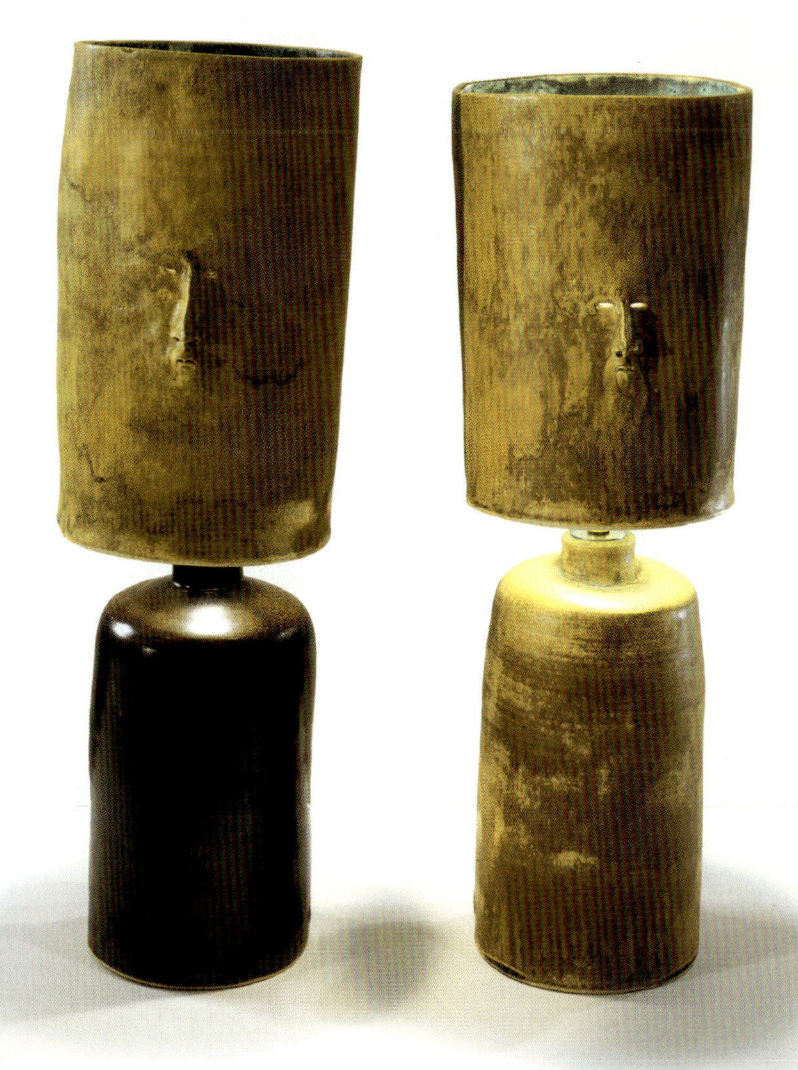

04

05

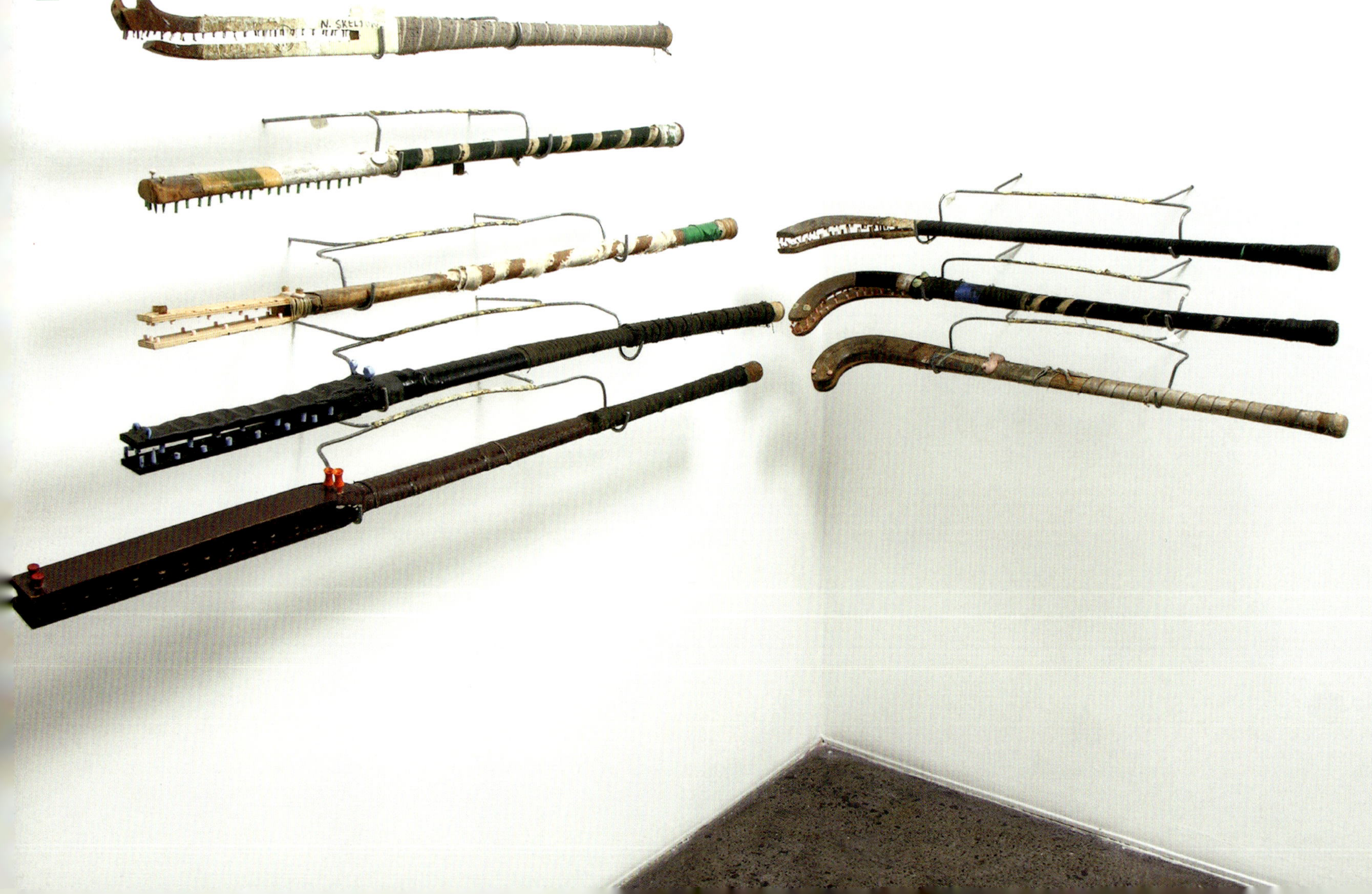

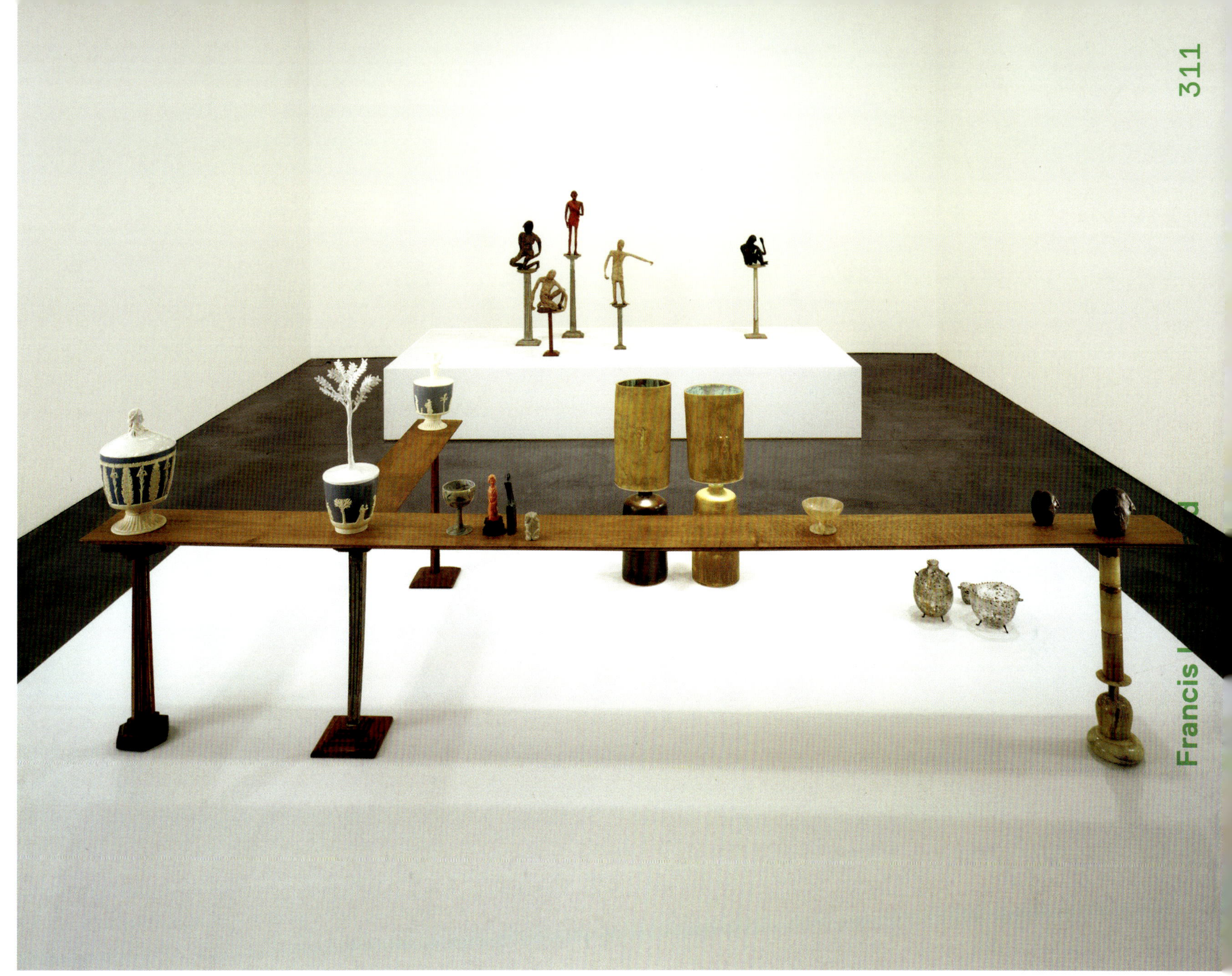

06

05 *Jealous Saboteurs*, 2005
Found sports sticks, modelling material
Each length approx. 92 cm

06 *Torcello and Balata Figures*, 2005
Various found objects, ceramic,
modelling materials, balata
rubber, wooden stands
Dimensions variable

Engendering bold physicality as well as a poetic lightness, Rebecca Warren builds her sculptural practice on knowing art historical references and poignant revisions. Her figurative sculptures in unfired clay affect an air of instability in their quick and messy finish, a style that she also brings to her works in bronze, while her vitrines reflect careful deliberation in the arrangement of found objects. Imbuing her clay and bronze figures with visceral and physical mass, she thrusts them just beyond a position of stability. Modelling awkward poses and exaggerated features, Warren elicits the sense of embarrassment and vulnerability in the experience of form and body. At the same time, her vitrines, enigmatic arrangements of non-figurative elements — wood, wire, cotton balls and neon tubes — hold back from instant legibility. Likewise, the vitrines are bound firmly to walls or plinths while the bronzes and clay works often perch precariously atop a set of wheels.

Her work straddles a range of media and history, yielding a collage of references. Mixing the robust forms of Auguste Rodin with the intimate poses of Edgar Degas, the comic-book audacity of R. Crumb and the monumental nudes photographed by Helmut Newton, Warren's figurative sculptures can seem to be an aggressive reconfiguration of form and composition. In *Helmut Crumb* (1998), for example, she pairs R. Crumb's thick, caricatured proportions with the sultry fashion photography pose celebrated by Newton. For *Croccioni* (2000) she again mobilizes the muscular limbs favoured in Crumb's illustrations, arranging them in the futuristic stance of Umberto Boccioni's *Unique Forms of Continuity*. Meanwhile, the juxtaposition of diverse elements in her vitrines, as in Robert Rauschenberg's *Combines*, fractures a unified reading of the works, complicating the possibility of illusion through a diffusion of signification.

Beneath a profusion of overdeveloped secondary sexual characteristics — bulbous hips, calves and breasts — the representation of the female body is clearly at stake in her work. *She* (2003) and *Dark Passage* (2004), in addition to their voluptuous volumes and erotic poses, evoke cinematic representations of women, referencing Ursula Andress in the 1965 *She* and Lauren Bacall in 1947's *Dark Passage*. Needless to say, if Warren's figures are wearing anything, it's mini-skirts, high heels or panties around their knees. Even her vitrines, especially in her consistently playful treatment of the plinth, that lingering art-world phallus (she typically paints it a pale pink), challenge the stubborn language and signs of gender and sexuality. The short, slightly curving pieces of pale green or rose-coloured neon placed in many of the vitrines make a symbolic yet direct link to the central crease in *Helmut Crumb*. In both works, Warren is presenting images of the cleft — in the fullest sense of Doris Lessing's use of the term.

Deliberate in her selection of material for her sculptures and vitrines, Warren implicates gestures within her compositions. The unfired clay allows her a certain freedom or open-endedness of construction, a looseness of form echoed in the bronzes. This visible malleability also allows Warren to reveal the subjectivity of figuration. At the same time, her vitrines, recalling the sacred arrangements of medieval reliquaries, seem charged with a devotional significance. Their contents would typically have been considered waste, and in their recovery and enshrinement she mobilizes acts of grace and redemption — precisely what her cast of leading ladies seem to be grasping for. [Lillian Davies]

01

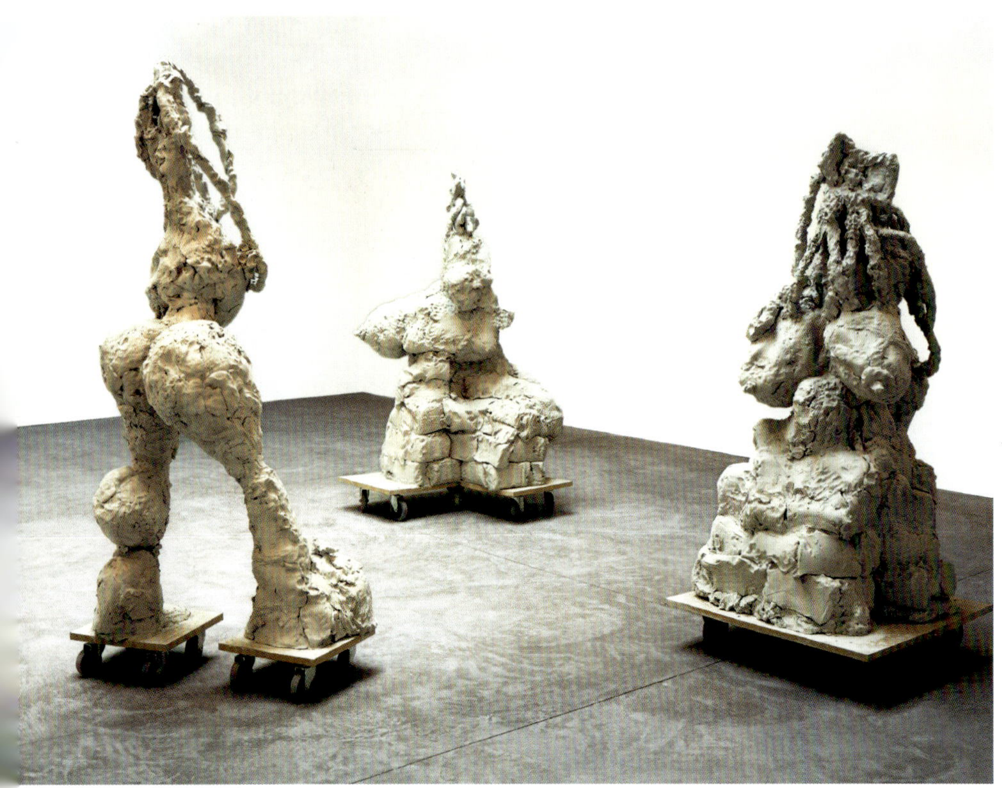

02

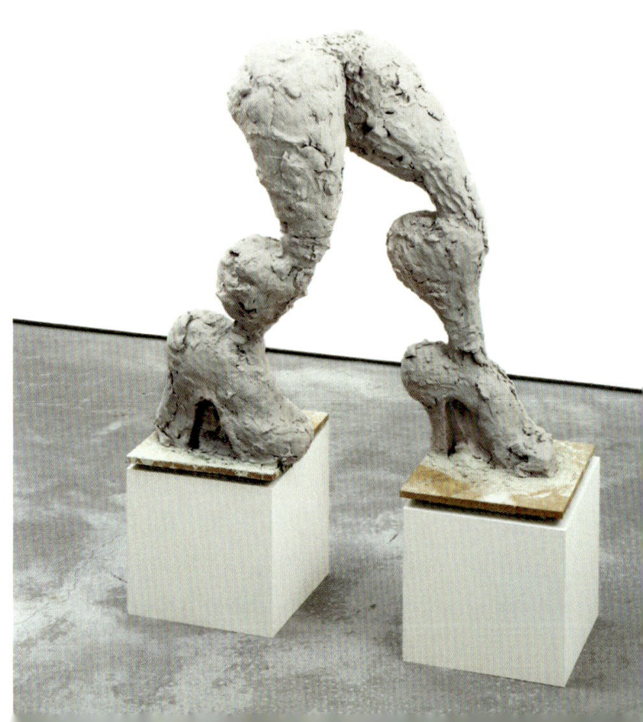

03

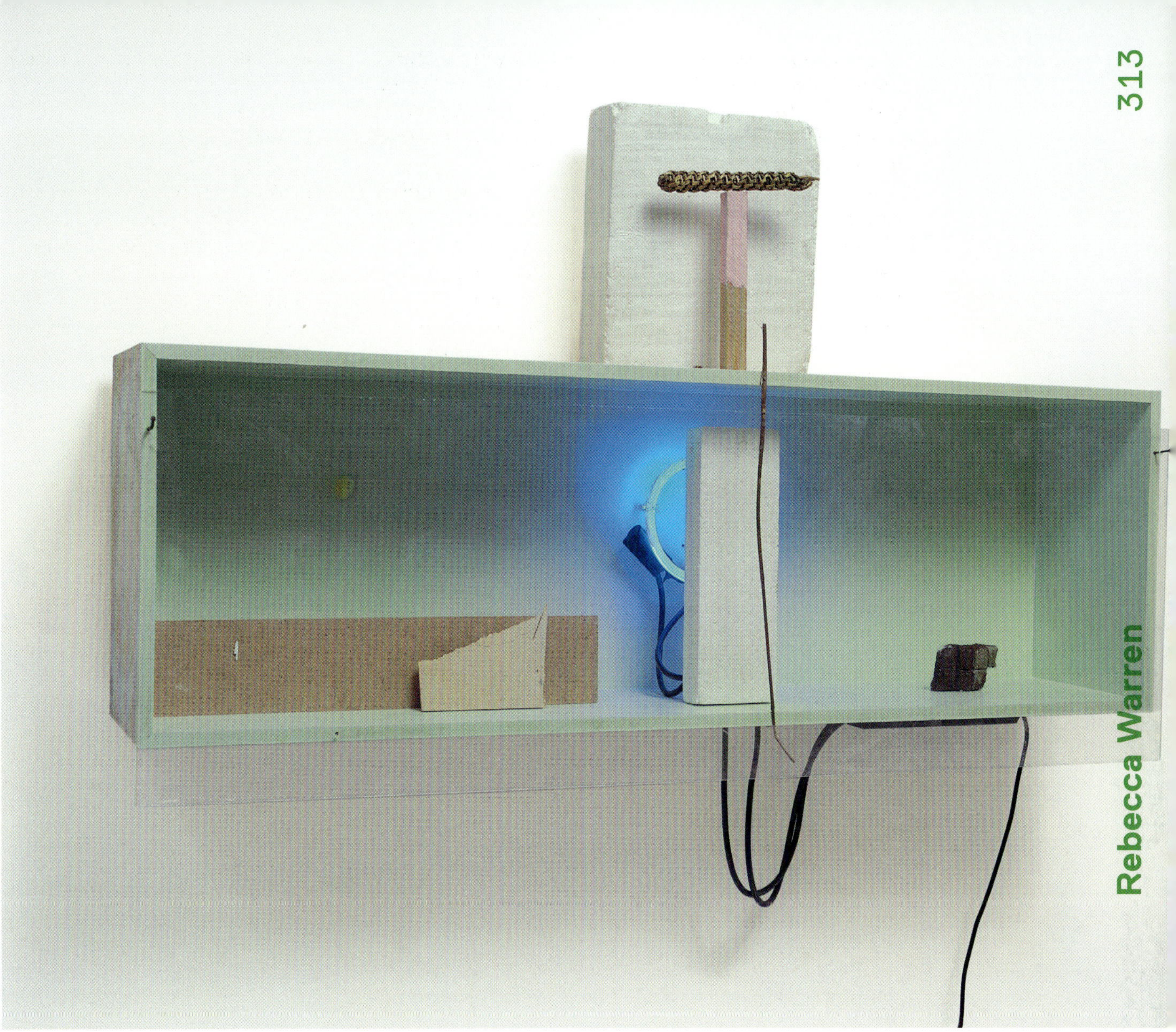

04

01 from left:
→ *Teacher (M.B.)*, 2003
Reinforced clay, MDF, wheels
214 × 102 × 74 cm
→ *Teacher (W)*, 2003
Self-firing clay, MDF, wheels
190 × 96 × 109 cm
→ *Teacher (R)*, 2003
Self-firing clay, MDF, wheels
189 × 88 × 88 cm

02 *Croccioni*, 2000
Reinforced clay, plinths
85 × 34 × 84 cm

03 *Man in the Dark*, 2005
Polystyrene, MDF, pom-poms, twig, neon, painted clay, wicker, hardboard, nails, perspex, painted MDF
103 × 123 × 28 cm

04 *Helmut Crumb*, 1998
Reinforced clay, MDF, stacked plinths
196 × 30 × 30 cm

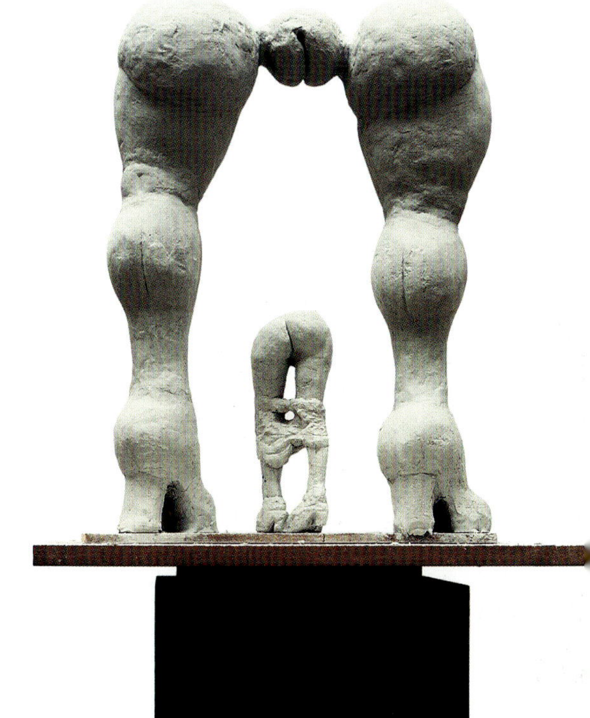

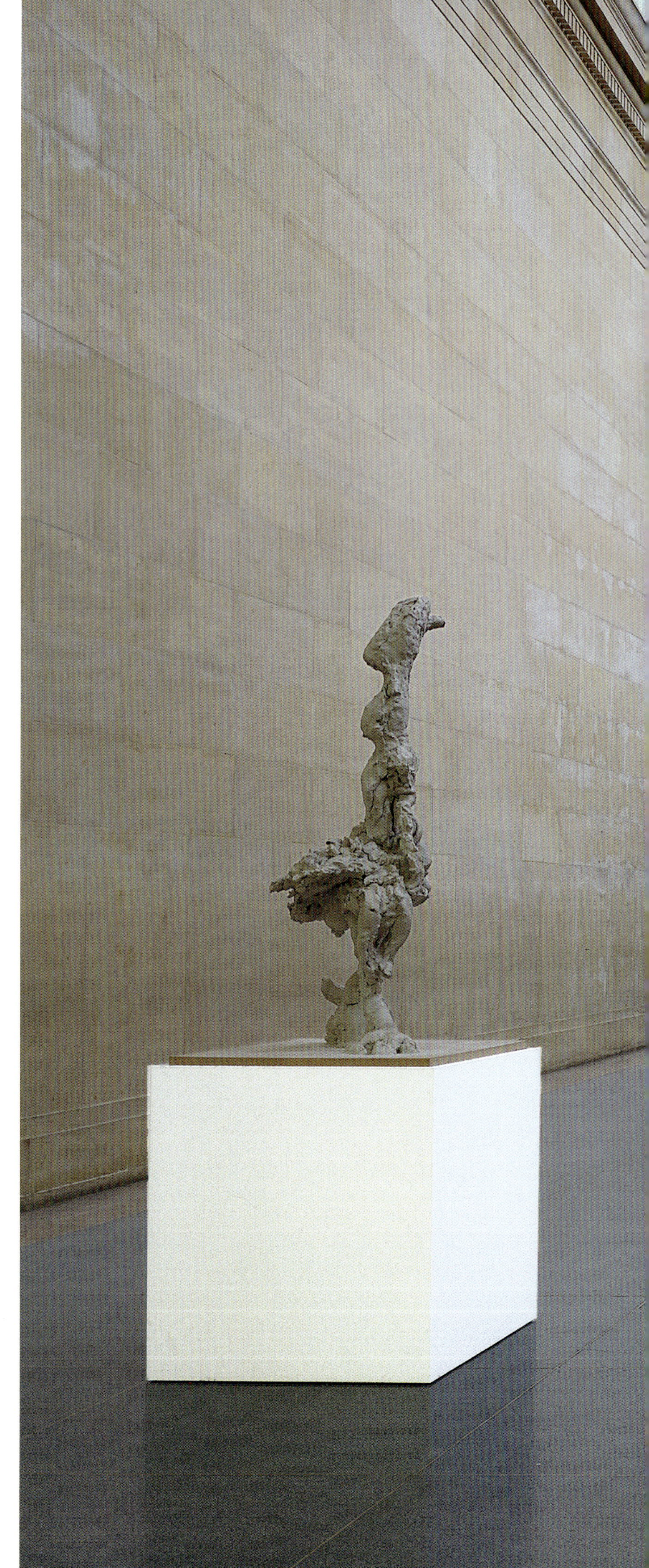

05 from left:
→ *The Hostess*, 2006
Reinforced clay, plinth
250 × 86 × 95 cm
→ *Cube*, 2006
Bronze, MDF, wheels
51 × 35 × 37 cm
→ *Come Helga*, 2006
Reinforced clay, paint,
plinth, Perspex
215 × 61 × 154 cm
→ *Fido*, 2006
Reinforced clay,
wood, plinth, Perspex
198 × 87 × 45 cm
→ *H*, 2006
Reinforced clay, MDF, wheels
180 × 85 × 85 cm

05

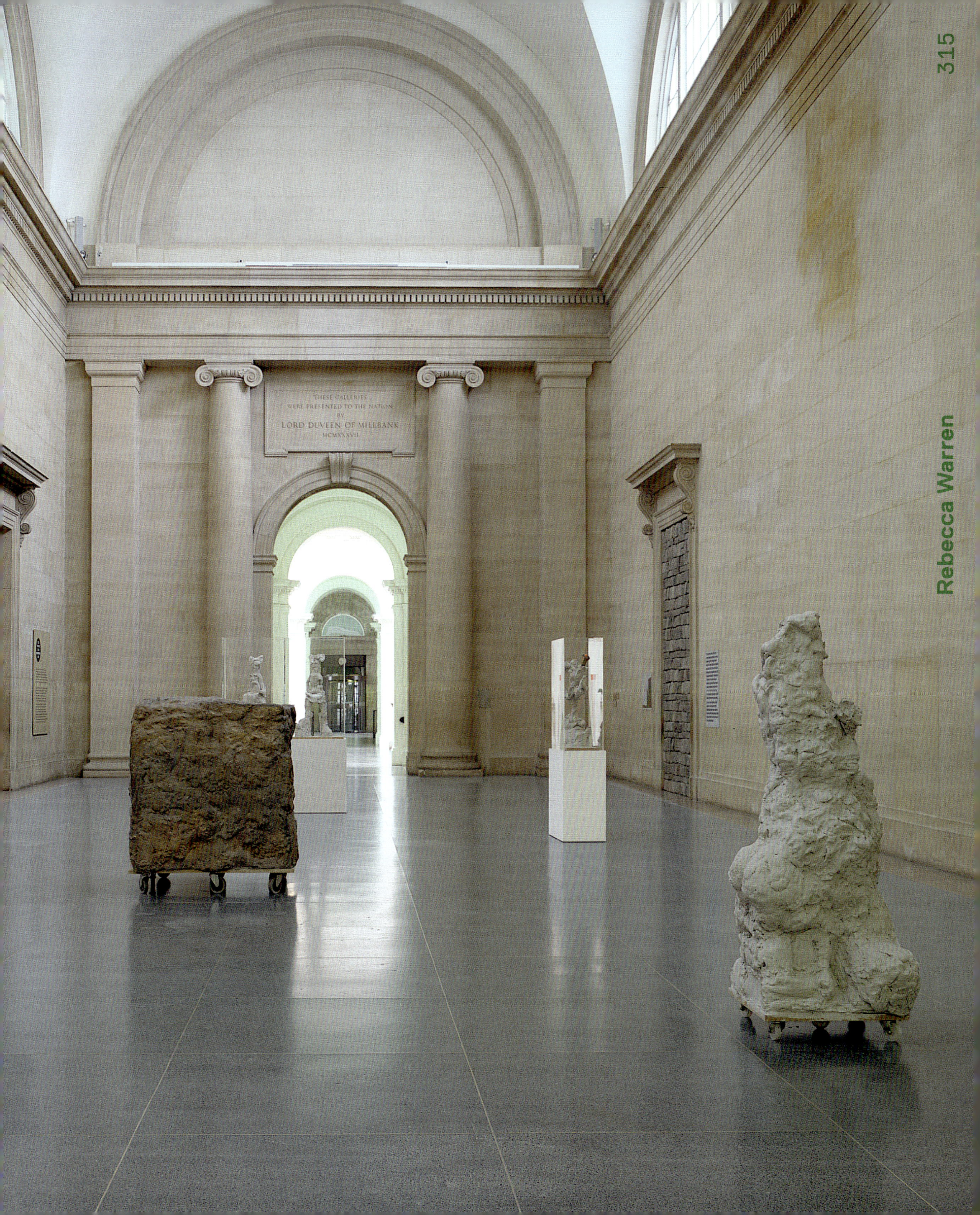
THESE GALLERIES
WERE PRESENTED TO THE NATION
BY
LORD DUVEEN OF MILLBANK
MCMXXXVII

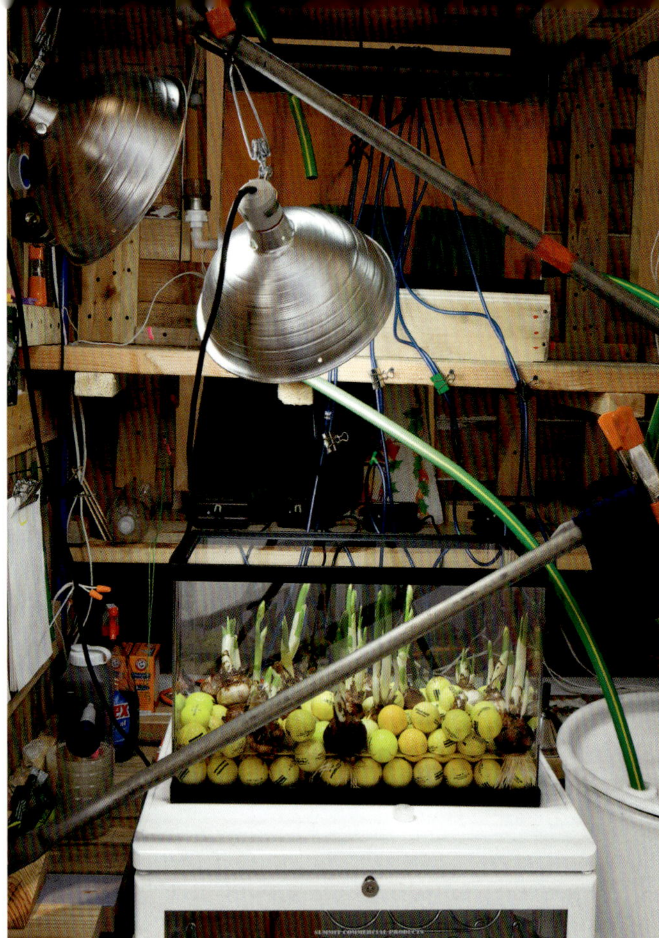

01

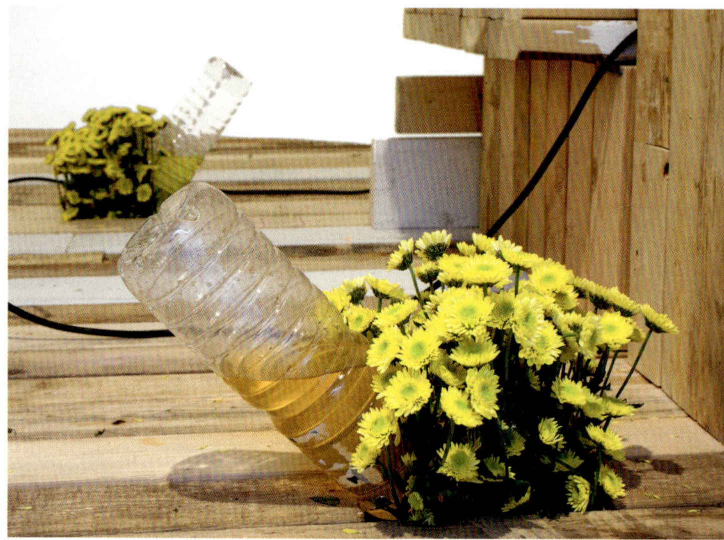

02

01, 02, 03, 04 *While Enhancing a Diminishing Deep Down Thirst, the Juice Broke Loose (the Birth of a Soda Shop)*, 2008
Mixed media
335 × 427 × 601 cm

05 *Tickle the Shitstem*, 2008
Mixed media
Main structure 358 × 696 × 475 cm
Overall dimensions variable

The absurdist systems that have most recently animated Pheobe Washburn's large-scale architectural installations are emblematic of some of the foremost contemporary sculptural concerns: a projected, dispersed composition (and thus practice) that defies a complete understanding of the whole; a constant shifting of viewpoints (overhead to ground, micro to macro); and a tension between immersive, spatio-temporal experience and near-formalist arrangement within a single installation.

A work such as *Regulated Fool's Milk Meadow* (2007) embodies these ideas. A mechanized but seemingly jerry-built grass-growing factory, 'the sculpture is the industry producing its own parts', says the artist. It is thus simultaneously both object and process. A huge structure housing a closed system of conveyor belts, water and grow lamps for producing the sod, the factory was built in Washburn's characteristic style. Found and recycled wood was elegantly shingled into form, accented with colour via other industrial materials (paint, tape, coloured tools, pencils and at other times golf balls), and living, growing terrariums were inserted throughout. As the sod grew, it became the roofing material for the sculpture, dying over the course of the show and thus creating its own cycle of production and waste while also embedding time and history in its actual form.

To borrow a phrase used to describe the sculptural practice of Jason Rhoades — an artist deeply influential on contemporary sculpture — Washburn's recent work tends to incorporate within itself 'the anticipation and preparation of a form, the form itself, and the interaction with the form'. Both a sculptural installation and a functional site, Washburn's installation for the 2008 Whitney Biennial *While Enhancing a Diminishing Deep Down Thirst, the Juice Broke Loose (the Birth of a Soda Shop)* (2008) continues in what Washburn has termed her 'anti-industrious' vein, referring to the irrationality of the 'clumsy, labored events' produced. Assembled on site and designed to interact specifically with its location in the museum (directly in front of an enormous Marcel Breuer trapezoidal window, thus enhancing the inside/outside, public/private dialogue typical of her work), Washburn's machine performs a simple task in an indirect, convoluted manner. Gatorade is prepared in the 'workroom' and used to grow flowers, which are then employed to adorn the exterior of the stepped sculpture. The sugar content in the liquid accelerates both the growth and flowering of the paperwhites, as well as their death — an 'organism' as she calls the work, mocking capitalist ideas of speed and efficiency mitigated by the formal balance of the overall composition she creates.

In Tickle the Shitstem (2008) Washburn has developed a functional environment that spreads throughout all the rooms of the gallery in which it is displayed. As before, the system generates its own products — including beverages, pencils, coloured sea urchins and T-shirts — which are then sold to viewers as they navigate the unruly, complex sculptural masses. As viewers wend their way around the hulking central souvenir shop and into the smaller back rooms, they trace the cycle of the factory itself, following its products backwards along their lifeline to the original materials being constantly refined and recycled anew. Like the other works, the installation unfolds in time — that of the exhibition but ever more so that of the viewer's experience as well —creating a peformative space that implicates us in the artist's exuberantly faux-industrious exploration of process and decay. [Shamim M. Momin]

Overleaf:

06 *Tickle the Shitstem*, 2008
Mixed media
Overall dimensions variable
Main structure
358 × 696 × 475 cm

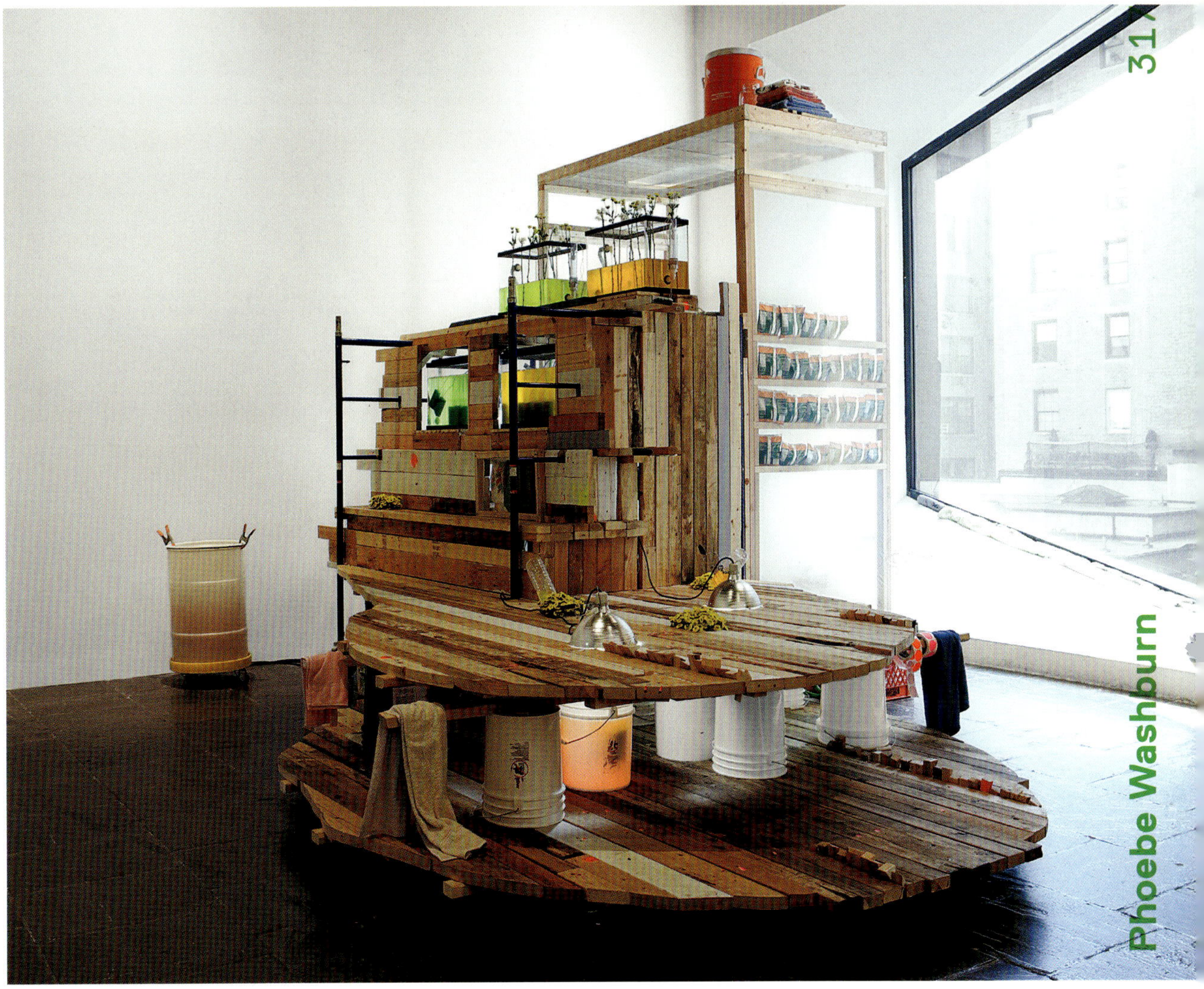

03

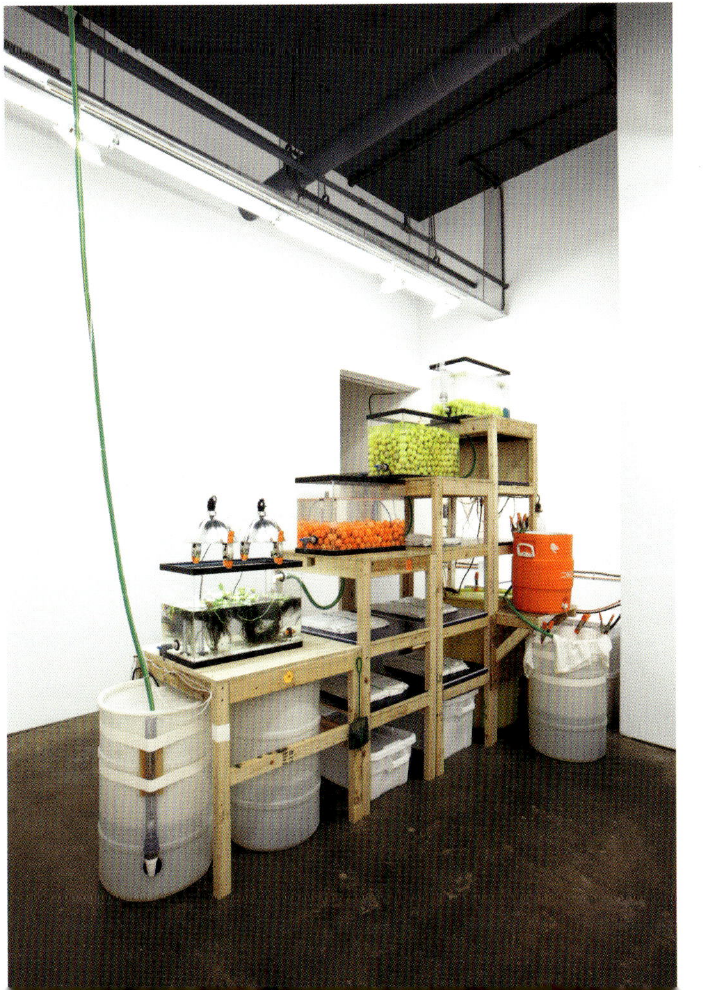

04

05

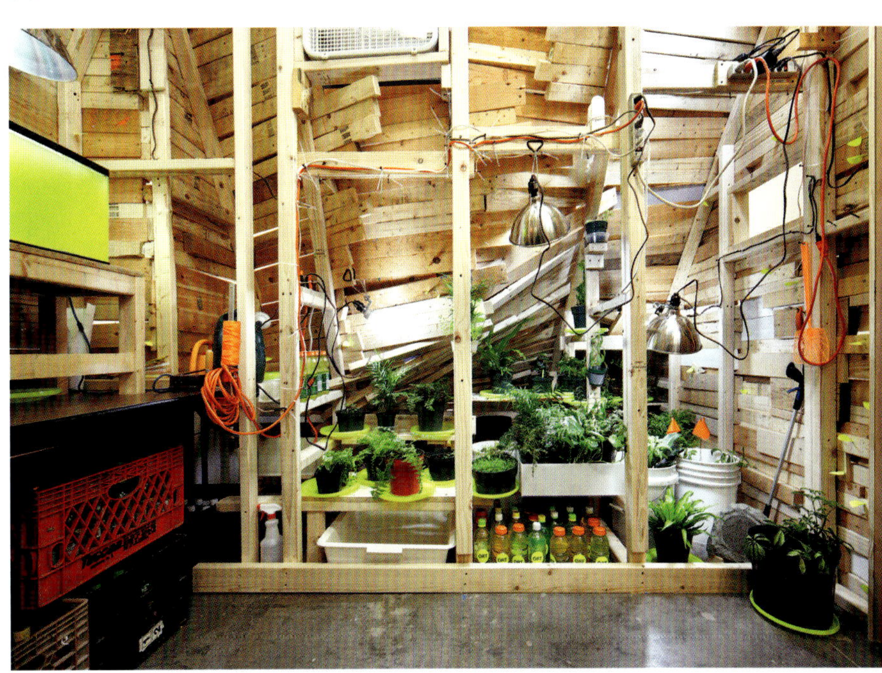

Phoebe Washburn

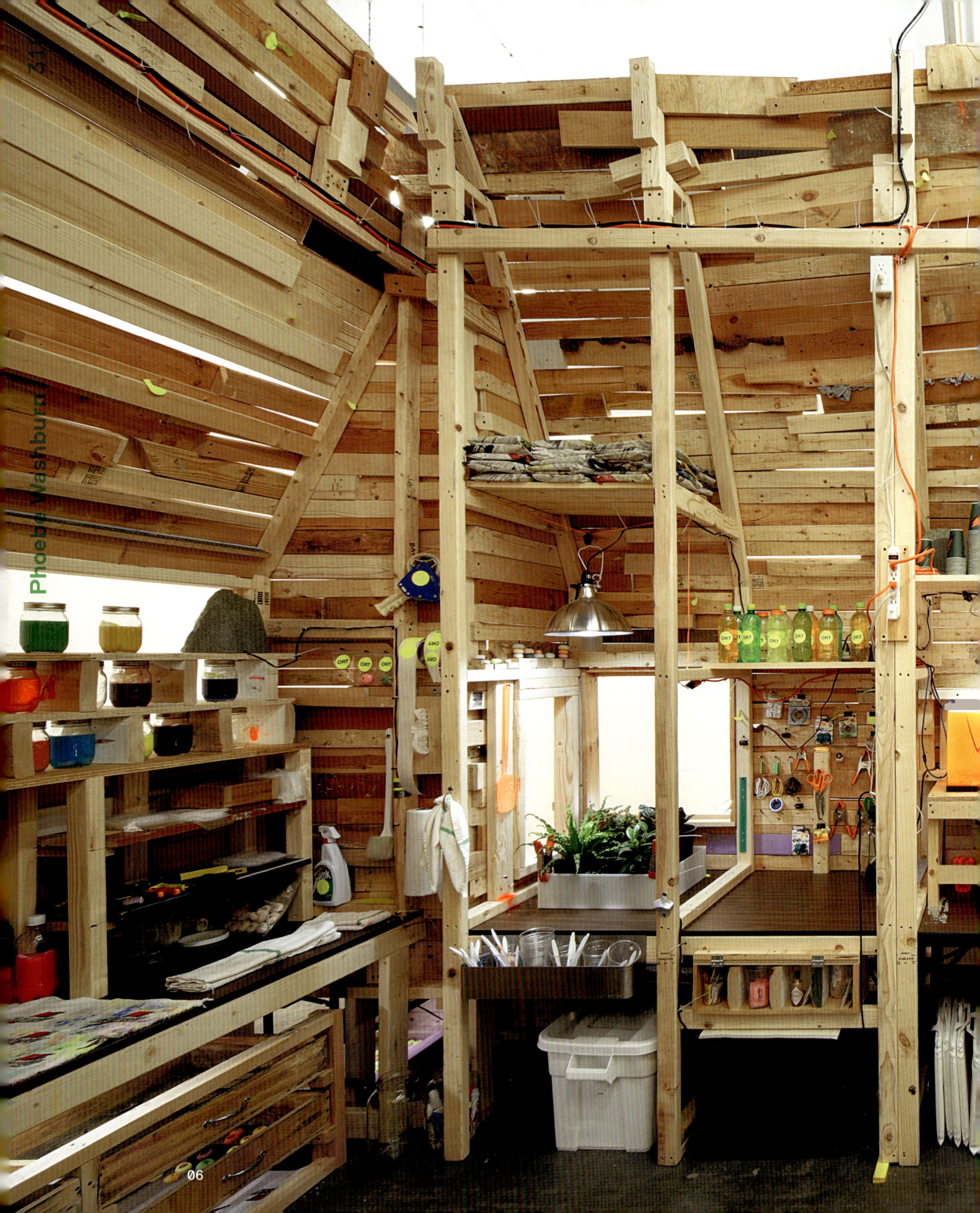

06

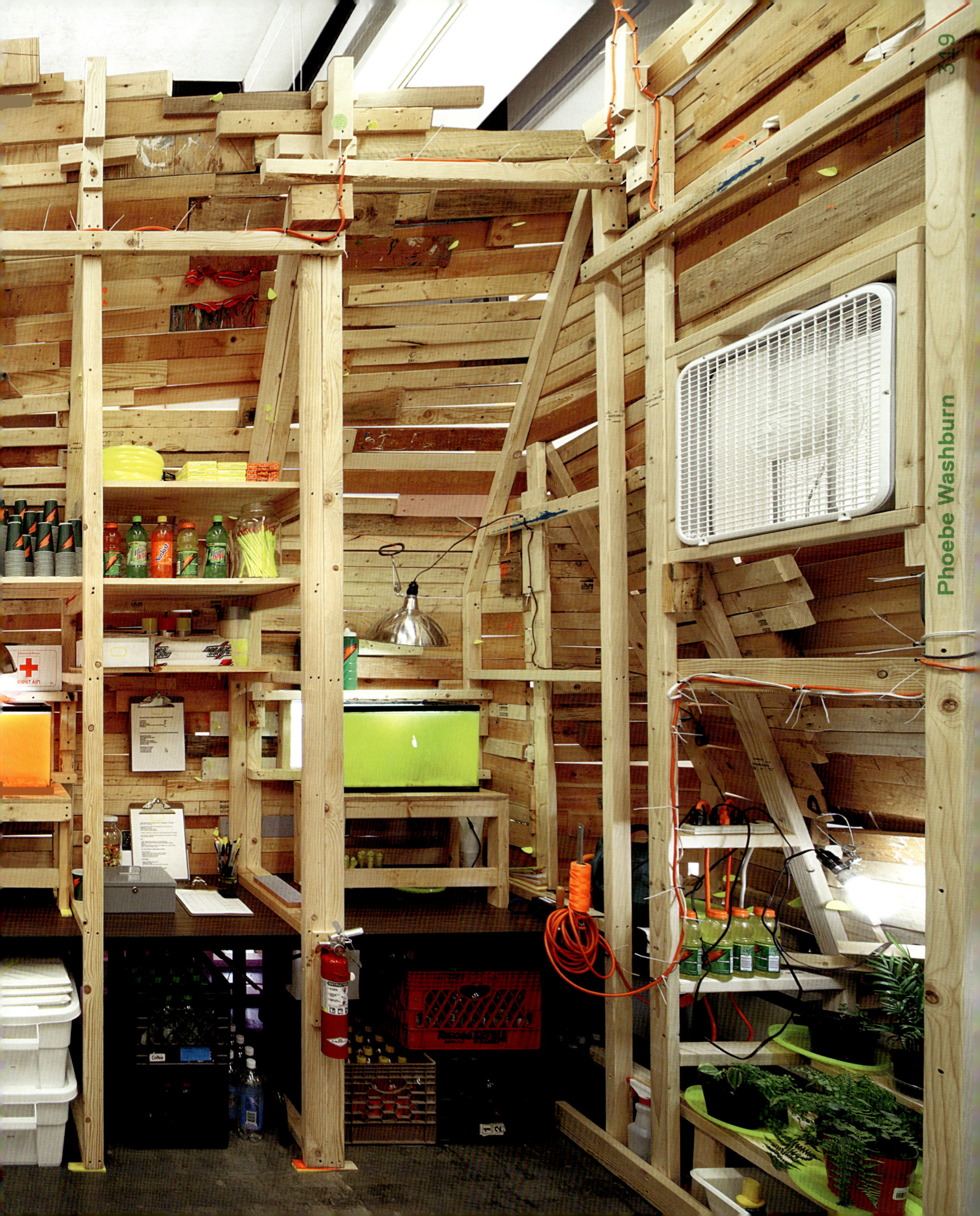

You could expend acres of text on describing one of Gary Webb's sculptures, but it would be a joyless task. His conglomerations of form, texture and colour are evocative and sensual, pulling together to suggest something elusive yet associatively rich. Reducing them to a description of shape and position would destroy the intangible connections that form as you walk around a piece, and deaden the soulful process of pinpointing likenesses: the horseyness of *The Creator Has a Master Plan* (2004), for instance, or the hint of snouted creatures in conversation over a perfume counter in *Paranoid Mountain* (2001).

Reaching an associational essence by boiling off excess details is a prime methodology of twentieth-century abstraction; Webb's approach to these essences is so additive it is almost baroque. While each piece appears to retain the autonomy of mid-twentieth-century British sculpture by the likes of Anthony Caro and Phillip King, the accumulation of parts that constitutes the whole is in an unstable state, its associative make-up threatening to unravel or cancel itself out. Webb is not seeking essence either as a metaphysical proposition or a formal interlude, but collecting and piling up material moments from the quotidian world for the joy of it.

02

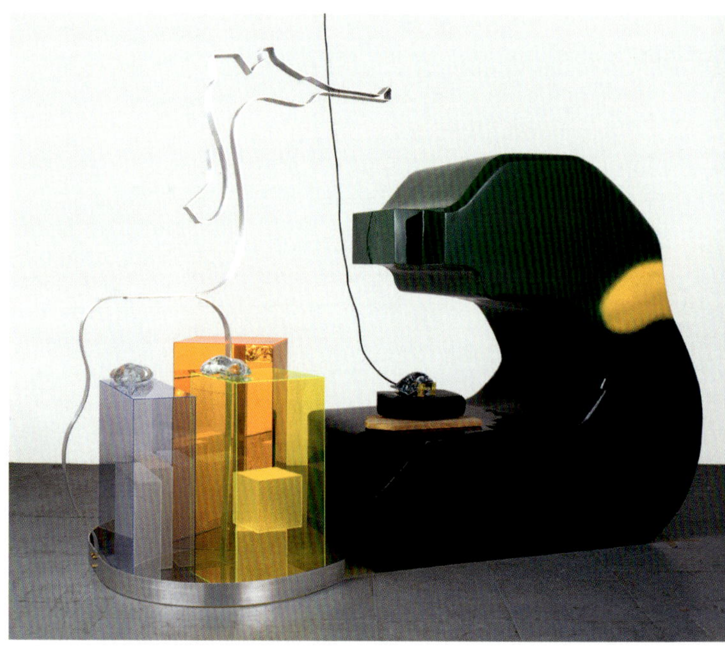

01

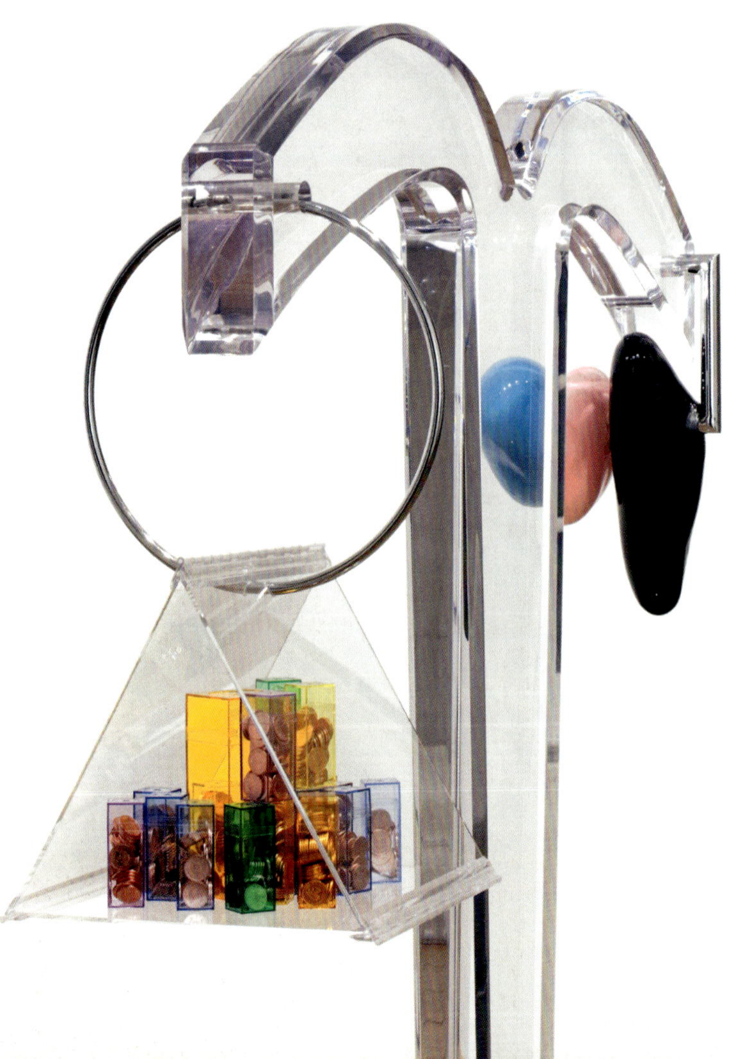

The overt use of currency and baubles in *The Penny One* (2008), while lending a pendulous organic quality to what looks like an overwrought desk novelty, refers wryly back to the sculpture's value as art an object. Indeed, an element of consumerist critique creeps throughout Webb's practice with its industrial and commercial references, although this is perhaps a condition of our times, rather than a strategic intention of the artist. His shiny surfaces and sensual curves speak the language of the desirable object, while their component-like structures seem to be designed for mass manufacturing. The possibility of their reproducibility is implied, so that their uniqueness as one-offs seems even more valuable.

Despite frequent comparisons between his work and modernist sculpture, Webb is not an art-historically reflexive artist. His references are wholly contemporary, capricious and appropriational rather than eulogistic. The incorporation of audio into some works, such as human beatbox sounds in *Paranoid Mountain*, shatters any illusion of the sculpture's reverence towards its forebears, since its single purpose is to declare itself, like a siren on the rocks or a flashy handbag on a shelf. It is as though Webb hijacks modernism to give credibility to his evocations of shopping, consumerist desire and the faint whiff of disappointment masked by shininess, musak and other techniques of distraction. [Sally O'Reilly]

01 *Libra Dos*, 2006
Perspex, chrome, coins, coloured glass, plastic
165 × 132 × 46 cm

02 *Paranoid Mountain*, 2001
Steel, Perspex, glass, sprayed Q-cell, wood
350 × 250 × 300 cm

03 *The Penny One*, 2008
Powder coated steel, chromed aluminium, bronze
176 × 181 × 61 cm

Overleaf:

04 *Double Bubble*, 2008
Sprayed aluminium, polished bronze, plastic
200 × 140 × 60 cm

05 *Revolution Oil*, 2008
Powder-coated aluminium, resin
170 × 134 × 60 cm

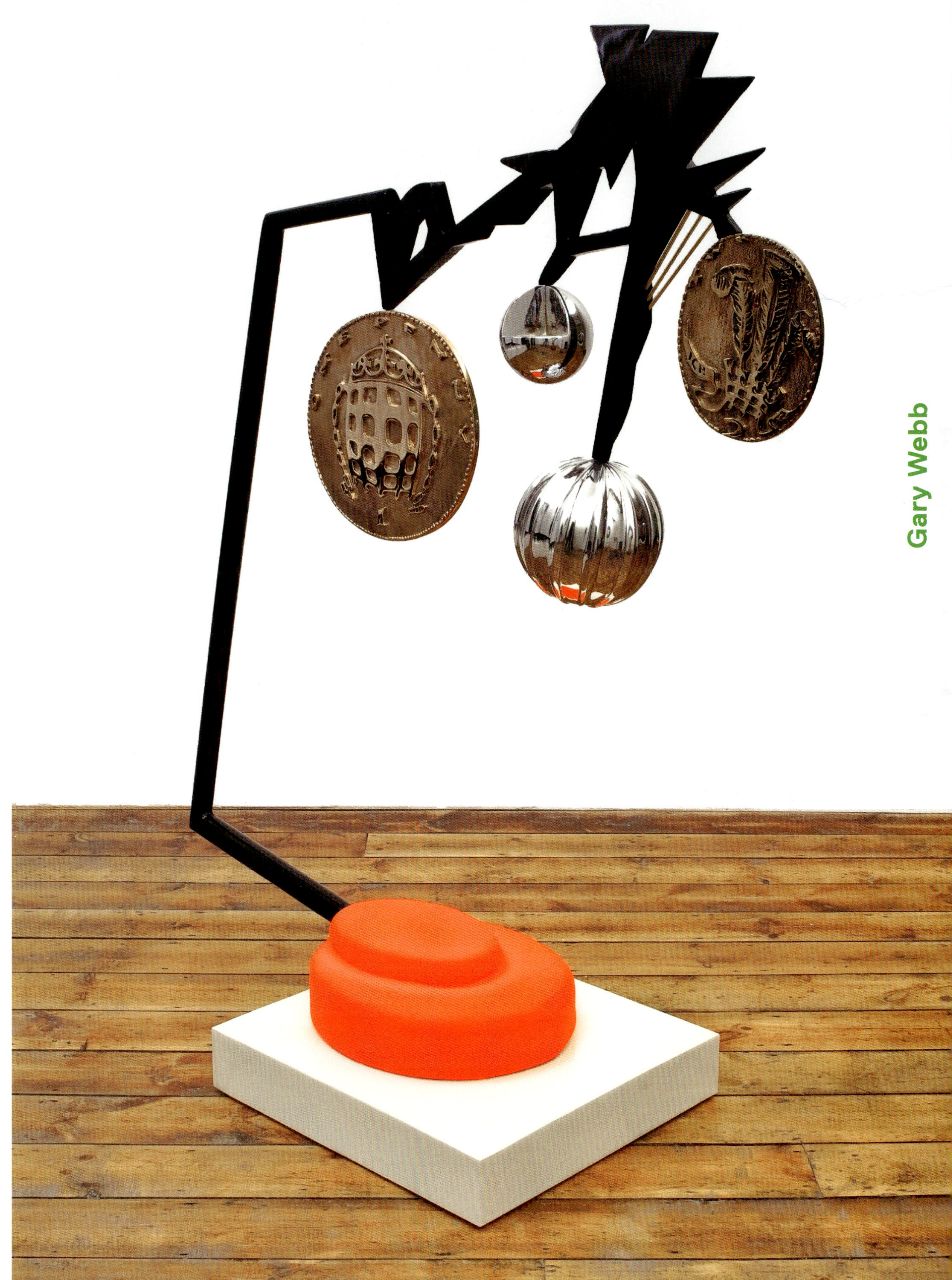

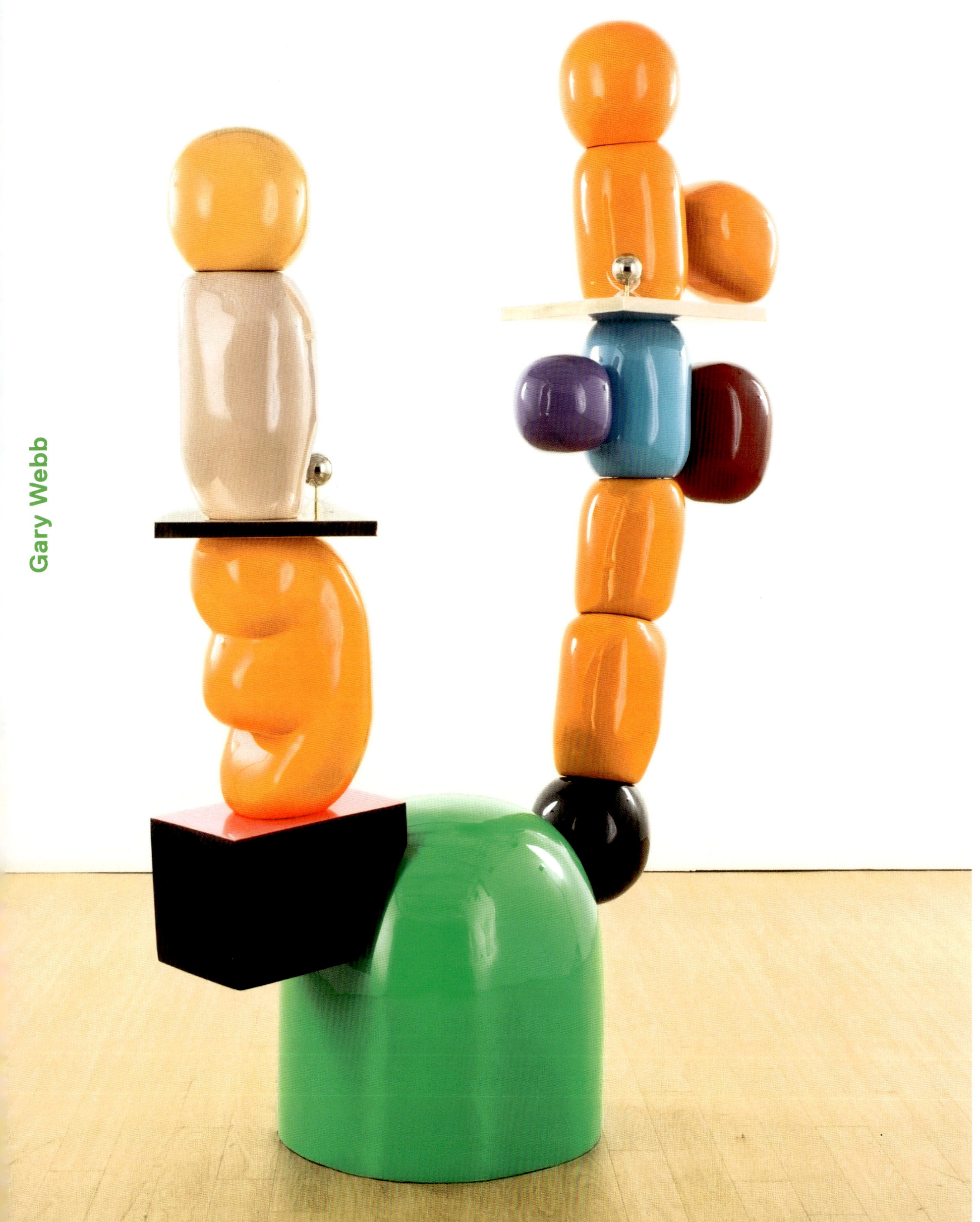

04

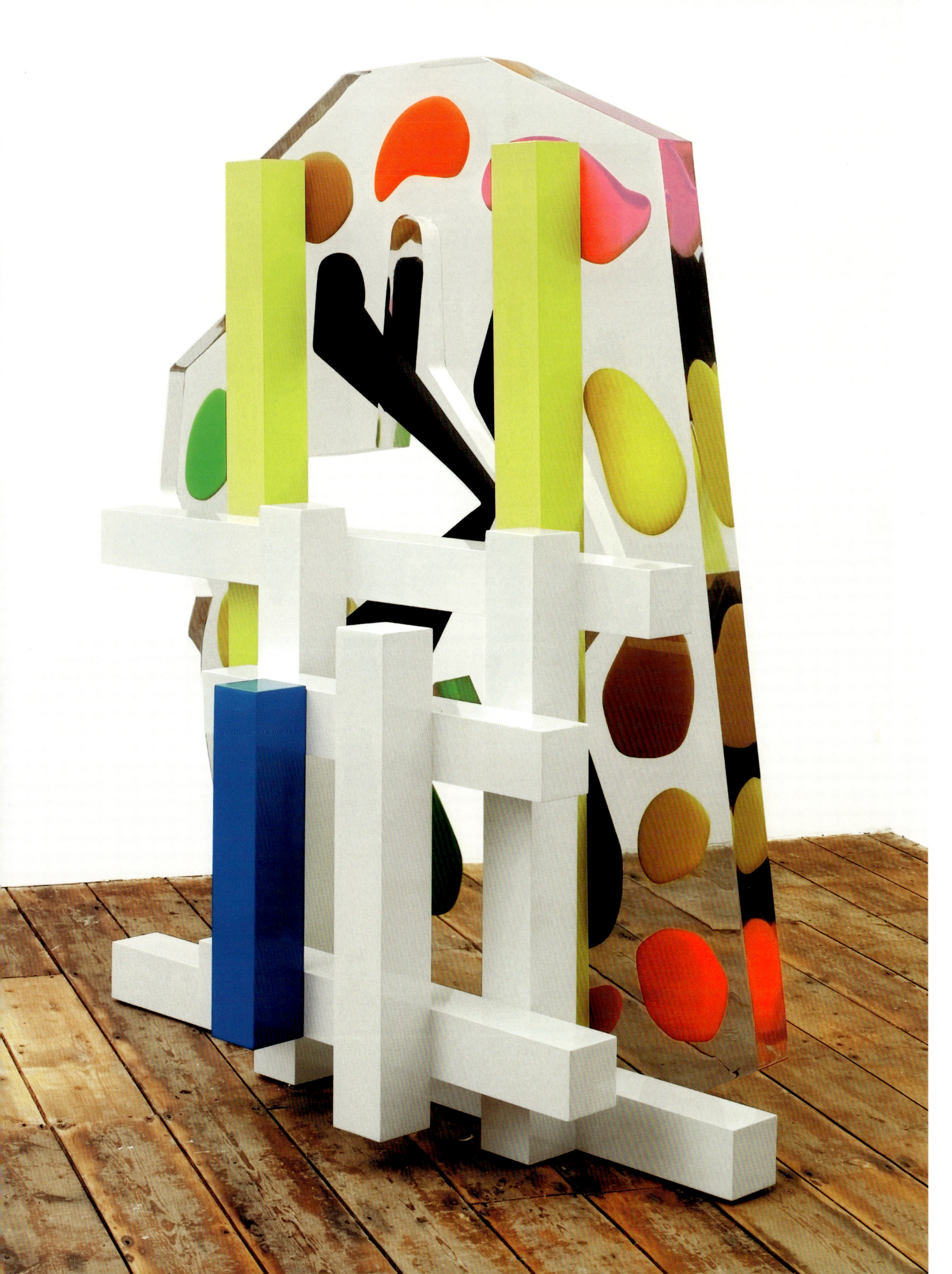

05

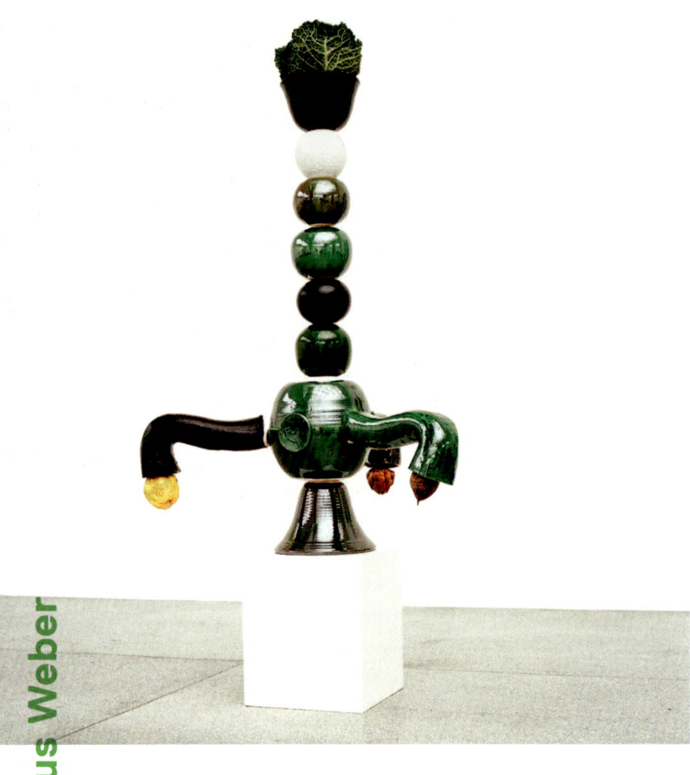

01

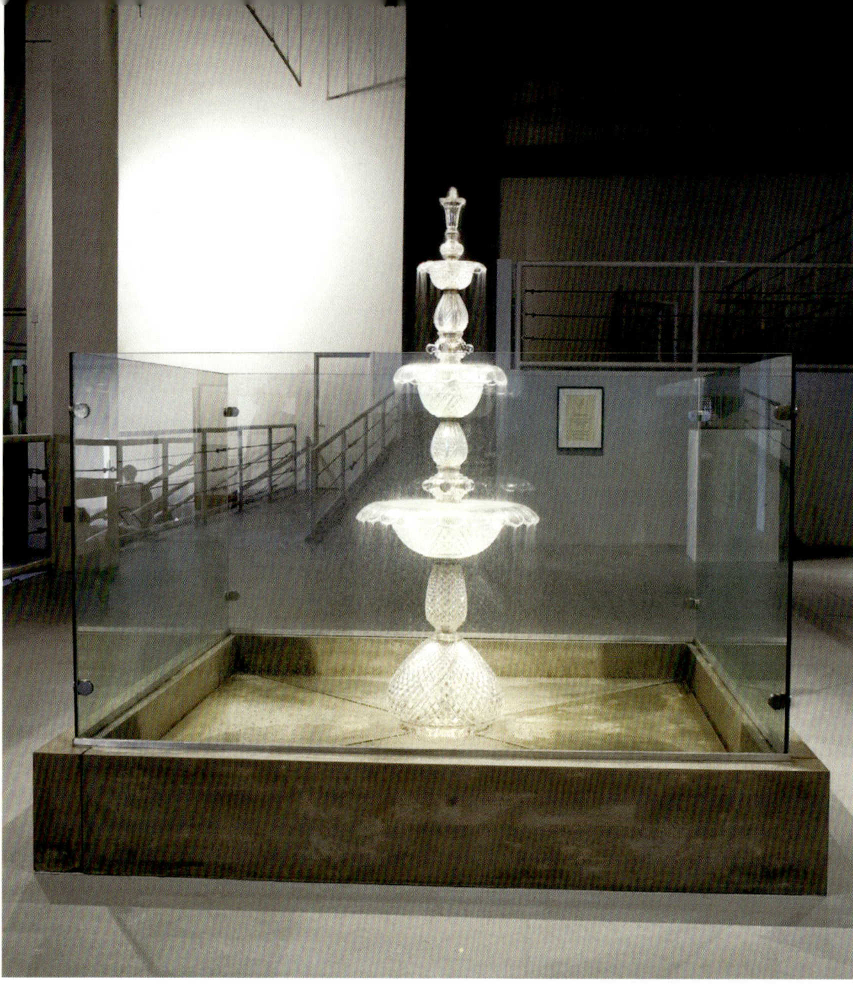

02

A three-tiered neo-Victorian crystal fountain, from which a tinkling cascade of water falls, is a good preparation for Klaus Weber's works. Its classically attractive form is easy to assimilate within a range of aesthetic, civic and cultural perspectives. But its innocuously pleasant appearance is undermined by the fact that the liquid in this *LSD Fountain* (2003) is, as its title suggests, potentized lysergic acid.

The potential for transformation — both psychic and civic — that this sculpture implies, is a central aspect of Weber's work, which twists social or institutional conventions by introducing foreign, unpredictable forces into otherwise familiar forms. Often natural elements, such as wind, water, plants or insects, these forces have a destabilizing effect that accesses an alternative, imaginary space of unconstrained possibility which is at once liberating and threatening. In an early piece entitled *Brutstube* (2002), for instance, Weber sowed the spores of a particularly aggressive species of mushroom beneath a swath of freshly applied tarmac in central Berlin, where he lives. As the mushrooms grew, they pushed up through the pavement, rupturing the smooth urban surface with their bulbous white forms. Germinating ferociously, they spread and expanded to grotesque proportions. The utopian idea of nature biting back at its urban oppressors quickly gave way to a nightmare of uncontrollable fecundity.

Through minor interventions, Weber seeks to re-establish links between the artificial and the natural where they have long been ignored. In an exhibition at the Secession in Vienna, the hermeticism of the stark white gallery space was punctured by a number of works suspended from gaps in the gallery's glass-tiled suspended ceiling. Fluffy jungle vines hung down like giant feather boas to form living (and ever growing) partition screens (*Tilandsienwaende*, 2008). The drooping arms and extended necks of a pair of comically anthropomorphic ceramic sculptures, each entitled *Eve* (both 2008), sprouted vegetables instead of a head and hands, as though they were harvest deities. A small octagonal object of angled mirrors (*Sonnenorgel*, 2008) received a beam of light channeled from a heliostat on the museum's roof. This in turn was sent by way of the mirrors towards the separate exhibited works, providing each with a natural sun-spotlight, linking them all together while connecting them physically with the natural world at large.

Weber's work, however, does not present the artificial and the natural, or the institutional and the individual, as simply dichotomous. Rather it suggests a fresh approach to reality, by seeing instability, rupture or turbulence as productive forces, and by engaging the dull architecture of the institutional or societal in unpredictable and playful ways. It aims to carve a liberated personal micro-climate from within an oppressively controlling cultural climate. This is not always a case of rose-tinted spectacles, however, as *rainisacageyoucanwalkthrough* (2008) demonstrates. In this car with a sprinkler system fixed to its roof you always see the world through a rainy windscreen, whatever the weather outside. [Kirsty Bell]

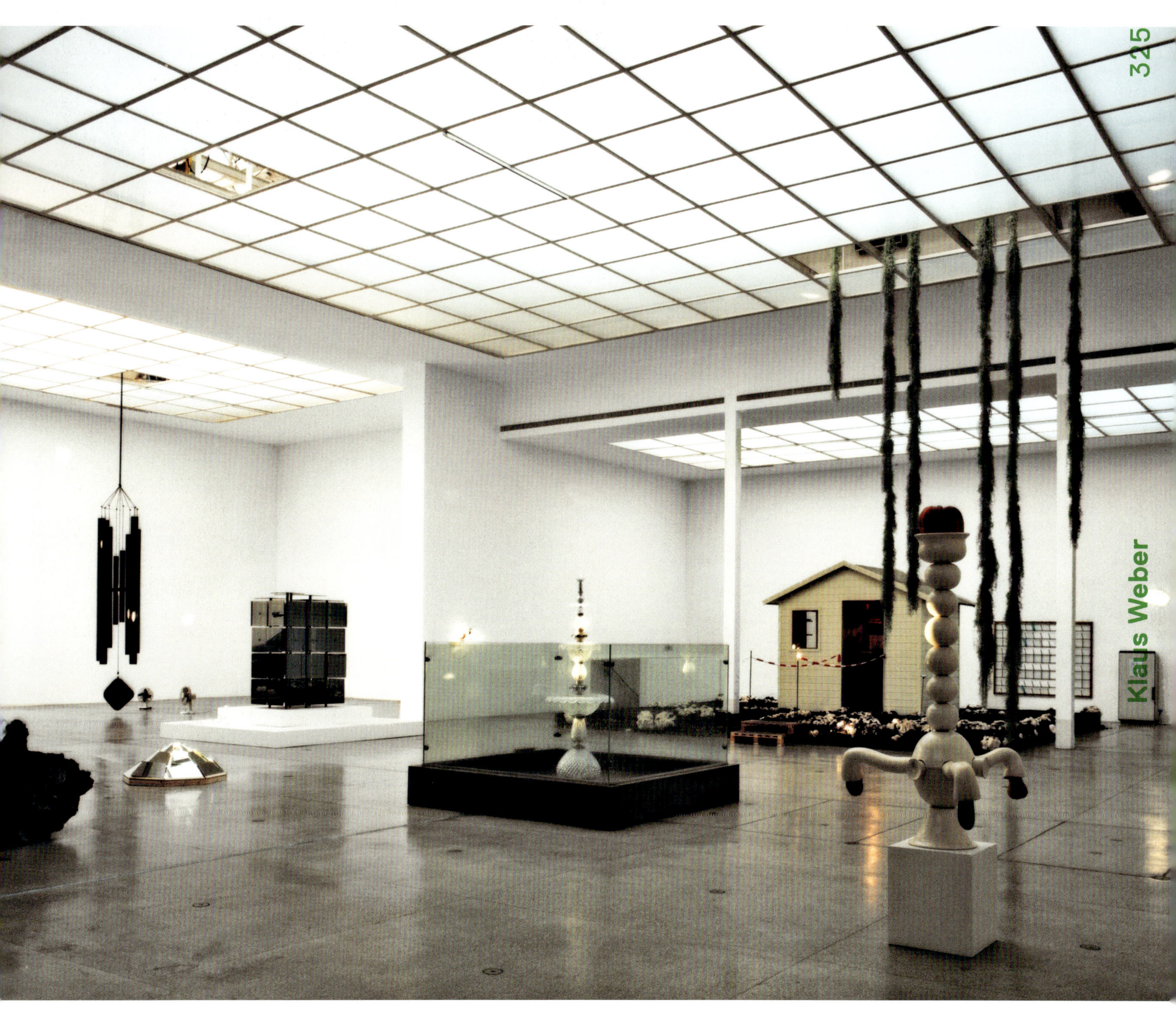

03

01 *EvE (Colour)*, 2008
Ceramics, fruit, vegetables
90 × 90 × 130 cm

02 *LSD Fountain*, 2003
Victorian lead crystal glass, concrete, toughened glass, metal, potentized LSD
210 × 210 × 180 cm

03 from left:
→ *Untitled (BECKENSTEIN)*, 2008
Scoria, ceramic washbasin
100 × 153 × 90 cm
→ *Large Dark Wind Chime*, 2008
Powder-coated aluminium, stainless steel, high polymer plastic, ventilators
428 × 150 × 150 cm
→ *Sonnenorgel*, 2008
Heliostat, mirror, wood
Dimensions variable
→ *Breeder*, 2007
Steel, mirrored spy glass, butterfly pupae, butterflies
106 × 177 × 144 cm
→ *LSD Fountain*, 2003
Victorian lead crystal glass, concrete, toughened glass, metal, potentized LSD
210 × 210 × 180 cm
→ *Unfolding Cul-de-Sac*, 2002–08
Asphalt, compost, mushroom spawn, garden hut
Dimensions variable
Hut 106 × 177 × 144 cm
→ *EvE (Colour)*, 2008
Ceramics, fruit, vegetables
90 × 90 × 130 cm

Writing in 1960 of the diminishing returns of an irrelevant avant-garde, Guy Debord decried the 'practical reduction of [an artist's] realm of real action to zero'. Against this farcical 'decay in art', he argued that true modern art must be 'the revolutionary claim to other professions'. Debord's idea has become commonplace in the art of the twenty-first century, with restless artists moving parasitically or collaboratively into other still bounded areas of knowledge, including anthropology, natural sciences, literature, academic research, information management, design and so on.

Nowhere has this claim been so dramatized — and ironized — as in the work of Eric Wesley, for whom it is imagined as a drive towards rogue expertise in a range of disciplines. Pursuing the activities of the set designer, manager, manufacturer, entrepreneur, social worker and professor, his productions are often the artefacts of an autodidactic and hard-won acquisition of skill. This practice presents, in his words, 'a social encoding [...] which remains an encoding', even as it acts as 'a vehicle for the real'.

Such encoding is particularly absurdly over-determined in the world of commodity exchange. Wesley uses a version of sculpture, through the irreverent lens of Pop art, to work over both the signs and objects of this world. Take, for example, his *Remix [Stage Coach]* (2008), a bronze sculpture, in the style of Frederick Remington, of the famous logo of Wells Fargo Bank. A prescient riff on capitalism's fatal attraction to destabilization and liquidity, as well as the stagecoach's role in conquering the American West, the work presents its coach upended, apocalyptically disordered — a negation of the values for which the mascot elliptically stands.

Frit Display (2007) is both a prank — gold jewellery in the form of French fries and onion rings, cheap food elevated to symbols of status — and a meditation on the primitive basis of exchange value: a sort of binary code of deep-fried ones and zeros. Proceeds for the fried jewellery go to ending slave labour in Africa — a way of both mapping out and commenting on what Wesley calls the 'haphazard symbiotic relationship' between the production of reified objects for consumption and display, and real-world causes and struggles.

Real space is a second line of attack, and guerrilla architecture another position that Wesley inhabits. Producing or befouling built spaces with a negative verve, he makes visible the way in which architectural form structures social relationships. For one untitled project, made in 1994, he built, transformed and destroyed a crude six-foot cinderblock cube on the campus of the University of California, Los Angeles, where he was a student. The structure was connected formally to the dumpsters, sheds and power generators that subsist beneath the ideal order of the campus landscape. In contrast to the edifying public nature of the university, it was an outpost of privacy and muddy dis-enlightenment: an industrial-primitive edifice where the artist could learn physics on his own terms.

Located on the campus of Caltech, in Pasadena, *Two Story Clocktower* (2000) was a 'frontier' monument — a common symbol of civilized mastery over land, nature and time — with a subterranean clubhouse and miniature casino in its foundation. Simply constructed, the work was metaphorically rich. Above ground was a technocratic universe of controlled time and civic myth, subtended by a basement where time disappeared. The structure also worked as a sniper platform, with targets suspended in the surrounding trees. By invoking campus shooting rampages, Wesley upended the deceptive symbolism of such structures, even as he made space for disruptive play. [Julian Myers]

01

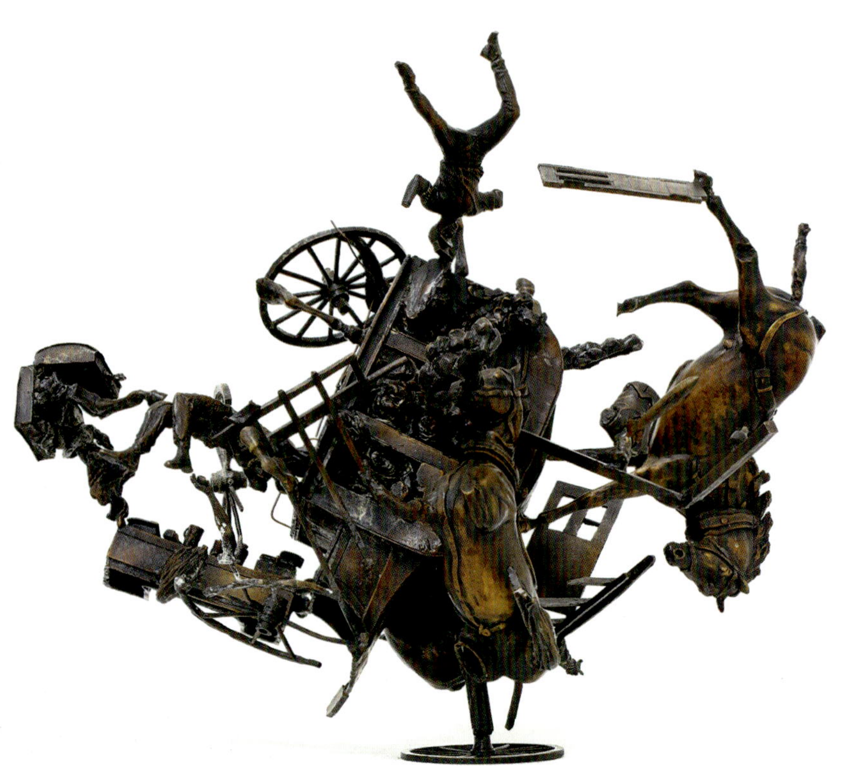

01 *Remix (Stage Coach)*, 2008
Cast bronze
46 × 46 × 40 cm

02 *Audi*, 2004
Wood, metal, motors
25 × 305 × 305 cm

03 *Onion Ring*, 2008
from the series *Frit Display*
Gold plated
Britannia metal
3.2 × 1.3 × 1.3 cm

04 *Two Story Clocktower*, 2003
Wood, building materials
244 × 244 × 610 cm

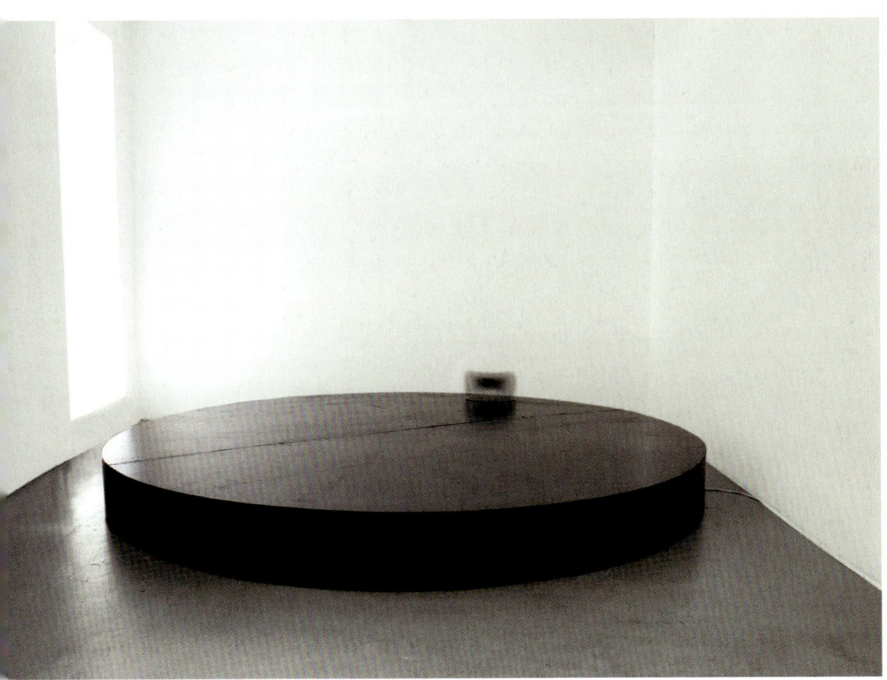

02

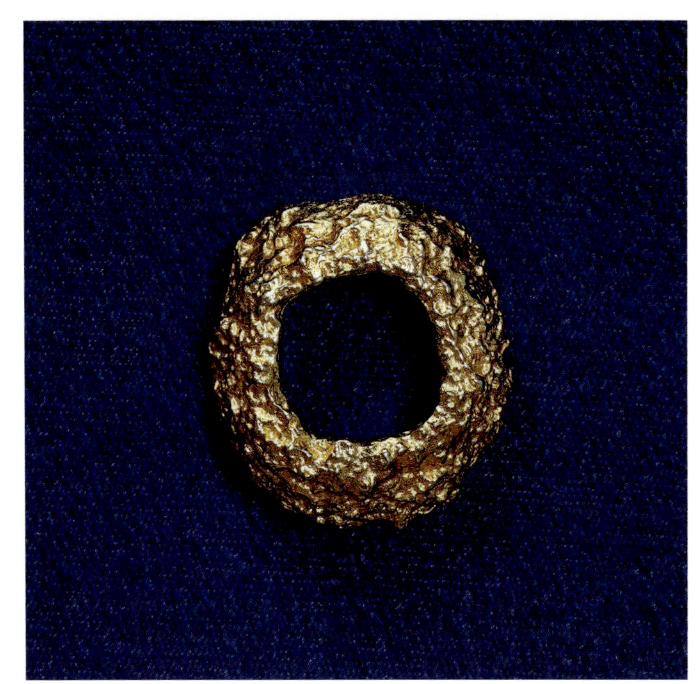

03

04

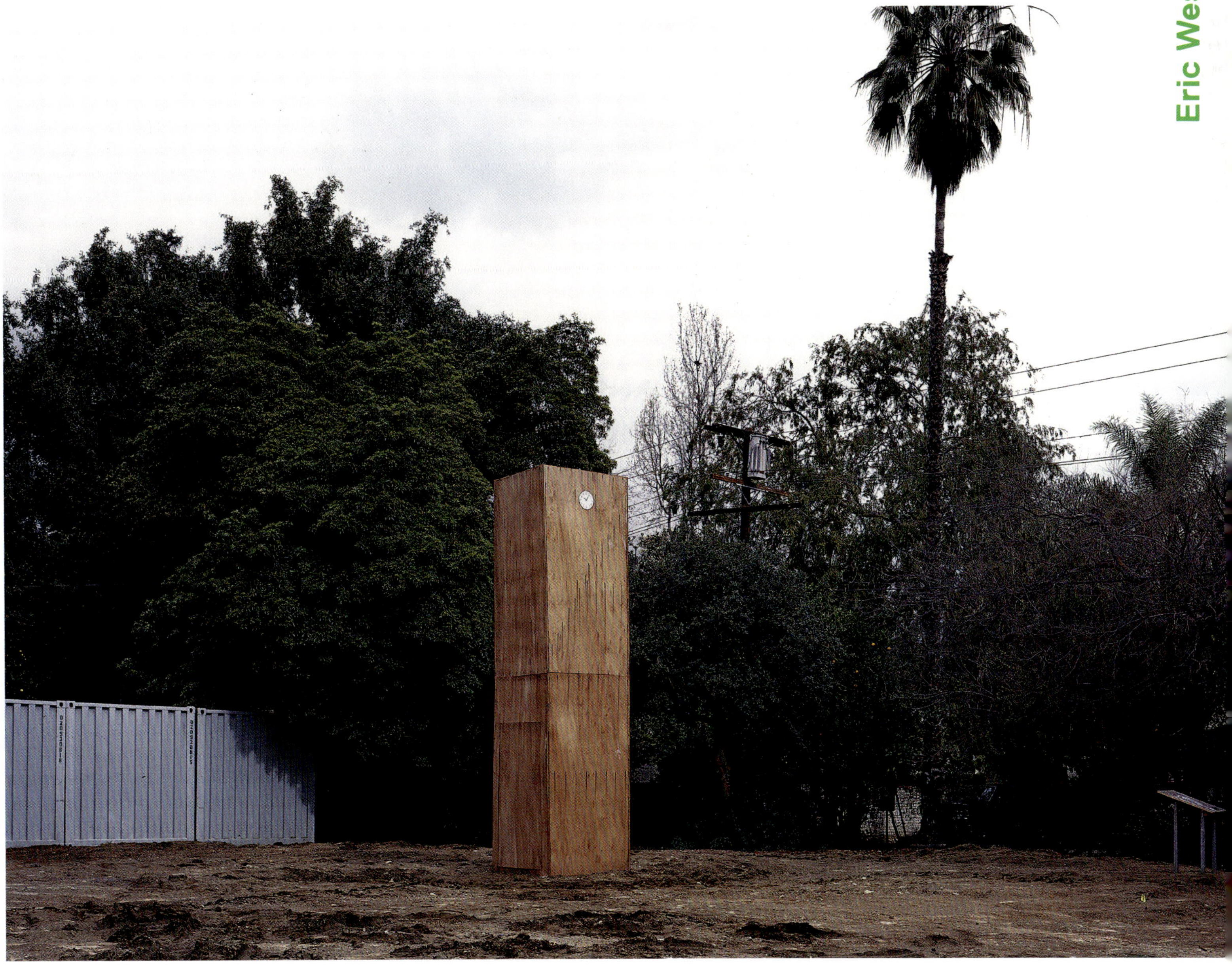

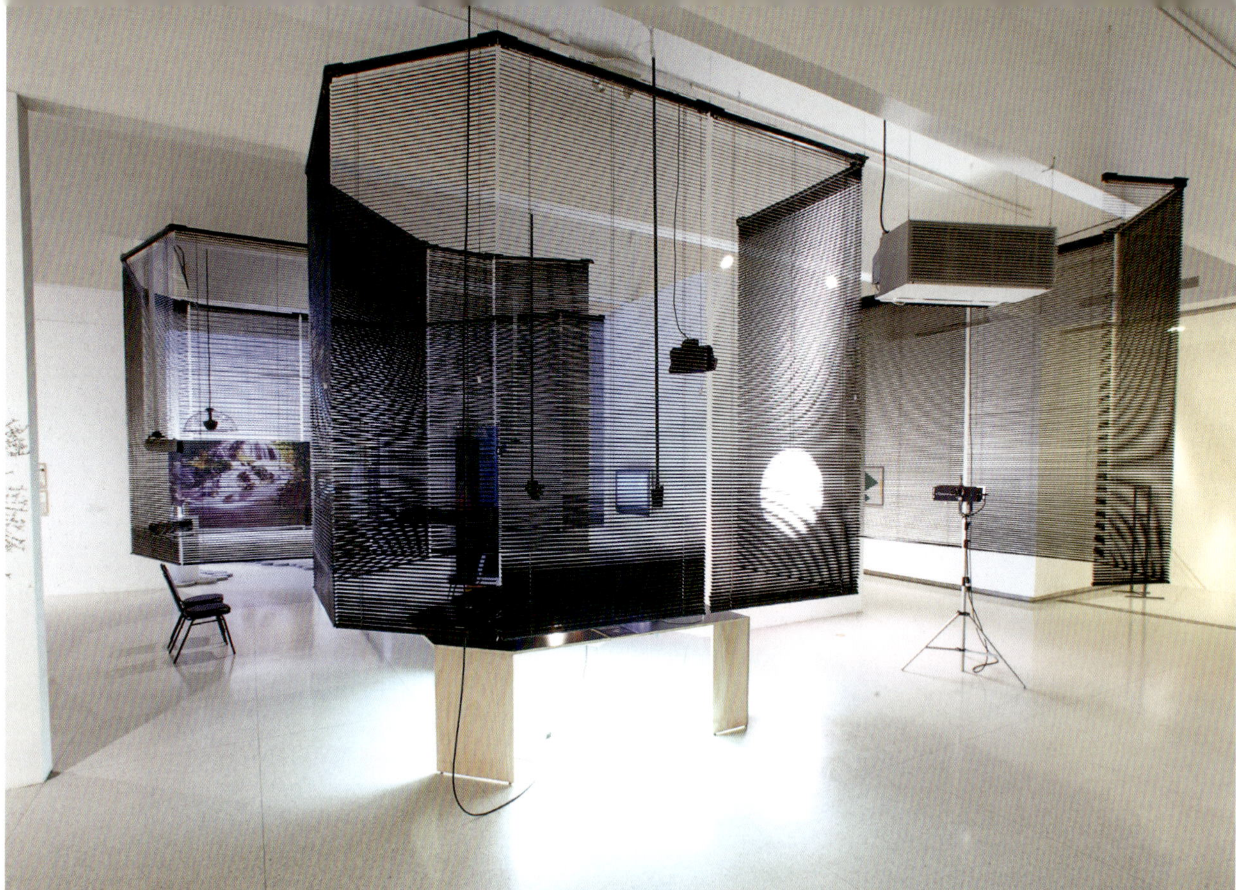

01

In Maurice Blanchot's *Unavowable Community* he locates 'community' not in what a group has in common but in the distance that separates its individual members, the dissymmetrical experience of the other that allows for 'unknown spaces for freedom' to exist in the moment of coming apart. This sense of community is something that Haegue Yang has been thinking through in her installations of everyday, functional objects, which articulate a consciousness of the tensions that arise between the individual and the social, fostering the idea of Blanchot's 'community of absence'.

For her *Series of Vulnerable Arrangements* (2006) Yang gathered an incongruous group of modified electrical devices. Heaters, fog machines, spotlights and scent dispensers, each triggered by the movements of visitors, released bouts of glowing warmth, feint wafts of vapour and breeze that displaced familiar sensations. With no clear functional relation to one another, they stood as an oddly animated group, connected by a sprawling system of wires that held them in a sustained struggle between autonomy and dependency. In contrast, the video works *Unfolding Places* (2004) and *Restrained Courage* (2004), made over the course of her travels through various cities, tell melancholic, self-reflexive accounts of the sense of disjointedness that results when mobility prevents one from being part of a community in the conventional sense.

These dichotomies of independence and connectedness resonated strongly in Yang's first solo exhibition in Korea, 'Sadong 30' (2006). She forwent the safe confines of an art institution in favour of staging her work in a derelict traditional house in Incheon (a satellite city of Seoul) that had once belonged to a member of her family. Besides a series of carefully placed objects — electrical devices, coloured origami, an oscillating fan, a covered clothes drying rack and strands of lights — the main intervention to the house was the reconnection of its power supply. Thus while set apart it again became connected to a social network.

Over the course of 2008 Yang realized a series of works in different exhibitions that were memorials to individuals who have stood for particular social or political concerns, including the novelist Marguerite Duras and the Korean freedom-fighter Kim San. Each installation was comprised of Venetian blinds, theatre lights and mirrors. *Lethal Love* (2008) was inspired by the activist founder of the German Green Party, Petra Kelly, who was shot dead in her sleep by her lover. Here blinds were suspended before a large mirror, filtering a roving theatrical spotlight, shifting between transparency and reflectivity, preventing a fixed view. As curator Bart van der Heide wrote in the accompanying statement, 'instead of communicating a social, cultural or political position, the installations seem to hide one,' perhaps collectively creating Blanchot's 'community of absence.' Embodying many of the dialectical relationships that consistently surface within Yang's work — between positive and negative space, individual and social behaviour, acts of speech and silence, autonomy and dependency, isolation and engagement — they embed a social and political consciousness within a highly subjective, abstract, aesthetic language. [Emily Pethick]

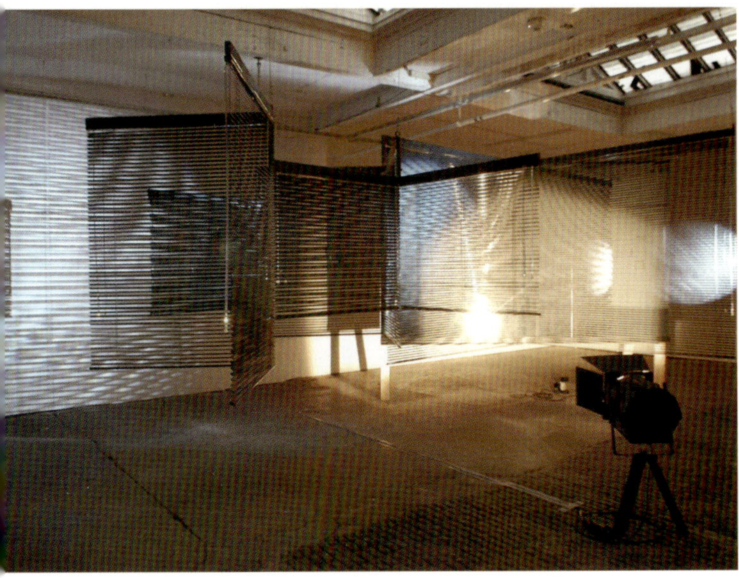

02

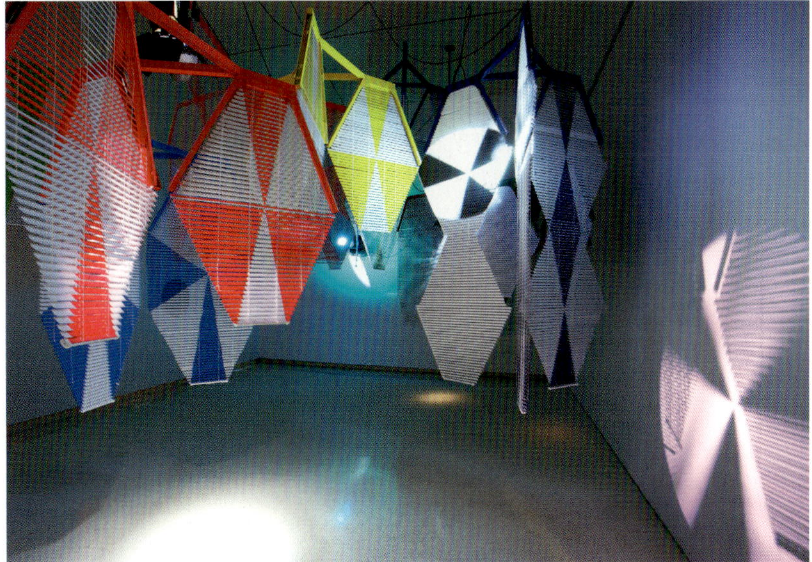

03

01 *Series of Vulnerable Arrangements — Blind Room*, 2006
Black aluminium venetian blinds, three video essays (*Trilogy* 2004–06), MDF, spotlight, mirror, humidifier, infrared heater, air ventilator, scent emitters ('Wood Fire' and 'Fresh Linen' scents), origami, photocopies, found objects, seating
Dimensions variable

02 *Lethal Love*, 2008
Perforated, gun metal aluminum venetian blinds, mirror, wood, flood spotlight, moving light, two scent emitters ('Wild flower' and 'Gunpowder' scents)
Dimensions variable

03 *Three Kinds*, 2008
Aluminium venetian blinds, three Arri flood lights, three Martin Mac 250-plus moving lights
Dimensions variable

04 *Sadong 30*, 2006
Various light sources (hanging light bulbs, strobes, light chain), mirror, origami objects, drying rack wrapped in fabric, fan, viewing terrace, cooler filled with bottles of mineral water, chrysanthemums and garden balsams, wood bench, wall clock, glow-in-the-dark paint, wood piles, spray paint
Dimensions variable
Incheon, Korea

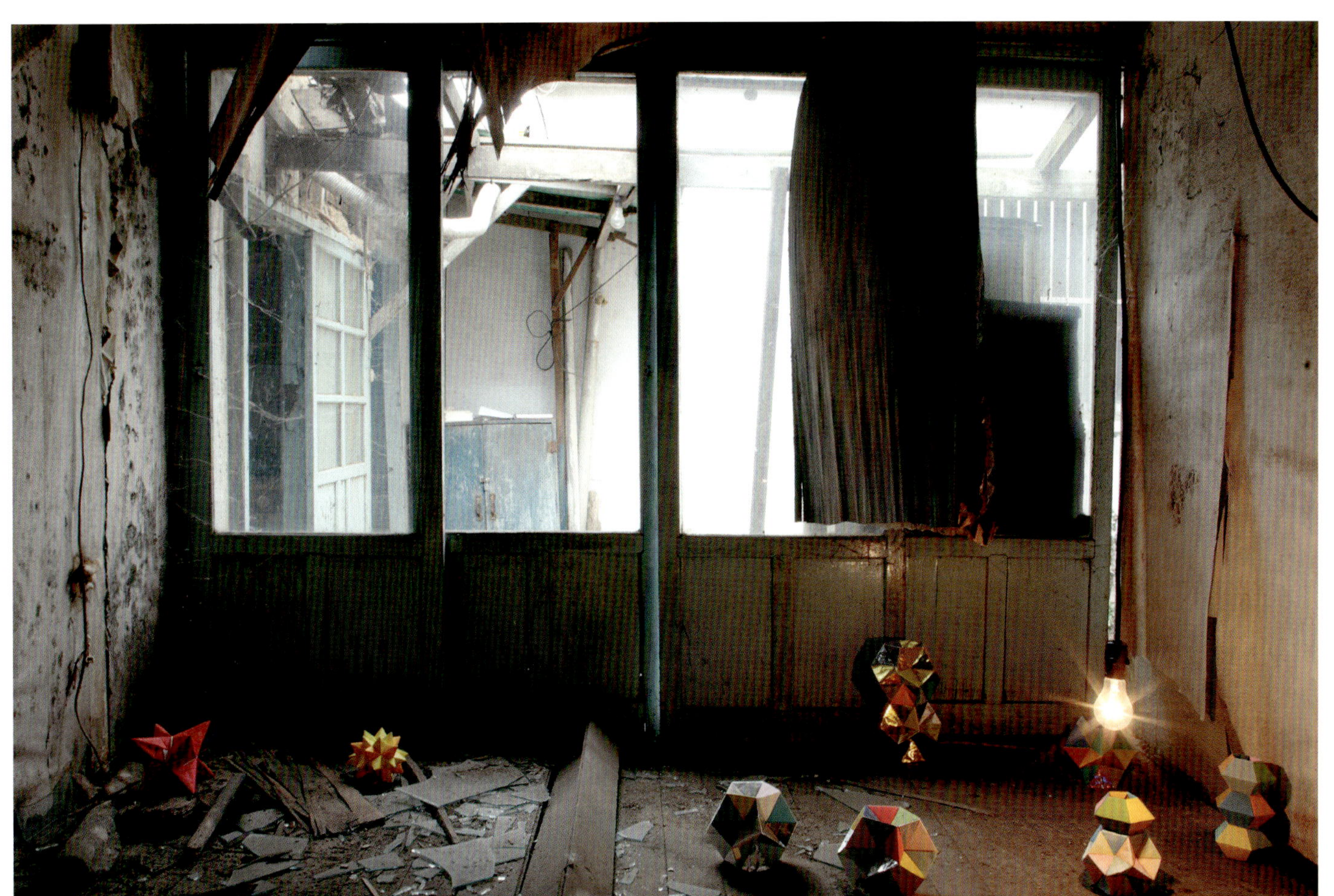

04

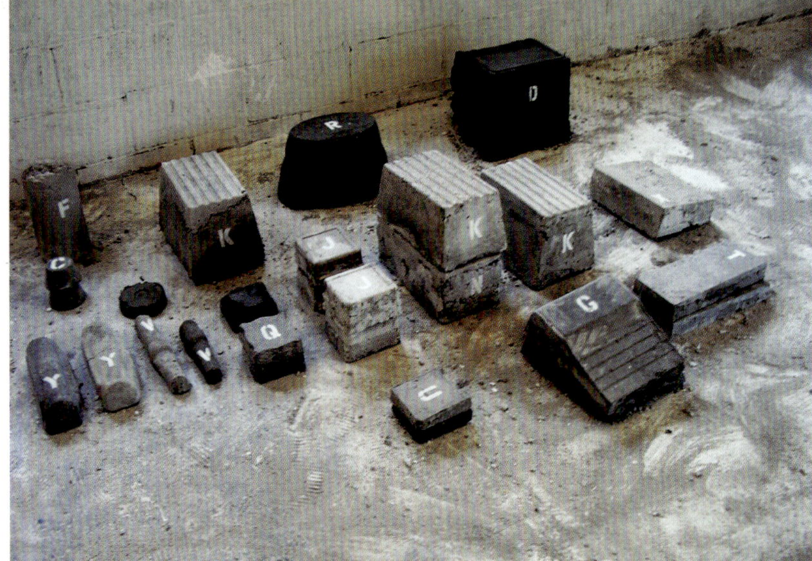

01

01 *BCADY2K dig-it-al*, 2006
Concrete and spray paint,
Approx. 120 × 180 × 120 cm

02 *Time Machine: Remembering Tomorrow*, 2004–07
Cast stone, vitrine
Approx. 30 × 27 × 35 cm

03, 04 *Monument X*, 2007
Concrete, plaster, metal frame, spray paint
Approx. 500 × 700 × 250 cm

'Away with the monuments!' Nietzsche once proclaimed, infuriated by the tendency of traditional monuments to deform or idealize the past. Since Nietzsche's attack, many philosophers, historians and artists have added their voice to the critique of memorial sites.

Tarek Zaki's *Monument X* (2007) proposes an alternative genre of artistic production that challenges the very premise of the monument and that could be termed the 'countermonument'. First presented in Cairo's Townhouse Gallery, this large-scale installation consists of an assemblage of objects arranged to mimic the site of an archaeological excavation. The displaced casts of plaster and cement — chiselled columns, disembodied horse's legs, an extended arm — can be imaginatively pieced together like a three-dimensional puzzle to reform the dismantled monument. Contrary to a traditional monument, which ostentatiously and permanently glorifies an ideology or a historical fact, *Monument X* presents the possibility for a playful and personal monumental construction, one that also holds the potential for multiple archaeologists to read and re-read traces of the past. If the installation fragments the past, it also dislocates our heritage. Confronted with Zaki's work in the Egyptian gallery or later at Liverpool's Blue Coat Art Centre, one wonders where history comes from and to whom it belongs.

If Zaki's interest in deconstructing monumental forms emerged as a result of the myriad of socio-political tensions in the Middle East, and in Egypt in particular, it also conveys his interest in the historical implications that a sculpture bears in general. Contrary to the photograph's ability to document a framed, present moment, sculpture reveals the existence of an object via successive layers. Zaki's participation in the exhibition 'Haunted by Detail', which took place at De Appel, in Amsterdam, in 2002 consisted of a bathroom moulded in white plaster. The many layers of plaster that form the furniture and accessories could suggest an accumulation of temporal strata in which various traces become sandwiched and without physical intervention remain hidden from human view indefinitely. At the same time, Zaki's familiar solidified creations — a bathtub, slippers, a mirror and so on — acquire a troubling otherness that transforms his sculptures into crystallizations of psychological memory.

02

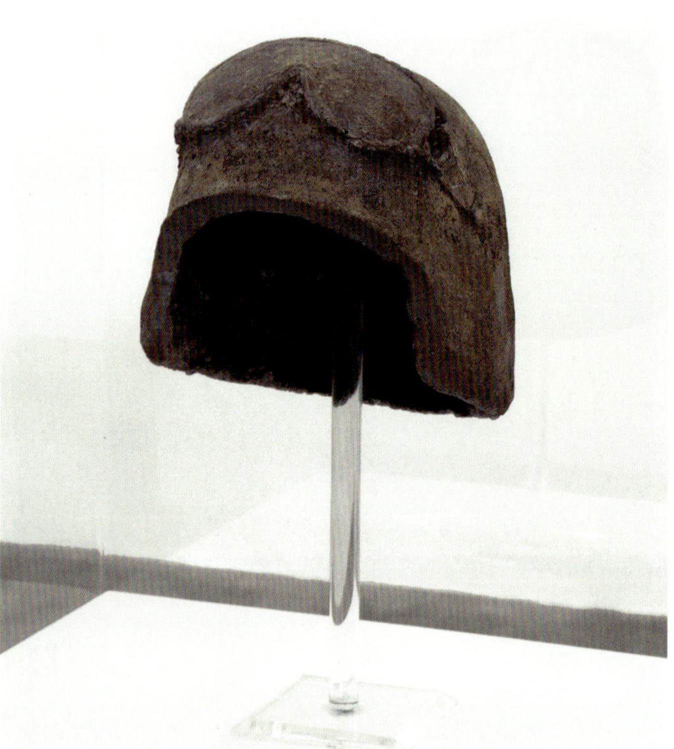

The project *Time Machine: Remembering Tomorrow* (2004) focuses more specifically on the issue of archiving memory. The installation is composed of technological accessories that include an electrical circuit, keyboard and rocket, all fossilized by Zaki and displayed in museum-like vitrines. The trompe-l'oeil effects of the casts appear even more beautiful than their original sources, and their formal presentation consecrates them as archaeological discoveries or artworks. Sublimated, these objects comment on our current globalized and computerized state of affairs, while raising the question of what tomorrow's heritage might be.

If Zaki's sculpture thus reveals a sharp analytical ability, not to mention an original and perfectly controlled technique, it is ultimately the concept of time that the artist explores. 'Time is such an elusive thing. Time is also everything,' the artists explains. 'We [try] to fight or tame nature, climate, gravity, but when it comes to time, we are clueless.' [Devrim Bayar]

03

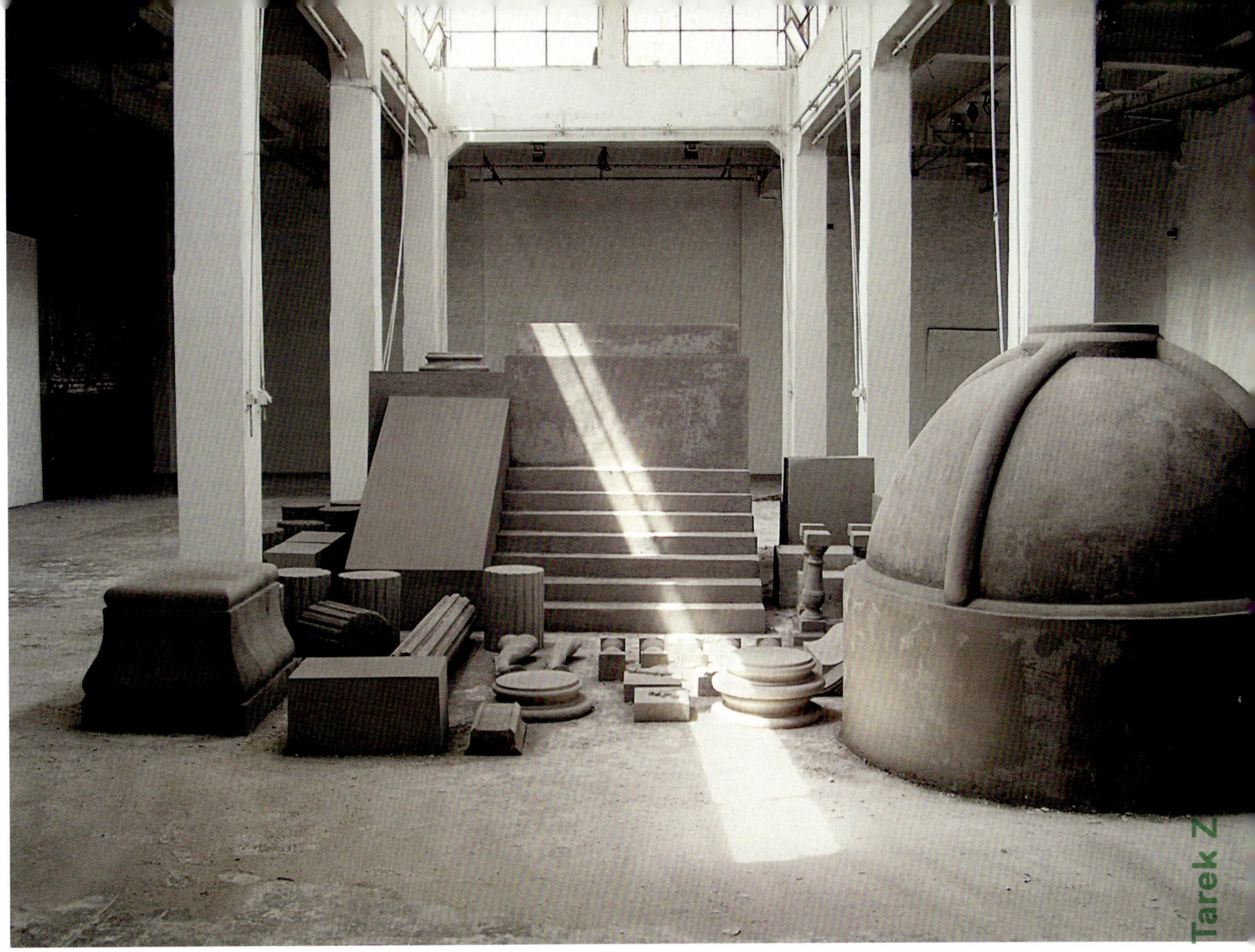

04

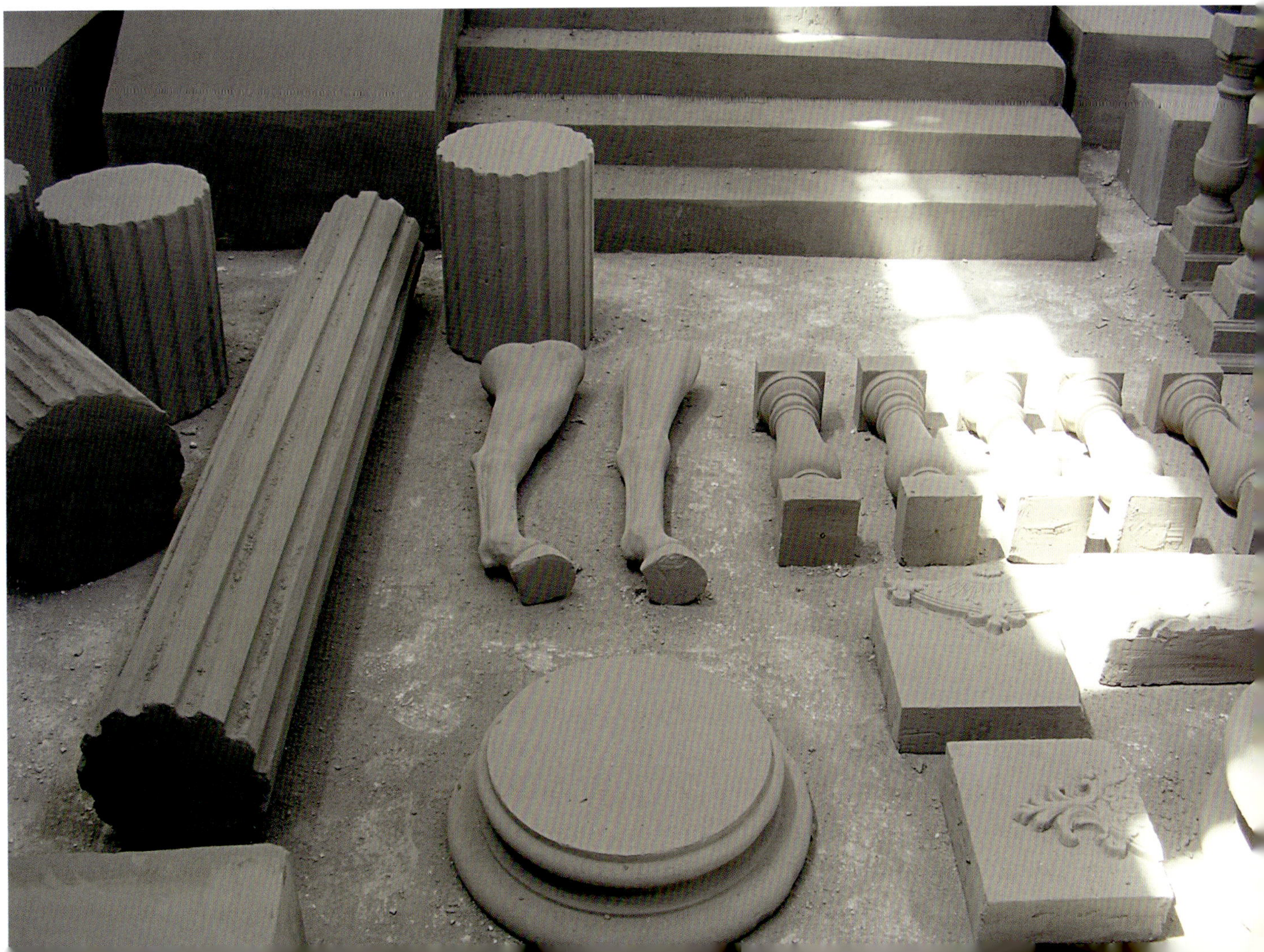

Some artists are difficult to encapsulate, hard to contain, choosing instead to rebel constantly. Thomas Zipp is one such artist. His exhibitions include brooding canvases of dark, nocturnal mountainscapes, collages and assemblages of numbers and symbols, all overseen by photocopied portraits with thumbtacks for eyes — undead watchers leering out from the past. Stone carvings, inscriptions, photographs, chandeliers, painted globes, hastily scrawled manifestos and, occasionally, a chapel, stage or mechanized instrument are bound together into Wagnerian gesamtkunstwerke in which Zipp and his band DA (Dicke Arsche), may also appear, playing their improvised and anarchic 'Rock music in a free, avant-garde Jazz mindset'.

The apparently chaotic energy of Zipp's chimerical practice hides within it a chain of associations that draws on moments of creation bound together with destruction in violent Dionysian acts. It's a language of signs and symbols divined from past avant-gardes transmogrified by the artist. In *Planet Caravan. Is there Life after Death? A Futuristic World Fair* (2007), Zipp trawls the shadows cast by history, particularly the Enlightenment and modern Germany, and traces a genealogy of the radicalized movements that spawned there, for better or for worse. Looking back to the explosive creative moments that set out to transform society, he unearths the zombified remains of Dada, National Socialism, nuclear physics, astronomy, Lutheran Christianity and experimental psychology that linger on, often discredited and redundant, in the recesses of today's culture.

While drawing from the past, Zipp is no historian per se; his research is more eccentric and arcane, more experiential than experimental. He eschews academia in favour of conspiracy and contradiction, his methodology following the same failures of logic, reason and morality as those that drive his subjects — transgressive individuals and decadent subversives from science, music, philosophy or politics who go beyond social norms. This is a rock-and-roll spirit distilled into a fiery challenge to convention, law and order.

Zipp wields his cultural scalpel with the unhealthy zeal of a young boy hovering over a captive spider. Not only does he adopt Dada and Surrealism's methods of cut, paste and collage, he turns them on themselves, using their oeuvres, histories, fantasies and beliefs as raw material. Such a search for an authentic connection to a modernist zeitgeist, particularly one rooted in times past, may now seem anachronistic. Indeed, Zipp's installations often carry the sense of a forgotten, faded museum or world fair left derelict — totalizing visions of historic and future triumphs, now an obsolete dream. However, there is also something deeply contemporary in his flare for the gothic, the cultic, the cryptic and the corrupt that lingers in adolescent low culture, an adoption of shock and horror as quotidian spectacle that was once reserved for those whose challenge to authority and convention was more politicized. In their extreme subjectivity, his works become dissections of reason, ideology and belief. [Kit Hammonds]

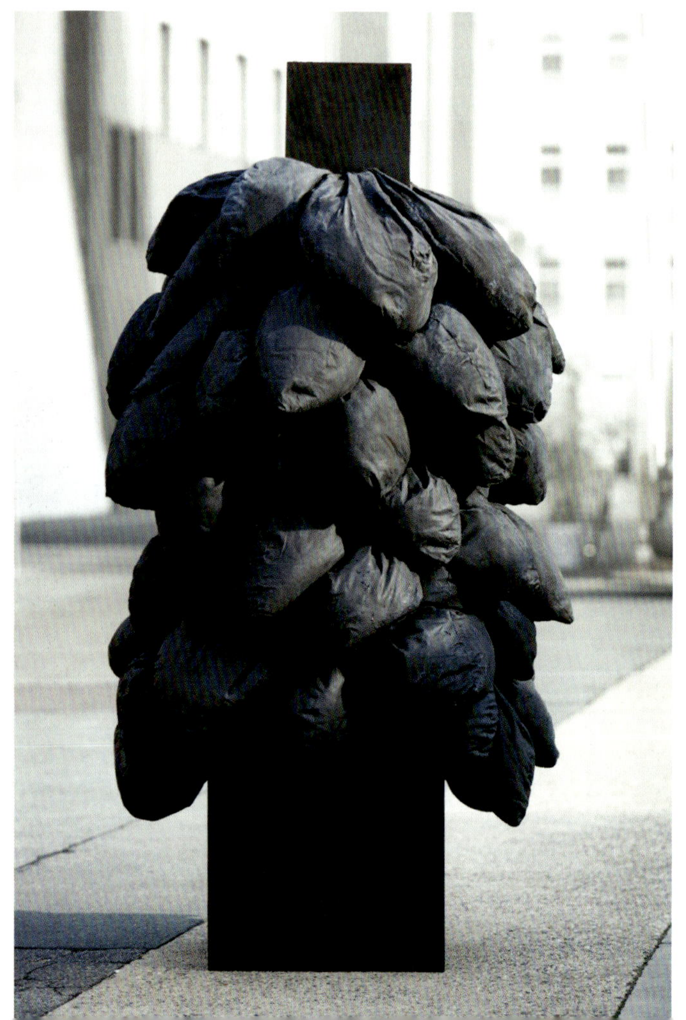

01

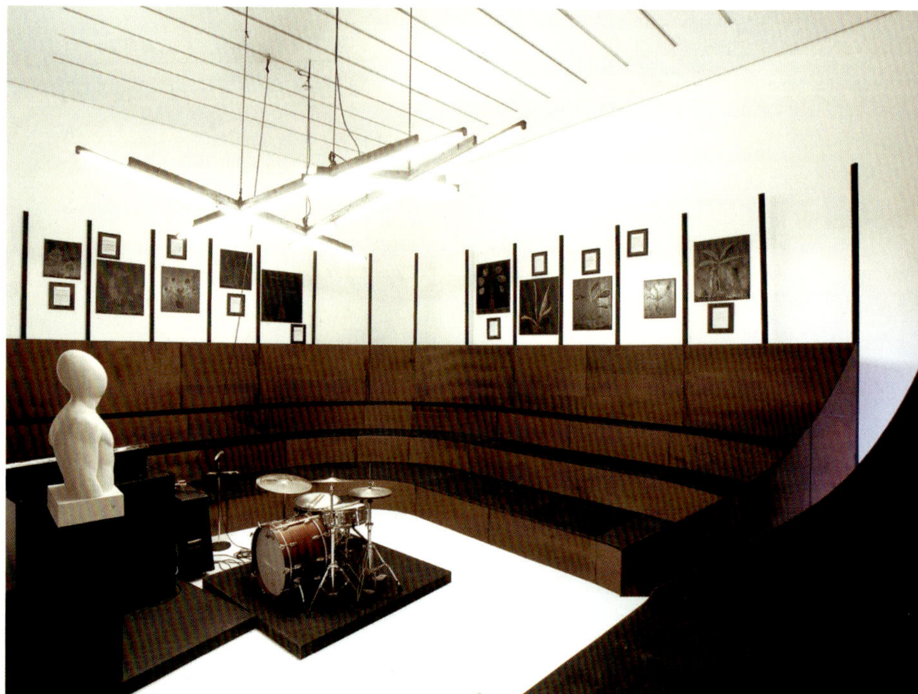

02

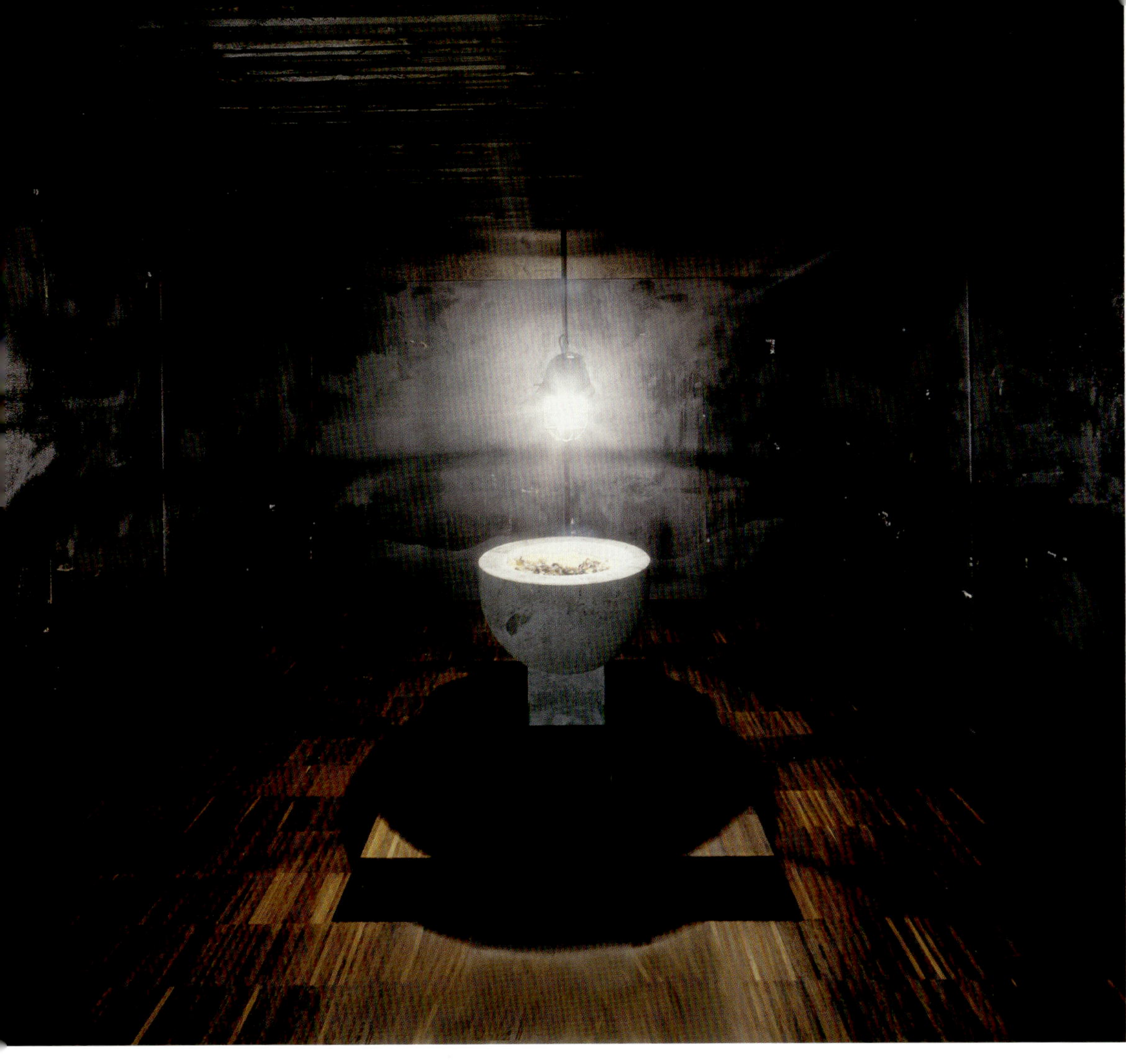

03

01 *Pollock 66*, 2008
Bronze
250 × 150 × 150 cm

02 *White Dada*, 2008
Mixed media
Dimensions variable

03 *Mushroom Chapel*, 2007
Acrylic and oil on canvas, wood, parquet, marble, mushrooms, lightbulb
300 × 450 × 650 cm

04 *The Family of Raumplan*, 2007
Mixed-media, mixed-media on paper
Dimensions variable

05 *Black Pattex*, 2008
Shell limestone, wood, acrylic
28 × 46 × 45 cm
Plinth
88 × 88 × 134 cm

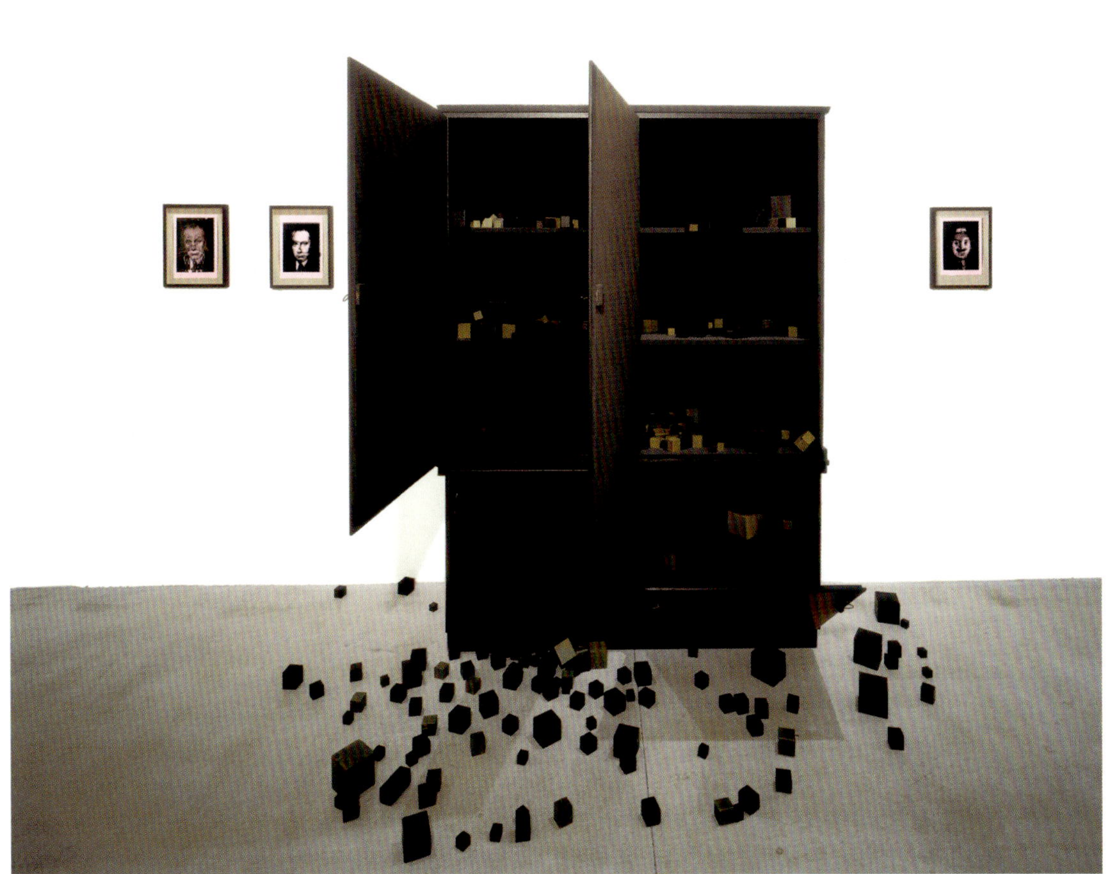

04

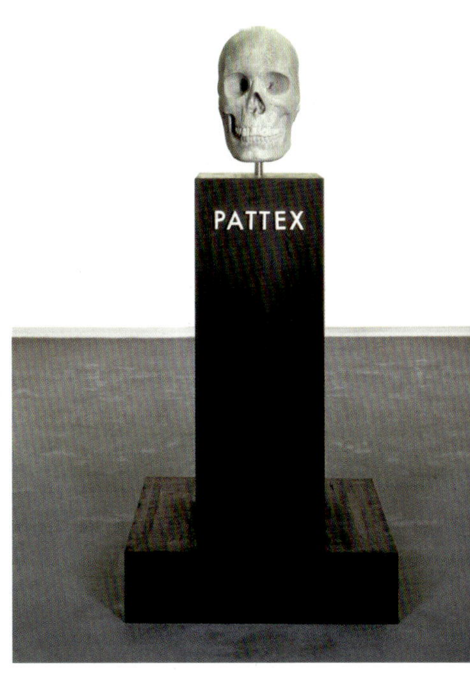

05

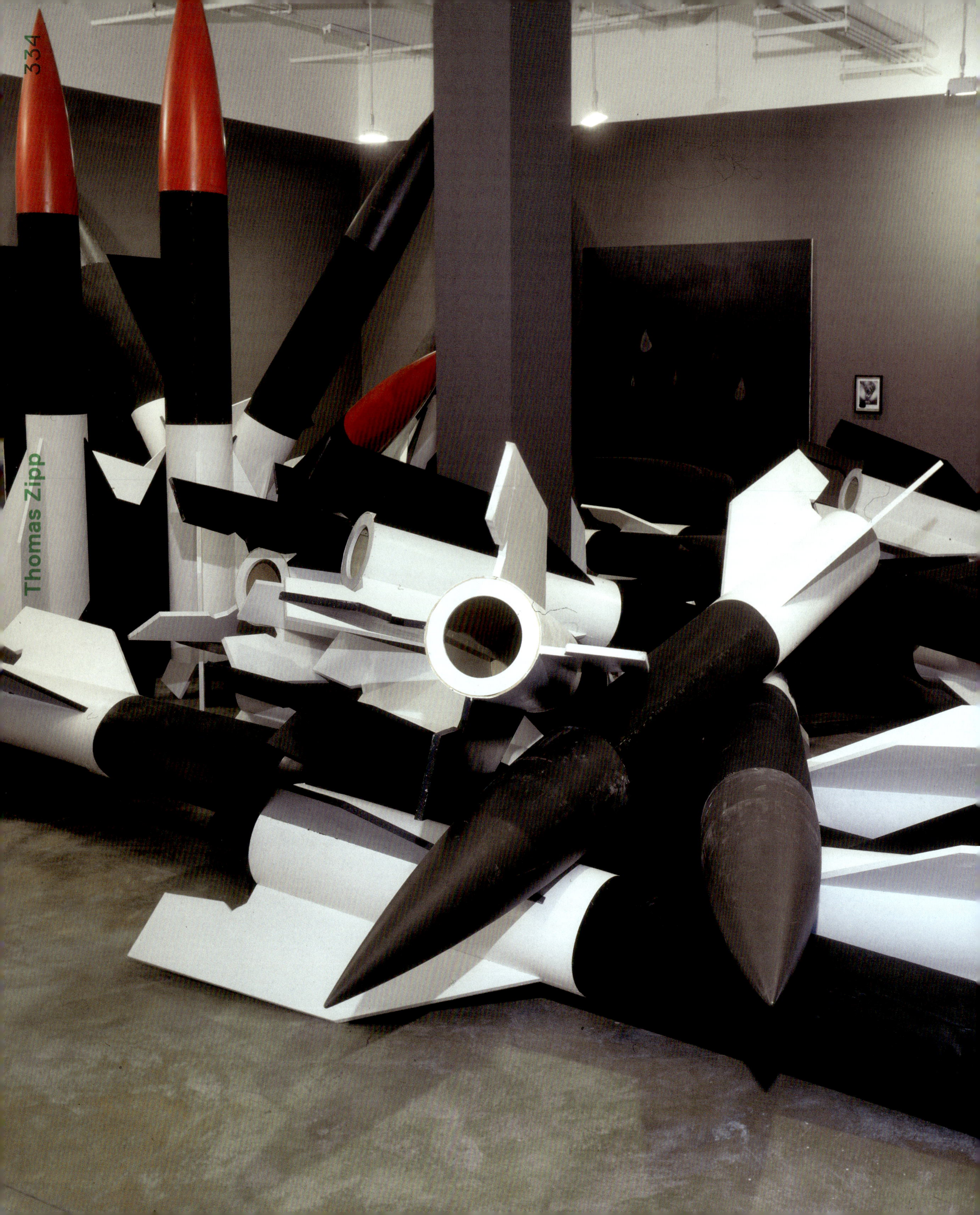

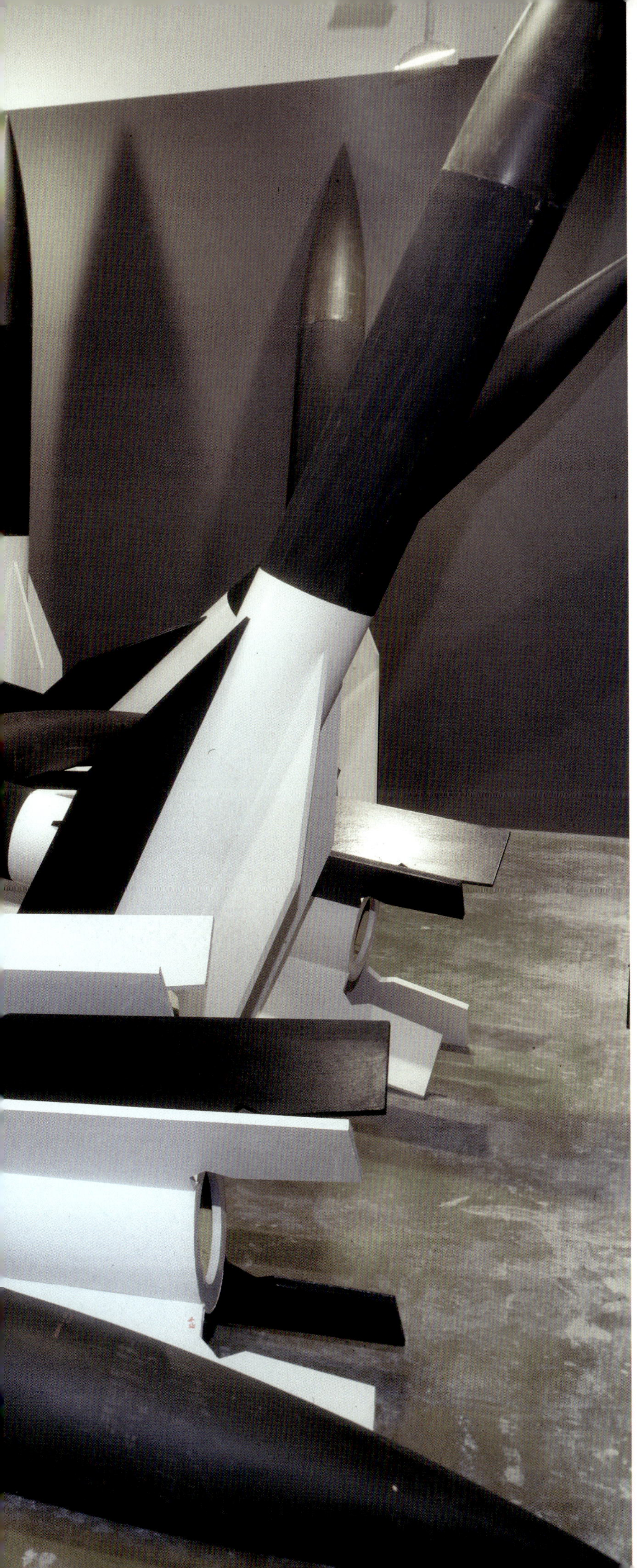

06 *Dwarf Nose*, 2008
Mixed-media installation
Dimensions variable

Adel Abdessemed Born 1971, Constantine, Algeria. Lives in Paris, France

— **Selected solo exhibitions** 2009 David Zwirner, New York / 2008 List Visual Arts Center, MIT, Cambridge, MA, USA / 2007 P.S.1 Contemporary Art Center, New York / 2005 Ikon Gallery, Birmingham, UK / 2004 Musée d'art moderne et contemporain (MAMCO), Geneva

— **Selected group exhibitions** 2009 'Transmission Interrupted, Modern Art Oxford / 2008 'Traces du sacré: Art and Spirituality of the 20th and 21st Centuries', Centre Pompidou, Paris / 2008 'Flow', The Studio Museum in Harlem, New York / 2007 Venice Biennale / 2007 Istanbul Biennial / 2006 São Paulo Biennial / 2006 'Notre Histoire', Palais de Tokyo, Paris

— **Selected bibliography** 2008 Neville Wakefield and Alanna Heiss, *Adel Abdessemed: Dead or Alive*, P.S.1 Contemporary Art Center, New York / 2008 Mai Abu El Dahab, *Flow*, The Studio Museum in Harlem, New York / 2007 Philippe-Alain Michaud and Elisabeth Lebovici, *Adel Abdessemed: À L'attaque*, JRP Ringier, Zurich / 2007 Mark Rappolt, 'Adel Abdessemed', *Art Review*, Mar. / 2006 Guitemie Maldonado, 'In the "Global Bordello" with Adel Abdessemed', *Parachute*, no. 124

Ai Weiwei Born 1957, Beijing, China. Lives in Beijing, China.

— **Selected solo exhibitions** 2009 Philips de Pury, London / 2008 'Go China! Ai Weiwei', Groniger Museum, Netherlands / 2008 Hyundai Gallery, Seoul / 2008 Sherman Contemporary Art Foundation, Sydney / 2008 Mary Boone Gallery, New York / 2007 Galerie Urs Meile Beijing–Lucerne, Lucerne / 2007 AedesLand, Berlin

— **Selected group exhibitions** 2008 Liverpool Biennial / 2008 'Half-Life of a Dream', San Francisco Museum of Modern Art / 2007 Documenta 12, Kassel / 2007 'China Welcomes You ... Desires, Struggles, New Identities', Kunsthaus Graz / 2007 'The Real Thing: Contemporary Art from China', Tate Liverpool, Institu Valencià d'Art Modern (IVAM) / 2007 Moscow Biennial / 2006 'MoCA Envisage / Entry Gate: Chinese Aesthetics of Heterogeneity', Museum of Contemporary Art Shanghai / 2006 Sydney Biennial / 2006 'Territorial: Ai Weiwei and Serge Spitzer', Museum für Moderne Kunst (MMK), Frankfurt

— **Selected bibliography** 2009 Karen Smith, Hans Ulrich Obrist and Bernard Fibicher, *Ai Weiwei*, Phaidon Press, London / 2008 Adam Jasper, 'Critical Mass: Ai Weiwei', *Art Review*, May / 2008 Carol Lu, 'Mr. Big', Frieze, June–Aug / 2008 Nataline Colonello, 'Ai Weiwei', *Contemporary*, no. 96 / 2007 Philip Tinari, 'Some Simple Reflections on an Artist in a City 2001–2007'; Jacques Herzog, 'Concept and Fake'; Charles Merewether, 'Made in China', *Parkett*, no. 82 / 2007 Ai Weiwei, 'Production Notes', *Artforum*, Oct. / 2007 Philip Tinari, 'A Kind of True Living', *Artforum*, Summer

Allora & Calzadilla
Jennifer Allora born 1974, Philadelphia, PA, USA.
Guillermo Calzadilla born 1971, Havana, Cuba.
Live in San Juan, Puerto Rico.

— **Selected solo exhibitions** 2008 Haus der Kunst, Munich / 2007 Kunsthalle Zürich / 2007 Serpentine Gallery, London / 2007 Renaissance Society, University of Chicago / 2007 Centre for Contemporary Art, Kitakyushu / 2006 Palais de Tokyo, Paris / 2006 Stedelijk Museum voor Actuele Kunst (SMAK), Ghent

— **Selected group exhibitions** 2008 Sydney Biennial / 2008 'After Nature', New Museum, New York / 2008 'Greenwashing', Fondazione Sandretto Re Rebaudengo, Turin / 2007 Lyon Biennial / 2007 Istanbul Biennial / 2007 'Uncertain States of America', Astrup Fearnley Museum of Modern Art, Oslo; Musée d'Art Moderne de la Ville de Paris; Center for Curatorial Studies, Bard College, Annandale-on-Hudson, NY; Reykjavík Art Museum; Serpentine Gallery, London / 2006 Whitney Biennial, New York

— **Selected bibliography** 2008 Julienne Lorz (ed.), *Stop, Repair, Prepare: Variations on Ode to Joy for a Prepared Piano*, Haus Der Kunst, Munich and Walther König, Cologne / 2007 Hannah Feldman, 'Sound Tracks: Hannah Feldman on the Art of Allora & Calzadilla', *Artforum*, May / 2007 Patricia Falguieres, 'Archipelago', *Parkett*, no. 80 / 2007 Sally O'Reilly, 'Trumpets and Turtles', *Frieze*, June / 2006 Jennifer Allora and Guillermo Calzadilla, *Land Mark*, Palais de Tokyo, Paris

David Altmejd Born 1974, Montreal, Canada. Lives in New York, NY, USA.

— **Selected solo exhibitions** 2008 Andrea Rosen Gallery, New York / 2007 Fundació La Caixa Museum, Barcelona / 2007 Canadian Pavilion, Venice Biennale / 2006 Stuart Shave Modern Art, London / 2005 Xavier Hufkens, Brussels / 2003 Galerie SKOL, Montreal

— **Selected group exhibitions** 2009 'Everyday Above Ground is a Good One: Reflections of the Underworld', Reg Vardy Gallery, Sunderland, UK / 2008 Liverpool Biennial / 2008 'Intrus/Intruders', Musée National des Beaux-Arts du Québec, Quebec City / 2006 'The Eighth Square', Museum Ludwig, Cologne / 2006 'The Guggenheim Collection', Kunsthalle Bonn, Germany

— **Selected bibliography** 2007 Louise Déry, *David Altmejd: The Index*, Galerie de l'UQAM, Montreal / 2007 Silvia Sauquet, *David Altmejd: Stages*, Fundació La Caixa, Barcelona / 2005 Max Hollein and Martina Weinhart (eds.), *Ideal Worlds: New Romanticism in Contemporary Art*, Hatje Cantz, Ostfildern / 2005 Christopher Miles, 'David Altmejd', *Frieze*, Feb. / 2004 Pamela M. Lee, 'Crystal Lite', *Artforum*, May

Micol Assaël Born 1979, Rome, Italy. Lives in Rome, Italy.

— **Selected solo exhibitions** 2008 Kunsthalle Fridericianum, Kassel / 2008 Edicola Notte, Rome / 2007 Kunsthalle Basel / 2005 Zero, Milan / 2004 Fondazione Sandretto Re Rebaudengo, Turin

— **Selected group exhibitions** 2008 São Paulo Biennial / 2008 'After Nature', New Museum, New York / 2008 Sydney Biennial / 2007 'Silence: Listen to the Show', Fondazione Sandretto Re Rebaudengo, Turin / 2006 Berlin Biennial / 2005 Venice Biennale / 2005 'Work Time / Life Time/Material Time', Reykjavík Arts Festival / 2005 Moscow Biennial

— **Selected bibliography** 2008 Massimiliano Gioni, 'Micol Assaël', *Art Review*, Mar. / 2007 Ester Coen and Adam Szymczyk, *Chizhevsky Lessons*, Kunsthalle Basel and Electa, Milan / 2007 Polly Staple, 'Risk Assessment', *Frieze*, Oct. / 2007 Adam Szymczyk, 'Micol Assaël', *Flash Art*, Oct.–Nov. / 2004 Carolyn Christov-Bakargiev, 'Carolyn Christov-Bakargiev on Micol Assaël', *Artforum*, Jan.

Nairy Baghramian Born 1971, Isfahan, Iran. Lives in Berlin, Germany.

— **Selected solo exhibitions** 2008 Kunstverein Aachen, Germany / 2008 Staatliche Kunsthalle, Baden Baden, Germany / 2007 Kunstverein Nürnberg, Nuremburg / 2006 Kunsthalle Basel / 2005 Galerie Christian Nagel, Cologne

— **Selected group exhibitions** 2008 Berlin Biennial / 2008 'Draw a Straight Line and Follow it', Tate Modern / 2007 Skulptur Projekte Münster / 2007 'Devotee', Cabinet, London / 2007 'Door Slamming Festival', Mehringdamm 72, Berlin / 2006 'Time Lines', Kunstverein für die Rheinlande und Westfalen, Dusseldorf

— **Selected bibliography** 2008 Dominic Eichler, Karola Grässlin and André Rothmann, *The Walker's Day Off*, Staatliche Kunsthalle Baden-Baden and Walther König, Cologne / 2008 Juliane Rebentisch, 'Im Glaushaus', *Texte Zur Kunst*, May / 2007 Manfred Herms, 'Nairy Baghramian: Deserted frames, whispery voices; marquees, mirrors and steel earrings', *Frieze*, May

Claire Barclay Born 1968, Paisley, UK. Lives in Glasgow, UK.

— **Selected solo exhibitions** 2009 Fruitmarket Gallery, Edinburgh / 2008 Camden Arts Centre, London / 2007 Kunstverein Braunschweig, Germany / 2005 Stephen Friedman Gallery, London / 2005 Doggerfisher, Edinburgh / 2004 Tate Britain, London / 2003 Dundee Contemporary Arts, UK

— **Selected group exhibitions** 2008 'Group', Doggerfisher, Edinburgh / 2007 'Sculpture in the Close', Jesus College, Cambridge, UK / 2005 British Art Show 6, Baltic Centre for Contemporary Art, Gateshead / 2003 'This Was Tomorrow', New Art Centre, Salisbury, UK

— **Selected bibliography** 2008 Andrea Tarsia, *Claire Barclay: File Note*, Camden Arts Centre / 2007 Dominic Eichler and Janneke De Vries, *Fault on the Right Side*, Walther König, Cologne / 2006 Rebecca Fortnum, 'Contemporary British Women Artists', I.B. Tauris, London / 2003 Katrina Brown and Penelope Curtis, 'Ideal Pursuits', Dundee Contemporary Arts,UK

Michael Beutler Born 1976, Oldenburg, Germany. Lives in Berlin, Germany.

— **Selected solo exhibitions** 2008 Bonniers Konsthall, Stockholm / 2007 Portikus, Frankfurt / 2006 Lufthansa Aviation Center, Frankfurt Main Airport / 2005 Sprengel Museum, Hanover / 2005 IASPIS, Stockholm / 2004 Oldenburger Kunstverein, Germany / 2004 Kunstverein Heilbronn, Germany / 2004 Kunstverein Braunschweig, Germany

— **Selected group exhibitions** 2008 'Psycho Buildings', Hayward Gallery, London / 2008 'Personal Protocols and other Preferences', Centre for Curatorial Studies, Bard College, Annandale-on-Hudson, NY / 2007 'Kunstmaschinen Maschinenkunst', Schirn Kunsthalle, Frankfurt; Tinguely Museum, Basel / 2007 'Modelle für Morgen', European Kunsthalle, Cologne / 2006 Berlin Biennial / 2006 'Don Quixote', Witte de With, Rotterdam / 2006 Gwangju Biennial / 2006 'Housewarming', Swiss Institute, New York

— **Selected bibliography** 2008 Sara Arrhenius, Kim Einarsson and Polly Staple, *Kottgubbar*, Bonniers Konsthall, Stockholm / 2006 Thomas Bayrle, Maria Lind, Ariane Müller, Nicolaus Schafhausen and Katja Schroeder, *Michael Beutler: Pecafil*, Sternberg Press, Berlin and New York / 2005 Karola Grässlin, *Flip*, Kunstverein Braunschweig, Germany / 2002 Matthias Hermann, Stefanie Keelfeld and Gregory Williams, *Michael Beutler*, Vienna Secession

Frank Benson Born 1978, Norfolk, VA, USA. Lives in New York, NY, USA.

— **Selected solo exhibitions** 2008 Sadie Coles HQ, London / 2005 Taxter & Spengemann, New York / 2001 Miami Art Museum

Selected group exhibitions 2008 'Scene Seen: Recent Acquisitions from the Luckman Fine Arts Complex Permanent Collection, 1979–2006', Luckman Fine Arts Complex, Los Angeles / 2006 'Red Eye: Los Angeles Artists from the Rubell Family Collection', Rubell Family Collection Museum, Miami / 2006 'Uncertain States of America', Astrup Fearnley Museum of Modern Art, Oslo; Musée d'Art Moderne de la Ville de Paris; Center for Curatorial Studies, Bard College, Annandale-on-Hudson, NY; Reykjavík Art Museum; Serpentine Gallery, London / 2005 'Make It Now: New Sculpture in New York', SculptureCenter, New York

—— **Selected bibliography** 2007 Dan Cameron, *New York Interrupted*, PKM Gallery, Beijing / 2006 Georg Leutner (ed.), *World's Best New Art: Unreal Projects*, Verlag für Moderne Kunst, Nuremberg / 2006 Nathaniel McBride, 'Uncertain States of America and USA Today', *Flash Art*, Fall / 2005 Roberta Smith, 'The Many Shades of Now Explored in Three Dimensions', *The New York Times*, 27 May / 2005 Daniel Birnbaum(ed.) et al., *Uncertain States of America*, Astrup Fearnley Museum of Modern Art, Oslo

Huma Bhabha Born 1962, Karachi, Pakistan. Lives in Poughkeepsie, NY, USA.
—— **Selected solo exhibitions** 2008 Aldrich Contemporary Art Museum, Ridgefield, CT, USA / 2007 Salon 94, New York / 2007 Greener Pastures Contemporary Art, Toronto / 2006 Mario Diacono Gallery, Boston / 2004 ATM Gallery, New York
—— **Selected group exhibitions** 2008 Gwangju Biennial / 2008 'After Nature', New Museum, New York / 2008 'Nina in Position', Artists Space, New York / 2007 'Every Revolution is a Roll of the Dice', Ballroom Marfa, TX, USA / 2006 'USA Today', Royal Academy of Arts, London / 2006 'Remember Who you Are', Mary Boone Gallery, New York
—— **Selected bibliography** 2007 Brian Sholis, 'Huma Bhabha', *Artforum*, Dec. / 2007 Nancy Princenthal, 'Blasted Allegories', *Art in America*, Dec. / 2007 Merrily Kerr, 'Ouverture', *Flash Art*, Winter / 2006 Adrian Searle, 'Culture', *The Guardian*, 5 Oct.

Alexandra Bircken Born 1967, Cologne, Germany. Lives in Cologne, Germany.
—— **Selected solo exhibitions** 2009 Herald St, London / 2008 Ursula Blickle Stiftung, Kraichtal-Unteröwisheim, Germany / 2008 Docking Station, Stedelijk Museum, Amsterdam / 2007 Gladstone Gallery, New York / 2006 BQ, Cologne / 2005 Herald St, London
—— **Selected group exhibitions** 2008 Brussels Biennial / 2008 'Borders', Museum Boijmans Van Beunigen, Rotterdam / 2008 'Martian Museum of Terrestrial Art', Barbican Art Gallery, London / 2007 'Unmonumental', New Museum, New York / 2007 'Um-Kehrungen', Kunstverein Braunschweig, Germany / 2006 'Dereconstruction', Gladstone Gallery, New York / 2006 'Kn'-yan', Galerie Christine Mayer, Munich
—— **Selected bibliography** 2008 Nicolas Schafthausen and Florian Waldvogel, *Alexandra Bircken*, Ursula Blickle Stiftung, Kraichtal-Unteröwisheim, Germany / 2007 Richard Flood et al., *Unmonumental*, Phaidon Press, London / 2006 Peter Abs, 'Alexandra Bircken', *Spex*, no. 10 / 2006 Alexandra Bircken, *Klötze*, BQ, Cologne

Karla Black Born 1972, Alexandria, UK. Lives in Glasgow, UK.
—— **Selected solo exhibitions** 2009 Mary Mary, Glasgow / 2009 Migros Museum für Gegenwartskunst, Zurich / 2009 Modern Art Oxford / 2009 Inverleith House, Edinburgh / 2008 West London Projects / 2008 Galeria Gisela Capitain, Cologne / 2008 Longside Gallery, Yorkshire Sculpture Park, Wakefield, UK / 2007 Ibid Projects, London / 2006 Galerie Sandra Buergel, Berlin / 2006 Outpost, Norwich
—— **Selected group exhibitions** 2008 'Wollust: The Presence of Absence', Columbus Art Foundation, Leipzig / 2008 'Strange Solution', Tate Britain, London / 2008 'Group Show', Stuart Shave Modern Art, London / 2007 'Poor Thing', Kunsthalle Basel / 2007 'Untitled: Works on Paper', Art: Concept, Paris / 2005 'Like It Matters', Centre for Contemporary Arts, Glasgow
—— **Selected bibliography** 2008 Jonathan Griffin, 'Karla Black', *Frieze*, Sep. / 2008 Karla Black, *Mistakes Made Away From Home*, Mary Mary, Glasgow / 2008 Michael Archer 'Karla Black', *Artforum*, Mar. / 2007 Barry Schwabsky, 'Karla Black: Mother Sculpture', *Map Magazine*, Winter

Carol Bove Born 1971, Geneva, Switzerland. Lives in New York, NY, USA.
—— **Selected solo exhibitions** 2008 Dennis Kimmerich, Dusseldorf / 2007 Maccarone inc, New York / 2007 Art Gallery of Ontario, Toronto / 2006 Blanton Museum, Austin, TX, USA / 2004 Institute of Contemporary Art, Boston / 2005 Kunsthalle Zürich / 2003 Kunstverein in Hamburg
—— **Selected group exhibitions** 2009 'Contemporary Fine and Applied Arts: 1928–2009', Tate St Ives, UK / 2008 Whitney Biennial, New York / 2008 'Murder Letters', Galeria Filomena Soares, Lisbon / 2007 'Unmonumental', New Museum, New York / 2007 'Multiplex: Directions in Art 1970 to Now', The Museum of Modern Art, New York / 2007 'Every Revolution is a Roll of the Dice', Ballroom, Marfa, TX, USA / 2007 'Learn to Read', Tate Modern, London
—— **Selected bibliography** 2007 David Rimanelli, 'Best of 2007 Carol Bove, Maccarone, Inc. New York', *Artforum*, Jan. / 2007 Thomas Kuhn, 'Carol Bove: Vintage', *Kunstforum*, May–June / 2007 Shamim M. Momin, 'Carol Bove', *Ice Cream*, Phaidon Press, London / 2005 Barry Schwabsky, 'Shelf life: The Art of Carol Bove', *Artforum*, Dec. / 2005 Tom Morton, 'Come Together', *Frieze*, Mar.

Martin Boyce Born 1967, Hamilton, UK. Lives in Glasgow, UK.
—— **Selected solo exhibitions** 2008 Ikon Gallery, Birmingham, UK / 2008 Westfälischer Kunstverein, Munster / 2007 Centre d'Art Contemporain, Geneva / 2006 Fonds Régional d'Art Contemporain (FRAC) des Pays de la Loire, Carquefou, France / 2005 Kabinett fur aktuelle Kunst, Bremerhaven, Germany / 2004 Galerie Eva Presenhuber, Zurich
—— **Selected group exhibitions** 2008 '5 minutes later', KW Institute for Contemporary Art, Berlin / 2007 'Unmonumental', New Museum, New York / 2007 'The Third Mind', Palais de Tokyo, Paris / 2006 'How to Improve the World: 60 Years of British Art', Hayward Gallery, London / 2006 'Strange I've Seen That Face Before', Museum Abteiberg, Moenchengladbach, Germany / 2005 'Body: New Art from the UK', British Council, London; Vancouver Art Gallery; Ottawa Art Gallery; Oakville Galleries; Edmonton Art Gallery; Art Gallery of Nova Scotia, Halifax
—— **Selected bibliography** 2008 John-Paul Stonard, 'The Third Mind, Palais de Tokyo', *Artforum*, Mar. / 2007 Richard Flood et al., *Unmonumental*, Phaidon Press, London / 2006 Axel Haubrock, 'Der Konzeptioner', *Spike*, no. 10 / 2006 Martin Herbert, 'All That is Solid', *Frieze*, Oct. / 2003 *Martin Boyce: This Place is Dreaming*, Contemporary Art Gallery, Vancouver, Tramway, Glasgow

Matti Braun Born 1968, Berlin, Germany. Lives in Cologne, Germany.
—— **Selected solo exhibitions** 2009 Kunstmuseum Liechtenstein, Vaduz / 2008 'Özurfa', Museum Ludwig, Cologne; Museum of Modern and Contemporary Art, Bolzano, Italy / 2008 BQ, Cologne / 2007 Galleria S.A.L.E.S, Rome / 2007 'Lota', Ester Schipper, Berlin
—— **Selected group exhibitions** 2009 'Le Travail de Rivière', Le Credac, Ivry-sur-Seine, France / 2008 'Santhal Family: Positions Around Indian Sculpture', Museum van Hedendaagse Kunst Antwerpen (MuHKA), Antwerp / 2007 'HIRAM', Galeria Antonio Ferrara, Reggio Emilia, Italy / 2007 'L'homme nu', Maison populaire, Montreuil, France / 2006 'If it Didn't Exist You'd Have to Invent it: A Partial Showroom History', The Showroom, London / 2006 'Absolute Democracy', Galleria Antonio Ferrara, Reggio Emilia, Italy
—— **Selected bibliography** 2008 Nina Guelicher and Kasper König (eds.), *Özurfa*, Museum Ludwig, Cologne, Museum of Modern and Contemporary Art, Bolzano, Italy and Walther König, Cologne / 2008 GeORGIO Verzotti, 'Matti Braun at Galleria S.A.L.E.S', *Artforum*, Jan. / 2007 Axel Lapp, 'Matti Braun at Esther Schipper', *Art in America*, Sep. / 2006 Andreas Schlaegel, 'Matti Braun: The Alien', *Flash Art*, Oct.

Berlinde De Bruyckere Born 1964, Ghent, Belgium. Lives in Ghent, Belgium.
—— **Selected solo exhibitions** 2009 Galleria Continua, San Gimignano, Italy / 2008 Yvon Lambert, New York / 2008, Espace Claude Berri, Paris / 2007 'Berlinde De Bruyckere: Schmerzensmann', Museum Moderner Kunst Kärnten, Klagenfurt, Austria / 2007 'Berlinde De Bruyckere: Schmerzensmann V', Bijloke Campus, Ghent / 2006 'Schmerzensmann', Hauser and Wirth, London / 2006 'Under Cover', Kunsthalle Düsseldorf
—— **Selected group exhibitions** 2008 'Life? Biomorphic Forms in Sculpture', Kunsthaus Graz / 2008 'After Nature', New Museum, New York / 2008 'God and Goods', Villa Manin Centre for Contemporary Art, Udine, Italy / 2007 'Schmerz / Pain', Nationalgalerie im Hamburger Bahnhof, Museum für Gegenwart, Berlin / 2007 'Berlinde De Bruyckere, Jenny Saville, Dan Flavin', Kunstmuseum Lucerne
—— **Selected bibliography** 2009 Berlinde De Bruyckere and Tommy Devriendt, *Berlinde De Bruyckere: In the Woods There Were Chainsaws*, Steidl, Göttingen / 2006 Gregor Muir and Ali Subotnick, *Berlinde De Bruyckere: Der Schmerzensmann*, Steidl, Göttingen and Hauser and Wirth, London and Zurich / 2006 Ulrike Groos, Georg Imdahl and Beate Söntgen, *Under Cover: Berlinde De Bruyckere und Martin Honert*, Kunsthalle Düsseldorf

Christoph Büchel Born in 1966, Basel, Switzerland. Lives in Basel, Switzerland.
—— **Selected solo exhibitions** 2008 Kunsthalle Fridericianum, Kassel / 2008 Palais de Tokyo, Paris / 2007 Museum für Gegenwartskunst, Basel / 2006 Hauser and Wirth Coppermill, London / 2006 Massachusetts Museum of Contemporary Art, North Adams, USA / 2005 Kunsthalle Basel
—— **Selected group exhibitions** 2008 'Shifting Identities: (Swiss) Art Now', Kunsthaus Zürich; Contemporary Art Centre, Vilnius / 2008 Sydney Biennial / 2007 Romanian Pavilion, Venice Biennale / 2007 'Memorial to the Iraq War', Institute of Contemporary Arts, London / 2007 'Une question de génération', Musée d'Art Contemporain de Lyon / 2006 'In den Alpen', Kunsthaus Zürich / 2006 'Denial is a River', SculptureCenter, New York
—— **Selected bibliography** 2008 Mirjam Varadinis (ed.), *Shifting Identities: (Swiss) Art Now*, JRP Ringier, Zurich / 2008 Christoph Büchel and Giovanni Carmine, *CEAU*, Steidl, Göttingen / 2008 Judith Rodenbeck, 'Christoph Büchel', *Artforum*, Sep. / 2008 Door Rein Wolfs, 'Het hart van "Hole": Christoph Büchel', *Metropolis M*, Feb.–Mar. / 2007 Markus Brüderlin and Julia Wallner, *Swiss Made: Präzision und Wahnsinn*, Hatje Cantz, Ostfildern / 2007 Dan Fox, 'Christoph Büchel', *Frieze*, May / 2007 Alison M. Gingeras, 'Christoph Büchel', *Artforum*, Jan. / 2005 Christoph Büchel and Giovanni Carmine, *PSYOP Post-9/11 Leaflets*, JRP Ringier, Zurich

Michał Budny Born 1976, Leszno, Poland. Lives in Warsaw, Poland.
—— **Selected solo exhibitions** 2008 Kronika Gallery, Bytom, Poland / 2008 Galerie Naechst St Stephan, Vienna / 2007 Johnen + Schöttle Galerie, Cologne / 2006 Centre for Contemporary Art, Warsaw / 2006 Galerie Annex 14, Bern / 2004 Centre for Contemporary Art Ujazdowski Castle, Warsaw

—— **Selected group exhibitions** 2008 'Illusion and consequence', Kunsthalle Mainz, Germany / 2008 Manifesta 7, Trentino, South Tyrol, Italy / 2008 Art Sheffield, UK / 2008 SITE Santa Fe Biennial / 2006 'Spiralen der Erinnerung', Hamburg Kunstverein / 2006 'Museum as a Luminous Object of Desire', Museum of Art, Łodz / 2006 'Is it better to be a good artist or a good person?', Raster at Rental Gallery, Los Angeles / 2006 'Manipulations: On Economies of Deceit', Laznia Centre for Contemporary Art, Gdansk —— **Selected bibliography** 2007 Karolina Grabowicz (ed.), *Manipulations: On Economies of Deceit*, Laznia Centre for Contemporary Art, Gdansk / 2006 Michał Budny and Zbigniew Rogalski, *Projekcja,* Zachęta Narodowa Galeria Sztuki, Warsaw / 2005 Krinzinger Projekte (ed.), *Revange on realism: The fictitious moment in current polish art*, Krinzinger Projekte, Vienna

Tom Burr Born 1963, New Haven, CT, USA. Lives in New York, NY, USA. —— **Selected solo exhibitions** 2009 Städtische Galerie im Lenbachhaus und Kunstbau, Munich / 2009 Museum für Gegenwarts-kunst, Basel (with Monica Bonvincini) / 2008 SculptureCenter, New York / 2007 Swiss Institute, New York (with Walter Pfeiffer) / 2007 Secession, Vienna / 2006 Cantonal des Beaux-Arts de Lausanne / 2002 Whitney Museum of American Art, New York —— **Selected group exhibitions** 2007 'Walk!', Kunstraum Kreuzberg Bethanien, Berlin / 2007 'Oh Girl, It's a Boy!', Kunstverein München, Munich / 2007 'Body Politicx', Witte de With, Rotterdam / 2007 'Unmonumental', New Museum, New York / 2007 'Pale Carnage', Arnolfini, Bristol; Dundee Contemporary Arts, UK / 2006 'Wieder und Wider', Museum moderner Kunst Stiftung Ludwig Wien (MUMOK), Vienna / 2004 Whitney Biennial, New York —— **Selected bibliography** 2008 Joshua Decter, 'Tom Burr Talks About "Addict-Love"', *Artforum*, Feb. / 2007 Mark Rappolt, 'The Man Who Wasn't There', *Art Review*, Apr. / 2007 George Baker, 'The Other Side of the Wall', *October*, no. 120 / 2007 Anke Kempkes, *Tom Burr: Moods*, Secession, Vienna and Walther König, Cologne / 2006 Florence Derieux, *Tom Burr: Extrospective,* Musée Cantonal des Beaux-Arts de Lausanne, JRP Ringier, Zurich

Jedediah Caesar Born 1973, Oakland, CA, USA. Lives in Los Angeles, CA, USA. —— **Selected solo exhibitions** 2008 Galerie Nathalie Obadia, Paris / 2007 D'Amelio Terras, New York / 2007 Blanton Museum of Art, Austin, TX, USA / 2007 Susanne Vielmeter Los Angeles Projects / 2004 Black Dragon Society, Los Angeles —— **Selected group exhibitions** 2008 'Multiverse', Claremont Museum of Art, CA, USA / 2008 'Red Wind', Blum & Poe, Los Angeles / 2008 Whitney Biennial, New York / 2007 'Circumventing the City', D'Amelio Terras, New York / 2007 'Paper Bombs', Jack Hanley Gallery, Los Angeles / 2006 'Trace', Whitney Museum of American Art at Altria, New York / 2005 'Thing', Hammer Museum, Los Angeles —— **Selected bibliography** 2008 Holly Myers, 'Contradictions and Complexities', *Los Angeles Times*, 18 July / 2008 Christopher Knight, 'California Biennial at the Orange County Museum of Art', *The Los Angeles Times*, 4 Nov. / 2008 Gregory Volk, 'Spring in Dystopia', *Art in America*, May / 2007 Roberta Smith, 'In These Shows, Material Is the Message', *The New York Times*, Aug. 10 / 2006 Anne Rochette and Wade Saunders, 'Place Matters: Los Angeles Sculpture Today', *Art in America*, Nov.

Valentin Carron Born 1977, Martigny, Switzerland. Lives in Geneva, Switzerland. —— **Selected solo exhibitions** 2009 303 Gallery, New York / 2009 Galerie Eva Presenhuber, Zurich / 2008 l'Espace Lausannois d'Art Contemporain, Lausanne / 2007 Kunsthalle Zürich / 2006 Swiss Institute, New York / 2006 Chisenhale Gallery, London (with Mai-Thu Perret) / 2005 Galerie Francesca Pia, Berne —— **Selected group exhibitions** 2008 'Blasted Allegories: Works from the Ringier Collection', Kunstmuseum Lucerne / 2008 'Less is less and more is more', CAPC Musée d'Art Contemporain, Bordeaux / 2007 'The Third Mind', Palais de Toyko, Paris / 2007 'The Freak Show', Musée d'Art Contemporain, Lyon / 2007 'The Happiness of Objects', SculptureCenter, New York / 2007 'Kunstpreis der Böttcherstrasse in Bremen', Kunsthalle Bremen / 2006 'In den Alpen', Kunsthaus Zürich —— **Selected bibliography** 2007 Adam Jasper, 'Valentin Carron: Alpine aesthetics and Modernism; imitation and a boar's head', *Frieze*, May / 2007 Beatrix Ruf, 'Valentin Carron', *Monopol*, Jan. / 2006 Katya Garcia-Anton and Beatrix Ruf, *Valentin Carron*, JRP Ringier, Zurich / 2006 Eva Scharrer, 'Valentin Carron', *Artforum*, Mar. / 2006 Cathérine Hug, 'Valentin Carron', *Tema Celeste*, no. 113

Marcelo Cidade Born 1979, São Paulo, Brazil. Lives in São Paulo, Brazil. —— **Selected solo exhibitions** 2008 'Brazileños: Intervenciones', La Casa Encendida, Madrid / 2008 'Acidentes não acontecem', Fundação Ascensão, Vale do Anhangabaú, São Paulo / 2008 'Outro Lugar', Galeria Vermelho, São Paulo —— **Selected group exhibitions** 2008 'TRANSFER_cultura urbana', Santander Cultural, Porto Alegre, Brazil / 2008 'An Unruly History of the Readymade', Fundación Colección Jumex, Mexico City / 2007 'Whenever it starts it is the right time strategies for a discontinuous future', Frankfurter Kunstverein / 2007 'FLUX', les Abattoirs, Avallon, Brazil / 2006 São Paulo Biennial / 2006 'Moderne Cite II', Le Grand Café Saint Nazaire Centre d'Art Contemporain, France —— **Selected bibliography** 2008 Jessica Morgan, 'Marcelo Cidade', *Art Review*, Mar. / 2006 Glória Ferreira, 'Fronteiras Móveis', *Critica de Art no Brazil: Temáticas Contemporâneas*, Funarte, Rio de Janeiro / 2006 Fernando Oliva, 'Marcelo Cidade', *Lapiz*, no. 222 / 2005 Betti-Sue Hertz, 'The Mobility of the Fragment: Architectural Out-takes and Photographic Cuts of the Urban', *InSite_05 / Farsite > Sitios Distantes*, Frienses Book Division, San Diego

Steven Claydon Born 1969, London, UK. Lives in and works in London, UK. —— **Selected solo exhibitions** 2009 David Kordansky Gallery, Los Angeles / 2009 Galleria Massimo De Carlo, Milan / 2008 'Osram and Omar', Hotel, London / 2008 'The Ancient Set', International Project Space, Birmingham / 2008 '*a & not a*', Galerie Dennis Kimmerich, Dusseldorf / 2006 'Courtesy of the Neighbourhood Watch', White Columns, New York —— **Selected group exhibitions** 2008 Busan Biennial / 2008 'Strange Events Permit Themselves the Luxury of Occurring', Camden Arts Centre, London / 2007 'Sympathy for the Devil: Art and Rock and Roll Since 1967', Museum of Contemporary Art, Chicago; Museum of Contemporary Art, North Miami / 2007 'Old School', Hauser and Wirth, London; Zwirner and Wirth, New York / 2007 'Pale Carnage', Arnolfini, Bristol; Dundee Contemporary Arts, UK / 2006 'Rings of Saturn', Tate Modern, London / 2006 'Dereconstruction', Barbara Gladstone Gallery, New York —— **Selected bibliography** 2008 Tom Morton, 'Back to the Future', *Frieze*, Sep. / 2008 Alessio Ascari, 'Interview', *Mousse*, Jan. / 2007 Martin Coomer, 'Introducing: Steven Claydon', *Modern Painters*, Dec.–Jan. / 2005 Catherine Wood, 'Fear of a Planet at Hotel', *Frieze*, Sep.

Peter Coffin Born 1972, Berkeley, CA, USA. Lives in New York, NY, USA. —— **Selected solo exhibitions** 2009 The Curve, Barbican Art Gallery, London / 2008 'Yellow Outline', Fri-Art, Centre d'Art Contemporain, Fribourg, Switzerland / 2007 Galerie Emmanuel Perrotin, Paris / 2007 'Model of the Universe (e.g. sweet harmonica solo, e.g. the idea of the sun, e.g. Frisbee dog catch in mid air, e.g. brightly colored gem stones, e.g. the desire for a tropical drink, e.g. dance sweat)', Galerie Emmanuel Perrotin, Miami / 2007 'The Idea of the Sun', le Confort Moderne, Poitier Cedex, France / 2007 'Tree Pants', The Horticultural Society of New York —— **Selected group exhibitions** 2009 Tate Triennial, London / 2008 'The Possibility of an Island', Museum of Contemporary Art, North Miami / 2008 Manifesta 7, Trentino, South Tyrol, Italy / 2008 'Untamed Paradises', Museo de Arte Contemporanea de Vigo (MARCO), Spain / 2007 'The Office', Tanya Bonakdar Gallery, New York / 2007 'Learn to Read', Tate Modern, London / 2007 Moscow Biennial —— **Selected bibliography** 2008 Jerry Saltz, 'Critic's Pick: Peter Coffin "You Are Me"', *New York Magazine Online*, Apr. 11 / 2008 Roberta Smith, 'Peter Coffin You Are Me', *The New York Times*, Apr. 25 / 2007 Maurizio Cattelan, 'Peter Coffin, A Heap of Language', *Flash Art*, Oct.

William Cordova Born 1971, Lima, Peru. Lives in Houston, TX, Miami, FL, and New York, NY, USA. —— **Selected solo exhibitions** 2009 'More than Bilingual', Fleming Museum of Art, University of Vermont / 2008 'pachacuti, pachachti, pachacuti', OK Mountain, Austin, TX, USA / 2008 'Moby Dick (Tracy)', Artpace, San Antonio, TX, USA / 2008 'The house that Frank Lloyd Wright built for Atahulpa, Fred Hampton y Mark Clark', Threewalls, Chicago / 2007 'Pachacuti (stand up next to a mountain)', Arndt & Partner, Zurich / 2006 'Drylongso (Pichqa Suyo)', P.S.1 Contemporary Art Center, New York —— **Selected group exhibitions** 2008 Whitney Biennial, New York / 2008 'Street Level', MIT, Boston / 2008 'NeoHooDoo', Menil Collection, Houston; P.S.1 Contemporary Art Center, New York; Miami Art Museum / 2007 'Street Level', Nasher Museum, Duke University, Durham, NC, USA / 2005 'Scratch', The Studio Museum in Harlem, New York —— **Selected bibliography** 2008 Lori Waxman, 'Threewalls Review', *Artforum*, Apr. / 2007 Miguel Amago, 'Street Level', *Contemporary*, no. 94 / 2007 Trevor Schoonmaker, *Street Level*, Duke University Museum of Art, Durham, NC, USA / 2006 Gesine Borcherdt, 'Ground Zero', *Monopol*, Oct.–Nov. / 2005 Holland Carter, 'Scratch', *The New York Times*, 24 July

Abraham Cruzvillegas Born 1968, Mexico City, Mexico. Lives in Mexico City, Mexico, and Paris, France. —— **Selected solo exhibitions** 2009 'The Exhibition Formerly Known as Passengers: Abraham Cruzvillegas', CCA Wattis Institute for Contemporary Arts, San Francisco / 2008 'Autoconstrucción: The Soundtrack', Centre for Contemporary Arts Glasgow / 2007 'Autoconstrucción' Jack Tilton Gallery, New York / 2006 'Ici', Château de Tours, France —— **Selected group exhibitions** 2009 Havana Biennial / 2008 'God and Goods', Villa Manin Centre for Contemporary Art, Udine, Italy / 2008 'Mexico: Expected / Unexpected: Colección Isabel and Agustin Coppel', La Maison Rouge, Paris / 2007 'Unmonumental', New Museum, New York / 2007 'Stay forever and ever and ever', South London Gallery / 2007 'Trinchera', Museo Raúl Anguiano, Guadalajara / 2006 'The Exotic Journey Ends', Foksal Gallery Foundation, Warsaw —— **Selected bibliography** 2008 Abraham Cruzvillegas and Francis McKee, *Autoconstrucción*: *Abraham Cruzvillegas*, Centre for Contemporary Arts, Glasgow /

2007 J.R Widholm, *Escultura Social: a New Generation of Art from Mexico City*, Museum of Contemporary Art Chicago / 2006 Tom Morton, 'Found and Lost', *Frieze*, Oct. / 2006 Abraham Cruzvillegas and Dr. Lakra, *Los Dos Amigos: Abraham Cruzvillegas and Dr. Lakra*, A&R Press, Mexico

Alexandre da Cunha Born 1969, Rio de Janeiro, Brazil. Lives in London, UK.
— **Selected solo exhibitions** 2008 Vilma Gold, London / 2008 Galeria Luisa Strina, São Paulo / 2008 Sommer & Kohl, Berlin / 2007 'Passengers', CCA Wattis Institute for Contemporary Arts, San Francisco / 2007 Neuer Aachener Kunstverein (NAK), Aachen, Germany / 2006 Paco das Artes, São Paulo / 2005 Museu de Arte da Pampulha, Belo Horizonte, Brazil
— **Selected group exhibitions** 2008 'This is not a void', Galeria Luisa Strina, São Paulo / 2008 'The Gentle Art of Collapsing the Expanded Field', Cardenas Bellanger, Paris / 2008 'Procedente', Museu de Arte da Pampulha, Belo Horizonte, Brazil / 2007 'Fortunate Objects', Cisneros Fontanals Art Foundation, Miami / 2007 'Close to me', Studio Guenzani, Milan / 2007 'CTRL_C + CTRL_V', SESC Pompeia, São Paulo
— **Selected bibliography** 2008 Nicola Harvey, 'Alexandre da Cunha', *Frieze*, June / 2007 Jens Hoffmann, *Poor Materials with Rich Meaning*, CCA Wattis Institute for Contemporary Arts, San Francisco / 2007 Judith Collins, *Sculpture Today*, Phaidon Press, London / 2006 Rodrigo Moura, *Economies of Desire*, Paco das Artes, São Paulo / 2006 Jens Hoffmann, *Around the World in 80 Days*, Institute of Contemporary Arts, London

Jan De Cock Born 1976, Brussels, Belgium. Lives in Brussels, Belgium.
— **Selected solo exhibitions** 2008 'Modern is Changing fig. 1', Galerie Fons Welters, Amsterdam / 2008 'Modern is Changing fig. 3', Luis Campana Gallery, Cologne / 2008 'Modern is Changing fig. 4', Stella Lohaus Gallery, Antwerp / 2008 'Denkmal 11', The Museum of Modern Art, New York / 2007 'Denkmal 70', Sint-Lukas Hogeschool, Paleizenstraat 70, Brussels / 2006 'Denkmal 4' (with Daniel Buren), Casa del Fascio, Como; Galleria Francesca Minini, Milan; Galleria Massimo Minini, Brescia / 2006 'Denkmal 25', Haus Konstruktiv, Zurich
— **Selected group exhibitions** 2008 Le Havre Biennial / 2007 'Twee en twintig duizend vijfhonderd: De Collectie Almere, aanwinsten 01–07', Museum De Paviljoens, Almere, Netherlands / 2004 'Mouse on Mars', Kunsthalle Düsseldorf / 2004 Manifesta 5, San Sebastian, Spain
— **Selected bibliography** 2008 Jan De Cock, *Denkmal isbn 9789080842441, The Museum of Modern Art, New York*, Atelier Jan De Cock, Brussels / 2008 Daniel Buren, Jan De Cock, *Denkmal isbn 9789080842434*, Atelier Jan De Cock, Brussels / 2008 Monica Amor, 'Jan De Cock', *Artforum*, Apr. / 2006 Jan De Cock, *Denkmal isbn 9080842427, Tate Modern, London*, Atelier Jan De Cock, Brussels / 2006 Angela Madesani, 'Daniel Buren and Jan De Cock', *Artforum*, Oct.

Thea Djordjadze Born 1971, Tbilisi, Georgia. Lives in Cologne, Germany.
— **Selected solo exhibitions** 2008 Galerie Monika Sprüth Philomene Magers, Cologne / 2008 Kunstverein Nürnberg, Nuremburg / 2007 'History of an Encounter', Galerie Micky Schubert, Berlin / 2007 'Possibility Nansen', Studio Voltaire, London
— **Selected group exhibitions** 2008 'Un soir, j'ai assis la beauté sur mes genoux' (with Rosemarie Trockel), Galerie Monika Sprüth Philomene Magers, Munich / 2008 Berlin Biennial / 2008 'On Interchange: Zwischenspiele einer Sammlung', Museum Kurhaus Kleve, Germany / 2008 'Élégance', Kölnischer Kunstverein, Cologne / 2007 Lyon Biennial / 2007 'Objects', Karma International, Zurich / 2006 'Modus', Kunsthalle St Gallen / 2006 'The New Vernacular: Contemporary art meets popular culture', Zentrum Paul Klee, Bern
— **Selected bibliography** 2008 Mark von Schlegell, Nora Schulz and Catherine Wood, *Thea Djordjadze*, Verlag für Moderne Kunst, Nuremburg / 2008 Daniel Völzke, 'Thea Djordjadze baut in Nürnberg krumme Dinger', *Monopol*, no. 6 / 2007 Stéphanie Moisdon and Hans Ulrich Obrist (ed.), *Lyon Biennial: History of a Decade that Has not yet Been Named*, JRP Ringier, Zurich / 2007 Dan Fox, 'Thea Djordjadze', *Frieze*, Nov.

Trisha Donnelly Born 1974, San Francisco, CA, USA. Lives in San Francisco, CA, USA.
— **Selected solo exhibitions** 2008 Centre d'Édition Contemporain, Bâtiment d'Art Contemporain, Geneva / 2008 Institute of Contemporary Art, Philadelphia / 2008 Renaissance Society, University of Chicago / 2008 Douglas Hyde Museum, Dublin / 2007 Modern Art Oxford
— **Selected group exhibitions** 2009 'The Quick and the Dead', Walker Art Center, Minneapolis / 2008 'I Love the Horizon', Centre National d'Art Contemporain, Grenoble / 2008 'The World as a Stage', The Institute of Contemporary Art, Boston; Tate Modern, London / 2008 'Gravity', The Museum of Modern Art, New York / 2008 'The Sound of Things: Unmonumental Audio', New Museum, New York / 2007 'The Third Mind', Palais de Tokyo, Paris / 2007 'Depth of Field: Modern Photography at the Metropolitan', Metropolitan Museum of Art, New York
— **Selected bibliography** 2008 Jenelle Porter, *Trisha Donnelly*, Institute of Contemporary Art at the University of Pennsylvania, Philadelphia / 2008 Jonathan Griffin, 'Trisha Donnelly', *Frieze*, Jan.–Feb. / 2007 Martin Herbert, 'Trisha Donnelly', *Artforum*, Sep. / 2006 Laura Hoptman, Bruce Hainley and Beatrix Ruf, 'Trisha Donnelly' *Parkett*, no. 77

Tara Donovan Born 1969, New York, NY, USA. Lives in New York, NY, USA.
— **Selected solo exhibitions** 2008 Institute of Contemporary Art, Boston; Lois and Richard Rosenthal Center for Contemporary Art, Cincinnati, OH; Des Moines Art Center, IA; Museum of Contemporary Art, San Diego / 2008 Metropolitan Museum of Art, New York / 2007 'Tara Donovan: Colony', Berkeley Art Museum, University of California / 2006 'Tara Donovan: Drawings and Sculpture', Barbara Krakow Gallery, Boston / 2006 'Currents 98: Tara Donovan', Saint Louis Art Museum, MO, USA
— **Selected group exhibitions** 2008 'Second Lives: Remixing the Ordinary', Museum of Arts and Design, New York / 2008 'Gravitas: Tara Donovan, Deborah Hede, Rebecca Holland and Susan York', Dorsky Gallery, New York / 2008 'Found!', Barbara Krakow Gallery, Boston / 2008 'Attention to Detail', Flag Art Foundation, New York / 2008 'Sheldon Survey: An Invitational', Sheldon Memorial Art Gallery, Lincoln, NE, USA / 2007 'Visions of Concern', Daniel Weinberg Collection, Chicago
— **Selected bibliography** 2009 Suzanne Hudson, 'Tara Donovan', *Artforum*, Jan. / 2008 Carol Kino, 'The Genius of Little Things' *The New York Times*, 28 Sep. / 2008 Holly Hotchner, David Revere McFadden and Lowery Stokes Sims, *Second Lives: Remixing the Ordinary*, Museum of Arts and Design, New York / 2008 Nicholas Baum, Jen Mergel and Lawrence Weschler, *Tara Donovan*, Monacelli Press, New York / 2007 Robert Hobbs, *Contemporary, Cool and Collected*, Mint Museum of Art, Charlotte, NC, USA

Jim Drain Born 1975, Cleveland, OH, USA. Lives in and works in Miami, FL, USA.
— **Selected solo exhibitions** 2007 'I Would Gnaw on My Hand', Greene Naftali Gallery, New York / 2005 'I Wish I Had a Beak', Greene Naftali Gallery, New York / 2004 'Eldorado (1 of 5)', Drantmann Gallery, Brussels / 2004 'theskywasfilledwitha1000starswhilethesunkissedthemountainsblueand11moonsplayedacrosstherainbows', Peres Projects, Los Angeles
— **Selected group exhibitions** 2007 'Sympathy for the Devil: Art and Rock and Roll Since 1967', Museum of Contemporary Art, Chicago; Museum of Contemporary Art, North Miami / 2006 'Wunderground: Providence, 1995 to the present', RISD Museum of Art, Providence / 2006 'Uncertain States of America', Astrup Fearnley Museum of Modern Art, Oslo; Musée d'Art Moderne de la Ville de Paris; Center for Curatorial Studies, Bard College, Annandale-on-Hudson, NY; Reykjavík Art Museum; Serpentine Gallery, London
— **Selected bibliography** 2007 Sara Agniel, Maya Allison, Gary Panter and Judith Tannenbaum, *Wunderground: Providence, 1995 to the present*, Museum of Art, RISD, Providence / 2007 Mark Beasley, 'Wunderground', *Frieze*, May / 2006 Martin Herbert, 'Jim Drain', *Modern Painters*, May

Latifa Echakhch Born 1974 in El Khnansa, Morocco. Lives in Paris, France, and Martigny, Switzerland.
— **Selected solo exhibitions** 2009 Kunsthalle Fridericianum, Kassel / 2009 Bielefelder Kunstverein, Germany / 2009 Galerie Kamel Mennour, Paris / 2008 'Speakers' Corner', Level 2 Gallery, Tate Modern, London / 2008 'Vita Kuben', Norrlandsoperan, Umeå, Sweden / 2007 'Fifty Fifty Fantasia', Karma International, Zurich / 2007 'Il m'a fallu tant de chemins pour parvenir jusqu'à toi', Le Magasin, Grenoble
— **Selected group exhibitions** 2009 'The space between', Gävle Konstcentrum, Museum Anna Norlander, Skelleftea, Sweden / 2008 'Transformational grammars', Francssca Kaufmann, Milan / 2008 Manifesta 7, Trentino, South Tyrol, Italy / 2008 'Shifting Identities: (Swiss) Art Now', Kunsthaus Zürich, Contemporary Art Centre, Vilnius / 2008 'Flow', The Studio Museum in Harlem, New York / 2007 'Revolution!', La Passerelle, Brest; Mucsarnok, Kunsthalle, Budapest / 2007 'Global Feminisms', Brooklyn Museum, New York / 2007 'Where ever we go', San Francisco Art Institute
— **Selected bibliography** 2009 Michele Robecchi, 'Latifa Echakhch', *Flash Art*, Jan.–Feb. / 2009 Nicolas Tremblay, 'L'envers du décor', *Numéro*, Dec.–Jan. / 2008 Coline Miliard, 'Latifa Echakhch: Speakers' Corner' *Art Review*, Dec. / 2008 Sarah Valdez, 'Report from the Diaspora', *Art in America*, Sep. / 2007 Maura Reilly and Linda Nochlin, *Global Feminisms*, Brooklyn Museum, New York / 2007 Miklos Erhardt, *Revolution!*, Mucsarnok Kunsthalle, Budapest

Iran do Espírito Santo Born 1963, Mococa, São Paulo, Brazil. Lives in São Paulo, Brazil.
— **Selected solo exhibitions** 2008 'Deposition', Sean Kelly Gallery, New York / 2008 'En Passant', Galeria Fortes Vilaça, São Paulo / 2007 'Uma Visão Geral', Estação Pinacoteca, São Paulo / 2007 Irish Museum of Modern Art, Dublin / 2006 Museo Nazionale delle Arti del XXI Secolo, Rome / 2004 Museo de Arte Carrilollo Gil, Mexico City
— **Selected group exhibitions** 2008 Inhotim Instituto Cultural, Brumadinho, Brazil / 2008 São Paulo Biennial / 2007 Venice Biennale / 2007 'MAM na Oca', Pavilhão Lucas Noqueira Garcez, São Paulo / 2006 'Transforming Chronologies: An Atlas of Drawings, Part One', The Museum of Modern Art, New York / 2000 'F(r)icciones', Museo Nacional Centro de Artes Reina Sofia, Madrid

—— **Selected bibliography** 2006 Paolo Colombo (ed.), *Iran do Espírito Santo*, Electa, Milan ⁄ 2006 Seán Kissane and Lilian Tone, *Iran do Espírito Santo*, Irish Museum of Modern Art, Dublin ⁄ 2004 Marisol Argüelles, *Iran do Espírito Santo,* Museo de Arte Carrillo Gil, Mexico City

Chris Evans Born 1967, Eastrington, UK. Lives in Brussels, Belgium, and London, UK.

—— **Selected solo exhibitions** 2008 'Point at it, like a farmer at a pig', Galerie Juliette Jongma, Amsterdam ⁄ 2007 'What's the point of revolution without copulation, copulation, copulation', Lüttgenmeijer, Berlin, Artpace; San Antonio, TX, USA ⁄ 2007 'As simple as your life used to be', British School at Rome; Store, London ⁄ 2007 'The Freedom of Negative Expression', Chapter, Cardiff ⁄ 2007 'Bent Aura', Outpost, Norwich ⁄ 2007 'Militant Bourgeois', International Project Space, Birmingham, UK; Stedelijk Museum Bureau, Amsterdam ⁄ 2006 'Radical Loyalty', Studio Voltaire, London

—— **Selected group exhibitions** 2009 'Lapdogs of the Bougeoisie', Arnolfini, Bristol ⁄ 2008 'The Impossible Prison', Nottingham Contemporary ⁄ 2008 'Hey, Hey, Glossolalia', Creative Time, New York ⁄ 2007 Athens Biennial ⁄ 2007 'Memorial to the Iraq War', Institute of Contemporary Arts, London

—— **Selected bibliography** 2008 Chris Evans, *Radical Loyalty*, Platform, UK ⁄ 2007 Alex Farquharson, Robert Garnett and Jan Verwoert, *Militant Bourgeois*, Black Diamond, New York ⁄ 2007 Andrew Bonacina, 'Focus: Chris Evans', *Frieze,* Apr. ⁄ 2007 JJ Charlesworth, 'Future Greats', *Art Review*, March ⁄ 2007 Rosemary Heather, 'Chris Evans: REC Project Space at Esther Schipper', *Flash Art*, Mar.–Apr.

Geoffrey Farmer Born 1967, Eagle Island, Canada. Lives in Vancouver, Canada.

—— **Selected solo exhibitions** 2008 Witte de With, Rotterdam ⁄ 2008 Musée d'Art Contemporain de Montréal ⁄ 2007 The Drawing Room, London ⁄ 2007 Spacex, Exeter, UK ⁄ 2005 The Power Plant, Toronto ⁄ 2002 Contemporary Art Gallery, Vancouver ⁄ 2000 Art Gallery of Ontario, Toronto

—— **Selected group exhibitions** 2009 'Nomads', National Gallery of Canada, Ottawa ⁄ 2008 Brussels Biennial ⁄ 2008 'Caught in the Act: Viewer as Performer', National Gallery of Canada, Ottawa ⁄ 2008 Sydney Biennial ⁄ 2008 'The World as a Stage', Institute of Contemporary Art, Boston; Tate Modern, London ⁄ 2007 Montreal Biennial ⁄ 2007 'Gasoline Rainbows', Contemporary Art Gallery, Vancouver ⁄ 2006 'Make Believe', Art Gallery of Alberta ⁄ 2005 'Intertidal: Vancouver Art and Artists', Museum van Hedendaagse Kunst Antwerpen (MuHKA), Antwerp

—— **Selected bibliography** 2008 Zoë Gray, Nicolaus Schafhausen and Monika Szewczyk (eds.), *Geoffrey Farmer*, Witte de With, Rotterdam ⁄ 2008 Pierre Landry, Jessica Morgan and Scott Watson, *Geoffrey Farmer*, Musee d'Art Contemporain de Montréal ⁄ 2008 Monika Szewczyk, 'Changes in the work of Geoffrey Farmer', *Anthology of Exhibition Essays 2006⁄2007*, CJ Press, Vancouver ⁄ 2007 Andrew Bonacina, 'Entrepeneur alone returning back to sculptural form', *Uovo,* no. 13 ⁄ 2006 Jessica Morgan, 'First Take: Jessica Morgan on Geoffrey Farmer', *Artforum*, Jan.

Mounir Fatmi Born 1970, Tangier, Morocco. Lives in Paris, France.

—— **Selected solo exhibitions** 2008 Brussels Biennial ⁄ 2008 'Fuck Architects: Chapter II', Centre d'Art Contemporain le Creux de l'Enfer, Thiers, France ⁄ 2008 'Connexion 02', Galerie Delacroix, Tangiers ⁄ 2007 'In Search of Paradise', Ferdinand van Dieten Gallery, Amsterdam ⁄ 2007 'Something is Possible', Shoshana Wayne Gallery, Los Angeles ⁄ 2007 'J'aime l'Amérique', La Maison Rouge, Fondation Antoine de Galbert, Paris ⁄ 2007 'Sans Histoire', Musée Picasso, La Guerre et la Paix, Vallauris, France

—— **Selected group exhibitions** 2008 'Flow', The Studio Museum in Harlem, New York ⁄ 2008 'Traces du sacré', Centre Pompidou, Paris ⁄ 2008 'Visionary Tales of a Balanced Earth', Te Papa Museum, New Zealand ⁄ 2008 'Traversia', Centro Atlántico de Arte Moderno (CAAM), Canary Islands ⁄ 2008 'Attempt to exhaust an African place', Santa Monica Art Centre, Barcelona ⁄ 2007 Venice Biennal ⁄ 2007 'Frontier(s)', Musée d'Art et d'Histoire, Saint-Brieuc, France ⁄ 2007 Sharjah Biennial ⁄ 2007 'Africa Remix', Johannesburg Art Gallery ⁄ 2007 Luanda Triennial, Angola

—— **Selected bibliography** 2008 Angela Lampe and Jean de Loisy, *Traces du Sacré*, Centre Pompidou, Paris ⁄ 2008 Jérôme Sans (ed.), *In the Arab World Now*, Galerie Enrico Navara, Paris ⁄ 2008 Martina Corgnati (ed.), *The Gates of Mediterranean*, Palazzo del Piozzo Rivoli, Turin ⁄ 2008 Claire Gilman, 'Mounir Fatmi', *Frieze*, Apr. ⁄ 2008 Vali Murtaza, 'Mounir Fatmi, Fuck Architects: Chapter 1', *Art Review*, Jan.

Lara Favaretto Born 1973, Treviso, Italy. Lives in Turin, Italy.

—— **Selected solo exhibitions** 2007 Frieze Projects, Frieze Art Fair, London ⁄ 2006 'Non ho creduto in niente', Galleria Franco Noero, Turin ⁄ 2006 'Cominciò ch'era finita', Galerie Klosterfelde, Berlin ⁄ 2005 'I poveri sono matti ⁄ The poor are mad', Castello di Rivoli Museo d'Arte Contemporanea, Rivoli, Turin

—— **Selected group exhibitions** 2008 Turin Triennial ⁄ 2008 Sydney Biennial ⁄ 2008 'Perplexed in Public', Lisson Gallery; Chelsea College of Art and Design, London ⁄ 2008 'Italia Italie Italien Italy Włochy', Museo d'Arte Contemporanea Sannio (ARCOS), Benevento, Italy ⁄ 2007 'Où?: Scènes du Sud', Palais de Tokyo, Paris ⁄ 2006 'Une seconde une année', Palais de Tokyo, Paris ⁄ 2006 'Trial Balloons ⁄ Globos Sonda', Museo de Arte Contemporáneo de Castilla y León (MUSAC), Spain

—— **Selected bibliography** 2007 Marco Meneguzzo', 'Lara Favaretto', *Artforum*, Feb. ⁄ 2006 Olga Gambari, 'Lara Favaretto', *Flash Art*, Nov.–Dec. ⁄ 2006 Max Andrews, 'Trial Balloons', *Frieze*, Oct. ⁄ 2005 Alessandro Rabottini, 'Lara Favaretto: il future ritrovato', *Flash Art*, Nov.–Dec.

Vincent Fecteau Born 1969, Islip, NY, USA. Lives in San Francisco, CA, USA.

—— **Selected solo exhibitions** 2008 Art Institute of Chicago ⁄ 2006 Galerie Daniel Buchholz, Cologne ⁄ 2005 greengrassi, London ⁄ 2004 'Journal #7', Van Abbemuseum, Holland (with Tomma Abts) ⁄ 2003 Pasadena Museum of California Art, Pasadena, CA, USA

—— **Selected group exhibitions** 2007 'Good Morning, Midnight', Casey Caplan, New York ⁄ 2007 'You Always Move in Reverse', Leo Koenig Inc., New York ⁄ 2007 'A Point in Space Is a Place for an Argument', David Zwirner, New York ⁄ 2007 'Exit Music (For a Film)', Grimm ⁄ Rosenfeld, New York ⁄ 2006 Barbara Gladstone Gallery, New York ⁄ 2006 Armory Centre for Arts, Pasadena, CA ⁄ 2006 'Pure Land: Fecteau-Hill-Pederson', Ratio 3, San Francisco

—— **Selected bibliography** 2005 J.J. Charlesworth, 'Vincent Fecteau: greengrassi', *Modern Painters*, July–Aug. ⁄ 2005 Jennifer Thatcher, 'Vincent Fecteau', *Art Monthly*, Apr. ⁄ 2004 Bruce Hainley, 'Best of 2004', *Artforum*, Dec. ⁄ 2003 Bruce Hainley and Siobhan McDevitt, *Ishstar*, Midway Contemporary Art, Minneapolis

Urs Fischer Born 1973, Zurich, Switzerland. Lives in New York, NY USA, and Zurich, Switzerland.

—— **Selected solo exhibitions** 2009 New Museum, New York ⁄ 2008 Kunstnernes Hus, Oslo ⁄ 2008 'Blurry Renoir Debussy', Galerie Eva Presenhuber, Zurich ⁄ 2007 'Agnes Martin', Regen Projects, Los Angeles ⁄ 2007 'Uh…', Sadie Coles HQ, London ⁄ 2007 'you', Gavin Brown's Enterprise, New York ⁄ 2006 'Paris 1919', Museum Boijmans van Beuningen, Rotterdam ⁄ 2006 'Marry Poppins', Art Museum of the University of Houston

—— **Selected group exhibitions** 2008 'Sammlung ⁄ Collection', Migros Museum für Gegenwartskunst, Zurich ⁄ 2008 'The Hamsterwheel', Malmö Konsthall ⁄ 2008 'Blasted Allegories. Works from the Ringier Collection', Kunstmuseum Lucerne ⁄ 2007 'Sequence 1', Pinault Collection, Palazzo Grassi, Venice ⁄ 2007 'Traum and Trauma: Works from The Dakis Joannou Collection', Museum Moderner Kunst Stiftung Ludwig Wien (MuMok), Vienna; Kunsthalle Vienna ⁄ 2007 'The Third Mind', Palais de Tokyo, Paris ⁄ 2007 'Unmonumental', New Museum, New York

—— **Selected bibliography** 2008 Bob Nickas, 'Urs Fischer', *Artforum*, Dec. ⁄ 2008 Gavin Brown, 'Interview with Urs Fischer', *Interview*, Dec.–Jan. ⁄ 2007 Maurizio Cattelan, 'Maurizio Cattelan interviews Urs Fischer', *Mousse*, Nov. ⁄ 2006 Rein Wolfs, *Paris 1919*, JRP Ringier, Zurich ⁄ 2004 Mirjam Varadinis (ed.), *Kir Royal*, JRP Ringier, Zurich

Daphne Fitzpatrick Born 1964, Long Island, New York. Lives in New York, NY, USA.

—— **Selected solo exhibitions** 2007 'A Roll in the Hay', Bellwether, New York

—— **Selected group exhibitions** 2009 'The Shape of Things to Come: New Sculpture', Saatchi Gallery, London ⁄ 2008 'Jekyll Island', Honor Fraser, Los Angeles ⁄ 2007 'Future 86', Parksville, New York ⁄ 2007 '07⁄08', Bellwether, New York ⁄ 2007 'Shared Women', Los Angeles Contemporary Exhibitions ⁄ 2006 'Ridykeulous', Participant Inc., New York ⁄ 2005 'Part Three: Last Minute', Orchard47, New York

—— **Selected bibliography** 2007 Jerry Saltz, 'Daphne Fitzpatrick: Critics' Pick', *New York Magazine*, Nov. ⁄ 2007, Andrea Scott, 'Daphne Fitzpatrick', *The New Yorker*, 12 Nov. ⁄ 2007, Holland Cotter, 'Daphne Fitzpatrick: A Roll in the Hay', *The New York Times*, 2 Nov. ⁄ 2007 Chris Bors, 'A Duchampian Sanford and Son', *Artslant New York*, Oct. ⁄ 2007 Helen Molesworth, 'Worlds Apart', *Artforum*, May

Ryan Gander Born 1976, Chester, UK. Lives in London, UK.

—— **Selected solo exhibitions** 2008–09 'Heralded as the new black', Museum Boijmans Van Beuningen, Rotterdam; Ikon, Birmingham, UK; South London Gallery ⁄ 2008 'Something Vague', St Gallen Kunstverein; Bonner Kunstverein, Bonn ⁄ 2007 'Passengers', CCA Wattis Institute for Contemporary Arts, San Francisco ⁄ 2007 'Short cut through the trees' Museum moderner Kunst Stiftung Ludwig Wien (MUMOK), Vienna ⁄ 2007 'The Last Work', Stedelijk Museum, Amsterdam ⁄ 2007 'Cinema Verso', Whitechapel East Wing, London

—— **Selected group exhibitions** 2009 'The Space of Words', Musée d'Art Moderne (MUDAM), Grand-Duc Jean ⁄ 2009 Museo Arte Contemporánea de Vigo (MARCO), Spain ⁄ 2008 'Wouldn't it be nice', Centre d'Art Contemporain, Geneva ⁄ 2008 Sydney Biennial ⁄ 2008 'The flight of the Dodo', Project Arts Centre, Dublin ⁄ 2007 Performa, New York 2007 Lyon Biennial ⁄ 2007 'You have not been honest', Museo D'Arte Donnaregina, Naples ⁄ 2007 'Whenever It Starts It Is The Right Time', Frankfurter Kunstverein

—— **Selected bibliography** 2008 Dan Fox, 'Where to Begin?', *Frieze*, June–July ⁄ 2008 Rebecca May Marston, Nigel Prince and Brian Sholis, *Heralded as the new black*, Ikon Gallery, Birmingham, UK ⁄ 2008 Diana Baldon, 'Ryan Gander: South London Gallery', *Artforum*, Oct. ⁄ 2007 Charles Esche, Francesco Manacorda and Hans-Ulrich Obrist, *Ryan Gander: Intellectual Colours*, Silvana Editoriale S.p.A.,

Mila and Dena Foundation for Contemporary Art, Paris / 2007 Bice Curiger, 'The Prolific Pleasures of Paradox', *Parkett*, no. 80

Gelitin Wolfgang Gantner, born 1971, Wiener Neustadt, Austria / Ali Janka, born 1970, St Poelten, Austria / Florian Reither, born 1968, Bruck an der Muhr, Austria / Tobias Urban, 1966, Lueneburg, Germany. Live in Vienna, Austria.
— **Selected solo exhibitions** 2008 'La Louvre Paris', Musée d'Art Moderne de la Ville de Paris / 2007 'The Dig Cunt: Six Actions for New York City', Creative Time, New York / 2006 'Chinese / Synthese / Leberkäse', Kunsthaus Bregenz, Austria / 2006 'Hugris', Kling & Bang Gallery, Reykjavík / 2005, 'Tantamounter 24/7', Leo Koenig Inc., New York; 'Sweatwat', Gagosian Gallery, London
— **Selected group exhibitions** 2008 'Psycho Buildings', Hayward Gallery, London / 2007, 'Stellungswechsel 500', Hamsterwheel, Venice Biennale / 2005 Performa, New York / 2005 Moscow Biennial
— **Selected bibliography** 2008 Gelitin, *Gelitin's acb*, Walther König, Cologne / 2008 Gelitin, *monalisa*, Walther König, Cologne / 2007 gelitin, *Das Kakabet*, Walther König, Cologne / 2007 Herbert Lachmayer, 'Inspiring Decadence', *Parkett*, no. 796 / 2005 Christina Romano, 'Gelitin: Hase', *Domus*, no. 885

Loris Gréaud Born 1979, Eaubonne, France. Lives in Paris, France.
— **Selected solo exhibitions** 2008 'Cellar Door, Once is Always Twice', Institute of Contemporary Arts, London / 2006 'Cellar Door', Palais de Tokyo, Paris / 2006 'Illusion is a Revolutionary Weapon', Swiss Institute, New York; Institute of Contemporary Arts, London; Centro Culturale Francese (CCF), Milan; Omote Sando, Tokyo / 2005 'Silence Goes More Quickly When Played Backwards', Le Plateau, Paris / 2005 'Devils Tower', Centre Pompidou; Musée National d'Art Moderne, Paris
— **Selected group exhibitions** 2009 Tate Triennial, London / 2008 Turin Triennial / 2008 'The Wizard of Oz', CCA Wattis Institute for Contemporary Art, San Francisco / 2008 'Martian Museum of Terrestrial Art', Barbican Art Gallery, London / 2006 'Repeat Redux', Whitney Museum of American Art, New York
— **Selected bibliography** 2008 Raimundas Malasauskas and Aaron Schuster, *Cellar Door*, JRP Ringier, Zurich / 2008 Claire Moulène, 'Cellar Door', *Artforum*, Summer / 2008 Vivian Rehberg, 'Doors of Perception', *Frieze*, June–July / 2008 Amy Serafin, 'The Taste of Nothing, The Smell of Mars', *The New York Times*, 9 Mar. / 2006 Loris Gréaud (ed.), *End Extend*, Editions HYX, Orléans, France

Rachel Harrison Born 1966, New York, NY, USA. Lives in New York, NY, USA.
— **Selected solo exhibitions** 2009 Center for Curatorial Studies, Bard College, Annandale-on-Hudson, NY; Portikus, Frankfurt / 2008 'Lay of the Land', Le Consortium, Dijon / 2007 'Voyage of the Beagle', Migros Museum für Gegenwartskunst, Zurich / 2007 Kunsthalle Nürnberg, Nuremburg / 2006 'When Hangover Becomes Form' (with Scott Lyall), Contemporary Art Gallery, Vancouver; Los Angeles Contemporary Exhibitions
— **Selected group exhibitions** 2008 'Plug In #38', Vanabbemuseum, Eindhoven / 2008 Whitney Biennial, New York / 2007 'Unmonumental', New Museum, New York / 2006 'The Uncertainty of Objects and Ideas: Recent Sculpture', Hirshhorn Museum and Sculpture Garden, Washington, DC, USA / 2006 Berlin Biennial
— **Selected bibliography** 2008 George Baker, 'Mind the Gap' / 2008 Ina Blom, 'All Dressed Up' / 2008 Allison M. Gingeras, '(Un) Natural Selection' and Richard Hawkins, 'Enigmarelle: The Statuesque', *Parkett*, no. 82 / 2007 John Kelsey, Heike Munder and Ellen Seifermann, *If I Did It*, Migros Museum für Gegenwartskunst, Zurich, Kunsthalle Nürnberg, Nuremburg and JRP Ringier, Zurich / 2007 Jennifer Allen, 'Moving Targets', *Frieze*, Oct. / 2005 Brian Sholis, 'Two Into One' and Catherine Wood, 'The Stuff: Rachel Harrison's Sculpture', *Afterall*, no. 11

Jay Heikes Born 1975, Princeton, NJ, USA. Lives in Minneapolis, MN, USA.
— **Selected solo exhibitions** 2007 Project Space, Institute of Contemporary Art, Philadelphia / 2007 Marianne Boesky Gallery, New York / 2006 Shane Campbell Gallery, Chicago / 2005 P.S.1 Contemporary Art Center, New York
— **Selected group exhibitions** 2008 'Depositions', Galerie Francesca Pia, Zurich / 2008 'Martian Museum of Terrestrial Art', Barbican Art Gallery, London / 2007 'Sympathy for the Devil: Art and Rock and Roll Since 1967', Museum of Contemporary Art, Chicago / 2007 Museum of Contemporary Art, North Miami / 2007 'The Office', Tanya Bonakdar Gallery, New York / 2006 'Ordinary Culture: Heikes / Helms / McMillan', Walker Art Center, Minneapolis / 2006 Whitney Biennial, New York
— **Selected bibliography** 2008 Nick Stillman, 'Jay Heikes', *Artforum*, Jan. / 2007 Philippe Vergne, 'Jay Heikes', *Ice Cream: Contemporary Art in Culture*, Phaidon Press, London / 2006 Claire Barliant, 'Emerging Artists: Jay Heikes', *Modern Painters*, Oct.

Jeppe Hein Born 1974, Copenhagen, Denmark. Lives in Copenhagen, Denmark, and Berlin, Germany.
— **Selected solo exhibitions** 2009 Århus Kunstmuseum, Denmark / 2009 Indianapolis Museum of Art, IN, USA / 2009 Vancouver Art Gallery, Vancouver / 2008 Bonner Kunstverein, Bonn / 2007 'Objects in the mirror are closer than they appear', Carré d'Art, Musée d'Art Contemporain de Nimes, France / 2007 'Illusion', SculptureCenter, New York / 2007 'Distance', The Curve, Barbican Art Gallery, London
— **Selected group exhibitions** 2008 Institut d'Art Contemporain Villeurbanne, Lyon / 2008 Singapore Biennial / 2008 'Museum as Medium', Museo de Arte Contemporánea (MARCO), Vigo, Spain / 2008 'Reconstruction #3', Sudeley Castle, Winchecombe, UK / 2008 'Fluid Street: Alone, Together', Kiasma Museum, Helsinki / 2008 'The World as a Stage', Institute of Contemporary Art, Boston; Tate Modern, London / 2007 'Just Use it!', Nordjyllands Kunstmuseum, Ålborg, Denmark / 2007 'The Freak Show', Musée d'art Contemporain, Lyon / 2007 'Made in Germany', Kunstverein Hanover
— **Selected bibliography** 2008 Dmitry Komis, 'Jeppe Hein', *Flash Art*, May–June / 2007 Michel Gauthier and Jeppe Hein, *Reflectingly Yours: Jeppe Hein Objects in the mirror are closer than they appear*, Carré d'Art Musée d'Art Contemporain de Nîmes, France / 2006 Francesco Bonami, Michel Gauthier and Ilina Koralova, *Jeppe Hein: Until Now*, Walther König, Cologne / 2006 Francesco Stocchi, 'Jeppe Hein', *Artforum*, Oct.

Roger Hiorns Born 1975, Birmingham, UK. Lives in London, UK.
— **Selected solo exhibitions** 2008 Corvi-Mora, London / 2008 Jerwood Artangel Open, Harper Road, London / 2007 Church of Saint Paulinus, Richmond, UK / 2007 Camden Arts Centre, London / 2007 Marc Foxx, Los Angeles / 2006 Cubitt Gallery, London / 2006 Milton Keynes Gallery
— **Selected group exhibitions** 2008 Busan Biennial / 2008 'Thyssen-Bornemisza Art Contemporary: As Aleph', Kunsthaus Graz / 2007 'If Everybody had an Ocean: Brian Wilson An Art Exhibition', CAPC Musée d'Art Contemporain, Bordeaux / 2007 'Good Morning, Midnight', Casey Kaplan, New York; Athens Biennial / 2006 'How to Improve the World: 60 Years of British Art', Hayward Gallery, London
— **Selected bibliography** 2008 Tom Morton and Roger Hiorns, 'Seizure: Roger Hiorns', *Frieze*, Sep. / 2008 Skye Sherwin, 'The Asphalt Jungle: Artangel', *Art Review*, July–Aug. / 2008 Bruce Hainley, 'Roger Hiorns', *Artforum*, Mar.

Evan Holloway Born 1967, La Mirada, CA, USA. Lives in Los Angeles, CA, USA.
— **Selected solo exhibitions** 2009 The Approach W2, London / 2008 'Projects Series: #35', Pomona College Museum of Art, Claremont, CA, USA / 2007 'Scripted and Scored', Raucci Santamaria, Naples / 2006 '$ocial Epi$temology', Harris Lieberman Gallery, New York / 2005 'Analog Counter-revolution', The Approach E2, London / 2004 'I Don't Exist', Marc Foxx, Los Angeles; San Francisco Museum of Modern Art
— **Selected group exhibitions** 2008 'The Wizard of Oz', CCA Wattis Institute for Contemporary Art, San Francisco; 'The Impossible Prison', Nottingham Contemporary / 2007 'Ensemble', Institute of Contemporary Art, Philadelphia / 2006 'The Uncertainty of Objects and Ideas', Hirshhorn Museum and Sculpture Garden, Washington, DC, USA; 'Gone Formalism', Institute of Contemporary Art, Philadelphia / 2005 'Sculpture d'Appartment', Musée Department d'Art Contemporain de Rochechouart, France
— **Selected bibliography** 2008 Christopher Knight, 'Low-tech, yet high on wow', *Los Angeles Times*, 2 May / 2007 Michelle Kuo, 'The Uncertainty of Object and Ideas', *Artforum*, Feb. / 2005 Dan Adler, 'Evan Holloway at Marc Foxx', *Art in America*, May / 2004, Dennis Cooper and Lee Trimming, 'Evan Holloway: Third Space', *Flash Art*, Nov.–Dec.

Christian Holstad Born 1972, Anaheim, CA, USA. Lives in New York, NY, USA.
— **Selected solo exhibitions** 2009 Victoria Miro Gallery / 2009 Galleria Nazionale d'Arte Moderna, Rome / 2007 Galleria Massimo deCarlo, Milan / 2006 'Christian Holstad: The Terms of Endearment', Museum of Contemporary Art, Miami / 2006 'Leather Beach', Prince Deli (Daniel Reich Gallery), New York
— **Selected group exhibitions** 2008 Yokohama Triennial / 2008 'Art and Entrepeneurship', Chelsea Art Museum, New York / 2008 'The Dark Fair', Swiss Institute, New York / 2007 'Unmonumental', New Museum, New York / 2007 Lyon Biennial / 2007 Moscow Biennial / 2006 'Panic Room: Works from the Dakis Joannou Collection', Deste Foundation, Athens
— **Selected bibliography** 2008 Nick Weist, 'All that Glitters', *Tokion*, vol. 2 / 2007 Rosalee Goldberg, *Performa: New Visual Art Performance*, David Krut Publishing, New York / 2006 Maurizio Cattelan, 'Christian Holstad', *Flash Art*, Nov. / 2006 Holland Cotter, 'Christian Holstad', *The New York Times*, 24 Mar. / 2006 Christopher Bollen, 'Christian Holstad', *Artforum*, May / 2004 Christian Holstad, *Dignity (Pressed Flowers)*, Snoeck-Ducaju & Zoon NV Publisher, Gent / 2004 Aurel Scheibler, Berlin and Cologne

Thomas Houseago Born 1972, Leeds, UK. Lives in Los Angeles, CA, USA.
— **Selected solo exhibitions** 2008 'Serpent', David Kordansky Gallery, Los Angeles / 2008 'When Earth Fucks With Space', Xavier Hufkens, Brussels / 2008 'Bastard', Herald St, London / 2007 'A Million Miles Away', The Modern Institute, Glasgow
— **Selected group exhibitions** 2008 'Black Swan', Michael Werner Gallery, London / 2008 'Kabul 3000: Love Among the Cabbages', Zero, Milan / 2008 'Grandeur: Sonsbeek 2008', Arnhem, Netherlands / 2007 'Strange things

permit themselves the luxury of occurring', Camden Arts Centre, London / 2006 'Red Eye: Los Angeles Artists from the Rubell Family Collection', Rubell Family Collection, Miami — **Selected bibliography** 2008 Hans Werner Holzwarth (ed.), *Art Now 3*, Taschen, Cologne / 2007 Mark Coetzee, Michael Darling, Michael Holte and Jason Rubell, 'Red Eye: Los Angeles Artists from the Rubell Family Collection,' Rubell Family Collection, Miami / 2007 Skye Sherwin, 'Future Greats: Thomas Houseago', *Art Review*, Mar.

Matthew Day Jackson Born 1974 Panorama City, CA, USA. Lives in New York, NY, USA. — **Selected solo exhibitions** 2008 'Terranaut: Paintings and Sculpture' Peter Blum Chelsea, New York / 2008 'Drawings from Tlön', Nicole Klagsbrun, New York / 2007 'Diptych', Mario Diacono at Ars Libri, Boston / 2007 'The Lower 48', Perry Rubenstein Gallery, New York / 2007 'Paradise Now! (The Salvage)', Workspace, Blanton Museum of Art, Austin, TX, USA / 2006 'Paradise Now! (Limbo)', Cubitt, London / 2006 'Paradise Now!' Portland Institute of Contemporary Art — **Selected group exhibitions** 2008 'Matthew Day Jackson and Sara Krajewski: The Violet Hour', Henry Art Gallery, University of Washington, Seattle / 2008 'The Old, Weird America', Contemporary Arts Museum Houston / 2008 'Martian Museum of Terrestrial', Barbican Art Gallery, London / 2008 'Heartland', Van Abbemuseum, Eindhoven / 2007 'To Build a Fire', Rivington Arms, New York / 2007 Athens Biennial / 2006 'USA Today', Royal Academy of Arts, London — **Selected bibliography** 2008 Jen Graves, 'The Lunatic is on the Grass: Pink Floyd, a Crashed Corvette, and Brutalist Architecture at the Henry Capturing the Angst of an Era', *The Stranger*, 28 Aug. / 2006 Kristin M. Jones, 'Matthew Day Jackson', *Frieze*, Mar. / 2006 John Motley, 'Matthew Day Jackson', *PICA*, Sep. / 2005 Clemence de Cambourg, 'The History Man', *Art Review*. Nov.

Koo Jeong-A Born 1967, Seoul, Korea. Lives in Berlin, Germany, London, UK, and Paris, France — **Selected solo exhibitions** 2008 Yvon Lambert, Paris / 2008 Maribel Lopez Gallery, Berlin / 2008 Pinksummer, Genoa / 2007 'oussseux', Centre International d'Art et du Paysage, Ile de Vassiviere / 2007 Aspen Museum, CO, USA / 2007 'Temporary Measures', Associates, London / 2004 'Wednesday', Portikus, Frankfurt / 2004 'club koo', Centre Pompidou, Paris — **Selected group exhibitions** 2009 'Your Bright Future', Museum of Fine Arts, Houston; Los Angeles County Museum of Art (LACMA) / 2009 Performa 09, New York / 2008 'God and Goods', Villa Manin Centre for Contemporary Art, Udine, Italy; Turin Triennial / 2007 'Wherever we go', San Francisco Art Institute; 'Various Small Fires', Royal College of Art Galleries, London — **Selected bibliography** 2008 Vivian Rehberg, 'Koo Jeong-A', *Frieze*, Apr. / 2004 Christine Macel, *Koo Jeong-A, livre numéro 1*, Centre Pompidou, Paris / 2003 Brigitte Huck, 'Koo Jeong-A: Secession', *Artforum*, June / 2002 Matthias Herrmann and Cedric Price, *Koo Jeong-A*, Secession, Vienna

Daniel Joglar Born 1966, Mar del Plata, Argentina. Lives in Buenos Aires, Argentina. — **Selected solo exhibitions** 2007 Panamerican Art Projects, Dallas / 2006 'Cosas sin hacer, cosas para hacer mañana', Artist's Space, New York / 2006 'Nothing in my hands, nothing up my sleeves', Centro Colombo Americano, Bogotá / 2005 'Sonidas Distantes', Dabbah Torrejon Gallery, Buenos Aires — **Selected group exhibitions** 2008 'Releve', Andrew Edwin Gallery, New York / 2008 'Visions from abroad', Flushing Town Hall Gallery, New York / 2008 'Fantasma', Universidad Torcuato di Tella, Buenos Aires / 2007 'Red Badge of Courage', The National Newark Building, New York / 2007 'Ouro Sentimental', Museum of Modern Art of Niteroi, Rio de Janeiro / 2007 'Off Fora', Pontevedra Biennial, Centro Cultural Recoleta, Buenos Aires / 2006 'MALBA, donaciones, adquisiciones y comodatos', Museo de Arte Latinoamericano de Buenos Aires — **Selected bibliography** 2007 Maria Rosa Ramirez, 'Daniel Joglar: Centro Colombo Americano', *Art Nexus*, no. 63 / 2006 Tamara Stuby, 'Daniel Joglar', *Contemporary*, no. 79 / 2006 Ines Katszenstein, 'South of the South', *Untitled*, no. 37 / 2005 Eva Grinstein, 'Daniel Joglar', *Arte Contexto*, no. 8 / 2004 Maria Gainza, 'La vida sobre la mesa', *Pagina 12*, June

Matt Johnson Born 1978, New York, NY, USA. Lives in Los Angeles, CA, USA. — **Selected solo exhibitions** 2009 Taxter & Spengemann, New York / 2006 Blum & Poe, Los Angeles / 2005 Taxter & Spengemann, New York / 2004 Taxter & Spengemann, New York — **Selected group exhibitions** 2007 'All about laughter', Mori Art Museum, Tokyo / 2007 'Makers and Modelers', Gladstone Gallery, New York / 2007 'Time Difference', Frank Cohen Collection, Initial Access Gallery, Wolverhampton / 2005 'Thing', Hammer Museum, Los Angeles — **Selected bibliography** 2007 Sally O'Reilly, 'Funny Guys: All About Laughter', *Art Review*, Jan. / 2006 Sonia Campagnola, 'Focus on Los Angeles', *Flash Art*, Jan. – Feb. / 2006 Mariuccia Casadio, 'Intimacy', *Vogue Italia*, Feb. / 2006 Christopher Knight, 'Daring to tread on the turf of a master', *Los Angeles Times*, 6 Oct.

Brian Jungen Born 1970, Fort St John, Canada. Lives in Vancouver, Canada. — **Selected solo exhibitions** 2009 Fonds Régionaux d'Art Contemporain, Orléans, France / 2007 Museum Villa Stuck, Munich / 2006 Witte de With, Rotterdam / 2006 Level 2 Gallery, Tate Modern, London / 2006 Vancouver Art Gallery, Vancouver / 2006 Musée d'Art Contemporain de Montréal / 2005 New Museum, New York — **Selected group exhibitions** 2008 'Hard Targets: Sport and Contemporary American Masculinity', Los Angeles County Museum of Art (LACMA) / 2008 'NeoHooDoo: Art For a Forgotten Faith', The Menil Collection, Houston; P.S.1 Contemporary Art Center, New York / 2008 Sydney Biennial / 2008 'Martian Museum of Terrestrial Art,' Barbican Art Gallery, London / 2007 Lyon Biennial / 2007 Montreal Biennial / 2006 '274 East 1st', Catriona Jeffries, Vancouver — **Selected bibliography** 2008, Brian Sholis, 'Brian Jungen: Casey Kaplan Gallery', *Artforum*, Summer / 2008 Candice Hopkins, 'Ruptures on the Architectural Grid: Brian Jungen's Treaty Project ...', *Informal Architecture: Space and Contemporary Culture*, Black Dog Publishing, London / 2007 Nat Muller, 'Brian Jungen', *Springerin*, Winter / 2006 Homi Bhabha et al., *Brian Jungen*, Witte de With, Rotterdam / 2005 Daina Augaitis, et al., *Brian Jungen*, Vancouver Art Gallery and Douglas & McIntyre

Kitty Kraus Born 1976, Heidelberg, Germany. Lives in Berlin, Germany. — **Selected solo exhibitions** 2008 'blauorange 2008: Kunstpreis der Deutschen Volks und Raiffeisenbanken', Kunstverein Heilbronn, Germany / 2008 Kunsthalle Zürich / 2007 Galerie Senn, Vienna / 2006 Galerie Neu, Berlin — **Selected group exhibitions** 2009 'Modern Modern Art', Chelsea Art Museum, New York / 2008 'The Skat Players', Vilma Gold, London / 2008 'Act so that I can speak to you', Galerie Kamm, Berlin / 2008 'MD 72', Mehringdamm 72, Berlin / 2008 'Porzadki Uronje: So ist es und anders', Muzeum Sztuki, Lodz Museum Abteiberg, Moenchengladbach / 2007 'Filaturen', Sies + Höke Galerie, Dusseldorf / 2006 'Optik Schröder: Werke aus der Sammlung Schröder', Kunsthalle Braunschweig, Germany — **Selected bibliography** 2008 Christy Lange, 'Kitty Kraus: Identical dimensions and precarious constellations', *Frieze*, Oct. / 2008 Daniel Völzke, 'Malewitschs Enkel', *Monopol*, no. 2 / 2007 Ursula Maria Probst, 'Exzentrischer Minimalismus', *Spike*, Fall / 2006 Jennifer Allen, 'o.T', *Artforum*, Nov.

Gabriel Kuri Born 1970, Mexico City, Mexico. Lives in Brussels, Belgium and Mexico City, Mexico. — **Selected solo exhibitions** 2009 Franco Noero, Turin / 2008 'Model for a Victory Parade', Sadie Coles HQ, London / 2007 'Space made to measure object, made to measure space', Esther Schipper, Berlin / 2007 'Reforma Fiscal 2007', Galería Kurimanzutto, Mexico City / 2006 'and thanks in advance', Govett-Brewster, New Plymouth / 2006 'dato duro, dato blando, dato ciego', Galleria Franco Noero, Turin — **Selected group exhibitions** 2009 'The Space of the Work and the Place of the Object', SculptureCentre, New York / 2008 Berlin Biennial / 2007 'Unmonumental', New Museum, New York / 2007 'Brave New Worlds', Walker Art Center, Minneapolis — **Selected bibliography** 2008 Katerina Gregos, 'Between Hard Facts and Soft Information', *Janus*, Jan. / 2007 Gabriel Kuri, *and thanks in advance*, Govett Brewster Art Gallery, New Plymouth / 2006 Jessica Morgan, *Gabriel Kuri: Suggested Taxation Scheme*, Roma Publications, Amsterdam / 2006 Gabriel Kuri, *En Cuenta*, Imschoot Publishers, Ghent / 2005 Maxine Kopsa and Dieter Roelstraete, *Compost Index*, Roma Publications, Amsterdam

Robert Kusmirowski Born 1973, Lodz, Poland. Lives in Lublin, Poland. — **Selected solo exhibitions** 2008 Guido Costa Projects, Turin / 2008 'P.A.P.O.P.', Museum Dhondt-Dhaenens, Deurle, Belgium / 2007 'DATAmatic 880', Galerie Magazin, Berlin / 2006 Migros Museum für Gegenwarts-kunst, Zurich / 2006 'Ornamente der Anatomie, Band II', Kunstverein in Hamburg / 2006 'At the Very Centre of Attention 7', (with Rafal Bujnowski) Centre for Contemporary Art Ujazdowski Castle, Warsaw — **Selected group exhibitions** 2008 Turin Triennial / 2008 'After Nature', New Museum, New York / 2008 Folkestone Triennial / 2008 'Go for it! Olbricht Collection (a sequel)', Neues Museum Weserburg, Bremen, Germany / 2008 'Of this Tale I cannot guarantee a single word', Royal College of Art Galleries, London / 2007 'Mot Tiden / Against Time', Bonniers Konsthall, Stockholm / 2007 'Rockers Island', Olbricht Collection, Museum Folkwang, Essen / 2007 'On Tectonics of History', Wyspa Institute of Art, Gdansk — **Selected bibliography** 2007 Sara Arrhenius and Magnus Bergh (eds.), *Anachronisms*, Bonniers Konsthall, Stockholm, Albert Bonniers Förlag, Stockholm / 2007 Katerina Gregos, 'Robert Kusmirowski: A 20th Century History', *Flash Art*, Jan.–Feb. / 2007 Yannis Tsitsovits, 'Robert Kusmirowski', *Stimulus respond*, Oct.–Nov. / 2005 Yilmaz Dziewior (ed.), *Robert Kusmirowski, The Ornaments of Anatomy*, Kunstverein in Hamburg, Hatje Cantz, Ostfildern

Lisa Lapinski Born 1967, Palo Alto, CA, USA. Lives in Los Angeles, CA, USA. — **Selected solo exhibitions** 2008 'Linz Wedding Song', Richard Telles Fine Art,

Los Angeles / 2008 'MOCA Focus: Lisa Lapinski, The Fret and Its Variants', Museum of Contemporary Art, Los Angeles / 2007 'Linz Wedding Song', Midway Contemporary Art, Minneapolis / 2006 'Fine Evening, Sir!', Johann König, Berlin
—— **Selected group exhibitions** 2008 'Zuordnungsprobleme', Johann König, Berlin / 2007 'Pure Self-Expression', Kölnischer Kunstverein, Cologne / 2007 'Uneasy Angel/ Imagine Los Angeles', Sprüth Magers Projekte, Munich / 2007 'Good Morning, Midnight', Casey Kaplan Gallery, New York / 2007 'LA Desire (Part 2)', Galerie Dennis Kimmerich, Dusseldorf / 2006 Whitney Biennial, New York / 2006 'The Swan is very Peaceful...', Richard Telles Fine Art, Los Angeles
—— **Selected bibliography** 2008 Bennet Simpson, *MOCA Focus: Lisa Lapinski: The Fret and its Variants*, The Museum of Contemporary Art, Los Angeles / 2007 Maria Muhle, 'Die Kunst des Handwerks — or risking your life for tautology', *Text Zur Kunst*, Mar. / 2007 Aurélie Voltz, 'Lisa Lapinski', *Flash Art*, Mar.–Apr. / 2006 Terry Meyers, 'freezer burn', *Modern Painters*, May

Camilla Løw Born 1976, Oslo Norway. Lives in Glasgow, UK.
—— **Selected solo exhibitions** 2008 'New Ruins', Bergen Kunsthall, Norway / 2008 'Embraced Open Reassembled', Sutton Lane, London / 2008 'Straight Letters', Dundee Contemporary Arts; Pier Art Centre, Orkney, UK / 2007 'Broken Windows', Elastic Gallery, Malmö, Sweden
—— **Selected group exhibitions** / 2008 'Idealismusstudio', Grazer Kunstverein / 2007 'Language of Vision', Middlesbrough Institute of Arts, UK / 2007 'Dump: Postmodern Sculpture in the Dissolved Field', The National Museum of Art, Architecture and Design, Oslo / 2006 'How to Improve the World: 60 Years of British Art', Hayward Gallery, London, Gas Hall, Birmingham / 2006 'Try Again Fail Again Fail Better', Momentum 4th Nordic Festival of Contemporary Art, Moss / 2006 'Sixty Years of Sculpture in the Arts Council Collection', Longside Gallery, Yorkshire Sculpture Park, Wakefield, UK
—— **Selected bibliography** 2008 Michael Archer and Sarah Lowndes, *Straight Letters*, Dundee Contemporary Arts / 2007 Randi Godø, Andrea Kroksnes and Marianne Yvenes, *Dump: Postmodern Sculpture in the Dissolved Field*, The National Museum of Art, Architecture and Design, Oslo / 2006 Marjorie Allthorpe-Guyton, Michael Archer and Roger Malbert, *How To Improve The World, 60 Years of British Art: Arts Council Collection*, Hayward Gallery, London

Renata Lucas Born 1971, Ribeirão Preto, Brazil. Lives in São Paulo, Brazil.
—— **Selected solo exhibitions** 2007 'Resident', Gasworks, London / 2007 'Falha', Gallery at REDCAT, Los Angeles / 2006 'Atlas', Galeria Milan Antonio, São Paulo / 2005 'Gentileza', Galeria A Gentil Carioca, Rio de Janeiro / 2003 'Cruzamento', Castelinho do Flamengo, Rio de Janeiro / 2003 'Antifogo-Falha', Paco das Artes, São Paulo
—— **Selected group exhibitions** 2008 Sydney Biennial / 2008 'The World as a Stage', The Institute of Contemporary Art, Boston; Tate Modern, London / 2008 'God is Design', Galeria Fortes Vilaça, São Paulo / 2007 'Positions in Context: 2007 Cifo Grants Program Exhibition', Cisneros Fontanals Art Foundation, Miami / 2007 'For Sale', Galeria Cristina Guerra, Lisbon / 2006 São Paulo Biennial
—— **Selected bibliography** 2008 Eva Fabris, 'Manipulating Architecture', *Mousse*, Jan. / 2007 Clara Kim, Adriano Pedrosa and Lynn Zelevansky, *Renata Lucas*, Gallery at REDCAT, Los Angeles / 2007 Jessica Morgan and Catherine Wood, *The World as a Stage*, Tate Publishing, London / 2007 Jens Hoffmann, *For Sale*, Galeria Cristina Guerra, Lisbon / 2007 Christopher Bedford, 'Renata Lucas', *Artforum*, Nov. / 2007 Lisette Lagnado, 'Turning so many corners', *Frieze*, May

Nathan Mabry Born 1978, Durango, CO, USA. Lives in Los Angeles, CA, USA.
—— **Selected solo exhibitions** 2008 Cherry and Martin, Los Angeles/ 2006 Cherry and Martin, Los Angeles
—— **Selected group exhibitions** 2008 'LA Now', Las Vegas Art Museum / 2008 'Take Me There (Show Me The Way)', Haunch of Venison, New York / 2008 'Weighing and Wanting: 25 Years of Collecting', Museum of Contemporary Art San Diego / 2008 'Idle Youth', Gladstone Gallery, New York / 2008 'Kabul 3000: Love Among The Cabbages', Zero, Milan / 2008 'Past Forward', 176, London / 2007 'Hammer Contemporary Collection: Part II', Hammer Museum, Los Angeles / 2006 'Red Eye: Los Angeles Artists from the Rubell Family Collection', Rubell Family Collection, Miami
—— **Selected bibliography** 2008 Russell Ferguson, *Idle Youth*, Gladstone Gallery, New York / 2008 Christopher Bedford, 'Nathan Mabry', *Frieze*, June–Aug. / 2008 Ben Borthwick et al., *Past Forward*, 176, London / 2008 Shana Nys Dambrot, 'Nathan Mabry at Cherry and Martin', *Artweek*, no. 39 / 2008 James Scarborough, 'Nathan Mabry at Cherry and Martin', *Art in America*, May

Goshka Macuga Born 1967, Warsaw, Poland. Lives in London, UK.
—— **Selected solo exhibitions** 2009 Kunsthalle Basel / 2009 Whitechapel Gallery, London / 2008 Galerie Rüdiger Schöttle, Munich / 2007 Tate Britain, London / 2006 A Foundation, Liverpool / 2006 Kate MacGarry, London
—— **Selected group exhibitions** 2008 Turner Prize, Tate Britain, London / 2008 'The Great Transformation: Art and Tactical Magic', Frankfurter Kunstverein / 2008 Berlin Biennial / 2008 'Martian Museum of Terrestrial Art', Barbican Art Gallery, London / 2008 'Santhal Family: Positions Around an Indian Sculpture', Museum van Hedendaagse Kunst Antwerpen (MuHKA), Antwerp / 2006 'The Past is a Foreign Country: They do Things Differently There, Mathilda is Calling', Institut Mathildenhöhe, Darmstadt, Germany
—— **Selected bibliography** 2009 Monika Szewczyk, 'Goshka Macuga', *Afterall*, no. 20 / 2008 Bryony Bond (ed.), *Goshka Macuga: Sleep of Ulro*, Veenman, Rotterdam / 2008 Arifa Akbar, 'Shortlist for Turner Prize promises end to male domination', *The Independent*, 14 May / 2007 Jonathan Griffin, 'Goshka Macuga', *Frieze*, July / 2007 Skye Sherwin, 'Goshka Macuga, The New Museum: Constructing Cultural Identity', *Art Review*, May / 2007 Michael Wilson, 'Goshka Macuga', *Artforum*, Apr.

Mark Manders Born 1968, Volke, Netherlands. Lives in Arnhem, Netherlands, and Ronse, Belgium.
—— **Selected solo exhibitions** 2007–09 'The Absence of Mark Manders', Kunstverein Hanover; Stedelijk Museum, Amsterdam; Bergen Kunsthall, Norway; Kunsthaus Zürich / 2006 'Short Sad Thoughts', Baltic Centre for Contemporary Art, Gateshead
—— **Selected group exhibitions** 2008 'Life on Mars', 55th Carnegie International, Carnegie Museum of Art, Pittsburgh / 2006 Berlin Biennial / 2004 Manifesta 5, San Sebastian, Spain / 2002 Documenta 11, Kassel / 2002 'Drawing Now: Eight Propositions', The Museum of Modern Art, New York
—— **Selected bibliography** 2007 Stephan Berg, Douglas Fogle, Mark Manders and Mirjam Varadinism, *The Absence of Mark Manders*, Hatje Cantz, Ostfildern / 2006 Melissa Gronlund, 'Mark Manders', *Frieze*, June / 2005 James Cuno et al., *Mark Manders: Eucaryote Tarp*, Roma Publications, Amsterdam / 2002 Laura Hoptman, Loretta Yarlow, Marije Langelaar and Mark Manders, *Mark Manders: Singing Sailors*, Art Gallery of York University, Toronto and Roma Publications, Amsterdam

Marepe Born 1970, Santo Antônio de Jesus, Bahia, Brazil. Lives in Santo Antônio de Jesus, Brazil.
—— **Selected solo exhibitions** 2008 Galerie Max Hetzler, Berlin / 2007 Galeria Luisa Strina, São Paulo / 2007 'Veja meu Bem', Tate Modern, London / 2005 Centre Pompidou, Paris / 2005 Museu de Arte da Pampulha, Belo Horizonte, Brazil
—— **Selected group exhibitions** 2007 'Panorama da Arte Brasileira', Museu de Arte Moderna de São Paulo / 2007 'Alien Nation', Manchester Art Gallery; Sainsbury Centre for Visual Arts, Norwich / 2006 'Alien Nation', Institute of Contemporary Arts, London / 2006 São Paulo Biennial / 2006 'MAM na OCA', Museu de Arte Moderna de São Paulo / 2006 Sydney Biennial / 2006 'Tropicália: A Revolution in Brazilian Culture', Barbican Art Gallery, London; The Bronx Museum of the Arts, New York; Museum of Contemporary Art, Chicago; Museu de Arte Moderna, Rio de Janeiro
—— **Selected bibliography** 2007 Galerie Max Hetzler and Galerie Luisa Strina, *Marepe*, Holzwarth Publications, Berlin / 2007 Rosa Olivares (ed.), *100 Latin American Artists*, Exit Publications, Madrid / 2006 John Gill, Jens Hoffmann and Gilane Tawadros (eds.), *Alien Nation*, Institute of Contemporary Arts, London / 2005 Museu de Arte da Pampulha (ed.), *Marepe*, Museu de Arte da Pampulha, Belo Horizonte / 2005 Carlos Basualdo (ed.), *Tropicália: A Revolution in Brazilian Culture*, Museum of Contemporary Art, São Paulo

Kris Martin Born 1972, Kortrijk, Belgium. Lives in Ghent, Belgium.
—— **Selected solo exhibitions** 2008 CCA Wattis Institute for Contemporary Arts, San Francisco / 2008 'Eldorado: Kris Martin Inter pares', Galleria d'Arte Moderna e Contemporanea (GAMeC), Bergamo, Italy / 2008 White Cube, London / 2007 P.S.1 Contemporary Art Center, New York / 2006 'Deus ex machina', Johann König, Berlin / 2005 Neuer Aachener Kunstverein (NAK), Germany
—— **Selected group exhibitions** 2009 'The Quick and the Dead', Walker Art Center, Minneapolis / 2008 'Heavy Metal', Kunsthalle zu Kiel, Germany / 2008 'Fade In / Fade Out', Bloomberg Space, London / 2008 'Traces du sacré', Centre Pompidou, Paris / 2008 'Speicher fast voll: Sammein und Ordnen in der Gegenwartkunst', Kunstmuseum Solothurn, Switzerland / 2008 'All-Inclusive: Die Welt des Tourismus', Schirn Kunsthalle, Frankfurt / 2007 'Passengers', CCA Wattis Institute for Contemporary Art, San Francisco
—— **Selected bibliography** 2008 Sies + Höke (ed.), *Kris Martin*, Sies + Höke, Dusseldorf / 2008 Jens Hoffmann, 'In the Hands of God', *Frieze*, May / 2008 Jessica Morgan, 'Kris Martin: Time Bomb', *Art Review*, Jan. / 2008 Friedhelm Mennekes, 'L'art dans L'Espace sacré', *Traces du sacré*, Éditions du Centre Pompidou, Paris / 2007 Penelope Curtis and Stephen Feeke (eds.), *Towards a New Laocoön*, Henry Moore Institute, Leeds, UK

Josephine Meckseper Born 1964, Lilienthal, Germany. Lives in New York, NY, USA.
—— **Selected solo exhibitions** 2009 Migros Museum für Gegenwartskunst, Zurich / 2009 Blaffer Gallery, Art Museum of the University of Houston / 2008 'New Photography 2008: Josephine Meckseper and Mikhael Subotzky', The Museum of Modern Art, New York / 2008 Arndt & Partner, Berlin / 2008 Elizabeth Dee Gallery, New York / 2008 Gesellschaft für Aktuelle Kunst (GAK), Bremen, Germany / 2007 Kunstmuseum Stuttgart

— **Selected group exhibitions** 2009 'Shape of Things to Come: New Sculpture', Saatchi Gallery, London / 2009 'Kaderstimmung: Ost-West Überblick', Künstlerhaus Bethanien, Berlin / 2009 'Man Son', Hamburger Kunsthalle / 2008 Prospect, New Orleans / 2008 'That Was Then ... This is Now', P.S.1 Contemporary Art Center, New York / 2008 'Steirischer Herbst', Landesmuseum Joanneum, Graz / 2007 'Brave New Worlds', Walker Art Center, Minneapolis / 2007 'Resistance Is', Whitney Museum of American Art, New York
— **Selected bibliography** 2008 Gabriele Mackert, Sylvère Lotringer and Mona Schieren, *Quelle International: Josephine Meckseper*, Gesellschaft für Aktuelle Kunst (GAK), Bremen / 2007 Marion Ackermann, Christian Höller and Okwui Enwezor (ed.), *Josephine Meckseper*, Hatje Cantz, Ostfildern / 2007 Julia Bryan-Wilson, 'Josephine Meckseper: Display, the female form and protest culture', *Frieze*, Mar. / 2006 Sylvère Lotringer, *The Josephine Meckseper Catalogue No. 2*, Sternberg Press, New York and Berlin

Michaela Meise Born 1976 in Hanau, Germany. Lives in Berlin, Germany.
— **Selected solo exhibitions** 2009 Greene Naftali, New York / 2009 Badischer Kunstverein, Karlsruhe / 2008 Richard Telles Fine Art, Los Angeles / 2008 'Das schwache Haus', Basis, Frankfurt / 2007 Johann König, Berlin / 2007 'Spazieren', Standard, Oslo / 2006 'Bank und Bleibe', Verein zur Förderung von Kunst und Kultur am Rosa Luxenburg-Platz, Berlin
— **Selected group exhibitions** 2008 'Madonna und wir', Galerie Christian Nagel, Berlin / 2007 'Die Sammlung Rausch', Portikus, Frankfurt / 2007 'Construction time again', Lisson Gallery, London / 2006 'Cooling Out: On the Paradox of Feminism', Kunsthaus Basel; Halle für Kunst, Lüneburg, Germany / 2006 Lewis Glucksman Gallery, Cork, Ireland / 2006 Berlin Biennial / 2005 'Zur Vorstellung des Terrors: Die RAF-Ausstellung', KW Institute for Contemporary Art, Berlin
— **Selected bibliography** 2007 Sarina Basta, 'Gentle Vandalism', *Texte Zur Kunst*, Mar. / 2006 Ingeborg Wiensowski, 'Skulpturen für Denker', *Kulture Spiegel*, May / 2005 Henning Bohl, Karola Grässlin and Ursula Panhans-Bühler, *Michaela Meise: Finding my Balance*, Walther König, Cologne / 2005 Dominic Eichler, 'A worldly post-Minimalism, understatement, a singer's lament, dissonance and Feminism', *Frieze*, Jan.

Matthew Monahan Born 1972, Eureka, CA, USA. Lives in Los Angeles, CA, USA.
— **Selected solo exhibitions** 2008 Anton Kern Gallery, New York / 2007 'MOCA Focus: Matthew Monahan', Los Angeles Museum of Contemporary Art / 2007 Douglas Hyde Gallery, Dublin / 2006 Stuart Shave Modern Art, London / 2005 Anton Kern Gallery, New York / 2005 Galerie Fons Welters, Amsterdam
— **Selected group exhibitions** 2008 'Grandeur: Sonsbeek 2008', Arnhem, Netherlands / 2008 'Martian Museum of Terrestrial Art', Barbican Art Gallery, London 2007 'Unmonumental', New Museum, New York / 2007 'USA Today', Royal Academy of Arts, London / 2007 'Fractured Figures', Deste Foundation, Athens / 2007 'Eden's Edge: Fifteen LA Artists', Hammer Museum, Los Angeles / 2006 Berlin Biennial
— **Selected bibliography** 2008 Jonathan Griffin, 'Matthew Monahan', *Frieze*, Oct. / 2007 Ari Wiseman, *Five Years Ten Years Maybe Never*, Museum of Contemporary Art, Los Angeles / 2007 Malik Gaines, 'Under the Volcano: History and What We Make of it in the Work of Matthew Monahan', *Modern Painters*, Oct. / 2005 Elizabeth Schambelan, 'Matthew Monahan', *Artforum*, Oct.

Mike Nelson Born 1967, Loughborough, UK. Lives in London, UK.
— **Selected solo exhibitions** 2008 Villa Arson, Nice / 2007 'A Psychic Vacuum', Creative Time, New York / 2006 'Lonely Planet', Australian Center for Contemporary Art, Melbourne / 2006 'After Jack Kerouac', Centre d'Art Santa Monica, Barcelona / 2006 Frieze Projects, Frieze Art Fair, London / 2005 'Spanning Fort Road and Mansion Street: Between a Formula and a Code', Turner Contemporary, Margate, UK
— **Selected group exhibitions** 2008 'Eclipse: Art in a Dark Age', Moderna Museet, Stockholm / 2008 'Reality Check', Statens Museum for Kunst, Copenhagen / 2008 'Psycho Buildings', Hayward Gallery, London / 2007 The Turner Prize', Tate Liverpool / 2007 'Breaking Step / U Raskoraku', Museum of Contemporary Art, Belgrade / 2006 'A Secret Service: Art, Compulsion, Concealment', Hatton Gallery, Newcastle upon Tyne; Hayward Gallery, London
— **Selected bibliography** 2008 Brian Dillon, Jane Rendell and Ralph Rugoff, *Psycho Buildings: Artists Take on Architecture*, Hayward Publishing, London / 2005 Richard Grayson, Peter Eleey and Ralph Rugoff, *Mike Nelson: Between a formula and a code*, Turner Contemporary, Margate / 2002 Rachel Withers, 'A Thousand Words: Mike Nelson' *Artforum*, Feb.

Ernesto Neto Born in Rio de Janeiro, Brazil, 1964. Lives in Rio de Janeiro, Brazil.
— **Selected solo exhibitions** 2009 Musée des Beaux-arts de Nantes, France / 2008 Museu d'Arte Contemporanea di Roma / 2008 Galeria Elba Benitez, Madrid / 2008 Gallerí I 8, Reykjavík / 2008 Tanya Bonakdar Gallery, New York / 2007 'É a vida, o espaço interior', Galeria Artur Fidalgo, Rio de Janeiro / 2007 'Otheranimal', Merce Cunningham Dance Company, Museum of Contemporary Art, Miami / 2007 Marugame Genichiro-Inokuma Museum of Contemporary Art, Kagawa
— **Selected group exhibitions** 2009 'When Lives Become Form: Creative Power from Brazil', Hiroshima City Museum of Contemporary Art / 2008 '19 Desarranjos: Panorama da Arte Brasileira 2003', Museo de Arte del Banco de la Republica Bogotá / 2008 'Blooming Now! Brazilian Contemporary Art', Toyota Municipal Museum of Art / 2008 'Container Art', Parque Vila Lobos, São Paulo, Brazil / 2008 'Poética da Percepção', Museu de Arte Moderna do Rio de Janeiro / 2008 'Psycho Buildings', Hayward Gallery, London
— **Selected bibliography** 2008 Brian Dillon, Jane Rendell and Ralph Rugoff, *Psycho Buildings: Artists Take on Architecture*, Hayward Publishing, London / 2007 Jean-Marc Prevost, *Ernesto Neto: Léviathan Thot*, Éditions du Regard, Paris / 2006 Paulo Herkenhoff, Rodrigo Moura and Victor Zamudio-Taylor, *Seduções: Ernesto Neto, Valeska Soares, Cildo Meireles*, Hatje Cantz, Ostfildern / 2006 Philip Ursprung, Paulo Herkenhoff and Yuko Hasegawa, 'Ernesto Neto', *Parkett*, no. 78 / 2006 Lars Grambye, *Ernesto Neto: The Malmö Experience*, Malmö Konsthall, Sweden

Rivane Neuenschwander Born, 1967, Belo Horizonte, Brazil. Lives in Belo Horizonte, Brazil.
— **Selected solo exhibitions** 2009 New Museum, New York / 2008 South London Gallery / 2008 Stephen Friedman Gallery, London / 2007 'Coisa de Ninguém Coisa de Todos', Galeria Fortes Vilaça, São Paulo / 2007 'Forum 60: Rivane Neuenschwander', Carnegie Museum of Art, Pittsburgh / 2007 'Black Box: Rivane Neuenschwander', Hirshhorn Museum and Sculpture Garden, Washington, DC, USA
— **Selected group exhibitions** 2008 'All-Inclusive: A Tourist World', Schirn Kunsthalle, Frankfurt / 2007 'Comic Abstraction: Image-Breaking Image-Making', The Museum of Modern Art, New York / 2007 'Organizing Chaos', P.S.1 Contemporary Art Center, New York / 2007 'The Shapes Of Space', Guggenheim Museum, New York / 2007 'Panorama da Arte Brasileira', Museu de Arte Moderna de São Paulo / 2007 Mercosul Biennial, Porto Alegre, Brazil / 2006 'Tropicalia', Barbican Art Gallery, London; Centro Cultural de Belem, Lisbon; Bronx Museum, New York / 2006 Havana Biennial
— **Selected bibliography** 2007 Margot Heller, *Rivane Neuenschwander: Suspension Point*, South London Gallery, London / 2007 Kristin M. Jones, 'Rivane Neuenschwander', *Frieze*, Jan. / 2007 Roxana Marcoci, *Comic Abstraction: Image-Breaking, Image-Making*, The Museum of Modern Art, New York / 2006 Roberta Smith, 'Other Stories and Stories of Others', *The New York Times*, 22 Sep. / 2006 Liz Linden (ed.), *The Best Surprise is No Surprise*, JRP Ringier, Zurich

Ruben Ochoa Born 1974, Oceanside, CA, USA. Lives in Los Angeles, CA, USA.
— **Selected solo exhibitions** 2009 SITE Santa Fe Biennial / 2008 Susanne Vielmetter Berlin Projects / 2007 Hallwalls Contemporary Arts Center, Buffalo, NY / 2006 LA><ART, Los Angeles / 2004 The Project, Los Angeles
— **Selected group exhibitions** 2008 Whitney Biennial, New York / 2008 'Phantom Sightings', Los Angeles County Museum of Art / 2007 'Multifaceted Lens', Minnesota Center for Photography, Minneapolis / 2007 'Viva Mexico!', Zachęta National Gallery of Art, Warsaw / 2006 'An Image Bank for Everyday Revolutionary Life', Gallery at REDCAT, Los Angeles
— **Selected bibliography** 2008 Julia Bryan-Wilson, 'Phantom Sightings: Art After the Chicano Movement', *Artforum*, July / 2007 Sonia Campagnola, 'Live from Los Angeles', *Flash Art*, Nov.–Dec. / 2007 Holly Myers, 'When nature and urban life conflict', *Los Angeles Times*, Sep. 14 / 2006 Clara Kim, 'Ruben Ochoa: Extracted', *Contemporary*, no. 88

Damián Ortega Born 1967, Mexico City, Mexico. Lives in Berlin, Germany, and Mexico City, Mexico.
— **Selected solo exhibitions** 2008 Centre Pompidou, Paris / 2007 'Man is the Controller of the Universe', DAAD Gallery, Berlin / 2007 'Being', Ikon Gallery, Birmingham / 2007 'Nine Types of Terrain', White Cube Gallery, London / 2007 'Obelisco transportable', Public Art Fund, Central Park, New York / 2005 'Damián Ortega: The Beetle Trilogy and Other Works', Gallery at REDCAT, Los Angeles / 2005 'The Uncertainty Principle', Tate Modern, London
— **Selected group exhibitions** 2008 'An Unruly history of the Readymade', Colección Jumex, Mexico City / 2008 'That Was Then ... This Is Now', P.S.1 Contemporary Art Center, New York / 2008 'A Skate in the Mud, a Hole in the Referent: Land Art's Expanded Field 1968–2008', Museo Tamayo, Mexico City / 2007 'Preis Der Nationalgalerie für Junge Kunst', Hamburger Bahnhof Museum für Gegenwart, Berlin / 2007 'Escultura Social: A New Generation of Art from Mexico City', Museum of Contemporary Art, Chicago / 2007 'Hidden in Plain Sight: Contemporary Photographs from the Collection', Metropolitan Museum of Art, New York
— **Selected bibliography** 2007 Friedrich Meschede (ed.), *Survival of the Idea, Failure of the Object: Sketches and Projects 1991–2007* Hatje Cantz, Ostfildern / 2007 Susan May, *Damián Ortega: Nine Types of Terrain*, White Cube, London / 2007 Julie Rodrigues Widholm (ed.), *Escultura Social: A New Generation of Art from Mexico City*, Museum of Contemporary Art, Chicago / 2007 Jonathan Griffin, 'Damián Ortega', *Frieze*, Oct. / 2006 Adam Szymczyk, *Hugo Boss Prize*, Solomon R. Guggenheim Foundation, New York / 2006 Euridice Arratia,

'Damián Ortega', *100 Latin American Artists*, Exit Publications, Madrid

Mitzi Pederson Born 1976, Stuart, FL, USA. Lives in San Francisco, CA, USA.

— **Selected solo exhibitions** 2009 World Class Boxing, Miami / 2008 Hammer Museum, Los Angeles / 2007 Nicole Klagsbrun Gallery, New York / 2006 Duchess, Chicago / 2006 White Columns, New York / 2005 Ratio 3, San Francisco

— **Selected group exhibitions** 2009 'Lotte Gertz and Mitzi Pederson', The Approach E2, London / 2008 'What's it to you?', Aspen Art Museum, CO, USA / 2008 Whitney Biennial, New York / 2008 'Update', White Columns, New York / 2007 'Artists of Invention: A Century of CCA', Oakland Museum of California / 2006 'Louis Morris', Atlanta Contemporary Art Center, GA, USA / 2006 'SECA Art Award', San Francisco Museum of Modern Art

— **Selected bibliography** 2007 Janet Bishop and Tara McDowell, *2006 SECA Art Award*, San Francisco Museum of Modern Art / 2007 Glen Helfand, 'Mitzi Pederson', *Artforum*, May / 2006 Marisa Olson, 'Mitzi Pederson at Ratio 3', *Artweek*, vol. 36, 4 / 2006 Megan Ratner, 'Mitzi Pederson', *Frieze*, Sep.

Mai-Thu Perret Born 1976, Geneva, Switzerland. Lives in Geneva, Switzerland.

— **Selected solo exhibitions** 2008 San Francisco Musuem of Modern Art / 2008 The Kitchen, New York / 2008 Kunsthalle St Gallen / 2007 Bonnefanten Museum, Maastricht, Netherlands / 2006 Renaissance Society, University of Chicago / 2006 Chisenhale Gallery, London (with Valentin Carron) / 2005 Centre d'Art Contemporain, Geneva (with Valentin Carron)

— **Selected group exhibitions** 2008 'Shifting Identities: (Swiss) Art Now', Kunsthaus Zürich; Contemporary Art Centre, Vilnius / 2007 'Eurocentric', Rubell Family Collection, Miami / 2007 Lyon Biennial / 2007 'Pure Self-Expression', Kölnischer Kunstverein, Cologne / 2006 'Shiny', Wexner Art Center, Columbus, OH, USA / 2005 'Again For Tomorrow', Royal College of Art Galleries, London / 2003 'Form/Kontext/Troja', Secession, Vienna

— **Selected bibliography** 2008 Fabrice Stroun and Hamza Walker, *Land of Crystal*, JRP Ringier, Zurich / 2008 Andrew Bonacina, 'Focus: Mai-Thu Perret', *Frieze*, Mar. / 2006 Lionel Bovier, 'Mai-Thu Perret', in *Mai-Thu Perret: Cahiers d'artistes*, Periferia Edizioni, Cosenza and Pro Helvetia, Lucerne, Zurich / 2006 Hannah Feldman, 'Desert of the Real: Hannah Feldman on the Art of Mai-Thu Perret', *Artforum*, June

Falke Pisano Born 1978, Amsterdam, Netherlands. Lives in Amsterdam, Netherlands.

— **Selected solo exhibitions** 2008 Hollybush Gardens, London (with Benoît Maire) / 2008 Croy-Nielsen, Berlin (with Benoît Maire) / 2008 Galerie Balice Hertling, Paris / 2008 Ellen de Bruijne Projects, Amsterdam

— **Selected group exhibitions** 2008 Yokohama Triennial / 2008 Manifesta 7, Trentino, South Tyrol, Italy / 2008 'Word event', Kunsthalle Basel / 2008 Berlin Biennial / 2006 'Feminist Legacies and Potentials in Contemporary Art Practice: If I Can't Dance, I Don't Want To Be Part Of Your Revolution Edition II', Museum van Hedendaagse Kunst Antwerpen (MuHKA), Antwerp; De Appel, Amsterdam; Kunsthalle Basel / 2007 'Imagine Action', Lisson Gallery, London / 2007 'Elephant Cemetery', Artists Space, New York / 2006 'Just in Time', Stedelijk Museum, Amsterdam

— **Selected bibliography** 2008 Christophe Gallois, 'Words and Objects', *Metropolis M*, no. 2 / 2008 Lillian Davis, 'Affecting Abstractions', *Uovo*, no. 17

Wilfredo Prieto Born 1978, Sancti Spiritus, Cuba. Lives in Barcelona, Spain, and Havana, Cuba.

— **Selected solo exhibitions** 2008 Stedelijk Museum, Amsterdam / 2008 Galerie Martin Van Zomeren, Amsterdam / 2007 Nogueras Blanchard, Barcelona / 2007 Artists' Web Projects, Dia Art Foundation, New York / 2007 Lennon Park, Havana / 2006 Kadist Art Foundation, Paris / 2006 McMaster Museum of Art, Hamilton, Canada

— **Selected group exhibitions** 2008 'That Was Then ... This is Now', P.S.1 Contemporary Art Center, New York / 2008 'The Disobedients', Annet Gelink, Amsterdam / 2008 'States of Exchange: Artists from Cuba', Institute of International Visual Arts (INIVA), London / 2008 'Greenwashing', Fondazione Sandretto Re Rebaudengo, Turin / 2007 'Territorios', Latin-American Pavilion, Venice Biennale / 2007 'Extraordinary Rendition', Nogueras Blanchard, Barcelona / 2007 'Errore di sistema-System error', Palazzo delle Papesse, Siena, Italy

— **Selected bibliography** 2008 Martí Peran, 'Wilfredo Prieto', *Artforum*, Mar. / 2008 Gerardo Mosquera, 'Wilfredo Prieto: The tension of the image', *Art Nexus*, no. 69 / 2007 Rose Olivares (ed.), *100 Latin American Artists*, Exit Publications, Madrid / 2007 Max Andrews, 'Wilfredo Prieto: A lot of noise and not many nuts; dysfunction and barred humour', *Frieze*, Oct. / 2006 Cuauhtemoc Medina, *Mute*, McMaster Museum of Art, Hamilton, Canada

Tobias Putrih Born 1972, Kranj, Slovenia. Lives in New York, USA.

— **Selected solo exhibitions** 2009 Baltic Centre for Contemporary Art, Gateshead / 2009 Boijmans Van Beuningen, Rotterdam / 2009 Espace 315, Centre Pompidou, Paris / 2008 Kunsthaus, Zurich (with Runa Islam) / 2008 Galeria Civica, Modena (with Runa Islam) / 2007 Neuberger Museum of Art, Purchase, NY, USA / 2006 Laumeier Sculpture Park, Saint Louis, MO, USA

— **Selected group exhibitions** 2008 'Psycho Buildings', Hayward Gallery, London / 2008 'Multiplex: Directions in Art, 1970 to Now', The Museum of Modern Art, New York / 2008 'Peripheral Vision and Collective Body', Museum of Modern and Contemporary Art, Bolzano, Italy / 2007 Slovenian Pavilion, Venice Biennale / 2007 'Forms of Resistance', Van Abbemuseum, Eindhoven / 2006 'Erzählungen, ~35/65+ Zwei Generationen', Kunsthaus Graz

— **Selected bibliography** 2008 Milovan Farronato, Maeem Mohaiemen, Igor Spanjol and Angela Vettese, *Runa Islam Lost Cinema Lost Tobias Putrih*, Galleria Civica di Modena, Italy / 2008 Francesco Manacorda, 'Tobias Putrih', *Psycho Buildings: Artists Take on Architecture*, Hayward Publishing, London / 2008 Giorgio Verzotti, 'Lost Cinema Lost: Galleria Civica', *Artforum*, Apr. / 2007 Mara Ambrozic, Aleksander Bassin, Francesco Manacorda and Natasa Petresin, *Tobias Putrih: Venetian Atmospheric*, Slovenian Pavilion, Venice Biennale / 2006 Billy Nolan, 'Rules to be Broken: Interview with Tobias Putrih', *Frame*, Nov.–Dec.

Michael Queenland Born 1970, Pasadena, CA, USA. Lives in New York, NY, USA.

— **Selected solo exhibitions** 2007 LA><ART, Los Angeles / 2007 Harris Lieberman, New York / 2006 Daniel Hug Gallery, Los Angeles / 2005 Institute of Contemporary Art, Maine College of Art, Portland, ME / 2005 Massachusetts College of Art, Boston / 2005 The Studio Museum in Harlem, New York

— **Selected group exhibitions** 2008 'Idle Youth', Gladstone Gallery, New York / 2008 'Act so that I can speak to you', Galerie Kamm, Berlin / 2008 Whitney Biennial, New York / 2008 'Nina in Position', Artists Space, New York / 2006 'Civil Restitutions', Thomas Dane Gallery, London / 2006 'Trace', Whitney Museum of American Art at Altria, New York / 2005 'Frequency', The Studio Museum in Harlem, New York / 2004 'Fade: A Survey of African American Art 1990–2003', Luckman Gallery, Los Angeles

— **Selected bibliography** 2008 Russell Ferguson, *Idle Youth*, Gladstone Gallery, New York / 2007 Roberta Smith, 'Michael Queenland: Bread and Balloons', *The New York Times*, 9 Mar. / 2006 Barbara Pollack, 'Michael Queenland at Daniel Hug Gallery', *Artforum*, Sep. / 2005 Thelma Golden, 'Extremes: A Dialogue Between Michael Queenland and Thelma Golden', *Frequency*, The Studio Museum, New York

Michael Rakowitz Born 1973, Great Neck, NY, USA. Lives in Chicago, IL, USA.

— **Selected solo exhibitions** 2007 'The invisible enemy should not exist', Lombard-Fried Projects, New York / 2006 'Return', Creative Time, New York / 2006 'The Visionaries', Trafo Gallery, Budapest / 2006 'Endgames', Galleria Alberto Peola, Turin / 2006 'Percent for Art Program Commission', Department of Cultural Affairs, New York

— **Selected group exhibitions** 2008 Sydney Biennial / 2008 'Second Lives: Remixing the Ordinary', Museum of Art and Design, New York / 2008 'The Greenroom: Reconsidering the Documentary and Contemporary Art', Center for Curatorial Studies, Bard College, Annandale-on-Hudson, NY / 2008 'Heartland', Van Abbemuseum, Eindhoven / 2008 'Shelter X Survival: Alternative Homes for Fantastic Lives', Hiroshima City Museum of Contemporary Art / 2007 'An Atlas of Events', Calouste Gulbenkian Foundation, Lisbon / 2007 'Consuming War', Hyde Park Art Center, Chicago / 2007 'Instant Urbanism', Swiss Architecture Museum, Basel / 2007 Istanbul Biennial / 2007 Sharjah Biennial

— **Selected bibliography** 2008 Miguel Amado, 'An Atlas of Events', *Artforum*, Feb. / 2008, Hannah Feldman, 'Michael Rakowitz and the tactics of being in-between and everywhere else', *Art & Australia*, Winter / 2007 Regine Basha, 'Return: A Project by Michael Rakowitz', *ARTL!ES*, Spring / 2007 Brian Boucher, 'Babylon Without Borders', *Art in America*, Apr. / 2007 Frances Richard, 'Michael Rakowitz, Lombard-Freid Projects', *Artforum*, Apr.

Lisi Raskin Born 1974, Miami, FL, USA. Lives in New York, USA.

— **Selected solo exhibitions** 2009 Riccardo Crespi, Milan / 2009 Blanton Museum, University of Texas at Austin, TX, USA / 2008 Milliken Gallery, Stockholm / 2008 Center for Curatorial Studies, Bard College, Annandale-on-Hudson, NY / 2008 Park Avenue Armory, New York / 2007 Gavle Konstcentrum, Sweden / 2006 'Jack Shack', P.S.1 Contemporary Art Center, New York

— **Selected group exhibitions** 2008 'Soft Manipulation or Who's Afraid of the New Now', Casino Luxembourg / 2008 'The Possibility of an Island', Museum of Contemporary Art, North Miami / 2007 'Pensée Sauvage', Frankfurter Kunstverein / 2006 'Written in Light', Art in General, Bloomberg HQ, New York / 2005 'Hunch and Flail', Artist Space, New York

— **Selected bibliography** 2009 Lisi Raskin, *Lisi Raskin: Mobile Observation*, Center for Curatorial Studies, Bard College, Annandale-on-Hudson, NY and Riccardo Crespi, Milan / 2007 Holland Cotter, 'Lisi Raskin: Switchyard', *The New York Times*, 11 May / 2007 Julia Bryan-Wilson, 'Julia Bryan-Wilson on Lisi Raskin', *Artforum*, May / 2007 Barbara Casavecchia, 'Lisi Raskin at Riccardo Crespi', *Flash Art*, Dec.–Jan.

David Renggli Born 1974, Zurich, Switzerland. Lives in Zurich, Switzerland.

— **Selected solo exhibitions** 2008 'Ivresse au cognac', Galerie Chez Valentin, Paris / 2007

'You're Only Once, Twice my Age', ausstellungsraum25, Zurich / 2007 'Arm Holds Hand', Alexandre Pollazzon Ltd, London / 2007 'Du Dein Psychiater, Kannst Du den empfehlen', Via Farini, Milan / 2007 Galerie Klerkx, Milan / 2006 Galerie Chez Valentin, Paris / 2006 Gallery Willem van Zoetendaal, Amsterdam / 2006 'Leihgabe ans Nichts', Kuntsthalle Winterthur, Switzerland
—— **Selected group exhibitions** 2008 'The way in witch it landed', Tate Britain, London / 2008 'Shifting Identities: (Swiss) Art Now', Kunsthaus Zürich; Contemporary Art Centre, Vilnius / 2008 'Sammlung / Collection', Migros Museum für Gegenwartskunst, Zurich / 2008 'Ready Made', Yvon-Lambert, Paris / 2007 'Our Magic Hour', Arario, Seoul / 2007 'Nouvelles acquisitions / Volet 1', Fonds régional d'art contemporain (FRAC) Nord-Pas de Calais, Dunkerque, France / 2006 'Housewarming', Swiss Institute, New York
—— **Selected bibliography** 2008, Milovan Farronato, 'From Dusk Till Dawn', *Tema Celeste*, July / 2007 Joanne Bernstein, 'Double Take', *UBS Young Art*, UBS Zurich / 2007 Christoph Doswald and Dorothea Strauss, *David Renggli: Cage Writes Bird*, Codax Publishers and JRP Ringier, Zurich / 2006 Giovanni Carmine, 'Ein sehr schöner Titel', 'David Renggli: Du kannst mir auch Du sagen', *Collections Cahiers d'Artistes*, Periferia Edizioni, Cosenza and Pro Helvetia, Lucerne, Zurich

Lili Reynaud-Dewar Born 1975, Nantes France. Lives in Bordeaux, France.
—— **Selected solo exhibitions** 2009 Centre d'Art Parc Saint-Leger, France / 2009 Mary Mary, Glasgow / 2008 'LOVE = U.F.O.', Frac-Collection, Aquitaine, France / 2008 'The Race', Civica Montevergini di Siracusa, Italy / 2006 'The Center and Eyes', Zoo Galerie, Nantes, France / 2006 'Power, Corruption and Lies', Galerie RLBQ, Marseilles
—— **Selected group exhibitions** 2009 'Latifa Echakhch / Lili Reynaud-Dewar', Karma International at James Fuentes, New York / 2009 'Born under a bad sign', The Power House, Memphis, TN, USA / 2008 'Explorations in French psychedelia 1968', CAPC Musée d'Art Contemporain, Bordeaux / 2008 'Prix Ricard', Fondation d'Entreprise Ricard, Paris / 2008 Berlin Biennial / 2007 Lyon Biennial / 2007 'Ultramoderne', Hall Paul Wurth, Luxembourg / 2007 'Freak Show', Museum of Contemporary Art, Lyon
—— **Selected bibliography** 2008 Nicolas Bourriaud, *La consistance du visible, 10ème prix de la fondation Ricard*, Fondation d'entreprise Ricard, Paris / 2008 Didier Arnaudet, 'Lili Reynaud-Dewar', *Art Press*, no. 344 / 2008 Judicael Lavrador, 'Lili Reynaud-Dewar et la manière rastaquouère', *Beaux-Arts Magazine*, no. 285 / 2007 Emilie Renard and Yann Chateigné, *Madame la baronne etait plutôt maniérée, assez rococo et totalement baroque*, Centre d'art Mira Phalaina, Paris

Mandla Reuter Born 1975, Nqutu, South Africa. Lives in Berlin, Germany.
—— **Selected solo exhibitions** 2009 Mezzanin Gallery, Vienna / 2008 Neue Alte Brücke, Frankfurt / 2006 rraum, Frankfurt
—— **Selected group exhibitions** 2008 'Disarming Matter', DKH, Helsingbor / 2008 Gwangju Biennial / 2008 SITE Santa Fe Biennial / 2008 'Word Event', Kunsthalle Basel / 2007 'Pensée Sauvage', Frankfurter Kunstverein / 2007 'The Four Colour Contingency', The Approach, London
—— **Selected bibliography** 2007 Chris Sharp, *The Image Itself*, Wiens Verlag, Berlin / 2007 Lars Bang Larsen, 'Dialectics of Space', *Neue Heimat: Berlin Contemporary*, Berlinische Galerie, Berlin / 2006 Mandla Reuter (ed.), *Pigment Piano Marble*, Revolver, Berlin / 2004 Mandla Reuter, *Tokyo Panda*, Revolver, Berlin / 2001 Michael Pfrommer and Mandla Reuter, *Frühe Arbeiten*, Verlag Bernd Slutzky, Frankfurt

Eva Rothschild Born 1972, Dublin, Ireland. Lives in London, UK.
—— **Selected solo exhibitions** 2007 South London Gallery / 2007 303 Gallery, New York / 2006 Galerie Eva Presenhuber, Zurich / 2005 Douglas Hyde Gallery, Dublin / 2005 Stuart Shave Modern Art, London / 2004 Kunsthalle Zürich / 2003 The Modern Institute, Glasgow
—— **Selected group exhibitions** 2008 'A Life of Their Own', Lismore Castle, Ireland / 2007 'Unmonumental', New Museum, New York / 2006 'All Hawaii Entrées / Lunar Reggae', Irish Museum of Modern Art, Dublin / 2006 'How to Improve the World: 60 Years of British Art', Hayward Gallery, London / 2006 Tate Triennial / 2006 'Strange Powers', Creative Time, New York
—— **Selected bibliography** 2008 Michael Archer, 'Eva Rothschild: South London Gallery', *Artforum*, Jan. / 2007 Ian Hunt, 'They don't unpack: Eva Rothschild interviewed by Ian Hunt', *Art Monthly*, Nov. / 2007 Kristin M. Jones, 'Eva Rothschild', *Frieze*, Oct. / 2006 Clarrie Wallis, *Tate Triennial*, Tate Publishing, London / 2005 Grant Watson, *Eva Rothschild*, The Douglas Hyde Gallery, Dublin / 2004 Will Bradley, Eva Rothschild and Beatrix Ruf (eds.), *Eva Rothschild*, Kunsthalle Zürich, JRP Ringier, Zurich

Heather Rowe Born 1970, New Haven, CT, USA. Lives in New York, NY, USA.
—— **Selected solo exhibitions** 2007 'On Returning', D'Amelio Terras, New York / 2006 'Green Desert', D'Amelio Terras, New York / 2006 'Shadows of a Doubt', Galerie Michael Zink, Munich
—— **Selected group exhibitions** 2008 'Only Connect', Art in General, New York / 2008 'Slow Glass', Lisa Cooley Fine Art, New York / 2008 Whitney Biennial, New York / 2007 'Undone', Whitney Museum of American Art at Altria, New York / 2006 'Open Walls #2', White Columns, New York / 2006 'Bunch Alliance and Dissolve', Contemporary Arts Center, Cincinnati, OH, USA / 2006 'Mystic River', Southfirst, New York; Arcadia University Art Gallery, Glenside, PA, USA
—— **Selected bibliography** 2008 Adam Weinberg and Shamim M. Momin, *Whitney Museum of American Art at Altria: 25 Years*, Yale University Press, London and New Haven, CT, USA / 2008 Cecilia Alemani, 'Whitney Girls', *Mousse*, no. 13 / 2008 Lisa Turvey, 'Heather Rowe', *Whitney Biennial 2008* Whitney Museum of American Art, Yale University Press, London and New Haven, CT, USA / 2008 Jonathan T.D. Neil, 'Heather Rowe: On Returning', *Art Review*, Jan. / 2007 Holland Cotter, 'Art in Review: Heather Rowe and Leslie Hewitt', *The New York Times*, 17 Dec. / 2007 Suzanne Hudson, 'Stubborn Materials', *Artforum*, Nov.

Sterling Ruby Born 1972, Bitburg, Germany. Lives in Los Angeles, CA, USA.
—— **Selected solo exhibitions** 2008 'Zen Ripper', Galleria Emi Fontana, Milan / 2008 'Grid Ripper', Galleria d'Arte Moderne e Contemporanea, Bergamo, Italy / 2008 'Spectrum Ripper', Sprüth Magers, London / 2008 'Supermax 2008', Museum of Contemporary Art, Los Angeles / 2008 'Kiln Works', Metro Pictures, New York / 2008 'Chron', The Drawing Center, New York / 2007 'Slasher Posters & Pillow Works', Bernier / Eliades, Athens
—— **Selected group exhibitions** 2008 'Dirt on Delight', Institute of Contemporary Art, Boston; Walker Art Center, Minneapolis / 2008 'Begin Again Right Back Here', White Columns, New York / 2008 'If You Destroy The Image You Destroy The Thing Itself', Bergen Kunsthall, Norway / 2008 'Substraction', Deitch Projects, New York / 2008 'Stray Alchemists', Ullens Centre of Contemporary Art, Beijing / 2007 'Imagine Los Angeles', Galerie Sprüth Magers, Munich
—— **Selected bibliography** 2008 Lisa Max, *Sterling Ruby: Supermax*, Museum of Contemporary Art, Los Angeles / 2008 Roberta Smith, 'Substraction', *The New York Times*, 25 Apr. / 2008 Roberta Smith, 'Sterling Ruby: Chron & Kiln Works', *The New York Times*, 21 Mar. / 2007 Mark Coetzee, Michael Darling, Michael Holte and Jason Rubell, *Red Eye: LA Artists from the Rubell Family Collection*, Rubell Family Collection, Miami

Tomas Saraceno Born 1973, Tucumán, Argentina. Lives in Frankfurt, Germany.
—— **Selected solo exhibitions** 2009 Walker Arts Center, Minneapolis, / 2008 Tanya Bonakdar Gallery, New York / 2008 'On Clouds (Air-Port-City)' Towada Art Center / 2007 'Biosphere MW32', Pinksummer, Genoa / 2007 'Opening', Aerea, Stockholm / 2007 'Air-Port-City', De Vleeshal, Middelburg, Netherlands / 2006 Centre d'Art Santa Monica, Barcelona / 2006 The Curve, Barbican Art Gallery, London
—— **Selected group exhibitions** 2008 'Psycho Buildings', Hayward Gallery, London / 2008 'Greenwashing', Fondazione Sandretto Re Rebaudengo, Turin / 2008 'Grandeur: Sonsbeek 2008', Arnhem, Netherlands / 2008 Liverpool Biennial / 2008 Turin Triennial / 2007 'Brave New Worlds', Walker Art Center, Minneapolis / 2007 Lyon Biennial / 2007 Sharjah Biennial / 2007 'Entrada al Presente', El Museo de Arte Contemporaneo de Monterrey
—— **Selected bibliography** 2008 Brian Dillon, Jane Rendell and Ralph Rugoff, *Psycho Buildings: Artists Take on Architecture*, Hayward Publishing, London / 2007 Luca Cerizza, 'Temporary Communities', *Tema Celeste*, no. 119 / 2006 Martha Schwendener, 'Tomas Saraceno: Tanya Bonakdar Gallery', *Artforum*, Oct. / 2006 Sally O'Reilly, 'Tomas Saraceno', *Frieze*, Sep. / 2005 Hans Ulrich Obrist and Stefano Boeri, 'Interview with Tomás Saraceno', *Domus*, July–Aug.

Bojan Šarčević Born 1974, Belgrade, Serbia. Lives in Paris, France, and Berlin, Germany.
—— **Selected solo exhibitions** 2008 'Only After Dark', Kunstverein in Hamburg / 2007 'Already vanishing', Galleria d'Arte Moderna di Bologna / 2007 'Kissing the back of your hand sounds like a wounded bird', Bawag Foundation, Vienna / 2006 'To what extent should an artist understand the implications of his or her findings?', Project Arts Centre, Dublin; The Model Arts and Niland Gallery, Sligo, Ireland / 2006 'Sometimes a man gets carried away', Kunstverein Heilbronn, Germany
—— **Selected group exhibitions** 2008 'Eurasia: Geographic cross-overs in art', Museo d'Arte Moderna e Contemporanea di Trento e Rovereto, Italy / 2008 'Many challenges lie ahead in the near future', Kölnischer Kunstverein, Cologne / 2008 'Der große Wurf: Faltungen in der Gegenwartkunst', Kaiser Wilhelm Museum, Krefeld, Germany / 2008 'Wenn ein Reisender in einer Winternacht: Variationen über Max Bill', Museum Marta Herford / 2007 'Point de vue', Albrecht Dürer Gesellschaft, Kunstverein Nürnberg, Nuremburg / 2007 'Aprés la pluie', Musée Départemental d'Art Contemporain de Rochechouart, France / 2007 'The Secret Theory of Drawing', The Drawing Room, London
—— **Selected bibliography** 2008 Caoimhín Mac Giolla Léith, Marcus Steinweg and Andrea Viliani, *Already Vanishing*, Museo d'Arte Moderna di Bologna and Skira, Milan / 2008 Jennifer Allen, 'Social Patterns', *Frieze*, Sep. / 2007 Christine Kintisch (ed.), *Bojan Šarčević: Kissing the back of your hand makes a sound like a wounded bird*, Bawag Foundation, Vienna / 2006 Christy Lange, 'Une Heureuse Régression', *Frieze*, Mar.

Arcangelo Sassolino Born 1967, Vincenza, Italy. Lives in Vincenza, Italy.
—— **Selected solo exhibitions** 2008 'Critical Mass', Feinkost, Berlin / 2008 'Superdome', Palais de Tokyo, Paris / 2007 Nicola van Senger, Zurich / 2006 'Momento', Galleria Galica, Milan / 2004 'Rimozione', Galleria Arte Ricambi, Verona, Italy
—— **Selected group exhibitions** 2008 'Deleted Scenes', Feinkost, Berlin / 2008 'Disarming Matter', Dunkers Kulturhus, Helsingborg, Sweden / 2008 'Palais de Fontainebleau / Chateau de Tokyo', Chateau de Fontainbleau / 2008 'Visionary Collection Vol. 6', Haus Konstruktiv, Zurich / 2007 'What You See Is What You Get', Fonds Régional d'Art Contemporain (FRAC) Champagne-Ardenne, Reims, France
—— **Selected bibliography** 2008 Jasper Sharp (ed.), *Arcangelo Sassolino*, JRP Ringier, Zurich / 2008 Dan Halpern, 'Intimidation Factory', *Men's Vogue*, Aug.

Felix Schramm Born 1970, Hamburg, Germany. Lives in Dusseldorf Germany.
—— **Selected solo exhibitions** 2008 'Savage Salvage', De Vleeshal, Middelburg, Netherlands / 2008 Galerie Sfeir-Semler, Hamburg / 2007 San Francisco Museum of Modern Art / 2006 Soft Corrosion, Hamburger Bahnhof Museum für Gegenwart, Berlin / 2006 Galerie Thomas Flor, Dusseldorf
—— **Selected group exhibitions** 2007 'Less Roses', Gallery Sfeir-Semler, Beirut / 2007 Kunsthalle St Gallen / 2007 Kunstverein Lübeck, Germany / 2006 'Eigenheim', Kunstverein Göttingen, Germany / 2006 Gallery Anna Hellwing, Los Angeles
—— **Selected bibliography** 2008 Michael Zeeman, *Savage Salvage*, De Vleeshal, Middelburg / 2008 Brigitte Kölle, 'Break on Through (To the Other Side)', in *Skulptur!*, Kulturstiftung Hartwig Piepenbrock, Berlin / 2007 Apsara Diquinzio, *New Work: Felix Schramm*, San Francisco Museum of Modern Art / 2007 Sabine von Fischer and Burkhard Meltzer, *Umbau / Modification*, Kunsthalle St Gallen / 2006 Adina Popescu, *Soft Corrosion*, Kulturstiftung Hartwig Piepenbrock, Berlin

Nora Schultz Born 1975, Frankfurt, Germany. Lives in Berlin, Germany.
—— **Selected solo exhibitions** 2008 Dépendance, Brussels / 2008 Reena Spaulings, New York / 2007 Galerie Isabella Bortolozzi, Berlin / 2007 Sutton Lane, London / 2007 Kjubh, Cologne / 2006 Galerie Meerrettich, Berlin
—— **Selected group exhibitions** 2008 'One Season in Hell', Mehringdamm 72, Berlin / 2008 'Non-Solo Show, Non-Group Show', Gallery Franco Soffiantino, Turin / 2008 'On Interchange: Zwischenspiele einer Sammlung', Museum Kurhaus Kleve, Germany / 2007 'The Four Colour Contingency', The Approach, London / 2007 'No Ideas Without Bodies', Egypted, Vienna 2006 'Societe des Nations ...', Circuit, Lausanne / 2005 'Wer von diesen sieben...', Kunstverein Braunschweig, Germany
—— **Selected bibliography** 2008 Rudi Fuchs, Roland Mönig and Guido de Wird, *On Interchange: Zwischenspiele einer Sammlung*, Museum Kurhaus Kleve / 2007 Charles Danby, 'Nora Schultz', *Untitled*, no. 43 / 2007 Michelle Cotton, 'Michelle Cotton on Nora Schultz at Sutton Lane, London', *Texte zur Kunst*, Oct.

Anna Sew Hoy Born 1976, Auckland, New Zealand. Lives in Los Angeles, CA, USA.
—— **Selected solo exhibitions** 2008 'Look-see', Renwick Gallery, New York / 2008 '*Pow!*', LA><Art, Los Angeles / 2007 'Hook & eye', Karyn Lovegrove Gallery, Los Angeles / 2003 'Broken arm', Peres Projects, Los Angeles / 2002 'Wash My Bike', Massimo Audiello Fine Art, New York
—— **Selected group exhibitions** 2009 'An Expanded Field of Possibilities', Santa Barbara Contemporary Arts Forum, CA, USA / 2008 California Biennal, Orange County Museum of Art, Los Angeles / 2008 'Sew Hoy, Lutker, Youngblood', University Art Museum, University of California, Santa Barbara, CA, USA / 2008 'Now You See It', Aspen Art Museum, CO, USA / 2008 'Against the Grain', Los Angeles Contemporary Exhibitions / 2008 'Living Flowers', Japanese American National Museum, Los Angeles / 2007 'Edens Edge: Fifteen LA Artists', Hammer Museum, Los Angeles
—— **Selected bibliography** 2008 Scarlet Cheng, 'How their roots intertwine', *Los Angeles Times*, 6 July / 2008 Holly Myers, 'Future Greats', *Art Review*, no. 20 / 2008 Christopher Miles, 'Anna Sew Hoy', *ArtForum*, Feb. / 2006 Roberta Smith, 'A mélange of Asian roots and shifting identities', *The New York Times*, 8 Sep. / 2003 Christopher Miles, 'Anna Sew Hoy', *Artforum*, Dec.

Mindy Shapero Born 1974, Louisville, KY, USA. Lives in Los Angeles, CA, USA.
—— **Selected solo exhibitions** 2008 Anna Helwing Gallery, Los Angeles / 2007 The Breeder Project, Athens / 2006 CRG Gallery, New York / 2004 Anna Helwing Gallery, Los Angeles
—— **Selected group exhibitions** 2008 'The Plural Dimensionality of Rapture', Arthouse, Austin, TX, USA / 2008 'Currents: Recent Acquisitions', Hirshhorn Museum, Washington, DC, USA / 2007 'Like color in pictures', Aspen Art Museum, CO, USA 2006 'LA Trash and Treasure', Milliken Gallery, Stockholm / 2006 'The Uncertainty of Objects and Ideas', Hirshhorn Museum, Washington, DC, USA / 2006 'Diptych: Mindy Shapero and Jockum Nordström', Wexner Center for the Arts, Columbus, OH, USA
—— **Selected bibliography** 2008 Rosa Albertini, 'Mindy Shapero', *Flash Art*, May–June / 2007 Michelle Kuo, 'The Uncertainty of Objects and Ideas: Recent Sculpture', *Artforum*, Feb. / 2006 Jerry Saltz, 'Dot-Mistress', *The Village Voice*, 16 Nov. / 2006 Anne Rochette and Wade Saunders, 'Place Matters: Los Angeles Sculpture Today', *Art in America*, Nov. / 2005 Christopher Miles, 'Truth to materials: the mundane and the amazing', *Frieze*, Nov.

Ranjani Shettar Born 1977, Bangalore, India. Lives in Bangalore, India.
—— **Selected solo exhibitions** 2009 San Francisco Museum of Modern Art / 2008 'Focus: Ranjani Shettar', Modern Art Museum, Fort Worth, TX, USA / 2008 'Momentum 10: Ranjani Shettar', Institute of Contemporary Art, Boston / 2006 Talwar Gallery, New York / 2005 'Transition and Transformation', Fine Arts Center, University of Massachusetts, Amherst
—— **Selected group exhibitions** 2008 'Life on Mars: 55th Carnegie International', Carnegie Museum of Art, Pittsburgh / 2007 Lyon Biennial / 2007 Sharjah Biennial / 2006 Sydney Biennial / 2006 'Artist in Residence', Artpace San Antonio, TX, USA / 2005 'J'en reve (Dream on)', Fondation Cartier pour l'art Contemporain, Paris / 2005 'Out there', Sainsbury Centre for Visual Arts, Norwich
—— **Selected bibliography** 2008 Max Andrews, 'Ranjani Shettar', *Life on Mars: 55th Carnegie International*, Carnegie Museum of Art, Pittsburgh / 2008 Michael Wilson, 'Worldly Concerns', *Artforum*, May / 2008 Emily Moore Brouillet, *Ranjani Shettar: Sun-sneezers blow light bubbles*, Institute of Contemporary Art, Boston / 2008 Zehra Jumabhoy, 'New Delhi: Ranjani Shettar', *Artforum*, Feb.

Sudarshan Shetty Born 1961, Mangalore, Karnataka, India. Lives in Mumbai, India.
—— **Selected solo exhibitions** 2008 'Leaving Home', Galerie Krinzinger, Vienna / 2008 'Saving Skin', Jack Tilton Gallery, New York / 2006 'Love', Galleryske, Bangalore; Bodhi Art, Mumbai / 2005 'Eight corners of the world', Galleryske, Bangalore / 2004 'Statics', Chemould Gallery, Mumbai
—— **Selected group exhibitions** 2008 'The Destruction Party', The Royal Monceau Hotel, Paris / 2008 'Affair', 1 × 1 Gallery, Dubai / 2005 'Shift', Philips Contemporary, Mumbai / 2005 'Bombay Boys', Palette Art Gallery, New Delhi / 2005 'Configurations', Anant Art Gallery, New Delhi
—— **Selected bibliography** 2008 Niharika Dinkar, 'The Cold-Blooded World of Machines', *ART India*, vol. XIII, 1 / 2007 Gopal Mirchandani, 'Recent Works by Sudarshan Shetty, Mattress Factory Pittsburgh', *Art & Deal*, vol. IV, 25 / 2007 Anupa Mehta (ed.), *India 20 : Conversations With Contemporary Artists*, Mapin Publishing, Ahmedabad / 2006 Marta Jakimowicz, 'The Secret Life of Objects', *ART India*, vol. XI, 1 / 2006 Vyjayanthi Rao, *Love*, Galleryske, Bodhi Art, Mumbai

Gedi Sibony Born 1973, New York, USA. Lives in New York, USA.
—— **Selected solo exhibitions** 2009 The Contemporary Art Museum, Saint Louis, MO, USA / 2008 Galerie Neu, Berlin / 2008 Greene Naftali Gallery, New York / 2008 Zero, Milan / 2007 Kunsthalle St Gallen / 2007 Fonds Régional d'Art Contemporain (FRAC) Champagne-Ardenne, Reimsm France / 2007 Midway Contemporary Art, Minneapolis
—— **Selected group exhibitions** 2008 'Now You See It', Aspen Art Museum, CO, USA / 2007 'Genesis I'm Sorry', Greene Naftali Gallery, New York / 2007 'Unmonumental', New Museum, New York / 2006 'A Broken Arm', 303 Gallery, New York / 2006 'Gedi Sibony and Josh Smith', Harris Lieberman, New York / 2006 Whitney Biennial, New York / 2005 'Make It Now', SculptureCenter, New York
—— **Selected bibliography** 2008 Giovanni Carmine, Francois Quintin and Philip Vergne, *Gedi Sibony: If Surrounded by Foxes*, Kunsthalle St Gallen and JRP Ringier, Zurich / 2008 Karen Rosenberg, 'Gedi Sibony', *The New York Times*, 2 May / 2008 Jonathan T.D. Neil, 'Legibility of Effort', *Art Review*, Jan. / 2007 Ann Klefstad, 'Minneapolis: Gedi Sibony', *Sculpture*, Oct. / 2006 Gedi Sibony and Philippe Vergne, 'Gedi Sibony', *Flash Art*, July–Sep.

Lucy Skaer Born 1975, Cambridge, UK. Lives in Glasgow and London, UK.
—— **Selected solo exhibitions** 2008 Longside Gallery, Yorkshire Sculpture Park, Wakefield, UK / 2008 Fruitmarket Gallery, Edinburgh / 2008 Chisenhale Gallery, London / 2005 Frankfurter Kunstverein / 2004 doggerfisher, Edinburgh
—— **Selected group exhibitions** 2008 Berlin Biennial / 2007 Venice Biennale / 2006 'If I Can't Dance, I Don't Want to be Part of Your Revolution', De Appel, Amsterdam / 2006 'Momentum', Nordic Festival of Contemporary Art, Moss, Norway / 2005 The British Art Show 6, Baltic Centre for Contemporary Art, Gateshead
—— **Selected bibliography** 2008 Will Holder, *F.R. David*, De Appel, Amsterdam / 2008 Stacy Boldrick, Fiona Bradley, Lizzie Carey-Thomas and Ilsa Leaver-Yap, *Lucy Skaer*, Fruitmarket Gallery, Edinburgh / 2007 Isla Leaver-Yap, 'Drawing Close: Isla Leaver-Yap and Lucy Skaer in Conversation,' *Map Magazine*, no. 10 / 2007 Melissa Gronlund, 'Mining for Gold', *Frieze*, Nov.

Monika Sosnowska Born 1972, Ryki, Poland. Lives in Warsaw, Poland.
—— **Selected solo exhibitions** 2007 Talbot Rice Gallery, University of Edinburgh / 2006 'Projects 83: Monika Sosnowska', The Museum

of Modern Art, New York / 2006 'Interventions 41', Sprengel Museum, Hanover / 2006 *The Corridor*, Museo de Arte Contemporáneo de Castilla y León (MUSAC), Spain / 2005 'Display', Foksal Gallery Foundation, Warsaw / 2005 'The Tired Room', Sigmund Freud Museum, Vienna / 2004 De Appel, Amsterdam / 2004 Serpentine Gallery, London
—— **Selected group exhibitions** 2007 '1:1', Polish Pavilion, Venice Biennale / 2007 'Stay Forever and Ever and Ever', South London Gallery / 2006 'Ideal City: Invisible Cities', Zamość, Potsdam, Germany / 2006 'Centres of Attraction', Constitution Square 4, Warsaw / 2006 'Longing balloons are floating around the world', Green Light Pavilion, Berlin / 2006 'Phantom', Charlottenberg Museum, Copenhagen / 2006 'ARS 06: Sense of the Real', Kiasma Museum, Helsinki / 2006 'Satellite of Love', Witte de With, Rotterdam
—— **Selected bibliography** 2008 Elizabeth, Schambelan, 'Andrea Zittel and Monika Sosnowska 1:1', *Artforum*, May / 2008 Kirsty Bell, 'Time and Space', *Frieze*, Dec. / 2008 Malgorzata Jurkiewicz (ed.), *Monika Sosnowska: 1:1*, Galeria Zacheta and Walther König, Cologne / 2007 Will Bradley, et al., *Monika Sosnowska: Loop*, Walther König, Cologne

Simon Starling Born 1967, Epsom, UK. Lives in Copenhagen, Denmark.
—— **Selected solo exhibitions** 2008 'The Nanjing Particles', Massachusetts Museum of Contemporary Art, North Adams, USA / 2008 'Plant Room', Kunstraum Dornbirn, Germany / 2008 'Cuttings (supplements)', The Power Plant, Toronto / 2007 'Nachbau', Städtischen Kunstmuseum zum Museum Folkwang, Essen, Germany / 2007 Presentation House Gallery, Vancouver / 2006 Heidelberger Kunstverein, Germany
—— **Selected group exhibitions** 2008 'Reality Check', Statens Museum for Kunst, Copenhagen / 2008 'Greenwashing', Fondazione Sandretto Re Rebaudengo, Turin / 2008 'History in the making: a restropective of the Turner Prize', Mori Art Museum, Tokyo / 2008 'Amateurs', CCA Wattis Institute for Contemporary Arts, San Francisco / 2007 Lyon Biennial / 2007 'Turner Prize: A Retrospective', Tate Britain, London / 2007 'Des mondes perdus', CAPC Musée d'Art Contemporain, Bordeaux / 2007 Sharjah Biennial / 2007 Moscow Biennial
—— **Selected bibliography** 2008 Gregory Burke, Mark Godfrey, Reid Shier, Sarah Stanners and Simon Starling, *Simon Starling: Cuttings [Supplement]*, The Power Plant, Toronto / 2007 Simon Starling, 'Replication: Some Thoughts, Some Works', *Tate Papers: Special Issue on Replication*, Autumn / 2007 Simon Starling, 'Simon Starling', *domus*, July–Aug.

Katja Strunz Born 1970, Ottweiler, Germany. Lives in Berlin, Germany.
—— **Selected solo exhibitions** 2008 Contemporary Fine Arts, Berlin / 2007 Galerie Almine Rech, Brussels / 2007 The Modern Institute, Glasgow / 2007 Artpace, San Antonio, TX, USA / 2006 Museum Haus Esters, Krefeld / 2006 Gavin Brown's Enterprise, New York
—— **Selected group exhibitions** 2008 'Material Presence: Sculpture and Installation from the Zabludowicz Collection', 176, London / 2008 'Life on Mars', Carnegie Museum of Art, Pittsburgh / 2008 'Boros Collection', Sammlung Boros, Berlin / 2007 'Delusive Orders', Muzeum Sztuki, Lodz
—— **Selected bibliography** 2008 Heather Pesanti, 'Katja Strunz', *Life on Mars: 55th Carnegie International*, Carnegie Museum of Art, Pittsburgh / 2007 Elke Buhr, 'Blechshcirme und Batmans Mantel', *Frankfurter Rundschau*, 9 Jan. / 2007 Suzanne Hudson and Lutz Niethammer, *Katja Strunz*, Walther König, Cologne / 2006 Katrin Wittneven, 'Preview: Ein Blick ins Atelier von Katja Strunz vor ihrer Retrospektive in Krefeld', *Monopol*, no. 5

Ricky Swallow Born 1974, San Remo, Australia. Lives in Los Angeles, CA, USA.
—— **Selected solo exhibitions** 2008 Marc Foxx, Los Angeles / 2007 'Younger Than Yesterday', Project Space, Kunsthalle Vienna / 2007 Douglas Hyde Gallery, Dublin / 2006 'Long Time Gone', Stuart Shave Modern Art, London / 2006 P.S.1 Contemporary Art Center, New York / 2006 'The Past Sure Is Tense', Art Gallery of Western Australia, Perth
—— **Selected group exhibitions** 2007 'Goth: Reality of the Departed World', Yokohama Museum of Art / 2007 'Sculptors Drawing', Aspen Art Museum, CO, USA / 2005 'Getting Emotional', The Institute of Contemporary Art, Boston / 2005 Venice Biennale
—— **Selected bibliography** 2007 Jon Bywater and Gerald Matt, *Younger Than Yesterday*, Kunsthalle Vienna / 2007 Robert Tufnell, *Ricky Swallow*, Douglas Hyde Gallery, Dublin / 2006 Reuben Keehan, Robert Cook and Jenepher Duncan, *Ricky Swallow: The Past Sure Is Tense*, Art Gallery of Western Australia, Perth / 2005 Charlotte Day, Jennifer Higgie and Tom Nicholson *This Time Another Year*, The Australia Council, Sydney

Mika Tajima Born 1975, Los Angeles, CA, USA. Lives in New York, NY, USA.
—— **Selected solo exhibitions** 2008 The Kitchen, New York / 2008 Centre for Opinions in Music and Art, Berlin / 2007 Circuit, Lausanne / 2007 Elizabeth Dee Gallery, New York
—— **Selected group exhibitions** 2008 Whitney Biennial, New York / 2008 'One Way or Another: Asian American Art Now', Japanese American National Museum, Los Angeles / 2007 'Sympathy for the Devil: Art and Rock and Roll Since 1967', Museum of Contemporary Art, Chicago; Museum of Contemporary Art, North Miami / 2007 'Uncertain States of America', Astrup Fearnley Museum of Modern Art, Oslo; Musée d'Art Moderne de la Ville de Paris; Center for Curatorial Studies, Bard College, Annandale-on-Hudson, NY; Reykjavík Art Museum; Serpentine Gallery, London / 2006 'Bunch, Alliance and Dissolve', Contemporary Arts Center, Cincinnati / 2006 'Music is a Better Noise', P.S.1 Contemporary Art Center, New York
—— **Selected bibliography** 2008 Gary Carrion-Murayari, 'Production Anxiety,' *Domus*, no. 915 / 2008 Henriette Huldisch and Shamim M. Momin, *Whitney Biennial*, Yale University Press, London and New Haven, CT, USA / 2007 Dominic Molon, *Sympathy for the Devil: Art and Rock and Roll Since 1967*, Yale University Press, London and New Haven, CT, USA / 2006 Linda Shearer et al., *Bunch Alliance and Dissolve*, Public-Holiday Projects, New York and Contemporary Art Center, Cincinnati

Tatiana Trouvé Born 1968, Cosenza, Italy. Lives in Paris, France.
—— **Selected solo exhibitions** 2009 Kunstverein in Hamburg / 2008 Centre Pompidou, Paris / 2007 Villa Arson, Nice / 2004 Musée d'Art Moderne et Contemporain (MAMCO), Geneva / 2003 CAPC Musée d'Art Contemporain de Bordeaux
—— **Selected group exhibitions** 2008 Turin Triennial / 2008 Manifesta 7, Trentino, South Tyrol, Italy / 2007 Venice Biennale / 2007 'Airs de Paris', Centre Pompidou, Paris / 2006 'Notre Histoire', Palais de Tokyo, Paris / 2006 'Re-opening', Musée d'Art Moderne de la Ville de Paris / 2005 'Configurations Modèles', Musée d'art Moderne et Contemporain (MAMCO), Geneva
—— **Selected bibliography** 2008 Vivian Rehberg, 'Tatiana Trouvé', *Frieze*, May / 2008 Catherine Millet, Richard Shusterman and Robert Storr, *Tatiana Trouvé*, Walther König, Cologne / 2007 Catherine Gonnard and Elisabeth Lebovici, *Femmes artistes, Artistes Femmes*, Hazan, Paris / 2005 Hans Ulrich Obrist, *Djinns*, Centre National de l'Estampe et de l'Art Imprimé, Chatou, France

Luca Trevisani Born 1979, Verona, Italy. Lives in Berlin, Germany.
—— **Selected solo exhibitions** 2008 Giò Marconi, Milano / 2008 Mehdi Chouakri, Berlin / 2008 Kunstlerhaus Bethanien, Berlin / 2006 Pinksummer, Genoa
—— **Selected group exhibitions** 2008 Turin Triennial / 2008 Manifesta 7, Trentino, South Tyrol, Italy / 2008 'Peripheral vision and collective body', Museion, Bozen, Italy / 2007 'Space for your future: Recombining the DNA of Art and Design', Museum of Contemporary Art, Tokyo / 2006 'L'immagine del Vuoto: Una Linea di Ricerca dell'Arte in Italia 1958–2006', Museo Cantonale d'Arte, Lugano, Switzerland
—— **Selected bibliography** 2008 Luca Cerizza, Dominic Eichler and Simone Menegoi, *Luca Trevisani: The effort took its tools*, Argobooks, Berlin / 2006 Daniela Lotta, 'Praticare L'esperienza', *Flash Art*, Aug.–Sep.

Oscar Tuazon Born 1975, Seattle, WA, USA. Lives in Paris, France, and Tacoma, WA, USA.
—— **Selected solo exhibitions** 2009 Kunstmuseum, Tønsberg / 2009 Standard, Oslo / 2009 Galerie Isabella Bortolozzi, Berlin / 2008 Fortescue Avenue Jonathan Viner, London / 2008 St Louis Museum of Contemporary Art (with Alex Hubbard), MO, USA / 2008 Seattle Art Museum / 2007 Palais de Tokyo, Paris
—— **Selected group exhibitions** 2008 'A Town (Not a City)', Kunsthalle St Gallen / 2008 'Degrees of Remove', SculptureCenter, New York / 2008 'dragged down into lowercase', Zentrum Paul Klee, Bern / 2008 'You Complete Me', Western Bridge, Seattle / 2007 'Leave Me Be', Seattle Art Museum / 2006 'Down By Law', The Wrong Gallery, Whitney Biennial, New York
—— **Selected bibliography** 2006 Clementine Deliss and Oscar Tuazon (eds.), *Metronome Nº10: 'Future Academy' (Oregon) Shared, Mobile, Improvised, Underground, Hidden, Floating*, Metronome, Paris / 2004 Roberta Smith, 'Slouching Towards Bethlehem', *The New York Times*, 13 Aug.

Francis Upritchard Born 1976, New Plymouth, New Zealand. Lives in London, UK.
—— **Selected solo exhibitions** 2009 Venice Biennale / 2008 Artspace, Sydney / 2008 Gertrude Contemporary Art Spaces, Melbourne / 2008 Govett-Brewster Art Gallery, New Plymouth / 2007 Ivan Anthony Gallery, Auckland / 2006 Kate McGarry, London / 2005 Andrea Rosen Gallery, New York
—— **Selected group exhibitions** 2009 'Feierabend: Francis Upritchard, Martino Gamper and Karl Fritsch', Kate McGarry, London / 2008 'Martian Museum of Terrestrial Art', Barbican Art Gallery, London / 2007 'Effigies', Stuart Shave Modern Art, London / 2006 The Walters Prize, Auckland Art Gallery / 2006 'Around The World In Eighty Days', South London Gallery / 2005 'The Way We Work Now', Camden Arts Centre, London
—— **Selected bibliography** 2008 Anthony Gardner, 'Francis Upritchard', *Artforum*, Dec. / 2008 Natasha Conland, 'Francis Upritchard', *Art World* (UK), Aug.–Sep. / 2008 Justin Paton, 'Mixed Feelings, Francis Upritchard's 1970s Show', *Art & Australia*, Spring / 2006 Hari Kunzru, *Francis Upritchard: Human Problems*, Kate McGarry, London and Veenman Publishers, Rotterdam

Rebecca Warren Born 1965, London, UK. Lives in London, UK.
— **Selected solo exhibitions** 2009 Serpentine Gallery, London / 2009 Matthew Marks Gallery, New York / 2007 Galerie Max Hetzler, Berlin / 2004 Kunsthalle Zürich / 2003 Maureen Paley, London / 2003 Donald Young Gallery, Chicago
— **Selected group exhibitions** 2008 'Martian Museum of Terrestrial Art', Barbican Art Gallery, London / 2007 'The Third Mind', Palais de Tokyo, Paris / 2007 'Unmonumental', New Museum, New York / 2006 Tate Triennial, London / 2005 'The British Art Show', Hayward Gallery, London / 2004 'Sculpture, Precarious Realism between the Melancholy and the Comical', Kunsthalle Wien, Vienna
— **Selected bibliography** 2007 Barry Schwabsky, 'Rebecca Warren', *Artforum*, Nov. / 2006 Neal Brown, Martin Herbert and Catherine Lampert, 'Rebecca Warren', *Parkett*, no. 78 / 2006 Julian Keeling, 'Shapes of Things to Come', *Harper's Bazaar*, Nov. / 2004 Gregorio Magnami and Beatrix Ruf, *Rebecca Warren*, Kunsthalle Zürich and JRP Ringier, Zurich

Phoebe Washburn Born 1973, Poughkeepsie, NY, USA. Lives in New York, NY, USA.
— **Selected solo exhibitions** 2008 Zach Feuer Gallery, New York / 2007 Deutsche Guggenheim, Berlin / 2007 Institute of Contemporary Art, Philadelphia / 2005 Hammer Museum, Los Angeles / 2004 Weatherspoon Art Gallery, Greensboro, NC, USA
— **Selected group exhibitions** 2008 Whitney Biennial, New York / 2006 'Burgeoning Geometries', Whitney Museum of American Art at Altria, New York / 2006 'Ping Pong Diplomacy', Kemper Museum, Kansas City, MO, USA / 2005 'The Bench', Kunsthalle St Gallen / 2005 'Make It Now', SculptureCenter, New York
Selected bibliography 2008 Henriette Huldisch and Shamim M. Momin, *Whitney Biennial 2008*, Yale University Press, London and New Haven, CT, USA / 2005 James Trainor, 'Rubbish isn't always a dead-end, sometimes it's a beginning', *Frieze*, Oct. / 2005 Michael Amy, 'Phoebe Washburn at LFL', *Art in America*, Jan. / 2004 Melissa Pearl Friedling, 'Phoebe Washburn', *Flash Art*, Nov.–Dec.

Gary Webb Born 1973, Bascombe, UK. Lives in London, UK.
— **Selected solo exhibitions** 2008 Pilar Parra and Romero, Madrid / 2008 The Approach W1, London / 2008 Kukje Gallery, Seoul / 2005 Kunsthaus Glarus, Switzerland / 2005 Le Consortium, Dijon / 2005 Centre d'Arte Contemporain, Geneva / 2004 Chisenhale Gallery, London / 2004 Mead Gallery, Warwick / 2003 The Approach, London
— **Selected group exhibitions** 2007 'Back to Nature', Ruzicska, Salzburg / 2007 'Sublime Experiences and Perceptions in Contemporary Sculpture', Pilar Parra and Romero, Madrid / 2005 The British Art Show 6, Baltic Centre for Contemporary Art, / 2005 'Sculptures d'Apartement', Musee d'Art Contemporain de Rochechouart, France
— **Selected bibliography** / 2008 Colin Perry, 'Gary Webb: The Approach W1', *Frieze*, June / 2005 Anne Pontegnie, 'Gary Webb, Chisenhale Gallery', *Artforum*, Feb. / 2005 Lee Trimming, 'Gary Webb', *Flash Art*, Jan.–Feb. / 2005 Eliza Williams, 'Gary Webb, Chisenhale Gallery', *Art Monthly*, Dec.–Jan.

Klaus Weber Born 1967, Sigmaringen, Germany. Lives in Berlin, Germany.
— **Selected solo exhibitions** 2008 Secession, Vienna / 2007 'Shape of the Ape', Andrew Kreps Gallery, New York / 2007 'The Big Giving', Hayward Gallery, London / 2006 'The Big Giving (small group)', Herald St, London / 2005 'Allee der Schlaflosigkeit', Kunstverein in Hamburg / 2004 'Unfolding cul-de-sac', Cubitt Gallery, London / 2003 'Public Fountain LSD Hall', Frieze Projects, Frieze Art Fair, London
— **Selected group exhibitions** 2008 'Eine bessere Welt', Bonner Kunstverein, Bonn / 2008 'Der Blinde Fleck', Neue Gesellschaft für Bildende Kunst (NGBK), Berlin / 2008 Manifesta 7, Trentino, South Tyrol, Italy / 2008 'Kabul 3000: Love Among the Cabbages', Zero, Milan / 2007 'Memorial to the Iraq War, Institute of Contemporary Arts, London / 2006 'Faster! Bigger! Better!', Zentrum für Kunst und Medientechnologie (ZKM), Karlsruhe
— **Selected bibliography** 2009 Alex Farquharson and Clemens Krümmel, *Klaus Weber*, Secession, Vienna / 2008 Jonathan Griffin, 'Klaus Weber', *Frieze*, Apr. / 2008 Tobias Rüther, 'Was vom Störkopf übrig bleibt', *FAZ*, 17 Nov. / 2007 Martha Schwendener, 'Shape of the pe', *The New York Times*, 28 Dec.

Eric Wesley Born 1973, Los Angeles, CA, USA. Lives in Los Angeles, CA, USA.
— **Selected solo exhibitions** 2007 Bortolami, New York / 2007 Galeria Franco Noero, Turin / 2007 Foundation Morra Grecco, Naples / 2006 Meyer-Riegger Gallery, Karlsruhe / 2006 China Art Objects, Los Angeles / 2006 Museum of Contemporary Art, Los Angeles
— **Selected group exhibitions** 2008 'Los Angeles Confidential', Centre d'Art Contemporain, Pougues-les-Eaux, France / 2008 'Amateurs', CCA Wattis Institute for Contemporary Art, San Francisco / 2007 'Darling, Take Fountain', Kalfayan Galleries, Athens / 2006 'Axis of Praxis', Midway Contemporary Art, Minneapolis, MN, USA / 2006 'Alien Nation', Institute of Contemporary Arts, London / 2006 'The Gold Standard', P.S. 1 Contemporary Art Center, New York
— **Selected bibliography** 2008 Paul Schimmel, 'Future Greats', *Art Review*, Mar. / 2008 Johanna Burton, 'Eric Wesley', *Artforum*, Mar / 2007 Sonia Campagnola, 'Eric Wesley', *Flash Art*, Mar.–Apr. / 2007 Emily Verla Bovina, 'Eric Wesley: Fondazione Morra Greco', *Frieze*, Oct. / 2006 Anne Rochette and Wade Saunders, 'Place Matters: Los Angeles', *Art in America*, Nov. / 2002 Julian Myers, 'Just for Kicks,' *Frieze*, Jan.

Haegue Yang Born 1971, Seoul, Korea. Lives in Berlin, Germany, and Seoul, Korea.
— **Selected solo exhibitions** 2010 Artsonje Centre, Seoul / 2009 Korean Pavilion, Venice Biennale / 2009 Walker Art Center, Minneapolis / 2008 Cubitt Gallery, London / 2008 Kunsthalle Hamburg / 2008 Portikus, Frankfurt / 2008 Gallery at REDCAT, Los Angeles / 2008 Sala Recalde, Bilbao / 2006 Sadong 30, Incheon, Korea / 2006 Basis voor Actuele Kunst (BAK), Utrecht
— **Selected group exhibitions** 2009 'Your Bright Future: 12 Korean Artists', Los Angeles County Museum of Art; Museum of Fine Arts, Houston; Freer Sackler Gallery, Washington, DC, USA / 2008 'Whose History', Hamburger Kunstverein / 2008 Guangzhou Triennial / 2008 Turin Triennial / 2008 'If We Can't Get It Together', The Power Plant, Toronto / 2007 'Brave New Worlds', Walker Art Center, Minneapolis / 2007 'Feminist Legacies and Potentials in Contemporary Art Practice', Museum van Hedendaagse Kunst Antwerpen (MuHKA), Antwerp
— **Selected bibliography** 2006 Lars Bang Larsson, Binna Choi and Nina Möntmann, *Haegue Yang*, BAK, Utrecht and Revolver Frankfurt / 2003 Charles Esche, *Why is everyday life so different, so appealing?*, Art Sonje Center, Seoul / 2006 Emily Pethick, 'Fog machines, scent dispensers and origami; sci-fi tower blocks and urban detritus', *Frieze*, Nov. / 2003 Daniel Birnbaum, 'First Take: Daniel Birnbaum on Haegue Yang', *Artforum*, Jan.

Tarek Zaki Born 1975, Riyadh, Saudi Arabia. Lives in Cairo, Egypt.
— **Selected solo exhibitions** 2007 Townhouse Gallery, Cairo / 2004 Townhouse Gallery, Cairo / 2002 Townhouse Gallery, Cairo
— **Selected group exhibitions** 2008 'Antekhana: Museum as Hub', New Museum, New York / 2008 'New Ends Old Beginnings', Bluecoat Gallery, Liverpool / 2007 'Out of Place', Sfeir-Semler Gallery, Beirut / 2007 'Focus Agypten', Roemer-und-Pelizaeus Museum, Germany / 2006 'Downloads from Future', Kunsthalle Winterthur, Switzerland / 2004 'Under Construction', Mayrau Museum, Vinařice, Czech Republic / 2002 'Haunted by Detail', De Appel, Amsterdam
— **Selected bibliography** 2008 Kaelen Wilson-Goldie, 'Monument X', *Bidoun*, no. 14 / 2008 Fiona Fox, 'Made in Cairo: Time and Time Again', *Contemporary Practices*, Apr. / 2002 Mai Abu El Dahab et al., *Haunted by Detail*, De Appel, Amsterdam

Thomas Zipp Born 1966, Heppenheim, Germany. Lives in Berlin, Germany.
— **Selected solo exhibitions** 2008 'White Dada', Alison Jacques Gallery, London / 2008 'S.S.B.S.M. (sick souls by sick minds)', Galerie Guido W. Baudach, Berlin / 2008 Sommer Contemporary Art, Tel Aviv / 2008 'Dwarf Nose', Gallery Harris Lieberman, New York / 2007 'Planet Caravan? Is There Life After Death? A Futuristic World Fair', Museum Dhondt-Dhaenens, Deurle, Belgium; South London Gallery; Kunsthalle Mannheim, Germany; Museum in der Alten Post, Muehlheim, Germany
— **Selected group exhibitions** 2007 'Sympathy for the Devil: Art and Rock and Roll Since 1967', Museum of Contemporary Art, Chicago; Museum of Contemporary Art, North Miam / 2007 'Mystic Truths', Auckland Art Gallery / 2006 'Defamation of Character', P.S.1 Contemporary Art Center, New York / 2006 'Rings of Saturn', Tate Modern, London / 2006 'Faster! Bigger! Better!', Zentrum für Kunst und Medientechnologie (ZKM), Karlsruhe
— **Selected bibliography** 2008 Ossian Ward, 'Thomas Zipp, South London Gallery', *Modern Painters*, Feb. / 2007 Sandra Rehme, 'Thomas Zipp, South London Gallery', *Artforum*, Dec. / 2007 Melissa Gronlund, 'Thomas Zipp', *Art Review*, Mar. / 2005 Zdenek Felix et al. (eds.), *Thomas Zipp: Achtung! Vision: Samoa and The Family of Pills and the Return of the Subreals*, Hatje Cantz, Ostfildern

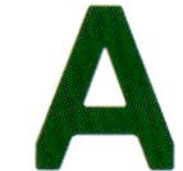

Q

R

S

T

U

V

W

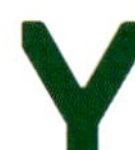

Y

Z